MANAGEMENT CONTROL SYSTEMS

Performance Measurement, Evaluation and Incentives

Third Edition

Kenneth A. Merchant
University of Southern California

Wim A. Van der Stede
London School of Economics

Financial Times
Prentice Hall
is an imprint of

Harlow, England • London • New York • Boston • San Francisco • Toronto
Sydney • Tokyo • Singapore • Hong Kong • Seoul • Taipei • New Delhi
Cape Town • Madrid • Mexico City • Amsterdam • Munich • Paris • Milan

Pearson Education Limited
Edinburgh Gate
Harlow
Essex CM20 2JE
England

and Associated Companies throughout the world

Visit us on the World Wide Web at:
www.pearson.com/uk

First published 2003
Second edition published 2007
Third edition published 2012

© Pearson Education Limited 2003, 2007, 2012

ISBN: 978-0-273-73761-2

British Library Cataloguing-in-Publication Data
A catalogue record for this book is available from the British Library

Library of Congress Cataloging-in-Publication Data
A catalog record for this book is available from the Library of Congress

10 9 8 7 6 5 4 3 2
15 14 13 12

Typeset in 10.5/12pt Times by 35
Printed and bound in Great Britain by Ashford Colour Press Ltd, Gosport, Hampshire

TO OUR FAMILIES

Gail, Abbidee, Madelyn (KM)

Ashley, Emma, Erin (WVDS)

BRIEF CONTENTS

Supporting resources

Visit **www.pearsoned.co.uk/merchant** to find valuable online resources:

For instructors
- A complete, downloadable Instructor's Manual
- PowerPoint slides that can be downloaded and used for presentations

For more information please contact your local Pearson Education sales representative or visit **www.pearsoned.co.uk/merchant**.

CONTENTS

Contents

Section III
FINANCIAL RESULTS CONTROL SYSTEMS

7 Financial Responsibility Centers   261

8 Planning and Budgeting   306

9 Incentive Systems   367

Section IV
PERFORMANCE MEASUREMENT ISSUES AND THEIR EFFECTS

10 Financial Performance Measures and Their Effects   413

11 Remedies to the Myopia Problem   445

12 Using Financial Results Controls in the Presence of Uncontrollable Factors   503

Section V
CORPORATE GOVERNANCE, IMPORTANT CONTROL-RELATED ROLES, AND ETHICS

Section VI
SITUATIONAL INFLUENCES ON MANAGEMENT CONTROL SYSTEMS

PREFACE

This book provides materials for a comprehensive course on management control systems (MCSs). MCSs are defined broadly to include everything managers do to help ensure that their organization's strategies and plans are carried out or, if conditions warrant, that they are modified. Thus, the book could be used in any course that focuses on topics related to strategy implementation or execution.

While the treatment of the MCS subject is broad, the primary focus of the book is on what we call *results controls*, which involve motivating employees to produce the outcomes the organization pursues. This type of management control, which requires performance measures and evaluations and the provision of incentives, dominates in importance in the vast majority of organizations. When we use the word *incentives*, we are not referring solely to monetary incentives, such as bonuses and stock options, we are also referring to any of a variety of non-monetary incentives, such as praise, recognition, and autonomy.

Because management control is a core function of management, all students interested in business or management can benefit from this book. However, courses based on the materials in this book should be particularly useful for those who are, or aspire to be, managers, management consultants, financial specialists (for example, controllers, financial analysts, auditors), or human resource specialists (for example, personnel directors, compensation consultants).

This book includes 71 cases for classroom use. The cases have been selected because of their interest and educational value in stimulating useful class discussions. Some of them are also suitable for use in examinations. We view these cases as an essential part of the textbook. Case studies that stimulate learning through the analysis of often complex situations in the "real world" are generally recognized to be the best pedagogical conduit for teaching a MCSs course. Because MCSs, the contexts in which they operate, and the outcomes they produce, are complex and multi-dimensional, simple problems and exercises cannot capture the essence of the issues managers face in designing and using MCSs. Students must develop the thinking processes that will guide them successfully through decision tasks with multiple embedded issues and large amounts of relatively unstructured information. They must learn to develop problem-finding skills, as well as problem-solving skills, and they must learn how to articulate and defend their ideas. Case analyses, discussions, and presentations provide the best method available for simulating these tasks in a classroom.

The discussions in this book assume a basic level of knowledge of financial accounting (for example, how financial statements are put together), management accounting (for example, variance analysis), and core MCS elements (for example, budgeting). The book was designed primarily for use by graduate students and practicing professionals. It can also be used successfully by undergraduate students who have had a prior management accounting course, but it should be recognized that some of the cases in this book might be too challenging for undergraduate students. Cases for use in an undergraduate course have to be chosen judiciously.

This book is different from other MCS texts in a number of important ways. First, the basic organizing framework is different. The first major module of the book discusses management controls based on the object of control: results, actions, or personnel/culture.

The object-of-control framework has considerable advantages over other possible organizing frameworks. It has clean, clearly distinguishable categories. It is also relatively all-inclusive in the sense that the reader can relate many management controls and other control classifications and theories (for example, proactive vs. reactive controls, prevention vs. detection controls, and agency theory concepts such as monitoring vs. incentives) to it. It is also intuitive; that is, students can easily see that managers must make choices from among these categories of management control. Thus, using the object-of-control focus, the overall structure of the book can be summarized as being organized around a framework that describes the core management control problems that need to be addressed, the MCSs that can be used to address those problems, the most important situational factors that can cause managers to choose one set of management controls over another, and the outcomes that can be produced, both positive and negative.

Second, the book's treatment of management control is broad. Like all MCS textbooks, this book focuses intensively on the use and effects of financial performance measures, which dominate in importance at managerial levels in most organizations. However, this book also provides a broader treatment of management controls (organized around the object-of-control framework) to put the financial results controls in proper perspective. For example, the book describes many situations where financial results controls are not effective and discusses the alternatives that managers can use in those situations (such as nonfinancial performance indicators, centralization of authority, management audits, or the creation of a team-oriented culture).

Third, the book provides considerable discussion on the causes and remedies of the most common and serious management control-related problems, including myopia, suboptimization, uncontrollability, and gameplaying.

Fourth, the book provides a whole chapter of ethics coverage. This makes it perhaps unique among accounting and control textbooks. There are many management control-related ethical issues, and the recent debacles at, for example, Enron, WorldCom, Parmalat, Lehman Brothers, and Bear Stearns, clearly suggest the need to develop managers' and prospective managers' ethical reasoning skills more fully. Related to this is coverage of corporate governance, to which we devote another whole chapter.

Fifth, the important concepts, theories, and issues are not discussed just in abstract terms. They are illustrated with a large number of real-world examples, far more than typically included in any other MCS textbook. The examples make the textual discussion more concrete and bring the subject to life.

Finally, the mix of cases included in this book is different from those included in other MCS textbooks in four important ways:

- A high proportion of the cases are real and undisguised (that is, they describe the facts of the actual situations and use the companies' real names). Reality and lack of disguise enhance student interest and "secondary" learning (that is, about named industries, companies, and individuals).

- Most of the cases include rich descriptions of the context within which the MCSs are operating. The rich descriptions give students opportunities to try to identify and address management control problems and issues within the same multi-dimensional situations that practicing managers face.

- Most of the cases are of relatively recent vintage, and the set of cases has been chosen to ensure coverage of the latest MCSs topics and issues, such as how to stress test budgets; how to minimize management myopia; how to motivate all employees to create sustainable value; and whether to use the EVA™ or Balanced Scorecard measurement approaches, just to name a few.

- The cases are descriptive of the operations and issues faced by companies located in many different countries and regions around the world, including Asia, Europe, Latin America, as well as North America.

The cases in this book permit the exploration of the management control issues in a broad range of settings. Included in the book are cases on both large and small firms, manufacturing and service firms, domestic-focused and multinational firms, and for-profit and not-for-profit organizations. The cases present issues faced by personnel in both line and staff roles at corporate, divisional, and functional levels of the organization, as well as by members of boards of directors. Instructors can use this set of cases to teach a management control course which is broad in scope or one which is more narrowly focused (for example, MCSs in service organizations by focusing on the cases from the healthcare, education, financial, and other service sectors).

The cases provide considerable scheduling flexibility. Most of the cases cut across multiple topic areas because MCSs are inherently multi-dimensional. For example, the classroom focus for the new Statoil case in Chapter 11 might be on performance measurement, as Statoil uses a key-performance-indicator (KPI) structure that is Balanced Scorecard-like. Or it could be on Statoil's planning and budgeting system, which separates the functions of target setting, forecasting, and resource allocation using the principles of "Beyond Budgeting". Students also have to consider the industry characteristics, the organization structure, the characteristics of the people in key positions, and the company's history (for example, a recent merger), so instructors can choose to use this case when they wish to focus on the effects of one or more of these factors on the design of MCSs. As a consequence, the ordering of the cases in the book is not intended to be rigid. Many alternatives are possible. A case overview sheet in the accompanying Instructors Manual to this textbook provides a matrix that helps instructors disentangle the various relevant topics for which each case could be fruitfully used.

In this third edition of the book, we made a number of substantive updates, most obviously in those areas where the world has been moving fast during the past few years, particularly since the 2008–2009 financial crisis and subsequent economic recession. This includes changes in incentive systems (Chapter 9) and corporate governance (Chapter 13). Throughout the book, we incorporated discussions of some of the most important recent research findings and updated the survey statistics and examples provided. We also added some new, exciting cases. Eleven of the 71 cases included in this edition are new, and an additional three were revised or brought up to date. Some of the new cases cover cutting-edge topics, such as stress testing (scenario budgeting) (VisuSon, Inc.), enterprise risk management (Entropic Communications, Inc.), and "Beyond Budgeting" (Statoil). Others were intended to address the topics in new and different settings, such as Raven Capital LLC (a hedge fund), Family Care Specialists Medical Group, Inc. (a medical group), and Game Shop, Inc. (a billings system "scorecard").

In developing the materials for this third edition of our book, we have benefited from the insightful comments, helpful suggestions, and cases of many people. Ken owes special thanks to the two professors who served as his mentors at the Harvard Business School: William Bruns and Richard Vancil.

Ken also appreciates the valuable research assistance from David Huelsbeck, Sahil Parmar, and Michelle Spaulding, and useful suggestions from Jong Hwan Kim, all currently or formerly at USC. Wim is especially grateful to Renuka Fernando for her capable assistance with updating the many examples throughout this book. We also appreciate the punctual administrative assistance from Ingrid McClendon and Linda Ramos at USC, and Justin Adams and Liz Venning at LSE. At Pearson Education, we are indebted to Katie Rowland (Acquisitions Editor, Accounting) and Gemma Papageorgiou (Assistant Editor, Higher Education Division). David Hemsley made helpful suggestions in copyediting the manuscript.

We thank Harvard Business School Publishing for granting permission to use the Harvard cases that are included in this text. Tad Dearden, Permissions Coordinator, was very efficient in helping us through the permissions process. Requests to reproduce cases copyrighted by Harvard Business School should be directed to the Permissions Department, Harvard Business School Publishing, 60 Harvard Way, Boston, MA 02163 (permissions@hbsp.harvard.edu). We also thank the Asia Case Research Center at the University of Hong Kong for granting permission to use two of their Poon Kam Kai Series cases, and especially Neale O'Connor for his help with this. Finally, we wish to thank the authors of several cases included in this book, the names of whom are listed with the cases inside this book.

In closing, we wish to acknowledge that there is certainly no one best way to convey the rich subjects related to MCSs. We have presented one useful framework in the best way we know how, but we welcome comments about the content or organization of the book, or regarding specific errors or omissions. Please direct them to us.

Kenneth A. Merchant
Deloitte & Touche LLP Chair of Accountancy
Leventhal School of Accounting
Marshall School of Business
University of Southern California
Los Angeles, CA 90089-0441
USA

Phone: (213) 821-5920
Fax: (213) 747-2815
E-mail: kmerchant@marshall.usc.edu

Wim A. Van der Stede
CIMA Professor of Accounting and
Financial Management
London School of Economics
Department of Accounting
Houghton Street
London WC2A 2AE
UK
Phone: (020) 7955-6695
Fax: (020) 7955-7420
E-mail: w.van-der-stede@lse.ac.uk

We are grateful to the following for permission to reproduce copyright material:

Figures

Figure 15.6 from Tech firm's Korean growth raises eyebrows, *The Wall Street Journal*, 08/08/2000, p. C1 (Maremont, Mark, Eisinger, Jesse and Song, Meeyoung), The Wall Street Journal by News Corporation. Copyright 2000. Reproduced with permission of Dow Jones & Company, Inc. in the format Textbook via Copyright Clearance Center; Figure 15.6 from Lernout & Hauspie Seeks Bankruptcy Protection – Company struggles to repay millions to banks *The Wall Street Journal*, 30/11/2000, p. A3 (Carreyrou, John, and Maremont, Mark), The Wall Street Journal by News Corporation. Copyright 2000. Reproduced with permission of Dow Jones & Company, Inc. in the format Textbook via Copyright Clearance Center; Figure 15.6 from KPMG, Former Auditor of L&H, May Draw Investor Ire, *The Wall Street Journal*, 18/01/2001, p. C1 (Maremont, Mark), The Wall Street Journal by News Corporation. Copyright 2001. Reproduced with permission of Dow Jones & Company, Inc. in the format Textbook via Copyright Clearance Center; Figure 17.1 from USC Financial Report 2010, University of Southern California, reproduced with permission

Tables

Table 16.4 from BOVAG Autodealers, 2006, reproduced with permission.

Text

Case Study 3.3 from Chris S. Paddison and Associate Professor Kenneth A. Merchant, Copyright © 1987 by the President and Fellows of Harvard College. Harvard Business School Case 9-187-197; Case Study 4.2 from Norman Fast under the direction of Professor Norman Berg, Copyright © 1975 by the President and Fellows of Harvard College. Harvard Business School Case 376-028; Case Study 4.3 from Grace Lao under the supervision of Professor Neale O'Connor, Copyright © 2010. The University of Hong Kong. This material is used by permission of The Asia Case Research Center at The University of Hong Kong (http://www.acrc.org.hk). This case study is a single piece of work. Reproduction of the case study does not constitute fair use under 17 USC 107 or equivalent provisions in other laws; Case Study 5.2 from Grace Lao under the supervision of Professor Neale O'Connor © 2010 The University of Hong Kong. This material is used by permission of The Asia Case Research Center at The University of Hong Kong (http://www.acrc.org.hk). This case study is a single piece of work. Reproduction of the case study does not constitute fair use under 17 USC 107 or equivalent provisions in other laws; Case Study 6.4 from Research Associate Carleen Madigan under the direction of Professor Brian Hall, Copyright © 2000 by the President and Fellows of Harvard College. Harvard Business School Case 9-800-269; Case Study 8.1 from Professor Kenneth A. Merchant, Copyright © 1984 by the President and Fellows of Harvard College. Harvard Business School Case 9-185-061; Case Study 8.2 from Lourdes Ferreira and Professor Kenneth A. Merchant, Copyright © 1988 by the President and Fellows of Harvard College. Harvard Business School Case 9-189-096; Case Study 11.2 from Professor Robert S. Kaplan with the assistance of Michael Nagel of the Balanced Scorecard Collaborative Copyright © 2001 President and Fellows of Harvard College. Harvard Business School Case 9-104-042; Case Study 13.5 from Professor Paul Healy, Copyright © 2005 President and Fellows of Harvard College. Harvard Business School Case 9-105-082; Extract 15.6 from Tech firm's Korean growth raises eyebrows, *The Wall Street Journal*, 08/08/2000, p. C1 (Maremont, Mark, Eisinger, Jesse and Song, Meeyoung), The Wall Street Journal by News Corporation. Copyright 2000. Reproduced with permission of Dow Jones & Company, Inc. in the format Textbook via Copyright Clearance Center; Case Study 16.2 from Jamie O'Connell under the direction of Professor Christopher A. Bartlett, Copyright © 1998 by the President and Fellows of Harvard College. Harvard Business School Case 9-398-095; Case Study 17.3 from Prepared by Professor Robert S. Kaplan and doctoral student Dennis Campbell, Copyright © 2001 President and Fellows of Harvard College. Harvard Business School Case 9-101-111

In some instances we have been unable to trace the owners of copyright material, and we would appreciate any information that would enable us to do so.

Section I

THE CONTROL FUNCTION
OF MANAGEMENT

Chapter 1

MANAGEMENT AND CONTROL

Management control is a critical function in organizations. Management control failures can lead to large financial losses, reputation damage, and possibly even to organizational failure. Here are some recent examples:

- In the Autumn of 2010, during the trial of Jérôme Kerviel, a rogue trader who almost bankrupted Société Générale, France's second-biggest bank, the French court pondered the competing descriptions of whether Mr. Kerviel was "a country bumpkin from Brittany, seduced by a corrupt banking system and the avarice of his bosses, or 'a crook, a fraud and a terrorist'?"[1] On October 5, 2010, the court ruled that Mr. Kerviel was guilty, sentencing him to five years in jail, thus judging him to be "a fraud." The court also ordered that Mr. Kerviel repay the bank €4.9 billion, the amount that it lost due to his fraudulent trades. Although the court's sentence essentially implied that Société Générale did not share the blame for Mr. Kerviel's fraudulent trading by looking the other way when his positions were profitable, the bank did not go entirely blameless either. For example, Britain's Financial Services Authority (FSA), the regulator, fined the bank for weaknesses in its record-keeping and reporting because weak oversight allowed a relatively junior employee to place bets worth more than the bank's entire capital. Société Générale has since spent €130 million tightening its controls. Although this may be an extreme case, several other banks have been fined for similar transgressions. As *The Economist* reports, Société Générale's "experience sounds a loud warning to all investment banks and their regulators that they need to pay more attention to the boring old back office. The case of Mr Kerviel – like that of Nick Leeson, whose bets almost two decades ago destroyed Barings Bank – should not obscure wider questions, [such as] how to remunerate legitimate traders who stand to earn bucket loads if they make successful bets but lose little if they suffer losses is prime among them."[2] This is an important question which we will discuss in this book extensively under the rubric of so-called results controls, of which incentive systems are an important part. We introduce results controls in Chapter 2 and discuss incentive systems in Chapter 9, although both results controls and incentive systems are a recurrent theme across many other chapters throughout the book as well.

- In October 2009, London stockbroker Seymour Pierce was fined £154,000 by the FSA for failing to prevent an employee fraud. Weak compliance controls at the broker allowed an employee to steal approximately £150,000 from the firm's private client accounts spread, and then cover up the theft, over 36 separate transactions between 2003 and 2006. The employee was dismissed before the discovery of the fraud, which only came to light when his replacement noticed serious accounting discrepancies. Seymour Pierce managers said that once the fraud was discovered it immediately referred the matter to the authorities. Margaret Cole, the FSA's Director of Enforcement and Financial Crime, stated: "This is a serious failure on Seymour Pierce's part. The frauds were not sophisticated and could have been detected at a much earlier stage if the proper procedures had been in place. Fraud seriously undermines the integrity of our markets, so this fine is a timely reminder of the consequences for firms that fail to have in place robust systems and controls to prevent unlawful transactions of this sort." Simon Morris, a financial services partner at law firm CMS Cameron McKenna, added: "All firms should heed this latest warning and redouble their efforts to ensure that their systems and controls are adequate to safeguard against both internal and external misfeasance."[3] We discuss internal controls as one type of what we call action controls in Chapter 3, and discuss how tightly they should be applied in Chapter 4.

- In the Autumn of 2010, all 50 US states started a joint investigation into whether mortgage firms were wrong to repossess hundreds of thousands of homes, following allegations that the lenders, among them venerable banks, such as Bank of America and JP Morgan Chase, often mishandled documents when people that had fallen behind on their mortgage payments had their houses taken from them. At the heart of the issue is the accuracy and legitimacy of the documents that lenders used to evict people from their properties, suggesting that bank employees signed off on repossession documents without reading them. Iowa Attorney General Tom Miller said: "This is not simply about a glitch in paperwork; it's also about some companies violating the law and many people losing their homes."[4] How can companies, banks in this case, ensure that their employees carry out their jobs properly? As we will see in this book, what we call action controls, among other control system elements, are important to consider in respect to this question.

- In April 2005, employees at the 75-year-old California-based not-for-profit Gemological Institute of America (GIA), the world's largest grader of diamonds, were accused of accepting bribes from large diamond dealers to inflate diamond grades. Large diamond dealers would submit proportionally high bids, often 20 to 30% higher than prevailing bids for rough stones, knowing that they would be able to sell these stones at a profit because they bribed GIA staff to get a higher-than-deserved grade. A small difference in grade can mean a huge difference in price, often hundreds of thousands of dollars on larger diamonds. The size of the bribes is unknown, but the probe into the allegations mentions cash, theater tickets, and other gifts. What is known, however, is that the bribes gave the large dealers enough of a financial edge to control the market and reap excess profits. As such, the scandal reverberated throughout the $80 billion diamond-jewelry industry around the world, as many customers overpaid for their diamonds and many diamond dealers, particularly smaller ones, were forced to leave the industry or were considering it.[5] This leads to a similar question as in the example above, but in reverse: how can companies not only ensure that employees do not fail to do something they should do, but also guard against the possibilities that employees will do something the organization does not want them to do? This is, as we will see in the remainder of this chapter, a key question related to management control.

- On that note, more examples abound. In 2002, two clerical workers at the Laguna Niguel, California-based service center of the US Immigration and Naturalization Service (INS) were accused of destroying thousands of immigration documents, including visa applications, passports, and other papers. According to the probe, the clerks started shredding unprocessed paperwork in early 2002 after an inventory revealed a processing backlog of about 90,000 documents. A month later, in March 2002, the backlog was reported to be zero. The shredding allegedly went on for about another month to keep the backlog at zero, until INS officials discovered the shredding spree during an evening shift.[6] Although it is not entirely clear what the clerical workers' motives were, this example illustrates that money is not always the motive for wrongdoing. There were no bonuses involved here, and maybe the employees were just trying to keep their job, but their actions were undesirable nonetheless, and thus control systems are needed to mitigate undesirable behaviors.

● But not every control problem involves fraud. Control systems must also prevent mistakes. For example, in July 2009, an employee at Westpac, an Australian bank, accidentally credited a client's account with a $10 million overdraft when he had asked for just $100,000. Westpac had recovered some of the money, but $3.8 million remained outstanding. The employee who made the mistake had more than 30 years' banking experience, and he should have been considered at least somewhat trustworthy. Yet controls should have been in place to prevent this mistake.[7]

The examples described above show the importance of having good management control systems (MCSs) and the types of problems – thefts, frauds, and unintentional errors – they can address.

However, having *more* controls in place does not always guarantee *better* control. As the next example illustrates, when copious MCSs are stifling, they can exacerbate rather than mitigate control problems:

In 2003, the European Union's (EU) anti-fraud office discovered an allegedly "vast enterprise of looting" at Eurostat, the statistical service of the European Commission. The probe focused on secret bank accounts in which senior managers at Eurostat allegedly funneled an estimated €900,000 of EU taxpayers' cash to contractors, including companies that they themselves had helped set up, by artificially inflating the value of the contracts or by creating fictitious contracts. Some noted that this was just a confirmation of the popular prejudice that the "Brussels bureaucracy" is rife with corruption, lax financial controls, complacency, and cronyism, a reputation that the European Commission had earned in the late-1990s when several other corruption scandals broke. However, others argued that it was not certain that the accounts set up by the Eurostat officials were used for the personal enrichment of those involved, at least not initially. They argued instead that these accounts may originally have been set up to give Eurostat a way to pay for research quickly without going through the Commission's cumbersome procedures. Ironically, while the Commission has elaborate procedures to prevent financial fraud, these procedures may not only have proved insufficient, they may actually have made the problem worse. Due to the tortuous form-filling that is required for funding requests, the number of bureaucratic hoops fund requesters have to jump through to get anything approved, and the notoriously slow delivery of the funds, commission officials and staff may have got used to cutting corners and finding "creative" ways to speed up the process. But even though there might be a strong suspicion that the secret accounts were at first intended to serve legitimate purposes, they may have been abused as time went on. While the jury was out on the validity of the conjectures on each side of the argument, some argued that perhaps the most essential problem at the Commission was its lack of a *culture of responsibility*.[8]

It is widely accepted that good MCSs are important. Comparing the books and articles written on management control is difficult, however, because much of the MCS language is imprecise. The term "control" as it applies to a management function does not have a universally accepted definition. An old, narrow view of a MCS is that of a simple *cybernetic* or *regulating* system involving a single feedback loop analogous to a thermostat that measures the temperature, compares the measurement with the desired standard, and, if necessary, takes a corrective action (turn on, or off, a furnace or air conditioner). In a MCS feedback loop, managers measure performance, compare that measurement with a pre-set performance standard, and, if necessary, take corrective actions.[9]

In this book, however, we take a broader view. Many management controls in common use, such as direct supervision, employee selection and retention, and codes of conduct, do not focus on measured performance. They focus instead on encouraging, enabling or, sometimes, forcing employees to act in the organization's best interest. Moreover, some management controls are *proactive* rather than *reactive*. Proactive means that the controls are designed to *prevent* problems before the organization suffers any adverse effects on performance. Examples of proactive controls include planning processes, required expenditure approvals, segregation of duties, and restricted access. Management control, then, includes all the devices or systems managers use to ensure that the behaviors and decisions of their employees are consistent with the organization's objectives and strategies. The systems themselves are commonly referred to as the *management control systems* (MCSs).

Designed properly, MCSs influence employees' behaviors in desirable ways and, consequently, increase the probability that the organization will achieve its goals. Thus, the primary *function* of management control is to influence behaviors in desirable ways. The *benefit* of management control is the increased probability that the organization's objectives will be achieved.

MANAGEMENT AND CONTROL

Management control is the back end of the management process. This can be seen from the various ways in which the broad topic of management is disaggregated.

Management

The literature includes many definitions of management. All relate to the processes of organizing resources and directing activities for the purpose of achieving organizational objectives.

Inevitably, those who study and teach management have broken the broad subject into smaller, more discernable elements. Table 1.1 shows the most prominent classification schemes. The first column identifies the primary management functions of the value chain: product or service development, operations (manufacturing products or performing services), marketing/sales (finding buyers and making sure the products and services fulfill customer needs), and finance (raising money). Virtually every management school offers courses focused on only one, or only part of one, of these primary management functions.

The second column of Table 1.1 identifies the major types of resources with which managers must work: people, money, machines, and information. Management schools also offer courses organized using this classification. These courses are often called human resource management, accounting and finance, production, and information systems, respectively. These are sometimes also referred to as the support management functions.[10]

The term *management control* appears in the third column of Table 1.1, which separates the management functions along a *process* involving objective setting, strategy formulation, and management control. Control, then, is the back end of the management process. The way we use the term management control in this book has the same meaning

TABLE 1.1 Different ways of breaking down the broad area of management into smaller elements

Functions	Resources	Processes
Product (or service) development	People	Objective setting
Operations	Money	Strategy formulation
Marketing/sales	Machines	Management control
Finance	Information	

Source: K. A. Merchant, *Modern Management Control Systems: Text and Cases* (Upper Saddle River, NJ: Prentice Hall, 1998), p. 3.

as the terms *execution* and *strategy implementation*. In most organizations, focusing on improving MCSs will provide higher payoffs than will focusing on improving strategy. A *Fortune* study showed that seven out of ten CEOs who fail do so not because of bad strategy but because of bad execution.[11]

Many management courses, including business policy, strategic management, and management control systems, focus on elements of the management process. To focus on the control function of management, we must distinguish it from objective setting and strategy formulation.

Objective setting

Knowledge of *objectives* is a prerequisite for the design of any MCS and, indeed, for any purposeful activities. Objectives do not have to be quantified and do not have to be financial, although that is how they are commonly thought of in for-profit organizations. A not-for-profit organization's primary objective might be to provide shelter for homeless people, for example. But many for-profit organizations also have nonfinancial objectives, such as related to sustainability or personnel development and wellbeing. In any organization, however, employees must have a basic understanding of what the organization is trying to accomplish. Otherwise no one could claim that any of the employees' actions are purposive, and no one could ever support a claim that the organization was successful.

In most organizations, the objectives are known. That is not to say that all employees always agree unanimously as to how to balance their organizations' responsibilities to all of their stakeholders, including owners (equity holders), debtholders, employees, suppliers, customers, and the society at large). They rarely do.[12] That said, organizations develop explicit or implicit compromise mechanisms to resolve conflicts among stakeholders and reach some level of agreement about the objectives they will pursue. As Jason Luckhurst, managing director of Practicus, a UK-based project-management recruitment firm, argues:

> [To achieve organizational success], it takes a clear vision around which the entire business [can] be designed, [and I] think it is something you should be able to communicate simply to everyone, whether a client or [an employee]. Having a simple and easily understood statement of intent is vital for setting clear objectives and targets.[13]

Strategy formulation

Having set the firm's strategic intentions or objectives, *strategies* then define how organizations should use their resources to meet these objectives. A well-conceived strategy guides employees in successfully pursuing their organizations' objectives; it conveys to employees what they are supposed to be doing. Or, as Mr. Luckhurst at Practicus states: "All the planning in areas as diverse as marketing, branding, financing and training, is designed around [our] objective – as are [our] incentive [systems]. We have a detailed road map, but it starts with a simple vision that everyone can understand and buy into. Everything else we do comes on the back of those goals. In effect, we can reverse-engineer the business to those objectives."[14]

Many organizations develop formal strategies through systematic, often elaborate, planning processes (which we discuss further in Chapter 8). Put differently, they have what can be called an *intended strategy*. However, strategies can sometimes be left largely unspecified. As such, some organizations do not have formal, written strategies; instead they try to respond to opportunities that present themselves. Major elements of these organizations' strategies *emerge* from a series of interactions between management, employees, and the environment; from decisions made spontaneously; and from local experimentation designed to learn what activities lead to the greatest success. Nonetheless, if some decision-making consistency exists, a strategy can be said to have been formed, regardless of whether managers planned or even intended that particular consistency. In that sense, strategic visions sometimes come about through dynamic organizational processes rather than through formalized *strategizing*.[15]

Not even the most elaborate strategic visions and statements are complete to the point where they detail every desired action and contemplate every possible contingency. However, for purposes of designing MCSs, it is useful to have strategies that are as specific and detailed as possible, if those strategies can be kept current. The formal strategic statements make it easier for management both to identify the feasible management control alternatives and to implement them effectively. The management controls can be targeted to the organization's critical success factors, such as developing new products, keeping costs down, or growing market share, rather than aiming more generally at improving profitability in otherwise largely unspecified ways.

Formal strategic statements are not a sufficient condition for success, however. As Adrian Grace, managing director of Bank of Scotland – Corporate, states:

> I have seen businesses with 400-page documents outlining their strategy and it's clear they should have spent less time outlining the vision and more time thinking about how they will deliver on it. You can have the best vision in the world but if you can't put it into effect, you are wasting your time.[16]

It is on the execution side of the management process that MCSs play a critical role. Jason Luckhurst explained:

> The difference between merely having a strategic vision and achieving strategic success is having a detailed understanding of what that vision means for every level of the business – how much funding you need, the branding and marketing strategy, which channels you will develop, how many people you need in which areas and when and what the organizational structure will be. It is also important to revisit the vision often and be aware of how close you are to achieving it at any given stage. This helps everyone in the company to stay focused.[17]

Management control versus strategic control

In the broadest sense, control systems can be viewed as having two basic functions: strategic control and management control. *Strategic control* involves managers addressing the question: Is our strategy valid? Or, more appropriately in changing environments, they ask: Is our strategy still valid, and if not, how should it be changed? All firms must be concerned with strategic control issues, but the concern that a strategy may have become obsolete is obviously greater in firms operating in more dynamic environments.[18] That said, strategic options sometimes may be limited. For example, When Archie Norman, the new executive chairman of ITV, a major television concern, laid out his vision for the company in March 2010 in a thoroughly businesslike presentation, he told analysts that he saw a future where ITV was freed from burdensome regulation, made more money from its online activities and, most importantly, improved the quality of programs. However, one analyst reacted to it by stating: "It's true, but it is the same strategy that Michael [Grade, his predecessor] laid out some years ago. The key is execution." Another analyst added: "The headlines are not all that different, but that is because there is not much else you can do."[19]

Management control focuses on execution, and it involves addressing the general question: Are our employees likely to behave appropriately? This question can be decomposed into several parts. First, do our employees understand what we expect of them? Second, will they work consistently hard and try to do what is expected of them; that is, will they pursue the organization's objectives in line with the strategy? Third, are they capable of doing a good job? Finally, if the answer to any of these questions is negative, what can be done to solve the management control problems? All organizations who must rely on their employees to accomplish organizational objectives must deal with these basic management control issues.

The tools for addressing strategic and management control issues are quite different. Managers addressing *strategic control* issues have a focus primarily external to the organization; they examine the industry and their organization's place in it. They contemplate how the organization, with its particular combination of strengths, weaknesses, opportunities, and threats, can compete with the other firms in its industry. Managers addressing *management control* issues, on the other hand, have primarily an internal focus; they reflect how they can influence employees' behaviors in desired ways.

From a management control perspective, strategies should be viewed as useful but not absolutely necessary to the proper design of MCSs. When strategies are formulated more clearly, more control alternatives become feasible, and it becomes easier to implement each form of management control effectively. Managers can, however, design and operate some types of MCSs without having a clear strategy in mind. As Adrian Grace, managing director of Bank of Scotland – Corporate, proffers: "If you don't have [a strategy] but you know how to deliver, you might still make it. Success in business is 25% strategy but 75% execution."[20] Or, the other way around, to devise a strategy and write it down is one thing; it is another thing entirely to make the plan work in practice.[21] That said, there is some evidence that organizations with formal systems for managing the execution of strategy outperform those that do not.[22]

Behavioral emphasis

Management control involves managers taking steps to help ensure that the employees do what is best for the organization. This is an important purpose because it is people in the organization who make things happen. Management controls are necessary to guard against the possibilities that people will do something the organization does not want them to do, or fail to do something they should do. For example, aiming to achieve greater cost control is open to question without reference to people because costs do not control themselves; people control them. As many examples throughout the book will illustrate, employees can work against, or around, systems, thereby leaving many objectives to remain unmet or to have unintended consequences.

This behavioral orientation has long been recognized by practitioners. For example, when Bill McElroy, finance director and board member of the Toyota Motor Corporation of Australia, was asked what he would study if given the opportunity for some formal learning, he replied:

> I would like to know more about psychology – in terms of why people are the way they are and why they behave the way they behave. If I had studied this in my university days, I think I would have gained significant benefits all the way through my career.[23]

If all employees could always be relied on to do what is best for the organization, there would be no need for an MCS. But employees are sometimes unable or unwilling to act in the organization's best interest, so managers must take steps to guard against the occurrence, and particularly the persistence, of undesirable behaviors and to encourage desirable behaviors.

CAUSES OF MANAGEMENT CONTROL PROBLEMS

Given the behavioral focus of controls, the next logical question to ask is: What is it about the employees on whom the organization must rely that creates the need to implement MCSs? The causes of the needs for control can be classified into three main categories: lack of direction, motivational problems, and personal limitations.

Lack of direction

Some employees perform inadequately simply because they do not know what the organization wants from them. When this *lack of direction* occurs, the likelihood of the desired behaviors occurring will be haphazard. Thus, one function of management control involves informing employees as to how they can direct their contributions to the fulfillment of organizational objectives.

Lack of direction is not a trivial issue in many organizations. For example, survey evidence collected in 2005 by KPMG from approximately 4,000 US employees spanning all levels of job responsibility across a wide range of industries and organizational sizes revealed that 55% of the sample respondents had a lack of understanding of the standards that applied to their jobs.[24] Moreover, a 2004 study of 414 World-at-Work members in mostly managerial positions at large North-American companies suggested that 81% of the respondents believe that senior managers in their organizations understand the value drivers of their business strategy; 46% say that middle management understands these drivers; but just 13% believe nonmanagement employees understand them. This indicates that organizational goals are not cascading down to all levels in the organization. And, while 79% of the respondents in this study believed that their employees' goals are aligned with organizational goals, 44% also stated that employees set goals based on their own views rather than direction from leadership.[25]

Motivational problems

Even when employees understand what is expected of them, some do not perform as the organization expects because of *motivational problems*. Motivational problems are common because individual and organizational objectives do not naturally coincide – individuals are self-interested.[26]

Employees sometimes act in their own personal interest at the expense of their organization's interest. Frederick Taylor, one of the major figures in the *scientific management* movement that took place in the early twentieth century wrote: "Hardly a competent worker can be found who does not devote a considerable amount of time to studying just how slowly he can work and still convince his employer that he is going at a good pace."[27] Such *effort aversion* and *other self-interested behaviors* are still a problem today, and recently likely to be even growing. Gary Gill, the author of KPMG's most recent Fraud Barometer for Australia published in 2010, believes that broad economic conditions have a significant effect on fraud levels: "It goes up following a boom period. People want to maintain their standard of living, even if it means criminal activity."[28] Another survey suggests that fraud is on the increase in the UK's public sector as austerity programs imply personnel reductions and fewer resources being spent on internal controls, according to a report from PricewaterhouseCoopers.[29]

Overall, survey evidence suggests that wasting, mismanaging, and misappropriating organizational resources, among other types of employee misconduct, are prevalent in most organizations.[30] Even ostensibly inconsequential forms of wasting time on the job can have high costs. Surfing the Internet while on the job, for example, was estimated in 2001 to have cost US employers $63 billion per year.[31] The advent of social network technologies, such as Facebook, is likely to have increased these costs. All told, survey participants in the most recent report by the Association of Certified Fraud Examiners estimated that the typical organization loses 5% of its annual revenue to fraud. Applied to the estimated 2009 Gross World Product, this figure translates to a potential global fraud loss of more than $2.9 trillion.[32] Staggering as these statistics may be, they suggest that it should not be taken for granted that employees will always, and automatically, act with the best interest of their organizations in mind, and that because of this issue, the costs to organizations, whether explicit or implicit, are nontrivial.

Indeed, the most serious forms of employees' misdirected behaviors, such as fraud, can have severe impacts, including deteriorated employee morale, impaired business relations, lost revenues from damaged reputations, investments in improving control procedures, legal fees and settlements of litigation, fines and penalties to regulatory agencies, and losses from plummeting stock prices.[33] While some of these impacts may seem far-fetched, they are not. Nearly two-thirds of the executives polled in the most recent KPMG Fraud Survey reported that fraud and misconduct pose a significant risk for their business, with 71% of them having the greatest concern for the potential loss of public trust at a time when market confidence is at a premium.[34]

These huge fraud costs can be traced back to human weaknesses (and, as we will see later in this book, to the lack of effective MCSs). Anecdotal assertions abound. For example, one manager claimed that "every single person in your [business] is trying to steal from you."[35] Another manager's estimate was more conservative, but still, it suggests that:

> Between 10 and 20% of a company's employees will steal anything that isn't nailed down. Another 20% will never steal; they would say it is morally wrong. The vast majority of people are situationally honest; they won't steal if there are proper controls.[36]

These estimates are consistent with research findings and the surveys of practice.[37] A special form of "stealing" occurs when employees manipulate their performance reports, either by falsifying the data or by taking decisions that artificially boost performance, with the intention of earning higher, but undeserved, incentive pay. The surveys of practice invariably show that financial reporting fraud has the highest cost per incident (with cost estimates varying from anywhere between $10 and $100 million in some studies to as high as $250 million per incident in other studies), even though it occurs relatively infrequently.[38] MCSs are obviously needed to protect organizations against these behaviors.

Employees, particularly managers, are also prone to make decisions that serve their interests, but not those of their organization. They tend to overspend on things that make their lives more pleasant, such as on office accoutrements and other perks. They often engage in *gamesmanship* such as "earnings management" to make their performance reports look good even when they know that the actions they are taking have no economic value to the company and, in some cases, are actually harmful. And they sometimes tend to be excessively risk averse and reluctant to make even good investments because of fear that if the investments do not pay off, they may lose their job. We discuss these and related problems in detail in Chapter 5 and in the chapters in Section IV of this book.

But in addition to focusing on how MCSs can be used to avoid or mitigate these *negative* or *dysfunctional* behaviors, this book's emphasis is also, even primarily, on how MCSs can be employed to motivate *positive* or *productive* behaviors; that is, how they can encourage employees to work consistently hard to accomplish organizational objectives. The role of MCSs in *motivating* employees to perform to their best abilities involves, among other subjects, the study of *incentives* (Chapter 9) in a *results control context*, which we introduce in Chapter 2.

Personal limitations

The final behavioral problem that MCSs must address occurs where employees who know what is expected of them, and who may be highly motivated to perform well, are simply unable to perform well because of any of a number of other limitations. Some of these limitations are person-specific. They may be caused by a lack of aptitude, training, experience, stamina, or knowledge for the tasks at hand. An example is the too-common situation where employees are promoted above their level of competence. When employees are "over their heads," problems are nearly inevitable. Sometimes jobs just are not designed properly, causing even the most physically fit and apt employees to get tired or stressed leading to on-the-job accidents and decision errors.

Regarding lack of training, for example, Illinois-based Ace Hardware was forced to restate its earnings for fiscal years 2004, 2005, and 2006, and correct its numbers for fiscal 2007, because of a $152 million accounting error made by a poorly trained employee, who incorrectly entered accounts in ledgers in the Finance department at company's headquarters. Ace CEO Ray Griffith stated: "We are embarrassed by it. We did not provide the training, oversight or checks and balances to help that person do [the] job."[39]

Moreover, psychology-based research suggests that all individuals, even intelligent, well-trained, and experienced ones, face limitations in their abilities to perceive new problems, to remember important facts, and to process information properly. For example, in looking to the future, it has been shown that people tend to overestimate the likelihood of common events and events that have occurred relatively recently (both of which are easier to remember) as compared with relatively rare events and those that have not occurred recently. Sometimes training can be used to reduce the severity of these limitations, but in most situations multiple biases and limitations remain. These limitations are a problem because they reduce the probability that employees will make the correct decisions or that they will correctly assess the problems about which decisions should be made. Researchers are just beginning to explore the management control implications of these limitations.[40]

These three management control problems – lack of direction, motivational problems, and personal limitations – can obviously occur simultaneously and in any combination. However, all that is required to call for the necessity of effective MCSs, is that at least one of these problems occurs, which will almost inevitably be the case in complex organizations as the above arguments and examples have suggested.

CHARACTERISTICS OF GOOD MANAGEMENT CONTROL

To have a high probability of success, organizations must therefore maintain good management control. *Good control* means that management can be reasonably confident that no major unpleasant surprises will occur. The label *out of control* is used to describe a situation where there is a high probability of poor performance, either overall or in a specific performance area, despite having a sound strategy in place.

However, even *good* management control still allows for some probability of failure because *perfect control* does not exist except perhaps in very unusual circumstances. Perfect control would require complete assurance that all control systems are foolproof and all individuals on whom the organization must rely always act in the best way possible. Perfect control is obviously not a realistic expectation because it is virtually impossible to install MCSs so well designed that they guarantee good behaviors. Furthermore, because MCSs are costly, it is rarely, if ever, cost effective to try to implement *enough* controls even to approach the idealized perfect control.

The cost of not having a perfect control system can be called a *control loss*. It is the difference between the performance that is theoretically possible given the strategy selected and the performance that can be reasonably expected with the MCSs in place. More or better MCSs should be implemented only if the benefits by which they would reduce the control loss exceed the costs. *Optimal control* can be said to have been achieved if the control losses are expected to be smaller than the cost of implementing more controls. Because of control costs, perfect control is rarely the optimal outcome; what is optimal is control that is good enough at a reasonable cost. The benchmark therefore is adequate control rather than perfect control.

Assessing whether good control has been achieved must be future-oriented and objectives-driven. It must be *future-oriented* because the goal is to have no unpleasant surprises in the future; the past is not relevant except as a guide to the future, such as in terms of experiences or lessons learned from control failures. It must be *objectives-driven* because the objectives represent what the organization seeks to attain. Nonetheless, assessing whether good control has been achieved is difficult and subjective. It is difficult because the adequacy of management control must be measured against a future that is inevitably difficult to predict, as are predictions of possible unintended consequences of the controls. Good control also is not established over an activity or entity with multiple objectives unless performance on *all* significant dimensions has been considered. As difficult as this assessment of management control is, however, it should be done because organizational success depends on a good MCS.

As the examples at the beginning of this chapter illustrate, organizations that fail to implement adequate MCSs can suffer loss or impairment of assets, deficient revenues, excessive costs, inaccurate records, or reports that can lead to poor decisions, legal sanctions, or business disruptions. At the extreme, organizations that do not control performance on one or more critical dimensions can fail.

CONTROL PROBLEM AVOIDANCE

Implementing some combination of the behavior-influencing devices commonly known as MCSs is not always the best way to achieve good control; sometimes the problems can be avoided. *Avoidance* means eliminating the possibility that the control problems will occur. Organizations can never avoid all their control problems, but they can often avoid some of them by limiting exposure to certain types of problems and problem sources, or by reducing the maximum potential loss if the problems occur. Four prominent avoidance strategies are activity elimination, automation, centralization, and risk sharing.

Activity elimination

Managers can sometimes avoid the control problems associated with a particular entity or activity by turning over the potential risks, and the associated profits, to a third party through such mechanisms as subcontracts, licensing agreements, or divestment. This form of avoidance is called *activity elimination*.

Managers who are not able to control certain activities, perhaps because they do not have the required resources, because they do not have a good understanding of the required processes, or because they face legal or structural limitations, are those most likely to eliminate activities. For example, in July 2010, after 28 years of joint administration, BP, the UK giant oil company, handed over the operation of the Cupiagua field in Colombia to its partner, state-controlled oil firm Ecopetrol. BP had operated the field and had a 31% stake in the venture, while Ecopetrol had 50%, and French Total held the remaining 19%. BP did so as part of a plan to sell assets to cover the huge costs related to the company's deep-sea oil leak in the Gulf of Mexico, to raise cash to cover its liabilities but also to refocus its business following the disaster.[41]

When managers do not wish to avoid completely an area that they cannot control well, they are wise at least to limit their investments, and hence (some of) their risks, in that area. An example is cloud computing, which means that companies obtain computing resources (processing, storage, messaging, databases, and so on) from outside, and paying only for what they use, rather than developing their own computing infrastructure and running their own systems. With the increase in demand for servers to store and process data, many companies would need to multiply their server capacity manyfold, for which they some-times have neither the money nor the skills, or the interest, because doing so falls outside most companies' core competencies. By using cloud computing services, firms can leave all that to be managed by those who have the competencies, and, hence, can provide the essential control over the process. Whereas this does not eliminate all risks, it partially avoids some control problems related to data management and all that it entails.[42]

The economics-based literature that focuses on whether specific activities (transactions) can be controlled more effectively through *markets* or through organizational *hierarchies* is known as *transaction cost economics*. A detailed examination of the theories and evidence in this field of study is outside the scope of this book.[43] We just note that the fact that all organizations of any size struggle with management control issues is testament to the limitations of arms-length, market-based transactions with entities external to the firm to solve all control problems satisfactorily. As such, organizations will always have to rely on MCSs, which have been found to be effective in a broad range of settings. The worldwide growth and success of large diversified organizations has depended to a large extent on good MCSs.

Automation

Automation is a second avoidance possibility. Managers can sometimes use computers, robots, expert systems, and other means of automation to reduce their organization's exposure to some control problems. These automated devices can be set to behave appro-priately, and, when they are operating properly, they usually perform more consistently than do humans. Computers eliminate the human problems of inaccuracy, inconsistency, and lack of motivation. Once programmed, computers are consistent in their treatments of transactions, and they never have dishonest or disloyal motivations.

As technology has advanced, organizations have substituted machines and expert systems for people who have been performing quite complex actions and making sophisticated judgments and decisions. In hospitals, artificial intelligence systems are able to perform many of the tasks doctors and nurses previously had to perform. These systems monitor the patients' conditions and trends and alert the medical staff of possible problems; they assist in making diagnoses; they order the needed drugs; and they check for potential drug interactions and allergic reactions.[44] These systems allow hospitals to avoid one of the behavioral problems – the personal limitations of the medical staff. In the vast majority of situations, these systems are more likely than are medical personnel to recall all the details of every condition, medication, and possible complications to initiate the proper response. The system makes it more likely that no major, unpleasant surprises will occur; in this case, avoidable medical errors.

Similarly, many legal tasks, although sometimes quite complex, are variations on a theme, where the production of certain types of legal documents, such as a trademark registration or a lease, does not differ vastly from one instance to another. Legal firms are therefore increasingly using what is called *document assembly software*, allowing them to reduce the time needed to create these documents to a fraction of the time that an employee would require and, possibly, do it more consistently and accurately. Moreover, automating these onerous processes reduces costs and allows lawyers to spend more time dealing with their clients.[45]

In most managerial situations, however, automation can provide only a partial control solution at best. One limitation is *feasibility*. Humans have many talents – particularly those involving complex, intuitive judgments – that no machines or decision models have been able to duplicate. A second limitation is *cost*. Automation often requires major invest-ments that may be justifiable only if improvements in productivity, as well as in control, are forthcoming.[46] Finally, automation may just replace some control problems with others. Computer automation often increases control risks. The elimination of source documents can obscure the audit trail; the concentration of information in one location can increase security risks; and placing greater reliance on computer programs can expose the company to the risks of programmer errors or fraud.

Centralization

Centralization of decision-making is a third avoidance possibility, which is a key element of almost all organizations' MCSs. High degrees of centralization, where all the key decisions are made at top management levels, are common in small businesses, particu-larly when they are run by the founder or owner. High degrees of centralization also exist in some large businesses whose top managers sometimes have reputations for being "detail oriented" or "control freaks". When that is the case, top management reserves the important, and sometimes the not-so-important, decisions for themselves, and in so doing, they avoid having the lower-level employees make poor judgments.

Centralization inevitably exists to some extent in all organizations, as well as at all levels of management within organizations, as managers tend to reserve for themselves many of the most critical decisions that fall within their authority. Common candidates for centralization are decisions regarding major acquisitions and divestments, major capital expenditures, negotiation of pivotal sales contracts, organization changes, and hiring and firing of key personnel. However, in most organizations of even minimal size, it is not possible to centralize all critical decisions, and other control solutions are necessary. As we will see, results controls play a critical role when decisions are decentralized. When decisions are decentralized, results controls need to be in place to hold the managers who enjoy the decision authority accountable for the results of their decisions. Accountability for results is what makes delegated authority legitimate. We discuss this in depth in Chapter 2.

Risk sharing

A final, partial avoidance possibility is risk sharing. Sharing risks with outside entities can bound the losses that could be incurred by inappropriate employee behaviors. Risk sharing can involve buying *insurance* to protect against certain types of potentially large losses the organization might not be able to afford. Many companies purchase fidelity bonds on employees in sensitive positions (such as bank tellers) to reduce the firm's exposure. These insurance contracts pass at least a portion of the risk of large losses and errors to the insurance providers. Another way to share risks with an outside party is to enter into a *joint venture* agreement. This shares the risk with the joint venture partner.

These avoidance alternatives are often an effective partial solution to, or bounding of, many of the control problems managers face. It is rarely possible to avoid all risks because firms are rewarded for bearing risk, but most firms use some forms of elimination, automation, centralization, and risk sharing in order to limit their exposure to the management control problems.

CONTROL ALTERNATIVES

For the control problems that cannot be avoided, and those for which decisions have been made not to avoid, managers must implement one or more control mechanisms that are generally called *management controls*. The collection of control mechanisms that are used is generally referred to as a management control system (MCS), which were discussed earlier.

MCSs vary considerably among organizations and among entities or decision areas of any single organization. Figures 1.1 and 1.2 show some of the controls used in a manufacturing firm and a computer facility, respectively. The MCSs of some organizations consist primarily of trying to hire people who can be relied upon to serve the organization well. Other organizations provide modest performance-based incentives, and still others offer incentives that are highly leveraged. Some organizations base incentives on the accomplishment of targets defined in terms of accounting numbers, others use nonfinancial measures of performance, and still others evaluate performance only subjectively. Some organizations have elaborate sets of policies and procedures that they expect employees to follow, whereas others have no such procedures or they allow the procedures that were once in place to get out of date. Some organizations make extensive use of a large professional internal audit staff, while others only ensure to be in minimal compliance with regulatory requirements in this regard. These are just examples. The distinctions that can be made among the MCSs in use are numerous.

Figure 1.1 Examples of controls used in a manufacturing firm

1. The cash payment and cash receipt functions are segregated.
2. A check protector is used, and signature plates are kept under lock and key.
3. The accounting department matches invoices to receiving reports or special authorizations prior to payment.
4. Checks are mailed by someone other than the person making out the check.
5. The accounting department matches invoices to copies of purchase orders.
6. The blank stock of checks is kept under lock and key.
7. Imprest accounting is used for payroll.
8. Bank reconciliations are to be accomplished by someone other than the one who writes checks and handles cash.
9. Surprise counts of cash funds are conducted periodically.
10. Orders can be placed with approved vendors only.
11. All purchases must be made by the purchasing department.

Source: K. A. Merchant, *Modern Management Control Systems: Text and Cases* (Upper Saddle River, NJ: Prentice Hall, 1998), p. 13.

FIGURE 1.2 Examples of controls used in a computer facility

1. Written standards exist for documentation of systems, operations, and administration.

2. Access to the computer system and all online data terminals is restricted at all times to authorized personnel only.

3. Data are secured through tape file protection rings, file labels, cryptographic protection, duplication procedures, and requirement of storage of duplicates at a remote site.

4. Hardware controls include duplicate circuitry, dual reading, echo checks, preventive maintenance, and uninterruptible power systems.

5. Major risks are insured against.

6. Backup systems and procedures are developed.

Source: K. A. Merchant, *Modern Management Control Systems: Text and Cases* (Upper Saddle River, NJ: Prentice Hall, 1998), p. 14.

Managers' control choices are not random. They are based on many factors. Some controls are not effective, or are not cost-effective, in certain situations. Some types of controls are better at addressing particular types of problems, and different organizations and different areas within each organization often face quite different mixes of control problems. Some types of controls have some undesirable side effects that can be particularly damaging in some settings. And some controls merely suit particular management styles better than others. A major purpose of this book is to describe the factors affecting management control choice decisions and the effects on the employees and the organization when different choices are made.

OUTLINE OF THIS BOOK

The book discusses MCSs from several different angles, each the focus of one major section of the book. Section II distinguishes controls based on the *object of control*, which can focus on the results produced (*results control*), the actions taken (*action control*), or the types of people employed and their shared norms and values (*personnel and cultural control*).[47] Chapters 2–6 in Section II discuss each of these forms of control, the outcomes they produce (which can be both positive and negative), and the factors that lead managers to choose one object of control over another.

Section III focuses on the major elements of *financial results control systems*, an important type of results control in which results are defined in financial terms. This section includes discussions of financial responsibility structures (Chapter 7), planning and budgeting systems (Chapter 8), and incentive systems (Chapter 9).

Section IV discusses some major problems managers face when they use financial results control systems and, particularly, the performance measurements that drive them. These problems include the tendency of accounting measures to cause managers to be excessively short-term oriented (myopic), the tendency for return-on-investment measures of performance to cause bad investment and performance evaluation decisions, and the likelihood of negative behavioral reactions from managers who are held accountable for factors over which they have less than complete control. Throughout Chapters 10, 11, and 12, we also discuss several approaches organizations can rely on to mitigate these problems.

Section V of the book discusses some key organizational control roles, including those of controllers, auditors, and audit committees of the board of directors. It also discusses recent developments in corporate governance, as well as common control-related ethical issues and how to analyze them.

The final section of the book, Section VI, discusses some of the contextual factors that have significant effects on either the choices of MCSs or their effectiveness in specific settings. Chapter 16 discusses the effects of three of the most important factors that cause control systems to be different: environmental uncertainty, organizational strategy, and multinationality. Chapter 17 focuses on some control problems unique to not-for-profit organizations.

Notes

1. "All His Fault: A Harsh Sentence for Jérôme Kerviel," *The Economist* (October 7, 2010), p. 110.
2. Ibid.
3. "Seymour Pierce Fined over Staff Fraud," *The Times* (October 8, 2009), online (www.thetimes.co.uk).
4. "US-wide Probe into Home Repossessions," *BBC* (October 13, 2010), online (www.bbc.co.uk/news).
5. "Diamond Group Widens Probe of Bribe Charges," *The Wall Street Journal* (March 8, 2006), p. B1.
6. "Two Accused of INS Shredding Spree," *The Los Angeles Times* (January 31, 2003), p. B5.
7. "Westpac Worker Fears Axe over Multi-million Dollar Error," *The New Zealand Herald* (July 19, 2009), online (www.nzherald.co.nz).
8. "The Road to Perdition: Are the EU's Financial Controls so Exasperating that They Force its Own Staff to Evade Them?," *The Economist* (July 24, 2003), p. 39.
9. For a recent academic article on the various concepts of management control, see T. Malmi and D. A. Brown, "Management Control Systems as a Package – Opportunities, Challenges and Research Directions," *Management Accounting Research*, 19, no. 4 (December 2008), pp. 287–300.
10. See, for example, M. E. Porter, *Competitive Advantage: Creating and Sustaining Superior Performance* (New York: The Free Press, 1985), Chapter 2.
11. "Why CEOs Fail," *Fortune* (June 21, 1999), online (www.businessbuilders.bz/why-ceos-fail.pdf).
12. "Shareholders vs. Stakeholders: A New Idolatry," *The Economist* (April 24, 2010), pp. 65–66. See also R. E. Freeman, *Strategic Management: A Stakeholder Approach* (Cambridge University Press, 2010).
13. "Keep Sight of Your Vision," *The Sunday Times* (March 23, 2008), online (www.business.timesonline.co.uk).
14. Ibid.
15. A seminal framework for "strategy analysis" is that by M. E. Porter, *Competitive Strategy: Techniques for Analyzing Industries and Competitors* (New York: The Free Press, 1980). A seminal contributor to the "emergent strategy" view is H. Mintzberg, "Crafting Strategy," *Harvard Business Review*, 65, no. 4 (July–August 1987), pp. 66–75. For a recent edition of a textbook on strategic management, see R. M. Grant, *Contemporary Strategy Analysis*, 7th edn. (Wiley, 2010).
16. "Keep Sight of Your Vision," op. cit.
17. Ibid.
18. For an early, seminal article on strategic control, see G. Schreyögg and H. Steinmann, "Strategic Control: A New Perspective," *Academy of Management Review*, 12, no. 1 (1987). For a recent article, and a perspective on the links between strategic and management control, see P. van Veen-Dirks and M. Wijn, "Strategic Control: Meshing Critical Success Factors with the Balanced Scorecard," *Long Range Planning*, 35, no. 4 (August 2002), pp. 407–427.
19. "Strategy Execution Key in World of Limited Options," *The Financial Times* (March 4, 2010), online (www.ft.com).
20. "Keep Sight of Your Vision," op. cit.
21. "Missing Link between Thinking and Doing," *The Financial Times* (August 28, 2010), online (www.ft.com).
22. R. S. Kaplan and D. P. Norton, *Execution Premium* (Boston, MA: Harvard Business School Press, 2008).
23. W. Birkett, "The Changing Role of the CFO: An Interview with Bill McElroy," *A View of Tomorrow: The Senior Financial Officer in the Year 2005* (New York: International Federation of Accountants, 1995).
24. *KPMG 2005/2006 Integrity Survey* (KPMG LLP, 2005).
25. World-at-Work, Sibson, and Synygy, *The State of Performance Management* (Survey Report, August 2004); and J. Kochanski and A. Sorensen, "Managing Performance Management," *Workspan* (September 2005), pp. 21–26.
26. Many management accounting and management control textbooks refer to lack of *goal congruence* as a general problem category which subsumes both lack of direction and lack of motivation.
27. F. Taylor, *The Principles of Scientific Management* (New York: Harper, 1929).
28. "Employee Fraud is a Growing Problem, Survey Shows," *The Australian* (June 25, 2010), online (www.theaustralian.com.au).
29. "PWC Survey Shows Rise in Fraud by Public-sector Staff," *The Independent* (July 4, 2010), online (www.independent.co.uk).
30. *KPMG 2005/2006 Integrity Survey*, op. cit.
31. S. Pruitt, "Are Employees Wasting Time Online?" *PCWorld.Com* (August 2, 2001).
32. *Association of Certified Fraud Examiners – 2010 Report to the Nations* (ACFE, 2010).
33. *PricewaterhouseCoopers 2005 Global Economic Crime Survey* (PricewaterhouseCoopers LLP, 2005).

34. *KPMG 2008/2009 Fraud Survey* (KPMG LLP, 2010).

35. "Thou Better Not Steal," *Forbes* (November 7, 1994), p. 170.

36. "Crime is Headed Up – And so is Business," *Boston Globe* (February 15, 1983), p. 47.

37. *KPMG 2005/2006 Integrity Survey*, op. cit.; *PricewaterhouseCoopers 2005 Global Economic Crime Survey*, op. cit.; *KPMG 2008/2009 Fraud Survey*, op. cit.

38. Ibid.

39. "Ace Employee Makes $152 Million Error," *CFO.com* (January 14, 2008), online (www.cfo.com).

40. See, for example, M. H. Bazerman, *Judgment in Managerial Decision Making*, 6th edn. (New York: John Wiley & Sons, 2005); S. L. Schneider, *Emerging Perspectives on Judgment and Decision Research* (Cambridge Series on Judgment and Decision Making, Cambridge University Press, 2003); and R. H. Ashton and A. H. Ashton, *Judgment and Decision-Making Research in Accounting and Auditing* (Cambridge Series on Judgment and Decision Making, Cambridge University Press, 1995).

41. "BP Hands Over Colombia's Cupiagua Oil Field to Ecopetrol," *The Wall Street Journal* (July 1, 2010), online (http://online.wsj.com).

42. "Cloud Computing: So You Don't Have to Stand Still," *The New York Times* (May 25, 2008), online (www.nytimes.com).

43. Oliver Williamson is generally recognized as the most prominent theoretical contributor in the area of transaction cost economics, and went on to win the Nobel Prize in Economics for it in 2009. For a layman's overview of some of the key ideas behind his seminal contributions, see "Reality Bites," *The Economist* (October 15, 2009), p. 92.

44. "Take Two Aspirin; the Computer Will Call in the Morning," *Forbes* (March 14, 1994), pp. 110–11.

45. "Curbing those Long, Lucrative Hours," *The Economist* (July 22, 2010), p. 66.

46. See, for example, "Hospital Heeds Doctors; Suspends Use of Software," *The Los Angeles Times* (January 22, 2003), p. B1.

47. This framework was discussed by W. Ouchi, "A Conceptual Framework for the Design of Organizational Control Mechanisms," *Management Science*, 25, no. 9 (September 1979), pp. 833–48. It was elaborated by K. A. Merchant, *Control in Business Organizations* (Cambridge, MA: Ballinger, 1985). Section II of this book presents a refined and expanded discussion of this framework.

Case Study

Leo's Four-Plex Theater

Leo's Four-Plex Theater was a single-location, four-screen theater located in a small town in west Texas. Leo Antonelli bought the theater a year ago and hired Bill Reilly, his nephew, to manage it. Leo was concerned, however, because the theater was not as profitable as he had thought it would be. He suspected the theater had some control problems and asked Park Cockerill, an accounting professor at a college in the adjacent town, to study the situation and provide suggestions.

Park found the following:

1. Customers purchased their tickets at one of two ticket booths located at the front of the theater. The theater used general admission (not assigned) seating. The tickets were color coded to indicate which movie the customer wanted to see. The tickets were also dated and stamped "good on day of sale only." The tickets at each price (adult, child, matinee, evening) were prenumbered serially, so that the number of tickets sold each day at each price for each movie could be determined by subtracting the number of the first ticket sold from the ending number.

2. The amounts of cash collected were counted daily and compared with the total value of tickets sold. The cash counts revealed, almost invariably, less cash than the amounts that should have been collected. The discrepancies were usually small, less than $10 per cashier. However, on one day two weeks before Park's study, one cashier was short by almost $100. ▶

This case was prepared by Professor Kenneth A. Merchant.

3. Just inside the theater's front doors was a lobby with a refreshment stand. Park observed the refreshment stand's operations for a while. He noted that most of the stand's attendants were young, probably of high school or college age. They seemed to know many of the customers, a majority of whom were of similar ages, which was not surprising given the theater's small-town location. But the familiarity concerned Park because he had also observed several occasions where the stand's attendants either failed to collect cash from the customers or failed to ring up the sale on the cash register.

4. Customers entered the screening rooms by passing through a turnstile manned by an attendant who separated the ticket and placed part of it in a locked "stub box." Test counts of customers entering and leaving the theater did not reconcile either with the number of ticket sales or the stub counts.

Park found evidence of two specific problems. First, he found a few tickets of the wrong color or with the wrong dates in the ticket stub boxes. And second, he found a sometimes significant number of free theater passes with Bill Reilly's signature on them. These problems did not account for all of the customer test count discrepancies, however. Park suspected that the ticket collectors might also be admitting friends who had not purchased tickets, although his observations provided no direct evidence of this.

When his study was complete, Park sat down and wondered whether he could give Leo suggestions that would address all the actual and potential problems, yet not be too costly.

Case Study

Wong's Pharmacy

Thomas Wong was the owner/manager of Wong's Pharmacy, a small, single-location drugstore. The store was founded by Thomas's father, and it had operated in the same location for 30 years. All of the employees who worked in the store were family members. All were hard workers, and Thomas had the utmost trust in all of them.

Although the store thrived in its early years, performance in the last few years had not been good. Sales and profits were declining, and the problem was getting worse. The performance problems seemed to have begun approximately at the time when a large drugstore chain opened a branch two blocks away.

This case was prepared by Professor Kenneth A. Merchant.

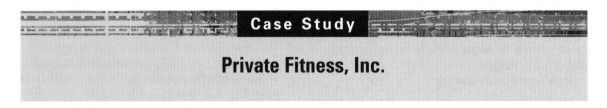

Case Study

Private Fitness, Inc.

"I don't know how much money I might have lost because of Kate. She is a long-time friend whom I thought I could trust, but I guess that trust was misplaced. Now I've got to decide whether or not to fire her. And then I've got to figure out a way to make my business work effectively without my having to step in and do everything myself."

This case was prepared by Professor Kenneth A. Merchant.

Rosemary Worth was talking about the consequences of a theft that had recently occurred at the business she owned, Private Fitness, Inc. Private Fitness was a small health club located in Rancho Palos Verdes, California, an upscale community located in the Los Angeles area. The club offered personal fitness training and fitness classes of various types, including aerobics, spinning, body sculpting, air boxing, kickboxing, hip hop, step and pump, dynamic stretch, pilates, and yoga. Personal training clients paid $50 per hour for their instructor and use of the club during prime time. During slower times (between 9:00 a.m. and 4:00 p.m.) the price was $35 per hour. The price per student for each hour-long fitness class was $12. Some quantity discounts were offered to clients who prepaid. Unlike the large health clubs, Private Fitness did not offer memberships for open access to fitness equipment and classes.

Prior to starting Private Fitness Rosemary had been working as an aerobics instructor and fitness model. She had won many local fitness competitions and was a former finalist in the Ms. Fitness USA competition. She wanted to go into business for herself to increase her standard of living by capitalizing on her reputation and knowledge in the growing fitness field and to have more time to spend with her two young children. Private Fitness had been operating for six months.

To open the club, Rosemary had to use almost all of her personal savings, plus she had to take out a bank loan. The building Rosemary rented, located in a convenient strip mall with ample parking, had formerly been operated as a fresh food market. Rosemary spent about $150,000 to renovate the facility and to buy the necessary fitness equipment. The club was comprised of five areas: an exercise room, a room containing aerobic equipment (e.g. treadmills, stair climbers, stationary bicycles, cross-country ski machines), a room containing weight machines and free weights, men's and ladies' locker rooms, and an office.

Rosemary contracted with five instructors she knew to run the classes and training sessions. The instructors were all capable of running personal training sessions, but they each tended to specialize in teaching one or two types of fitness class. Rosemary herself ran most of the spinning classes and some of the aerobics classes. The instructors were paid on commission. The commission, which ranged between 20% and 50% of revenue, varied depending on the instructor's experience and on whether the instructor brought the particular client to Private Fitness.

As manager of the business, Rosemary hired Kate Hoffman, one of the instructors and a long-time friend. Kate's primary tasks included marketing, facility up-keep, scheduling of appointments, and record keeping. Kate was paid a salary plus a commission based on gross revenues. During normal business hours when Kate was teaching a class one of the other instructors, or sometimes a part-time clerical employee, was asked to staff the front desk in return for an hourly wage. Private Fitness was open from 5:30 a.m.–9:00 p.m., Monday through Friday. It was also open from 6:00 a.m.–noon on Saturday and noon–3:00 p.m. on Sunday.

Rosemary was still in the process of building the volume necessary to operate at a profit. Typically one or two private fitness clients were in the facility during the prime early morning and early evening hours. A few clients came in at other times. Classes were scheduled throughout the times the club was open. Some of these classes were quite popular, but many of them had only one or two students, and some classes were cancelled for lack of any clients. However, Kate's marketing efforts were proving effective. The number of clients was growing, and Rosemary hoped that by the end of the year the business would be earning a profit.

As the quote cited above indicates, however, Rosemary gradually realized that Kate Hoffman was stealing from the club. On one occasion when Rosemary came to the club she noticed $60 in the cash drawer, but she noticed when she was leaving that the drawer contained only $20. She asked Kate about it, and Kate denied that there had been $60 in the drawer. Rosemary wondered if other cash amounts had disappeared before they had been deposited at the bank. While some clients paid by credit card or check others, particularly those attending fitness classes, often paid cash.

Rosemary became very alarmed when, during a casual conversation with one of the other instructors, the instructor happened to mention to Rosemary some surprising "good news." The good news was that Kate had brought in a new private fitness client who was working out in the 1:00–2:00 p.m. time period on Monday, Wednesday, and Friday. Kate was doing the training herself. However, Rosemary checked the records and found no new revenues recorded because of this new client. She decided to come to the club during the period to see if this client was indeed working out. Since the client was there and no revenue entry had been made, she confronted Kate. After first explaining that she had not yet got around to making the bookkeeping entry, Kate finally admitted that this client had been writing her checks out to Kate directly, in exchange for a discount. Kate said that she was very sorry and that she would never be dishonest again.

Rosemary realized she had two major problems. First, she had to decide what to do with Kate. Kate was a valuable instructor and a long-time friend, but her honesty was now in question. Should she forgive Kate

or fire her? Second, Rosemary also realized that she had an operating problem. She did not want to step in and assume the managerial role herself because she had significant family responsibilities to which she wanted to be able to continue to attend. But how could she ensure that her business received all the revenues to which it was entitled without being on-site at all times herself? Should she leave Kate, who promised not to steal again, in the manager position? Or should she hire one of the other instructors, or perhaps a non-instructor, to become the manager? And in either case, were there some procedures or controls that she could use to protect her business's assets?

Case Study

Atlanta Home Loan

In late 2002, Albert (Al) Fiorini was becoming more and more frustrated and depressed. In September 2002, he had taken a leave of absence to return to school to earn his MBA, and he had trusted some employees to run the mortgage lending business he had founded. Now it was clear to Al that those employees had schemed to wrest control of the business away from him. And amazingly, they seemed to have been successful. Al lamented, "They didn't just steal some of my assets. They stole my whole business!" Being 2,500 miles away and busy with his studies, Al felt nearly powerless to stop them. He had spent many sleepless nights wondering what he could and should do to get his business back. He also thought about where he went wrong – what he should have done to prevent this problem from happening in the first place.

THE COMPANY

Atlanta Home Loan (hereafter AHL) was a mortgage lending and financing company based in Atlanta, Georgia. Al Fiorini founded the company in April 2002, with an initial investment of about $40,000. He started operating the company from his home.

Al had many years of experience in the mortgage banking industry. He had worked for several different companies and had also served a year as president of the Orange County Chapter of the California Association of Mortgage Brokers. Under his direction, AHL's business grew rapidly in its first quarter of operation. By the summer of 2002, the company consisted of four telemarketers and eight loan officers, all of whom worked from their homes. "Telecommuting" was convenient for the employees because Atlanta was a large city with heavy traffic.

Al established banking relationships that allowed AHL clients to borrow money at wholesale rates. The actual loan terms varied depending on the clients' FICO scores.[1] In summer 2003, banks might offer an AHL client with a very high FICO score (over 620)

---

[1] FICO® scores provide a numeric representation of an individual's financial responsibility, based on his or her credit history. FICO scores are based on a scale from 300–900. Most individuals actually have three FICO scores, one from each national credit bureau (Equifax, Experian, TransUnion). These three FICO scores are the measure that most lenders look at when evaluating credit or loan applications. FICO is an acronym for Fair Isaac Credit Organization, the developer of the credit-rating analytics.

This case was prepared by Professors Kenneth A. Merchant and Wim A. Van der Stede, and research assistant Clara (Xiaoling) Chen.

Copyright © by Kenneth A. Merchant and Wim A. Van der Stede.

a rate of 6.25–6.75% on a fixed 30-year mortgage. This rate provided the bank with an operating margin of 1.5–2.0%. AHL earned a fee of 1.50% of the loan amount for every loan funded. This provided AHL with an average revenue per loan of $3,200.

AHL bought leads from list brokers for $0.20 per name. These lists provided information as to whether the individuals owned their homes, and if so when they bought their homes and when, if ever, they had refinanced their mortgages.

The telemarketers called people on the lead lists to assess their interest in refinancing. Al knew from industry experience that telemarketers should generate a minimum of one lead per hour. They were paid a combination of an hourly wage plus a performance bonus ($10.00) for each lead produced. Since most of them worked part-time, AHL's telemarketers generated, on average, about four new leads per person per day.[2] They gave the leads, the potential clients' names, to Al Fiorini. Al distributed the names to AHL's loan officers.[3]

The loan officers helped the prospective clients to fill out their loan applications and to assemble the needed back-up documents, such as W-2's, pay stubs, and bank statements. After the clients' information had been collected, office support personnel, called "loan processors," would order an appraisal and a credit report, open escrow, and independently verify the financial information. After all the information was collected and verified, the completed file would then be submitted to the prospective lenders either electronically or in paper form.

AHL did not yet have electronic links to the processors' files that would allow monitoring of the progress of the applications before they were submitted. Capabilities for those links were being put into place. However, each application required a credit inquiry, so Al monitored the activities of his loan officers by tracking the number of credit inquiries each requested. This provided him with an early indication of how many applications were being submitted. The loan application/lead ratios varied from 5–20% depending on the skill of the loan officer. Al also closely monitored these ratios and their trends.

In the mortgage lending industry, a 30% "fallout ratio" (the proportion of loans submitted to processing that were not funded) was typical. AHL's fallout ratio was slightly less than 30%.

Once approved, the legal loan documents were prepared. At that time Al knew the revenue due to his company and the fees due to the loan officer involved. AHL paid the loan officers 40% of this total loan revenue on loans that AHL originated, and 60% on loans they originated (by generating their own leads). At closing, AHL received its funds directly from the proceeds. A broker's check would be overnight mailed to AHL's office, or the money would be wired directly into AHL's general account.

BACK TO SCHOOL

For years Al had been thinking about earning an MBA degree. In June 2002, he was admitted to the executive MBA (EMBA) program at the University of Southern California in Los Angeles, and he decided to enroll. While in California, he planned to start another mortgage lending company.

Al had several options for AHL. He could find someone to run it; he could try to sell it; or he could shut it down. If he chose to shut it down, he would turn the unfunded applications over to a contract processing firm. The contract processing firm would be responsible for ordering credit reports and appraisals and for interfacing with the escrow companies and attorneys until the loans were funded. For its services, this firm would charge AHL $300–400 per contract.

But Al decided that he did not want to close AHL. It was a profitable business with considerable growth potential. In September 2002 alone, AHL loan officers were preparing to submit 30–40 new applications to banks for funding, and the volume of business was continuing to grow. Al enlisted the services of a business broker who placed a value of $600,000 on the company. However, Al doubted that he had enough time to find a buyer before he left for California. He decided to find someone to operate the company in his absence.

A PARTNER

Joe Anastasia[4] was one of AHL's loan officers. He had 20 years' experience in the mortgage lending

---

[2] AHL also developed leads from the Internet, as it operated the website www.lowerrate.com.

[3] In Georgia, unlike in some other states, loan officers are not licensed.

---

[4] All names, with the exception of Al Fiorini's, are disguised.

business. Although Al had known him for only about two months, his initial judgments about Joe were quite favorable. Joe seemed to have excellent sales ability; he was people-oriented; and he was knowledgeable about all areas of mortgage lending and financing. On his resume, he described himself as "dependable and honest." Before joining AHL, Joe had worked for ten years as vice president of operations for a sizable financial corporation and had previously operated his own mortgage service company for three years. Since Joe joined AHL, he had closed a higher loan volume than any of the other loan officers.

Impressed by Joe's background and performance, Al decided to make Joe a deal to be his partner. In July 2002, Al and Joe reached a verbal partnership agreement. Joe would invest $8,400, which was used to rent an office and to purchase some office equipment, and Joe and Al would share AHL's profits equally.

Curiously, however, on the day when the two partners were to meet their new landlord, Joe did not show up for the meeting. Al could not find him for two days.[5] In the first 10 working days after becoming Al's partner, Joe showed up in the office only three times.

Al did not feel comfortable letting Joe continue to run the company. Two weeks after their partnership agreement had been struck, he made Joe a deal. In exchange for terminating their agreement, Al agreed to pay Joe 100% of the fees earned on loans that Joe closed. Al then brought in an acquaintance, one with banking experience, to run AHL in his absence, but this manager lasted only three days before quitting. Faced with limited options and desperate to find someone to run the company before he left for Los Angeles the next day, Al turned again to his first option – Joe. Joe apologized for his absences with the admittedly weak excuse that "he had been partying, but it wouldn't happen again." So Al and Joe reinstated the previous agreement. When Al left for Los Angeles in August 2002, AHL had 90 loan applications in the pipeline, constituting nearly $300,000 in potential revenue.

Al started monitoring AHL from afar. He learned that in the following two weeks Joe went to the office only four times. One day he took a large batch of loan files home and did not return to the office for three days.

A NEW PARTNER AND LICENSING AGREEMENT

In September 2002, Al made a final decision that he could not trust Joe. He turned to Wilbur Washington, to whom Al had been introduced by Joe several months earlier. Like Al and Joe, Wilbur had considerable experience in mortgage banking. Al judged quickly that Wilbur would be quite good at sales. He had the requisite knowledge, and "he was smooth." On the basis of these quick judgments, on September 1, 2002, Al signed a written partnership and licensing agreement with Wilbur. This agreement stated that Al would offer Wilbur the use and privileges of AHL as an ongoing business until he returned, and Wilbur would provide AHL with his management services. AHL would make commission payments to Wilbur at 100% on all loans closed less a monthly licensing fee of $5,000 or 10% of all revenue, whichever was greater. Wilbur would also be responsible for interviewing and hiring all new loan officers, paying the expenses of running the office, and managing the entire staff.

Wilbur asked for authority to sign checks written against AHL's main bank account, but Al refused. Instead, as a gesture of good faith Al left with Letitia Johnson (the office manager) four signed, blank checks written against the main account. Al's instructions to Letitia were that the checks were not to be used without Al's permission.

Letitia had been with Al since May 2002. She had effectively managed the telemarketers and had demonstrated her loyalty to Al. In August 2002, because of slow funding loans, Al was unable to pay Letitia her full salary. He asked her whether she would like to find employment elsewhere or to go through the hardship with AHL. Letitia responded that she would like to stay with AHL. Al promised to pay Letitia the deferred part of her salary as soon as some loans got funded, which they did in September. Al trusted Letitia.

Later that month, when Joe found out what was happening, he became quite upset. Not only was he no longer the managing partner of AHL, he thought Al owed him quite a lot of money. He wanted his $8,400 investment back. But Al refused to pay him until he returned all of AHL's leads and loan files in his possession. Not only had his dereliction of duty caused

---

[5] Al found out later that Joe had a problem with alcoholism.

AHL great harm, none of Joe's loans had closed since August, which Al found suspicious.[6] In response, Joe filed a civil lawsuit demanding payment.[7]

MONITORING FROM CALIFORNIA

While he was no longer managing the day-to-day operations of the company, Al continued to monitor AHL's operations closely. Daily, or as soon as the information was available, he tracked the employee head count, the number of leads produced, credit inquiries requested, loan applications funded, office expenses, and bank activity. Al was also on the phone 3–4 hours per day talking with employees and, particularly, loan officers. He thought that this would allow him to monitor the employees' emotional states, an important leading indicator of forthcoming company performance. Al also had all of AHL's corporate mail forwarded to his California address. Al was particularly concerned about Wilbur keeping overhead expenses in line with production levels so that he would be able to pay the employees, to whom Al continued to feel a responsibility, as well as Al himself.

In late September, Wilbur hired a new loan processor. Al knew from experience that every loan officer believes that there is never enough processor time available to get "his" particular loan documents completed on a timely basis. But Al's experience also told him that each processor should be able to fund 20 loans per month, so the company needed only one processor for every four loan officers. Al thought that Wilbur was now employing one, or maybe even two, too many processors and/or salaried, overhead personnel. He sent Wilbur a note telling him that his processor-to-loan-officer ratio was too high. But Wilbur reacted angrily. He told Al "not to tell him what to do," that he was managing the company in the best way he saw fit.

SUBSEQUENT EVENTS

At the time Wilbur took over the operation of AHL, four loans, which would generate total revenues of $11,700, were about to be funded. This amount was supposed to be wired into AHL's main corporate checking account at Bank of America (BofA). When the loans funded, however, on October 1, 2002, without Al's permission, Wilbur personally collected the four checks himself from the closing attorneys, pooled them together, and deposited them into BofA. After depositing the checks, Wilbur immediately wrote checks to himself and Letitia for the entire amount of $11,700 using the four pre-signed checks Al had left.[8] However, since Wilbur wrote the checks against uncleared funds, the checks bounced.

Al had been monitoring the activity in the BofA account on the Internet from Los Angeles. He noticed that the four checks had been written without his knowledge and that they had all bounced. He immediately called Wilbur for an explanation. Wilbur told Al that he had withdrawn money from the account to pay the employees. Al did not believe this explanation, in part because the checks were made out to Wilbur and not run through the payroll account where payroll taxes would be withheld if the checks were meant for employees. On October 7, 2002, Al sent a fax and certified letter to Wilbur and Letitia and also spoke directly to them, ordering them not to write any more checks without his permission and to make sure that there were sufficient funds in the account to cover the checks they wrote. With the returned check charges, the main AHL account was already $1,533.09 overdrawn.

Al also called BofA to stop payments on the four checks and asked the bank to transfer the funds from the general checking account to a side payroll account to which Wilbur would not have access. However, Wilbur managed to release the stop payments on the checks. He transferred the money from the payroll account back into the general account and cashed the checks. Bank personnel apparently assumed that Wilbur had authority over the account since he had deposited the funds in the first place.

Angry and frustrated, Al decided that he could no longer trust Wilbur and could not do business with him. On October 9, 2002, Al asked a friend of his who used to be a sales manager in the mortgage company that Al had worked for previously to act as his agent. The friend was to go to AHL's office and fire all the employees. Among other things, Al was particularly concerned that AHL had over 100 client

---

[6] Al later also found out that Joe had used a friend to close his loans, which violated legal regulations for the mortgage business. Another reason for Al's suspicion was that one of AHL's loan officers had originated a loan and asked Joe to bring it to the office, but Joe never brought it in.

[7] The court dismissed this lawsuit on December 5, 2002.

[8] Al found out later that Wilbur and Letitia were actively dating.

files with sensitive personal information that might be misused. However, when Al's agent went to the AHL premises to fire the employees, they all refused to go. Al called in the police to support the firing action, but when they arrived Wilbur told the police that he was the owner, not Al. Not knowing who was telling the truth, the police just left.

On October 14, 2002, Al sent a letter to all 100+ AHL clients whose loans were in process that the company had to drop their applications. The key phrase in the letter was, "We are no longer going to be able to service your application."

On October 15, Wilbur opened a new account at Citizens Bank & Trust (CBT) in Atlanta, a bank where he did his personal business and where he knew the manager personally. Wilbur wired the funds being held in AHL's corporate name at the offices of the closing attorneys into this new bank account. He now had signing authority over the checks.

Al discovered the second bank account when a "Welcome" letter from CBT arrived to his California address. Al was outraged that personnel at CBT did not ask Wilbur for any corporate documents:

> Wilbur showed no documentation whatsoever . . . You would expect highly regulated institutions like banks to provide better protection for the public, but . . .

Al immediately called bank personnel and informed the manager that Wilbur had opened a fraudulent account with CBT. But CBT refused to freeze the account or return the money. As a last resort, Al informed the Atlanta police and the FBI, thinking that they might be interested in this identity theft case. However, possibly due to the relatively small amount of money involved, neither the police nor FBI gave the case any attention.

To make things worse, the day Wilbur opened the fraudulent bank account at CBT he also filed two applications for warrants for Al's arrest. Wilbur claimed that Al was the one who had taken the proceeds received from the closing attorneys out of the company's accounts. Al had to return twice to Atlanta to defend himself. Both cases were dismissed, but Al incurred over $7,500 in legal fees and travel costs, and he wasted substantial time and energy dealing with these frivolous lawsuits.

During all this time, the AHL personnel were maintaining their daily routines. Wilbur renegotiated a lease with the landlord and established AHL as his own company. Al suspected that Wilbur had used all of his means of persuasion to mislead the employees in order to break their bonds with Al. Al received his $5,000 licensing fee in September, but that was the last money he received. By December, Al realized that he had already lost at least $15,000 in licensing fees, and possibly more that might have been realized from the funding of the loans in the pipeline. Moreover, he had lost his company. Al said, sadly, "I have no idea how much revenue ended up being taken in my name."

Sensing defeat, Al finally asked the Georgia Department of Banking and Finance to withdraw AHL's mortgage banking license. Not only had he lost his business and his income, he had also lost his credit rating since he had incurred bills that he was unable to pay. And in February 2003, Al was forced to sell his home.

In the summer of 2003, Al had still not decided what he should do. Should he fight to regain control over AHL? But what was left of it? Perhaps only about $25,000 worth of equipment. Or should he give up, let these crooks get away with it, and try to rebuild somewhere else?

Al also pondered how he had gotten into this mess. What might he have done to prevent this disaster from happening?

Section II

MANAGEMENT CONTROL ALTERNATIVES AND THEIR EFFECTS

Chapter 2

RESULTS CONTROLS

If asked to think about powerful ways to influence behavior in organizations, most people would probably think first about pay-for-performance, which is no doubt an effective motivator. For example, at Thor Industries, a large recreational vehicle manufacturer, Wade Thompson, the CEO, attributes much of the company's success to its incentive compensation system. Among other things, the company shares 15% of each division's pretax profits with the division managers, because, Mr. Thompson explained, "I want every one of our company heads to feel like it is their business, in their control. If they don't perform, they don't get paid very much. If they do, there is no cap to what they can make."[1] Indeed, Vicky Wright, managing director at Hay Group, a compensation consultancy firm, argues:

> [Many] companies on the Most Admired list [a list of companies produced annually by *Fortune*] have chief executives who understand what performance measurement is all about. It's about learning how to motivate people – how to link those performance measures to rewards."[2]

Pay-for-performance is a prominent example of a type of control that can be called *results control* because it involves rewarding employees for generating good results. Identifying what are *good* results, as we will see, is crucial. The recent financial crisis has thrown pay-for-performance, especially in banks, into sharp relief, where rather than producing good results, pay-for-performance systems were said to have bred "bonus cultures" of *greed* and *short-termism*. Nonetheless, in the aftermath of the financial crisis, US Treasury Secretary Tim Geithner did not call to do away with pay-for-performance; rather he heralded to work with Congress to pass legislation designed to tie executive compensation *more closely* to *sound* performance. "Compensation should be tied to performance in order to link the incentives of executives and other employees with long-term value creation," Mr. Geithner said.[3]

Results controls of the pay-for-performance variety are also increasingly being used in the not-for-profit sector. For example, the National Health and Hospitals Reform Commission in Australia argued that the fee-for-service system of healthcare rebates often fails to promote the most effective treatments because doctors get paid for each consultation or clinical activity regardless of whether the patient recovers well or not. In considering how to reform this system, the Commission recommended to link the pay of doctors and nurses to measures of how well they treat their patients, or how quickly they are seen.[4]

Despite the increasing emphasis on pay-for-performance in many contexts, the rewards that can be linked to results go far beyond monetary compensation. Other rewards that can be usefully tied to measured performance include job security, promotions, autonomy, plum assignments, and recognition. (We discuss the vast array of rewards that can be given more fully in Chapter 9.)

Results controls create *meritocracies*. In meritocracies, the rewards are given to the most talented and hardest working employees, rather than those with the longest tenure or the right social connections. The combinations of rewards linked to results inform or remind employees as to what result areas are important and motivate them to produce the results the organization rewards. Results controls influence actions or decisions because they cause employees to be concerned about the *consequences* of their actions or decisions. The organization does not dictate to employees what actions or decisions they should take; instead employees are *empowered* to take those actions or decisions they believe will best produce the desired results. Results controls also encourage employees to discover and develop their talents and to get placed into jobs in which they will be able to perform well.

For all these reasons, well-designed results control systems can help produce the results desired. A review of a number of studies on the use of incentives to motivate performance found an average gain in performance of about 22% stemming from the use of incentive programs.[5] Like all other forms of controls, however, results controls cannot be used in every situation. They are effective only where the desired results can be clearly defined and adequately measured by the organization, and where the measured results can be sufficiently controlled by the employee.[6] We discuss the conditions for the effective use of results controls in more depth in this chapter.

PREVALENCE OF RESULTS CONTROLS

Results controls are commonly used for controlling the behaviors of employees at many organizational levels. They are a necessary element in the employee *empowerment* approach to management, which became a major management trend starting in the 1990s.[7] Results controls are particularly dominant as a means of controlling the behaviors of *professional employees*; those with *decision authority*, like managers. Reengineering guru Michael Hammer even defines a professional as "someone who is responsible for achieving a result rather than [for] performing a task."[8]

Results controls are consistent with, and even necessary for, the implementation of decentralized forms of organization with largely autonomous entities or responsibility centers (which we discuss in more detail in Chapter 7). For example, business pioneer Alfred Sloan observed that he sought a way to exercise effective control over the whole corporation yet maintain a philosophy of decentralization.[9] At General Motors (and numerous other companies that followed), the results controls under Sloan's leadership were built on a return-on-investment (ROI) performance measure (which we discuss in more detail in Chapter 10). By using this type of control system, corporate management could review and judge the effectiveness of the various organizational entities while leaving the actual execution of operations to those responsible for the performance of those entities – the entity managers.

DuPont, Merrill Lynch, Boeing, Coca-Cola, Alcoa, and many other large corporations have gone through the process of instituting more decentralized forms of organization with a concurrent increased emphasis on results control. In 1993, DuPont's CEO replaced a complex management hierarchy by splitting the company into 21 *strategic business units* (SBUs), each of which operates as a free-standing unit. The SBU managers were given greater responsibility and asked to be more entrepreneurial and more customer-focused. They were also asked to bear more risk, because a large portion of SBU managers' compensation was based on SBU performance (sales and profitability). The managers noticed the change. For example, one SBU manager said, "When I joined DuPont [21 years ago], if you kept your nose clean and worked hard, you could work as long as you wanted. [But today] job security depends on results."[10] The change was perceived as being successful: a *Business Week* article noted that, "The image of DuPont has morphed from giant sloth to gazelle."[11]

In 2010, Sanofi-Aventis, a large pharmaceutical company, divided its vast resources into decentralized disease-based units, each with its own departments for research and development, regulatory affairs, marketing, and sales – a plan designed to identify promising drugs more quickly and weed out failures before large amounts of money were spent on them. One industry expert noted that "the [model of] fully-independent units, operating under the parent company's umbrella, [constitutes] a break from the traditional big pharma business model, and represents companies' interest in duplicating the flexibility and cost-efficiencies of small biotech and biotech-like companies."[12] By establishing accountability for a fully-integrated entity's results, where the entity manager closest to the business makes the tradeoffs and takes responsibility over the entity's budget, the company aims to instill a "performance culture" that encourages both operating discipline (efficiency) and greater responsiveness to local business needs (flexibility).

In other words, decentralization attempts to replicate an "entrepreneurial model" within typically large corporations, where entity managers are given decision authority but then held responsible for the results that their decisions produce. Paul O'Neill, Alcoa's chairman at the time, and later US Treasury Secretary during President George W. Bush's first term, summarized this idea as follows:

> We cannot succeed if we persist in our use of the traditional command-and-control system of management where many thousands of people believe their only responsibility is to do what they are told to do.[13]

Similarly, when Nick Reilly took the helm as CEO in late 2009 of troubled Opel, the German car manufacturer owned by General Motors, he announced that he wanted to encourage an entrepreneurial spirit at Opel by delegating most decisions to country heads and by dismantling GM's bureaucratic style of centralized management that fostered a "debilitating culture of passing the buck." "It might seem obvious, but it isn't the way GM was managed and there was definitely some confusion about who was accountable," he said. "From the top line of revenue to the bottom line of profit, this is now the responsibility of the managing directors of the major entities."[14]

However, managers will act in an entrepreneurial manner necessary to thrive in competitive environments not only if they are subjected to the same market forces and pressures that drive independent entrepreneurs, but also if they are promised commensurate rewards for the risks they bear from doing so. As such, Richard Chandler, founder of Sunrise Medical, a medical products company, defended his company's decentralized organization and lucrative incentives by stating that "people want to be rewarded based on their own efforts. [Without divisional accountability] you end up with a system like the US Post Office. There's no incentive [for workers to excel]."[15]

Thus, *decentralization* or "delegation of decision rights" to managers, and the design of *incentive systems* to motivate these managers to generate the desired results, are two critical organizational design choices in a results-control context; they are part of what organizational theorists call the *organizational architecture*. This literature maintains that organizational choices about decentralization and incentive systems should be made *jointly*, and that concentrating on one element to the exclusion of the other will lead to poorly designed organizations.[16]

Results controls need not be limited to management levels only; they can also be driven down to lower levels in the organization, as many companies have done with good effects.[17] Lincoln Electric, a worldwide leader in the production of welding products, serves as the poster child of companies that use results controls down to the lowest organizational level. Lincoln Electric provides wages based solely on piecework for most factory jobs and lucrative performance-based bonuses that can more than double an employee's pay.[18] This incentive system has created such high productivity that some of the industry giants (General Electric, Westinghouse) found it difficult to compete in Lincoln Electric's line of business (arc welding) and exited the market. A *Business Week* article observed that "in its reclusive, iconoclastic way, Lincoln Electric remains one of the best-managed companies in the United States and is probably as good as anything across the Pacific."[19] And even though Lincoln's legendary *Incentive Performance System* has essentially remained the same since it was installed in 1934, the company is still acclaimed for its systems and performance today, such as in a recent book titled *The Modern Firm.*[20]

Whereas decentralization is an effective way to empower employees in a results-control context, there can, and even should, be limits to empowerment in certain circumstances. For example, when pursuing rapid growth in China, French hypermarket Carrefour faced systemic corruption among its management ranks at the local levels. Unlike the centralized approach to management that Wal-Mart employed in China, Carrefour empowered local managers to take charge of virtually all aspects of running their stores, including product pricing and promotions, supplier selection, and store design. Whereas this high degree of flexibility gave ample leeway for managers to expand fast in the early stages of building the chain, it also encouraged widespread bribe-taking at the local level and, over time, led to higher operating costs and reputation risk than would a centralized system.[21]

RESULTS CONTROLS AND THE CONTROL PROBLEMS

Results controls provide several preventive-type benefits. Well-defined results inform employees as to what is expected of them and encourages them to do what they can to produce the desired results. In this way, the results controls alleviate a potential lack of direction. Results controls also can be particularly effective in addressing motivational problems. Even without direct supervision or interference from higher up, the results controls induce employees to behave so as to maximize their chances of producing the results the organization desires. This motivational effect arises particularly when incentives for producing the desired results also further the employees' own personal rewards. Finally, results controls also can mitigate personal limitations. Because results controls typically promise rewards for good performers, they can help organizations to attract and retain employees who are confident about their abilities. Results controls also encourage employees to develop their talents to position themselves to earn the results-dependent rewards.

The performance measures that are a part of the results controls also provide some non-motivational, detection-type control benefits of a cybernetic (feedback) nature, as was mentioned in Chapter 1. The results measures help organizations answer questions about how various strategies, organizational entities, and employees are performing. If peformance fails to meet expectations, organizations can consider changing the strategies, processes, or the employees.[22] Investigating and intervening when performance is deviating from expectations is the essence of a *management-by-exception* approach to management, which is in common use in large organizations.

ELEMENTS OF RESULTS CONTROLS

The implementation of results controls involves four steps: (1) defining the dimension(s) on which results are desired; (2) measuring performance in the chosen dimensions; (3) setting performance targets for employees to attain for each of the measures; and (4) providing rewards for target attainment to encourage the behaviors that will lead to the desired results. Whereas these steps are easy to list, executing them effectively can be challenging.

Defining performance dimensions

Defining the right performance dimensions is challenging and involves balancing an organizations' responsibilities to all of their stakeholders, including owners (equity holders), debtholders, employees, suppliers, customers, and the society at large. Should a firm's sole aim be to maximize shareholder returns, or should it also, or even primarily, be customer or employee focused? Are these performance foci mutually exclusive or are they rather mutually reinforcing?[23] Where do performance dimensions such as innovation and sustainability belong? And so on.

As challenging as defining the desired performance dimensions may be, it is equally critical to choose performance measures that are *congruent* or *aligned* with the chosen performance dimensions because the goals that are set and the measurements that are made will shape employees' views of what is important. Phrased differently, *what you measure is what you get*. For example, firms may define one of their desired performance dimensions to be shareholder value creation, yet measure performance in terms of accounting profits. This implies that employees are likely to try to improve the *measured performance* (in this example, accounting profits) regardless of whether or not it contributes to the *desired performance* (in this example, shareholder value). We discuss this problem, and the difficulties related to this particular example, further in Chapters 5, 10, and 11.

Similarly, firms may aim to pursue innovation, yet they end up measuring patents filed. Anxious to promote innovation, many companies offer incentives to their employees to come up with patentable ideas, and such incentives are likely to produce results; that is, the number of patents filed is likely to increase. But as Tony Chen, a patent attorney with Jones Day in Shanghai notes, "patents are easy to file, but gems [can be] hard to find in a mountain of junk."[24] Indeed, what you measure may be what you get.

This important congruence problem also is prevalent in the not-for-profit sector. For example, a study by the UK Home Office found that organized trafficking was a "thriving industry" that "makes a killing," amassing healthy profits with little risk of detection. The study suggested that one of the reasons for this was the ill-defined performance targets that the police had to meet. Solving high volumes of simple crimes such as petty thefts and home burglaries is easier and cheaper than the long-drawn-out and expensive police work that is needed to crack down on trafficking rings. Even though the goal was to reduce crime, the result may have been that hardened criminals were let off.[25]

Hence, not only do firms need to decide what is desired, they also must ensure that their measurements of the desired performance dimensions are aligned with them. If they are not, the results controls are likely to encourage employees to produce *undesired* results. The results controls can then be said to have *unintended consequences*.

Measuring performance

As per the above, then, measurement is a critical element of a results control system. The object of the measurement is typically the performance of an organizational entity or an employee in a specific time period. Many *objective* financial measures, such as net income, earnings per share, and return on assets are in common use. So too are many objective nonfinancial measures, such as market share, customer satisfaction, and the timely accomplishment of certain tasks. Some other measurements involve *subjective* judgments. For example, qualities such as "being a team player" or "developing employees effectively" might be assessed on a five-point measurement scale.

Performance measures typically vary across organizational levels. At higher organizational levels, most of the key results are defined in either market (such as stock price) and/or financial (such a return on equity) terms. Lower-level managers, on the other hand, are typically evaluated in terms of operational measures that are more controllable at the local level. The key result areas for a manager in charge of a manufacturing site, for example, might be a combination of measures focused on production efficiency, inventory control, product quality, and delivery time. The variation in the use of financial and operational performance measures between higher- and lower-level management creates a *hinge* in the management hierarchy. That is, at some critical middle organizational level, often a profit center level (see Chapter 7), managers must translate financial goals into operational goals. These managers' goals are primarily defined by financial measures, so their communications with their superiors are primarily in financial terms. But because their subordinates' measures are primarily operational, their downward communications are primarily in operational terms.

If managers identify more than one result measure for a given employee, they must attach *weightings* to each measure so that the judgments about performance in each result area can be aggregated into an overall evaluation. The weightings can be additive. For example, 60% of the overall evaluation is based on return on assets and 40% is based on sales growth. The weightings can also be multiplicative. For example, Browning-Ferris Industries multiplies a score on achievement of profit and revenue goals by a score assessed based on environmental responsibility.[26] If the environmental responsibility score is less than 70%, the multiplier is zero, yielding no bonus. Sometimes, organizations make the weightings of performance measures *explicit* to the employees, as in the example just presented. Often, however, the weightings are partially or totally *implicit*, such as when the performance evaluations are done subjectively. Leaving the weighting implicit blurs the communication to employees about what results are important. Employees are left to infer what results will most affect their overall evaluations.

Setting performance targets

Performance targets are another important results control element because they affect behavior in two ways. First, they improve motivation by providing clear goals for employees to strive for. Most people prefer to be given a specific target to shoot for, rather than merely being given vague statements like "do your best" or "work at a reasonable pace."[27] Second, performance targets allow employees to assess their performance. People do not respond to feedback unless they are able to interpret it, and a key part of interpretation involves comparing actual performance relative to target. The targets distinguish strong from poor performance. Failure to achieve the target signals a need for improvement. (We discuss performance targets and target setting processes in more detail in Chapter 8.)

The following example illustrates both points. Maria Giraldo, a nurse in the intensive care unit at Long Island Jewish Medical Center, used to be evaluated on such criteria as leadership, respectfulness, and how well she worked with others. A few years ago, her hospital implemented a new computer-based performance system that broke down her job description into quantifiable goals, such as to keep infection rates for her unit low and patient satisfaction scores high, all relative to specific target levels. Ever since this new system was implemented, at review time the discussion does not linger on about how Ms. Giraldo had performed. She hit the targets or she did not. The clarity about measures and goals, and the reviews "by the numbers" that they allow, changed Ms. Giraldo's views about success and what she needs to do to get ahead in her career, all for the better, she believed.[28] (In Chapter 9, we discuss the drawbacks of relying exclusively on objective, formulaic performance evaluations in more detail.)

Providing rewards

Rewards or *incentives* are the final element of a results control system. The rewards included in incentive contracts can be in the form of anything employees value, such as salary increases, bonuses, promotions, job security, job assignments, training opportunities, freedom, recognition, and power. Punishments are the opposite of rewards. They are things employees dislike, such as demotions, supervisor disapproval, failure to earn rewards that colleagues manage to earn or, at the extreme, the threat of dismissal.

Organizations can derive motivational value from linking any of these valued rewards to results that employees can influence. For example, organizations can use any of a number of *extrinsic rewards*. They can grant additional monetary rewards, such as in the form of cash or stock. They can use non-monetary rewards, such as by granting high performing employees public recognition and additional decision authority. Alternatively, in entities where performance is mediocre or poor, they can threaten to reduce the decision authority and power managers derive from managing their entities or decline to fund proposed projects.

Results measures can provide a positive motivational impact even if no rewards are explicitly linked to results measures. People often derive their own internally generated *intrinsic rewards* through a sense of accomplishment for achieving the desired results. For example, when William J. Bratton became the New York City Police Commissioner in the 1990s, he gave his police force one clear, simple goal: cut crime.[29] (Previously the thinking had been that crime was due to societal factors beyond the department's control, so the police were largely measured by how quickly they responded to emergency calls.) He also implemented a results control system. He decentralized the department by giving the 76 precinct commanders the authority to make most of the key decisions in their police units, including the right to set personnel schedules, and he started collecting and reporting crime data daily. Even though Commissioner Bratton legally could not award good performers with pay raises or merit bonuses, the system was tremendously successful. In 1994, major felonies in New York fell by 12%, and in the first three quarters of 1995, they fell another 18% below 1994 levels. This success clearly was not attributable to pay-for-performance in the strictest sense; it was instead due, at least in part, to providing officers with clear goals and empowering them to go about fighting crime. Seeing the results of their initiatives gave police officers a sense of accomplishment and, presumably, an intrinsic motivation to perform well.

The motivational strength of any of the extrinsic or intrinsic rewards can be understood in terms of several motivation theories that have been developed and studied for nearly 50 years, such as *expectancy theory*. Expectancy theory postulates that individuals' motivational force, or effort, is a function of (1) their *expectancies* or their belief that certain outcomes will result from their behavior (e.g., a bonus for increased effort); and (2) their *valences* or the strength of their preference for those outcomes. The *valence* of a bonus, however, is not always restricted to its monetary value, it also may have *valence* in securing other valued items, such as status and prestige.[30]

Organizations should promise their employees the rewards that provide the most powerful motivational effects in the most cost effective way possible. But the motivational effects of the various reward forms can vary widely depending on individuals' personal tastes and circumstances. Some people are greatly interested in immediate cash awards, whereas others are more interested in increasing their retirement benefits, increasing their autonomy or improving their promotion possibilities. Reward tastes also vary across countries for a number of reasons, including differences in cultures and income tax laws.[31] However, if organizations can tailor their reward packages to their employees' individual preferences, they can provide meaningful rewards in a cost efficient manner. But tailoring rewards to individuals or small groups within a large organization is not easy to accomplish. A tailored system will likely be complex and costly to administer. When poorly implemented it can easily lead to employee perceptions of unfairness and potentially have the opposite effects of those intended: demotivation and poor employee morale. We discuss the choice of different forms of incentives and incentive system design in more detail in Chapter 9.

CONDITIONS DETERMINING THE EFFECTIVENESS OF RESULTS CONTROLS

Although they are an important form of control in many organizations, results controls cannot always be used effectively. They work best only when *all* of the following conditions are present:

1. organizations can determine what results are desired in the areas being controlled;

2. the employees whose behaviors are being controlled have significant influence on the results for which they are being held accountable; and

3. organizations can measure the results effectively.

Knowledge of desired results

For results controls to work, organizations must know what results are desired in the areas they wish to control, and they must communicate the desired results effectively to the employees working in those areas. *Results desirability* means that more of the quality represented by the results measure is preferred to less, everything else being equal.

As we alluded to above, one might argue that (one of) the primary objective(s) of for-profit organizations is to maximize shareholder value. However, it does not follow that, because this overall objective is understood, the desired results will also be known at all intermediate and lower levels in the organization. The disaggregation of overall organizational objectives into specific expectations for all employees lower in the hierarchy is often difficult. Different parts of the organization face different tradeoffs.

For example, purchasing managers create value by procuring good-quality, low-cost materials on time. These three result areas (quality, cost, and schedule) can often be traded off against each other, and the overall organizational objective to maximize shareholder value does not provide much guidance in making these tradeoffs. The importance of each of these results areas may vary over time and among parts of the organization depending on differing needs and strategies. For example, a company (or entity) short of cash may want to minimize the amount of inventory on hand, which may make scheduling the dominant consideration. A company (or entity) with a cost leadership strategy may want to emphasize the cost considerations. A company (or entity) pursuing a unique product quality image or differentiation strategy may emphasize meeting or exceeding the specifications of the materials being purchased. Thus, to ensure proper purchasing manager behaviors, the importance orderings or weightings of these three results areas must be made clear.

If the wrong results areas are chosen, or if the right areas are chosen but given the wrong weightings, the combination of results measures will not be *congruent* with the organization's intended objectives. Using an incongruent set of results measures may then result in motivating employees to take the wrong actions. In the above setting, for example, ill-guided cost considerations may damage the company's pursued product quality reputation.

Ability to influence desired results (controllability)

A second condition that is necessary for results controls to be effective is that the employees whose behaviors are being controlled must be able to affect the results in a material way in a given time period. This *controllability principle* is one of the central tenets of responsibility accounting (which we discuss in more detail in Chapters 7 and 12). Here are some representative expressions that have stood the test of time of this perennial principle:

> It is almost a self-evident proposition that, in appraising the performance of divisional management, no account should be taken of matters outside the division's control.[32]

> A manager is not normally held accountable for unfavorable outcomes or credited with favorable ones if they are clearly due to causes not under his control.[33]

The main rationale behind the controllability principle is that results measures are useful only to the extent that they provide information about the desirability of the actions or decisions that were taken. If a results area is totally uncontrollable, the results measures reveal nothing about what actions or decisions were taken. Partial controllability makes it difficult to infer from the results measures whether or not good actions or decisions were taken.

In most organizational situations, of course, numerous uncontrollable or partially uncontrollable factors affect the measures used to evaluate performance. These uncontrollable influences hinder efforts to use results measures for control purposes. As a consequence, it becomes difficult to determine whether the results achieved are due to the actions or decisions taken, or rather, to uncontrollable factors. Good actions and decisions will not necessarily produce good results. Bad actions or decisions may similarly be obscured.

In situations where many, large uncontrollable influences affect the available results measures, results control is not effective. Managers cannot be relieved of their responsibility to respond to relevant environmental factors, but if these factors are difficult to separate from the results measures, results controls do not provide good information either for evaluating performance or for motivating good behaviors. We discuss the methods organizations use to cope with uncontrollable factors in results control systems in more detail in Chapter 12.

Ability to measure controllable results effectively

Ability to measure the controllable results effectively is the final constraint limiting the feasibility of results controls. Often the controllable results the organization desires, and the employees involved can affect, cannot be measured effectively. In virtually all situations *something* can be measured – often, however, the key results areas cannot be measured *effectively*.

The key criterion that should be used to judge the effectiveness of results measures is the ability to evoke the desired behaviors. If a measure evokes the right behaviors in a given situation – that is, if the measure can be said to be *congruent* with the desired results area – then it is a good control measure. If it does not, it is a bad one, even if the measure accurately reflects the quantity it purports to represent; that is, even if the measurement has little measurement error.

To evoke the right behaviors, in addition to being *congruent* and *controllable*, results measures should be *precise*, *objective*, *timely*, and *understandable*. And even when a measure has all of the above qualities, it should also be *cost efficient*; that is, the costs of developing and using the measure should be considered.

Precision

Measurements inevitably contain error; some random, some systematic. Error makes the measurement inaccurate. Measurement *accuracy* refers to the degree of closeness of measurements of a quantity to its actual (true) value. *Precision* is the degree to which repeated measurements under similar conditions show the same result; if they do, the measurements can be said to be *reliable*. Using a bullseye analogy, *accuracy* describes the closeness of arrows (measurement) to the target (true value). When all arrows are grouped tightly together, the cluster of arrows (measurement) is considered *precise* since they all struck close to the same spot, even if not necessarily near the bullseye.

Reducing systematic error (or *bias*) improves accuracy but does not change precision. However, it is not possible to achieve accuracy in measurement without precision; that is, when the measures contain mostly random error or, thus, when they are unreliable. In other words, and in the bullseye analogy, if the arrows are not grouped close to one another, they cannot all be close to the bullseye. Therefore, lack of precision is an undesirable quality for a results measure to have. But even precise measures that are biased (i.e. that contain systematic error) may not be of great use for control purposes. If the degree of the systematic error is not known; then the measurement will be systematically *biased* by either showing greater or lesser values than the actual value (see below – *objectivity*).

It is obvious that some aspects of performance (such as social responsibility, leadership acumen, personnel development) are difficult, or even impossible, to measure precisely, either because the measurements contain random error or are systematically biased (such as may be the case when subjective performance evaluations are used). Precision therefore is an important quality because without it the measure loses much of its information value. Imprecise measures increase the risk of misevaluating performance. Employees will react negatively to the inequities that will inevitably arise when equally good performances are rated differently.

Objectivity

An *objective* measure should be taken to mean here that it is not influenced by personal feelings or interpretations – hence, that it is *unbiased*. Measurement objectivity is low where either the choice of measurement rules or the actual measuring is done by the persons whose performances are being evaluated. Low objectivity is likely, for example, where performance is self-reported or where evaluatees are allowed considerable discretion in the choice of measurement methods. Indeed, and referring to the above definition related to measurement precision, low objectivity is likely to introduce systematic error (e.g. the reported performance is systematically higher than its true value). If that is the case, the measurement may be precise, but it will not be accurate. Good measures for control purposes therefore should be both precise (reliable) and objective (unbiased).

There are two main ways to increase measurement objectivity. The first alternative is to have the measuring done by people independent of the process, such as by personnel in the controller's department. The second alternative is to have the measurements verified by independent parties, such as auditors.

Timeliness

Timeliness refers to the lag between the employee's performance and the measurement of results (and the provision of rewards based on these results). Timeliness is an important measurement quality for two reasons. The first is motivational. Employees need repeated performance pressure to perform at their best. The pressure helps ensure that the employees do not become complacent, sloppy, or wasteful. Measures, and thus rewards, that are delayed for significant periods of time lose most of their motivational impact. The sustained pressure can also stimulate creativity by increasing the likelihood that employees will be stimulated to repeatedly search for new and better ways of improving results.

A second advantage is that timeliness increases the value of interventions that might be necessary. If significant problems exist but the performance measures are not timely, it might not be possible to intervene to fix the problems before they cause (more) harm.

Understandability

Two aspects of *understandability* are important. First, the employees whose behaviors are being controlled must understand what they are being held accountable for. This requires communication. Training, which is a form of communication, may also be necessary if, for example, employees are to be held accountable for achieving goals expressed in new and different terms, such as when an organization shifts its measurement focus from accounting income to, say, economic value added.

Second, employees must understand what they must do to influence the measure, at least in broad terms. For example, purchasing managers who are held accountable for lowering the costs of purchased materials will not be successful until they develop strategies for accomplishing this goal, such as improving negotiations with vendors, increasing competition among vendors, or working with engineering personnel to redesign certain parts. Similarly, employees who are held accountable for customer satisfaction must understand what their customers value and what they can do to affect it.

When employees understand what a measure represents, they are empowered to work out what they can do to influence it. In fact, this is one of the advantages of results controls: good control can be achieved without knowing exactly how employees will produce the results.

Cost efficiency

Finally, measures should be *cost efficient*. A measure might have all of the above qualities yet be too expensive to develop or use (e.g. when it involves third-party surveys of customers, say, to collect the data), meaning that the costs exceed the benefits. When that is the case, the firm may need to settle for an alternative, more cost efficient measure.

Overall, many measures cannot be classified as either clearly good (effective) or poor (ineffective). Different tradeoffs among the measurement qualities create some advantages and disadvantages. For example, measures can often be made more congruent, controllable, precise, and objective if timeliness is compromised. Thus, in assessing the effectiveness of results measures, many difficult judgments are often necessary. These judgments are discussed in more detail throughout several chapters of this book.

CONCLUSION

This chapter described an important form of control, results control, which is used at many levels in most organizations. Results controls are an indirect form of control because they do not focus explicitly on the employees' actions or decisions. However, this indirectness provides some important advantages. Results controls can often be effective when it is not clear what behaviors are most desirable. In addition, results controls can yield good control while allowing the employees whose behaviors are being controlled high autonomy. Many people, particularly those higher in the organizational hierarchy, value high autonomy and respond well to it.

Results controls are not effective in every situation, however. Failure to satisfy all three effectiveness conditions – knowledge of the desired results, ability to affect the desired results, and ability to measure controllable results effectively – will render results controls impotent. It will also probably precipitate any of a number of dysfunctional side effects, which we discuss in later chapters.

Results controls usually are the major element of the MCS used in all but the smallest organizations. However, results controls often are supplemented by action and personnel/cultural controls, which we discuss in the next chapter.

Notes

1. "Lord of the Rigs," *Forbes* (March 29, 2004), p. 68.
2. "Measuring People Power," *Fortune* (October 2, 2000), p. 186.
3. "Geithner: Link Executive Pay to Performance," *The Washington Times* (June 10, 2009), online (http://washingtontimes.com).
4. "Performance Pay Likely for Doctors," *The Australian* (May 6, 2009), online (www.theaustralian.com.au).
5. S. J. Condly, R. E. Clark, and H. D. Stolovitch, "The Effects of Incentives on Workplace Performance: A Meta-Analytic Review of Research Studies," *Performance Improvement Quarterly*, 16, no. 3 (2003), pp. 46–63. For some examples of empirical research studies on the effects of incentives on performance, see R. D. Banker, S. Y. Lee, G. Potter and D. Srinivasan, "An Empirical Analysis of Continuing Improvements Following the Implementation of a Performance-Based Compensation Plan," *Journal of Accounting and Economics*, 30, no. 3 (December 2000), pp. 315–350; and R. D. Banker, S. Y. Lee, and G. Potter, "A Field Study of the Impact of a Performance-Based Incentive Plan," *Journal of Accounting and Economics*, 21, no. 3 (April 1996), pp. 195–226.
6. As an example of several results control issues that can arise when these conditions are not met, see S. Kerr, "The Best-Laid Incentive Plans," *Harvard Business Review*, 81, no. 1 (January 2003), pp. 27–40.
7. See, for example, K. H. Blanchard, J. P. Carlos, and W. A. Randolph, *The 3 Keys to Empowerment* (San Francisco, CA: Berrett-Koehler Publishers, 1999). For a recent empirical research study in this area, see S. E. Seibert, S. R. Silver, and W. A. Randolph, "Taking Empowerment to the Next Level: A Multiple-Level Model of Empowerment, Performance, and Satisfaction," *Academy of Management Journal*, 47, no. 3 (June 2004), pp. 332–49. For a theoretical study on the feasibility and limitations of empowerment and decentralization, see G. Baker, R. Gibbons, and K. J. Murphy, "Bringing the Market Inside the Firm," *American Economic Review*, 91, no. 2 (May 2001), pp. 212–18.
8. M. Hammer, *Beyond Reengineering: How the Process-Centered Organization is Changing Our Work and Our Lives* (New York, NY: Harper Business, 1996).
9. A. P. Sloan, *My Years with General Motors* (New York, NY: Doubleday, 1964).
10. "For DuPont, Christmas in April," *Business Week* (April 24, 1995), p. 130.
11. Ibid., p. 129.
12. "Sanofi Seeks Efficiencies with New Model," *The Boston Globe* (August 16, 2010), online (www.boston.com).
13. "Changes at Alcoa Point Up Challenges and Benefits of Decentralized Authority," *The Wall Street Journal* (November 7, 1991), p. B7.
14. "In Break with Past, No More Passing the Buck at Opel," *Reuters* (December 6, 2009), online (www.reuters.com).
15. R. H. Chandler, quoted in "Sunrise Scam Throws Light on Incentive Pay Programs," *The Los Angeles Times* (January 15, 1996), p. D3.
16. J. Brickley, C. Smith, and J. Zimmerman, *Managerial Economics and Organizational Architecture* (Boston, MA: McGraw-Hill Irwin, 2001); D. A. Nadler, M. S. Gerstein, and R. B. Shaw, *Organizational Architecture: Designs for Changing Organizations* (New York: Jossey-Bass, 1992); and P. Milgrom and J. Roberts, *Economics, Organization and Management* (Englewood Cliffs, NJ: Prentice Hall, 1992).

17. "Employee Autonomy Results in Enhanced Profitability," *Manufacturing & Distribution Issues*, 7 (Summer 1996), pp. 3–4.

18. The details of Lincoln Electric's legendary *Incentive Performance System* are described in two cases about Lincoln Electric at the end of Chapters 4 and 16 in this book. See also "Ohio Firm Relies on Incentive-Pay System to Motivate Workers and Maintain Products," *The Wall Street Journal* (August 12, 1983), p. 23; and "Lincoln Electric: Where People Are Never Let Go," *Time* (June 18, 2001), p. 40.

19. "This is the Answer," *Business Week* (July 5, 1982), pp. 50–2.

20. J. Roberts, *The Modern Firm: Organizational Design for Performance and Growth* (New York, Oxford University Press, 2004).

21. "Carrefour Contends with Bribes in China," *Forbes* (August 27, 2007), online (www.forbes.com).

22. See, for example, D. Campbell, S. Datar, S. L. Kulp, and V. G. Narayanan, "Testing Strategy with Multiple Performance Measures: Evidence from a Balanced Scorecard at Store24," *Working Paper* (Harvard Business School, 2008).

23. "Shareholders vs. Stakeholders: A New Idolatry," *The Economist* (April 24, 2010), pp. 65–6.

24. "Patents, Yes; Ideas, Maybe," *The Economist* (October 14, 2010), pp. 78–9.

25. "Making a Killing," *The Economist* (July 16, 2009), p. 36.

26. Institute of Management Accountants, *Implementing Corporate Environmental Strategies*, Statement of Management Accounting (Montvale, NJ: Institute of Management Accountants, July 31, 1995).

27. G. P. Latham, "The Motivational Benefits of Goal-Setting," *Academy of Management Executive*, 18, no. 4 (November 2004), pp. 126–129.

28. "Performance Reviews by the Numbers," *The Wall Street Journal* (June 29, 2010), online (online.wsj.com).

29. "A Safer New York City," *Business Week* (December 11, 1995), p. 81.

30. V. H. Vroom, *Work and Motivation* (New York: Wiley, 1964).

31. E. P. Jansen, K. A. Merchant and W. A. Van der Stede, "National Differences in Incentive Compensation Practices: The Differing Roles of Financial Performance Measurement in The United States and The Netherlands, *Accounting, Organizations and Society*, 34, no. 1 (January 2009), pp. 58–84.

32. D. Solomons, *Divisional Performance: Measurement and Control* (Homewood, IL: Richard D. Irwin, 1965), p. 83.

33. K. J. Arrow, "Control in Large Organizations," in M. Schiff and A. Y. Lewin (eds.), *Behavioral Aspects of Accounting* (Englewood Cliffs, NJ: Prentice Hall, 1974), p. 284.

Case Study

Armco, Inc.: Midwestern Steel Division

In January 1991 management of the Kansas City Works of Armco's Midwestern Steel Division began implementing a new performance measurement system. Bob Nenni, Director of Finance for the Midwestern Steel Division, explained:

> With our old system, our managers spent more time explaining why changes in costs were caused by problems with our accounting system than they did fixing the problems. The new performance measurement system is designed to give us better management focus on the things that are most important for them to worry about, earlier warning of problems, and improved commitment to achieve objectives.

In the summer of 1991 the new system was still being implemented and its design refined. But Bob Nenni believed that the new system would be successful at the Kansas City Works, and he hoped that its use would spread throughout Armco.

BACKGROUND OF ARMCO AND THE KANSAS CITY WORKS

Armco, Inc. was a producer of stainless, electrical, and carbon steels and steel products. Through joint ventures the company also produced coated, high strength and low-carbon flat rolled steels and oil ▶

This case was prepared by research assistant Patrick Henry and Professor Kenneth A. Merchant.

field machinery and equipment. In 1990 Armco was the sixth largest steel manufacturer in the United States with slightly over $1.7 billion in net sales, and operating profits of $77 million. Exhibit 1 shows a three-year history of Armco's financial results.

Armco's Midwestern Steel Division generated $550 million in sales in 1990. (A division organization chart is shown in Exhibit 2.) Within the division, the Kansas City Works was by far the largest entity, accounting for approximately $250 million in sales. Like that of most of the firms in the US steel industry, business at the Kansas City Works had declined significantly in the last decade. Employment was down from 5,000 employees in 1980 to 1,000 in 1990.[1] The Works had recorded significant losses in the decade of the 1980s, but it had been marginally profitable since 1988.

The Kansas City Works produced two primary products: grinding media and carbon wire rod. Grinding media were steel balls used for crushing ore in mining operations. Carbon wire rod was used to make shopping carts, bed springs, coat hangers, and other products. In 1990 the Kansas City Works sold 700,000 tons of steel: 200,000 tons of grinding media and 500,000 tons of rods. Armco was recognized as the leading supplier of grinding media products in the United States. Armco's balls had proven themselves to be the most durable, and Armco received fewer customer complaints about its balls than did its competitors. Carbon wire rods, on the other hand, were basically a commodity product. Armco's rod mill, which used relatively old technology, was not cost competitive, so rods were not a profitable product. But the rods did generate volume and helped cover some of the fixed costs of the plant.

The Kansas City Works was not a low-cost manufacturer. Its union labor costs in Kansas City were higher than those of some of its nonunion competitors, particularly those located in the southeastern United States and non-US locations. And the Works had an inefficient plant infrastructure because the plant was designed to accommodate five times as many employees as were currently working there. Instead of being efficiently laid out, the buildings still being used were spread across a 900-acre plant site.

Because of the plant's cost disadvantage, the Work's managers looked for ways to differentiate

their products and to develop new higher-value products, and they had had some success in doing so. Each year approximately 10% of the shipments of the Kansas City Works were of new higher value, high carbon content products.

All salaried employees in the Works were eligible for cash incentive awards based on a performance evaluation made by their immediate superior and, ultimately, Rob Cushman, the division president. The incentive award potentials ranged from approximately 5–30% of annual salary depending on the individual's organization level. The performance evaluations were subjective but were based on, typically, three measures of performance applicable to the position. For example, Rob Cushman described the criteria he used for evaluating the performance of Charlie Bradshaw, the Works Manager, as being based approximately one third on plant safety, one third on hard production numbers (particularly productivity and quality), and one third on his evaluation of Charlie's "leadership" (i.e. "Do I hear good things and see good things going on?").

THE MANUFACTURING PROCESS AT THE KANSAS CITY WORKS

The manufacturing process used for making both rods and grinding media included four basic steps. First, scrap steel was melted in the ladle arc furnaces. Second, the melted steel was poured into a continuous caster that produced solid bars 30 feet in length with a 7″ by 7″ cross-section. Third, the 19″ mill pressed the steel bars between two large cylindrical rollers to give them either a square or circular shape and with either 3″ or 4″ cross-sections.[2] Finally, the bars were processed into finished rods or balls. The rod mill shop worked with square cross-section bars. It reduced the bars' diameter to between $1/4″$ and $5/8″$ and coiled them into 2,000-pound bundles for shipment to customers. The rods were further reduced in size ("cold drawn to wire") at the customers' facilities for use in their products. The grinding media shop worked with the circular cross-section bars produced by the 19″ mill. It formed them into spheres using a roll-forming machine. Finished balls ranged in size from 1″ to 5″ in diameter.

---

[1] Over the same period, Armco Inc. decreased in size from 70,000 to 23,000 employees.

[2] The distance from center to center of the two pressing rolls was 19 inches. Hence, the name for the process.

CRITICAL SUCCESS FACTORS IN THE WORKS

A. The melt shop

The melt shop, which included the ladle arc furnace and the continuous caster, produced molten steel in 167-ton batches known as "heats." The shop's goal was to run three "turns" (shifts) a day, seven days a week, 50 weeks a year, excluding the eight hours a week used for preventive maintenance. The other two weeks of the year were used for extensive preventive maintenance and installation of new equipment. The melt shop could theoretically produce about 110 heats/week, but the best quarter it had ever achieved was an average of 99 heats/week.

For a number of reasons, good performance in the melt shop was critical to the performance of the Kansas City Works as a whole. First, the melt shop was the "bottleneck" operation, so output from this phase of manufacturing process determined the output of the plant as a whole.

Second, the melt shop costs accounted for nearly 40% of the total steel conversion costs incurred in the plant. The largest expenditures in the melt shop were for labor, production materials of various types, and energy. Energy alone accounted for approximately 10% of the melt shop costs. Works managers were working toward computer control of energy, but in 1991 the melt shop manager still made most decisions about the heat used in the furnace, a major energy consumer. In 1988 Armco made an $8 million investment in a new ladle arc furnace that significantly changed the melting furnace technology used in the plant, and costs were declining as the melt shop managers learned how best to use the new technology.

Third, the quality of raw steel produced by the melt shop was an important component in determining whether the finished products met the required specifications. Quality was affected by the grades of scrap steel and nonmetallic materials used in the process. Nonmetallic materials were consumable items added to batches to remove contaminants from the steel. Armco managers purchased a variety of grades of scrap steel and nonmetallic materials, and they used different proportions of scrap to nonmetallic materials depending on the grades of scrap and nonmetallics being used; lower grades of scrap typically contained more contaminants. Some of the production processes were standardized, with the addition of some nonmetallics done either by automated equipment or by production employees following standardized recipes. Other processes, however, required the manufacturing manager and his technical supervisors to exercise judgment.

B. Rolling and Finishing

Personnel in the Rolling and Finishing areas were asked to make parts to specification while controlling yields and costs. Customer specifications for rods usually contained physical property requirements, such as for ductility and elasticity. One specification for balls required a two-story drop test. If the test ball cracked into parts on impact after being dropped from two stories, then the product was rejected on quality grounds. In addition, the lives of the balls were tested in Armco's customers' actual grinding operations. Those tests had shown that Armco's balls were more than competitive; they lasted up to 15% longer than did its closest competitor's balls. The rolling areas were heavily capital intensive. Significant costs in the finishing areas were for labor, energy, maintenance, and yield losses.

C. Maintenance

Maintenance was also an important determinant of success in the Kansas City Works. The goal of maintenance was to maximize equipment up-time while controlling maintenance expenditures. Organizationally, the maintenance activities were divided into three groups. Teams of electrical and mechanical maintenance employees were assigned to each manufacturing cost center. A third group operated a centralized maintenance shop. The cost of maintenance was significant, as approximately 40% of the 700 hourly employees in the plant were maintenance workers.

THE OLD PERFORMANCE MEASUREMENT SYSTEM

The manufacturing areas of the Kansas City Works were divided into five responsibility centers: melting, casting, the 19″ mill, the rod mill department, and the grinding media department. Each responsibility center was comprised of one or more cost centers.

Before changes were made in 1991 the performances of the cost center managers and their superiors in the plant were evaluated in terms of cost control and safety. The key cost performance measure was a summary measure called "Cost Above" which included the cost added per ton of steel at each production stage and for the entire plant. Cost Above and the items that comprised it were reported to the manufacturing managers on an Operating Statistics Report that was produced on approximately the 15th day following each month end.

The Operating Statistics Reports provided a five-year history, monthly and year-to-date actuals, and monthly and year-to-date objectives and variances from objectives for each of the factors that determined total Cost Above for each cost center. Exhibit 3 shows a portion of the Operating Statistics Report for one cost center – the #2 melt shop.[3] (The entire report, printed on five computer pages, included detailed information about 46 separate expense categories.) The report also gave cost per net ton ($/NT) for many of the cost categories. The Total Cost Above/NT is shown in the next to last column of page 3 of Exhibit 3.

The Operating Statistics Reports used the same accounting information that was used for financial reporting and inventory valuation purposes, so the figures included allocations of indirect manufacturing costs. For example, to provide smoother cost patterns, the charge for the two-week plant maintenance shutdown was spread over the 50 weeks of operations. These costs, which included labor and material, were shown on the Operating Statistics Report as "S-Order" costs.

The operating managers had become accustomed to the Operating Statistics Report and in general they liked it. For example Gary Downey, the Melting Operations manager, said that he looked at 95% of the information presented in the report, although he acknowledged that some of the items were quite small in dollar value. Paul Phillips, the Rolling and Finishing Manager, liked having the monthly and annual trends and the information comparing actual costs with objectives. Paul felt that the Operating Statistics report was "the minimum amount of detail necessary." He would have preferred to have the Operating Statistics Report on a weekly basis and in his hands on Monday morning because, for example, "If we see that fuel consumption is unusually high, we can go and look for the cause."

The accounting department also provided other reports showing the detail behind the figures for some of the cost elements on request. For example, one report showed the cost for nonmetallic materials broken down by the specific materials used.

THE NEW PERFORMANCE MEASUREMENT SYSTEM

A. The goals of the new system

Bob Nenni, the director of finance, had been working on a performance measurement system since 1989, but due to staff constraints he had been unable to design and implement the new system while keeping the old system going. On November 1, 1990 Rob Cushman was appointed as president of the Midwestern Steel Division, and Rob sponsored the implementation of a new performance measurement system. He allowed Bob Nenni to discontinue production of the Operating Statistics Report in January 1991 in order to implement the new system.

Rob Cushman observed:

The old system wasn't working. People were relying on something that was not adequate . . .

Enough companies are using good performance measurements as building blocks to excellence. I don't want to go against the grain. I want to give my managers the information they need. And I want to have good measures that tell us how we've done. I'm not using the performance measures as a threat. I'm trying to make it fun so that when we determine we've done well we can celebrate our successes . . .

If this plant does everything right, we should be able to make $30 million per year. But we're not doing it. This system is part of a spirit of change that has to happen. We will give people more responsibility . . . and more latitude to fail.

Bob Nenni added:

The cost part of our old performance measurement system was built for accountants. It was designed to produce financial statements, operating reports, and product cost reports. One system can't do all these things well.

The new system was designed both as a means of providing middle- and lower-level managers with a greater understanding of how their actions related to the implementation of the division's business strategies and as an improved method for managers

---

[3] The #1 melt shop contained obsolete equipment and was no longer used.

at all levels to assess the extent to which the desired results were being achieved. The vision and goals of the organization were to be translated into key success factors which would be disaggregated into department and individual objectives that would be compared with measures of actual results. The basic philosophy is illustrated in chart form in Exhibit 4.

Rob Cushman and Bob Nenni thought that the new system promised two major improvements. First, the new system was designed so that managers would focus on the few key objectives that largely determine the success of the Kansas City Works and not get involved in the detail until a problem existed. As Bob Nenni observed:

> When managers get too much data, they can easily get unfocused. The new system will cause them to focus on the five or six things that cause 80% of the costs, not the 40 that cause 100%.

Second, the new system was designed to provide an improved basis for evaluating operating managers and manufacturing supervisors. The system would include a balanced set of performance measures, including quality, schedule achievement, and safety, in addition to costs. And the cost reports would be improved because they would include only those costs deemed controllable by each individual operating manager. They would not be distorted by volume changes as in the old system.

B. The design of the new system

The new system design process began early in 1990. Rob Cushman, Charlie Bradshaw, Bob Nenni, Gil Smith (commercial director), and others defined 10 key performance measures for the Kansas City Works:

1. heats per week
2. tons per man hour
3. disabling injury index
4. total quality index
5. spending
6. maintenance performance
7. cash flow
8. product mix
9. inventory days on hand
10. sales price minus cost of net metal.

Performance measure 1, heats per week, was only relevant to the melt shop. However, since the melt shop was the bottleneck operation, heats per week was a critical measure for the Works as a whole. Measures 2 through 6 were applicable to all manufacturing areas. Tons per man hour was a productivity measure. The disabling injury index was a safety measure. The total quality index was the product of three measures: physical yield, percentage of product meeting specification, and percentage on-time shipment. Spending was the accumulation of all expenses incurred by the people reporting directly to a manager. The maintenance performance measures had not yet been clearly defined by the middle of 1991, but maintenance labor cost and material cost were being measured. Performance measures 7 through 10 were plant-wide (not cost center) measures. Cash flow was measured monthly for the plant. Product mix was the percentage of high carbon products sold compared to low carbon. Inventory days on hand was tracked monthly. Accountability for inventory performance was shared among plant purchasing managers, manufacturing managers, and commercial managers. Sales price minus net metal, a measure of value added, was tracked monthly.

The design group discussed the components of each performance area and the ways in which each measure could be disaggregated to guide performance at lower management levels. For example, the cascading of goals relating to total quality is illustrated in Exhibit 5. Total quality at the Works level was affected by the proportion of products meeting customer specifications, the yields, and the percentage of on-time shipments; and each of these indicators could be disaggregated further. The intent was to measure each of these areas of performance at the lowest relevant level of the organization.

One of the most significant changes was the elimination of the Cost Above measure. Production managers were no longer held accountable for all costs incurred in or allocated to their respective areas so, in effect, they were no longer cost center managers. The cost detail in the new performance reports was reduced considerably. In the new system the only cost figure on which managers were evaluated was the spending by the employees in their organizations. For example, in January 1991 spending on maintenance in the melt shop was $300,000, but only $30,000 of this amount was spent by people reporting in Gary Downey's organization. Thus, Gary's report included only the $30,000 figure. The other $270,000 was reported to other managers, particularly those of maintenance and purchasing.

C. The implementation process

On January 1, 1991 Bob Nenni discontinued the Operating Statistics Report system. He believed that the new system would have had no chance if "the managers kept using the old data and never seriously considered improvements that could be made." The accounting department began the process of producing new sets of reports. As the entire task could not be accomplished immediately they focused their attention on producing some pilot reports for a subset of the measures. They focused first on heats per week, tons per man hour, physical yield (a component of the total quality index), and spending. Exhibit 6 gives an example of a report for the Melting Operations Manager.

The operating managers' initial reaction to the sample reports they were given was dissatisfaction. The early reports did not provide the line-item expense detail to which they had become accustomed. In addition, they were no longer given Cost Above information, so they asked, "Where are my spending numbers?" In early April 1991 Charlie Bradshaw told Bob Nenni, "I've received nothing of use from your department since you discontinued the old reports." Another manager complained, "It almost seems like the operating managers finally understood the old report, so they decided to change it."

In late April the accounting group backed off their initial implementation plan. They started to provide spending numbers for the entire cost center in addition to the spending initiated by a manager's direct reports. This change was made to give the operating managers a number that they could compare to their budgeted spending targets which had been prepared using the old measurement philosophy. Starting in 1992, however, they promised that the reports would reflect only the new cost performance philosophy. By then the performance targets would be set using that same philosophy.

In June 1991 Bob Nenni reflected on nine months since the design meetings began. He was convinced

that the company was on the right track even though some of the managers were uncomfortable with the new system. And he knew that the delays in the implementation process had frustrated both the information users and his accounting staff. He noted:

> We're trying to change the way the managers think. The new system is not yet part of their mentality. Changing mindsets is ultimately more important and more challenging than the technical job of producing the reports.
>
> But we in accounting feel we will now be more useful to the organization. We were spending 60% of our time in accounting on the non-value-added chores of inventory valuation for financial reporting purposes. We have now reduced that to 20%.

REMAINING ISSUES

In 1991 two related performance evaluation/incentive issues arose in discussion. One was an issue about how to evaluate managers' performances in situations where the numbers were distorted by uncontrollable factors. For example, early in 1991 the melt shop suffered two transformer failures, apparently because of fluctuations in the line voltages provided by the local utility, Kansas City Power and Light. Such failures had happened nearly every year, but shop managers had recently upgraded some of their electrical switches to try to eliminate the problem. Nonetheless, the failures occurred again, and by April Gary Downey knew that his goal to average 101 heats per week was impossible. The failure of the melt shop to achieve its plan would mean that the Kansas City Works as a whole would not be able to achieve its plans for 1991. Rob Cushman knew that at the end of the year he would have to decide whether or not to let this, and perhaps other similar occurrences, affect the evaluations of his operating managers.

The second was an issue as to whether to increase the proportion of total compensation that was linked to individual performance evaluations. In other words, how much of total compensation should be provided in fixed salary, and how much should be paid only to those who were good at getting things done and done well?

Exhibit 1 Three-year financial history of Armco, Inc.[1]

(Dollars and shares in millions, except per share data)			
	1990	*1989*	*1988*
Sales[2]	1,735.2	2,422.7	3,277.3
Operating profit[3]	76.9	239.8	222.3
Net income (loss)[4]	(89.5)	165.0	145.4
Net income (loss) per share – primary	(1.10)	1.78	1.57
Capital expenditures	85.8	169.7	120.2
Number of shares of common stock outstanding	88.5	88.4	87.8
Number of employees[5]	9,800	10,500	19,500
Total domestic retirees	15,700	15,900	21,400

[1] Certain amounts in the prior periods have been reclassified to conform to the 1990 presentation.

[2] Effective May 13, 1989. Armco sold certain assets and a portion of its Eastern Steel Division's business to Kawasaki Steel Investments, Inc. in exchange for cash and a partnership interest in a joint venture. This division had annual revenues in excess of $1 billion.

[3] Includes special credits (charges) of $80.7 and $(35.0) in 1989 and 1988 respectively.

[4] Includes the cumulative effect of accounting changes in 1988 of $37.4 or 43 cents per share.

[5] Excludes discontinued operations, associated companies, and Armco Financial Services Group.

Exhibit 2 Organization chart, Midwestern Steel, March 1991

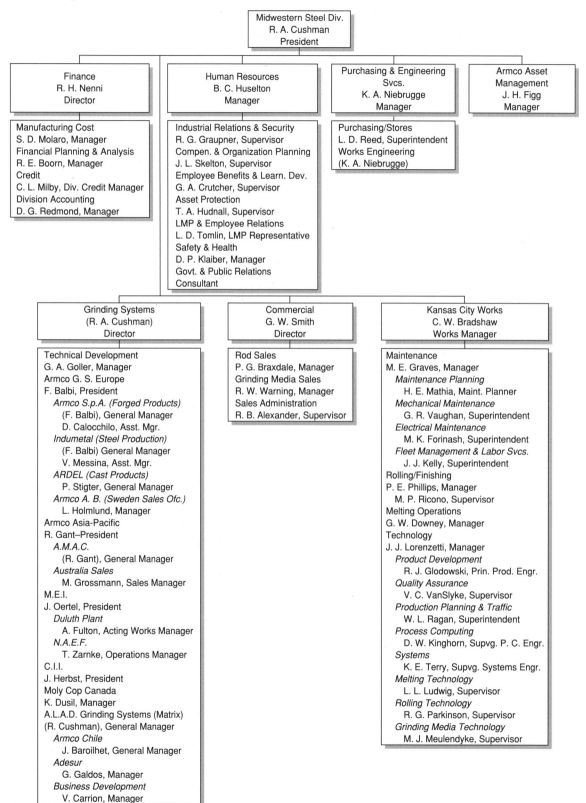

Midwestern Steel Div.
R. A. Cushman
President

Finance
R. H. Nenni
Director

Manufacturing Cost
S. D. Molaro, Manager
Financial Planning & Analysis
R. E. Boorn, Manager
Credit
C. L. Milby, Div. Credit Manager
Division Accounting
D. G. Redmond, Manager

Human Resources
B. C. Huselton
Manager

Industrial Relations & Security
R. G. Graupner, Supervisor
Compen. & Organization Planning
J. L. Skelton, Supervisor
Employee Benefits & Learn. Dev.
G. A. Crutcher, Supervisor
Asset Protection
T. A. Hudnall, Supervisor
LMP & Employee Relations
L. D. Tomlin, LMP Representative
Safety & Health
D. P. Klaiber, Manager
Govt. & Public Relations
Consultant

Purchasing & Engineering Svcs.
K. A. Niebrugge
Manager

Purchasing/Stores
L. D. Reed, Superintendent
Works Engineering
(K. A. Niebrugge)

Armco Asset Management
J. H. Figg
Manager

Grinding Systems
(R. A. Cushman)
Director

Technical Development
G. A. Goller, Manager
Armco G. S. Europe
F. Balbi, President
  Armco S.p.A. (Forged Products)
  (F. Balbi), General Manager
  D. Calocchilo, Asst. Mgr.
  Indumetal (Steel Production)
  (F. Balbi) General Manager
  V. Messina, Asst. Mgr.
  ARDEL (Cast Products)
  P. Stigter, General Manager
  Armco A. B. (Sweden Sales Ofc.)
  L. Holmlund, Manager
Armco Asia-Pacific
R. Gant–President
  A.M.A.C.
  (R. Gant), General Manager
  Australia Sales
  M. Grossmann, Sales Manager
M.E.I.
J. Oertel, President
  Duluth Plant
  A. Fulton, Acting Works Manager
  N.A.E.F.
  T. Zarnke, Operations Manager
C.I.I.
J. Herbst, President
Moly Cop Canada
K. Dusil, Manager
A.L.A.D. Grinding Systems (Matrix)
(R. Cushman), General Manager
  Armco Chile
  J. Baroilhet, General Manager
  Adesur
  G. Galdos, Manager
  Business Development
  V. Carrion, Manager

Commercial
G. W. Smith
Director

Rod Sales
P. G. Braxdale, Manager
Grinding Media Sales
R. W. Warning, Manager
Sales Administration
R. B. Alexander, Supervisor

Kansas City Works
C. W. Bradshaw
Works Manager

Maintenance
M. E. Graves, Manager
  Maintenance Planning
  H. E. Mathia, Maint. Planner
  Mechanical Maintenance
  G. R. Vaughan, Superintendent
  Electrical Maintenance
  M. K. Forinash, Superintendent
  Fleet Management & Labor Svcs.
  J. J. Kelly, Superintendent
Rolling/Finishing
P. E. Phillips, Manager
  M. P. Ricono, Supervisor
Melting Operations
G. W. Downey, Manager
Technology
J. J. Lorenzetti, Manager
  Product Development
  R. J. Glodowski, Prin. Prod. Engr.
  Quality Assurance
  V. C. VanSlyke, Supervisor
  Production Planning & Traffic
  W. L. Ragan, Superintendent
  Process Computing
  D. W. Kinghorn, Supvg. P. C. Engr.
  Systems
  K. E. Terry, Supvg. Systems Engr.
  Melting Technology
  L. L. Ludwig, Supervisor
  Rolling Technology
  R. G. Parkinson, Supervisor
  Grinding Media Technology
  M. J. Meulendyke, Supervisor

Exhibit 3 Excerpts from Operating Statistics Report, 2711–#2 Melt Shop

	Tons	Yield	Tons/ Tap/Tap Hour	Non-Metallics		Salaries		Hourly Supervision	
				Tons	$/NT	MH	$/NT	MH	$/NT
1985	706,237	93.64	36.01	0.04056	3.43	0.0815	1.67	0.0000	0.00
1986	737,380	93.38	37.40	0.04304	3.58	0.0818	1.73	0.0000	0.00
1987	741,234	93.85	39.17	0.04536	3.58	0.0756	1.63	0.0013	0.03
1988	800,581	92.79	41.30	0.04776	3.74	0.0822	2.06	0.0006	0.02
1989	870,768	94.42	45.15	0.04224	4.58	0.0649	1.53	0.0023	0.07
MONTHLY STATISTICS									
JAN	69,920	93.88	42.71	0.0411	6.50	0.0620	1.58	0.0057	0.19
FEB	68,106	91.41	44.81	0.0471	7.69	0.0628	1.57	0.0047	0.15
MAR	68,240	95.74	49.58	0.0512	7.75	0.0625	1.55	0.0038	0.12
APR	83,797	95.30	46.33	0.0398	5.57	0.0442	1.14	0.0033	0.11
MAY	74,507	95.50	46.96	0.0593	7.50	0.0433	1.30	0.0046	0.15
JUN	80,190	96.18	44.44	0.0532	6.56	0.0462	1.28	0.0047	0.15
JUL	76,513	94.58	44.37	0.0409	4.95	0.0486	1.27	0.0032	0.10
AUG	32,489	96.32	43.84	0.0851	11.18	0.1140	3.10	0.0047	0.15
SEP	70,475	95.54	51.03	0.0578	5.90	0.0525	1.34	0.0038	0.13
OCT	85,128	95.21	52.66	0.0466	5.76	0.0430	1.21	0.0014	0.04
NOV	85,992	96.47	54.48	0.0546	5.85	0.0426	1.13	0.0037	0.12
DEC	85,945	94.15	54.48	0.0400	5.72	0.0427	1.24	0.0038	0.13
YEAR-TO-DATE STATISTICS									
FEB	138,026	94.91	43.72	0.0441	7.09	0.0625	1.58	0.0052	0.17
MAR	206,268	95.72	44.00	0.0464	7.30	0.0625	1.57	0.0047	0.15
APR	290,065	96.10	45.48	0.0445	6.81	0.0572	1.44	0.0043	0.14
MAY	364,572	96.32	45.65	0.0475	6.94	0.0543	1.41	0.0044	0.14
JUN	444,761	96.57	45.88	0.0486	6.88	0.0529	1.39	0.0044	0.14
JUL	521,274	96.55	45.66	0.0474	6.59	0.0523	1.37	0.0043	0.14
AUG	553,763	96.63	45.59	0.0496	6.86	0.0559	1.47	0.0043	0.14
SEP	624,238	96.70	45.38	0.0506	6.75	0.0554	1.46	0.0042	0.14
OCT	709,366	96.73	45.99	0.0501	6.63	0.0540	1.43	0.0039	0.13
NOV	795,358	96.86	46.63	0.0506	6.55	0.0528	1.40	0.0039	0.13
DEC	881,303	96.79	47.30	0.0495	6.47	0.0518	1.38	0.0039	0.13
OBJECTIVES									
DEC	80,910	92.75	48.10	0.0000	4.18	0.0537	0.83	0.0005	0.02
YEAR	942,114	92.75	48.10	0.0000	4.18	0.0600	0.85	0.0005	0.02
VARIANCE FROM OBJECTIVES									
DEC	5,035	0.41	5.38	−0.0400	−1.536	0.0111	−0.41	−0.0033	−0.11
YTD	−60,811	1.24	−1.80	−0.04952	−2.288	0.0083	−0.53	−0.0034	−0.11

Note: Figures are disguised.

	Tons	Repair Labor MH	Repair Labor $/NT	S-Order Labor MH	S-Order Labor $/NT	S Order Matl	Maint Matl	Maint Outage	Electricity KWH	Electricity $/NT
1985	706,237	0.0671	2.06	0.0005	0.01	0.01	2.41	0.00	528.3264	20.90
1986	737,380	0.0670	2.25	0.0047	0.14	0.17	2.60	0.00	494.3517	19.23
1987	741,234	0.0749	2.22	0.0000	0.00	0.19	1.57	0.00	479.9061	18.41
1988	800,581	0.0862	2.86	0.0000	0.00	0.61	2.53	0.00	469.7077	18.37
1989	870,768	0.0685	2.32	0.0021	0.06	0.12	2.47	0.00	455.1210	18.99
MONTHLY STATISTICS										
JAN	69,920	0.0848	2.97	0.0006	0.01	0.54	3.50	0.84	497.9036	19.20
FEB	68,106	0.0686	2.38	0.0013	0.04	0.99	4.27	0.86	507.3894	19.82
MAR	68,240	0.0722	2.48	0.0020	0.06	1.06	3.73	0.86	522.4422	18.34
APR	83,797	0.0563	2.01	0.0030	0.10	0.74	2.81	0.70	491.3568	18.01
MAY	74,507	0.0749	2.71	0.0035	0.11	0.83	2.89	0.79	512.6357	20.43
JUN	80,190	0.0521	1.92	0.0050	0.16	0.71	2.68	0.73	516.9778	18.51
JUL	76,513	0.0338	1.25	0.0061	0.20	0.72	2.92	0.77	511.5135	19.89
AUG	32,489	0.3352	12.40	0.0174	0.57	1.81	8.66	−19.91	540.0536	28.03
SEP	70,475	0.0472	1.76	0.0010	0.03	1.19	2.42	0.83	540.4950	21.54
OCT	85,128	0.0504	1.84	0.0007	0.02	1.99	3.40	0.69	528.3277	18.66
NOV	85,992	0.0526	1.96	0.0003	0.01	2.07	1.79	0.68	533.7443	19.51
DEC	85,945	0.0347	1.40	0.0001	0.00	1.02	2.18	0.68	510.6142	18.95
YEAR-TO-DATE STATISTICS										
FEB	138,026	0.0768	2.68	0.0009	0.03	0.76	3.89	0.85	456.8288	19.50
MAR	206,268	0.0752	2.61	0.0013	0.04	0.86	3.84	0.86	462.1852	19.12
APR	290,065	0.0698	2.44	0.0018	0.06	0.83	3.54	0.81	458.1932	18.80
MAY	364,572	0.0708	2.50	0.0021	0.07	0.83	3.41	0.81	459.7953	19.13
JUN	444,761	0.0674	2.39	0.0026	0.08	0.81	3.28	0.79	461.6315	19.02
JUL	521,274	0.0625	2.22	0.0031	0.10	0.79	3.22	0.79	462.1277	19.15
AUG	553,763	0.0785	2.82	0.0040	0.13	0.85	3.54	−0.42	463.7972	19.67
SEP	624,238	0.0750	2.70	0.0036	0.12	0.89	3.42	−0.28	466.9283	19.88
OCT	709,366	0.0720	2.60	0.0033	0.11	1.02	3.41	−0.17	468.5328	19.73
NOV	795,358	0.0699	2.53	0.0030	0.10	1.14	3.24	−0.07	470.3372	19.71
DEC	881,303	0.0665	2.42	0.0027	0.09	0.93	3.13	0.00	469.7382	19.64
OBJECTIVES										
DEC	80,910	0.0552	1.95	0.0048	0.15	0.34	1.75	0.00	445.5000	19.15
YEAR	942,114	0.0552	1.95	0.0048	0.15	0.34	1.75	0.00	445.4858	19.15
VARIANCE FROM OBJECTIVES										
DEC	5,035	0.0205	0.55	0.0047	0.15	1.36	−0.43	−0.68	−18.69472	0.20
YTD	−60,811	−0.0113	−0.47	0.0047	0.07	−0.59	−1.38	0.00	−24.25236	−0.48

	Tons	Natural Gas MMBTU	Natural Gas $/NT	Gas & Diesel Fuel	Lubricants	Loco Cranes Hrs	Loco Cranes $/NT	Total Cost Above	Total Cost
1985	706,237	0.0147	0.06	0.02	0.00	0.0000	0.00	76.06	168.70
1986	737,380	0.1766	0.50	0.01	0.00	0.0000	0.00	79.38	164.20
1987	741,234	0.2242	0.60	0.01	0.01	0.0000	0.00	76.30	173.78
1988	800,581	0.2408	0.70	0.02	0.03	0.0003	0.03	79.03	216.37
1989	870,768	0.2180	0.52	0.02	0.03	0.0002	0.02	79.40	211.40
				MONTHLY STATISTICS					
JAN	69,920	0.1530	0.31	0.01	0.16	0.0002	0.02	89.62	198.21
FEB	68,106	0.1419	0.33	0.00	0.03	0.0001	0.01	93.82	207.92
MAR	68,240	0.2234	0.81	0.00	0.12	0.0001	0.01	90.68	202.70
APR	83,797	0.2002	0.54	0.01	0.00	0.0000	0.00	81.56	193.05
MAY	74,507	0.2033	0.55	0.01	0.00	0.0000	0.00	94.82	211.44
JUN	80,190	0.2094	0.57	0.01	0.21	0.0001	0.00	89.58	204.01
JUL	76,513	0.2698	0.72	0.01	−0.15	0.0002	0.02	90.10	204.57
AUG	32,489	0.3314	0.74	0.04	0.11	0.0005	0.04	142.82	251.19
SEP	70,475	0.9326	2.06	0.00	0.04	0.0003	0.02	99.91	216.90
OCT	85,128	−0.6225	−0.98	0.01	0.04	0.0000	0.00	93.99	205.63
NOV	85,992	0.0847	0.20	0.02	0.05	0.0001	0.02	86.31	195.64
DEC	85,945	0.0888	0.23	0.01	−0.02	0.0001	0.00	80.60	194.33
				YEAR-TO-DATE STATISTICS					
FEB	138,026	0.1475	0.32	0.01	0.10	0.0002	0.02	91.69	203.01
MAR	206,268	0.1726	0.48	0.01	0.11	0.0001	0.02	91.35	202.91
APR	290,065	0.1806	0.50	0.01	0.08	0.0001	0.01	88.53	200.06
MAY	364,572	0.1852	0.51	0.01	0.06	0.0001	0.01	89.82	202.38
JUN	444,761	0.1896	0.52	0.01	0.09	0.0001	0.01	89.78	202.68
JUL	521,274	0.2014	0.54	0.01	0.05	0.0001	0.01	89.82	202.95
AUG	553,763	0.2090	0.56	0.01	0.06	0.0001	0.01	92.92	205.79
SEP	624,238	0.2907	0.73	0.01	0.05	0.0001	0.01	93.72	207.04
OCT	709,366	0.1811	0.52	0.01	0.05	0.0001	0.01	93.76	206.87
NOV	795,358	0.1707	0.49	0.01	0.05	0.0001	0.01	92.95	205.66
DEC	881,303	0.1627	0.46	0.01	0.05	0.0001	0.01	91.74	204.57
				OBJECTIVES					
DEC	80,910	0.2192	0.51	0.02	0.03	0.0002	0.02	76.36	
YEAR	942,114	0.2192	0.51	0.02	0.03	0.0002	0.02	76.53	
				VARIANCE FROM OBJECTIVES					
DEC	5,035	0.1304	0.28	0.01	0.05	0.0001	0.01	−4.24	
YTD	−60,811	0.0565	0.05	0.01	−0.02	0.0001	0.01	−15.21	

Exhibit 4 Vision management process

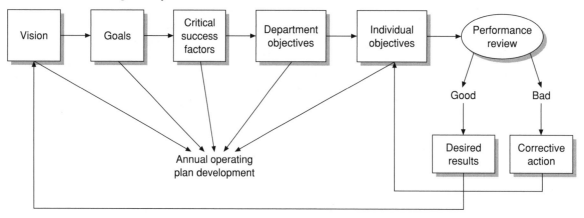

Exhibit 5 Cascading of total quality goals

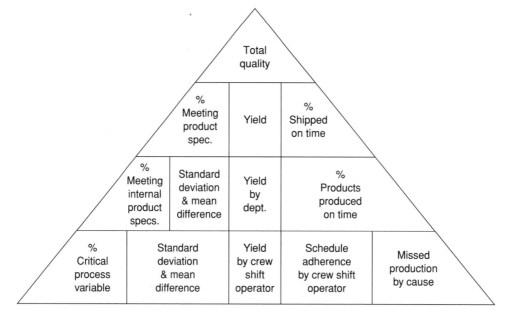

Exhibit 6 New system pilot performance report

	1990	Actual						Plan June	Var June	YTD Actual	YTD Plan	YTD Var
		Jan	Feb	Mar	Apr	May	June					
PRODUCTIVITY												
EAF/LAR[1]: Tons	587,535	58,080	46,624	55,532	57,281	46,706	56,188	58,832	(3,302)	320,359	347,564	(34,007)
Tap to tap hrs	12,164	1,152	982	1,133	1,149	956	1,143	1,102	(53)	6,517	6,617	100
Tons/hr	38.64	40.30	37.97	39.19	39.86	37.44	39.32	42.75	(4.29)	39.32	42.02	(3.37)
Heats/wk		79.20	70.40	75.20	78.40	61.60	77.60	81.60	(5)	73.60	80.00	(8)
HIT rate												
CASTER: Tons	572,704	56,901	44,655	54,201	56,246	45,751	55,272	57,361	(2,611)	313,030	338,876	(32,310)
Hours	6,346.40	563.20	512.00	563.20	550.40	556.80	550.40	550.40	0	3,296.00	3,308.80	12.80
Tons/hr	72.19	80.82	53.78	76.99	81.75	65.74	80.34	83.38	(3.80)	75.98	81.94	(7.44)
LABOR												
EAF/LAR: Man hours	107,307	9,837	8,929	10,236	9,806	9,806	10,000	9,514	(608)	58,632	55,629	(3,753)
Prod tons/manhr	4.38	4.72	4.17	4.34	4.03	3.81	4.66	4.94	(0.56)	4.37	5.00	(0.78)
CASTER: Man hours	78,110	6,683	6,089	6,724	4,964	6,938	6,724	6,567	(196)	39,724	39,616	(136)
Prod tons/manhr	6.01	6.81	5.86	6.45	6.86	5.27	6.58	6.98	(0.51)	6.30	6.84	(0.87)

[1] Electric arc furnace/ladle arc furnace.

Exhibit 6 *continued*

	1990	Actual Jan	Feb	Mar	Apr	May	June	Plan June	Var June	YTD Actual	YTD Plan	YTD Var
YIELD												
EAF/LAR: Reported	95.5%	96.4%	96.6%	97.0%	96.3%	97.9%	96.0%			96.7%		
Applied		95.4%	95.3%	95.6%	94.3%	95.0%	95.0%	95.0%	0.0%	95.2%	95.0%	0.2%
CASTER:	97.5%	96.0%	95.6%	97.6%	96.2%	98.1%	98.4%	97.5%	0.9%	97.7%	97.5%	0.2%
SPENDING												
EAF (electric arc furnace)		1,443,067	1,243,625	1,329,800	1,499,361	1,386,807	1,421,037	1,658,740	236,102	8,325,300	9,870,859	1,545,559
LAF (ladle arc furnace)		116,149	68,427	79,751	46,168.80	136,724	92,687	115,669	22,982	539,908	693,743	153,835
CASTER		351,824	290,937	305,132	313,962	312,456	289,136	325,392	36,255	1,863,450	1,936,292	72,842
TOTAL SPENDING												
Total$		1,909,441	1,602,990	1,714,684	1,859,492	1,835,987	1,804,461	2,099,801	295,340	10,728,658	12,500,895	1,772,236
$/NT		26.87	28.72	25.31	26.45	32.10	26.12	29.29	3.17	27.42	29.51	2.10
ADDITIONAL MEASURES												
EAF: KWH/NT	3.41	342.40	353.60	344.00	331.20	353.60	342.40	332.00	(13)	344.00	332.00	(15)
Electrodes/NT:	4.94	5.41	5.52	4.86	5.07	5.30	4.73	4.73	0.00	4.11	3.78	(0.51)
MMBTU's/NT	0.16	0.09	0.49	0.46	0.48	0.56	0.39	0.18	(0.25)	0.40	0.19	(0.26)
LAR: KWH/NT	28.80	20.80	23.20	25.60	27.20	28.80	25.60	28.80	3.20	25.60	29.60	4.00
Electrodes/NT:	0.78	0.54	0.45	0.63	0.00	1.46	0.60	0.80	0.20	0.59	0.80	0.21

Loctite Company de México, S.A. de C.V.

Corporate managers of the Loctite Company, a US-based specialty chemical company, allowed the general managers of their foreign subsidiaries to tailor their employees' compensation packages to the local environments. José Monteiro, general manager of Mexico, valued this autonomy, but he admitted that performance evaluations and compensation structures caused him considerable concern:

> One of the most difficult management areas in Mexico is compensation. When the [Mexican] borders opened, every company found itself in a special situation, and usually worse off. The lowering of tariffs, an important part of President Salinas's plan to bring down inflation and bring investment to the country to enable Mexico to compete globally, has caused a notable increase in foreign competition. For example, the tariff on cianoacrylate adhesives, a product we manufacture in Mexico, has been lowered from 37% to 15%.
>
> Everybody needs good people to compete effectively in this environment, so we have seen a tremendous increase in the competition for labor. The demand for skilled employees and executives far outstrips the supply. Bilingual employees, in particular, are being tempted by other companies, mostly US companies expanding their operations in the Mexican market. So I pay a lot of attention to how much we pay our employees as well as the bases for and the forms and timing of the payments. Loctite is a young company in Mexico, and if you want to grow, you must compensate your people appropriately.

In 1992 José faced a special compensation problem. Faced with a sales slowdown, some of the salespeople in the Mexico City area were working with distributors within their territories to capture sales, and hence commissions, from outside their territories. José had to decide whether to tolerate this intracompany competition or to take steps to eliminate either the salespeople's prerogatives to cross territory boundaries and/or their incentives to do so.

LOCTITE CORPORATION

Loctite Corporation was founded as American Sealants Co. in 1953 in Hartford, Connecticut by Dr. Vernon Krieble, a retired Trinity College chemistry professor. Its first product was an anerobic[1] sealant called Loctite. Over the years the company maintained a dominant (85% in 1992) market share in the world market for anerobic sealants, and it grew both internally and by acquisition. In 1992 Loctite was a worldwide company specializing in a broad range of sealant and adhesive products. Among the applications for Loctite's sealant products were to seal porosity in metal castings to stop leak paths, to seal bolts and nuts so that they would not come loose, and to seal transmissions to prevent oil leakage (i.e. liquid gaskets). Loctite's adhesives (e.g. gasket eliminator, *super* glue) were used for both manufacturing and repairs.

Loctite's 1991 sales ranked it 477th on the *Fortune* 500 list of the largest US industrial corporations, and it employed 3,500 people. The company's 10-year annual earnings-per-share growth rate of 22.4% was the 18th highest among the *Fortune* 500. (See financial highlights in Exhibit 1.) Company managers were proud that the company's *diversity without diversification* had allowed it to continue to grow through difficult economic times. They identified four elements to the diversity:

1. **Geographic.** Loctite had operating units in 33 countries around the world, and representative offices and joint ventures in many other countries, so its risk was spread across a range of national economic environments.

2. **End use markets.** Company managers recognized six major market areas: original equipment manufacturing (OEM), industrial maintenance, repair and

---

[1] Anerobic sealants cure without air.

This case was prepared by Professor Kenneth A. Merchant and Professors Francisco Arenas and Pedro Suãrez.

Copyright © by Kenneth A. Merchant and Pedro Suãrez.

overhaul (MRO), automobile manufacture, auto repair, auto body repair, and consumer.

3. **Product usage.** Many of Loctite's products could be used for multiple purposes and, in fact, the company had relatively high expense-to-sales ratio because Loctite engineers developed solutions tailored to individual industrial customer needs.

4. **Product diversity.** Loctite's R&D efforts had resulted in new technologies (e.g. specialty silicones) that broadened and expanded the company's sales offerings.

The company was organized into four geographical groups: North America, Europe, Latin America, and Asia/Pacific. North America and Europe were the largest groups by far, accounting for 46% and 39% of Loctite's total sales respectively. José Monteiro, general manager of Loctite's Mexican subsidiary, reported to Gerry Briels, president of the North American Group.

In the vast majority of its markets, Loctite competed on the basis of the superiority of its products. In the United States, competitors often undercut Loctite prices by 20–40%, and Loctite's price disadvantage was even more pronounced in many other countries, including Mexico.

LOCTITE'S MEXICAN SUBSIDIARY

Loctite's Mexican subsidiary, headquartered in Mexico City, was founded in 1958 by a US engineer formerly employed by Ford Motor Company. He imported a sealant product from a US company, Permatex, Inc., bottled it in Mexico, and sold it to the local Ford manufacturing plant. Permatex bought this Mexican distributor in 1964, and it became part of Loctite in 1973 when Loctite acquired Permatex.

In 1992 Loctite's Mexican subsidiary was still small but was growing rapidly. Sales had grown from $3.1 million in 1987 to a level expected to be slightly below $9 million in 1992. In the near term, growth was expected to continue in the Mexican market, which was less mature than that of the United States, at the annual rate of 15% in sales and 20% in profits.

Loctite operated two small manufacturing facilities in Mexico which, in 1992, employed a total of 45 people. The company started manufacturing anerobics in 1978 and cianoacrylate (instant)

adhesives in 1980, both for the Mexican market only. But José Monteiro expected that eventually Loctite would not do any manufacturing in Mexico because costs were increasing four to five times faster than the peso's devaluation relative to the dollar, and the small size of the subsidiary's manufacturing operations precluded economies of scale.

The subsidiary was organized functionally (see Exhibit 2). All but two of the 119 employees were Mexican nationals. The two exceptions were Luis Riquelme, the controller, who was from Argentina, and José Monteiro, the general manager, who was from Portugal. José had worked for Loctite for several years in the United States as a consolidation accountant; he had been the controller in both the Brazilian and Mexican subsidiaries; and he had been the general manager of the Mexican subsidiary since 1988.

The sales function was divided into two areas: Industrial and Permatex. The Industrial sales force, reporting to Larry Goldsmith,[2] was comprised of two separate groups, one which sold products direct to OEMs, mostly in the automotive industry, and the other which sold through distributors to MRO users. The Permatex salesforce, reporting to Victor Moreno, sold products directly to distributors and retailers (e.g. hardware stores). In all cases, the salespeople were assigned to territories designed to be approximately equal in sales potential. (In some remote territories, Industrial salespeople sold both OEM and MRO products.) Prices were set by José Monteiro; the salespeople had no pricing authority.

Because the product markets and distribution networks were quite different, the appropriate sales approaches were also quite different. All of the industrial salespeople worked both directly with users and through distributors, but the mix of their activities varied. OEM salespeople spent most (60–70%) of their time working directly with users; MRO salespeople split their time working with distributors and giving in-plant maintenance seminars. The sales cycle for large OEM sales was relatively long, often six months or more. MRO and Permatex sales, on the other hand, were made almost immediately. Most MRO sales were made at in-plant sales seminars given to corporate audiences. Permatex

---

[2] Larry Goldsmith had five American and three Mexican sales managers reporting to him. He was based in Dallas, Texas, and reported on a dotted-line basis only to José Monteiro.

products were sold primarily through direct calls to retailers and wholesalers.

The best OEM salespeople sold their products by inventing new applications for existing Loctite products. They studied customers' products and production processes and suggested ways in which Loctite products could help. As Javier Marron, OEM sales manager, emphasized, "We don't sell products. We sell solutions."

Specification of Loctite products could be influenced by engineering, production, or maintenance managers. The salespeople sometimes approached these people directly; sometimes they worked through the purchasing department; and sometimes they worked through the training function, usually located in human resources departments, and gave product seminars. The salespeople's inventiveness, however, only helped generate the first few sales. After a new application had been developed it was easy for competitors to suggest that their products, which were usually cheaper, be substituted. So to retain their customers the salespeople had to continue to provide superior service.

PERFORMANCE-DEPENDENT COMPENSATION

Compensation of Loctite de México employees was dependent on performance in three ways.[3] All employees were eligible for both company profit sharing and semiannual salary increases. Salespeople and manager-level personnel were eligible for commissions or bonuses based on individual performances.[4]

1. Profit sharing

All Mexican companies were required by law to distribute 10% of their pretax income to employees based on days worked and earnings (up to a maximum approximately equal to a salesperson's base salary). José considered the profit sharing payments to be incentive compensation, but he admitted that he had had less than complete success in convincing his employees that these payments provided an incentive for superior performance. He said, "They take [the payments] for granted."

2. Salary increases

Employee salaries were increased semi-annually.[5] José Monteiro wanted to offer excellent compensation packages to enhance his ability to attract and retain good people, but he found that it was not easy to judge the competition because every Mexican company's compensation package was somewhat unique. For sales personnel, for example, some companies paid salary only; some paid salary plus commission; some based their sales commissions on growth while others based them on the absolute level of sales; some provided a car while others did not; and the fringe benefit packages also varied considerably. But with the help of a compensation consulting firm, José conducted a study to identify a comparison group of Mexican companies that were considered *aggressive* in their compensation practices, and he set his salary and total compensation scales to be competitive with this group. As a result, Loctite's recent salary increases had been far above inflation.

The bases for the salary increases were determined subjectively by each employee's immediate superior. It was generally felt that the bases for which salary increases were given were quite similar to those that determined incentive compensation (described later).

Despite the high compensation levels, Loctite de México had still experienced considerable turnover. Loctite employees were seen as having received good training and experience, so they had many job opportunities presented to them. Turnover was particularly high in industrial sales – 78% in 18 months – and in each of the last two years the top salesperson had left the company to take a more lucrative position.

INCENTIVE COMPENSATION PLANS

Loctite de México offered different incentive compensation plans for salespeople, sales managers,

---

[3] Manufacturing line employees were given small bonuses (one day's pay) for coming to work on time every day for an entire month, but they were promised no production incentives. Studies have shown that piece rates are not very successful in Mexico because of adverse effects on the quality of the work done.

[4] The fringe benefit package was the same for all employees, with one exception: plant employees were provided with free lunches. They considered this an important benefit, and the company received a direct benefit in that the employees were healthier, in particular less likely to become ill from parasites.

[5] When inflation in Mexico was high (greater than 70%), Loctite gave its employees quarterly salary increases.

first-line managers (i.e. those reporting directly to the general manager), and the general manager.

A. Salespeople

The company's sales commission plan was designed to encourage the salespeople to work hard and to spend their time where the company's profit potential was greatest. About salespeople in general, José Monteiro said: "The tendency of most salespeople is to talk to people, to be liked, to do what they are comfortable with. The company needs to encourage them to have perseverance and to do tough things, such as to make the high value-added sales."

The plan paid a commission based on sales growth, as measured in liters/kilograms of product sales. José did not believe in paying a commission based on the absolute level of sales: "The biggest nonsense practiced in Mexican companies is to pay a straight commission on sales. That's a royalty, not a commission for performance." Payments were made on a bimonthly basis. The standard for each bimonthly period was the total prior year sales divided by six. No adjustments were made for seasonality because it was not considered to be an important factor.

Table 1 shows the commission chart for OEM salespeople. This chart shows that higher commission rates were earned for higher levels of growth and that the amount of growth needed for each level of commission varied depending on whether or not an MRO salesman was assigned to the same territory.

The salespeople were paid commissions bimonthly, rather than on an annual basis as was done in Loctite's US locations. José chose a shorter evaluation period because: "Mexico is a less mature market [than the United States]. If you want to grow at the rate we do, you need to look at very short periods of time. You get more focus and more rapid feedback." To

TABLE 1 OEM salesperson commission chart

Volume[a] growth in territory without MRO salesman	Volume[a] growth in territory including MRO salesperson	Commission (% revenue growth)
1–30	1–50	5
31–65	51–95	6
66–110	96–140	7
>111	>141	8

[a] Measured in liters/kilograms.

reduce the incidence of gameplaying, sales in any bimonthly period below the base were added to the base for the following bimonthly period (except in the last period of the year).

Although Loctite product gross margins varied significantly, from approximately 30% for equipment sales to 95% for some product sales (the average for industrial products was approximately 70%), commissions were based on sales, not gross margins, as was done in Loctite's US locations starting in 1992, because the subsidiary did not yet have a good cost accounting system. One problem was that the Mexican production processes were relatively new, so the production standards were not yet accurate. A second problem was that for many sales the Mexican subsidiary paid product transfer prices to Loctite's US subsidiaries that had a profit margin built into them. This intercompany profit was rebated to Mexico only in a lump sum that was not disaggregated to the product level.

Salespeople were also eligible for four other forms of incentive payments:

1. **Commission on house account sales.** House accounts were large OEM accounts (mostly automotive), the product specifications for which were set at corporate headquarters. Commissions on house account sales were paid at a lower rate, reflecting the salesperson's lack of control over those sales. The house account commission rate was set at 1% on sales below the base (last year's levels); 4.5% commission up to 14% growth over base; and higher commissions (up to 6%) for higher growth.

2. **New orders.** Permatex salespeople were paid an extra 2% commission on the first order from a new customer, defined as one to which there were no sales in the last six months.

3. **Achievement of SOP targets.** Salesmen could earn up to one month's salary each year for achievement of SOP (standards of performance) targets set in 13 performance areas (importance weighting shown in parentheses):

- in-plant seminars (15%)
- out-plant seminars (15%)
- new product ideas (10%)
- distributor visits (10%)
- sales (8%)
- special attention to major customers (8%)
- new prospects (8%)
- mailings (7%)
- new customers to database (7%)

- on-time monthly reports (4%)
- preparation of budget (3%)
- expenses within budget (3%)
- quarterly reports (2%).

SOP performances were evaluated quarterly, and up to one quarter of one month's salary was paid at that time. In a typical year, SOP ratings averaged 75–80% of maximum, and an average salesperson SOP bonus was approximately two thirds of one month's salary.

4. **Top performance.** Each year the top OEM and MRO salespeople were each given a vacation trip and a ring.

There was no limit to the amount of compensation a salesperson could earn, and the top salespeople earned quite handsome commissions. For example, in one 1992 bimonthly period, one salesman earned a commission of 19 million pesos.[6] Because of the economic slowdown, however, which caused the slowest period of growth ever for Loctite de México, about 75% of the salespeople earned no commission in the first half of 1992. Commission payments were not adjusted to offset bad (or good) luck because José believed, "Luck always seems to accompany those who are good."

B. Sales managers

The commission and SOP bonus plans for sales managers were quite similar to that for salespeople. Commission payments were based on sales growth over the preceding year, but the marginal rates for payment were lower than those provided to salespeople, as is shown in the representative schedule in Table 2. Also, payments were made quarterly, rather than bimonthly. There was no limit to what could be earned, but successful sales managers typically earned commissions totalling approximately 60–80% of salary.

Like the salespeople, sales managers could earn up to one month's salary for SOP performance. The list of SOP areas was quite similar to that for salespeople except that some targets were for activities unique to the sales manager role, such as conduct of SOP reviews of salespeople and conduct of regional sales meetings. The average SOP rating for the sales managers was typically above 90%.

---

[6] In 1992, a typical bimonthly commission for a salesperson was slightly less than 3 million pesos.

TABLE 2 Representative bonus function for an OEM sales manager

% Growth over last year base (in liters/kilograms)	Commission paid (% revenue growth)
1–10	2.0
11–20	2.5
21+	3.0

C. First-line managers

Incentive payments made to the managers reporting directly to the general manager were based on performance in SOP areas specific to their areas of responsibility. For example, Larry Goldsmith (manager of industrial sales) had 23 SOP objectives that were weighted approximately equally in importance. Some of the first-line managers also received small grants of restricted stock.

D. General manager

José Monteiro was included in a general manager's plan administered from the United States. José's annual bonus was based on sales and profit performance as compared with annual plan, both measured in terms of US dollars (not pesos), and performance in a few key areas (including day's receivables, cash self-sufficiency, implementation of statistical process control, use of participative management style). If the Mexican subsidiary achieved its annual profit and sales plan, José would earn a cash bonus of 40% of salary. If the plan was not achieved, no bonus was given, regardless of performance in the other areas. If the financial plans were achieved but some or all of the performance targets were not achieved, up to 25% of the bonus amount could be forfeited.

If the subsidiary's performance was *exceptional* (i.e. the plan was exceeded by a substantial margin), José would also be given some stock options to be exercised within a five-to-ten-year window. This had happened in two of the four years José had been in the general manager's job. The value of the options, of course, depended on the performance of Loctite stock. In recent years Loctite stock had performed quite well, and José expected that each of the two options awards he had been given would be worth significantly more than an annual bonus award in a successful year.

COMPETITION AMONG SALESPEOPLE IN MEXICO CITY TERRITORIES

In 1992 a problem arose in the Mexico City area, an area that was divided into four relatively small geographic territories. The sales slowdown was causing the integrity of the territorial system to break down. The most common problem was that some salespeople began to travel into territories other than those to which they were assigned to sell products to users serviced by distributors located within their territories. Loctite used 12 major distributors in the Mexico City area, and the distributors were free to sell wherever they wanted. But out-of-territory selling activity by salespeople was not good for Loctite because the salespeople spent time and money traveling outside their territories, and Loctite's sales efforts were sometimes duplicated. Another, relatively infrequent, violation of territories involved salespeople who were having a bad year *giving* sales to another salesperson or distributor in return for a sharing of the commission.

Daniel Rivera, an OEM salesman in a Mexico City territory, expressed some representative concerns:

Right now the situation is very tough, and the bonus system does not give us any motivation. The product almost sells by itself, but I am the fourth salesman who has been assigned to this territory in a very short period of time. We could sell a lot more if we didn't have as much turnover of salesmen.

I have to accomplish a 3,300 Lt/Kg base before I earn my first bonus. The growth commission is a doubly sharp knife. It is particularly tough because our competitors sell at lower prices, and our distributors compete against us to make their quotas. They don't have any territories as we, Loctite salesmen, do.

In my territory there are big companies, such as Black & Decker, Hewlett-Packard, and General Electric. I have to serve them, and there are at least 40 more prospects to whom we could sell, but at times like this you have to follow-up with your clients to make the sale.

It's not fair that at times like this, when customers are reducing their purchases, competitors are lowering their prices, and our distributors are competing with us unloyally, I have to sell at increased prices and generate sales growth in order to make a bonus. Other companies' salesmen, like the ones from 3M, earn as much as three times my pay check.

Comments from Javier Marron, OEM sales manager in Mexico City:

I really don't know how many customers we are serving. Neither the distributors nor the salesmen will tell me honestly because they fear I will keep some of the customers as house accounts. But my estimate is that within the Mexico City area, we have at least 3,000 potential customers.

I think our incentive system is good. It motivates the salespeople to sell and to serve old customers, because if you don't, our competitors will take them from you. But it is true that we have lost some salesmen with high sales bases who concluded that growth from that level is difficult.

One idea we had to eliminate the piracy problems between territories is to establish one joint territory within the Mexico City area. Then the bonus pool would depend on performance within the entire area, and we would allocate the pool to each individual based on SOP performance.

Exhibit 1 Loctite Corporation – 10-year financial highlights

Year ended	Net sales		Net earnings	
	$ millions	% incr.	$ millions	% incr.
1991	561.2	1	71.9	7
1990	555.2	17	67.4	16
1989	473.9	8	58.2	22
1988	438.9	14	47.6	30
1987	383.4	31	36.7	45
1986	292.4	22	25.3	32
1985	239.9	(2)	19.1	(26)
1984	243.8	7	25.7	16
1983	228.1	7	22.2	63
1982	212.6	(3)	13.6	(9)

Exhibit 2 Organization chart

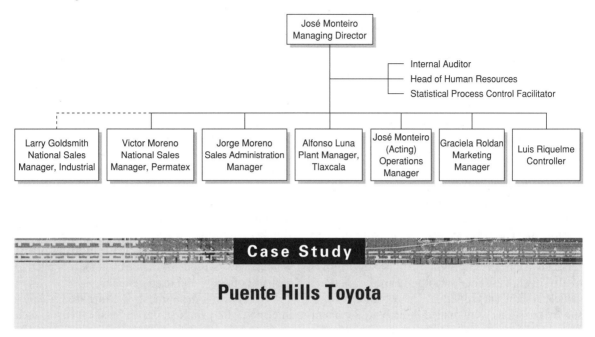

Case Study

Puente Hills Toyota

In December 2003, Howard Hakes, vice president of Hitchcock Automotive Services, reflected on some of the challenges his team faced in managing his company's stable of automobile dealerships. He illustrated his points by discussing the challenges faced at Puente Hills Toyota, Hitchcock's largest dealership, although all of the Hitchcock dealerships faced essentially the same problems.

> This is very much a people business. It's people who give us our biggest successes as well as our biggest challenges. At our Toyota store, in sales, I would say that about 20% of our people are loyal to the company and really want to do a good job. The other 80% are just in this for the money . . . and they can make more money here than anywhere else. Our compensation attracts some very talented people. But some of these people are sharks who try to get away with whatever they can. Others have personal problems. They live from paycheck to paycheck; that is their mentality. Still others are cancers whose bad habits can spread. We coach and counsel; we give written notices; and for most of the employees, once they get the message that is the end of the problems. But for some others . . .

> I think the key to management in this business is all about managing attitude. How can we keep the team moving in the same direction, to get everybody to be part of the team, and prevent the cancers from spreading?

THE COMPANY AND INDUSTRY

Hitchcock Automotive Services was a privately held corporation comprised of seven automobile dealerships – three Toyota dealerships and one each for Volkswagen, Ford, Hyundai, and BMW – and a large body shop. All of the entities were located in southern California. Four of the dealerships, including Puente Hills Toyota, were situated adjacent to each other in City of Industry, California, about 25 miles east of Los Angeles. The others were located in Anaheim, Hermosa Beach, and Northridge.

It was important for the dealerships to keep two important constituencies – manufacturers and customers – happy. The manufacturers allocated larger numbers of their best-selling models to their better performing dealers. The manufacturers ▶

This case was prepared by Professors Kenneth A. Merchant and Wim A. Van der Stede of the University of Southern California and Pieter Jansen of the University of Groningen (the Netherlands).

evaluated their dealers in terms of their abilities to fulfill their market potential: to meet sales targets the manufacturers set for each geographical trading area, known as the *primary market area*. The dealerships also had to satisfy the manufacturers' licensing and certification standards. The manufacturers regularly performed compliance audits to evaluate dealership practices in comparison with the established standards. However, Howard Hakes believed that short of flagrant violations of standards (e.g. selling competing brands under the same roof) fulfilling market potentials was the primary factor affecting the dealers' relationships with the manufacturers.

Customer satisfaction was obviously important in obtaining repeat sales and, hence, future profits. Customer satisfaction surveys were given to every customer who bought or leased a vehicle or had one serviced at a dealership. A copy of the survey given to all Toyota customers who purchased or leased a vehicle is shown in Exhibit 1.[1] The responses to these survey questions were mailed directly to the manufacturer and aggregated into a *customer satisfaction index* (CSI) to which considerable attention was paid both by the manufacturer and dealership managers. Manufacturers sometimes changed dealership vehicle allocations when CSI ratings fell below acceptable levels in three consecutive years.

PUENTE HILLS TOYOTA

Puente Hills Toyota (PHT) was a large Toyota dealership. Annual sales were about $85 million, including approximately $10 million from the body shop, which provided services to all of the Hitchcock dealerships in City of Industry. PHT had a total of 145 employees, and annual profits totaled about $1.8 million.

PHT had won many awards for excellent performance. For example, the dealership had been awarded Toyota's President's Award for overall excellence in each of the prior 13 years.

In 2003, PHT moved into a new, state-of-the-art, $13 million facility with 119,000 square feet of space. The new building provided the latest in customer amenities, including a children's play area, a movie

theatre, efficient work layout areas, and room for growth.

PHT's organization structure was fairly typical in the industry. Reporting to the dealership general manager were a general sales manager, whose organization included both new and used vehicle sales, a service manager, body shop manager, parts manager, and a director of finance and insurance (F&I) (see Exhibit 2). The one unique feature of the organization was the combined new and used vehicle sales department. Only about one in five auto dealerships, typically the smaller ones, had such a combined vehicle sales department. More typically, the managers of the new and used vehicle sales departments reported directly to the dealership general manager. But PHT managers liked the flexibility of having their sales personnel sell whatever vehicle customers wanted, new or used, and some customers wanted to look at both new and used vehicles.

Each of PHT's departments was managed as a profit center. Many indirect or overhead expenses, such as dealership administrative salaries and dealership advertising expenditures, were assigned or allocated to the departments. Only some infrastructure-related expenditures (e.g. rent and equivalent) and some other expenditures over which the department managers had little or no control (e.g. insurance, taxes, legal and auditing) were not allocated to them.

Exhibit 3 shows one page of the financial statement report that PHT was required to submit monthly to Toyota Sales Corporation. The other pages in this report called for an extensive array of information, including the profitability of the other departments, balance sheet data, unit sales by model, personnel counts by department and category, and a variety of performance ratios (e.g. total bonuses as a percentage of sales, gross profit average per unit of each model sold).

The profitability of PHT's departments varied widely. As in most dealerships, new vehicle sales at PHT were only marginally profitable. Used vehicles provided a better profit source, as Howard Hakes explained:

> This is one of the last barter businesses left. For some new vehicles, however, there is only an $800 difference between the window sticker price and dealer cost, so there is not much margin and not much room for bargaining. In used vehicles, we have a little more profit opportunity. We can sometimes take a trade-in for $2,000, put $1,500 worth of work in it, and sell it for $6,000.

---

[1] Toyota also required the use of a *service* survey, which asked service customers a comparable set of questions focused on satisfaction with (1) making the service appointment, (2) writing up the service order, (3) work quality, (4) work timeliness, (5) price, and (6) the facilities.

The service department was consistently PHT's most profitable department, with margins typically in the range of 15–20%. (See comparison statistics from an industry consulting report shown in Appendix A.)

As required by Toyota, PHT managers kept separate records for new and used vehicle sales, as if they were separate departments, even though all PHT salespeople could sell both new and used vehicles. The separation of new and used vehicle profits required some allocations of expenses. With rare exceptions, all items of expense were split 70% to new vehicles and 30% to used vehicles, an allocation formula that was typical in the industry. Howard Hakes knew that this formula was somewhat arbitrary. For example, he knew that some forms of advertising, such as half-hour television shows or "infomercials" on Spanish television stations, were solely aimed at selling used vehicles. But, he explained, "I'll bet we aren't off by more than 5% with the 70–30 split. Maybe it's 65–35, one way or the other, but we won't be further off than that."[2]

All interdepartmental transfers were done at market prices. Thus, for example, when PHT's used vehicles were serviced in the PHT shop, the sales department paid full retail price for parts and labor. This policy gave the used vehicle manager some negotiating power in the service area. Paying full retail price ensured that internal used vehicle service jobs would not be given lower priority.

Valuations of used vehicle trade-ins sometimes created disagreements. These valuations were important primarily because the sales personnel earned commissions based on the profits of the "deals" they closed. Such disagreements were common in dealerships because new car salesmen were often motivated to *over*pay the customer for trade-ins to secure the new car sale. And at PHT, and indeed all dealerships, needed repairs on trade-ins were sometimes not spotted at the time of the sales deal. This could happen anytime, but at PHT it was most likely to happen on Sundays when the service department

was closed and no service advisor could be called in for a second opinion on estimated trade-in repair costs. As Howard explained:

> On Mondays, we often have animated discussions between sales and service about the repairs that the service department claims are required on trade-ins. But we stick to the market price rule! If the costs of repair are higher than what the salesmen had anticipated on Sunday, it eats into their deal profit. If they don't agree with the service repair cost estimate, they are free to sell the trade-in "as-is" on the wholesale market. Sometimes they even get lucky when the repair problem isn't spotted there either. That's why some used vehicles come to be called "lemons."

PERFORMANCE MEASURES AND INCENTIVES

Compensation of line personnel at PHT was high, particularly given the employees' generally relatively modest education levels. Even young salespeople, those still in their early 20s, could earn $6,000–7,000 per month if they hustled and followed up effectively with customers. Top sales personnel could earn $20,000 per month, or even more. Some service technicians earned over $10,000 per month. Performance-based incentives were a significant part of the compensation of all line personnel.

A. Incentives in the sales department

All personnel in the sales department were paid a relatively modest base salary plus incentive pay. The *salesmen* and *assistant sales managers* earned commissions on the deals they closed. The average commission rate was 20% and 7% of deal gross profit for salesmen and assistant sales managers, respectively. The *general sales manager, used vehicle sales manager*, and *sales desk managers'* bonuses were based on a proportion of departmental profit after overhead expenses but before taxes (line 59 in Exhibit 3). The general sales manager and desk sales managers were paid 2.25% and 1.2–1.5% of this amount for the total sales department, respectively. The *used vehicle sales manager* was paid 5% of this amount for the used vehicle department only.

The bonuses, which were typically 250–300% of the sales employees' base salaries, provided a significant proportion of total compensation. The salaries were paid semi-monthly, and commissions and bonuses were paid monthly.

---

[2] The industry consulting report showed that for FY 2002, the average overhead expenses (equivalent to line 57 in Exhibit 3) in the industry were $2.6 million for new vehicle departments, or 7.22% of sales (equivalent to line 1 in Exhibit 3) or 94.48% of new vehicle department profit (equivalent to line 33 in Exhibit 3). For used vehicle departments, average overhead expenses in the industry amounted to $1.4 million, or 8.12% of sales or 85.78% of used vehicle department profit.

Howard Hakes explained that one side-benefit of having a combined new and used vehicle sales department was that combined the department was generally profitable, whereas new vehicle sales departments alone often were not.[3] Howard wondered how managers provided "profit-based" incentives in sales departments that were losing money.

All of the sales managers' bonus plan contracts also included the following wording:

Adjustments. "Any cancelled sales or subsequent changes to the account as a result of a returned product will be calculated into the commissionable gross profit and will be used to calculate your commissions earned for each month. Adjustments may also be made to correct errors, or for rewrites to the deal; unwinds, null and voided deals; customer receivables not collected (including, but not limited to down payments, drive-off fees, insurance coverage, or penalties on trade-in), or policy adjustments."

Other Factors. "Other factors such as the Customer Satisfaction Index (CSI)[4] and Employee Satisfaction Index (ESI)[5] score may be taken into account in determining bonuses."

How these nonfinancial performance indices were taken into account for bonus determination was left vague. They could be used in a positive sense, to provide "discretionary" bonus awards, or they could be used to limit the formula bonuses. However, no one at PHT could remember any situations where they had made a substantive difference in the bonuses awarded, perhaps because at PHT the indices had never fallen below acceptable levels.

For comparison purposes, Appendix B provides excerpts from a consulting report showing vehicle dealership department manager compensation data. In this appendix, Schedule 1 shows data about the amounts and forms of monetary compensation given to department managers. Schedule 2 shows the measures used in allocating formula bonuses.

Schedule 3 shows the incidence and size of discretionary (nonformula) bonuses.

B. Incentives in the service department

The *service technicians* were paid from \$10–23 per "flag hour" of work completed. The actual hourly rate depended on each individual's technical specialty and their certifications (e.g. master technician). Flag hours were standards set by the manufacturer for the accomplishment of specific tasks. The standards were set so that an average qualified technician could achieve them. However, it took technicians at PHT, who were generally very experienced, about 45 minutes on average to do one flag hour of work. For some technicians the disparity between flag and actual hours was much higher. Jesus Barragan, PHT's service manager, said "Our top guy, who is a 'natural,' beats the flag time by 600%." The disparity also varied by area.

The *service advisors* earned a base salary of approximately \$2,000 per month. They also earned bonuses as follows:

- 8% commission on customer-paid labor and parts;
- 6% commission on manufacturer-paid labor under warranty;
- 6% commission on labor and parts paid for internally at PHT.

The PHT *service* manager was paid a base salary of \$3,000 per month plus a bonus based on a percentage of the service department gross profit (before overhead expenses). The percentage was 3.75% if the gross profit figure was \$195,000 or below in any given month; the percentage rose to 4% if gross profit exceeded \$195,000. The \$195,000 was the total annual budgeted amount divided by 12.

C. Gameplaying temptations in the service area

Because they were paid by the job, service technicians had temptations to cut corners. For instance, for a typical Electronic Engine Control (EEC) repair, the technician might be required to diagnose the problem, replace the defective electronic module, hook up a test recorder, and test-drive the vehicle. The flag rate for this job might be 48 minutes. A technician who wanted to cut corners might skip the test drive. Knowing that a supervisor would check

---

[3] The consulting report showed that about one in three new vehicle sales departments incurred a loss (see note (2) in Appendix A).

[4] CSI was explained earlier in the case. The sales customer survey form is shown in Exhibit 1.

[5] ESI was calculated from the results of a survey designed by a consulting firm given annually to all PHT employees. Each employee was asked to indicate the level of agreement, on a scale from 1 (strongly disagree) to 5 (strongly agree), with 26 statements, such as "I feel my work is valued by the dealership" and "Overall the managers are honest and fair in their treatment of employees."

the vehicle's mileage-in and mileage-out, he would have to put the vehicle up on a hoist and run it for, perhaps, three minutes to increase the odometer mileage. But by cutting corners, he might be able to complete the entire job in less than 15 minutes.

PHT managers had two types of controls over these gaming behaviors. First, if the time spent on a job was very low, service managers asked the technician for an explanation of the anomaly. Second, management monitored the number of "re-checks," instances where the problem was "not fixed right the first time." In the industry, a one percent re-check rate was considered good. The re-check rate usually could not go to zero because some of the re-checks were not the technician's fault. The cause might be simply that a needed part was unavailable.

Technicians who cut corners were "written up," that is, given notice, and their ticket was deducted. "Bad habits can be corrected; bad mechanics can't," Jesus Barragan observed.

Howard Hakes had some confidence that this gaming problem was under control because the service area at PHT was averaging only about four re-checks per month for approximately 700 completed service jobs. If service technicians were cutting corners in a significant way, he estimated that the recheck rate would be significantly higher.

The service technicians at PHT were very loyal to the company, because "we treat them as people, not mechanics," Jesus said. "We also train and pay them well." Turnover was virtually zero.[6] But the mechanics had to buy their own tools. Jesus Barragan noted that "one of our guys has bought well over $535,000 worth of tools during his 36-year career with us, but then, he makes $130,000 per year too."

Management issues

Howard Hakes knew that his PHT management team had not solved all their problems. He lamented

about the fact that, in general, sales personnel were not effective at following up with customers. Follow-up means that the sales staff keeps in touch with potential customers with whom there has been an initial contact. Follow-up includes outreaches (e.g. phone calls, thank you cards) to customers who visited the sales department but have not yet decided to purchase a vehicle, as well as sales approaches to customers who are driving an older vehicle that has recently been serviced at PHT. PHT had established regular processes for both types of follow-up. For example, service advisors were encouraged to explain to customers which service costs were likely to occur on their older vehicle in the coming years and to invite the client to visit the sales department. However, these activities consumed time, and the service advisors regularly ignored them. Could incentives be provided to encourage follow-up and referral behaviors?

Howard also worried that the CSI measure, which could provide useful information, sometimes had questionable validity. Howard had heard that some dealerships regularly "gamed" the measures because they had become so important. The CSI ratings were important inputs for the influential ratings of automobile reliability published by the firm J.D. Power & Associates and, as mentioned above, the manufacturers used those ratings to allocate their vehicles. As a consequence, in the quest for "perfect" ratings, customers were regularly "coached" on how to complete the questionnaire at the time they purchased a new vehicle. And, sometimes, dealerships asked customers to drive to the dealership when they received the questionnaire from the manufacturer. When they arrived, the customer would give the questionnaire to a dealership employee and receive a present, such as a full tank of gas. The employee would complete the questionnaire and send it to the manufacturer. Howard was not sure whether some of his "shark" salesmen also engaged in such practices, and if they did, what he should do about it.

Despite these issues, Howard was confident that PHT was one of the best managed dealerships in the country.

---

[6] This is in stark contrast with turnover in the sales department, which Howard described as "horrid" (about 60% per year, as opposed to only about 5% in service).

Exhibit 1 Puente Hills Toyota: customer satisfaction survey

TOYOTA *Purchase/Lease Survey*

- To respect your privacy, we will not share individual survey results with dealerships without your permission.
- Please use pencil or blue or black ink to fill in the box with an X. | Example: ☒ |

Our records show you purchased/leased your   **2002 SIENNA VIN# 1A2BC34D56E00000 at Anytown Toyota on March 18, 2002**

Do you own/lease this vehicle? ☐ Yes (Continue) ☐ No ☐ Never owned *(if you marked no or never owned, please return survey in envelope provided)*

Did you purchase/lease at this dealership? ☐ Yes (Continue) ☐ No *(Please return survey in envelope provided)*   0203271015547

Product presentation

1   Please rate your **SALESPERSON** on each of the following: ■

	Excellent	Good	Average	Fair	Poor	Not Applicable
Prompt initial greeting	☐	☐	☐	☐	☐	
Courtesy/friendliness	☐	☐	☐	☐	☐	
Integrity	☐	☐	☐	☐	☐	
Matched vehicle to your needs	☐	☐	☐	☐	☐	
Considerate of your time	☐	☐	☐	☐	☐	
Ability to answer your questions	☐	☐	☐	☐	☐	☐
Test drive	☐	☐	☐	☐	☐	
Knowledge of models/features						

Comments on question 1:

Negotiation

2   During your price/payment **NEGOTIATION** experience, how would you rate the following?

	Excellent	Good	Average	Fair	Poor	
Simple and straightforward	☐	☐	☐	☐	☐	
Honesty	☐	☐	☐	☐	☐	
Your comfort with the process	☐	☐	☐	☐	☐	■
Consideration for your time	☐	☐	☐	☐	☐	
Knowledge of purchase/finance options	☐	☐	☐	☐	☐	

Comments on question 2:

Final paperwork

3   Thinking about the **PERSON WHO COMPLETED YOUR FINAL PAPERWORK** (financing/leasing, registration, insurance, service contracts) how would you rate the following?

	Excellent	Good	Average	Fair	Poor	
Concern for your needs	☐	☐	☐	☐	☐	
Courtesy/friendliness	☐	☐	☐	☐	☐	
Integrity	☐	☐	☐	☐	☐	
Knowledge of products/services offered	☐	☐	☐	☐	☐	
Explanation of documents/paperwork	☐	☐	☐	☐	☐	■
Ability to answer your questions	☐	☐	☐	☐	☐	
Consideration for your time	☐	☐	☐	☐	☐	
Accurately completed your paperwork	☐	☐	☐	☐	☐	
Fulfilled negotiated commitments	☐	☐	☐	☐	☐	

Comments on question 3:

Receiving your vehicle

4   When you picked up your new Toyota **(VEHICLE DELIVERY)**, how would you rate the following?

	Excellent	Good	Average	Fair	Poor	Not Applicable
Provided all accessories as promised	☐	☐	☐	☐	☐	☐
Explanation of features/controls	☐	☐	☐	☐	☐	
Explanation of maintenance schedule and warranty	☐	☐	☐	☐	☐	
Ability to answer your questions	☐	☐	☐	☐	☐	
Consideration for your time	☐	☐	☐	☐	☐	
Expressed appreciation for your business	☐	☐	☐	☐	☐	

Comments on question 4:

Elite-View™ forms by NCS Pearson MM243702-4 654321 Printed in U.S.A.   ②   373232

(Continued on next page)

Exhibit 1 *continued*

5 When you picked up your new Toyota **(VEHICLE DELIVERY)**, did the following occur...   Yes No Not Applicable

Offered a scheduled time for delivery .... ☐ ☐ ☐
If yes, kept to scheduled time .... ☐ ☐
Received a full tank of gas or a gas voucher .... ☐ ☐
Vehicle delivered clean .... ☐ ☐
Introduced to service area/personnel (if department was open) .... ☐ ☐ ☐

6 Did you have any concerns with your vehicle **WHEN YOU PICKED IT UP** from the dealership?
☐ No *(Skip to Question 7)*
☐ Yes
➡ 6b If yes, please check the appropriate box and describe the concern in the blank: *(Check all that apply)*
☐ Noise/rattle: _____ ☐ Wheel alignment/steering: _____
☐ Malfunction: _____ ☐ Missing item: _____
☐ Not clean: _____ ☐ Other: _____
☐ Chip/scratch/dent: _____

6c Has the dealership resolved the concern? ☐ Yes ☐ No

Dealership communications

7 After your purchase/lease, did the dealership phone, mail or e-mail you to determine your satisfaction with your purchase/lease experience?
☐ No *(Skip to Question 8)*
☐ Yes ⟶ 7b

If yes, how would you rate the follow-up contact?	Excellent	Good	Average	Fair	Poor
	☐	☐	☐	☐	☐
Please explain:					

8 At any point during or after the purchase/lease process, did you ask the dealership to resolve any concerns?
☐ No *(Skip to Question 9)*
☐ Yes ⟶ 8b

If yes, how would you rate the following?	Excellent	Good	Average	Fair	Poor
Efforts of dealership personnel to resolve the concern	☐	☐	☐	☐	☐
Outcome of the contact	☐	☐	☐	☐	☐
Please explain:					

Facilities

9 Please rate the following: Excellent Good Average Fair Poor

Cleanliness of dealership facilities .... ☐ ☐ ☐ ☐ ☐
Ease/convenience of parking at the dealership .... ☐ ☐ ☐ ☐ ☐

Overall

10 How would you rate your **OVERALL PURCHASE/LEASE EXPERIENCE** at this dealership?
☐ Excellent ☐ Good ☐ Average ☐ Fair ☐ Poor

11 Would you: Yes No Undecided

RETURN to this dealership to purchase/lease another Toyota? .... ☐ ☐ ☐
RECOMMEND this dealership to a friend or relative as a place to purchase/lease a Toyota? .... ☐ ☐ ☐
SERVICE your new Toyota at this dealership? .... ☐ ☐ ☐

Please explain why or why not: _____

12 What aspects of your purchase/lease experience did you **LIKE MOST**? ....

13 What aspects of your purchase/lease experience **COULD HAVE BEEN IMPROVED**? ....

14 Although we do not identify you with your individual check box results to the dealership, may we associate your name with your written comments?
☐ Yes, you can identify me when sharing my comments with the dealer
☐ No, I do not wish to share any information on this survey with the dealership

373233

Exhibit 2 Puente Hills Toyota: organization structure

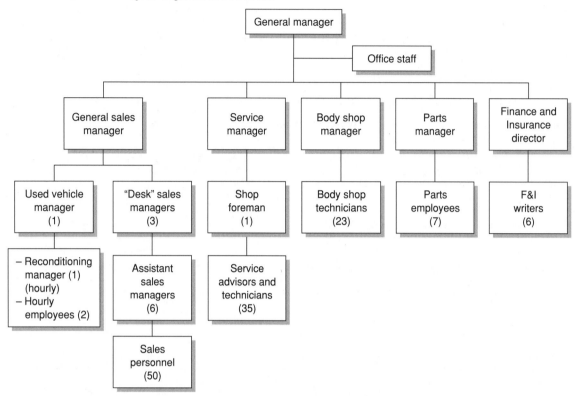

EXHIBIT 3 Puente Hills Toyota: sample page of financial reporting package

Total income and expenses

	NAME OF ACCOUNT	DEALERSHIP		NEW CAR DEPT		USED CAR DEPT	
		MONTH	YTD	MONTH	YTD	MONTH	YTD
1	**TOTAL SALES**						
2	**TOTAL GROSS PROFIT**						
3	**DEPARTMENTAL SELLING EXPENSES**						
4	Sales Compensation						
5	Sales Compensation – Scion only						
6	Supervision Compensation						
7	Supervision Compensation – Scion only						
8	Delivery Expenses						
9	Financing, Insurance & Service Center Commissions						
10	Financing, Insurance & Service Center Commissions – Scion only						
11	Advertising – Departmental						
12	Interest – Floor Plan						
13	**TOTAL SELLING EXPENSES** (Lines 4 to 12 incl.)						
14	**DEPARTMENTAL OPERATING EXPENSES**						
15	Policy Adjustments						
16	Claims Adjustments						
17	Demos & Company Vehicles – Departmental						
18	Inventory Maintenance						
19	Personnel Training						
20	Outside Services – Departmental						
21	Freight						
22	Supplies & Small Tools						
23	Laundry & Uniforms						
24	Equipment & Vehicles – Departmental						
25	Equipment Maintenance, Repair & Rental – Departmental						
26	Miscellaneous Expenses						
27	Salaries & Wages						
28	Clerical Salaries						
29	Vacation & Time Off Pay						
30	**TOTAL OPERATING EXPENSES** (Lines 15 to 29 incl.)						
31	**TOTAL SELLING & OPER. EXPS.** (Lines 13 & 30)						
32	**TOTAL SELL. & OPER. EXPS. % OF GROSS PROFIT**						
33	**DEPT. PROFIT (LOSS)** (Line 2 Less Line 31)						

(Continued on next page)

Exhibit 3 *continued*

	NAME OF ACCOUNT	DEALERSHIP		NEW CAR DEPT		USED CAR DEPT	
		MONTH	YTD	MONTH	YTD	MONTH	YTD
34	**OVERHEAD EXPENSES**			PRORATION OPTIONAL			
35	Rent & Equivalent						
36	Salaries & Wages – Administrative & General						
37	Owners Salaries						
38	Payroll Taxes						
39	Employee Benefits						
40	Pension Fund/Profit Sharing						
41	Advertising – General & Institutional						
42	Stationery & Office Supplies						
43	Data Processing Services						
44	Outside Services – General & Institutional						
45	Company Vehicles – Administration						
46	Contributions						
47	Dues & Subscriptions						
48	Telephone						
49	Legal & Auditing						
50	Postage						
51	Travel & Entertainment						
52	Heat, Light, Power & Water						
53	Furniture, Signs & Equip.-Depreciation, Maint., Repair & Rental						
54	Insurance – Other than Buildings & Improvements						
55	Taxes – Other than Real Estate Payments & Income Taxes						
56	Interest – Other than Floor Plan & Real Estate Mortgage						
57	**TOTAL OVERHEAD EXPENSES** (Lines 35 to 56 incl.)						
58	**TOTAL EXPENSES** (Lines 31 & 57)						
59	**ADJUSTED DEPT. PROFIT (LOSS)** (Line 2 Less 58)	■	■				
60	**OPERATING PROFIT (LOSS)** (Line 2 Less 58)			■	■	■	■
61	**NET ADDITIONS OR DEDUCTIONS** (Pg. 2 Line 77)						
62	**NET PROFIT (LOSS) BEFORE BONUS** (Line 60 Less 61)						
63	Bonuses – Employees						
64	Bonuses – Owners						
65	**NET PROFIT (LOSS) BEFORE TAXES** (Line 62 Less 63, 64)						
66	Estimated Income Taxes						
67	**NET PROFIT (LOSS) AFTER TAXES** (Line 65 Less 66)						

APPENDIX A Puente Hills Toyota: excerpts from Consulting Report showing automobile dealership and department data (FY 2002)[1]

	1st Quartile	Median	3rd Quartile	**Average**	St. Dev.
1. NEW VEHICLE DEPARTMENT					
Sales ($000)	17,217	27,134	42,470	**36,479**	34,585
Net profit ($000)[2]	−49.7	197.2	706.7	**530.0**	1,195.7
Return on sales	−0.002	0.008	0.021	**0.009**	0.020
2. USED VEHICLE DEPARTMENT					
Sales ($000)	10,000	14,533	21,016	**17,240**	11,601
Net profit ($000)[2]	−22.7	20.0	451.4	**258.6**	470.4
Return on sales	−0.003	0.014	0.026	**0.013**	0.025
3. SERVICE DEPARTMENT					
Sales ($000)	1,560	2,257	3,594	**32,846**	1,926
Net profit ($000)[2]	54.8	180.8	346.3	**246.6**	324.1
Return on sales	0.028	0.081	0.130	**0.072**	0.093
4. TOTAL DEALERSHIP					
Sales ($000)	34,326	49,933	73,502	**62,236**	47,286
Net profit ($000)[2]	43.4	100.2	1772.0	**1,443.9**	1,742.8
Return on sales	0.015	0.020	0.022	**0.031**	0.015

[1] Data obtained from 256 dealerships. The sum of the sales and profits of the service and the new and used vehicle departments do not add up to the dealership totals because sales and profits associated with body and parts are not included.

[2] 30.2% of the new vehicle departments, 27.8% of the used vehicle departments, 16.9% of the service departments, and 5.1% of the dealerships incurred a loss.

Appendix B Puente Hills Toyota: excerpts from Consulting Report showing department manager compensation data (FY 2002)

Schedule 1: Department Manager Compensation: Total and Breakdown into Components – Base Salary, Formula Bonuses, and Discretionary Bonuses (overall averages)

	Base salary	Formula bonus	Discretionary bonus
NEW VEHICLE DEPARTMENT MANAGERS			
(*Average total compensation = $78,428*)[1]			
Average ($)	$31,901	$44,829	$5,104
Percent receiving	79.23%	64.48%	23.50%
Average % of total compensation	44.89%	36.77%	4.26%
USED VEHICLE DEPARTMENT MANAGERS			
(*Average total compensation = $72,195*)[1]			
Average ($)	$31,672	$40,376	$4,046
Percent receiving	85.04%	66.14%	27.56%
Average % of total compensation	47.12%	38.32%	5.03%
SERVICE DEPARTMENT MANAGERS			
(*Average total compensation = $61,422*)[1]			
Average ($)	$33,278	$30,575	$2,302
Percent receiving	90.00%	68.00%	20.00%
Average % of total compensation	56.00%	34.26%	3.53%
ALL DEPARTMENT MANAGERS COMBINED			
(*Average total compensation = $70,189*)[1]			
Average ($)	$32,379	$37,993	$3,739
Percent receiving	84.90%	66.27%	23.14%
Average % of total compensation	49.80%	36.17%	4.17%

[1] TOTAL COMPENSATION consists of any or all of the following components: BASE SALARY, FORMULA BONUSES (maximum of three), DISCRETIONARY BONUS, and SPIFFS.

Definitions:

- Formula Bonuses are based on quantitative performance measures (e.g. department profit). Some contracts have up to three formula bonuses, although the majority of the managers (60%) receive one formula bonus only. Across departments, the first formula bonus is on average 85% of the total formula bonus. Also, the first formula bonus is on average more than seven times larger than the second formula bonus.

- DISCRETIONARY BONUSES are based on the supervisor's subjective judgments of the managers' performances.

- SPIFFS are miscellaneous rewards (not reported above), which are difficult to characterize in a standard way. Common examples are the use of promotional vehicles and certain incentives provided by the vehicle manufacturers (e.g. vacation trips). Although receipt of spiffs is common (about 63% of the managers receive them), their economic significance is relatively low (about $4,593 for those who receive spiffs, compared at $15,000 to $20,000 for those who receive a discretionary bonus).

APPENDIX B *continued*

Schedule 2: Dealership Performance Measure Used in Department Manager Formula Bonuses (as a percentage of all formula contracts)

		Formula bonus	#1	#2	#3
Dealership	Gross profit		1.8	1.7	0.0
	Net profit		27.0	10.9	20.0
New vehicle sales	Gross profit		6.4	6.9	0.0
	Net profit		5.8	1.7	2.9
	Inventory		0.0	1.1	0.0
	Unit sales		0.0	6.3	2.9
Used vehicle sales	Gross profit		5.9	4.6	14.3
	Net profit		2.2	5.2	8.6
	Inventory		0.2	2.9	14.3
	Unit sales		0.5	7.5	2.9
New + used	Gross profit		14.5	4.6	2.9
	Net profit		8.6	6.9	11.4
	Inventory		0.0	0.0	5.7
	Unit sales		0.3	8.6	2.9
Parts	Gross profit		2.7	1.1	0.0
	Net profit		1.9	2.3	0.0
	Revenue		0.2	0.0	0.0
Service	Gross profit		9.4	4.0	0.0
	Net profit		8.6	6.9	5.7
	Revenue		0.8	0.0	0.0
Body, parts & service	Gross profit		2.6	5.7	2.9
	Net profit		0.6	10.9	2.9
	% Gross profit		43.3	28.7	20.0
	% Net profit		54.8	44.8	51.4

Schedule 3: Average Discretionary Bonus for Managers Who Receive a Discretionary Bonus (dollars and percentage of total compensation)

		Average discretionary bonus	
	Pct. receiving	Dollars	% tot. comp.
New vehicle department managers	23.5%	$21,958	18.1%
Used vehicle department managers	27.6%	$15,719	18.3%
Service department managers	20.0%	$11,801	17.7%
All department managers	23.1%	$16,664	18.0%

Case Study

Houston Fearless 76, Inc.

In late 2000 M.S. Lee, president/CEO of Houston Fearless 76, Inc. (HF76), was considering making a major change in the company's sales incentive system:

> We need revenue growth and consistent profitability, and right now we don't have them. I think our primary problem relates to sales, which have slowed. Some of this is due to market conditions, but I also think that our sales effort and sales support can be improved. I want to take care of our people and give them opportunities to be successful, but I also want the company to get to the next level of performance. Are our structures set up to motivate them to do that?

> I think we have a range of problems. We're clearly not doing enough to develop new markets, to expand our existing markets, or to develop synergies among our markets. We have an obvious mismatch between our company objectives and our sales force incentives because our commissions are based on sales, not product profitability. We use different compensation structures for different products, and I have heard some grumbling among the sales people about equality. And our sales forecasts are inconsistent. Forecast accountability is not strong since there is no downside for salespersons for overstating forecasts. This sometimes causes production planning problems.

> So we need to make some changes to improve performance. We need better systems now more than ever because we are entering some new markets that are more competitive than those to which we have been accustomed.

With these concerns in mind, Mr. Lee asked his son, James (who joined HF76 in 1998 and later became head of corporate development and operations, and who was attending the University of Southern California Executive MBA Program), to critically evaluate HF76's sales function and to revamp the sales incentive plan. M.S. and James Lee planned to present a proposal for change at the annual sales meeting to be held in mid-December 2000.

COMPANY HISTORY

Houston Fearless 76, Inc. was a privately held company headquartered in Compton, California. Annual company sales were approximately $15 million. The company had 120 employees. HF76 was a worldwide leader in the design, manufacturing, marketing and service of high quality micrographic products, photographic film and paper processors, photographic chemical handling equipment, and photographic quality control accessories.

HF76's roots dated back to 1939 when H.W. Houston, one of Howard Hughes's movie-making business partners, founded a company around the development of the first automatic roll film processor. Most of the H.W. Houston Co.'s early customers were closely connected to the motion-picture industry. Later in the 1940s the company went public and expanded into a manufacturing company that produced a wide range of products, including film processors, hair-clips, turbine blades, and radar. At one time it was one of the largest manufacturing companies in the Los Angeles area. In 1950 the company merged with Fearless Camera Corporation of Culver City and became known as the Houston Fearless Corporation. Later, however, the company faced many problems, and it was forced to file for bankruptcy and to liquidate its assets.

In 1976 M.S. Lee, a former Houston Fearless employee, and two partners bought the Houston Fearless Photo Division. They named their company Houston Fearless 76, Inc., both to take advantage of the excellent reputation the company had developed, especially in film processing circles, and to commemorate the year of their acquisition. Mr. Lee later acquired all of his partners' shares.

HF76 prospered in the 1970s and 1980s. In the 1990s, however, film-based product markets experienced a dramatic decline. Many corporate customers,

---

This case was prepared by Professors Kenneth A. Merchant and Wim A. Van der Stede and Research Assistant Liu Zheng.

including those in the banking, health care, and movie industries, were moving toward digital production and record-retention technologies. Facing the declining market demand, several of HF76's competitors had exited the film-product market. Mr. Lee believed, however, that "the demise of film was greatly exaggerated." He wanted the company to continue serving its traditional film-based market, particularly in good niche markets, as it repositioned itself in faster-growing markets.

In the 1990s Mr. Lee aggressively expanded in both the traditional film market and growing digital market through a series of acquisitions. In 1990 HF76 acquired Extek Microsystems, an innovator of film duplicating technology that served a customer base similar to that of HF76's in the micrographics marketplace. Extek's operations were integrated into HF76's Compton facility. In 1997, HF76 acquired Houston International, Inc. which manufactured large volume, specialized (e.g. long roll) film processors. This division was renamed HF International, but its operations were not moved from its Yuma, Arizona location. In 1999, HF76 acquired 80% of Mekel Engineering, located in Brea, California, which produced scanners that converted microfilm and microfiche to digital format, lightweight film and video cameras, heads-up display units for fighter aircraft, and traffic photo-citation analyzers.

For over 30 years HF76 also had a government division, called HF North, that supported the US Air Force through a variety of special projects that involved film processors, power distribution systems, mobile shelters, climate control units, and pollution control systems. This division was located at Beale AFB, near Sacramento.

HF76 was also attempting to diversify its product line by capitalizing on potentially sizable commercial applications of the pollution control systems developed by HF North originally for the US Air Force. These innovative pollution control systems separated practically all kinds of water contaminants, from heavy metals to toxic biohazardous waste. A production facility for these systems had just been started in the Compton location.

THE COMPANY IN 2000

After the 1999 Mekel acquisition, HF76 was organized into four product divisions (see Exhibit 1). Each division operated as a profit center. Corporate staff provided support and coordination of activities. The pollution control business was being developed at the corporate level under the purview of James Lee.

The HF76 culture was close-knit, family-like, and casual. M.S. Lee, the president/CEO, was a former local "entrepreneur of the year." He was a strong central figure, but he was also perceived as being highly caring, honest, and nurturing. Staff were given recognition and periodic awards (e.g. parties, logo merchandise).

M.S. Lee described the company's strategy as follows:

> We now have products at different market stages. We have some emerging products, particularly pollution control systems and traffic photo-citation analyzers. We have some potentially high growth markets for some of our scanner products. And we have a lot of mature products, such as our processors and duplicators.
>
> Each market requires a different strategy. For example, for products in the emerging and growing markets, we need our sales force to identify new customers and new markets. For products in the mature markets, our sales force should capitalize on our brand name and maintain as much volume as possible in the niche market, probably through targeting local government and accounting firms and through special trade-in programs to stimulate the replacement of old machines.

The HF76 divisions each did their own manufacturing. Most product lines had some standard products, or at least subassemblies. In these cases, HF76 would build to inventory, based on demand forecasts. In the microfilm and motion picture film processing markets, customers typically waited about 30 days for delivery of machines that required some customization. Largely custom products were built after the order was booked, and the wait in such cases could be several months.

HF76 suffered from the sales/operations frictions common to many companies. Operation managers often complained that sales people were not aware of the required lead times and that some of their rush orders imposed significant overtime labor costs. Sales, on the other hand, complained that they sometimes lost orders because their operations department could not meet the required delivery schedule.

HF76 product gross margins averaged approximately 28%, but they varied significantly across product lines and models. Relatively low profit margins (10–15%) were earned on processors and pollution control systems. Duplicator sales were relatively profitable (30–35% margins). However, HF76's managers were selling some specific models of their older product lines at minimal, or even negative, gross margins. They did so because they wanted to retain their customer base in order to earn profits on forthcoming replacement part sales, the margins on which were usually in excess of 40%.

Industry performance benchmarks were difficult to establish accurately because HF76's smaller competitors were all privately held and their larger competitors (e.g. Eastman Kodak, Bell & Howell) were so large that they could bury their HF76-relevant financial results in aggregated financial statements. However, HF76's managers believed that their company's performance was lagging behind that of its major competitors on all dimensions. For example, in 1999 HF76's profit margin (as a percent of sales) was only 0.04%, while the industry benchmark, as given to HF76 management by a management consulting firm, was 5.7%. HF76's inventory turnover was 2.6 compared to the industry benchmark of 4.9. The HF International division, which was operating at a loss, was creating concern.

MARKETING AND SALES EFFORTS

All of the HF76 products, with the exception of replacement parts, sold for significant prices, so they were capital equipment for the buyers. For example, a typical new photo processing machine, one of HF76's low-end products, sold for approximately $60,000, and some of the high-end products sold for several hundred thousand dollars. Thus, the sales process usually involved more than just taking an order. For many of the products, the sales cycle was lengthy, a year or more. In many cases, particularly for the more advanced products, the salespeople had to serve as consultants, helping their customers to solve problems.

Until the last few years, most of HF76's sales were made through a network of dealers (sometimes referred to as "strategic partners") and independent sales representatives. The dealers and reps provided HF76 with a professional sales effort, local customer knowledge and, in the case of the dealers, sales of complementary products and a service capability, with little or no fixed costs. However, most of the dealers and reps did no pro-active marketing; they merely responded to inquiries. Further, having the dealers and reps do the selling was expensive because

HF76 had to offer them significant price concessions (typically 40% off list price) or high commission rates (typically 7–10%). One active independent rep was also paid a fixed retainer fee. She was somewhat like an employee, but with a lower salary and no benefits, and a higher commission rate. She also had no obligation to serve HF76's interests (e.g. market development) if she did not believe that those efforts would lead to her own commissions.

To provide a more effective and more company-focused selling effort and, secondarily, to cut costs, HF76 managers were trying to build up the company's own internal sales force. All of HF76's competitors sold all their products direct to customers. For internal sales, HF76's goal was to keep the sales costs (compensation and expenses) to less than 10% of total sales, but they did not always achieve that goal.

The tasks required to sell the various HF76 products varied significantly depending on a number of factors, including the product characteristics, the market conditions, and the company's customer relationships. Despite some redundancy (e.g. some of HF76's salespeople for different equipment lines called on the same customers), HF76 managers did not think that they could organize the company's sales effort entirely geographically. Selling the HF76 products required considerable technical knowledge, for example about optics, micrographics, and software. Little of that knowledge was consistent across product lines.

The **photo processing** business (HF International) was mature. Most sales in this market involved replacement of existing equipment and replacement parts, so the potential customer base was quite well known. The US photo processing market had 1,000–1,500 potential customers, mostly those who did wholesale photo finishing (e.g. school portraits, weddings). One HF76 salesperson, Brett Hutchins, covered the eastern half of the country. Sales in the western half were made through independent sales reps.

The **micrographics** and **motion picture processing** markets (Extek) were also mature. Most of the microfilm customers were local government entities. (Most corporations had moved to digital storage of documents.) The vast majority of sales in this market were made through a network of approximately 125 dealers, only some of which were active. HF76 had one salesman, Matt Petilla, working in the micrographics and motion picture markets. Matt was also given the task of culling the dealer list to a smaller number. HF76 managers wanted their dealers to be more aggressive. They were planning to require the dealers to do some significant selling in order to remain on the dealer list. In return they were going to promise some exclusive territory protection.

The **scanner** business (Mekel), which had more high-tech products with higher growth potential, used all the sales channels. The company had two in-house salespeople. Jim Mancini sold throughout the United States. Ryan Chase was responsible for Asia and Latin America. And some sales were made through dealers and independent reps. One rep, Stephanie Eller, described earlier as being on retainer, generated almost one sixth of Mekel's total scanner sales in 2000. HF76 managers estimated that its customer base for scanner products numbered about 300–400, but it did not know the names of all its customers because some distributors did not share their lists.

One HF76 salesman, Mark Fogarty, was responsible for selling **pollution control** systems. Mark was a technical person with little sales experience. By late 2000, HF76 had just gotten to the point that it could build the pollution control systems in any volume, and only one system had been sold.

One constant across all the divisions was that the salespeople were not, by themselves, actively developing new customers. They generally relied on a list of regular customers to contact and on company advertising to interest customers. They then responded to telephone and e-mail inquiries.

The in-house salespeople reported to Bob Smith (VP Sales), although in reality they worked relatively independently. The salespeople were geographically spread across the country. For example, Brett Hutchins (Houston International) lived in Maryland; Matt Petilla (micrographics) lived in St. Louis; Bob Smith (VP Marketing) lived in Atlanta. All of the salespeople traveled extensively to meet with their customers. The salespeople had the authority to discount up to 5% off list price. Larger discounts had to be proposed to and approved by Mr. Lee.

Assistants at both corporate and division levels provided support to the sales force. Among other things, they made some follow-up telephone calls to customers, maintained the databases, delivered the sales contracts to production, designed the company's advertisements, and set up the marketing shows. They also helped alleviate some of the salespeople's weaknesses. For example, one salesperson has no typing or computer skills. Thus he needed more support in preparing sales contracts.

Bob Smith managed the sales function primarily by monitoring the weekly sales reports. He also periodically observed salespersons' behaviors on sales trips and trade shows. About the evaluation process, Bob noted: "I can distinguish good performers from poor ones through the ways they deal with clients. But more directly, their performances are reflected automatically in the reports of items shipped to their territory." Bob also noted that HF76 had not had formal performance evaluations in two years. He said, "We can't afford raises, so why bother evaluating people?"

HF76 had gradually been computerizing its sales tracking systems. Previously all tracking had been manual.

SALES FORECASTS

The sales personnel were asked to provide an annual sales forecast at the beginning of each year. Then they were asked to update their forecasts on 30-, 60-, and 90-day rolling bases. The forecasts were important for production planning purposes, for example for decisions about which parts to buy and what subassemblies to produce to inventory.

However, according to Mr. Lee, the sales forecasts were inconsistent:

> Forecast accountability does not really exist in our current compensation structure. There is no mechanism to prevent salespersons from overstating forecasts or sandbagging. Thus, the salespeople tend to be optimistic, and efficient production planning sometimes becomes very difficult.

Bob Smith, on the other hand, thought that the sales forecasts were reasonably accurate. He noted:

> Last year our sales goals were too tough. We worked hard, but the market was soft. This year's targets are more realistic, so I think we'll do better. But we can't control all of the results. Things happen. For example, some sales get held up past the period end. This year one of our big customers, Olin Mills, cut their budget at the last minute, and we did not get a large order that we expected. On the other hand, we sometimes get a "bluebird" [a large order that was not forecast]. We surely have to be out there working with our customers to know what is going to happen, but even so we can't control everything.

Ryan Chase (Scanner Product Sales – Pacific Rim) explained the forecasts from his perspective:

> I don't have an annual forecast because I'm relatively new on the job. I have no basis for a forecast. I guess if they forced me, I would forecast 10 scanners per year. I got lucky last year with sales of 14, but my big sale took me two years of effort. The year before last I sold only two scanners . . . In my forecasts, I wouldn't mention the name of a company if the probability of the sale is less than 80% or 90%. You often don't get a solid answer from international customers until the last minute.

THE OLD SALES INCENTIVE PLAN

Up through 2000, all of the salespeople, except Mark Fogarty,[1] were paid a base salary plus commission. The salespersons' base salaries looked relatively low, typically $40,000–$60,000, but the total compensation packages and their structure were industry competitive. Commissions were set at a defined percentage of sales, measured as revenue from items shipped within the salesperson's assigned territory. The commission rate differed across salespeople on a negotiated basis with specific attention paid to product characteristics and market situation. Two salesmen, Brett Hutchins and Matt Petilla, earned a 4% commission. Ryan Chase earned a 2% commission because he was relatively new in his job. Bob Smith earned 1% on all company sales within the United States, Canada and Mexico. The actual commissions the salespeople earned were typically in the range of 50% of base salary, but they could be substantially more.

The sales assistants shared a small bonus pool if HF76 met its overall sales goals. In 1999 each assistant was given approximately $1,000. One assistant, Eva Colton (Mekel) described her reaction to the bonus.

> I had forgotten about the bonus. The $1,000 came as a total shock . . . If we make this year's goal, and right now we're behind, it'll be great. But there is not much I can do to help us get there.

---

[1] Mark Fogarty had been assigned to the job of marketing and sales of pollution control systems only recently, and he had not yet been included in the current incentive plan. However, he was lobbying for inclusion, and a decision on that had to be made soon.

A NEW INCENTIVE PLAN BEING CONTEMPLATED

M.S. Lee wondered what could be done to improve the company's marketing and sales efforts. He explained:

> Some causes of our low profits and cash flows are obvious, such as a declining film-based product market and our decision to invest strategically for future gains. However, I believe that we are not fully exploiting market and profit opportunities for either our traditional products or our new products. In particular, our sales force has not done what I want them to do. I want them to open new markets, to sell in more profitable markets, and to give us more lead time for better operational planning.

After a series of discussions, M.S. and James Lee concluded that they needed to make a major change in the company's sales incentive plan to attempt to alter behaviors in the desired ways. James observed:

> It was pretty clear that the old incentive plan was not working. The commissions were exclusively based on sales volume. While we tried to tell the sales force which products were most profitable, they seemed to be willing to push sales at any cost or price. They also were paying little attention to other strategic goals, such as the opening of new markets or accounts or improving the accuracy of their forecasts. This is perhaps natural because they were not evaluated on those factors. In addition, the linkage between efforts and rewards was unclear. Sales people received compensation for items shipped within their territory regardless of whether they were instrumental in making the sales or not. So, overall, the old incentive plan created distorted incentives.

To overcome the problems in the old system, M.S. and James were considering a quite different incentive plan that they thought would translate HF76 missions and strategies into sales actions. They planned to leave base salaries at current levels but were planning to implement a new incentive plan consisting of three elements: (1) a commission based on product gross margins, but with no commissions paid until gross margins exceeded 70% of forecast; (2) a bonus based on forecast accuracy; and (3) a bonus based on achievement of individual management-by-objectives targets.

The objective of basing **commissions on product gross margins** was to encourage salespeople to focus their effort where company profit potentials were greatest. M.S. and James hoped that the salespeople's knowledge of product gross margins, combined with the incentive reinforcements, would affect their sales behaviors beneficially.

One unsolved issue: M.S. and James had not yet decided what commissions they should pay on negative and low gross margin products. They thought that it was sometimes in the company's strategic interest to make some of these sales. Should they report "phoney" gross margins to the salespeople to motivate them to sell these low margin products? Or should they weight the commission payouts according to the "strategic importance" of the sale? If the latter, how should strategic importance be defined, and how should it be explained to the salespeople?

The actual commission slopes would be set for each individual so that at 100% of plan, each salesperson could expect to earn in commission slightly more under the new plan than they would have earned under the old plan. This feature was considered essential for securing the salespersons' easy acceptance of the change. However, the **commission structure** (see Exhibit 2) would be quite different. No commissions would be paid for sales up to a minimum performance standard, defined as 70% of the annual gross margin forecast. This feature was intended to allow for greater payout leverage at high performance levels. Between 70% and 100% of the planned annual gross margin, commissions would be paid at rates that were much higher than would be the case if commissions were paid on all sales. That is, if commissions were paid on all sales, the commission rate (as a percentage of gross margin) would be in the range of 10–12% on high margin sales and 30–35% on low margin sales. Because of the leverage provided by the minimum performance standard, the actual commission rate paid on gross margins earned above the 70% threshold could be raised to 30–100%. For sales above 100% of the annual gross margin plan, the slope on the commission curve would be 25% higher than in the 70–100% range, to encourage the higher performers to develop new markets and customers effectively. No cap was placed on the maximum commissions that could be earned. Salespeople were to be paid commissions on an annual basis, but monthly cash advances would be paid at a rate of 80% of annual plan to allow the salespeople to smooth out their cash flow.

To encourage the salespeople to take their sales forecasts seriously, a second element of the plan

promised an extra bonus based on the **accuracy of the sales forecasts**. The salespeople would earn an extra 5% of base salary if their total gross margins were within 10% (plus or minus) of the annual gross margin forecasts. M.S. and James Lee hoped that this "truthinducing" feature of the plan would motivate the salespeople to reveal their best estimates of their market prospects, rather than being optimistic, as had been typical in the past, or conservative, as might be expected with the new 70%-of-forecast minimum performance standard.

The third element of the contemplated new plan, the **MBO targets**, was designed to facilitate communication and reinforcement of management desires and expectations in any of a variety of areas. The target areas and specific targets would be negotiated between each individual and management. Typical MBO targets might include items such as the following:

- adding a significant number of new customers;
- coordinating well with production;
- keeping annual travel expenses below travel expense forecasts;
- strengthening ties with professional associations;
- improving communications through effective use of e-mail;
- learning and utilizing Microsoft Office and other software.

Assessment was subjective and intended to lean in favor of the employee. If top management deemed the salesperson's performance in all of the defined areas as satisfactory, the salesperson would be given an extra 5% of base salary.

No changes were planned to the bonus system for the sales assistants.

CONCERNS

M.S. and James were preparing to present their proposal for the new sales incentive plan at the company's annual sales meeting, to be held on December 13, 2000. However, both of them were concerned. They knew that changes of this magnitude could be made only rarely, so it was important that this change be made correctly. They were offering to pay their salesmen significantly more money. Would they be getting at least equivalent value in return? And even more importantly, was this plan what the company needed to push itself to a higher level of performance?

EXHIBIT 1 Houston Fearless 76, Inc., corporate organization chart, 2000

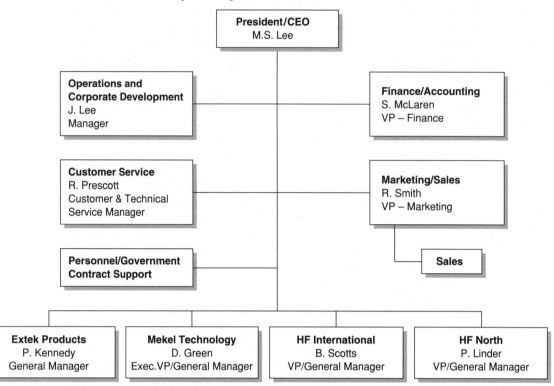

EXHIBIT 2 Comparison of old and new commission structure

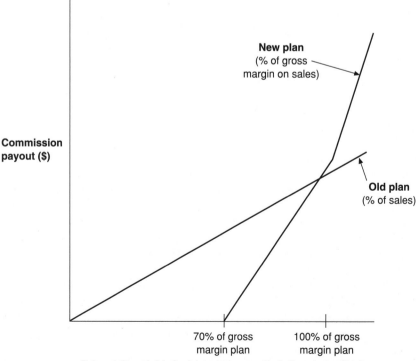

Chapter 3

ACTION, PERSONNEL, AND CULTURAL CONTROLS

Results controls are not the only form of control. Organizations can supplement or replace results controls with other forms of control that aim to make it more likely that employees will act in the organization's best interest. One such type of control, *action controls*, involves ensuring that employees perform (do not perform) certain actions known to be beneficial (harmful) to the organization. Although action controls are commonly used in organizations, they are not effective in every situation. They are feasible only when managers know what actions are (un)desirable and have the ability to ensure that the (un)desirable actions (do not) occur. Second, *personnel controls* are designed to make it more likely that employees will perform the desired tasks satisfactorily *on their own* because the employees are experienced, honest, and hard working, and derive a sense of self-realization and satisfaction from performing tasks well. Finally, *cultural controls* exist to shape organizational behavioral norms and to encourage employees to monitor and influence *each other*'s behaviors. Action, personnel, and cultural controls are a part of virtually every MCS. In some organizations, they are so important they can be said to be the dominant form of control.

ACTION CONTROLS

Action controls are the most direct form of management control because they involve taking steps to ensure that employees act in the organization's best interest by making their actions themselves the focus of control. Action controls take any of four basic forms: behavioral constraints, preaction reviews, action accountability, and redundancy.

Behavioral constraints

Behavioral constraints are a "negative" or, as the word suggests, a "constraining" form of action control. They make it impossible, or at least more difficult, for employees to do things that should not be done. The constraints can be applied physically or administratively.

Most companies use multiple forms of *physical constraints*, including locks on desks, computer passwords, and limits on access to areas where valuable inventories and sensitive information are kept. Some behavioral constraint devices are technically sophisticated and often expensive, such as magnetic identification card readers and fingerprint or eyeball pattern readers. In situations where a high degree of control is desired, such as in facilities where radioactive materials are processed, secret service agencies where classified information is gathered, or casino count rooms where cash is handled, the benefits of such sophisticated controls outweigh their costs. But physical constraints are important in more everyday settings, too, such as retailing. For example, a study by the Center for Retail Research indicated that theft by employees is the second largest source of "inventory shrinkage" – that is, losses stemming from shoplifting, theft by employees, supplier/vendor fraud, or accounting errors. According to this study, in the year to June 2010, retailers spent $26.8 billion (or 0.34% of sales) on preventing theft.[1] Effective physical constraints are also crucial in other contexts, especially due to increased data protection and privacy concerns faced by virtually all organizations, both private and public, that electronically store information about their clients, customers, patients, or citizens. For example, venerable HSBC's Swiss private bank arm had to embarrassingly apologize to its clients whose data were stolen by a former employee who should not have had, but did retain, access to client information.[2]

Administrative constraints can also be used to place limits on an employee's ability to perform all or a portion of specific tasks or actions. One common form of administrative control involves the restriction of decision-making authority. Managers at a low organizational level may be allowed to approve expenditures of up to $1,000; those at a higher level up to $5,000; and so on. Above those limits, the purchasing department is instructed not to place the order. The senior managers who restrict the decision-making authority in this way are trying to minimize the risk that resources are being disbursed by employees who are not trusted to do the job effectively.

Another common form of administrative control is generally referred to as *separation of duties*. This involves breaking up the tasks necessary for the accomplishment of certain sensitive duties, thus making it impossible, or at least difficult, for one person to complete the entire task on their own. There are many examples of separation of duties. One common example involves making sure that the employee who makes the payment entries in the accounts receivable ledger is not the employee who receives the checks. If an employee who is diverting company checks to a personal account only has the payment-entry duties, that is, opening the mail and listing, endorsing, and totaling incoming checks, customers will eventually complain about being dunned for amounts they had already paid. But a person with both check receiving and payment-entry duties could divert the checks and cover the action by making fictitious entries of returns of goods or, perhaps, price adjustments.

Separation of duties is one of the basic requirements of what is known as *internal control*, which is the control-oriented term used by the auditing profession. The effectiveness of separation of duties is limited, however, as it cannot completely eradicate possible *collusion*, such as between those with the check-receiving and payment-entry duties. Although collusion requires devious employees to reveal their fraudulent intentions to other employees whom they seek to engage in the scheme, survey evidence suggests that it occurs commonly nonetheless, either by collusion between employees and third parties or by collusion among employees or management themselves.[3] Inadequate internal controls heighten the risks of fraud and misconduct. Two-thirds of executives surveyed by *KPMG* admitted that when fraud and misconduct go unchecked in their organizations, it is likely due to *inadequate internal controls*.[4]

Sometimes physical and administrative constraints can be combined into what has been labeled as *poka-yokes* that are designed to make a process or system *foolproof*.[5] A poka-yoke is a step built into a process to prevent deviation from the correct order of steps; that is, where a certain action must be completed before the next step can be performed. A simple mechanical poka-yoke example is the inclusion of a switch in the door of a microwave oven so that the oven cannot be operated with the door open. Similar mistake-preventing poka-yokes can also be built into some production and administrative processes. For example, airlines make their pilots use *idiot-proof* software on laptops or handheld devices in the cockpit instead of letting them make manual preflight calculations that are error-prone. The software does not slip up on the math and flashes a warning if an out-of-range number is entered, such as a 10-ton mistake in the weight of the plane or fuel load.[6] Similarly, signature-verifying software can be used to authorize a cash distribution. Only after all the required signatures have been recognized by the software will the order be released or the transaction be approved.

It is often difficult to make behavioral constraints foolproof, especially when the organization is dealing with disloyal, deceitful employees. For example, despite reasonable safeguards, a former secretary at Bear Stearns, a global investment firm, used disappearing ink to write checks that her boss requested. After the manager signed the checks, she would erase the name of the payee and rewrite the checks for cash. In her eight months with the firm, she made more than $800,000 vanish from her boss's bank accounts.[7] As is common, "fraud often starts small and, as fraudsters find they can get away with it, gets bigger and bigger."[8]

Preaction reviews

Preaction reviews involve the scrutiny of the action plans of the employees being controlled. Reviewers can approve or disapprove the proposed actions, ask for modifications, or ask for a more carefully considered plan before granting final approval. A common form of preaction review takes place during planning and budgeting processes characterized by multiple levels of reviews of planned actions and budgets at consecutively higher organizational levels. We discuss planning and budgeting processes in more detail in Chapter 8.

Action accountability

Action accountability involves holding employees accountable for the actions they take. The implementation of action accountability controls requires: (1) defining what actions are acceptable or unacceptable; (2) communicating those definitions to employees; (3) observing or otherwise tracking what happens; and (4) rewarding good actions or punishing actions that deviate from the acceptable.

The actions for which employees are to be held accountable can be communicated either administratively or socially. *Administrative* modes of communication include the use of work rules, policies and procedures, contract provisions, and company codes of conduct. It is common in chains of fast-food franchises, such as McDonald's, to prescribe and communicate in writing, and clarify and reinforce through training, how virtually everything should be done, including how to handle cash, how to hire personnel, where to buy supplies, and what temperature to keep the oil while frying chips.[9] Similarly, nurses use preoperative checklists to help ensure that they prepare patients thoroughly for surgery. These checklists remind them to check on the patient's allergies, drug-taking history, and time of last meal. Train operators are provided with detailed sets of procedures communicated through Safety Rules and Procedures handbooks that they must know and follow. The importance of the procedures is reinforced through training and examinations.

The desired actions do not have to be communicated in written form, however. They can be communicated face-to-face in meetings or in private. For example, Andrew Grove, Intel's former chief executive officer (CEO), recognized that to keep "his generals and troops marching in the same direction requires constant cajoling and quarreling up and down the ranks."[10]

Sometimes the actions desired are not communicated explicitly at all. In many operational audits, post audits of capital investment decisions, and peer reviews of auditors, lawyers, doctors, and managers, individuals are held accountable for their actions that involve *professional judgment*. The desirability of the actions of professionals generally cannot be clearly delineated in advance. Nonetheless, these individuals are held accountable for their actions under the premise that they should "act professionally."

Although action accountability controls are most effective if the desired actions are well communicated, communication is not sufficient by itself to make these controls effective. The affected individuals must understand what is required and be confident that their actions will be noticed and rewarded or punished.

Actions can be tracked in several ways. Employee actions can be observed directly and nearly continuously as is done by direct supervisors on production lines. This is called *direct supervision* or *monitoring*. They can be tracked periodically, such as retail stores do when they use undercover *mystery shoppers* to evaluate the service provided by store clerks.[11] They can also be tracked by examining evidence of actions taken, such as activity reports or expense documentation. Examining evidence about compliance with pre-established action standards is a key function of *internal audit* (which we discuss in more detail in Chapter 14).

Action accountability is usually implemented with negative reinforcements. That is, the actions defined are more often linked with punishments than with rewards. For example, manufacturing firms sometimes devise "negative incentives" which stipulate that employees late for their shift lose a day's bonus, and those who miss their shift lose their bonus for the week. At Home Depot, managers are required to use an in-house personnel-screening system when hiring new employees. When five managers failed to use the system, they were fired.[12]

Redundancy

Redundancy, which involves assigning more employees (or equipment) to a task than is strictly necessary, or at least having backup employees (or equipment) available, also can be considered an action control because it increases the probability that a task will be satisfactorily completed. Redundancy is common in computer facilities, security functions, and other critical operations. However, it is rarely used in other areas because it is expensive. Further, assigning more than one employee to the same task usually results in conflict, frustration, and/or boredom.

ACTION CONTROLS AND THE CONTROL PROBLEMS

Action controls work because, like the other types of controls, they address one or more of the three basic control problems. Table 3.1 shows the types of problems addressed by each of the action controls.

Behavioral constraints are primarily effective in eliminating motivational problems. Employees who might be tempted to engage in undesirable behaviors can be prevented from doing so.

Preaction reviews can address all three of the control problems. Because they often involve communications to the employees about what is desired, they can help alleviate a lack of direction. They can also provide motivation, as the threat of an impending review of an employee's actions usually prompts extra care in the preparation of an expenditure proposal, a budget, or an action plan. Preaction reviews also mitigate the potentially costly effects of the personal limitations, since a good reviewer can add expertise if it is needed. The reviews can prevent mistakes or other harmful actions from happening.

Action accountability controls can also address all of the control problems. The prescriptions of desired actions can help provide direction and alleviate the types of personal limitations due to inadequate skills or experience. The rewards or punishments help provide motivation.

Redundancy is relatively limited in its application. It is primarily effective in helping to accomplish a particular task if there is some doubt as to whether the employee assigned to the task is either motivated to perform the task satisfactorily or capable of doing so.

TABLE 3.1 Control problems addressed by each of the action control types

	Control problem		
Type of action control	Lack of direction	Motivational problems	Personal limitations
Behavioral constraints		x	
Preaction reviews	x	x	x
Action accountability	x	x	x
Redundancy		x	x

Source: K. A. Merchant, *Modern Management Control Systems: Text and Cases* (Upper Saddle River, NJ: Prentice Hall, 1998), p. 30.

PREVENTION VERSUS DETECTION

Action controls can also be usefully classified according to whether they serve to *prevent* or to *detect* undesirable behaviors. This distinction is important because controls that prevent the undesired actions from occurring are, when they are effective, the most powerful form of control because the costs and harm stemming from the undesirable behaviors will be avoided. Detection-type action controls differ from prevention-type controls in that the former are applied *after* the occurrence of the behavior. Still, they can be effective if the detection is made in a timely manner and if the detection results in a cessation of the behavior and a correction of the effects of the harmful actions. Also, the promise of prompt detection of harmful actions is itself preventative; it discourages individuals from purposefully engaging in such behaviors.

Most action controls are aimed at preventing undesirable behaviors. The exception is action accountability controls. Although action accountability controls are designed to motivate employees to behave appropriately, it cannot be verified whether the appropriate actions were taken until evidence of the actions is gathered. However, if the evidence gathering is concurrent with the activity, as it is with direct supervision, then action accountability control can approach the desired state of prevention of undesired actions. Table 3.2 shows examples of common forms of action controls classified according to whether their purpose is to prevent or detect problems.

TABLE 3.2 Examples of action controls classified by purpose

	Control purpose	
Type of action control	Prevention	Detection
Behavioral constraints	Locks on valuable assets Separation of duties	N/A
Preaction reviews	Expenditure approvals Budget reviews	N/A
Action accountability	Prespecified policies linked to expectations of rewards and punishments	Compliance-oriented internal audits Cash reconciliations Peer reviews
Redundancy	Assigning multiple people to an important task	N/A

Source: K. A. Merchant, *Modern Management Control Systems: Text and Cases* (Upper Saddle River, NJ: Prentice Hall, 1998), p. 31.

CONDITIONS DETERMINING THE EFFECTIVENESS OF ACTION CONTROLS

Action controls cannot be used effectively in every situation. They are effective only when both of the following conditions exist, at least to some extent:

1. organizations can determine what actions are (un)desirable; and
2. organizations are able to ensure that the (un)desirable actions (do not) occur.

Knowledge of desired actions

Lack of knowledge as to what actions are desirable is the constraint that most severely limits the use of action controls. This knowledge is often difficult to obtain. Although it may be easy to define relatively completely the actions required of employees on a production line, the definitions of preferred actions in highly complex and uncertain task environments, such as those of salespeople, research engineers, or managers, often is incomplete or imprecise. Most organizations do not have a good idea as to how employees in these roles *should* best spend their time.

Knowledge of the desired actions can be discovered or learned in two ways. One is by analyzing the action patterns in a specific situation or similar situations over time to learn what actions produce the best results. For example, loan approval decisions are often highly structured. Over time, lenders observe which borrowers are likely to fail their loan payments. In so doing, they can develop a loan approval protocol, delegate the decision to lower-level employees, and control employee behaviors by monitoring their adherence to the desired decision protocol. Another way organizations can learn which actions are desirable is to be informed by others, especially for strategic decisions. Indeed, this is a major role played by consultants who have detailed knowledge of best practices.

It is important that the actions for which employees are to be held accountable are, in fact, the actions that will lead to the highest probability of accomplishment of one or more of the organization's goals, or at least the proper implementation of the strategy that is being pursued. As with results controls, as we discussed similarly in Chapter 2, many organizations have actually found themselves encouraging employees to take the *wrong* actions, which happens, for example, when policies and procedures are not kept up-to-date.

Ability to ensure that desired actions are taken

Knowing what actions are desirable is not sufficient by itself to ensure good control; organizations must have some ability to ensure or observe that the desired actions are taken. This ability varies widely among the different action controls.

The effectiveness of the *behavioral constraints* and *preaction reviews* varies directly with the reliability of the physical devices or administrative procedures the organization has in place to ensure that the (un)desired actions are (not) taken. In many cases, these devices and procedures are not effective. For example, a rogue currency trader at Allfirst Financial, who had lost about $700 million in foreign exchange trading, was said to have "targeted every control point in the system and systematically found a way around them." When called aside by managers for going over his trading limits, the trader complained that the computerized risk-monitoring system he used to check his risk exposure during the day was too cumbersome. He got away with it.[13] To cover up his losses, the trader allegedly started selling bogus option contracts. This practice was not detected in a timely manner either, in part because the responsibility for the monitoring and reporting of the trader's foreign-exchange risks was given to a junior, relatively inexperienced, staff member.[14]

At Lehman Brothers, the now defunct investment bank, a star stockbroker managed to keep a personal computer on his office desk, despite rules prohibiting this practice, and allegedly despite the fact that some senior executives were aware of it. The broker used his personal computer, rather than a Lehman office computer, to create fake account statements with inflated stock prices. He then diverted the real account statements to post office boxes that he controlled, rather than to his clients who instead received the phony statements he generated. Clients say the broker forged their authorizations to send their statements to the post office boxes. What's more, the broker supervised the compliance staff whose job it was to help police the office brokers. Over a 15-year period, this broker stole $125 million from his unsuspecting customers.[15]

Examples such as these are consistent with the findings of numerous fraud surveys that suggest that frauds occur and go undetected because of poor internal controls (many of which fall into the category of what we call *behavioral constraints*). Worse, another common reason why frauds go undetected in organizations is due to *management override* of the controls.[16] Quoting one such survey, "As indicated by nearly 60% of our respondents, companies find that one of the greatest challenges in countering fraud is that unscrupulous management may override otherwise effective internal controls."[17]

Action tracking often provides a significant challenge that must be faced in making *action accountability* controls effective. Usually some actions can be tracked even where employees' actions cannot be observed directly. But this tracking is not always effective. The criteria that should be used to judge whether the action tracking is effective are precision, objectivity, timeliness, and understandability (as we also discussed in Chapter 2 in a results control context). If any of these measurement qualities cannot be achieved, action accountability control will not be effective in evoking the desired behaviors.

Precision refers to the amount of error in the indicators used to tell what actions have taken place. If action tracking involves direct supervision, can the supervisors accurately distinguish good from bad actions? If action tracking involves scrutinizing transaction records, do those records reliably tell whether the proper actions were taken? For example, an initiative aimed at tracking whether salespeople spend enough time on market development activities, as opposed to direct sales activities, is doomed to fail until precise definitions can be developed as to which actions fall into each of these two areas. A similar precision failure of an action control exists within the context of the US Foreign Corrupt Practices Act. This act was intended to make "bribes" to foreign officials illegal, but it allowed "facilitating payments" to lower-level officials. The distinction between bribes and facilitating payments is not precise, however, causing concern for company officers who cannot be sure that their real-time interpretations of the actions by company personnel in foreign countries will match those made by independent observers (such as a jury) at a later date in lawsuits of bribe allegations.

Objectivity, or freedom from bias, is a concern because reports of actions prepared by those whose actions are being controlled cannot necessarily be relied upon. Project- and sales-oriented personnel are frequently asked to prepare self-reports of how they spend their time. In most cases, these reports are precise, as the allocations may be in units of time as small as by the minute. But the reports are not objective. If the personnel involved want to obscure the true time patterns, perhaps to cover a bad performance or to allow some personal time, it is relatively easy for them to report that most of their time was spent on productive activities. Most companies use direct supervisors and internal auditors to provide objectivity checks on such reports. Without objectivity, management cannot be sure whether the action reports reflect the actual actions taken, and the reports lose their value for control purposes.[18]

Timeliness in tracking actions also is important. If the tracking is not timely, interventions are not possible before harm is done. Further, much of the motivational effect of the feedback is lost when the tracking is significantly delayed.

Finally, it is important that the actions for which individuals are to be held accountable are *understandable*. Although employees presumably can easily understand prescriptions to arrive at work on time or to not steal, understanding and consistently acting in full compliance with the detailed rules and regulations contained in procedures handbooks, is obviously much more challenging. Forensic investigations indeed suggest that accidents are often due to a lack of employees' understanding (and hence, compliance with) all of the necessary detail of such procedures.

Implementing action controls where one of these action-tracking qualities cannot be achieved will lead to some undesirable effects. (These are discussed further in Chapter 5.) However, like results controls, action controls usually cannot be made near-perfect, or at least it is prohibitively expensive to make them near-perfect. As a consequence, organizations use personnel and cultural controls to help fill in some gaps. These controls motivate employees to control their own behaviors (*personnel controls*) or to control each other's behaviors (*cultural controls*).

PERSONNEL CONTROLS

Personnel controls build on employees' natural tendencies to control or motivate themselves. Personnel controls serve three purposes. First, some personnel controls help clarify expectations. They help ensure that each employee understands what the organization wants. Second, some personnel controls help ensure that each employee is able to do a good job; that they have all the capabilities (e.g. experience, intelligence) and resources (e.g. information and time) needed to do the job. Third, some personnel controls increase the likelihood that each employee will engage in self-monitoring. *Self-monitoring* is an innate force that pushes most employees to want to do a good job, to be naturally committed. Self-monitoring is effective both because most people have a conscience that leads them to do what is right and are able to derive positive feelings of self-respect and satisfaction when they do a good job and see their organization succeed. Self-monitoring has been discussed in the management literature under a variety of labels, including *intrinsic motivation* and *loyalty*.

Personnel controls can be implemented through (1) selection and placement, (2) training, and (3) job design and resourcing. In other words, finding the right people to do a particular job, training them, and giving them both a good work environment and the necessary resources is likely to increase the probability that the job will be done properly.

Selection and placement

Organizations devote considerable time and effort to employee selection and placement. A large literature studies and describes how that should best be accomplished. Much of this literature describes possible predictors of success, such as education, experience, past successes, and personality and social skills.[19]

Employee selection often involves reference checks on new employees, which many organizations have stepped up in recent years in response to the heightened worries over workplace security.[20] According to a 2010 survey by the Society for Human Resource Management, about 73% of major employers report that they always check on applicants' criminal records, while 19% do so for select job candidates.[21] But beyond screening new employees to mitigate security issues, organizations primarily focus on matching job requirements with job applicants' skills. For example, Home Depot, the large American retailer of home improvement and construction products and services, has an in-house computer system that contains the names of pre-screened candidates who have the right skills and experience. This allows managers to find qualified candidates quickly when the need arises. But the automated system also provides cues about what interview questions to ask, what answers to listen for, and even what advice to give the interviewees.[22]

More exotic employee-selection techniques have also been developed and used. Some organizations have resorted to analyzing potential employees' handwriting or using polygraph tests to try to weed out high-risk individuals. Dell Computer, General Electric, Motorola, and other companies require job candidates to undergo lengthy interviews with outside human resource service providers, or to take paper-and-pencil tests, or both. While these evaluations are expensive, their cost is far less than the costs associated with hiring someone who is a "poor fit" with the company.[23]

Training

Training is another common way to increase the likelihood that employees do a good job. Training can provide useful information about what actions or results are expected and how the assigned tasks can be best performed. Training can also have positive motivational effects because employees can be given a greater sense of professionalism, and they are often more interested in performing well in jobs they understand better.

Many organizations use formal training programs, such as in classroom settings, to improve the skills of their personnel. The Los Angeles Unified School District wanted to decentralize and give school principals more decision-making authority. District managers concluded, however, that the principals would not know how to use their increased authority. They decided to put the principals through a formal mini-MBA program to teach them how to improve the educational process and manage school costs. The principals attended classes over an 18-month period and several follow-up workshops. The program was judged so successful that its use was expanded to other school districts in the San Francisco Bay area and the East Coast.[24]

In a recent study, Stephen Dorgan of McKinsey, a consultancy, and John Van Reenen of the London School of Economics, investigated why, from America to Sweden, the best hospitals in developed countries outperformed the rest. They found that competition, hospital size and independence, and professional management and decision autonomy, were among the most important factors that explain hospital performance.[25] As in the schools example above, however, factors such as professional management and decision autonomy require, or need to be accompanied with, training to help develop the skills for managers to perform well.

Much training takes place informally, such as through employee mentoring. For example, every month, new *and* some existing franchisees for The Pita Pit, a quick-service sandwich chain with 180 stores across the United States, assemble in Coeur d'Alene, Idaho, for several days of training. Peter Riggs, vice president of The Pita Pit, however, wants to make sure that the franchisees also share their experiences after it is completed. "Anyone can learn systems," he said, but then hinted at the need to continually transfer knowledge among employees, which he saw as perhaps the most important aspect of the training and the way it was provided.[26] At Jaburg Wilk, a law firm in Phoenix, Arizona, junior colleagues have two monthly mentoring meetings for 30 minutes to an hour each with a senior colleague, which is seen as an effective way to help the junior colleagues improve their marketing and networking efforts to attract more sophisticated clients. Scott Allen, a consultant, notes that through mentoring "you will get insights [from the] one-on-one face time that no market research report could ever give you; and if the mentor is lucky, [s/he] may even learn a thing or two [too]."[27]

Job design and provision of necessary resources

Another way to help employees act aptly is simply to make sure that the job is designed to allow motivated and qualified employees a high probability of success. Some organizations do not give all their employees a chance to succeed. Some jobs are too complex. Salespeople may be assigned too many accounts to handle effectively. Employees also need a particular set of resources available to them in order to do a good job. Resource needs are highly job-specific, but they can include such items as information, equipment, supplies, staff support, decision aids, or freedom from interruption. In larger organizations, particularly, there is a strong need for transfer of information among organizational entities so that the coordination of well-timed, efficient actions and decisions is maintained. This latter point was illustrated pertinently in the example of The Pita Pit above, where the purpose of training, and the way in which it was delivered, also included and facilitated ways to allow transfer of knowledge, experiences, and best practices.

CULTURAL CONTROLS

Cultural controls are designed to encourage mutual monitoring; a powerful form of group pressure on individuals who deviate from group norms and values. In some collectivist cultures, such as Japan, incentives to avoid anything that would disgrace oneself and one's family are paramount. Similarly, in some countries, notably those in Southeast Asia, business deals sometimes are sealed by verbal agreement only. In those instances, the dominant social and moral obligations are stronger than legal contracts. But strong cultural controls produced by mutual-monitoring processes also exist within single organizations. Cultural controls are most effective where members of a group have social or emotional ties to one another.

Cultures are built on shared traditions, norms, beliefs, values, ideologies, attitudes, and ways of behaving. The cultural norms are embodied in written and unwritten rules that govern employees' behaviors. Organizational cultures remain relatively fixed over time, even while goals and strategies necessarily adapt to changing business conditions. To understand an organization's culture, ask long-time employees questions like: What are you proud of around here? What does it take to get ahead? How do you stay out of trouble? If a strong organizational culture exists, the vast majority of long-time employees will have consistent answers to these questions even when the answers are not written down. When that is the case, strong, functional organizational cultures prompt employees to work together in a synergistic fashion. It also implies, however, that despite the benefits of direction and cohesiveness, strong cultures sometimes can be a source of inertia, which can get in the way of needed change and adaptation in rapidly evolving environments.

Organizational cultures can be shaped in many ways, both in words and by example, including by way of codes of conduct, group rewards, intra-organizational transfers, physical and social arrangements, and tone at the top.

Codes of conduct

Most organizations above minimal size attempt to shape their organizational culture through what are known, variously, as codes of conduct, codes of ethics, organizational credos, or statements of mission, vision, or management philosophy. These formal, written documents provide broad, general statements of organizational values, commitments to stakeholders, and the ways in which management would like the organization to function. The codes are designed to help employees understand what behaviors are expected even in the absence of a specific rule; that is, they are to some extent principle-based rather than merely rule-based. They may include important messages about dedication to quality or customer satisfaction, fair treatment of employees and customers, employee safety, innovation, risk taking, adherence to ethical principles, open communications, and willingness to change. To be effective, the messages included in these statements should be reinforced through formal training sessions and through informal discussions or mentoring meetings among employees and their superiors.

Codes of conduct can vary considerably in form across firms.[28] In addition to general policy statements, which almost all codes of conduct necessarily elaborate, some codes provide guidance on specific issues. If such guidance is included, then the detailed behavioral prescriptions provide a form of action accountability control because employees who violate the prescriptions will be reprimanded.

Recent evidence indicates that the vast majority (86%) of Fortune Global 200 companies have a business code; that the rate of code adoption has doubled over the past 10 years; and that older codes are being updated. Specifically, two-thirds of the companies that have had a code for longer than three years have updated their codes during the past three years. The survey also indicates that the three most common drivers for code adoption are to comply with legal requirements; to create a shared company culture; and to protect or improve the corporate reputation. The most commonly cited values embedded in the codes are integrity, teamwork, respect, innovation, and client focus. The codes are most often directed at employees; corporate responsibilities to shareholders are discussed in less than half of the codes. More than 70% of the codes discuss the responsibilities of employees regarding confidential information, accuracy of reporting (fraud), protection of corporate property, and dealing with gifts and entertainment. Finally, most codes contain a combination of principles and rules: 13% of the codes are principle-based, 35% are rule-based; the other 52% are a mix of the two.[29]

The survey also suggests that American companies have taken more measures to implement their codes than their European or Asian counterparts. More than 80% of the companies use e-learning modules to implement the code and have an ethics hotline and whistle-blower mechanisms to detect misconduct. More than 80% of the companies have policies to enforce their codes and to investigate violations. However, less than half of the companies monitor compliance with the code in their business units or have external reporting on compliance.[30]

Do codes of conduct work? The evidence is equivocal. One study found that employees who work for companies with codes of ethics were much more likely to rate the commitment to ethical conduct by colleagues as "about right." They were also 88% more likely to rate their firm's fulfillment of its ethical obligations as "exceptional."[31] However, other evidence suggests that employee misconduct arises because their company's code of conduct is not taken seriously.[32]

Some codes of conduct indeed are dormant, meaning that employees perceive the codes as mostly public relations and not something to be taken seriously. Some codes of conduct fail because they are not supported by strong leadership and proper tone from the top.

Top managers do not always appear committed to them, or worse, set bad examples themselves through inappropriate conduct. For example, in August 2010, the Board of HP, the multinational information technology corporation, asked for CEO Mark Hurd's resignation "in large part because of the conflict between his actions and the company's code of conduct, which he publicly championed in 2006 following a boardroom scandal."[33] As another case in point, Enron managers were proud of their company's code of ethics, but it failed to prevent the major problems that led to the company's bankruptcy. Clearly, having a code is not quite the same as living by it. That said, intelligently designed and functionally implemented codes of conduct are likely to be indispensible for organizations to try and shape desired behaviors.[34]

Group rewards

Providing rewards or incentives based on collective achievement also encourages cultural control. Such incentive plans based on collective achievement can come in many forms. Common examples are bonus, profit-sharing or gain-sharing plans that provide compensation based on overall company or entity (rather than individual) performance in terms of accounting returns, profits, or cost reductions. Encouraging broad employee ownership of company stock, with effective corporate communications to keep employees informed and enthusiastic, encourages all employees to think like owners. According to Sarah McCartney-Fry, Member of Parliament and a member of the All Party Parliamentary Group on Employee Ownership, there is a "growing interest in . . . businesses [that] are substantially or majority owned by its employees, [because] co-owned firms appear adept at managing innovation and change and are underpinned by very high levels of productive employee engagement."[35]

Indeed, evidence suggests that group-based incentive plans create a culture of "ownership" and "engagement" to the mutual benefit of organizations and their employees.[36] Specifically, a review of 70 studies over a 25-year period found that both employee ownership and profit-sharing programs improved employee productivity, company performance, and company survivor rates.[37] According to a 2010 employee engagement study by the Corporate Executive Board's Corporate Leadership Council, employees most committed to their organizations put forth 57% more effort and are 87% less likely to leave their company than employees who consider themselves disengaged. The study concluded that, "it should be no surprise then that employee engagement, or lack thereof, is a critical factor in an organization's overall financial success."[38]

Group rewards are discussed here as a type of cultural control rather than as a results control (as we do in Chapter 9) because they are quite different in character from rewards given for individual performance. With group rewards, the link between individual efforts and the results being rewarded is weak, or at least weakened. Thus, motivation to achieve the rewards is not among the primary forces affected by group rewards; instead communication of expectations and mutual monitoring are. That is not to suggest that group rewards cannot have positive effects on motivation, even if only indirectly. Group rewards can encourage teamwork, on-the-job training of new employees (when assigned to teams that include experienced colleagues), and the creation of peer pressure on individual employees to exert themselves for the good of the group. Panhandle Eastern Corporation, a natural gas company, installed a gain-sharing plan that called for all employees to receive a bonus if corporate earnings exceeded $2 per share. This group-performance plan created a cost-cutting culture throughout the organization and turned "employees from top to bottom . . . into cost-cutting vigilantes."[39]

Other evidence of the success of group rewards comes from work that describes companies' experiences with programs known as *open book management* (OBM), of which group rewards are an important ingredient. The goal of an OBM program is to create a clear line of sight between each employee's actions/decisions and company financial performance, thereby instilling an incentive for the employees to behave in the company's best interest and to make useful suggestions for improvement. OBM programs involve: (1) regular sharing of the company's financial information and any other information that will help the employees work together with management towards organizational success; (2) training, so that employees understand both what that information means and how they themselves can contribute to company performance; (3) rewards linked to company performance; and (4) if necessary, a cultural change away from a top-down culture to ensure that employee ideas are both encouraged and considered fairly. Most commonly, OBM incentives involve tying a portion of each employee's compensation to key corporate financial indicators, usually in the form of an employee stock-ownership plan or a profit-sharing plan.[40] The earliest program given the OBM label was that implemented at the Springfield Remanufacturing Company in the early 1980s, credited for turning around a near-failing company. The idea has spread and there are now a number of examples explaining how OBM programs have yielded significant improvements in productivity and profits.[41]

All told, group rewards essentially delegate the monitoring of employees' behaviors to employees' co-workers. This is the essence of *mutual monitoring*. Managers know whether their group reward schemes are working when they hear diligent employees urging on their sluggish colleagues with statements like, "Get on, you're hurting my profit sharing!"

Other approaches to shape organizational culture

Other common approaches to shape organizational culture include intra-organizational transfers, physical and social arrangements, and tone at the top.

Intra-organizational transfers or *employee rotation* help transmit culture by improving the socialization of employees throughout the organization, giving them a better appreciation of the problems faced by different parts of the organization, and inhibiting the formation of incompatible goals and perspectives. Transfers also potentially mitigate employee fraud by preventing employees from becoming "too familiar" with certain entities, activities, colleagues, and/or transactions.

Physical arrangements, such as office plans, architecture, and interior decor, and *social arrangements*, such as dress codes, institutionalized habits, behaviors, and vocabulary, can also help shape organizational culture. Some organizations, such as technology firms in Silicon Valley, have created informal cultures, with open office arrangements and casual dress codes that deliver messages about the importance of innovation and employee equality. Steve Jobs, founder and CEO of Apple, the well-known company that designs and markets consumer electronics, computer software, and personal computers, serves as a good example of how corporate cultures can be shaped (and as a good example of "tone at the top" as we discuss next). When Mr. Jobs takes the stage in his trademark turtleneck, jeans, and sneakers for his "Apple Announcements" that are streamed live over the internet, he undoubtedly portrays an image of creativity and innovation. As some commentators note, he has "made culture cool" and "turned the most boring event in the catalog of boring events – a corporate press conference – into a global cultural phenomenon to rival rock star concerts or big sports events."[42] But many other companies also have, and are reputed for, their unique cultures. At Disneyland, employees are called *cast members*; being on the job is being *onstage* (off the job is *offstage*); a work shift is a *performance*;

and a job description is a *script*. This vocabulary, which is imparted on joining the company and is reinforced through training, separates Disney employees from the rest of the world, brings them closer together, and reminds them that they are performers whose job is to help fulfill the company's mission – that is, that "every product tells a story" and that "entertainment is about hope, aspiration and positive resolutions."[43]

Finally, management can shape culture by setting the proper *tone at the top*. Their statements should be consistent with the type of culture they are trying to create and, importantly, their actions and behaviors should be consistent with their statements. Managers serve as role models and, as the various surveys quoted earlier in this chapter suggest, are a determining factor in creating a culture of integrity in their organizations.[44] Management cannot say one thing and do another.

Management sometimes sets the *wrong* tone by not responding appropriately to matters brought to their attention, such as ethics concerns or reports of malpractice. All too common, *whistle-blowers* (employees who draw attention to suspected malpractice) are often ignored, such as Sherron Watkins was initially at Enron.[45] To correct such a situation, Abbey National, a British bank, set the right tone by producing a booklet about whistle-blowing and by providing contacts inside and outside the firm for employees who are concerned about malpractice.[46] In so doing, management set the tone that honesty and integrity are valued and rewarded by the organization. Several studies, however, paint a rather gloomy picture of tone at the top. For example, a study by the Treadway Commission that examined accounting scandals that brought down companies found that fraud started at the top in 70% of the cases.[47]

PERSONNEL/CULTURAL CONTROLS AND THE CONTROL PROBLEMS

Taken together, personnel/cultural controls are capable of addressing all of the control problems although, as shown in Table 3.3, not each type of control in this category is effective at addressing each type of problem. The lack-of-direction problem can be minimized, for example, by hiring experienced personnel, by providing training programs, or by assigning new personnel to work groups that will provide good direction. The motivational problems, which may be minimal in organizations with strong cultures, can

TABLE 3.3 **Control problems addressed by the various ways of effecting personnel and cultural controls**

	Lack of direction	Motivational problems	Personal limitations
Ways of effecting personnel controls			
Selection and placement	x	x	x
Training	x		x
Job design and provision of necessary resources			x
Ways of effecting cultural controls			
Codes of conduct	x		x
Group-based rewards	x	x	x
Intraorganizational transfers	x		x
Physical arrangements			x
Tone at the top	x		

Source: K. A. Merchant, *Modern Management Control Systems: Text and Cases* (Upper Saddle River, NJ: Prentice Hall, 1998), p. 130.

be minimized in other organizations by hiring highly motivated people or by assigning people to work groups that will tend to make them adjust to group norms. Personal limitations can also be reduced through one or more types of personnel controls, particularly the selection, training, and provision of necessary resources.

EFFECTIVENESS OF PERSONNEL/CULTURAL CONTROLS

All organizations rely to some extent on their employees to guide and motivate themselves. Some corporate control systems are dominated by personnel controls. William F. Cronk, now-retired president of Dreyer's Grand Ice Cream (since acquired by Nestlé), said at the time that, "We consider hiring the most important decision we can make. We hire the smartest, most inspired people we can find, give them the resources they need, then get out of their way."[48] Cultural controls can also, by themselves, dominate a control system.[49] The best chance to create a strong culture, however, seems to be early in an organization's life when a founder can imbue the organization with a distinctive culture.[50] Cultural controls often have the advantage of being relatively unobtrusive. Employees may not even think of the shared norms or "the way we do things around here" as being part of the "control" system. As such, organizational cultures can substitute for other formal types of controls. Or, as Peters and Waterman observed, "the stronger the culture . . . the less need there is for policy manuals, organization charts, or detailed procedures and rules."[51]

As such, personnel/cultural controls can have distinctive advantages over results and action controls. They are usable to some extent in almost every setting; their cost is often lower than more obtrusive forms of controls; and they might produce fewer harmful side effects. Moreover, "soft" personnel/cultural controls have also been shown to make "economic sense" as surveys and evidence suggest that "it *pays* to be nice to employees."[52] For example, in an 800-store study, Sears, the giant US retailer, found that if employee attitudes (such as about workload and treatment by bosses) improve by 5%, customer satisfaction will jump by 1.3%, driving a half percentage point increase in revenues.[53] At the SAS Institute, the large privately held software and business intelligence systems company, employee loyalty is instilled with an unusual array of perks for its roughly 3,000 headquarter employees, such as through a profit-sharing plan; a free health clinic; daycare centers; private offices for everyone; flexible 35-hour weeks; free sodas, fresh fruit, and pastries in the coffee-break rooms; and even a pianist in the subsidized lunch and recreation room. SAS's turnover rate has been about 4% for years, compared to an industry average of about 20%. Stanford University professor Jeffrey Pfeffer concluded, "The roughly $50 million per year that SAS saves with its low turnover pays for all the family-friendly stuff. And, while the free company clinic costs $1 million per year to operate, that is $500,000 less than what it would cost the company if employees were treated elsewhere."[54]

But, the degree to which personnel/cultural controls are effective can vary significantly across individuals, groups, communities, and societies. Some people are more honest than others, and some communities and societies have stronger emotional ties among their members. Cultures that are "too strong" can also be a disadvantage, especially when they need changing.

CONCLUSION

In this chapter, we provided an overview of the most direct type of controls, *action controls*, which take any of several different forms: behavioral constraints, preaction reviews, action accountability, and redundancy. Action controls are the most direct type of management control because they ensure the proper behaviors of the people on whom the organization must rely by focusing directly on their actions.

We also described *personnel* and *cultural controls*, which managers implement to encourage either or both of two positive forces that are normally present in organizations: self- and mutual-monitoring. These forces can be encouraged in a number of ways, including effective personnel selection and placement, training, job design and provision of necessary resources, codes of conduct, group rewards, intra-organizational transfers, physical and social arrangements, and tone at the top.

Personnel and cultural controls, which are sometimes referred to as *soft* controls, have become more important in recent years. Organizations have become flatter and leaner. Managers have wider spans of control, and elaborate hierarchies and systems of action controls (bureaucracies) have been dismantled and replaced with empowered employees.[55] In this environment, shared organizational values have become a more important tool for ensuring that everyone is acting in the organization's best interest.[56]

Notes

1. "Five-Fingered Discounts," *The Economist* (October 23, 2010), p. 80.
2. "HSBC Swiss Private Bank Posts 1H Net New Money After Data Theft," *The Wall Street Journal* (August 26, 2010), online (http://online.wsj.com).
3. *KPMG 2003 Fraud Survey* (KPMG LLP, 2003); *KPMG 2008/2009 Fraud Survey* (KPMG LLP, 2010).
4. *Effectiveness of Fraud Risk Management Efforts* (KPMG LLP, 2009).
5. D. Stewart and R. Chase, *Mistake-Proofing: Designing Errors Out* (Portland, OR: Productivity Press, 1995). *Poka-yoke* is the Japanese term for *foolproof*. It was introduced to the management literature by the Japanese quality guru Sigeo Shingo.
6. "At Some Airlines, Laptops Replace Pilots' 'Brain Bags'," *The Wall Street Journal* (March 26, 2002), p. B1.
7. "Bear Stearns Ex-Staffer Pleads Guilty to Taking Funds in Check Scheme," *The Wall Street Journal* (February 26, 2002), p. C14.
8. "Employee Fraud is a Growing Problem, Survey Shows," *The Australian* (June 25, 2010), online (http://theaustralian.com.au).
9. "Memorable Memo: McDonald's Sends Operations to War on Fries," *The Wall Street Journal Interactive Edition* (December 18, 1997).
10. "How to Plan for 1995," *Fortune* (December 31, 1990), p. 74.
11. "McDonald's Asks Mystery Shoppers What Ails Sales: Undercover Customers to Rate Service and Food Quality," *The Wall Street Journal* (December 17, 2001), p. B1.
12. "To Hire a Lumber Expert, Click Here," *Fortune* (April 3, 2000), p. 268.
13. "Allfirst Officials Raised Concern about Trader in a 1999 Memo," *The Wall Street Journal* (February 25, 2002), p. C16.
14. "Controls at Allied Irish's Allfirst Likely Failed in Important Ways," *The Wall Street Journal* (February 20, 2002), p. C1.
15. "Lehman Broker in Alleged Swindle Also Supervised the Compliance Officer," *The Wall Street Journal* (February 20, 2002), p. C1; C. Gasparino, "Rogue Broker Costs Lehman, Cowen a Bundle; Regulators Press Firms to Pay up to $100 Million to Investors Who Were Gruttadauria Victims," *The Wall Street Journal* (December 4, 2002), p. C1.
16. *KPMG 2003 Fraud Survey*, op. cit.; *KPMG 2008/2009 Fraud Survey*, op. cit.
17. *Driving Ethical Growth: New Markets, New Challenges* (Ernst & Young 11th Global Fraud Survey, 2010).
18. "Curbing those Long, Lucrative Hours," *The Economist* (July 22, 2010), p. 66.
19. See, for example, B. Smart, *How Leading Companies Win by Hiring, Coaching and Keeping the Best People* (New York: Portfolio Hardcover, Penguin Group USA, 2005); and M. Brannick and E. Levine, *Job Analysis: Methods, Research and Applications for Human Resource Management in the New Millennium* (Thousand Oaks, CA: Sage Publications, 2002).
20. "Check, Please," *The Wall Street Journal* (March 11, 2002), p. R11; "Employers Dig Deep Into Workers' Pasts, Citing Terrorism Fears," *The Wall Street Journal* (March 12, 2002), p. A1.
21. "Some Job-Screening Tactics Challenged as Illegal," *The Wall Street Journal* (August 11, 2010), online (http://online.wsj.com).
22. "To Hire a Lumber Expert, Click Here," op. cit., pp. 267–70.
23. "Does This Man Need a Shrink," *Fortune* (February 5, 2001), pp. 205–7.
24. "School Inc.: Principals Taught to Act Like CEOs," *The Wall Street Journal* (October 16, 1996), p. CA1.

25. "How to Save Lives," *The Economist* (October 23, 2010), p. 72.

26. "Improve Your Employee Training Sessions," *Business Week* (February 2, 2010), online (www.businessweek.com).

27. "Mentors Make a Business Better," *Business Week* (March 20, 2008), online (www.businessweek.com).

28. The codes of conduct of large, well-known corporations are often available on their websites. See, for example, Johnson & Johnson's "Credo" at www.jnj.com/connect/about-jnj/jnj-credo.

29. "Business Codes of the Global 200: Their Prevalence, Content and Embedding," KPMG (June 16, 2008).

30. Ibid. See also, "Code of Conduct Survey Reveals Serious Weaknesses," *CSR Wire* (January 16, 2008), online (www.csrwire.com).

31. "Employees Say It's Hard to be Ethical in Some Organizations," *Internal Auditor* (February 1995), p. 9.

32. *KPMG 2005/2006 Integrity Survey* (KPMG LLP, 2005).

33. "Mark Hurd Neglected to Follow HP Code," *The Wall Street Journal* (August 8, 2010), online (http://online.wsj.com).

34. See, for example, *Ethics & Workplace Survey* (Deloitte, 2010).

35. "Employee Benefits: Share Ownership Schemes – Should You CoCo?," *HR Magazine* (September 1, 2008), online (www.hrmagazine.co.uk).

36. C. Rosen, J. Case, and M. Staubus, *Equity: Why Employee Ownership is Good for Business* (Boston, MA: Harvard Business School Press, 2005).

37. J. Blasi, D. Kruse, and A. Bernstein, *In the Company of Owners: The Trust about Stock Options (and Why Every Employee Should Have Them)* (New York, NY: Basic Books, 2003).

38. "The Role of Employee Engagement in the Return to Growth," *Business Week* (August 13, 2010), online (www.businessweek.com).

39. "Gas Company's Gain-Sharing Plan Turns Employees into Cost-Cutting Vigilantes," *The Wall Street Journal* (September 29, 1995), p. B1.

40. Jack Stack, CEO of Springfield Remanufacturing, is credited with pioneering the OBM technique in the 1980s, which is described in more detail in J. Stack, *The Great Game of Business* (New York, NY: Doubleday, 1992).

41. See, for example, "To Beat the Recession, Open Your Books," *Business Week* (July 7, 2009), online (www.businessweek.com).

42. "Apple Announcement: How Steve Jobs Made Geek Culture Cool," *The Wall Street Journal* (September 1, 2010), online (http://online.wsj.com).

43. See company website: http://corporate.disney.go.com/careers/culture.

44. See, for example, *KPMG 2003 Fraud Survey*, op. cit. and *KPMG 2008/2009 Fraud Survey*, op. cit.; see also "Employees Lack Trust in Mangers, Survey Finds," *World-At-Work Newsline* (April 19, 2010), online (www.worldatwork.org).

45. M. Swartz and S. Watkins, *Power Failure: The Inside Story of the Collapse of Enron* (New York, NY: Doubleday, 2004).

46. "Why Honesty is the Best Policy: Corporate Deceit is a Slippery Slope," A Survey of Management, *The Economist* (March 9, 2002), pp. 9–13.

47. "One More Dirty Job for Accountants: Take the Blame," *The Wall Street Journal* (March 20, 2002), p. A23.

48. Quoted in D. Ferguson, "Do Entrepreneurial Companies Lose Their Innovative Spark as They Grow Larger?" *Cal Business* (Fall 1995), p. 12.

49. "New Atmosphere: Inside Southwest Airlines, Storied Culture Feels Strains; Spirit of Fun and Hard Work is Clouded by Picketing and Employee Complaints; No Longer the Underdog," *The Wall Street Journal* (July 11, 2003), p. A1.

50. See, for example, "Keeper of the Flame: How Tony Hsieh of Zappos.com Keeps the Dotcom Spirit Alive," *Economist.com* (April 16, 2009), online only (www.economist.com).

51. T. J. Peters and R. H. Waterman, *In Search of Excellence* (New York: Harper & Row, 1982), p. 75.

52. "Companies Are Finding It Really Pays to Be Nice to Employees," *The Wall Street Journal* (July 22, 1998); "Is Optimism a Competitive Advantage?," *Business Week* (August 13, 2009), online (www.businessweek.com). "Marco Equation: Happy Employees Equal Happy Customers," *Star Tribune* (August 22, 2010), online (www.startribune.com); For a contrarian view, see "Memo to CFOs: Don't Trust HR," *CFO Europe* (March 10, 2009), online (www.cfo.com).

53. A. Rucci, S. Kirn, and R. Quinn, "The Employee-Customer-Profit Chain at Sears," *Harvard Business Review* (January–February, 1998), pp. 82–97.

54. "An Idyllic Workplace under a Tycoon's Thumb," *The Wall Street Journal* (November 23, 1998).

55. *Tailored to the Bottom Line*, Deloitte Review (2010), online (www.deloitte.com).

56. For a recent academic perspective and overview of the control literature in the area of what we call personnel/cultural controls, see M. Loughry, "Peer Control in Organizations," in S. Sitkin, L. Cardinal, and K. Bijlsma-Frankema, *Organizational Control* (New York, NY: Cambridge University Press, 2010), Chapter 11.

The Platinum Pointe Land Deal

In early December 2006, Harry Hepburn, president of the Southern California Division of Robinson Brothers Homes, was faced with a significant challenge. The markets his division served had slowed considerably. To sell its homes, the division often had to make significant price concessions. But construction costs were continuing to rise, so margins were getting squeezed. It was clear that the division was not going to achieve its 2006 sales and profit plan. But what was worse, corporate executives were recommending a significant downsizing of the division in 2007 to wait until the housing market rebounded. Harry resisted this idea. He thought he had assembled a great employee team. The division's performance had been outstanding during the good years in the early 2000s. He wanted to keep his team intact. But that required finding a continuing stream of good projects for them to work on.

One promising project on the horizon was called Platinum Pointe. It was a large project that promised to provide over $100 million in revenue and nearly $14 million in profits in the 2008–11 time period. It would keep a lot of employees productively busy. Harry really wanted to do the project. However, the financial projections suggested that the project would not quite earn the returns that the corporation required for projects with this level of risk. He contemplated preparing projections that were a "little more optimistic" to ensure that the project would be approved.

THE COMPANY

Robinson Brothers Homes (RBH) was a medium-sized homebuilder. The company built single-family and higher-density homes, such as townhouses and condominiums. By 2006, RBH built almost 2,000 homes per year. Because it was much smaller than the largest homebuilders who had economies-of-scale advantages,[1] RBH focused on building higher quality/ higher price homes for first and second move-up buyers. In 2006, the average closing sales price for an RBH home was slightly more than $400,000.

RBH's stock had been traded publicly since 1995. The company had been highly profitable throughout the past decade, but finances were expected to be much tighter in 2007 because of the homebuilding slowdown that had started in early 2006. The stock price had declined almost 50% from the all-time peak in 2005.

RBH's organization was comprised of a headquarters staff located in Denver, Colorado, and 15 divisions located in most of the metropolitan areas of the Central, Mountain, and Southwest areas of the United States. The headquarters staff was small, comprised mainly of specialists in the areas of finance, accounting, legal, information systems, sales and marketing, and customer service, and their staffs.

Each division was largely self-contained, with its own construction supervision, customer care, purchasing, sales and marketing, land development, land acquisition, and accounting staffs. The only major function that was outsourced was construction. RBH's construction superintendents supervised the general contractors who built the homes to RBH's specifications.

Exhibit 1 shows the organization chart for the Southern California division. This division, one of RBH's largest, employed approximately 120 people. In 2006, it was projected to sell 637 homes, generating $235 million in revenue and $40 million in net income.

---

[1] For example, D. R. Horton, Inc., the largest homebuilder in the United States, was building over 50,000 homes per year.

This case was prepared by Professor Kenneth A. Merchant.

Copyright © by Kenneth A. Merchant.

LAND ACQUISITION

Land acquisition was a key function in the home-building business. RBH's land acquisition personnel had to find land on which the company could build homes that could be sold at a good profit. The lag between acquisition of the land and sale of the final house built was typically three–five years. Sometimes the permit-acquisition process itself dragged on for years, with the company fighting lengthy, emotional battles with city councils and other permit-granting organizations. On the other hand, sometimes land was acquired at "retail price," with all the permits already having been granted.

As a standard part of the land acquisition process, RBH's land acquisition personnel were required to prepare a detailed land acquisition proposal. These proposals provided detailed information on:

- the nature of the request;
- the location;
- entitlements;
- infrastructure;
- product design;
- market overview;
- environmental considerations;
- development fees and costs;
- special assessments and homeowner association dues (if any);
- school information;
- project milestones;
- risk evaluations; and,
- financial projections.

Many of the detailed proposals were 100 or more pages in length and often included detailed maps, product sketches, and excerpts from consultants' reports.

An important part of the proposal-writing process was a detailed evaluation of the project's risk in four areas: political, development, market, and financial. The risk in each area was evaluated subjectively into three categories: low, moderate, or high. The risk assessments in these areas were translated into a minimum internal rate of return (IRR) requirements for the project, according to the procedure shown in Exhibit 2.

Many land acquisition ideas failed to progress to the approval stage for any of a number of reasons, including inadequate financial returns, excess risk in the permit-granting process, or a mismatch between the needs of the market and the company's capabilities. If the proposals were approved by the division president and RBH's CEO and CFO, the division president then presented them to the Executive Land Committee of the Board of Directors for final approval. Only then could the monies be released.

THE PLATINUM POINTE SITE

The Platinum Pointe site was identified by Michael Borland, the vice president of land acquisition for the Southern California Division. The Platinum Pointe site was located in the Emerald Estates master planned community being developed by Jackson Development Company.

Jackson Development was recently formed by Tom Jackson, who had formerly worked as division president of one of RBH's competitors. Michael Borland and Tom Jackson were long-time friends, back to their time together as fraternity brothers at San Diego State University. Michael called Tom soon after he learned of the formation of Jackson Development. He looked forward to developing some projects jointly with Tom.

Michael discussed with Tom several sites in the planned Emerald Estates community. They finally settled on a 21-acre site on the northeast corner of the master planned community. The proposed purchase price was $22,500,000 plus a profit participation by Jackson Development in the amount of 50% above 9% net profit, with a soft cost allowance of 20%.[2]

Michael's experience suggested to him that higher density housing, rather than single-family detached homes, would provide the best use of this site. Over the forthcoming several months, he fleshed out the idea with the division and corporate specialists, particularly in the areas of sales and marketing and construction. He also contracted for special studies from two outside consulting firms. One consulting firm prepared a report detailing projections of the costs needed to develop the site. The other prepared a marketing study that provided pricing and absorption rate estimates based on analyses of competitive

---

[2] Soft costs are costs related to items in a project that are necessary to complete the nonconstruction needs of the project, which typically include such items as architecture, design, engineering, permits, inspections, consultants, environmental studies, and regulatory demands needing approval before construction begins.

offerings and forecasts of market trends in the geographical area.

Michael wrote a detailed proposal for building 195 homes in two formats: a triplex townhome and a six-plex cluster home. Other RBH divisions had produced similar homes, but the format had not been previously offered in Southern California, and some modifications were made to appeal to southern California buyers. The homes would range from 1,628 to 2,673 square feet and be priced from $445,000 to $705,000. The executive summary of the detailed proposal, with the required risk assessments and financial projections, is shown in Exhibit 3.

Michael was disappointed when he saw the projected IRR for the project. It was only 21%, which was below the minimum required for a project with this level of risk – 24.5%. He decided to discuss the problem with Harry Hepburn to see what, if anything, could be done.

WHAT TO DO?

Harry, too, was disappointed. He had hoped that the Platinum Pointe project would provide a significant proportion of the revenues and profits that the division would need over the next four-year period. He still wanted to do the project. So he and Michael sat down to take another look at the detailed proposal. What modifications could they make to lower the required IRR or to raise the projected IRR to ensure that the project would be approved?

Exhibit 1 Robinson Brothers Homes, Southern California Division, organization chart

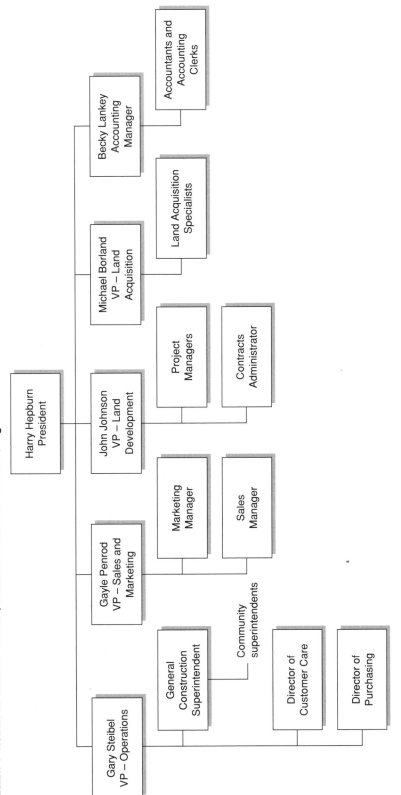

Exhibit 2 IRR requirements

Land acquisition opportunities and the related product choices continue to expand for Robinson Brothers Homes. Given that risks can vary greatly from opportunity to opportunity, guidelines to assess risk and the required minimum returns have been established. The risks to be assessed are as follows:

1. Political/Entitlement – ability to achieve expected entitlements and timing;

2. Development – site conditions and ability to accurately project development costs;

3. Market – experience with proposed product type, product price points, buyer types, current market conditions both current and future;

4. Financial/Financing – ability to achieve projected results and obtain proposed financing.

Based on these factors, a minimum unleveraged IRR is to be established. Risk ratings are to be assessed based on the projects' specific characteristics. Each area is to be rated as *Low*, *Moderate*, or *High*. A numerical value is to be attached to assessment as follows:

	Low	*Moderate*	*High*
Political	5.0	6.5	8.0
Development	5.0	6.5	8.0
Market	5.0	6.0	7.0
Financial/Financing	4.0	5.0	6.0

The minimum IRR for the project is assessed as the sum of the ratings assigned in each of the four assessment areas.

Exhibit 3 Platinum Pointe investment proposal – executive summary (initial draft)

The Southern California Division is requesting approval to acquire the 21-acre site known as Platinum Pointe in Carlsbad, CA. The site will yield 198 detached and attached homes. The purchase price is $22,500,000. The projected IRR is currently 21%, and the required IRR is 24.5%. Close of escrow is projected to occur in June 2007.

LOCATION

The site is located on the east side of Interstate 5 in the City of Carlsbad, located 30 miles north of San Diego. The site is in the Emerald Estates community being master planned by Jackson Development Company, Inc. The master planned community is comprised of just over 200 acres to yield approximately 1,000 units. The community will have a range of product from townhomes to duplexes, as well as single-family homes on lots ranging in size from 4,500–7,500 s.f.

PURCHASE

The Seller is Jackson Development Company, Inc. The purchase price of the property is $22,500,000 for 21 net acres. The purchase price is not tied to unit count. We are currently projecting construction of 123 townhome units and 72 cluster units. The Master Development Plan approval is a closing contingency. Should the Master Development Plan not be approved, we have the option to waive the condition or terminate the Agreement. The close of escrow is targeted for June 1, 2007. We have the option to purchase two non-refundable nonapplicable 30-day extensions should our tentative tract map not yet be approved. Should the Seller cause a delay that would prevent us from processing our entitlements in a timely manner, we will be granted the right to have the extensions without payment of the extension fee. This project includes profit participation by the Seller for the amount of 50% above 9% net profit, with a soft cost allowance of 20%. We have run multiple scenarios to include interest rate increases, financing options, construction delays, and a slow down in absorption. We are comfortable that we will stay below the 20% threshold.

Exhibit 3 *continued*

We have explored the option of negotiating this deal with no profit participation. Jackson was open to negotiations where we would increase the land price and move forward with no profit participation on the back end of the deal. But the increase in land price would decrease the projected IRR on the project.

RISK EVALUATION

▶ Political

The property is located within the Emerald Estates Master Plan area. It is zoned PCD (Planned Community Development). The Seller is preparing a detailed Master Development Plan (MDP) that will be submitted to the City of Carlsbad in early January 2007. Our proposed project will be part of that submission. The Seller has been working with the City throughout the creation of the MDP and has gained support of the project. If one contingency – preservation of habitat for the Western Speckled Toad possibly located in the area – can be solved, the Seller projects that the guidelines will be approved by the City in March 2007. A neighbor claims that the site is habitat for the Toad, but the Environmental Impact report has not yet been completed. If the Toad issue is real, we will have to place a permanent habitat on the property. We think we can do this without losing any buildable lots.

With the approval of the MDP, our review by the Design Review Committee will be expedited. Our proposed project will be designated R-M (Medium Residential, 8–10 duplexes/acre). Our current site plan shows a total of 195 units, which is approximately 9.29 duplexes/acre. We have met with the Director of Development Services three separate times. We believe that our latest site plan incorporates the City's requests. We will need to process a tentative map and to obtain approval from the Design Review Board for the site plan and architecture. The tentative map is expected to be received by May 2007, and all appeal periods are expected to expire before we close in June 2007.

- Overall political risk is moderate.

▶ Development

Site Development

The site is currently raw land, but it will be delivered as a mass-graded pad. The Seller received the grading permit on November 7, 2006, and has started grading. Grading will be completed in January 2007. The Seller will construct all offsite backbone sewer, water, storm drain, dry utility, street improvements, and perimeter landscaping. The street and storm drain plans are approved, as well as the sewer and water plans. Backbone utility plans are currently being designed. The Seller will provide utility stubs to the site if we are able to give them fixed entry locations prior to their installing the improvements. Otherwise, we will have to connect to the systems. The Emerald Estates master development infrastructure will not be completed prior to our close, but the Seller will soon begin the improvements. The improvements are being funded by the CFD [Community Facilities District]. Should the Seller fail to make the improvements in the timeline presented in the agreement and their failure to complete the improvements affects our site specifically, we have the right to assume responsibility for completion of the remaining Seller work, and Seller shall reimburse Buyer at 110% of the third party direct costs. In addition to cooperating with Buyer without limitation, Seller shall insure that Buyer is able to draw against or obtain reimbursement from the CFD for completing the remaining improvements.

As mentioned above, the CFD will be funding the entire infrastructure for the site. The CFD has an approved Resolution of Intent. The Resolution of Formation went to City Council and was continued to January 12, 2007. The CFD is confident that the formation will be heard at the January 13th meeting. The bonds will be sold in two issues. The first bond sale, expected to be $30–35 million will cover backbone infrastructure, including sewer, water, streets, and storm drain. This is expected to occur in March 2007. The second bond sale will occur approximately six months later and will include dry utilities and landscaping. The CFD has told us that the appraisal is underway and should be completed shortly. They do not see any issues with the appraisal meeting the 3:1 coverage requirement. The bid package for the first bond sale is complete and will be submitted for City review in January/February 2006. Furthermore, the City of Carlsbad is the lead agency and is pushing to get the backbone infrastructure constructed. The improvement plans have been through multiple plan checks and the tax rate will be approximately 1.8%.

In addition to the infrastructure, the CFD will be funding certain impact fees. We are expecting to receive a $8,500 plus credit per unit from the CFD to cover a portion of the fees. The fees that will be covered by the CFD include webbed toed lizard, drainage fees, signalization fees, sewer and water connection fees, supplemental water fees, and Art in Public Places fee. Our in-tract development costs are derived from a cost estimate based on our current site plan, which was prepared for us by the Evensen Group. These costs, including fees and net of the planned CFD reimbursement, come to $63,088 per unit. This total includes a 15% contingency on construction items and a 10% contingency on fees.

▶

EXHIBIT 3 *continued*

A site visit was performed by an environmental consultant and previous Phase I report were also reviewed. Other than the possible Western Speckled Toad issue, there are no potential environmental concerns and no additional assessment appears to be necessary. A geotechnical investigation concluded that the site was suitable for the intended use.

The Seller will also be establishing a Master Homeowners Association to maintain the perimeter and median landscaping. We will create our own sub-association to maintain our on-site landscaping detention basin and recreation facilities.

The Seller will be mass grading the well and park sites and designing the park. We will be responsible for constructing the well site improvements, excluding the well itself, and construction of the park. We have included $1.0 million for the park and well site. The well site improvements consist of a block perimeter wall, some landscaping iron drive gates and drive approach. The park improvements are in the preliminary planning stages and are expected to include landscaping, a tot lot, picnic tables, shade structures, walkways and lighting, and possible restroom facilities. The costs of the park and well site will be initially funded from equity in the short term but will be reimbursed through the CFD. The well site will be deeded to the Carlsbad Water District (CWD), and the park will be deeded to the City of Carlsbad. Both the well site and the park will be maintained by each entity respectively.

Direct Construction

The townhome product consists of new plans that we have not built before and direct construction costs continue to rise. However, the cluster product is a modification of product our Phoenix Division has built before. The direct construction estimates we have used are derived from our actual costs in building the 10-plex product in El Cajon, which is coming in at about $80 psf. There we added an additional $10 psf to account for the increased specs we are including in these new townhomes.

Overall we conclude that the risks associated with both site development and direct construction are moderate.

- Overall development risk is moderate.

▶ Competitive Analysis/Market Risk

We will be building two product types, a triplex townhome and a six-plex cluster product. The triplex townhome ranges in square footage from 1,753 square feet to 2,442 square feet and will be priced from $445,000 to $595,000. We feel this product will appeal to buyers who work in north San Diego County and second home owners (weekend or seasonal) who are attracted to a low maintenance home with a larger yard. The cluster will range in square footage from 1,628 square feet to 2,673 square feet and be priced from $450,000 to $705,000. These pricing projections are the exact prices recommended from our marketing consultant, the Blackfield Group. This is an upgrade version of a product that was very successful in Phoenix. It will be highly amenitized. The master baths have been revised to meet the new "wow" factor that is pervasive in this submarket. There is currently very little competition for attached or mid-density product in the Carlsbad area. We are currently unaware of any other 8–10 units/acre development projected within the City of Carlsbad at this time, but we continue to monitor new development projects within the City. We have a completed marketing study by the Blackfield Group that supports our product type and pricing. We are comfortable with the absorption recommendation from Blackfield given the two very separate product lines. The models in our estimates are currently slated to open in July 2008. Our absorption would maintain 15 homes per month average as recommended by the Blackfield Group. But there is risk. The north San Diego County market has experienced a noticeable downturn in the last 12–18 months. If interest rates continue to increase and if prices in markets throughout north San Diego County continue to moderate, we may not be able to maintain our absorption rate, or we will have to shave our margins.

- The risk associated with the market is moderate to high.

▶ Financial/Financing Risk

All indications are that interest rates will continue to rise. In the event that interest rates increase substantially during the life of this project, our product will still be positioned in a more affordable segment of the market. Given the size of the transaction ($48 million at March 2009), some form of outside capital will be used. Lot option and or joint venture will be considered and leads to the moderate financial risk.

- The financial/financing risk is moderate given the previously discussed political and development risks.

Exhibit 3 *continued*

IRR REQUIREMENTS

Based on the above analysis and assessed risk, the IRR requirements are as follows:

Political	Moderate	6.5
Development	Moderate	6.5
Market	Moderate/High	6.5
Financial	Moderate	5.0
	Required IRR	24.5%

FINANCIAL SUMMARY

Total Sales Revenue:	$112,050,000
Profit ($):	$13,707,000
Profit (%):	12.2%
Equity Required:	$8,722,000
Home Size Triplex:	2,151 sf weighted average
Home Size Cluster:	2,126 sf weighted average
Direct Costs Triplex:	$93/sf weighted average
Direct Costs Cluster:	$82/sf weighted average
Base Sales Price Triplex:	$531,667/unit weighted average
Base Sales Price Cluster:	$571,667/unit weighted average
Base Sales Price Triplex: ($/sf)	$247.17/sf weighted average
Base Sales Price Cluster: ($/sf)	$268.89/sf weighted average
IRR Leveraged:	41.4%
IRR Unleveraged:	21.0% (Required 24.5%)
TOTAL PEAK EQUITY	$11,809,000

Case Study

Axeon N.V.

In October 1998 Anton van Leuven, managing director of Axeon N.V., a large Dutch chemical company, was faced with a difficult decision. Ian Wallingford, managing director of Axeon's British subsidiary, Hollandsworth, Ltd., and Jeremy Noble, a member of Hollandsworth's board of directors, were frustrated that an investment proposal that had been presented some time ago had not yet been approved. The board member had even threatened to resign his post. But Mr. van Leuven had received advice from some of his other managers to reject the Hollandsworth proposal.

This case was prepared by Professors Kenneth A. Merchant and Wim A. Van der Stede, with the research assistance of Xiaoling (Clara) Chen.

THE COMPANY

Axeon N.V. was headquartered in Heerlen, in the southern part of the Netherlands. Axeon produced an extensive product line of industrial chemicals in 24 factories.

Early in its history, Axeon had a simple functional organization structure, with just one manufacturing division and a sales division. Over the years, however, Axeon acquired some foreign companies. These included Saraceno, S.p.A., in Milan, Hollandsworth, Ltd., in London, and KAG Chemicals, AB, in Gothenburg, Sweden (Exhibit 1). To take advantage of the geographical expertise in these acquired companies, each of these subsidiaries was asked to assume responsibility for sales of all Axeon products in their assigned territory: southern Europe for Saraceno, the United Kingdom for Hollandsworth, and Scandinavia for KAG. Southern Europe, the United Kingdom, and Scandinavia, respectively, accounted for 8%, 14%, and 6% of Axeon's total sales. All other sales were handled by Axeon's organization in the Netherlands.

The style of Axeon's top-level managers was to emphasize a high degree of decentralization. Hence, the subsidiary managers had considerable autonomy to decide what to sell in their territories. For products produced in the Netherlands, the Axeon Dutch sales organization would quote the subsidiaries the same prices as they quoted agents in all countries. The subsidiaries could bargain, but if, in the end, they did not like the price, they did not have to sell the product.

In some cases the foreign subsidiaries produced products that competed with those produced by Axeon factories in the Netherlands. To date, little attempt had been made to rationalize the company's production. The subsidiaries were allowed to continue to produce whatever mix of products they deemed appropriate. The subsidiary managers were also encouraged to propose the development of new products, and they were allowed to build their own manufacturing plants if they could justify the investment in their own markets.

Management personnel were included in a bonus plan that provided rewards based on achievement of divisional revenue growth and "economic profit" targets set as part of the company's annual planning and budgeting process. Economic profit was defined as operating profits less a capital charge on the division's average assets, computed monthly. The capital charge was adjusted annually based on Axeon's weighted average cost of capital. In 2002, the annual charge was set at 10%. In prior years, it had been as high as 14%. Achievement of the annual targets could earn divisional managers bonuses of 50% or more of base salary. If they exceeded their targets, they could more than double their base salaries.

HOLLANDSWORTH, LTD

Hollandsworth was purchased by Axeon in 1992. During the first three years of Axeon's ownership, Hollandsworth's sales were in slow decline. In 1996, they totaled £111 million. Hollandsworth's board of directors[1] decided that the company needed a new management team and a major overhaul. Mr. Ian Wallingford, a 39-year-old with university degrees in engineering and commerce, was hired. Ian had experience as a manufacturing engineer, a marketing manager for a British subsidiary of a US company, and a profit center manager in a large UK industrial company.

In the first four years of Ian's presidency, Hollandsworth's sales increased to £160 million, and profits improved markedly, to levels that Axeon's management deemed acceptable. The board concluded that a number of factors contributed to Hollandsworth's turnaround. An important part was Ian's ambition, hard work, and management skill. Ian made some good personnel appointments and implemented a number of effective changes in production methods, marketing strategy, market research, financial planning, and organization structure. In addition, industrial activity in the United Kingdom increased significantly during this period.

In 1998, in an article in a local English business publication, Ian was quoted as saying:

> This has been an enjoyable challenge. When I took the job, I had several offers from other companies, and I am still getting calls from executive recruiters, but I thought that Hollandsworth had potential. The Axeon management team promised me considerable freedom to make the changes that I thought were necessary. And I was able to put into practice many of the modern

---

[1] The outsiders on the Hollandsworth board included Anton van Leuven from Axeon; Jeremy Noble, a prominent London banker; and James Bedingfield, the managing director of a large industrial company located outside of Manchester, England.

management practices that I learned in my previous jobs. I know that if I do a good job here, I will have the confidence of the executives in Heerlen, and succeeding here will make me an even better manager.

THE PROPOSAL

In 1998, Ian informed the Hollandsworth board that he proposed to study the feasibility of constructing a factory in England to manufacture a protective coating chemical known as AR-42. He explained that Hollandsworth's product engineers had developed a new way of helping users to store and apply this coating. In his judgment, Hollandsworth could develop a market in the United Kingdom that would be almost as large as Axeon's present worldwide market for AR-42. Approximately 600 tons of AR-42 was then being produced annually in an Axeon plant in the Netherlands, but none of this output was being sold in the United Kingdom. Ian observed that the board seemed enthusiastic at this initial meeting, but they wanted to see the detailed plan.

Hollandsworth managers developed the proposal over the following six months. They interviewed potential customers and conducted trials in the factories of three of them and proved that the large cost savings would indeed materialize. In the end, they estimated the total UK market potential for AR-42-like coatings at 800 tons per year. If they could sell the product for £3,700 per ton, they would capture half of the total market, or 400 tons per year, within a three-year period.

Ian asked the head of the Corporate Engineering Division in Heerlen for help in designing a plant to produce 400 tons of AR-42 per year and in estimating the cost of the investment. A team comprised of engineers from both Corporate Engineering and Hollandsworth estimated that the plant could be built for £1,400,000.

In July 1998, Ian presented the results of the analysis, the net-present-value calculations and supporting explanations (Exhibits 2–5) at a Hollandsworth board meeting. With Ian were his directors of manufacturing, sales, and finance. Here are some excerpts from Ian's presentation:

- "You can see from the summary chart [Exhibit 2] that this is a profitable project. We will obtain a rate of return of 20% and a present value of £916,000 for an initial investment of £1,400,000 for equipment and £160,000 for working capital. I used an

8% discount rate because I can borrow money in England at that rate to fund this project . . ."

- "The second chart [Exhibit 3] shows the operating cash flows that we expect from the AR-42 project in each of the seven years. The sales forecast for the first seven years is shown in row (2). We did not extend the forecast beyond seven years because our engineers estimate that production technologies will continue to improve, so major plant renovations will be called for around the end of the seventh year. Actually, we see no reason why demand for this particular product, AR-42, will decline after seven years . . ."

- "The estimated variable cost of £2,000 per ton, shown in row (3), is our estimate of the full operating cost of manufacturing AR-42 in England. This figure takes into account out-of-pocket fixed costs such as plant supervision, but excludes depreciation. These fixed costs must, of course, be included because they are incremental to the decision . . ."

- "As row (4) shows, we are confident that we can enter the market initially with a selling price of £4,000 per ton, but in order to gain market share and achieve full market penetration, we will reduce the selling price to £3,700 at the beginning of the second year . . ."

- "These figures result in variable profits shown in rows (5) and (6). Row (7) presents the marketing expenditures that are needed to promote the product and achieve the forecasted sales levels. Row (8) shows the net operating cash flows before tax, based on figures in the preceding columns . . ."

- "The cost of the plant can be written off for tax purposes over a five-year period. As shown in row (9), the taxable income figures are computed by subtracting this amount from the before-tax cash flow. The tax in row (10) is then subtracted from the before-tax cash flow to yield the after-tax cash flow in row (11) . . ."

- "My third chart [Exhibit 4] summarizes our estimates of the requisite investment in working capital. We'll need about £160,000 to start with. We'll need small additional amounts of working capital in the next two years. These amounts are shown in row (4). Altogether, our working capital requirements will add up to £190,000 by the end of our second full year of operations . . ."

- "The last chart [Exhibit 5] shows some asset recovery values. At the end of seven years, the plant should be worth £1,400,000, at the very worst. We'd have to pay tax on that because the plant would be fully depreciated, but this would still leave us with a positive cash flow of £840,000. The working capital should also be fully recoverable. So the total value at the end of seven years would thus be £1,030,000 . . ."

- "Gentlemen, it seems clear from these figures that we can justify this investment in England on the basis of sales to the UK market. It meets your policy of having all new investments yield at least 12%. This particular proposal promises to return 20%. My management team and I strongly recommend this project."

Ian and his managers answered the few questions raised by the board members.

At the end of the meeting, Ian and his team went to a neighborhood pub to celebrate. They all felt that the meeting went extremely well. Soon thereafter they were pleased to learn that the proposal was placed on the agenda for the next meeting of the Axeon board of directors, which was scheduled in three weeks' time.

THE BOARD MEETING

The presentation to the Axeon board also went well. Ian explained:

It took only an hour. Mr. van Leuven said in the meeting that the decision seemed to be clear.

Some board members asked some interesting questions, mainly about the likelihood that we would eventually be able to sell more than 400 tons of AR-42 per year and about how we would finance the project. I explained that we in the United Kingdom believed strongly that we would reach 400 tons per year even in the first year, but we felt constrained to show a conservative estimate and a conservative transition period. We also showed how we could finance further expansions through borrowings in the United Kingdom. If our 400 tons were reached quickly, banks would easily lend any further expansion. The UK member of the board supported our conclusion.

At the end of the hour, the Axeon board voted unanimously to allow construction of the plant.

DISPUTE BETWEEN PARENT AND SUBSIDIARY

About a week later, Mr. van Leuven called Ian and said, "Since the board meeting, I have been through some additional discussions with the product and marketing people here in the Heerlen. They agree with your engineering design and plan cost projections, but they think you are too optimistic on your sales forecast. I must ask you to justify this more."

Ian pushed for an immediate meeting, which was scheduled for the following week. The meeting was attended by Ian and his key functional directors and four Axeon managers based in Heerlen: Anton van Leuven, Willem Backer (senior vice president Dutch operations), Marc Oosterling (director of manufacturing), and Geert De Rijcke (director of sales).

Ian described the meeting from his perspective:

It was one of the most frustrating meetings of my life. It lasted all day. Mr. De Rijcke said that from their sales experience in other countries our estimates of the UK market potential and our share were too optimistic. I explained to him several times how we arrived at our figures, but he wouldn't change his over-optimism argument. He said that Axeon's current total worldwide market for AR-42 for Axeon was only 600 tons a year, that it was being produced in the Netherlands at this level, and that it was inconceivable that the United Kingdom alone could take 400 tons.

Then Mr. Oosterling started preaching that AR-42 production is complicated and that he had had difficulties producing it in the Netherlands, even with trained workers who have long experience. I told him I only needed five trained workers and that he could send me two men for two months to train our people to do the job. I told him that, "If you can manufacture it in the Netherlands, you can manufacture it for us in England until we learn, if you don't have confidence in English technology." But he kept saying over and over that the difficulties in manufacturing were great. I stressed to him that we were prepared to learn and to take the risk, but for some reason I just couldn't get him to understand.

At 6 p.m., everybody was exhausted. Mr. Backer had backed up his two functional directors all day, repeating their arguments. Mr. van Leuven seemed just to sit there and listen, occasionally asking questions. I can't understand why he did not back me up. He had seemed so agreeable in the previous meetings, and he had seemed so decisive. Not so at this meeting. He seemed distant and indecisive. He stopped the meeting without a solution and said that he hoped all concerned would do more investigation of this subject. He vaguely referred to the fact that he would think about it himself and let us know when another meeting would be held.

Ian returned home to London and reported the meeting to his own staff and to the two English members of his board. They were all extremely disappointed. One of the Hollandsworth staff members said, "Axeon's management seems to talk decentralization, but at the same time they act like emperors."

Mr. Noble, the English banker on the Hollandsworth board, expressed surprise:

I studied this proposal very carefully. It is sound business for Hollandsworth, and AR-42 will help to build one more growth company in the English economy. Somehow the management in Heerlen has failed to study this, or they don't wish the English subsidiary to produce it. I have today dictated a letter to Mr. van Leuven telling him that I recognize that the Dutch managers have the right to their own thoughts, but I don't understand why the proposal is being delayed and possibly rejected. I am prepared to resign as a Hollandsworth director. It is not that I am angry or that I believe I have a right to dictate decisions for the whole worldwide Axeon. It is simply that if I spend my time studying policy decisions and my judgments do not serve the right function for the business, then it is a waste of my time to continue.

In the meeting with Mr. Noble, Ian said:

While I certainly wouldn't say this in a broader meeting, I think that those Dutch production and sales people simply want to build their own empire and make the money in Axeon Netherlands. They don't care about Hollandsworth and the United Kingdom. Theirs is a slippery way to operate. We have the ideas and initiative, and they are trying to take them and get the payoff.

After Mr. van Leuven received Mr. Noble's letter, he contacted Messrs. Backer, Oosterling, and De Rijcke and Arnold Koonts (Axeon's vice president finance). He told them that the English AR-42 project had become a matter of key importance for the whole company because of its implications for company profits and for the autonomy and morale of subsidiary management. He asked them to study the matter and report their recommendations in one month. Meanwhile, he sent Ian the following e-mail: "Various members of the division and corporate headquarters are studying the proposal. You will hear from me within about six weeks regarding my final decision."

REPORT OF THE DIRECTOR OF MANUFACTURING

A month later, Marc Oosterling (director of manufacturing) sent Mr. van Leuven a memorandum

explaining his reasons for opposing the UK AR-42 proposal, as follows:

At your request, I have reexamined thoroughly all of the cost figures that bear on the AR-42 proposal. I find it highly uneconomical to manufacture this product in England for two reasons: overhead costs and variable costs would both be higher than projected.

As to the former, we can produce AR-42 in the Netherlands with less overhead cost. Suppose that Hollandsworth does sell 400 tons per year so that our total worldwide sales increase to 1,000 tons. We can produce the whole 1,000 tons in the Netherlands with basically the same capital investment as we have now. If we produce 1,000 tons, our fixed costs will decrease by £240 per ton.[2] That means £144,000 in savings on production for domestic and export to countries other than the United Kingdom and £240,000 for worldwide production including the United Kingdom (1,000 tons).

Regarding the variable costs, if we were to produce the extra 400 tons in the Netherlands, the total production of 1,000 tons per year would allow us to have longer production runs, lower set-up costs, and larger raw material purchases, which lead to mass purchasing and material handling and lower purchase prices. My accounting department has studied this and concludes that our average variable costs will decrease from £1,900 to £1,860 per ton (Exhibit 6). This £40-per-ton difference would save us £24,000 on Dutch domestic production and £40,000 on total worldwide production, assuming that the United Kingdom takes 400 tons per year. There would be some additional shipping and duty costs, but these would be negligible. Taxes on these added profits are about the same in the Netherlands as in the United Kingdom.

So I conclude that the UK plant should not be built. Ian is a bright young man, but he does not know the coatings business. He would be over his head with costly production mistakes from the very beginning. I recommend that you inform Hollandsworth management that it is in Axeon's interest to buy their AR-42 product from the Netherlands.

REPORT OF THE VICE PRESIDENT FINANCE

The same day, Mr. van Leuven received the following memorandum from Arnold Koonts (vice president finance):

---

[2] The total fixed cost in the Netherlands is the equivalent of £360,000 per year. Divided by 600, this equals £600 per ton. If the cost were spread over 1,000 tons, the average fixed cost would be £360 per ton.

I am sending you herewith estimates of the working capital requirements if Axeon increases its production of AR-42 in our Dutch plant from 600 to 1,000 tons per year (Exhibit 7). Initially we will need £120,000, mostly for additional inventories. By the end of the second year, this will have increased to £160,000. I have also looked at Marc's calculations for the fixed and variable manufacturing costs, and I am in full agreement with them.

IAN'S THOUGHTS AT THE TIME

In an interview at about this same time, Ian expressed impatience.

I have other projects that need developing for Hollandsworth, and this kind of long-range planning takes a lot of time and energy. It's not like this is all I have to do. I also have to keep on top of a lot of normal operating problems. Sometimes I feel like giving up, telling them just to go and sell AR-42 themselves.

Exhibit 1 Axeon N.V. organization chart

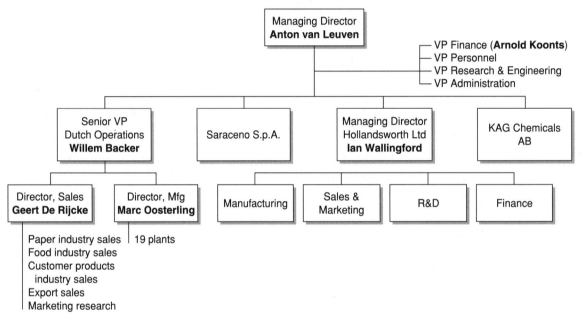

Exhibit 2 Proposal for manufacture of AR-42 in England – financial summary (£000s)

Year	0	1	2	3	4	5	6	7	Total
Equipment	(1,400)								
Working capital	(160)	(10)	(20)						
Cash operating profit		196	328	460	460	460	348	348	
Recovery value of equipment and working capital								1,030	
TOTAL	(1,560)	186	308	460	460	460	348	1,378	2,040

Net present value (@ 8%)	£916,000
Payback period	4½ years
Internal rate of return	20%

Exhibit 3 Estimated operating cash flows from manufacture and sale of AR-42 in England (figures in rows (3)–(5) in £s; rows (6)–(11) in £000s)

(1)	Year	1	2	3	4	5	6	7	Total
(2)	Sales (in tons)	200	300	400	400	400	400	400	2,500
(3)	Variable costs per ton	2,000	2,000	2,000	2,000	2,000	2,000	2,000	
(4)	Sales price per ton	4,000	3,700	3,700	3,700	3,700	3,700	3,700	
(5)	Variable profit margin per ton (4) − (3)	2,000	1,700	1,700	1,700	1,700	1,700	1,700	
(6)	Total variable profit margin (2) × (5)	400	510	680	680	680	680	680	4,310
(7)	Promotion costs	260	150	100	100	100	100	100	910
(8)	Net operating cash flows before tax (6) − (7)	140	360	580	580	580	580	580	3,400
(9)	Depreciation	280	280	280	280	280	–	–	1,400
(10)	Tax 40% of (8) − (9)	−56	32	120	120	120	232	232	800
(11)	Net cash flow after tax (8) − (10)	196	328	460	460	460	348	348	2,600

Exhibit 4 Estimated working capital required for manufacture and sale of AR-42 in England (£000s)

	Year	0	1	2	3 and later	Total
(1)	Inventory at cost	160	180	200	200	
(2)	Other current assets less current liabilities	0	−10	−10	−10	
(3)	Working capital (1) + (2)	160	170	190	190	
(4)	Change from previous year	160	10	20	0	190

Exhibit 5 Estimated end-of-life value of UK assets

Plant	£1,400,000	
Less: tax on gain if sold at this price	560,000	
Net value of plant		840,000
Working capital recapture		190,000
Net value of UK assets after 7 years		£1,030,000

Exhibit 6 Estimated variable cost of manufacturing AR-42 in the Netherlands for shipment to the United Kingdom

Variable costs per ton:	
Manufacturing	£1,860
Shipping from Netherlands to UK	100
UK import duty	100
Total variable cost per ton	£2,060
Total variable cost, 400 tons to UK	£824,000

Exhibit 7 Estimated working capital required for manufacture of AR-42 in the Netherlands for sale in the United Kingdom (£000s)

	Year	0	1	2	3 and later	Total
(1)	Inventory at cost	100	110	120	120	
(2)	Other current assets less current liabilities	20	30	40	40	
(3)	Working capital (1) + (2)	120	140	160	160	
(4)	Change from previous year	120	20	20	0	160

Case Study

Alcon Laboratories, Inc.

In early 1985, George Leone, senior vice president of Science and Technology at Alcon Laboratories, Inc., reflected on his concerns about the challenges his company faced in measuring the productivity of its research and development (R&D) activities:

> R&D is perhaps the most critical part of Alcon's business; the company will thrive only if we are effective at developing new breakthrough products. In managing the research function, we have to address three difficult but important issues. The first is how much to spend on R&D. The second is how to allocate the resources among the various programs and projects. The third is how to ensure that the resources are used effectively. The combination of answers to these three questions determine how productive our research activity will be.
>
> While all three questions are important, I am especially concerned about the third one – how to control the use of our resources. What causes me concern is that I don't think we do a very good job of measuring our productivity, and that can limit our managerial effectiveness. At the time we are spending our resources, both money and time, and even for some time after they have been spent, it is very difficult to tell how productive we are being and have been. We could be missing some important information about problems we might be having. I feel we should do some thinking about this issue and what we can do to improve the tracking of our R&D productivity.

THE COMPANY AND ITS PRODUCTS

Alcon Laboratories was founded in 1947 in Fort Worth, Texas by two pharmacists, William C. Conner and Robert D. Alexander, who saw a need for more accurate, sterile and stable ophthalmological drugs (that is, those used in the treatment of defects and diseases of the eye). At the time, 85% of all eye care drugs were being compounded in retail drug stores.

The founders' judgments proved to be correct, and within two decades Alcon had become an international leader in the research, development, manufacturing, and marketing of a wide range of products for the diagnosis and treatment of ophthalmic disorders. The company marketed both prescription and nonprescription drugs, a wide variety of products for use in ophthalmic surgery, products for the care of hard, soft and gas-permeable lenses, and a few dermatological products. In 1984, Alcon sold products in over 100 countries; worldwide sales totalled almost $400 million. A corporate organization chart is shown in Exhibit 1.

In 1977, Alcon was purchased by Nestlé S.A., the giant Swiss-based multinational corporation. Nestlé provided increased funding and gave Alcon management a mandate to increase new product development. The increased research fueled very

This case was prepared by Research Assistant Chris S. Paddison and Associate Professor Kenneth A. Merchant.

rapid growth: Alcon's sales tripled over the period between 1977 and 1984, and over 25% of 1984 sales were from products released in the past five years.

THE R&D ORGANIZATION

Alcon's research and development facilities were located in a modern complex adjacent to the corporate headquarters on the southern edge of Fort Worth. The R&D department, headed by Dr. Dilip Raval, included 350 people: 290 scientists (80 of whom had PhD degrees), and 60 support staff.

The purpose of the R&D organization was to develop new, marketable eye care products that would fuel the company's growth. Alcon's board of directors established broad research policies based on the long-term strategies of the marketing divisions, but the board depended heavily on Mr. Leone and Dr. Raval to provide the guidance and direction necessary to ensure effective research activities.

Mr. Leone and Dr. Raval complemented each other well in terms of knowledge and experience. Mr. Leone had an in-depth knowledge of Alcon's products and markets because he had advanced through the sales organization. He joined Alcon in 1950 and spent 21 years in sales, including eight years as national sales manager. He was made vice president of Science and Technology in 1971. Dr. Raval was a chemist. He joined Alcon in 1971 and was made vice president of Research and Development in 1976.

The R&D department was organized in matrix form (see Exhibit 2). On one dimension of the matrix were four medical specialty groups: ophthalmology, optical, dermatology, and basic research. Personnel in these groups specialized in particular types of diseases. The basic research group was distinguished from the other three medical specialty groups in that its work took place early in the drug development cycle (described later). On the other dimension of the matrix were four preclinical science departments: microbiology, chemistry, toxicology, and pharmaceutical sciences. Personnel in these departments were experts in one of these scientific fields.

The matrix form of organization was used because of the need for interactions among the people with highly specialized knowledge. Each research program and project was managed by a medical specialty expert. The preclinical science personnel were assigned to programs and projects

when needed, and they often had more than one assignment at any particular time.

The personnel on the research staff had needs and characteristics that were different from those of employees in other parts of the organization, and managers in the R&D department had to be sensitive to those differences. Bill York, a senior director in the basic research group explained:

> We're not an organization comprised of conformists, and we don't want to be; the other companies can have those people. Good researchers are unique. They are creative and intelligent, and although they can be lazy, they will work their tails off when they get on a project they like. But their feelings are easily hurt. It's very easy to kill ideas. We have to be careful because if we use punishment or discouragement, we may never get another idea.

PRODUCT DEVELOPMENT CYCLE

The product development cycle in pharmaceutical companies such as Alcon was long, typically totalling up to 15 years for a totally new drug and from three to five years for a simple product. Often the cycle started with some basic research designed to provide a better understanding of the basic biochemistry of the disease processes at the molecular level. For example, in 1985 doctors treated glaucoma by reducing interocular pressure, but Alcon researchers were trying to understand the biochemical basis of lesion of glaucoma with the goal of discovery of a more effective therapy. In 1985, Alcon had five basic research programs underway, all in the area of ophthalmology: inflammation, immunology, glaucoma, diabetic retinopathy/cataracts, and drug delivery.

When a new product concept was formed, the product development cycle was said to begin. Development consisted of a number of relatively distinct steps. First was the discovery phase of development, the purpose of which was to identify compounds with potential commercial applications. Scientists designed and tested new drug compounds against the characteristics of the diseases they were studying both in test tubes and later in live animal subjects, generally rabbits, dogs, and monkeys. For most new drug concepts, these screening and testing activities would last from two to five years.

When the compounds moved into the discovery phase of development, Alcon management assigned the effort a development program number, and this number identified the effort until the product entered the clinical phase of testing. In 1985, Alcon had a total of 11 development programs underway, four each in ophthalmology and optical, and three in dermatology.

A successful culmination of the discovery phase of development was marked by the identification of a compound that showed promise. Such compounds were moved into the optimization phase of development. This phase usually involved one to two years of studies of how the compound may act in the body. Scientists would study how the compound was absorbed, distributed, metabolized and excreted in animal subjects. They would do some exploratory testing of toxicity (i.e. harmful side effects) and stability (i.e. length of time the drug retains its effectiveness when stored). By the end of this phase of development, the scientists would prescribe a preliminary chemical formulation and make a preliminary packaging decision (i.e. mode of delivery and size of dosage).

Drugs continuing to show promise were moved into the preclinical phase of development. This phase involved better controlled laboratory experiments to validate the results of the exploratory tests conducted in the optimization phase of development. The preclinical phase of development usually lasted about six to twelve months. The drugs that continued to show promise were filed as IND (Investigation of a New Drug) candidates with the US Food and Drug Administration (FDA). At this point, a reasonably complete composition and specification existed, and a manufacturing procedure suitable for the preparation of clinical supplies was in place.

Once the IND was filed, the project moved into the clinical phase of development. This phase involved toxicity and stability testing of a longer-term nature than had been done previously. The testing was performed on live subjects: first normal human subjects and then diseased human subjects. During this testing, the scientists would make judgments of the safety and efficacy of the drug candidates and make final decisions about the dosages and modes of delivery to be used.

The clinical phase of development generally lasted between five and eight years. When a product entered the clinical phase of development, a project number was assigned, and this number would stay with the effort until the product received FDA approval or the effort was abandoned. In 1984, Alcon had a total of 30 active projects.

A drug that passed clinical testing was filed as an NDA (New Drug Application) with the FDA. The FDA approval process took from one to three years, and approval was needed before the drug could be marketed in the US. The product could be sold in many countries after it had passed clinical testing.

Exhibit 3 shows an overview of the product development cycle. The times shown in the exhibit for completion of each of the phases in the cycle are for development of major drugs. For fairly simple drugs and optical devices, the times were considerably shorter. For these products, INDs were often filed within 12 months, and clinical testing took between 12 and 18 months.

A SHIFT IN EMPHASIS

In 1985, Alcon management was contemplating a fairly significant shift in the R&D efforts to emphasize more basic research. Up to 1985, Alcon had been relying heavily on other pharmaceutical companies not involved in ophthalmic markets as sources of new product ideas. Alcon scientists would screen compounds developed from these companies, and if they showed promise, Alcon would license the compounds and introduce tailored forms of them into ophthalmic markets. Compounds screened in such a manner were entered into the product development process in the preclinical phase of development because the properties of the compounds were already understood.

Mr. Leone felt that the licensing source of new product would become less important over time. The ophthalmic markets were getting large, and as they continued to grow, it became more likely that other companies would enter some of Alcon's market segments. These companies would then be less likely to offer Alcon their newest compounds.

Alcon had already begun shifting its emphasis in recent years toward more basic research. The research focus had been evolving toward larger-scale, longer-term studies of more complex, sophisticated diseases of the eye. This is because the company already had a broad product line covering most niches in the eye care market, and to meet the company's aggressive growth targets, new breakthrough products were needed. The inevitable shift toward more basic research made Mr. Leone and Dr. Raval even more concerned about having measures of research productivity available for control purposes because the investments in basic research were longer-term and riskier.

DRUG INVESTMENTS AND PAYOFFS

New product development involved high risk investments for potentially lucrative payoffs. Across the industry, only about one of every 10,000 compounds investigated in the early exploratory research stages eventually proved to be commercially successful. The probabilities of failure of a typical compound in each of the phases of the product development cycle were approximately as shown in Table 1.

TABLE 1

Phase	Probability of failure
Discovery	90%
Optimization	50%
Preclinical	25%
Clinical	70%
FDA & patent	Negligible

The payoffs from the research were highly dependent on the size and term of the competitive advantage Alcon enjoyed when the new products were developed. Some drugs were breakthrough products which provided significant advantages over the competition in large market segments. Others were either minor modifications of already existing Alcon products or were aimed at small market segments. Sometimes competing firms developed alternatives to commercially successful new drugs in periods as short as two to three years, while on other occasions, Alcon products were sold for 20 years or more with little or no competition.

To a large extent, the timing of the development efforts was critical. If the development of a particular drug was pursued too early, the company could be subject to a high probability of failure and/or significant extra development expenses, and if problems were found after introduction, possible legal liability expenses. If the development was pursued too late, the result would be a "me-too" product.

PLANNING AND BUDGETING

Alcon used a well-developed set of management systems to help manage its R&D effort. Planning and budgeting was done on an annual cycle that took place from mid-July to mid-September. Planning was an iterative process. Mr. Leone and Dr. Raval began the process by setting program and project objectives and priorities and by outlining an overall budget for the R&D department. In establishing these guidelines, Mr. Leone and Dr. Raval met with Alcon directors and top-level managers to ensure that they had a good understanding of market trends and the amount of resources the company (and Nestlé) were willing to spend on R&D. Then directors and managers in each medical specialties group and each preclinical science department determined the labor hours and resources required to satisfy project and program objectives. This process was accomplished through a multitude of meetings between directors and managers.

Plans for the basic research programs were easier to prepare than were those for the development projects in that the programs used very few resources from the preclinical science departments, so very little cross-organizational coordination was required. Most development projects required the assistance of all, or at least most, of the preclinical science groups, so many meetings between the managers of the medical specialty groups and Dr. Charles Robb, director of Preclinical Sciences, were required to ensure that resources were allocated appropriately and, if necessary, that steps were taken to procure additional resources.

After the plans were prepared, Dr. Raval re-viewed them and made suggestions and adjustments as necessary. Then the plans were consolidated and compared with the overall targets, and sometimes further adjustments were necessary.

By February, all Alcon employees were required to develop, in consultation with their immediate supervisor, personal objectives for the year. The company did not require the use of a standardized form or format for documenting these objectives, but the objectives had to be written down, and this document had to be signed by both the employee and the supervisor.

During the year, budget analyses were prepared on a quad (every four months) basis consistent with the planning schedule used at Nestlé. The budget analysis process, like the annual planning processes, was very informal because, as Dr. Raval explained:

We do not expect the scientists to act like businessmen when they plan new product activity. We want to encourage them to develop new ideas without many constraints, and they don't like a lot of paperwork.

A research program manager explained his dislike for paperwork requirements:

> We work only on programs with payoffs so large that a monkey can run the figures showing the payoff. The trick is to score, not to try to figure out that a new breakthrough therapy for glaucoma will pay off. It will!

Mr. Leone had two main concerns about the planning process. First, he wondered if too much detail was still being required. And second, he wondered if requiring numbers about the research activities made the managers and scientists conservative in presenting their ideas. Given the company's need for good ideas, he thought it was important that no administrative barriers to ideas were erected.

MEASUREMENT AND REPORTING

Accounting in the R&D department was done on a full absorption cost basis. All direct expenses, both labor and materials, were charged to specific programs and projects. Labor was charged on the basis of time sheets completed weekly by R&D personnel. Costs not specifically identifiable with a particular project or program were allocated monthly on the basis of direct labor hours.

Alcon produced an extensive set of cost reports. Many of the reports were on a project, program, or medical specialty basis. They showed costs compared to budget and were available on a monthly basis (an example is shown in Exhibit 4). Another set of reports, were on a cost center basis; the R&D department was divided into 75 cost centers. Exhibit 5 shows an example of a cost center report. The cost reports were summarized at various levels of aggregation, such as by type of medical specialty and by type of project or program. The program/project cost accounting system provided the information necessary to monitor the flow of resources to medical specialty areas, research versus development, and for long-term versus short-term purposes.

The project/program and cost center reports were sent to the managers responsible for the costs. The managers reviewed the reports, but they were not required to explain variances. This was because most of the variances were caused by changes in the scope or timing of the project/program, and

such changes were almost always preapproved by Mr. Leone and/or Dr. Raval.

Alcon management recognized that the cost reports were not very useful for measuring the productivity of the R&D activity. Traditional accounting measures, such as return on investment, were not very meaningful because the lag between the investment in R&D and the returns generated from those investments was usually at least several years.

To date Mr. Leone and Dr. Raval had focused their attention on the consolidated financial summary (actual vs plan) and on the major achievements of the year. In the last few years, these achievements were as follows:[1]

	1984	1983	1982
INDs filed	3	4	3
NDAs filed	6	5	3
Research publications	25	19	17
Patent applications filed	15	9	8
Patents indicated allowable	7	8	5
Patents issued	5	6	4

Mr. Leone and Dr. Raval realized, however, that none of these indicators was a totally reliable indicator of forthcoming commercial success.

INCENTIVE PLANS

Alcon used two formal incentive plans which offered cash awards for good performance, one for scientists and one for senior-level managers. The scientist incentive plan was introduced in the R&D department in 1983. Four cash awards of $5,000 each were made annually for technical excellence. The awards were split between scientists doing basic research and those involved in development activities.

Candidates for the scientist award were nominated by director-level managers in the R&D department. The candidates' accomplishments were judged by a seven-person committee which included four working-level scientists, two director-level managers, and one person from outside R&D (e.g. from corporate marketing). The committee assigned the awards based on "perceptible contributions or unusual problem solving capabilities which are perceptible to fellow workers."

---

[1] These numbers are disguised.

The management incentives were provided through a companywide program which provided stock options and bonuses to senior managers down to the director level of the firm. Each year an incentive award pool was assigned to the R&D department based on a predetermined percentage of Alcon profits. This pool was allocated by R&D management to R&D employees included in the plan in conjunction with the annual performance review.

TABLE 2

Category of achievement	Percent so evaluated	Average award (% of salary)
DP	<1	30–35
SP	50–60	15–20
GSP	40–50	10

For purposes of assigning the awards in the R&D department, R&D employees were classified into three categories of achievement: (1) distinguished performance (DP), (2) superior performance (SP), and (3) good solid performance (GSP). (A fourth category called "Needs Improvement" was also used on occasion but, as Dr. Raval observed, "Those people don't get to stay very long.") Table 2 shows the approximate percentage of people who were classified in each category of achievement and the bonuses that could be expected in an average year in each of the categories.

The evaluations were based on a weighted average of three factors: (1) meeting the technical milestones in the annual plan, (2) discovering new product candidates, and (3) contribution provided from new products and getting new products through FDA approvals. The factors used for weighting accomplishments in each of these areas were preestablished at the beginning of the year. In general, the highest weightings were given to the accomplishments that could be measured in a tangible fashion in the next 12 months.

The weighting factors varied significantly among the various areas of the department. For example, managers in development areas (as opposed to those in basic research) were expected to have products progress through the FDA approvals, but they were not expected to generate many new product leads.

The standards used to assess performance also varied significantly among the areas, reflecting the probability of payoffs of the various activities. For example, managers of basic research activities might be expected to achieve 40% of their objectives for the following year to be evaluated as SP (superior performance). For managers of ophthalmology drug development activities, however, the achievement of 50% of their objectives might qualify only as GSP, while SP might require the achievement of 70%. For product development managers in optical, GSP might require achievement of 60% of their objectives, and SP might require achievement of 80%.

MANAGEMENT CONCERNS

Alcon managers felt they had an excellent research team that had produced many new products that had fueled the company's growth. They were concerned, however, that they did not have a good early warning system in place to signal potential problems on a timely basis because of the difficulty in measuring R&D productivity, and this might be particularly costly as the emphasis shifted toward more basic research.

Here are some of their observations.

Mr. Leone:

What's important in conducting research is to keep achieving progress on a daily basis. When it takes 10 years to develop a product, you can't wait until tomorrow to get the work done. The important questions are: Are we doing everything we can to ensure that we are being productive every day? And how can I tell if we're being productive?

Eighty percent of the really good ideas – those that lead to breakthrough products – come from 20% of our people. It is important for us to hire as many of those good people as we can, and perhaps even more important not to lose any we've already employed. But it is very difficult to tell who the really good people are until their accomplishments are apparent, but that may not be for some years after they were hired.

From my perspective, it's not very important whether a product costs $30 million or $60 million to develop. When we are working on a drug that will give us a billion dollars in sales over 15 years and a 25% cost of goods sold, overspending a little on research doesn't matter much as long as the drug gets created.

Dr. Raval:

I think we have an excellent scientific team. In 1984 we filed more regulatory submissions [INDs and NDAs] than ever before, and we expect to surpass that record in 1985. But we still need a better way to measure our performance among other things to prove to Alcon and Nestlé management that the R&D department is very productive. It's important, however, that the measures be simple enough to assemble and use without devoting too much time away from the job at hand.

We now have 16 programs and 30 projects underway, and the growth has made coordination of the groups more difficult. It is increasingly difficult to keep up with the status of each program and project well enough to be able to decide priority issues. In the last six months, we have started an effort to try to identify a set of standard product development mile-stones and decision points around which a computerized information system could be built and used for control purposes. Because of the great variance among projects, however, not everybody in the organization is convinced as to the worth of trying to organize an information system around a conceptualization of a standardized process.

Even in defining what we mean by productivity, we have to be careful in how we define our terms and use the measures that could result. For example, we rarely terminate projects, but we do adjust priorities and let some of them sit in an inactive state until a solution to a particular problem surfaces. Should the inactive projects reflect negatively on our productivity?

Exhibit 1 Alcon Laboratories, Inc., corporate organization

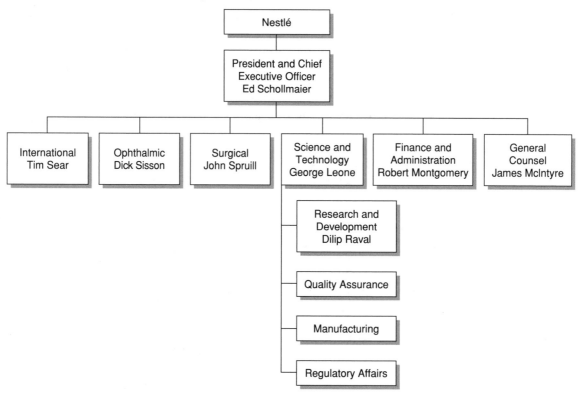

EXHIBIT 2 Alcon Laboratories, Inc., organization of R&D Department

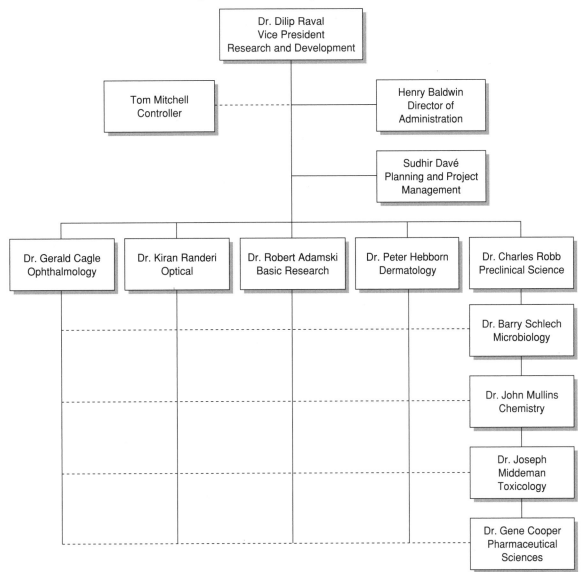

Exhibit 3 Alcon Laboratories, Inc., product development cycle

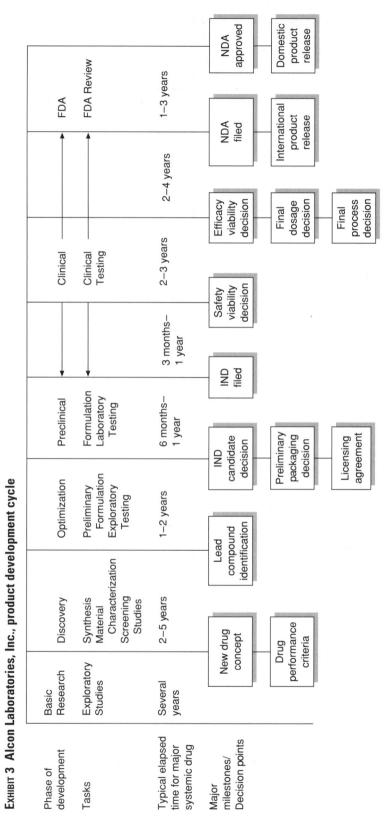

Phase of development	Basic Research	Discovery	Optimization	Preclinical		Clinical		FDA	
Tasks	Exploratory Studies	Synthesis Material Characterization Screening Studies	Preliminary Formulation Exploratory Testing	Formulation Laboratory Testing		Clinical Testing		FDA Review	
Typical elapsed time for major systemic drug	Several years	2–5 years	1–2 years	6 months–1 year	3 months–1 year	2–3 years	2–4 years	1–3 years	
Major milestones/Decision points	New drug concept / Drug performance criteria	Lead compound identification	IND candidate decision / Preliminary packaging decision / Licensing agreement		IND filed	Safety viability decision	Efficacy viability decision / Final dosage decision / Final process decision	NDA filed / International product release	NDA approved / Domestic product release

Exhibit 4 Alcon Laboratories, Inc., example of medical specialty cost report

Research and Development
December 1985

	Account	Medical Specialty Ophthalmic (220000) Actual	Budget	Variance	Quad Act	Quad Bud	Variance	Year Act	Year Bud	Variance
1. Dirct Chg	Consultants	4,929	4,900	−29	9,182	14,000	4,818	17,281	30,000	12,719
	Contract Service	43,638	32,856	−10,781	104,286	94,018	−10,268	261,657	343,500	81,843
	Contract Research	67,160	24,675	−42,485	113,410	70,500	−42,910	225,640	182,500	−43,140
	Clinical Studies	60,099	122,150	62,051	167,021	349,000	181,978	396,361	704,000	307,639
	Supplies	21,777	4,875	−16,302	119,746	19,500	−100,246	245,560	80,000	−165,560
	Other Controllable	633	8,963	8,329	14,397	35,850	21,453	56,445	97,850	41,405
	Fixed Expenses	0	0	0	0	0	0	−1,928	0	1,928
*Total 1. Dirct Chg		197,636	198,419	783	528,043	582,868	54,825	1,201,015	1,437,850	236,835
2. Allocated	Payroll	225,779	255,487	29,708	912,934	1,024,043	111,109	2,847,194	2,917,348	70,153
	Consultants	5,872	2,759	−3,114	5,872	8,555	2,682	6,213	15,205	8,991
	Contract Service	6,420	9,361	2,941	20,623	28,346	7,724	54,518	89,334	34,816
	Contract Research	0	0	0	0	0	0	182	0	−182
	Clinical Studies	0	0	0	0	0	0	857	0	−857
	Supplies	33,132	42,646	9,514	101,933	172,021	70,088	340,529	481,876	141,347
	Other Controllable	40,058	28,630	−11,427	150,263	114,606	−35,657	382,385	341,906	−40,479
*Total 2. Allocated		311,261	338,882	27,621	1,191,624	1,347,570	155,946	3,631,878	3,845,667	213,789
3. Var. O/H	Payroll	108,707	66,619	−42,088	318,091	272,892	−45,199	903,191	679,617	−223,574
	Consultants	5,231	131	−5,100	8,682	464	−8,218	16,017	2,477	−13,540
	Contract Service	9,210	4,806	−4,404	13,680	13,798	118	38,278	36,783	−1,495
	Contract Research	16	5,739	5,723	16	23,033	23,017	−72	31,916	31,989
	Supplies	8,927	4,061	−4,866	19,140	17,113	−2,027	61,655	37,590	−24,065
	Other Controllable	101,347	23,218	−78,130	178,064	93,844	−84,220	283,723	234,093	−49,629
*Total 3. Var. O/H		233,438	104,574	−128,865	537,673	421,144	−116,529	1,302,792	1,022,476	−280,315
4. Fix O/H	Contract Service	10,170	9,476	−695	30,919	27,151	−3,768	83,425	75,636	−7,789
	Supplies	7,900	3,345	−4,555	16,023	13,425	2,598	55,785	37,392	−18,392
	Other Controllable	3,481	3,062	−419	7,576	12,290	4,714	15,760	33,959	18,179
	Fixed Expenses	157,350	119,695	−37,655	469,885	480,809	10,924	1,427,039	1,349,593	−77,447
*Total 4. Fix O/H		178,902	135,578	−43,324	524,403	533,674	9,272	1,582,010	1,496,561	−85,449
*Total MEDSPEC 220000		921,236	777,453	−143,783	2,781,743	2,885,257	103,514	7,717,694	7,802,555	84,860

Exhibit 5 Alcon Laboratories, Inc., example of cost center expense report

Report Number GLCP0020R07 Final   Alcon Science and Technology   Domestic   April 1985
Page Number   123 Run Date = 05/08/85   Budget vs Actuals by Territory   Performance Ledger   3921-3621
Variance is Budget – Actual (– = Over)   Degenerative Disease Programs   Amounts are in US Dollars

Account description	Account code	April 1985 Actual	April 1985 Variance	Current quad to date Actual	Current quad to date Variance	Current year to date Actual	Current year to date Variance
Salaries	61,100	17,399.63	2,042.37	72,711.56	5,056.44	72,711.56	5,056.44
Profit sharing trust	61,500	1,913.96	46.96–	7,649.96	181.96–	7,649.96	181.96–
Payroll tax. group insurance	61,600	2,696.94	122.06	11,090.96	185.04	11,090.96	185.04
Temporary labor costs	61,800		1,250.00		5,000.00		5,000.00
Payroll costs	Total	22,010.53	3,367.47	91,452.48	10,059.52	91,452.48	10,059.52
Travel and entertainment	62,000		2,175.00		8,700.00		8,700.00
Meals	62,100	58.04	58.04–	1,003.88	1,003.88–	1,003.88	1,003.88–
Entertainment	62,200			121.94	121.94–	121.94	121.94–
Auto mileage and rental	62,300	267.75	267.75–	521.98	521.98–	521.98	521.98–
Air other transportation	62,500	50.60	50.60–	6,361.10	6,361.10–	6,361.10	6,361.10–
Lodging	62,600	248.14	248.14–	1,378.34	1,378.34–	1,378.34	1,378.34–
Parking and tolls	62,700	31.00	31.00–	46.55	46.55–	46.55	46.55–
Misc travel & entertainment	62,800	168.37	168.37–	533.25	533.25–	533.25	533.25–
Meetings, seminars, & conventions	62,900	100.00	100.00–	1,041.27	1,041.27–	1,041.27	1,041.27–
Travel and entertainment	Total	923.90	1,251.10	11,008.31	2,308.31–	11,008.31	2,308.31–
Domestic consulting	63,110	83.95	1,666.05	4,363.85	636.15	4,363.85	636.15
Contr SVC – general	63,211	200.00	200.00–	1,688.57	1,688.57–	1,688.57	1,688.57–
Contr SVC – prof	63,212	2,500.00	11,815.00	5,798.06	35,101.94	5,798.06	35,101.94
Contr SVC & labor	Total	2,700.00	11,615.00	7,486.63	33,413.37	7,486.63	33,413.37
Contr RESH – domes	63,221	24,741.00	3,274.00–	58,784.00	2,549.00	58,784.00	2,549.00
Contr RESH – forgn	63,222		3,500.00		10,000.00		10,000.00
Contract research	Total	24,741.00	226.00	58,784.00	12,549.00	58,784.00	12,549.00
Contract services & labor	Total	27,441.00	11,841.00	66,270.63	45,962.37	66,270.63	45,962.37
Professional & commercial SVCS	Total	27,524.95	13,507.05	70,634.48	46,598.52	70,634.48	46,598.52
Printing	64,400	43.96	43.96–	115.96	115.96–	115.96	115.96–
Freight & postage	66,000		250.00		1,000.00		1,000.00
Freight in	66,100	481.50	481.50–	566.77	566.77–	566.77	566.77–
Freight out	66,200			9.50	9.50–	9.50	9.50–
Postage	66,300	51.27	51.27–	100.27	100.27–	100.27	100.27–
Freight & postage	Total	532.77	282.77–	676.54	323.46	676.54	323.46
General supplies	67,100	1,036.32	536.32–	6,146.58	4,146.58–	6,146.58	4,146.58–
Supplies – lab	67,410	660.68	589.32	2,512.01	2,487.99	2,512.01	2,487.99
Supplies	Total	1,697.00	53.00	8,658.59	1,658.59–	8,658.59	1,658.59–
Rental – equipment	68,200	491.03	258.97	2,359.59	640.41	2,359.59	640.41
Lease – equipment	68,300			1,178.33	1,178.33–	1,178.33	1,178.33–
Purchased software	68,400		500.00	1,321.20	678.80	1,321.20	678.80
Rents & leases	Total	491.03	758.97	4,859.12	140.88	4,859.12	140.88
Employment expense	69,100	14.49	735.51	14.49	2,985.51	14.49	2,985.51
Recruiting (excl field sales)	69,111			40.00	40.00–	40.00	40.00–
Employment expense	Total	14.49	735.51	54.49	2,945.51	54.49	2,945.51
Employee relations	69,200		1,625.00	1,040.00	5,460.00	1,040.00	5,460.00
Telephone & telegraph	69,300	164.90	2,085.10	851.53	8,148.47	851.53	8,148.47
Repair & maintenance	69,400	20.02	3,904.98	342.04	15,357.96	342.04	15,357.96
Professional dues	69,500		150.00	435.00	165.00	435.00	165.00
Professional literature	69,600	46.11	203.89	531.88	468.12	531.88	468.12
Miscellaneous expense	Total	245.52	8,704.48	3,254.94	32,545.06	3,254.94	32,545.06
Controllable expense	Total	53,469.66	27,315.34	190,660.42	85,584.58	190,660.42	85,584.58
Depr – lab equip & fixtures	74,400	409.77	6,182.23	1,254.94	25,113.06	1,254.94	25,113.06
Depr – office furn/fixt/equip	74,500		189.00	68.54	687.46	68.54	687.46
Depr – information systems	74,600	70.91	1,229.09	70.91	5,129.09	70.91	5,129.09
Depr – other than bldg	Total	480.68	7,600.32	1,394.39	30,929.61	1,394.39	30,929.61
Cost center total	Total	53,950.34	34,915.66	192,054.81	116,514.19	192,054.81	116,514.19

Chapter 4

CONTROL SYSTEM TIGHTNESS

The benefit of any management control system (MCS) is derived from the increase in the likelihood that the organizational objectives will be achieved relative to what could be expected if the MCS were not in place. This benefit can be described in terms of MCS *tightness* (or *looseness*). Tighter MCSs should provide more assurance that employees will act in the organization's best interest.

How tightly to apply management controls is a major management decision that has received relatively little attention in the literature, and, when it has, it has been primarily discussed in a results-control context. The concept of tight control can certainly be applied to results controls. Tight results controls might involve detailed (often line-by-line) and frequent (monthly or even weekly) budget reviews of performance as well as lucrative incentives.[1] But there are many other ways to effect tight management control, both with other forms of control and with reinforcing combinations of control types.

Conceptually, effective implementation of tight control requires that management has a good understanding of how one or more of the control objects – results, actions, and personnel/culture – relate and contribute to the overall organizational objectives. The following sections describe how each of the management control types can be used to generate tight control.

TIGHT RESULTS CONTROL

The achievement of tight results control depends on characteristics of the definitions of the desired result areas, the performance measures, and the reinforcements or incentives provided.

Definitions of desired results

For management control to be considered tight in a results control system, the results dimensions must be congruent with the "true" organizational objectives; the performance targets must be specific; the desired results must be effectively communicated and internalized by those whose behaviors are being controlled; and if results controls are used exclusively in a given performance area, the measures must be complete.

Congruence

Chapter 2 discussed congruence as one of the main determinants of the effectiveness of results controls. Results control systems may suffer congruence problems either because managers do not understand well the organization's true objectives or because the performance dimensions on which the managers choose to measure results do not reflect the true objectives well.

For many types of organizations, and for many specific areas within organizations, it is a reasonable assumption that the true objectives are well understood. For example, it is clearly desirable for production workers to be more efficient and for sales personnel to sell more, everything else being equal. In many other organizations, however, a good understanding of the true objectives and/or how they should be prioritized is not a reasonable assumption.[2] In many types of government agencies and not-for-profit organizations, key constituents often disagree as to the organization's objectives. Is the primary objective of a government agency to provide more services or reduce its costs (and tax burden)? Where objectives are not clear, congruence becomes a limiting problem.

Moreover, choosing measurable performance dimensions that reflect an organization's true objectives is often challenging. For example, are annual profits a good indicator of the success of a company with significant growth prospects? Is the number of patents granted a good indicator of a research and development entity's ability to create value, most of which comes from developing commercially successful ideas for new products?[3] Is the number of visitors a good indicator of the success of a museum? If the chosen measurable performance dimensions are not good indicators of the organization's true objectives, then the results control system cannot be tight, regardless of any of the other system characteristics.

Specificity

The degree of tightness of results control also depends on having performance expectations described in specific terms. Specificity of performance expectations, or targets, requires disaggregation and quantification, such as a 15% return on assets per year, less than 1% customer complaints, or $2.29 labor costs per unit of production. Organizations usually can, and do, set such specific, quantified targets in financial terms. Indeed, in many performance areas, such as with respect to sustainability and environmental performance, control is loose(r) because organizations do not set specific, quantified targets and merely evaluate the global performance area subjectively. "Profits are easy to measure; the many and often conflicting demands [arising from corporate social responsibility] are not."[4] Control in the difficult-to-measure areas can be tightened by disaggregating the global performance area into its various components, such as energy usage, volume and type of waste generated, and extent of recycling. In some performance areas, however, detailed and specific targets and measures are not feasible. It is difficult to be specific about how many cases a lawyer should handle in a year or about what is meant by ethical behavior or social justice. Nonetheless, specificity of expectations is one of the elements necessary for the implementation of tight results controls.

Communication and internalization

For results controls to be tight, performance targets must also be communicated effectively and internalized by those charged with their accomplishment. Only then can the results controls influence performance. The degree to which goals are understood and internalized is affected by many factors, including the qualifications of the employees involved, the perceived degree of controllability over the measured results areas, the reasonableness of the goals, and the amount of participation allowed in the goal-setting processes. Internalization is likely to be low when employees perceive they lack the ability to perform well in the expected performance area, when they consider the desired results to be unduly affected by factors outside of their control, when they believe the goals are unachievable, or when they were not allowed to participate in setting the goals. We discuss the conditions for effective target setting further in Chapter 8.

Completeness

Completeness is the final requirement for tight results controls. Completeness means that the result areas defined in the MCS include all the areas in which the organization desires good performance and for which the employees involved can have some impact. What is not measured becomes less visible, or perhaps even invisible. Thus, when the defined result areas are incomplete, employees often allow performance in the unmeasured areas to slip. For example, purchasing personnel evaluated solely on meeting cost standards might allow quality to slip. Similarly, salespeople who are asked to meet sales volume quota are likely to strive for volume, at the expense, possibly, of smaller but more profitable sales.

Thus, results control systems should capture, as completely as possible, all information about employees' effects on firm value, weighted properly, so that employees' efforts are appropriately balanced across the multiple dimensions of their job. At managerial levels, however, where jobs are complex, results controls are almost inevitably incomplete. Commonly, then, managers direct their efforts only to measured tasks and may ignore other important-but-unmeasured tasks (such as by focusing on improving short-term profits at the expense of long-term customer relations).[5] This is a typical example of *managerial myopia* due to incomplete results controls, which we discuss further in Chapters 10 and 11.

When the results controls are incomplete, other types of control, including action and personnel/cultural controls, should be designed to try to fill the void left by the incomplete results controls. Examples of *complementary* control mechanisms are action controls that include quality controls, or cultural controls that aim to instill a mindset towards sustainable performance or innovation to counter myopic results-driven behaviors.

Performance measurement

Tight results control also depends on the adequacy of the performance measures that are used. As discussed in Chapter 2, results controls rely on measures that are precise, objective, timely, and understandable. A results control system that is used to apply tight control requires that all of these measurement qualities are met to a high degree. If the measurements fail in any of these areas, the control system cannot be characterized as tight because behavioral problems are likely. Chapters 10, 11, and 12 deal with the complex nature of designing effective performance measurement systems.

Incentives

Results controls are likely to be tighter if meaningful rewards are directly and definitely linked to the accomplishment of the desired results. A *direct* link means that the accomplishment of results translates explicitly and unambiguously into rewards. A *definite* link between results and rewards means that no excuses are tolerated. Both elements are pertinently illustrated in a quote from a former president at Bausch & Lomb: "Once you sign up for your target number, you are expected to reach it." Managers who failed to achieve annual profit targets by even a small amount received "paltry" bonuses, while those who exceeded them earned "hefty" payouts.[6] Equally, in the public sector, the head of the Philippines' Bureau of Internal Revenue, the tax authority which brings in most of the government's revenues, resigned over the agency's "failure to meet its targets." Upon announcing the resignation, the president's office stated: "He has not performed well and he said he takes responsibility for it."[7]

Although there appears to be a trend in most organizations, including not-for-profit and public sector organizations, towards making the link between incentive compensation and performance more direct and more definite, there is much debate and controversy about this important topic. We discuss the key factors that determine the effectiveness of, and issues arising from, performance-linked incentives in more depth in Chapter 9.

The system used to monitor drivers' performance at United Parcel Service (UPS) provides a good example of a tight results control system. UPS pays good wages but pushes its drivers hard. Management compares each driver's performance (how many miles, how many deliveries, how many pickups) every day with a computerized projection of what performance should have been. Drivers who cannot meet the standards are assigned a supervisor to ride with them to provide suggestions for improvement, and those who do not improve can be warned, suspended, and eventually dismissed.[8] This control system meets every characteristic of tight results control. The results measures seem to be congruent with the company's goal of maximizing shareholder value because the company has been consistently successful. The measures seem to be complete at the driver level. Drivers have no other significant responsibilities other than to deliver packages efficiently. The performance targets are specific; measurement is thorough and done on a frequent (daily) basis; and the rewards, which include job security and sizable amounts of money, are significant to the employees involved.

TIGHT ACTION CONTROLS

Since the action control types are quite different from each other, we discuss the ways in which each action control type might be used to achieve tight control separately. Overall, action control systems should be considered tight only if it is highly likely that employees will engage consistently in all of the actions critical to the operation's success and will not engage in harmful actions.

Behavioral constraints

Behavioral constraints, either physical or administrative, can produce tight control in some areas of an organization. Physical constraints come in many forms, ranging from simple locks on desks to elaborate software and electronic security systems. No simple rules can be provided as to the degree of control they provide except, perhaps, that extra protection usually costs more.

Administrative constraints also provide widely varying degrees of control. *Restricting decision authority* to higher organizational levels provides tighter control if it can be assumed that higher-level personnel will make more reliable decisions than lower-level personnel. At Super Micro Computer, a California-based 15-year-old computer maker that has grown to about 850 employees, Charles Liang, the company's co-founder and CEO, "obsesses over every detail of the business, from approving the custom orders that are the company's specialty to dictating the environmentally themed, green neckties that executives wear to customer meetings." Despite its peculiarities, Super Micro is a thriving, publicly traded business that sells about $600 million worth of servers annually, beating its competitors to market by three to six months and offering the fastest, most compact, energy-efficient computers to demanding corporate customers such as eBay and Yahoo. The company has seen its sales grow by about 20% in recent years, and its stock has outperformed competitors, such as Sun Microsystems. "[Mr. Liang] is the person who approves and looks at everything the company is doing – every new product, marketing effort, sales effort, anything you want to do or promote," said Scott Barlow, a former sales manager at Super Micro. "If [Mr. Liang] says a product will be on schedule, it will be on schedule," added Don Clegg, a vice president. However, despite the seemingly effective control arising from centralized decision making, Mr. Liang "is considered so vital to the operation that the company warns investors in regulatory filings that his loss could derail the company's business, culture and strategic direction."[9]

Separating duties between two (or more) employees, which is another type of administrative constraint, makes the occurrence of a harmful activity less likely because one person cannot accomplish the entire undesirable task. Good separations of duties make the control system tighter. The critical assumption here is that those who do not have authority for certain actions or decisions cannot violate the constraints that have been established. Evidence suggests, however, that both *overrides* of internal controls and *collusion* among employees are significant contributors to fraud in organizations.[10] Indeed, Richard Powell, a partner at KPMG Forensic in the UK, said: "Companies clearly have a challenge on their hands: over 60% of the perpetrators [of fraud] are members of senior management, whose status in the company makes it easier for them to bypass internal controls and inflict greater damage on the company."[11]

Preaction reviews

Preaction reviews can make MCSs tight if the reviews are frequent, detailed, and performed by diligent, knowledgeable reviewers. Preaction reviews are invariably tight in areas involving large resource allocations because many investments are not easily reversible and can, by themselves, affect the success or failure of an organization. Tight preaction reviews of this kind involve formal scrutiny of business plans and requests for capital by experts in staff positions, such as in the Finance Division, and multiple levels of management, including top management. But some organizations also use tight preaction reviews before employees can spend even small amounts of money. L. A. Gear, the sport shoe manufacturer, was described as a *tight-fisted company* because senior management had to approve any expenditure greater than $2,500.[12] At Disney under former CEO Michael Eisner, Eisner antagonist Roy Disney complained that "Nobody is empowered to do anything on their own; everything goes up to Michael if it costs more than a dime."[13] Tight preaction controls can also be exercised at the level of the board of directors. For example, Ted Turner, chairman of Turner Broadcasting, has made decisions that several times pushed his company close to insolvency. As a consequence, his board of directors would not let him spend more than $2 million, a tiny amount for such a large company, without approval of the board.[14]

The extent to which organizations tighten their controls also often varies with their fortunes. For example, as Citigroup sought to recover from its crippling losses following the financial crisis, it tried many fixes, some involving the restructuring of its organizational charts and the consequent layoffs. But the banking giant apparently wasn't satisfied. A memo by John Havens, head of Citigroup's Institutional Clients Group (ICG), urged employees to be much more frugal in their expenses. "Managing our expenses is not only a critical aspect of our strategy, it is also an important part of our jobs," Mr. Havens wrote. "Each of us must do our part to manage our expenses by challenging every dollar we spend to ensure that it is truly necessary and in compliance with our policies." Many of the policy changes include stricter controls on who gets a BlackBerry, how much bankers can spend on client meetings, and how often executives can call upon management consultants. "Our current usage of management consultants is too high," Mr. Havens wrote; "Management consultants should only be engaged for those limited instances where a specific expertise which does not reside within our organization is absolutely required." He also noted that "color presentations are unnecessary for internal purposes, therefore [. . .] color copying and printing should only be used for client presentations. Also whenever possible, presentations should be printed double sided to reduce unnecessary paper usage." He emphasized that these "expense policies and pre-approval procedures will take effect immediately [and that] these policies and procedures apply to all ICG employees and the functional support areas dedicated to ICG, in all regions."[15]

The requirement of reviews by top-level officers or committees or even the board of directors does not, however, automatically signify that the preaction control is tight. Many busy top managers and even capital committees do not take the time to examine carefully all expenditure proposals, particularly smaller ones. They merely *rubber stamp* them.

Action accountability

Action accountability controls produce tight control in a manner quite similar to tight results controls. The amount of control generated by action accountability controls depends on characteristics of the definitions of desirable (and undesirable) actions, the effectiveness of the action-tracking system, and the reinforcements (rewards or punishments) provided.

Definitions of actions

To achieve tight action accountability control, the definitions of actions must be congruent, specific, well communicated, and complete. *Congruence* means that the performance of the actions defined in the control system will indeed lead to the achievement of the true organizational objectives.

Tighter control can also be affected by making the definitions of actions *specific* in the form of work rules (such as prohibiting alcoholic beverages during work) or policies (such as the requirement to obtain three competing bids before releasing a purchase order), as opposed to relying solely on less specific guidance (such as to exercise good judgment or to treat colleagues and customers with respect).

Tight action control depends on the *understanding* and *acceptance* of the work rules, policies or guidance by those whose behaviors are being controlled. If the employees involved do not understand the rules, policies, or guidance, they will be inconsequential. If the employees do not accept the rules, they may try to find ways to avoid them. Understanding and acceptance can be improved through communication and training and by allowing employees to participate in the development of the rules, policies, or guidance.

If the MCS relies extensively on action accountability, the definitions of (un)desired actions must be *complete*. Completeness means that all the important, acceptable (and unacceptable) actions are well defined. "We have procedures for everything" is an indicative comment from someone who is working in a tight action-accountability environment. Indeed, in the words of a manager at a care home for the elderly:

> We have procedures for everything . . . including a policy on confidentiality; a staff complaint procedure; a comprehensive job description; a record of training in care; and company rules. [The company rules] include a variety of policies from health and safety to smoking, and a section on gross misconduct.[16]

The co-owner at another care home for young people stated:

> A disciplined environment underpins everything that we do; adherence to regulations and procedures is part and parcel of everyone's work. Government regulations on care home and child protection require documentary evidence on most aspects of our day to day operations. I can tell you what a child resident ate on a particular day six years ago, what mood he got up in, what social worker s/he was with . . . The social workers have to write all this down; it all gets typed up. We keep the records for 10 years.[17]

Although tight action controls can be relied on extensively for the proper functioning of organizations in certain environments, such as banks, nuclear power facilities, hospitals, and critical health care homes, they are not effective in all circumstances, such as in situations where the desired actions cannot be defined nearly completely because the tasks are complex and require considerable discretion or creativity. When the desired actions cannot be properly defined, action accountability controls will not produce tight control; they may even be counterproductive as they are likely to limit professional judgment, stifle creativity, and cause decision delays and slow strategic responses to changing market conditions. At SAP America, a division of the world's largest provider of enterprise resource planning (ERP) software, the tight control exercised by SAP's headquarters in Germany was seen as utterly irritating.[18]

Action tracking

Control in an action accountability control system can also be made tighter by improving the effectiveness of the action-tracking system. Employees who are certain that their actions will be noticed, and noticed relatively promptly, will be affected more strongly by an action accountability control system than will those who feel that the chance of being "caught" is small. Constant direct supervision is one tight action-tracking method. Detailed audits of action reports is another (e.g. detailed reviews of expense reports). After Cendant Corporation uncovered accounting irregularities in one of its divisions, corporate management created three new senior Finance positions "to make sure that we never, ever have another accounting surprise."[19] Creating the three positions helped the company provide better action tracking to screen out the undesirable gameplaying activities.

Action reinforcement

Finally, control can be made tighter by making the rewards or punishments more significant to the employees affected. In general, significance varies directly with the size of the reinforcement. Whereas rewards (incentives) are the most common form of reinforcement that organizations provide in results control settings, punishments (disciplinary actions) are common in action control settings because they often involve employee violations of rules and procedures. And although, like with rewards, different individuals react differently to identical punishments, one type of significant disciplinary action – the threat of dismissal – is likely to be universally understood.

The way commercial airlines control the actions of their pilots provides a good example of a tight action-accountability control system. The pilots are given detailed checklists specifying nearly all required actions, not only for normal operations but also for all conceivable contingencies, such as engine failure, fire on board, wind shear, and hijacking. Intensive training helps ensure that the procedures are understood, and frequent checking and updating help ensure that they remain in the pilot's active memory. The tracking of deviant actions is precise and timely as all potential violations are thoroughly screened by objective investigators. Finally, reinforcement is significant because pilots are threatened with severe penalties, including loss of profession, not to mention the fear for loss of life when accidents do happen.

Even the most detailed action specifications can be undercut by the lack of action tracking and reinforcement. For example, rules and procedures will not be followed if top management does not show interest in having them followed. Thus, for action accountability to be tight, *all* of the elements of the action control system – definitions of actions, action tracking, and reinforcement – must be properly designed. Moreover, action controls are sometimes seen as hindering efficiency. As such, reengineering efforts focused on improving efficiency sometimes imprudently downgrade preaction reviews, segregation of duties, paper trails, and reconciliations as *non-value-added*. While these controls might seemingly not add value, they can help prevent the dissipation of value the company may have otherwise generated, and they can, hopefully, prevent major losses that might arise from corruption scandals or accidents.

Surveys of practice, however, suggest that sophisticated frauds have been on the rise, in part explained by an increase in computer-based transactions as part of complex information technology (IT) systems that handle virtually all company transactions including sales accounts, cost accounts, personnel administration, and general ledger. Although computer-based transactions are now commonplace in most organizations, control of such transactions is sometimes loose (compared to control of "old-economy" paper-based transactions). There is no reason why control of computer-based transactions cannot be tight, even tighter than paper-based transactions, but due to system complexity, companies do not always fully understand the control risks involved. Moreover, and as a recent study by KPMG pointed out, "although IT systems form a core part of [most business], many organizations suffer from not having people in the business clearly identified to be responsible and accountable for their usage." The study showed that more than two thirds of the executives surveyed believe that effective control is hampered because they put too much focus on technology and fail to address the organizational and procedural changes that are required.[20] This can lead to major security breaches such as those that took place at French bank Société Générale, mentioned earlier in this book, where Jérôme Kerviel, the perpetrator, was able to move from the middle office to the front office while retaining his previous access rights so that he could circumvent systems that were in place to enforce compliance policies.

It is such high-profile scandals, such as those in the early 2000s at Enron and WorldCom, that have put the spotlight back on the importance of internal controls. For example, Section 404 of the Sarbanes-Oxley Act of 2002 (see also Chapter 13) requires that publicly traded companies in the United States provide in their annual reports a statement by management on the effectiveness of the company's system of *internal controls*, many of which are of the action-control type. Section 404 further stipulates the responsibilities of the company's independent auditor in performing an audit of the internal controls in conjunction with an audit of financial statements.[21] As a consequence of the required compliance with Section 404 of the Act, many public companies in the United States have both improved the documentation of their internal controls and tightened them up.

TIGHT PERSONNEL/CULTURAL CONTROLS

In some situations, MCSs dominated by personnel/cultural controls also can be considered tight. In charitable and voluntary organizations, personnel controls usually provide a significant amount of control, as most volunteers derive a keen sense of satisfaction just from doing a good job, and thus are motivated to do well. Tight personnel/cultural controls can also exist in for-profit businesses. They are common in small family run companies where personnel/cultural controls may be effective because of the overlap or congruence between the organizational interests and those of the individuals on whom it must rely for pursuing them.

Some organizations use multiple forms of personnel/cultural controls which, in combination, produce tight control. For example, among the controls used in production areas of Wabash National Corporation, a truck-trailer manufacturer located in Lafayette, Indiana, are:[22]

- *walk and talk* interviews in which job applicants get to observe the *frenetic factory pace*;
- group incentive plans, including a profit-sharing plan that gives employees 10% of after-tax earnings and a retirement plan that bases contributions on profit margins;
- required training: new employees are strongly encouraged to take two specified Wabash improvement classes on their own time and are rewarded with pay raises for doing so. Supervisors are promoted only after they take special classes and pass a test.

Performance at Wabash has been consistently outstanding since the company was founded. An executive who recently visited Wabash remarked that, "I've never seen a work force that motivated."

In many instances, however, the degree of control provided by personnel/cultural controls is less than tight. In most firms, the natural overlap between individual and organizational objectives is smaller than that in family firms. It is also unstable. An impending divergence between the individual and organizational objectives often comes unexpectedly. As a survey by KPMG Forensic suggests, "the typical company fraudster is a trusted male executive who gets away with over 20 fraudulent acts over a period of up to five years or more."[23] Clearly, organizations should, ironically, not put all their trust in "trusted" employees, even ones who seemingly never show any signs of dishonesty and get on well with colleagues. The steps that might be taken to increase the strength of personnel controls are difficult to assess and potentially unreliable. Factors such as education, experience, and personality cannot always predict future performance.[24]

Cultural controls, on the other hand, are often more stable. Organizational cultures can be strong because they derive from deeply held and widely shared beliefs and values. Electronic Data Systems, Hewlett-Packard, Johnson & Johnson, Motorola, Nordstrom, The Walt Disney Company, WalMart, Nike, and Procter & Gamble are among the companies generally considered to have a strong culture.[25] Many large companies have weak cultures, however, because of their diversity and dispersion of people, some caused by mergers of dissimilar entities, as well as because of the lack of training and reinforcement needed to instill and maintain a strong culture.

Except for companies with strong cultures, tight control probably cannot be affected with the use of personnel/cultural controls alone. They can break down quickly if demands, opportunities, or needs change, and they provide little or no warning of failure.

CONCLUSION

This chapter focused on an important characteristic of MCSs: their degree of tightness. We defined tight control in terms of a high degree of assurance that employees will behave in the organization's best interests. All of the control types, i.e. those discussed in Chapters 2 and 3, can be used to provide tight control, depending on the situation. Table 4.1 presents a summary of the characteristics of each of the control types that can be varied to affect tight control.

TABLE 4.1 A summary of the characteristics that make a control "tight"

Type of control	What makes It tight
Results or action accountability	Definition of desired results or actions: ● Congruent with true organizational skills ● Specific ● Effectively communicated and internalized ● Complete (if accountability emphasized) Measurement of results or tracking of actions: ● Congruent ● Precise ● Objective ● Timely ● Understandable Rewards or punishments: ● Significant to person(s) involved ● Direct and definite link to results or actions
Behavioral constraints	Reliable Restrictive
Preaction reviews	Frequent Detailed Performed by informed person(s)
Personnel/cultural controls	Certainty and stability of knowledge linking personnel/cultural characteristics with desired actions

Source: K. A. Merchant, *Modern Management Control Systems: Text and Cases* (Upper Saddle River, NJ: Prentice Hall, 1998), p. 166.

In some organizations, a particular type of control is replaced with another type that provides a better fit with the situation for the purpose of tighter controls. Some companies tighten their controls by replacing "gentlemanly attitudes" (personnel control) with "hard-nosed" performance-based incentives (results controls). Other companies tighten controls by deemphasizing results controls and emphasizing instead detailed preaction reviews (action controls). But managers are not just limited to tinkering with the characteristics of one form of control or to replacing one with another. To tighten controls, organizations must often rely on multiple forms of controls and *align* them with one another. The controls then either reinforce each other or overlap, thus filling in gaps so that they, in combination, provide tight control over all of the factors critical to the organization's success. Lincoln Electric, whose case study is included in this book, is a good example of a company that effectively uses multiple overlapping and mutually reinforcing controls at the results, action, and personnel/cultural level.

It should also be recognized that organizations sometimes deliberately choose to *loosen* their controls. They do so because an inappropriate use of controls causes harmful side effects, such as operating delays or employee frustration and demotivation. It is these side effects that cause many people to have negative feelings when they hear the mere mention of tight control. The example of SAP America discussed above serves as a case in point, where layers of oversight and bureaucracy were dismantled to allow the firm to become more responsive in its rapidly changing environment.[26] In the next chapter, we discuss more fully the costs and negative side effects associated with some control types and, particularly, with imperfect, overly tight, or inappropriate uses of controls.

Notes

1. W. A. Van der Stede, "Measuring Tight Budgetary Control," *Management Accounting Research*, 12, no. 1 (March 2001), pp. 119–37.

2. "Shareholders vs. Stakeholders: A New Idolatry," *The Economist* (April 24, 2010), pp. 65–6.

3. "Patents, Yes; Ideas, Maybe," *The Economist* (October 14, 2010), pp. 78–9.

4. "Companies Aren't Charities," *The Economist* (October 21, 2010), p. 82.

5. W. A. Van der Stede, "The Pitfalls of Pay-for-Performance," *Finance & Management* (December 2007), pp. 10–13; W. A. Van der Stede, "Designing Effective Reward Systems," *Finance & Management* (October 2009), pp. 6–9; see also J. Roberts, *The Modern Firm* (New York, NY: Oxford University Press, 2004), and other work by John Roberts and colleagues.

6. "Blind Ambition: How the Pursuit of Results Got Out of Hand at Bausch & Lomb," *Business Week* (October 23, 1995), p. 81.

7. "Manila's Tax Chief Resigns for Not Meeting Targets," *Forbes* (November 2, 2009), online (www.forbes.com).

8. "Behind the UPS Mystique: Puritanism and Productivity," *Business Week* (June 6, 1983), pp. 66–73.

9. "Super Micro Computer: A One-Man, or at Least One-Family, Powerhouse," *The New York Times* (November 23, 2008), online (www.nytimes.com).

10. *KPMG 2003 Fraud Survey* (KPMG LLP, 2003), p. 7; *KPMG 2008/2009 Fraud Survey* (KPMG LLP, 2010).

11. "Adequate Procedures Report – Blessing in Disguise," *KPMG* (July 10, 2010), online (www.kpmg.co.uk).

12. "Getting Beyond a Market Niche," *Forbes* (November 22, 1993), pp. 106–7.

13. "Mouse Hunt," *Fortune* (January 12, 2004), p. 110.

14. R. Goldberg and G. Goldberg, *Citizen Turner: The Wild Rise of an American Tycoon* (Harcourt Brace, 1995).

15. "Trimming Expenses, Citi Holds Back on Color Copying," *The New York Times* (August 26, 2008), online (www.nytimes.com).

16. Quoted in P. Edwards, M. Ram, and J. Black, *The Impact of Employment Legislation On Small Firms: A Case Study Analysis*, Employment Research Series No. 20 (London, UK: Department of Trade and Industry September 2003), p. 52.

17. Ibid., p. 128.

18. "SAP's U.S. Chief Plans Reorganization of Unit," *The Wall Street Journal* (May 26, 2000), p. B7.

19. "Cendant Creates Three Finance Jobs to Tighten Control," *The Wall Street Journal* (April 29, 1998), p. B11.

20. "Too Much Faith in Technology Leads to Lapses," *KPMG* (June 16, 2008), online (www.kpmg.co.uk).

21. Sarbanes-Oxley Act of 2002 (One Hundred Seventh Congress of the United States of America, January 23, 2002).

22. This example taken from "Hard Driving: A Productivity Push at Wabash National Puts Firm on a Roll," *The Wall Street Journal* (September 7, 1995), p. A1.

23. "Profile of a Fraudster: Trusted Male Manager – And Getting Away with it for Years," *KPMG* (April 17, 2007), online (www.kpmg.co.uk).

24. For a comprehensive article on deviant workplace behaviors, see B. E. Litzky, K. A. Eddleston, and D. L. Kidder, "The Good, the Bad, and the Misguided: How Managers Inadvertently Encourage Deviant Behaviors," *The Academy of Management Perspectives*, 20, no. 1 (February 2006), pp. 91–103.

25. See, for example, J. Collins and J. Porras, *Built to Last: Successful Habits of Visionary Companies* (New York: Harper Business, 1994).

26. "SAP's U.S. Chief Plans Reorganization of Unit," op. cit.

Case Study

Controls at the Bellagio Casino Resort

In our world, good controls mean good business. A lot of our controls are dictated to us by the Nevada Gaming Control Board, but we would institute most of the same controls they require anyway. The State wants its share of the revenue. We want to earn profits.

Trent Walker, Bellagio Casino Controller

MGM MIRAGE AND ITS PROPERTIES

The Bellagio was one of 23 properties of MGM MIRAGE (NYSE: MGM), one of the world's leading hotel and gaming companies. In addition to the 23 properties shown in Exhibit 1, MGM MIRAGE was also developing a major resort in Macau (with a joint-venture partner) and a new multibillion dollar "urban metropolis" on 66 acres of land on the Las Vegas strip. At the end of 2005, the company had over 66,000 employees and total assets of over $20 billion (see Exhibits 2 and 3).[1]

MGM MIRAGE operated primarily in one industry segment, the operation of casino resorts, which included gaming, hotel, dining, entertainment, retail, and other resort amenities. All the MGM MIRAGE casino resorts operated 24 hours a day, every day of the year. Over half of the company's net revenue was derived from nongaming activities, a higher percentage than many of MGM MIRAGE's competitors.

Primary casino operations were owned and managed by the company. Other resort amenities sometimes were owned and operated by the company, owned by the company but managed by third parties for a fee, or leased to third parties. The company, however, generally had an operating

philosophy that preferred ownership of amenities, since guests had direct contact with staff in these areas and the company preferred to control all aspects of the guest experience. However, the company did lease space to retail and food and beverage operators in certain situations, particularly for branding opportunities.

As a resort-based company, MGM MIRAGE's operating philosophy was to provide a complete resort experience for guests, including nongaming amenities that commanded a premium price based on quality. The company's operating results were highly dependent on the volume of customers at its resorts, which in turn impacted the price it could charge for hotel rooms and other amenities. MGM MIRAGE also generated a significant portion of its operating income from the high-end gaming segment, which also caused variability in operating results. Results of operations tended not to be highly seasonal in nature though, but a variety of factors could affect the results of any interim period, including the timing of major Las Vegas conventions, the amount and timing of marketing and special events for high-end customers, and the level of play during major holidays, including New Year and Chinese New Year. However, the company's significant convention and meeting facilities allowed it to maximize hotel occupancy and customer volumes during off-peak times such as midweek or during traditionally slower leisure travel periods, which also allowed better labor utilization.

MGM MIRAGE's casino resorts generally operated in highly competitive environments. They competed against other gaming companies as well as other hospitality and leisure and business travel companies. At the end of 2005, Las Vegas, for example, had approximately 133,200 guestrooms.

The principal segments of the Las Vegas gaming market were leisure travel; premium gaming customers;

---

[1] In April 2005, MGM MIRAGE acquired Mandalay Resort Group at a total acquisition cost of approximately $7.3 billion. As a result of the acquisition, MGM MIRAGE became a much larger company with, for example, over 66,000 employees versus 40,000 and total assets of over $20 billion versus $11 billion (see Exhibit 3).

This case was prepared by Professors Kenneth A. Merchant, Leslie R. Porter, and Wim A. Van der Stede.

conventions, including small meetings and corporate incentive programs; and tour and travel. The company's high-end properties, which included Bellagio, MGM Grand Las Vegas, Mandalay Bay, and The Mirage, appealed to the upper end of each market segment, balancing their business by using the convention and tour and travel segments to fill the midweek and off-peak periods.[2] The company's primary methods of competing successfully in the high-end segment consisted of:

- locating resorts in desirable leisure and business travel markets, and operating at superior sites within those markets;
- constructing and maintaining high-quality resorts and facilities, including luxurious guestrooms along with premier dining, entertainment, and retail amenities;
- recruiting, training, and retaining well-qualified and motivated employees to provide superior and friendly customer service;
- providing unique, "must-see" entertainment attractions; and
- developing distinctive and memorable marketing and promotional programs.

A key element of marketing to premium gaming customers was personal contact by marketing personnel. Direct marketing was also important in the convention segment. MGM MIRAGE maintained Internet websites that informed customers about its resorts and allowed customers to book hotel rooms and make restaurant and show reservations. The company also operated call centers to service customers by phone to make hotel, restaurant, and show reservations. Finally, MGM MIRAGE utilized its world-class golf courses in marketing programs. The company's major Las Vegas resorts offered luxury suite packages that included golf privileges, such as golf packages at special rates or on a complimentary basis for premium gaming customers.

In this environment, the company's key revenue-related performance indicators were:

- *Gaming revenue indicators*, such as table games *drop* and slot machines *handle* (volume indicators) and *win* or *hold* percentages (profitability indicators). These performance indicators are discussed in detail in the later sections of the case.

- *Hotel revenue indicators*, such as hotel occupancy (volume indicator), average daily rate (ADR – a price indicator), and revenue per available room (REVPAR – a summary measure of hotel results that combined ADR and occupancy rate).

Most of MGM MIRAGE's revenue was cash-based. Customers typically wagered with cash or paid for nongaming services with either cash or credit cards. The business, however, was capital intensive and the company relied heavily on the ability of its resorts to generate operating cash flow to repay debt financing, fund maintenance capital expenditures, and provide excess cash for future developments.

MGM MIRAGE was making increasing use of advanced technologies to help maximize revenue and operational efficiency. For example, the company was in the process of combining its player-affinity programs, the Players Club and Mandalay's One Club, into a single program. This integration would link all MGM MIRAGE's major resorts and consolidate all slots and table games activity for customers with a Players Club account. Under the combined program, customers qualified for benefits ("comps") across all of the company's resorts, regardless of where they played. This program enabled the company to get to know its better customers and to market to them more effectively.

A significant portion of the slot machines at the MGM MIRAGE resorts operated with the EZ-Pay™ cashless gaming system, including the Mandalay resorts that had recently converted its slot machines. This system enhanced both the customer experience and increased the revenue potential of the slot machines.

Technology was a critical part of MGM MIRAGE's strategy in nongaming operations and administrative areas as well. For example, the hotel systems included yield management modules that allowed maximizing occupancy and room rates. Additionally, these systems captured most charges made by customers during their stay, including allowing customers of any of the company's resorts to charge meals and services at other MGM MIRAGE resorts to their hotel accounts. In short, this system enhanced guest

[2] MGM MIRAGE's marketing strategy for Treasure Island, New York-New York, Luxor, and Monte Carlo was aimed at attracting middle- to upper-middle-income guests, largely from the leisure travel and, to a lesser extent, the tour and travel segments. Excalibur and Circus Circus Las Vegas generally catered to the value-oriented and middle-income leisure travel and tour and travel segments.

service and improved yield management across the company's portfolio of resorts.

The Bellagio

The Bellagio, located in the heart of the Las Vegas strip, was widely recognized as one of the premier casino resorts in the world. Inside the richly decorated resort was a conservatory filled with unique botanical displays that changed with the season. In front was an eight-acre lake featuring over 1,000 fountains that performed a choreographed ballet of water, music, and lights. Amenities and entertainment options at the Bellagio included an expansive pool, a world-class spa, exquisite restaurants, a luxuriant nightclub and several bars and lounges, shows by Cirque du Soleil, as well as a gallery of fine arts. The Bellagio also featured 200,000 square feet of convention space.

In the casino operations area, the Bellagio operated 2,409 coin-operated gaming devices (slot machines) and 143 game tables (see Exhibit 1), slightly over half of which were blackjack tables. The other table games included primarily baccarat, craps, and roulette. The casino also operated a keno and poker area. The games operated on a 24/7 basis in three shifts per day: day (8 a.m.–4 p.m.), swing (4 p.m.–midnight), and graveyard (midnight–8 a.m.) shifts. Approximately 1,000 people were employed in casino operations.

As in most companies in this industry, the gaming (casino) and nongaming operations in each of the MGM MIRAGE properties such as the Bellagio were run as separate profit centers. Exhibit 4 shows the Table Games Division organization chart. Bill Bingham, vice president of table games, reported directly to Bill McBeath, Bellagio's president/CEO. The vice president of the separate Slot Machines Division of the casino also reported directly to Bill McBeath.

The unique feature of a casino resort organization, as compared to that in most corporations, was the relatively large size of the finance staff. In the Bellagio, about 1,000 of the total of approximately 4,000 employees were in the finance organization, reporting in a direct line to Jon Corchis, executive vice president/CFO (Exhibit 5). Strict separation was maintained between operations and recordkeeping. The finance organization was large because it had responsibility for cash control and recordkeeping, both important functions in the casino and food and beverage parts of the business, particularly. Thus, the finance organization included credit operations personnel, casino change personnel (cage operations), pit clerk personnel, and count room personnel, in addition to people who were normally part of a finance organization, such as accounting clerks and financial analysts.

Laws and regulations over gaming activities

This case is focused on the controls used in the casino, especially in the difficult to control table games areas such as the blackjack pits. Many of these controls were legally mandated because the gaming industry was highly regulated. Each company had to maintain its licenses and pay gaming taxes to be allowed to continue operations. Each casino was subject to extensive regulation under the laws, rules, and regulations of the jurisdiction where it was located. These laws, rules, and regulations generally concerned the responsibility, financial stability, and character of the owners, managers, and persons with financial interest in the gaming operations. Violations of laws in one jurisdiction could result in disciplinary action in other jurisdictions. Exhibit 6 shows a more detailed description of some of these regulations as applied in the State of Nevada.

In connection with the supervision of gaming activities at the company's casinos, specifically, MGM MIRAGE maintained stringent controls on the recording of all receipts and disbursements. These controls included:

- locked cash boxes on the casino floor;
- daily cash and coin counts performed by employees who were independent of casino operations;
- constant observation and supervision of the gaming area;
- observation and recording of gaming and other areas by closed-circuit television;
- timely analysis of deviations from expected performance; and
- constant computer monitoring of slot machines.

These controls used in the casino were intended to ensure that the casino and the various governmental entities each kept their fair share of the money that was wagered.

Some of the regulations required extensive training of casino personnel to ensure compliance. For example, the last paragraph of the regulations shown in Exhibit 6 dealt with the reporting of so-called *suspicious activities* related to money laundering and/or the structuring of transactions by customers to avoid reporting to the US Internal Revenue Service (IRS) tax authority. This regulation, particularly, had regained importance subsequent to the signing into law of the US Patriot Act of 2001 following the terrorist attacks on the US. Because a casino is not a bank where every transaction can be more easily traced, and because the law required the reporting of any cash transaction in excess of $10,000 *as a result of one or a combination of transactions over a 24-hour period*, the company provided extensive training to standardize the handling, aggregation, and reporting of same type or dissimilar cash transactions by single customers on a single or multiple visits within a 24-hour period.

The company's businesses were also subject to various other federal, state, and local laws and regulations in addition to gaming regulations. These laws and regulations included, but were not limited to, restrictions and conditions concerning alcoholic beverages, environmental matters, employees, currency transactions, taxation, zoning and building codes, and marketing and advertising.

The game of blackjack and the roles of dealers

In a short case, it is not possible to describe all of the many controls that were employed in the casino. To simplify the discussion, all references will be to the table game of blackjack.[3] The following section provides a brief description of blackjack and the personnel involved in running it.

Blackjack is a very popular card game where up to seven patrons play against the house. The players' object is to draw cards whose total is higher than the dealer's total without exceeding 21.

Each blackjack table was run by a dealer whose job was to sell chips to customers, deal the cards, take losing wagers, and pay winning wagers. Dealing was a skilled profession that required some training

and considerable practice. Experience was valuable, as the dealer's value to the casino increased with the number of games that could be dealt within a given time period, and speed usually increased with experience. Experience was also valuable in identifying players who might be cheating.

Dealers assigned to a table worked for one hour and then were replaced by a *relief dealer* during their 20-minute break. Relief dealers worked at three different tables. The frequent breaks were required because the job was mentally and physically taxing – dealers were required to be standing up while they dealt; they had to maintain intense concentration, as errors in paying off bets were not tolerated; and they had to maintain good humor under sometimes difficult conditions (e.g. dealing to players who became irritable because they were losing).

Bill Bingham, vice president of table games, described a good dealer as follows:

> A good dealer makes a minimum number of mistakes and is productive in terms of hands per hour. But we don't clock our dealers. We believe that customers gravitate towards a dealer they are comfortable with, and that means different things for every customer. Some players prefer a slower pace.
>
> We only hire experienced dealers, and so we assume that they have mastered the technical aspect of dealing. For us, *customer satisfaction* is key, meaning that dealers have to be welcoming and engaging. They smile; they make eye contact and conversation with the players; and they wish them well. We also value attendance. Dealers with perfect attendance over a six-month period earn an extra vacation day.
>
> Regarding speed, you may have noticed as you walked through the casino that some tables have only one or two customers. You might ask why I don't close these tables. As a matter of fact, a low number of customers at a table doesn't worry me at all. If a good dealer can do 60 hands per hour on a table with, say, five customers, then that same dealer probably can do nearly 300 hands with just one customer! And, as I said, some customers don't like to join a busy table, and so it all works out in the end.

Bellagio dealers were paid well. While they earned a base wage of only $6.15 per hour, their total compensation was usually in the range of $85,000–$100,000 per year, including *tokes* (tips), which were shared equally among all dealers. Because the total compensation was high, perhaps among the top two or three casinos in Las Vegas, the Bellagio was seen a desirable place to work.

---

[3] This is done with little loss of generality. Control over all the table games in the Bellagio was nearly identical. The one major exception was that one extra level of supervision (*box person*) was used at the crap tables (see Exhibit 4). In the slot machines area, control was simpler because machines eliminated the human element (dealers). The machines did, however, have to be inspected regularly for evidence of tampering.

The company hired only dealers with a minimum of two years' experience. Dealer turnover was low – less than 3%.

The blackjack tables at Bellagio were spread across six *pits* containing 16 to 30 blackjack tables each. *Floor supervisors* (also called *floor persons*) supervised three to six blackjack tables, depending on the so-called *table minimum* (i.e. the minimum dollar amount to be wagered at the table). Each shift was also staffed by three to five *pit managers* (also called *pit bosses*), as well as a *shift manager* and an *assistant shift manager*. Hence, for example, when fully operating during a busy day shift, pit number 4, which contained 30 blackjack tables, employed about 30 dealers (depending on the number of tables that were open in the pit), 10 relief dealers, up to 10 floor persons, and one pit manager (plus relief).[4] In total, the Bellagio employed about 775 dealers, 225 floor (and box) supervisors, and 16 pit managers. Because they did not share in tokes, floor persons and pit managers earned less than dealers; on average about $62,000 and $85,000 per year, respectively.

Controls over cash and credit

Because most of the casino business was conducted in terms of cash or cash equivalents (i.e. chips), having good control over the many stocks of cash and chips located within the casino and over movements of these stocks without loss was essential. Moreover, because *marker play* (play on credit) represented a significant portion of the table games volume at Bellagio, the company also maintained strict controls over issuing credit. Overall, then, Bellagio's cash and credit control system can be described in terms of four main elements: (1) individual accountability for cash and (cash equivalent) stocks; (2) formal procedures for transfers of cash; (3) strict controls over credit issuance; and (4) tight control in the count rooms.

A. Individual accountability for cash stocks

All cash stocks – with the exception of those kept at a game table or those taken from a game or slot machine for counting – were maintained on an *imprest* basis. This meant that most personnel who

dealt directly with cash, such as change personnel, coin redemption personnel, cashiers, and chip fill bank personnel, were held individually accountable for a specific sum of money that was charged out to them. These personnel were required to turn in the exact amount of money for which they were given responsibility, and any large shortages or persistent patterns of shortages were grounds for dismissal.

B. Formal procedures for transfers

Strict procedures had to be followed when transferring cash or chips to or from *nonimprest* funds (e.g. a game table). All transfers required the creation of formal transactions signifying the transfer of accountability for the money involved. These procedures can be illustrated by describing the so-called *drop standards* and what was required to move cash or chips to and from a blackjack table.

When the Bellagio casino opened in 1998, the *drop box* affixed to each table was removed and its contents were counted at the end of each shift. But little or no use was made of the shift-by-shift information, so in 2004, the practice was changed to just one drop per day, a so-called *24-hour drop*.

The drop for each table had to be reconciled with other recorded transactions that occurred during the day. First, at the close of each shift, the incoming and outgoing pit managers proceeded through their pits and counted the chips (for blackjack) on each table, and recorded them on a *table inventory sheet* (see Exhibit 7). Table inventory sheets indicated the date, shift, game table number, and count by denomination and in total. Both the incoming and outgoing pit managers were required to sign the table inventory sheet verifying the accuracy of the count. When completed, one copy of the table inventory sheet was dropped in the pit drop box and the duplicate copy was delivered to the casino cage,[5] where the cage cashier or cage supervisor entered the table inventory amount (by denomination and in total) for each table into the computer system. Pit managers did not have access to the computer system that would allow them to add, change, or delete table inventory amounts.

As the game was played, several transactions could take place. One involved players buying chips from the dealer for cash or credit. Cash was deposited

---

[4] This pit also contained a few other table games, such as roulette wheels.

[5] This was a secure work area within the casino where the casino bankroll was kept.

immediately in the drop box. Players could not make reverse exchanges (chips for cash) at the tables. They had to take their chips to the casino cage where this type of exchange was made. Credit had to be approved by checking the customer's credit authorization limit through the use of a computer terminal located in the pit. If the credit was approved, a so-called *marker* was prepared. This process is described in the next section.

Transfers of chips to and from a gaming table were also common. Chip transfers to a table took place each time a table was opened for play or when additional chips were needed at an already open table. When the pit boss decided to open a blackjack table, or a floor person noticed that additional chips were needed at a table, a request for a particular mix of chips was input into the computer terminal in the pit (using a so-called *input form*) and relayed to the fill bank cashier in the casino cage, where a four-part, serially numbered *fill slip* was printed (see Exhibit 8). The fill bank cashier then summoned a security guard and filled the order in the guard's presence. Both the chip bank cashier and the security guard then signed copies 1, 2, and 3 of the fill slip. Copy 4 of the fill slip was retained by the cage to forward to casino accounting daily. The security guard then transported copies 1 and 2 of the fill slip and the fill to the table where the fill was required. The chip bank cashier retained copy 3 of the fill slip. The guard then gave copies 1 and 2 of the fill slip to the pit manager and placed the fill on the table. The dealer counted the fill by breaking down the chips in public view, agreed the count to the fill slip, and signed copies 1 and 2 of the fill slip. The pit manager also signed copies 1 and 2 of the fill slip. The dealer then placed the fill in the table tray and inserted copy 2 of the fill slip and copy 2 of the input form into the drop box. Copy 1 of the fill slip was given to the security guard who returned it to the chip bank cashier in the cage. Copies 1 and 3 of the fill slip were later forwarded to the casino accounting department.

A similar process was followed when a table was closed or an overabundance of chips had to be transferred to the cage, in which instance the transaction was traced through the use of an *input form* and *credit slip* (instead of a *fill slip*).

The so-called *drop* procedure, the process through which the table drop box was removed at the end of each gaming day, operated as follows. At least two security guards first obtained the soft count room key, locked storage carts with empty drop boxes, and the drop box release keys from the cage. They then proceeded to the table game pits where they unlocked the cart padlocks utilizing the drop box storage cart keys, removed the empty drop boxes, and placed them on their respective table. Pit managers and security guards observed the empty drop boxes from the time they were removed from the carts until placed on their respective gaming table. After setting out the empty drop boxes, the security guards removed the full drop boxes from the table using the drop box release keys. Empty drop boxes were then locked on the tables and the full drop boxes were immediately stored in carts. When the drop was complete but prior to transport, the carts were secured with a different padlock designated for carts with full drop boxes. Neither security guards nor pit managers had access to the keys for this padlock. At a minimum, two security guards and one pit manager transported the full drop boxes in the locked carts to the soft count room where they were secured until the count took place. Multiple drop teams were utilized such that each made only one trip to and from the casino floor for the placement and collection of drop boxes. The security guards completed the drop cycle by returning the keys to the cage.

C. Strict controls over credit issuance

When players wanted to gamble with money borrowed from the casino, as was common, they were issued what was called a *marker* (or *counter check*). Players' credit limits had to be preapproved.

Strict controls were applied over the issuance of markers. Marker paperwork contained multiple parts; (1) the original, which was maintained in the pit until the marker was settled, after which it was transferred to the cage; (2) an *issuance stub*, signed by the dealer and floor supervisor and inserted into the table drop box when the marker was issued; and (3) a *payment stub*. If the marker was paid in the pit, the payment stub was signed by the dealer and floor supervisor and inserted in the table game drop box. If paid at the table, there were strict rules for the dealer to follow when advancing the chips in the amount of the marker to the customer (e.g. the dealer had to break down the chips in full public view (and, obviously, in full view of the surveillance camera overhead) prior to advancing the chips). If the marker was not paid, the payment stub was transferred to the cage with the original marker. All these documents contained a check number, customer number, shift, pit number, type of table game, table number, date and time, and the approved dollar amount, in addition to the required employee signatures and ID numbers. There was also a time limit (30 minutes) within which the marker issuance process had to be completed, as well as strict rules for voiding markers.

Because marker play represented a significant portion of the table games volume at Bellagio, the company also aggressively pursued collection from those customers who failed to pay their marker balances timely. These collection efforts were similar to those used by most large corporations when dealing with overdue customer accounts, including the mailing of statements and delinquency notices, personal contacts, the use of outside collection agencies, and civil litigation. A significant portion of the company's accounts receivable, for amounts unpaid resulting from markers which were not collectible through banking channels, was owed by major casino customers from Asia. In this instance, the collectibility of unpaid markers was affected by a number of factors, including changes in currency exchange rates and economic conditions in the customers' home countries.

D. Tight security in count rooms

Wins (or losses) on a particular game table could not be determined until the funds in the drop box were counted. All counting from table games was done in the soft count room,[6] a highly secure room located adjacent to the casino cage. Tight security and supervision was necessary in the count rooms to ensure that the winnings were tallied accurately and that all the money to which the casino was en-titled was added to stores in the casino cage.

All cash and chips inventory storied in the soft count room was secured from unauthorized access at all times. Access to the count room during the count was restricted to members of the drop and count teams, authorized observers, supervisors for resolution of problems, authorized maintenance personnel,

and personnel performing currency transfers. Access to stored table game drop boxes, full or empty, was restricted to authorized members of the drop and count teams. When counts from various revenue centers occurred simultaneously in the soft count room with the table game count, each count table could contain funds from only one revenue center and the tables had to be adequately spaced to prevent commingling of funds. During the count, a minimum of three persons had to be in the count room until the monies were transferred and accepted into cage accountability. Full time count personnel independent of the pit department and the subsequent accountability of count proceeds had to be maintained by the casino to ensure the staffing of a count team with at least three members each day.

The count began with the opening of the first table game drop box and ended when a member of the cage signed the *master games worksheet* and assumed accountability of the drop proceeds. During the actual counting process, very strict procedures were followed, as described in Exhibit 9. The counting process was filmed by the cameras located in the room. After the money was counted, it was transferred to the casino cage.

Only after the cash and markers in the drop box had been counted was it possible to calculate the winnings for each table. Specifically, the win for a particular gaming table was calculated by determining the total drop (= cash + markers in the drop box) adjusted for table inventory (= beginning table inventory + fills – credits – ending table inventory), as illustrated in the following (simplified) example taken from the Bellagio *master games worksheet* for January 17, 2006:[7]

```
GAME: BJ
SHIFT: ALL
PIT: ALL
DATE: 01/17/06
TOTAL BEGINNING INVENTORY      29,497,800.00
TOTAL FILLS                     3,923,960.00
TOTAL CREDITS                       21,500.00
TOTAL ENDING INVENTORY         32,548,000.00
TOTAL CASH DROP                   583,008.00
TOTAL COUNTER CHECKS              626,500.00
WIN (LOSS)                        357,248.00
```

---

[6] This money was mostly bills and markers; hence the name *soft count* room. Coins taken from the slot machines were counted in the *hard count* room, which was about to disappear due to the use of slot machine tickets, rather than coins.

[7] Numbers in this example were disguised to safeguard company restrictions on the release of internal operating data.

As illustrated in this example for the blackjack game, the results for all games for each shift were reported on the *master games worksheet*, which was produced daily and summarized by type of game. The uses of this document as a control report are described further in a later section of the case.

Control of games

As discussed, the table games and the slot machines provided the only ways by which the casino made money. The table games were particularly difficult to control because of the need to rely on people who might be tempted by the extremely large amounts of money that could exchange hands very quickly.

In response to this difficult control problem, multiple forms of control were required by the Nevada Gaming Control Board (GCB) and used in the Bellagio to help ensure that the casino kept the cash to which it was entitled. These included: (1) licensing of casino personnel; (2) standardization of actions of personnel running the games; (3) careful supervision and surveillance of the actions taking place at the table; (4) monitoring of results; and (5) strict auditing procedures. These are discussed in the following sections.

A. Licensing

All employees of the casino (referred to by the GCB as *gaming employees*)[8] had to be registered with the GCB. The casino was required to submit a report to the GCB containing the name, social security number, position held, and date of hire of each gaming employee hired during the previous month. In addition, a registration packet had to be submitted for each employee. The key contents of the registration packet were the *gaming employee registration application* (which contained all the basic information about the employee (name, address, social security number) and employer), the *gaming employee questionnaire* (which contained additional information relating to the background of the applicant), and the *fingerprint form*. The registration process itself essentially involved a background check of gaming employees against police department records. When applicants did not pass the registration process, they

could not be kept in employ by the casino. Successful registration, on the other hand, resulted in the issuing of a *gaming card* (essentially a gaming work permit), which expired after five years at which time a new application had to be filed.

Similarly, on or before the 15th of the month after a calendar quarter, the casino was required to submit a report to the GCB containing the name, social security number, position held, and date of termination of each gaming employee terminated or separated from service within the previous quarter.

The Bellagio, however, performed its own employee screenings independent of the required registration process. The intent of these background checks was to avoid hiring people who had been involved in crimes or violations of casino rules, or those who might be attracted because of a need for quick cash. In the words of Bill Bingham, vice president of table games, "We know from experience that dealers with addiction issues, either alcohol, drugs, or gambling, are the ones to watch out for; they need cash to satisfy their addiction, and there is plenty of cash around here."

Moreover, Robert Rudloff, vice president of internal audit, noted that, "Dealers who, say, steal at one casino could still get in under the radar screen at another casino if the stealing was not reported to the police, which is basically what the GCB checks against. Our own preemployment screening hopefully can catch this." Trent Walker, casino controller, added: "What we really need though is a casino-wide system, kind of like an alert system, that links the whole city."

While the required background checking for gaming employees was relatively simple, checks on so-called *key employees* were more elaborate. Key employees included any executive, employee, or agent of a gaming establishment having the power to exercise a significant influence over decisions concerning any part of the gaming operation. The GCB required key employees to be licensed, a process that involved comprehensive background checks and extensive information, including the scrutiny of employment history, personal financial statements, and tax returns.

B. Standardization of actions at the tables

At the gaming tables, most of the dealers' physical motions were standardized in order to make supervision and surveillance easier. For example:

---

[8] Simply put, *gaming employees* essentially included all casino personnel except bartenders, cocktail waitresses, or other persons engaged exclusively in preparing or serving food or beverages.

1. All cash and chip exchanges were to be made in the middle of the gaming table in full public view to make them easier to see by supervisory personnel and the surveillance camera overhead.

2. Tips were to be accepted by tapping the cash or chips on the table and placing them in a clear, locked *toke box* attached to the gaming tables. This was done to distinguish these exchanges from wagers.

3. Before dealers left their tables, they were required to place their hands in the middle of the table and to show both the palm and back of their hands. This was done to prevent them from *palming* money or chips in order to take it from the table as they left. Dealers were also required to wear attire that was designed to make it more difficult for them to pocket cash or chips.

C. Supervision and surveillance

Front-line gaming personnel (e.g. dealers) were subjected to multiple forms of supervision and surveillance. Direct supervision was provided by the floor persons and pit bosses. One of their primary functions was to watch the gaming activity and spot events that were out of the ordinary. As highly experienced gaming people, they had a keen sense of the activity going on around them and, thus, were generally good at spotting nonroutine events, such as dealers paying losing bets in blackjack or customers marking cards in blackjack or switching dice in craps.

Extra surveillance of the table games was provided through a system of closed-circuit cameras, one fixed above each gaming table. In total, the Bellagio employed 2,000 cameras located throughout the property. The cameras had lenses powerful enough to zoom in to view objects as small as the date on a dime on the table. The pictures were viewed in a security room located on the mezzanine level of the casino. The system provided the capability to record the activities shown on videotape for later viewing, or, if necessary, as evidence (e.g. if malfeasance was suspected). The tapes from each camera were retained for a minimum of seven days. But in some cases where problems were identified, the tapes were retained indefinitely. To ensure that the surveillance was done objectively, strict separation was maintained between the personnel working on the casino floor and those working in the surveillance areas.

The Bellagio also used *mystery shoppers* to evaluate the dealers. A mystery shopper evaluated each dealer at least once every 1.5 years. The mystery shoppers evaluated only customer service, not speed. Each dealer was rated as *superior*, *expected*, *needs improvement*, or *unsatisfactory*. Eighty-five percent of the dealers were rated superior or expected. The mystery shoppers revisited the other 15% at a later time. No dealer was ever fired based on the mystery shopper ratings. If the poor performance persisted, supervisors worked with the dealer to improve. Dealers that consistently performed poorly usually did not need to be told; they usually did not get as many customers at their table. Bill Bingham explained, "The mystery shopper program is geared more towards keeping our customer orientation in check rather than being a performance evaluation tool of dealers *per se*."

The levels of casino management above the pit bosses, such as shift managers and the vice president of table games, did little direct supervision of the gaming activity. They were mainly involved in trouble shooting (e.g. resolving cases of malfeasance), keeping good customers happy, resolving special problems that arose (e.g. staffing issues), and improving the casino operations.

D. Monitoring of results

The *master games worksheet* provided three key indicators of the results of the gaming activity: drop, win, and hold percentage.

1. The *drop*, which was essentially the sum of *cash drop* and credit amounts (*markers*), was interpreted as the total amount of money the customers were willing to bet against the casino. However, the drop number had some limitations as an activity indicator of some table games (e.g. blackjack) as it was biased upward when table game players exchanged money for chips at the table but did not bet, thereby creating what was called *false drop*; and it was biased downward when players gambled with chips bought at another table, perhaps even on another shift or day. A better indicator of activity would have been the *handle*, the total value of wagers made, but there was no way to determine this number for blackjack and some other table games.

2. The *win* was the casino's gross profit number. It was calculated as shown in the example above.

3. The *hold* percentage was the primary measure of casino profitability. It was defined as the win divided by the drop.

An example of a *master games worksheet* summary report is shown in Exhibit 10. However, a comprehensive set of reports also was produced that provided these performance measures in various levels of detail, by table, shift, and time period. One such report is shown in Exhibit 11.

Bellagio's management watched the total drop and hold numbers carefully. The drop number was the best available measure of the volume of betting activity, and as such, it was useful as an indicator of the success of the company's marketing strategies and credit policies.

The hold percentage was the best available measure of casino profitability. Using these numbers, Bellagio's management looked for patterns. They knew that each table game should maintain a certain hold percentage; for example, Bellagio's normal table games win percentages were in the range of 18–22% of the table games drop.[9] If the hold percentage was low across the casino table games operation, on all shifts and all tables, and that pattern persisted for a period of, say, several days, the managers in casino operations, including the vice president of table games, had a hard look at the operations and control system to try and tie down the root cause of the unfavorable trend in the hold percentage. Moreover, the drop, win, and hold percentage measures were standard throughout the gaming industry, and competitive analyses were facilitated because summaries were prepared and distributed through several industry sources and trade associations.

The managers in casino operations also looked at the hold generated on each shift in each pit and at each table, but dealers and floor people were not always assigned to the same tables, so management did not have information to tie them to hold percentages. Also, because of the 24-hour drop procedure described above, at least six dealers were at a given table during that time period (that is, at least one dealer and one relief dealer during each shift, times three shifts), and sometimes personnel did not work exact shifts. Thus, Bellagio management did no analysis of results – hold percentage – at the table level. Bill Bingham explained, "We used to monitor the reports on a table-by-table basis, but we never caught anybody doing anything. We did

use surveillance on one dealer whom we suspected, but to no avail."

Pit bosses had to make independent estimates of the drop by shift for each table in their pit, which were reconciled with the actual count. This was done on a so-called *cash drop variance report*, as shown in Exhibit 12. When unusual deviations were observed, game table supervisory personnel, such as the shift manager or even the vice president of table games, could go back and ask the pit personnel to explain why the deviation occurred. Sometimes, the reason for the deviation was just due to a high roller on a hot streak, but if there were any doubts about the explanation, or the deviation could not be pinpointed easily, extra surveillance was called in. Estimated vs. actual data were also aggregated on a daily basis for the Table Games Division as shown in Exhibit 13. This report, as mandated by the GCB, required that a deviation between the actual and estimated drop exceeding +/−10% had to be investigated and explained.

Finally, the GCB required the casino controller to investigate on a monthly basis all statistical fluctuations by game type in excess of +/−5% resulting from the comparison of the previous calendar year to that of the current month. Reasons for the deviations could include the activity of customers whose play materially affected the results of the month (the so-called *high-roller-on-a-hot-streak* explanation); the effects of any changes to the rules, types of wagers, or game play procedures; the effect of any errors or mistakes made during the operation of the game during the month; the effect of any thefts or other improper acts by employees or patrons; or any other unusual occurrences during the month being reviewed.

E. Auditing procedures

As a final control mechanism, personnel independent of the transactions and the accounting thereof were assigned to perform stringent and frequent auditing procedures. There were audits of all types of transactions and their accompanying documentation, such as of transfers and their accompanying fill and credit slips, for one day of each month. The audits involved reconciling each document's multi-part stubs, checking their proper completion and the propriety of signatures, verifying their sequential numbering, and tracing their amounts to the master games worksheet. Any issues, such as unaccounted

---

[9] Normal win percentages in the slot machines area were in the range of 6.5 to 7.5% of slots handle.

for slips or variances between the source documents and the master games worksheet, were investigated, documented, and retained. Other audits involved, for example, the recalculation of the win (loss) for one day of each week. Because of the extensive internal auditing procedures, the internal audit organization of MGM MIRAGE, headed by Robert Rudloff, vice president of internal audit, employed about 63 people.

Bonuses

Results measures were considered in bonuses paid to management personnel. Most executives received annual bonuses averaging about 30% of salary based both on the bottom-line performance of the casino and a set of individual performance objectives. For example, Bill Bingham's annual bonus was based on growth in volume (drop) supplemented with factors that were more difficult to quantify, such as customer relations, employee relations, and/or the successful completion of a casino floor reconfiguration, depending on the focus in any given year. For reasons including lack of control no bonuses were based on win. Bob Rudloff explained, "We obviously don't want games where the win is *too high*, as that might jeopardize the enjoyment guests derive from gambling and coming into our casino in the first place."

Even though the standard measures of performance were important indicators of success, corporate executives were careful not to place too much emphasis on them because they didn't want to encourage casino managers to sacrifice everything for annual bottom-line growth. A good example of a situation where a careful tradeoff was required was customer relations. If a customer had a complaint, casino personnel had to take care to make the customer happy, even at some immediate cost, so that the customer would come back.

There were no bonuses for any other casino personnel, who received only salary and, where applicable, *tokes* (tips). But there were some non-monetary awards, such as employee of the month and employee of the year. For example, dealers with consistently superior mystery shopper ratings could earn this award. Employees of the year were invited to an annual gala honoring all outstanding employees from across all MGM MIRAGE properties.

Future controls

In response to a request for a speculation as to what controls in the casino might look like in the future, Trent Walker, casino controller, responded:

In the table games area, we don't have a detailed understanding of what happens at the tables *as it happens* because we can't track the play at the table. We don't really know how much money we have until we count. In other words, we have no way to account for the inventory of cash when it comes to us; we can only do that 24 hours or so later when the cash comes through the count room. The ultimate form of control for us would be to track every play at the tables, as we can with the slot machines because they are *machines*. If a slot machine over- or underperforms, we can shut it down and fix it. Controls in the slot world are virtually real time.

But even slot machines, I must add, are not without their control failures. A couple of years ago, for example, we encountered a slot scam where an individual had figured out a way to put bills in a slot machine, get them validated, thus receiving credit to play, and yet got the machine to spit the bill back. We just have to live with the fact that there are always people out there trying to rip us off. That's just the nature of this business.

Bill Bingham, vice president of table games, added:

There are new technologies out there that potentially could alter and improve the control environment in the table games area. For example, we could use RFID (radio frequency identification) technology in our chips. If that technology were perfected, that could allow us to track every transaction by every customer at the gaming tables. Then we'd be able to capture a lot of information that would be very valuable for decision-making purposes; e.g. average bets, wins and losses, time played. The better we can identify players' betting patterns, the better we can market to our better customers. But RFID is now only about 75% accurate. We'd need it to be close to (if not exactly) 100% accurate to make it worthwhile.

Bob Rudloff, vice president of internal audit, explained:

We should be able to improve our player ratings. There are essentially four parameters to determine player profiles: the theoretical odds of the game (which we know), the average bet, time played, and the number of decisions (hands) per hour. With this information, we can determine how much a player *should* have won. We currently use this *theoretical* number to comp players. To the extent that we could tie these parameters with precision, however, the better our comp program would perform. A combination of player cards and RFID technology, for example, would make that possible. We would also be able to easily detect counterfeit chips. These are just some of the potential benefits. With these benefits in mind, some casinos have already begun experimenting with RFID.

But we currently have a wait-and-see attitude, as the costs may outweigh the benefits. One obvious cost is the nontrivial expense of replacing all our chips. But there are probably some more subtle, indirect costs too. For example, what will be the *customer impact* of RFID? Having *too much* information – knowing to the penny who wins or loses how much – isn't always the best for the customer. At some point the customers might lose some entertainment value if we monitor every little thing that happens. And we're not sure that we understand all the privacy implications of this just yet. What if the IRS comes to us and asks for this information? We are in the entertainment business, and so we shouldn't do anything that diminishes customer enjoyment.

Control issues and areas for improvement were always being addressed or contemplated, however. Trent Walker explained:

In the surveillance area, our controls are possibly now about as good as they are going to get. We have cameras trained on every game table, and we cover just about every square inch of the casino floor. This has allowed us to do away with certain old-style controls such as pocketless dealer uniforms and human supervision from overhead catwalks or through one-way mirrors. If we suspect foul play by employees or customers, we can always go back to the tape and verify. We are currently digitizing the surveillance recordings. That will allow us to get rid of the tens of thousands of tapes we currently handle, and it will facilitate the streaming and archiving of the recordings.

In the slot machine area, the *hard count* is about to disappear as everything is almost completely ticket-based now. Eliminating the human element in handling and counting coins is both more efficient from a cost perspective and more effective from a control perspective.

But, there are always the inevitable human errors, such as pit personnel signing a marker for the wrong person. Even though this doesn't happen more than a few times a year, it does happen, and the risk of it happening is higher when volumes are up. We don't fire people for making human errors; instead we work with them to prevent the errors from happening again.

As I said, however, there always are, and will be, people trying to rip us off. There are a lot of hands in the pot – dealers, counters, and money strappers. But we are also getting smarter in catching them. For example, dealers and customers working together have pulled off scams where the dealer *simulates* the shuffle so that the customer can count cards. We've done away with that problem through automatic shufflers and regular updates of the shuffle programs. Customers have tried to scratch key cards with a tiny piece of glass glued to their finger. Improved camera surveillance now can catch that too. All in all, I'd say that our controls are very good. We have gone above and beyond mere compliance with what is required by the GCB. We have learned many valuable lessons where we have been burned over the years.

Bob Rudloff concluded with the following observation:

The industry has changed a lot in the last decade or two. Customers used to be interested in the Las Vegas that offered $2.99 buffets and $49.99 rooms, which were part of a gig to tease people onto the casino floor to gamble. In that era, gaming was where the money was made. Today, most of the MGM MIRAGE properties, and many of the properties of our competitors on the Vegas Strip, don't offer such deals anymore. Now we have the $26.99 buffets and $229.99 rooms, yet occupancy rates have stayed about the same, which is remarkable given that total room numbers have gone up dramatically. This tells me that customer tastes have changed. They don't just come to Vegas anymore to gamble; rather, they are attracted by shopping, dining, spas, shows, and entertainment. They want to have a good time; not just gamble. This has resulted in a shift in revenues from gaming to nongaming. Good controls obviously will always be critical in the gaming side of our business, no matter what the shift in proportion of total revenues; it's just good business sense. Strategically, however, our business is not just about controlling the gaming part of revenues any longer.

Exhibit 1 MGM MIRAGE operating casino resorts

Name and location	Number of guestrooms and suites	Approximate Casino square footage	Slots[1]	Gaming tables[2]
Las Vegas Strip, Nevada[3]				
Bellagio	3,933	155,000	2,409	143
MGM Grand Las Vegas	5,044	156,000	2,593	172
Mandalay Bay[4]	4,756	157,000	1,949	127
The Mirage	3,044	118,000	2,056	109
Luxor	4,403	100,000	1,778	88
Treasure Island ("TI")	2,885	90,000	1,800	64
New York-New York	2,024	84,000	1,867	85
Excalibur	3,990	100,000	1,762	73
Monte Carlo	3,002	102,000	1,726	74
Circus Circus Las Vegas[5]	3,764	133,000	2,364	92
Subtotal	36,845	1,195,000	20,304	1,027
Other Nevada				
Primm Valley Resorts (*Primm*)[6]	2,642	137,000	2,854	94
Circus Circus Reno (*Reno*)	1,572	69,000	1,369	52
Silver Legacy – 50% owned (*Reno*)	1,710	87,000	1,707	68
Gold Strike (*Jean*)	811	37,000	737	15
Nevada Landing (*Jean*)	303	36,000	733	14
Colorado Belle (*Laughlin*)	1,173	50,000	1,167	39
Edgewater (*Laughlin*)	1,356	57,000	1,099	33
Railroad Pass (*Henderson*)	120	13,000	347	6
Other domestic operations				
MGM Grand Detroit (*Detroit, Michigan*)	N/A	75,000	2,841	72
Beau Rivage (*Biloxi, Mississippi*)[7]	N/A	N/A	N/A	N/A
Gold Strike (*Tunica, Mississippi*)	1,133	40,000	1,345	48
Borgata – 50% owned (*Atlantic City, New Jersey*)	2,000	125,000	3,572	133
Grand Victoria – 50% owned (*Elgin, Illinois*)	N/A	34,000	1,100	37
Grand total	49,665	1,955,000	39,175	1,638

This table provides certain information about MGM MIRAGE casino resorts as of December 31, 2005. Except as otherwise indicated, MGM MIRAGE wholly owns and operates the resorts.

[1] Includes slot machines, video poker machines and other electronic gaming devices.

[2] Includes blackjack ("21"), baccarat, craps, roulette and other table games; does not include poker.

[3] Excludes Boardwalk, which closed in January 2006.

[4] Includes the Four Seasons Hotel with 424 guest rooms and THEhotel with 1,117 suites.

[5] Includes Slots-a-Fun.

[6] Includes Primm Valley, Buffalo Bill's and Whiskey Pete's, along with the Primm Center gas station and convenience store.

[7] Beau Rivage sustained significant damage in late August 2005 as a result of Hurricane Katrina and has been closed since. We expect to reopen Beau Rivage in the third quarter of 2006.

Source: MGM MIRAGE 2005 Form 10-K.

Exhibit 2 MGM MIRAGE operating results – detailed revenue information

Year ended December 31	2005 $ (000)	Pct. change	2004 $ (000)	Pct. change	2003 $ (000)
Casino revenue, net:					
Table games	$1,140,053	21%	$943,343	9%	$866,096
Slots	1,741,556	43%	1,218,589	9%	1,115,029
Other	100,042	61%	62,033	10%	56,389
Casino revenue, net	2,981,651	34%	2,223,965	9%	2,037,514
Non-Casino revenue:					
Rooms	1,673,696	84%	911,259	9%	833,272
Food and beverage	1,330,210	58%	841,147	11%	757,278
Entertainment, retail and other	1,098,612	58%	696,117	7%	647,702
Noncasino revenue	4,102,518	68%	2,448,523	9%	2,238,252
Total revenue	7,084,169	52%	4,672,488	9%	4,275,766
Less: Promotional allowances	(602,202)	39%	(434,384)	5%	(413,023)
	6,481,967	53%	4,238,104	10%	3,862,743

Table games revenue, including baccarat, was flat on a same-store basis in 2005. A 4% increase in table games volume was offset by a slightly lower hold percentage, though hold percentages were within the normal range for all three years presented. In 2004, table games volume increased 9%, with particular strength in baccarat volume, up 18%. In both 2005 and 2004, key events such as New Year, Chinese New Year and other marketing events, were well-attended.

Slots revenue increased 8% on a same-store basis, following a 9% increase in 2004. Additional volume in 2005 was generated by the Spa Tower at Bellagio – Bellagio's slots revenue increased over 30% – and the traffic generated by KÀ and other amenities at MGM Grand Las Vegas, where slots revenue increased almost 10%. In both periods, MGM MIRAGE benefited from the continued success of our Players Club affinity program and marketing events targeted at repeat customers.

Hotel revenue increased 19% on a same-store basis in 2005. MGM MIRAGE had more rooms available as a result of the Bellagio expansion and 2004 room remodel activity at MGM Grand Las Vegas, and company-wide same-store REVPAR increased 13% to $140 (REVPAR = Revenue per Available Room). This was on top of a 10% increase in 2004 over 2003. The increase in REVPAR in 2005 was entirely rate-driven, as same-store occupancy was consistent at 92%. The 2004 increase was also largely rate-driven.

Source: MGM MIRAGE 2005 Form 10-K.

Exhibit 3 MGM MIRAGE selected financial data

| | For the years ended December 31 (in thousands, except per share data) | | | | |
	2005	2004	2003	2002	2001
Net revenues	$6,481,967	$4,238,104	$3,862,743	$3,756,928	$3,699,852
Operating income	1,357,208	950,860	699,729	746,538	599,892
Income from continuing operations	443,256	349,856	230,273	289,476	160,440
Net income	443,256	412,332	243,697	292,435	169,815
Basic earnings per share					
Income from continuing operations	1.56	1.25	0.77	0.92	0.51
Net income per share	1.56	1.48	0.82	0.93	0.53
Weighted average number of shares	284,943	279,325	297,861	315,618	317,542
Diluted earnings per share					
Income from continuing operations	1.50	1.21	0.76	0.90	0.50
Net income per share	1.50	1.43	0.80	0.91	0.53
Weighted average number of shares	296,334	289,333	303,184	319,880	321,644
At yearend					
Total assets	20,699,420	11,115,029	10,811,269	10,568,698	10,542,568
Total debt, including capital leases	12,358,829	5,463,619	5,533,462	5,222,195	5,465,608
Stockholders' equity	3,235,072	2,771,704	2,533,788	2,664,144	2,510,700
Stockholders' equity per share	11.35	9.87	8.85	8.62	7.98
Number of shares outstanding	285,070	280,740	286,192	309,148	314,792

In June 2003, MGM MIRAGE ceased operations of PLAYMGMMIRAGE.com, the company's online gaming website ("Online"). In January 2004, MGM MIRAGE sold the Golden Nugget Las Vegas and the Golden Nugget Laughlin including substantially all of the assets and liabilities of those resorts (the "Golden Nugget Subsidiaries"). In July 2004, MGM MIRAGE sold the subsidiaries that owned and operated MGM Grand Australia. The results of Online, the Golden Nugget Subsidiaries and MGM Grand Australia are classified as discontinued operations for all periods presented. The Mandalay acquisition occurred on April 25, 2005.

Source: MGM MIRAGE 2005 Form 10-K.

Exhibit 4 **Bellagio Casino Resort: table games organization chart**

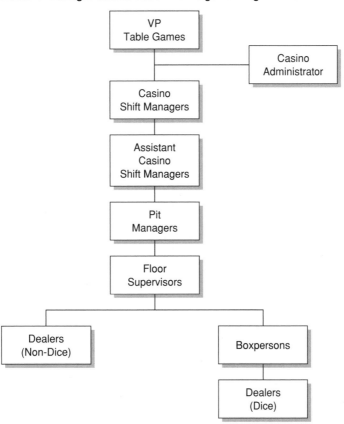

Exhibit 5 Bellagio Casino Resort: finance organization chart

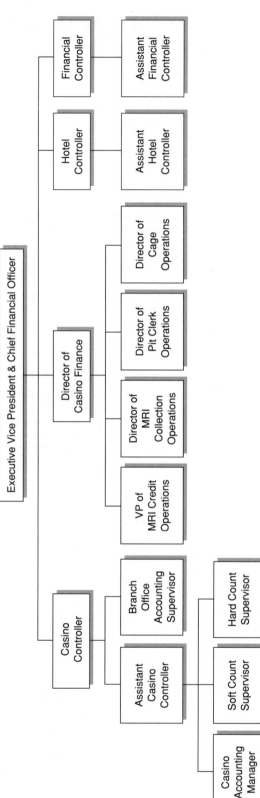

Exhibit 6 Description of Regulations and Licensing by the Nevada Gaming Authorities

The ownership and operation of our casino gaming facilities in Nevada are subject to the Nevada Gaming Control Act and the regulations promulgated thereunder (collectively, the "Nevada Act") and various local regulations. Our gaming operations are subject to the licensing and regulatory control of the Nevada Gaming Commission (the "Nevada Commission"), the Nevada State Gaming Control Board (the "Nevada Board") and various county and city licensing agencies (the "local authorities"). The Nevada Commission, the Nevada Board, and the local authorities are collectively referred to as the "Nevada Gaming Authorities."

The laws, regulations and supervisory procedures of the Nevada Gaming Authorities are based upon declarations of public policy that are concerned with, among other things:

— The prevention of unsavory or unsuitable persons from having a direct or indirect involvement with gaming at any time or in any capacity;

— The establishment and maintenance of responsible accounting practices;

— The maintenance of effective controls over the financial practices of licensees, including the establishment of minimum procedures for internal fiscal affairs and the safeguarding of assets and revenues;

— Providing reliable record keeping and requiring the filing of periodic reports with the Nevada Gaming Authorities;

— The prevention of cheating and fraudulent practices; and

— Providing a source of state and local revenues through taxation and licensing fees.

. . . . .

The Nevada Gaming Authorities may investigate any individual who has a material relationship to, or material involvement with, the registered corporations or any of the licensed subsidiaries to determine whether such individual is suitable or should be licensed as a business associate of a gaming licensee. Officers, directors and certain key employees of the licensed subsidiaries must file applications with the Nevada Gaming Authorities and may be required to be licensed by the Nevada Gaming Authorities. Officers, directors and key employees of the registered corporations who are actively and directly involved in the gaming activities of the licensed subsidiaries may be required to be licensed or found suitable by the Nevada Gaming Authorities. The Nevada Gaming Authorities may deny an application for licensing or a finding of suitability for any cause they deem reasonable. A finding of suitability is comparable to licensing, and both require submission of detailed personal and financial information followed by a thorough investigation. [. . .]

If the Nevada Gaming Authorities were to find an officer, director or key employee unsuitable for licensing or to continue having a relationship with the registered corporations or the licensed subsidiaries, such company or companies would have to sever all relationships with that person. In addition, the Nevada Commission may require the registered corporations or the licensed subsidiaries to terminate the employment of any person who refuses to file appropriate applications. [. . .]

. . . . .

We are required to maintain a current stock ledger in Nevada that may be examined by the Nevada Gaming Authorities at any time. [. . .]

. . . . .

License fees and taxes, computed in various ways depending on the type of gaming or activity involved, are payable to the State of Nevada and to local authorities. Depending upon the particular fee or tax involved, these fees and taxes are [. . .] based upon either:

— A percentage of the gross revenues received;

— The number of gaming devices operated; or

— The number of table games operated.

The tax on gross revenues received is generally 6.75%. A live entertainment tax is also paid on charges for admission to any facility where certain forms of live entertainment are provided.

. . . . .

▶

EXHIBIT 6 *continued*

Because we are involved in gaming ventures outside of Nevada, we are required [. . .] to comply with certain reporting requirements imposed by the Nevada Act. We would be subject to disciplinary action by the Nevada Commission if we:

– Knowingly violate any laws of the foreign jurisdiction pertaining to the foreign gaming operation;

– Fail to conduct the foreign gaming operation in accordance with the standards of honesty and integrity required of Nevada gaming operations;

– Engage in any activity or enter into any association that is unsuitable because it poses an unreasonable threat to the control of gaming in Nevada, reflects or tends to reflect discredit or disrepute upon the State of Nevada or gaming in Nevada, or is contrary to the gaming policies of Nevada;

– Engage in any activity or enter into any association that interferes with the ability of the State of Nevada to collect gaming taxes and fees; or

– Employ, contract with or associate with any person in the foreign gaming operation who has been denied a license or a finding of suitability in Nevada on the ground of personal unsuitability, or who has been found guilty of cheating at gambling.

· · · · ·

[. . .] Pursuant to a 1985 agreement with the United States Department of the Treasury (the "Treasury") and provisions of the Money Laundering Suppression Act of 1994, the Nevada Commission and the Nevada Board have authority, under Regulation 6A of the Nevada Act, to enforce their own cash transaction reporting laws applicable to casinos which substantially parallel the federal Bank Secrecy Act. Under the Nevada Act, the licensed subsidiaries are required to monitor receipts and disbursements of currency related to cash purchases of chips, cash wagers, cash deposits or cash payment of gaming debts in excess of $10,000 in a 24-hour period, and file reports of such transactions with the United States Internal Revenue Service. The licensed subsidiaries are required to file suspicious activity reports with the Treasury and provide copies thereof to the Nevada Board, and are also required to meet the reporting and record keeping requirements of Treasury regulations amended by the USA PATRIOT Act of 2001.

Source: Excerpts from MGM MIRAGE 2005 Form 10-K.

EXHIBIT 7 Bellagio Casino Resort: master games inventory sheet

PIT *4*   SHIFT *swing/gyd*   DATE *1-17-06*

GAME	IOU	100,000	25,000	5,000	1,000	500	100	25	5	1	TOTAL
RW1					77,000	41,500	17,500	6,100	1,200	100	143,400
RW2					67,000	39,000	16,900	7,925	1,285	90	132,200
BJ1					44,000	25,500	12,900	4,100	600	100	87,200
BJ2						21,000	9,200	2,500	900	100	33,700
BJ3					47,000	22,000	10,000	4,100	1,000	100	84,200
BJ4					39,000	26,500	9,600	2,000	600	100	77,800
BJ5					53,000	33,500	8,500	2,000	700	100	97,800
BJ6					48,000	22,000	11,600	3,175	1,230	95	86,100
BJ7											
BJ8					56,000	27,000	9,100	2,200	1,200	100	95,600
BJ9											
BJ10					42,000	23,500	9,400	2,675	770	55	78,400
BJ11					40,000	31,500	10,100	2,200	700	100	84,600
BJ12					52,000	21,500	11,400	1,300	1,100	100	87,400
BJ13					36,000	30,000	9,500	2,975	1,120	105	79,700
BJ14					33,000	17,000	11,900	2,200	700	100	64,900
BJ15					49,000	21,500	9,200	2,800	860	40	83,400
BJ16					42,000	26,000	8,900	2,325	940	35	80,200
BJ17					40,000	23,500	7,500	2,450	865	85	74,400
BJ18					50,000	20,000	10,300	2,850	740	110	84,000
BJ19					43,000	26,500	9,900	3,525	970	105	84,000
BJ20					57,000	27,500	10,800	3,675	495	130	99,600
BJ21					51,000	18,500	11,200	2,275	1,210	115	84,300
BJ22					50,000	23,000	10,000	4,100	730	70	87,900
BJ23					51,000	25,500	8,300	2,725	755	120	88,400
BJ24					34,000	23,000	9,400	2,125	1,155	120	69,800
BJ25					43,000	24,500	7,400	3,525	785	90	79,300
BJ26					59,000	18,000	7,400	2,425	790	85	87,700
BJ27					33,000	22,500	8,500	3,950	810	140	68,900
BJ28					37,000	27,500	10,200	2,625	470	105	77,900
BJ29					36,000	20,000	9,300	4,500	650	50	70,500
BJ30					50,000	24,500	9,800	4,400	785	115	89,600
WPT1					57,000	26,500	10,600	2,300	955	45	97,400
WPT2					44,000	18,500	10,400	1,900	1,400	100	76,300
WR1					52,000	17,000	8,200	2,200	900	100	80,400
TOTAL											*2,797,000*

Incoming *John. W. McIntyre 56941*

Outgoing *Beth. C. Chung 23587*

Note: Numbers on this form were disguised to safeguard company restrictions on the release of internal operating data.

Exhibit 8 Bellagio Casino Resort: fill slip

FILLS	BELLAGIO – RESTRICTED	COPY 1
		DOC. # 7734350

	PIT	02
CLERK ID: ROA	GAME	BJ
DATE: 1/17/06	TABLE	05
TIME: 12:58P	CASE SHIFT	D
	PIT SHIFT	D

	DENOMINATION	AMOUNT
@@@@@@@	100,000.00 ...	.00
@@@@@@@	25,000.00 ...	.00
@@	20,000.00 ...	.00
@@@@@	5,000.00 ...	.00
@@@@@	1,000.00 ...	20,000.00
@@	500.00 ...	10,000.00
@@	100.00 ...	6,000.00
@@	25.00 ...	1,000.00
	5.00 ...	.00
	1.00 ...	40.00
	.50 ...	.00
	.25 ...	.00
		TOTAL 37,040.00

*** NOTIFY SURVEILLANCE ***

Rob Arlington 25891	*Gilbert R. Hall 36582*
CHIP BANK CASHIER	SECURITY GUARD
Mary L. Comben 68752	*Kendall Brooke 65892*
DEALER / BOXPERSON	CASINO SUPERVISOR

F 37040

Note: Numbers on this form were disguised to safeguard company restrictions on the release of internal operating data.

Exhibit 9 Bellagio Casino Resort: soft count room procedures

The soft count supervisor and two count team members had to be present when the soft count room key was obtained from the cage. The soft count supervisor and two count team members had to be present when the keys to remove the full drop boxes from their cart and the keys to remove the drop box contents were obtained from the master vault. The count team then entered the soft count room.

A currency counter was used to count the table game drop proceeds. Immediately prior to beginning the count procedures, a test of the currency counter's accuracy was performed by two count team members using a precounted batch of currency obtained from the master vault consisting of all denominations. The results of the test were recorded on the *grand totals report* produced by the currency counter. The supervisor and one count team member had to sign the report. Quarterly, casino accounting personnel performed unannounced counter tests, the results of which were also documented and maintained.

Each drop box was individually opened and emptied on the count table. The contents of the subsequent drop box to be opened were prohibited from being emptied onto the count table until the previous box's contents had been entirely removed and stored to prevent the commingling of funds between drop boxes. The empty drop box was shown to another count team member and to the surveillance camera to verify that the box was empty. The empty box was then placed in a storage cart. When the storage cart was full of empty drop boxes, it was locked with a padlock. The count team members did not have access to the key for this padlock.

Each drop box's contents were segregated into stacks of currency, chips, and documents. The chips were counted and verified by two count team members, and the chip count was recorded on the back of the so-called *header card*. The header card contained a bar code wherein the table game's pit, game type, and table game number were encoded. The bar code on the header cards were then read by the currency counter's bar code reader and the chip count manually entered into the currency counter.

Currency was prepared for the currency counter and was placed in a rack with the header card. When full, the rack of currency was given to the count team member responsible for operating the currency counter, who placed the currency and header card into the hopper of the currency counter to start the counting. During the operation of the currency counter, count team members other than the count team member operating the currency counter had to witness the loading and unloading of all currency at the currency counter, including rejected currency.[10] The drop box count for each drop box was then individually recorded by denomination and in total in an electronic file generated by the currency counter.

Upon completion of the drop count (currency and chips), the currency counter generated a *master games sheet* that detailed the count by table, denomination, and in total. The master games sheet was then forwarded to a count team member who manually entered the drop count into the computerized *master games worksheet*.

A count team member also individually traced other documents obtained from the drop boxes (fill slips, credit slips, markers) to the master games worksheet. Fill or credit input forms were stapled to their corresponding fill or credit slip. Fill and credit slips also had to be inspected for correctness. Similarly, table inventory sheets reflecting chip inventory counts by table game were examined and traced to the master games worksheet.

Corrections to information, originally input in the computerized master games worksheet were made by inputting the correct figure. An audit trail of corrections was recorded in the computer. Count team members did not have access to the audit trail file. Correction to information originally recorded by the count team on manual soft count documentation were made by crossing out the error, entering the correct figure, and then obtaining the initials of at least two count team members who verified the change.

Upon conclusion of the table games drop count, the soft count supervisor and one other count team member verified and agreed the currency and chip count to the total count as recorded on the master games sheet and master games worksheet. If the totals did not agree, the error had to be located, corrected, and documented. All count team members then signed the master games worksheet certifying the accuracy of the count.

Currency transfers out of the soft count room during the table games soft count process were strictly prohibited. To prepare a transfer, a three-part *transfer slip* was completed with the amount (by denomination and in total) of funds being transferred, dated, and signed (all copies) by the soft count supervisor and one other count team member. Part 3 of the transfer slip was retained in the soft count room. The cash, chips, and parts 1 and 2 of the transfer slip were transferred to the cage where a cage cashier counted the cash and chips, agreed the total to the amount recorded on the transfer slip, and signed to verify that the amounts agree. The cage cashier retained part 2 of the transfer slip, which was later forwarded to the casino accounting department. Part 1 was returned to the soft count room by a soft count team member, matched and agreed to part 3, and both forwarded to casino accounting.

The cage cashier then agreed the currency and chip transfers as recorded on the transfer slip to the drop recorded on the master games worksheet and signed the master games worksheet verifying that the transfer and drop amounts agree. Any variances had to be reconciled and documented. The master games worksheet then had to be returned to the soft count room by a count team member. The cage cashier then assumed accountability of the drop proceeds.

After the entire count was completed, the soft count supervisor locked the soft count room and returned the drop box keys and drop box cart keys to the master vault, after which the soft count supervisor returned the soft count room keys and the master vault keys to the cage. A count member team then promptly transported the master games worksheet and all supporting documents including the transfer slip directly to casino accounting.

---

[10] There were also very stringent procedures to handle rejected currency, which we omit here due to space constraints.

Exhibit 10 Bellagio Casino Resort: master games worksheet summary report

GAME DESC	DROP/HANDLE	WIN/RESULT	%
CRAPS	168,552	9,452	5.61
BLACKJACK	727,508	−124,752	−17.15
PG POKER	78,278	104,748	133.82
RED DOG	0	0	.00
WHEELS	170,218	48,428	28.45
SINGLE RW	33,710	20,610	61.14
BIG SIX	3,364	1,864	55.41
BACCARAT	461,420	55,425	12.01
PAI GOW	5,800	−120	−2.07
MINI BAC	70,828	6,468	9.13
CARRIB ST	19,581	5,323	27.18
LET RIDE	19,815	4,435	22.38
CASINOWAR	13,632	1,312	9.62
3 CARD PK	56,315	14,155	25.14
SIC BO	0	0	.00
CRZY 4 PK	14,066	106	0.75
PYRMD PKR	0	0	.00
HOLD POKER	6,697	3,517	52.52
	1,849,784	**150,971**	**8.16**

Note: Numbers in this table were disguised to safeguard company restrictions on the release of internal operating data.

Exhibit 11 Bellagio Casino Resort: table games daily operating report

BELLAGIO
RESTRICTED – DAILY OPERATING REPORT   April 12, 2006 Wednesday

CASINO REVENUE	2006		2005			BUDGET		
	Today	M.T.D.	M.T.D.	Variance	Var.%	M.T.D.	Variance	Var.%
PIT	1,336,818	9,424,151	7,017,092	2,407,059	34.3	8,900,800	523,351	5.9
KENO	2,523	22,835	83,937	(61,102)	(72.8)	24,000	(1,165)	(4.9)

CASINO DATA	TODAY			2006 MONTH-TO-DATE			2005 MONTH-TO-DATE		
PIT GAMES:	DROP	WIN	WIN%	DROP	WIN	WIN%	DROP	WIN	WIN%
Baccarat	810,560	511,160	63.1	7,915,818	2,236,938	28.3	7,026,171	2,211,900	31.5
Blackjack	1,240,594	192,664	15.5	23,682,129	2,906,769	12.3	19,770,201	2,268,698	11.5
Craps	762,035	389,435	51.1	8,172,150	2,147,850	26.3	6,825,554	1,376,077	20.2
Mini-baccarat	220,602	8,422	3.8	2,303,889	874,109	37.9	1,648,907	268,340	16.3
Wheels	195,169	39,509	20.2	2,768,677	604,277	21.8	2,070,914	504,128	24.3
Single Wheels	96,865	92,765	95.8	977,110	362,110	37.1	466,963	29,458	6.3
Pai Gow	28,245	(16,305)	(57.7)	439,714	39,814	9.1	423,369	102,565	24.2
Pai Gow Poker	135,457	56,237	41.5	1,078,854	156,774	14.5	865,283	364,233	42.1
Caribbean Stud	20,020	7,465	37.3	321,004	81,570	25.4	384,669	102,279	26.6
Let It Ride	20,140	(1,240)	(6.2)	255,806	58,466	22.9	382,297	100,480	26.3
Casino War	10,760	3,500	32.5	249,191	67,061	26.9	279,498	80,066	28.6
Big Six	4,354	434	10.0	67,070	34,010	50.7	70,411	35,467	50.4
3 Card Poker	61,780	36,460	59.0	974,149	365,069	37.5	930,783	266,134	28.6
Crazy 4 Poker	28,645	7,905	27.6	290,074	72,294	24.9	284,393	74,328	26.1
Pyramid Poker	0	0	0.0	0	0	0.0	17,443	8,436	48.4
Hold 'Em Poker	13,587	8,407	61.9	215,928	61,048	28.3	23,275	0	0.0
Sic Bo	0	0	0.0	0	0	0.0	0	0	0.0
Total Pit Games	3,648,813	1,336,818	36.6	49,711,563	10,068,159	20.3	41,470,131	7,792,589	18.8
LESS:									
Discount Accruals		0			(371,008)			(775,107)	
Promotional Expenses		0			(273,000)			(390)	
Net Pit Games		1,336,818			9,424,151			7,017,092	
KENO	4,630	2,523	54.5	66,892	22,835	34.1	278,971	83,937	30.1
CREDIT DROP%	1,251,500	34.3%		17,935,325	36.1%		14,513,079	35.0%	

Note: Numbers in this table were disguised to safeguard company restrictions on the release of internal operating data.

EXHIBIT 12 Bellagio Casino Resort: table games cash drop variance report

| PIT/GAME | ------------------ESTIMATED DROP------------------ | | | | ACTUAL DROP | VARIANCE | VARIANCE % |
TABLE	GRAVE	DAY	SWING	TOTAL			
02 BJ 01	0	0	2,500	2,500	1,840	660	35.87
02 BJ 02	0	0	11,000	11,000	11,030	−30	−0.27
02 BJ 03	0	0	8,000	8,000	6,630	1,370	20.66
02 BJ 04	0	0	6,500	6,500	4,720	1,780	37.71
02 BJ 05	11,000	13,500	6,500	31,000	32,100	−1,100	−3.43
02 BJ 06	7,000	19,000	12,500	38,500	37,480	1,020	2.72
02 BJ 07	6,500	17,000	13,500	37,000	39,220	−2,220	−5.66
02 BJ 08	4,000	11,000	22,500	37,500	40,650	−3,150	−7.75
02 BJ 09	3,000	9,000	6,500	18,500	21,170	−2,670	−12.61
02 BJ 10	6,500	25,000	13,500	45,000	48,680	−3,680	−7.56
02 BJ 11	6,000	22,500	13,500	42,000	45,120	−3,120	−6.91
02 BJ 12	10,500	4,500	11,000	26,000	30,010	−4,010	−13.36
02 BJ 13	0	4,500	4,500	9,000	7,830	1,170	14.94
02 BJ 14	0	12,500	4,500	17,000	14,590	2,410	16.52
02 BJ 15	0	0	0	0	0	0	0.00
02 BJ 16	0	7,000	6,500	13,500	14,430	−930	−6.44
02 BJ 17	0	0	0	0	0	0	0.00
02 BJ 18	0	4,500	11,500	16,000	20,720	−4,720	−22.78
02 BJ 19	0	2,000	8,000	10,000	13,990	−3,990	−28.52
02 BJ 20	14,500	2,500	11,500	28,500	34,970	−6,470	−18.50
02 BJ 21	12,500	16,000	9,000	37,500	37,400	100	0.27
02 BJ 22	0	0	4,500	4,500	3,860	640	16.58
02 BJ 23	0	0	0	0	0	0	0.00
02 BJ 24	0	0	0	0	0	0	0.00

Note: Numbers in this table were disguised to safeguard company restrictions on the release of internal operating data.

Exhibit 13 Bellagio Casino Resort: table games cash drop estimate vs. actual comparison

Gaming Date: 10-Apr-06

Statistics:	DROP	CASH	Total WIN
Estimate	3,679,800	1,841,800	607,810
Actual	3,853,027	2,003,027	784,621
Estimate Variance:			
Dollars	(173,227)	(161,227)	(176,811)
Percentage	−4. 5%	−8.0%	−22.5%

Instructions: When the <u>Cash Drop</u> Variance Percentage exceeds 10%, the cause for the variance must be researched and the resulting findings explained in the space provided below. Your response should be received by Casino Accounting within two (2) days of your receipt of this report.

Cash Drop Variance Explanation:

Signature of Responding TG Executive: _____

Date: _____

Note: Numbers on this form were disguised to safeguard company restrictions on the release of internal operating data.

The Lincoln Electric Company

We're not a marketing company, we're not an R&D company, and we're not a service company. We're a manufacturing company, and I believe that we are the best manufacturing company in the world.

With these words, George E. Willis, president of The Lincoln Electric Company, described what he saw as his company's distinctive competence. For more than 30 years, Lincoln had been the world's largest manufacturer of arc welding products (Exhibit 1). In 1974, the company was believed to have manufactured more than 40% of the arc welding equipment and supplies sold in the United States. In addition to its welding products Lincoln produced a line of three-phase alternating-current industrial electric motors, but these accounted for less than 10% of sales and profits.

Lincoln's 1974 domestic net income was $17.5 million on sales of $232 million (Exhibit 2).

Perhaps more significant than a single year's results was Lincoln's record of steady growth over the preceding four decades, as shown in Figure 1.

During this period, after-tax return on equity had ranged between 10% and 15%. Lincoln's growth had been achieved without benefit of acquisition and had been financed with internally generated funds. The company's historical dividend payout policy had been to pay to the suppliers of capital a fair return each year for its use.

COMPANY HISTORY

Lincoln Electric was founded by John C. Lincoln in 1895 to manufacture electric motors and generators. James F. Lincoln, John's younger brother, joined the company in 1907. The brothers' skills and interests were complementary. John was a technical genius.

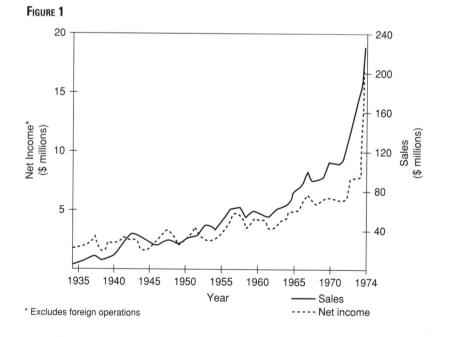

FIGURE 1

* Excludes foreign operations

Sales
Net income

This case was prepared by research assistant Norman Fast under the direction of Professor Norman Berg.

During his lifetime he was awarded more than 50 patents for inventions as diverse as an apparatus for curing meat, an electric drill, a mine-door-activating mechanism, and an electric arc lamp. James's skills were in management and administration. He began as a salesman but soon took over as general manager. The Lincoln Electric Company was undeniably built in his image.

In 1911, the company introduced its first arc welding machine. Both brothers were fascinated by welding, which was then in its infancy. They recognized it as an alternative use for the motor-generator sets they were already producing to recharge the batteries for electric automobiles. The success of Ford, Buick, and others indicated that the days of the electric auto might be numbered, and the brothers were anxious to find other markets for their skills and products.

John's mechanical talents gave the company a head start in welding machines which it never relinquished. He developed a portable welding machine (a significant improvement over existing stationary models) and incorporated a transformer to allow regulation of the current. As his biographer noted, "This functional industrial development gave Lincoln Electric a lead in the field that it has always maintained, although the two giants – Westinghouse and General Electric – soon entered the market."[1]

By World War II, Lincoln Electric was the leading American manufacturer of arc welding equipment. Because of the importance of welding to the war effort, the company stopped producing electric motors and devoted its full capacity to welding products. Demand continued to outpace production, and the government asked the welding equipment manufacturers to add capacity. As described by Lincoln's president, George Willis:

> Mr. Lincoln responded to the government's call by going to Washington and telling them that there was enough manufacturing capacity but it was being used inefficiently by everyone. He offered to share proprietary manufacturing methods and equipment designs with the rest of the industry. Washington took him up on it and that solved the problem. As a result of Mr. Lincoln's patriotic decision, our competitors had costs which were close to ours for a short period after the war, but we soon were outperforming them like before.

In 1955, Lincoln once again began manufacturing electric motors, and since then its position in the market had expanded steadily.

Through the years, Lincoln stock had been sold to employees and associates of the Lincoln brothers. In 1975, approximately 48% of employees were shareholders. About 80% of the outstanding stock was held by employees, the Lincoln family, and their foundations.

In its 80-year history, Lincoln had had only three board chairmen: John C. Lincoln, James F. Lincoln, and William Irrgang, who became chairman in 1972.

STRATEGY

Lincoln Electric's strategy was simple and unwavering. The company's strength was in manufacturing. Management believed that Lincoln could build quality products at a lower cost than their competitors. Their strategy was to concentrate on reducing costs and passing the savings through to the customer by continuously lowering prices. Management had adhered to this policy even when products were on allocation because of shortages in productive capacity. The result had been an expansion of both market share and primary demand for arc welding equipment and supplies over the past half century. Lincoln's strategy had also encouraged the exit of several major companies (including General Electric) from the industry and had caused others to seek more specialized market niches.

Management believed its incentive system and the climate it fostered were responsible in large part for the continual increase in productivity upon which this strategy depended. Under the Lincoln incentive system, employees were handsomely rewarded for their productivity, high quality, cost reduction ideas, and individual contributions to the company. Yearend bonuses averaged close to 100% of regular compensation, and some workers on the factory floor had earned more than $45,000 in a single year.[2]

Lincoln's strategy had remained virtually unchanged for decades. In a 1947 Harvard Business School case study on the company, James F. Lincoln described the firm's strategy as follows:

---

[1] Raymond Moley, *The American Century of John C. Lincoln* (New York: Duell, Sloan & Pearce, 1962), p. 71.

[2] By contrast, the median income for US manufacturing employees in 1974 was less than $9,200, according to Bureau of Labor Statistics data.

It is the job of The Lincoln Electric Company to give its customers more and more of a better product at a lower and lower price. This will also make it possible for the company to give to the worker and the stockholder a higher and higher return.

In 1975, Chairman William Irrgang's description was remarkably similar:

The success of The Lincoln Electric Company has been built on two basic ideas. One is producing more and more of a progressively better product at a lower and lower price for a larger and larger group of customers. The other is that an employee's earnings and promotion are in direct proportion to his individual contribution toward the company's success.[3]

Management felt it had achieved an enviable record in following this strategy faithfully and saw no need to modify it in the future. Lincoln Electric's record of increasing productivity and declining costs and prices is shown in Exhibit 3.

COMPANY PHILOSOPHY

Lincoln Electric's corporate strategy was rooted in the management philosophy of James F. Lincoln, a rugged individualist who believed that through competition and adequate incentives every person could develop to his or her fullest potential. In one of his numerous books and articles he wrote:

Competition is the foundation of man's development. It has made the human race what it is. It is the spur that makes progress. Every nation that has eliminated it as the controlling force in its economy has disappeared, or will. We will do the same if we eliminate it by trying to give security, and for the same reason. Competition means that there will be losers as well as winners in the game. Competition will mean the disappearance of the lazy and incompetent, be they workers, industrialists, or distributors. Competition promotes progress. Competition determines who will be the leader. It is the only known way that leadership and progress can be developed if history means anything. It is a hard taskmaster. It is completely necessary for anyone, be he worker, user, distributor or boss, if he is to grow.

If some way could be found so that competition could be eliminated from life, the result would be disastrous. Any nation and any people disappear if life becomes too easy. There is no danger from a hard life as all history shows. Danger is from a life that is made soft by lack of competition.[4]

Lincoln's faith in the individual was almost unbounded. His personal experience with the success of Lincoln Electric reinforced his faith in what could be accomplished under the proper conditions. In 1951 he wrote:

Development in many directions is latent in every person. The difficulty has been that few recognize that fact. Fewer still will put themselves under the pressure or by chance are put under the pressure that will develop them greatly. Their latent abilities remain latent, hence useless . . .

It is of course obvious that the development of man, on which the success of incentive management depends, is a progressive process. Any results, no matter how good, that come from the application of incentive management cannot be considered final. There will always be greater growth of man under continued proper incentive . . .

Such increase of efficiency poses a very real problem to management. The profit that will result from such efficiency obviously will be enormous. The output per dollar of investment will be many times that of the usual shop which practices output limitation. The labor cost per piece will be relatively small and the overhead will be still less.

The profits at competitive selling prices resulting from such efficiency will be far beyond any possible need for proper return and growth of an industry . . .

How, then, should the enormous extra profit resulting from incentive management be split? The problems that are inherent in incentive dictate the answer. If the worker does not get a proper share, he does not desire to develop himself or his skill. Incentive, therefore, would not succeed. The worker must have a reward that he feels is commensurate with his contribution.

If the customer does not have a part of the saving in lower prices, he will not buy the increased output. The size of the market is a decisive factor in costs of products. Therefore, the consumer must get a proper share of the saving.

Management and ownership are usually considered as a unit. This is far from a fact, but in the problem here, they can be considered together. They must get a part of the saving in larger salaries and perhaps larger dividends.

There is no hard and fast rule to cover this division, other than the following. The worker (which includes management), the customer, the owner, and all those

---

[3] *Employee's Handbook* (Cleveland: The Lincoln Electric Company, 1974).

[4] James F. Lincoln, *Incentive Management* (Cleveland: The Lincoln Electric Company, 1951), p. 33.

involved must be satisfied that they are properly recognized or they will not cooperate, and cooperation is essential to any and all successful applications of incentives.[5]

Additional comments by James F. Lincoln are presented in Exhibit 4.

COMPENSATION POLICIES

Compensation policies were the key element of James F. Lincoln's philosophy of "incentive management." Lincoln Electric's compensation system had three components:

- wages based solely on piecework output for most factory jobs;
- a yearend bonus which could equal or exceed an individual's full annual regular pay; and
- guaranteed employment for all workers.

Almost all production workers at Lincoln were paid on a straight piecework plan. They had no base salary or hourly wage but were paid a set "price" for each item they produced. William Irrgang explained:

> Wherever practical, we use the piecework system. This system can be effective, and it can be destructive. The important part of the system is that it is completely fair to the worker. When we set a piecework price, that price cannot be changed just because, in management's opinion, the worker is making too much money. Whether he earns two times or three times his normal amount makes no difference. Piecework prices can only be changed when management has made a change in the method of doing that particular job and under no other conditions. If this is not carried out 100%, piecework cannot work.
>
> Today piecework is confined to production operations, although at one time we also used it for work done in our stenographic pool. Each typewriter was equipped with a counter that registered the number of times the typewriter keys were operated. This seemed to work all right for a time until it was noticed that one girl was earning much more than any of the others. This was looked into, and it was found that this young lady ate her lunch at her desk, using one hand for eating purposes and the other for punching the most convenient key on the typewriter as fast as she could; which simply goes to show that no matter how good a program you may have, it still needs careful supervision.[6]

A Time Study Department established piecework prices which were guaranteed by the company, until methods were changed or a new process introduced. Employees could challenge the price if they felt it was unfair. The Time Study Department would then retime the job and set a new rate. This could be higher or lower but was still open to challenge if an employee remained dissatisfied. Employees were expected to guarantee their own quality. They were not paid for defective work until it had been repaired on their own time.

Each job in the company was rated according to skill, required effort, responsibility, and so on, and a base wage rate for the job was assigned. Wage rates were comparable to those for similar jobs in the Cleveland area and were adjusted annually on the basis of Department of Labor statistics and quarterly to reflect changes in the cost of living. In this way, salaries or hourly wages were determined. For piecework jobs, the Time Study Department set piece prices so that an employee producing at a standard rate would earn the base rate for his or her job.

The second element of the compensation system was a year-end bonus, which had been paid each year since 1934. As explained in the *Employee's Handbook*, "The bonus, paid at the discretion of the company, is not a gift, but rather it is the sharing of the results of efficient operation on the basis of the contribution of each person to the success of the company for that year." In 1974, the bonus pool totaled $26 million, an average of approximately $10,700 per employee, or 90% of prebonus wages.

The total amount to be paid out in bonuses each year was determined by the board of directors. Lincoln's concentration on cost reduction kept costs low enough that prices could generally be set (and not upset by competition) on the basis of costs at the beginning of the year to produce a target return for stockholders and to give employees a bonus of approximately 100% of wages. The variance from the planned profits was usually added to (or subtracted from) the bonus pool to be distributed at yearend. Since 1945, the average bonus had varied from 78% to 129% of wages. In the past few years, it had been between 40% and 55% of pretax, prebonus profit, or as high as twice the net income after taxes.

An individual's share of the bonus pool was determined by a semiannual "merit rating" which measured individual performance compared to that of other members of the department or work group.

[5] Ibid., pp. 7–11.
[6] William Irrgang, "The Lincoln Incentive Management Program," Lincoln Lecture Series, Arizona State University, 1972, p. 13.

Ratings for all employees had to average out to 100 on this relative scale. If, because of some unusual contribution, an individual deserved a rating above 110, he or she could be rewarded from a special corporate pool of bonus points, without any penalty to coworkers. Ratings above 110 were thus reviewed by a corporate committee or vice presidents who evaluated the individual's contribution. Merit ratings varied widely, from as low as 45 to as high as 160.

In determining an employee's merit rating, four factors were evaluated separately:

- dependability
- quality
- output
- ideas and cooperation.

Foremen were responsible for the rating of all factory workers. They could request help from assistant foremen (dependability), the Production Control Department (output), the Inspection Department (quality), and the Methods Department (ideas and cooperation). In the office, supervisors rated their people on the same items. At least one executive reviewed all ratings. All employees were urged to discuss their ratings with their department heads if they were dissatisfied or unclear about them.

Lincoln complemented its rating and pay system with a Guaranteed Continuous Employment Plan. This plan provided security against layoffs and assured continuity of employment. Every full-time employee who had been with the company at least two years was guaranteed employment for at least 75% of the standard 40-hour week. In fact, the company had not had any layoffs since 1951 when initial trials for the plan were put into effect. It was formally established in 1958.

The guarantee of employment was seen by the company as an essential element in the incentive plan. Without such a guarantee, it was believed that employees would be more likely to resist improved production and efficiency for fear of losing their jobs. In accepting the guaranteed continuous employment plan, employees agreed to perform any job that was assigned as conditions required, and to work overtime during periods of high activity.

The philosophy and procedures regarding the incentive plan were the same for management and workers, except that William Irrgang and George Willis did not share in the bonus.

EMPLOYEE VIEWS

To the researchers, it appeared that employees generally liked working at Lincoln. The employee turnover rate was far below that of most other companies, and once a new employee made it through the first month or so, he rarely left for another firm (see Exhibit 5). One employee explained, "It's like trying out for a high school football team. If you make it through the first few practices, you're usually going to stay the whole season, especially after the games start."

One long-time employee who liked working at Lincoln was John "Tiny" Carrillo, an armature bander on the welding machine line, who had been with the company for 24 years. Tiny explained why:

> The thing I like here is that you're pretty much your own boss as long as you do your job. You're responsible for your own work and you even put your stencil on every machine you work on. That way if it breaks down in the field and they have to take it back, they know who's responsible.
>
> Before I came here, I worked at Cadillac as a welder. After two months there I had the top hourly rate. I wasn't allowed to tell anyone because there were guys who still had the starting rate after a year. But, I couldn't go any higher after two months.
>
> I've done well. My rating is usually around 110, but I work hard, right through the smoke breaks. The only time I stop is a half hour for lunch. I make good money. I have two houses, one which I rent out, and four cars. They're all paid for. When I get my bills, I pay them the next day. That's the main thing, I don't owe anyone.
>
> Sure, there are problems. There's sometimes a bind between the guys with low grades and the guys with high ones, like in school. And there are guys who sway everything their way so they'll get the points, but they [management] have good tabs on what's going on . . .
>
> A lot of new guys come in and leave right away. Most of them are just mamma's boys and don't want to do the work. We had a new guy who was a produce manager at a supermarket. He worked a couple of weeks, then quit and went back to his old job.

At the end of the interview, the researcher thanked Tiny for his time. He responded by pointing out that it had cost him $7.00 in lost time, but that he was glad to be of assistance.

Another piece worker, Jorge Espinoza, a fine-wire operator in the Electrode Division, had been with the company for six years. He explained his feelings:

> I believe in being my own man. I want to use my drive for my own gain. It's worked. I built my family a house and have an acre of land, with a low mortgage. I have a car and an old truck I play around with. The money I get is because I earn it. I don't want anything given to me.
>
> The thing I don't like is having to depend on other people on the line and suppliers. We're getting bad steel occasionally. Our output is down as a result and my rating will suffer.
>
> There are men who have great drive here and can push for a job. They are not leaders and never will be, but they move up. That's a problem . . .
>
> The first few times around, the ratings were painful for me. But now I stick near 100. You really make what you want. We just had a methods change and our base rate went from 83 to 89 coils a day. This job is tougher now and more complex. But, it's all what you want. If you want 110 coils you can get it. You just take less breaks. Today, I gambled and won. I didn't change my dies and made over a hundred coils. If I had lost, and the die plugged up, it would have cost me at least half an hour. But, today I made it.

MANAGEMENT STYLE

Lincoln's incentive scheme was reinforced by top management's attitude toward the men on the factory floor. In 1951, James Lincoln wrote:

> It becomes perfectly true to anyone who will think this thing through that there is no such thing in an industrial activity as Management and Men having different functions or being two different kinds of people. Why can't we think and why don't we think that all people are Management? Can you imagine any president of any factory or machine shop who can go down and manage a turret lathe as well as the machinist can? Can you imagine any manager of any organization who can go down and manage a broom – let us get down to that – who can manage a broom as well as a sweeper can? Can you imagine any secretary of any company who can go down and fire a furnace and manage that boiler as well as the man who does the job? Obviously, all are Management.[7]

Lincoln's president, George Willis, stressed the equality in the company:

> We try to avoid barriers between management and workers. We're treated equally as much as possible. When I got to work this morning at 7:30, the parking lot was three quarters full. I parked way out there like anyone else would. I don't have a special reserved spot. The same principle holds true in our cafeteria. There's no executive dining room. We eat with everyone else.[8]

Willis felt that open and frank communication between management and workers had been a critical factor in Lincoln's success, and he believed that the company's Advisory Board, consisting of elected employee representatives, had played a very important role in achieving this. Established by James F. Lincoln in 1914, the board met twice a month, providing a forum in which employees could bring issues of concern to top management's attention, question company policies, and make suggestions for their improvement. As described in the *Employee's Handbook*:

> Board service is a privilege and responsibility of importance to the entire organization. In discussions or in reaching decisions Board members must be guided by the best interests of the Company. These also serve the best interests of its workers. They should seek at all times to improve the cooperative attitude of all workers and see that all realize they have an important part in our final results.

All Advisory Board meetings were chaired by either the chairman or the president of Lincoln. Usually both were present. Issues brought up at board meetings were either resolved on the spot or assigned to an executive. After each meeting, William Irrgang or George Willis would send a memo to the executive responsible for each unanswered question, no matter how trivial, and he was expected to respond by the next meeting if possible.

Minutes of all board meetings were posted on bulletin boards in each department and members explained the board's actions to the other workers in their department. The questions raised in the minutes of a given meeting were usually answered in the next set of minutes. This procedure had not changed significantly since the first meeting in

---

[7] James F. Lincoln. *What Makes Workers Work?* (Cleveland: The Lincoln Electric Company, 1951), pp. 3–4.

[8] The cafeteria had large rectangular and round tables. In general, factory workers gravitated toward the rectangular tables. There were no strict rules, however, and management personnel often sat with factory workers. Toward the center was a square table that seated only four. This was reserved for William Irrgang, George Willis, and their guests when they were having a working lunch.

1914, and the types of issues raised had remained much the same (see Exhibit 6).

Workers felt that the Advisory Board provided a way of getting immediate attention for their problems. It was clear, however, that management still made the final decisions.[9] A former member of the Advisory Board commented:

> There are certain areas which are brought up in the meetings which Mr. Irrgang doesn't want to get into. He's adept at steering the conversation away from these. It's definitely not a negotiating meeting. But, generally, you really get action or an answer on why action isn't being taken.

In addition to the Advisory Board, there was a 12-member board of middle managers which met with Irrgang and Willis once a month. The topics discussed here were broader than those of the Advisory Board. The primary function of these meetings was to allow top management to get better acquainted with these individuals and to encourage cooperation between departments.

Lincoln's two top executives, Irrgang and Willis, continued the practice of James F. Lincoln in maintaining an open door to all employees. George Willis estimated that at least twice a week factory employees took advantage of this opportunity to talk with him.

Middle managers also felt that communication with Willis and Irrgang was open and direct. Often it bypassed intermediate levels of the organization. Most saw this as an advantage, but one commented:

> This company is run strictly by the two men at the top. Mr. Lincoln trained Mr. Irrgang in his image. It's very authoritarian and decisions flow top down. It never became a big company. There is very little delegated and top people are making too many small decisions. Mr. Irrgang and Mr. Willis work 80 hours a week, and no one I know in this company can say that his boss doesn't work harder than he does.

Willis saw management's concern for the worker as an essential ingredient in his company's formula for success. He knew at least 500 employees personally. In leading the researcher through the plant,

he greeted workers by name and paused several times to tell anecdotes about them.

At one point, an older man yelled to Willis good-naturedly, "Where's my raise?" Willis explained that this man had worked for 40 years in a job requiring him to lift up to 20 tons of material a day. His earnings had been quite high because of his rapid work pace, but Willis had been afraid that as he was advancing in age he could injure himself working in that job. After months of Willis's urging, the worker switched to an easier but lower paying job. He was disappointed in taking the earnings cut and even after several years let the president know whenever he saw him.

Willis pointed out another employee, whose wife had recently died, and noted that for several weeks he had been drinking heavily and reporting to work late. Willis had earlier spent about half an hour discussing the situation with him to console him and see if the company could help in any way. He explained:

> I made a definite point of talking to him on the floor of the plant, near his work station. I wanted to make sure that other employees who knew the situation could see me with him. Speaking to him had symbolic value. It is important for employees to know that the president is interested in their welfare.

Management's philosophy was also reflected in the company's physical facilities. A no-nonsense atmosphere was firmly established at the gate to the parking lot where the only mention of the company name was in a sign reading:

> $1,000 REWARD for information leading to the arrest and conviction of persons stealing from the Lincoln Electric parking lot.

There was a single entrance to the offices and plant for workers, management, and visitors. Entering, one could not avoid being struck by the company motto, in large stainless steel letters extending 30 feet across the wall:

THE ACTUAL IS LIMITED
THE POSSIBLE IS IMMENSE

A flight of stairs led down to a tunnel system for pedestrian traffic which ran under the single-story plant. At the base of the stairs was a large bronze plaque on which were inscribed the names of the 8 employees who had served more than 50 years,

---

[9] In some cases, management allowed issues to be decided by a vote of employees. Recently, for example, employees had voted down a proposal that the company give them dental benefits, recognizing that the cost of the program would come directly out of their bonuses.

and the more than 350 active employees with 25 or more years of service (the Quarter Century Club).

The long tunnel leading to the offices was clean and well lit. The executive offices were located in a windowless, two-story cement-block office building which sat like a box in the center of the plant. At the base of the staircase leading up to the offices, a Lincoln automatic welding machine and portraits of J. C. Lincoln and J. F. Lincoln welcomed visitors. The handrail on the staircase was welded into place, as were the ashtrays in the tunnel.

In the center of the office building was a simple, undecorated reception room. A switchboard operator/receptionist greeted visitors between filing and phone calls. Throughout the building, decor was Spartan. The reception room was furnished with a metal coat rack, a wooden bookcase, and several plain wooden tables and chairs. All of the available reading material dealt with Lincoln Electric Company or welding.

From the reception room, seven doors each led almost directly to the various offices and departments. Most of the departments were large open rooms with closely spaced desks. One manager explained that "Mr. Lincoln didn't believe in walls. He felt they interrupted the flow of communications and paperwork." Most of the desks and files were plain, old, and well worn, and there was little modern office equipment. Expenditures on equipment had to meet the same criteria in the office as in the plant: the Maintenance Department had to certify that the equipment replaced could not be repaired, and any equipment acquired for cost reduction had to have a one-year payback.[10] Even Xerox machines were nowhere to be found. Copying costs were tightly controlled and only certain individuals could use the Xerox copiers. Customer order forms which required eight copies were run on a duplicating machine, for example.

The private offices were small, uncarpeted, and separated by green metal partitions. The president's office was slightly larger than the others, but still retained a Spartan appearance. There was only one carpeted office. Willis explained: "That office was occupied by Mr. Lincoln until he died in 1965. For the next five years it was left vacant and now it is Mr. Irrgang's office and also the Board of Directors' and Advisory Board meeting room."

PERSONNEL

Lincoln Electric had a strict policy of filling all but entry level positions by promoting from within the company. Whenever an opening occurred, a notice was posted on the 25 bulletin boards in the plant and offices. Any interested employee could apply for an open position. Because of the company's sustained growth and policy of promoting from within, employees had substantial opportunity for advancement.

An outsider generally could join the company in one of two ways: either taking a factory job at an hourly or piece rate, or entering Lincoln's training programs in sales or engineering.[11] The company recruited its trainees at colleges and graduate schools, including Harvard Business School. Starting salary in 1975 for a trainee with a bachelor's degree was $5.50 an hour plus a yearend bonus at an average of 40% of the normal rate. Wages for trainees with either a master's degree or several years of relevant experience were 5% higher.

Although Lincoln's president, vice president of sales, and personnel director were all Harvard Business School graduates, the company had not hired many recent graduates. Clyde Loughridge, the personnel director, explained:

> We don't offer them fancy staff positions and we don't pretend to. Our starting pay is less than average, probably $17,000–$18,000[12] including bonus, and the work is harder than average. We start our trainees off by putting them in overalls and they spend up to seven weeks in the welding school. In a lot of ways it's like boot camp. Rather than leading them along by the hand, we like to let the self-starters show themselves.

The policy of promoting from within had rarely been violated, and then only in cases where a specialized skill was required. Loughridge commented:

---

[10] Willis explained that capital projects with paybacks of up to two years were sometimes funded when they involved a product for which demand was growing.

[11] Lincoln's chairman and president both advanced through the ranks in Manufacturing. Irrgang began as a pieceworker in the Armature Winding Department, and Willis began in Plant Engineering. (See Exhibit 7 for employment history of Lincoln's top management.)

[12] In 1975, the median starting salary for Harvard Business School graduates who took positions in industrial manufacturing was $19,800.

In most cases we've been able to stick to it, even where the required skills are entirely new to the company. Our employees have a lot of varied skills, and usually someone can fit the job. For example, when we recently got our first computer, we needed a programmer and systems analyst. We had 20 employees apply who had experience or training in computers. We chose two, and it really helps that they know the company and understand our business.

The company did not send its employees to outside management development programs and did not provide tuition grants for educational purposes.

Lincoln Electric had no formal organization chart and management did not feel that one was necessary. (The chart in Exhibit 8 was drawn for the purposes of this case.) As explained by one executive:

> People retire and their jobs are parceled out. We are very successful in overloading our overhead departments. We make sure this way that no unnecessary work is done and jobs which are not absolutely essential are eliminated. A disadvantage is that planning may suffer, as may outside development to keep up with your field.

Lincoln's organizational hierarchy was flat, with few levels between the bottom and the top. For example, Don Hastings, the vice president of sales, had 37 regional sales managers reporting to him. He commented:

> I have to work hard, there's no question about that. There are only four of us in the home office plus two secretaries. I could easily use three more people. I work every Saturday, at least half a day. Most of our regional men do too, and they like me to know it. You should see the switchboard light up when 37 regional managers call in at five minutes to twelve on Saturday.

The president and chairman kept a tight rein over personnel matters. All changes in status of employees, even at the lowest levels, had to be approved by Willis. Irrgang also had to give his approval if salaried employees were involved. Raises or promotions had to be approved in advance. An employee could be fired by his supervisor on the spot for cause, but if the grounds were questionable, the decision had to be approved afterward by either Willis or Irrgang. Usually the supervisor was supported, but there had been cases where a firing decision was reversed.

MARKETING

Welding machines and electrodes were like razors and razor blades. A Lincoln welding machine often had a useful life of 30 years or more, while electrodes (and fluxes) were consumed immediately in the welding process. The ratio of machine cost to annual consumables cost varied widely, from perhaps 7:1 for a hand welder used in a small shop to 1:5 or more for an automatic welder used in a shipyard.

Although certain competitors might meet Lincoln's costs and quality in selected products, management believed that no company could match the line overall. Another important competitive edge for Lincoln was its sales force. Al Patnik, vice president of sales development, explained:

> Most competitors operate through distributors. We have our own top field sales force.[13] We start out with engineering graduates and put them through our seven-month training program. They learn how to weld, and we teach them everything we can about equipment, metallurgy, and design. Then they spend time on the rebuild line [where machines brought in from the field are rebuilt] and even spend time in the office seeing how orders are processed. Finally, before the trainees go out into the field, they have to go into our plant and find a better way of making something. Then they make a presentation to Mr. Irrgang, just as if he were one of our customers.
>
> Our approach to the customer is to go in and learn what he is doing and show him how to do it better. For many companies our people become their experts in welding. They go in and talk to a foreman. They might say, "Let me put on a headshield and show you what I'm talking about." That's how we sell them.

George Ward, a salesman in the San Francisco office, commented:

> The competition hires graduates with business degrees (without engineering backgrounds) and that's how they get hurt. This job is getting more technical every day . . . A customer in California who is using our equipment to weld offshore oil rigs had a problem with one of our products. I couldn't get the solution for them over the phone, so I flew in to the plant Monday morning and showed it to our engineers. Mr. Willis said to me, "Don't go back to California until this problem is solved . . ." We use a "working together to

---

[13] The sales force was supplemented in some areas by distributors. Sales abroad were handled by wholly owned subsidiaries or Armco's International Division.

solve your problem" approach. This, plus sticking to published prices, shows you're not interested in taking advantage of them.

I had a boss who used to say: "Once we're in, Lincoln never loses a customer except on delivery." It's basically true. The orders I lost last year were because we couldn't deliver fast enough. Lincoln gets hurt when there are shortages because of our guaranteed employment. We don't hire short-term factory workers when sales take off, and other companies beat us on delivery.

The sales force was paid a salary plus bonus. Ward believed that Lincoln's sales force was the best paid and hardest working in the industry. He said, "We're aggressive, and want to work and get paid for it. The sales force prides itself on working more hours than anyone else ... My wife wonders sometimes if you can work for Lincoln and have a family too."

MANUFACTURING

Lincoln's plant was unusual in several respects. It seemed crowded with materials and equipment, with surprisingly few workers. It was obvious that employees worked very fast and efficiently with few breaks. Even during the 10-minute smoke breaks in the morning and afternoon, employees often continued to work.

An innovative plant layout was partly responsible for the crowded appearance. Raw materials entered one side of the plant and finished goods came out the other side. There was no central stockroom for materials or work-in-process. Instead, everything that entered the plant was transported directly to the work station where it would be used. At a work station, a single worker or group operated in effect as a subcontractor. All required materials were piled around the station, allowing visual inventory control, and workers were paid a piece price for their production. Wherever possible, the work flow followed a straight line through the plant from the side where raw materials entered to the side where finished goods exited. Because there was no union, the company had great flexibility in deciding what could be performed at a work station. For example, foundry work and metal stamping could be carried out together by the same workers when necessary. Thus, work could flow almost directly along a line through the plant. Intermediate material handling

was avoided to a great extent. The major exception arose when multiple production lines shared a large or expensive piece of machinery, and the work had to be brought to the machines.

Many of the operations in the plant were automated. Much of the manufacturing equipment was proprietary,[14] designed and built by Lincoln. In some cases, the company had modified machines built by others to run two or three times as fast as when originally delivered.

From the time a product was first conceived, close coordination was maintained between product design engineers and the Methods Department; this was seen as a key factor in reducing costs and rationalizing manufacturing. William Irrgang explained:

> After we have [an] idea ... we start thinking about manufacturing costs, before anything leaves the Design Engineering Department. At that point, there is a complete "getting together" of manufacturing and design engineers – and plant engineers, too, if new equipment is involved.
>
> Our tooling, for instance, is going to be looked at carefully while the design of a product is still in process. Obviously, we can increase or decrease the tooling very materially by certain considerations in the design of a product, and we can go on the basis of total costs at all times. In fact, as far as total cost is concerned, we even think about such matters as shipping, warehousing, etc. All of these factors are taken into consideration when we're still at the design stage. It's very essential that this be done: otherwise, you can lock yourself out from a lot of potential economies.[15]

In 1974, Lincoln's plant had reached full capacity, operating nearly around the clock. Land bordering its present location was unavailable and management was moving ahead with plans to build a second plant 15 miles away on the same freeway as the present plant.

Over the years, Lincoln had come to make rather than buy an increasing proportion of its components. For example, even though its unit volume of gasoline engines was only a fraction of its suppliers, Lincoln purchased engine blocks and components and assembled them rather than buying completed

---

[14] Visitors were barred from the Electrode Division unless they had a pass signed by Willis or Irrgang.

[15] "Incentive Management in Action," *Assembly Engineering*, March 1967. Reprinted by permission of the publisher © 1967 by Hitchcock Publishing Co. All rights reserved.

engines. Management was continually evaluating opportunities for backward integration and had not arbitrarily ruled out manufacturing any of Lincoln's components or raw materials.

ADMINISTRATIVE PRODUCTIVITY

Lincoln's high productivity was not limited to manufacturing. Clyde Loughridge pointed to the Personnel Department as an example: "Normally, for 2,300 employees you would need a personnel department of about 20, but we have only 6, and that includes the nurse, and our responsibilities go beyond those of the typical personnel department."

Once a year, Loughridge had to outline his objectives for the upcoming year to the president of the company, but as he explained, "I don't get a budget. There would be no point to it. I just spend as little as possible. I operate this just like my home. I don't spend on anything I don't need."

In the Traffic Department, workers also seemed very busy. There, a staff of 12 controlled the shipment of 2.5 million pounds of material a day. Their task was complex. Delivery was included in the price of their products. They thus could reduce the overall cost to the customer by mixing products in most loads and shipping the most efficient way possible to the company's 39 warehouses. Jim Biek, general traffic manager, explained how they accomplished this:

> For every order, we decide whether it would be cheaper by rail or truck. Then we consolidate orders so that over 90% of what goes out of here is full carload or full truckload, as compared to perhaps 50% for most companies. We also mix products so that we come in at the top of the weight brackets. For example, if a rate is for 20,000 to 40,000 pounds, we will mix orders to bring the weight right up to that 40,000 limit. All this is computed manually. In fact, my old boss used to say, "We run Traffic like a ma and pa grocery store."

As in the rest of Lincoln, the employees in the Traffic Department worked their way up from entry level positions. Jim Biek had become general traffic manager after nine years as a purchasing engineer. He had received an MBA degree from Northwestern after a BS in mechanical engineering from Purdue, started in the engineering training program, and then spent five years in Product Development and Methods before going to Purchasing and finally to Traffic. Lack of experience in Traffic was a disadvantage,

but the policy of promoting from within also had its advantages. Biek explained:

> One of my first tasks was to go to Washington and fight to get welders reclassified as motors to qualify for a lower freight rate. With my engineering experience and knowledge of welders, I was in a better position to argue this than a straight traffic man . . .
>
> Just about everybody in here was new to Traffic. One of my assistant traffic managers had worked on the loading platform here for years before he came into the department. He had to go to night school to learn about rates, but his experience is invaluable. He knows how to load trucks and rail cars backwards and forward. Who could do a better job of consolidating orders than he does? He can look at an order and think of it as rows of pallets.
>
> Some day we'll outgrow this way of operating, but right now I can't imagine a computer juggling loads like some of our employees do.

Lincoln's Order Department had recently begun computerizing its operations. It was the first time a computer had been used anywhere in the company (except in engineering and research), and according to Russell Stauffer, head of the Order Department, "It was a three-year job for me to sell this to top management." The computer was expected to replace 12 or 13 employees who would gradually be moved into new jobs. There had been some resistance to the computer, Stauffer noted:

> It's like anything new. People get scared. Not all the people affected have been here for the two years required to be eligible for guaranteed employment, and even though the others are assured a job, they don't know what it will be and will have to take what's offered.

The computer was expected to produce savings of $100,000 a year, and to allow a greater degree of control. Stauffer explained:

> We're getting information out of this that we never knew before. The job here is very complex. We're sending out more than two million pounds of consumables a day. Each order might have 30 or 40 items, and each item has a bracket price arrangement based on total order size. A clerk has to remember or determine quickly whether we are out of stock on any items and calculate whether the stock-out brings the order down into another bracket. This means they have to remember the prices and items out of stock. This way of operating was okay up to about $200 million in sales, but now we've outgrown the human capability to handle the problem.

Although he had no previous experience in computers, Stauffer had full responsibility for the conversion.

> I've been here for 35 years. The first day I started, I unloaded coal cars and painted fences. Then I went to the assembly line, first on small parts, then large ones. I've been running the Order Department for 12 years. Since I've been here, we've had studies on computers every year or two and it always came out that we couldn't save money. Finally, when it looked like we'd make the switch, I took some courses at IBM. Over the last year and a half, they've totaled eight and a half weeks, which is supposed to equal a full semester of college.

To date, the conversion had gone well, but much slower than anticipated. Order pressure had been so high that many mistakes would have been catastrophic. Management thus had emphasized assuring 100% quality operations rather than faster conversion.

LINCOLN'S FUTURE

The 1947 Harvard Business School case study of Lincoln Electric ended with a prediction by a union leader from the Cleveland area:

> The real test of Lincoln will come when the going gets tough. The thing Lincoln holds out to the men is high earnings. They work like dogs at Lincoln, but it pays off . . .
> I think [Mr. Lincoln] puts too much store by monetary incentives – but then, there's no denying he has attracted people who respond to that type of incentive. But I think that very thing is a danger Lincoln faces. If the day comes when they can't offer those big bonuses, or his people decide there's more to life than killing yourself making money, I predict the Lincoln Electric Company is in for trouble.

Lincoln's president, George Willis, joined the company the year that this comment was made. Reflecting on his 28 years with the company, Willis observed:

> The company hasn't changed very much since I've been here. It's still run pretty much like Mr. Lincoln ran it. But today's workers are different. They're more outspoken and interested in why things are being done, not just how. We have nothing to hide and never did, so we can give them the answers to their questions.

Looking forward, Willis saw no need to alter Lincoln's strategy or its policies:

> My job will continue to be to have everyone in the organization recognize that a common goal all of us can and must support is to give the customer the quality he needs, when he needs it, at the lowest cost. To do this, we have to have everyone's understanding of this goal and their effort to accomplish it. In one way or another, I have to motivate the organization to meet this goal. The basic forms of the motivation have evolved over the last 40 years. However, keeping the system honed so that everyone understands it, agrees with it, and brings out disagreements so improvements can be made or thinking changed becomes my major responsibility.
> If our employees did not believe that management was trustworthy, honest, and impartial, the system could not operate. We've worked out the mechanics. They are not secret. A good part of my responsibility is to make sure the mechanics are followed. This ties back to a trust and understanding between individuals at all levels of the organization.
> I don't see any real limits to our size. Look at the world with a present population of just under four billion now and six and a quarter billion by the year 2000. Those people aren't going to tolerate a low standard of living. So there will be a lot of construction, cars, bridges, oil and all those things that have got to be to support a population that large.
> My job will still be just the traditional things of assuring that we keep up with the technology and have sufficient profit to pay the suppliers of capital. Then, I have to make sure communication can be maintained adequately. That last task may be the biggest and most important part of my job in the years ahead as we grow larger and still more complex.

Exhibit 1 Arc welding

Arc welding is a group of joining processes that utilize an electric current produced by a transformer or motor generator (electric or engine powered) to fuse various metals. The temperature at the arc is approximately 10,000° Fahrenheit.

The welding circuit consists of a welding machine, ground clamp, and electrode holder. The electrode carries electricity to the metal being welded and the heat from the arc causes the base metals to join together. The electrode may or may not act as a filler metal during the process; however, nearly 60% of all arc welding that is done in the United States utilizes a covered electrode that acts as a very high quality filler metal.

The Lincoln Electric Company manufactured a wide variety of covered electrodes, submerged arc welding wires and fluxes, and a unique self-shielded, Flux-cored electrode called Innershield. The company also manufactured welding machines, wire feeders, and other supplies that were needed for arc welding.

Exhibit 2 Financial statements

**Statement of Financial Condition
(Foreign subsidiaries not included)**

December 31	1974
ASSETS	
Current assets	
Cash and certificates of deposit	$5,691,120
Government securities	6,073,919
Notes and accounts receivable	29,451,161
Inventories (LIFO basis)	29,995,694
Deferred taxes and prepaid expenses	2,266,409
Total	73,478,303
Other assets	
Trustee – notes and interest receivable	1,906,871
Miscellaneous	384,572
Total	2,291,443
Intercompany	
Investment in foreign subsidiaries	4,695,610
Notes receivable	0
Total	4,695,610
Property, plant, and equipment	
Land	825,376
Buildings[a]	9,555,562
Machinery, tools, and equipment[a]	11,273,155
Total	21,654,093
Total assets	$102,119,449
LIABILITIES AND SHAREHOLDERS' EQUITY	
Current liabilities	
Accounts payable	$13,658,063
Accrued wages	1,554,225
Taxes, including income taxes	13,262,178
Dividends payable	3,373,524
Total	31,847,990
Shareholders' equity	
Common capital stock, stated value	281,127
Additional paid-in capital	3,374,570
Retained earnings	66,615,762
Total	70,271,459
Total liabilities and shareholders' equity	$102,119,449

[a] After depreciation.

Exhibit 2 *continued*

Statement of Income and Retained Earnings

Year ended December 31	1974
Income	
Net sales	$232,771,475
Interest	1,048,561
Overhead and development charges to subsidiaries	1,452,877
Dividend income	843,533
Other income	515,034
Total	236,631,480
Costs and Expenses	
Cost of products sold	154,752,735
Selling, administrative, and general expenses and freight out	20,791,301
Yearend incentive bonus	24,707,297
Pension expense	2,186,932
Total	202,438,265
Income before income taxes	34,193,215
Provision for Income Taxes	
Federal	14,800,000
State and Local	1,866,000
	16,666,000
Net income	$ 17,527,215

Exhibit 3 Lincoln Electric's record of pricing and productivity

A. Lincoln prices[a] relative to commodity prices[b], 1934–71

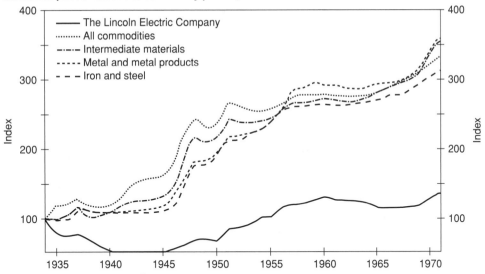

— The Lincoln Electric Company
······· All commodities
–·–·– Intermediate materials
------ Metal and metal products
– – – Iron and steel

[a] Index of annual selling prices of $3/16$-inch diameter electrode in No. 5 and No. 5P in 3,000-pound quantities.
[b] Indexes of wholesale prices.

B. Lincoln prices[c] relative to wholesale machinery and equipment prices, 1939–71. 1939 = 100

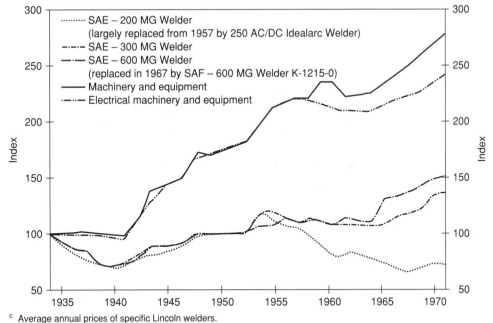

········· SAE – 200 MG Welder
    (largely replaced from 1957 by 250 AC/DC Idealarc Welder)
–·–·– SAE – 300 MG Welder
–·–· SAE – 600 MG Welder
    (replaced in 1967 by SAF – 600 MG Welder K-1215-0)
— Machinery and equipment
–··– Electrical machinery and equipment

[c] Average annual prices of specific Lincoln welders.

Exhibit 3 *continued*

C. Productivity of Lincoln production workers relative to workers in manufacturing and durable goods industries, 1934–71

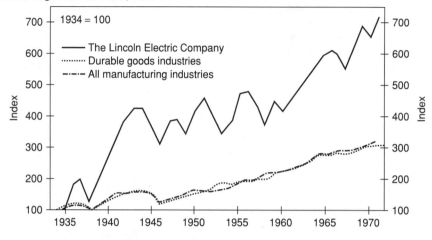

D. Lincoln productivity relative to three other companies: sales value[d] of products per employee, 1934–71

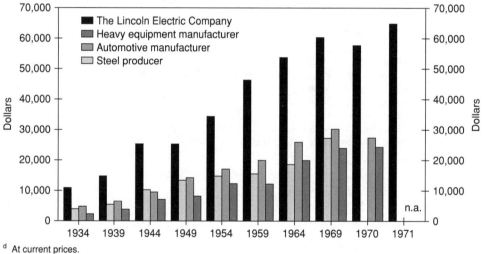

[d] At current prices.
n.a. Not available.

Source: Company records.

Exhibit 4 James F. Lincoln's observations on management

- Some think paying a man more money will produce cooperation. Not true. Many incentives are far more effective than money. Robert MacNamara gave up millions to become Secretary of Defense. Status is a much greater incentive.

- If those crying loudest about the inefficiencies of labor were put in the position of the wage earner, they would react as he does. The worker is not a man apart. He has the same needs, aspirations, and reactions as the industrialist. A worker will not cooperate on any program that will penalize him. Does any manager?

- The industrial manager is very conscious of his company's need of uninterrupted income. He is completely oblivious though, to the worker's same need. Management fails – i.e. profits fall off – and gets no punishment. The wage earner does not fail but is fired. Such injustice!

- Higher efficiency means fewer manhours to do a job. If the worker loses his job more quickly, he will oppose higher efficiency.

- There never will be enthusiasm for greater efficiency if the resulting profits are not properly distributed. If we continue to give it to the average stockholder, the worker will not cooperate.

- Most companies are run by hired managers, under the control of stockholders. As a result, the goal of the company has shifted from service to the customer to making larger dividends for stockholders.

- The public will not yet believe that our standard of living could be doubled immediately if labor and management would cooperate.

- The manager is dealing with expert workers far more skillful. While you can boss these experts around in the usual lofty way, their eager cooperation will not be won.

- A wage earner is no more interested than a manager in making money for other people. The worker's job doesn't depend on pleasing stockholders, so he has no interest in dividends. Neither is he interested in increasing efficiency if he may lose his job because management has failed to get more orders.

- If a manager received the same treatment in matters of income, security, advancement, and dignity as the hourly worker, he would soon understand the real problem of management.

- The first question management should ask is: What is the company trying to do? In the minds of the average worker the answer is: "The company is trying to make the largest possible profits by any method. Profits go to absentee stockholders and top management."

- There is all the difference imaginable between the grudging, distrustful, half-forced cooperation and the eager, whole-hearted, vigorous, happy cooperation of men working together for a common purpose.

- Continuous employment of workers is essential to industrial efficiency. This is a management responsibility. Laying off workers during slack times is death to

efficiency. The worker thrown out is a trained man. To replace him when business picks up will cost much more than the savings of wages during the layoff. Solution? The worker must have a guarantee that if he works properly his income will be continuous.

- Continuous employment is the first step to efficiency. But how? First, during slack periods, manufacture to build up inventory; costs will usually be less because of lower material costs. Second, develop new machines and methods of manufacturing; plans should be waiting on the shelf. Third, reduce prices by getting lower costs. When slack times come, workers are eager to help cut costs. Fourth, explore markets passed over when times are good. Fifth, hours of work can be reduced if the worker is agreeable. Sixth, develop new products. In sum, management should plan for slumps. They are useful.

- The incentives that are most potent when properly offered are:

  Money in proportion to production.
  Status as a reward for achievement.
  Publicity of the worker's contributions and skill.

- The calling of the minister, the doctor, the lawyer, as well as the manager, contains incentive to excel. Excellence brings rewards, self-esteem, respect. Only the hourly worker has no reason to excel.

- Resistance to efficiency is not normal. It is present only when we are hired workers.

- Do unto others as you would have them do unto you. This is not just a Sunday school ideal, but a proper labor–management policy.

- An incentive plan should reward a man not only for the number of pieces turned out, but also for the accuracy of his work, his cooperation in improving methods of production, his attendance.

- The progress in industry so far stems from the developed potentialities of managers. Wage earners, who because of their greater numbers have far greater potential, are overlooked. Here is where the manager must look for his greatest progress.

- There should be an overall bonus based on the contribution each person makes to efficiency. If each person is properly rated and paid, there will not only be a fair reward to each worker but friendly and exciting competition.

- The present policy of operating industry for stockholders is unreasonable. The rewards now given to him are far too much. He gets income that should really go to the worker and the management. The usual absentee stockholder contributes nothing to efficiency. He buys a stock today and sells it tomorrow. He often doesn't even know what the company makes. Why should he be rewarded by large dividends?

- There are many forms and degrees of cooperation between the worker and the management. The worker's attitude can vary all the way from passivity to highly imaginative contributions to efficiency and progress.

Source: *Civil Engineering*, January 1973, p. 78. Reprinted by permission.

Exhibit 5 Stability of employment

A. Lincoln and industry labor turnover rates, 1958–70

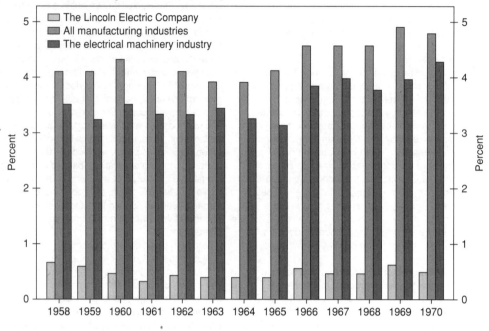

B. Employee distribution by years of service, 1975

Employee's years of service	Number of employees
Less than 1	153
1	311
2	201
3	93
4	34
5	90
6–10	545
11–20	439
21–30	274
31–40	197
41–50	27
51 or more	1
Total	2,365

Exhibit 6 Management Advisory Board minutes

September 26, 1944

Absent: William Dillmuth

A discussion on piecework was again taken up. There was enough detail so it was thought best to appoint a committee to study it and bring a report into the meeting when that study is complete. That committee is composed of Messrs. Gilletly, Semko, Kneen, and Steingass. Messrs. Erickson and White will be called in consultation, and the group will meet next Wednesday, October 4th.

The request was made that the members be permitted to bring guests to the meetings. The request was granted. Let's make sure we don't get too many at one time.

The point was made that materials are not being brought to the operation properly and promptly. There is no doubt of this difficulty. The matter was referred to Mr. Kneen for action. It is to be noted that conditions of deliveries from our suppliers have introduced a tremendous problem which has helped to increase this difficulty.

The request was made that over-time penalty be paid with the straight time. This will be done. There are some administrative difficulties which we will discuss at the next meeting but the over-time payment will start with the first pay in October.

Beginning October 1st employees' badges will be discontinued. Please turn them in to the watchmen.

It was requested that piecework prices be put on repair work in Dept. J. This matter was referred to Mr. Kneen for action.

A request was made that a plaque showing the names of those who died in action, separate from the present plaques, be put in the lobby. This was referred to Mr. Davis for action.

The question was asked as to what method for upgrading men is used. The ability of the individual is the sole reason for his progress. It was felt this is proper.

J. F. Lincoln
President

September 23, 1974 (Excerpts)

Members absent: Tom Borkowski. Albert Sinn

Mr. Kupetz had asked about the Christmas and Thanksgiving schedules. These are being reviewed and we will have them available at he next meeting.

Mr. Howell had reported that the time clocks and the bells do not coincide. This is still being checked.

Mr. Sharpe had asked what the possibility would be to have a time clock installed in or near the Clean Room. This is being checked.

Mr. Joosten had raised the question of the pliability of the wrapping material used in the Chemical Department for wrapping slugs. The material we use at the present time is the best we can obtain at this time . . .

Mr. Kostelac asked the question again whether the vacation arrangements could be changed, reducing the fifteen year period to some shorter period. It was pointed out that at the present time, where we have radically changing conditions every day, it is not the time to go into this. We will review this matter at some later date . . .

Mr. Martucci brought out the fact that there was considerable objection by the people involved to having to work on Saturday night to make up for holiday shutdowns. This was referred to Mr. Willis to be taken into consideration in schedule planning . . .

Mr. Joosten reported that in the Chemical Department on the Saturday midnight shift they have a setup where individuals do not have sufficient work so that it is an uneconomical situation. This has been referred to Mr. Willis to be reviewed.

Mr. Joosten asked whether there would be some way to get chest x-rays for people who work in dusty areas. Mr. Loughridge was asked to check a schedule of where chest x-rays are available at various times . . .

Mr. Robinson asked what the procedure is for merit raises. The procedure is that the foreman recommends the individual for a merit raise if by his performance he has shown that he merits the increase . . .

Chairman
William Irrgang: MW
September 25, 1974.

Exhibit 7 Employment history of top executives

William Irrgang, Board Chairman
1929	Hired, Repair Department
1930	Final Inspection
1934	Inspection, Wire Department
1946	Director of factory engineering
1951	Executive vice president for manufacturing and engineering
1954	President and general manager
1972	Chairman of the board of directors

George E. Willis, President
1947	Hired, Factory Engineering
1951	Superintendent, Electrode Division
1959	Vice president
1969	Executive vice president of manufacturing and associated functions
1972	President

William Miskoe, Vice President, International
1932	Hired, Chicago sales office
1941	President of Australian plant
1969	To Cleveland as vice president, international

Edwin M. Miller, Vice President and Assistant to the President
1923	Hired, factory worker
1925	Assistant foreman
1929	Production Department
1940	Assistant department head, Production Department
1952	Superintendent, Machine Division
1959	Vice president
1973	Vice president and assistant to the president

D. Neal Manross, Vice President, Machine and Motor Division
1941	Hired, factory worker
1942	Welding inspector
1952	General foreman, Extruding Department and assistant plant superintendent
1953	Foreman, Special Products Department, Machine Division
1956	Superintendent, Special Products Division
1959	Superintendent, Motor Manufacturing
1966	Vice president, Motor Division
1973	Vice president in charge of Motor and Machine Divisions

Albert S. Patnik, Vice President of Sales Development
1940	Hired, sales student
1940	Welder, New London, Conn.
1941	Junior salesman, Los Angeles office
1942	Salesman, Seattle office
1945	Military service
1945	Reinstated to Seattle
1951	Rural Dealer Manager, Cleveland sales office
1964	Assistant to the vice president of sales
1972	Vice president

Donald F. Hastings, Vice President and General Sales Manager
1953	Hired, sales trainee
1954	Welding engineer, Emeryville, Calif.
1959	District manager, Moline office
1970	General sales manager, Cleveland
1972	Vice president and general sales manager

Exhibit 8 Organization

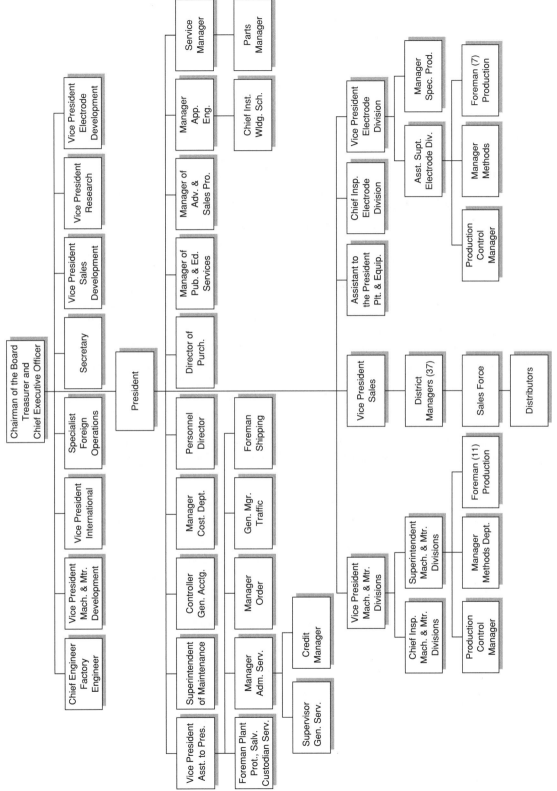

Exhibit 9 Lincoln comment on the case

After reading the 1975 Harvard case study Richard S. Sabo, manager of publicity and educational services, sent the following letter to the casewriter:

July 31, 1975
To: Mr. Norman Fast
Dear Mr. Fast:

I believe that you have summarized the Incentive Management System of The Lincoln Electric Company very well; however, readers may feel that the success of the Company is due only to the psychological principles included in your presentation.

Please consider adding the efforts of our executives who devote a great deal of time to the following items that are so important to the consistent profit and long range growth of the Company.

I.   Management has limited research, development and manufacturing to a standard product line designed to meet the major needs of the welding industry.

II. New products must be reviewed by manufacturing and all production costs verified before being approved by management.

III. Purchasing is challenged to not only procure materials at the lowest cost, but also to work closely with engineering and manufacturing to assure that the latest innovations are implemented.

IV. Manufacturing supervision and all personnel are held accountable for reduction of scrap, energy conservation, and maintenance of product quality.

V.   Production control, material handling and methods engineering are closely supervised by top management.

VI. Material and finished goods inventory control, accurate cost accounting and attention to sales costs, credit and other financial areas have constantly reduced overhead and led to excellent profitability.

VII. Management has made cost reduction a way of life at Lincoln and definite programs are established in many areas, including traffic and shipping, where tremendous savings can result.

VIII. Management has established a sales department that is technically trained to reduce customer welding cost.

This sales technique and other real customer services have eliminated nonessential frills and resulted in long-term benefits to all concerned.

IX. Management has encouraged education, technical publishing and long-range programs that have resulted in industry growth, thereby assuring market potential for The Lincoln Electric Company.

Richard S. Sabo

bjs

Case Study

PCL: A Breakdown in the Enforcement of Management Control

PCL was a leading European consumer electronics, lifestyle, and healthcare company that had entered the Chinese market in 1985. While its consumer electronics business grew steadily in China, the costs of returned sets in its TV division amounted to 5% of the division's total sales in 2008. Even more worrying was that 37% of the returned TVs were of good quality and had been returned without good reason. PCL taskforces set up to study the situation found that control measures designed to handle returns were simply not being carried out by staff and third-party after-sales service centres. What could PCL do to remedy the situation?

THE CONSUMER ELECTRONICS INDUSTRY IN CHINA

With a population of 1.3 billion and rising disposable incomes, China had become the second-largest market for consumer electronics in the world.[1] Analysts forecasted a compounded annual growth rate of 9.8% through to 2014 for consumer electronics, with growing demand for TV sets and computers in smaller cities and rural areas being the main driver.[2] As the market in the big cities had become saturated, market competition had moved increasingly to smaller cities and rural areas. Sales of consumer electronics products in these markets were further enhanced by the government's subsidy programme, which offered rebates for purchases of consumer electronic goods in rural areas. Another government programme that allowed consumers to trade in old electronic appliances for new ones in

nine provincial areas since 2009 had also helped to stimulate demand.

The television market in China

It was no surprise that China, a country that produced 42% of the world's total shipment of TV sets,[3] had a strong TV market. Domestic manufacturers alone accounted for three-quarters of its liquid-crystal display (LCD) TV market in 2009.[4] Driven by consumers' preference for large-sized TVs and by falling prices, China was forecasted to surpass North America as the largest LCD TV market in the world, with sales reaching 29 million units in 2010, translating to more than 30% in growth year-on-year.[5] The growth would be driven by consumers replacing their cathode ray tube (CRT) sets with LCD sets, especially in third- and fourth-tier cities.[6] International brands faced fierce competition from domestic brands, which enjoyed advantages in both cost control and distribution, and price wars were common as domestic brands lowered their prices to increase their market share. Large retail chains played a critical role in the retail market for consumer electronics in China, and competition for shelf space in such chains was fierce. Manufacturers became involved with the promotions, marketing, and supply chain management of these chain stores in order to

[1] "Consumer Electronics in China," *Euromonitor* (April 2009), online, www.euromonitor.com/Consumer_Electronics_in_China (accessed 20 June 2010).

[2] "China Consumer Electronics Report Q3 2010," *Business Monitor International* (2010) online, www.pr-inside.com/china-consumer-electronics-report-q-r1905491.htm (accessed 10 June 2010).

[3] K. Zhang, "China TV Market to Enjoy Solid Growth in 2014," *iSuppli* (April 26, 2010), online, www.isuppli.com/Display-Materials-and-Systems/MarketWatch/Pages/China-TV-Market-to-Enjoy-Solid-Growth-in-2014.aspx (accessed 20 June 2010).

[4] Ibid.

[5] "Corning: China to Become World's Biggest LCD TV Market," *SinoCast Business Beat* (April 14, 2010), online, www.tradingmarkets.com/news/stock-alert/glw_dtek_corning-china-to-become-world-s-biggest-lcd-tv-market-910387.html (accessed 20 June 2010).

[6] "Overview of China's LCD Market," *GfK Retail and Technology* (March 29, 2010) online, www.gfkrt.com/news_events/market_news/single_sites/005606/index.en.html (accessed 30 June 2010).

▶

This case was prepared by Grace Loo under the supervision of Professor Neale O'Connor.

build relationships with them.[7] Others opened their own branded stores so they could have a direct hand in shaping consumers' purchase experience.

PCL Consumer Electronics – background

PCL was a high-tech multinational company based in Europe. Since its establishment in the late nineteenth century, it had diversified into multiple industry segments. The diversification strained its resources and consequently PCL reshaped the organization to focus on the healthcare and electronics sectors. In 2010, it had a sales and service presence and manufacturing sites in more than 100 countries around the world.

PCL's consumer electronics division (PCL Consumer Electronics) was a global player in digital and electronic devices, bringing the latest technology and human-centered designs to the market. Its product portfolio included colour TV sets, DVD players, audio products, PC monitors, and PC peripherals. PCL Consumer Electronics had a sales and service presence in more than 50 countries and manufacturing sites in France, Hungary, Belgium, Brazil, Mexico, and Argentina even though it outsourced its production heavily. PCL Consumer Electronics placed a strong emphasis on emerging markets such as China and India. It entered China in 1985, and by 2008 its sales organization on the mainland had grown to 550 people with annual sales of US$752 million. (See Exhibit 1.)

REPAIRING THE BROKEN SYSTEM

Returned sets

In 2008, the handling of returned TV sets cost PCL an average of US$6 million, equal to about 5% of its annual TV sales. The costs covered freight from the dealer to PCL's warehouse, repair, and refurbishment at the factory workshop. While PCL spent a hefty sum each year servicing returned goods, about 37% of the returned goods were no-fault-found (NFF) returns, translating to a loss of US$2.2 million for PCL. NFF returns also included demo sets and

slow-moving goods that were not supposed to be returned (see Exhibit 2).

The TV return process

After-sales service for PCL's TV division was handled by authorized service centres (ASCs), which were third-party service centres authorized and managed by PCL's after-sales service team. Under China's consumer law, consumers could return a defective TV set to the retailer from whom they made the purchase within five days or exchange it for a new one within 15 days. Retailers sent PCL sets returned by customers to the company's ASCs, which would decide whether to accept the return and repair them. If the defect was serious, the ASC would send the set back to PCL's factory for repair.

Investigation

In response to the high volume of returned sets and high NFF returns, PCL's management appointed the product marketing manager of the TV division, who was also familiar with the return process, to look into the matter so appropriate actions could be taken. He formed a taskforce that brought together the sales operation manager, the service manager, and the financial controller of the TV business. The team set out to investigate the situation and uncovered a number of causes for the problem.

Neither retailers nor ASCs had been trained in educating customers about product performance or the criteria for accepting returns. Retail stores usually used high-definition signals for product demonstrations, but most consumers used cable TV at home. As a result, consumers often became dissatisfied with the picture quality after they took the TV set home and would try to exchange it for a new set or simply return it. While PCL had established return criteria that were as stringent as those of its competitors, retailers and ASCs often failed to execute them properly, accepting returns without proper screening.

Chain retailers were significant players in China's consumer electronics market, and consumer electronics companies could not maintain their market share without selling through them. Because no international TV brand possessed unique product features or technical advantages that differentiated its products in the market, the manufacturers' best

[7] I. B. Von Morgenstern and C. Shu, "Winning the Battle for the Chinese Consumer Electronics Market," (September 2006), online, www.mckinseyquarterly.com/High_Tech/Hardware/Winning_ the_battle_for_the_Chinese_consumer_electronics_market_1855 (accessed 20 June 2010).

option was to make concessions in their negotiations with chain stores in order to maintain good relationships with them and in turn receive higher visibility at the point of sale. PCL, for instance, cut its profit margins and accepted returns of slow-moving models and demo sets in order to secure prominent display locations in the stores. In addition, PCL salespeople had to meet sales targets and required the support of dealers to achieve these targets. This made it hard for many salespeople to say no to unreasonable returns because doing so might jeopardize their relationship with the dealers. Moreover, they put little effort into investigating the returns, despite established approval procedures for returned goods.

PCL's after-sales service team, which was responsible for overseeing the ASCs, did not report to the TV division directly, but instead reported to the general manager of the organization, a line of reporting that reduced the incentive for the after-sales team to control TV returns or to monitor the third-party ASCs stringently. Not only did the ASCs fail to inspect the returned sets carefully, they sometimes faked their inspection records instead of rejecting the return of TV sets. The situation was further aggravated by the fact that PCL had no punishment policy for fraud or incompliance on the part of ASCs.

Action

The team came up with a series of actions based on their initial assessment of the situation. The sales team's annual performance appraisals would be linked with TV returns and the cost of servicing returns, and this new measure was communicated by the TV sales director to all the salespeople. The service manager also communicated to ASCs a new policy whereby they would be fined three times the labor charge for each fake inspection record discovered.

The project team forecasted that their plan would reduce the return rate to 3.5% and the NFF rate to 20% within two months, but their projection did not materialise. In fact, the NFF return rate went up to 40% after two months. Upon further investigation, the general manager and the production manager of the TV division discovered two reasons for the rising rate of NFF returns, despite their efforts. First, the sales team was under enormous pressure to meet their sales targets, which was set at 132% of the sales of the previous year, a rate that exceeded actual market growth. In order to reach their targets, they put pressure on the dealers to increase their purchase volumes, leading to higher inventory levels and tighter cash flow. To counter these problems, dealers negotiated with salespeople to accept returns and to allow exchanges of demo sets and slow-moving goods for new models. The second reason was that the after-sales service team had failed to take punitive action against the ASCs for fake inspection records. There was little incentive for the service team to respond to the ASCs' transgressions, as it did not report to the TV division and its performance indicators were not linked to the amount of goods returned.

Second try

Dissatisfied with the outcome, the general manager of PCL Consumer Electronics appointed the service director, who reported directly to him, to lead the taskforce. The service director was also given the authority to handle issues that did not usually fall within his scope of responsibilities in order to tackle the problem. Once appointed, the service director put together a new cross-functional team, with each member responsible for a specific area for improving the return rate and NFF return rate, as follows:

- service director – served as team leader;
- service manager – managed the ASC network;
- chief financial officer – responsible for the financial results of the team;
- TV sales operation manager – engaged in dealer management;
- service financial controller – performed service cost computation and analysis;
- TV product manager – concerned with process implementation and improvement.

The team set specific targets:

- TV NFF return rate to be reduced from 40% to 20%;
- TV return and exchange rate to be reduced from 5% to 3.5%;
- total savings of US$1.13 million within six months.

The service director also applied for some US$4,500 as a bonus for the team, to be used for an outing or teambuilding exercise if it could meet its targets. The general manager of the consumer electronics division endorsed the proposal and also incorporated the project targets into the bonus scheme of the team members such that they would lose their annual bonuses if the targets were not met.

The team analyzed the situation and the following actions were drawn up to remedy the situation:

- Given that both the sales team and the ASCs were failing to enforce the established criteria for accepting returned goods, PCL had ended up being more accepting of returned goods than its competitors. To manage the situation, the TV sales operation manager was put in charge of rotating the regional sales managers and salespeople geographically in order to prevent the sales team from becoming too friendly with the dealers.

- The TV sales operation manager and service director were put in charge of ensuring that no models that had been phased out for more than six months would be accepted for return.

- The TV sales operation manager and service director were also put in charge of defining clear and sound criteria for the inspection and acceptance of returned merchandise.

- The TV product marketing manager and service director were put in charge of organizing training on the return process and criteria for all individuals involved in making decisions in the return process.

The team quickly got to work, defining the criteria and monitoring measures to control the return process:

- For goods that were defective upon arrival at the dealers' warehouses, PCL would accept return only if they were functionally defective or there were serious cosmetic failures vis-à-vis PCL's standards for finished goods.

- For defective goods returned within 15 days after purchase by consumers, only functional failures would be accepted as grounds for return.

- Returned goods were to be accepted only after approval by cross-functional personnel.

- Returned goods would be required to come in their original PCL packaging, with all the original accessories.

- Models that had been phased out for more than six months would not be accepted for return or exchange.

PCL's regional service managers and engineers would also visit the top 10 ASCs for returned goods – which together were responsible for 40% of monthly returns – and provide training sessions with detailed working instructions to the ASCs. A new incentive and penalty scheme for ASCs was also drawn up, with the following mandates:

- increased labor charges for inspection of returns;

- penalties for NFF returns;

- quarterly bonuses to those with the highest levels of compliance.

On the sales team side, the TV sales operation manager worked closely with the TV sales directors to draw up a detailed rotation plan. Field salespeople were required to visit top dealers within their respective regions on a weekly basis to solicit feedback and to implement follow-up actions. The plan was fulfilled after seven months and extended to 52% of the salespeople.

The project team met every two weeks for reviews as remedy measures were implemented. Immediate actions were taken to correct any weaknesses that had materialized and warnings were issued to those responsible for them. The team was able to adhere closely to the project schedule.

After six months, the NFF return rate was reduced to 12%, surpassing the team's target of 20%. The return and exchange rates dropped to 3.2%, surpassing the team's 3.5% target. The team did not meet the target of US$1.13 million in savings, though it came quite close at US$1.1 million, and thus the team was awarded its bonus.

EPILOGUE

After the hard work of PCL's two taskforces, PCL finally managed to bring the issue of the high return rate of its TV sets under control. The work of the two taskforces had revealed a major issue in enforcement within the organization. Even the best strategy or business plan could only be effective if it was properly executed. What could PCL do to ensure that internal control measures would be enforced properly to achieve organizational objectives in the future?

Exhibit 1 PCL Consumer Electronics in China: organization chart

Exhibit 2 Flow of TV sales and returns

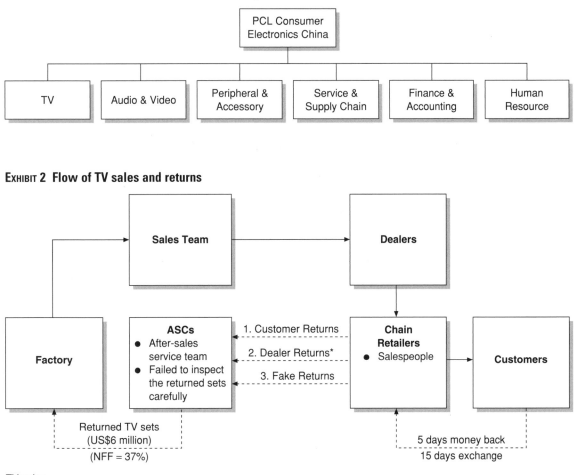

Chapter 5

CONTROL SYSTEM COSTS

Management control systems (MCSs) provide one primary benefit: a higher probability that employees will pursue organizational objectives. Managers are willing to incur sometimes significant direct, out-of-pocket costs to try to derive this benefit. But managers must also consider some other, indirect costs that can be many times greater than the direct costs. Some of these indirect costs arise from negative side effects that are inherent in the use of specific types of controls. Others are caused either by a poor MCS design or by implementation of the wrong type of control in a given situation. To make informed cost-benefit judgments, managers must understand these side effects, their causes, and their consequences (costs).

DIRECT COSTS

The direct costs of an MCS include all the out-of-pocket, monetary costs required to design and implement the MCS. Some direct costs, such as the costs of paying cash bonuses (arising from incentive compensation for results control) or the costs of maintaining an internal audit staff (needed to ensure compliance with action control prescriptions) are relatively easy to identify. Other costs, however, such as those related to the time employees spend in planning and budgeting activities or preaction reviews can only be estimated. Many organizations often are unaware of, or do not bother to calculate accurately the size of, all of these direct costs. But it is known, for example, that the costs of complying with the provisions of the Sarbanes-Oxley Act in the United States, which requires an organization to document processes that have a significant impact on the financial statements and to test key controls embedded in these processes, have totaled many millions of dollars for some companies (see also Chapter 13).

INDIRECT COSTS

Challenging as estimating the direct costs of control may be, they can be dwarfed by indirect costs of control caused by any of a number of harmful side effects, including behavioral displacement, gamesmanship, operating delays, and negative attitudes, which we discuss below. Chapters 10 and 11 discuss in more detail some of the harmful side effects that commonly arise from the use of financial results controls, especially managerial short-termism or myopia.

Behavioral displacement

Behavioral displacement is a common MCS-related side effect that can expose organizations to significant indirect costs; it occurs when the MCS produces, and actually encourages, behaviors that are not consistent with the organization's objectives. Behavioral displacement is most common with accountability-type controls (either results or action accountability) where the specification of the results or actions desired is *incongruent*. But some forms of personnel/cultural control can also produce the problem.

Behavioral displacement and results controls

In a results control system, behavioral displacement occurs when an organization defines sets of results measures that are incongruent with the organization's "true" objectives. Some examples are given below.

- When companies give their salespeople monthly sales quotas, the salespeople tend to work on the easiest sales, which are not necessarily the most profitable sales or sales with the highest priority.

- When brokerage firms reward their brokers through commissions on client trades, some brokers respond by *churning accounts*; engaging in more transactions than are in the customers' best interests and that run the risk of client dissatisfaction and turnover.

- When companies reward their computer programmers for output measured in lines of code per day, the programmers tend to generate programs with lengthy code even when the company's problems can be better addressed by simpler programs or by off-the-shelf applications.

- When software testers are evaluated in terms of the number of "bugs" they find, the bug count goes up. But more of the bugs found will be minor. Bug counts also create incentives for superficial testing, penalizing testers to take the time either to look for the harder-to-find but more important bugs or to document their findings thoroughly. Bug counts also penalize testers who support others testers through coaching, helping, and auditing.

- When companies reward their research scientists for the number of patents filed, they are likely to see an increase in the number of patents filed. However, this incentive may lead only to patent proliferation. It does not enhance researchers' concerns for the eventual commercial success of their discoveries.

Why do organizations, then, use measures that are not congruent with their true objectives? Most commonly, incongruence arises because organizations focus on easily quantifiable results that lead them to *incompletely* capture all of the desired results. When that is the case, employees are induced to concentrate on the results that are rewarded by the control system and to snub other desired but unmeasured result areas.[1] For example, when a major personal computer (PC) maker started paying its sales reps higher commissions for selling add-on services than for selling PCs, the sales reps became lax about selling no-frills PCs. Sometimes they would even hang up on customers who did not want add-ons. As a result, customer satisfaction went down as did the referral business on which the company had relied for its growth in a highly competitive market.[2]

Similarly, when city officials wanted to tackle overtime in their garbage collection service, they offered the garbage collectors an incentive scheme where they would be paid full time even if they reported back early. It worked! Garbage collectors came back consistently early and received full pay for the shift. Despite this good effect on overtime reduction, however, there was an increase in preventable traffic accidents, missed pick-ups of garbage, and trucks filled over the legal weight limit. By emphasizing time in the incentive scheme, the city was delivering the message that time is essentially all that mattered, even at the expense of safety, service, and obeying work rules.[3]

Garbage collection is not exactly what comes to mind when thinking of *multitasking*, yet even this job is presumably complex enough to be subject to the effects of *distorted incentives* (a form of behavior displacement as we call it here). Consider then the complexity involved in determining appropriate weights on the multiple dimensions of, say, managerial jobs, and one can see how easy it is for incentives to have potentially displacing effects. All told, there are very few jobs, even presumably simple jobs, where what is counted is all that counts – in other words, results controls are almost invariably *incomplete*. If the relative importance of the various aspects of the job is not captured correctly, employees are unlikely to allocate their efforts appropriately, and outcomes will be distorted.

A major cause of the incompleteness in results control systems, as the examples above illustrate, is a tendency to concentrate on results areas that are concrete and easily quantifiable, rather than intangible and difficult to quantify, despite their importance for organizational success. Avoiding quantified indicators is not the general solution to this problem, however, because quantified indicators are not inherently bad. They do have advantages, particularly with regard to the clarity with which performance targets and results can be communicated. One solution to the results control-induced displacement problem is to find or develop indicators of the results areas that may be missing (customer service, safety, etc.), for which the measures are often nonfinancial. (We discuss the use of nonfinancial performance measures in Chapter 11.)

However, situations do exist where quantified measures cannot be used. For example, it may not be possible to develop good measures of the success of research scientists, at least in the short-run.[4] There is also the ever-present tendency that quantified measures will be overused; that is, used when they do not provide an acceptably close representation of the actual result desired. Indeed, organizations are prone to appear to want what they can measure, rather than trying to more adequately measure what they really want. When the measurement causes distortions of the behavioral displacement sort, sometimes the best, or only, remedy is to rely *less* on results controls.[5]

Behavioral displacement and action controls

Behavioral displacement can also occur with action controls. One form of action control-related displacement is often referred to as *means-ends inversion*, meaning that employees pay attention to what they do (the means) while losing sight of what they are to accomplish (the ends). For example, managers who are given an approval limit for capital expenditures have been known to invest in a series of small projects, each of which falls just within their authorization limits. Although the action-accountability controls may not be breached, the resulting pattern of small, incremental investments may be suboptimal.

Sometimes action control-related displacement occurs simply because the defined actions are *incongruent*. As with results controls, this problem arises in an action-accountability context. For example, the PC maker mentioned above also implemented a policy to put a time limit on customer service calls. Specifically, customer service reps who spent more than 13 minutes talking to a customer would not get their monthly bonuses. Not surprisingly, service reps began doing just about anything possible to get customers off the phone, such as pretending that the line was not working or merely hanging up. As a result, the company's customer satisfaction ratings, once the best in the industry, dropped dramatically and fell below the industry average.[6]

Some action controls cause behavioral displacement because they promote compliant yet *rigid, non-adaptive behaviors*, a pathology commonly associated with *bureaucratic* organizations. For example, US automobile manufacturers focused on elaborate action prescriptions for their assembly workers to try to optimize assembly line operations. On

Japanese assembly lines, in contrast, the control systems in use for assembly workers were much more flexible. Workers were encouraged to experiment with different ways of doing their jobs, for example, by putting the doors on the car before the locks were installed, and then to alternate the order to see which was more efficient. By giving their workers more flexibility, the Japanese gained a competitive advantage. Similarly, at Continental Airlines, there used to be a rule for just about everything conceivable in the nine-inch thick procedures manual known as the "Thou Shalt Not" book. As one company observer noted, "No one could possibly know everything in [the book], so most employees played it safe by doing nothing at all." To overcome the undesired rigidity fostered over time by the rule book, the new management team ceremoniously burned the "Thou Shalt Not" book in the company parking lot to provide a clear signal that from then onwards employees had "permission to think for themselves."[7] Action controls and bureaucratization can be good in stable environments with considerable centralized knowledge about what actions are desired because they help establish compliant, reliable, and efficient work routines. In changing environments, however, they may hinder the needed change that is required to stay competitive.

Behavioral displacement and personnel/cultural controls

Behavioral displacement can also occur with personnel/cultural controls. It can arise from recruiting the wrong type of employees or from providing insufficient training. Strong cultures can also cause displacement when the behavioral norms that groups use to guide the behaviors of their members, or the measures used to provide group rewards, are not in line with what the organization desires. When that is the case, it causes incongruence. For example, many organizations operate on the belief that research scientists are highly professional and will control themselves better than the organization could by implementing formal controls. Although this belief may be correct to some extent, many scientists also are motivated to conduct research that contributes to their individual reputations even when that research might have little or no immediate application for their organization.

When personnel/cultural controls are implemented in the wrong setting, they will be rendered ineffective and encourage unintended behaviors. For example, when Levi Strauss wanted to raise productivity and reduce costs, particularly those incurred by injured workers pushing to make piecework goals, it turned to teamwork, which Levi's felt would be more humane, safe, and exemplary of workplace standards in an industry notorious for poor working conditions. The old piecework system – under which a worker repeatedly performs a specialized task (such as attaching pockets or belt loops) and gets paid by the amount of work completed – was abandoned and replaced by teams consisting of 10 to 35 workers who shared the tasks and were paid according to the total amount of trousers the group completes.

Despite these praiseworthy intentions, the nature of the work at Levi's may not be well suited for teamwork, however. Garment manufacturing consists of a series of specific tasks (pocket setting, belt looping). The speed of these tasks relates directly to a worker's skill for the grueling, repetitive motions involved in stitching fabric. Some workers are much faster than others. Although teamwork was expected to reduce monotony, enable workers to perform different tasks, and reduce repetitive injuries, it was a failure. When skilled workers were pitted against slower co-workers, the wages of top-performers fell while those of lower-skilled workers went up. This not only eliminated savings for Levi's but also caused infighting among co-workers. Longtime friendships were dissolved, and faster workers tried to banish slower ones. Morale was damaged, efficiency dropped, and labor and overhead costs surged. The teamwork concept did not fit the context.[8]

Gamesmanship

We use the term *gamesmanship* to refer generally to the actions that employees take to improve their performance indicators without producing any positive economic effects for the organization. Gamesmanship is a common harmful side effect faced in situations where accountability forms of control, either results or actions accountability, are used. We discuss two major forms of gamesmanship: slack creation and data manipulation.

Creation of slack resources

Slack involves the consumption of organizational resources by employees in excess of what is required; that is, consumption of resources by employees that cannot be justified easily in terms of its contribution to organizational objectives.

The propensity to create slack often takes place when tight results controls are in use; that is, when employees, mostly at management levels, are evaluated primarily on whether or not they achieve their budget targets. Managers who miss their target face the prospect of interventions in their jobs, the loss of organizational resources, the loss of annual bonuses and pay raises, and sometimes even the loss of their job. Under these circumstances, managers may look for ways to protect themselves from the downside risk of missing budget targets and the stigma attached to underachievers. One way in which managers keep tight results control from hurting them is by negotiating highly achievable targets; that is, targets that are deliberately lower than their best-guess forecast of the future. This is called *budget slack*; it protects the managers against unforeseen contingencies and improves the probability that the budget target will be met, thus increasing the likelihood of receiving a favorable evaluation and associated performance-dependent rewards (incentive pay).[9]

There is little doubt that slack creation is a common practice in most organizations.[10] That said, slack should not be seen as producing only negative effects.[11] On the positive side, slack can reduce manager tension and stress, increase organizational resiliency to change, and make available some resources that can be used for innovation. On the negative side, slack obscures true underlying performance and, hence, distorts the decisions based on the obscured information, such as performance evaluations and resource allocation decisions.

In most situations, slack is nearly impossible to prevent. Theoretically, slack is feasible only where there is *information asymmetry*, where superiors have less-than-complete knowledge about what can be accomplished in a given area, and where subordinates are allowed to participate in setting the performance targets for that area. Thus, where performance can be accurately forecast, or be set in a top-down manner, it should be possible to prevent, or at least mitigate, slack. But these conditions exist only in rare situations – highly stable environments. If accountability controls are used in other situations, slack must be considered to be almost inevitable.

We discuss the issue of slack creation further in the context of target setting in budgeting in Chapter 8. We also discuss various ethical considerations related to slack creation in Chapter 15.

Data manipulation

Data manipulation involves fudging the control indicators. It comes in two basic forms: falsification and data management. *Falsification* involves reporting erroneous data, meaning that the data are changed. *Data management* involves any action undertaken to change the reported results, such as sales numbers, reported earnings, or a debt/equity ratio, while providing no real economic advantage to the organization and, sometimes, even causing harm. Data management actions are typically undertaken to make performance look better, such as to achieve a budget target or to increase stock price. However, data management actions can also be undertaken to make performance look worse. Sometimes managers "save sales" for a future period when the current-year bonus has reached its cap. Sometimes they "take a bath" – that is, they make results look worse in bad times (when there are no bonus payouts anyway) to get a head start on recording an improvement in the subsequent period. Sometimes they report abnormally poor results to try to lower the stock price to coincide with, say, a stock option grant.[12]

Data management can be accomplished through either accounting or operating means. *Accounting methods* of data management involve an intervention in the measurement process. Individuals engaging in accounting methods of data management sometimes violate accounting rules, but more frequently they use the flexibility available in either the selection of accounting methods or the application of those methods, or both, to "manage earnings" as it is often called.[13] To boost earnings, for example, managers might shift from accelerated to straight-line depreciation or change their judgments about accounting estimates (such as about reserves, allowances, and write-offs). IBM corporation used revenues from patent licenses and profits from asset sales to understate the company's reported general and administrative (G&A) expenses, to make the company look "lean" as observers and investors expected it to be.[14] A *Fortune* article called accounting treatments like these, which are consistent with generally accepted accounting principles, "legal, but lousy."[15]

Similarly, in 2010, computer maker Dell agreed to pay $100 million to settle charges from the Securities & Exchange Commission (SEC) concerning how it manipulated payments from Intel, a chip maker. The SEC complaint alleged a pattern of accounting manipulation that calls into question Dell's apparent financial success from 2002 to 2006. During much of that time, Dell's share price nearly doubled, which observers and investors were led to believe was due to the company's ultra-efficient supply chain and direct-sales strategy. Instead, it is alleged that Dell's executives used larger payments from Intel to hit financial goals while publicly crediting "cost reduction initiatives" and "declining component costs" as the reason for Dell's growing profit margins, even though they presumably knew the increase was due to Intel's payments.[16]

Operating methods of data management involve the altering of operating decisions. To boost earnings in the current period, managers can, say, try to delay the timing of discretionary expenditures (such as maintenance) and/or try to accelerate sales. These methods affect the size and/or timing of cash flows, as well as reported earnings. Several companies have been charged with booking revenues on sales to distributors (as opposed to waiting until the products have been sold by the distributor), thus taking advantage of the ambiguity in accounting rules on revenue recognition. This ambiguity in accounting rules makes "channel stuffing" tempting by persuading distributors to take more product than they really need or want, particularly towards the end of a poor quarter, to help earnings look better than they really are.

For example, at contact lens manufacturer Bausch & Lomb, the culture was a mirror image of Daniel Gill, the company's longtime chairman and chief executive: "tenacious, demanding – and very numbers-oriented."[17] Pressure to maintain double-digit annual profit growth led division managers to sell products to gray-market distributors, force distributors to take large quantities of unwanted products, ship goods before customers ordered them, run large promotions at every quarter-end, and give customers abnormally long payment terms in exchange for large orders.[18] An operations manager at Bausch & Lomb's sunglass distribution center said, "We'd ship 70% of the month's goods in the last three days."[19]

Because altering decisions can have adverse effects on real economic value, even when they improve reported accounting income, operating methods of data management can be harmful to the firm in the long-term. The actions can harm customer satisfaction (arising from the aggressive sales tactics), employee productivity (arising from the unneeded overtime at quarter's end), and/or quality (arising from postponed maintenance or reduced quality inspections). Manipulation is a serious problem because it can render an entire control system ineffective. If the data are being manipulated, it is no longer possible to determine whether a company, entity, or employee has performed well. The effects of manipulation can also go far beyond the MCS because it affects the accuracy of an organization's information system. If that is the case, management's ability to make good, facts-based decisions will be jeopardized. Thus, even though various data manipulation methods are not illegal, they can be costly – that is, harmful to the firm in the long-term. No wonder, then, that an article in the *Harvard Business Review* called the "earnings game" something that "everyone plays, [but] nobody wins."[20]

Some data manipulation schemes involve outright fraud, however. At Sunrise Medical, four employees at one of the firm's major divisions, including its general manager, were involved in falsifying financial reports. The scheme was intended to disguise a deteriorating financial situation. The company's bonus plan was seen as a major cause of the fraud. The plan paid annual cash bonuses worth up to 50% of salary, but it paid no bonuses in divisions that failed to record a year-on-year earnings increase. Many observers were shocked that such a fraud could occur at Sunrise which "has long presented itself as a values-conscious health-care firm whose employees carry lofty corporate precepts about customers, shareholders and social responsibility on wallet cards."[21] When such frauds come to light, their financial impact can be huge. Reputations are ruined and billions of dollars of shareholder value can be destroyed, as was the case in Enron and WorldCom.

Despite these costs, data manipulation schemes are often fostered by excessive short-term performance pressures and inadequate controls to prevent the dysfunctional side effects (see also Chapter 15). A *Business Week* article on the Bausch & Lomb situation above noted that, "Bausch & Lomb's performance-oriented ethos delivered outstanding results for many years, [. . .] but when the company's markets slowed at the same time that several acquisitions soured, Bausch & Lomb's culture was a train wreck waiting to happen."[22] In many other situations, investigators lay much of the blame on the failure of auditors to perform their functions well. Auditors do not always understand the company's business or its accounting methods well enough or they do not pursue some of the observed improprieties far enough, perhaps in part because of a lack of independence from their clients.[23]

Evidence indicates that detection of performance manipulations and misrepresentations of financial reports is on the rise. This is due, in part, to the increased scrutiny of financial statements in the wake of the collapse of Enron and WorldCom and other major financial reporting scandals in the United States and elsewhere that have spawned heightened regulatory and legislative scrutiny and enforcement by lawmakers and stock exchanges. The recent financial crisis has nudged regulators even further towards stepping up their investigations of alleged irregularities.[24] Most of these regulatory and legislative reforms focus on the roles and responsibilities of management and boards of directors in financial reporting as well as the roles and responsibilities of independent auditors in performing their audits of the financial reports. This falls broadly under the realm of corporate governance, which we discuss further in Chapters 13. The role of auditors is discussed further in Chapter 14.

Operating delays

Operating delays often are an unavoidable consequence of the preaction review types of action controls and some of the forms of behavioral constraints. Delays such as those caused by limiting access to a stockroom or by requiring the typing of a password before using a computer system are usually minor. However, other control-caused delays can be major, such as those arising from approvals requiring multiple signatures from managers at various levels in the hierarchy or from endless memos through layers of higher-ups before anything gets cleared. In these circumstances, required approvals sometimes *straitjacket* operations and, hence, market and customer responsiveness.

To enhance the market responsiveness of its North-American operations, Toyota Motor Corporation's president Fujio Cho had the following message for its American division: "It's all yours." In response, Jim Press, executive vice president of Torrance, California-based Toyota Motor Sales USA noted that, "These days, we don't need so many approvals from Japan; we have more autonomy." The American management used to have to go down to the docks to greet the boats to find out what the new-model-year cars looked like. Now, many Toyota cars and their interiors are designed in the United States. Toyota's president Cho called this a "reinvention" of the carmaker, necessary because the market, especially in the United States, is so competitive. "Any company not willing to take the risk of reinventing itself is doomed," Cho said.[25]

Obviously, where fast action is important, as it is in many competitive markets, decision delays can be quite costly. Delays are a major reason for the negative connotation associated with the word "bureaucracy." In organizations that tend to place more emphasis on action controls and, as a consequence, suffer these bureaucratic operating delays, many MCS changes are motivated by a desire to reduce the burdens caused by these types of controls, which are often typified as "killing entrepreneurship."

Control-caused operating delays are not an independent problem; they can cause other managerial reactions that are potentially harmful, such as gameplaying, or that are undermining the behaviors the controls were designed to keep in check. For example, one study of general managers in a well-run diversified corporation found that 74% obtained the required approvals *after* the money was spent in order to speed up the process.[26]

Negative attitudes

Even when the sets of controls being used are well designed, they can sometimes cause negative attitudinal effects, including job tension, conflict, frustration, and resistance. Such attitudes are important not only because they are indicators of employee welfare, but also because they are coincident with many behaviors that can be harmful, such as gameplaying, lack of effort, absenteeism, and turnover.

The causes of negative attitudes are complex. They may be precipitated by a large number of factors such as economic conditions, organization structure, and administrative processes, alone or in combination. Furthermore, these factors affect different types of employees differently.

Negative attitudes produced by results controls

Results controls can produce negative attitudes. One cause of negative attitudes arises from a lack of employee commitment to the performance targets defined in the results control system. Most employees are not committed to *targets* they consider too difficult, not meaningful, not controllable, injudicious, or imprudent (and, of course, illegal or unethical). In the example of a tight results control system at UPS in Chapter 4, commitment sometimes was low because the targets were too difficult. Some of the drivers compared their working conditions with those in a "Roman galley."[27] The company avoided major labor problems apparently because it provided generous salaries. However, a gradual shift by UPS towards more part-time employment and subcontracting in the late-1990s triggered a major strike. The union claimed that part-time workers put in 35 hours or more each week without getting paid full-time rates, which were nearly double. At that time, about 57% of UPS employees worked part time, compared with the national average of 20%.[28]

Negative attitudes may also stem from problems in the *measurement* system. It is common to hear managers complain that their performance evaluations are not fair because they are being held accountable for things over which they have little or no control. (We discuss this issue in more detail in Chapter 12.) Other potential causes of negative attitudes may be associated with the *rewards* (or punishments) associated with the MCS. Rewards that are not perceived to be equitable, and perhaps most forms of punishment, tend to produce negative attitudes. Even the target setting and evaluation processes themselves may produce negative attitudes, particularly when they are implemented with people-insensitive, non-supportive leadership styles. Allowing employees to participate in setting their targets often reduces negative feelings toward results-oriented control systems.[29]

The collection of factors affecting attitudes is complex. There is some evidence that poor performers may react more negatively to better control systems because the limitations in their abilities are easier to discover. More critical, however, are system flaws that could cause negative attitudes in good performers. Attitudes are important MCS outcomes to monitor not only because they have their own value as indicators of employee welfare, but also because the presence of these negative attitudes may indicate the propensity to engage in any of a number of harmful behaviors, such as data manipulation or other forms of gamesmanship, withdrawal, or even sabotage. Clearly, the design of the MCS alone does not guarantee its success; the implementation of the system is an equally important, if not more important, determinant.

Negative attitudes produced by action controls

Most people, particularly professionals, react negatively to the use of action controls. Preaction reviews can be particularly frustrating if the employees being reviewed do not perceive the reviews as serving a useful purpose. For example, the European investment banking business at Bank of America Merrill Lynch was locked in a clash as former Merrill Lynch managers and Bank of America's top executives argued over how the business should be run. At stake was whether the combined investment business will be run using the Merrill Lynch-style decentralized model or Bank of America's centralized "command and control" model. Specifically, attempts by global banking head Brian Moynihan from Bank of America to remove individual managers' power to rule on matters such as staff compensation and to impose the Bank of America model on Merrill Lynch has caused widespread dissent. Prior to the takeover by BofA, Merrill Lynch's investment banking business in Europe was largely left to run itself. One London-based former Merrill Lynch manager said: "Moynihan's view is 'we'll do it the Bank of America way and no other,' even though that got them nowhere in European investment banking for the past five years, whereas the Merrill Lynch model, which delegated a lot of authority, has proven very successful over the past 10 years." The spat has led to the resignations of more than 40 senior managing directors in London and New York with more expected to follow in the coming months.[30]

At 7-Eleven, the global convenience store chain, some managers describe the action controls in use in the Japanese locations as "draconian." The company's point-of-sale computer system, which registers every sale at each store location, is used to monitor how much time each manager uses the analytical tools built into the cash register system. Stores are ranked by how often their operators use the system, and if they are not using it "enough" the store managers are told to "shape up." One manager complained: "Sometimes I don't know who's really running the store. It's like being under 24-hour surveillance; it's like being enslaved."[31] Even though 7-Eleven Japan has been called "the world's best-run convenience store chain,"[32] efforts to import the computer-focused action control system to stores in the United States met with stiff resistance because it "goes against American workers' desire for independence."[33] Moreover, although employee monitoring software (some call it "spyware") may provide what seems useful information, it may undermine employee morale and mutual trust. "If you have to check up on employees all the time, then you probably have bigger issues than just productivity," notes Peter Cheese, managing director of Accenture's talent and organization practice.[34]

Action controls can also annoy lower-level personnel. At Value Line, CEO Jean Bernhard Buttner barraged employees with memos regulating virtually every aspect of their work life. An example of such a highly restrictive, perhaps even petty, action control was that department heads [must] file a "clean surfaces report" at the end of each workday certifying that all desktops in their areas are clean.[35] At Gateway Computers, two widely hated policies dictated what posters employees could put up in their cubicles and the exact time employees could go to lunch. (Some employees had their lunch hour set at 9:30 in the morning.) The result, not surprisingly, is a demoralized, embittered workforce and high turnover. Or, as some employees groused at Gateway Computers: "It's the ultimate AT&T-ification of business"[36] (referring to the culture at the former US telecommunications giant that was renowned for its elaborate bureaucracy).

CONCLUSION

The implementation of virtually all controls requires companies to incur some direct, out-of-pocket costs. But sometimes those direct costs are dwarfed by the indirect costs caused by any of a number of harmful side effects.

We can make four general observations about the occurrence of these side effects. First, as Table 5.1 summarizes, the harmful side effects are not unique to one form of control. However, the risk of side effects does seem to be smaller with personnel controls. Second, some of the control types have negative side effects that are largely unavoidable. It is difficult, or even impossible, for people to enjoy following a strict set of procedures (action accountability) for a long period of time, although the negative attitudes can probably be minimized if the reasons for them are well communicated and if the list is kept to a minimum. Third, the likelihood of severe harmful side effects is greatest when there is either a failure to satisfy one or more of the desirable design criteria or a misfit between the choice of type(s) of control and the situation. Fourth, when controls have design imperfections or when they are inappropriately used, the tighter the controls are applied, the greater are both the likelihood and the severity of harmful side effects.

What makes dealing with these potential side effects difficult is that there is not always a simple one-to-one relationship between the control type and the effect. Furthermore, the existence of the side effects is often difficult to detect. For example, a failure to make the measurement processes objective in a results- or action-accountability control system just only offers the *opportunity* for data manipulation. However, *actual* manipulation may not occur until an employee has a personal need for more money, poor performance

TABLE 5.1 Control types and possible harmful side effects

Type of control	Behavioral displacement	Gamesmanship	Operating delays	Negative attitudes
Results controls				
Results accountability	x	x		x
Action controls				
Behavioral constraints			x	x
Preaction reviews			x	x
Action accountability	x	x		x
Redundancy				x
Personnel/cultural controls				
Selection and placement	x			
Training	x			
Provision of necessary resources				
Creation of a strong organizational culture	x			
Group-based rewards	x			

Source: K. A. Merchant, *Modern Management Control Systems: Text and Cases* (Upper Saddle River, NJ: Prentice Hall, 1998), p. 224.

creates additional pressure to perform, or leadership creates a motivation to manipulate.[37] That said, the better organizations can alleviate both the opportunity and motivation for undesired behaviors, the more likely their control systems will have predominantly desired effects and, hence, lower costs.

Notes

1. This problem is also known as *multi-tasking* – see J. Roberts, *The Modern Firm* (New York, NY: Oxford University Press, 2004), and other work by John Roberts and colleagues; see also W. A. Van der Stede, "The Pitfalls of Pay-for-Performance," *Finance & Management* (December 2007), pp. 10–13; W. A. Van der Stede, "Designing Effective Reward Systems," *Finance & Management* (October 2009), pp. 6–9.

2. "I Built This Company, I Can Save It," *Fortune* (April 30, 2001).

3. This example is taken from J. Pfeffer and R. Sutton, *Hard Facts, Dangerous Half-Truths and Total Nonsense* (Boston, MA: Harvard Business School Press, 2006), p. 120.

4. "Look Who's Doing R&D: Big Corporate Labs Are Cutting Back on Research When They Don't See a Quick Payoff," *Fortune* (November 27, 2000), p. 232.

5. See note 1.

6. "I Built This Company, I Can Save It," op. cit.

7. "Just Think: No Permission Needed," *Fortune* (January 8, 2001), pp. 190–2.

8. "Jeans Therapy: Levi's Factory Workers Are Assigned to Teams, And Morale Takes a Hit," *The Wall Street Journal* (May 20, 1998), p. A1.

9. See W. A. Van der Stede, "The Relationship Between Two Consequences of Budget Controls: Budgetary Slack Creation and Managerial Short-term Orientation," *Accounting, Organizations and Society*, 25, no. 6 (August 2000), pp. 609–22.

10. See, for example, M. Jensen, "Corporate Budgeting is Broken: Let's Fix It," *Harvard Business Review* (November 2001), pp. 94–101; and M. Jensen, "Why Pay People to Lie?," *The Wall Street Journal* (January 8, 2001), p. A32.

11. Van der Stede, "The Relationship Between Two Consequences of Budget Controls," op. cit.

12. For various manifestations of such practices, see, for example, M. Jones, *Creative Accounting, Fraud and International Accounting Scandals* (Wiley, 2010).

13. See, for example, M. Nelson, J. Elliott, and R. Tarpley, "How Are Earnings Managed? Examples from Auditors," *Accounting Horizons*, 17 (Supplement 2003): pp. 17–35.

14. "Full Disclosure," *Forbes* (April, 2002), pp. 36–8.

15. "Legal – But Lousy," *Fortune* (September 2, 2002), p. 192.

16. "'A Bad Way to Run a Railroad': Dell Pays Big to Settle Fraud Charges," *The Wall Street Journal* (July 23, 2010), online (http://blogs.wsj.com).

17. "Blind Ambition: How the Pursuit of Results Got Out of Hand at Bausch & Lomb," *Business Week* (October 23, 1995), p. 80.

18. Ibid., pp. 78–92.

19. Ibid., p. 82.

20. H. Collingwood, "The Earnings Game: Everyone Plays, Nobody Wins," *Harvard Business Review*, 79, no. 6 (June 2001), pp. 5–13.

21. "Sunrise Scam Throws Light on Incentive Pay Programs," *The Los Angeles Times* (January 15, 1996), p. D1.

22. "Blind Ambition," op. cit., p. 80.

23. "EU Markets Chief Barnier Plans Radical Overhaul of Audit Industry," *The Telegraph* (October 13, 2010), online (www.telegraph.co.uk); see also J. Coffee, *Gatekeepers: The Professions and Corporate Governance* (New York, NY: Oxford University Press, 2006), Chapter 5.

24. "A Farewell to Pussyfooting," *The Economist* (July 8, 2010), p. 27; "The Gauge of Innocence," *CFO Europe* (April 2009), pp. 42–4.

25. "In the Driver's Seat at Toyota: US Execs Get More Independence as the Automaker Focuses on Asia and Europe," *The Los Angeles Times* (October 19, 2004), p. C1.

26. K. A. Merchant, "The Effects of Financial Controls on Data Manipulation and Management Myopia," *Accounting, Organizations and Society*, 15, no. 4 (1990), pp. 297–313.

27. "Behind the UPS Mystique: Puritanism and Productivity," *Business Week* (June 6, 1983), p. 68.

28. "A look at the Core Issues of the UPS Strike," *CNN Interactive US News Story Page* (August 18, 1997).

29. See, for example, G. Latham, "The Motivational Benefits of Goal-Setting," *Academy of Management Executive*, 18, no. 4 (2004), pp. 126–9.

30. "Power Struggle at BofA Merrill Lynch," *Market Watch* (April 19, 2009), online (www.marketwatch.com).

31. "7-Eleven Operators Resist System to Monitor Managers," *The Wall Street Journal* (June 16, 1997), p. B1.

32. A. Ishikawa and T. Nejo, *The Success of 7-Eleven Japan: Discovering the Secrets of the World's Best-Run Convenience Store Chain* (Singapore: World Scientific, 2002).

33. "7-Eleven Operators Resist System to Monitor Managers," op. cit.

34. "Big Brother Bosses," *The Economist* (September 10, 2009), pp. 71–2; see also "Monitoring the Monitors," *The Wall Street Journal* (August 16, 2010), online (http://online.wsj.com).

35. "Value Line: Too Lean, Too Mean?" *Business Week* (March 16, 1992), p. 105.

36. "I Built This Company, I Can Save It," op. cit.

37. B. Litzky, K. Eddleston, and D. Kidder, "The Good, the Bad, and the Misguided: How Managers Inadvertently Encourage Deviant Behaviors," *The Academy of Management Perspectives*, 20, no. 1 (February 2006), pp. 91–103.

Case Study

Philip Anderson

It was three days to month end. Philip Anderson, the Phoenix branch manager of Stuart & Co., the largest brokerage firm in town, was dreading the monthly teleconference meeting with his bosses in New York. Once again his team had failed to deliver on some of the specific product sales targets set for them in the company's sales budget. Specifically, the ratio of in-house to outside product sales of items such as mutual funds and insurance product offerings had not improved from the prior month; his team had not been successful in pushing equity issues syndicated or underwritten by the parent firm to the levels set by his boss a few months earlier; and his team had not increased the overall balance of margin accounts. On the positive side, the number of margin accounts had increased, new clients had

been signed up, and overall branch revenues had increased. But Phil questioned how long he would be able to justify not meeting some of the specific targets the firm had given his branch.

Phil began his sales career right after college. His first job was with a cereal producer, as an inside salesman. He switched to the brokerage business after just two years, lured by the potential for higher income and the opportunity to have direct contact with retail clients. Phil was an outgoing individual who had a talent for financial matters, and he looked forward to a job that would allow him to interact with clients directly. Just five months ago, Phil had celebrated his thirtieth year in the brokerage industry and his twenty-first year with Stuart & Co. Although he truly enjoyed being a manager and working with ▶

This case was prepared by Research Assistant Juan Jimenez and Professors Kenneth A. Merchant and Wim A. Van der Stede.

his team, some of the other demands of the job were beginning to wear on him. Things had not turned out as he had expected. Phil thought of himself as a hard-working and loyal employee, a good manager, and an ethical businessman. The "compromises" that his career seemed to demand were beginning to trouble him. He did not consider himself a saint, and he knew that his job required balancing conflicting goals, but he wondered how far he could bend without breaking.

Phil started his brokerage career with one of the largest firms in the industry. He moved to Stuart & Co., then a boutique firm, in the hope of breaking free from the high-pressure sales-oriented attitude prevalent in the industry. He thought that the perception that the large firms tried to perpetuate – that their advisors are experts at providing unbiased financial advice – is for the most part wrong. Phil learned firsthand that brokers are paid, first and foremost, to sell products and services. Meeting the financial needs of their clients was not paramount.

Stuart & Co. seemed to be different. It was a firm that emphasized the development of long-term client relationships based upon rendering expert independent financial advice. Its investment advisors were to be trusted counselors to clients on all financial matters. But Phil was also lured by Stuart's compensation package, which included a relatively large fixed salary and a bonus based upon overall branch revenues, growth in the number of ties or relationships (financial, insurance, investment) developed with each customer, and the number of business referrals to other branches.

However, things had changed since he had joined the firm. As the investment and analysis units expanded, the demand on the branch managers to push specific products began to be in-corporated into their annual sales budgets. Phil felt that those changes had compromised his ability to deliver investment options suited to his clients' financial situations. They risked the many long-term relationships with clients that he had worked hard to develop and created ethical dilemmas for him and his staff. Phil felt that pursuing some of the new budget goals could result in future financial losses for some of his clients. However, Phil had worked in the brokerage industry and at Stuart & Co. long enough to know that it was dangerous to openly express those concerns to his boss. Additionally, Phil was troubled with the recent scandals in the industry. It was mostly low-level employees like him who were the object of criminal prosecution, not the top executives.

As Phil saw it, his job was to develop and nurture profitable relationships with as many clients as possible, and the specific products and services sold to clients should be dictated by the needs of those clients. Consequently, he could never bring himself to pushing his team to adhere to the firm directives, and this approach had negatively impacted his total compensation in the last few years. Invariably, his annual bonus lagged behind those of other managers at Stuart & Co., even though his branch was one of the largest in the firm in terms of clients, sales volume, and net profits. Phil felt his current situation was unfair. He also was beginning to worry that his failure to meet specific product sales targets was eroding whatever measure of job safety his overall results had given him. To compound the situation, Stuart & Co. had recently been bought by one of the largest brokerage firms in the country, and it seemed that the new hierarchy did not take well to independent-minded managers like Phil who did not aggressively pursue the objectives set out by corporate.

Phil was getting tired of the game but could not see how he could avoid playing it. He was almost 54 years old and was the sole provider for his family. His wife had retired a year before from her teaching job to take care of their three teenage sons. They had just recently bought a 4,000 square feet home in an exclusive neighborhood of Scottsdale. And last fall, Phil had fulfilled a college dream by buying for himself a brand new red Corvette. Phil feared that if he allowed his team of advisors to continue focusing on meeting their clients' needs with little regard for corporate targets, more than his discretionary compensation would be at risk.

Phil had many questions and doubts and few answers. Was he right in allowing his clients' financial goals to take precedence over his own family's financial security? Was he being unreasonable, naive, or impractical? Was there somewhere a proper balance? Was he being too ethical at a time when his family's future should be his primary concern? Or perhaps it was time for him to find another employer that shared Phil's philosophy, if one existed in the brokerage industry? But could he find another good job at his age? Or should he even bother? After all, he had done his part. Maybe it should be the job of some younger managers to champion the cause of service to clients and continue the battle.

Sunshine Fashion: Fraud, Theft, and Misbehavior Among Employees

Shenzhen-based Sunshine Fashion was a Sino-Japanese venture that had grown from merely an OEM export manufacturer of cashmere sweaters to also a retailer with a chain of 220 retail points across China in 2010. In order to manage its retail operation, it had set up regional as well as branch offices to handle stock as well as support and monitor its retail points. Nonetheless, fraudulent behavior among employees had cost the retail chain almost 5% of its domestic sales revenues. The implementation of an ERP system for tracking goods and sales had improved the situation somewhat. What were the challenges that Sunshine face in trying to control fraudulent behavior among its staff? What additional measures should the management undertake and how should the remedial measures be implemented to achieve its target?

COMPANY BACKGROUND

Shenzhen-based Sunshine Fashion Co. Ltd. was a Sino-Japanese joint venture founded in 1993. It started out as an OEM[1] export manufacturer of cashmere sweaters and eventually grew to become an integrated manufacturer and retailer with activities that included material sourcing, spinning, dyeing, design, distribution, marketing, and retailing. By 2010, it had three factories, located in Shenzhen, Shanghai, and Taiyuan of Shanxi province; 220 sales counters in departmental stores across the country; and a workforce of more than 1,000 employees.

Sunshine produced some 300,000 pieces a year for domestic sales, which enjoyed a considerably higher profit margin than its export business. With a turnover of RMB 150 million, domestic sales made up more than two-thirds of Sunshine's business. Sunshine was positioned as a high-end fashion brand in the domestic market with design being the leading factor in determining the sales of its goods. At RMB 3,000 a piece,[2] Sunshine's cashmere sweaters were considered a luxurious item in China.[3]

> We are concerned with the price at which we sell, not how many garments we sell. Volume is nothing for us. If we sell a lot of garments but at a very low price, there is no profit.
>
> *Kitty Li, Sales Manager of Sunshine*

Since the customers of Sunshine were fashion conscious, the value of out-of-season items could fall to as low as one-third of their original price. Sunshine's vertically integrated organization gave it a competitive edge over its competitors. It could complete the product cycle from design to distribution within 20 days as compared with the three months it took for its major competitor Edor.

THE OPERATION

Sunshine's 220 retail counters in departmental stores across the country were managed by 14 branch offices that reported to three regional offices in Beijing, Chongqing, and Nanjing. The three regional offices were all former branch offices promoted to regional offices.

> Before the head office controlled almost everything, the price, the quantity, which branch office was to be allocated how much goods . . . These decisions and

---

[1] OEM stands for original equipment manufacturer. It refers to manufacturers who produce products for another company that will be retailed under the brand name of that company.

[2] RMB 3,000 = US$451.35 at an exchange rate of $US1 = RMB 6.65.

[3] China's national average GDP per capita of 2007 was RMB 18,665. (Source: Statistical Communiqué of the People's Republic, dated February 28, 2008.)

▶

This case was prepared by Grace Loo under the supervision of Professor Neale O'Connor

coordination was concentrated with one person. With three regional companies, [the work] can be separated and it reduces the load on this one person.

Kitty Li, Sales Manager of Sunshine

Sunshine had franchised some retail points outside of the major cities but remained cautious about expanding its franchise network out of concern for operational control and brand integrity.

Stock

At the beginning of each season, Sunshine's head office would prepare the stock, tagging each item with barcodes with prices, and send it to the branch offices. The branch offices were responsible for distributing the sweaters to the 220 retail counters and for replenishing the stock at each counter throughout the season. The head office sent the goods to the branch offices by air and sometimes also by courier. Roughly 3% of the goods was lost during transportation. At the end of each season, the branch offices were required to return all leftover stock to the head office and they would be refunded the cost of the returned goods. Over a two month period each year the head office would put ten people to work, counting and inspecting the returned items, repackaging them, and changing the barcodes to a new price if necessary ready for sale in the following season (see Exhibit 1).

Sales

The branch offices and retail points reported information about stock and sales to the head office manually until 1998 when Sunshine implemented an RFID/ERP system. The system networked the branch offices and head office together, and this allowed the head office to receive updates on sales at all the retail points every four hours. Sunshine's RFID/ERP system also stored information about inventory at the branch offices and retail counters, but the information had to be input manually by staff.

THEFT AND FRAUD BY EMPLOYEES

In 2008, Sunshine faced serious fraud and misbehavior problems by employees with estimated losses of between RMB 9.3 million and RMB 10.5 million, translating to more than 5% of Sunshine's total domestic sales. Although Sunshine's RFID/ERP system provided the head office with an updated point-of-sales situation every four hours, managers who wanted to cheat took advantage of the head office's inability to control discounts and stock at the local level. Sunshine's head office was responsible for setting the price and determining promotional time-frames but these time-frames were not necessarily followed by all the branch managers. Some branch managers postponed the start date of the promotional period without informing the head office so they could sell sweaters at the original price and pocketed the difference between the sale price and the discounted price, which was remitted to the head office. Other branch managers reported a higher discount rate to the head office than what was actually the case and pocketed the difference. The situation was further complicated by the fact that the market situation varied widely across China and each department store had its own policy with regard to the timing of sales promotions.

> It depends on the different department stores. They each have different sales and celebrations and other things. It's hard to control from the head office, they are far away from the office.

Kitty Li, Sales Manager of Sunshine

Sunshine had no choice but to allow some autonomy for decisions over promotions and discounts rates at the local level, a practice that increased the risk of managers engaging in fraudulent behavior. The branch offices also engaged in a small amount of cash sales and there was no way for the head office to control such sales. The branch managers had total discretion over how much discount they wanted to give in such instances.

Fraudulent behavior was also encouraged by the fact that Sunshine had no mechanism in place to control stock at the local level. While the head office knew how many pieces it sent out to each branch office at the beginning of the season, it had no information how many of those pieces were at the branch office and how many had been distributed to each retail point at any moment in time. The branch office sent pieces to the retail points almost every day depending on their needs. This made it difficult for the head office to control promotions.

> To check the stock before each promotion is impossible. The promotion each time depends on the different holidays and the policy of each departmental store . . .

It's hard to take stock before each promotion. We only control the inventory.

Kitty Li, Sales Manager of Sunshine

Sunshine's ERP system could not update stock information automatically. It stored stock information but that information had to be input and updated manually. This meant that staff could input the stock information only after a promotion started, giving them an opportunity to sell the sweaters at the original price and pocket the difference. Loss arising from such misbehavior was estimated to cost Sunshine RMB 3 million.

While barcoding the sweaters helped Sunshine to track its products, it had found that the barcodes of some of the sweaters had been changed, which altered the price upwards by as much as 50% when the unsold goods were returned to the head office at the end of the season.

> For example, given two garments priced at 1000 yuan and 500 yuan, respectively, the salesman might sell one piece of 1000 yuan, and return 500 yuan piece to the head office at the end of the season. The head office knows that the salesman has 1000 yuan earning. But, if the salesman changes the barcode of the 500 yuan garment to the 1000 yuan barcode, then on returning the garment and barcode to the head office, the head office thinks that the salesman has only 500 yuan earning (cash). When auditing at the end of the season, the total quantity is not less, but the amount difference who knows?
>
> Every year we have a big quantity and amount of sale, and the price changes all the time (because of festivals, shop anniversary, discount season . . .) it's a huge workload to check every barcode, or the boss thinks that is it worth to do so? It's another big cost . . .

Kitty Li, Sales Manager of Sunshine

Loss due to changed barcodes was estimated at RMB 1.5 million. Sunshine's accounting department visited the branch offices once or twice a year during the sales season to check their stock and their accounts and the head office also arranged random visits to the retail counters, but to little avail.

Another misbehavior that Sunshine encountered was managers who used the relationship they built up with departmental stores as Sunshine managers to sell their own goods or brands.

> . . . these managers, they use their own relationship with the department store manager to begin their own brand and business. Maybe they give money to the manager every year, but this money is from Sunshine,

you know, so they use the company's money to set up their own relationship. That's the problem.

Kitty Li, Sales Manager of Sunshine

To counter such misbehavior, the president of Sunshine regularly visited department stores with Sunshine retail counters around the country to reinforce the Sunshine brand and to build up a personal relationship with the department stores himself.

> We don't want the branch managers to get too close to one store manager. Once they have good relationship [with the departmental store manager], even better relationship than the general managers from our head office . . . they can begin their own brand easily, use this relationship to begin their own business may be at the same time.

Kitty Li, Sales Manager of Sunshine

Sunshine rotated the branch managers among the different branches periodically to control their power.

A number of organizational factors also contributed to the rampant fraudulent misbehavior among employees. *Guanxi*, or relationship, with the departmental stores was critical for brands to set up retail points within departmental stores in China, and Sunshine branch managers were often recruited based on the strength of their relationships with the departmental stores rather than their management ability or integrity. With branch managers having an average tenure of two years and a yearly turnover rate of 20%, their weak sense of belonging and loyalty to Sunshine encouraged greed and opportunistic behavior. Branch managers, leveraging the relationships they built with department stores while they worked at Sunshine, often became agents of other brands when they left, turning into competitors of Sunshine.

Branch managers received a fixed monthly salary of between RMB 3,000 and RMB 4,000 and a year-end bonus that was decided solely at the discretion of the general manager. While the standard of living and wage level varied widely across China, the salary of Sunshine's branch managers was generally set on par with Shenzhen, where Sunshine's head office was located and which had one of the highest wage levels in China.[4] Nonetheless, the year-end bonus

---

[4] According to the *China Statistical Yearbok 2009*, Shenzhen has the fifth highest average wage and salary level among the major cities in China after Shanghai, Beijing, Lhasa, and Guanzhou. The average wage and salary of Shenzhen is RMB 43,731, compared to RMB 56,565 in Shanghai. Kunming, which ranks 36th, has an average wage and salary level of RMB 22,432.

was decided solely at the discretion of the general manager and the lack of transparency into how decisions over the bonuses were made gave branch managers little motivation to act in the best interest of the company. To remedy the situation, Sunshine had begun setting sales targets for the branch managers each June based on their location, and the square footage and sales history of the retail points, and awarding year-end commissions to branch managers who could meet their sales target. Under the new system, branch managers could receive commission that was as high as their annual salary if their sales performance was good.

ANNUAL REVIEW

Sunshine's management was due to meet soon for its annual review meeting, and employee fraud and misbehavior was on the meeting's agenda. The CEO had decided on a target of reducing the fraudulent behavior to 2% of retail sales. The implementation

of the ERP system had given the head office better control over its retail operation, but fraud and misbehavior among employees continued. Li knew that it was impossible to control everything.

> If the manager knows you are to come, he will do something about it. Everything we do is to reduce risk but we cannot control perfectly. If you control them perfectly, they will resign.
>
> *Kitty Li, Sales Manager of Sunshine*

But there must be more that could be done to control such misbehavior. What were the root causes of the staff's misbehavior? What were the strengths and weaknesses of Sunshine's current internal control system? Most of all, what could Li propose to the management to improve the situation? What measures should the management undertake and how should the remedial measures be implemented? In what order would you implement the recommended actions for Sunshine?

EXHIBIT 1 Sunshine's operational flow for its retail business

	Head office	Regional offices	Branch offices	Retail points
Flow of goods at the beginning of the season	Prepare stock with bar codes and send out at the start of each season.		Branch office responsible for replenishing retail points throughout the season.	
Flow of goods not sold at the end of the season	Head office inspects, counts, and change barcodes if necessary after receiving goods returned.		Branch offices sent goods not sold back to head office at the end of the season.	
Flow of retail sales information	Receives information via ERP system.	Receives information via ERP system.	Receives information via ERP system.	ERP system records sales information. Inventory information has to be input/ updated manually.
Discounts/promotions	Determines discounts and promotions.		Branch offices engage in some direct sales and branch managers have discretion in giving discounts in such sales.	Department stores in which retail points are located also make their own discounts/promotion policies.

Fit Food, Inc.

Our shareholders are demanding better performance from us. Our market valuation has been basically flat for most of the last decade. At the same time, we need to be making larger investments in our future, to develop new products and to augment our sources of organic ingredients. So we need to ratchet up the performance pressure. We need to do better.

Sean Wright, CEO, Fit Food, Inc.

Sean made this pronouncement in May 2008 at a management meeting held just after the Fit Food annual shareholders' meeting. The division managers responded to Sean's call to action, but not all of their responses were what Sean had in mind.

THE COMPANY

Sean Wright founded Fit Food, Inc. (FFI) in 1972. Sean had been working as the VP R&D in a large food company, but he had always wanted to start his own business. In his spare time, he developed a new line of cookies, called "Smart Cookies," that he could advertise as being healthier because they were lower in fat and calories. After many struggles to get Smart Cookies placed in major supermarket chains, by 2000 Sean and his growing team were able to declare proudly that the Smart Cookie brand was being distributed nationally. With more products in development, and taking advantage of the good stock market environment in 2000, Sean launched an FFI IPO. The company's stock was listed on NASDAQ.

By the year 2009, FFI was a medium-sized food company that targeted "tasty-but-healthier" market segments. In 2001 Sean introduced several new snack products and started a Savory Snacks Division. In 2003 he acquired an energy drink company, which became FFI's Sport and Energy Drinks division. By 2009, FFI's annual revenues were approaching $500 million. The company was consistently profit-able but heavily leveraged, as Sean had funded the energy-drink acquisition by increasing the company's debt load significantly.

FFI used a divisionalized organizational structure (see Exhibit 1). The general managers of the three relatively autonomous divisions – Cookies & Crackers, Savory Snacks, and Sports & Energy Drinks – reported directly to Sean, the CEO. Each division had its own sales and marketing, production, and R&D departments and a controller. The corporate staff included human resources, MIS, finance, R&D, and legal departments. FFI did not have an internal auditing function. It had outsourced the documentation and testing work needed to comply with the Section 404 requirements of the Sarbanes-Oxley Act. Recently, however, Joe Jellison, FFI's CFO, had suggested that the company was becoming large enough that it should start bringing this work in-house.

In 2008 Kristine Trodden was assigned as the external auditing firm partner on the FFI account. Kristine considered FFI not to be a particularly desirable client because of persistent requests to reduce auditing fees amid threats to solicit bids from competing firms.

FFI's board of directors included five members. Sean was the chair. The other outside directors included a small company CEO, a CFO of a medium-sized public company, a vice president of marketing at a large supermarket chain, and a practitioner in holistic nutrition. All of the outside directors had been suggested by Sean but approved by the board's nominating and governance committee. The board met in person four times a year and also by conference call as needed.

PLANS, REVIEWS, AND INCENTIVES

FFI's planning process began in August when corporate managers sent to each division economic ▶

This case was prepared by Professor Kenneth A. Merchant and research assistant Michelle Spaulding.

Copyright © by Kenneth A. Merchant.

forecasts, other planning assumptions, and preliminary sales targets. The sales targets reflected investor expectations of steady growth. Typically each division was expected to increase annual revenues and profits by at least 5%.

Over the following two months, division management created formal strategic plans, which included both a strategic narrative and a high-level summary profit and loss statement. The strategic plans were approved by corporate managers in early October. Then division managers developed the elements of their Annual Operating Plans (AOP) for the coming year, which included detailed marketing and new product development plans and pro forma income statements and balance sheets.

Developing the AOPs required many discussions between corporate and division management. The division managers typically argued that they needed to increase their expense budgets to be able to achieve their sales goals, and corporate typically wanted to squeeze expenses to generate increased profits. A fairly standard planning exercise was to ask each division what programs or plans they would cut if their profit budget was cut by 10%. Once these programs were identified, the division managers had to justify adding them back into the budget. Tensions between division and corporate management increased in 2008 because corporate was asking the divisions to increase their growth rates to 7% to allow some new corporate investment initiatives to be funded internally. At the end of the negotiation processes, the AOPs were presented to the board of directors for approval at its meeting held in early December.

During the year, performance review meetings were held quarterly. The focus of the meetings tended to be on explaining variances between revenue and profit performance goals and actual performance. The meetings were quick and painless when performance matched or exceeded expectations, but the tone was dramatically different when the quarterly profit goals were not achieved. Catherine Elliot (marketing manager, Cookies and Crackers Division) explained:

> Corporate pushes us hard to make our numbers. There is never a good reason for not making our goals. We're paid to be creative and come up with solutions, not excuses. Sean calls it "no excuses management."

Division presidents and their direct management reports could earn annual bonuses based on achievement of AOP profit targets. The target bonuses ranged from 25% to 100% of the manager's base salary, depending on organization level. No bonuses were paid if division profits fell below 85% of AOP plans. Maximum bonuses of 150% of the target bonus amounts were paid if profits exceeded AOP by 25%. Average bonuses exceeded target bonus levels in seven of the first eight years of FFI's history as a public corporation.

Some corporate managers and division presidents were also included in a stock option plan. FFI stock had performed well in the early 2000s, but virtually all of the gains were lost in the stock market downturn of 2008–09. Most of the options were underwater.

The recession of 2008–09 stressed company operations at the same time that Sean was calling for better financial performance. The Savory Snacks Division performed well and achieved the higher growth rates called for in both 2008 and 2009. The other two divisions experienced more challenges, however, as is explained below. (Summary income statements for these divisions are shown in Exhibit 2.)

SPORTS & ENERGY DRINK DIVISION

The Sports & Energy Drinks Division (Drink Division) was formed in 2003 when FFI acquired a successful, regional energy drink brand. As part of the deal, Jack Masters, the former CEO of the acquired company, became president of the division. Performance in the first few years after the acquisition was good. The targeted drink categories continued to grow; two brand extensions were successfully launched; and Drink Division sales nearly doubled between 2003 and 2006. The division achieved its AOP profit targets easily, and Jack was able to operate without much interference from corporate.

By early 2007, however, Jack saw some clouds on the horizon. The energy drink category was becoming more and more competitive as more players, including some large, well-capitalized corporations, entered the category. At the same time, retailers were consolidating and becoming more powerful, increasing pressure on manufacturers to lower prices. Jack began to worry that he might not be able to deliver the growth that was expected of his division.

2007

Despite Jack's worries, 2007 was another stellar year, with sales growth exceeding even Sean's increased expectations. The category momentum continued, and Jack's brands gained market share, due in part to a successful grassroots advertising campaign.

With performance far exceeding the AOP targets and excellent bonuses assured for the year 2007, Jack thought it would be prudent to try to position the division for success in the future. He met with his management team to discuss his concerns and to come up with ideas to get better control over reported profits. Jack and his team decided on three courses of action. The first was to declare a shipping moratorium at the end of the year, which shifted some sales that would normally have been recorded in 2007 into 2008.

Not all of Jack's managers were happy with the shipping moratorium plan of action. The production team was unhappy because the moratorium would cause scheduling problems. Some employees would have to be furloughed temporarily at the end of the year to minimize the build-up in inventory. Then in early 2008 they would have to incur some over-time costs both to accelerate production and to ship the orders that had accumulated. The sales department was concerned that they would have to deal with customer complaints about shipment delays and product outages. Nevertheless, Jack decided to move forward with the shipping moratorium regardless of the costs, which he considered relatively minor.

The second plan was to build up accounting reserves against accounts receivable and inventory balances. In 2007 the Drink Division controller was able to provide a justification for increasing reserves by $1,000,000 over 2006 levels.

The third plan was to prepay some expenses that would have normally been incurred in 2008. Among other things, some facility maintenance programs were accelerated, and supplies inventories were replenished before the end of the year. These items were not material, amounting to expenditures of only about $100,000. But, as Jack noted, "Every little bit helps."

2008

In 2008 some of Jack's fears were realized. As the economy slowed down, consumers became more frugal. The once exploding energy drink category began to stagnate; competition for market share grew fierce; and margins declined. In addition, there were rumblings of an impending soft drink "obesity" tax that could put even more pressure on profits.

The division was able to make its annual revenue targets in 2008, but the division managers did so by offering an "early order program" developed by the Sales and Marketing Department. Customers were offered discounts and liberal payment terms if they placed orders scheduled to be delivered before the year ended. Discounts ranged from 5–20% and customers were given 120 days to pay their invoices without incurring interest, rather than the traditional 30 days. However, Jack learned later that some of the more aggressive salespeople had told customers to accept the shipments now and "just pay us whenever you sell the product."

While sales remained strong, profit margins decreased significantly. In order to make sure the Division would hit its AOP profit target, Jack and his controller began to liquidate some of its accounting reserves in the third quarter, and by the end of the year the reserves were reduced by a total of $1.7 million. The auditors noticed and questioned the change, and brought it to the attention of Joe Jellison, FFI's CFO. Joe looked into the issue and concluded that the new reserve levels seemed justified based on historical performance levels.

2009

Sales started out slowly in 2009, but in the second quarter the sales team landed a major new national account. Because of the uptake in demand, Jack had now become more concerned about meeting production schedules than he was about achieving sales goals. Thus, the early order program and almost all other promotions and discounts were eliminated.

Jack also told his controller to rebuild reserves, and a total of $2 million in reserves were restored in 2009. Once again the auditors questioned the change, but the controller provided a justification based on uncertainty in the economy and irregularities in some new customers' payment patterns, Jack believed that his division was well positioned for success going into 2010.

COOKIES & CRACKERS DIVISION

The Cookies & Crackers Division (Cookie Division) was built around the "Smart Cookie" product, once

FFI's flagship brand. But the Smart Cookie product had been struggling for the last several years. Cookies was a low growth, low margin product category with a strong private label presence, though quality health-oriented brands commanded a small price premium. The biggest problem for the Cookie Division, however, was a shift in consumer mindset. In recent years "healthy" was less likely to be associated with low fat, and more likely to be associated with healthful ingredients such as whole grains, nuts, and natural anti-oxidants, a trend that the Cookie Division management had largely missed.

Scott Hoyt, the Cookie Division president, had been with FFI since its inception. Scott had a strong background in sales and was credited with selling Smart Cookie to national accounts, but he was perceived as resistant to change, and his accounting and finance knowledge was relatively weak.

The Cookie Division traditionally relied heavily on a variety of seasonal trade promotions to achieve their volume targets. By 2008, Catherine Elliott, head of the Marketing Department, was concerned that the new required 7% growth rate was probably not attainable without both some aggressive marketing and development of some good new products. During the annual planning process, she made a case for increasing the division's advertising and new product development budgets, but her requests were denied. Sean explained that he did not think the advertising was necessary. He also believed that the projects being funded at the corporate level would yield better returns than the proposed investments in Cookies, and FFI could not afford both investments.

2008

It became obvious early in the first quarter of 2008 that Cookie sales were falling well below the levels forecast in the AOP. The Cookie sales department initiated a promotion to meet the first quarter goals. The specifics of the program were similar to those of the early order program being used in the Drink Division – generous discounts and extended payment terms for early orders. The early order program was implemented aggressively. The sales team was told to contact all of their customers and convince them to take early delivery of product. Many of these contacts were successful. In most cases, the sales staff received written authorization from their customers, but in some cases the authorizations were only verbal.

In the final days of the first quarter, Catherine and Mitch Michaels, head of the Sales Department, asked shipping to work around the clock to ship as much product as possible before the quarter end. In the last hours of the quarter, trucks filled with cookies drove a few blocks away from the loading docks and parked, so that product was technically "shipped" and sales could be booked.

The heavy sales volume at the end of the quarter attracted the auditors' attention. They concluded, however, that the accounting treatment conformed to GAAP since ownership of the product officially changed at the time of shipment.

In the second quarter of 2008, Scott, Catherine, and Mitch knew they had a problem. Second-quarter orders were predictably slow given the amount of extra product that had been shipped in the first quarter. The three managers then decided to ship additional, unordered product to their customers. The additional order volumes were generated either by increasing the quantities of actual orders or by entering orders into the company's billing system twice. When customers complained about the unordered shipments, blame was attributed to human errors, and the sales team was charged with the task of making the unordered shipments "stick." They were offered a number of tools toward that end, such as special pricing and credit terms and product exchanges.

The program worked surprisingly well. Returns increased, but the program still effectively increased revenue by $2.3 million and profit by $460,000. Scott, Catherine, and Mitch were encouraged by the results and praised the sales team for their heroic efforts. They continued the program throughout 2008, being careful to rotate the "mistaken" shipments between customers. At the end of the year, the team managed to deliver 97% of the AOP sales and profits.

2009

During the 2009 AOP process Scott, along with Catherine and Mitch, made a strong plea to reduce the Cookie Division's revenue goals. They argued that given the weak economy and sluggish category growth, a flat revenue goal, or at most 2% growth, was a more reasonable target. However, Sean was unwilling to lower the goal. He understood the difficulties in the category, but he believed that the setting of aggressive goals and a commitment to achieve them were cornerstones of FFI's success over the years, and he knew that FFI shareholders would be demanding better performance than that.

After the disappointing AOP meeting, Scott called a meeting with his management team to develop new ideas for increasing sales. He thought if the division could make it through 2009 successfully, they would face smoother sailing in 2010 because some new, promising products would be ready for launching. A decision was made to continue the programs used in 2008.

Irene Packard, head of the Production Department, came up with another idea. She thought she could decrease expenses significantly by rewriting contracts with suppliers who supplied both machines and parts. If she could convince suppliers to decrease the costs of parts, and charge the difference to machines, she would be able to capitalize costs that would otherwise have been expensed. Irene estimated that she could reduce expenses by $2.3 million, or

$2 million after depreciation. Scott thought this was a good idea. He noted that the cost savings could bring them within striking range of the division's profit goals.

In September, though, one of the junior accountants in the division was feeling unduly pressured to make accounting entries that she felt were not good practice, particularly related to some of the billings that seemed to lack adequate supporting documentation. The managers' justifications for these entries seemed to her to be capricious rather than facts-based. She took it upon herself to discuss the issue with Joe Jellison, FFI's CFO. Joe had one of his assistant controllers examine the accounting practices in the Cookie Division, and he reported finding multiple problems with potentially material financial statement effects. Joe had to decide what to do next. Should he have his people calculate the size of the errors, make the adjusting entries, and fix the processes, or should he, at this point, inform the external auditors and/or the audit committee of the board of directors?

EXHIBIT 1 Fit Food, Inc.: organization chart

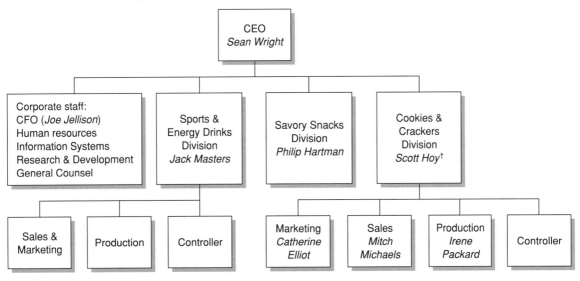

EXHIBIT 2 Fit Food, Inc.: income statements for Sports & Energy Drinks and Cookies & Crackers Divisions, FYs ending December 31 ($ millions)

Sports & Energy Drinks Division

	2007		2008		2009	
	AOP	*Actual*	*AOP*	*Actual*	*AOP*	*Actual*
Revenue	$110.0	$125.3	$130.3	$130.5	$137.0	$146.2
Cost of goods	64.0	73.6	75.5	76.6	79.5	87.5
Gross margin	$46.0	51.7	54.8	53.9	57.5	58.7
R&D expense	0.8	1.0	1.0	0.8	1.1	1.0
SG&A expense	18.0	20.0	20.0	19.2	21.0	22.0
Operating Profit	$28.2	30.7	33.8	33.9	35.4	35.7

Cookies & Crackers Division

	2007		2008		2009	
	AOP	*Actual*	*AOP*	*Actual*	*AOP*	*Actual*
Revenue	$130.0	124.5	131.0	127.3	133.0	127.1
Cost of goods	80.6	77.2	81.2	80.2	82.5	76.7
Gross margin	$49.4	47.3	49.8	47.1	50.5	50.4
R&D expense	0.4	0.3	0.4	0.3	0.4	0.3
SG&A expense	20.8	18.8	20.0	18.3	19.0	19.2
Operating profit	$28.2	28.2	29.4	28.5	31.1	30.9

Chapter 6

DESIGNING AND EVALUATING MANAGEMENT CONTROL SYSTEMS

The preceding chapters described the range of management controls that can be used and how they affect behaviors. This chapter discusses a general framework that can be used to design management control systems (MCSs) or to improve those already in use.

The process of designing and improving MCSs requires addressing two basic questions: *What is desired?* and *What is likely to happen?* If what is likely is different from what is desired, then managers must subsequently address the following two MCS-design questions: *What controls should be used?* and *How tightly should each be applied?* The following sections in this chapter describe how to address each of these questions. The chapter concludes with some observations about common management control issues faced when designing or improving MCSs.

WHAT IS DESIRED? AND *WHAT IS LIKELY?*

MCSs cannot be designed or evaluated without an understanding of what it is the organization wants the employees to do. *Objectives* and, more importantly, *strategies* that are derived from a good understanding of the organization's objectives often provide important guides to the actions that are expected. A better understanding of objectives and strategies yields a larger set of feasible control alternatives, provides a better chance of being able to apply each alternative tightly (if so required), and reduces the chance of producing behavioral displacement problems.

Not only must organizations determine what is desired, they also need to try to assess what is likely to happen. This essentially amounts to assessing the likelihood that each of the control problems are present or will occur: lack of direction, motivational problems, or personal limitations. In other words, organizations should ask whether their employees understand what they are expected to do (key actions) or to accomplish (key results), whether they are properly motivated, and whether they are able to fulfill their required roles.

If the likely actions or results are different from the desired actions or results, more or different MCSs might be called for, depending on the severity of the problems and the costs of the MCSs that could be used to solve the problems. In this situation, managers should then address the questions about what MCSs to use and how tightly to apply them.

CHOICE OF CONTROLS

The different types of management controls are not equally effective at addressing each of the management control problems. Table 6.1 provides a summary of the control problems

TABLE 6.1 Control types and control problems

	Control problems		
Control types	Lack of direction	Motivational problems	Personal limitations
Results controls			
Results accountability	x	x	
Action controls			
Behavioral constraints		x	
Preaction reviews	x	x	x
Action accountability	x	x	x
Redundancy			x
Personnel/cultural controls			
Selection and placement	x	x	x
Training	x		x
Provision of necessary resources			x
Creation of a strong organizational culture	x	x	
Group-based rewards	x	x	

Source: K. A. Merchant, *Modern Management Control Systems: Text and Cases* (Upper Saddle River, NJ: Prentice Hall, 1998), p. 253.

each of the types of management controls addresses. It shows, for example, that behavioral constraints do not help solve lack-of-direction problems; hence, if direction is a significant problem in the area of concern, managers will have to consider other forms of control.

The specific set of management controls to be selected from the feasible alternatives should be those that will provide the greatest net benefits (i.e. benefits less costs). The benefits of an MCS are derived from the increased probability of success. Since management controls are not costless to implement and operate, these costs must be put against the expected benefits of improved control.

Personnel/cultural controls as an initial consideration

In deciding among the many management control alternatives, managers should start by considering whether personnel or cultural controls will be sufficient. Personnel/cultural controls are worthy of first consideration because they have relatively few harmful side effects and relatively low out-of-pocket costs. In some cases, such as small organizations, personnel/cultural controls may provide effective management control by themselves.

Even in settings where personnel/cultural controls are not sufficiently reliable by themselves, it is useful to focus on them first because they will have to be relied upon to some extent no matter what other forms of management control are used. Considering personnel/cultural controls first allows organizations to consider how reliable these forms of management control are and assess the extent to which they should consider using other forms of control.

For example, when Marc Brownstein, president of the Brownstein Group, a small family-run advertising and public relations firm in Philadelphia, decided to take advice from his managers to tackle high turnover (30% per year among a 20-plus-person agency) and low employee morale, he was perplexed when he learned what his employees were asking for. They were not greatly concerned with the levels of salaries or bonuses (although there were some requests for better employee benefits and some "perks" such as office decorations and technology updates). Instead they wanted to get more involved with the business, such as by having a say about which new accounts the firm should solicit. They also wanted better communication from top management. They felt that Mr. Brownstein did not listen very well and offered little performance feedback. In other words, the important requests were more about communication and decision-making involvement (personnel and cultural controls) than about money (results control). Mr. Brownstein heeded his personnel's advice, which seemed to have had at least some effect. Soon after changes were made, the company's billings were at record levels, turnover dropped by half, and, for the first time in its history, the agency won the "Oscar" of the ad world.[1]

However, personnel/cultural controls are sufficient only if employees understand what is required in their particular roles, are capable of performing well, are supported by the requisite organizational structures and systems, and are motivated to perform well without additional reinforcements provided by the organization. Rarely are all four conditions satisfied so thoroughly that managers can conclude that the personnel/cultural controls are sufficiently reliable by themselves. In other words, rarely can organizations rely exclusively on employees who are so "fascinated by their assignments; jumping out of their skins with excitement about what's next; eagerly pursuing better solutions and new initiatives" that they can rule out using any other types of controls, although some organizations are trying to achieve this ideal as closely as possible.[2]

That said, many examples exist to show the risks of relying excessively on personnel/cultural controls. Allen Robbins, owner of the Plastic Lumber Company, which converts old milk and soda bottles into fake lumber, initially relied mostly on personnel/cultural controls to build his business. Wanting to be an "enlightened employer," he offered all his employees a friendly, supportive working environment and a generous benefits package and largely relied on them to do a good job for the company. Mr. Robbins even offered cold beers at the end of a shift, granted some employees personal loans to help them out, and gave his lowest-tier workers multiple opportunities to prove themselves, even after they had made serious missteps. But his control strategy backfired. Absenteeism and drug and alcohol use on the job were a major problem, and many employees sued for injury, discrimination, or unemployment compensation claims. Learning the limitations of a freewheeling atmosphere the hard way, Mr. Robbins quickly reverted to a zero-tolerance policy toward alcohol in the workplace and stopped making loans to employees. He also implemented a thick employment manual built around a point system with points lost for any violation of work rules (such as reporting late to work, fighting, or drinking on the factory floor). This helped to bring discipline in the workplace and helped build cases against problem workers who were subsequently terminated.[3]

Moreover, organizational cultures can be fickle and cause turmoil. For example, the "HP Way" at Hewlett-Packard was once heralded as the paragon of Silicon Valley's innovation model. The HP culture was engineering-led and encouraged top executives to mingle with lower-level employees and engineers to discover fresh ideas, resulting in a flow of popular, affordable, and utilitarian products. Until it became synonymous with complacency and high costs, that is. When Carly Fiorina took the helm as CEO in 1999, she tried to shift to a marketing-led culture, which generated strong sales but demoralized employees. Mark Hurd, who succeeded her in 2005, however, intended to restore tradition and reinvigorate the company's 30,000 engineers.[4] It remains questionable, however, as to whether Mr. Hurd, who was subsequently fired in an ethics scandal, was successful. As one of the workers put it, "we had an office party this Monday at HP HQ to celebrate the resignation of CEO Mark Hurd." This worker was apparently not the only disgruntled employee, as dozens of readers identifying themselves as HP employees or ex-employees left comments on Deal Journal cheering Hurd's resignation. "Morale was at an all-time low at lunch last Friday," wrote one employee; "Jodie [the dealings with whom were at the center of Mr. Hurd's scandal] will likely get about 300,000 Thank

You notes." "Thanks Mark for making me take all that ethics training – looks like *you* were the one who needed it," said another one. Mr. Hurd may have been admired by Wall Street (HP's stock tumbled 8% on the day he was fired although it rose more than fourfold during his five-year tenure at the HP helm) but he was not loved by everybody inside the technology giant where he had implemented draconian cost cuts, including laying off thousands of people.[5] For over a decade now, clearly, the "HP Way" has not been as strong a guide for employee behavior as it once was believed to be.

All told, it is rare that personnel/cultural controls are, by themselves, sufficient. As one author put it, "If nobody stole cars, no car would have to be locked. But if no car were locked, somebody would start stealing them."[6] While most employees are probably honest most of the time, there will always be some who are less than totally honest. Even honest employees might be tempted into undesirable behaviors if they perceive the control system so weak that their chances of being caught are nil. Opportunity makes the thief, as the old saying goes. Thus, organizations perhaps should not fully rely on the absolute righteousness or trustworthiness of their employees. Therefore, in most cases, it will be necessary to supplement personnel controls with controls over actions, results, or both.

Knowing the limitations of personnel/cultural controls, choices among the various forms of action and results controls should depend on the particular advantages and disadvantages each has in the specific setting in question.

Advantages and disadvantages of action controls

Perhaps the most significant advantage of action controls is that they are the most direct form of control. If it is absolutely essential that an action be performed properly the first time (e.g. a significant investment decision), perhaps because the decision is not easily reversible, action controls usually provide the best control because the control-action link is direct. Further, if controls over the actions themselves are judged to be adequate, there is no need to monitor results.

Action controls also provide several other advantages. Action controls tend to lead to documentation of the accumulation of knowledge as to what works best. The documents that are produced (e.g. policies and procedures) are an efficient way to transfer knowledge to the employees who are performing the actions. They also act as a form of organizational memory, so that the knowledge is not lost if, for example, key employees leave the organization.

Action controls, particularly in the form of policies and procedures, also are an efficient way to aid organizational coordination. They increase the predictability of actions and reduce the amount of inter-organizational information flows required to achieve a coordinated effort. As such, they are a key element in bureaucratic forms of organization in a positive sense; that is, in settings where standardization and routinization are desirable organizational attributes.

But action controls have a number of significant disadvantages. First, there is a severe *feasibility limitation*. As we discussed earlier, excellent knowledge of what actions are desirable exists only for highly routinized jobs. Moreover, there is a tendency, with action accountability controls in particular, to focus on known or established actions of lesser importance that are easy to monitor, thereby potentially causing *behavioral displacement*, such as the means-ends inversion we discussed in Chapter 5.

Second, most action controls also often discourage creativity, innovation, and adaptation. Employees often react to action controls by becoming passive. They develop their work habits based on the work rules they are given. This adaptation may be so complete that they begin to depend on the rules, cease to think how the processes could be improved, and become resistant to change. In some cases, however, creativity is not required, or indeed not desired. For example, creativity from pilots is rarely a desired feature. But in other cases, action controls cause significant opportunities for improvement and innovation to be foregone.

Third, action accountability, in particular, can cause sloppiness. Employees who are accustomed to operating with a stable set of work rules are prone to cut corners. For example, airplane accidents have been commonly traced to checklist errors, meaning that the pilots carelessly rushed through their pre-takeoff and pre-landing procedures.[7] As such, action controls often just encourage compliance of the "check-the-box" type, rather than the required scrutiny and care to ensure fail-proof operations.

Another situation of sloppiness often arises when various software applications and computer systems require too many different passwords. The users then start saving their passwords within spreadsheets or e-mail messages, or change their system preferences to allow them to automatically log into, or stay logged on, the various systems. Circumventing the authentication systems in this way obviously leaves a security gap, the exact opposite result of what was intended. To prevent this from happening, organizations have had to roll out software packages specifically designed so that users can save their passwords securely.[8]

Fourth, action controls often cause negative attitudes. Some, perhaps even most, people are not happy operating under them. Some people, especially the more independent, creative people, may leave to find other jobs that allow more opportunity for achievement and self-actualization.

As an example, perhaps a bit extreme, but factual nonetheless, consider how managers at *The South Bend Tribune*, a newspaper from Michiana, Indiana, ordered newsroom staff to start writing daily memos detailing their every activity. They did this as the newspaper was scrambling to keep their remaining staffers motivated and productive in the midst of the chaos following a round of layoffs. The purpose of the daily staff memos presumably was to improve communication in order to make the organization as "productive as possible." This was targeted at all reporters, who were instructed to send a daily e-mail to their most immediate editor (and five others) as the last thing they did before leaving for the day. These e-mail "memos" would lay out specifically what the reporters accomplished that day, what they needed to finish or follow up on the next day, and what they planned to do the next day. As such, management believed (or rather hoped) that the organization would benefit from encouraging communication and sharing information. The editor would be able to tell how busy the reporters had been and, more importantly, what they had accomplished and what they were struggling with. From that, it was expected that "[our] morning planning meetings can be even more efficient." In her guidance as to what the organization was looking for in the memos, assistant managing news editor Virginia Black provided an example of what she wanted by means of a 375-word sample memo that was "mind-numbing in its minute detail." Needless to say, this turned out to be received with skepticism among the reporters. As one of them pointed out, "followed to its logical conclusion, this productivity memo thing would produce a never-ending memo loop. Think about it: the last item on your memo must be, 'wrote a memo about how I spent my day,' which, of course, requires you to then write, 'updated my memo to account for memo,' and so on." The reporters could not see how these memos would make the morning planning meetings more efficient. In the meantime, Ms. Black's memo quickly spread through the blogosphere, stirring up plenty of counter-memos (of the sarcastic sort, that is). Someone summarized the ill-fated idea as follows: "Who thought this was a good idea? It would be faster to just tell [us] directly that they believe every single one of [us] is lazy, incompetent and untrustworthy."[9]

Clearly, the intended action-accountability measure had created ill will and negative reactions from the independent, creative-minded reporters.

Similarly, in a "battle of humans versus machines," equity traders in one brokerage firm were resisting a push by their firm to impose an ever-increasing amount of computer-based analysis on their trades. Although management may see such "electronic control regimes" as helpful when it comes to monitoring trading desk performance and ensuring regulatory compliance, others argue that they inevitably will have unintended consequences – one observer noted that traders, who are typically independent-minded, will be tempted to "game the system to produce results that maximize compensation" regardless.[10] Or, as another observer noted, "The traders will be back saying to their compliance officers: There's too much control; let us make money."[11]

Finally, some action controls, particularly those that require preaction reviews, are costly. The reviews must usually be performed by individuals who are as well, or more, qualified than those who are taking the actions. Thus the reviewers must be highly knowledgeable, and their time and services are costly. If they do not take, or have, the time to perform their reviews thoroughly, then the intended control purposes will be rendered moot.

Advantages and disadvantages of results controls

Results controls also have several advantages and disadvantages. One common advantage is feasibility. Results controls can provide effective control even where knowledge as to what actions are desirable is lacking. This situation is typical of many (even most) of the important roles in many organizations.

Another advantage of results controls is that employee behaviors can be influenced even while the employees are allowed significant autonomy. This is particularly desirable when creativity is required because autonomy allows room for new and innovative ways of thinking. But even where creativity is not important, allowing autonomy has some advantages. It usually yields greater employee commitment and motivation because higher-level personal needs (such as the need for self-accomplishment) are brought into play. Results controls can also provide on-the-job training. Employees learn by doing and by making mistakes. It also allows room for idiosyncratic styles of behavior (such as a unique sales approach), which can provide better results than standardization of one approach.

A final advantage of results controls is that, as compared to some forms of action control, they are often relatively inexpensive. Performance measures are often collected for reasons not directly related to management control, such as for financial reporting, tax reporting, or strategy formulation, and if these measures can be used or easily adapted for results controls, the incremental expense of the control can be relatively small.

Results controls, however, have some disadvantages or limitations. First, results measures usually provide less than perfect indications of whether good actions had been taken when the measures fail to meet one or more of the qualities of good measures: congruence, precision, objectivity, timeliness, or understandability. As discussed earlier (Chapter 2), it is often difficult to fix, and sometimes even to recognize, these measurement problems.

Second, when results are affected by anything other than the employee's own skills and efforts, as they almost always are, results controls impose risk on the employees. This risk is caused by measurement "noise" created by any of a number of likely uncontrollable factors (which we discuss further in Chapter 12), including environmental uncertainty, organizational interdependencies, and sometimes just bad luck. Subjecting employees to this risk is often problematic because employees are, to varying degrees, *risk averse*. When organizations make their employees bear risk, they must offer them a higher expected level of compensation (a *risk premium*) compared to when the employees do not bear the risk. Failure to provide the correct premium for the risk borne is likely to lead to employee dissatisfaction, frustration, and perceptions of unfairness, making it difficult for the organization to attract and retain talented employees. Moreover, regardless of whether the correct risk premium is offered, the organization will have to guard against employees' tendencies to take some risk-reducing, rather than value-maximizing, actions.

Third, it is usually impossible to optimize the performance targets set as part of result control systems (such as budget targets). The targets are often asked to fulfill multiple important, but competing, control functions. One is *motivation-to-achieve*. For this function, it is best for the targets to be *challenging but achievable*. Another is planning. The targets are used to make decisions about levels of cash and inventory to have on hand. For this function, the targets should be *realistic*. A third function is *coordination*. Plans are often treated as commitments and passed among the various entities in an organization so that each entity knows what to expect from the other entities. For this function, the targets should be a *best guess*, or maybe even slightly *conservative*, to make sure they are achieved and no (wasteful) over-commitments of resources take place. Obviously, one set of targets cannot serve all purposes equally well. One or more purposes must be sacrificed if results controls are used.[12] We refer to Chapter 8 for a more detailed treatment of this important target-setting issue and how organizations address it.

Aside from the difficulty involved in setting the right target for the right performance area(s), the measures themselves can be conflicting, and certainly overwhelming, when they are (too) numerous. For example, the Royal College of Nursing told an influential group of Members of Parliament (MPs) in the UK that "the number of performance targets forced on healthcare professionals must be reduced from 400 to about 15 because staff were being 'bullied' into working harder," and that "the government's demands were 'crazy' and demoralized staff." To remedy the situation, RNC executive director Alison Kitson called on the MPs to scrap many targets and introduce instead focused standards based on skill mix, patient dignity, and clinical outcomes.[13] As we discussed in Chapters 2 and 4, a proliferation of measures can lead to confusion and conflicts, making it more likely that the combination of measures will be less congruent with the truly desired results. There clearly is a tradeoff to be made between measurement completeness and congruence.

Finally, not all employees like being empowered to produce results as they best see fit. Some employees simply have no desire for autonomy; that is, they do not enjoy the responsibility that these controls impart on them nor the risks they subject them to. However, (self-)selection of employees into jobs that match their skills and ambitions, a form of personnel controls, should try to mitigate this problem.

CHOICE OF CONTROL TIGHTNESS

The decision as to whether controls should be applied more or less tightly in any particular organization, or area within the organization, depends on the answer to three questions: (1) *What are the potential benefits of tight controls?*; (2) *What are the costs?*; and (3) *Are any harmful side-effects likely?*

In any organization, tight control is most beneficial over the areas most critical to the organization's success. The *critical success factors* vary widely across organizations. For example, inventory control is critical in retail superstores because "carrying heavy inventories without tight controls is, of course, a recipe for bankruptcy."[14] Tight inventory control can be implemented by focusing on *key results* if employees can be trusted to determine how to keep inventory near the required service levels, or *key actions* that involve detailed inventory procedures and decision rules. But inventory control is of only minor importance in other situations. In airlines, seat capacity utilization is one of the critical success factors. Most airlines achieve tight control in this area through extensive preaction reviews over airplane acquisition and replacement decisions.

The potential benefits of tight controls also tend to be higher when performance is poor. For example, in reference to CEO Jack Welch's management style at General Electric, a former manager said, "If you're doing well, you probably have more freedom than most CEOs of publicly traded companies. But the leash gets pulled very tightly when a unit is underperforming."[15]

What are the costs involved in implementing tight controls? Some forms of control are costly to implement in tight form. As we discussed above, tight action controls in the form of preaction reviews, for example, can require considerable top management time. Tight results controls might require extensive studies to gather useful performance standards, or they might require sophisticated information systems to collect and analyze all the required performance data. Chapter 5 dealt exclusively with the costs of management control systems; both direct and indirect costs.

Are any harmful side effects likely? All the conditions necessary to make a type of control feasible, such as knowledge about how the control object relates to the desired ends, may not be present. If so, harmful side effects are likely if the control is implemented, *especially* if the control is implemented in tight form. For example, if the environment is unpredictable and the need for creativity is high, such as in hi-tech firms, good knowledge does not exist about either the actions that are needed or the results that should be accomplished. Therefore, neither action nor results control can be said to be clearly effective, and the implementation of either in tight form is likely to cause problems. Tight action controls would likely cause behavioral displacement and stifle creativity. Tight results controls would likely cause problems to select the right results measures and set adequately challenging targets, both of which are difficult in rapidly changing environmental conditions.[16]

Simultaneous tight-loose controls

In a now-dated but still-seminal management book, *In Search of Excellence*, Peters and Waterman observed that a number of companies they defined as "excellent" employed what they called *simultaneous tight-loose controls*.[17] They observed that the MCSs used in these companies can be considered *loose* in that they allow, and even encourage, autonomy, entrepreneurship, and innovation. But these same control systems can also be called *tight* because the people in the company share a set of rigid values (such as focus on customer needs). Peters and Waterman observed that policies and procedures and other types of controls are not necessary in these companies because "people way down the line know what they are supposed to do in most situations because the handful of guiding values is crystal clear"[18] and "culture regulates rigorously the few variables that do count."[19] In other words, the MCSs in these organizations are dominated by personnel or cultural control; or, they can be said to be tight on objectives and core values, but loose on procedures.

It sounds like nirvana: let culture provide a high degree of reliance that the employees are acting in the organization's best interest and avoid most of the harmful side effects. But this desirable state is difficult to achieve, as several examples earlier in this chapter have suggested. Many companies are dealing with employees who do not share a single set of values. Then what do managers of organizations without strong cultures do?

It may be possible to approach a similar type of simultaneous tight-loose control even where a strong culture does not exist. This can be accomplished by using tight controls over the few key actions or results that have the greatest potential impact on the success of the organization. More control should be exercised over strategically important areas than over minor areas, regardless of how easy it is to control the latter. None of the controls that might be substituted for culture can be assumed to be free of harmful side effects, but selective use of tight controls may limit these effects. Most individuals can tolerate a few restrictions if they are allowed some autonomy in other areas. In the context of a results control example mentioned above, an organization probably does not need 400 measures if 15 will suffice, and even that may be too many in most situations.[20]

ADAPTING TO CHANGE

Most organizations emphasize one form of management control at a given point in time, but they often change their emphasis from one form to another as their needs, capabilities, and environments change. Small companies can often be controlled adequately through the supervisory abilities of their founding leaders who develop a staff of loyal employees, centralize most key decisions, and involve themselves personally in detailed reviews of budgets and expenditures. As organizations grow, however, these forms of personnel/ cultural and action control may have to be replaced, or supplemented, with other forms of control. As a consequence, organizational growth typically pushes management controls in the direction of increased formalization of procedures for action accountability purposes and/or development of more elaborate information systems for results control purposes.[21] In addition to growth, many other situational factors (such as intensifying competition, global expansion, or technological change) cause organizations to adapt their management control systems to their changing environments. We discuss the effects of situational factors on management control system design in more detail in Chapter 16.

KEEPING A BEHAVIORAL FOCUS

What makes the analysis of management controls so difficult is that their benefits and side effects are dependent on how employees will react to the controls that are being considered. Predicting these behaviors is far from an exact science. Significant behavioral differences exist among people in different countries, in different parts of a single country, in different organizations, as well as in different areas of the same organization, and managers must be aware of such differences because the effectiveness of the management controls used will vary depending on the reactions of the employees involved. As examples above have suggested, "creative types," such as advertising executives, traders, and design engineers, tend to react more negatively to action controls than do employees working in production scheduling or accounting. Equally, some employees seem to be relatively highly interested in, and hence motivated by, money as a reward, whereas others are more attracted to stimulating work, autonomy, and challenge.[22]

These differences make the implementation of MCSs particularly challenging, and it is crucial to emphasize that *no one form of control is optimal in all circumstances*. What works best in one organization, or area within an organization, may not work in another. However, it is still important to keep the focus on the people involved because it is their responses that will determine the success or failure of the MCS. The benefits of management controls are derived only from their impacts on behaviors.

MAINTAINING GOOD CONTROL

What causes control problems so serious that an organization is "out of control"? Although this seemingly shattering term, this condition is not rare. In addition to the many organizations that no longer exist because their MCSs failed, the list of surviving organizations that have been criticized for poor (or lax) controls is long and often includes even the most "admired" companies by the business press at some point in their history (e.g. "Apple Computer" in the 1990s, which made a remarkably successful and famous return from the brink in the early-2000s to the present day, a transformation marked by a name change to just "Apple Inc.").[23]

The causes of the problems these companies have faced are often diverse. One cause is an imperfect understanding of the setting and/or the effect of the management controls in that setting. An imperfect understanding of the situation is often associated with rapid growth and/or "transformational change" in their markets. Rapid growth and transformational change often precipitates control problems because it causes the key factors that need to be controlled tightly to change.

Another cause is management's inclination to subjugate the implementation of management controls to other, often more pressing, business demands. This, again, often happens in growth and change situations, which cause managers to delay the development of adequate MCSs, usually while they choose to emphasize marketing. The aforementioned example of HP from an engineering-led approach to a marketing-focused approach serves as a case in point.[24] Personal style also makes some managers unwilling to implement proper, or the most suitable, management controls. The example of HP under the leadership of Carly Fiorina again serves as a plausible case in point.[25] Entrepreneurs, particularly, often find it difficult to relinquish the centralized control they exerted when their firm was small and wholly owned by them.

Criticisms, however, should be made carefully. While many organizations may have faced MCS weaknesses of various magnitudes, knowing what should be criticized is not unproblematic (including in the examples given above). It is not easy to keep a finely tuned set of MCSs in place over long periods of time, particularly when the organization is operating in a rapidly changing environment. Further, some MCSs that are seemingly inadequate may actually be quite effective because they minimize some harmful side effects. Clearly, there is a tension between trying to fully "regulate" behaviors and allowing some "ambiguity" in the roles of relatively autonomous managers in decentralized entities, where it is difficult for organizations to always make the seemingly correct trade-off between *control* and *autonomy*.[26] Organizations often oscillate between one and the other, sometimes over-doing it one way, to then drift back the other way. In that sense, "optimality" is easy to say, but hard to achieve in constantly changing environments.

Hence, criticisms of MCSs must be made with caution. Controls that seem quite loose may have some unseen benefits, such as in terms of high creativity, a healthy spirit of cooperation, or low cost. Even the suffering of ill effects due to the occurrence of one or more of the control problems does not necessarily imply that a poor MCS was in place. MCSs only reduce the probability of poor performance; they do not eliminate it. Most criticisms should be leveled only after a thorough investigation of the situation. Control is a complex part of the management function. There is no perfect MCS. There is no single best way to accomplish good control. There are many control benefits and costs that are hard to discern, but for control systems to have desirable effects, organizations must inevitably fine tune them as the situation calls for, using the best assessments, knowledge, and insights available.

Notes

1. "Self-Evaluation Brings Change to a Family's Ad Agency: Executive Learns to Listen to Employees and Adopt New Work Habits," *The Wall Street Journal* (January 6, 1998).

2. "Why I Put My Employees Ahead of My Customers," *Forbes* (June 18, 2010), online (www.forbes.com).

3. "A Factory Owner's Idealism Fades amid Personnel Troubles," *The Wall Street Journal* (January 14, 1998).

4. "HP's Cultural Revolution," *Business Week* (November 15, 2007), online (www.businessweek.com).

5. "Jodie [Fisher] Will Likely Get 300,000 Thank You Notes," *The Wall Street Journal* (August 10, 2010), online (http://online.wsj.com).

6. "A Cure for Selfishness," *The Wall Street Journal Europe* (April 15, 1997), p. 8.

7. "Don't Count Your Chickens," *Forbes* (February 27, 1995), p. 102.

8. "Société Générale Bolsters Internal Controls," *Search Security* (May 27, 2008), online (http://searchsecurity.com).

9. "Memo Madness, Or, Does Busy Work Increase Productivity?," *Business Week* (February 2, 2009), online (www.businessweek.com).

10. "Traders Sceptical of Electronic Monitoring," *The Globe and Mail* (June 3, 2009), online (www.theglobeandmail.com).

11. "Société Générale Trial Begins This Week," *The New York Times* (June 6, 2010), online (www.nytimes.com).

12. See, for example, S. C. Hansen and W. A. Van der Stede, "Multiple Facets of Budgeting: An Exploratory Analysis," *Management Accounting Research*, 15, no. 4 (December 2004), pp. 415–39.

13. "Too Many NHS Targets Are 'Bullying' Staff, MPs Told," *Nursing Standard* (January 29, 2003).

14. "Here Comes a Cat Killer," *Business Week* (April 22, 1996), p. 52.

15. "Jack: A Close-up Look at How American's #1 Manager Runs GE," *Business Week* (June 8, 1998), p. 104.

16. See, for example, T. Davila, M. Epstein, and R. Shelton, *The Creative Enterprise* (Westport, CT: Praeger, 2007); T. Davila, M. Epstein, and R. Shelton, *Making Innovation Work: How to Manage It, Measure It, and Profit from It* (Philadelphia, PA: Wharton Business School Publishing, 2006).

17. T. J. Peters and R. H. Waterman, *In Search of Excellence* (New York, NY: Harper & Row, 1982).

18. Ibid., p. 76.

19. Ibid., p. 105.

20. "Too Many NHS Targets are 'Bullying' Staff, MPs Told," op. cit.

21. See, for example, L. E. Greiner, "Evolution and Revolution as Organizations Grow," *Harvard Business Review*, 76, no. 3 (May–June 1998), pp. 55–64; E. Flamholtz and Y. Randle, *Growing Pains: Transitioning from an Entrepreneurship to a Professionally Managed Firm* (San Francisco, CA: Jossey-Bass, 2000).

22. See, for example, A. Falk and M. Kosfeld, "The Hidden Cost of Control," *American Economic Review*, 96, no. 5 (2006), pp. 1611–30; B. Frey and R. Jegen, "Motivation Crowding Theory," *Journal of Economic Surveys*, 15, no. 5 (2001), pp. 589–611; and R. Benabou and J. Tirole, "Intrinsic and Extrinsic Motivation," *Review of Economic Studies*, 70 (2003), pp. 489–520.

23. "The Fall of an American Icon," *Business Week* (February 5, 1996), p. 39.

24. "HP's Cultural Revolution," op. cit.

25. Ibid.

26. See, for example, D. Marginson and S. Ogden, "Coping with Ambiguity Through the Budget: The Positive Effects of Budgetary Targets on Managers' Budgeting Behaviors," *Accounting, Organizations and Society*, 30, no. 5 (July 2005), pp. 435–56.

Case Study

Diagnostic Products Corporation

This incentive program is still in its infancy stages, but we believe that we are on the right path. What has amazed us throughout this process is just how difficult it is to achieve a performance bonus program that truly inspires and acknowledges strong performance. I believe that for this reason most enterprises either "settle" for programs that look great on paper but are ineffective in practice, or avoid this type of a program altogether in favor of compensation mechanisms that do not really examine individual performance metrics that are (ironically) most essential to the success of the business plan. Though no plan is perfect, we are determined to develop this program in a way that is first and foremost a benefit to our customers, while addressing our values as a corporation.

James Sorensen, Field Service/Support Manager,
Diagnostic Products Corporation

In the second quarter of 2004, Diagnostic Products Corporation implemented a new Performance Bonus Program for its US-based Field Service Engineers (FSEs). The new program provided rewards to FSEs based on their accomplishments, rather than for merely working long hours. The new program was still work in progress, however. Managers were still considering how some of the elements of the program should be structured, and they were not yet able to measure objectively the FSEs' performances in all of the critical aspects of their jobs.

DIAGNOSTIC PRODUCTS CORPORATION

Diagnostic Products Corporation (DPC) designed, manufactured, and marketed laboratory instruments and reagents designed for immunodiagnostic testing. The tests were for the diagnosis, monitoring, management, and prevention of various diseases, including thyroid disorders, reproductive disorders, cardiovascular disorders, allergies, infectious diseases, and

certain types of cancer. All of DPC's tests were performed in vitro, which is through samples removed from the body, such as blood, urine, tissues, or other bodily fluids.

DPC's products were sold to hospitals, independent clinical laboratories, and physician office laboratories, as well as forensic, research, references, and veterinary laboratories. The company sold its products through independent distributors as well as through its own sales force.

Historically, foreign sales accounted for more than 70% of revenues, although in recent years domestic sales growth had outpaced foreign sales growth. In 2003, the company generated slightly in excess of $60 million in profit after tax on revenues of nearly $400 million (see Exhibit 1). DPC stock was listed on the New York Stock Exchange (symbol: DP).

DPC's primary instrument offering was the IMMULITE series of instruments, which were first introduced in 1993. IMMULITE systems were fully automated, computer-driven modular systems that used specialized proprietary software to provide rapid, accurate test results to reduce the customers' labor and reagent costs. DPC's IMMULITE provided the capacity for walk-away processing of up to 120 samples per hour, on a random access basis, meaning that it could perform any test, or combination of tests, on any patient sample at any time.

DPC had two principal immunoassay platforms (see Exhibit 2). DPC's IMMULITE 2000 addressed the needs of high-volume laboratories, while the IMMULITE served lower volume facilities and niche markets.

The IMMULITE 2000 had an innovative service feature that included a remote diagnostic capability. DPC's service facility could access any IMMULITE 2000 worldwide for the purpose of diagnosing

---

This case was prepared by Professors Kenneth A. Merchant and Wim A. Van der Stede. Some facts and names have been disguised.

system problems. In 2002, DPC introduced Real Time Service (RTS) on the IMMULITE 2000 system. RTS enabled the IMMULITE 2000 to monitor itself and to proactively contact DPC's service facility if it sensed a potential problem. In this way, DPC was sometimes able to solve a problem before a customer was even aware that it existed.

In early 2004, DPC launched the IMMULITE 2500. This instrument was similar to the IMMULITE 2000 but reduced the time it took to get a result from certain tests, most importantly tests used in emergency rooms to aid in the diagnosis of cardiac conditions. DPC also expected to launch an enhanced version of the Sample Management System (SMS) that would connect to two IMMULITE 2000s or 2500s. The SMS would eventually function as a universal robotic interface that could be linked to almost any of the automated systems available.

The IMMULITE instruments were closed systems, meaning that they would not perform other manufacturers' tests. Accordingly, an important factor in the successful marketing of these systems was the ability to offer a broad menu of individual assays and assay groups; that is, tests which jointly represent decision-making panels for various disease states, such as thyroid disorders or infertility. DPC managers believed that the IMMULITE and IMMULITE 2000 had the most extensive menus of any automated immunoassay systems on the market. In 2004, DPC manufactured over 400 immunodiagnostic test kits (also called reagents or assays). DPC's research and development (R&D) activities continued to focus on expanding the test menus, giving special attention to complete implementations of clinically important assay groups, as well as on developing new generations of instrumentation and software.

In addition to breadth of menu, major competitive factors for the IMMULITE instruments included time-to-results (how quickly the instrument performs the test), ease of use, and overall cost effectiveness. Because of these competitive factors and the rapid technological developments that characterized the industry, DPC devoted approximately 10% of its annual revenues to R&D activities.

DPC was organized functionally (see Exhibit 3). Headquarters were located in Los Angeles, California. Manufacturing facilities were located in New Jersey, California, Wales, and China. DPC also had a distribution network in over 100 countries.

THE FIELD SERVICE ORGANIZATION

DPC's field service organization was part of its Instrument Systems Division (ISD), based in Flanders, New Jersey. ISD was comprised of DPC's largest manufacturing facility, its instrument R&D function, and its service organizations, which included technical services, service quality management, and US-based field service/support (see Exhibit 4). Technical services personnel provided telephone support to DPC customers and distributors on a 24/7 basis. The service quality management maintained client databases and automated reporting systems, managed regulatory affairs, and administered customer satisfaction surveys.

The field service organization provided on-site support to customers and distributors. The goal of the field service organization was to be on site where needed within 4–6 hours on a 24/7 basis. The visits served multiple purposes, including repairs, installations, preventive maintenance, and instrument removals.

The US field service organization, which included 86 field service engineers (FSEs) based in 32 states, was organized into six regions. Most of the FSEs had an associate degree in a technical field, but some had bachelor degrees and/or were trained in the military. Their ages ranged from 25 to 60+. Their average base salary was slightly less than $50,000.[1] The orientation of the DPC field service organization was different from that of some of the company's competitors. DPC operated its field service organization as a cost center, with the emphasis on providing "total customer satisfaction." Some of DPC's competitors ran their field service organizations as profit centers, which sometimes caused them to focus more on cost-cutting rather than customer service.

Field service managers monitored their organization's performance with an extensive array of data that they summarized by product, region, and FSE. These data included repair rates, productivity, call back rates, incomplete call rates (with reasons), return call rates, MTTR (mean time to repair), MTBF (mean time before failure), travel expense per call, and on-site response time. These data were reported monthly at a Quality Management Meeting.

Preventive maintenance (PM) procedures were an important part of the FSEs' jobs. If a PM was done on time, there was a better chance of the customer

---

[1] This figure and certain other facts in the case have been disguised.

having no problems with the instrument. If a PM was not completed to standard, the chance of a "call back" increased significantly, which caused a disgruntled customer and caused DPC to incur more costs. A PM on an IMMULITE instrument took an average of 3.5 hours to complete. On an IMMULITE 2000, a PM took 5.5 hours. Most FSEs completed 5–7 PMs per month. The total cost of a service call was significant, as it included direct labor costs, labor-related benefits, travel, and often other field service expenses.

Completing a job on the first visit was another important performance factor. Most customers could not afford to have an instrument down for a few days, or sometimes even for a few hours. If the FSEs did not understand the job they would face in the field, they will not finish it on the first day, and customer satisfaction would be adversely affected. To be prepared, the FSEs should schedule the visit with the customer to reduce the chances that a failure to complete the job was caused by customer time constraints. And they should download the error log and look at the instrument's service history so that they would have the parts they needed with them. As James Sorensen, manager of field service/support, expressed it, "The better the FSEs screen the job, and so the more thorough they are up front, the more likely they are to complete the call on the first visit. Ideally, the FSEs get the 'oh by the ways' on the phone, not at the site."

After each visit FSEs left a short (five-question) satisfaction survey for customers to complete and return. If the customer comments were favorable, they were always shared with the FSE and management. Unfavorable comments were invariably addressed with the customer and FSE. The vast majority of the field service ratings (over 99%) were in the "very good" and "excellent" categories. But the customer survey return rate was only just above 25%.[2] To get better feedback, DPC hired an outside vendor to conduct phone follow-ups with a random sample of customers starting in January 2005.

PERFORMANCE-DEPENDENT COMPENSATION

Because DPC FSEs were exempt employees who were not eligible for overtime, DPC created a Variable Compensation Plan. This plan provided quarterly payments to FSEs for time worked beyond regular

working hours. One part of the plan paid the FSEs a monetary "comp unit" for every period of time where a FSE worked for 12 hours or was away from home for 24 straight hours. Long days were common for FSEs as customers' needs were paramount, and some FSEs had to cover customers spread over large regions so travel time was significant. Extra compensation was also paid for weekend work or for being "on call" during a weekend. In 2003, these extra payments totaled nearly 7% of the FSEs' base pay.

As DPC grew, the field service organization also grew. Approximately 15–20 FSEs were being added each year. The additional staff decreased the need for travel and, consequently, reduced the need to pay comp units.

DPC managers still wanted to provide their FSEs an opportunity to earn extra money, but they thought that the money would be better spent in paying for performance, rather than for hours worked. Managers were particularly concerned that some FSEs who were merely spending too much time on their jobs were earning comp units, while the better FSEs were finishing their jobs early. Sunil Das, manager of regional field service engineering, explained a motivation for change: "We want to acknowledge those who work at a 'superior' level." As a consequence, they designed a new Performance Bonus Program, which was implemented in the second quarter of 2004. The objective of the program was defined as follows:

> The Bonus Program is designed to measure critical performance metrics of a Field Service Engineer as it pertains to aspects of the job that lead to total customer satisfaction. These metrics target the key facets that increase DPC's value to our customers.

The new Performance Bonus Program awarded field service engineers both points and money. The money was designed to replace the compensation that was formerly paid in comp units and, hence, to leave the total-compensation packages at competitive levels. But the change was phased in. The comp unit values were reduced by 50% in the third and fourth quarters of 2004 and were eliminated in 2005. The points portion of the program was to be introduced to the field in 2005. Management wanted to take "baby steps" in the implementation of the program and manage each quarter manually until they had a full understanding of the ups and downs of the data.

The awards of points and/or money were based on the FSEs' performance in six areas:

---

[2] DPC field service managers believed that the average return rate for similar paper surveys across all industries was less than 10%.

1. **Cross training**. Engineers were awarded 10 "base" points for each instrument that they were qualified to service – IMMULITE, IMMULITE 2000, IMMULITE 2500, SMS – for a maximum of 40 points.

2. **Preventive maintenance (PM) completion**. FSEs earned two points for each PM completed. To earn the points, the PMs had to be both scheduled with the customer and completed on time.

James Sorenson was confident that the FSEs could not easily manipulate the number of PMs completed, such as by reporting PM completion without actually having done the work. Each PM required a checklist of critical parts that must be changed, and each PM call was automatically tracked in the software. And, Sunil Das added, "When FSEs do a poor job at preventative maintenance, it 'bites them back' in the call back rate" (see below).

3. **Teamwork factor for PMs**. If the region met the specified PM goals for the quarter for instruments covered by warranty and/or service agreement, each FSE in that region would receive the following:

90–96% completed	1% of base quarterly salary, plus 5 points
97–100% completed	2% of base quarterly salary, plus 10 points

4. **Complete first visit**. Complete first visits were defined as service events completed on the first day of the visit. The following proportions of complete first visits were rewarded as follows:

PMs	Repairs
90–99% 2–11 points	85–95% 1–11 points
100% 20 points	96–98% 18–20 points
	99–100% 24–25 points

Sunil Das explained that completing service calls on the first day was not always possible, "no matter how hard one tries," due to parts delivery delays and other uncontrollable factors. The DPC national average first-day-completion of PMs was 97%; for repairs it was 93%.

5. **Call back rate**. Call back rates were defined as multiple visits within 30 days of each other where: (1) the same module was worked on; (2) non-PM visits were for the same problem; (3) the subsequent visit was within three days of a PM; and (4) initial and subsequent visits were associated with the same client call. However, subsequent visits in the following categories were not considered call backs: (1) moves; (2) installations; (3) removals; (4) PM; (5) service check list; (6) proactive repair; (7) retrofit; and (8) peripheral.

Some of these exceptions were added after the bonus program was initially implemented. In their early experiences with the program, managers noticed that some of the FSEs that they thought were among their best did not have the lowest call back rates. Sunil Das gave an example:

One of our sharp engineers noticed during a PM that the hinge on an instrument was a little weak. He went back the next week to fix it, but then we "dinged" him for a call back. So unintentionally we were penalizing an opportunity to "shine" before the customer. Now we exclude this type of procedure as a proactive repair. It doesn't affect the customer, and the machine is not down. We're trying to get this right. But even the best engineers won't have a 0% call back rate. We do get some "hard" instrument failures that have nothing to do with the quality of their work.

The rewards for call back rate proportions were set as follows:

IMMULITE			IMMULITE 2000		
Call back rate proportions (%)	Points	% base quarterly salary	Call back rate proportions (%)	Points	% base quarterly salary
10–9	2–3	1.33	20	2–4	1.33
8–7	4–5	1.67	19–17	5–7	1.67
6–5	6–7	2.0	16–14	8–10	2.0
4	10	2.33	13–12	11–12	2.33
3	20	2.67	11–10	13–14	3.33
2	25	3.0	9–7	20–25	4.0
1	40	3.33	6–5	30–35	4.67
0	60	4.0	4–3	40–45	5.33
			2–1	50–55	6.0
			0	60	6.67

A minimum of nine service visits per instrument type had to be attained each given quarter for eligibility. The DPC national average for call backs was approximately 10%, which was less than the industry average of slightly less than 20%.

The new instruments (IMMULITE 2500 and SMS) were not included in this reward schedule. They were too new to have well-established failure rates that distinguished inevitable start-up problems from FSE-related service quality issues. At the end of 2004, only seven FSE specialists were qualified to work on these new products.

6. **Administrative functions**. Managers evaluated each FSE in each of the following performance areas:

1. Customer satisfaction	0–25 points
2. Expense reports	0–25 points
3. Service reports completion	0–25 points
4. Dispatch feedback	0–25 points
5. Synchronization	0–25 points
6. Company car maintenance	0–25 points
7. Conference call roll call	0–25 points
8. Inventory management	0–25 points

The evaluations were based on subjective judgments of data that were monitored centrally. Managers considered several factors deemed important in each area. For example, the *customer satisfaction* ratings were based on both the averages from the customer survey as well as the return rate. The idea was to watch trends in customer survey return rates per FSE (relative to the overall average of about 25%), as some FSEs sometimes neglected to leave a survey for the customer to complete. Past experience had shown, particularly, that some FSEs had tended to "forget" to leave a survey with the customer when they suspected that the customer was dissatisfied about their work. *Dispatch feedback* was based on reports from the service dispatchers. Which FSEs were not accepting calls? Which were "grabbing" them? *Synchronization* ratings reflected the extent to which the FSEs were inputting their service data to the centralized database within 48 hours. FSEs who were never "delinquent" ordinarily received 25 points for synchronization; those who showed a pattern of delinquencies would receive no points and be called in for corrective action.

James Sorensen, manager of field service/support, explained that, "No dollar bonus amounts were attached to performance in the administrative function areas to remove the possibility for perceived favoritism. All we were trying to do when we came up with this was to assess, at the margin, whether someone had put in an honest day's work."

Exhibit 5 shows a quarterly bonus calculation for a hypothetical FSE. This FSE would be paid a bonus of 6.33% of his/her quarterly base salary and would also have earned 261 bonus points.

Field service managers were monitoring the point accumulations as indicators of successes and failures both of their function and those of individual FSEs. They used this feedback to make improvements, such as in the content of training courses and the mentoring of individual FSEs, but they had not yet decided how to attach reward values to the points earned. One possibility that had been mentioned was to invite the top FSE point earner to the annual sales meeting, which was held in the winter in either Hawaii or Arizona. Other possibilities were an awards plaque, a monetary award and/or a mention in the service newsletter that was distributed company-wide.

EARLY EXPERIENCES AND PLANS FOR THE FUTURE

At the end of 2004, field service managers were pleased with the initial effects of the new bonus program. From their perspective, the bonus program had introduced a lot more objectivity in the system. Managers had a quarterly, quantitative snapshot of the performance of each FSE. The managers also thought that the bonus program had had positive influences on FSEs' behaviors. They saw, for example, decreases in call back rates, which they attributed to the FSEs paying more care to their jobs and not "trying to rush through the calls."

The field service managers continued to compare the data against the performances of the FSEs whom they thought were the best to make sure the new bonus program was not critically flawed. That's how they discovered, and subsequently added, the new call back exceptions, as was described above.

At the end of 2004, after much debate, FSE managers decided to make a substantive change. They decided to combine the instrument groups to calculate one overall call back rate per FSE. They concluded that as far as the company was concerned, a call back, (regardless of instrument model) is a call back: The expenses incurred are the same, and customers are upset with a call back regardless of the type of instrument they have. The field service managers also decided to have the payout increase based on the number of calls the FSE makes in a given quarter. So FSEs were promised higher payouts for more calls (productivity) and fewer callbacks (customer responsiveness), as follows (minimum of 10 calls per quarter):

Calls per quarter	Call back rate (%)	Payout (% base quarterly salary)	Calls per quarter	Call back rate (%)	Payout (% base quarterly salary)
10	20	1.0	31–40	20	5.0
	19–15	1.33		19–15	5.67
	14–10	1.67		14–10	6.67
	9–5	2.33		9–5	8.33
	4–0	3.33		4–0	10.0
11–20	20	1.33	41–50	20	6.67
	19–15	2.0		19–15	8.33
	14–10	2.67		14–10	10.0
	9–5	4.0		9–5	11.67
	4–0	5.33		4–0	13.33
21–30	20	3.33	50+	20	8.0
	19–15	4.0		19–15	9.33
	14–10	5.0		14–10	10.67
	9–5	5.67		9–5	12.0
	4–0	6.67		4–0	13.33

While they had proposed the schedule shown above, the field service managers were not yet sure if the payout levels were correct. They were withholding their bonus recommendations to the payroll department while they examined the data further. The fourth quarter payments were to be made by the end of February 2005.

DPC's field service managers knew that there was "still some wariness" among the FSEs regarding the new program. Many FSEs had expressed concerns. Some FSEs were concerned that the company had "taken something away from them." Others were not sure that they were being held accountable for something "real." And some complained that they were placed at an unfair advantage, as compared to other FSEs, because of their customer mix.

The field service managers knew that they would have to continue to "tweak and massage" the program to get it right, and feedback from the field service force would help the process. They knew that they had to decide how to reward the FSEs' accumulations of "points," something they had promised to do by 2005. And they knew that they had to enhance their performance metrics and, hopefully, move some of the performance areas, such as parts inventory, out of the subjectively assessed "administration" category.

Exhibit 1 Diagnostic Products Corporation: income statements for years ending December 31 (all data in millions)

	2003	2002	2001	2000
Net sales	381.39	324.09	283.13	247.61
Cost of goods sold	164.36	137.75	120.69	110.52
Gross profit	**217.02**	**186.34**	**162.44**	**137.08**
Research and development expenditures	40.68	36.82	31.45	26.46
Selling general and administrative expenses	99.02	84.15	76.47	70.52
Income before depreciation and amortization	**77.33**	**65.37**	**54.52**	**40.10**
Depreciation and amortization	n/a	n/a	n/a	n/a
Nonoperating income	11.11	3.84	3.30	2.42
Interest expense	n/a	1.22	.01	n/a
Income before tax	**88.44**	**67.99**	**57.82**	**42.52**
Provision for income taxes	26.28	21.08	17.81	12.86
Minority interest	.36	(.40)	.98	1.41
Net income before extra items	**61.80**	**47.31**	**39.03**	**28.25**
Extra items discontinued operations	n/a	n/a	n/a	n/a
Net income	**61.80**	**47.31**	**39.03**	**28.25**

Exhibit 2 Diagnostic Products Corporation: IMMULITE products

IMMULITE 1000

IMMULITE 2000 with Sample Management System (SMS)

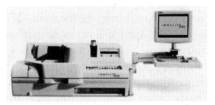

Exhibit 3 Diagnostic Products Corporation: corporate organization chart

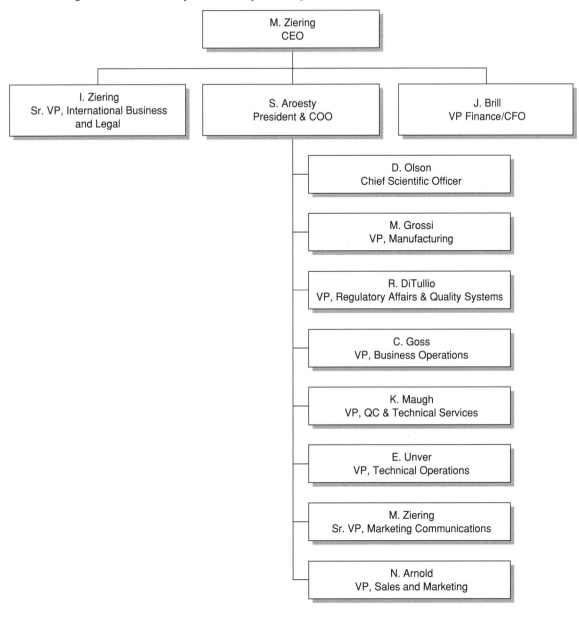

Exhibit 4 Diagnostic Products Corporation: field service organization

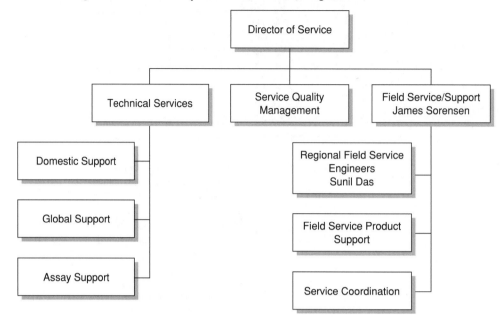

Exhibit 5 Diagnostic Products Corporation: bonus program reward calculation for a hypothetical FSE

		Points earned	Payout (% base quarterly salary)
Base points	Qualified on IMMULITE and IMMULITE 2000	20	–
PMs completed	10	20	–
Teamwork	97%	10	2
Complete first visit	PMs 95%	7	–
	Repairs 90%	6	–
Call back rate	IMMULITE 5%	7	2
	IMMULITE 2000 13%	11	2.33
Administration		180	–
Total for quarter		261	6.33%

Game Shop, Inc.

David McDonald, financial analyst for Game Shop, Inc. (GSI), had just hand-delivered invoices to ExcitoVision, Inc. (EVI), one of GSI's largest customers. He did not have to make such deliveries often, and he hated the task, but he thought this trip was necessary to keep EVI happy. EVI had always been a difficult client to deal with, but the relationship had become much more prickly since GSI had accidentally over-billed EVI for almost $1 million in a recent quarter. The over-billings occurred because of a series of errors, particularly double billings and incorrect calculations of rebates. In fact, GSI almost lost EVI as a customer as a result of this incident. David felt that when he delivered the invoices, he needed to greet the EVI managers "with a bow, and roses and chocolates." In the past few months, David believed that he had made a lot of progress in mending the relationship with EVI and also with some other companies that had suffered because of errors in GSI's billing system.

GSI management knew that the company's billing system needed to be improved significantly. In early 2010, top management had assigned David the task of improving GSI's billing process. He had largely completed the first phase of that task. He had designed new processes, conducted a series of training sessions, and started monitoring billing performance using a new "Billings Scorecard" that contained an extensive array of billing-related performance metrics. David hoped that the new, improved billing system would prove to be effective. The goal was perfection. He noted: "Expectations are high; even one mistake can have huge consequences."

COMPANY BACKGROUND

GSI, founded in 2002, was a leading video game servicing house, providing services to video game publishing companies. GSI converted games from template backgrounds, video, and computer code into finished digital products, mostly DVDs and secure downloadable files. GSI also provided related services such as menu creation, international dubbing, and audio enhancement.

GSI's customers, video game publishing companies, developed or licensed video games, and then financed, distributed, and marketed the games around the world. The video game publishing industry was an oligopoly; it consisted of a handful of very large companies that dominated the market, as well as many much smaller, niche companies. Six game publishing companies accounted for 90% of GSI's revenue.

GSI was divided into 17 profit centers or business units (BUs) (see Exhibit 1). Seven of the BUs were organized around customers, six of them focused exclusively on the projects of a single, large customer. The other ten BUs focused on an area of expertise, such as Creative Content Production and International Dubbing, and worked on projects for numerous customers. The BU managers reported to Kevin Brink, senior vice president of Worldwide Operations and Business Execution, who, in turn, reported to the CEO. Functional departments, such as finance, sales and marketing, legal, and human resources reported directly to the CEO.

The video game industry was dynamic. GSI employees had to work hard to stay on top of increasingly complex and rapidly changing game features, specifications, and requirements. GSI had a reputation both for production quality and for being able to tackle difficult projects. Kevin Brink explained:

> Throughout our business we try to create a culture of excellence. One of the signs on my wall says, "Perfect, that is all." Our expectation is perfection, because our reputation can be ruined with just one mistake. Six sigma isn't good enough. We have to operate at 15 sigma, or we go out of business. ▶

This case was prepared by Professor Kenneth A. Merchant and research assistant Michelle Spaulding.

Copyright © by Kenneth A. Merchant.

Every month Kevin's office published a 50-page Management Review, which was available to all employees on the company's intranet. The report consisted of dozens of scorecards, focused primarily on product quality. The report created transparency and allowed employees to learn from the reports of failures. Failures were measured and also addressed with a Corrective Action Report (CAR). The CAR outlined the reason for the failure, named the department and/or individual(s) responsible, and prescribed corrective action. CARs linked to an individual employee became part of that employee's permanent record.

Kevin also managed a World Wide Knowledge Base that gave employees around the world access to the most recent work instructions, check lists, forms, and policies. He discouraged employees from sending outdated e-mails or storing outdated instructions on their PCs. Often when CARs were issued, the failure was at least partially addressed by updating instructions in the Knowledge Base. Kevin believed in knocking out failure modes with smart controls, or as he explained, "I minimize discretion so that a process cannot continue until the right choices are made. I try to force things to be right."

BILLINGS AND REVENUE RECOGNITION

GSI project managers (PMs) were responsible for managing customer projects from start to finish. Their responsibilities included billing. Most PMs had no financial or technical background. All were high school graduates, and some also had a college degree, usually in a liberal arts field. The best of the PMs were smart generalists who were able to juggle multiple priorities.

In addition to the PM, a typical project involved at least eight employees, most of whom had a technical specialty, such as video compositing. Projects required quality control personnel as well, usually two focused on the incoming stage of the project and two or three focused on the outgoing stage. Quality control checks were built into the process.

GSI's policy was that no project was to be started without first securing a purchase order (PO) from the customer. The PMs regularly violated that policy, however, with tacit approval from corporate. As one PM explained, "[The big customers] are temperamental. We don't want to upset them." Even starting a project with a PO in hand did not solve all the billing problems. Not all the project contingencies could be foreseen, and overages above the amount specified in the initial purchase order were common in the industry.

Revenue was recognized when it was earned. PMs would estimate the amount they would eventually bill for the work that had been done to date and enter it as accrued revenue. Once the project was billed, the amount changed from accrued revenue to an account receivable. Each PM was responsible for tracking time spent on projects, changes to the projects, and overages. Once the project shipped, the PM was also responsible for compiling a billing packet that the billing department sent to the customer for approval and payment.

Bills, and in some cases even the billing processes, were tailored to each customer. For example, one customer did not allow overages, so they would not sign a PO until the project was completed. The PO, shipping document, and invoice were all sent to this customer at the same time. In a practice somewhat unique to the industry, many customers were not billed when the project shipped, but were given a period of time to review and approve charges after the project was shipped. The period of time allowed varied by customer. Kevin noted, "Sometimes it's as difficult to bill the thing as to build the thing."

ACCURACY AND TIMELINESS ISSUES

Billing accuracy and timeliness had become increasingly important as the company matured. Kevin was concerned that GSI's reputation for billing was not up to par with its reputation for delivering quality products, and billing problems were causing frictions with important customers. Partly because of the financial reporting and internal control requirements of the Sarbanes-Oxley Act of 2002, most customers were now requesting better invoice accuracy. In addition, as GSI grew, its need for working capital also grew, so it was imperative to get invoices delivered and receivables collected as promptly as possible.

Friction with large customers had revealed some billing issues, and there was additional evidence that problems existed. The PM's accrual estimates could be wildly inaccurate, and there were often several months of accrued revenue sitting on the books. In late 2010, GSI had over $5 million of working capital "trapped in accruals older than 60 days," almost twice GSI's average monthly revenue.

THE IMPROVEMENT PROCESS

David was assigned the task of improving the billing system. He was given clear project goals: achieve 98% accuracy in accrued revenue calculations and reduce accruals to a maximum of 30 days of sales. If David's project was successful, the accrued revenue amount would decrease from over $5 million to $1.3 million.

In early 2010, GSI management had a brainstorming session to identify the issues. They found that a lot of controls were missing. As a result, some billings were not being turned in. Many that were turned in were inaccurate. Sometimes customers were double billed. PMs were a major cause of the problems. This was understandable, as Kevin noted, "They are busy people. Sometimes they don't get all the details right."

To understand all the root causes of the problem, David built a "fault tree" (see Exhibit 2). The purpose of the fault tree was to diagnose the problem in enough detail so that the solutions would follow from the detailed diagnoses. David's fault tree exercise exposed nearly 100 causes of the inaccuracies and revenue accrual build-ups. These issues could be categorized as system or process issues, customer issues, and management issues.

System/process issues

The billing system had several flaws. Billing paperwork could only be submitted once a week, and reports could take upwards of ten minutes to download onto a PM's computer. There was also no redundancy in the process. A single employee's vacation could hold up the entire company's billing cycle.

Theoretically these issues could be addressed with changes to the system, but both the billing and IT departments were resistant to change. David thought that billing department resistance stemmed both from familiarity and comfort with the existing system and, probably, fear of job loss. Billing department personnel had also been burned once by the IT department when it tried to force a new alpha version of a system on them. This system was untested and full of bugs, so hard feelings had been created. The IT department had always given billing projects low priority. Historically, the IT focus had always been on systems designed to improve operations. Financial systems had always been an afterthought.

Customer issues

GSI's policy was that nothing could be shipped without a PO, but some customers refused to issue a PO. They wanted to make changes along the way and have the bill from GSI reflect what was actually shipped. Even where POs were used, they often quickly became obsolete as changes were made to the work orders. Some customers insisted on a lengthy review process before they would approve a bill even though the order had already shipped. Some projects shipped over a long period of time, upwards of one year, but customers would not accept a bill until the final stage of the project was complete.

David accepted that customer behavior could not be controlled completely, but he also believed that PMs and managers could do more to try to influence customer behavior. PMs could try to insist on getting a customer PO. They could also try to get authorization to bill for parts of a job instead of waiting for the entire job to be complete. For example, one BU was able to persuade a customer to pay for international dubbing before the Japanese version, by far the most technical and time consuming dubbing task, was complete. This shortened the billing cycle on this job from over a year to just four months.

Management issues

Perhaps the biggest issue was that many GSI PMs did not track project changes and simply did not turn in billing paperwork in a timely manner. Some just accrued things randomly. For example, they would declare certain tasks as having been completed, forget what they had done in the prior period, and then bill for them again.

David discovered several causes of this problem. GSI did not have a set of written billing instructions, and many managers did not know how to use the billing tools available to them. In general, PMs did not understand the importance of correct and timely billing, and often were not aware that there was a problem; they assumed several months of accruals were the norm. Managers were also not terribly motivated to spend time on billing. They were much more focused on production. The problem was aggravated during the busy season when some managers complained that they were already in the office until past 11 p.m. every night making sure orders were shipped. Forced to choose between spending time on shipping or billing issues, they chose shipping.

While some of the problems could be seen as failures of specific individuals, David decided to focus on improving the process, rather than focusing on specific individual's failures. He provided training sessions that included instruction on billing and time management, and he added detailed billing instructions to the World Wide Knowledge Base.

BILLINGS SCORECARD

To focus attention on billing performance, David developed a new "Billings Scorecard," a monthly report that tracked each BU's billing performance. David hoped the Billings Scorecard would provide increased visibility about billing performance. Many PMs, and even their bosses, had not cared about billing-related performance in large part because it was not measured or reported. He noted, "We are metrics centric in our culture." David hoped that the scorecard would motivate better billing performance and, in the end, provide the basis for assessing the overall success of his project.

The Billings Scorecard (see Exhibit 3) rated each BU's billing performance in terms of four measures (described below). David converted each of the scores into a 0 to 4 point scale, or "grade."

1. **Percent of sales invoiced = monthly dollars invoiced/monthly dollars sold**
   A perfect score of 1 would mean that every dollar sold was also invoiced. This measure was converted into a grade by multiplying by 4.
2. **Adjusted number of weeks of sales accrued = accruals/(3 months of sales/13) – approval delay**
   A week of sales was approximated using a 13-week average to smooth the value. The measure was adjusted by an approval delay factor that was specific to each customer. Most customers had an approval delay built into their payment systems that allowed them a certain period of time to approve bills before they could be officially billed. The adjusted number of weeks accrued was calculated by subtracting the weeks a customer was allowed for approval from the number of weeks accrued. For example, if a business unit had 6 weeks of sales accrued, but their customer was allowed 3 weeks to approve bills, the BU's adjusted weeks of accruals would be three (i.e., 6 − 3). BUs were allowed one week of slack. For each additional week or fraction thereof, one grade point was subtracted from a perfect 4.0 to convert the measure into a grade. So using the example above, a score of 3 would produce a 2.0 or C grade (i.e., 4 − (3 − 1)).

3. **Percent of sales shipped without a PO = sales shipped without PO/sales shipped**
   This measure was only available for the five BUs that used GSI's standard order management system. A perfect score for this measure would be 0; i.e., nothing shipped without a PO. The measure was converted to a grade by subtracting it from 1 and multiplying the result by 4.
4. **Percent of accruals less than 30 days old**
   This measure was a rough estimate of accrual aging. A perfect score of 100% (or 1 in decimal points) would mean that all of the accruals on the books were less than 30 days old. The measure was converted to a grade by multiplying the decimal score by 4 (i.e., 75% or 0.75 would yield a score of 3).

The four grades were weighted equally to produce an overall average. The scores for each BU were published in an e-mail message that was distributed to all BU directors, vice presidents, and senior vice presidents.

DETENTION

The managers of BUs with a grade of C and below (less than or equal to a 2.0 grade) were called to a "detention" meeting with Tyler Pizer, GSI's vice president of Finance. Kevin and David also attended these meetings. During the detention meetings, the participants went through each accrual in detail to determine what was causing a delay. If the delay was caused by client behavior, the problem was noted and communicated to the sales department. If it was caused by managers who were "too busy to bill," David would seek a commitment from the BU director to bill during the current period. Sometimes meeting participants uncovered "phantom" accruals, such as a project that had already been billed or a non-billable project with no accruable value.

Despite the punitive nomenclature, detention meetings were intended to be productive. Sometimes grades were adjusted if it was determined that the poor grades were either caused by incomplete information or were not the fault of the BU employees. David explained,

> The purpose of the detention meetings is to understand and correct the issues in the business unit. The Scorecard is a dialogue opener. In fact often after discussing a particular BU's performance during detention we realized that we needed to make a grade change. Sometimes they didn't deserve the D because we were

missing the right information. The detention discussions are part of the measurement system analysis.

For example, in June, the BU for Customer 7 received a D grade, mostly because of its very low score on Measure #4 (percent of accruals less than 30 days old). But the BU director, Quinton Ruiz, explained that though there was a low percentage of accruals less than 30 days old, 100% of accruals were less than 60 days old. "We fell a little bit behind because of the busy season, but it hasn't spun too far out of control." The BU's grade was adjusted upward by removing the offending items from the calculation.

Managers of the Creative International Menu BU complained that it was not possible for them to improve their grade on Measure #4. The BU built menus several months in advance of a project completing, but most customers insisted on receiving the bill for menu charges together with the final project. David agreed to factor the menu charges out of Measure #4 in the future.

The Localization BU had similar issues. They could not bill until an entire project with dozens of languages and elements was complete, but they recognized accruals language by language, piece by piece. Tyler and David ultimately decided that due to the nature of their work, the Localization BU could not be expected to earn a grade above 2.0; it was acceptable for them to have significant unbilled accruals.

Sometimes the detention process uncovered simple clerical errors. One business unit called into detention had actually turned in a box of invoices that was misplaced by the billing department, so their grade was also adjusted upward.

P-CARS

David had one other motivational tool at his disposal; he could issue P-CARs (Process Corrective Action Reports) to managers who made billing errors. P-CARs were used to identify software glitches and broken procedures. The P-CARs described where a process went wrong, who the responsible parties were, and what corrective actions should be prescribed. Unlike CARs, which were administered by the human resources department, P-CARs were not noted in an employee's personnel file. The focus of a P-CAR was on the process, rather than the person. Still, no one who was issued a P-CAR was pleased about it.

At the time of the case, David was issuing an average of a few P-CARs per month. He expected that

number to decline over time as the broken elements in the processes were repaired. Eventually, he expected most of the errors to come from human mistakes more than from software or process design flaws.

EARLY RESULTS

David was generally pleased with the early results of his billing process improvements and, in particular, the BU managers' responses to the scorecard. He said:

> Their first reactions might be defensive, but they really do want to understand. They are curious. They want their metrics to go up, and they are intelligent enough to realize that they need to understand the metrics to improve them.

David expected that the scorecard grades would eventually be used as a "bonus modifier." That is, the grades would be considered by managers in making their judgments about performance. In normal economic conditions, PMs earned an average annual bonus of 20% of salary. However, because the recession of 2008–09 had adversely affected GSI's performance, nobody within the company had earned any bonuses in the last two years.

In the three months since David had implemented the scorecard and related processes, deferred revenue accruals had dropped by half. Billing error rates had dropped to 0.3%, much lower than the 15% error rates of a year earlier. David expected that billing grades for the following month would be improved, partly because the busy season was over, but mostly because the GSI's CEO had warned BU directors that there would be "dire consequences" if their grades did not increase.

David knew that his mission was far from being complete. The scorecard was still new, and he was open to suggestions for refinements. He still wondered if the scorecard was built on the best measures, and if it made sense to weight them all evenly. He was particularly concerned about Measure #1 because it was distorted by seasonal sales spikes. For example, the BU for Customer #5 had managed to increase its grade to a B– in August, but David knew the improvement was mostly due to declining sales and lagging invoices, not improved billing practices. More generally, David wondered if he would be able to meet his ambitious quantitative project goals without changing customer behaviors. He also wondered if even achievement of those goals would be sufficient in the long run, as the true objective was perfection.

Exhibit 1 Game Shop, Inc.: organizational chart

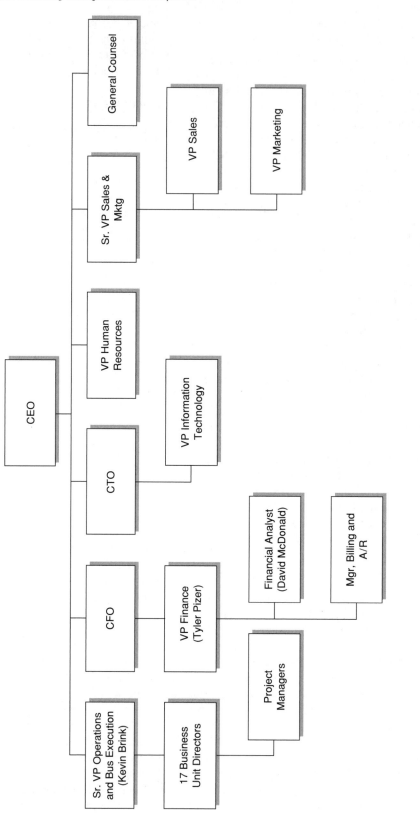

EXHIBIT 2 Accrual fault tree

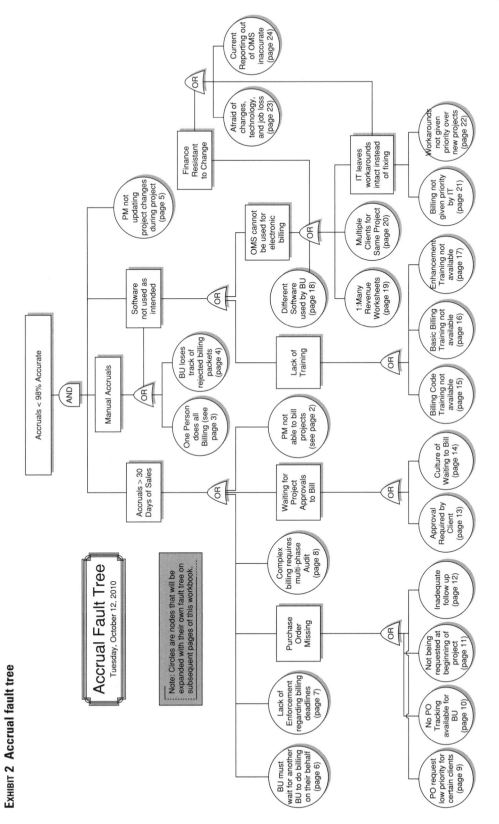

Game Shop, Inc.

Accrual Fault Tree
Tuesday, October 12, 2010

Note: Circles are nodes that will be expanded with their own fault tree on subsequent pages of this workbook.

Accruals < 98% Accurate

AND

Accruals > 30 Days of Sales

Manual Accruals

Software not used as intended

PM not updating project changes during project (page 5)

Finance Resistant to Change

Afraid of changes, technology, and job loss (page 23)

Current Reporting out of OMS inaccurate (page 24)

OR

One Person does all Billing (see page 3)

BU loses track of rejected billing packets (page 4)

OR

Different Software used by BU (page 18)

OMS cannot be used for electronic billing

1:Many Revenue Worksheets (page 19)

Multiple Clients for Same Project (page 20)

OR

IT leaves workarounds intact instead of fixing

Billing not given priority by IT (page 21)

Workarounds not given priority over new projects (page 22)

Lack of Training

Billing Code Training not available (page 15)

Basic Billing Training not available (page 16)

Enhancement Training not available (page 17)

OR

PM not able to bill projects (see page 2)

Waiting for Project Approvals to Bill

Approval Required by Client (page 13)

Culture of Waiting to Bill (page 14)

OR

Complex billing requires multi-phase Audit (page 8)

Purchase Order Missing

PO request low priority for certain clients (page 9)

No PO Tracking available for BU (page 10)

Not being requested at beginning of project (page 11)

Inadequate follow up (page 12)

OR

Lack of Enforcement regarding billing deadlines (page 7)

BU must wait for another BU to do billing on their behalf (page 6)

235

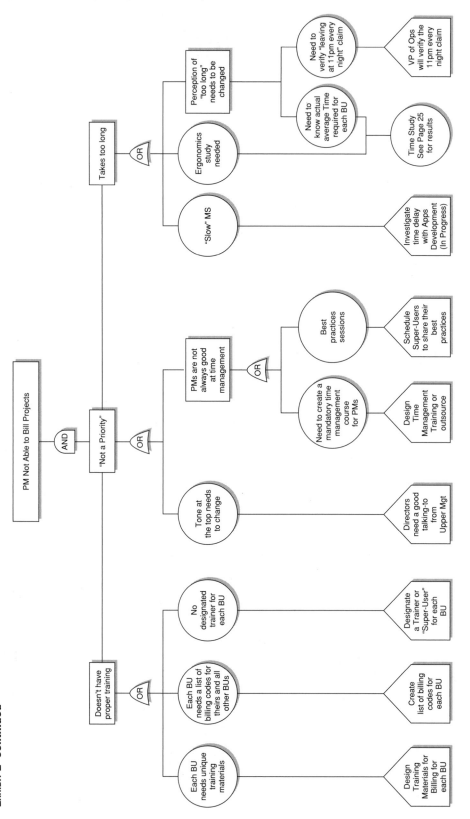

Exhibit 2 *continued*

EXHIBIT 3 The Billings Scorecard (June)

Business unit	June invoiced	June sales	% of sales invoiced	GPA 1	Weeks of sales accrued	Customer approval delay	Adjusted weeks of sales accrued	GPA 2	% shipped w/o PO	GPA 3	% accruals <30 days Old	GPA 4	Overall GPA	Grade
Customer 1	803.84	2,668.47	0.30	1.20	4.5	3.0	1.5	3.51	38%	2.48	54.7%	2.19	2.34	C+
Customer 2	345.88	762.40	0.45	1.81	9.0	3.0	6.0	0.00	9%	3.65	46.7%	1.87	1.83	C–
Customer 3	1,683.97	1,954.20	0.86	3.45	0.6	0.0	0.6	4.00	0%	4.00	100.0%	4.00	3.86	A
Customer 4	93.28	370.44	0.25	1.01	0.0	0.0	0.0	4.00	41%	2.37	100.0%	4.00	2.84	B–
Creative International Menu	74.82	134.81	0.55	2.22	5.1	5.0	0.1	4.00		n/a	73.8%	2.95	3.06	B
Creative Content Production	295.65	282.19	1.05	4.00	2.9	1.0	1.9	3.11		n/a	61.4%	2.45	3.19	B+
Creative Design	218.48	144.74	1.51	4.00	5.0	3.0	2.0	3.04		n/a	52.9%	2.12	3.05	B
Network Services	197.25	499.41	0.39	1.58	6.6	0.3	6.3	0.00		n/a	59.5%	2.38	1.32	D+
Digital Reference Services	152.13	152.13	1.00	4.00	0.0	0.0	0.0	n/a		n/a	100.0%	n/a	4.00	A+
Audio Services	137.33	137.33	1.00	4.00	0.0	0.0	0.0	n/a		n/a	100.0%	n/a	4.00	A+
International Dubbing	310.46	310.46	1.00	4.00	0.0	0.0	0.0	n/a		n/a	100.0%	n/a	4.00	A+
Customer 5	261.17	275.32	0.95	3.79	11.2	0.3	10.9	0.00		n/a	33.0%	1.32	1.70	C–
Customer 6	94.96	94.96	1.00	4.00	0.0	0.3	–0.3	4.00		n/a	100.0%	4.00	4.00	A+
Customer 7	504.78	763.12	0.66	2.65	17.0	3.0	14.0	0.00	39%	2.42	13.9%	0.56	1.41	D+
Design, Eng. & Mfg 1	2,098.85	1,515.81	1.38	4.00	0.0	2.0	–2.0	4.00		n/a	100.0%	4.00	4.00	A+
Design, Eng. & Mfg 2	–	418.93	–	0.00	2.7	2.0	0.7	4.00		n/a	100.0%	4.00	2.67	B–
Localization	918.26	1,827.66	0.50	2.01	7.6	4.0	3.6	1.39		n/a	34.0%	1.36	1.59	C–

Exhibit 4 Scorecard early trends (June–August)

Business unit	GPA 1 – % of sales invoiced			GPA 2 – adjusted weeks of sales accrued			GPA 3 – % shipped with PO			GPA 4 – % accruals <30 days old			Overall grade		
	JUN	JUL	AUG	JUN	JUL	AUG	JUN	JUL	AUG	JUN	JUL	AUG	JUN	JUL	AUG
Customer 1	1.20	3.19	2.12	3.51	4.00	1.60	2.48	3.39	3.54	2.19	2.72	2.20	C+	B+	C+
Customer 2	1.81	2.42	3.45	0.00	0.00	0.10	3.65	3.65	3.70	1.87	2.94	2.31	C–	C+	C+
Customer 3	3.45	4.00	3.99	4.00	4.00	4.00	4.00	4.00	4.00	4.00	4.00	4.00	A	A+	A+
Customer 4	1.01	2.59	3.94	4.00	3.52	3.60	2.37	4.00	0.00	4.00	4.00	4.00	B–	A–	B
Creative International Menu	2.22	4.00	3.32	4.00	3.97	3.05	n/a	n/a	n/a	2.95	2.75	3.11	B	A–	B+
Creative Content Production	4.00	4.00	2.53	3.11	4.00	2.92	n/a	n/a	n/a	2.45	1.34	1.98	B+	B+	B–
Creative Design	4.00	4.00	4.00	3.04	2.82	3.40	n/a	n/a	n/a	2.12	2.24	1.94	B	B	B
Network Services	1.58	4.00	3.31	0.00	0.76	0.00	n/a	n/a	n/a	2.38	2.72	0.87	D+	B–	D+
Digital Reference Services	4.00	4.00	4.00	n/a	n/a	n/a	n/a	n/a	n/a	n/a	n/a	n/a	A+	A+	A+
Audio Services	4.00	4.00	4.00	n/a	n/a	4.00	n/a	n/a	n/a	n/a	n/a	n/a	A+	A+	A+
International Dubbing	4.00	3.95	3.47	n/a	n/a	4.00	n/a	n/a	n/a	n/a	n/a	n/a	A+	A	A
Customer 5	3.79	3.46	4.00	0.00	0.00	2.44	n/a	n/a	n/a	1.32	1.88	1.97	C–	C–	B–
Customer 6	4.00	4.00	4.00	4.00	4.00	4.00	n/a	n/a	n/a	4.00	4.00	4.00	A+	A+	A+
Customer 7	2.65	4.00	4.00	0.00	0.00	0.00	2.42	3.44	3.34	0.56	1.47	0.51	D+	C+	C
Design, Eng. & Mfg 1	4.00	4.00	1.48	4.00	4.00	2.84	n/a	n/a	n/a	4.00	3.58	3.91	A+	A	B–
Design, Eng. & Mfg 2	0.00	4.00	4.00	4.00	4.00	4.00	n/a	n/a	n/a	4.00	4.00	4.00	B–	A+	A+
Localization	2.01	3.86	2.82	1.39	0.18	0.00	n/a	n/a	n/a	1.36	1.60	1.02	C–	C	D+

Family Care Specialists Medical Group, Inc.

On the afternoon of Saturday, January 9, 2010, Dr. Luis Samaniego, president of Family Care Specialists Medical Group, Inc. (FCS) pondered his proposal to revise the FCS physician compensation system. On the following Monday, the six physicians who comprised the Board of FCS would meet to discuss the Group's accomplishments for 2009 and to consider, among other issues, improvements to the compensation system.

The Group's pay scheme had been a continuing topic of discussion for years. FCS had used two very different incentive plans over the past ten years and management had spent a year discussing possible revisions, but Dr. Samaniego still had concerns. While he recognized that no scheme could be perfect and that whatever choices the Board made would involve tradeoffs, Dr. Samaniego knew that the scheme chosen would have real impacts on the physicians, the Group, and, most importantly, their patients.

FAMILY MEDICINE

Family physicians together with internists comprised the overwhelming majority of primary care physicians in the United States. Primary care physicians normally served as the first point of contact for a patient with an undiagnosed, non-emergent health concern. In addition to acting as the first point of contact, primary care physicians provided ongoing care and facilitated coordination of care for patients who required the services of other medical specialists. In short, they are the people that most of us think of when we think of our trusted family doctor.

Though sometimes referred to as general practice, family medicine is a recognized medical specialty. In the United States, upon receiving medical degrees, newly graduated doctors had to complete a medical residency program before they could be awarded licenses by their state board. Medical schools provided would-be physicians with general medical knowledge and some clinical skills. The residency programs provided more specialized knowledge and clinical skills through years of intensive work treating patients under the close supervision of an attending physician. Across all specialties including family medicine, residency programs were associated with, and primarily conducted in, hospitals.

In March of 2009, the Health Resources and Service Administration (HRSA) of the US Department of Health and Human Services designated 6,080 Health Professional Shortage Areas (HPSAs) with an aggregate population of 65 million. The HRSA calculated that an additional 16,585 practitioners would be required to adequately service this underserved population. The American Academy of Family Physicians calculated that to meet the anticipated needs for primary care physicians over the next decade, the United States would need to train 4,449 each year with the goal of increasing the number of family physicians by 39% over the next ten to 15 years. However, in 2007, the number of medical students choosing family care residency programs actually declined by 8% from the previous year to just over 1,100.

The consensus explanation for the growing shortage was money. Due to the prevailing system of medical reimbursements in the United States, which primarily paid providers for performance of specific procedures, the average compensation for family physicians was the lowest of any specialty. A study published in the September 9, 2008, issue of the *Journal of the American Medical Association* documented a high correlation between average annual compensation and the number of filled residency positions by specialty. At the low end with average compensation and percentage of filled residency positions was family medicine with $185,740 and ▶

This case was prepared by Professor Kenneth A. Merchant and research assistant David P. Huelsbeck.

42%. These compared unfavorably to radiology ($414,875) and orthopedic surgery ($436,481) with percentage of filled residency positions of 89% and 94%, respectively. These findings were hardly surprising given current studies estimating that the average graduating medical student carried $140,000 in student loan debt.

WEALTH AND HEALTHCARE IN LOS ANGELES

In 2009, Los Angeles County, California, claimed nearly 10.4 million residents. In their 2008 annual report on America's millionaires, TNS Financial Services reported that Los Angeles County again topped the list with 261,081 households with net worth exceeding $1 million, excluding the value of their primary residences. The county boasted 108 licensed general acute care hospitals with a total of more than 27,000 beds. Yet, at the same time, the HRSA database listed over 300 of its more than 6,000 Health Professional Shortage Areas within Los Angeles County. For physicians and other health care providers, the Los Angeles area offered a wide range of communities and facilities in which to practice. The choice of where to practice and whom to serve significantly affected compensation.

FAMILY CARE SPECIALISTS

In 1988, Dr. Samaniego together with six other Latino family physicians formed FCS with the mission of providing high quality primary care to underserved communities in East Los Angeles (see Exhibit 1). The FCS physicians' strategy for fulfilling their mission developed along two main, complementary lines. First, the Group reached out to the community by growing into four clinical locations: one each in Montebello and Highland Park, as well as two clinics on the grounds of White Memorial Medical Center (WMMC) in the Boyle Heights neighborhood. The larger of the two Boyle Heights clinics provided the physical presence for the other line of the FCS physicians' strategy, which was to provide the faculty for a Family Medicine Residency program.

Indeed, a number of FCS physicians also served as faculty for the Family Medicine Residency program at WMMC. Dr. Samaniego served as the program's director. In 2008, the three-year residency program was ranked first in California by the Office of Statewide Health Planning and Development (OSHPD) for the third straight year. FCS physicians supervised the clinical training of 21 new doctors, graduating seven family medicine specialists each year with the training to meet the needs of underserved communities. Among the two dozen physicians currently in the FCS Group, five were graduates of the WMMC residency program.

The FCS clinicians – 24 physicians, five physician assistants, three mental health practitioners, and one family nurse – together with the 21 WMMC residents served roughly 45,000 patients, including 32,000 HMO patients, tallying 80,000 individual patient encounters per year.[1] FCS clinicians at all four locations, together with residents at the WMMC Family Health Clinic, saw patients on a pre-scheduled basis between 8:30 a.m. and 5:00 or 6:00 p.m., Monday through Friday. The Montebello and Highland Park clinics were also open for scheduled appointments each Saturday from 8:30 or 9:00 a.m. until noon. The Family Health Center was open all day, from 8:30 a.m. until 6:00 p.m. on Saturdays (see Exhibit 2).

Across the four clinics there were just over 200 half-day Saturday sessions annually that required coverage, or roughly eight Saturday sessions per physician per year. As a service to the Medical Residency Program, FCS attending physicians provided weekend and off-shift on-call service to the Medical Center. Each on-call shift required the services of two doctors. The role of first on-call attending was more demanding, requiring the attending to field all calls from the residents. The second on-call attending was required only for rounds. Newly-hired physicians in their first year with the Group were required to carry a greater number of on-call shifts, as they were deemed necessary for these new physicians to "learn the ropes." Though all FCS physicians carried some on-call shifts, the requirement to do so decreased with seniority.

Though its clinicians participated in more than 20 private insurance networks, nearly 40% of FCS patients were covered by Medicare and roughly 30% by Medi-Cal, the designation for the State of California Medicaid program (see Exhibit 3). Reimbursement rates from these public programs were generally lower than those from private payers,

---

[1] Some of the company-specific data presented in this case have been disguised for confidentiality reasons.

but these were the constituents that FCS had been formed to serve. For their contribution to the residency program, FCS received a fixed contribution of $1.6 million each year from WMMC. While teaching was a major part of the FCS mission, on an hourly basis it generated less revenue for the Group than clinical care. First-year residents could see on average just four patients per day. Second-year residents could see seven to eight, and third-year residents eight to nine. An FCS attending physician was required to act as a preceptor, supervising the patient care provided by the residents.

In addition to work in FCS clinics and teaching at WMMC, the terms of FCS employment agreements with its physicians required each physician to maintain privileges at a number of other area hospitals. To do so, each physician was required by the hospitals to attend and participate in medical staff meetings and other activities in these facilities, in addition to rendering patient care. Within FCS clinics, the physicians were required to attend medical staff meetings and site quality improvement (QI) program meetings. Beyond the walls of the clinics and hospitals, FCS physicians were expected by the Group to volunteer in the community for about one week each year. All physicians in California were required by the Medical Board of California to complete 50 hours of continuing medical education biannually in order to maintain licensing and certification.

Thus FCS physicians' time was a precious commodity and there was a limit to the number of hours each physician could devote to the clinical care that produced revenue for the Group. On average, FCS physicians worked five to six 3.5-hour clinical sessions per week across an average of 46 to 47 weeks per year per physician. Full-time clinical physicians might see patients as many as seven or eight sessions per week, while physicians with more educational or managerial responsibilities might see patients as few as two or three sessions per week. Other full-time clinicians, such as the Physician Assistants (PAs), saw patients during as many as ten sessions per week, though PAs saw, on average, ten or fewer patients per session.

Nonetheless, it was not uncommon for physicians to work part-time outside of their main practice. This "moonlighting" was common throughout the industry, not just amongst physicians. Primarily due to concerns about quality and image control, the FCS Group employment contract barred its clinicians from moonlighting except with explicit permission from the practice executive. Dr. Samaniego routinely granted such permission, as the Group's clinicians knew what it took to make requests that would not raise concerns. A moonlighting physician could earn as much as $500 for taking a half-day shift on a holiday, making moonlighting attractive even for very busy physicians.

Not all of the Group's operating margin could be paid out to the physicians and other clinicians. On occasion, unfavorable changes in payers' reimbursement schedules or increases in operating costs forced the Group to operate at a deficit while the Group's management implemented steps to mitigate the problem. During these periods, reserves established during better periods maintained the Group's solvency. Financing constraints dictated that the Group build reserves in order to fund major capital investments in facilities and technology. For example, upgrading its IT infrastructure and purchasing software systems to implement electronic medical record systems could cost a practice the size of FCS on the order of $1 million. Consequently, the total pool available to fund any clinician compensation program was limited.

THE EVOLUTION OF THE FCS PHYSICIAN COMPENSATION SCHEME

In the early days, FCS clinicians were paid fixed salaries. Those more recently hired and less experienced were paid less; the experienced senior clinicians more. However, the salary range had always been relatively narrow. A physician could reach the upper end of the salary scale in five years with the Group. Over time the Group's leadership came to believe that incentives would help drive better achievement of the FCS mission of service and benefit the Group.

Starting in 1994 and for the next six years, FCS operated what they called the Quality Improvement Incentive Program (QIIP). The stated purpose of the QIIP was "to reward behavior that reflects the highest standards in Family Medicine, medical education, and health care service to [FCS] patients and [the] community." The program assigned possible points (weights) to seven categories of quality improvement activities (see Exhibit 4). By design, the total points across the seven categories for each clinician totaled 100. Based on both objective and subjective criteria determined in advance for each category, the clinic medical directors in collaboration with the Residency Program co-directors scored each clinician's degree of achievement in each area.

For example, an individual clinician might have ten points allocated to the category Provider Meetings. Achievement in this category would be judged by the objective criterion of attendance at both FCS and site provider meetings. Clinicians in attendance were required to sign-in at such meetings and the records were maintained and provided to the practice executives. At the same time, increasingly subjective criteria would also be considered, such as volunteering for special projects, active participation in meetings, and assumption of leadership and responsibility for projects assigned. Hypothetically, the clinician might have been awarded nine of the ten possible points for this category. The process would be repeated for each category and the points summed, yielding a score or percentage achievement for that clinician for the period.

Dr. Samaniego and others at FCS believed that small rewards were unlikely to motivate clinicians to modify their behavior. They believed that a figure of one fifth to one quarter of compensation was necessary to motivate different behavior. Thus, a fraction of each clinician's potential total compensation equal to between 20% and 25% would be multiplied by the total QIIP score for the period to determine payout of the at-risk portion of that clinician's compensation.

While Dr. Samaniego was satisfied with the motivational dimension of the QIIP, with time it became evident that the program was failing FCS on other dimensions. The WMMC Family Medicine Residency Program was achieving its stated mission, placing nearly half of its graduates into family medical practice in East Los Angeles and most others into underserved communities outside the immediate area, FCS itself was experiencing more difficulty in the competition for its associated program's own graduates. The Group also lost senior clinicians to larger and better funded competitors in the local market, especially the national leader in managed care, Kaiser Permanente, which employed more than 14,000 physicians and covered more than 3 million patients in Southern California by 2008. Dr. Samaniego was himself a product of Kaiser's residency program.

Under competitive pressure to attract and retain increasingly scarce family medical specialists, FCS scrapped the QIIP in 2001 in favor of a new scheme that rewarded physicians willing to take extra initiative and responsibility in return for higher compensation. Under the new system, FCS would permit its clinicians to work extra hours for FCS, placing the Group on a more even footing with its local competitors for its clinicians' time.

Under the new program, physicians seeking to increase their compensation could indicate their desire for extra sessions prior to the start of each scheduling period. Sessions were scheduled by the practice executive semi-annually, from January through June and from July through December. Schedules were prepared and posted one month prior to the start of each six-month period. Physicians who requested an increased number of weekend sessions at FCS clinics would be paid for these extra sessions at a rate comparable to rates for moonlighting at non-FCS facilities. Further, the "extra" sessions assigned to these physicians would be deducted from the total pool to be shared among all physicians. That is, if five physicians requested an average of four extra weekend sessions for one six-month period, this reduced the pool of sessions to be shared by 20 sessions bringing the total shared pool to about 80. Consequently, the base number of weekend sessions required of all physicians would be reduced from about four to about three. For their extra effort, the "volunteering" five physicians might increase their compensation by as much as 7% to 10% for the six-month period. Likewise, on-call shifts would be compensated, though the rate of compensation for on-call shifts ranged from about 85% to less than 50% of that for Saturday clinic sessions, depending on factors such as holidays and first vs. second on-call rolls.

To provide a productivity incentive for all of its physicians, with the new program FCS established targets for the number of patients each physician would serve in a typical half-day clinical session. The target number was set at 14 patients per session. On a monthly basis the Group's information systems began generating a productivity report showing the number of total patient encounters, the number of clinical sessions, and the average number of encounters per session for each physician (see Exhibit 5). Based on the average number of patients per session, a monthly bonus was computed according to the formula $250, $750, or $1000 when the average was

12, 13, or 14, respectively. The total monthly productivity bonus was pro-rated by the percentage of time each individual physician dedicated to clinical care each month. So, for example, a physician who consistently achieved a productivity average of 13 encounters/session while devoting half of her time to clinical duties would earn a total productivity bonus of $4,500 over the course of a year.

Under the new plan it was possible for an ambitious doctor to earn compensation roughly equal to that of physicians employed by larger local competitors. However, base compensation for FCS doctors remained at about the 50th percentile for family physicians in comparable markets based on recent salary surveys while physicians at the larger local competitors were closer to the 90th percentile. The difference was slightly more than 20% of total compensation. Dr. Samaniego believed that FCS offered other advantages over some larger competitors in the form of greater flexibility and intrinsic rewards, but the Group's continuing challenges with retention left him wondering whether the new compensation system was doing all it could. At the same time, he felt somewhat nostalgic for the QIIP, with its greater emphasis on the FCS's mission.

CONSTRAINTS

The number of patients seen was an imperfect measure of clinical productivity. Some cases were more complex and required more time to deliver high quality care. Some FCS clinicians specialized in treating certain types of patients who required on average more or less time per patient encounter. OB/GYN cases, for example, took somewhat less time while geriatric cases required more. Also, the financial effect of seeing an additional patient varied widely. Private payers generally compensated FCS at higher rates than Medicare, while Medi-Cal payments were typically only a fraction (e.g., 30%) of private rates. FCS was paid for managed care (HMO) patients primarily on a monthly basis with relatively little or no additional payments for specific patient encounters. Billings were prepared in batches, as many as six weeks apart. When combined with the time payers took to respond to billings, collections lagged treatments by a matter of months. In many cases, collections were received in the name of the patient's primary physician of record, even though the patient may have been seen by another

clinician. In any case, FCS would not provide different levels of care to patients with different health plans, making any incentive system based on billings or collections questionable regardless of the practical problems of implementation.

Moreover, clinicians had more control over the number of patients seen in each session than over the payer mix or average case complexity. Clinicians were given discretion over the maximum number of patients to schedule for a session as well as whether or not to accept patients arriving late for scheduled appointments and those seeking treatment at short notice. Some Saturday clinics were operated on a walk-in basis. However, FCS maintained a policy of not significantly overbooking despite a no-show rate that often averaged as high as 30%.

Direct measurements of the quality of care provided by a given clinician were expensive to collect. As part of each clinic's Quality Improvement program, so-called chart reviews were conducted on a weekly basis. These peer reviews of a very small sample of each clinician's patient encounters were considered to be very powerful motivators, though they were not linked to compensation. In the words of Dr. Samaniego, "It's like a dagger through your heart when one of your peers says 'Hey Louie, you forgot to do X here'."

Various payers measured the quality of care provided based on metrics such as the proportion of diabetic patients covered by the payer's plan that received annual eye exams or of women in targeted groups receiving scheduled mammograms. Bonuses paid to FCS for achieving targeted levels or improvements on such metrics had totaled as much as hundreds of thousands of dollars to as little as a few tens of thousands of dollars in some years. However, achievement of such targets depended heavily on patient compliance as well as on clinical diligence. As with collections, the fact that the same patient might be seen by multiple clinicians made linkage of performance on such metrics to the actions of individual clinicians practically impossible. Likewise, achievement on patient satisfaction surveys were seen as measures of the clinics as a whole more than as measures of individual clinicians.

A BETTER WAY?

These constraints notwithstanding, Dr. Samaniego believed that the FCS compensation scheme had become overly focused on clinical productivity. Like a number of the other Board members, he felt that the original QIIP had been more balanced and better aligned with the Group's mission. However, patient volume, payer mix, staffing, and productivity drove financial results and, ultimately, what the Group could afford to pay clinicians and staff. Even in the not-for-profit world of hospitals like WMMC there was a popular aphorism that without margin there is no mission, and despite the importance of their shared mission, FCS had never been a not-for-profit enterprise.

Dr. Samaniego questioned whether the current scheme was effective in achieving even its relatively narrow purpose. While some clinicians now requested additional Saturday sessions and even additional on-call shifts, only a few achieved bonus levels of average patients seen per session on a monthly basis. Further, while the new scheme had helped to narrow the gap between physician compensation at FCS and the local market level, periodic departures of experienced clinicians seeking better pay or hours and the perennial competition to recruit new physicians only highlighted the fact that serving their target communities would never be as lucrative as treating the average patient population in the LA area. Dr. Samaniego felt certain that the FCS compensation scheme could be improved, but he was less certain of how to achieve the right balance.

Exhibit 1 Mission statement

Family Care Specialists (FCS) Medical Corporation

Mission Statement

Family Care Specialists Medical Corporation is dedicated to the maintenance, restoration, and improvement of each family member's health. The medical group provides high quality, compassionate and culturally responsive medical care, and is dedicated to improving community health and the education of family physicians.

Exhibit 2 Locations and hours

Boyle Heights	8:30 a.m.–5:00 p.m. Monday–Friday
Highland Park	8:30 a.m.–5:00 p.m. Monday–Friday 9:00 a.m.–Noon Saturday
Montebello	8:30 a.m.–6:00 p.m. Monday–Friday 8:30 a.m.–Noon Saturday
White Memorial Medical Center Family Health Clinic	8:30 a.m.–6:00 p.m. Monday–Saturday

EXHIBIT 3 Patient mix

Patient mix by payer and type

	Percentages		*Patients*
Managed care			
Medicare HMO	17%		7,650
Medi-Cal HMO	5%		2,250
Private HMO	<u>43%</u>	65%	19,350
Fee-for-service			
Medicare/Medi-Medi *	13%		5,850
PPO	10%		4,500
Medi-Cal	5%		2,250
Other	<u>7%</u>	<u>35%</u>	<u>3,150</u>
		100%	45,000

EXHIBIT 4 Quality Improvement Incentive Plan (1994–2001)

Quality Improvement Incentive Plan (QIIP)

"To reward behavior that reflects the highest standards in Family Medicine, medical education and health care service to our patients and community."

Provider Meetings	10 points
Medical Staff Meetings	10 points
Community Service	10 points
Clinic Site Quality Improvement Program	20 points
Patient Satisfaction Survey	15 points
Site Medical Director	<u>35 points*</u>
Medical Education	
TOTAL	100 points

* Allocated by percentage of physician time spent in clinical vs. education.

EXHIBIT 5 Sample productivity report

Clinic B: Monthly summary

	Providers	*Total Patients seen*	*Number of sessions*	*Patients/session*
1.	*Clinician One*, MD	45	4	11.25
2.	*Clinician Two*, MD	250	23	10.87
3.	*Clinician Three*, MD	255	21	12.14
4.	*Clinician Four*, MD	349	29	12.03
5.	*Clinician Five*, MD	210	19	11.05
6.	*Clinician Six*, MD	331	18	18.39
7.	*Clinician Seven*, PA-C	321	32	10.03
8.	*Clinician Eight*, PA-C	315	33	9.55
	Totals	**2,076**	**179**	**95.32**

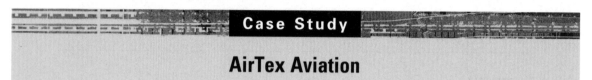

Case Study

AirTex Aviation

"Hello, Sarah. This is Ted Richards." Ted was on his way to resign from his job. He and his business partner Frank Edwards had just bought AirTex Aviation, a floundering enterprise on the verge of bankruptcy, and were excited about putting their business school education to work. The two had scraped together $500,000 so that AirTex would have at least a little cash to pay some bills. With the amount they had contributed, AirTex had a total of $515,000 in the bank.

"Oh, Mr. Richards," Sarah said, "I'm so glad you called. When will you be in? I have a few checks for you to sign."

"I should be in tomorrow. What are the checks for?"

"I've written checks for only our most pressing bills," she said. "I tried very hard to make sure that only those that are most important be paid."

"That's fine," Ted replied. "What's the total of the checks you've written?"

"$510,000," she said.

Ted nearly dropped the phone. "Let's discuss this when I get into the office."

He drove down to AirTex the next morning to speak with Sarah Arthur, the company's accountant. As it turned out, his first day owning his own company would not turn out exactly as he had planned:

I had envisioned that when I bought my company, I would walk in the front door the next morning, and everyone would bow down to me. There would be a brass band playing, or something. Instead, I walk in through the back door (a) realizing that I have a crisis on my hands, (b) hoping no one is going to see me so I can deal with this crisis, and (c) of course, not really knowing how I'm going to deal with it. What I did was say to Sarah Arthur, "We are not going to pay these bills." Well, she was shocked. "But you have to

pay them!" she said. I looked at this woman, who had been with the company for 20 years, and said, "No, I will decide what bills we are going to pay." She sat back and said, "Okay," convinced that I was going to make a fool of myself. That was my first day.

THE PURCHASE

Ted Richards and Frank Edwards met in 1986 when they were students at Harvard Business School. Although planning on initially working for large companies, they eventually wanted to own their own business. Upon graduation in 1988, Frank took a job in the corporate finance department of a large electronics company in Los Angeles, and Ted went to the Los Angeles branch of a well-respected consulting firm.

As they were located in the same city, the two met often for lunch. Whenever they met, they talked about going into business together. Instead of starting an entirely new business, Ted and Frank really wanted to find a "fixer-upper" – they wanted to purchase and "turn around" a failing business that showed a lot of potential. "In good business school fashion," said Frank, "we established some criteria, which were:

1. The company couldn't cost much, since we didn't have much money.

2. The company had to need what we had to offer – which we thought at that time were managerial skills.

3. The industry had to be fragmented and non-oligopolistic. We didn't want to be a small fish in a big pond.

4. We needed to be able to see our way clear to have the company grow at a rate of 20% per year the first five year-period."

This case was prepared by Research Associate Carleen Madigan under the direction of Professor Brian Hall. It is an updated version of Assuming Control at Altex Aviation (HBS Case 9-183-058), originally authored by Professors Neil C. Churchill (SMU), Edmund M. Goodhue (MIT), and Kenneth A. Merchant. Some names, dates, and numbers have been changed.

Ted and Frank looked at a number of businesses over the next year and a half and in early fall of 1989, located a fixed-base operation[1] at San Miguel Airport in Texas that was losing money and looking for a buyer. After four months of negotiation, on December 29, 1989, Ted, just 26 years old, and Frank, 28, purchased the stock of the company for $100,000, assumed the lease on the building (and all the assets and liabilities) and were in business.

The lease on the facilities had a purchase option at a price considerably less than the market value. By exercising the option and then selling and leasing back the building, Ted and Frank were able to raise the $500,000 for working capital.

Ted and Frank discussed the organizational structure at AirTex, and agreed to decentralize its operations by making each operating activity a profit center and grouping them by departments. Each departmental manager would be given authority over his operations, including granting of credit, purchasing to a predetermined limit, setting policies, and collecting receivables. He or she would also be held responsible for its results. Frank was concerned, however:

> I agree with our decision to decentralize this authority, but I am concerned whether now is the time to do it. We'll have a tough time when we first walk in the door and I don't know if the departmental managers can be taught some of these management techniques fast enough. After all, some have never finished high school. Maybe we should begin by making all these decisions ourselves for a month or two. I realize that we don't know the aviation business yet, but even though neither of us has been a line manager, maybe we can learn the aviation business faster than some of our managers can learn formal management skills. Either way, we're putting the company on the line and the two-minute warning whistle has already blown.

During the four months they were negotiating the deal, Frank and Ted spent virtually every weekend together. Of this period, Ted commented:

> We spent something on the order of ten hours a week, of which maybe two or three hours would be trying to understand Sarah Arthur's accounting system and

accounting statements, and another two or three discussing pro forma financial projections and the rest on what we would do when we acquired the company. Frank basically did the financial projections and I designed the accounting system. Actually, I dreamed it up one afternoon at work. I sat down at my computer and designed the forms myself. Frank's projections for the next ten years showed that things were really tight. Even with the $500,000 from the sale and leaseback of the facilities, Frank projected that we were going to run out of money near the end of the first year. We knew this when we were negotiating for the company, and it made us a bit nervous.

Well, three days before the closing, Frank came to me, white as a sheet, and confessed that we had made a structural error in the projections. He was computing accounts payable on the wrong basis, and we were going to run out of money in three months. We had a little discussion as to whether we should blow the whole deal right there, knowing that we couldn't survive. We decided to go ahead with the deal. We knew it would be an impossible job, no matter how we sliced it, but we were prepared to go through with it.

AIRTEX AVIATION PRIOR TO PURCHASE

AirTex was one of eight fixed-base operations at San Miguel Airport, which served Center County, Texas – one of the most rapidly growing communities in the nation. AirTex had a loss of $500,000 on sales of $10 million in fiscal year 1989, and this left the company with a negative net worth (see Exhibit 1). The company conducted activities through six informal departments (see Exhibit 2).

Fuel line activity

The activity employed twelve unskilled fueling people, with an average tenure with the company of eight months, and three dispatchers who coordinated their activities via two-way radio. It was managed by Will Leonard, a man in his mid-30s, who had been the construction foreman for Bill Dickerson when Bill was a real estate developer. When Dickerson bought AirTex in 1980, he brought Will Leonard with him to manage the "line crew." Will was enthusiastic about his job, extremely loyal to Dickerson, and well-liked by his employees. Although lacking in any theory of management (he had a high school diploma and some junior college credits), Will was a good first line manager who was instinctively people-conscious while holding them in line.

---

[1] Fixed-base operations are companies located on an airport that service the non-airline aviation market. They generally sell, fuel and maintain aircraft as well as provide flight instruction and charter services. These companies can range from small family operations to multiple-location companies with sales exceeding $500 million.

The fuel activity encompassed five operations:

Retail Fueling – A Phillips Petroleum franchise of underground storage of 60,000 gallons of jet fuel, 20,000 gallons of "AV-Gas," and five fuel trucks to serve locally based and transient aircraft.

Wholesale Fueling – Service of a fuel farm for Texas Air, a regional airline connecting San Miguel with cities in Texas, Louisiana, Arkansas and Oklahoma. AirTex bought its own fuel separately.

Fuel Hauling – An over-the-road fuel truck and a Texas Public Utilities permit to haul fuel on public roads. The truck, in essence, served Phillips, at a price, by delivering its fuel to AirTex.

Rental Cars – An agency of a local automobile rental company, mainly used as a service to transient pilots.

Tie-Downs – Storage of transient and San Miguel-based aircraft in six hangars and 50 open tie-downs.[2]

The fuel activity was open 18 hours a day, seven days a week, year-round.

Service and parts

The service activity repaired, maintained, and over-hauled aircraft. It employed six mechanics and a departmental secretary. The parts activity, a separate accounting entity, employed one person and was managed by the head of service, as sales went almost entirely to the service activity.

The manager of these operations was Carl Green, a man in his 60s, who had been chief mechanic for Dove Aircraft at Love Field in Dallas prior to moving to AirTex. Before that, he was the mechanic/copilot for a Dallas oil executive. Carl had a high school diploma, aircraft and power plant licenses, and multi-engine and commercial pilot certificates. He knew airplanes, engines and aircraft mechanics. He was, in Ted's words, "not a self-starter, had a bit of retirement mentality, and avoided conflict except when it came to quality. You would never worry about anything he rolled out of his shop."

Flight training

The flight training activity was managed by Roy Douglas, whose pilot license was signed by one

of the Wright Brothers. Roy had held several world records in aviation's early days, and was highly respected by the aviation community. He spent a lot of time "hangar flying" with old cronies and, while he didn't manage the department in any real day-to-day sense, he hired the seven instructor pilots and three dispatchers, gave check rides to students prior to their FAA [Federal Aviation Administration] flight exam, and set safety policies. He and his chief dispatcher, who now had been with him for over ten years, were intensely loyal to both AirTex Aviation and the flying community. They had, however, "seen everything and were surprised by nothing," and they were very resistant to change, be it new aircraft technology, aviation teaching methodology, or accounting systems.

The flight training activity, which had lost money each year, had two types of operations:

Flight School – Flight training in 18 single-engine light aircraft from eight flight instructors coordinated by three dispatchers. Flight ratings were offered from private pilot through air transport ratings.

Pilot Shop – Sales of flight supplies, such as logbooks, navigational charts, and personal and training flight supplies. Sales were made from three display counters by the flight school dispatchers.

Avionics

Avionics was a single-person activity conducted by Leon Praxis. Leon was a college-trained electronics technician whose responsibilities included repairing radios and electronic navigational equipment. He started at eight every morning and left promptly at five, so that he could spend time working on other interests at home.

Aircraft sales

AirTex had been a Piper Aircraft dealer until two months before its sale. The owner, Bill Dickerson, was unable to finance the number of aircraft Piper required to be carried in inventory, so he lost the franchise, fired his two salespeople, and closed down the department.

Accounting

The Accounting Department was central to the company in two ways. First, it was located in a

---

[2] A tie-down is an area of asphalt or concrete with ropes, where an aircraft is parked by tying it down to prevent it from rolling away or from sustaining wind damage.

glass-enclosed office in the center of the building, where it could be seen by everyone and everyone could be seen from it (see Exhibit 3). The second part of its centrality was the role that its manager, Sarah Arthur, played in AirTex. Sarah had worked for Bill Dickerson for more than 20 years. In his absence, which was frequent, Sarah managed the company. While her title was accountant, she had no accounting training of any kind, and her idea of running the company was to be the central repository of all information. She received and opened all the mail – not just mail for her department – and she would distribute it to the department heads as she saw fit. What she distributed, in Ted's words, "was typically nothing – bills would come and she would keep them. Checks would come and she would keep them. And, at the end of the day, she would collect cash from all the departments and keep it." Sarah managed all the receivables and payables.

All accounting information was Sarah's, and nothing left her office. The department managers knew nothing about the profitability of their operations. All they knew was that airplanes would fly and that Sarah Arthur would come around at the end of each day and collect their money. Then, occasionally, she would berate the department managers for their high receivables. Of course, they had no idea how big their receivables were, or who they represented. They would just "be beaten over the head."

As Ted described it:

> The management system that was in place when we bought the company was one woman who magically kept everything in her head. There was a limited and almost incomprehensible formal system. There were basic financial statements and a set of reports that were produced for and according to Piper Aircraft's specifications each month, but they helped Piper, not the management. We may have negotiated with Bill Dickerson, but we were going to take over the management of the company from Sarah Arthur.

ASSUMING MANAGEMENT RESPONSIBILITIES

The roles of Ted and Frank

Frank and Ted took over the business not only as full and equal partners, but as best friends who understood each other very well. Frank assumed the chairmanship, and turned his attention to specific and critical projects, the first being the reestablishment of aircraft sales – potentially a major profit area. Ted took the title of president and chief operating officer, and began to manage the rest of the business. As Ted said later:

> I knew Frank wouldn't be right at my side at every decision, but I made sure that four times a day I could walk into his office and say, "Frank, I don't really know what I'm doing," and he would give me a pat on the back and put my head in order.

Frank, in turn, depended on Ted for operational inputs and intellectual support. They both worked 12-hour days, five days a week, with Ted, not married, putting in 10–12 hours each day on weekends as well. Frank, who had a family, tried to put in three or four hours a day on the weekends.

Management and control

Beyond the immediate cash crisis, Ted viewed his three most important tasks as:

1. Revamping the management of AirTex.

2. Installing a control system that would both support the management and provide information needed in order to make decisions.

3. Wresting *de facto* control of the company from Sarah Arthur promptly.

Frank and Ted believed that it was very important to provide an environment where the departmental managers could make correct decisions on their own, since they had decided they could not make all the decisions themselves. They had neither the time nor the technical knowledge. As Ted put it:

> One of the things I was very concerned about was how to manage by providing an environment that encouraged the managers to make decisions the way I would want them made. That was very, very important to me. I wanted to provide a framework that didn't limit their actions but certainly provided very fast feedback as to how they were doing and made it personally worthwhile for them to do the right things. I spent a lot of time thinking about how to do that, and it occurred to me that there were really two ways to do that. I recognize that there has to be the black hat and the white hat in any of these situations, and so I decided to make the control system represent reality and my personal role would then be that of an emotional leader as opposed to a task leader. I would let the control system be the task leader, and then I could exert more avuncular personal leadership.

I also realized that I didn't have the time to train everyone in the management approach we wanted to use at AirTex. Nor did I have the guts to fire everyone and bring in new talent, and that wouldn't have been a good idea anyway. I also realized that unless I changed the basic attitudes in the company, we would never survive. In order to do that, we needed to do a lot of education, and that would be my personal role. But, if I was going to do that successfully, I couldn't at the same time be berating them about the receivables, so it was necessary to take the nitty-gritty daily tasks of banging people over the head and put them somewhere else. I didn't really feel that Frank should do that, and so to provide this environment for decentralized decision making was very, very important.

Ted began to implement a management control structure, incorporating the following policies:

1. Profit centers would be established for each major activity. These profit centers would be combined where appropriate into departments.

2. Revenues and expenses would be identified by profit center and communicated to the profit center manager.

3. Departmental managers would be responsible for their profit centers, and would receive a bonus of 10% of their profit center profits after administrative allocation.

4. The profit center managers would have pricing authority for their products or services, both internally and externally. The fuel department manager could, and did, charge the Flight School retail price for the fuel they used, whereas he charged the Service Department his cost for its oil.

5. The profit center managers could buy products externally rather than internally, if it was in their best interests to do so. The Flight School manager could, and did, have his aircraft repaired outside AirTex's shop when it was unable to fulfill his service needs.

6. The profit center managers could buy needed capital equipment and operating supplies on their own authority within established purchase order limits.

   Ted recalled one of the first times this decentralized authority was tested:

   When we bought the company, it had an old, rotten, obsolete copier. It was under the control of Sarah Arthur, and everyone who wanted a copy of anything had to go to Sarah, the Witch of the North,

and plead – which was really an awful thing to do. I remember one day, Will Leonard, the manager of the Fuel Department, said, "Can't I get a copier?" I said, "Will, you can do anything you want within the limitations of the PO." So, he bought the smallest copier he could find, and he let everyone in the company make copies, charging them 10 cents a copy. At the end of the month, he would present bills to every department for the copies they used. He made money on his copier because everyone else was scared to death to walk into the Accounting Department and face the Witch of the North. Here was a classic entrepreneurial example, and it became almost a cause célèbre. People were saying, "How did he get a copier? What right does he have to charge me for the copier?" I would say, "If you want a copier, go get one." But with one here at 10 cents a copy, they realized they couldn't really afford one themselves, so they grumbled and went about their business.

7. The profit center managers had the authority to hire, fire, and administer the salary schedule in their departments quite independent of the rest of the company.

CASH MANAGEMENT

Cash and accounts payable

When Ted arrived at AirTex on the first day of his ownership, he gathered up the checks Sarah had written and pulled up the accounts payable file on the computer, called in his departmental managers one by one and said, "Who are your most important suppliers?" He looked at the individual accounts to see how old the balances were and called up each of the suppliers, saying, "I'm the new owner of AirTex Aviation, and I would like to come down and talk to you about our credit arrangements." He later said:

Over the next six months, I got on good terms with the suppliers. I talked to them, took them out to lunch, and let them take me out to lunch. We paid them a little bit here and a little bit there, and we stayed out of serious trouble.

A direct result of Ted's assumption of the accounts payable decision was that Sarah Arthur began to view her stay at AirTex as being limited to the four months agreed upon. As it became clear that Ted was not going to let her make the management decisions anymore, she limited her work for the company strictly to the four-month transition period agreed upon in the purchase agreement. As Ted put it:

> She effectively said, "I will work from 11:00 a.m. to 2:00 p.m. every day. I will answer your questions and that is all." That was fine with me. I hired a new accounting clerk to be Sarah's assistant. She worked from 8 in the morning until 7 at night. I hired her; she worked for *me*. And when Sarah Arthur quietly packed up and left, the departure was easy.

Cash and accounts receivable

With the accounts payable crisis on the road to a solution, Ted turned his attention to cash inflow. In his words:

> My biggest worry was how we were going to control cash, or rather, how I was going to provide a system that would motivate the departments to manage cash. The solution I came up with was to take the receivables and give them back to the departments. That was very controversial. Everybody in the whole company fought me on that. Frank didn't like it – I was totally alone. First of all, the managers didn't understand it. They had never seen receivables, they didn't know what they were. They felt as though they were playing with dynamite. "Here they are, but what do I do with them?" Frank, on the other hand, was concerned that things would get totally out of control because our most important asset – our incoming cash flow – had suddenly been handed out to amateurs. Sarah Arthur may not have been perfect, but she had a lot of experience.
>
> In the Fuel Department, I handed the receivables to the dispatcher, a 20-year-old surfer who had dropped out of college after two years. In the Flight School, I also gave them to the dispatcher, a 55-year-old, loyal employee. These were the only two departments with significant accounts receivable. In Service and Avionics, I gave them to the managers, but these were not significant.
>
> One Saturday morning, I sat down at the computer and printed up all of the balances, and physically presented them to these two women – the *de facto* department heads. Then I sat down and showed them how to input the correct information using the current week's transactions. So, we started to collect data on the accounts receivable.

To motivate the department heads to manage their accounts receivable, Ted gave them the credit-granting authority and the responsibility for collections. He also established the following monthly charges against their departmental profits:

Receivables	60 days old or less	1% of the balance
Receivables	60–90 days old	3% of the balance
Receivables	90–120 days old	6% of the balance
Receivables	over 120 days old	charged the balance to the profit center

Cash and the banks

When Frank and Ted acquired AirTex, they also acquired short-term bank notes payable of $300,000 from the Center National Bank. The notes had been outstanding for several years, and Ted was concerned, since if the bank called the notes, it would put the company into bankruptcy. As Ted recalled:

> One of the people I called just before we bought the company was Hal Lattimer, the manager of the branch we did business with. I took him out to dinner, and over dinner, I told him about the company and how it was doing, as well as some of my plans for the future. I said, "But we have this problem of the $300,000 I owe you. I would love to convert that to a 24-month note to get it out of the short-term category, so as to increase our working capital to make us more attractive to our suppliers. That way, we can get better terms from them." He looked at me and, without thinking it over, said, "Fine, I'll do it."
>
> He had made a gut decision based upon some good vibes, and I was shocked, since I was prepared to negotiate with him. I thought to myself, "The basis upon which business is done, at least with this man, is total candor and honesty." So, I started this program of giving the bank our internal financial reports every month, along with a cover letter summarizing what I was doing. Hal's reaction was great. He thought it was the best thing he'd ever seen. No customer had ever done that to him before. The result was that whenever I went to him – we paid off the loan ahead of time – and said, "Hal, it looks as if I'm going to need $500,000 for 60 days," he would say, "Yes, I've been following it. I've been watching your receivables growing because of your extra business. I know a growing business needs money from time to time. It's no problem – I'll put the money in your account this afternoon."

THE ACCOUNTING SYSTEM

By the end of the second month, AirTex was producing a profit and loss statement on the activities of each department. Each department kept account of its own sales, receivables, inventories, expenses and, through the PO system, expenses initiated by the department.

In order to provide a predictable, and simple method of cost allocation which still would be understood and "managed" by the department heads, Ted established an Administration Profit Center which paid taxes, borrowed money, paid interest, utilities, bills, and other general administrative expenses. The Administrative Department in turn levied a series of monthly charges to each department as follows:

- Social Security taxes, health insurance, and other fringe benefits were charged to departments as a predetermined percent of wages. Thus, when a manager took on a new employee, he or she knew that it would cost the department, say, 125% of the wage.

- Accounts receivable – a monthly charge based on the amount and age of the receivables.

- Operating assets – including the Parts Department inventory and the Service Department's shop equipment – were charged to the departments using them on a predetermined percent of the asset's cost.

- Rent, fire and occupancy insurance, building maintenance and depreciation, and other occupancy costs were charged as predetermined rental per square foot of floor or ramp space occupied.

- A predetermined percentage of sales which represented the cost of Ted's office and the Accounting Department was also charged.

As all the charges were predetermined, calculated and announced twice a year, the managers would control their expenses by managing their receivable balances, conserving on equipment purchases, and varying the square footage they occupied. There were never any unanticipated expenses, and the charging rates were set for breakeven. As Ted put it:

There was an interesting example of the effects of this system. AirTex had a total of 5.2 acres of land, of which approximately 3 were for tie-downs that accommodated approximately 60 aircraft. The fuel Department always wanted more space because it meant that they could accommodate more transient aircraft. The Flight School always wanted more space to make it easier to manage their comings and goings. The Shop always wanted more space as a service and convenience to customers leaving or dropping off aircraft to be serviced.

Before the departments were charged for the area they occupied there was no way to intelligently resolve

this conflict. Bill Dickerson, the former owner, or Sarah would have to make what was essentially an arbitrary decision. With our system, however, there was a definite price to be paid for demanding more space. And with the manager's bonus system, 10% of that price came right out of the manager's pocket.

The result was that we had very few of these discussions that did not reach a natural compromise. And when, over time, each department truly needed more space and was more and more willing to pay the rent, we raised the rent until demand equaled supply. It was great to see a free market in action!

THE TASK GUIDANCE SYSTEM

As an aid towards educating departmental managers in the management of their operations and for keeping them aware of their activities, responsibilities and results, Frank and Ted instituted a Daily Department Report, which required the departments to submit internally consistent operating and accounting information. Each department kept the customer account information, and central accounting kept only receivables control accounts, which would balance to each department's detail. The managers would account for their daily activity in units and in dollars.

For example, the Flight School's DDR was prepared each morning by 11:00 a.m. and reported the activity of the preceding day. The first set of entries on the report (see Exhibit 4) detailed the sales made by the Flight Department by each type of sales. The total represented all the revenue that was credited to Sales (indicated by (1) on the DDR). The second set of numbers categorized the flow of funds into the Flight Department by type – cash, credit card slips, or reductions in the block accounts[3] or leaseback payments due. The total of these funds (indicated by (2) on the DDR) are the charges (debits), to cash, accounts receivable or the block accounts payable.

The final group of items details the direct costs incurred in the production of revenue. These were:

---

[3] A block account represented prepaid flying lessons or aircraft rental. Cash was received in advance and recorded as an accounts payable by AirTex. The customer's flying activities were then charged (debited) to this account as they occurred. AirTex leased most of its instructional aircraft from private owners. AirTex contracted to pay them so much per hour for use of the aircraft. Some leases were "wet," meaning that the aircraft owner furnished the fuel. Other were "dry," meaning that AirTex paid for the fuel used.

- The expenses incurred in utilizing leased training aircraft. These were, by contract, a fixed amount per actual hour of aircraft use.

- The wages due to the flight instructors. These instructors were paid a contractual amount for each hour of instruction given. If the flight student was charged $60.00 per instructional hour by AirTex, AirTex would then owe the instructor $40.00 for that hour.

- Cost of supplies – the direct cost of the items sold in the Pilot Shop.

The total, (3) on the DDR, represented the direct costs of the Flight Department for that day.

Cash received in the mail and cash collected by the departments was deposited daily. Photocopies of the checks were given to the departments for identification of source and inclusion on their DDRs. Ted commented:

> We would deposit the check and send the photocopies around to the departments. Sometimes a check would come into AirTex from someone and no one would know who it was. Sometimes it would take two or three weeks to find out what it was for. It was passed around the various departments, but in the meantime, we had the money. We couldn't account for it, so we put it in a little suspense account. And, interestingly enough, sometimes no one accounted for it, and it became administrative profit.

The detail of charge slips, photocopies of checks, and physical currency would be attached to the DDR and by 11:00 a.m. each department would turn them into Accounting – with sales balanced against receipts, inventory against fuel flows, and receivables proven-out. There were still errors, but they got corrected at the departmental level, although at least one department had to hire an additional person to do the DDR.

The system left the Accounting Department with a simple task. They had DDRs from each department, but only one sales figure from each. Thus, their postings were trivial. All they had to do was to post the DDRs and then worry about other corporate issues, like taxes. Now, only one person was needed in accounting, and the detail was where it should be – in the departments where it could be used.

Similar systems were put in place for the Flight School, Service Department and Parts Department. For example, in Parts, a physical card was maintained for each inventory item. To purchase, the Parts Department would issue a purchase order. When the parts and invoice arrived, the total inventory balance was increased by the invoice amount, and a copy of the invoice was sent to the Parts Department. They would update their card balances for sales made. At the end of each month, Accounting would balance its control account against the sums shown on the parts cards.

Another control was the requirement for each department to submit aging of their accounts receivables to Accounting. Accounting would compare these amounts against their control totals. As Ted put it, "We balanced the aging provided by the departments against the books in central accounting down to the penny. That gave us our basic control."

Aircraft sales

While Ted was implementing the control system, educating the managers, dealing with the creditors, and establishing a better relationship with the bank, Frank was dealing with aircraft sales. Frank began by reestablishing AirTex's relationship with the Piper Aircraft Corporation. He convinced them that AirTex was on its way to financial stability and could not only sell but be able to inventory the requisite number of aircraft to maintain dealer status. Frank negotiated the terms with Piper, involving Ted only with Piper's reporting requirements.

A few years before, AirTex had been the largest Piper dealer in the territory, so Piper was interested in the potential of the new management. Things went well until Piper brought up the subject of their standard accounting reports. Frank and Ted were willing to commit to purchase five aircraft in the first six months, but they balked at the standardized reporting requirements which Ted characterized as "factory-oriented." He stated:

> I wanted to be basically independent. The reports weren't all that onerous. It might have been childish, but it was partly, "I own this place and no one is going to tell me what to do." It was also partly a feeling that I wanted to establish an equal relationship with Piper. I did not want to come to them as a supplicant. For the past several years, AirTex had always been begging Daddy Piper for handouts. I wanted to establish a relationship with them that was one of equals. It was psychological, but I also didn't want to waste the time of my people on something that I didn't think would

be productive. I told them they could have access to any of our reports that they wanted, but that we wouldn't use their forms. They didn't like it, but they bought it.

After obtaining the Piper franchise, Frank rehired the old salesmen, but personally shepherded the first aircraft sales through. The first one was, in Frank's word, "memorable." He continued:

Our first sale was to a local car dealer. He wanted to buy the aircraft, but he wouldn't pay for it until it arrived at San Miguel, saying, "In my business, you don't pay for a car until you see it." Now we had to pay for it when we picked it up at the factory, so I asked Ted how we stood. He said, "We have enough money although if he doesn't pay for it, we won't make the next payroll, and we'll be out $200,000 for however long it takes to get the airplane from Vero Beach to here. But I'm willing to do it. Go do whatever you have to do." So we did. I engaged the son of the air-craft salesman to fly the airplane. Unfortunately, there was horrible weather that grounded him in Tuscaloosa, Alabama for a week. I nearly lost my mind. I had committed every last cent the company had, and it was sitting in Tuscaloosa. That's how tight things were.

Profitability of the aircraft sales activity proved to be highly variable between months. For example, while losses were shown in May and August 1990, several very high-margin sales, accounting for nearly $500,000 in operating profit, were made in the June–July 1990 period. (See Exhibits 5–7.)

MANAGEMENT STYLE

In running the company, Ted took an active role both through long hours of planning and managing, and also through learning and doing. He learned to fly and got a multi-engine commercial license, changed the oil in the shop, and worked on the engines. It was, as Ted said:

a part of the process of being an avuncular, emotional leader. In the first couple of years, I deliberately set out to make my role a teacher. The first thing I did in my office was to put up a blackboard, and arrange the furniture so that there was a sofa facing the blackboard and a chair turned towards it as well. My desk was at right angles to the blackboard – all of us could see it. When departmental managers would come to me with a problem, rather than focusing on the problem, we would talk about the process. I would say, "Where is your accounting data? Where are your profit center reports? What do your profit center reports tell you about this problem? What thought processes did you go through to extract information from the profit center reports that would help you solve this problem? What alternatives did you consider?" And I did this in a typical Socratic teaching process. Through Frank's and my personal involvement in the company, and through this teaching approach, we could not only obviate Frank's forecast of bankruptcy in three months, but we could rely on our managers and build for the future.

Exhibit 1 Balance sheet for AirTex Aviation (000s)

Assets	8/26/89	1/1/90	Liabilities and net worth	8/26/89	1/1/90
Cash and marketable securities	$40	$440	Accounts payable – trade	$310	$250
Accounts receivable	125	245	Accounts payable – Phillips oil	560	580
Contracts receivable – current	255	75	Contracts payable – current	155	165
Financing commissions due	100	100	Customer deposits	–	10
Receivables from officers and employees	340	–	Notes payable	440	155
Other receivables	70	–	Accrued expenses	160	175
Inventory:			Deferred block time	25	20
Aircraft	165	515	Other current liabilities	10	10
Parts and flight supplies	250	225	**Total current liabilities**	1,660	1,365
Fuel	65	125	Contracts payable – long term	205	450
Work in progress	35	10	Long-term debt	2,120	170
Prepaid expenses	35	150	**Total liabilities**	3,985	1,985
Total current assets	1,480	1,885	Net worth	(85)	310
Fixed assets (net)	2,185	135	**Total liabilities and net worth**	$3,900	$2,295
Contracts receivable – long term	–	130			
Investments	145	145			
Other	90	–			
Total assets	$3,900	$2,295			

Exhibit 2 Prepurchase organizational chart

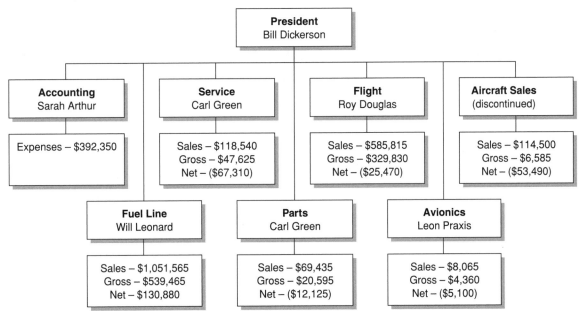

Sales, Gross Profit Margin, and Net Income were for the four months preceding purchase – September–December, 1989. Profit was calculated from the extant accounting system, which fully allocated administrative costs.

Exhibit 3 Floorplan of AirTex Aviation

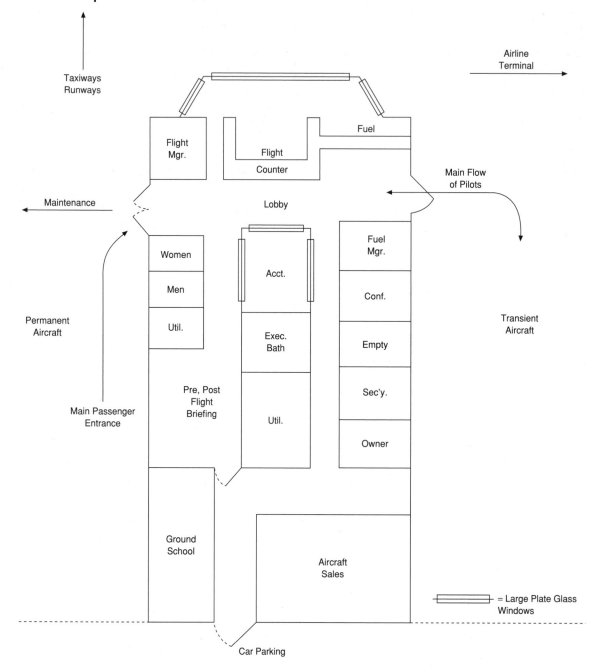

Exhibit 4 Flight Department daily report

Sales

Primary Ground School

Flight Instruction

Leaseback Owner's Rental

Rental (Solo)

Flight Supplies and Over Counter Sale – Retail Sales

Sales Tax Collected

Check Rides

Waiver

Car Wash and Aircraft Wash, and Tie-Downs

Student Tuition Refund Fee

Enrollment Fee

Interest Service Charges

| | TOTAL | $_____(1) |

Receipts

Cash

Credit Card Payment

Block Accounts and Block Account Supplies

AirTex Charges and AirTex Charge Supplies

Master Charge and Visa

Leaseback Refunds

| | TOTAL | $_____(2) |

Direct Cost of Sales

Leaseback Expenses

Instructor Wages

Cost of Supplies Sold Today

| | TOTAL | $_____(3) |

Exhibit 5 Summary income statements by activity – January–February 1990 ($000)

	Parts and Service	Avionics	Flight training	Fuel activity	Aircraft sales
Sales	78.5	0	125.5	313	439.5
Cost of product	28.5	7	52	204.5	382
Salaries & commissions	17.5	–	30	39	2.5
Payroll-related expenses	3.5	–	5.5	5	–
	49.5	7	87.5	248.5	384.5
Gross margin	29	(7)	38	64.5	55
Other expenses	34	.5	22.5	55	39.5
Operating profit	(5.0)	(7.5)	15.5	9.5	15.5

Exhibit 6 Summary income statements by activity – May 1990 ($000)

	Parts and service	Flight training	Fuel activity	Aircraft sales	Charter*
Sales	65	207	315.5	225.5	8
Cost of product	19.5	109.5	166.5	214.5	7
Direct payroll	25	46.5	41.5	–	–
Commissions	–	–	5	–	–
Payroll-related expenses	4	5.5	9.5	–	–
	48.5	161.5	222.5	214.5	7
Gross margin	16.5	45.5	93	11	1
Other expenses	32.5	33	49	31	.5
Operating profit	(16)	3.5	44	(20)	.5

* Charter activity started in May.

Exhibit 7 Summary income statements by activity – August 1990 ($000)

	Parts and service	Flight training	Fuel activity	Aircraft sales	Charter
Sales	132.5	177	327.5	111.5	61.5
Cost of product	46.5	93	168.5	99.5	34
Direct payroll	23	39	7.7	–	3
Payroll-related expenses	4.5	4.5	13.5	–	–
	74	136.5	220.5	99.5	37
Gross margin	58.5	40.5	107	12	24.5
Other expenses	33.5	30	14	43	12.5
Operating profit	25	10.5	93	(31)	12

FINANCIAL RESULTS CONTROL SYSTEMS

Chapter 7

FINANCIAL RESPONSIBILITY CENTERS

The vast majority of organizations control the behaviors of many of their employees, particularly their managers, through *financial results control systems*. In financial results control systems, results are defined in monetary terms, most commonly in terms of accounting measures such as revenues, costs, profits, or returns (e.g. return on equity). At higher organization levels, financial results control systems often are the most pervasive and dominant form of control.

Financial results control systems have three core elements: (1) *financial responsibility centers*, which define the apportioning of accountability for financial results within the organization; (2) *planning and budgeting systems*, which are used for a number of control-related purposes including the setting of performance targets for evaluating performance; and (3) *incentive contracts*, which define the links between results and various rewards.

This chapter describes the advantages of financial results control systems and then discusses in depth one important element of these systems: financial responsibility centers. It also describes one common problem faced by organizations using multiple financial responsibility centers: the transfer pricing problem. We discuss the other two financial results control system elements (planning and budgeting systems and incentive systems) in Chapters 8 and 9, respectively.

ADVANTAGES OF FINANCIAL RESULTS CONTROL SYSTEMS

Several good reasons explain the ubiquity of financial results control systems in organizations. First, financial objectives are paramount in for-profit firms. Profits and cash flows provide returns to investors and are among the primary measures outsiders use to evaluate for-profit firm performance. Thus, it is natural that managers of for-profit firms monitor their success in financial terms and use the financial measures to direct their employees' actions toward important organizational ends. Managers of not-for-profit organizations, too, must monitor finances closely because cash flows usually create significant constraints for their organizations.

Second, financial measures provide a *summary measure* of performance by aggregating the effects of a broad range of operating initiatives across a possibly broad range of markets, products/services, or activities into a single (or a few) measure(s). In so doing, they enhance the comparability of the effects of the initiatives and reduce the possibility of conflicting signals about their importance. The financial measures remind employees that the various operating initiatives they take on, such as initiatives to improve response times, defect rates, delivery reliability, or customer satisfaction ratings, benefit the organization only if they result in improved financial performance. Because financial measures are a comprehensive summary measure of performance, they provide a relatively easy, standardized, and inexpensive way for the organization to evaluate the results of a variety of operational initiatives without necessarily needing to obtain and evaluate the intricate detail of each of the initiatives.

The ubiquity and usability of financial measures is particularly valuable for the management of complex, diversified firms. Management in these organizations can usually set corporate goals in financial terms, decompose the corporate goals into multiple financial responsibility centers, and then monitor only one (or just a few) results measures – such as accounting profits or returns and their components (revenues, costs, assets, and liabilities) – which provide a good summary of the effects of most of the actions or decisions needing to be controlled. The managers then do not need to track either the actions that are affecting financial performance (e.g. how time was spent, how specific expenditures were made) or the specific line items that comprise the summary measures of performance (e.g. revenues by product line, cost line items) until problems (such as failures to achieve performance targets) appear in the summary measures. The process of getting involved only when problems appear is also known as *management-by-exception*. In this way, financial results controls reduce the amount of information that top managers need to assimilate. At the same time, financial results controls provide a relatively unobtrusive form of management control; that is, they provide control while allowing those being controlled considerable autonomy.

Third, most financial measures are relatively precise and objective. They generally provide significant measurement advantages over *soft* qualitative or subjective information and over many other quantifiable alternatives (e.g. quality or customer satisfaction measures). Cash flow – the primitive financial measure – is relatively easy to observe and measure. Accounting rules, on which most financial measures are built, limit the managers' measurement discretion, improve measurement objectivity, and facilitate the verification of the resulting measures.

Finally, the cost of implementing financial results controls is often small relative to that of other forms of management control. This is because the core financial results control measurement elements are largely in place. Organizations already routinely prepare and transmit elaborate sets of accounting information to government agencies, creditors, shareholders, and other constituencies on either a mandated or voluntary basis. This information can be readily and inexpensively adapted for control uses. In Chapter 10, we provide a further in-depth analysis of the features, as well as the limitations, of financial measures of performance.

TYPES OF FINANCIAL RESPONSIBILITY CENTERS

Financial responsibility centers are a core element of a financial results control system. The term *responsibility center management* denotes the apportioning of responsibility (or accountability) for a particular set of outputs and/or inputs to an employee (usually a manager) in charge of an organizational entity (the *responsibility center*). Responsibilities can be expressed in terms of quantities of inputs consumed, physical units of output generated, particular characteristics of the production or service process (e.g., defects, schedule attainment, customer satisfaction), or financial indicators of performance in these areas.

Financial responsibility centers are responsibility centers in which the assigned responsibilities are defined at least partially in financial terms. There are four basic types

TABLE 7.1 Typical examples of financial responsibility centers

Selected financial statement line items	Revenue center	Cost center	Profit center	Investment center
Income statement				
Revenue	x		x	x
Cost of goods sold		x	x	x
Gross margin			x	x
Advertising and promotion		x	x	x
Research and development		x	x	x
Profit before tax			x	x
Income tax			x	x
Profit after tax			x	x
Balance sheet				
Accounts receivable				x
Inventory				x
Fixed assets				x
Accounts payable				x
Debt				x

Note: x signifies that the responsibility center manager is (or could be) held accountable for some elements included in that financial statement line item.

Source: K. A. Merchant, *Modern Management Control Systems: Text and Cases* (Upper Saddle River, NJ: Prentice Hall, 1998), p. 303.

of financial responsibility centers: investment centers, profit centers, revenue centers, and cost centers. Table 7.1 shows that these centers are distinguishable by the financial statement line items for which the managers are held accountable in each type of center.

Investment centers

Investment centers are responsibility centers whose managers are held accountable for both some income statement and some balance sheet line items; that is, for both the accounting returns (profits) and the investments made to generate those returns. A corporation is an investment center, so top-level managers in most organizations, such as the chief executive and group vice presidents, are evaluated as investment center managers. So are the managers of many subsidiaries, operating groups, and divisions in large, decentralized organizations.

Accounting returns can be defined in many ways, but they typically involve a ratio of the profits earned to the investment capital used. The varying definitions cause many different labels to be put on the investment centers' *bottom line*, such as return on investment (ROI), return on equity (ROE), return on capital employed (ROCE), return on net assets (RONA), return on total capital (ROTC), risk adjusted return on capital (RAROC), and many other variations.

Profit centers

Profit centers are responsibility centers whose managers are held accountable for some measure of profits, which is the difference between the revenues generated and the costs of generating those revenues. Business terminology often is not precise, and many firms refer to their investment centers as profit centers. But there is a conceptual distinction between profit and investment centers: profit center managers are held accountable for profits but not for the investments made to generate them.

Profit and investment centers are an important control element of the vast majority of firms above minimal size. Profit centers, however, come in many different forms, some of which are considerably more limited in their scope of operation than others. In deciding whether or not a responsibility center manager truly has profit center responsibility, the critical question to ask is whether the manager has significant influence over both revenues and costs. Take Bonnaroo, a 100-band jamboree Music and Arts Festival on a farm outside of Nashville, which is run as 16 on-site profit centers, including concessions, merchandise, and even paid showers. The managers of each of the on-site profit centers are not only responsible for gross revenues, but also for the costs they incur to generate the revenues. Maybe due to linking revenues and costs so directly, and assigning responsibility at the profit level, Bonnaroo has been one of the most financially successful music festivals in North America during the last decade.[1]

But there are variations of fully fledged profit responsibility that organizations can play with. One such limited form of profit center is created when *sales-focused* entities are made into profit centers by charging the entity managers the standard cost of the products sold, thus making them accountable for *gross margin*. Even this limited assignment of costs provides the manager with useful information. Decisions, such as about sales and marketing direction and intensity, will be made based on the incremental contribution to the firm (i.e. gross margins) rather than just gross revenues.

Another limited form of profit center is created where *cost-focused* entities are assigned revenues based on a simple function of costs. A typical example exists where manufacturing and administrative departments supply unique products or services, for which sometimes external market prices cannot be determined, to internal customers only. Revenues for these entities might be calculated as cost plus a markup. Are these cost-focused entities profit centers? It depends on the extent to which the employees in these entities can influence the revenue figure. If their internal customers can outsource their purchases, then the employees in the supplying entities probably do have considerable influence over the revenue that will be assigned to them. At least, they are motivated to produce quality products or services, to provide superior delivery schedules, and to provide friendly, hassle-free customer service in order to keep the business and, hence, to generate *allocated* or *assigned* revenues. Thus, even though the revenues are artificially imputed in these cost-focused profit centers, the main idea is to transmit the competitive pressures faced by a firm in the marketplace to its internal service groups. Internal profit centers that do not directly interface with the market and have no control over revenues in a competitive sense are also sometimes called *micro* profit centers.[2] If the employees do not have significant control over the revenues assigned, however, these entities are merely *pseudo* profit centers. Assigning revenues to these entities to allow a profit figure to be shown is merely a way to charge the buying entities a cost-based approximation of a market price so that their profits are not overstated and can be compared more easily with entities that source externally.

In deciding whether an entity is a profit center, it is *not* important to consider either whether the entity's goal is to maximize profits or whether any revenues are generated from outside the organization. The financial goal of profit centers, such as those in not-for-profit organizations, can be merely to break even. For example, hospitals can adopt a "profit center" structure to relate the costs of patient care in various clinical groups directly to revenues received either from the patient, through insurance payments, from government subsidies or other sources (e.g. grants). The primary goal of the "profit centers" in this case is not to maximize profit; instead it is to assess and manage the costs of medical care within the constraints applied by the funds available. Because the managers of these entities allocate resources (costs) in relation to the funds available (revenues), and thus essentially make cost–revenue tradeoffs, they should be considered "profit center" managers, even though that term is rarely used in the not-for-profit sector. Similarly, it is not necessary that a profit center generates revenues from outside the organization. Many profit centers derive most, or even all, of their revenues by selling their products or services to other entities within the same organization. These sales are made at *transfer prices*, which we discuss in detail later in this chapter.

Revenue centers

Revenue centers are responsibility centers whose managers are held accountable for generating revenues, which is a financial measure of output. Common examples are sales managers and, in not-for-profit organizations, fundraising managers.

Revenues, rather than profits, provide a simple and effective way to encourage sales managers to attract and retain customers. However, it will encourage them to make profitable sales if, and only if, it can be ascertained that all sales are approximately equally profitable. But if all revenues are not equally "endowed," controlling with a revenue center structure can encourage employees to make "easy" sales, rather than those that are most profitable.

Most revenue center managers are also held accountable for some expenses. For example, many sales managers are accountable for their salespeople's salaries and commissions and perhaps some travel, advertising, and promotional expenses. These managers could be said to manage a *net revenue* center. But while these managers are held accountable for both revenues and some costs, they should not be considered profit center managers because there is no profit calculation relating outputs to inputs; that is, these revenue centers are not charged for the cost of the goods or services they sell.

Cost centers

Cost (or expense) centers are responsibility centers whose managers are held accountable for some elements of cost. Costs are a financial measure of the inputs to, or resources consumed by, the responsibility center.[3] In *standard cost centers* (sometimes called *engineered cost centers*), such as manufacturing departments, the causal relationship between inputs and outputs is direct, and both inputs and outputs are easy to quantify. Thus, control can be exercised by comparing a standard cost (the cost of the inputs that *should have been consumed* in producing the output) with the costs that were *actually incurred*.

In *discretionary cost centers* (sometimes called *managed cost centers*), such as research and development departments and administrative departments (e.g. personnel, purchasing, accounting, estates), the outputs produced are difficult to value in monetary terms. In addition, the relationship between inputs and outputs is not well known. Thus, evaluations of discretionary cost center managers' performances often have a large subjective component to them. Control is usually exercised by ensuring that the discretionary cost center adheres to a budgeted level of expenditures while successfully accomplishing the tasks assigned to it.

Variations

While the four categories of financial responsibility centers can be distinguished, there is considerable variation within each financial responsibility type. For example, Table 7.2 shows four quite different responsibility centers, each of which is a profit center even though the breadth of responsibility, as reflected in the number of income statement line

TABLE 7.2 Four types of profit center

Selected financial statement line items	Gross margin center	Incomplete profit center	Before-tax profit center	Complete profit center
Income statement				
Revenue	x	x	x	x
Cost of goods sold	x	x	x	x
Gross margin	x	x	x	x
Advertising and promotion		x	x	x
Research and development			x	x
Profit before tax			x	x
Income tax				x
Profit after tax				x

Note: x signifies that the responsibility center manager is held accountable for that financial statement line item.
Source: K. A. Merchant, *Modern Management Control Systems: Text and Cases* (Upper Saddle River, NJ: Prentice Hall, 1998), p. 306.

items for which the managers are held accountable, varies considerably. *Gross margin center* managers may be salespeople who sell products of varying margins and who are charged with the standard cost of the goods they sell. The "profit" measure gives them an incentive to sell higher margin products, rather than merely generating additional, possibly unprofitable, revenues. The *incomplete profit center* managers may be managers of product divisions but without authority for all of the functions that affect the success of their products, such as research and development or advertising. *Complete profit center* managers may be business unit managers who are accountable for all aspects of the worldwide performance of their business segment. Similar variations are also common among the other responsibility center types as the managers are held accountable for more or fewer financial statement line items.

CHOICE OF FINANCIAL RESPONSIBILITY CENTERS

The four financial responsibility center types can be contrasted in a hierarchy reflecting the breath of financial responsibility, or the number of financial statement line items for which the manager is held accountable, as was shown in Table 7.1. Revenue and cost center managers are held accountable for only one, or sometimes a few, income statement line items. Profit center managers are held accountable for some revenue and some expense line items. Investment center managers are held accountable for a measure of profit that is related directly to performance in areas reflected on the balance sheet.

One important point to keep in mind is that the lines between the financial responsibility center types are not always easy to discern, so responsibility center labels are not always informative. In actual practice, financial responsibility centers can be arrayed on an almost seamless continuum from cost or revenue centers to investment centers. For example, consider the case of manufacturing managers who are held accountable for meeting customer specifications, production quality standards, and customer delivery schedules, in addition to costs. In combination, these non-cost factors may largely determine the company's success in generating revenues, and these managers clearly have to make tradeoffs between costs and factors that affect revenues. But, technically, these managers are cost center managers.

Much more important than the labeling of financial responsibility centers are the decisions that have to be made in designing financial responsibility structures. The

FIGURE 7.1 **Typical financial responsibility centers in a functional organization**

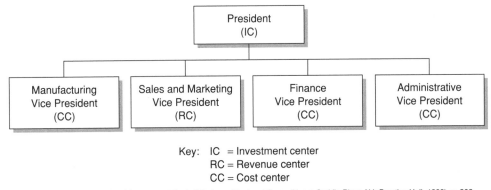

Key: IC = Investment center
RC = Revenue center
CC = Cost center

Source: K. A. Merchant, *Modern Management Control Systems: Text and Cases* (Upper Saddle River, NJ: Prentice Hall, 1998), p. 308.

important question to answer is: Which managers should be held accountable for which specific financial statement line items? These choices are obviously important because they affect behavior. Managers pay attention to the measures for which they are held accountable. Thus, from a behavioral angle, the answer to the question is relatively straightforward: Hold managers accountable for the line items you want them to pay attention to.

To a large extent, firms' financial responsibility center structures are coincident with the managers' areas of authority. Areas of authority are defined by organization structures and policies that define managers' *decision rights*. In a typical functional organization (Figure 7.1), none of the managers has significant decision-making authority over *both* the generation of revenues and incurrence of costs, so revenues and costs (including the costs of investments) are brought together in a return measure only at the corporate level. The manufacturing, engineering, and administrative functions are typically cost centers, and the sales function is a revenue center. In a typical divisionalized organization (Figure 7.2), division managers are given authorities to make decisions in all, or at least many, of the functions that affect the success of their division. Consistent with this broad authority, each division is a profit center (or investment center) comprised of multiple cost and revenue centers.

Decisions about an organization's structure do not necessarily precede decisions about the type of responsibility centers that should be used; the responsibility structure decision can come first. For example, the desire to have managers make tradeoffs between revenues and costs may lead to the choice of a divisionalized organization structure. As such, there should be a close relationship between decisions about organizational structure and responsibility centers, as that is where *decision authority* and *results accountability* meet.

The desire to have managers pay attention to a particular line item does not necessarily mean that the managers need to have direct and *complete* control over the item, although it should mean that the managers have *some influence* over the line item. Some managers are purposely held accountable for line items over which they have no direct control, such as corporate administrative expenses, to empower them to influence the behaviors of the managers with direct control. We discuss this further in more depth in Chapter 12.

Specific strategic concerns sometimes also affect the choice of responsibility center structure. A strategy focused on providing superior customer service may dictate that the managers of responsibility centers with direct customer interfaces (such as customer support) should be held accountable for revenue or profit because having these

Figure 7.2 Typical financial responsibility centers in a divisionalized organization

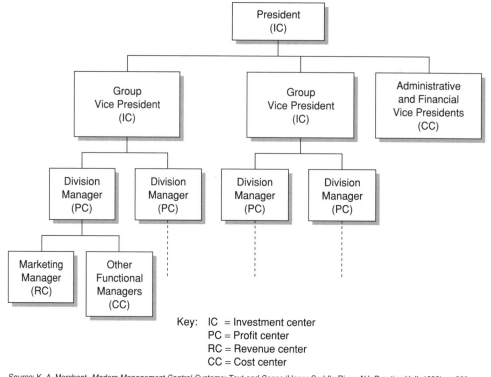

Key: IC = Investment center
PC = Profit center
RC = Revenue center
CC = Cost center

Source: K. A. Merchant, *Modern Management Control Systems: Text and Cases* (Upper Saddle River, NJ: Prentice Hall, 1998), p. 309.

managers just focus on costs could cause behaviors that conflict with the company's strategy (such as behaviors that reduce costs by skimping on customer service). Alternatively, these managers could be held accountable for costs plus a measure of customer satisfaction.

Some strategies might even suggest that some managers not be held accountable for line items over which they clearly have some influence. It may be desirable *not* to charge entity managers for the costs of certain activities (such as research and development costs or information technology costs) in order to stimulate greater use of them. If the entity's strategy depends on technological leadership, for example, corporate managers might not want the entity managers to make rigid cost–benefit tradeoffs on every expenditure in this critically important strategic area.

Finally, as business models change, so should responsibility center structures. For example, innovative corporations today are starting to look at energy in a different way, focusing on how energy management can help the business rather than treating it just as a cost. Specifically, companies are finding that they can reduce energy use by investing in projects that can earn tax incentives, create new lines of business, and in many countries qualify as a tradable asset in financial markets. A shift in energy management from an "environmental cost" to an "environmental asset" calls for turning a cost into a profit through recycling waste into a source of energy (the excess of which can be sold) as well as through reducing energy usage, which not only saves costs, but also can earn tax incentives and carbon credits that can be worth millions a year. This approach to energy management, in turn, creates the need for a profit center structure where there were previously only costs and risks.[4]

THE TRANSFER PRICING PROBLEM

Profit (or investment) centers often supply products or services to other profit centers within the same firm. When that happens, some mechanism for determining the prices of the transfers must be established.[5] *Transfer prices* directly affect the revenues of the selling (supplying) profit center, the costs of the buying (receiving) profit center and, consequently, the profits of both entities. The impact of these transfer prices depends largely on the number and magnitude of internal transfers relative to the size of each entity. When the amount of transfers is significant, failure to set the right transfer prices can have significant effects on a number of important decisions, including those regarding production quantities, sourcing, resource allocations, and evaluations of the managers of both the selling and buying profit centers.

Purposes of transfer pricing

Transfer prices have multiple organizational purposes, and these purposes often conflict. One purpose of transfer prices is to provide the proper economic signals so that the managers affected will make good decisions. In particular, the prices should properly influence both the selling profit center managers' decisions about how much product/ service to supply internally and the buying profit center managers' decisions about how much product/service to buy internally.

Second, the transfer prices and subsequent profit measurements should provide information that is useful for evaluating the performances of both the profit centers and their managers. Transfer prices directly affect the profits of both the selling and buying entities. Ideally, the transfer prices should not cause the performance of either entity to be either over- or understated. Misleading profitability signals can adversely affect allocations of resources within the firm. They can also severely undercut profit center managers' motivations because the managers will argue that they are not being treated fairly.

Third, transfer prices can be set to purposely move profits between firm locations. Several factors can motivate managers to use transfer prices in this way. When firms are operating in multiple tax jurisdictions (countries or states), their managers might be motivated to use transfer prices to move profits between jurisdictions to minimize taxes. Corporate income tax rates differ significantly across countries, and managers can set transfer prices to earn profits in relatively low-tax localities to maximize after-tax world-wide profits.[6] Although this particular aspect of the transfer pricing problem is beyond the scope of this chapter, evidence suggest that the maximization of global profits remains a critical consideration of transfer pricing policies in multinational corporations.[7]

Profit repatriation limitations also provide a motivation for companies to use transfer prices to move profits between entities across country borders. For a number of reasons, including balance of payments problems and a scarcity of foreign currency reserves, some governments prohibit repatriation of profits, either directly or indirectly. Indirect forms of restrictions include distorted exchange rates or high withholding tax rates. When companies are unable to repatriate profits from their entities in foreign countries, they are motivated to set transfer prices to minimize profits in those countries.

Companies also sometimes set transfer prices to shift profits between wholly owned subsidiaries and entities where the profits are shared with, say, joint venture partners. As a matter of fact, transfer prices are for this reason often strictly included and set out in great detail in the joint venture contract to avoid possible expropriation. Sometimes transfer prices are set to move profits to an entity which is being positioned for divestment in hopes of increasing its valuation, and hence, its selling price.

These multiple transfer pricing purposes often conflict.[8] Except in rare circumstances, tradeoffs are necessary because no single transfer pricing method serves all the purposes well. The usual desire to have transfer pricing mechanisms operate automatically between entities, without frequent interventions from corporate management, provides another transfer pricing complication. Transfer pricing interventions undermine the benefits of decentralization. They reduce profit center (entity) autonomy and cause decision-making complexity and delay. They also increase organizational costs, particularly in terms of the management time needed to review the facts and to reach a transfer pricing "ruling" acceptable to all entities involved. Thus, firms seek to set transfer pricing policies that work without producing major exceptions and disputes.

Transfer pricing alternatives

Most firms use any of five primary types of transfer prices. First, transfer prices can be based on *market prices*. The market price used for internal transfers could be the listed price of an identical (or similar) product or service, the actual price the selling entity charges external customers (perhaps less a discount that reflects lower selling costs for internal customers), or the price a competitor is offering. Second, transfer prices can be based on *marginal costs*, with marginal costs approximated as the variable or direct cost of production. Third, transfer prices can be based on the *full costs* of providing the product or service. Both marginal and full cost-based transfer prices can reflect either standard or actual costs. Fourth, transfer prices can be set at *full cost plus a markup*. Finally, transfer prices can be *negotiated* between the managers of the selling and buying profit centers. Information about market prices and either marginal or full production costs often provide input into these negotiations, but there is no requirement that they do so.

On balance, surveys of practice across sources and time seem to suggest that transfers at marginal cost are rarely used and that most companies internally transfer goods or services at either market prices or variations of full costs (e.g. full cost plus markup). In other words, what emerges is that both market price and "cost-plus" methods are the most widely used. Perhaps due to the increased scrutiny and enforcement by the tax authorities of the presumed *arm's-length* principle (see below), most companies use market-based transfer prices for international transfers more often than either cost-based or negotiated transfer prices.[9] We discuss each of the transfer pricing methods next.

Market-based transfer prices

In the relatively rare situation where a perfectly (or at least highly) competitive external market exists for internally traded goods or services, it is optimal for both decision making and performance evaluation purposes to set transfer prices at competitive market prices. A *perfectly* competitive market exists where the product is homogenous and no individual buyer or seller can unilaterally affect its price.

The case for using market-based transfer prices under competitive conditions is apparent. If the selling profit center cannot earn a profit by selling at the external market price, then the firm is better off shutting that profit center down and buying from an outside supplier, all else equal. Similarly, if the buying profit center cannot earn a profit by buying its inputs at the prevailing market price, then the firm should shut that profit center down and have its selling profit center sell all its outputs to outsiders in the market. Hence, if transfer prices are set at market price, managers of both the selling and buying profit centers are likely to make decisions that are optimal from the firm's perspective, and reports of both of their performances will provide good information for evaluation purposes.

Entities within organizations, however, rarely operate as they would as stand-alone firms in the open market.[10] Therefore, many firms use *quasi* market-based transfer prices by allowing deviations from the observed market prices. The deviations allow for adjustments that reflect differences between internal and external sales. These differences can reflect the savings of marketing, selling and collecting costs, the costs of special terms offered only to external customers (e.g. warranties), or the value of special features, special services provided or differences in quality standards. Adjustments in market prices also may reflect the belief that the price quoted by the external supplier is not a sustainable competitive price. The price quoted might just be a low-ball bid designed merely to get the first order. The greater the number and size of these adjustments, however, the more the market-based transfer prices are like cost-based prices and the more difficult the transfer pricing tradeoffs become.

Marginal cost transfer prices

When intermediate products and services are exchanged internally at marginal cost, it is easy to determine the total contribution generated by the final product or service to the firm as a whole. The total contribution is simply equal to the selling price of the final product or service minus the marginal cost of the last production or service process stage. Although this might be an appealing feature from a cost accounting perspective, and sometimes from a price-setting perspective for short-term pricing decisions, it creates a problem when viewed from a responsibility center perspective. The reason is that the total contribution is not easily traceable to each of the supplying entities, nor do any of the supplying entities even recuperate their full costs, which makes it unfeasible to evaluate them as profit centers. At best, they can be *standard variable cost centers*; that is, their performance evaluation depends on the extent to which their *actual* variable costs for a given output are at or below the standard variable cost. As we have discussed above, this obviously is a very limited form of financial results accountability.

This perhaps explains why the survey sources mentioned above indicate that companies rarely use marginal cost transfers. Indeed, the rarity of use of this method is likely due to the fact that marginal cost transfers provide poor information for evaluating the economic performance of either the selling or buying profit centers. The selling profit center will typically have to record losses because it bears the full cost of production or provision while receiving in revenue only the marginal costs. Conversely, the profits of the buying profit center will be overstated because it does not have to pay for even the full cost of the transferred goods or services.

Marginal cost transfer prices also are sometimes difficult to implement. Relatively few companies can measure marginal costs accurately. Direct costs (direct material, direct labor) are not the problem; indirect costs are. Companies that use marginal cost transfer pricing usually define marginal costs as standard variable costs, but there is no clean break between variable and fixed indirect costs. Indirect cost allocations sometimes are quite arbitrary. Marginal costs also are not always constant over the range of output. Sharp increases in marginal costs may occur if the selling profit center is operating near a capacity constraint.

Full cost transfer prices

Transfers at *full cost* or *full cost plus a markup* are more widely used. Full-cost transfer prices offer several advantages. First, they provide a measure of long-run viability. For a product or service to be economically sustainable, its full cost, and not just its marginal cost, must be recuperated, actually even generating a margin above full cost. Second, full cost transfers are relatively easy to implement because firms have systems in place to calculate the full costs of production (goods) or provision (services). Finally, full cost transfers are not as distorting for evaluation purposes since the selling profit center is allowed to recover at least the full cost of production or provision.

Full cost transfer prices are not a panacea, however. The full cost rarely reflects the actual, current cost of producing the products or the services being transferred. Some of the distortions are caused by poor cost accounting systems that involve arbitrary over-head cost allocations. In addition, strictly full cost transfer prices do not provide an incentive for the selling profit center to transfer internally since they include no profit margin. If internal transfers are a significant part of the selling profit center's business, then that entity's profit will be understated. Transfers at *full cost plus a markup*, however, do allow the selling profit centers to earn a profit on internally transferred products or services. They also provide a crude approximation of the market price that can be used in situations where no competitive external market price exists. But because the markup is internally set, such transfer prices are not responsive to changes in market conditions.

Negotiated transfer prices

Another transfer pricing alternative is to allow the selling and buying profit center managers to negotiate between themselves. This policy can be effective only if the profit centers are not *captive* to one another; that is, the selling profit center has some possibilities to sell its product outside the company and the buying profit center has some outside sources of supply. Captivity obviously erodes bargaining power and undermines the negotiations.

However, negotiated transfer prices often cause several other problems. Negotiating a potentially large number of transactions is costly in terms of management time. Negotiation often accentuates conflicts between profit center managers, and resolution of the conflicts often requires mediation from corporate management. The outcome of the negotiations often depends on the negotiating skills and bargaining power of the managers involved, rather than it likely being economically optimal. If one of the entities has reasonably good outside selling or sourcing possibilities but the other does not, the bargaining power will be unequal. The unequal bargaining power will be magnified if the transaction is a relatively small proportion of the business of one of the entities and a relatively large proportion of the business of the other. The managers of the small-proportion entity will have considerable bargaining power because they can walk away from the trans-action without bearing serious consequences. And managers' egos and self-interest can sometimes lead them to try to gain an upper hand in the negotiations over peers with whom they compete for recognition, bonuses, and promotions, even at the expense of the corporation's best interest.

Variations

Researchers have proposed several variations of one or more of the primary transfer pricing methods. All of these variations have some merit, so they are worth mentioning, although their actual usage may vary in importance and with circumstances. One possibility is to transfer at *marginal costs plus a fixed lump-sum fee*. The lump-sum fee is designed to compensate the selling profit center for tying up some of its fixed capacity for producing products that are transferred internally. This method has some obvious appeal. It preserves goal congruence because additional unit transfers are made at marginal cost. It preserves information for evaluation purposes because the selling division can recover its fixed costs and a profit margin through the lump-sum fee. It also stimulates intra-firm planning and coordination because the selling and buying entities must discuss the bases for the lump-sum fee.

The major problem with the marginal-cost-plus-lump-sum method is that the managers involved must predetermine the lump-sum fee based on an estimate of the capacity that each internal customer will require in the forthcoming period. If these estimates are incorrect, then the charges will be inaccurate, and the capacity will not be assigned to the most profitable uses. If the selling entity changes all the lump-sum charges after the fact to reflect each customer's actual use of capacity, then the result will be nearly identical to transferring at the full cost of production.

Dual-rate transfer prices are another variation. In this case, the selling profit center is credited with the market price (or an approximation of it), but the buying profit center pays only the marginal (or full) costs of production. This scheme double counts the profits the corporation earns on each transaction. The accounting entries are balanced by putting the difference in a holding account at corporate which is eliminated at the time of financial statement consolidation.

Dual-rate transfer prices have two basic advantages. First, the managers of both the selling and buying profit centers receive the proper economic signals for their decision-making. The seller receives the market price and is thereby not discouraged to transact internally. The buyer pays only the marginal (or full) cost, and thus, should normally be encouraged to buy internally. As such, the dual-rate transfer pricing method almost ensures that internal transactions will take place, making it possible to maintain a vertically integrated production process.

However, dual-rate transfer prices have disadvantages. Dual-rate transfer pricing can destroy the internal entities' proper economic incentives. Since the buying profit centers pay only marginal (or full) cost, they have little incentive to negotiate with outside suppliers for more favorable prices. Hence, the selling profit centers find it easy to generate internal sales because the transfer pricing policy shields them from competition. Many corporations also do not like to double count profits because it is often difficult to explain to the profit center managers how the double counting has overstated their entity profits. Equally, when the dual rates involve bookings across national borders, the corporation may wish to avoid alarming the tax authorities by the double counting and the retrospective adjustments to the accounts. What may seem merely to be an internal accounting adjustment may not be seen this way by the tax authorities or regulators, and, for this reason, it is also not favored by the firm's external auditors.

Simultaneous use of multiple transfer pricing methods

One potential response to the need to serve multiple transfer pricing purposes is to use multiple transfer pricing methods. However, it is virtually impossible to use two different transfer pricing methods and simultaneously serve both the decision making and evaluation purposes because managers make decisions in light of the numbers for which they are being evaluated. Tradeoffs here are usually inevitable.

When firms do use multiple transfer pricing methods, they typically use one method for internal purposes – both decision making and evaluation – and another method to affect taxable profits across jurisdictions. But the countries in which multinational corporations operate obviously have incentives not to allow these firms to manipulate reported profits through transfer prices, as they will suffer tax losses if profits are moved out of their jurisdiction.[11] Or they may suffer decreased market competitiveness if the firm manipulates its transfer prices to maintain a monopoly position as a supplier. Therefore, laws often require an *arm's-length* transfer price; that is, a price charged to the associated entity as the one between unrelated parties for the same transactions under the same circumstances. In the United States, there are no restrictions on domestic transfer pricing methods, but the Internal Revenue Service (the US tax authority) disallows the shifting of income with international subsidiaries to avoid US taxes. This is true for many other countries as well. All told, then, it is easier for managers to claim that they are not manipulating reported income to evade taxes if they use the same transfer pricing method for tax purposes as is used for internal purposes. For this reason, and for reasons of system simplicity, multinational firms sometimes avoid using different transfer pricing methods for domestic and international transfers.

CONCLUSION

This chapter has provided an introduction to financial responsibility centers and transfer pricing. Financial responsibility centers are one of the core elements of financial results control systems. The definitions of financial responsibility centers are important because they provide managers with signals about what financial statement line items they are expected to pay attention to. We discussed how the financial responsibilities usually are congruent with the managers' authorities or decision rights, but there are exceptions. Sometimes managers are held accountable for financial statement line items over which they have no direct authority because the accountability empowers them to influence the actions of those who do have direct authority.

This chapter also discussed how the pricing of goods or services that are transferred from one organizational entity to another often causes problems in the measurement of an entity's financial performance. Except in the rare situation where there is a perfectly competitive external market for the internally traded good or service, no transfer pricing approach can guide profit center managers to make decisions which are optimal from the corporation's perspective and simultaneously provide good information for evaluation. Incentives to move profits between firm locations with different tax jurisdictions cause additional transfer pricing considerations. Transfer pricing methods based on market prices or full costs, and variations thereof, are in common use, but some companies also use negotiated transfer prices. No method is superior in all settings; each has its advantages and disadvantages.

The next chapter discusses planning and budgeting systems, the second core element of financial results control systems. Planning and budgeting systems also have several control purposes, some of which are, like transfer pricing purposes, sometimes conflicting.

Notes

1. "Who Says the Music Industry is Kaput," *Business Week* (May 27, 2010), online (www.businessweek.com).
2. R. Cooper and R. Slagmulder, "Micro Profit Centers," *Management Accounting*, 79, no. 12 (1998), pp. 16–18.
3. The term *cost center* also has a cost accounting meaning that is different from its meaning here in the context of responsibility center management. Most firms are comprised of many cost centers set up for cost accounting purposes to collect like-type costs and assign them to products and services, but these are not responsibility centers because the former focus on cost categorizations rather than lines of authority over expenses by managers in charge of organizational entities with accountability for a cost budget. Firms typically use many more cost

centers for cost accounting purposes than for responsibility center control purposes.
4. "Why Energy Management Matters to CIOs," *Forbes* (September 15, 2010), online (www.forbes.com).
5. Transfer pricing also applies to transfers involving cost centers. Transfers can be made, for example, at actual or standard cost or at full or variable cost between cost centers. Since most transfer pricing problems involve profit (or investment) centers, however, this chapter will, for reasons of simplicity, refer to both the supplying and buying entities as *profit centers*.
6. See, for example, "Glaxo in Major Battle with IRS over Taxes on Years of US Sales," *The Wall Street Journal* (June 11, 2002), p. A1; "IRS Accepts Settlement Offer

in Largest Transfer Pricing Dispute," *Internal Revenue Service* (September 11, 2006), online (www.irs.gov); "Dodge $60 Billion in Taxes Even Tea Party Condemns," *Business Week* (May 13, 2010), online (www.businessweek.com).

7. J. Elliot and C. Emmanuel, *International Transfer Pricing: A Study of Cross-Border Transactions* (London: CIMA Publishing, 2000); *Global Transfer Pricing Survey* (Ernst & Young, 2009).

8. M. Cools and R. Slagmulder, "Tax-Compliant Transfer Pricing and Responsibility Accounting," *Journal of Management Accounting Research*, 21 (2009), pp. 151–78.

9. Elliot and Emmanuel, *International Transfer Pricing*, op. cit.; *Global Transfer Pricing Survey*, op. cit.

10. "The Nobel Prize for Economics: The Bigger Picture," *The Economist* (October 12, 2009), online (www.economist.com); "Reality Bites," *The Economist* (October 15, 2009), p. 92.

11. See, for example, "Glaxo in Major Battle with IRS over Taxes on Years of US Sales," op. cit.; "IRS Accepts Settlement Offer in Largest Transfer Pricing Dispute," op. cit.; "Dodge $60 Billion in Taxes Even Tea Party Condemns," op. cit.

Case Study

Kranworth Chair Corporation

In July 2003, Kevin Wentworth, CEO of Kranworth Chair Corporation (KCC), was considering a major reorganization – a divisionalization – of his company's organization structure:

> Like many entrepreneurs, I have always been focused on top-line sales growth, and I have constantly been impressing on my managers to drive sales. My belief was that if you do that, everything else takes care of itself. Up until recently, I think our approach made sense. We had very little competition, and our margins were huge.
>
> Now things are changing. We've got some major competitors who are making headway. I think we needed to take a fresh management approach to find opportunities to do things better. Our new divisionalized organization structure should help us serve our customers better and maybe force us to eliminate certain markets or products that are not producing results.
>
> But I'm not sure it's working very well. We're seeing some finger pointing between the managers of the newly created divisions and the managers in charge of corporate departments. There is a lot of politics involved in defining the roles, responsibilities, . . . and rights, of each of the responsibility centers, and it's not clear to me yet exactly where to draw the lines.

THE COMPANY

In the early 1980s, Weston Krantz, an avid outdoors person, developed a new design for a lightweight, portable chair that could be stored in a bag and carried anywhere. Convinced that his design had commercial value, in 1987 Weston cofounded Kranworth Chair Corporation (KCC) with his long-time friend, Kevin Wentworth, who had an MBA degree and financial expertise. (The corporation's name was a contraction of the founders' names: Krantz and Wentworth.) KCC was headquartered in Denver, Colorado, in the foothills of the Rocky Mountains. KCC produced a broad line of high-quality and fashionable portable, folding chairs, which were branded as various models of the Fold-it! brand. In its early years, KCC sold its products exclusively to distributors.

Since its inception, KCC had been organized functionally. In 2003, reporting to the cofounders were vice presidents in charge of sales, supply chain, and finance and administration, plus staff managers responsible for advertising and research and development (Exhibit 1).   ▶

This case was prepared by Professors Kenneth A. Merchant, Wim A. Van der Stede, and research assistant Clara (Xiaoling) Chen.

Over the years, KCC expanded its product offerings. In 2003, it offered an extensive line of folding chairs. The chairs were produced in various sizes and models, including both adult and child chairs, single chairs and loveseats, and full- and beach-height chairs. Some chairs had additional features, such as cup holders, storage pockets, and trays. The chairs were produced at several price points, with varying fabrics, designs (e.g. single vs. double layer), and frame materials. KCC also offered some related products, such as folding tripod stools, ottomans, cots, and stadium seats. KCC also produced custom-designed products. It employed screen-printing artists and seamstresses who applied custom logos, graphics, and lettering to the nylon. KCC products were often seen at corporate trade shows and tailgate parties at sporting events. The company kept track of approximately 1,500 stock keeping units (SKUs) – finished products and various piece parts that the company sold – although about 85–90% of the sales stemmed from only about 40 of the SKUs.

Gradually, KCC built sales by investing in more advertising and by adding other distribution channels. By 2003, it sold some products directly to major retail chains (Wal-Mart, K-Mart, Target), as well as other retailers (e.g. sporting goods stores) of various sizes. It sold to retailers using the KCC sales force, outside reps, and distributors. It also sold custom products directly to corporations and high school or university bookstores and athletic departments. The retail channels provided the highest sales volumes, but those sales were made at lower margins.

In the 1990s, KCC moved its core manufacturing facilities to Mexico and China to take advantage of lower labor rates. Only some assembly ("kitting") and customizing facilities were retained in the Denver location.

In the company's first decade of existence, KCC had little competition. Its chair designs were protected by more than 20 patents. Sales grew rapidly, and average margins were high, in the range of 40–50%, although some margins were sacrificed in later years in order to generate sales from large retail chains.

In 1999, KCC borrowed $30 million because the founders, particularly Kevin, wanted to take a significant amount of cash out of the company. Kevin had become interested in ranching, and he wanted to buy a significantly larger ranch. Ranching had become his passion, and he was spending less and less time at KCC. (For years Weston had spent only a small portion of his time at KCC as he traveled and pursued his various avocations.) The debt service on the loan reduced KCC managers' margin for error. Cash flow was tight, particularly at the slow time of the year – October to January.

Starting in the late 1990s, some significant competitors, mostly from Asian countries, entered the market with comparable chair designs. Despite the fact that most customers perceived KCC as having superior designs and higher quality, and customer satisfaction was high, the higher competition and the worldwide recession of the early 2000s caused sales to flatten and profits to drop. The company's management incentive plan did not pay out in either 2001 or 2002. In 2003 performance was slightly improved. KCC's total revenues were projected to be approximately $70 million, up from $68 million in 2002, and profits were expected to be slightly positive.

MOTIVATION FOR DIVISIONALIZATION

In 2002, Kevin began to think about changes that might stem from a change in organization structure. He thought that the KCC managers needed to focus more on the quality, and not just the quantity, of sales. To illustrate the point, he described an example in which KCC personnel had aggressively sought business from Target, the large retail chain. In order to develop this retail account, KCC designed a special chair model for Target and offered a special price with a lower gross margin. While Target did sell some Fold-it! chairs, they did not sell many. Part of the reason for the poor sales was that many of Target's outlets did not display the Fold-it! chairs effectively. Instead of displaying them in the sporting goods department, they shelved them wherever they had room. Kevin explained, "I walked into a Target store in a suburb of Denver and found that our products were sitting on the bottom shelf horizontally in the back corner of the Automotive department, where nobody could ever see them!" Because of the "growth at all costs" philosophy, KCC incurred significant product development and marketing costs and ended up carrying a large amount of inventory, so overall the Target account, and some others like it, were very unprofitable. But to develop more focus on the quality of sales, KCC had to develop a stronger customer focus, to understand better customers' needs and wants, and to improve customer service levels.

Kevin also thought that divisionalization, if implemented properly, could help KCC improve its efficiency and asset utilization. He thought that with an improved customer focus, it was almost inevitable that the company could reduce its SKUs, possibly outsource more functions, and generally learn to serve customer needs better while tying up less capital.

DIVISIONALIZATION ALTERNATIVES

What kind of divisionalization would be best? Kevin thought first about the relatively conservative approach of merely making the sales function a profit center. This approach would involve charging Sales for the full costs (or, perhaps, full costs plus a mark-up) of the products they sold. Sales would have to pay for the costs of customizing products and holding inventory. This approach would make Sales more aware of the cost implications of their decisions and, hence, more motivated to generate profitable sales.

But Kevin concluded that KCC should probably go further to create true product divisions. The KCC managers had frequent debates about what products and sales channels were most profitable, but those debates were not informed with hard data. A divisionalization would require some disaggregation of total costs and would facilitate profitability analyses.

If this was done, however, the KCC managers would have to consider how self-contained the new operating entities should be. Kevin wondered, "Should [the product divisions] each have their own supply chain management, sales force, R&D, and human resources functions, or should those resources be shared?"

The obvious product split in KCC was between Retail Products and Custom Products. The Retail Division would focus on the higher volume, standard product sales to retail outlets. The Custom Products Division would focus on the smaller volume custom sales.

In the approach that Kevin was planning to present to his management team, the two product divisions were to become profit centers. Each entity would be dedicated to its focused core business, but their managers would be free to choose how they did business and what they incorporated into their business model. Reporting to each of the division managers would be managers responsible for sales and marketing, purchasing and inventory control, and finance and accounting. Supply chain, R&D, human resources, and advertising would still be centralized, although these functions would clearly have to work closely with division managers.

Kevin hoped that this new structure would allow the Retail and Custom Products divisions to make some bold, new decisions. The new company focus would also be on creating value, rather than merely growing. For the divisions, creating value could easily mean contracting sales to eliminate unprofitable or marginally profitable products and customers. The best customers, for example, were probably those that bought the most profitable products, placed inventory requirements on KCC that were reasonable and predictable, had a strong credit standing and payment history, and were relatively easy to serve. The divisions might also decide that they should outsource some functions, such as warehousing, which might allow KCC to provide better customer service during the busy seasons and to employ fewer people and assets in the low seasons.

On July 28, 2003, Kevin presented his divisionalization ideas to his management team. Figure 1 shows an excerpt from the presentation he gave.

Some of the KCC managers were enthusiastic about the proposed change. Others thought that the ideas were radical. A few managers were bewildered, as they had never worked in an organization with a divisional structure and had trouble visualizing how it would work. In the ensuing discussion, many questions arose, such as relating to the specifics as to who would be responsible for what and how performance would be measured and rewarded. It was decided that the idea needed more specifics.

A follow-up meeting was held two weeks later. By then most of the managers realized that top management had already made this decision; the company was going to be divisionalized. They then became highly interested in shaping the details of the change. The focus of the second meeting was on defining division management responsibilities.

FIGURE 1 Excerpt from presentation given by Kevin Wentworth

The new product divisions will be lean, mean fighting machines with a direct purpose and the vision to carry that purpose out. With our [corporate managers'] help, they will look at how they do business now and what they can do better. They will have the opportunity to dream. If we were to start a new product-line business, think of the questions that would have to be answered:

1. How should we staff?
2. How should we source?
3. How should we warehouse?
4. How should we sell?
5. How should we ship?
6. How should we finance?

These are just some of the many questions that a new company has to address.

We have a certain advantage since we already have a baseline. But we also carry along a disadvantage. We have become entrenched in our ways and are the costliest product in the market. If we forced ourselves to completely reevaluate the business, could we significantly reduce costs, provide better customer service, and yield higher operating profits? That answer must be "yes" in order to stay in business in the future. Think of the fabulous business opportunity in front of us!

After considerable discussion, there was general agreement regarding the following general division of responsibilities:

Responsibilities of top management and corporate staff:

1. Overall vision and strategy for the company.
2. Financing and other high-level financial matters.
3. Engineering, design, and R&D.
4. Facilities.
5. Legal and intellectual property.
6. Supply chain and quality.
7. Corporate identity (e.g. public relations, some general advertising).
8. Human resources.
9. Information technology.
10. Acquisitions and joint ventures.

Responsibilities of division management:

1. Overall vision and strategy for their respective markets.

2. Development and implementation of divisional annual budgets.
3. Staffing.
4. Operations, including purchasing of parts and materials specific to respective markets, receiving, warehousing, shipping, and inventory management.
5. Controllership and accounting.
6. Product-specific advertising and collateral material.
7. Information technology support.

With this general understanding of the distribution of responsibilities in the company in place, the next task was the development of ideas regarding performance measurement and incentives. This task was assigned to Robert Chang, VP – Finance and Administration.

PERFORMANCE MEASUREMENT AND INCENTIVES

Robert developed a measure that he called *controllable returns*, which was defined as operating income (before tax) divided by controllable assets. To get to operating income, all the division direct expenses were subtracted from division revenues, as were as many of the corporate expenses that could be reasonably allocated to the divisions. The assets deemed controllable by the divisions included their receivables, inventories, and an assigned cost of facilities they used.

Robert proposed an incentive plan that provided 22 managers, down to the director level (one level below division manager), with a cash award based on achievement of annual targets set for controllable return at the divisional and corporate levels. For corporate managers, the bonuses would be based solely on corporate performance. For managers assigned to a division, the bonuses would be based 75% on division performance and 25% on corporate performance.

Robert proposed that the expected payouts be set initially at relatively modest levels. If the annual performance targets were achieved, Kevin and Weston would be paid an award of 40% of salary, division managers would be paid 30%, and managers lower in the hierarchy would be paid 15–20%. No payouts would be made if actual performance was below plan.[1]

---

[1] If the division (corporate) plan was met, but the corporate (division) plan was not, division management would still receive the divisional (corporate) portion of the bonus.

If actual performance exceeded plan, the payouts could be increased by up to 50%, at the discretion of top management and the company's board of directors.

Robert explained that he proposed the relatively modest awards because the costs of this plan would probably be in excess of $500,000, a significant additional expense for the company. Maintaining competitive total compensation levels was not an issue because KCC managers were currently not accustomed to earning a bonus, since the old sales growth-based incentive plan had not paid out anything in either 2001 or 2002. Plus Robert thought the company needed to get some experience with setting division-level performance targets and measuring and evaluating performance in a new way before ratcheting the performance-dependent rewards upward while, probably reducing the proportion of total compensation paid as fixed base salaries.

These suggestions were discussed in a staff meeting held on October 13, 2003.[2] The major point of dissension was regarding the proposed assignment of some of the corporate expenses to the divisions. Some of the personnel who were slated for assignment to a division complained that they could not control the terms of deals that corporate staff negotiated for them, such as for insurance. Kevin headed off this discussion by explaining that these cost assignments would be built into the performance targets, so they would not affect the actual vs. targeted return comparison. Further, division managers would have near complete freedom of sourcing. If they did not like the services provided to them by corporate staffs, they were free to purchase those services from outside the company.

A follow-up meeting was scheduled for October 27, 2003. That meeting was intended to be used primarily to design the new organization – who would be assigned to what division and in what role (see Exhibit 2). It was hoped that the new divisionalized structure would be completely in place by January 1, 2004, and the first incentives based on controllable return would be paid based on 2004-performance.

---

[2] Sales personnel were still included in a sales-based commission plan. At this meeting the idea came up that the sales commissions should be weighted based on product profitability, but detailed discussion of this idea was deferred.

HOPES AND CONCERNS FOR THE FUTURE

Kevin was convinced that the new divisionalized organization structure would give KCC its best chance for future success:

> Most of us are now convinced that this is a good idea. Although it creates a more complex organization, it will make most of our managers feel more empowered. It will also force us to be more focused on returns, rather than revenues and cost control.

Privately, however, Kevin expressed concern that this major turning point in the company's history was quite risky.

> I'm delegating considerable decision-making power to the division managers. If they make mistakes, our business can go down the tubes. The managers will make out all right; they can go find another job. But the fortunes of my family and those of the other major owners would be devastated.

He had a specific concern about one manager, Joe Yarmouth, the current VP-sales who would be appointed as general manager of the Retail Division.

> Joe is in his early 50s, and he has a lot of experience. But most of the experience is in sales, rather than marketing and other functions, and all of his experience before KCC was in big companies – Clorox, Hershey's. Culturally he does not have the small company mindset. He has no experience in understanding costs, cash flows, and returns. I think he should have been able to set up more deals that don't require any working capital investment, but he just doesn't think that way.

So Kevin, and indeed most of the KCC managers, looked to the future with both eager anticipation and trepidation.

EARLY EXPERIENCES

KCC's early experiences with the divisionalized structure created more concern. The first major initiative of Ed Sanchez, the manager of the new Custom Division, was to propose the procurement of a more sophisticated fabric cutting machine. This machine would allow the fabric to be cut more efficiently and lower both material and labor costs slightly. A discounted cash flow analysis suggested that this machine was a worthwhile investment. But, Kevin explained:

In my opinion, this investment does not address the real issue in the Custom Division. Our real issue is turnaround time. We have plenty of margin in custom work, but we need to reduce our turnaround time to serve our customers better. I think Ed is turning the wrong dials.

Kevin also knew that in Retail, the newly installed division manager Joe Yarmouth, who had good contacts in the advertising world through his prior jobs, was talking with a new advertising agency about the possibility of a new campaign to advertise retail products more aggressively. Kevin wondered whether this was in the best interest of the company. He commented:

I'm worried about losing economies of scale from dealing with different ad agencies and about what this "go-it-alone" advertising will do to our corporate identity. And in any case, lack of advertising was not the problem we faced at Target; it was product placement!

Joe, in turn, had already been grumbling to Robert about late deliveries and missed sales, as well as product returns due to quality problems, which were caused, in his opinion, by vendor problems that were under the purview of Carrie Jennings, the corporate head of Supply Chain and Quality. In the new organization structure, Supply Chain was responsible for obtaining and maintaining an adequate vendor group, primarily in Asia and Mexico, to secure both high-quality subassemblies and on-time delivery, while reducing dependency on any given vendor. The divisions had responsibility only for placing the day-to-day purchasing orders (POs) with these vendors. Joe complained:

If I keep having delivery and quality issues due to problems with our overseas vendors, over which I have no control, I'm sure going to miss my performance target for the year. *I* am the one – not *Carrie* – who feels the pain of lower sales and higher costs due to product returns, because it directly affects the numerator of my controllable returns measure, and thus, *my* bonus that is totally based on it. I have already lobbied corporate to let me have control over vendor negotiations. If they won't do that, they should at least adjust my targets so that my evaluations aren't affected by others' failures. But so far they don't seem to want to listen to me.

Robert estimated that the divisions had about 85% control over their own P&L results. He believed that was significant enough:

Joe's arguments have some merit, but no manager ever controls everything. Our managers need to work with others in the organization within the constraints in which they are placed, to react to a lot of changing conditions, and to deliver the needed results. If Joe can't do this, then we'll find someone else who can.

Robert did not think that corporate managers should make any changes either to the assigned responsibilities or the bonus plan.

Joe had also proposed some other ideas for a leaner Retail business that could potentially affect the design of the Supply Chain function. He wanted to enter into arrangements with large retailers that would provide favorable pricing in return for commitments to take delivery of full containers of finished products right at the port of entry (from either Asia or Mexico). This would eliminate further kitting in the Denver plant and reduce inventory significantly. Kevin thought this could be a good idea, but he was not sure who should take responsibility for working out the details. He was also worried about the politics involved in redrawing the lines of responsibility so early into the new divisionalization.

Another issue that had arisen involved the R&D function. Corporate R&D was responsible for new product designs and refinements. Even though most ideas for new products or product improvements came from the division managers and their sales people in the field, division management did not have much control over which R&D initiatives received priority. Joe Yarmouth commented:

There is too much filtering by corporate R&D of the ideas that we feed them. We can't get anything done without Ken Simmons' [R&D manager] blessing, and Ken really takes his orders from Weston [Krantz]. We ought to have more influence. We know our markets better than anyone else in the company, and we are paying for the function. We [the divisions] each fund 50% of the corporate R&D budget. I'm about to take a $150,000 hit for corporate R&D in my 2004 P&L, and what do I get for that? And why do we [the divisions] each have to share the burden equally? I'm also annoyed that Custom is getting a lot more R&D support than I do. Certainly Retail is much larger than Custom, but we're not getting much support from R&D. All they're doing for us are a few tweaks on our standard products.

Ed Sanchez [Custom], in turn, was complaining that R&D was much too "reactive" to new product features already introduced by competitors, despite the fact that he and his sales people has proposed many ideas for more radical changes.

Under this pressure from the division managers, Kevin was considering whether KCC should allow the divisions to do their own R&D. He knew doing so would solve the problems the divisions managers were complaining about, but he wasn't sure which new problems it might create. Kevin did not like the whining. But he also did not want to undercut the local initiative that the new organization promised to bring to KCC. And in any case, there were pressing issues to attend to on his new ranch.

Exhibit 1 **Kranworth Chair Corporation: 2003 organization structure**

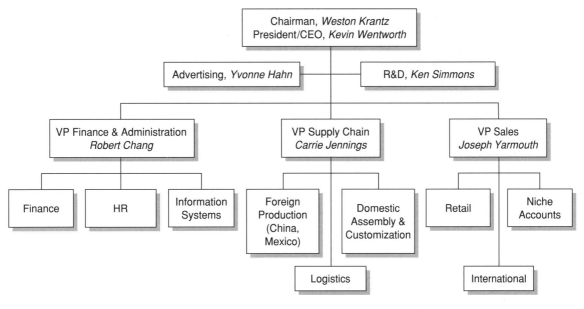

EXHIBIT 2 Kranworth Chair Corporation: 2004 organization structure

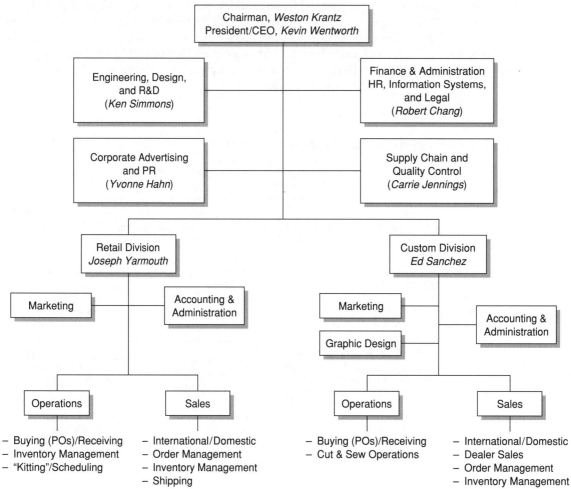

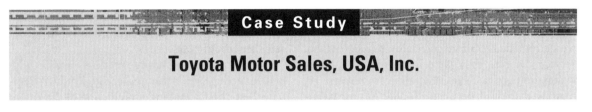

Case Study

Toyota Motor Sales, USA, Inc.

In 1991, top-level managers at Toyota Motor Sales, USA, Inc. (TMS) were discussing the merits of a significant organizational change that would increase the authority and responsibility given to TMS's regional general managers (GMs). The proponents for change argued that the GMs should be given authority for most of the activities that determined the success or failure of their region. The activities included finance, marketing, human resources, and possibly even port-of-entry operations, in addition to the dealer-support functions they already had. If these changes were made, then it would make sense to evaluate the GMs in terms of profit, rather than primarily sales.

Opponents of the change, however, feared that a profit target would force the regional GMs to focus excessively on short-term profit and sacrifice TMS's goals of growth in the US market and long-term commitment to customers. They were also afraid that the regional managers were experienced with sales-related functions but lacked some of the experience necessary to fill a profit center manager's role effectively.

THE COMPANY

TMS was a wholly owned subsidiary of Toyota Motor Corporation of Japan (TMC), the third largest automobile manufacturer in the world (after General Motors and Ford). TMS was founded in 1957 to operate as TMC's US marketing and sales organization. TMS bought vehicles from TMC manufacturing plants in Japan (and, later, when plants were established, in the United States and Canada), sold them to Toyota dealers within the US, and helped the dealers sell them to customers. In 1990, TMS was the largest seller of import cars and trucks in the United States, with sales of over one million units (market share of 7.6%), revenues

of approximately $14 billion, and approximately 5,000 employees.[1]

Exhibit 1 shows the TMS organization chart. It shows that all of the TMS car-related functions reported to Bob McCurry, executive vice president. Most of the finance and administrative functions reported to Yale Gieszl, senior vice president.

TMS's primary function was to provide vehicles, parts, and service and sales support to Toyota and Lexus dealers within the United States, all of which were independently owned and operated. The support for the 1,200 Toyota dealers was provided by nine regional offices and three distributorships with which TMS had contracts.[2] The nine regional offices, which were operated under a wholly owned TMS subsidiary, Toyota Motor Distributors (TMD), were located in the metropolitan areas of Portland (Oregon), San Francisco, Los Angeles, Denver, Kansas City, Chicago, Cincinnati, New York, and Boston. The three distributorships were Gulf States Toyota (Houston), Southeast Toyota (Deerfield Beach, Florida), and Central Atlantic Toyota (Baltimore) (see Exhibit 2). Gulf States Toyota and Southeast Toyota were privately owned distributors. Central Atlantic Toyota was formerly a privately owned distributor that TMS acquired in 1990.

THE REGIONAL GENERAL MANAGER ROLE

The TMD regional GMs, who reported to Al Wagner (group vice president, Toyota Sales), had three

---

[1] In North America, TMC also operated manufacturing facilities, located in California, Kentucky, and Canada; technology centers, located in Michigan and California; and a design center located in California. These entities were not part of TMS's operations.
[2] Operations in Hawaii were contracted to an outside corporation which was not affiliated with TMS. Sales of Lexus vehicles were coordinated through four area offices reporting to the Group vice president, Lexus Sales.

This case was prepared by research assistant Patrick Henry and Professor Kenneth A. Merchant.

Copyright © by Kenneth A. Merchant.

primary responsibilities. First, they were responsible for all dealer-related activities in their regions,
which included retail vehicle sales, parts sales, and
service. Second, they were responsible for supervising, training, and evaluating their employees. The
regions employed between 40 and 70 employees,
including field travelers (sales representatives),
staff personnel, and regional management. (Exhibit
3 shows an organization chart for a representative
region.) And third, they were responsible for
achieving sales penetration, customer satisfaction,
and operating budget objectives. A typical region
had an annual operating budget of $12–16 million
dollars. The regional operating budget was not a
significant expense from the corporate standpoint
because the amounts were small as compared with
the national promotional budget, but expense control was still considered an integral part of the
regional GM's job.

The ways in which the regional GMs allocated
their time varied significantly depending, for example,
on their management style, the size of the region, the
market conditions, and the quality of the regional
dealer network. However, dealer-related activities,
particularly involving new retail car and truck
sales, usually took precedence over the GMs' other
roles. Most GMs spent more than 50% of their
time on dealer-related matters, such as assisting
in designing sales programs and improving dealer
operations. According to Al Wagner, the group
vice president for Toyota Sales, regional GMs had
to be *cheerleaders* in good economic times and
firefighters in bad economic times. He explained
that cheerleaders motivate and inspire their people
and those of their dealers, while a firefighter attacks
problems. The biggest potential problem in the
firefighting role was dealer cash flow. Dealers
financed their own inventories, and if sales were
down it was sometimes difficult for them to make
interest payments. In bad economic times this lack
of cash could put dealers out of business and cause
fewer Toyotas to be sold.

SALES FORECASTS AND PLANS

Accurate sales forecasts by car line/by region were
important because Toyota vehicles were earmarked
for a specific US region on the production floor.
Sales forecasts were prepared as part of Toyota's
two formal planning processes: the first resulted in

the preparation of a strategic plan with a horizon of
five years or longer. The second produced an annual
sales and profit plan.

The *strategic planning* process began with
managers in TMS's Strategic and Product Planning Department making a prediction of the future
automobile market segments. They based these
predictions on demographic information, knowledge of forthcoming governmental regulations, and
estimates of competitor plans, such as for model
changes and new introductions. Second, they selected
the segments in which TMS wanted to participate.
And finally, they worked with TMC in Japan to
formulate plans for the design of new models. (All
production mix decisions were negotiated with
Japan.) The strategic plan was reviewed in detail by
TMS's board of directors.

The *annual planning* process involved several
steps. First, TMS managers prepared a target for
total unit sales and market share in the next year.
This target, which was set by the end of July, was
based on total market size estimates prepared by
TMS corporate staff planners. Second, managers
in the TMS Sales Administration and Marketing
Departments developed a sales plan designed to
achieve the unit sales target. They looked for growth
areas among the models offered in their product
lines and established pricing and incentive policies
and advertising and promotion programs designed
to effect the desired sales growth. They prepared
sales projections by car line, region, and month.

The regional managers were not greatly involved
in the sales planning process for two basic reasons.
Some of the planning could be done more efficiently at the TMS level because vehicle sales were
greatly affected by broad macroeconomic factors,
seasonality, and corporate marketing plans that tended
to influence all regions roughly equally. And the
accuracy of the regional managers' plans had been
found to be inconsistent in the past.

The third element in the annual planning process
involved preparation of an expense budget. This
budget, which was prepared by regional personnel
based mostly from history, and the sales projections
were reviewed by corporate and regional managers in
a series of meetings held in August and September.
The TMS plans were then sent to Japan at the end
of September for comparison with sales plans that
had been prepared by TMC corporate managers.
Differences were ironed out, and TMC managers

sent a revised, detailed sales plan to TMS managers in October. During the year, TMS managers updated their plans quarterly to reflect changes in market conditions and strategies.

CONSTANT PRODUCTION RATE POLICY

TMC had a policy of maintaining steady production rates in its manufacturing operations. This policy was established because it provided greater and more efficient utilization of fixed asset and labor resources and eased the suppliers' scheduling problems. TMC, like most large Japanese companies, offered its employees lifetime employment. This meant that labor costs were fixed, for all practical purposes: TMC did not lay off full-time employees even when sales were slow. In addition, TMC had to support its supplier network with a consistent demand schedule. TMC relied heavily on its supplier network because TMC's plants operated a just-in-time (JIT) or *kanban* inventory system, and these systems required reliable sources of supply. TMC had an extensive supplier network in Japan that required long lead times to supply some parts, and many of these companies depended on TMC for their survival. Constant production rates greatly facilitated their ability to meet TMC's needs.

ALLOCATION OF AUTOMOBILES TO REGIONS

TMC plants required a four-month vehicle order forecast lead time. The four months were necessary to allow the preparation of orders to its suppliers and the establishment and completion of the production schedules. Production of a particular grade could be shifted only very little in a three-month time frame. A major shift in production could take up to eight months.

One month before TMC plants shipped the completed vehicles, TMS would give the plant managers a firm order based on the current market conditions. If the four-month forecast was significantly incorrect, TMC might not be able to satisfy the revised order mix. The TMC system did not allow for redistribution of units among the regions after the order was placed. The regions could trade vehicles with each other after arrival at the ports, but this was rarely done because of the expense involved.

The assembled vehicles were shipped to one of the US ports of entry. The port operations reported to H. Imai, group vice president, manufacturing liaison and distribution. When the cars reached the port, port personnel took them off the ship, added a window label and perhaps some accessories that had been ordered by the dealer but that the dealer did not want to install (e.g. roof rack), washed them, and loaded them on trucks or trains for shipment to the dealer. The ports were cost centers. Port personnel were responsible for maintaining good facilities, shipping vehicles on a timely basis, and minimizing labor costs (particularly overtime), port storage charges, and yard damage to the vehicles.

TMS managers were working with TMC plant managers to provide greater vehicle ordering flexibility. They wanted the plants to allow the shifting of the following month's production plus or minus 10% five days before the start of the month. This would allow the changing of August production on July 25. TMS managers were also lobbying to reduce the four-month required lead time to three months.

DEALER INCENTIVES

Like most automobile manufacturers, Toyota used dealer incentives to help sell the vehicles that had been allocated to the regions. TMS offered its dealers incentives for achieving predetermined sales volume targets by car line, and sometimes by grade (e.g. a four-door model only). The incentives were primarily in the form of cash paid to the dealership, but sometimes cash or incentive trips were given to individual dealer sales people or sales managers. In 1990, the total cost of the Toyota dealer incentive program in the United States was approximately $250 million, or about $250 per vehicle sold. The incentive programs were generally run on a 60-day cycle. Thus, there was a January/February program, a March/April program, and so on.

Most national dealer incentive programs were tiered. Here is a hypothetical example of such a program:

The Joe Jones Toyota dealership has a TMS-set target to sell 40 pickup trucks in July/August. The incentives promised to the dealership are tiered, with greater unit incentives provided at higher sales levels.

Pickups sold	Incentive/vehicle ($)
1–24	250
25–32	350
33–40	450
Over 40	550

Toyota, and other car manufacturers, also frequently offered *fast start* incentives. Such incentives might be provided as follows:

> The Joe Jones Toyota dealership has a 60-day incentive to sell 40 pickups. If it sells 16 pickups in the first 30 days of the incentive program, then the dealer gets an additional $100 for each pickup sold in the second 30 days of the program.

Starting in 1991, TMS managers gave regional GMs the authority to allocate about $75 per vehicle in dealer incentives as they wished. These regionalized incentives were expected to total about $70 million, slightly over 30% of the total dealer incentive money budgeted for 1991. This change was made to allow the regional general managers to enhance the national incentive programs or to structure their own regional incentive programs to respond to local conditions (e.g. to move particular slow-moving products).

The regional general managers liked having some authority over dealer incentives. For example, Bob Weldon, GM of the Cincinnati region, explained:

> In the June/July period, the national incentive program focused on trucks. But our dealers were overstocked on Camrys, so we put extra incentives on Camry sales. It worked. We had two very strong sales months, and we are now ready for the transition to the new model year. The dealers made money, and we are in a good position.

EVALUATION OF REGIONAL GENERAL MANAGERS

The nine regional GMs were evaluated by Al Wagner. Al's evaluations were often subjective, coming as a result of judgments made throughout the year based on Al's observations of the operation of the region.

Al did have access to considerable quantitative data that he could use to help him make his evaluations, however. For example, Exhibit 4 shows the sales and stock summary report for June 1991 for each of the 12 sales areas and TMS in total (listed across the top). This report provided detail on car and truck sales, and it ranked the regions according to their percentage achievement of their retail sales objectives. Exhibit 5 shows a summary of various customer satisfaction indices for June 1991 and year to date. Exhibits 6 and 7 provide regional budget reports showing actual sales and expenses compared to plan and supporting details about the expenses. Monthly, Al also had full access to dealer records.

Only the expense line items shown with an asterisk on Exhibit 7 were deemed controllable by the GMs. Some other expenses were not even allocated to the regional level. These included a LIFO inventory provision, the costs of employee benefits (e.g. group insurance, bonuses), some advertising and promotional costs (e.g. regional contributions to Toyota dealer associations, fleet incentives), and TMS administrative expenses.

Al said that he tended to evaluate the GMs in terms of four primary criteria: total unit sales, market penetration, customer satisfaction, and dealer profit. He did not like to rank the regions' performances against each other. He preferred to rate the managers as compared with their own region's history. He said,

> I don't like rankings. I dropped all rankings when I took this job. How can I compare a manager in Boston with one in Los Angeles? I cannot come up with meaningful, equal targets. And, furthermore, I don't want Boston to worry about what Los Angeles is doing.

GMs earned performance bonuses annually, but at midyear they were paid an advance of approximately 45% of their projected bonus for the year. In a typical year the highest performing regional manager would earn a bonus of approximately 25% of salary, while the lowest performing manager's bonus would be approximately two thirds of that amount. The bonus amounts varied somewhat depending on the manager's salary grade and TMS's sales and profit performance for the year but, according to Yale Gieszl, Toyota's bonus awards were "not as volatile as those in a typical US car company which tend to be feast or famine." In recent years the total bonus awards had varied only slightly from *normal*, because of TMS's overall performance.

Al Wagner did not think the relatively weak link between performance and bonuses caused Toyota to attract people with any less talent. He said:

People have gratifications other than money. After a few years, the other things become more important. For example, we give our people recognition and a sense of participation in what we're doing. Once a month we have a sales meeting with the GMs. They make a report and can talk all they want to the president and other executives in the company. That doesn't happen at General Motors, Ford, or Chrysler. It's a whole different climate here. That may sound corny, but it's very real. There are 50–60 people in the room. It means a lot.

THE CENTRAL ATLANTIC TOYOTA EXPERIMENT

As an experiment, TMS management was giving the management of Central Atlantic Toyota (CAT) more autonomy and operating flexibility than it allowed the nine TMD regional managers. CAT's operations were different from those of the TMD regions in three primary ways. First, CAT had its own finance, marketing, information systems, human resources, and port processing departments. Second, CAT managers had a profit plan and was thus more accountable for all of its costs than were the regional managers. And third, CAT's manager was given the title of subsidiary president. As a consequence, the eight-member TMS executive committee, rather than the group vice president of sales, evaluated his performance. In effect, CAT was a hybrid between a TMD region and a private distributor.

This experiment seemed to have noticeable effects on the attitudes of CAT's management team. Dennis Clements, CAT's president/GM believed that he had more of a bottom-line mentality than when he was at GM. He said, "As president of CAT, I am always thinking of the financial implications of what goes on. For example, now when I leave a meeting, I turn out the lights because I know the costs have an effect on profitability."

A PROPOSAL FOR CHANGE

Some TMS managers believed that the regions should be made more like CAT. They wanted to give the regional GMs more authority and bottom-line (profit-and-loss) responsibility. They worried about the growing bureaucracy at TMS headquarters, and they believed that making the regions profit centers was a logical way to get the company to respond more quickly and more reliably to local market conditions. By making the regions into profit centers, these managers felt that the regional GMs could affect TMS profits and that the managers should be made aware of the costs and trade-offs associated with various administrative functions (e.g. finance, marketing, human resources) and port functions (e.g. work scheduling, accessorizing). They also believed that the current set of regional GMs was capable of balancing the necessary priorities and that making the regions into profit centers would further develop the GMs' managerial abilities. Yale Gieszl believed that, "They will step up to the challenge."

Other TMS corporate managers, however, argued that the regional managers should not have profit responsibility. Some believed that the profit measure would discount the importance of the other performance measures. Some feared that a profit target would force the regional GMs to focus excessively on short-term profit and sacrifice TMS's goals of growth in the US market and long-term commitment to customers. Some believed that the change would cause significant operating and accounting issues. These managers pointed out that port operations would be a particular problem because the relationship between a port and a sales region was rarely one-to-one. For example, the Long Beach port facilities provided Toyotas to both the Los Angeles and Denver regions and Lexus automobiles to 70% of the United States. Some opposing managers were also afraid that the regional managers were not capable of broader responsibilities. They noted that these managers were experienced with sales-related functions but might lack some of the experience necessary to assume a broader role. And, finally, some managers noted that the CAT experiment had not necessarily proven to be a success: Eight out of nine TMD regions had a higher share of the imported car market than did CAT during the 1991 recession.

Everybody agreed that a certain amount of decentralization to the regions was good and that the establishment of regionalized dealer incentives was a positive step. The remaining question was, as one manager put it, "When do you have too much of a good thing?" Some cynics also noted that even if more decentralization was desirable, they doubted that top management would be willing to let go since they had operated so long with centralized control.

EXHIBIT 1 Toyota Motor Sales organization chart

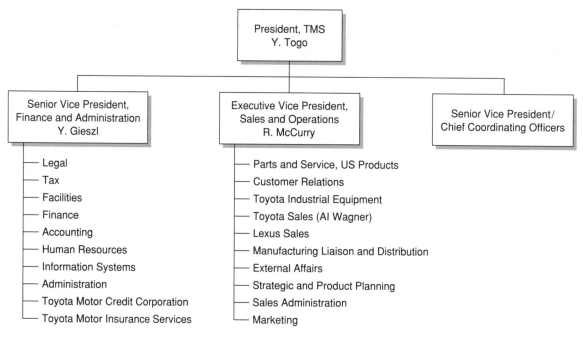

```
                        ┌─────────────────────┐
                        │   President, TMS    │
                        │      Y. Togo        │
                        └─────────────────────┘
```

Senior Vice President, Finance and Administration Y. Gieszl	Executive Vice President, Sales and Operations R. McCurry	Senior Vice President/ Chief Coordinating Officers

Senior Vice President, Finance and Administration — Y. Gieszl
- Legal
- Tax
- Facilities
- Finance
- Accounting
- Human Resources
- Information Systems
- Administration
- Toyota Motor Credit Corporation
- Toyota Motor Insurance Services

Executive Vice President, Sales and Operations — R. McCurry
- Parts and Service, US Products
- Customer Relations
- Toyota Industrial Equipment
- Toyota Sales (Al Wagner)
- Lexus Sales
- Manufacturing Liaison and Distribution
- External Affairs
- Strategic and Product Planning
- Sales Administration
- Marketing

EXHIBIT 2 Location of TMS facilities

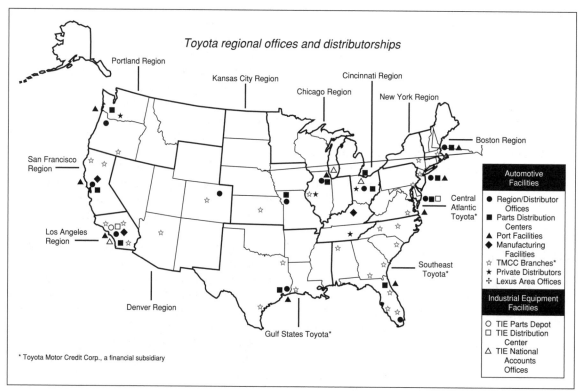

Toyota regional offices and distributorships

Portland Region
Kansas City Region
Cincinnati Region
Chicago Region
New York Region
Boston Region
San Francisco Region
Los Angeles Region
Denver Region
Central Atlantic Toyota*
Southeast Toyota*
Gulf States Toyota*

Automotive Facilities
- ● Region/Distributor Offices
- ■ Parts Distribution Centers
- ▲ Port Facilities
- ◆ Manufacturing Facilities
- ☆ TMCC Branches*
- ★ Private Distributors
- ⊹ Lexus Area Offices

Industrial Equipment Facilities
- ○ TIE Parts Depot
- □ TIE Distribution Center
- △ TIE National Accounts Offices

* Toyota Motor Credit Corp., a financial subsidiary

EXHIBIT 3 Representative regional organization chart

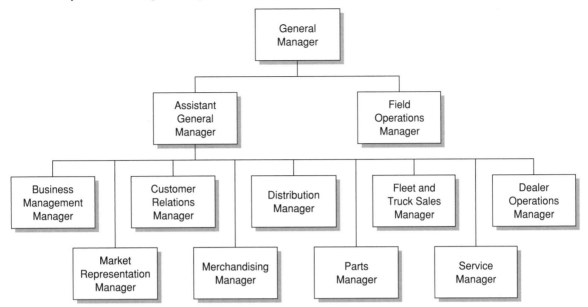

Exhibit 4 Sales and stock summary

V539DX-T10885
**** Total Car ****

07/02/91
100.00% OF MONTH REPORTED

	BOS	CHI	PTL	S.F.	N.Y.	CINN	K.C.	DEN	L.A.	SET	GST	CAT	190th	USA
Daily retail sales	563	957	271	329	1,296	1,059	460	324	655	601	630	1,182	0	8,327
MTD retail sales	3,033	5,279	2,139	3,811	8,305	6,094	2,183	2,576	6,708	7,735	4,769	6,877	113	59,622
Retail objective	2,950	4,510	2,110	3,920	8,080	5,260	1,870	2,290	7,200	7,020	4,470	5,520	0	55,200
% Retail objective	102.8	117.1	101.4	97.2	102.8	115.9	116.7	112.5	93.2	110.2	106.7	124.6	.0	108.0
% Obj. rank in USA	8	2	10	11	9	4	3	5	12	6	7	1		
Retail dealer stock	4,580	7,164	4,241	6,777	11,253	8,530	3,447	4,442	9,358	12,573	9,430	9,755	92	91,642
Retail days supply	38	34	50	44	34	35	39	43	35	41	49	35	20	30
% Retail sales/avail	39.8	42.4	33.5	35.9	42.4	41.6	38.7	36.7	41.7	38.0	33.5	41.3	.0	39.4
MTD total sales	3,314	5,587	2,241	4,094	8,764	6,699	2,272	2,977	7,035	8,164	5,022	8,425	113	64,707
Total objective	3,090	4,690	2,190	4,020	8,165	5,560	1,930	2,540	7,300	7,345	4,625	7,045	0	58,500
% total objective	107.2	119.1	102.3	101.8	107.3	120.5	117.7	117.2	96.4	111.2	108.6	119.6	.0	110.6
Memo: MTD fleet (J)	281	308	102	283	459	605	89	401	327	429	253	1,548	0	5,085
Memo: fleet obj	140	180	80	100	85	300	60	250	100	325	155	1,525	0	3,300
Memo: % fleet obj	200.7	171.1	127.5	283.0	540.0	201.6	148.3	160.4	327.0	132.0	163.2	101.5	.0	154.0
**** Total truck ****														
Daily retail sales	52	79	126	95	93	172	121	145	182	108	134	197	0	1,504
MTD retail sales	294	498	1,187	1,587	619	918	464	959	2,172	1,229	1,191	1,150	0	12,268
Retail objective	370	700	1,050	1,570	800	910	420	900	2,190	1,490	1,059	1,050	0	12,500
% Retail objective	79.5	71.1	113.0	101.1	77.4	100.9	110.5	106.6	99.2	82.5	113.4	109.5	.0	98.1
% Obj. rank in USA	10	12	2	6	11	7	3	5	8	9	1	4		
Retail dealer stock	631	1,132	1,880	2,507	1,693	1,271	657	1,557	3,393	2,563	1,571	2,027	41	20,923
Retail days supply	54	57	40	39	68	35	35	41	39	52	33	44	0	43
% retail sales/avail	31.7	30.5	38.7	38.7	26.7	41.9	41.3	38.1	39.0	32.4	43.1	36.1	.0	36.9
MTD total sales	295	504	1,217	1,603	618	923	607	972	2,310	1,268	1,218	1,153	0	12,687
Total objective	370	705	1,065	1,585	805	915	560	905	2,280	1,500	1,060	1,050	0	12,800
% total objective	79.7	71.5	114.3	101.1	76.8	100.9	108.4	107.4	101.3	84.5	114.9	109.7	.0	99.1
Memo: MTD fleet (J)	1	6	30	16	1-	5	143	13	138	39	27	2	0	419
Memo: fleet obj	0	5	15	15	5	5	140	5	90	10	10	0	0	300
Memo: % fleet obj	.0	120.0	200.0	106.6	20.0-	100.0	102.1	260.0	153.3	390.0	270.0	.0	.0	139.6

Exhibit 5 National customer relations owner satisfaction index, June 1991

National

Region	Current month NVSDS INDEX/ RESPONSE		NVSDS RECMD/ RESPONSE		TSS INDEX/ RESPONSE		TSS RECMD/ RESPONSE		OSI INDEX/ RESPONSE		Year to date NVSDS INDEX/ RESPONSE		NVSDS RECMD/ RESPONSE		TSS INDEX/ RESPONSE		TSS RECMD/ RESPONSE		OSI INDEX/ RESPONSE	
Los Angeles	94.5	3,357	91.9	3,331	92.9	1,357	89.9	1,345	90.9	4,676	94.4	20,613	91.9	20,475	92.3	8,648	89.5	8,579	90.7	29,054
San Francisco	92.1	1,947	90.4	1,935	92.3	803	89.2	796	89.8	2,731	92.1	12,326	90.0	12,255	92.0	5,526	89.3	5,468	89.7	17,723
Portland	93.4	1,412	90.9	1,387	91.2	632	87.2	626	89.1	2,013	93.4	8,793	90.7	8,718	91.1	4,750	88.2	4,709	89.5	13,427
Denver	92.9	1,315	89.6	1,304	90.4	633	86.9	627	88.3	1,931	93.2	8,498	90.0	8,446	91.6	4,665	88.6	4,610	89.3	13,056
New York	91.4	3,515	88.8	3,493	90.5	1,874	88.0	1,846	88.4	5,339	91.4	21,578	88.5	21,454	90.3	12,509	87.9	12,380	88.2	33,834
Boston	94.2	1,595	91.0	1,580	91.8	955	90.3	950	90.7	2,530	93.8	9,535	91.2	9,483	91.7	6,789	89.9	6,735	90.6	16,218
Chicago	93.9	2,442	92.0	2,414	91.6	1,492	89.7	1,479	90.9	3,893	93.9	14,752	91.6	14,653	91.4	10,423	89.1	10,336	90.4	24,989
Cincinnati	93.9	2,748	92.6	2,698	92.2	1,410	89.9	1,397	91.3	4,095	94.1	17,326	92.4	17,244	91.8	9,288	89.8	9,212	91.1	26,456
Kansas City	95.1	1,112	92.5	1,067	92.0	576	89.8	571	91.2	1,638	94.6	7,057	92.1	7,011	92.6	4,287	90.0	4,246	91.1	11,257
Southeast	93.8	4,370	93.3	4,308	93.4	1,769	92.4	1,753	92.9	6,061	93.7	25,234	92.8	25,090	93.3	11,630	92.1	11,547	92.5	36,637
Gulf States	92.9	2,653	91.7	2,542	92.2	1,159	90.8	1,146	91.3	3,600	93.1	15,726	91.5	15,656	91.1	7,624	89.1	7,564	90.3	23,220
Cen. Atlantic	93.6	3,446	90.8	3,376	92.4	1,397	90.0	1,383	90.4	4,759	93.5	20,188	90.5	20,060	92.7	9,393	90.0	9,393	90.3	29,364
National	93.4	29,912	91.4	29,435	92.0	14,057	89.8	13,919	90.6	43,354	93.4	181,626	91.2	180,545	91.8	95,532	89.5	94,690	90.4	275,235

The OSI is a combination of NVSDS and service survey recommend questions.

NVSDS	-0.1 BELOW MAY MTD	NVSDS NO CHANGE FROM MAY YTD
TSS	-0.3 BELOW MAY MTD	TSS NO CHANGE FROM MAY YTD
OSI	NO CHANGE FROM MAY MTD	OSI +0.1 ABOVE MAY YTD
		NVSDS, TSS, OSI YTD BEST EVER

Exhibit 6 Budget report for a representative region for year ended September 30, 1991 ($000)

	Actual	Plan	Variance fav (unfav)
Units	86,987	89,760	(2,773)
Sales	$1,045,000	$1,060,000	$(15,000)
Gross profit	$21,312	$21,852	$(540)
Expenses			
Personnel	2,815	2,920	105
Operating	2,785	2,714	(71)
Advertising & promotion	7,175	7,337	162
Occupancy	1,837	1,845	8
General	2	1	(1)
Total expenses	14,714	14,917	203
Operating income	$6,598	$6,935	$(337)

Exhibit 7 Expense detail for a representative region for year ended September 30, 1991 ($000)

	Actual	Plan	Variance fav (unfav)
Personnel			
Salaries, wages and payroll taxes	$2,749	$2,856	$107
*Overtime	11	15	4
*Temporary help	21	17	(4)
Temporary help – disability related	10	–	(10)
*Other	24	32	8
	2,815	2,920	105
Operating			
*Travel and transportation	1,029	963	(66)
*Telephone and telegraph	365	350	(15)
*Meetings	324	362	38
*Supplies	78	75	(3)
*Postage	111	113	2
*RL Polk	120	120	–
*Dealer training expense	100	108	8
*Company car	440	406	(34)
*Other	218	217	(1)
	2,785	2,714	(71)
Advertising and promotion			
*Vehicle incentives	6,959	7,181	222
*Local promotion – parts	129	37	(92)
*Local promotion – service	37	33	(4)
*Recognition and awards	11	19	8
*Other	39	67	28
	7,175	7,337	162
Occupancy			
Rent expenses – Intercompany	589	589	–
* – equipment	26	29	3
Depreciation	19	26	7
Port storage	970	970	–
*Utilities	83	73	(10)
*Security service	13	15	2
Property taxes – real/personal	114	114	–
*Janitor/refuse service	21	20	(1)
*Other	2	9	7
	1,837	1,845	8
*General	102	101	(1)
Total expenses	$14,714	$14,917	$203

* These expenses are deemed "controllable." It is the responsibility of the regional General Manager to maintain spending within the planned level.

Case Study

Zumwald AG

In August 2002, a pricing dispute arose between the managers of some of the divisions of Zumwald AG. Mr. Rolf Fettinger, the company's managing director, had to decide whether to intervene in the dispute.

THE COMPANY

Zumwald AG, headquartered in Cologne, Germany, produced and sold a range of medical diagnostic imaging systems and biomedical test equipment and instrumentation. The company was organized into six operating divisions. Total annual revenues were slightly more than €3 billion.

Zumwald managers ran the company on a highly decentralized basis. The managers of each division were allowed considerable autonomy if their performances were at least on plan. Performance was evaluated, and management bonuses were assigned, based on each division's achievement of budgeted targets for return on invested capital (ROIC) and sales growth. Even though the company was partly vertically integrated, division managers were allowed to source their components from external suppliers if they so chose.

Involved in the dispute mentioned above were three of the company's divisions: the Imaging Systems Division (ISD), the Heidelberg Division (Heidelberg), and the Electronic Components Division (ECD).

- ISD sold complex ultrasound and magnetic resonance imaging systems. These systems were expensive, typically selling for €500,000–1 million.
- Heidelberg sold high-resolution monitors, graphics controllers, and display subsystems. Approximately half of its sales were made to outside customers. ISD was one of Heidelberg's major inside customers.

- ECD sold application-specific integrated circuits and subassemblies. ECD was originally established as a captive supplier to other Zumwald divisions, but in the last decade its managers had found external markets for some of the division's products. Because of this, ECD's managers were given profit center responsibility.

THE DISPUTE

In 2001, ISD designed a new ultrasound imaging system, called the X73. Hopes were high for X73. The new system offered users advantages in processing speed and cost, and it took up less space. Heidelberg engineers participated in the design of X73, but Heidelberg was compensated for the full cost of the time its employees spent on this project.

After the specifications were set, ISD managers solicited bids for the materials needed to produce X73 components. Heidelberg was asked to bid to supply the displays needed for production of the X73 system. So were two outside companies. One was Bogardus NV, a Dutch company with a reputation for producing high-quality products. Bogardus had been a long-time supplier to Zumwald, but it had never before supplied display units and systems to any Zumwald division. Display Technologies Plc was a British company that had recently entered the market and was known to be pricing its products aggressively in order to buy market share. The quotes that ISD received were as follows:

Supplier	Cost per X73 system (B)
Heidelberg Division	140,000
Bogardus NV	120,500
Display Technologies Plc	100,500

▶

This case was prepared by Professors Kenneth A. Merchant and Wim A. Van der Stede.

After discussing the bids with his management team, Conrad Bauer, ISD's managing director, announced that ISD would be buying its display systems from Display Technologies Plc. Paul Halperin, Heidelberg's general manager was livid. He immediately complained to Mr. Bauer, but when he did not get the desired response, he took his complaint to Rolf Fettinger, Zumwald's managing director. Mr. Fettinger agreed to look into the situation.

A meeting was called for August 29, 2002. Mr. Halperin asked Christian Schönberg, ECD's GM, to attend this meeting to support his case. If Heidelberg got this order from ISD, it would buy all of its electronic components from ECD.

At this meeting, Mr. Bauer immediately showed his anger:

> Paul wants to charge his standard mark-up for these displays. I can't afford to pay it. I'm trying to sell a new product (X73) in a very competitive market. How can I show a decent ROIC if I have to pay a price for a major component that is way above market? I can't pass on those costs to my customers. Paul should really want this business. I know things have been relatively slow for him. But all he does is quote list prices and then complain when I do what is best for my division.
>
> We're wasting our time here. Let's stop fighting amongst ourselves and instead spend our time figuring out how to survive in these difficult business conditions.

Mr. Fettinger asked Mr. Halperin why he could not match Display Technologies' price. Paul replied as follows:

> Conrad is asking me to shave my price down to below cost. If we start pricing our jobs this way, it won't be long before we're out of business. We need to price our products so that we earn a fair return on our investment. You demand that of us; our plan is put together on that basis; and I have been pleading with my sales staff not to offer deals that will kill our margins. Conrad is forgetting that my engineers helped him design X73, and we provided that help with no mark-up over our costs. Further, you can easily see that Zumwald is better off if *we* supply the display systems for this new product. The situation here is clear. If Conrad doesn't want to be a team player, then you must order him to source internally! That decision is in the best interest of all of us.

In the ensuing discussion, the following facts came out:

1. ISD's tentative target price for the X73 system was €340,000.[1]

2. Heidelberg's standard manufacturing cost (material, labor and overhead) for each display system was €105,000. When asked, Mr. Halperin estimated that the variable portion of this total cost was only €50,000. He treated Heidelberg's labor costs as fixed because German laws did not allow him to lay off employees without incurring expenses that were "prohibitively" high.

3. Because of the global business slowdown, the production lines at Heidelberg that would produce the systems in question were operating at approximately 70% of capacity. In the preceding year, monthly production had ranged from 60–90% of total capacity.

4. Heidelberg's costs included €21,600 in electronic subassemblies to be supplied by ECD. ECD's full manufacturing costs for the components included in each system were approximately €18,000, of which approximately half were out-of-pocket costs. ECD's standard policy was to price its products internally at full manufacturing cost plus 20%. The mark-up was intended to give ECD an incentive to supply its product internally. ECD was currently operating at 90% capacity.

Near the end of the meeting, Mr. Bauer reminded everybody of the company's policy of freedom of sourcing. He pointed out that this was not such a big deal, as the volume of business to be derived from this new product was only a small fraction (less than 5%) of the revenues for each of the divisions involved, at least for the first few years. And he also did not like the potential precedent of his being forced to source internally because it could adversely affect his ability to get thoughtful quotes from outside suppliers in the future.

THE DECISION

As he adjourned the meeting, Mr. Fettinger promised to consider all the points of view that had been expressed and to provide a speedy judgment. He wondered if there was a viable compromise or if, instead, there were some management principles involved here that should be considered inviolate.

---

[1] The cost of the other components that go into X73 is €72,000. IDS's conversion cost for the X73 system is €144,000, of which €117,700 is fixed.

Case Study

Global Investors, Inc.

I have a basic "gut" discomfort with the proposition that investment management as a profitmaking function exists only in New York.

Alistair Hoskins, Chairman/CEO,
Global Investors, London

Bob Mascola, CFO of Global Investors, Inc. (GI), took a last look at his notes as he walked into the conference room where he and the other members of the transfer pricing task force would meet with Gary Spencer, GI's CEO. The transfer pricing task force supervised by Mascola was meeting with Spencer to discuss the latest transfer pricing models that the task force members had identified. Mascola hoped the meeting would result in a final decision about the transfer-pricing method that should be used to recognize profits in GI's subsidiaries.

Mascola knew that the meeting would be difficult. On repeated occasions, two of the members of the transfer-pricing task force, Alistair Hoskins and Jack Davis, had engaged in heated debates about which transfer pricing model should be selected. Hoskins, the Chairman/CEO of GI's London office, believed that regional offices – or at least the regional office he led – should be treated as largely autonomous profit centers so that the value created by these offices would be reflected in their financial statements. However, Davis, GI's corporate vice president of operations argued that virtually all of the investment strategies used to manage the clients' funds were designed by the research team located in New York. Consequently, Davis believed that the revenues generated by investment activities should be recognized in New York, even if a few investment services were offered by a regional office. The essence of Hoskins' reply to Davis was that expressed in the epigraph.

THE COMPANY

Global Investors, founded in 1965, was a privately owned investment management company headquartered in New York. A number of directors and executives based in New York, Spencer among them, held majority ownership of GI's outstanding stock. GI, started as a domestic equity investment management firm, had grown to manage US$160 billion for a variety of clients, including corporations, insurance companies, public and private pension funds, endowments, foundations, and high-net-worth individuals.

GI focused on two activities: investment management (which included research, portfolio management, and trading) and client services (which included marketing and investor advisory services provided to institutional investors and independent brokers/dealers). Although the company initially focused on direct sales to institutional investors (such as endowments and pension funds), it was increasingly selling its investment products through independent brokers/dealers who both served wealthy individual investors and invested in GI funds on their behalf (see Exhibit 1). GI generated its investment management revenues by charging a percentage fee for the amount each of its clients invested in GI funds.

GI's investment philosophy differentiated the firm from most of its competitors. Since its inception, GI based all of its investment strategies on financial market theories emerging from academic research. The company developed a prominent New York-based research team comprised mostly of PhD-qualified investment experts, who were supported by contracted-for advice from some of the world's most highly regarded academic financial economists.

▶

This case was prepared by Professors Kenneth A. Merchant and Tatiana Sandino.

The company's investment philosophy revolved around the theory that markets are affected by judgmental biases of the market participants. That is, under certain circumstances and for certain time periods, investors, and hence markets, over-react or underreact to information that is publicly available regarding companies' expected risks and returns. Instead of focusing on the valuation of individual securities and actively selecting securities based on their estimated value (as most of its competitors did), GI developed its different funds by focusing more directly on the types of securities that academic research had shown to be under-valued by the market.

As part of its strategy, GI was also committed to lowering its trading costs through economies of scale, technological investments aimed at increasing liquidity, and crossing activities (that is, matching clients' buy and sell requests).

GI focused mostly on equity investments in countries committed to free markets and with reasonably well-functioning capital markets, but it also invested in fixed income and commodity securities. Over the years, GI had expanded its activities throughout Asia, Europe, and the Americas (as shown in Exhibit 2).

GI'S SUBSIDIARIES

Most of GI's 415 employees were located in New York, but GI also offered its services through four remote subsidiaries (see Exhibit 3). The largest subsidiaries located in Tokyo and London employed 52 and 40 employees, respectively. The other two subsidiaries located in Singapore and San Francisco employed fewer than a dozen individuals each. About 80% of the personnel employed in these offices were dedicated to trading financial assets following guidelines established by headquarters, 15% were dedicated to selling GI's funds, and the rest were involved in operations. Recently, three highly competent senior portfolio managers in Tokyo and four in London had started both to act as subadvisors for the Japanese, Pacific Rim, and European portfolios and to manage a series of trusts for their regional clientele. Many of the sales personnel at those subsidiaries were using these local funds to attract new clients. However, all clients attracted by the subsidiaries, regardless of the location

of the subsidiary or the fund they invested in, were assigned a contact person in New York in addition to their local representative. They also received timely information resulting from the internal and sponsored research generated in New York.

GI's subsidiaries were separately incorporated companies. Their ownership composition resembled that of GI's parent company, but additional shares were issued to the subsidiaries' chairmen/CEOs. The chairman/CEO of GI London (Hoskins) owned 23% of the London subsidiary; the chairman/CEO of GI Tokyo (Paul Hashi) owned 5% of the Tokyo subsidiary; and the chairmen/CEOs of GI Singapore and GI San Francisco each owned 3% of their respective subsidiaries.

GI's subsidiaries had historically been treated as cost-focused profit centers, while the administrative departments providing support were treated as cost centers. Expenses and revenues were recorded according to the following accounting model:

1. Expenses (see Exhibit 4, presenting the format of a consolidated statement):

   ● Any expenses that could be traced directly to the subsidiaries or the cost centers were recorded in the Direct Controllable Cost category. When expenses could not be directly traced, an allocation method was followed. (The last column of Exhibit 4 describes the allocation bases.)

   ● Royalty expenses (paid to academics for developing trading strategies) were charged to the New York office, the center of the firm's investment management activities.

   ● Allocations from the cost centers were based on cost center manager estimates of the proportions of the cost centers' services that were consumed by each of the center's internal "clients" (other cost centers or subsidiaries).

   ● After the proportions of each cost center's expenses were established, GI utilized a reciprocal cost allocation method, using a system of simultaneous equations, to identify the total costs incurred by each cost center and the dollar amount that should be allocated from each cost center to its "internal clients," both cost centers and subsidiaries.

2. Revenues

   ● GI New York retained all of the revenues generated worldwide (from fixed fees charged to the clients based on the amount of money they invested in GI) and assigned GI's subsidiaries a portion of the revenue based on local costs (direct controllable costs and other costs allocated to the subsidiaries) plus a 10% mark-up over the direct controllable costs.

A report of GI subsidiaries' profits for 2006 is presented in Exhibit 5. The cost-plus revenue-allocation method resulted in a small profit for all subsidiaries. This profit guaranteed that the subsidiaries would comply with capital requirements imposed by local financial authorities. The subsidiaries also used these profit reports both as a benchmark to calculate their taxes and as disclosures to institutional investor clients interested in learning about the financial health of the subsidiary holding their investments. On a few occasions where GI executives discussed the possibility of selling the firm or a subsidiary, the executives also used subsidiary profits to obtain a rough estimate of the worth of each subsidiary (calculated as a multiple of their EBITDA).

Subsidiary profits were not explicitly tied to the managers' compensation. A bonus pool based on GI's total profits was allocated to each executive based on the relative number of bonus points that each had earned. The compensation committee (comprising three members of the board of directors and the vice president of human resources) assigned these bonus points to each executive at the beginning of the year based on its subjective assessments of both the executive's performance in the prior year and his or her contribution to the company.

ALTERNATIVE TRANSFER-PRICING MODELS

Some subsidiary CEOs expressed discomfort with the way the firm was calculating their units' profits. During the last quarter of 2006, Hoskins had been particularly vocal in pointing out to Spencer that treating GI's subsidiaries as cost-focused profit centers was wrong. He argued that the resulting profits did not portray a fair picture of the subsidiaries' performance, which could have an adverse effect on the subsidiaries' sales prices, if they were ever spun off. The inaccurate profits also could be viewed negatively by financial and tax

regulators in the countries where the subsidiaries were located.[1]

Gary Spencer was not convinced that the current structure created problems that were worth fixing. However, in December 2006, primarily to appease Hoskins, he asked Mascola to create a committee to evaluate the situation, to address both Hoskins' and the tax concerns and, if appropriate, to propose an improved transfer pricing system. Mascola was selected to lead the evaluation process because of his financial expertise, his independence (he did not own any GI stock), and his personality (he was widely regarded as being thoughtful and impartial).

Right after his meeting with Spencer, Mascola began recruiting the people that he believed needed to participate in the process if a new transfer pricing model were to be both well designed and successfully implemented throughout the company. Every person invited accepted the invitation to become part of what became known as the Transfer-Pricing Model Task Force. Mascola chaired the task force, which also included Jack Davis (operations vice president), Michael Freeman (research director), plus Hashi (GI Tokyo) and Hoskins (GI London).

The task force met periodically over a seven-month period. During that time, they evaluated a number of different transfer-pricing alternatives. In an early meeting, Hoskins took the initiative by proposing that GI revenues should be allocated to the subsidiaries using "assets under management" as the allocation base and that the subsidiaries pay a royalty of (around) 50% to New York as compensation for the R&D and trading strategies developed by headquarters. According to his model, the London office would receive 20% of total revenues, since it managed $32 of the $160 billion

---

[1] Many countries' tax authorities were concerned that multinational corporations use transfer prices to shift income out of their country to countries with lower income taxes. Consequently, laws in the United States as well as other countries constrained transfer-pricing policies. For example, Section 482 of the US Internal Revenue Code required that transfer prices between a company and its foreign subsidiaries equal the price (or an estimate of the price) that would be charged by an unrelated third party in a comparable transaction. Regulators recognized that transfer prices can be market-based or cost-plus based, where the plus should represent margins on comparable transactions.

Tax rates varied significantly across countries: In GI's case, Singapore had the lowest effective tax rate (approximately 20%), followed by the United Kingdom and Japan (25–30%). The United States' subsidiaries paid the highest tax rates (around 40%).

of assets under management at GI (see Exhibit 2). Thus, according to Hoskins, the London office would have been allocated the following revenues in 2006:

	London subsidiary revenues ($000)
Allocated revenues	20% * 619,949.1 = 123,989.8
Minus royalty expense	50% * $123,989.8 = 61,994.9
Net revenues	61,994.9

However, Davis and Freeman did not agree that London should record all of those revenues. They argued that the fact that London was managing those funds did not mean they were generating a significant proportion of the value associated with them. Davis argued that, in fact, most of the assets managed by the subsidiaries belonged to New York clients. Further, to manage those assets, the subsidiary employees were just following instructions from headquarters, since the investment management research group in New York was the unit in charge of developing GI's trading strategies. Instead of allocating revenues based on assets under management, Davis believed a more accurate way of allocating revenues would be based on the origin of the clients (the source of the fixed fee revenues generated at each subsidiary), distributed as follows in 2006:

Subsidiary	Asset distribution based on the origin of the clients ($bn)
New York	150.6
London	2.2
Tokyo	4.2
Singapore	1.0
San Francisco	2.0
Total	160.0

Under this proposal, GI London's 2006 revenue would have declined from its actual $26.5 million to a mere $8.5 million and would have resulted in a subsidiary loss of over $16 million.

Totally dissatisfied with Davis' counter-proposal, which he considered ridiculous, Hoskins decided to conduct some research to learn whether (and how) GI's competitors were allocating revenues to their subsidiaries. Hoskins learned that the industry standard was to split fee revenues 50:50 between Client Services and Investment Management. Thus, he proposed, GI's business units should be split into these two categories. Half of the revenue would be allocated to Client Services (including two business units: Institutional Investor Sales, and Independent Broker/Dealer Sales) and the other half would be allocated to the Investment Management unit. This would allow GI to treat both activities separately.

Hoskins went on to propose that 50% of the fee revenues be assigned to Client Services based on the revenues generated in each subsidiary (or equivalently, based on the origin of clients which were directly proportional to the revenues in each subsidiary), while the 50% assigned to Investment Management be allocated based on assets under management. He proposed still to pay a 50% royalty to New York. Under this proposed scheme, Hoskins calculated GI London's 2006 revenues as follows:

	London subsidiary revenues ($000)
Client revenues	1.375% * 50% * 619,949.1 = 4,262.1
Investment management revenues	20% * 50% * 619,949.1 = 61,994.9
Minus royalty expense	50% * $61,994.9 = 30,997.5
Net revenues	35,259.6

Hoskins' new proposal also met with the disapproval of most of the task force members. Although most agreed with the concept of the subsidiaries' recording of revenues from Client Services, Davis reiterated that Investment Management should be considered a New York business unit only, since almost all of the investment strategies were developed at headquarters. Consequently, Davis and Freeman proposed that the fee revenues corresponding to Investment Management (50% of total revenues) be fully recognized by the headquarters office. The subsidiaries, on the other hand, would be reimbursed by headquarters for any expenses related to investment management activities in their units plus a 10% mark-up if these expenses qualified as direct controllable costs. Using the 2006 financial results, Davis and Freeman estimated that the operating incomes recorded for the different subsidiaries under their proposed model, would be those shown in Exhibit 6.

This model was unacceptable to Hoskins. He argued that the London and Tokyo subsidiaries were actively participating in investment management, and they should be rewarded for the value these activities created. He explained:

> Clearly there is activity under the broad banner of Investment Management in London and Tokyo. The issue is whether our offices add value or not. We are building resources in London on the basis that GI London is at least responsible for the investment management function for locally sourced clients. We have established an Investment Committee to oversee policies for our fixed income portfolios in the UK and continental Europe as well as for the Irish funds, and we have initiated the development of a local research function. I accept that the local activity is primarily, though not exclusively, one of policy tailoring and implementation rather than original intellectual capital investment, but most companies would regard this as a source of added value.

Hashi supported Hoskins by adding,

> Local value-added is not the same for all products or for all clients. It is clear, for example, that GI Tokyo adds little when it simply implements programs of trades suggested by GI New York, but it is also clear that it adds a significant share of value when it is managing money for its own clients in products designed specifically for them using local inputs.

Hoskins also expressed a concern about the effect that not recording the investment management revenues at the subsidiary level would have on external parties. Hoskins believed that local tax authorities might disapprove such treatment, as the profitability from investment management operations would be constrained to 10% or less. He claimed that, in practice, it seemed acceptable that support services (such as those provided by the cost centers) would be transferred at cost (or at a slight markup), but functions that formed part of a group's offering to clients (in this case, client services and investment management) were expected to be transferred in exchange for a proportion of revenues, following an "arms-length standard."[2] Departures from arm's-length prices could be interpreted by the local authorities as an attempt to

shift taxable income out of their countries. Hoskins explained:

> Our main competitors in the UK allocate revenues to the location actually carrying out the fund management. The alternative of a cost-plus arrangement, such as we have historically maintained, is probably no longer tenable where we now have local clients from whom we are receiving revenues for local investment activities.

Another external party that Hoskins worried about was his own clients. Hoskins believed that key local clients would be hesitant to appoint GI London to manage their assets if they knew their funds were considered to be managed in New York.

Davis disagreed with Hoskins' and Hashi's contentions. He believed that the contributions made to the local investments managed in London and Tokyo were minimal. Davis argued that the majority of operations at the subsidiaries consisted of selling the investment funds managed in the headquarters or executing a few investment operations, following strategies and guidelines developed by the investment management unit in New York.

Although Freeman agreed that the transfer pricing model should adhere to tax regulations, he believed that the model he and Davis proposed was appropriate. It should not trigger regulators' concerns since it already allowed the subsidiaries to record revenues for the services provided to institutional investor and independent broker/dealer clients (which he considered the main value-added activity performed by the subsidiaries). Additionally, GI's executives believed that the model used to prepare the subsidiaries' financial statements was not all that crucial to other financial regulators since GI was required to report consolidated (rather than subsidiary) financial statements.

THE MEETING

As Mascola prepared for the meeting with Spencer, he recognized the tensions among the task force members. He had carefully considered the advantages and disadvantages of the models proposed by Hoskins and by Davis and Freeman. He wondered how he could direct the meeting towards a final selection of a transfer pricing model that would both benefit the firm and be accepted by all, or at least most, members of the task force.

---

[2] "Arms-length" prices are those charged after bargaining between unrelated persons or those charged between related persons that approximate the result of independent bargaining.

Exhibit 1 Global Investors, Inc.: total assets under management

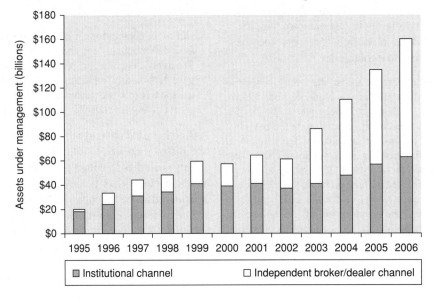

Exhibit 2 Global Investors, Inc.: types of funds (December 2006)

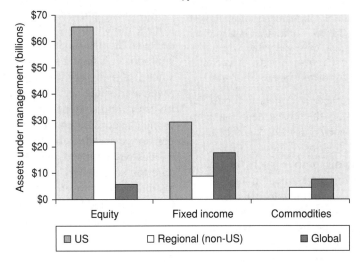

Assets under management by subsidiary
(in billions of dollars, as of December 2006)

Subsidiary managing the assets	Equity	Fixed income	Commodities	Total
New York	70.2	36.3	5.9	112.4
London	14.5	14.5	3.0	32.0
Tokyo	6.2	4.0	2.2	12.4
Singapore	2.1	0.3	0.0	2.4
San Francisco	0.0	0.2	0.6	0.8
Total	93.0	55.3	11.7	160.0

Exhibit 3 Global Investors, Inc.: organizational structure

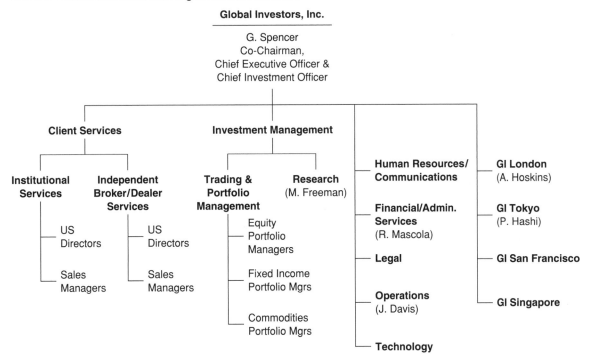

Exhibit 4 Consolidated statement following traditional transfer-pricing model

	Business units Headquarters and subsidiaries	Trading	Research	Technology	Financial services	Legal	Operations	Admin.	HR & commun.	Allocation if actual is not available
Fee revenue	yyy	n/a	n/a	n/a	n/a	n/a	n/a	n/a	n/a	Fixed percentage of fee revenues
Less: royalties (NY office only)	zzz	n/a	n/a	n/a	n/a	n/a	n/a	n/a	n/a	
Direct controllable costs										
Sales commissions	xxx	xxx	xxx	xxx	xxx	xxx	xxx	xxx	xxx	50% of the clients' first year fees
Salaries	xxx	xxx	xxx	xxx	xxx	xxx	xxx	xxx	xxx	Actual
Bonuses	xxx	xxx	xxx	xxx	xxx	xxx	xxx	xxx	xxx	Actual
Payroll taxes	xxx	xxx	xxx	xxx	xxx	xxx	xxx	xxx	xxx	Actual
Employee benefits	xxx	xxx	xxx	xxx	xxx	xxx	xxx	xxx	xxx	Actual
Professional fees	xxx	xxx	xxx	xxx	xxx	xxx	xxx	xxx	xxx	Actual
Occupancy (rent/utilities)	xxx	xxx	xxx	xxx	xxx	xxx	xxx	xxx	xxx	Pro rata based on sq. ft.
Depreciation office equipment	xxx	xxx	xxx	xxx	xxx	xxx	xxx	xxx	xxx	Actual
Maintenance	xxx	xxx	xxx	xxx	xxx	xxx	xxx	xxx	xxx	Actual
Travel expenses	xxx	xxx	xxx	xxx	xxx	xxx	xxx	xxx	xxx	Based primarily on reason for trip
Other administrative:										
Equipment rentals	xxx	xxx	xxx	xxx	xxx	xxx	xxx	xxx	xxx	Actual
Advertising	xxx	xxx	xxx	xxx	xxx	xxx	xxx	xxx	xxx	Actual, or else pro-rata based on revenue
Bank charges	xxx	xxx	xxx	xxx	xxx	xxx	xxx	xxx	xxx	Charge to Financial area
Stationery & supplies	xxx	xxx	xxx	xxx	xxx	xxx	xxx	xxx	xxx	Pro rata based on sq. ft.
Meetings	xxx	xxx	xxx	xxx	xxx	xxx	xxx	xxx	xxx	Pro rata based on sq. ft.
Gifts	xxx	xxx	xxx	xxx	xxx	xxx	xxx	xxx	xxx	Pro rata based on sq. ft.
Postage	xxx	xxx	xxx	xxx	xxx	xxx	xxx	xxx	xxx	Pro rata based on sq. ft.
Miscellaneous admin.	xxx	xxx	xxx	xxx	xxx	xxx	xxx	xxx	xxx	Pro rata based on sq. ft.
Total direct controllable costs	DCCbu1:DCCbu5	DCCtr	DCCres	DCCtech	DCCfin	DCCleg	DCCop	DCCad	DCChc	
Other allocated costs										
Trading	a1:a5	–	a7	a8	a9	a10	a11	a12	a13	
Research	b1:b5	b6	–	b8	b9	b10	b11	b12	b13	
Technology	c1:c5	c6	c7	–	c9	c10	c11	c12	c13	
Financial services	d1:d5	d6	d7	d8	–	d10	d11	d12	d13	
Legal	e1:e5	e6	e7	e8	e9	–	e11	e12	e13	
Operations	f1:f5	f6	f7	f8	f9	f10	–	f12	f13	
Administration	g1:g5	g6	g7	g8	g9	g10	g11	–	g13	
HR & communications	h1:h5	h6	h7	h8	h9	h10	h11	h12	–	
Total direct and allocated costs	TCbu1:TCbu5	A	B	C	D	E	F	G	H	
Reimbursement to cost centers		–A	–B	–C	–D	–E	–F	–G	–H	
Profit or loss	Profit or loss	0	0	0	0	0	0	0	0	

GI employed a reciprocal allocation method (a system of simultaneous equations) to find the cost allocations (a1, . . . , h12) and the total costs of the cost centers (A, B, . . . , H), using for each cost center the following equation:

$$\text{Total} = \left(\begin{array}{c}\text{Direct controllable} \\ \text{costs}\end{array}\right) + \left(\begin{array}{c}\text{Other alloc.} \\ \text{costs}\end{array}\right)$$

e.g. $A = DCCtr + b6 + c6 + d6 + e6 + f6 + g6 + h6$. In turn, each cost center got reimbursed by allocating its total costs to its "internal" clients (business units or other cost centers)

e.g. $A = a1 + a2 + a3 + \ldots + a13$

EXHIBIT 5 Operating income using traditional transfer-pricing model ($000)

	Business units Headquarters or subsidiaries	Cost centers Trading	Research	Technology	Financial services	Legal	Operations	Admin.	HR & communic.	Totals
New York										
Global fee revenue	619,949.1									619,949.1
Reimbursement to subsidiaries	(59,529.0)									(59,529.0)
Royalties expense	(41,587.0)									(41,587.0)
Direct controllable costs	(151,411.0)	(27,654.1)	(10,519.1)	(5,966.5)	(6,287.1)	(12,283.7)	(4,620.2)	(2,399.5)	(58,943.0)	(280,084.2)
Other allocated costs to	(111,650.5)	(6,766.5)	(6,315.4)	(2,968.4)	(3,529.5)	(8,866.5)	(2,938.3)	(2,040.5)	(13,071.2)	(158,146.8)
Other allocated costs away	0.0	34,420.6	16,834.5	8,934.9	9,816.6	21,150.2	7,558.5	4,440.0	72,014.3	175,169.5
Operating income	255,771.6	0.0	0.0	0.0	0.0	0.0	0.0	0.0	0.0	255,771.6
London										
Reimbursement from parent[a]	26,507.0									26,507.0
Direct controllable costs	(7,903.7)	(5,231.7)	(163.3)	(23.4)	(1,494.0)	(647.5)	(33.3)	(402.7)	(1,686.4)	(17,586.1)
Other allocated costs to	(16,844.6)	(664.0)	(72.3)	(3.6)	(11.7)	(15.8)	(4.0)	(113.1)	(330.8)	(18,059.9)
Other allocated costs away	0.0	5,895.8	235.6	27.0	1,505.7	663.3	37.3	515.8	2,017.2	10,897.6
Operating income	1,758.6	0.0	0.0	0.0	0.0	0.0	0.0	0.0	0.0	1,758.6
Tokyo										
Reimbursement from parent[a]	20,180.1									20,180.1
Direct controllable costs	(6,452.2)	(6,165.6)	0.0	0.0	(1,028.0)	0.0	(565.3)	(290.6)	(2,707.2)	(17,208.9)
Other allocated costs to	(12,007.0)	(113.9)	(89.3)	(67.6)	(232.8)	(1,080.2)	(417.1)	(96.8)	(1,465.0)	(15,569.7)
Other allocated costs away	0.0	6,279.5	89.3	67.6	1,260.8	1,080.2	982.4	387.4	4,172.2	14,319.4
Operating income	1,720.9	0.0	0.0	0.0	0.0	0.0	0.0	0.0	0.0	1,720.9
Singapore										
Reimbursement from parent[a]	4,776.1									4,776.1
Direct controllable costs	(1,613.0)	0.0	0.0	0.0	0.0	0.0	0.0	0.0	0.0	(1,613.0)
Other allocated costs to	(3,001.8)	0.0	0.0	(16.9)	(58.2)	(270.1)	(104.3)	(24.2)	(366.3)	(3,841.6)
Other allocated costs away	0.0	0.0	0.0	16.9	58.2	270.1	104.3	24.2	366.3	839.9
Operating income	161.3	0.0	0.0	0.0	0.0	0.0	0.0	0.0	0.0	161.3
San Francisco										
Reimbursement from parent[a]	8,065.9									8,065.9
Direct controllable costs	(2,233.5)	0.0	0.0	0.0	0.0	0.0	0.0	0.0	0.0	(2,233.5)
Other allocated costs to	(5,609.0)	0.0	0.0	(1.1)	0.0	(289.7)	(3.6)	(56.0)	(178.6)	(6,138.0)
Other allocated costs away	0.0	0.0	0.0	1.1	0.0	289.7	3.6	56.0	178.6	529.0
Operating income	223.3	0.0	0.0	0.0	0.0	0.0	0.0	0.0	0.0	223.3
Consolidated operating income	259,635.7	0.0	0.0	0.0	0.0	0.0	0.0	0.0	0.0	259,635.7

a The reimbursement from parent is equal to the total costs of the subsidiaries plus 10% of the total direct controllable costs incurred in the subsidiaries.

EXHIBIT 6 Operating income using Davis and Freeman's proposed transfer-pricing model ($000)

Fee revenues by subsidiary

	Institutional	Indep. broker/dealer
New York	227,003.4	356,370.6
London	7,512.0	1,110.5
Tokyo	3,630.4	12,620.6
Singapore	907.6	3,155.2
San Francisco	4,342.3	3,296.5
Total fee revenues	**619,949.1**	

	Business units		Investment management						Cost centers			
	Institutional sales	Indep. Broker/ dealer sales	General	Trading	Research	Technology	Financial services	Legal	Operations	Admin.	HR & communic.	Totals
New York												
Fee revenues			619,949.1									619,949.1
Commission revenue/ (expense)[a]	113,501.7	178,185.3	(309,974.5)									(18,287.6)
Investment management reimbursement to subsidiaries			(19,027.7)									(19,027.7)
Royalties expense			(41,587.0)									(41,587.0)
Direct controllable costs	(38,897.6)	(53,415.7)	(59,097.7)	(27,654.1)	(10,519.1)	(5,966.5)	(6,287.1)	(12,283.7)	(4,620.2)	(2,399.5)	(58,943.0)	(280,084.2)
Other allocated costs to	(23,922.9)	(19,229.3)	(68,498.3)	(6,766.5)	(6,315.4)	(2,968.4)	(3,529.5)	(8,866.5)	(2,938.3)	(2,040.5)	(13,071.2)	(158,146.8)
Other allocated costs away	0.0	0.0	0.0	34,420.6	16,834.5	8,934.9	9,816.6	21,150.2	7,558.5	4,440.0	72,014.3	175,169.5
Operating income	50,681.3	105,540.2	121,763.8	0.0	0.0	0.0	0.0	0.0	0.0	0.0	0.0	277,985.3
London												
Commission revenue/ (expense)[a]	3,756.0	555.3										4,311.3
Investment mgmt reimb from parent[b]			11,068.5									11,068.5
Direct controllable costs	(3,829.5)	(4,074.2)	0.0	(5,231.7)	(163.3)	(23.4)	(1,494.0)	(647.5)	(33.3)	(402.7)	(1,686.4)	(17,586.1)
Other allocated costs to	(2,735.7)	(3,579.9)	(10,529.0)	(664.0)	(72.3)	(3.6)	(11.7)	(15.8)	(4.0)	(113.1)	(330.8)	(18,059.9)
Other allocated costs away	0.0	0.0	0.0	5,895.8	235.6	27.0	1,505.7	663.3	37.3	515.8	2,017.2	10,897.6
Operating inome	(2,809.3)	(7,098.9)	539.5	0.0	0.0	0.0	0.0	0.0	0.0	0.0	0.0	(9,368.6)

EXHIBIT 6 *continued*

	Business units		Investment management						Cost centers			
	Institutional sales	Indep. Broker/ dealer sales	General	Trading	Research	Technology	Financial services	Legal	Operations	Admin.	HR & communic.	Totals
Tokyo												
Commission revenue/ (expense)[a]	1,815.2	6,310.3										8,125.5
Investment mgmt reimb from parent[b]			4,906.1									4,906.1
Direct controllable costs	(1,862.4)	(4,589.7)	0.0	(6,165.6)	0.0	0.0	(1,028.0)	0.0	(565.3)	(290.6)	(2,707.2)	(17,208.9)
Other allocated costs to	(2,682.6)	(5,034.8)	(4,289.6)	(113.9)	(89.3)	(67.6)	(232.8)	(1,080.2)	(417.1)	(96.8)	(1,465.0)	(15,569.7)
Other allocated costs away	0.0	0.0	0.0	6,279.5	89.3	67.6	1,260.8	1,080.2	982.4	387.4	4,172.2	14,319.4
Operating income	(2,729.8)	(3,314.3)	616.6	0.0	0.0	0.0	0.0	0.0	0.0	0.0	0.0	(5,427.5)
Singapore												
Commission revenue/ (expense)[a]	453.8	1,577.6										2,031.4
Investment mgmt reimb from parent[b]			1,072.4									1,072.4
Direct controllable costs	(465.6)	(1,147.4)	0.0	0.0	0.0	0.0	0.0	0.0	0.0	0.0	0.0	(1,613.0)
Other allocated costs to	(670.6)	(1,258.7)	(1,072.4)	0.0	0.0	(16.9)	(58.2)	(270.1)	(104.3)	(24.2)	(366.3)	(3,841.6)
Other allocated costs away	0.0	0.0	0.0	0.0	0.0	16.9	58.2	270.1	104.3	24.2	366.3	839.9
Operating income	(682.4)	(828.6)	0.0	0.0	0.0	0.0	0.0	0.0	0.0	0.0	0.0	(1,511.0)
San Francisco												
Commission revenue/ (expense)[a]	2,171.1	1,648.3										3,819.4
Investment mgmt reimb from parent[b]			1,980.7									1,980.7
Direct controllable costs	(18.6)	(2,214.9)	0.0	0.0	0.0	0.0	0.0	0.0	0.0	0.0	0.0	(2,233.5)
Other allocated costs to	(192.2)	(3,436.1)	(1,980.7)	0.0	0.0	(1.1)	0.0	(289.7)	(3.6)	(56.0)	(178.6)	(6,138.0)
Other allocated costs away	0.0	0.0	0.0	0.0	0.0	1.1	0.0	289.7	3.6	56.0	178.6	529.0
Operating income	1,960.3	(4,002.7)	0.0	0.0	0.0	0.0	0.0	0.0	0.0	0.0	0.0	(2,042.4)
Consolidated Operating income	46,420.1	90,295.8		122,919.8								259,635.7

a Commission revenue is equal to 50% of the fee revenues generated by the clients of the subsidiary. In New York, the commission expense is equal to 50% of the total fee revenues (allocated to the subsidiaries).

b The investment management reimbursement from parent is equal to the total investment management costs of the subsidiaries plus 10% of the investment management direct controllable costs (general/trading).

Chapter 8

PLANNING AND BUDGETING

Planning and budgeting systems are another important element of financial results control systems. One important output of a planning and budgeting system is a written plan that clarifies where the organization wishes to go (objectives), how it intends to get there (strategies), and what results should be expected (performance targets).

Many of the organizational benefits of planning and budgeting come from the processes of developing the plans. Planning processes force managers and employees to think about the future, to discuss their ideas with others in the organization, to prepare their projections carefully, and to be committed to achieve objectives that will serve the organization's interests. The issue is not whether to prepare a plan or budget, but rather *how* to do it.

Planning and budgeting systems vary considerably across organizations. Some are more formal than others. Some are more elaborate and time-consuming. Some require considerable top management involvement, while others operate more on a bottom-up, management-by-exception basis. There are many ways in which to design planning and budgeting systems, but not all of them are equally effective, and some features work better in certain settings than do others.

This chapter discusses the multiple purposes of planning and budgeting systems, including the setting of financial performance targets used for performance evaluation and incentive purposes. We also discuss some of these systems' most important characteristics, as well as some of the factors that can lead organizations to use planning and budgeting systems with differing characteristics.

PURPOSES OF PLANNING AND BUDGETING

Planning and budgeting systems serve four main purposes. Quite obviously, the first purpose is *planning*; that is, decision making in advance. Employees tend to become preoccupied quite naturally with their seemingly urgent, day-to-day exigencies. Unless they are encouraged to, they often fail to engage sufficiently in strategic, long-term thinking. Planning and budgeting systems provide the needed encouragement. They serve as a potent form of *action control* forcing managers to propose plans of action when thinking about the future, considering business prospects, resource constraints, and risks. In doing the forward thinking, the managers develop a better understanding of their organization's opportunities and threats, strengths and weaknesses, and the effects of possible strategic and operational decisions. This forward-thinking decision-making process sharpens the organization's responses and reduces risk.

Decisions regarding strategies, staffing and operational tactics can be adjusted based on predictions of outcomes before the organization suffers major problems. This is a classic example of what is called *feedforward control*. Effective planning processes make control systems *proactive*, not just *reactive*. They help managers shape the future, not just respond to the conditions they face and performance they observe.[1] For example, Davis Service Group, a large public UK-based service contractor that sources, cleans and maintains industrial textiles, protective clothing and textiles, continued to be a profitable company despite the severe recession of 2008, presumably "as the result of careful budgeting, [which] involves making detailed financial plans for every aspect of the business, identifying risks and ensuring that managers are committed to the outcomes that they have agreed."[2]

A second purpose is *coordination*. The planning and budgeting processes force the sharing of information across the organization. The processes involve a top-down communication of organizational objectives and priorities, as well as bottom-up communication of opportunities, resource needs, constraints and risks. They also involve lateral communication that enhances the abilities of organizational entities (e.g. business units, divisions, functional areas, administrative units) working together toward common objectives. Everyone involved becomes more informed, so the process is more likely to result in decisions that consider all perspectives. The sales plan is coordinated with the production plan so that shortages or surpluses of inventory and personnel are less likely and synchronized as needed. The production plans are coordinated so that the potentials for bottleneck constraints are minimized. Plans for growth and investments are communicated to the finance function, which takes steps to ensure the needed capital. And so on.

A third purpose is facilitating *top management oversight*. This oversight occurs in the form of *preaction reviews* (a type of action control) as plans are examined, discussed and approved at successively higher levels in the organization before actions are taken. Top management also uses plans as the performance standards used to implement the *management-by-exception* form of control (a type of results control). The planning and budgeting processes provide a forum that allows the organization to arrive at challenging but realistic performance targets by balancing top managers' wishes for desired performance with lower-level managers' information about possibilities. Negative variances – that is, measured performance below target levels – provide top managers an early warning of potential problems and justification for either reconsidering the organization's strategy or for interfering in the operating affairs of subordinate managers.

The final purpose is *motivation*. The plans and budgets become targets that affect manager motivation because the targets are linked to performance evaluations and, in turn, various organizational rewards. As mentioned briefly in Chapter 2, merely telling employees to "do their best" is not nearly as motivating as asking them to attain specific performance targets that are neither too easy nor too difficult to achieve. While all performance targets can provide these benefits, this chapter focuses on financial performance targets, which are the most common type of targets derived from firm's annual budgeting processes.

PLANNING CYCLES

Organizations often use three hierarchical, sequential planning cycles called *strategic planning*, *capital budgeting* (or *programming*), and (*operational*) *budgeting*.

Strategic planning

Strategic planning includes the relatively broad processes of thinking about the organization's missions, objectives, and the means by which the missions and objectives can best be achieved (i.e. *strategies*). Strategic planning processes typically involve senior executive corporate and entity managers who are the most broadly informed. It also involves both analyses of the past and forecasts of the future. Although a detailed treatment is outside the scope of this chapter, strategic planning typically involves developing: (1) an overarching vision or mission and objectives for the organization as a whole; (2) an understanding of the organization's present position, its strengths and weaknesses, and its opportunities and risks; (3) an agreement about the types of activities or businesses the organization should (and should not) pursue; and (4) a strategy for each of the core activities or businesses the organization has decided to pursue; that is, a plan that sets out the path of action by which each business or entity's objectives will be achieved by building on its strengths.[3]

A complete, formal strategic planning process leads to the establishment of the organization-wide strategy, as well as, where applicable, strategies for various entities within the organization, identification of resource requirements, and statements of tentative performance goals, usually projected 3–5 or 10 years into the future. Strategic planning provides a framework for the more detailed planning that takes place in the planning cycles that follow.

Capital budgeting

Capital budgeting (also sometimes called *programming*) involves the identification of specific action programs (projects to be implemented or investments to be made) over the next few years (usually 1–3 or 5 years) and specification of the resources each will consume. Programs should translate each entity's strategy, which is generally focused externally, into an internally focused set of activities designed to implement the strategy and, in turn, to lead to the achievement of the entity's goals. Programs can be developed at various levels of detail ranging from a complex program covering all the activities necessary to allow an entity to sell its products in a new geographical territory down to the simple purchase of a single new machine for an existing production line. Capital budgeting is constrained in that the program options considered must be consistent with the tentative agreements reached during the strategic planning process. Capital budgeting often involves many people with expert knowledge, such as related to investment analyses, forecasting, and financing. Capital budgeting also typically requires substantially more planning detail than does strategic planning.

The capital budgeting process usually starts with discussions between the entity managers and their subordinates about the programs needed in the near future. As part of this process, managers must inevitably review ongoing programs to judge whether they are fulfilling their intended purposes and whether they should be modified or discontinued. Scarce resources are then allocated to specific programs. Much of the existing theory of resource allocation focuses on allocation of *capital funds*, where the screening and comparisons of potential investments is structured in financial terms using discounted cash flow or similar finance-based analyses. However, rarely is resource allocation a mechanical process dependent solely on the financial calculations. Other resources, which may be scarce in the time period being considered and which are more difficult to quantify in financial terms – such as *talent* (human resources), essence of *timing* to reap potential first-mover advantages, and considerations arising from *escalating commitment* due to prior investments – often also influence the final allocation decisions.[4] Moreover, the outcomes of capital budgeting processes are likely also dependent on the track record, preparation, arguing skill, and political power of the managers involved. Managers have to compete for resources. Those making the most persuasive arguments and presentations are generally those whose requests are supported.

A subset of corporate managers is usually involved in reviewing larger program or investment proposals, often as part of a capital or resource allocation committee. These reviews allow the corporate managers another opportunity to communicate corporate priorities to entity managers (helping to alleviate potential *lack-of-direction* problems) and to exercise another preaction review (an action-type control). They also serve to help lower-level managers, particularly functional managers, understand how their activities fit into the organizational portfolio of activities and how they influence or relate to initiatives in other parts of the organization (again, addressing potential *lack-of-direction* problems). But the reviews also have an important bottom-up communication function: they serve as a forum for lower-level managers to communicate opportunities, threats, and requests for capital funds to the corporate managers. If capital budgeting is done well, the programs receiving resources are individually consistent with corporate objectives and strategies and mutually consistent with other related programs.

(Operational) budgeting

Operational (or annual) budgeting – *budgeting* for short – involves the preparation of a short-term financial plan, a *budget*, usually for the next fiscal year. Budgets match the organization's responsibility structure (see Chapter 7) and provide as much revenue, expense, asset, and liability line-item detail as appropriate. Budgeting is a near-universal organizational process. In the most comprehensive survey available, the vast majority (97%) of respondents reported that their organization had a formal budgeting process. Of these, 91% reported that their budget was annually; 3% semi-annually; and 1% quarterly. In budgeting, quantitative (particularly financial) data are emphasized.[5]

Every effectively-run organization performs the functions of each of the three planning cycles – strategic planning, capital budgeting (programming), and budgeting – although the formality and distinguishability of the cycles vary greatly from one organization to the next. In smaller firms, particularly, one or more of these cycles are usually relatively informal, and many firms combine two, or sometimes all, of these cycles as part of one planning or budgeting process, which they typically do annually. As organizations grow, however, a more elaborate and formal planning process evolves; one closer to a full three-cycle system. In not-for-profit organizations, the planning processes may be less focused on capital funds, although for them, too, capital is often a major constraint, equally forcing them to consider tradeoffs among various programs and designate available funds annually in their operating budget to well-chosen courses of action that help further their charitable objectives (see Chapter 17).

TARGET SETTING

Beyond producing written plans that clarify the organization's goals, strategies, and expected results, plans and budgets become *targets* that affect managers' motivation because the targets are linked to performance evaluations and, often, various incentives (which we discuss in Chapter 9). The use of pre-set performance targets in business organizations is almost universal.[6] Performance targets, and especially BHAGs (big hairy audacious goals), are thought to stimulate employees' competitive juices.[7] In addition, budgets are the primary performance target to evaluate performance at managerial levels and to award incentives. Review discussions, which tend to focus on variances between actual performance and targets, can lead to improved understanding of what is, and what is not, working and provide a useful forum for intra-organizational communication. Even in the absence of explicit incentives, managers are motivated to achieve their performance targets if for no other reason than to avoid having to explain to their bosses and colleagues why they missed their targets. For example, China's Haier, the large consumer appliances company, not only made pay 100% performance-based, it also makes extensive use of naming and shaming. Photographs of managers are prominently displayed throughout the company with a red smiley face for good performance and a yellow frowning one for those doing poorly.[8] Moreover, in committing to a target, managers choose to direct attention toward goal-relevant activities. Targets also motivate managers to use the knowledge they have, or discover the needed knowledge, to help them attain the goal.

The most commonly used performance targets at management levels in for-profit organizations arise during the budgeting process; the last stage of the full three-cycle planning system as discussed above. As mentioned there, and in this context, budgeting targets are typically financial in nature; they are typically expressed on a fiscal-year or annual basis; they match the firm's responsibility center structure; and they typically tie into the annual performance reviews and incentive contracts of their managers. For example, the financial targets of profit center managers are defined in terms of profit or at least in terms of selected line items of controllable revenues and expenses in some combination. For these reasons, our focus in this section is primarily on financial performance targets in a budgeting context.

Types of financial performance targets

Financial performance targets can be distinguished in a number of ways; that is, whether the targets are (1) model-based, historical, or negotiated; (2) fixed or flexible; or (3) internal or external.

Model-based, historical and negotiated targets

Performance targets can be (1) derived from a quantitative model of what performance should be; (2) based on historical performance; or (3) derived from a process of negotiation between lower- and higher-level managers.

Model-based targets are derived from predictions of the performance that is possible in subsequent measurement periods. When model-based targets are used in areas where activities are *programmable* (where there is a direct and relatively stable, deterministic causal relationship between inputs and outputs) they are said to be *engineered* targets. For example, in production departments, which are often cost centers, input–output relationships for materials and labor, say, can often be derived directly from the product(ion) specifications. The physical quantities for material and labor requirements can then be turned into financial targets by multiplying the standard quantities by their standard unit costs. But models are also used to try to derive performance targets in contexts other than standard costing applications. For example, firms often develop quantitative models of profit plans at the organization or entity levels, which are built on a financial accounting model and other inputs. Such models inevitably require many forecasts and planning assumptions, such as about the total available market, competitor actions, product mix, prices, and so forth. However, the target that is ultimately adopted arising from such models is often negotiated (see below) based on the range of outcomes that the model predicts before being committed to by the managers as the "final" target.

Historical targets are derived directly from performance in prior periods. They sometimes involve what is called *ratcheting*, such as when, for example, a profit center manager is asked to increase profits by 10% over last year's numbers.

At managerial levels, however, most performance targets are *negotiated* between hierarchical superiors and subordinates, such as when division managers negotiate their profit (or investment) center budgets with corporate. Negotiation is common due to the limitations of model-based approaches and the planning assumptions that they inevitably incorporate (see above), as well as due to *information asymmetry* in decentralized organizations. Higher-level managers generally are more knowledgeable about the overall organization's objectives and resource constraints. Lower-level managers generally have superior knowledge about the business prospects and constraints at the operating level. Negotiations about performance targets, therefore, should allow making use of each level's relative information advantage and induce superiors and subordinates to share at least some of their information.

Tight results control is easiest to implement when targets are engineered because the link between effort and results is direct. Consumption of inputs greater than, or production of outputs lower than, an engineered target indicates a performance problem with high probability. Managers can also use historical targets to affect tight results control if the processes being controlled are stable over time. Tight results control is more difficult when important assumptions about the future are necessary or if negotiation is used, unless the negotiation is tightly constrained by good performance models or good historical performance data. In these latter situations, performance variances from the target might indicate a performance problem, but they also might indicate that the original assumptions were wrong or that the negotiation process was biased.

Fixed versus flexible targets

Another way to distinguish targets is in terms of whether they are fixed or flexible. *Fixed* targets do not vary over a given time period. *Flexible* targets are changed according to the conditions faced during the period. The targets may be set to vary, for example, with changes in the volume of activity, the price of inputs (e.g. oil or rare minerals), interest rates, or currency exchange rates.

A survey of budgeting practices indicates that only a minority of firms (28%) report using flexible budgets.[9] By implication, financial targets are fixed in most firms, at least at profit center and corporate levels, which means that managers are held accountable for achieving their budgets regardless of the business conditions they face. If they fail to do so, they stand to lose some important forms of rewards, such as their annual bonus. Where targets are made flexible, this would tend to be done at lower organizational levels. Manufacturing (standard cost center) managers, for example, are usually not held accountable for achieving a fixed total cost budget. Instead, their total cost budgets are typically flexible, meaning that their budget varies with the volume of production (e.g. $350,000 for production of 100,000 units), or involves the use of unit cost standards (e.g. $3.50 per unit).

Targets can also be made flexible by stating them in terms of *relative performance*; that is, relative to the performance of others facing identical, or at least similar, conditions. This means that any given manager's performance is evaluated not in terms of the absolute level of his or her own performance, but relative to the performance of others. Most typically, the comparisons are relative to managers in the organization in charge of like entities (e.g. fast food outlets or bank branches of similar size in similar demographic locations). We discuss relative performance evaluations in more detail in Chapter 12.

Internal versus external targets

Almost all planning and budgeting processes involve target-setting approaches that are *internally* focused. Managers consider what is possible within the organization and focus on period-over-period, continuous improvements. But planning and budgeting processes can also involve target-setting approaches that are *externally* focused. This is the case when an organization uses relative performance evaluations and benchmarks its performance and practices with those of other organizations.

Evidence suggests, perhaps not surprisingly, that many firms in competitive environments engage at least in some form of *benchmarking*.[10] For example, Corus, a large steel maker from Europe, used to rely on "tons of steel rolled" as the key measure of performance in its steel plants. This measure did not show, however, whether it met customer needs or whether the steel needed rework because it did not meet quality standards. Therefore, Corus started to monitor and measure how its operations compare with other producers and competitors in the steel industry. This process of benchmarking means that Corus is continually reviewing its activities to try to become best-in-industry. Corus also shares relevant information internally across entities to drive improvement, and it reciprocally makes information available across the steel industry through industry associations such as the International Iron and Steel Institute.[11]

Benchmarking can involve comparing the organization's performance against the *best-in-industry* (direct competitors), as in Corus, or *best-in-class* (companies generally recognized for superior performance on the dimension of interest; that is, companies known for their *best practice*). Any of many aspects of performance can be benchmarked, including specific product or service characteristics (e.g. mean time between failures), specific activities or processes (e.g. customer service), or overall organizational outcomes (e.g. return on assets). When the benchmarking focus is on organizational outcomes (*performance*), rather than on *best practices*, the benchmarks are often used as performance standards for purposes of relative performance evaluations. The idea is that if one aspires to become the best, performance should be compared with the best. (In Chapter 12, we also discuss the use of relative performance evaluations for another purpose; that of filtering uncontrollable factors from measured performance.)

Common financial performance target issues

The effects of any results control system can be undermined if the wrong targets are set or if the targets are not set in the proper way. Two of the most important financial performance target issues are related to (1) the appropriate amount of challenge in a target, and (2) the appropriate amount of influence to allow subordinates in setting targets.

How challenging should financial performance targets be?

The first financial performance target-setting issue is how difficult, or challenging, to make the targets. Should targets be set at *stretch* levels; should they be a *best guess* as to what will happen in the forthcoming periods; or should they be set *conservatively* to help ensure that they will be achieved? The answer to this question depends on the planning process purposes that are emphasized.

For planning purposes, budget targets should be an unbiased *best-guess*. They should equal expected performance; that is, in probabilistic terms, with a 50% chance of achievement, thus, as likely to be missed as to be exceeded. As such, the targets will provide the best decision-making guidance for managers who are planning resource levels without (or less) risk of over- or under-committing resources (such as employee hiring numbers, production levels, and financing) due to either optimistic or conservative performance expectations that may subsequently not be forthcoming or overshot.

For motivational purposes, however, appropriate target levels should have at least some *stretch* in them. This causes a tradeoff because, as one budgeting study showed, more

FIGURE 8.1 Relationship between performance target achievability and motivation/performance

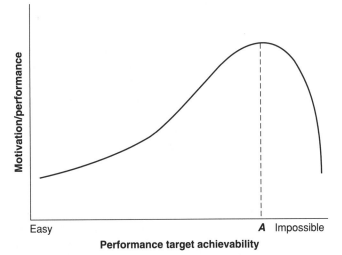

Source: K. A. Merchant, *Modern Management Control Systems: Text and Cases* (Upper Saddle River, NJ: Prentice Hall, 1998), p. 388.

than three-quarters of the surveyed companies use the same budget for planning and motivational purposes.[12] Thus, the budget system designer's problem is how to choose a target that either suits the primary purpose of budgeting, or provides a reasonable compromise between the planning and motivational purposes.

The theory regarding the effects of performance targets on motivation is complex. As both management gurus such as Jack Welch and Gary Hamel, as well as other pundits have pointed out, if organizations do not set high performance expectations, their employees will not produce superior results.[13] Challenging or *stretch* performance targets push employees to perform at a higher level. They lead to innovation, rather than just incrementalism.[14]

On the other hand, performance targets can be set too high. Findings from psychological research have shown a fairly consistent, nonlinear relationship between target difficulty and motivation (and hence, performance) as shown in Figure 8.1.[15] If the targets are perceived as quite easy to achieve, there is virtually no relationship between target difficulty and motivation. People's levels of aspiration (and hence, motivation and performance) are low because they are able to achieve their targets with a minimum of effort, persistence or creativity. Above a threshold level of difficulty, motivation seems to increase with target difficulty up to the point where people approach the perceived limits of their ability. After that, the relationship levels off and eventually turns down. At high levels of difficulty, most people get discouraged, lose their commitment to achieve the target, and exert less effort – they give up trying. Motivation is highest when performance targets are set at an intermediate level of difficulty, point A in Figure 8.1, which can be called *challenging, but achievable*.

Where, specifically, is the point of optimal motivation – the inflection point in the target difficulty-performance relationship? In other words, where do perceptions of excessive difficulty and, hence, lack of commitment to achieve the target, set in? The point varies undoubtedly depending on such things as the personalities (such as the degree of confidence and risk tolerance), capabilities, and experiences of the individuals involved. As we will see below, it also depends on the setting (such as the degree of uncertainty or the extent of uncontrollable factors affecting the environment in which the target needs to be achieved). This is why some research findings, or sometimes merely anecdotal claims, vary widely in the "recommended" level of challenge that targets should have for "optimal" motivation, ranging from as low as a 25 to 40% chance of achievement, to as high as an 80 to 90% chance.

Studies of practice suggest that at corporate and entity (profit center) levels in firms most annual profit targets are set to be highly achievable. The budget targets are set to be achievable 80 to 90% of the time by an effective management team working at a consistently high level of effort.[16] These targets should not be described as *easy* because they require competence and a consistently high level of effort. These highly achievable budget targets have many motivation, planning, and control advantages, as discussed below: increased manager commitment, protection against optimistic projections, higher achievement, reduced cost of interventions, and reduced gameplaying.

Increased manager commitment

Highly achievable budget targets increase managers' commitment to achieve the targets. Most managers operate in conditions of considerable uncertainty; their performance is affected by many unforeseen circumstances. Highly achievable targets protect the managers to a considerable extent from the effects of unfavorable, unforeseen circumstances and allow them few, if any, rationalizations for failing to achieve their targets. They have no choice but to *commit* to achieve their targets regardless of the business conditions faced. This increased commitment causes the managers to prepare their budget plans more carefully and to spend more of their time managing rather than preparing rationalizations to explain away failure to meet them.

Because of the lengthy budget performance period – typically one year in most firms – the costs of a lack of commitment to achieve budget targets are high. If highly difficult targets are set and some negative circumstances arise early in the year, the loss of commitment and decreased motivation may persist for many months. In contrast, if the budget targets are highly achievable, managers can withstand some adverse circumstances, even quite early in the period. They retain the motivation to try to make up for the unforeseen negative effects and are more confident that they will be able to get back on track.

Corporate managers have other possibilities for insuring managers against the effects of unforeseen, negative circumstances. They could shorten the planning horizon and set targets for periods shorter than a year. However, budget target-setting processes are expensive, and profit measures for short-time periods require many inter-period revenue and expense allocations. Another possibility is to *flex* the budget when unforeseen effects arise. However, most profit centers, and sometimes even cost centers, are affected by many unforeseen events, some positive and some negative. It is costly to analyze the effects of each unforeseen effect and make a judgment as to whether and to what extent it should be corrected for. For these reasons, highly achievable targets are often seen as the more appropriate approach, where managers are left to deal both with "the rough" and "the smooth" themselves while maintaining a reasonable expectation, and motivation, that they stand a chance to meet the target in the end, ups and downs notwithstanding.

Protection against optimistic projections

Highly achievable budget targets protect the organization against the costs of optimistic revenue projections. The first step in budgeting is usually preparation of sales forecasts. Production (or service) levels are then geared to the forecasted level of sales. If the budgets have optimistic revenue projections, managers will be induced to acquire resources in anticipation of revenue (activity) levels that may not be forthcoming. Some of these acquisition decisions are at least partially irreversible. It is often difficult and expensive to shed people and specific assets. It is usually safer to forecast sales and profits relatively conservatively and acquire additional resources only when their need is assured. This conservatism implies that budget targets should be highly, or at least reasonably, achievable.

Higher manager achievement

In the minds of most managers, budget achievement defines the line between success and failure. Highly achievable budget targets are motivating; they make most managers feel like "winners." Managers who achieve their budgets are given a package of rewards – bonuses, autonomy, and higher probability of promotion – and their self-esteem is given a boost. Organizations derive advantages when their managers have good self-esteem and feel like winners. Managers who feel good about themselves and their abilities are more likely, among other things, to be eager to work hard, to be entrepreneurial, and to increase their levels of aspiration for the future. In contrast, when managers fail to achieve their budget targets, they live with that failure for an entire year, and even beyond due to the stigma often associated with failure, where such frustration is likely to undermine their confidence and commitment, which can be quite costly to the organization.

Reduced costs of interventions

Highly achievable budget targets reduce the costs of needed interventions from higher up in the organizational hierarchy. Most corporations use a *management-by-exception* philosophy. Higher-level managers intervene in the affairs of their subordinate managers only when unfavorable variances from budget signal the need. When 80 to 90% of the managers are achieving their budgets, top management attention is directed to the relatively few situations where the operating problems are most likely and most severe.

This point is illustrated in Figure 8.2, which shows two probability distributions of forthcoming profits, one for an effective, hardworking manager and one for an ineffective, complacent (lazy) manager. Because the scaling shows better performance to the right, the distribution for the ineffective manager is to the left of that for the effective manager.

FIGURE **8.2 Probability distributions of forthcoming profits for effective and ineffective managers**

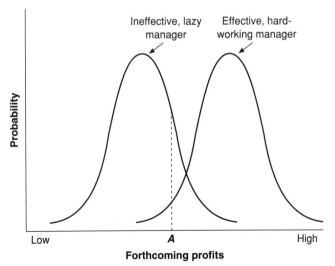

Source: K. A. Merchant, *Modern Management Control Systems: Text and Cases* (Upper Saddle River, NJ: Prentice Hall, 1998), p. 390.

If the budget target is set at point A, the vast majority, perhaps 90%, of effective hard-working managers will achieve their targets. But a much smaller proportion of ineffective managers, perhaps only 20% the way this curve is drawn, will get lucky enough to achieve their targets. Thus, higher-level managers will spend relatively little time intervening in the affairs of effective managers; instead, most of their intervention efforts will be directed at ineffective managers, where it probably should be directed.

Reduced gameplaying

Highly achievable budget targets also reduce the risk of gameplaying. The stakes associated with budget achievement in most firms, which include bonuses, promotions, and job security, are so significant that managers who are in danger of failing to achieve their budget targets have powerful motivations to play games, either with the numbers or through foolhardy decisions (that is, either through accounting or operating methods, as we discussed in Chapter 5). In other words, and in those circumstances, managers may engage in manipulative actions and decisions to make their performance indicators look more favorable while knowing that their actions or decisions are having no positive effects on real performance, and might actually be harming it.[17]

However, the primary risk organizations face by setting highly achievable budget targets is that manager aspirations, and hence motivation and performance, might be lower than they should be. The managers might as such not be encouraged to perform at their best. Whereas this is a potentially serious risk, organizations can protect themselves from it by giving managers incentives to *exceed* their budget targets. Figure 8.3 shows a typical results–reward function for entity (profit center) managers. It shows that managers earn all (or sometimes most) of their bonuses by exceeding their budget targets (up to a pre-specified maximum). If the rewards given for exceeding budget targets are sufficiently high relative to those given merely for achieving the budget targets, managers will have incentives not to slack off after the achievement of their budget targets is assured.

While the use of highly achievable budget targets is the typical observed practice, not all budget targets should be set to be highly achievable. If the firm is in danger of

FIGURE 8.3 Typical rewards/results function for a profit center manager

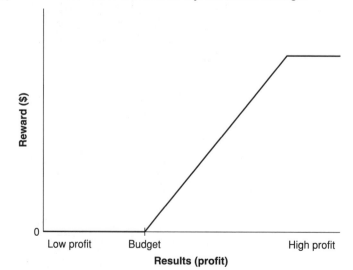

Source: K. A. Merchant, *Modern Management Control Systems: Text and Cases* (Upper Saddle River, NJ: Prentice Hall, 1998), p. 391.

failing or defaulting on a significant loan, corporate managers may set highly challenging profit targets to signal to operating managers the short-term exigency.[18] Top managers sometimes also set high profit targets to limit managers' discretionary investments, both as a way to provide a signal to lower-level managers that the strategy has changed (that is, that short-term profits now have priority over growth) and to enforce that change. They sometimes set high targets because they suspect organizational *fat* or because they want to set up a rationale to replace a manager. They may also set high targets to penalize managers for earning high bonuses in prior periods based solely on luck, rather than their own efforts.

Another budget target-setting possibility is to set multiple levels of targets, such as optimistic, realistic, and worst case, each designed to serve a different budget purpose (motivation, planning, or control). This is a budget-focused approach to *contingency*, *scenario*, or *what-if* planning. The key tension that these approaches try to address is, on the one hand, ensuring that target setting is flexible enough to incorporate uncertainty (to serve the planning purpose) while, on the other hand, trying to preserve the motivational effects of fixed targets (to try to meet the motivational and control purposes).[19]

How much influence should subordinates have in setting their targets?

Another important issue in designing a financial results control system when targets are negotiated is the extent of influence subordinates should be allowed in setting their targets; that is, to what extent should the planning and budgeting process be *top down* or *bottom up*? Many organizations lean towards bottom-up target-setting processes at managerial levels.[20] Allowing employees to participate and to have influence on the process of setting their performance targets can have several benefits.

Involvement in the setting of targets enhances the focal manager's *commitment to achieve the target*. Those who are actively involved in the process of setting their performance targets are more likely to understand why the targets were set at the levels they were, so they are more likely to accept the targets and be committed to achieve them. A second benefit is *information sharing*. As discussed above, target setting in most firms involves a process of sharing information about local business possibilities and corporate objectives and resources. Managers who are closest to the local business can provide useful information to superiors about both business potentials and risks. Corporate managers can provide information about corporate priorities and constraints. A third benefit is *cognitive*. Allowing participation in target-setting has the beneficial effect of clarifying expectations and encouraging managers to think about how best to achieve their targets.[21]

However, all employees, and not even all managers, should always be highly involved in planning and budgeting processes and, in particular, the setting of performance targets. Situations where target-setting processes can be completed effectively in a predominantly top-down manner include the following. First, targets can effectively stem from a top-down process when corporate management has sufficient knowledge of their entity business prospects and issues for setting properly challenging performance targets, or when corporate management has the knowledge that essentially subsumes the knowledge possessed by the entity managers. This occurs most commonly when a given activity or operation is programmable; where targets can be engineered or set exclusively by projecting historical trends. Related, knowledge can be sufficient for setting performance targets when corporate managers have a good understanding of the local business, perhaps because they formerly ran it and conditions have not changed much. But even when budgets are prepared in a seemingly bottom-up process, when higher-level managers have this knowledge, they exert greater influence on the final decisions about performance targets, as they might be less prone to listen to subordinates' arguments (or excuses) as to why performance targets cannot be raised.

Second, top-down target setting can be effective when higher-level managers have the information available for evaluating performance on a relative basis. For example, they may be managing a large number of relatively homogenous entities operating in a stable environment. These situations exist in some industries, such as where firms manage large numbers of like-concept retailing outlets, including fast food restaurants, car dealerships, or bank branches.

Third, top-down target setting can be effective, and should even be preferred, when lower-level managers are not good at budgeting. Top-down target setting is common in small businesses for just this reason. Small business operating managers are often technically skilled, but their management and financial education and experience might be limited.

Fourth, top-down target setting should be preferred when lower-level managers' thinking is dysfunctionally bound by historical achievements. Corporate management may know how to set standards according to a learning curve model that has proven accurate in the past or they may know that a new technology will cause structural changes in the business, thus obsolescing historical performance standards.

Finally, top-down target-setting can be used to try to mitigate biases that lower-level managers are prone to impart in the budgeting process. Biases can lead the organization to set performance targets either higher or lower than is desired. Most operating managers have a conservative bias and they use the opportunity of involvement in the target-setting processes to set lower targets. Lower targets increase the probability of target achievement, enhance the managers' reward potentials, and make it possible for them to achieve their targets with less effort. But some operating managers, particularly entrepreneurial and sales-oriented managers, may have an optimistic bias. Some managers want a challenge that will give them a feeling of accomplishment. Some want to signal to their bosses that they are aggressive, perhaps to compete for additional resources.

Sometimes top managers can control these biases. They can promote managers who have a greater reputation for truth telling, or they can implement some form of *truth-inducing incentive system*. Truth-inducing systems reward managers both for high performance and for minimizing the variance between actual and target performance. With such a system, managers are motivated to set high performance targets *and* to achieve them, thus overcoming the common tendency toward conservatism in target setting. The professional literature rarely mentions or discusses such schemes, however, suggesting that they are not commonly used in practice.

While top-down target setting has advantages in some settings, organizations who rely on this type of process must be careful not to forego too many of the benefits of a bottom-up process. Perhaps most importantly, they risk losing their managers' commitment to achieve the targets. Corporate managers may set targets that capable and consistently hardworking managers should be able to achieve with high probability, but if those asked to achieve those targets do not share that perception of achievability, they may be discouraged.[22] The resulting lack of motivation may lead to a low probability of achievement, in which case perception becomes reality.

PLANNING AND BUDGETING PRACTICES, AND CRITICISMS

The ways in which planning and budgeting systems are used reflect the outcome of a large number of management design and implementation decisions. Planning and budgeting systems can vary in terms of their planning horizon. Most firms' planning horizons are short: 1 year or less (34%), 2–3 years (20%), 4–5 years (38%), over 5 years (7%).[23] One key factor affecting firms' planning horizons is the length of the business cycle; that is, the lag between investments and their payoffs. Firms in different industries have very different planning horizons. Those in the power utility industry, for example, often plan quite far in the future, 25 years or more. Firms in the retail industry, however, might consider a one or two year plan adequate. Another key factor in determining the proper planning horizon is uncertainty. Sometimes the future is so uncertain that only short-term plans can be made. For example, a firm in the fashion industry might only be able to plan a season or two ahead.

There is also variation across firms in the timing of, and the time devoted to, planning and budgeting, with more variation in how firms run their long-range planning than in how they run their budgeting, which follows a rather standard, annually recurring pattern in most large firms. Most firms start their budgeting process four to six months before the end of the fiscal year and complete it during the last two months of the year. The budgeting process takes about four months to complete in most firms.[24] This suggests that budgeting consumes a nontrivial portion of time over a significant time period each year of many managers and their employees in both line and staff positions. Once the budget is set, firms are unlikely to revise it during the year for evaluation purposes, although they may frequently update it for planning purposes.[25] That is, they typically ask their managers to achieve their original budget targets, no matter what business conditions they face.

Budgeting is costly, particularly in terms of management time. It is not uncommon to hear managers complain that they spend so much time with the budget that they have little time to do any work. They never stop budgeting! That said, it is hard to envision any other way to run large, decentralized organizations with complex reporting structures that inevitably have a high need for coordination and that are mainly managed by the numbers (using results controls) through a management-by-exception approach. Nonetheless, some experts have suggested that firms should try to move "*beyond budgeting.*"

In the last few years, there indeed has been a spate of criticisms of planning and budgeting processes, including that they:

- are rife with politics and gameplaying;
- produce only incremental thinking, minor modifications to the plans and budgets prepared in the preceding periods, and are not responsive to changes in today's fast-moving economy;
- centralize power in the organization and stifle initiative;
- separate planning (thinkers) from execution (doers);
- cause too many costs for too few benefits.

The critics go on to make a number of suggestions for improvement. Some of these suggestions are for relatively minor modifications to traditional planning and budgeting processes, such as updating plans more frequently (*rolling plan* processes) or using relative performance standards rather than budgeted standards in evaluating performance and providing incentives. Some of the critics go further by imploring managers to abandon traditional budgeting and to move "*beyond budgeting.*"[26]

One of the budgeting-abandonment success stories cited by many critics is that of the Swedish-based Svenska Handelsbanken, which eliminated budgets in 1972 and has never looked back to re-introduce them. Svenska Handelsbanken has no annual budgeting process, and it produces no budgets; instead it evaluates the bank's and its managers' performances by comparing them with measures of competitors' performances on key performance dimensions, such as return-on-capital, cost-to-income ratio, and profit-per-employee. Whereas Svenska Handelsbanken has been successful in managing the firm without budgets, even so during the severe financial and economic crisis of 2008, it must be remembered, though, that most firms are not in an industry with such homogenous entities as banking. Therefore, many firms do not have such good relative performance data available to them. Moreover, Svenska Handelsbanken still has to engage in many of the standard planning and budgeting elements described above to fulfill all the other purposes, other than motivation, such as planning, coordination, and facilitation of top management oversight.

The critics are correct, though, that many firms' planning and budgeting processes are ineffective. Designing and implementing planning and budgeting systems is complex and difficult. The purposes for which the systems are needed often conflict, necessitating some difficult tradeoffs.[27] Business conditions are prone to shift, yet it is difficult to adapt plans and budgets quickly. And in any case, it is sometimes counterproductive to set performance targets because they can focus employees unnecessarily narrowly, and they can encourage unethical risk taking or earnings management (as will be discussed further in Chapter 15).[28] For example, in the early 2000s, General Motors set a goal to attain a 29% market share, which it had not reached in recent years. To reinforce the goal, employees started wearing goal lapel pins with the number 29 on it. Fixated on this target, managers made a series of bad decisions, such as attempts to buy market share by offering lots of buyer incentives that brought it to the brink of bankruptcy.

The spirit of the *beyond-budgeting* management model can be seen perhaps more as a management philosophy rather than a mere issue of planning and budgeting, or planning and budgeting alone. Its key aim, instead, is to increase the adaptability of organizations. Companies that follow the *beyond-budgeting* principles tend to have simple organizational structures (or aim to simplify them), flat hierarchies (or aim to make them flatter, less hierarchical), and flexible peer-to-peer networks used to provide and exchange the benchmarking data and share best practices. They operate with an assumption that organizations, like natural systems, are capable of self-organization and self-regulation. Their managers do not require negotiation of fixed performance targets, as is done in a traditional budgeting system. Allocations of resources are event-driven, not calendar-driven. Allocated resources are not treated as entitlements that must be spent. Unconstrained by a fixed and outdated plan, employees strive to improve their performance relative to their peers or some other benchmark. Creativity and rapid response to customer needs and unpredicted events are encouraged. However, the *beyond-budgeting* proponents caution that adopting a few principles while ignoring the others could lead to unsatisfactory outcomes.[29] There simply is no "quick fix" when it comes to improving an organization's adaptability and responsiveness in increasingly uncertain and turbulent environments. To improve the design of a planning and budgeting system, or whatever takes its place, managers must be aware of all of the purposes for which the system can be used and choose the best combination of system elements for their own setting.

The *beyond-budgeting* model has been developed and refined as its use has spread to several other organizations around the world, including Nokia, Southwest Airlines, Statoil, Toyota, and Whole Foods Markets. That said, many organizations continue to consider budgets as indispensable,[30] although many of them also continually struggle to make them more effective.[31]

CONCLUSION

Planning and budgeting systems are potentially powerful management tools that serve multiple purposes. They provide a way of converting managers' visions into an organized set of tactics that are employed throughout their organizations. They provide a standard that can be used to judge organizational success or progress. And they have many behavioral implications, such as regarding the effort invested in thinking about the future and commitment to achieve performance targets.

Many of the criticisms of planning and budgeting systems, such as those made by devotees of the so-called *beyond-budgeting* movement, focus on the flaws of negotiating performance targets. It is true that allowing target negotiations has drawbacks. The negotiating processes are costly, particularly in management time. Hence, firms are willing to engage in the processes relatively infrequently, typically annually. Targets that are fixed that far in advance can easily become obsolete, however, particularly in fast changing environments. Moreover, allowing negotiation of targets can also enhance gameplaying, such as the reluctance to share private information so as to be able to create budgetary slack and to maximize incentive payouts associated with achieving the targets.

Still, negotiating targets has its advantages, as this chapter has described. Although annual budgets have been criticized for inducing gameplaying behaviors and for being incapable of meeting managers' needs in rapidly changing environments, evidence suggests that they remain in widespread use and continue to play a crucial role in coordinating and motivating employee actions and behaviors.

However, just because an organization prepares a plan does not mean that it is engaging in useful planning. Frequent criticisms voice that strategic planning is overly bureaucratic and absurdly quantitative. Often plans are prepared but not used; they just take up shelf space. For plans to be effective, they must match the business conditions the firm is facing so that they can be used as a near-constant guide for employee actions. The plans should also assign responsibility and accountability for performance. This is an important role for budgets. Budgets turn plans into performance targets that affect employee motivation, particularly because the targets are often linked to performance evaluations and rewards, which we discuss in the next chapter.

Notes

1. See, for example, W. A. Van der Stede and T. Palermo, "Scenario Budgeting: Integrating Risk and Performance," *Finance & Management*, no. 184 (January 2011), pp. 10–13.
2. "Planning a Budget (Davis Case Study)," *Times 100* (2010), online (www.thetimes100.co.uk).
3. In large, diversified corporations, the question as to which businesses the corporation should (and should not) be in is often referred to as "(corporate) *diversification strategy*." The individual strategies for each of the businesses that the corporation has decided to pursue are, in turn, referred to as "(strategic business unit) *competitive strategies*."
4. See, for example, J. J. Gong, W. A. Van der Stede, and S. M. Young, "Real Options in the Motion Picture Industry: Evidence from Film Marketing and Sequels," *Contemporary Accounting Research* (2011), in press.
5. S. Umapathy, *Current Budgeting Practices in US Industry: The State of the Art* (New York, NY: Quorum, 1987), p. 137 and p. 140. For more recent, although less encompassing or more topically focused survey data on certain aspects of budgeting, see, for example, S. C. Hansen and W. A. Van der Stede, "Multiple Facets of Budgeting: An Exploratory Analysis," *Management Accounting Research*, 15, no. 4 (December 2004), pp. 415–39; T. Libby and R. M. Lindsay, "Beyond Budgeting or Budgeting Reconsidered? A Survey of North-American Budgeting Practices," *Management Accounting Research*, 21, no. 1 (March 2010), pp. 56–75.
6. A. Locke, "Goal-Setting Theory and Its Applications to the World of Business," *Academy of Management Executive*, 18, no. 4 (November 2004), pp. 124–5. See also, for example, A. Meekings, S. Briault, and A. Neely, "Are Your Goals Hitting the Right Target?," *Business Strategy Review* (Quarter 3, 2010), pp. 46–51.
7. J. Collins and J. Porras, "Building Your Company's Vision," *Harvard Business Review*, 74, no. 5 (September–October, 1996), pp. 65–77; G. Latham, "The Motivational Benefits of Goal-Setting," *Academy of Management Executive*, 18, no. 4 (November 2004), pp. 126–9.
8. "Grow, Grow, Grow," *The Economist* (April 17, 2010), Special Report, p. 13.
9. Umapathy, *Current Budgeting Practices in US Industry*, op cit, p. 149.
10. "How to Steal the Best Ideas Around," *Fortune* (October 19, 1992), pp. 102–6.

11. "Continuous Improvement as a Business Strategy: Target Setting (Corus Case Study)," *Times 100* (2010), online (www.thetimes100.co.uk).

12. Umapathy, *Current Budgeting Practices in US Industry*, op. cit., p. 149.

13. J. Welch, *Jack: Straight From the Gut* (New York, NY: Warner Business Books, 2001); G. Hamel, *Leading the Revolution* (Boston, MA: Harvard Business School Press, 2000); S. Kerr and S. Landauer, "Using Stretch Goals to Promote Organizational Effectiveness and Personal Growth: General Electric and Goldman Sachs," *Academy of Management Executive*, 18, no. 4 (November 2004), pp. 134–8.

14. "Grow, Grow, Grow," op. cit., pp. 12–13.

15. Edwin Locke and Gary Latham are renowned researchers in this area. For a recent reflection by them on research in the target-setting area, see E. Locke and G. Latham, "Building a Practically Useful Theory of Goal Setting and Task Motivation: A 35-year Odyssey," *American Psychologist*, 57 (2002), pp. 705–17.

16. See, for example, K. A. Merchant and J. F. Manzoni, "The Achievability of Budget Targets in Profit Centers: A Field Study," *The Accounting Review*, 64, no. 3 (July 1989), pp. 539–58; and K. A. Merchant, "How Challenging Should Profit Budget Targets Be," *Management Accounting* (November 1990), pp. 46–8.

17. See also M. Jensen, "Corporate Budgeting Is Broken: Let's Fix It," *Harvard Business Review* (November 2001), pp. 94–101; and M. Jensen, "Why Pay People to Lie?," *The Wall Street Journal* (January 8, 2001), p. A32.

18. See, for example, M. Matejka, K. A. Merchant, and W. A. Van der Stede, "Employment Horizon and the Choice of Performance Measures: Empirical Evidence from Annual Bonus Plans of Loss-Making Entities," *Management Science*, 55, no. 6 (June 2009), pp. 890–905.

19. Van der Stede and Palermo, "Scenario Budgeting," op. cit.; see also, N. Frow, D. Marginson, and S. Ogden, "Continuous Budgeting: Reconciling Budget Flexibility with Budgetary Control," *Accounting, Organizations and Society*, 35, no. 4 (May 2010), pp. 444–61; "Managing in the Fog," *The Economist* (February 26, 2009), pp. 67–8.

20. Umapathy, *Current Budgeting Practices in US Industry*, op. cit.

21. There is an extensive stream of research in the area of budget participation going back nearly half a century. For a recent example of a study that speaks to some of the benefits discussed here, among many other studies too numerous to list, see V. Chong and K. Chong, "Budget Goal Commitment and Informational Effects of Budget Participation on Performance: A Structural Equation Modeling Approach," *Behavioral Research in Accounting*, 14 (2002), pp. 65–86.

22. T. Libby, "The influence of Voice and Explanation on Performance in a Participative Budgeting Setting," *Accounting, Organizations and Society*, 24, no. 2 (February 1999), pp. 125–37.

23. Umapathy, *Current Budgeting Practices in US Industry*, op. cit., p. 145.

24. Ibid., p. 73.

25. Ibid., p. 139.

26. See, for example, J. Hope and R. Fraser, *Beyond Budgeting: How Managers Can Break Free from the Annual Performance Trap* (Boston, MA: Harvard Business School Press, 2003); B. Bogsnes, *Implementing Beyond Budgeting: Unlocking the Performance Potential* (London, UK: John Wiley & Sons, 2008). For an academic perspective, see S. C. Hansen, D. T. Otley, and W. A. Van der Stede, "Recent Developments in Budgeting: An Overview and Research Perspective," *Journal of Management Accounting Research*, 15 (2003), pp. 95–116; Libby and Lindsay, "Beyond Budgeting or Budgeting Reconsidered? op. cit.

27. Hansen and Van der Stede, "Multiple Facets of Budgeting," op. cit.

28. L. Ordonez, M. Schweitzer, A. Galinsky, and M. Bazerman, "Goals Gone Wild: The Systematic Side Effects of Overprescribing Goal Setting," *Academy of Management Perspectives*, 23, no. 1 (2009), pp. 6–16.

29. Hope and Fraser, *Beyond Budgeting*, op. cit.; Bogsnes, *Implementing Beyond Budgeting*, op. cit.

30. Libby and Lindsay "Beyond Budgeting," op. cit.; B. Ekholm and J. Wallin, "Is the Annual Budget Really Dead," *The European Accounting Review*, 9, no. 4 (2000), pp. 519–39; T. Libby and R. Lindsay, "Beyond Budgeting or Better Budgeting?," *Strategic Finance* (August 2007), pp. 47–51.

31. J. Orlando, "Turning Budgeting Pain into Budgeting Gain," *Strategic Finance* (March 2009), pp. 47–51.

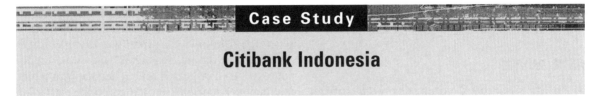

Case Study

Citibank Indonesia

In November 1983, Mehli Mistri, Citibank's country manager for Indonesia, was faced with a difficult situation. He had just received a memorandum from his immediate superior, David Gibson, the division head for Southeast Asia, informing him that during their just-completed review of the operating budgets, Citibank managers at corporate had raised the SE-Asia division's 1984 after-tax profit goal by $4 million. Mr. Gibson, in turn, had decided that Indonesia's share of this increased goal should be between $500,000 and $1,000,000. Mr. Mistri was concerned because he knew that the budget he had submitted was already very aggressive; it included some growth in revenues and only a slight drop in profits, even though the short-term outlook for the Indonesian economy, which was highly dependent on oil revenues, was pessimistic.

Mr. Mistri knew that to have any realistic expectation of producing profits for 1984 higher than those already included in the budget, he would probably have to take one or more actions that he had wanted to avoid. One possibility was to eliminate (or reduce) Citibank's participation in loans to prime government or private enterprises, as these loans provided much lower returns than was earned on the rest of the portfolio. However, Citibank was the largest foreign bank operating in Indonesia, and failing to participate in these loans could have significant costs in terms of relations with the government and prime customers in Indonesia and elsewhere. The other possibility was to increase the total amount of money lent in Indonesia, with all of the increase going to commercial enterprises. But with the deteriorating conditions in the Indonesian economy, Mr. Mistri knew that it was probably not a good time for Citibank to increase its exposure. Also, the government did not want significant in-creases in such offshore loans to the private

sector at this time because of their adverse impact on the country's balance of payments and services account.

So, Mr. Mistri was contemplating what he should do at an upcoming meeting with Mr. Gibson. Should he agree to take one or both of the actions described earlier in order to increase 1984 profits? Should he accept the profit increase and hope that the economy turned around and/or that he was able to develop some new, hitherto unidentified sources of income? Or should he resist including any of the division's required profit increase in his budget?

CITIBANK

Citibank, the principal operating subsidiary of Citicorp, was one of the leading financial institutions in the world. The bank was founded in 1812 as a small commercial bank in New York City, and over the years it had grown to a large, global financial services intermediary. In 1983, the bank had revenues of almost $5.9 billion and employed over 63,000 people in almost 2,600 locations in 95 countries.

Citibank's activities were organized into three principal business units: institutional banking, individual banking, and the capital markets group. The Institutional Banking units provided commercial loans and other financial services, such as electronic banking, asset-based financing, and foreign exchange, to corporations and governmental agencies around the world. The Individual Banking units, which operated in the US and 18 other countries, provided transactional, savings, and lending services to consumers. The capital markets group served as an intermediary in flows of funds from providers to users. With a staff of 3,500, this group was one of the largest investment banks in the world. (Exhibit 1 shows the relative size of these ▶

This case was prepared by Professor Kenneth A. Merchant.

Copyright © by the President and Fellows of Harvard College. Harvard Business School Case 185-061.

activities, and Exhibit 2 shows a summary corporate organization chart.)

MEHLI MISTRI

Mehli Mistri, Citibank's country corporate officer for Indonesia, joined Citibank as a management trainee in the Bombay office in 1960, just after finishing a BA degree in economics from the University of Bombay. Between 1960 and 1964, Mehli gained experience in a number of assignments in the Bombay office, and in 1965 he transferred to New York to work in the credit analysis division. He returned to Bombay in 1966, and then became manager of Citibank branches in Madras (1968), Calcutta (1969–71), New Delhi (1972), and Beirut (1973). In 1974, he was promoted to regional manager with responsibility for five countries in the Middle East (Turkey, Syria, Iraq, Jordan, Lebanon), and he held that position until 1979 when he was appointed the country head of Indonesia. He remained in that position up until the time of this case. In 1982, Mehli attended the Advanced Management Program at the Harvard Business School.

CONTROL OF INTERNATIONAL BRANCHES

Citibank managers used two formal management processes to direct and control the activities of the corporation's international branches: reviews of sovereign risk limits for each location and reviews of operating budgets and accomplishments.

Sovereign risk limits

Each year Citibank management set sovereign risk limits for its international branches based on country risk analyses. The term sovereign risk actually refers to a wide spectrum of concerns that would impair the bank's ability to recapture the capital it invested in foreign countries. These included macroeconomic risk, foreign exchange controls that the government of the host country might employ that would make it difficult for clients to pay their obligations, or, in the extreme, expropriation of assets. Once Citibank had opened a given branch, however, it intended to keep it open, so the reviews of sovereign risk were concerned only with setting limits of the amount of money a branch could lend in foreign currency.

The sovereign risk review process started in midyear with the country manager proposing a sovereign risk limit. This limit was discussed with division and group managers and was finally approved, on a staggered time schedule, by a senior international specialist on the corporate staff. The foreign currency lending limit for Indonesia had grown substantially as the branch had grown.

The sovereign risk limit set during these reviews was an upper guideline. When the economic conditions in a country changed in the period between sovereign risk reviews, country managers sometimes chose to operate their branches with self-imposed sovereign risk limits that were below the limits set by management in New York. Corporate managers encouraged this behavior because they knew that the managers on site often had a better appreciation of the risks in the local environment.

Budgeting

Budgeting at Citibank was a bottom-up process which started in July when headquarters sent out instructions to the operating units describing the timing and format of the submissions and the issues that needed to be addressed. The instructions did not include specific targets to be included in the budget, although it was widely recognized that the corporation's combined long-term goals were approximately as follows:

Growth	12 to 15% per annum
Return on assets	1.25% (125 basis points)
Return on equity	20%

The above norms were established for Citibank as a whole, but a number of international branches, including Indonesia, traditionally exceeded these norms, and these entities often established their own targets at higher levels.

At the time the operating managers received the budget instructions, they would have the results for half the year (through the end of June), and in the period from July until the end of September, they would prepare a forecast for the remainder of the current year and a budget for the following year. The starting point for the preparation of the budget was projections about each of the major account relationships, and discussions continued until the summation of the account relationship projections could be reconciled with the desired profit center bottom line. Then costs were considered. The budget submission form included all the line items shown in Exhibit 3. In some past years, the bank had prepared two- and five-year projections, but the numbers were seen to be very soft and not very useful.

Formal reviews of the annual budgets were held according to the following schedule:

Level of review	Timing
Division	end of September
Group	mid-October
Institutional Bank	end of October

If the sovereign risk review for a particular entity had not yet been held, the budgets were submitted with the assumption that the risk limits would be approved as submitted. If this assumption proved to be incorrect, the budget had to be revised before it was incorporated in the corporate consolidated budget.

Performance was monitored and compared against budget each month during the year. Every quarter a new forecast for the remainder of the year was made. Whether these were reviewed formally by division managers varied widely, depending on the division manager's style. Some managers held relatively formal on-site reviews of performance and budget revisions, and others communicated only by mail or by telephone.

Mr. Mistri was very comfortable with the review processes:

> Every level of management has a role to play, and there is a lot of horsetrading and give and take in the budget review processes. Usually there is more revision of the numbers at lower management levels, but revisions do not necessarily mean increased profit goals. I have seen cases where the division head thought the country head was being too aggressive and he asked for the budget to be lowered. The managers sitting further away are more objective, and the review processes are consultative, collegial, and constructive.

Budgets were taken very seriously at Citibank, not only because they were thought to include the most important measures of success, but also because incentive compensation for managers at Citibank was linked to budget-related performance. For a country manager, incentive compensation could range up to approximately 70% of base salary, although awards of 30 to 35% were more typical. Assignment of bonuses were based approx-

imately 30% on corporate performance and 70% on individual performance, primarily performance related to forecast. The key measures for assessing both corporate and international-branch performance were growth, profits, return on assets, and return on equity. However, in the analyses of individual performance for the purposes of assigning incentive compensation, considerable care was taken to differentiate base earnings from extraordinary earnings (or losses) for which the manager should not be held accountable.

CITIBANK IN INDONESIA

Indonesia was a relatively young country; it achieved independence only in 1949 after many years of being a Dutch colony. Citibank had operated in Indonesia only since 1968 when President Suharto allowed eight foreign banks to set up operations in Jakarta. From the point of view of the Indonesian government, the role of the foreign banks was to help develop a young economy by transferring capital into the country, establishing a modern banking infrastructure, attracting foreign investment, and developing trained people.

The foreign banking community operated in Indonesia with some important restrictions. The most serious constraints were that foreign banks were not allowed to open branches outside the Jakarta city limits, and local currency loans could be made only to corporations with headquarters and principal operations within the Jakarta city limits. But, on the other hand, the Indonesian government did not require any local ownership of equity; it set no lending quotas for the banks (e.g. requirements to lend specific amounts of money to certain types of businesses at favorable rates); and it valued and maintained a free foreign exchange system.

In explaining the goals of the government with respect to the foreign banks, Mr. Mistri commented:

> We consider ourselves privileged to be in Indonesia. We realize that the country wants to develop economically, and we know that the government sees us in the role of a development and change agent, attracting and developing not only capital, but also new financial products, services and techniques and trained managers and professionals for the financial services industry. The government also expects us and other international banks to participate in extensions of credit to both the public and private sectors.

Citibank and the other foreign banks were interested in operating in Indonesia for several reasons: (1) to serve their international and local customers, (2) to assist in the economic development of the country, and (3) to share in the potential for profits and growth the Indonesian economy offered. The Indonesian economy had tremendous potential: the country was the fifth largest in the world in terms of population, and the economy had shown excellent growth for many years, as the figures shown in Exhibit 4 illustrate. The country was rich in raw materials, particularly oil and tin, and the Indonesian government was very interested in developing the country's industrial activities.

In 1983, Citibank's Indonesian operation included activities in each of the three major lines of business – institutional, individual, and capital markets. Mehli Mistri was the Country Corporate Officer, and as such he was the primary spokesman for all of Citibank's activities in Indonesia. His prime line responsibility, however, was the Institutional Banking activity which provided by far the greatest proportion of revenues and profits. Other individuals headed the Individual Banking and Capital Markets activities in Indonesia, and they reported through separate management channels (see Exhibit 5).

Since its inception, Citibank's Indonesian operation had been very successful. Its growth paralleled that of the Indonesian economy.

THE SITUATION IN 1983

In 1983, Mr. Mistri was concerned about the risk–return ratio in his branch. He felt comfortable with Indonesia's long-term prospects, but the country, which was highly dependent on oil revenues, had slipped into a recession when oil prices decreased significantly. His concern was as to whether the government would take strong enough steps to correct its balance-of-payments problem.

Inside the bank, Mr. Mistri was faced with a problem of high staff turnover. High turnover had been a problem for Citibank for many years because the bank provided its people with training that was recognized as probably the best in

Indonesia, and local financial institutions had lured many Citibank people away with generous offers. This had happened so often that Citibank had been given labels such as "Citi-university" and "Harvard-on-wheels," and the government often held Citibank up as an example of how foreign banks could (and should) supply trained professionals to the country. To attempt to retain more of its trained people, Citibank had recently increased its compensation levels, but some people in the branch felt that the bank could not compete on the basis of salary because of its desire to be profitable, its limited domestic branch network, and significant career opportunities elsewhere.

The year 1983 was particularly difficult from a staff turnover standpoint, as the losses included Mr. Mistri's chief of staff and two senior officers. In mid-1983, the average account manager experience was under two years, and there were three unfilled slots at management levels. Mr. Mistri knew that the inexperience and people shortages in the branch were also serious constraints to growth.

Given these significant problems, Mr. Mistri thought that the budget he submitted, which projected modest growth, should be considered as aggressive. He wanted to submit an aggressive budget because

> we are an aggressive organization. We like to stretch because we feel the culture of our corporation and the will and desire of our people to succeed and excel can make up the difference.

In reflection of the fast-changing uncertainties in the economy and the personnel problems, however, Mr. Mistri decided to operate with a self-imposed sovereign risk limit that was somewhat lower than that which had been formally approved by management in New York. He knew that his responsibility was as much to manage risk as to generate profits.

In late October 1983, however, the budget for the whole Institutional Bank was reviewed at headquarters, and the consolidated set of numbers did not show the growth that top management desired. This led management to suggest some budget increases, and these increases presented Mr. Mistri with the dilemma described in the introduction to this case.

Exhibit 1 Selected Citicorp financial data – 1983 (dollars in millions)

	Citicorp Consolidated	Institutional Bank	Individual Bank	Capital Markets Group
Revenues	$5,883	$2,896	$2,380	$587
Net income	$860	$758	$202	$128
Return on shareholders' equity	16.5%	22.0%	17.7%	32.2%
Return on assets	.64%	.87%	.69%	1.26%

Source: Citicorp 1983 Annual Report.

Exhibit 2 Partial Citibank organization chart

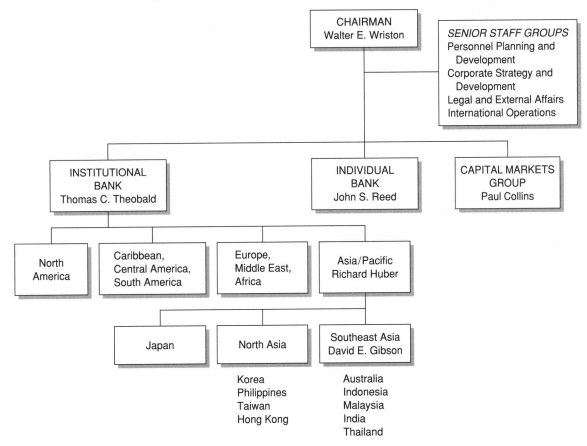

EXHIBIT 3 Line items on budget submission form

REVENUE/EXPENSE
Local Currency NRFF
Foreign Currency NRFF
Allocated Equity NRFF
BAD DEBT RESERVE EARNINGS
NET REVENUE FROM FUNDS
Exchange
Translation Gains/Losses
Trading Account Profits
Trade Financing Fees
Securities Gains/Losses
Fees, Commissions & Other. Rev.
Affiliate Earnings
Gross Write-offs
Gross Recoveries
Loan Provision Excess
Direct Staff Expenses
Direct Charges
Other Direct Expenses
Allocated Processing Costs
Minority Interest
Other Allocated Costs
Matrix Earnings
EBIT
Foreign Taxes
US Taxes
PROFIT CENTER EARNINGS

Equity Adj. – Translations
Placements (AVG.)
Total Staff (EOP)
Total Non-Performing Loans-EOP
Rev./Non-Performing Loans
Avg. Total Assets – Lcl Curr.
Avg. Total Assets – Fgn Curr.
Allocated Equity
LOCAL CURRENCY – AVG. VOL.
Loans
Sources – Non-Interest Bearing
Sources – Interest Bearing
FOREIGN CURRENCY – AVG. VOL.
Loans
Sources – Non-interest Bearing
Sources – Interest Bearing
END OF PERIOD (EOP)
Past Due Obligations
Interest Earned Not Collected
Loans
Assets

EXHIBIT 4 Indonesia gross domestic product (billions of rupiahs)

Year	Gross domestic product	Gross domestic product (1980 prices)
1968	2,097	18,493
1969	2,718	20,188
1970	3,340	21,499
1971	3,672	22,561
1972	4,564	24,686
1973	6,753	27,479
1974	10,708	29,576
1975	12,643	31,049
1976	15,467	33,187
1977	19,011	36,094
1978	22,746	38,925
1979	32,025	41,359
1980	45,446	45,446
1981	54,027	49,048
1982	59,633	50,150
1983	72,111	52,674

Source: International Financial Statistics Yearbook, 1984.

Exhibit 5 Organization chart – Citibank Indonesia

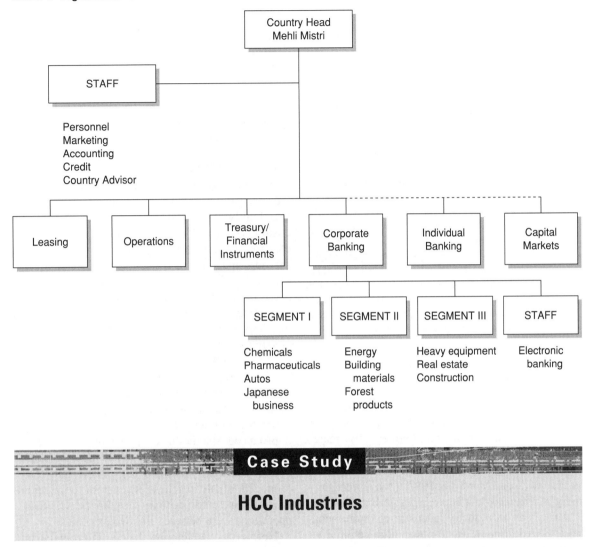

Case Study

HCC Industries

Until 1987, HCC Industries, a manufacturer of hermetically sealed electronic connection devices and microelectronic packages, operated with a philosophy of having *stretch* performance targets for its operating managers. This philosophy was based on the belief that aggressive targets would motivate the managers to perform at their highest possible levels. In planning for fiscal year 1988, however, this philosophy was changed. Andy Goldfarb, HCC's CEO explained:

[A large consulting firm] designed our old budgeting philosophy and the incentive compensation plan associated with it, but I'm not sure they understand companies smaller than the *Fortune 500*. They gave us "the great incentive plan of 1982," but it hasn't worked very well.

The problem is that if you're forecasting for stretch targets, you must be thinking optimistically. This concept might work well at some companies of a certain size that understand their markets well enough and are in a position to influence it. But we haven't ▶

This case was prepared by research assistant Lourdes Ferreira and Professor Kenneth A. Merchant.

been in that position. We have just been taking orders, not doing marketing. In the meantime, the corporation has been missing its plans. For four years now we have had some divisions do well and some do poorly, but the corporation never achieved its targets. As a public company, we need that to happen. Also, people at corporate haven't earned any bonuses.

Now we've changed our philosophy. We want to judge people first on whether they are hitting a "minimum performance standard." Only then can they start earning extra rewards. We've asked our managers to submit budgets with targets that are realistic and achievable, and to make sure the managers have got the message about the change, we made it clear to them that missing budget now could cost them their jobs.

Most of our general managers didn't like the change when we announced it. They worried that bonuses aren't automatic and that the amounts they could earn weren't large enough. They might be right, and we may make some changes. And as I look at the actual results for the first quarter of FY 1988, I'm concerned that we haven't yet implemented the new concept quite as we intended. Some of our divisions have missed their minimum performance standards by large margins.

THE COMPANY

HCC was a small publicly held corporation, headquartered in Encino, California, that designed, manufactured and marketed hermetically sealed electronic connection devices and microelectronic packages. Revenues totalled $36 million in fiscal year 1987 (ended March 28, 1987). (A five-year summary of financial data is presented in Exhibit 1.)

HCC was an industry leader in electronic connectors requiring glass-to-metal and ceramic-to-metal seals, and particularly those requiring un-usual or close tolerance machining and the sealing of exotic metals. Many of the company's products were used for aerospace and military applications requiring high reliability or operation in adverse conditions (such as high temperatures or pressures).

The company was organized into four primary operating divisions, each run by a general manager (see Exhibit 2). The general managers were each responsible for all the division's business functions except that the division controllers reported on a solid line to Chris Bateman, HCC's chief financial officer. Andy Goldfarb explained:

The division controllers are paid to be controllers. We don't want them to be motivated to *cook the books*.

That is a danger because we base bonuses on division results and because they work at quite a distance from headquarters and naturally develop an emotional attachment to the people with whom they work. The solid-line reporting to corporate helps remind them that their primary job is to protect the corporation's assets.

Three of the divisions – Hermetic Seal, Glasseal, and Sealtron – produced connectors of various types. Hermetite produced custom-designed, micro-electronic packages. Exhibit 3 shows some typical products. Exhibit 4 provides some summary information about each division.

The three connector divisions were similar in that they were profitable but growing slowly. Their industry was highly fragmented. The number of potential customers was huge because many products used electrical connectors. Many small competitors served some portions of the market. The connector divisions did not have a solid base of knowledge about their competitors' strengths and weaknesses, their market shares, and forthcoming business possibilities because of the dearth of readily available marketing information and limited size of their marketing staffs. Thus it was difficult for them to make accurate sales forecasts.

The primary difference among the connector divisions was in the degree of standardization of their product lines. Sealtron was at one extreme, as it produced standardized connectors in relatively large volumes. Hermetic Seal, on the other hand, operated primarily as a job shop that designed and produced small batches of custom connectors, predominantly for military customers. Glasseal's operations were between the two extremes.

Hermetite, which produced microelectronic packages, was different from the connector divisions in several important ways. First, its market and competitors were relatively well defined. Customer contacts were typically made at trade shows, and most customers and competitors were well known. There were five main competitors in the industry, and Hermetite's market share was third or fourth in rank. Second, Hermetite's potential for growth was great. In contrast with the connector market, which was stable, the packaging market was growing at 20 to 30% per year. Third, it faced tremendous price competition. A new competitor had entered the market in 1985 and had lowered prices to buy market share. The existing competitors responded by lowering their prices to attempt to fill their production capacity. Fourth, Hermetite faced significant production technology and control problems. The production processes were complex, and the division had had instability in its engineering and production organizations. This had resulted in half of its $3 million backlog being delinquent, even though on-time delivery was an important competitive factor. Because of the price competition and the production problems, Hermetite had been operating at a loss since before it was acquired in August 1985.

The divisions were all largely self-contained and independent of each other. They served different customers and had different part number systems, product standards, and accounting and information systems. Corporate management had never tried to force, or even encourage, synergy between the divisions. As Chris Bateman, HCC's CFO, explained it:

> We want to let the managers be managers. They will do the best for you that way. Decentralization is a sound business concept.

Corporate staff had always monitored nonoperating decisions closely (for example, corporate authorization was necessary for any capital acquisition in excess of $500). But they had been providing few direct services to the divisions, however. This was starting to change. In 1987, a corporate marketing function was created to assist the divisions with market research, advertising and promotions. And a corporate engineering service function was started to develop new product designs that might be used by any or all of the connector divisions. Chris Bateman observed that the division managers were generally not receptive to receiving this support: "Some of them say that corporate is now dictating when they should brush their teeth."

STANDARDS FOR EVALUATING THE DIVISIONS' PEFORMANCES

The divisions' performances were evaluated in terms of seven performance areas: (1) profit before tax, (2) bookings, (3) shipments, (4) returns (as percentage of total dollars shipped), (5) rework aging (number of jobs and percentage less than 30 days), (6) efficiency (net sales/number of employees), and (7) delinquencies (dollar volume and percentage of delinquent orders outstanding). Profit was

generally the most important evaluation criterion, but good performance in all of these performance areas was considered necessary for achievement of the profit targets.

Division and corporate management negotiated performance standards in each of these areas during HCC's formal planning process – an annual budgeting cycle. This process began in December (or early January) and concluded in mid-March, just before the start of the new fiscal year.

The process started with the division managers' preparation of sales forecasts. To prepare these numbers, they typically contacted their largest customers directly. Then they worked with their operating managers to prepare budgets for expenses, capital expenditures and cash flow. They summarized the numbers into thirteen-week quarters that were broken into *monthly* periods of four, four and five weeks.

In February, corporate officers visited the divisions and conducted thorough reviews of these preliminary targets. They looked at the detailed numbers, such as sales by customer and by product, and challenged the general managers' assumptions and numbers by account. Chris Bateman explained why they conducted such a thorough review:

> There are a couple of reasons. First, most of our managers are not very good at budgeting. They are engineers and generally do not have a lot of business training. Second, they tend not to play it straight with us. Some will submit conservative targets. Others will submit numbers they have little chance to make.

After this review, the revised targets were 95% ready. Typically the divisions just needed to work out a few details before their budgets were presented to the board of directors. The board formally approved the budget in March.

After the budget was approved, it became a fixed evaluation standard for purposes of awarding incentive compensation. The division managers were asked to send updated forecasts to corporate monthly, but these forecasts were used for planning purposes only. HCC managers did some planning for periods greater than one year, but these processes were handled almost exclusively at corporate. Al Berger explained:

> The general managers are not in a position to do what needs to be done two years down the road. They compete day-to-day. The corporation needs to do some

long-term things, such as improving our marketing and consolidating some of our efforts. We involve the general managers in some of those discussions only occasionally because they are not leading those efforts.

MONITORING OF PERFORMANCE

Corporate managers, particularly Al Berger, who was hired as COO in March 1987, monitored division performances closely. He was in frequent contact with the division managers and reviewed performance reports in detail when they were produced. Al was even monitoring quality reports from Hermetite on a daily basis because of the significance of that division's known production problems.

The division managers were acutely aware of the emphasis placed on quarterly results. Each quarter they had to write a commentary explaining their division's results as input to a formal budget review. Considerably less explanation was necessary if they exceeded their performance targets. For example, Mike Pelta, manager of Hermetic Seal noted that:

> If I miss a monthly target, I can always explain that something happened at the last minute, and they accept that explanation. If I miss a quarterly target, that's a big thing.

And Lou Palamara, manager of Sealtron, explained that:

> If I miss a quarterly budget, Al Berger will visit me immediately asking what I am doing about the problem.

PERFORMANCE TARGETS AND INCENTIVES UNDER THE *STRETCH* BUDGETING CONCEPT

Until 1987, HCC's philosophy was to have *stretch* performance targets based on the belief that aggressive targets would push managers to strive to do their best. These targets were "not unreachable, just tough." The intended probability of achievement was 75 to 80%.

The budget targets directly affected bonuses paid to those included in the bonus plan. Each person included in the plan was assigned a bonus potential which, for most division managers, was 30% of base salary. The bonuses paid were based half on profit before taxes (PBT) and half on a subjective rating of performance (which was also influenced by profit

performance). The objective portion of the award was paid according to the following schedule:

Actual division PBT (% budget)	Bonus paid (% bonus potential)
<60	0
60	80
100	100
140	150

The subjective portion of the evaluation was based primarily on top management's judgment of the degree of accomplishment of the targets in all seven performance areas. For example, if a division manager met the standards for five out of the seven performance criteria mentioned earlier, top management would have to judge the importance of the targets that were not met. If the two targets that were not met were judged to be critical, the manager might earn no subjective bonus.

Bonuses were paid based on annual performance, but payments were made quarterly. The interim (quarterly) payments were made only at 80% of the earned rate to protect the company from paying bonuses that might not eventually be earned.

DISSATISFACTION WITH THE STRETCH BUDGETING CONCEPT

Gradually corporate managers became dissatisfied with the stretch budgeting concept. Most important, they felt it was causing the corporation not to achieve its plans. Each year some divisions achieved their targets and some did not, but the corporation was consistently missing its targets. Chris Bateman explained:

> Since everybody knew that the *stretch* targets were too optimistic, it became "OK to miss budget." For example, from the time when I joined HCC in September 1986 until March 1987 I had to prepare eight budget reviews because the corporation was not achieving its plans. The problem was that at 60% of budget, the managers were still in bonus territory, so they didn't have to worry much about meeting budget. Their budgets were like a wish. They were too easily blown off.

There was also dissatisfaction with the bonus plan associated with the stretch budgets. The division managers, in particular, considered it to be too subjective and complex to communicate to their middle managers. Communication of the details of the plan was also hampered at two divisions because the division managers did not want to disclose division-level financial information to their personnel because they feared that the information might be leaked to competitors. As a consequence, most of the division personnel included in the plan never knew their bonus potential nor the bases on which the bonus awards were made.

Most managers were also dissatisfied with the plan because the awards were typically not made until three to four months after the end of the quarter. The delay was caused by the several levels of approvals that were necessary before the payments could be made.

THE CHANGE TO MINIMUM PERFORMANCE STANDARDS

In October 1986, Andy Goldfarb met with his division managers and corporate staff and announced that from then on the company would operate with a *minimum performance standard* (MPS) budgeting philosophy. MPS budgets were to be set so that the felt probability of achievement was 100%. In addition to the MPS, the managers were asked to set *targets* that reflected a performance level considered to be beyond normal capability. Al Berger explained that these targets might involve a 25 to 30% increase in something, rather than 5 to 10%. They represent a level that might be said to have only a 50% probability of achievement.

The change in level of difficulty of standards was coincident with a change in the incentive compensation plan. Under the new plan, a division bonus pool was created based on 20% of the amount by which actual division PBT exceeded the MPS, plus 25% of the amount by which it exceeded the target.

The most important performance measure for bonus purposes was still PBT, but bonuses could be affected by results in the other six performance areas. Al Berger explained:

If they make all their targets, they will be paid the full bonus pool. If they miss only a couple of targets, they may earn 100% or close to 100% of the pool. If they make only half their targets, they may earn only 60% of the pool. I left the details of the plan vague because the importance of particular targets varies over time

– for example, this year delinquencies and quality are even more important than profit – and some targets are more important in some divisions than in others. I did not want to quantify the relationships.

The division managers were given the discretion to decide (before the year started) which of their subordinates would share in the bonus pool and how the pool would be allocated among themselves and the others included. Corporate guidelines suggested that they reserve between 30% and 40% of the pool for themselves. At targeted performance levels, the division managers were expected to earn bonuses of approximately 20 to 25% of base salary.

Bonuses were still paid quarterly at a level of 90% of that earned. The remaining 10% was accrued to be paid at the end of the year contingent on annual performance.

THE 1988 BUDGET NEGOTIATION PROCESSES AND REACTIONS TO THE CHANGE IN BUDGETING PHILOSOPHY IN THE FOUR DIVISIONS

Hermetic Seal

Mike Pelta, general manager of Hermetic Seal, was a cofounder (with Jack Goldfarb, the current chairman) of HCC. Mike was a major HCC stockholder, owning 15% of the corporation's stock. He had been managing Hermetic Seal since January 1987, after having served a stint as general manager of Hermetite. Mike was known as an effective, hard-working manager, but one who had a tendency to be autocratic and ineffective at developing his subordinates. This limitation was becoming a more serious problem because Mike was nearing retirement age.

Mike's philosophy in setting performance targets was to be conservative:

Knock on wood, in my 33 years as a manager, I've never missed a budget. I'm not really sandbagging; I'm an upbeat person. When I get a target to meet, I go for it. I do have to be careful with the optimism of my subordinates, however. I often have to lower their estimates when putting together my budgets.

Mike's reasoning for wanting to achieve budget targets consistently:

If you keep missing budget, how do you feel? You feel like a failure. If you exceed a budget, you feel proud. You're going to project higher the next year. You can't keep beating down on people. You've got to build them up. Stretch budgets don't make me work harder. They can't make me do something I can't do. If the bookings are not there, the profit targets are impossible.

Consistent with his philosophy, Mike submitted a conservative budget for fiscal year 1988. Al Berger explained from his point of view:

> Mike was looking for a large bonus. He had good reasons for pessimism, bookings were terrible and the bookings rate had declined in the last three months of the year; they were shipping 25% more than they were booking; delinquencies were numerous, as production was inefficient. But he didn't explain his numbers in terms of these problems. He just said he was new in the job and was in the process of rebuilding. I listened to what he had to say and then we went through the customer list a number of times. We finally agreed on sales and bookings numbers, and then quality, delinquencies, and profit targets.

After the revisions were approved, Mike felt between 95% and 98% confident that he would achieve his sales target. And even if he missed the sales target, he expected to meet the profit goal. He explained:

> It would simply be a matter of digging into my backlog and cutting costs here and there. I know this business inside out, so I know what I have to do to make budget. I wouldn't do anything that could hurt the company in the long run, though.

He noticed the change in budgeting philosophy. He recalled that in the past he used to have only an 85 to 90% chance of making the *stretch* profit targets.

Glasseal

Carl Kalish was the manager of Glasseal. Carl had been vice president marketing for Glasseal at the time it was acquired by HCC. He was appointed general manager of Glasseal soon after the acquisition.

Carl considered it very important to prepare realistic forecasts:

> It's easy to sit in a staff position and be optimistic, but as a general manager, I have to be right. In the past four years I have been tremendously accurate in my market projections. You can't anticipate everything, though. For instance, in fiscal year 1987 we exceeded our profit budget by 12% primarily because

of unusual gains in sales volume. A major competitor was going through some crises, and we were able to pick up part of their share. We exceeded budget during each of the first three quarters, but in the last quarter our customers started deferring shipments to use up their inventory, and our sales decreased sharply. We expected our volume to go back to normal in 1988.

Carl's first budget projected $7.4 million in bookings and $7.2 million in shipments. Corporate managers told him to increase both targets by $200,000, based on their interpretation of market trends. They also increased his PBT target by almost 2%, up to $1.1 million.

Carl's reaction to these changes:

> Personally, I think that my initial forecast was right, but I'm committed to the new budget. It's a number that I'm trying to live with . . .
>
> [Under the old system] I used to feel 90% sure that I'd make budget in a given year. Now I'm still only 90% sure, but the difference is that my job depends on it . . .
>
> The old plan allowed for bonus payments if you missed budget, so we had something to shoot for even if we knew we would come out short, and the rewards were also greater than they are now. Furthermore, corporate was not so dictatorial when setting the targets. But I'm trying to stay openminded and see how it goes. I consider this first year as an experiment.

Sealtron

Lou Palamara, Sealtron's general manager, was recruited from outside HCC in January 1986. His background was as a ceramic engineer and engineering manager.

Lou's initial 1988 budget submission was for sales of $6.4 million and PBT of $900,000. This budget was rejected. Lou explained:

> Andy Goldfarb told me, "Your charter is to make $1 million in PBT next year. Show me a plan to make that much profit."

Lou then prepared a budget that increased the projected sales and reduced costs of advertising, promotions and other discretionary spending. He discussed this new budget with Chris Bateman (CFO). Neither Lou nor Chris were confident that the $1 million target would be achieved, so Chris agreed to propose the $900,000 PBT target again to

Andy. Andy would not budge. He sent Lou a letter stating that "Sealtron's target for 1988 must be $1 million."

Lou felt that while he had perhaps a 95% chance to achieve the $900,000 profit budget, his chance to achieve the $1 million MPS budget was only 60 to 65%. His PBT target was $1.1 million, a level that he considered impossible to achieve. Lou was somewhat discouraged:

Mine is a strange plan. If I make budget, which is an 18% increase from our last year actuals, I get no bonus. I really feel that if you put together a plan and don't hide anything and plan capital investments and expenditures for the future, and you feel comfortable with it, then that's the best plan. The plan must be realistic. My plan is a threat. I may even have to lay off some people that we will likely need later. But if I don't do it and I miss my minimum performance standards, I may get fired.

Lou was concerned because nobody at Sealtron expected a bonus in 1988. Missing budget also prevented salary increases. In fiscal year 1987, for example, nobody at Sealtron got a salary increase because the division did not make budget. This situation made him worry about employee retention:

If this salary freeze persists for two more years, I may lose some of my key employees. We missed our profit target last year mainly because I had to hire a new industrial engineer and a production control manager to get our manufacturing operations in shape. Now I know of a local company that wants to hire the industrial engineer, and he is just starting to put our systems in order. I think we should keep people happy if we want them to stay. They should be compensated for their effort.

Corporate managers' perspectives about the situation at Sealtron were somewhat different. Al Berger thought that the $1 million PBT budget was necessary to change the aspiration levels of Sealtron personnel. He explained that Sealtron's efficiency, measured in terms of sales per employee, was 50% below that of the other connector divisions even though its production processes were simpler. And Al was particularly annoyed that even though Sealtron had missed its budget by 30% in 1987, the number of employees in the division had actually grown. Al felt that with good management, Sealtron would be certain to achieve its $1 million PBT budget, but this would probably require cutting staff and shipping more product.

Chris Bateman rated the probability of Sealtron achieving the $1 million target at only 90%:

Because of the people. The people in that division have historically not been thinking much about costs. Their perspective has always been that they need sales to make money. We're trying to get the message to them that we can't afford any fat in the organization, and I'm not sure how fast they will learn to adjust.

Lou felt that personnel at Sealtron truly were concerned about costs:

I recognize that some good comes out of budget pressures. Everybody becomes conscious of overhead costs, and the pressures force expense cuts and productivity improvements faster. But I still feel that hiring the people I did was in the best long-term interest of the company.

Hermetite

Alan Wong, the general manager at Hermetite, was an MBA/CPA/lawyer who worked for a major public accounting firm before joining HCC as CFO. He accepted the job as general manager of Hermetite in August 1986, only four months before he had to submit his initial budget for 1988.

Alan's first budget showed projections of $13 million in sales, and PBT of $130,000. These figures compared with 1987 actual sales of $7 million and a loss of $2.8 million. Although he knew these were aggressive targets, Alan felt that it was important for him to be optimistic:

You have to be an optimist in a turnaround situation. If you don't set high standards, you'll never achieve high performance.

Alan thought that the pressure to make budget every year would encourage him and his personnel to become more efficient:

We may have to postpone maintenance or purchases of supplies in a tough quarter. If the profit is not there, you shouldn't spend the money. It is my job to provide the profits this quarter. And it is up to corporate to think long term.

Alan's initial budget submission was also based on a belief that corporate managers would not accept a budget that projected a loss. It had been two years since HCC acquired Hermetite and he felt that corporate managers were anxious for it to turn into a profitable operation. This belief was incorrect. Al Berger noted that:

> Alan thought the company wanted profit from him; he thought we would not survive without profit. So he based his budget on what was needed in order to break even or make a small profit. He was naive. I told him we would not accept a budget from him that showed a profit.

Al and the other corporate managers considered Alan's first budget *ludicrous* (a *pie in the sky*), and they felt that even his second submission (sales of $11 million) was still too optimistic. During a series of budget reviews, Hermetite's budget was revised sharply downward. The final MPS budget was for sales of $9.2 million and a loss of $400,000. The performance target was set at sales of $10.5 million and PBT of $67,000.

After these reviews, Al was certain that Hermetite had a budget that it would achieve. Alan was not as confident; he felt that he had only an 80% chance of achieving it. He commented:

> This concept of minimum performance standards may be OK for a normal business, but we're not normal. Nobody knows what is the standard for Hermetite. We could make $200,000 in profits or show many times that in losses. Hermetite's track record has been so bad that we don't know what to expect. Our motivating factor is just to keep our jobs.

Alan felt he had only a slight (perhaps 5%) chance of achieving his PBT target.

EARLY EXPERIENCES WITH THE NEW SYSTEM

As described earlier, the division managers were concerned that they were not assured of achieving their MPS budgets. Al Berger was certain that the division budgets were achievable, but, as is shown in Exhibit 5, others in the corporation were not as sure.

Events subsequent to the budget approvals caused Al to admit he was wrong in the case of Hermetite, which started the year 1988 very poorly. Only three weeks into the year, Al lowered Hermetite's performance targets (but not MPS) as a gesture of encouragement:

> At the time it was prepared, I was certain that Hermetite's budget would be achieved. But some good things didn't happen. Bookings were so low that we went dry in December and January. This was out of Alan's control. The delinquency problem, created by his predecessor, had caused the reputation of the company to go to pot, and customers weren't placing orders.
>
> I had to admit we were wrong. Although I had intended never to revise the standards, I lowered the performance target to $9 million in sales. The people needed to be reinforced during a difficult time. I wanted to be able to say "You're doing a good job" through bonuses.

The first quarter results, which were available in July 1987, caused more concern. As is shown in the summary presented in Exhibit 6, none of the divisions had achieved all of its MPS. These results caused Andy Goldfarb and other corporate managers concern about whether the new budgeting philosophy had been implemented properly.

Exhibit 1 Summary financial data (dollar amounts are in thousands, except per share data)

	1987	1986[a]	1985[a]	1984[a]	1983[a]
Operations					
Net sales from continuing operations	$35,552	$32,554	$25,262	$18,827	$11,177
Earnings (loss) from continuing operations					
before extraordinary items	(1,028)	793	1,236	735	808
Per common share					
Earnings (loss) from continuing operations					
before extraordinary items[b]	$(.58)	$.45	$.68	$.38	$.43
Cash dividends	.06	.06	.06	.06	.06
Stockholders' equity	4.98	6.38	6.24	6.05	5.50
Yearend financial position					
Current assets	$17,830	$20,993	$20,665	$24,067	$21,629
Working capital	12,145	12,856	14,577	17,166	17,579
Current ratio	3.14:1	2.58:1	3.39:1	3.49:1	5.34:1
Total assets	$32,495	$38,857	$33,039	$36,971	$30,007
Long-term debt	15,997	16,635	13,557	17,334	15,228
Stockholders' equity	8,851	11,332	11,405	11,554	10,512
Return on average stockholders' equity					
from continuing operations	(10%)	7%	11%	6%	8%
Shares outstanding (in thousands)	1,776	1,776	1,773	1,911	1,910

[a] Restated for discontinued operations.
[b] Based on weighted average number of shares outstanding.

Exhibit 2 Partial corporate organization chart

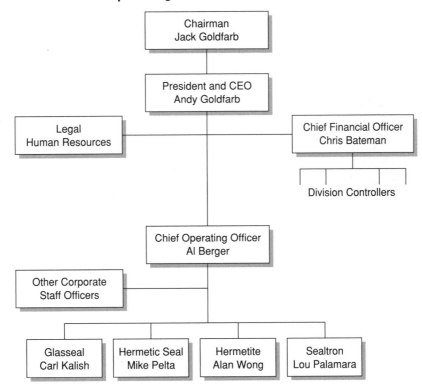

Exhibit 3 Typical products

Hermetically Sealed Connectors

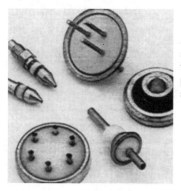

Hermetically sealed headers and terminals and ceramic-to-metal seals used in high temperature and pressure requirements such as jet fuel nozzles.

Connector used in deep-hole oil exploration.

Custom-designed Microelectronic Packages

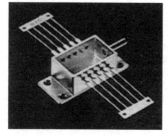

Kovar fiberoptics package with precisely dimensioned tube designed for telecommunications.

Microelectronic packages for hermetically sealed hybrid integrated semi-conductor applications such as in MX missiles.

Exhibit 4 Summary information about divisions

Division	Products	1987 Revenues ($ millions)	Location	Other
Hermetic Seal	Connectors	12	Rosemead, CA	The original HCC business
Glasseal	Connectors	6	Lakewood, NJ	Acquired in June 1983
Sealtron	Connectors	6	Cincinnati, OH	Was wholly owned subsidiary of Glasseal when acquired
Hermetite	Microelectronic packages	10	Avon, MA	Acquired in August 1985

Exhibit 5 Felt probability of budget achievement at time target was set (March 1987)

Division	Al Berger (COO)	Estimate from: Chris Bateman (CFO)	General Manager
Hermetic Seal	100%	100%	95%–98%
Glasseal	100	100	90
Sealtron	100	90	60–65
Hermetite	100	70	80

Exhibit 6 First quarter results – 1988

Criteria	Hermetic Seal			Glasseal			Sealtron			Hermetite		
	MPS	Target	Actual	MPS	Target	Actual	MPS	Target	Actual	MPS	Target	Actual
Sales												
Bookings	2,600	2,800	[2,844]	2,020	NA	(1,645)	1,500	1,600	1,513	1,811	2,000	(1,234)
Shipments	2,600	2,900	2,843	1,815	NA	(1,742)	1,400	1,450	1,442	2,351	2,200	(2,323)
Quality												
Returns (% of shipment)	10%	7%	(14.4%)	3%	NA	(3.5%)	3%	2%	[1.3%]	10%	5%	6.3%
Rework: number of jobs/ percent less than 30 days	60/ 85	40/ 92	(62/ 30)	10/ 80	NA	10/ 80	6/ 70	4/ 75	(9/ 67)	25/ 50	12/ 80	[10/ 82]
Productivity												
Profit (before tax)	650	800	[843]	283	300	(192)	167	175	[195]	(410)	(300)	[(188)]
Efficiency (sales/employee)	60	62	60	57	59	[67]	38	40	38.7	52	59	53
Delinquency ($,%)	220K 6%	0	(460K 10.4%)	80K	0	[48K]	70K	0	(151K)	250K	150K	(368K)

Key: ( ) Below MPS   [ ] Exceed target

Case Study

Patagonia, Inc.

In planning for their company's 1996 fiscal year (ending April 30), managers of Patagonia, Inc., which designed and marketed high-quality outdoor equipment and clothing, decided to implement a form of "open-book management." The Patagonia system, which was called the Workbook Process, was intended to be a single coordinated process that combined the company's strategic planning, budgeting, and quality improvement processes. But more importantly, the Process was designed to make information about all aspects of Patagonia's business available to all employees and to encourage the employees to be an active part of the company's planning, operating review, and decision-making processes.

In September 1997 Karyn Barsa, Patagonia's chief financial officer, reflected on the company's first two years' experience with the Process:

We think [the Workbook Process] has worked quite well. Among other things, we think employees understand better what we're trying to accomplish. We think most employees feel more empowered because we really are encouraging them to share their ideas, and we are listening to those ideas. We have created a language common to all departments. And we have created a much better spirit of teamwork within the company.

That is not to say we can't improve the Process. We don't have good participation from all of our people. Some people don't seem to understand the Process, or they don't want to be bothered by it. And the Process is unquestionably costly in time. We are looking at a number of options for improvement.

THE COMPANY

Patagonia's products were sold: (1) wholesale to specialty outdoor gear retailers in North America, Europe and Japan; (2) through mail order; (3)

through 22 company-owned retail stores in the United States, Japan, and Europe; and (4) through distributors in Italy, Argentina, Chile, Australia, and Korea. In FY 1997 Patagonia grossed over $158 million in sales and employed over 750 people.

Patagonia was founded in 1957 by Yvon Chouinard, an avid and renowned outdoorsman.[1] As a rock climber Yvon was known for having a long list of first ascents, including the North American Wall of El Capitan in Yosemite National Park. Yvon could not get pitons he liked, so he started producing climbing gear in his own blacksmith shop. Soon that shop grew into a machine shop and then into Chouinard Equipment, Ltd. Yvon reflected on the start,

I never intended for my craft to become a business, but every time I returned from the mountains, my head was spinning with ideas for improving the carabiners, crampons, ice axes, and other tools of climbing . . . My partner and I seemed to have a gift for good design.[2]

Yvon's pitons, for example, were made of hardened steel, not soft iron, so they were more reliable. And because they were intended to be removed and reused on a climb they allowed climbers to carry less gear. Others recognized the superiority of Yvon's designs, and by the late 1960s Chouinard Equipment had an estimated 80% of the US market for climbing hardware.

In the late 1960s Yvon shifted his attention to the sale of quality outdoor clothes. His company continued to grow slowly until 1972 when the clothing

---

[1] Much of this history is adapted from Patagonia, Inc., *Defining Quality: A Brief Description of How We Got Here* (1998).
[2] Y. Chouinard, *Patagonia: The Next Hundred Years* (Ventura, CA: Patagonia, 1995), p. 1.

This case was prepared by Professor Kenneth A. Merchant with the assistance of Xuyi (Marcella) Feng.

business took off. One of Yvon's early clothing successes stemmed from the sale of rugby shirts and canvas shorts he had brought back from England.

Over the years the clothing business, which was organized under the Patagonia, Inc. name, thrived. Patagonia added a broad range of company-designed-and-produced items, including rain gear, pile jackets, fleece vests, hats and gloves, sweaters, underwear, and children's clothing. The company produced clothing for just about every intense outdoor pursuit, including backcountry skiing, mountaineering, dog sled racing, whitewater kayaking, surfing, mountain biking, trail running, flyfishing, and sailing. All items of Patagonia clothing were designed for heavy use and built to last. By the late 1980s Patagonia's clothing products had proliferated into 375 different styles. Fueled by periodic breakthroughs that produced revolutionary new fabrics, company sales grew rapidly, as is shown in the revenue figures in Exhibit 1.

In 1984 Yvon and his wife, Malinda, organized the clothing lines, the mail order business, and a chain of retail stores that had been built up under an umbrella legal entity called Lost Arrow Corporation. (The company's 1997 legal structure is shown in Exhibit 2.) The Chouinards still owned 97% of the company.

COMPANY MISSION AND VALUES

Patagonia's mission statement and statement of values are shown in Exhibit 3. At a May 1996 Conference on Corporate Citizenship hosted by US President Clinton, Yvon Chouinard paraphrased Patagonia's mission statement as: "Make the best quality product and cause no unnecessary harm." At Patagonia, "quality" was not reflected just by how long the products lasted; the term described a whole way of doing business. At the Conference, Yvon explained:

It's linked: quality product, quality customer service, quality workplace, quality of life for your employees, even quality of life for all living things on this planet. If you miss any one piece there is a good chance you'll miss it all.

Yvon's efforts to reduce environmental damage began early in the company's history when, in 1971, he noticed the destruction of rock on climbing routes in Yosemite caused by climbers' pitons

being pounded into the rock. In response, starting with the company's 1972 catalog, he began to try to convince the US climbing community to switch to "clean climbing" techniques which involved use of chocks and stoppers which were wedged only by hand and then removed after use.

Yvon was also concerned that the company used up nonrenewable resources and created some pollution. To attempt to create less damage to the environment, Patagonia maintained an active program of environmental activities, including the promotion of environmental issues, design of environmentally responsible products, and encouragement of employee involvement in community affairs. The company set up grants programs mostly focusing on small, grassroots groups interested in wilderness, biodiversity, and habitat protection issues. In one program, Patagonia imposed on itself a tax of 1% of sales or 10% of pretax profit, whichever was greater, and used the money to safeguard and restore the natural environment. The establishment of this "Tithing Program" in 1985 changed the company forever because, as one company publication described it:

We could focus on the bottom line with pride – knowing that if we made money, others would as well. Our motivations for business success became more clear – an essential need in a company culture that resented traditional business regimes – and we were able to recruit from a more diverse pool of applicants.[3]

Through 1998 this program allowed Patagonia to give away more than $13 million to nearly 500 environmental organizations. Patagonia managers also set five-year and one-year environmental goals for each department, tracked environmental performance in considerable detail, and published an annual Environmental Assessment Report.

Rapid growth and maximization of corporate profits were not among Patagonia's goals. Yvon Chouinard explained publicly that the only reason he and Malinda had not sold the company was that they were "pessimistic about the fate of the world and felt a responsibility to do something about it."[4] The Chouinards' bottom-line reason for staying in business was to make money that they could give to

---

[3] Patagonia, p. 24.
[4] Chouinard, p. 6.

environmental causes.[5] They did not want "rampant and senseless growth." They did not want to "exploit the marketplace." They valued "sustainability." Thus they were comfortable with company growth in the 3–5% range.

In 1991 Yvon felt a need to reorient the company more toward "self-sustaining" principles, one of his core values. The Chouinards and key colleagues went on a three-week retreat in the Patagonia region of Argentina to discuss the company's "next 100 years." The group concluded that the company was growing too fast; at current rates of growth it would be a billion-dollar company in 11 years. Yvon said:

> Can a company that wants to make the best quality outdoor clothing in the world become the size of Nike? Can a three-star French restaurant with 10 tables retain its three stars and add 50 tables? Can a village in Vermont encourage tourism (but hope tourists go home on Sunday evening), be pro development, woo high-tech "clean" companies (so the local children won't run off to jobs in New York), and still maintain its quality of life? Can you have it all? I don't think so.[6]

When Yvon returned to Ventura, he wrote an essay that was published in the company's Fall 1991 catalog. The essay proclaimed, "We are limiting Patagonia's growth in the United States with the eventual goal of halting growth altogether."

The low-growth constraint became clear to everyone in the company when, after the end of the 1994 fiscal year, Patagonia's president announced the highest levels of growth in sales and profits in the company's history. But Yvon Chouinard changed the mood of the meeting when he announced, morosely, "This is really bad."

WORKPLACE AND ORGANIZATION

Patagonia had a unique culture. The corporation was comprised of many employees "who share [Yvon's] passion for the environment – and his thinly disguised contempt for conventional business."[7] (These employees often refer to themselves as "dirt bags" or "Patagoniacs.") The company's

dress code was ultra casual (mostly Patagonia attire). The cafeteria served only health foods at low prices. The company offered flexible work arrangements, such as flextime, job-sharing, and work-at-home programs. While the employees worked hard, they were allowed to take breaks during the day in order to climb, paddle, or surf. (Good surfing could be found only a few blocks from corporate headquarters, and employees were encouraged to store their surfboards on company grounds.)

Patagonia's relatively flat organization is shown in Exhibit 4. Dave Olsen, the CEO/president, joined Patagonia in June 1996. The top-management team consisted of eight managers. The company's middle management layer consisted of approximately 30 people.

The company culture favored minimum bureaucracy and maximum informality. No one in the company, not even Yvon Chouinard, who was still active in some company affairs, nor senior company officers, had a private office. Because of the lack of private offices many business meetings were held in the cafeteria. Top-level managers had little respect for organizational lines of authority, and they often dealt directly with employees at many organization levels. For example, as one first-level supervisor explained:

> I can walk right up to the CEO's desk. There are no walls. I can even walk up to the owner's desk anytime and talk to him. I don't need to go through secretaries. We don't have secretaries.

Every two weeks top management held an Open Forum. All employees were invited to attend. Management would provide company updates and answer questions.

Patagonia's headquarters site included a child daycare center that offered a variety of programs for children aged from eight weeks to 10-years old. Patagonia managers observed that most corporations assume the attitude of "That's their problem" when dealing with employees' parental responsibilities. At Patagonia, on the other hand, managers believed that quality childcare is a problem belonging to everyone. Thus, both parents were allowed two months paid leave after a birth. Mothers were encouraged to continue nursing when they were back at work. Parents were encouraged to take breaks and have lunch with their children. Parents were allowed to keep young babies right at their

---

[5] Ibid., p. 6.
[6] Ibid., pp. 3–4.
[7] E. O. Welles. "Lost in Patagonia," *INC*. (August 1992), p. 46.

desk. Eligible employees were even allowed to take up to five workdays off during the school year to participate in their child's classroom activities. The company believed that these policies were beneficial to the company, the employees, and the children. It created less anxiety and frustration in the parents and the children and, consequently, increased work satisfaction and productivity.[8]

EMPLOYEE COMPENSATION

Patagonia's system for allocating salary increases was quite typical. Each employee had individual annual MBO-type goals. Immediate superiors evaluated their subordinates' performances and gave them salary increases from a raise pool.

The company's bonus system was quite informal. If the company was performing well all employees were given a $1,000 bonus just before Christmas and another $1,000 at the end of the fiscal year.

In FY 1997, however, Patagonia managers eliminated the Christmas bonus because company sales were lagging behind plan. Dave Olsen thought that he could create a small bonus pool ($80,000) in the last four months of the year, and he recommended that this pool be divided among 25 worthy employees. This idea was discussed at one of the company's quarterly Open Forums, and many employees raised fairness concerns. They asked, for example, "Who will decide how this pool is allocated?" "What criteria will be used to allocate it?" "Shouldn't the allocation criteria be made public so that employees can understand what they must do to earn a portion of it?" Since answers to all of these questions were not immediately forthcoming, the employees decided that nobody should be given a bonus. They turned the $80,000 back to the company!

Company managers did not expect to move toward a more formal individually oriented bonus system anytime in the near future. Karyn Barsa, Patagonia's CFO, explained that, "We have a difficult time quantifying individual contributions. There are a lot of variables that make up individual performance, and we don't have the systems in

place to hold employees individually accountable."

Dave Olsen, in one of his first moves after joining Patagonia, did create a formal company-wide profit-sharing plan. This plan became effective in the 1997 fiscal year. A pool of 15% of adjusted[9] corporate profits before tax was allocated to departments proportionately based on base salaries. Department managers decided subjectively how to allocate their portion of the pool to individual employees. Dave wanted the department managers to allocate the pool to employees according to merit, but most chose instead to allocate it in equal percentages of base salaries.

PLANNING AND BUDGETING

Until the 1990s Patagonia did not have a formal planning process. Yvon focused on products, and demand almost always exceeded supply. Money was not scarce, and many expenditures were made on an intuitive basis. For example, Yvon was "notorious for hiring people on impulse – people he met surfing or fishing, people he believed could bring an unfettered, intuitive feel to the company."[10] A former Patagonia CEO was quoted as saying:

> Yvon has no respect for banking and accounting people – people who wear coats and ties. It's almost a loathing. But that stuff is part of business. It's almost like hating your left arm.[11]

Largely because of the lack of attention paid to financial affairs and business planning, Patagonia faced its first crisis, in 1991. The economy was in the midst of a recession, and the company was facing more significant competition. Mainstream apparel makers, specialized niche companies, and cataloguers such as L. L. Bean, Eddie Bauer, and Lands End were copying Patagonia's better-selling products, and some were offering their products at lower prices. Sales were flat; Patagonia had to dump inventory into the market below cost; and profits plunged. Patagonia's bank reduced the company's line of credit, forcing the company to look for alternative sources of credit.

---

[8] Patagonia was named in the 1993 book *The 100 Best Companies to Work for in America*. It has also made *Working Mother* magazine's list of the top 100 list of best companies to work for 10 consecutive times, and was listed in this magazine's top-10 list three times.

[9] The adjustment involved adding back Yvon and Malinda Chouinard's bonuses, but not their base salaries.
[10] Welles, p. 50.
[11] Ibid., p. 48.

The financial problems forced Patagonia managers to take a number of steps. They hired some more professional managers, kept a closer eye on credit, cut the number of clothing styles, and laid off 120 people, 20% of its work force. (The layoff, in particular, demoralized the work force.) They also opened the company's books to employees to show them why expenses needed to be cut.

The problems also forced Patagonia's managers to become more concerned about setting plans and allocating scarce resources effectively. The planning process and thinking was still quite centralized, with only the top management team deeply involved in it. Yvon and Malinda Chouinard, and others, were not pleased with the move toward more formal planning; one manager said, "[They] hate it." But company performance rebounded nicely: 1993 was a boom year and performance improved steadily from there.

In the summer of 1994 Alison May, Patagonia's then-general manager, conducted a Quality Survey within the company that asked employees, "What do we have to do to make your department 'a perfect 10'?" One of the findings was that nearly everyone in the company was unhappy with the company's budgeting process. Employees felt ignorant of the company's plans and other departments' activities and, generally, not in control of their destiny. The Workbook Process grew out of that discontent.

THE WORKBOOK PROCESS

The Workbook Process involved: (1) making every department's and the corporation's plans visible to all employees; (2) making monthly department and corporate financial and operating reports visible to all employees; (3) investing substantial time and resources to train every employee in financial management so that they would understand the information made available to them; (4) encouraging all employees to become actively involved in the planning and operating review processes.

The Workbook Process actually grew from an idea that was introduced only in the Mail Order Department for planning for FY 1995. The Mail Order experiment was judged to be a success, so the Process was extended company-wide the following year.

Patagonia managers hoped that the Workbook Process would provide multiple benefits:

1. Employees would better understand how their job fits within the strategy of the company. They would be more likely to think strategically because they would be allowed easy access to the highest levels of planning within the company and would have the knowledge to understand it.

2. Employees would be encouraged to take other groups' resources and objectives into consideration in their planning, both because all departments' goals and activities would be visible and because all departments would share a common language.

3. Employees would have an enhanced sense of control of their own destiny because they would be actively involved in the planning processes and could track their department's, and the corporation's, progress.

Many corporate managers resist the open sharing of information with employees. Traditionally they worry that an open book system might result in competitors gaining access to the company's important confidential information or that information highlighting the fact that some individuals and groups have missed their goals might be demoralizing. Sharing information also weakens managers' power base because selective disclosure of information can be used to control and manipulate people. These concerns did not arise at Patagonia, however. Patagonia's top-level managers, at least, embraced the open book system. They thought it was consistent with the company's culture and, particularly, the company's respect for employees and concern for employees' quality of life.

In preparation for FY 1996 planning, managers of each of the 24 workgroups into which the company had been divided were provided Workbook Process training. These managers, who were all middle-level managers or higher, in turn trained the members of their group. In November 1994 a planning manual, called the "Workbook Workbook," was sent to each of the workgroup heads. The 40-page Workbook explained the intent and goals of the Workbook Process and described the 11 steps in the Process. Here are descriptions of each of the 11 steps, taken from the Workbook Workbook:

Step 1: Create a mission statement

A mission statement addresses your work group's fundamental reason for being and specifies the functional role that the workgroup is going to play within Patagonia and the market as a whole. It should not describe your workgroup as it is, but rather it should present your vision for the workgroup. Among the suggestions for creating a successful mission statement are: (1) involve your workgroup, (2) keep it short, and (3) remember, this is only a first step. (Don't spend an inordinate amount of time creating the mission statement.)

Step 2: Develop FY '96 objectives

The objectives should follow as a natural next step. At the start, assume that your baseline operating expenses for FY '96 will be no greater than FY '95. In developing the objectives, decide what would be necessary to have your workgroup be rated as a perfect "10," identify objectives in each important area, and involve everyone in the workgroup. Finally, prioritize objectives and limit the number of objectives requiring resources above last year's budget to three.

[This section of the Workbook provided some information regarding Patagonia's corporate focus for FY '96. Listed were nine specific goals in the areas of product design, distribution, operations, environment, and personnel/training. Three of these goals were: (1) to have no industrially grown cotton in any company products by Spring '96; (2) complete the domestic warehouse relocation and move; and (3) complete development of an Asia distribution strategy. This section also listed preliminary financial objectives for sales, gross profit margin, operating expenses, and net profit.]

Step 3: Identify cross-functional objectives to send to appropriate departments

Separate your prioritized objectives into two lists: internal workgroup objectives (those requiring *no* assistance from a department outside your own), and cross-functional workgroup objectives (those requiring some assistance from other departments). Send cross-functional workgroup objectives to each department affected by them.

Step 4: Quantify objectives

For each internal objective, make your best guess as to the estimated capital expenditure, operating expense, and estimated return.

For each cross-functional objective *sent* to another department, meet with the senior manager of that workgroup. That senior manager will provide estimates of the cost and required resources (people, equipment, etc.) and the time involved to complete the objective. For each cross-functional objective *received*, meet with the affected parties and provide estimates of the total cost and time involved for your workgroup. Also let them know the priority your workgroup has assigned to the objective.

Step 5: Prioritize all objectives

Take the objectives your workgroup developed and reprioritize them with the cross-functional objectives you have received from other workgroups. Communicate back the priorities you have given the cross-functional objectives and the reasons for the priorities.

Step 6: Develop the objectives matrix

Develop the objectives matrix that is designed to organize the objectives and ensure that every aspect of them is considered. For each objective, show the person responsible, the cost, the financial return or benefit, and the timing. [Exhibit 5 shows some hypothetical objectives matrix examples.]

Step 7: The off-site senior managers' meeting

This meeting is designed to allow the senior managers to meet, discuss outstanding cross-functional issues, and allocate additional expense dollars.

Step 8: Modify objectives matrix based on feedback from off-site meeting

Each department should work on finalizing their mission statement and fiscal year objectives for inclusion in the Workbook.

Step 9: Complete budget worksheets

By now the senior managers group has agreed to budget priorities for FY '96. You are now ready to complete the process of defining your budget and completing the budget worksheets. Assume a baseline operating budget equal to FY '95 and a zero capital expenditure budget unless an increase or a capital expenditure was approved at the senior managers' off-site meeting. Complete the budget worksheets for personnel, monthly expense breakdown, capital expenditures, personal computers or other DP/MIS equipment, information services, travel and entertainment, and outside services (e.g. contract labor, consulting, legal).

Step 10: Develop back sections of the workbook

Consider which aspects of your business you would like to include in the back sections of your Workbook. The nature of these sections will depend entirely on the focus of each workgroup. [For example, Mail Order chose to include the following back sections in its Workbook: (1) marketing plan, (2) advertising plan, (3) customer service, (4) customer comments, (5) catalog comments, (6) product comments, (7) training notes, (8) personal performance notes, (9) team notes. The comments and notes sections provided space for employees to record observations in one centralized, convenient location.]

Step 11: Distribute and implement the workbooks

Senior managers should distribute copies of the Workbooks to all workgroup members and briefly describe each section and the purpose it serves. Then give your employees time to read the Workbook. Hold another meeting to allow them to ask specific questions.

The objectives and financial statements should be updated on a monthly basis. You will need to meet as a workgroup on a monthly basis. Go through each objective and have the responsible person report on its status. If the due date is not appropriate, consider how this will affects others' work and how you will deal with this impact. Update the financial figures. Go through the figures and show employees where there are differences, and discuss their impact.

Exhibit 6 shows a Gantt chart showing the timing of the Workbook Process for FY 1996.

Each month a reporting package was distributed to all employees. This package included income and cash flow statements compared with objectives. It also included a written commentary explaining trends and reasons for favorable and unfavorable variances. This commentary provided, for example, more detail on sales performance by line of business (e.g. wholesale, mail order, retail) and specific, major sources and uses of cash. Employees who did not understand the information were encouraged to direct questions to their superiors or to accounting staff.

During the year, the workgroups were supposed to hold one meeting each month to review actual financial and operating results and to monitor progress toward the achievement of their specific objectives. Some workgroups actually scheduled two meetings, one focused on the Workbook-objectives versus actual results comparison, the other a working session focused on new or different actions that might be taken. Other workgroups met less frequently.

FAVORABLE REACTIONS TO THE PROCESS

Most employees' reactions to the Workbook Process were favorable. Here are some representative reactions.

Sharon McAlexander (Manager of Logistics):

In the 1991 crisis, the company gathered everybody together, and ideas started flowing. The Workbook Process kept the ideas flowing. It causes a backflow of information from the people doing the day-to-day work to the top. People were encouraged to want to share their ideas, and they were given enough training that they could make educated suggestions. This is good because a lot of people at the top don't have a lot of knowledge as to how things work at the bottom . . .

It's hard to attribute specific actions we took to the Workbook Process. Our group is very savvy. We're right on top of things. But maybe the Process made our people understand their jobs better, and maybe it made them care more . . .

The main benefits of the Workbook Process are intangible. It created an interest in what was going on.

Last year, we achieved all of our objectives. That gave us a great deal of pride.

Julie Ringler (Production Department):

There is benefit to having access to the information. It has allowed me to ask questions, such as why are mail order sales so good or retail sales not so good? . . .

Every month we talk about it. If sales are down, I want to know why. The Process gives you a reason for asking. If the company is not doing well, maybe it's because I need to order materials earlier.

Megan Montgomery (Manager of Marketing Services):

We were all used to setting goals. But it was neat to be part of a team in setting goals. It's nice to have a plan, and it's nice to have group goals (in addition to individual goals). It's great for teamwork . . .

We got to see how all the pieces of the company work, to see how many "cooks it takes in the kitchen to get the meal made." . . .

Twice we discovered that we had the same goal as another department, such as to streamline a process. In both cases, we decided to work on the goal together . . .

Having a monthly meeting keeps you focused. We ask the question, "How's that goal coming?" . . .

Before the 1991 crisis, company finances and most company operations were a mystery to me. After the crisis, everybody pitched in. I can now make suggestions, and I can see the effect on the bottom line. I feel good about that.

Everybody here feels empowered because they feel they can make a difference. We don't want to lose that.

CONCERNS FOR THE FUTURE

Senior Patagonia managers were generally pleased with the Workbook Process, but they recognized it could be improved. They identified three changes that should be made as soon as possible:

1. Accelerate the preparation of the monthly financial figures. Currently, the numbers were reported only a month or two after the month end. This frustrated some employees because, as one said, "We're keyed up about December, but we can look only at October numbers."

2. Computerize the Process. Too much paperwork was required.

3. Offer more training. There was evidence that some nonfinancially oriented people, particularly, did not understand all the needed concepts. Some of their numbers were inconsistent. In addition, more training was needed to help employees understand how to spread their forecasts across the months. Most of the annual forecasts were reasonably accurate, but the monthly variances were sometimes large because employees had not previously been asked to forecast by month.

Other issues were more complex or more controversial. One concern was that while a majority of employees participated actively and well in the Workbook Process, some employees seemed not to want to participate. Some employees did not want to participate from the start. Most, however, were initially excited about the Process, and that excitement made it worthwhile for them to participate. But for some the excitement faded as time passed. By the end of the year, fewer employees were taking the time to refer to the Workbooks and follow through as they were supposed to. It was hard to schedule meetings and to initiate meaningful discussions when some employees did not make the Process a priority.

Employee participation was particularly poor where department heads did not believe in the Process. Top-level managers estimated that perhaps two thirds of the department heads were committed to the Process, but that one third were not. They held the required meetings, but they were just going through the motions. One manager thought the problem was just that some people, particularly those in more creative positions, are not "numbers-oriented" and do not like formal management structures. However, another manager said, "It's not a right brain/left brain issue. It's just an attitude. Some people seem not to understand the benefits. They don't think the Process is worth the time."

It is true that the Process was costly in time. The planning meetings were intensive; preparing the Workbooks required a lot of paperwork; doing a good job of reading other departments' Workbooks consumed a lot of time; and then workgroups and subgroups were supposed to meet monthly to monitor progress. Was the Process too complex? Could it be simplified? If so, how?

Some employees even advised top management to discontinue the Process or, possibly, to use it only periodically, perhaps every five years. They argued that the Process was a useful one-time experience because it helped many employees understand better how the company worked and how their jobs interfaced with others. However, they noted that most of the benefits had already been accrued, at least for the current work force, while most of the costs of the Process would continue unabated.

A second concern was in the quality of the objectives and plans that were set. It was easy to judge at the end of the year whether objectives in some areas were accomplished, but it was not so easy in some other areas. For example, it was relatively easy to judge the accomplishment of the following 1997 objectives:

- "Utilize tree-free paper in 80% of our non-catalog printed materials." (An Environmental Focus objective for the Art Services workgroup)

- "Identify five systems or values within the company that are not good representatives of our image and strive to correct them by suggesting alternatives" (An Image Focus objective for the Logistics workgroup)

- "Transition [the company's on-site corporate child-care center's] quality rating from an overall rating of '7' to '9'." (A Quality Focus objective for the Family Services workgroup)

On the other hand, it was difficult to judge the accomplishment of the following objectives:

- "Reduce amount of files here and off-site." (An Environmental Focus objective for the Legal workgroup)

- "Improve internal processes to speed project completion." (A Quality Focus objective for the Information Systems workgroup)

- "Expand our tracking system for worldwide inventory turn levels to better manage the planning and distribution of inventories." (An Inventory Focus objective for the Logistics workgroup)

Another issue in the quality-of-plans area concerned the number of objectives that were being set. Some workgroups identified only three objectives. Was that enough? Others did not follow directions and identified 20 or more objectives mentioning the accomplishment of specific projects and/or covering virtually all aspects of their operation, sometimes without any prioritization of those objectives. Was that too many? And with any list of objectives, was prioritization necessary, or should all identified objectives be considered equally important, or at least worthy of achievement?

A third concern related to the timing of what was an annual process. Should the company plan beyond a one-year horizon? Should the Process involve some kind of rolling planning, with periodic, formal updates to the full plan?

A final concern related to incentives. Does the company have the right mix of employee incentives? Should some compensation be linked to the accomplishment of Workbook Process goals?

Exhibit 1 Patagonia, Inc., Lost Arrow Corporation – consolidated net sales, FY 1980–97

Fiscal year ended	Sales (millions)	% change
June 1980	$3,125	
June 1981	5,020	60.6
June 1982	8,350	66.3
June 1983	16,383	96.2
June 1984	22,449	37.0
June 1985	31,156	38.8
June 1986	36,919	18.5
June 1987	46,508	26.0
June 1988	66,786	43.6
June 1989	73,561	10.1
June 1990	86,136	17.1
April 1991	103,725	20.4
April 1992	115,703	11.5
April 1993	112,194	(3.0)
April 1994	125,869	12.2
April 1995	148,642	18.1
April 1996	154,067	3.6
April 1997	158,476	2.9

Exhibit 2 Legal structure

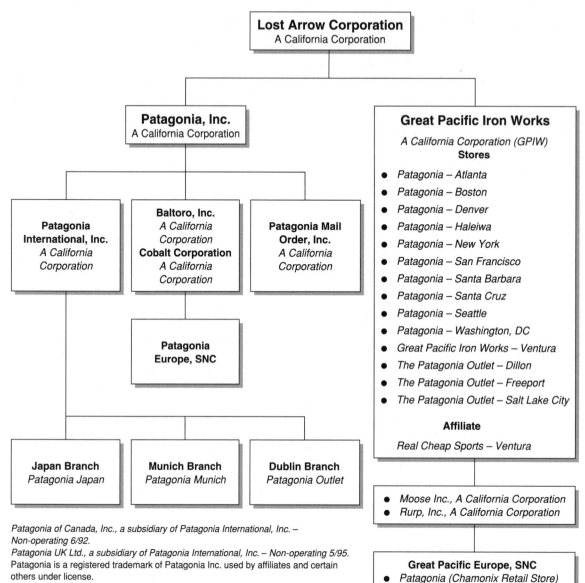

Lost Arrow Corporation
A California Corporation

Patagonia, Inc.
A California Corporation

Great Pacific Iron Works

A California Corporation (GPIW)
Stores

- Patagonia – Atlanta
- Patagonia – Boston
- Patagonia – Denver
- Patagonia – Haleiwa
- Patagonia – New York
- Patagonia – San Francisco
- Patagonia – Santa Barbara
- Patagonia – Santa Cruz
- Patagonia – Seattle
- Patagonia – Washington, DC
- Great Pacific Iron Works – Ventura
- The Patagonia Outlet – Dillon
- The Patagonia Outlet – Freeport
- The Patagonia Outlet – Salt Lake City

Affiliate

Real Cheap Sports – Ventura

Patagonia
International, Inc.
A California
Corporation

Baltoro, Inc.
A California
Corporation
Cobalt Corporation
A California
Corporation

Patagonia Mail
Order, Inc.
A California
Corporation

Patagonia
Europe, SNC

Japan Branch
Patagonia Japan

Munich Branch
Patagonia Munich

Dublin Branch
Patagonia Outlet

- Moose Inc., A California Corporation
- Rurp, Inc., A California Corporation

Great Pacific Europe, SNC
- Patagonia (Chamonix Retail Store)

Patagonia of Canada, Inc., a subsidiary of Patagonia International, Inc. –
Non-operating 6/92.
Patagonia UK Ltd., a subsidiary of Patagonia International, Inc. – Non-operating 5/95.
Patagonia is a registered trademark of Patagonia Inc. used by affiliates and certain
others under license.
Revised 7/96. Printed on recycled paper.

Exhibit 3 Mission statement and statement of values

PATAGONIA MISSION STATEMENT

To deliver innovative, excellent, useful products and service to our customers; to reduce or reverse the environmental harm we cause; to honor our obligations to each other and to our stakeholders; to earn a sufficient profit to achieve these objectives, but without the pursuit of growth for growth's sake.

PATAGONIA STATEMENT OF VALUES

We run a business in a time of environmental crisis and historic social change. This business is our reason for being together. We value our jobs. We value our products. But we also value the earth whose life is threatened.

This creates a moral dilemma for all of us. In pursuing our livelihood we create significant environmental harm. We consume irreplaceable resources. We pollute the earth's air, water and soil, and we do so daily. So what do we truly value: economic gain or the health of the earth?

This dilemma, like a Zen koan, won't resolve itself; it can't be talked through. In the meantime, we all have to make choices and act.

The Board has developed a statement of values: it is a moral framework for making decisions. It is as simple as it can be; with focus on the necessary rather than the desirable. It reflects values already at work here as well as values we need to strengthen:

- Everyone here, in the course of our ongoing daily work and as part of our individual and mutual job responsibility, works to reduce or reverse the harmful environmental impact of everything we do.
- Our products must be innovative, excellent, and useful. The world does not need more clutter.
- We will improve, or fight for the reversal of, the quality of life in all communities in which we participate.
- We will make a profit and yet be true to our principles.
- We tithe 1% of sales or 10% of profit, whichever is greater, as a self-imposed environmental tax.
- We promote environmental activism at all levels of the company.
- In management, we value collaboration, openness and maximum simplicity.

Exhibit 4 Organization structure (at the beginning of FY 1997)

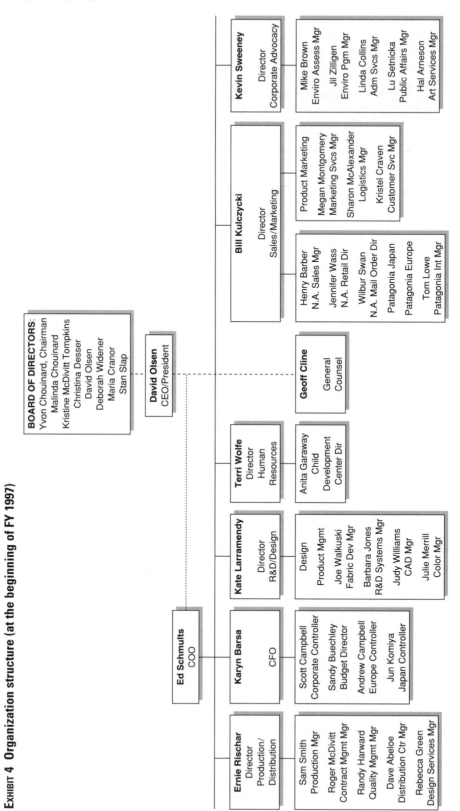

Exhibit 5 Objectives matrix – hypothetical examples

Example No. 1: Mail Order

Marketing Objectives

1) Lower cost per acquired customer by 10% to reduce Mail Order's operating expenses. Test more cost-effective methods (higher response rates, lower in-mail costs) to add customers to our file.

	Pers. Resp. (a)	Dept.'s Invld. (b)	Date Due	Date Comp.	Staff Req. (c)	Addit. Staff Req. (d)	Additional Cost (e)			Expected Return Benefit (i)	Overall Priority (j)
							Operating Expense (f)	Personnel Expense (g)	Capital Expend. (h)		
● Test Introductory Piece Fall '94	JT	Creative	8/1/94		3	0	$100.00	$100.00	$0.00	$200.00	1
● Improve ad design, placement	JT	Creative	9/1/94		3	0	$100.00	$0.00	$0.00	$200.00	3
● Refine internal reporting	JT	Log., DP	10/1/94		4	1	$100.00	$100.00	$0.00	$200.00	6

Operating Objectives

1) Upgrade computer hardware and software to improve customer service and reduce operating expense as a % of sales.

	Pers. Resp. (a)	Dept.'s Invld. (b)	Date Due	Date Comp.	Staff Req. (c)	Addit. Staff Req. (d)	Operating Expense (f)	Personnel Expense (g)	Capital Expend. (h)	Expected Return Benefit (i)	Overall Priority (j)
● Operationalize 2 homebase stations	DG		7/1/94		1	0	$100.00	$0.00	$100.00	$200.00	2
● Voice mail catalog requests	DG		8/1/94		1	0	$0.00	$0.00	$100.00	$200.00	7
● Move laser printer to CS area	SO		9/1/94		1	0	$0.00	$0.00	$100.00	$200.00	10

Example No. 2: Finance

Operating Objectives

1) Reduce no. of days required to produce monthly financial statements by five days.

	Pers. Resp. (a)	Dept.'s Invld. (b)	Date Due	Date Comp.	Staff Req. (c)	Addit. Staff Req. (d)	Operating Expense (f)	Personnel Expense (g)	Capital Expend. (h)	Expected Return Benefit (i)	Overall Priority (j)
● Install purchasing application	LN	DP	5/1/95		2	0	$xxxx.xx			#########	1
● Develop interface to A/P & MFG	KB	DP	7/31/95		2	1	$xxxx.xx	$xxxxx.xx	$xxxx.xx	#########	3
● Complete Euro VTA interface	SB/RH	DP	5/1/95		3	0	$xxxx.xx			#########	
● Complete B of A cash mgmt download	SB/TC		3/1/95		2	0	$0.00		$0.00	#########	

353

EXHIBIT 6 FY 1996 Workbook Process timeline

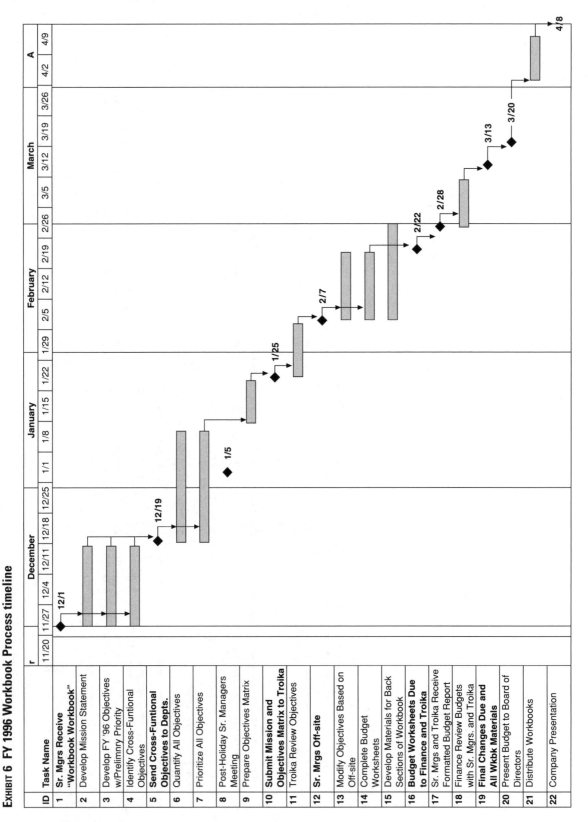

Case Study

VisuSon, Inc.: Business Stress Testing

On the evening of Friday, October 10, 2008, Linda Ott sat alone in her office contemplating the year to come. Linda was the founder of VisuSon, Inc. (VSI), a small manufacturer of medical ultrasound equipment, and the only CEO the company had ever had. Linda reflected on the meeting she had had that afternoon with Jonathon Foley, VSI's CFO. At the meeting, they reviewed the company's results for the third quarter just ended and discussed projections for the rest of 2008 and for 2009. The last item on the agenda – the look at 2009 – dominated their discussion and now occupied Linda's thoughts.

Sales were at a record high in the third quarter of 2008. Furthermore, the company's book of confirmed orders provided ample assurance that the fourth quarter, and 2008 as a whole, would continue VSI's established pattern of double-digit growth (see Exhibits 1–3).

But there were dark clouds on the horizon. The Dow Jones Industrial Average had just closed at 8,451, nearly 20% below its level of a week before and down 40% from a year ago. Of more direct importance to VSI, the February collapse of the auction-rate securities market produced some delays in orders and collections, while many US hospitals, VSI's largest group of customers, scrambled to replace their auction-rate debt with alternative sources of capital. Both Linda and Jon believed that this one problem had reduced sales growth for the year by several percentage points from what they had projected at the same meeting a year ago. Both Linda and Jon agreed that a wider credit crisis would negatively impact 2009 sales, but there was no historical precedent on which to base a reliable forecast.

Linda worried about the near-term impact on earnings and the long-term strategic impact of a slowdown while VSI prepared to release its first entirely new product platform in several years. The new platform accounted for nearly 30% of VSI's research and development budget plus more than $10 million in capital expenditures over the last two years. Jon, however, had cautioned against "fixating on sunk costs," as he put it. He believed the company should be focused on cash flow and VSI's own access to financing as much as customer demand. As Linda pored over the numbers and considered various scenarios, she wondered whether Jon might be right.

ULTRASONOGRAPHY

Medical devices for ultrasound imaging (ultrasonography) use high-frequency sound waves to generate graphical representations of soft tissue, organs and blood flow. This often can be accomplished non-invasively through the application of probes, called transducers, to the surface of the patient's skin. In some important applications, transducers are inserted into body cavities or even into blood vessels to produce better images. Modern ultrasonography equipment is capable of producing moving 3-D images of internal body structures in real time. With the use of so-called doppler technology and color display, the speed and direction of fluid flow can be accurately measured and displayed. Ultrasonography is generally a less expensive form of radiology than magnetic resonance imaging (MRI) and computed tomography (CT). In contrast to CT and X-Ray imaging, ultrasonography does not expose the patient to potentially harmful radiation. Consequently, ultrasonography has developed into the most common form of radiology for some areas of medicine. Cardiology and obstetrics/gynecology, for example, provide important applications for ultrasonography.

This case was prepared by Research Assistant David P. Huelsbeck and Professor Kenneth A. Merchant.

By 2008, the global market for ultrasonography equipment was dominated by four large medical device manufactures that were themselves divisions of global conglomerates. Industry analysts estimated that Philips Healthcare, Siemens Healthcare, GE Healthcare, and Toshiba together controlled approximately 80% of the worldwide market. But the medical ultrasound market remained quite dynamic and innovative with more than a dozen smaller competitors vying for the remaining share. In addition to new and niche competitors from North America and Europe, new entrants into the global market were emerging from other parts of the world, particularly China. Historically, as smaller competitors established themselves and grew, they were often acquired and absorbed by one of the four dominant players.

Rapidly developing technology and above average growth drove the dynamism of the ultrasonography equipment industry. The US domestic market for medical ultrasound had grown at 4 to 6% annually for the last decade. Certain segments, especially cardiology and so-called hand-carried ultrasound (HCU), were projected to grow much faster than the overall market. By 2008, industry analysts believed that the US market, which accounted for more than 40% of the global market, had reached saturation. New sales were primarily replacing older technology. In contrast, markets in the developing world were expected to grow at annual rates above 5% for at least the next five to seven years.

COMPANY BACKGROUND

VSI manufactured its ultrasonography systems at a plant in Apple Valley, California, and sold them worldwide through a network of independent distributors. The firm began as Visutech Partners in 1998, commercializing and licensing novel signal processing and visualization algorithms pioneered by Linda Ott's former academic research laboratory.

After several years of initial development efforts, the fledgling firm signed a licensing agreement with Bainbridge Manufacturing. At the time, Bainbridge was a contract manufacturer of components for the medical ultrasound market. It possessed considerable manufacturing expertise but lacked proprietary technology of its own. Bainbridge hoped to use the licensed technology to move up

from lower margin contract manufacturing into the more profitable market for integrated ultrasonography systems. By the time Bainbridge's new system had won approval from the US Food and Drug Administration, Visutech had merged with a unit of Bainbridge, forming VSI with Linda as the Chief Executive and the former head of the Bainbridge unit as the newly independent firm's Chief Operating Officer. Linda's former principal research collaborator, Dr. Simon Lee, was retained as Director of Engineering (see Exhibit 4).

As a new firm entering a market dominated by much larger firms, VSI chose to target a mid-tier niche. It focused on cardiology applications where it believed its proprietary technology conferred the greatest advantage. VSI targeted its initial offerings well. Within its first six years, its systems were in use in hospitals and medical practices across all 50 states and in most countries in Western Europe. One major competitor responded to VSI's entry into their market by negotiating an agreement under which they resold VSI's top-of-the-line system under their own brand. Though nearly 70% of its revenues still came from the domestic market, with the addition of two global distributors, VSI's expansion into Asia and Latin America had begun.

VISUSON, INC. IN 2008

By the start of 2008, VSI had grown to just over 200 full-time employees. Of this number, roughly half were in manufacturing. The engineering department employed a staff of 25 scientists and engineers supported by a dozen technicians. As most sales were handled through distributors, the sales and marketing staff totaled just 25 employees. The accounting and finance, information technology, human resources and payroll, and legal staffs, all reporting to Jon Foley, made up the remainder.

As medical diagnostic devices, VSI's products were subject to extensive regulations by a number of governmental authorities. Chief among these was the US Food and Drug Administration (FDA). In addition to its role of overseeing and approving pre-clinical testing of VSI's products, the FDA also oversaw registration of VSI's manufacturing facility and compliance with the FDA Quality System Regulation. Consequently, all of VSI's manufacturing employees were required to learn and maintain proficiency with the company's stringent quality control and recording systems. Together with the skills and training required for the manufacturing process, this slowed the process of bringing newly hired manufacturing employees up to full productivity and placed a premium on the retention of skilled employees. VSI's only seasonal or part-time employees were clerical. Accounting and legal temps were used to fill occasional staffing shortages.

Beyond the impact it had on the manufacturing process, regulation drove the new product release process. All of VSI's products were required to obtain pre-market clearance as FDA 510(k) Class II devices before they could be sold in the domestic market. Typically the process of pre-market notification and clearance for VSI's products required two to three months, but for the most innovative products it could take substantially longer. For example, the process of earning clearance for VSI's first intravenous transducer catheter required well over a year.

VSI's systems were modular platforms, enabling incremental expansion or enhancement of their functionality. As transducer technology advanced, VSI introduced new and improved probes. These new components could be added to existing platforms. Frequently this necessitated concurrent upgrades to the processing and control software. Less frequently, VSI upgraded the digital signal processing unit at the core of each system. Since the introduction of VSI's original platform, the Alpha-PD, it had introduced just one new platform, the smaller and less costly Delta-CV. In 2007, both platforms were enhanced and were now marketed as Alpha-PDx and Delta-CVx. Customers with older devices were able to purchase upgrades to bring their existing devices up to the latest standard.

Sales to new customers typically resulted from a lengthy process. In general the time from initial contact with a VSI distributor to the final delivery and acceptance was between 12 and 18 months. Existing customers periodically purchased new probes or other system upgrades, but even these smaller sales could normally be measured in months from inception to delivery. Platform sales to new customers and often to existing customers were competitive. It was not uncommon for customers to require competing vendors to place equipment at the customer's location for direct comparison and evaluation. For especially promising or demanding accounts, VSI provided not only equipment but

staff sonographers to augment the distributor representatives in demonstrating equipment and training customer personnel.

Due to the length of the sales cycle, VSI began each year with a strong indication of the volume of sales to be expected in the coming year. For more than two thirds of their annual platform sales, the sales cycle was already underway before the beginning of the year. Moreover, VSI kept careful track of its end customers. The company's knowledge of its customers and their applications for its systems were invaluable in forecasting the number who would purchase upgrades. This helped VSI develop quarterly and annual sales targets for its distributors.

THE BUDGETING PROCESS

The overall market for medical ultrasound equipment had historically expanded at an annual growth rate of 4–6%, and the market segments on which VSI focused grew at an even faster clip. Thus, from the early years of the firm, VSI's management systems were designed to allow the firm to cope with rapid growth. The budgeting process was a key element of the firm's management system. The budget provided the foundation for VSI's planning, control and incentive systems.

VSI's planning and budgeting cycle started 13 months prior to the start of the company's fiscal year (see Exhibit 5). It began with the annual meeting of the Radiological Society of North America (RSNA), which was held in late November of each year. This professional conference was well attended by radiologists and other physicians from across North America and beyond. It also featured an exhibit space where virtually all of the radiology equipment vendors came to show their latest offerings. The meeting was an opportunity for VSI to meet with its most important North American distributors, key customers and prospects. Initial feedback gathered at RSNA allowed VSI sales and marketing to develop business forecasts for the coming year.

Coincident with the RSNA meeting, industry analysts would release their annual updates of market growth, market share, and five-year forecasts. VSI did not rely on these market analyses for forecasting the next year's sales. The state of the sales pipeline and distributor quota commitments were far more useful for near-term sales forecasting. But the market analyses aided VSI's marketing team in planning and positioning the firm and its products for the years beyond.

Engineering managers, together with product managers from the marketing team, would begin finalizing specifics and features for any new products to be introduced at the next year's RSNA meeting shortly after they returned from the current year's meeting. This was necessary as the FDA pre-market certification process required months and needed to be successfully concluded ahead of the next meeting. A detailed understanding of the features of the product line was required in order to anticipate unit costs and relative market competitiveness as well as to develop pricing plans. Engineering personnel, together with specialists in the legal department, were responsible for the FDA 510(k) pre-market notification process. Typically VSI sought certification from the FDA before pursuing certification from foreign regulators.

By early February, on the basis of the plans provided by the engineering and marketing departments, the manufacturing department would begin to generate bills of materials, labor standards, and cost estimates. Capacity projections and capital equipment requirements were also developed by manufacturing as part of this process. Manufacturing would initiate negotiations with suppliers to meet their anticipated needs for components, subassemblies and any additional capital equipment required by the manufacturing process. Though underway by mid-year, these agreements would not be finalized before December when the budgets were finalized and then approved by VSI's board of directors.

While engineering was navigating the approval process and manufacturing was developing cost estimates, it fell to sales to begin working with the distributors. Although most distributor agreements were renewed each December as part of the quota commitment process, sales worked with the distributors throughout the year. In addition to monitoring current sales activity and achievements towards quota, the sales department worked through a formal review and evaluation process with each distributor of the partnership's performance over the previous year. At the same time, the distributors provided feedback on developing sales leads for the coming year. Together with the distributors, sales would formulate plans to support these sales efforts with VSI demonstration and training staff as well

as evaluation equipment. Sales would also begin providing distributors with advanced marketing information concerning forthcoming offerings in order to elicit feedback on anticipated volume and market pricing. Though most distribution and sales agreements included confidentiality clauses, the distribution network was a valuable source of competitive intelligence regarding expected features and pricing by competitors. This information was combined into a preliminary sales forecast provided to the budget committee by mid-August of each year.

On the basis of the preliminary forecast from sales and their own planning effort for any new products, manufacturing developed and submitted a draft labor budget to human resources (HR). The other departments also submitted staffing requests at this time, but the manufacturing labor budget was the most critical. HR was responsible for developing the staffing and training schedule for the coming year. As part of this process, HR reviewed the salary and wage surveys it purchased from consultants to ensure that VSI kept pace with the competitive labor markets. Salaries and wages were a significant cost category for VSI. This information was critical for developing department managers' merit pay budgets for the coming year as well as for refining the direct labor budget.

The most intensive phase of the budget process took place each September. By this point in the year, the volume of sales and product mix for the coming year was relatively predictable. Combining the updated sales forecast distributed by the sales department at the beginning of the month with salary, wage and staffing information provided by HR, department managers developed detailed budgets for their departments using a standardized spreadsheet produced by the Accounting department. The design of the spreadsheet largely automated the roll-up of department budgets to higher organizational levels. But in the budgeting review processes, changes were inevitably suggested, forcing negotiations and revisions. The budgeting review effort was intensive, but the process was not overly cumbersome because VSI's management consisted of fewer than 20 individuals. Finally, in December, VSI's executive committee, and then the board of directors, approved the consolidated budget.

Management of cash and working capital was a critical issue for this small, rapidly growing company. VSI management and its bankers agreed that the firm should typically hold six weeks of operating expenditures in its cash accounts. In an effort to be responsive to the needs of its distributors and customers, VSI maintained a policy of holding 30 to 40 days forward sales in finished goods inventory. Finished goods accounted for just more than 40% of the total value of inventory, with the remainder split about equally between work in process and raw materials. At the other end of its operating cycle, VSI's accounts receivable balance hovered between 60 and 80 days of trailing sales. In an effort to minimize net operating capital, VSI maintained accounts payable and accrued liabilities at the highest levels possible while still taking advantage of all available trade credits for prompt payment. Likewise, expenses were only prepaid when required. Nonetheless, its long operating cycle and high growth rate required VSI to finance this growing investment in working capital through short-term borrowing against the value of its accounts receivable and inventories. Thus, before any budget could be considered viable, it required review and approval by the finance department.

Anywhere from one-third to one-half of the managers' cash compensation was tied to achievement of objectives set by the executive committee and the board at the start of each year. For first-level managers, one-third of cash compensation was considered "at-risk," with the level rising to 50% for Linda. For most managers, achievement of budget objectives was weighted 50% in importance for determining the annual bonus. The remaining 50% was based on achievement of other quantified goals and/or a subjective evaluation of performance.

THE NEW CHALLENGE

The budget that Jon Foley delivered to Linda earlier in the day was based on an assumption of 10% revenue growth for 2009 (see Exhibits 6 and 7), a level that had been considered quite conservative just a month earlier. It included plans to bolster Asia/Pacific and Latin American sales support by hiring more account managers and sonographers and by devoting additional demonstration equipment to these markets. While it included no plans for major product releases in 2009, engineering and marketing planned to begin the FDA 510(k) process for approval of the new hand-carried

ultrasound (HCU) platform targeted for release in 2010. Recently, the HCU market had grown faster than the cart-based segment where VSI currently competed. Analysts were forecasting an acceleration of the shift towards greater use of HCUs. Linda and the board were eager to enter this new market segment.

With the assumption of 10% growth, most first-level management perceived that they would face tight resource constraints. Manufacturing headcount and manufacturing compensation were budgeted to grow by only 6.4% and 9.0%, respectively. Capital expenditures were actually budgeted to fall significantly as the firm more fully utilized existing capacity. Additional investments were expected to accompany the new HCU platform introduction in 2010. By far the most significant growth in operating expenses would come from expansion of the sales staff, with total compensation expense in sales and marketing budgeted to increase by slightly less than 40%. This was considered an investment required to maximize the potential growth from new product introductions in subsequent years. Growth in engineering head count of 12% and engineering compensation of just over 15% was in equal parts justified by growth in manufacturing capacity and the installed base and by development of the new product line. Finally, the roughly 12% growth in headcount and compensation expense within finance was deemed necessary to support growth in the other three functions.

However, while the strategic importance of growing into new markets and keeping ahead of the technology would not change, continuation of the market's and VSI's high rates of growth could not be assured. The US domestic market was dominated by private no-for-profit hospitals which rely in part on endowments like those of some private universities. The nearly 40% fall in equity market values was sure to adversely affect such investment portfolios. Government-owned hospitals were already anticipating funding shortages because the slowdown was reducing tax revenues. In addition, the crisis was likely to reduce demand for elective procedures, further reducing all hospitals' revenues and spending. Consequently, analysts were beginning to speculate about a decrease in capital spending by US hospitals of as much as 14% in 2009. Yet, it was unclear how capital spending on radiology generally, and sonography in particular, might be affected. As the bulk of sales in the domestic market were replacements for older technology, many customers could defer purchases.

Customers had already shifted purchases to later in the year during 2008. Linda and others at VSI feared that this pattern could become more pronounced due to the developing recession. With limited workforce flexibility, VSI would be forced to choose between building inventory early in 2009 or risking stocking out later in the year. Fortunately, the sales mix was expected to remain essentially fixed, as it was driven by customers' clinical requirements rather than by financial factors.

As Linda reviewed the spreadsheet Jon Foley had prepared for the 2009 budget, she considered his words of caution. Jon believed that in the short term VSI's fate could be determined by how well they managed cash and by their ability to access bank financing. He felt that all plans should be built upon an assumption of reduced gross debt levels and improved debt ratios. He suggested that they "prepare for the worst and hope for the best," and advocated beginning a policy of "deferring expen-

ditures and wringing cash out of the working capital accounts." Jon argued that committing to plans for growth was risky and that "modest cuts now [could] avert severe cuts later." While Linda had come to rely on Jon's financial expertise, her trusted friend and collaborator, Simon Lee, had privately criticized the CFO as overly cautious and Peter Beeson had on more than one occasion dismissed him as "just a bean counter." In contrast, Tom Nelson, VSI's COO, who had worked with Jon at Bainbridge, never made a significant proposal without having Jon first vet the numbers.

Linda knew that deferring planned investments, let alone cutting back, would limit the company's capacity for growth in 2009 and beyond. Recognizing that any course of action would create some controversy within the management team, she wondered how exposed VSI was to a decrease in sales, which might be imminent. How great a downturn could the company endure without having to make the sort of deep cuts that would choke off future growth? And might VSI's own survival be threatened if market conditions became really unfavorable?

Exhibit 1 Income statements

Income statement	2008 (estimated)	9 months ended 9/30/08	2007	2006
Revenues (net)	$59,766	$44,227	$52,994	$47,443
Cost of goods sold	27,269	20,224	24,806	22,930
Gross margin	32,498	24,003	28,188	24,513
Operating expenses				
Selling	10,663	7,921	9,581	8,705
R&D	7,566	5,744	6,646	5,856
General and administrative	7,458	5,611	7,028	6,673
Operating income	6,811	4,728	4,933	3,279
Interest expense	1,060	773	886	653
Income before tax	5,751	3,955	4,046	2,626
Tax	2,013	1,384	1,416	919
Income before extraordinary items	3,738	2,570	2,630	1,707
Extraordinary items (net of tax)	–	–		
Net income	$3,738	$2,570	$2,630	$1,707

Exhibit 2 Balance sheets

Balance sheet	2008 (estimated)	9 months ended 9/30/08	2007	2006	2005
Current assets					
Cash	$5,930	$5,448	$5,258	$4,701	$4,178
Accounts receivable (net)	12,898	12,153	11,436	10,238	9,093
Inventories	6,767	6,216	6,000	5,371	4,770
Prepaid expenses	2,030	1,835	1,800	1,611	1,431
Total current assets	27,625	25,652	24,494	21,922	19,472
Non-current assets					
Property, plant, and equipment	26,531	26,945	24,108	21,583	19,167
Less accumulated depreciation	6,323	6,353	6,356	6,430	6,483
	20,208	20,592	17,752	15,152	12,685
Other assets	4,282	4,209	3,522	2,988	2,466
	—	—			
Total assets	$52,115	$50,454	$45,767	$40,063	$34,624
Current liabilities					
Accounts payable	4,496	4,348	4,423	3,960	3,516
Notes payable	14,860	14,640	12,040	9,470	6,210
Tax payable	384	253	368	239	111
Accrued liabilities	2,437	2,357	2,397	2,146	1,906
Current portion of long-term debt	339	339	339	339	339
Total current liabilities	22,516	21,938	19,568	16,154	12,083
Non-current liabilities					
Long-term debt	348	433	687	1,027	1,366
Total liabilities	22,865	22,371	20,255	17,180	13,448
Owners' equity					
Common stock	189	189	189	189	189
Additional paid-in-capital	4,546	4,546	4,546	4,546	4,546
Retained earnings	24,516	23,348	20,777	18,147	16,440
Total owners' equity	29,251	28,083	25,512	22,882	21,175
Total liabilities and equity	$52,115	$50,454	$45,767	$40,063	$34,624

Exhibit 3 Statements of cash flows

Statement of cash flows	2008 (estimated)	9 months ended 9/30/08	2007	2006
OPERATIONS:				
Net income	$3,738	$2,570	$2,630	$1,707
Adjustments to reconcile:				
Depreciation and amortization	5,182	3,836	4,275	3,813
Accounts receivable	(1,462)	(717)	(1,198)	(1,146)
Inventories	(767)	(216)	(628)	(601)
Prepaid expenses	(230)	(35)	(189)	(180)
Accounts payable	73	(75)	463	443
Tax payable	15	(115)	129	128
Accrued liabilities	40	(41)	251	240
Cash flow from operating activities	6,590	5,208	5,734	4,405
INVESTING:				
Additions to PP&E	6,509	5,845	5,978	5,482
Acquisitions of technology licenses	1,889	1,519	1,430	1,321
Cash flow used for investing activities	8,398	7,364	7,409	6,803
FINANCING:				
Borrowing of notes payable	14,860	11,510	12,040	9,470
Repayments of notes payable	(12,040)	(8,910)	(9,470)	(6,210)
Long-term borrowing	–	–	–	–
Repayment of long-term debt	(339)	(254)	(339)	(339)
Cash dividends paid	–	–	–	–
Cash flow from (used by) financing	2,481	2,346	2,231	2,921
Net increase (decrease) in cash	$673	$190	$557	$523
Cash paid for income taxes	$1,621	$1,122	$1,287	$791
Cash paid for interest	$1,054	$780	$846	$614

Exhibit 4 VisuSon, Inc.: organization chart

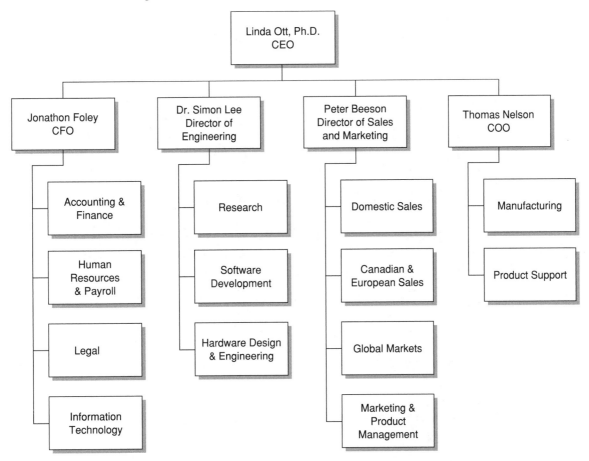

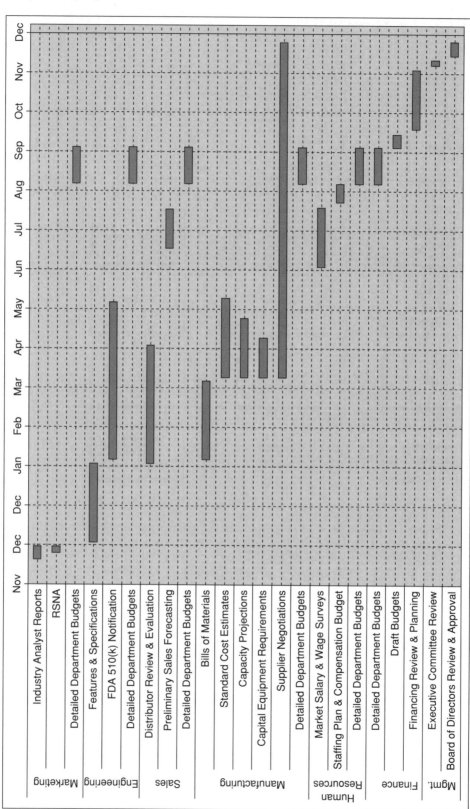

Exhibit 5 Budget timeline

Exhibit 6 Staffing

Staffing Budget	Current FTE	Estimated attrition	Requested FTE	Anticipated need (excess)	Estimated wage increase
Manufacturing:					
Management	4	–	4	–	3.0%
Supervisory	8	1	8	1	2.0%
Labor & Technical	92	4	98	10	2.0%
Clerical	5	1	6	2	0.0%
	109	6	116	13	
Engineering:					
Management	4	–	4	–	3.5%
Science	5	–	5	–	3.0%
Engineering	16	1	16	1	3.6%
Technical	11	1	14	4	2.6%
Clerical	6	1	8	3	0.0%
	42	3	47	8	
Sales & Marketing:					
Management	5	–	5	–	2.0%
Commissioned	4	1	5	2	1.5%
Professional	6	–	9	3	2.7%
Technical	10	2	15	7	3.0%
	25	3	34	12	
Finance Division:					
Management	5	–	5	–	3.0%
Professional	9	1	9	1	3.0%
Technical	6		8	2	1.8%
Clerical	12	2	13	3	0.0%
	32	3	35	6	
	208	15	232	39	

Exhibit 7 Summary budget

2009 Budgeted income summary				Comments and analysis
Revenues (net)			$65,743	10% growth
Cost of goods				
Direct materials		12,742		
Direct labor		6,959		
Manufacturing overhead				
Salary and wages	4,078			Includes $160 for management bonuses
Depreciation and amortization	3,148			Includes $596 on 2009 investments
Miscellaneous	2,919	10,145	29,846	Includes indirect materials, utilities, and maintenance: 74% fixed
Gross margin			35,897	
Operating expense				
Selling				
Salary and wages	2,807			Includes estimated commissions of $965 + $190 management bonus
Marketing and advertising	5,036			85% discretionary / 15% variable
Shipping	1,747			95% variable, based on estimated forward rates
Sales promotion funding	1,972	11,562		Discretionary-variable
Research and development				
Salary and wages	4,934			Includes $210 for management bonuses
Depreciation and amortization	1,712			Includes $430 on 2009 investments
Consulting	1,640			Discretionary
Miscellaneous	39	8,325		Discretionary
General and admin.				
Salary and wages	6,567			Includes $445 for management bonuses
Travel and training	2,060			Discretionary
Depreciation and amortization	791			
Miscellaneous	395	9,813	29,700	Includes $105 of contract labor: 20% variable
Operating income			6,197	
Interest expense			1,250	At assumed rate of working capital growth
Before tax income			$4,947	
Capital expenditure			$5,960	92% for replacements and license renewals

Chapter 9

INCENTIVE SYSTEMS

One of the primary principles of effective management is that rewards should be the third thing you work on. Measurements should come second, and both rewards and measurements should be subordinated to performance definition; i.e. clear and unambiguous articulation of what needs to be done.

Steven Kerr, chief learning officer, Goldman Sachs[1]

The third major element of financial results control systems deals with the provision of organizational rewards; that is, the design of incentive systems. As per the opening quote above, incentives follow performance definition. Performance definition described by Kerr as the "clear and unambiguous articulation of what needs to be done" includes both defining desired performance and assigning responsibility for achieving the desired results. Defining desired performance and setting adequately challenging performance targets in the desired performance areas are among the main purposes of planning and budgeting systems, which we discussed in Chapter 8. Designing responsibility centers, which we discussed in Chapter 7, determines the accountability for the desired result areas. Incentive systems, which we discuss in this chapter, tie rewards (and/or punishments) to the performance evaluations. Incentive systems are important because they reinforce the definitions of the desired result areas and motivate employees to achieve and exceed the performance targets. Section IV of this book focuses exclusively on the important topic of performance measurements, which drive the performance evaluations and associated incentives in most organizations.

Hereafter, we use the term *incentives* to refer primarily to things that employees value – (positive) *rewards*. That said, organizations can, and do, also provide some negative rewards, or *punishments*. In an organizational context, though, punishments commonly manifest themselves through an *absence* of positive rewards, such as not being paid a bonus or being passed over for a promotion. Naming and shaming is another type of unpleasant experience (hence, punishment) that employees would rather avoid. For example, at Black & Decker's semiannual meeting of division heads, managers who had met their budget targets sat on the left side of the room whereas those who had failed to meet their targets were asked to sit on the right in order to explain to the others why they had not met their targets. Mr. Archibald, the executive chairman, explained proudly: "They hate being over on the right. We think this kind of peer competition is motivational." In a similar fashion, China's Haier, the large consumer appliances company, uses naming and shaming by prominently displaying photographs of managers throughout the company with a red smiley face for good performance and a yellow frowning one for those doing poorly.[2]

TABLE 9.1 Examples of positive and negative rewards

Positive rewards	Negative rewards (punishments)
Autonomy	Interference in job from superiors
Power	Loss of job
Opportunities to participate in important decision-making processes	Zero salary increase
Salary increases	Assignment to unimportant tasks
Bonuses	Chastisement (public or private)
Stock options	No promotion
Restricted stock	Demotion
Praise	Public humiliation
Recognition	
Promotions	
Titles	
Job assignments	
Office assignments	
Reserved parking places	
Country club memberships	
Job security	
Merchandise prizes	
Vacation trips	
Participation in executive development programs	
Time off	

Source: K. A. Merchant, *Modern Management Control Systems: Text and Cases* (Upper Saddle River, NJ: Prentice Hall, 1998), p. 427.

Table 9.1 lists some of the types of rewards that organizations use. Note that many of these rewards are *nonmonetary*. Although it is widely accepted that individuals universally value money, it is equally correct to suggest that monetary rewards are not the only thing that people value. When properly chosen, nonmonetary rewards will be greatly appreciated by employees, and in many cases they place a smaller financial burden on the firm. Therefore, organizations typically do not rely on just a single form of rewards. In many for-profit firms, various monetary incentives in the form of cash or stock usually go up and down with performance. But a manager's power and recognition often do too. Corporate managers can (threaten to) reduce the decision autonomy of entity managers by refusing to fund investments in entities where performance is poor. In entities where performance is excellent, they can grant managers additional power and increase their recognition within the firm by publicizing the results. Employees who are doing notably well also often are given various *perks* (discretionary rewards), such as the opportunity to travel first class, to pick a larger office, to be given first choice for vacation scheduling, to have a preferred parking spot, or to enjoy some leisure activities (e.g. golf) on work time.

This chapter first describes the purposes of incentives. It then mainly focuses on monetary incentives to discuss various important incentive system decisions that organizations need to consider, such as about the extent to which the incentives are determined formulaically, the shape of the incentive-performance function, and the form and size of incentive pay. The chapter concludes by providing a set of criteria for evaluating incentive systems.

PURPOSES OF INCENTIVES

Performance-dependent rewards, or incentives, provide the impetus for the alignment of employees' natural self-interests with the organization's objectives. They provide three types of management control benefits. The first is *informational*. The rewards attract employees' attention and inform or remind them of the relative importance of often-competing results areas, such as cost, quality, customer service, asset management, and growth. Merely telling employees that customer service, for example, is important might have some effect on their behaviors. But including customer service measures in annual bonus plans is more likely to convince them to emphasize customer service. In other words, the rewards signal which performance areas are important and help employees decide how to *direct* their efforts. For this reason, the informational aspect of incentives is sometimes also referred to as the *effort-directing* purpose.

This informational purpose of incentives is pertinently illustrated by the case when Bob Dudley, the new chief executive at BP, vowed to improve BP's safety culture upon taking the helm following the company's deep-sea oil well disaster in the Gulf of Mexico. To make his point, Mr. Dudley announced that the company had decided that bonuses for the fourth quarter of 2010 would be based *solely* on how employees perform in terms of safety and risk management. BP would honor the existing performance contracts for the first three-quarters of the year, but the fourth quarter's performance would be measured "solely according to each business's progress in reducing operational risks and achieving excellent safety and compliance standards," he said. In so doing, Mr. Dudley signaled in no uncertain terms that the company was "absolutely clear that safety, compliance and operational risk management [was to be] BP's number one priority, well ahead of all other priorities."[3]

The second control benefit is *motivational*. Some employees need incentives to exert the extra effort required to perform tasks well; that is, to work hard, do a good job, and succeed.[4] In other words, this purpose of incentives is sometimes also called the *effort-inducing* purpose. Sometimes even hardworking employees need incentives to overcome their natural aversion to some difficult or tedious actions that are in their organization's best interest, such as working cooperatively with other divisions to resolve customer complaints, making cold sales calls to get more business, preparing paperwork, or training employees.

The third control benefit is *attraction and retention* of personnel. Performance-dependent rewards are an important part of many employees' total compensation package. Some rewards are promised because the organization wants to improve employee recruitment (*selection*) and retention either by offering a package that is comparable or superior to those offered by their competitors or by linking payments to an employee's continued employment. Some firms also overtly offer compensation packages with below average *base salaries* but with performance-dependent compensation elements (*variable pay*) that provide the opportunity to earn above average total compensation if excellent performance is forthcoming. These packages tend to appeal to employees who are entrepreneurial, rather than risk averse, and those who are confident about their abilities to produce superior results. These efforts to use compensation packages to attract and retain a higher quality set of employees often form a key element of firms' personnel control strategy, as was discussed in Chapter 3.

Finally, incentive systems also serve several *non-control purposes*. Incentive systems that are performance-dependent make compensation *more variable with firm performance*. This decreases cash outlays when performance is poor and, thus, smoothes earnings, because compensation expense is lower when profits are lower. Incentive system design choices can also affect a firm's *tax payments*. Some forms of compensation are not deductible for tax purposes, and some deductions are limited. For example, Section 162(m) of the US Internal Revenue Code of 1986 limits the deductibility of compensation in excess of $1 million paid to an employee unless the compensation qualifies as "performance-based." The intent of this law was to discourage high guaranteed payments to executives in situations where shareholders were not benefiting.

Government regulations also affect compensation arrangements in organizations, thus driving another important concern of incentive system design – *compliance*. Concerns for compliance were heightened following the financial crisis of 2008 when, for example, executive compensation in firms (banks) that participated in the Troubled Assets Relief Program (TARP) in the United States was directly restricted by law in size and form of payments.[5] As a consequence, at Wells Fargo, a large American bank, chairman and chief executive John Stumpf saw a shift in his 2009 compensation package towards salary, purportedly "because the company was unable to 'reward him appropriately' in other pay categories due to TARP-related restrictions."[6]

The intent of this particular TARP-regulation (as well as regulation of the same vintage in many other countries) is for the government to try to curtail (outrage at) lucrative (excessive) compensation packages in firms that benefited from so-called "taxpayer bailouts." Indeed, increased scrutiny by the press and activists of the pay packages of mainly well-paid top executives in large corporations, and banks particularly, has become commonplace.[7] Companies therefore must take utmost care to design effective incentive systems without being seen as excessive or triggering outrage. This can be tricky, as the following example illustrates. When UBS booked compensation costs that pushed its investment banking unit into the red in 2009, its chief financial officer was brutally honest to analysts: "We are a living example of a bank that experimented with not paying people [at competitive levels] and it didn't come off very well in 2008; as a consequence, we know that we are bound to pay people, to some extent, regardless of the performance of the bank." How do you explain high compensation (for retention purposes) in the face of poor performance?[8] Such forms of payments are not pay-for-performance; they are merely deferred salary.

While this chapter focuses on the management control benefits of incentives, it must be recognized that the control and non-control purposes of incentive systems can, and must, sometimes be traded off against each other. Consequently, observing organizations' incentive practices does not necessarily provide definitive clues as to which incentives they find to be most effective for control purposes.

MONETARY INCENTIVES

Money is an important form of reward that is often linked to performance, particularly at management levels in organizations. Monetary incentives certainly are not the only form of reward, and they may not even always be the best one, but their use is common. There are three primary ways through which monetary incentives can be provided: through performance-based salary increases, short-term incentive plans, and long-term incentive plans. Note that the term "performance-based" is key to distinguish incentives from entitlements. When we use incentives hereafter, we presume them to be performance- or merit-based, instead of amounts being awarded as cost-of-living adjustments or on the basis of seniority, custom (e.g. a holiday "bonus" depending on salary band rather than performance), or collective bargaining agreements.

Salary increases

All organizations give, or at least consider, salary increases to employees at all organizational levels, typically annually. These salary increases are minimally cost-of-living adjustments. But they can also be seen as an incentive when at least some portion of the total raise consists of merit-based increases. Salary increases are typically a small proportion of an employee's salary, but they have considerable value because they are not just a one-time payment; they provide an annuity that typically persists for many years because rarely are employees' salaries reduced (even though in years of austerity further increases may be put on hold).

Salary increases can be seen as an incentive when they are expected to be "earned" through performance or the acquisition of skills that promise improved performance in future periods. Indeed, higher salaries often come with higher expectations going forward; that is, those who performed well can expect to "earn" the highest raises, but with that also often come expectations of sustained performance.[9] Even the Vatican has apparently introduced an "element of incentive" into its salary system, as it takes into account issues such as "dedication, professionalism, productivity and correctitude" when awarding pay raises.[10]

Short-term incentives

Many organizations, especially those beyond minimal size in the commercial sector, but also increasingly those in the not-for-profit sector, in a growing number of countries, use short-term incentives, which include bonuses, commissions, and piece-rate payments. Indeed, incentives have become so widespread that some have claimed that they are "overused" and that they "emerge as the first answer to almost every problem" in the for-profit and not-for-profit sectors alike.[11]

The primary rationale for variable pay is to differentiate pay; that is, to provide rewards in accordance with an employee's contributions to the organization, hence the notion of *pay-for-performance* or *variable pay*. Moreover, by better recognizing employee contributions, organizations aim to more effectively encourage outstanding performance; that is, they try to encourage employees to go the "extra" proverbial mile for the "extra" compensation. Employees (of the right type) appreciate the opportunity to be rewarded for their performance, whereas their employer appreciates variable pay's *risk-sharing* feature that makes compensation expense more variable with performance. Another feature that employers value is that the variable payments are one-time payments, rather than annuities.

Short-term incentives typically provide cash payments based on performance measured over periods of one year or less. The awards are often called *annual incentive pay* or *bonuses*. The awards can be based on the performance of a single individual or that of a group of which an individual is a member, such as a work team, profit center, or even the firm as a whole. Probably the most commonly-used performance metrics in annual bonus plans are financial. For example, a manager's bonus could be calculated as the lesser of either 0.75% of the entity's controllable earnings (as defined in the bonus contract) up to 150% of annual salary. As another example, the bonus of a corporation's chief executive could be calculated as 0.6% of the firm's pretax income with an upper limit of $100,000 for each penny of the firm's fully diluted earnings per share (the exact terms of which are typically defined in the bonus contract in often great detail). These are just two examples of a virtually infinite number of possible *bonus formulas*, the key parameters of which we discuss in more detail in the later sections.

Usually in addition to financial measures of performance, annual incentive plans can also include bonus payments contingent on achievements in nonfinancial performance areas. For example, 30% of an entity manager's bonus could be based on meeting targets for customer satisfaction and a further 10% based on meeting targets for environmental performance. As a case in point, Telstra, the large Australian telecommunications and media company, is said to link up to 40% of employee's bonuses, including those for top executives and managers, to feedback from customers.[12]

When the bonus formula in annual incentive plans includes multiple performance dimension, managers (executives) can sometimes earn a bonus, often somewhat controversially, due to on-target performance in one or some areas despite poor performance in other areas, such as when their entity (or firm) is making losses and axing jobs, say. Companies that are concerned about this eventuality can make bonus payments contingent on minimum performance thresholds in all of the bonus formula components, and, thus, use one performance measure as condition or a *modifier* for the other. Again, the combinations of possibilities add up to a virtually infinite number of conceivable bonus formulas.

To add to the possible variety of bonus plans, some short-term incentive awards are calculated directly by formula, such as in the examples above (0.75% of the entity's controllable earnings for its manager; 0.6% of the firm's pretax income for the chief executive). But some short-term incentive awards are assigned in two separate steps. First a *bonus pool* is funded, often based on corporate performance; then the pool is assigned to individuals, usually through a rating system that provides higher awards to better performers.

A recent survey from Hay Group shows that, presumably as a fallout from the global recession, firms are moving away from "soft" performance metrics (such as employee satisfaction or turnover) in the design of their variable pay plans in 2010 and beyond. Instead, they are placing more emphasis on "hard" financial measures. Specifically, the study reports that 51% of the companies surveyed said they were using more financial metrics in performance-based pay, such as revenue, profit, and sales, with just 9% placing greater emphasis on employee satisfaction. Surprisingly, only 5% of the companies considered risk reduction as a major driver of change in their bonus plans. Thomas Haussmann, Variable Pay Leader for Hay Group EME commented that this is a "cause for concern," as "an emphasis on financial metrics can encourage employees to be focused on short-term financial gain without considering risks to long-term sustainability, company brand or broader social concerns. The most successful reward strategies encourage long-term goals, and recognize the need for a balance between financial, operational and employee satisfaction measures." The survey results also indicated that firms were making the performance targets in their bonus plans harder to achieve, to which Mr. Haussmann added: "At this time of change it is important that companies are aware of the serious impact that raising performance thresholds can have on employee engagement. Many employees have seen limited or no pay rises and bonus payments over the past two years. If the variable portion of their pay is made too difficult to earn, there is a danger they will disengage altogether, just when companies most need them on board."[13] This quote merely reiterates a key point we made in Chapter 8 about the importance of setting adequately challenging performance targets, although it suggests that adverse economic times appear to add to the challenge.[14]

All of the major compensation consulting firms (such as Aon Hewitt, Buck Consultants, Hay Group, Mercer, Towers Watson, and several others) provide data on reward practices collected from a large number of firms across industries in a large number of countries around the world.[15] These surveys are sometimes hard to compare (due to different sample composition in terms of type and size of companies as well as industry and country coverage, plus different survey instruments and incentive system categorizations and valuations taken at different times). Overall, however, the surveys suggest that short-term incentive pay is ubiquitous at higher management levels with eligibility conservatively estimated upwards of 75% and, when eligible, payouts easily upwards of 30% of base salary for on-target performance in normal years, with a noticeable trend of variable pay spreading around the world.[16] However, in addition to quite a wide variation across countries, industries,[17] and firm sizes and types,[18] the surveys also exhibit a wide spread in variable pay across organizational roles[19] and levels. Although virtually impossible to draw a line through these findings, Richard Semler, chairman of the Semler-Brossy Consulting Group, observes that, across organizational roles, employees with higher salaries typically receive larger bonuses as a result of having higher proportions incentive pay. In other words, the bonus proportions of compensation generally increase with organization levels; that is, as one moves up the organizational hierarchy.

Long-term incentives

Long-term incentive awards are based on performance measured over periods greater than one year. Their principal objective is to reward employees for their role in creating long-term value. In addition to motivating employees to contribute to the organization's long-term success, long-term incentive awards also aim to attract and retain key talent by making total expected compensation more attractive; by encouraging employee ownership (through equity-based features of the plan); and by tying incentive payouts to service period requirements (to address retention concerns). Long-term incentive awards often are restricted to relatively high levels of management based on the argument that executive decision making at these levels most directly impacts the long-term success of the organization, although some would object to this argument and call instead for a distributed responsibility for long-term success to everyone in the organization. We will come back to this point when we discuss group rewards.

Long-term incentive plans (LTIPs) come in multiple forms. The typical LTIP covers a 3–4 year period with a given performance target to be achieved by the end of the period. Some LTIPs measure performance in accounting terms, such as earnings per share (EPS), say. The target for these metrics can be *cumulative* over the LTIP period (such as by requiring EPS to be within a given range each year of the performance period in addition to meeting the target at the end of the period), or instead be stipulated as an *end-of-period* target (where the plan only requires that the EPS target is achieved at the conclusion of the performance period regardless of the actual fluctuations in EPS during the period). Some firms implement *consecutive* (end-to-end) LTIPs, meaning that a new cycle begins only at the completion of the previous one. Others opt for *overlapping* performance cycles, where a new plan begins each year, and, hence, multiple plans are running simultaneously, making it easier to tweak the long-term targets, or even the chosen metrics, each year. Overlapping LTIPs also facilitate enrolling newly eligible employees and new hires each year.[20]

Equity-based plans are another common way to provide long-term incentives. These plans provide rewards based on changes in the value of the firm's stock. Equity-based plans, too, come in many forms, including the following.

Stock option plans

Stock option plans give employees the right to purchase a set number of shares of company stock at a set price (i.e. the exercise or *strike* price) during a specified period of time (i.e. after the options vest but before they expire). Although stock option terms vary across firms, most options are granted *at the money* (i.e. the exercise price is equal to the stock price on the day of grant) with a 3–5-year vesting rate (i.e. one-third, one-fourth, or one-fifth of the options granted, respectively, vest at the end of each of the first three, four, or five years), and a 10-year maturity (i.e. the options expire 10 years after they are granted). When the stock price is above the option exercise price – that is, when the stock options are *in the money* – the employee can exercise the vested options and either hold the shares or sell them with a gain. However, when the strike price of vested options is higher than the stock price, the options are said to be *underwater*. Rather than having motivational effects, underwater options often are a source of morale and retention problems, particularly if the firm's stock price malaise is deemed to persist.

While employees might desire stock options because of the size of the potential gains, stock options also have several attractive features for the granting firms. From an incentive perspective, employees only benefit when the stock price goes up, so stock options motivate employees to increase their company's stock price. This improves incentive alignment as employees only benefit when shareholders benefit; that is, when the stock price goes up and presumably value has been created. Moreover, the potential for share ownership associated with stock options also affects alignment by tying some of the employee's wealth to the company's future. Finally, vesting schedules coupled with service-based restrictions that cause employees to forfeit unvested options when they leave the firm are believed to both enhance employees' long-term focus on the business as well as retention. Thus, stock options get employees to think more like owners while enhancing retention of talent. Stock options also allow the firm to provide incentive compensation without cash outlay, which makes stock options a particularly attractive arrangement for cash-constrained firms. As a matter of fact, stock options create a positive cash flow for the firm when employees exercise options (due to the purchase of shares, but also due to a tax deductible compensation expense in the amount of the difference between the exercise price of the options and the market price of the stock). And, until 2005, most stock option grants did not require the firm to take a charge against earnings. This flaw in the accounting rules provided powerful incentives for firms to grant options rather than to use other forms of compensation that require expensing. As of 2006, however, the most commonly applied accounting rules around the world, including International Financial Reporting Standards (IFRS) and US Generally Accepted Accounting Principles (GAAP), require that the fair value of the stock options at the grant date be estimated using an option pricing model. A detailed discussion of such non-control implications of stock options, however, is outside the scope of this book.

Against these advantages, stock options also have several disadvantages. Stock option grants represent a potential future issuance of shares, which creates *dilution* and puts a downward pressure on stock prices. Stock options also sometimes motivate managers to undertake riskier business strategies because the managers are rewarded for gains but not penalized for losses. Their risk-taking behavior can increase stock price volatility. Stock options also have been criticized for generating *windfall* compensation due to market-wide stock price improvements rather than strong firm performance. In reverse, however, stock options also can fall *underwater* due to bearish stock market conditions rather than poor firm performance and cause morale and retention problems. But also when the firm is performing poorly and the stock price is subdued, stock options are worth little, and, thus, are likely to erode the motivation to perform, ironically, just at a time when it is important for the executives and employees to be motivated the most. Moreover, given the relatively high liquidity of stock options (due to short vesting periods) and, often, the vast amounts of stock options held, executives may be encouraged to take actions that boost stock price in the short term but harm shareholders in the long run after the options have been cashed in. Considering these issues, the premise that stock options contribute to the creation of shareholder value has been actively debated, especially recently.[21]

Before they became so contested, however, stock options were the most prevalent form of stock-based incentives during the 1990s, by far, particularly in the United States, especially in certain industries (e.g. hi-tech).[22] Although stock options remained in play, the years 2003 and 2004 began to show declining grant rates, rising exercise rates, and declining eligibility as firms were increasingly considering alternatives to standard option plans, particularly below the executive/management level.[23] The decline in stock options' popularity around that time, particularly in the United States, coincided with the change in accounting rules that required stock option expensing. But there are other reasons that could help explain stock options' decline, such as the bear stock market in the United States that drove many stock options underwater, as well as investor activism against the ostensibly *excessive pay* that stock options helped provide during the boom. Investors also scorned the dilution effects of the large amounts of stock options that were being granted.

Differences in stock option use have existed, and continue to persist, across countries, however. Firms in Britain and France, for example, make use of stock options, whereas firms elsewhere in Europe have a preference for full-value share awards (see below). That said, use of stock options, never so widespread in Europe as in America, appears to be declining in most countries.[24] With the decline in stock option usage, however, other forms of equity-based compensation have become more prominent, including *restricted shares* and, especially, *performance awards*.

Restricted stock plans

Employees eligible for restricted stock do not have to spend cash to acquire the stock, but selling the stock that they are given is restricted for a specified period of time (typically 3–5 years) and is contingent upon continued employment. Restricted stock obviously provides a reward for increases in stock price, although the stock itself also has value when the stock price is flat or even declines (unlike stock options that only provide a reward when the stock price exceeds the exercise price). Because *full-value stock awards* like restricted stock have less risk than stock options, the firm can issue fewer shares as it would when using stock options instead, thus causing less dilution. On the other hand, restricted stock has been derided as a *giveaway* or pay-for-*pulse* (rather than pay-for-*performance*) because the stock has some value (even if the stock price declines) and the restrictions on selling the stock disappear merely with the passage of time and continued employment. For this reason, restricted stock is said to better serve *retention* purposes and benefits stemming from *ownership*, rather than *motivation* per se.

Performance stock or option plans

To eliminate the giveaway perception of restricted stock and accentuate pay-for-performance, some firms have resorted to *performance awards* by making their stock grants contingent on the achievement of stock or non-stock goals over a multi-year performance period. Here is an example from the Coca-Cola Company:[25]

> *Performance Share Units*. In 2008, we granted performance share units to approximately 4,600 employees. These were generally the same employees who received stock options. Performance share units provide an opportunity for employees to receive restricted stock if a performance criterion is met for a three-year performance period. [. . .] For the 2008–2010 performance period, the performance criterion is compound annual economic profit growth. Economic profit is our net operating profit after tax less the cost of the capital used in our business. The Compensation Committee chose this measure as it believed economic profit growth is a key metric for long-term sustainable growth. Over time, economic profit growth has proven to be highly correlated with the performance of our stock price.
>
> For the 2008–2010 performance period, the Compensation Committee set the target performance measure at 9% compound annual economic profit growth. The threshold award requires 6.5% growth and the maximum award is earned at 11% growth. If the minimum performance measure is not met, no shares are earned. In determining the minimum, target and

maximum economic profit growth levels, the Compensation Committee considers the circumstances facing the Company for the specific performance period. Actual grants, if any, range from 50% to 150% of the target number of performance share units awarded.

In February 2008, the Compensation Committee and the Audit Committee certified the results of the 2005–2007 performance period, which was based on compound annual growth in comparable earnings per share. The target was 5% compound annual growth in comparable earnings per share and the maximum award was earned at 7% compound annual growth in comparable earnings per share. The performance target was achieved at the maximum level and 150% of the target award was granted.

In February 2009, the Compensation Committee and the Audit Committee certified the results of the 2006–2008 performance period. The target was 8% compound annual growth in comparable earnings per share and the maximum award was earned at 10% compound annual growth in comparable earnings per share. The performance target was achieved at the maximum level and 150% of the target award was granted.

Performance options are yet another type of performance awards. Performance options stem from alternative stock option plans that make vesting or exercise of the options contingent on improvements in stock or non-stock goals. Performance options come in different forms. *Premium options* have exercise prices greater than the stock price on the grant date. *Indexed options* have exercise prices contingent on performance relative to a peer group of firms. *Performance-vested options* link the vesting of the options to the achievement of performance targets, such as return on equity, earnings per share, or other financial or operating measures (e.g. sales growth).

Here is an example. In fiscal year 2004, James N. Stanard, chairman and CEO of Renaissance Re Holdings (RenRe), a Bermuda reinsurance company, was awarded 2.5 million premium options, half of which at a strike price of $74.24, which was 50% higher than the market price of the stock on the day of grant, and the other half at a strike price of $98.98, which was double the market price on the day of grant. These options, which would become exercisable in 2009, clearly provided significant incentives for Mr. Stanard to improve the company's stock price over the next five years.[26] Up to this date, however, the company's stock price never traded even at the lower of the two thresholds, thus leaving the options underwater. In any event, the options never would have come to fruition anyway as Mr. Stanard resigned in 2005 following regulatory investigations of the reinsurer. (In 2009, he was found guilty on charges of fraud in connection with a sham transaction that deferred more than $26 million of RenRe's earnings from 2001 to later periods.)[27]

Examples can be varied, such as for performance stock option plans that contain both premium pricing and performance vesting. Regardless of the variations, the key idea behind these alternative stock option plans is to provide stronger incentives to maximize shareholder value by raising the bar for stock price improvements before the options become exercisable (as is the case with premium and indexed options) or by raising the bar on the conditions to vest, and, thus, earn the stock (as is the case with performance-vested options). But as is true for all incentive plans that require the setting of performance targets, triggers, or thresholds, doing so effectively is a key challenge. When the performance conditions are set too leniently, the performance stock or option plans will be seen as merely providing giveaways. But when they are set too tough, they can have other undesired consequences, such as excessive risk taking, discouragement, and/or turnover.

There are many other possible long-term incentive instruments, but most are variants of stock option, restricted stock or performance stock/option plans. For example, *Stock Appreciation Rights* (SARs) are similar to options in that the employee benefits from appreciation in the company's stock price. They are different in that the employee does not have to spend cash to acquire the stock. But like stock options, the employee typically can exercise the SAR at any point during the term (typically 10 years) after any specified vesting period. When the SAR is exercised, the firm pays the employee cash (cash SARs), stock (stock SARs), or a combination of both, in an amount equal to the stock's appreciation since the date of grant.

An analysis by Aon Hewitt of the fiscal year 2010 filings of Fortune 250 companies found that the most common LTIP mix consists of 40% stock options, 40% performance stock or options, and 20% restricted stock. The second most common mix is to allocate the LTIP into thirds across these three components. Furthermore, the analysis reveals that the prevalence of performance stock or option plans has steadily increased over the past seven years, from 18% in 2003 to 35% in 2009. This suggests that more companies are moving away from unrestricted grants and are establishing performance plans that require executives to hit specific business goals to pay out. David Hofrichter, principal and business development leader of Hewitt's Executive Compensation Consulting practice, proffered that, indeed, "Compensation Committees now want something for [their LTIP grants]; [which] they are expressing [. . .] through performance plans that target key metrics and support the strategy of the organization."[28]

INCENTIVE SYSTEM DESIGN

In this section, we discuss three related incentive system design choices: the extent to which the rewards are determined formulaically, the shape of the incentive-performance function, and the size of incentive pay.

Incentive formula

The types of rewards provided and the bases on which they are awarded are commonly communicated to the incentive plan participant by means of an *incentive formula* and described in an *incentive contract* that might be written in great detail. This is typically the case for annual bonus plans at most organizational levels. However, the incentive formulae and contract details are sometimes left completely or partially *implicit*; that is, the rewards are assigned *subjectively*. Subjectivity almost inevitably plays some role for decisions about promotions and job assignments. But subjectivity can also be part of annual bonus assignments in any of several ways: (1) all or part of the bonus can be based on subjective judgments about performance; (2) the weights on some or all quantitative measures can be determined subjectively; or (3) a subjective performance threshold or *override* can be used, in which case a subjective determination as to whether or not to pay a bonus is made.

Contract terms can be left implicit for a number of reasons. It may be difficult to describe the bases for the rewards and/or their weightings from a large set of evaluation criteria prior to the performance period. Keeping the contract flexible can mitigate motivating employees in directions that turn out to be no longer appropriate as conditions change. When the contract is left flexible, employees are encouraged to keep doing their best and not give up in the face of an impossible performance target or, in reverse, coast once the target is achieved. And, keeping the bases for rewards vague can reduce employees' propensities to manipulate the performance measures.[29]

The use of subjectivity in contracting, however, can affect employee risk. It can *decrease* risk if it allows adjustments for the effects of factors that are outside the employee's control. (We discuss this in greater detail in Chapter 12.) But the use of subjectivity can also *increase* employee risk. First, with implicit contracts, employees bear the risk that their evaluators might evaluate them on different bases than that they were assuming when they made their decisions; that is, subjective evaluations are prone to *hindsight biases*. Second, if employees do not *trust* their evaluators to make informed and unbiased performance assessments, they can result in employee frustration, demotivation, and friction. Finally, when evaluations are subjective, employees may attempt to inappropriately influence their evaluators for better evaluations. These problems, however, are reduced if the employee and the evaluator develop a working relationship with greater mutual trust, which has been shown to be critical for the effective implementation of completely or partially subjective performance evaluations.[30]

Shape of the incentive function

When the reward promises are *formulaic*, the link between rewards and the bases on which they are awarded is often determined by a rewards–results or *incentives–performance function*. This was illustrated in a budget setting in Chapter 8 (Figure 8.3), showing that bonuses are typically promised only over a restricted performance range; that is, the function has lower and upper reward cutoffs and it is linear in shape (although sometimes with kinks) between the cutoffs.[31]

At profit center levels, most firms set a *lower cutoff* or *threshold* in their short-term incentive contracts. Below some significant fraction (e.g. 80%) of targeted annual performance (which is typically the budget), managers are promised no incentive compensation for performance. Organizations set a lower cutoff because they do not want to pay any bonuses for performance they consider mediocre or worse. The fraction of the target set as the lower limit varies, among other things, with the predictability of the target; that is, it tends to be a lower fraction when predictability is lower. An *upper cutoff* or *cap* on incentive payments also is commonly used; it means that no extra rewards are provided for any additional performance above the cutoff. The caps are typically set at a percentage of the annual performance target, such as 150% of budget. Upper cutoffs can be considered for a number of reasons, including:

1. concern that the high incentive payments might not be deserved because of *windfall gains* (unforeseen good luck);
2. concern that employees will be unduly motivated to take actions to increase current period performance at the expense of the long-term – in other words, produce results that are unsustainably high;
3. desire not to pay hierarchically subordinate employees more than hierarchically higher employees or managers, thus maintaining *vertical compensation equity*;
4. desire to keep total compensation somewhat consistent over time so that employees are able to sustain their lifestyle, and, thus, to mitigate "feast-or-famine" volatility in pay year over year; and
5. concern about a possibly faulty plan design, the risk of which is greatest when the plan is new.

Size of incentive pay

Because employees almost invariably value money, a significant proportion variable pay should motivate them to achieve the performance goals. Further, compensation packages that offer significant performance-contingent pay (*at-risk pay* or *pay-for-performance*) are likely to attract employees who are confident about their abilities to produce superior results and/or more willing to accept risk. In that sense, the type of compensation package offered serve an *employee selection* role.

However, the most important consideration to the high use of variable pay is that if performance is not totally controllable by the employees, then the incentive system inevitably imposes risk on them (hence the term *at-risk pay*). Employees therefore will want to be compensated for bearing that risk; that is, their compensation *in expectation* must be higher than what it would be when offered a fixed salary. If the organization fails to provide the *risk premium*, which is an additional compensation expense, it will find itself unable to compete for talent in the labor markets.

CRITERIA FOR EVALUATING INCENTIVE SYSTEMS

To evaluate an incentive system, one can consider the following criteria. First, the rewards should be *valued*. Rewards that have no value will not provide motivation. However, reward tastes probably vary across individuals. As compared with top executives, lower-level managers are probably interested in protecting their autonomy and in improving their prospects for promotion in addition to just the size of their short-term income (after their base salaries are assured). Employees later in their careers are probably more concerned about job security. And so on. Overall, studies suggest that the reasons people join and stay with an organization are broader than compensation alone, including the satisfaction that comes from the work they do and the role they have, the long-term opportunities for development and advancement, and the feelings of belonging to an admirable organization that shares their values.[32] Reward tastes also vary across countries due to many factors, including culture, stage of economic development, and differences in tax and regulation, although evidence suggests that these differences are diminishing and that the world is getting flatter when it comes to incentive pay.[33] Nonetheless, some differences at various levels will remain, and, thus, if organizations can tailor their reward packages to their employees' preferences they could possible provide the control benefits of incentives more effectively. Such tailoring is costly, however, and firms often opt to administer a single organization-wide incentive system (or at most just a few systems).[34]

Second, the rewards should be large enough to have *impact*. If rewards that are valued are provided in trivial amounts, the effect can be counterproductive. Employees can be insulted and react with such emotions as contempt and anger.[35] Reward visibility may affect impact. If rewards are visible to others, the motivational effect is enhanced by a sense of pride and recognition. Third, rewards should be *understandable*. Employees should understand both the reasons for and the value of the rewards. Organizations can incur considerable expense in providing potentially valuable rewards, but if employees do not understand them well, the expense will not generate the desired motivational effects. Fourth, rewards should be *timely*. Delay in providing the rewards after the performance is said to dilute their motivational effects. Prompt rewards also increase the extent of any learning that takes place from receiving the reward and connecting it to the performance for which it was given. Fifth, the effects of the rewards should be *durable*. Rewards have greater value if the good feelings generated by the granting of a reward are long lasting; that is, if employees remember them. Sixth, rewards should be *reversible*. Performance evaluators often make mistakes, and some reward decisions are more difficult to correct than others. Promotions, for example, are difficult to reverse. Finally, rewards should be *cost efficient*; that is, all else equal, incentives should achieve the desired motivation at minimal cost.

Monetary incentives and the evaluation criteria

How well do the monetary rewards that many organizations provide satisfy the reward evaluation criteria? Monetary rewards can have potent impacts on employees' behaviors because virtually everyone values money. Money can be used to purchase goods and services that can satisfy each employee's most pressing desires. A vice president in a human resources consulting firm expressed this advantage in colorful terms, "You can't pay orthodonture bills with crystal from Waterford."[36] Money also has important symbolic values. It reflects achievement and success, and it accords people prestige and, some-times, power; it sometimes even serves as a proxy for some people's estimation of their self-worth. However, the observation that employees almost without exception value money does not necessarily imply that higher incentives will necessarily lead to higher performance. Indeed, recent studies suggest that there is an inverse U-shaped relation-ship between effort levels and incentive intensity, indicating that ever higher incentives may actually result in a decline in performance.[37]

Some monetary rewards fail the impact criterion. Merit raises are typically quite small for most employees, so total raises look small in times of low inflation. Moreover, the performance evaluations on which the merit raises are based typically are kept confidential or communicated to employees in quite vague terms, thus leaving them ambiguous (thereby affecting understandability) and possibly failing to provide a sense of recognition. Another common issue arises when firms that fall on hard times "flatten" pay, inadvertently or not. Because it is difficult to cut an employee's pay, poor performers are merely given no raises or bonuses, and the penalty to these employees is low. But lowering the payments to the top performers is where it hurts, often leading to perceptions of inequity, demotivation, and increased turnover, unhelpfully, among the most valuable employees.

On the other hand, some forms of monetary incentives, such as stock options, have been said to have "too much" impact. Stock options have often been granted in large numbers to, particularly, higher-level employees or executives. Due to the large number of stock options typically granted and held by top executives, and exacerbated by relatively short vesting periods, the executives may be encouraged to take actions that affect stock price in the short term but harm shareholders in the long run. For example, an action that can slightly affect stock price downwards at the time of a stock option grant, or boost stock price at the time of a stock option exercise, can make a huge difference for the stock options to be subsequently in the money or yield a greater payout at exercising, respectively, when applied to a very large number of stock options. In other words, pay can be significantly impacted by short-term movements in stock prices, thus encouraging executives to take measures to affect stock price rather than to maximize shareholder value in the long term (by which time they may have left the firm). In that sense, and due to the potential short-term impact that stock price may have on the potential value and payout from stock options, these instruments are in fact working against their intended purpose – that is, to have the executives focused on the long-term rather than to take actions that affect short-term. This illustrates that, indeed, impact is a powerful criterion for incentives to have, but, equally, when impact directs behaviors in ill-aligned ways, it can be detrimental.[38]

Because incentive contracts sometimes are quite complex (as are many long-term incentive plans, such as performance stock plans) or even ambiguous (when they include the use of subjectivity), and because performance-related feedback is incomplete or biased, employees often fail to understand the reasons why they are given the rewards (or the size of their rewards). When the rewards fail the understandability criterion, they are less likely to produce the desired effects. Stock options are often said to be ill-understood by employees, especially at lower organizational levels.

But many incentive arrangements are also ill understood by those to whom they matter too – shareholders. Many firms' compensation arrangements have been criticized for being insufficiently linked with performance, causing the executives to benefit even when shareholders do not and, importantly, for such "pay *without* performance" to be obscured or camouflaged from shareholders.[39] This has led to increased disclosure requirements by regulators and calls for "say on pay" by shareholders.[40] How effective such measures will be, however, remains to be seen.[41] In Britain, "say on pay" has been in place since 2004. "Shareholders now have a far better understanding of the structure of executive pay packages and their link with performance," says Peter Montagnon, Director of Investment Affairs at the Association of British Insurers, "but nothing stops the volume of payments, and the amounts seem to rise inexorably," he added.[42] As we will see below, it is indeed near impossible to determine the "correct" level of pay, which makes any judgment about another important criterion – the cost efficiency criterion – problematic.

Monetary rewards vary in their timeliness. Piece-rates used in some production settings are possibly the timeliest. Sales commissions are perhaps a close second. The most common period for performance reviews, however, such as for salary increases and bonuses, is annual. Long-term incentive awards, those based on multi-year performance, are less timely. It has been suggested that the mental discount rate employees apply to delayed rewards is greater than the time value of money. Or, as Peter Boreham, a director at Hay Group, puts it: "Once you go beyond three years [as is commonly the case with long-term incentive plans], the mental discount that executives put on rewards gets very large; any longer and it become a lottery ticket."[43] Hence, extending the time horizon of incentives, which has been increasingly called for to enhance a focus on the long term, is not costless given the rather large mental discount that people attach to delayed payouts.

Following the financial crisis of 2008, a common trend in the calls for change was to suggest to defer bonus payments because "deferring bonus payments helps companies to control short-termism," said Vicki Elliot, a worldwide partner at Mercer. "It means that a portion of the bonus is payable to employees in installments based on subsequent company and/or business unit performance. This *claw-back approach* sends the message that the bonus isn't finally determined until company or business unit performance is sustained."[44] In other words, deferring some of the bonus payments should prevent that employees pocket bonuses when they misleadingly appear to be doing well yet keep the booty when their firm subsequently suffers or even collapses, as was the case with some of the banks following the financial crisis, as even insiders were willing to admit. "There has been too much focus on payments that are very short-term focused, people who pick up the tab for short-term profits, without having to bear the costs of long-term impairments," said Stephen Green, Chairman of HSBC, a global bank.[45] Highlighting this trend towards longer-term compensation schemes on Wall Street, Bank of America (BofA) tied its chief executive's 2010 bonus to the bank's performance over the next four years. Specifically, BofA's chief executive, Brian Moynihan, will receive $9.1 million in restricted stock only if the bank's profits remain above 0.80% of its assets from 2011 to 2015.[46]

Another way to possibly mitigate the short-term focus of some incentive systems while circumventing the "mental discount" cost of deferred payments would be to consider *risk-adjusted measures* as the basis for bonus determination. However, the vast majority of banks (and likely non-financial firms as well) admitted in a recent study that "they still don't have reliable methods to measure the risks they are running" and "were still working out how to phase compensation to make sure it reflects the risks being taken over a long period."[47] As we will see in the next chapter, there are indeed no easy solutions to overcome the ubiquitous myopia problem.

Most monetary rewards, particularly small ones, are not durable. In many cases, salary increases are "lost in the paycheck." Similarly, many employees' bonuses are quickly spent and forgotten. One survey found that 29% of employees who earned bonuses used them to pay bills; 18% "admitted they couldn't remember where the money went." The report concluded that, for most employees, "[cash] bonuses have no lasting value."[48] Durability can perhaps be improved if the award is given but restricted for a period of time, such as with an award of restricted stock, because the employee can see the reward and can value it, but cannot spend it. This benefit of durability would also apply to the deferred bonus schemes that firms ponder, thus involving a tradeoff against the possible cost due to mental discounting. In contrast, some non-monetary rewards, such as a promotion, are quite durable (although they tend to be less reversible).

Indeed, monetary rewards also vary in their reversibility. Bonus awards are reversible because they are typically contingent on performance in a single period. Salary increases, on the other hand, provide an almost guaranteed annuity. But some question whether even bonuses are truly reversible. Employees come to expect them, and if there is no payout, they will be frustrated, especially if it happens because the company is not doing well. This is why managers at Svenksa Handelsbanken, one of Northern Europe's most successful banks, have been skeptical (not only of budgets as we discussed in Chapter 8, but also) of bonuses long before the financial crisis. "It doesn't make sense to pay bonuses in good times and then in bad times tell [employees] they have to work harder for 30% less money," said Par Boman, the bank's chief executive.[49]

Finally, monetary rewards tend to be expensive. The value provided to the employees is a direct cost to the firm. Some other forms of rewards, such as titles, recognition, interesting job assignments, or prized parking spots are much less expensive, yet they can have value to employees, although of course, to paraphrase, "you can't pay the bills with . . . the plaque on your wall."

Related, critics have argued that the high pay for, say, top executives is driven more by an ideology called the "talent myth" rather than by a reality that a small group of select employees who make a huge impact on their companies' success are hard to replace. Moreover, some argue that increased disclosures of pay may have contributed to this phenomenon as an executive can turn to his board and say, "look, I'm far better than such and so in the peer group, and yet he's paid more than me."[50] And even without such insistence by the executives themselves, boards are probably reluctant to signal that their executives would be seen as "worth less" than the peer group's 75th percentile, let alone less than the median. There is even some evidence that firms appear to select highly paid peers to justify their own firm's executive compensation, and that such is more likely where boards are weaker.[51] All told, a combination of myths, institutional forces, vested interests, and governance weaknesses may at least partly result in pay not being quite cost efficient.

As a contrarian example in such a context, Henry Engelhardt, head of the Admiral Group, a large Wales-based insurance company, and a strong performer throughout the recession, raised the following question with astonishment: "What can a [chief executive officer] do to warrant the kind of packages put together compared to the other people working in the organizations?" Every employee of Admiral is given free shares every six months. "It is important that people feel part of the organization – ownership is part of that – and it shouldn't just be restricted to top management," he added. Not only is Mr. Engelhardt said to be "the poorest paid boss in the FTSE 100," he also might hold the record for having the most cost-efficient pay package in our terms here. In 2009, the company reported a record pre-tax profit and also paid a record dividend.[52]

Although monetary rewards do not satisfy all the evaluation criteria equally well, the criteria are not all equally important either. As such, monetary rewards possibly are quite effective in satisfying the most important criteria. In particular, money is highly valued, so monetary awards attract most employees' attention. That is not to say that monetary rewards are not sometimes overused or that they could not be better designed.[53] As we have shown, such design considerations inevitably will involve tradeoffs among the various criteria.

GROUP REWARDS

Team or group rewards certainly have advantages; they were discussed in Chapter 3 as one of the methods by which personnel/cultural controls can be implemented. But they also have some significant disadvantages. Importantly, group rewards often do not provide direct and strong incentive effects. They provide a direct incentive only if the individuals to whom the rewards are promised perceive that they can influence the performance on which the rewards are based to a considerable extent. When the rewards are based on the performance of a large group (e.g. corporate performance), no individual, except perhaps the group leaders (e.g. the top executive team), is likely to have a material effect on the performance. For most other team members, the group rewards provide a *diluted* motivational effect at best. Group rewards also create the potential for *free rider* effects. In larger teams, particularly, some team members can slack off and suffer little adverse effects on the rewards earned; they are free riders on the efforts of their fellow team members.

As such, stock-based plans, one prominent form of group rewards, provide direct incentives only for the small number of managers at the very top of publicly held firms who presumably can influence their firm's stock price in a meaningful way. When lower-level employees are included in stock-based plans, their compensation is made more volatile and uncertain, but their motivation is not proportionally affected. With only rare exceptions, such as a research scientist who makes a breakthrough discovery, even if the lower-level employees perform heroically, their efforts will not have a significant influence on stock price.

Group rewards can produce a beneficial form of cultural control, however. Team members may monitor and sanction each other's behaviors and produce improved results. Comments like, "Get to work; you're hurting my profit sharing!" are evidence that cultural control – mutual monitoring – is working. It is this benefit and the avoidance of some dysfunctional effects of individual rewards that group rewards can provide.

Some firms have used group rewards very effectively over long periods of time. For example, all 70,000 employees (or "partners," as the company calls them) at John Lewis, a large UK retailer, share in the company's profit, which in 2009 (during the height of the recession) amounted to about eight weeks' salary for each employee. "Today's results reflect the collective hard work of our partners," said Charlie Mayfield, John Lewis' chairman. "While not a universal panacea, [our collective performance-based bonus plan] clearly underpins the partnership's performance," he added.[54]

CONCLUSION

Incentives are an important part of the results-control arrangements used to direct employees' behaviors. Rewards that can be linked to measures of performance or subjective performance evaluations come in many forms. It is widely, but not universally, believed that monetary rewards are important for motivation.[55] However, a wide range of other forms of rewards, such as praise, titles, recognition, promotions, and so on, also can be potent motivators while being cost efficient and having advantages in terms of satisfying the various other evaluation criteria that we discussed.

Incentive contract design presents problems that are far larger than just the choice of rewards, however. For example, tailoring rewards to employees' individual preferences would seem to be effective, but that benefit has to be weighed against the potential for employees' perceptions of inequities and the cost of contract administration. Similarly, it is well recognized that organizations' total compensation package must be competitive to attract and retain talented employees. If a portion of the compensation package, such as base salary, is not competitive, perhaps because cash is in short supply during the start-up phase of a new venture, then the incentives-performance function for the variable portion of pay may have to be adapted to compensate, or alternative forms of compensation such as stock options may have to be provided.

Perhaps the safest advice that can be proffered is that incentives should be sufficiently meaningful to offset other motives employees have to act in ways that are contrary to the organization's best interests, but the rewards should not be greater than those necessary to provide the needed motivation. An incentive system will not create value for the organization unless the incremental value of the increased performance generated by the incentives exceeds the associated compensation and administration expense. Organizations also have to worry about implementing an incentive system that encourages behaviors that do not lead to the desired outcomes. Many incentive systems have *unintended consequences* that can actually destroy value, such as by encouraging results that maximize incentive pay in the short term while jeopardizing the long-run viability of the organization. If that is the case, it may be better to have no incentive system than to have a bad one. The literature is littered with examples of where incentives have unintended consequences. This is, in a perverse sense, testimony that incentives work – that is, they encourage employees to produce results. But if poorly designed incentive systems encourage employees to produce the wrong results or do the wrong things in the wrong way, then strong incentives will only get the organization off track, and sometimes even ruin the firm, faster.

Notes

1. S. Kerr, "Executives Ask: How and Why Should Firms and Their Employees Set Goals," *Academy of Management Executive*, 18, no. 4 (November 2004), pp. 122–3.
2. "Cut-and-Build Archibald," *Forbes* (September 23, 1996), p. 46; "Grow, Grow, Grow," *The Economist* (April 17, 2010), Special Report, p. 13.
3. "BP Links Bonuses to Safety Performance," *Financial Times* (October 18, 2010), online (www.ft.com).
4. For a review of research examining the effects of monetary incentives on effort and performance, see for example S. E. Bonner and G. B. Sprinkle, "The Effects of Monetary Incentives on Effort and Task Performance: Theories, Evidence, and a Framework for Research," *Accounting, Organizations and Society*, 27, no. 4/5 (May–July 2002), pp. 303–45.
5. See, for example, "Amending the Executive Compensation Provisions of the Emergency Economic Stabilization Act of 2008 to Prohibit Unreasonable and Excessive Compensation and Compensation not Based on Performance Standards," 111th Congress of the House of Representatives, Report 111–64 (March 30, 2009).
6. "CEO Pay Drops, But . . . Cash is King," *Business Week* (March 25, 2010), online (www.businessweek.com).
7. Following the financial crisis of 2008, the press was filled with articles that indicate the heightened scrutiny of compensation practices by regulators, the press, and activists especially on the subject of executive pay. See, for example, "Attacking the Corporate Gravy Train," *The Economist* (May 28, 2009), pp. 71–3; "Nay on Pay," *The Economist* (May 13, 2010), pp. 70–1.
8. "Mutiny over Bounty," *The Economist* (November 6, 2010), p. 90.
9. "Why Everyone's Working So Hard?," *Business Week* (April 15, 2008), online (www.businessweek.com).
10. "Vatican Unveils Merit-Based Pay," *BBC* (November 22, 2007), online (www.bbc.co.uk).
11. J. Pfeffer and R. Sutton, *Hard Facts* (Boston, MA: Harvard Business School Press, 2006), p. 129.

12. "Telstra to Link Bonus to Customer Satisfaction, Review Reports," *Business Week* (August 15, 2010), online (www.businessweek.com).

13. Hay Group, *Variable Pay: What's the Winning Strategy?* (July 2010), see also: "Bonuses Are Back, But Not as We Know Them," *Hay Group* (July 7, 2010), online (www.haygroup.com).

14. See also M. Matejka, K. A. Merchant, and W. A. Van der Stede, "Employment Horizon and the Choice of Performance Measures: Empirical Evidence from Annual Bonus Plans of Loss-Making Entities," *Management Science*, 55, no. 6 (June 2009), pp. 890–905.

15. See, for example, Buck Consultants, *Recovery, Restoration, and Retention: 2010 Compensation Trends* (February 2010); Hay Group, *Top Executive Compensation in Europe* (2010); Mercer, *Executive Incentive Plan Snapshot Survey* (2010); Towers Watson, "Executive Pay Practices Around the World," *Remuneration Committee Briefing*, Europe (Autumn 2009), online (www.towerswatson.com).

16. See also K. Abosch, J. Schermerhorn, and L. Wisper, "Broad-Based Variable Pay Goes Global," *Workspan* (May 2008), pp. 56–62.

17. See, for example, Pearl Meyer & Partners, *Executive Pay in the New Economy* – Information Technology Edition (February 2009).

18. See, for example, B. Schindler, "Understanding Private Company Incentive Pay Practices," *Workspan* (March 2008), pp. 44–8.

19. See, for example, Financial Executives Research Foundation, *Financial Executive Compensation Survey* (2009).

20. See also M. Means, "Six Steps to Implementing Performance Metrics in LTI Plans," *Workspan* (May 2008), pp. 49–54.

21. See, for example, B. Deya-Tortella, L. Gomez-Meija, J. De Castro, and R. Wiseman, "Incentive Alignment or Perverse Incentives: A Behavioral View of Stock Options," *Management Research*, 3, no. 2 (Spring 2005), pp. 109–20; B. Hall and K. Murphy, "The Trouble with Stock Options," *Journal of Economic Perspectives*, 17, no. 3 (Summer 2003), pp. 49–71; "Do Stock Options Improve Performance?," *CalBusiness* (Spring/Summer 2010), pp. 8–9. See also D. Aboody, N. Johnson, and R. Kasznik, "Employee Stock Options and Future Firm Performance: Evidence from Option Repricings," *Journal of Accounting and Economics*, 50, no. 1 (May 2010), pp. 74–92; "Incentives for the Long Run: An Executive Compensation Plan that Looks Beyond the Next Quarter," *Knowledge@Wharton* (May 27, 2009), online (http://knowledge.wharton.upenn.edu); L. Becchuk, Y. Grinstein, and U. Peyer, "Lucky CEOs and Lucky Directors," *Journal of Finance*, 65, no. 6 (December 2010), pp. 2363–401.

22. See, for example, Watson Wyatt Worldwide, *Stock Option Overhang: Shareholder Boon or Shareholder Burden* (2001); Watson Wyatt Worldwide, *Strategic Rewards: Managing through Uncertain Times* (2002).

23. See, for example, Watson Wyatt Worldwide, *Stock Incentives: Moving Toward a Portfolio Approach* (2005); Deloitte & Touche USA LLP, *2005 Stock Compensation Survey* (2005).

24. "Pay Attention," *The Economist* (June 12, 2008), pp. 77–8.

25. The Coca-Cola Company, www.thecoca-colacompany.com/investors/2009_coca_cola_proxy.pdf.

26. "Goodbye to Pay for No Performance," *The Wall Street Journal* (April 11, 2005), p. R1.

27. "James N. Stanard, Former CEO of RenaissanceRe Holdings Ltd., Held Liable for Accounting Fraud," *Trading Markets Enforcement Proceedings* (February 2, 2009), online (www.tradingmarkets.com).

28. "Hewitt Study Shows Long-Term Incentives in Executive Compensation Packages Are Back – But With a Catch," *Aon Hewitt* (August 5, 2010), online (www.hewittassociates.com).

29. For an overview, see J. Bol, "Subjectivity in Compensation Contracting," *Journal of Accounting Literature*, 28 (2009), pp. 1–24.

30. For a detailed discussion and further references to this literature, see M. Gibbs, K. A. Merchant, W. A. Van der Stede, and M. E. Vargus, "Determinants and Effects of Subjectivity in Incentives," *The Accounting Review*, 79, no. 2 (April 2004), pp. 409–36.

31. See also K. J. Murphy, "Performance Standards in Incentive Contracts," *Journal of Accounting and Economics*, 30, no. 3 (December 2000), pp. 245–78; X. Zhou and P. Swan, "Performance Thresholds in Managerial Incentive Contracts," *Journal of Business*, 76, no. 4 (October 2003), pp. 665–96.

32. "Companies Using Employee Engagement to Attract, Retain Top Talent," *Industry Week* (July 2, 2010), online (www.industryweek.com); D. Scott and T. McMullen, *The Impact of Rewards Programs on Employee Engagement*, Hay Group & World-at-Work (June 2010).

33. Pearl Meyer & Partners, *Executive Pay in the New Economy*, op. cit.

34. "Multinational Firms Favor Global Approach to Compensation Management," *Workspan* (May 2005), pp. 24–5; Mercer, *What's Working* (June 2008), online (www.mercer.com/whatsworking); W. A. Van der Stede, "The Effect of National Culture on Management Control and Incentive System Design in Multi-Business Firms: Evidence of Intracorporate Isomorphism," *European Accounting* Review, 12, no. 2 (2003), pp. 263–85.

35. "41% of Employees Say They Would Be Insulted by a Low Bonus," *World-at-Work* (November 3, 2010), online (www.worldatwork.org).

36. "Bonus Question: Cash Rewards or Gifts? Experts Are Divided," *The Los Angeles Times* (May 30, 1999), p. C5.

37. See, for example, K. Pokorny, "Pay – But Do Not Pay Too Much: An Experimental Study on the Impact of Incentives," *Journal of Economic Behavior and Organizations*, 66, no. 2 (May 2008), pp. 251–64; D. Ariely, U. Gneezy, G. Loewenstein, and N. Mazar,

"Large Stakes and Big Mistakes," *Review of Economic Studies*, 76, no. 2 (April 2009), pp. 451–69.

38. See, for example, J. Efendi, A. Srivastava, and E. Swanson, "Why Do Corporate Managers Misstate Financial Statements? The Role of Option Compensation and Other Factors," *Journal of Financial Economics*, 85, no. 3 (September 2007), pp. 667–708.

39. See, for example, L. Bebchuk and J. Fried, *Pay without Performance: The Unfulfilled Promise of Executive Compensation* (Cambridge, MA: Harvard University Press, 2004).

40. See, for example, KPMG, "SEC Adopts Revised Executive Compensation Disclosures," *Defining Issues*, no. 06-24 (August 2006); D. R. Dalton and C. M. Dalton, "Corporate Governance in the Post Sarbanes-Oxley Period: Compensation Disclosure and Analysis (CD&A)," *Business Horizons*, 51 (2008), pp. 85–92.

41. See, for example, "How to Handle CEO Pay Before Dodd-Frank Hits?", *Business Week* (September 9, 2010), online (www.businessweek.com).

42. "Pay Attention," op. cit.

43. "Hard to Get," *CFO Europe* (April 2009), pp. 38–41.

44. "Financial Organizations Shuffling Compensation Programs," *World-at-Work* (January 14, 2010), online (www.worldatwork.org).

45. "HSBC Chief Backs Bank Pay Reform," *BBC* (September 13, 2008), online (www.bbc.co.uk).

46. "BofA Ties Chief's 2010 Bonus to Future Profits," *Financial Times* (February 1, 2011), online (www.ft.com).

47. "Banks, Aware of Discord on Pay, Work to Adjust, a Survey Finds," *The Wall Street Journal Europe* (March 30, 2009), p. 3.

48. "Bonus Question," op. cit.

49. "Bank Chief Champions Case for Fixed Pay," *Financial Times* (February 18, 2010), online (www.ft.com).

50. "Are Executives Worth their Huge Pay Packets?," *BBC* (September 15, 2010), online (www.bbc.co.uk).

51. M. Faulkender and J. Yang, "Inside the Black Box: The Role and Composition of Compensation Peer Groups," *Journal of Financial Economics*, 96, no. 2 (May 2010), pp. 257–70.

52. "Insurer Boss Attacks Fat Cat Pay?," *BBC* (September 4, 2009), online (www.bbc.co.uk).

53. Pfeffer and Sutton, *Hard facts*, op. cit.; see also W. A. Van der Stede, "Designing Effective Reward Systems," *Finance & Management* (October 2009), pp. 6–9.

54. "John Lewis Staff Get £151m Bonus," *BBC* (March 11, 2010), online (www.bbc.co.uk).

55. M. Beer and N. Katz, "Do Incentives Work? The Perception of A Worldwide Sample of Senior Executives," *Human Resource Planning*, 26, no. 3 (2003), pp. 30–44; W. A. Van der Stede, "The Pitfalls of Pay-for-Performance," *Finance & Management* (December 2007), pp. 10–13.

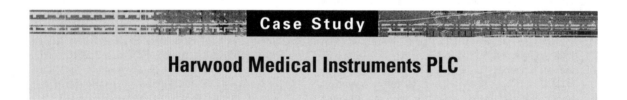

Case Study

Harwood Medical Instruments PLC

Harwood Medical Instruments PLC (HMI), based just outside of Birmingham, England, manufactured specialty medical instruments and sold them in market niches that were becoming increasingly competitive and price sensitive because of pressures to reduce health care costs. HMI was organized into nine divisions each run by a general manager. Over the years, HMI had grown both organically and by acquisition. Six of the divisions had been acquired by HMI within the past decade.

All of HMI's divisions sold medical products to hospitals, laboratories, and/or doctors, so the need for product quality and reliability was high. The divisions varied significantly, however, in terms of the degree to which their success depended on, for example, development of new products, efficiency of production, and/or customer service.

Bonuses for division general managers were paid semi-annually. Up to the year 2009, these bonuses were calculated as 1% of division operating profits.

HMI's managing director, Andy Guthrie, had concerns though that the operating profit measure was too narrowly focused. He had been reading

This case was prepared by Professor Kenneth A. Merchant.

Copyright © by Kenneth A. Merchant.

articles about performance measurement and decided to implement a "more balanced" scorecard. In November 2009, just before introducing a new bonus plan, Mr. Guthrie explained to his chief financial officer that he was willing to pay out higher bonuses than had been paid historically if improved performance warranted doing so.

The new plan provided a base bonus for division general managers of 1% of division operating profits for the half-year period. This base bonus was adjusted as follows:

- Increased by £5,000 if over 99% of deliveries were on time; by £2,000 if 95–99% of deliveries were on time; or by zero if less than 95% of deliveries were on time.

- Increased by £5,000 if sales returns were less than or equal to 1% of sales, or decreased by 50% of the excess of sales returns over 1% of sales.

- Increased by £1,000 for every patent application filed with the UK Intellectual Property Office.

- Reduced by the excess of scrap and rework costs over 1% of operating profit.

- Reduced by £5,000 if average customer satisfaction ratings were below 90%.

If the bonus calculation resulted in a negative amount for a particular period, the manager received no bonus. Negative amounts were not carried forward to the next period.

Exhibit 1 shows results for two representative HMI divisions for the year 2010, the first year under the new bonus plan. The Surgical Instruments Division (SID), one of HMI's original businesses, sold a variety of surgical instruments, including scissors, scalpels, retractors, and clamps. The markets for these products were mature, so growth was relatively slow. Not much innovation was needed, but controlling costs was critical. The Ultrasound Diagnosti Equipment Division (Ultrasound), which was acquired in 2007, sold and serviced ultrasound probes, transducers, and diagnostic imaging systems. The ultrasound market promised excellent growth and profits if the division could keep its sophisticated products on the cutting edge technologically and control both product development and production costs effectively.

In 2009, the total annual bonuses for the year earned by the managers of SID and Ultrasound were approximately £85,000 and £74,000, respectively.

Exhibit 1 Harwood Medical Instruments PLC

Operating results for the Surgical Instruments and Ultrasound Diagnostic Equipment Divisions, 2010 (£ in 000s)

	Surgical Instruments Division		Ultrasound Diagnostic Equipment Division	
	1st half of 2010	2nd half of 2010	1st half of 2010	2nd half of 2010
Sales	£42,000	£44,000	£28,600	£29,000
Operating profit	£4,620	£4,400	£3,420	£4,060
On-time deliveries	95.4%	97.3%	98.2%	94.6%
Sales returns	£450	£420	£291	£289
Patent applications filed	0	1	4	8
Scrap and rework costs	£51.1	£45.0	£39.7	£28.2
Customer satisfaction (average)	78%	89%	81%	91%

Case Study

Superconductor Technologies, Inc.

In October 2003, Martin (Marty) McDermut, Senior VP, CFO, and Secretary of Superconductor Technologies, Inc. (STI) was reflecting on some issues related to his company's compensation and incentive systems. He had multiple concerns. Marty knew that STI's most important asset was its people, and he was worried about employee retention. STI's stock price was stuck far below its historical highs, so most of the options that had been granted to employees were "underwater." Without the prospects of significant rewards, some of the company's key people might be "ready to bolt." He wondered, "What can we do so that these things that we have put in place don't vanish?"

Marty also worried that some of the incentive system elements might motivate some behaviors that were not in the shareholders' best interest. One specific concern of this type was that top management would be too motivated to try and sell the company to cash in the large numbers of options that they had been granted. He sighed:

> These things have tremendous motivational effects, but they can really get you in trouble if you don't think the issues all the way through.

COMPANY HISTORY AND STRATEGY

Superconductor Technologies, Inc. (STI) was founded in Santa Barbara, California, in 1987 by Nobel Prize winner Dr. J. Robert Schrieffer, who teamed up with three venture capitalists to form a company to capitalize on a scientific breakthrough known as high-temperature superconductivity (HTS) technology. In the mid-1990s, STI managers decided to focus their application of HTS technology on the wireless communications industry. In 1997, STI began the transformation to an operating company with the launch of its first commercial product, the SuperFilter®. M. Peter Thomas, a wireless-industry veteran, was hired as CEO.

By 2003, STI was the global leader in developing, manufacturing, and marketing HTS products for wireless communication networks. STI's products incorporated patented technologies that extended network coverage, increased capacity utilization, improved both the uplink and downlink radio frequency signals, thus lowering the incidence of dropped and blocked calls. They also enabled higher wireless transmission data rates while reducing operators' capital and operating costs. Over 3,000 STI systems had been installed worldwide, making STI the clear leader in the HTS wireless network optimization technology marketplace. STI's successes stemmed largely from its technological developments, including patented thin-film technologies and unique software design and simulation tools. It planned to exploit its management, engineering, and manufacturing expertise to maintain and expand its market leadership in radio frequency enhancement solutions.

In 2003, STI, which had nearly 300 employees, was organized into two main operating entities. One was located in Sunnyvale, California, at the former site of Conductus, a company acquired in December 2002. People at the Sunnyvale location were primarily involved in research, some of which was funded by the federal government on a cost-plus basis. The other operating entity was located in Santa Barbara, California. Personnel at the Santa Barbara location were responsible for the company's commercial applications.

STI management looked at the year 2002 as a "watershed year," even though STI reported a net loss of $19.5 million that year (see financial statements in Exhibits 1 and 2). The reason was the increased market acceptance of STI's products,

This case was prepared by Professors Kenneth A. Merchant and Wim A. Van der Stede. Financial support from the KPMG Foundation is gratefully acknowledged.

which was expected to fuel further revenue growth and bring the company closer to profitability. In its entire 17-year history, STI had never made a profit. In 2002, STI also completed a multimillion dollar expansion of its production facilities in Santa Barbara to ramp up production and further improve product quality.

Since 2001, STI revenues had grown quite rapidly. In 2003, revenues were expected to be nearly $50 million, up from $22 million in 2002. In both 2002 and 2003, STI was named one of the "Technology Fast 50" companies in the Los Angeles area.

STI was considered to be a consensus-driven company. As Marty McDermut phrased it, "People buy into our major decisions before we go ahead." Plans were developed on a bottom-up basis. Performance was reviewed monthly, and the forecasts for the remainder of the year were updated quarterly.

STI went public in March 1993 (NASDAQ: SCON), with 1.5 million shares offered at $10 per share. In an eight-week period in early 2000, STI's stock price shot up above $100, but it came down as quickly as it had risen. Most of the time since then the stock had been trading below $5 per share (see Exhibit 3).

Still, STI's future looked bright. In 2003, approximately 150,000 wireless communications base stations were deployed in the US alone, providing service to nearly 140 million people.[1] The number of US subscribers to mobile services had been growing at 14% per year, and the average monthly minutes of use per person was growing at an annual rate of 26%. The combined effect of more subscribers and more minutes of use resulted in an exponential increase in total wireless communications traffic. That growth was expected to continue, and the greater wireless traffic had also led to a rise in radio frequency interference, resulting in more dropped and blocked calls and origination failures, outcomes that negatively affect customer satisfaction. Consequently, the wireless operators' had continuing needs to find new, cost-effective ways to increase network traffic while improving network performance. STI's products, which could be employed at a fraction of the cost of building more

base stations, were designed to be part of the solution to the industry's delivery problems.

ELEMENTS OF MANAGEMENT COMPENSATION

The compensation package for STI's top 30 people, those down to the director level (one level below vice president), was comprised of three elements:

1. **Base salary**. STI set its salaries at competitive levels. For most employees, including top executives, annual salary increases were in the range of 0–5%.

2. **Cash bonuses**. All top STI executives were included in a bonus plan that provided cash awards based on the achievement of a weighted combination of corporate and individual objectives. The targeted bonus awards varied by organization level, from 25–40% of base salary.

Up through 2002, all bonuses were based exclusively on corporate performance. The compensation committee of the board of directors reached a judgment about corporate performance by comparing results measured in terms of the elements of a "performance scorecard" (see Table 1) with expectations.

The performance evaluation judgments did not automatically weight all the measurement elements equally in importance. Ken Barry, VP-Human Resources and Environmental Health & Safety, suspected that sales (revenue growth) was by far the most important criterion considered by the compensation committee. He postulated that the judgments about bonuses might come about as follows:

> Let's see . . . they met the revenue target; . . . they didn't earn as much profit as we'd expected; . . . but, they didn't have any major operational problems internally or externally, . . . and they signed a big deal . . . so, taken together, that probably warrants a bonus equal to potential for the year . . .

TABLE 1 Key elements of corporate "Performance Scorecard"

Cash	Number of employees
Sales	Warranty expenses
Profits	Inventory
Timing of sales	Yield
Receivables (days outstanding)	Gross margins
On-time delivery performance	Product reliability

[1] The global numbers were nearly one million base stations serving more than one billion customers.

Ken concluded that what it really came down to in normal years was for the compensation committee to decide whether to award a bonus at 80%, 100%, or 120% of the target bonus. Because the Board met with the key executives about four times a year, Ken believed that they had sufficient knowledge to make these bonus decisions, although the evaluations were undeniably subjective.

Before 2002, everyone received the same, undifferentiated bonus potential percentage. In 2002, however, the compensation committee concluded that some executives had performed better than others. They decided that these differences should be recognized by basing some of the bonus awards on individual performance. They decided to base the bonuses 75% on corporate performance and 25% on individual performance.

Each executive's individual performance was evaluated in terms of achievements in 4–9 performance areas tailored to the individual's areas of responsibility. Examples of achievements that were considered in the evaluations of specific individuals included:

● Successfully accomplish a project milestone;

● Reduce costs of products manufactured;

● Establish a needed line of credit;

● Maintain receivables at a level equal to or less than 28 days outstanding;

● Make significant new hires/retain valued employees;

● Maintain safe workplace (no lost-time accidents).

The evaluations of individual performance were linked to bonus awards as follows:

Evaluation	% of target bonus earned
Exceeded objectives	37.5
Met objectives	25
Partially missed objectives	12.5
Substantively missed objectives	0

When the compensation committee was not sure of its evaluations, they generally asked for more information or for an explanation from the "team leader," CEO Peter Thomas, before making the final call.

3. **Stock options**. Annually, almost all STI employees were given stock options. The purpose of the options was to promote the success, and enhance the value, of the company by linking the personal interests of participating employees to those of the company's stockholders and by providing such employees with an incentive for outstanding performance. The details of the stock option plan had been modified somewhat over the years, but all the options granted were 10-year options, and they vested over either four or five years.

The number of options granted varied depending on organization level, tenure, and individual performance. Lower-level employees were given only a few, perhaps only 200, options per year. Top management received thousands of options annually. Exhibits 3 and 4 provide detail on the option grants given to STI's top five executives.

Ken Barry estimated that in a normal year, about 10% of the workforce (30 employees, say) did not receive stock options, for one of three reasons each of which explained the treatment of about 10 of the excluded employees. The first reason was because some employees did not meet performance expectations. Ken added, "By not meeting performance expectations I mean that we usually let these employees go within the next year." Second, some employees were not given the annual allotment of options for equity reasons. Some of them, for example, had recently received extra options because they had been promoted. And third, extra options were not provided to employees hired during the last quarter of the year.[2]

IMPLEMENTATION OF THE COMPENSATION PLANS

In 2001, STI failed to achieve its revenue plan by a narrow margin. All STI executives were given 80% of their target bonus.

The year 2002 was not a good one. STI did not come close to achieving its aggressive revenue plan. The STI plan was set at $32 million, and the actual revenues for 2002 were $22 million. In July 2002, management implemented a salary cut of 10% for the top 10 executives. At the end of the year no bonuses were paid, and virtually all the options that had been granted previously were underwater.

---

[2] All employees were given stock options when they were first hired.

In March 2003, STI's board approved a 2003 Equity Incentive Plan that reserved six million shares for issuance to key employees, directors, and consultants of the company. Two million of these shares were reserved for the top 20 executives. This plan replaced other stock option plans created in 1992, 1998, and 1999. It was designed both to help ensure that STI did not lose its key employees and to drive employees to focus on having the company become profitable. Becoming profitable was important because management wanted to raise more money, but they were told that would be difficult until and if the company started earning profits.

The 2003 Equity Incentive Plan provided 10-year options to be awarded on January 1, 2004, with "cliff vesting" after five years.[3] However, this plan also included a unique feature, a promise of accelerated vesting – 50% on January 1, 2004, and 50% on January 1, 2005 – if the company was profitable in the fourth quarter of 2003 and if the profits were judged to be sustainable.[4]

In January 2003, the executives whose salaries had been cut had their salaries reinstated to prior levels. They were not given back pay, however.

ISSUES FOR THE FUTURE

Both Marty McDermut and Ken Barry raised issues about the incentive packages that STI should use in the future. If accounting rules regarding stock options were changed to require the immediate recording of the value of the options as an expense, as seemed likely to happen, should that cause the company either to discontinue the granting of options or to restrict their use, perhaps only for top executives? Should the company instead substitute restricted stock, or some combination of restricted stock and options? Marty did not think that the solution would be just to provide higher bonus payments because those payments would cause "a big hit to the P&L."

Particularly if the use of options was to be restricted, Ken Barry thought that the company would need more deferred compensation options, mechanisms that would allow the company to spread the employees' compensation over five, 10, or even 15 years. Deferred compensation approaches had tax benefits for the employees, and they allowed the company to save cash during its most rapid growth period.

Related was a concern about the appropriate short-term/long-term balance of the incentive package. Should STI link the much desired annual profit objective more strongly with incentives, or should the company continue to be patient in its positioning of the firm for long-term success? Ken also was not sure whether the assignments of the rewards should be less subjective after the firm became profitable.

Ken had also started thinking about issues that the company would face when it expanded internationally. STI had no foreign employees as yet, but Ken knew that incentive approaches varied markedly around the world. He wanted to be prepared to give recommendations to management when and if the international expansion took place.

---

[3] That is, all the options would vest on January 1, 2009.

[4] Without the cliff vesting feature, the accelerated vesting in this plan would have had a significant accounting implication. The original fixed price options did not require the recording of any compensation expense because the options were granted at the market price at the time of grant (*Accounting Principles Board Statement 25, Accounting for Stock Issued to Employees* (October 1972). However, without the cliff vesting provision, a change in terms, in this case the acceleration of vesting, if it happened, would require STI to record compensation expense in accordance with the "variable method" (*FASB Interpretation 44, Accounting for Certain Transactions Involving Stock Compensation: An Interpretation of APB Opinion No. 25* (March 31, 2000). Under variable accounting, compensation expense is recognized based on the excess of the underlying stock's market price over the exercise price on the exercise date. Then, prior to the exercise date, compensation expense is estimated each period. It varies with the movement in the price of the company's stock in comparison to the exercise price. Therefore, if a company changes the terms of its stock option grants, it is subject to the uncertainty of how much compensation expense it will have to record, not only during the vesting period of the option, but until the option is actually exercised by the employee. If the company's stock performs well, the company will probably have to take a hit to earnings.

Exhibit 1 Superconductor Technologies, Inc.: income statement data for years ending December 31 ($ millions)

	2002	2001	2000	1999	1998
Net sales or revenues	22.40	12.39	9.96	7.12	7.98
Cost of goods sold	17.36	8.49	13.92	5.54	10.79
Depreciation, depletion, and amortization	1.93	2.14	1.79	1.31	0.94
Gross income	**3.11**	**1.77**	**−5.75**	**0.27**	**−3.74**
Selling, general, & admin expenses	18.90	18.90	15.09	10.88	5.44
Other operating expenses	0.00	0.00	0.00	0.00	0.00
Other expenses – total	38.18	29.52	30.80	17.72	17.16
Operating income	−15.79	−17.13	−20.85	−10.60	−9.18
Extraordinary charge – pretax	3.80	0.98	0.13	0.00	0.00
Nonoperating interest income	0.22	1.05	0.81	0.02	0.08
Earnings before interest and taxes (EBIT)	**−19.37**	**−17.06**	**−20.17**	**−10.58**	**−9.10**
Interest expense on debt	0.15	0.15	0.48	0.30	0.06
Pretax income	−19.51	−17.20	−20.66	−10.88	−9.16
Income taxes	0.00	0.00	0.00	0.00	0.00
Net income before extra items/preferred div	**−19.51**	**−17.20**	**−20.66**	**−10.88**	**−9.16**
Extra items & gain(loss) sale of assets	0.00	0.00	−10.61	0.00	0.00
Net income before preferred dividends	−19.51	−17.20	−31.27	−10.88	−9.16
Preferred dividend requirements	1.76	2.60	2.20	1.36	0.27
Net income available to common	**−21.27**	**−19.80**	**−22.86**	**−12.24**	**−9.43**

Exhibit 2 Superconductor Technologies, Inc.: Balance Sheet Data for years ending December 31 ($ millions)

Assets	2002	2001	2000	1999	1998
Cash and ST investments	18.19	15.21	31.82	0.07	0.31
Receivables (net)	3.41	1.45	3.69	1.59	1.94
Total inventories	6.35	5.73	3.78	2.75	2.72
Raw materials	1.84	1.39	1.09	0.43	0.82
Work in progress	3.14	2.95	1.96	1.69	1.67
Finished goods	2.01	1.40	0.72	0.63	0.24
Progress payments & other	−0.65	0.00	0.00	0.00	0.00
Prepaid expenses	0.00	0.00	0.00	0.00	0.00
Other current assets	0.56	0.60	0.50	0.45	0.17
Current assets – total	28.50	22.98	39.79	4.85	5.14
Long-term receivables	0.82	0.00	0.00	0.00	0.00
Property, plant & equipment – net	11.09	5.22	4.99	4.10	5.11
Property, plant & equipment – gross	23.74	16.24	14.34	12.15	12.10
Accumulated depreciation	12.65	11.03	9.35	8.05	6.99
Other assets	25.74	1.96	1.98	2.14	2.25
Deferred charges	0.00	0.00	0.00	0.00	0.00
Tangible other assets	0.49	0.28	0.11	0.21	0.18
Intangible other assets	25.25	1.68	1.88	1.93	2.07
Total assets	**66.15**	**30.16**	**46.76**	**11.09**	**12.51**
Liabilities & shareholders equity					
Accounts payable	5.89	2.70	2.00	1.80	2.40
ST debt & current portion of LT debt	1.55	0.28	0.24	2.16	0.81
Accrued payroll	1.05	0.84	0.90	0.67	0.58
Income taxes payable	0.00	0.00	0.00	0.00	0.00
Dividends payable	0.00	0.00	0.00	0.00	0.00
Other current liabilities	3.50	0.41	0.46	0.24	0.00
Current liabilities – total	12.00	4.23	3.60	4.87	3.79
Long-term debt	0.57	0.27	0.51	0.75	0.93
Other liabilities	3.23	2.00	4.24	0.00	0.00
Total liabilities	**15.80**	**6.50**	**8.35**	**5.62**	**4.72**
Preferred stock	0.00	37.53	0.00	20.34	8.98
Common equity	50.34	−13.87	38.41	−14.87	−1.20
Common stock	0.06	0.02	0.02	0.01	0.01
Capital surplus	154.74	73.34	110.65	32.21	35.01
Other appropriated reserves	0.00	−2.28	−4.52	0.00	0.00
Retained earnings	−104.46	−84.95	−67.75	−47.09	−36.22
Total liabilities & shareholders equity	**66.15**	**30.16**	**46.76**	**11.09**	**12.51**
Common shares outstanding (thousands)	59,823.55	18,579.16	17,823.16	7,739.22	7,722.59

Exhibit 3 Superconductor Technologies, Inc.: stock performance

SUPER TECH as of 20-Feb-2004

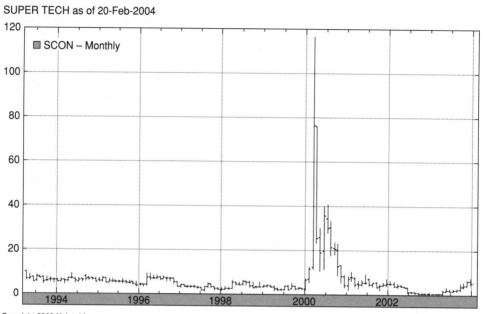

http://finance.yahoo.com/

Exhibit 4 Superconductor Technologies, Inc.: executive officer compensation

The following table sets forth all compensation received for services rendered to the Company in all capacities during the fiscal years ended December 31, 2002, 2001, and 2000 by the Company's Chief Executive Officer and the four executive officers other than the Chief Executive Officer whose total salary and bonus for fiscal year 2002 exceeded $100,000.

Name and principal position	Year	Annual compensation			Long-term compensation	
		Salary ($)	Bonus ($)	Other ($)[1]	Securities underlying options (#)	All other compensation ($)[2]
M. Peter Thomas	2002	303,854	–	–	125,000	1,980
President and Chief	2001	300,014	72,000	–	75,000	2,323
Executive Officer	2000	285,394	70,000	–	250,000	1,290
E. Ray Cotten	2002	194,997	–	–	57,750	6,180
Senior Vice President,	2001	209,467	30,172	–	7,300	7,250
Business Development	2000	195,582	28,080	–	20,000	3,810
Robert B. Hammond	2002	208,394	–	–	57,750	690
Senior Vice President and	2001	205,945	29,628	–	3,650	809
Chief Technical Officer	2000	194,613	27,675	–	40,000	690
Robert L. Johnson[4]	2002	186,267	–	–	66,000	690
President, STI Wireless	2001	182,163	26,244	–	38,350	809
Systems, North America	2000	116,462[4]	20,048	–	100,000	504
Martin S. McDermut[5]	2002	194,961	–	–	43,750	690
Senior Vice President,	2001	193,895	23,310	–	43,750	809
Chief Financial Officer	2000	167,212[5]	24,975	43,374[3]	100,000	398
and Secretary						
Charles E. Shalvoy[6]	2002	277,052	–	–	–	–
President and CEO	2001	264,992	56,644	–	153,000	–[7]
of Conductus	2000	250,185	66,250	–	200,000	–

[1] Excludes certain perquisites and other amounts that, for any executive officer, in the aggregate did not exceed the lesser of $50,000 or 10% of the total annual salary and bonus for such executive officer.

[2] Term life insurance premiums.

[3] One-time relocation expenses.

[4] Mr. Johnson joined the Company in April 2000.

[5] Mr. McDermut joined the Company in February 2000.

[6] Mr. Shalvoy joined the Company in December 2002. All compensation paid by Conductus prior to acquisition of Conductus by the Company. Mr. Shalvoy is the President of the Conductus subsidiary and an Executive Vice President of Superconductor Technologies, Inc.

[7] Because Conductus provided group term life insurance for its employees and named executive officers on an aggregate basis, Conductus is unable to determine the amount of term life insurance premiums paid by Conductus for Mr. Shalvoy during the 2002, 2001, and 2000 fiscal years.

Source: STI Proxy Statement, May 23, 2003.

Exhibit 5 Superconductor Technologies, Inc.: option grants to executives in 2002

The following table sets forth certain information regarding stock options granted during the fiscal year ended December 31, 2002, to each of the executive officers named in the table under "Executive Officer Compensation – Summary Compensation Table."

| | Individual grants | | | | Potential realizable value at assumed annual rates of stock price appreciation for option term[3] | |
Name	Number of securities underlying options granted[1]	% of Total Options granted to employees in fiscal year[2]	Exercise price ($/share)	Expiration date	5% ($)	10% ($)
M. Peter Thomas	125,000	15%	5.60	2/4/2012	385,930	950,563
E. Ray Cotten	57,750	7%	5.60	2/4/2012	178,300	439,160
Robert B. Hammond	57,750	7%	5.23	1/23/2012	178,300	439,160
Robert L. Johnson	66,000	8%	5.23	1/23/2012	190,307	468,736
Martin S. McDermut	43,750	5%	5.23	1/23/2012	126,151	310,715
Charles E. Shalvoy[4]	–	–	–	–	–	–

[1] Except as set forth herein, each option vests over a four-year period at the rate of $1/4$th of the shares subject to the option at the end of the first 12 months and $1/36$th of the remaining shares subject to the option at the end of each monthly period thereafter so long as such optionee's employment with the Company has not terminated.

[2] Total number of shares subject to options granted to employees in fiscal 2002 was 851,975, which number includes options granted to employee directors, but excludes options granted to nonemployee directors and consultants.

[3] The Potential Realizable Value is calculated based on the fair market value on the date of grant, which is equal to the exercise price of options granted in fiscal 2002, assuming that the stock appreciates in value from the date of grant until the end of the option term at the compounded annual rate specified (5% and 10%). Potential Realizable Value is net of the option exercise price. The assumed rates of appreciation are specified in rules of the SEC and do not represent the Company's estimate or projection of future stock price. Actual gains, if any, resulting from stock option exercises and common stock holdings are dependent on the future performance of the common stock and overall stock market conditions, as well as the option holders' continued employment through the exercise/vesting period. There can be no assurance that the amounts reflected in this table will be achieved.

[4] Mr. Shalvoy joined the Company in December 2002 and did not receive any options from the Company in 2002, although he did receive options from Conductus in 2002 prior to the acquisition.

Source: STI Proxy Statement, May 23, 2003.

Case Study

Tsinghua Tongfang Co. Ltd.

If Tsinghua Tongfang can keep its pace of development as it does now ... it will make one hundred ten millionaires and 1,000 millionaires within a period of at most three to five years.[1]

Lu Zhicheng, CEO, Tsinghua Tongfang Co. Ltd.

Historically, the vast majority of the corporations in the People's Republic of China used bureaucratic forms of control characterized by, for example, centralization of authority, subjective performance evaluations and, if any, only relatively small performance-based incentives. However, as China adapted to its new socialist market economy and competition in the global economy, Chinese corporations were changing their control systems rapidly. They were decentralizing their operations, developing more formal performance evaluation systems, and providing larger performance-related incentives. Still, subjective performance evaluations remained common and heavily weighted in many Chinese corporations in the early 21st century.

Tsinghua Tongfang Co. Ltd. (THTF), one of China's most successful high-tech companies, was different. A young company, it had a relatively well developed and objective performance measurement, evaluation, and incentive system. Significant bonuses were offered to most of the company's management-level employees based on performance measured in terms of return on investment (ROI).

THTF managers were generally pleased with their measurement/incentive system, although they knew that the system would have to evolve over time, as Meilan Han (chief financial officer) explained:

We've taken a conservative approach that is designed to prevent failures. We worry that if we have failures, we can ruin the reputation of the company and Tsinghua University [the company's largest shareholder]. Our conservative approach has been very successful. But as we continue to grow, it is inevitable that our systems will have to change.

One change that the company's managers were hoping to make as soon as possible was to add stock options to the compensation packages of at least some employees, if and when the Chinese government legalized their use.

COMPANY BACKGROUND

THTF, headquartered in Beijing, was one of China's leading high technology companies.[2] In 2002, the company's sales revenue was about 5.5 billion yuan,[3] 50% derived from the sale of computer products (e.g. personal computers and components), 31% from network, software, and systems integration products, and 19% from resource and environmental engineering and facilities products (e.g. energy economization systems, pollution control systems, large-scale container inspection systems). Net income in 2002 was 184 million yuan. Exhibit 1 presents a five-year summary of financial data.

THTF was created through the consolidation of ten enterprises owned by Tsinghua University. Tsinghua University was widely regarded as being China's premiere engineering-oriented university ("the MIT of China"). The association with Tsinghua University provided THTF with a reputation for high technology and high quality, which made its products easier to sell. THTF was particularly proud of its highly educated employees, many of

---

[1] "Bring Hundred Multimillionaires in Tsinghua Tongfang," *People's Daily*, August 1, 2000.

[2] A China Securities/Asian Commerce survey of the "Top 50 Highest Development Potential Chinese Companies," ranked THTF 6 (*SINO-US Weekly*, June 20, 2000).

[3] yuan = US$0.123.

This case was prepared by Professors Thomas W. Lin and Kenneth A. Merchant.

Copyright © by Thomas W. Lin and Kenneth A. Merchant.

whom had earned degrees in technical fields. Among its approximately 1,200 employees, 22% had masters degrees and 66% had bachelors degrees. Company brochures described THTF's philosophy as follows:

> Today's THTF is the successful combination of applying human and capital market resources to high technology. Tomorrow it will stand firmly as a world leader in developing technology and serving society with innovative products and services.

THTF launched its initial public stock offering on June 27, 1997, with 110.7 million shares issued at a price of 15.99 yuan. The stock was listed on the Shanghai Stock Exchange. After the IPO, Tsinghua University was the largest shareholder with 59.3% of the company's total shares.

Just before THTF's stock was listed, all of the company's 1,200 employees were given shares of THTF stock. The number of shares granted depending on each employee's organizational position. THTF stock subsequently appreciated significantly, to 67.5 yuan on January 15, 1998. As a consequence, some of the company's employees became quite wealthy. In summer 2001, the stock was trading in the range of 40–50 yuan. By 2001, because of the issuance of additional public shares, the university owned exactly 50% of the company's stock. The employees, all of whom were company stockholders, owned 3.8% of the company's shares.

ORGANIZATION AND MANAGEMENT STYLE

THTF was organized into more than ten subsidiary companies, almost all of which were growing rapidly. The company used a decentralized management philosophy. The general managers of the subsidiary company had substantial authority in all functional areas of their business except finance, which was centralized. (An organization chart is presented in Exhibit 2.)

THTF's corporate managers used a variety of management control mechanisms to ensure good corporate performance, including the following:

1. **Control of cash flow.** Each subsidiary company was given limits on total cash spending in any given month. In addition, if monthly cash flows were negative for six months in a row, then the subsidiary company would have to finance itself. It would be denied further loans from headquarters.

2. **Monthly spending limits.** Monthly expenditures on office expenses were limited to 7% of sales. Monthly spending on promotional expenses (e.g. samples, entertainment, travel, exhibitions, advertising) was limited to 10% of sales. R&D and technological change expenses were approved as part of the annual budgeting process.

3. **Control of accounts receivable.** Monthly ending balances of accounts receivable were limited to 15% of monthly sales.

4. **Control over inventory.** Ending monthly inventory balances were limited to 30% of monthly sales. The allowable ending inventory balance was reduced by 10% of the value of any finished goods inventory that did not move in a three-month period, by 20% of the value of any inventory older than four months, and so on.

5. **Fixed asset control.** The subsidiary company general manager could approve a purchase if it was within an approved budget line-item amount. However, every fixed asset purchase over 5,000 yuan needed an invoice and a voucher with signatures from the purchasing clerk, the subsidiary company fixed asset administrator, and the subsidiary company general manager.

   If the amount of expenditure exceeded the original budget amount, corporate approval was required. To obtain that approval, subsidiary managers were required to prepare a detailed investment proposal.

   All fixed asset dispositions, whether they were transfers to another subsidiary company or sales to an outsider, required approval by both the subsidiary company general manager and a corporate officer.

   At yearend, corporate and subsidiary company fixed asset administrators participated in a joint inspection of all fixed assets.

6. **All accounting people working in the subsidiaries were placed in their positions by corporate.**

7. **All employees were eligible for performance-dependent rewards** (see below).

Meilan Han (vice president and chief financial officer) estimated that perhaps two thirds of the subsidiary company managers accepted the control systems described above without complaint. However, some complained that the system was too restrictive.

PERFORMANCE EVALUATION SYSTEM

In 1998, THTF implemented a formal individual employee performance evaluation system consisting of three parts: self evaluation (20%), peer evaluation (20%), and direct superior's evaluation (60%). Each part of the evaluation was based on judgments in each of the following areas:

1. **Performance:** efficiency, effectiveness, and output quality.

2. **Dedication:** commitment, work attitude, and self motivation.

3. **Obedience** to superiors and cooperation with others.

4. **Knowledge:** technical and managerial skills, experience, and demonstration of competence.

5. **Discipline:** attendance, adherence to company rules and regulations, and good moral character.

Twice per year (in July and January), each rater assigned scores for each criterion on a 20-point scale with the following guidelines:

Excellent (a score of 17–20)
Good (13–16)
Adequate (9–12)
Need improvement (5–8)
Unacceptable (1–4)

For both the self evaluation and the direct superior's evaluation, the rater had to explain in writing the reasons for assigning a specific score for each criterion. After completing the self evaluation form, each employee also had to write down a plan for improvement in the next half year.

For the peer evaluation, each employee evaluated his/her immediate superior, colleagues, and subordinates. Typically employees rated five to 20 people, depending on the specific position the employee held.

INCENTIVE SYSTEM

The compensation packages for all employees included some performance-dependent elements. For example, for a subsidiary general manager, the average total annual compensation was comprised of approximately 30% base salary, 40% "discretionary bonus," and 30% formula bonus.

Salary increases were based on the semi-annual performance evaluations described above. About 50% of the importance weighting was placed on *performance*. The other criteria were weighted approximately equally.

The **discretionary bonus** was "almost guaranteed." While it could be withheld under exceptional

TABLE 1 Function linking subsidiary performance with annual bonus amounts

Actual ROI ÷ target ROI	Total bonus amount (%) (marginal % of excess profit)
<100	0
100–119.9	40
120–129.9	50
130–139.9	60
140–159.9	70
160–169.9	80
170–179.9	90
>180	100

circumstances, it never had been withheld at THTF. Thus, it was like another component of salary, and it increased proportionally with increases in base salary.

The **performance-dependent bonuses** for all subsidiary company employees were based on subsidiary company results – return on investment (ROI) and "excess profit." – as is shown in Table 1. Excess profit was defined as actual profit less profit based on target ROI.

Performance targets were set to be challenging-but-achievable. Since most of the subsidiary companies operated in highly uncertain markets, their performances as compared to targets varied. In a typical year approximately two (of the 10) subsidiary companies would not achieve the ROI target level. One would be at or near the target. The other seven would exceed the target, and some would do so by a wide margin.

The function shown in Table 1 defined the size of the bonus pool to be allocated among subsidiary company personnel. Subsidiary general managers decided how to allocate the pool to individual employees. Corporate managers did not prescribe a policy for making these allocations, but they did reserve the right to exercise some judgment to "smooth out" the allocations of bonuses. In recent years, the highest bonus given to any individual totaled 70% of that person's total compensation.

Bonuses for corporate-level managers and staff were based on corporate ROI performance, using a similar performance/reward function.

In addition to this bonus plan, THTF conducted an annual employee vote to select the top 1% "Star Employees" and the top 5% "Excellent Employees."

(Managers were not eligible.) These employees had the opportunity to get additional bonuses, promotions, overseas study opportunities, and new share issues.

EMPLOYEE STOCK OPTION PLAN

THTF managers regretted that they had been unable to add stock options to the mix of compensation offered to the company's employees. They viewed options as important for attracting and retaining the best employee talent. Historically, Chinese companies had not been allowed to issue stock options. Joint venture companies operating in China were allowed by law to use stock options and restricted stock grants, and some Chinese companies listed their stock on the Hong Kong stock exchange explicitly to evade the ban on the use of options. But THTF managers expected that a law permitting the company to use options would soon pass the People's Congress, as the Chinese government wanted to encourage, particularly, development of the country's information technology and software industries.

Anticipating the legalization of stock options, THTF designed a stock option plan with the following parameters for use when legal:

- The total number of stock options granted would be limited to 5% of total shares outstanding.

- The option term would be for a 10-year period.

- The stock options would be part of the company's incentive systems. Stock option grants would be announced once per year. The vesting of options would be limited to 30% after one year of the date of grant, 30% after two years, and 40% after three years. There would be two exercise windows per year.

- Only five types of employees would be eligible for option grants: (1) top management including CEO, CFO, COO, VP (to be given 15 to 20% of the grants awarded); (2) subsidiary company Presidents and VPs (15 to 20%); (3) special contribution employees such as senior managers, senior engineers, and department managers (50 to 60%); (4) R&D employees with

TABLE 2 Link between corporate performance and option grants to be awarded

If sales growth rate was:	Or profit growth rate was:	Then stock option grants as % of total shares outstanding would be:
≥100%	≥50%	1.0–1.5%
≥70%	≥30%	0.75–1.25%
≥50%	≥20%	0.5–1.0%
≥30%	≥10%	0.25–0.75%

successful new product developments (10 to 20%); and (5) new top management, senior engineers, or marketing managers who joined the THTF through a merger or acquisition.

- The above mentioned employees would be eligible only if their annual performance was rated as either "Excellent" or "Good."

- To protect shareholder interests, stock option grants would take place only in years when the company's previous year performance met all of the following criteria: (1) sales growth rate of 10% or more, (2) profit growth rate of 5% or more, and (3) ROA greater than 105% of the rate paid on government Treasury Bills.

- The total number of options to be granted would be linked to overall THTF performance using the schedule shown in Table 2.

- No company employee would be allowed to hold more than 5% of the company's total number of authorized shares.

- This proposed employee stock option plan was subject to approval by proper government authorities.

If they were able to grant options, THTF managers expected that they would reduce the size of the bonus potentials to keep the total compensation package amounts at current levels – competitive, but not excessive. But they also wanted key THTF employees to share in the company's success. They thought that an option program, particularly, would be important in attracting and retaining talented employees to THTF and in rewarding them for their efforts.

EXHIBIT 1 Tsinghua Tongfang Co. Ltd.: five-year financial data (unit = 1,000 Yuan)

	1998	1999	2000	2001	2002
Sales revenues	815,952	1,684,108	3,336,791	5,033,945	5,460,617
Cost of goods sold	614,548	1,278,953	2,729,206	4,157,496	4,644,226
Selling expenses	37,239	82,747	137,558	219,127	286,465
Administrative expenses	64,312	99,694	129,918	225,174	287,833
Interest expenses	−5,117	13,062	22,848	15,155	19,312
Operating income	105,033	209,652	317,261	416,993	222,780
Other income (expenses)	8,961	9,424	16,588	15,978	31,369
Minority interests	805	35,119	58,917	85,141	38,430
Income taxes	8,425	23,109	38,957	57,072	32,124
Net income	104,764	160,848	235,975	290,758	183,595
Current assets	912,294	1,703,306	3,877,716	4,228,184	4,303,856
Long-term investments	65,198	56,246	214,545	256,490	491,188
Fixed assets	266,625	543,473	772,293	1,217,670	1,209,500
Intangible & deferred assets	132,320	260,507	426,026	362,828	271,777
Total assets	1,376,437	2,563,532	5,290,580	6,065,172	6,276,321
Current liabilities	597,765	804,237	1,542,553	2,141,535	2,712,017
Deferred taxes			5,113	4,545	3,977
Long-term liabilities	108,748	183,682	261,170	235,147	152,564
Total liabilities	706,513	987,919	1,808,836	2,381,227	2,868,558
Minority interests	33,736	260,242	908,132	1,020,601	645,125
Stockholders' equity	636,188	1,315,371	2,573,612	2,663,344	2,762,637
Total liab. & equity	1,376,437	2,563,532	5,290,580	6,065,172	6,276,321
Total shares (000)	166,050	260,000	383,075	574,612	574,612

EXHIBIT 2 Tsinghua Tongfang Co. Ltd.: organization chart

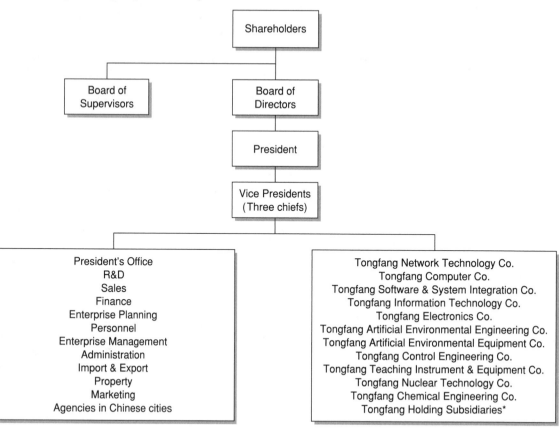

```
                          ┌──────────────┐
                          │ Shareholders │
                          └──────────────┘
              ┌──────────────────┴──────────────┐
      ┌──────────────┐                  ┌──────────────┐
      │   Board of   │                  │   Board of   │
      │  Supervisors │                  │   Directors  │
      └──────────────┘                  └──────────────┘
                                                │
                                        ┌──────────────┐
                                        │  President   │
                                        └──────────────┘
                                                │
                                     ┌────────────────────┐
                                     │  Vice Presidents   │
                                     │   (Three chiefs)   │
                                     └────────────────────┘
```

| President's Office
R&D
Sales
Finance
Enterprise Planning
Personnel
Enterprise Management
Administration
Import & Export
Property
Marketing
Agencies in Chinese cities | Tongfang Network Technology Co.
Tongfang Computer Co.
Tongfang Software & System Integration Co.
Tongfang Information Technology Co.
Tongfang Electronics Co.
Tongfang Artificial Environmental Engineering Co.
Tongfang Artificial Environmental Equipment Co.
Tongfang Control Engineering Co.
Tongfang Teaching Instrument & Equipment Co.
Tongfang Nuclear Technology Co.
Tongfang Chemical Engineering Co.
Tongfang Holding Subsidiaries* |

* Beijing Tsinghua Reftek Control Engineering Co. (60% owned by THTF), Beijing Advanced Systems Development Co. (51%), Beijing Tsinghua Golden-Profit Chemical Engineering Co. (51%), Beijing Dascom Network Security Co. (51%), Jiangxi Tsinghua Taiho Electronics Co. (51%), Jiangxi Radio Factory Co. (99%), Tsinghua Tongfang Optical Disc Co. (51%), Jiangxi Tsinghua Tongfang Pharmaceutical Co. (51%).

Case Study

Raven Capital, LLC

In late December 2009, portfolio managers at hedge fund Raven Capital, LLC had just finished delivering annual performance reviews and year-end bonuses to their staffs. They spent considerable time and effort trying both to allocate bonuses fairly and to keep employees happy. But those two goals were sometimes in conflict. Every year some employees were surprised by the amount of their bonuses. Some of the surprises were positive, but inevitably some were negative.

CFO Julie Behrens reflected on Raven's performance evaluation and incentive compensation plan:

This case was Prepared by Professor Kenneth A. Merchant and research assistant Michelle Spaulding.

Copyright © by Kenneth A. Merchant.

Hedge funds like ours have access to lots of data. We have many performance measures and indices that we can use for benchmarking purposes. But interestingly, our incentive plan is not purely quantitative. We consider the performance metrics, but none of them gives us a complete picture of an employee's contribution to the company. The management team makes our evaluation system work with painstaking qualitative adjustments. Still, I wonder if we should make at least a portion of our incentive plan more formulaic.

INDUSTRY BACKGROUND

Hedge fund managers pursue absolute returns on their underlying investments. The investments can be any combination of financial vehicles, including stocks, bonds, commodities, currencies, and derivatives. Sometimes hedge fund managers hold cash, sell short, and/or buy or sell options or futures.

The word "hedge" means to manage risk. Risks come in many forms, such as inflation risk, market risk, interest rate risk, currency risk, sector risk, and regional risk. Hedge fund managers are experts in designing hedging positions for most perceivable risks, making a true hedge fund less risky than a traditional long-only investment fund, at least in theory. But each hedge fund is unique. Different hedge funds use different mixes of investment vehicles, and their strategies vary significantly from conservative to highly speculative.

Hedge funds differ from other managed funds in a few key areas. Hedge fund investors are typically required to have high income, high net worth, and demonstrated investment knowledge. Because hedge funds manage money for a limited range of sophisticated, accredited investors, they operate with fewer regulations than other funds. They are less restricted in their use of leverage and are distinguished from mutual funds by a greater flexibility in investment strategies. Hedge fund management companies are typically organized as limited partnerships. The manager acts as the general partner, and the investors act as the limited partners.

Most hedge fund companies use the same business model. They derive revenue from two sources: management fees and incentive fees. Management fees, typically 1–2% of assets under management (AUM), are earned regardless of performance. Incentive fees, collected annually, are performance-based, typically totaling 20% of a fund's return above a "high water mark," the highest level of value the

fund ever had for each investor. If a fund loses money, its managers are not penalized, but they cannot collect further incentive fees until the fund surpasses its high water mark; i.e., until the losses are recovered. The high water marks are different for each investor, depending on the point at which they invested their monies. (See Exhibit 1 for a simple high water mark example.) Hedge funds typically use the management fees to cover their operating expenses. Incentive fees are normally distributed to staff as bonuses.

The year 2008 was an extremely challenging year for the hedge fund industry. The S&P 500 index dropped 37%, the credit markets tightened, and investors around the world fled to safe investments. AUM at hedge funds fell sharply due to trading losses and redemptions, as investors rushed to liquidate their assets. A record number of hedge funds closed in 2008. By 2009, the S&P 500 rose 24%, regaining some of the prior year's losses. According to several indexes that track hedge fund performance, hedge funds that survived 2008 were up 18% or more in 2009, making it the best year for hedge fund performance since 2003. However, almost half of all hedge funds were still below their high water marks at the end of 2009.

RAVEN CAPITAL, LLC

Investment strategy

Raven Capital, LLC was founded in 1999 by Maxwell (Max) Stoneman. Total AUM in 2009 were slightly less than $1 billion. Raven's funds bought and sold long and short positions in domestic equities. Raven managers focused their investments in industries – financial, energy, technology, consumer products, and healthcare – in which they had years of expertise and many management contacts. Their heaviest investment weights were in the financial and energy industries.

Almost half of Raven's AUM came from "funds of funds" – funds that invested in portfolios of different hedge funds. Another 33% came from pension and retirement funds, and 18% came from high net worth individuals. Only 1.5% came from foundations and endowments. (See Exhibit 2 for a chart of capital sources by investor type.)

As a traditional hedge fund, Raven made investment decisions based on fundamentals, not short-term momentum, arbitrage opportunities, or expectations of superior predictions of macroeconomic trends. Analytical horse power was considered key to Raven's success. Raven managers sought superior returns based on a thorough understanding of strategic, financial, and competitive dynamics of companies and industries, as well as selective entry and exit points. Specifically for long positions, Raven targeted both growth companies and solid companies that were currently out of favor. Raven also took short positions in companies that they perceived had fundamental problems, aggressive accounting and overstated earnings, and/or stock prices that reflected unrealistic earnings expectations.

Raven's approach was disciplined. Managers were cognizant of macro-economic trends, but macro trends did not materially alter the overall strategies, long/short exposures, or industry focus. As portfolio manager Jeffrey Lomintz put it, "We do what we say we're going to do within the bands that are prescribed because we want to have product integrity." Raven funds had tight net exposure targets (long exposure plus the absolute value of short exposure). Net exposure for their long/short funds was typically 40%–55%.

Organization

Raven's 17 employees were organized into two groups, Investment Management and Business Operations. Max Stoneman was the general manager and CIO of Raven. Together with Jeffrey Lomnitz, Max also managed the Investment Management Group. Max and Jeffrey acted as Raven's portfolio managers (PMs), managing 100% of the firm's assets. They supervised the analysts and traders who comprised the balance of Investment Management. Julie Behrens managed Business Operations. (See Exhibit 3 for an organization chart.)

The analysts were industry specialists who closely studied and monitored the publicly traded companies in their industry. They studied financial statements, interviewed management, and ran models, working to identify inflection points in companies' business models. Analysts frequently championed stocks for inclusion in Raven funds, and made entry and exit price recommendations. They were also responsible for monitoring stocks once investments had been made in them.

As PMs, Jeffrey and Max were responsible for "pulling the trigger" on stock picks. They considered

analysts' inputs, and decided which stocks to buy at what price, and how to size the positions. The analysts perceived the PM's investment styles as being somewhat different. One was described as wanting to be a "home run hitter." The other was said to take "smaller cuts at the ball because he did not like volatility."

The traders were responsible for executing buy and sell orders at the portfolio managers' target prices. Hitting target prices could be difficult, especially for illiquid stocks or to buy and sell orders large enough to move the stock price. Traders made use of relationships and negotiations with executing brokers to obtain favorable pricing.

Raven was a relatively small firm. Most of its employees lived in the same neighborhood, and knew each other socially as well as professionally. Employee tenure at Raven was higher than the hedge fund industry average.

Performance

For over a decade, the Raven Capital team had delivered superior risk adjusted returns for the investors who entrusted their monies to the company. For example, Raven's Flagship Fund (the Fund), the firm's oldest, had an annualized return since inception of 14.8%, as compared to a 7.3% annualized return for the S&P 500 firms in that period. In approximately 70% of the months when the market was down, the Fund's values either increased or were down less than the market declined. (See Exhibit 4 for the Fund's monthly fund risk report.)

But 2008 was a year for the record books on the downside. Though Raven funds beat the overall market, they lost significant absolute value. The Fund dropped 27% (the S&P dropped 37%). While technically the job of a hedge fund was to participate when the market went up, and lose less when the market went down, many clients had an expectation that the fund would never lose money, let alone a significant amount of money.

Raven's liquidity terms were much more liberal than those of many hedge funds. Raven funds did not have lock-ups or gates.[1] For example, if a fund had a gate of 15%, and investors requested withdrawals totaling 25% of the fund's assets, fund managers could

---

[1] *Lock-ups* restricted withdrawals of the original investment in a hedge fund for a period of time. *Gates* limited the percentage of a fund's assets that could be withdrawn during any redemption period.

legally refuse all withdrawals exceeding 15%. Investors desperate for cash sold their assets that were liquid regardless of performance, and the funds entrusted with Raven were liquid. That liquidity policy contributed significantly to the decline of Raven's AUM in 2008 as investors needed to get cash fast.

By the end of 2009, both the markets and Raven funds turned a corner. The Fund was up 36%, and had exceeded its high water mark. But despite the investment gains, the firm's AUM had not returned to anything near their historical levels. By the end of 2009, Raven's AUM were only 41% of what they had been at the beginning of 2008.

ANALYST COMPENSATION

Raven analysts earned a minimum base salary of $180,000 plus an annual bonus granted at the discretion of management. Bonuses fluctuated significantly but generally ranged from approximately $150,000 upwards to several million dollars.

Raven's incentive fees earned became the annual bonus pool. The bonus pool was split two-thirds to Investment Management and one-third to Business Operations, as was traditional in the industry. Within Investment Management, the PMs typically took a standard percentage of the pool, and the balance was allocated to the other employees.

The bonus allocation decisions were made subjectively by the management team, Max and Jeffrey (the two PMs) and Julie (CFO). They considered many quantitative measures but applied considerable judgment in deciding what quantitative factors to consider and how to weight the multiple indicators in importance. Jeffrey explained, "Most importantly we need a process that is fair and repeatable."

The bonuses were awarded based on a combination of company, team, and individual performance. For evaluating analysts, the primary quantitative evaluation measure was an analyst performance report (see Exhibit 5) that was updated monthly and closely tracked by all members of the Raven team. The performance of every stock that an analyst "touched" was coded, and the monthly profits or losses from those stocks were tracked in the report.

Though the management team knew that at least some analysts would prefer to be awarded bonuses based entirely on quantitative measures, they recognized several difficulties with a strictly formulaic approach. First, analysts could only choose stocks within their industry of expertise, so their performance could be helped or hindered by industry performance. Though theoretically their performance could be measured against an industry benchmark, managers believed that in practice it was very difficult to find a robust index.

Second, exposure to short or long positions could have a significant effect on performance as well. It may well have been in an analyst's best interest to take only long positions in a rising market, but Raven strategy often required somebody to "take shorts for the team."

Finally, analysts could "touch" stocks in several ways that were not reflected in the stock performance report. For example, if an analyst made a stock recommendation, but the PM chose not to buy a position, the stock was not tracked on the report. Several analysts kept track of those stocks on their own, to receive credit for good picks even if they didn't become part of a fund. Equally, if an analyst made a "save" by recommending getting out of a position, it was not directly reflected in the report either. Analysts could clearly also make bad calls that the PM chose not to implement. Jeffrey explained, "I could follow an analyst's recommendation to buy a stock at $10 and ignore his recommendation to sell at $15. If I ultimately sell at $18, who gets the credit? The analyst had a good idea but he told me to sell the stock earlier, and I didn't, so we made even more money. That's one area where the performance evaluations get murky."

Ultimately, company performance drove bonuses, since the company couldn't pay out more than it earned in incentive fees. Max explained,

> There are years where everyone is overpaid. If the firm has a great year and you have horrible performance, you'll be overpaid. But in years like this year, everyone is underpaid. You may have done well, but fees were lower because we had to get up to our high water marks again. There were not as many dollars to go around. But my memory is not that short.

Management used a "mental carry forward" to compensate people they felt had been overpaid or underpaid in prior years. Managers also adjusted bonuses based on qualitative factors. For example, they considered whether analysts wasted time with poor recommendations. Jeffrey explained, "Some analysts use a dart board approach. If you throw enough darts, you'll eventually hit the board, but it puts the burden on the PMs to sort through all those ideas."

From the analysts' perspective, Raven's evaluation method, while not perfectly visible, was generally seen as fair. The analysts were not oblivious to the economics of the business. They were aware of how much the company earned each year, and had a general idea of what they deserved as a bonus. While they sometimes believed their bonus award was not completely fair compared with other analysts, the differences were generally not huge. As analyst Winston Hill put it, "we're not underpaid by 50%." Winston explained further,

> I don't know the mad science behind how Max comes up with some of his performance metrics. I'm sure he runs the numbers a number of different ways. There is an art to this as well as a science . . . Everyone thinks that Max and Jeffrey are fair people. This model would not work if there wasn't a trust factor.

Having such a subjective process was not the industry norm. Many other hedge funds did use a formulaic approach, most typically awarding a pre-negotiated percentage of fund returns as an annual bonus. Winston reflected, "The great thing about that is you know exactly what you make."

CONCERNS

Each year seemed to present unique evaluation challenges. Julie listed some of the questions that had to be addressed:

What is the firm making? How are the funds doing? How should we evaluate employee contribution? Should we pay for tenure? How much of the bonus pool should go to those working in administration?

Reflecting on the 2009 year-end performance reviews, the Raven management team had some concerns. They feared that bonus expectations had become unmanageable. They valued their analysts and wanted to keep them happy. High water marks had made this year unusually difficult for Raven and for hedge funds in general. But because fund returns were high, some analysts felt entitled to bonuses similar to the record amounts earned in 2007. And, as Max and Jeffrey both noted, "Most employees overrate their performances and overvalue their worth." In the past, it was not uncommon for analysts who were unhappy with their compensation to jump to companies with more assets or to start hedge funds of their own, but that possibility had become far less likely given the state of the industry.

Max and Jeffrey were also concerned that they were not accomplishing much in the way of evaluating and improving performance through the review process. During their reviews, analysts paid careful attention to the bonus award, but were unable to focus on anything else. One possibility that Julie had suggested was to move performance reviews to September, to separate performance discussions from the awarding of bonuses, which would still be done in December.

Exhibit 1 Hypothetical high water mark example

	Pool at beginning of period	% return	$ return	Pool at end of period	Incentive fee earned at rate of 20% of fund returns
Year 1	$800,000	+25%	+$200,000	$1,000,000	$40,000*
Year 2	$1,000,000	−20%	−$200,000	$800,000	$0
Year 3	$800,000	+10%	+$80,000	$880,000	$0
Year 4	$880,000	+25%	+$220,000	$1,100,000	$20,000**

* ($1,000,000 − $800,000) × 0.2 = $40,000

** ($1,100,000 − $1,000,000) × 0.2 = $20,000

EXHIBIT 2 Raven assets under management by investor type (as of 7/1/2009)

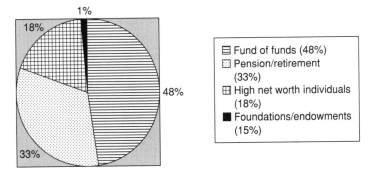

Legend:
- ⊟ Fund of funds (48%)
- ▧ Pension/retirement (33%)
- ⊞ High net worth individuals (18%)
- ■ Foundations/endowments (15%)

EXHIBIT 3 Organizational chart

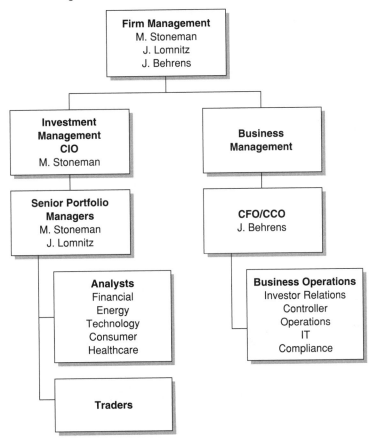

Exhibit 4 The fund risk report

STATISTICAL HIGHLIGHTS		
Firm AUM	$732M	
Fund AUM	$128M	
Returns Since Inception	**Fund**	**S&P 500**
Cumulative	687.50%	182.70%
Annualized	15.11%	7.34%
General Summary	**MV**	**Delta Adj.**
Equity ($)	$131,557,936	–
LMV ($)	$119,262,214	$131,035,077
SMV ($)	($61,414,565)	($73,739,807)
Gross Exposure	$180,676,779	$204,774,884
Net Exposure	$57,847,649	$57,295,270
LMV (% Equity)	90.65%	99.60%
SMV (% Equity)	(46.68%)	(56.05%)
Gross Exposure (% Equity)	137.34%	155.65%
Net Exposure (% Equity)	43.97%	43.55%
1 day VaR 95%	$1,392,438	–
1 day VaR 99%	$2,111,171	–
Position Info.	**Long**	**Short**
Top 25 positions	74.88%	(30.21%)
# of Positions	53	63
Days Liquidity (Fund)	0.70	0.12
Turnover	15.58%	35.68%
Risk Metrics	**Fund**	**S&P 500**
Standard Dev.	3.87%	4.60%
Standard Dev. Ann.	13.42%	15.94%
Sharpe Ratio	0.85	0.55
Downside Dev.	2.53%	3.49%
Sortino Ratio	1.30	0.30
Benchmark Comps	**Fund**	**S&P 500**
R2	54.44	1.00
Beta	0.62	1.00
Alpha (Since Inception)	574.63%	–
Correlation	0.74	1.00

Exhibit 4 *continued*

Definition of risk metrics

Alpha	The Y-intercept of the security characteristics line. The specific benchmark used in the Monthly Fund Risk Reports is the S&P 500 with dividends reinvested.
Annualized standard deviation	(Monthly standard deviation) × (square root of 12).
Beta	With ra denoting the rate of return of asset A and rp denoting the rate of return of referencing benchmark, beta can be expressed as beta(a) = covariance (ra,rp)/variance (rp).
Correlation coefficient	Correlation coefficient pX,Y between two random variables X and Y, with standard deviations sigma (X) and sigma (Y) is defined as pX,Y = covariance (X,Y)/(sigmaX sigmaY).
Downside deviation	The standard deviation of the returns that are less than the minimum acceptable return (MAR).
Hard to borrow	This is defined by our broker as MV of short equities for which we receive less than our cold rate.
Liquidity	The day's liquidity for each position is calculated by dividing the shares held by 30% of the average 20-day trading volume. The day's liquidity for the firm or fund is based on the weighted average of firm or fund holdings.
R^2	R-squared, coefficient of determination, in linear regression, which is employed here, r-squared is simply the square of the correlation coefficient.
Sortino Ratio	Investment return-risk free (ROR)/downside deviation. The downside deviation is relative to a user-specified minimum acceptable return (MAR), which in the case of the fund risk report is 0.
Standard deviation	The square root of variance.

Exhibit 5 Analyst performance report

Long portfolio

Month to month profit/loss in $ millions (profit and loss defined as realized plus changes in unrealized)

Analyst	Jan	Feb	Mar	Apr	May	Jun	Jul	Aug	Sep	Oct	Nov	Dec	2009
MS	22.6	−1.3	29.3	21.7	8.1	−13.4	−11	7.7	32.6	30.5	−31.4	−8	87.4
BS	5.4	0.5	7.1	1.8	13.3	−5.6	−6.2	7.3	5.3	10.7	2.5	−1.2	40.8
JL	9.8	−1.5	13.8	11.7	16.1	7.8	−17	24	22.1	16.6	−30.4	1.6	74.6
NK	3.7	−0.5	−4.3	2.8	0.7	4.2	−9.8	3.1	4.6	9.7	−0.2	−3.0	11.07
WH	8	2.1	−1	8.3	12.1	−10.7	−2	−1.2	−1.1	−0.6	−1.6	−1.4	11.02
CF	0.2	−0.1	−0.1	0.1	−0.01	−0.2	−0.1		−0.1	0.1	−0.03	0.1	−0.31
CIM	−1.4	−0.4	2.3	2.5	3.4	0.5	0.7	−0.8	0.02	1.2	−0.6	−0.01	7.4
IPOS		0.27			0.2	0.4	0.5	0.3	−0.01	0.05	0.09		1.73
GOLD	−1.2		−0.8	−0.1	−0.4	−0.3	0.5	−0.5					−2.8
TOTAL	46.8	−0.7	46.4	49.1	53.2	−17.3	−44.7	40.7	64.1	71.4	−61.2	−12.3	235.4

EXHIBIT 5 *continued*

Short portfolio

Month to month profit/loss in $ millions (profit and loss defined as realized plus changes in unrealized)

Analyst	Jan	Feb	Mar	Apr	May	Jun	Jul	Aug	Sep	Oct	Nov	Dec	2009
MS	−8.8	8.3	0.6	−17.2	−2.3	3.8	30.8	6.1	3.5	19.7	36.2	17.8	98.5
BS	−4.4	−1.3	−7.3	−7.7	−8.4	4.7	14	2.3	1.5	4.7	8.6	1.3	8.0
JL	−7.2	11.1	3	−7.7	−4.7	6.8	1.8	3.4	−8.2	−11.9	16.5	11.2	14.1
NK	−0.3	2	1.9	−3.2	−2.4	−1.1	1.2	−2.5	−1.4	−3.4	9	−2.6	−2.8
WH	−4.2	2.9	−1	−10.6	−10	−1.3	3.6	0.8					−19.7
CF													
CIM	0.03	0.1	−0.3	−0.4	−0.5	0.4	0.2	0.03	−0.2	0	0.5	−0.2	−0.3
NC													
SPYS	−3.5	4.4	−3.8	−7.5	−6.6	1.9	7.2	−3.2	−3.6	−0.01	5.6	0.7	−8.5
TOTAL	−28.4	27.3	−6.9	−54.3	−34.7	15.6	58.9	6.7	−7.3	8.6	79	29	93.6

Total portfolio

Month to month profit/loss in $ millions (profit and loss defined as realized plus changes in unrealized)

Analyst	Jan	Feb	Mar	Apr	May	Jun	Jul	Aug	Sep	Oct	Nov	Dec	2009
MS	13.8	6.9	29.9	4.5	5.8	−9.7	19.8	13.8	36.2	50.2	4.8	9.8	185.8
BS	0.9	−0.8	−0.3	−5.9	4.9	−0.9	7.8	9.6	6.9	15.3	11.1	0.1	48.8
JL	2.6	9.6	16.9	4	11.4	14.5	−15.2	27.4	13.9	4.7	−14	12.8	88.7
NS	3.3	1.5	−2.4	−0.4	−1.7	3.1	−8.6	0.7	3.2	6.4	8.8	−5.6	8.3
WH	3.8	5	−2	−2.4	2.1	−11.9	1.7	−0.3	−1.1	−0.6	−1.6	−1.4	−8.7
CF	0.2	−0.1	−0.1	0.1	−0.01	−0.2	−0.1		−0.1	0.1	−0.03	0.1	−0.3
CIM	−1.3	−0.3	2	2.1	2.9	0.9	0.8	−0.8	−0.2	1.2	−0.1	−0.2	7.1
IPOS		0.3			0.2	0.4	0.5	0.3	−0.01	0.1	0.1		1.7
GOLD/SPYS	−4.7	4.4	−4.5	−7.5	−7	1.6	7.7	−3.7	−3.6	−0.01	5.6	0.7	−11.3
TOTAL	18.3	26.6	39.5	−5.2	18.5	−1.6	14.2	47.4	56.8	80	17.8	16.9	329

Analyst	2009 profit	% of 2009 profit	Allocated capital ($ millions)	% of allocated capital	% return on allocated capital
MS	234.59	71.3%	800	33%	29.3%
JL	88.71	27.0%	800	33%	11.1%
NS	8.31	2.5%	300	12%	2.8%
WH	−8.66	−2.6%	300	12%	−2.9%
CF	−0.31	−0.1%	2	0%	−15.3%
CIM	7.09	2.2%	30	1%	23.6%
IPOS	1.73	0.5%		0%	
GOLD/SPYS	−11.26	−3.4%	190	8%	−5.9%
TOTAL	329.03	100%	2422	100%	13.6%

Section IV

PERFORMANCE MEASUREMENT ISSUES AND THEIR EFFECTS

Chapter 10

FINANCIAL PERFORMANCE MEASURES AND THEIR EFFECTS

The primary objective of for-profit organizations is to maximize shareholder (or owner) value, or *firm value* for short. Thus, the results-control ideal would be to reward employees for their contributions to firm value. However, because direct measurements of the contributions by employees to value creation are rarely possible, firms have to look for measures that proxy for this ultimate objective and resort to results-control alternatives to either reinforce desired behaviors where the proxies leave gaps or mitigate undesired consequences that may arise from relying on the proxies.

A commonly cited management axiom is: *what you measure is what you get*. As discussed in Chapter 9, this axiom is particularly pertinent when the performance measures are linked to incentives that reinforce the attainment of the measured performance. But which performance measure(s) should be used? At managerial levels in organizations, job responsibilities are both broad and varied. In common jargon, managerial jobs are said to be *multi-tasking* in nature. Reflecting this task variety, the list of measures used in practice to motivate and evaluate managerial performance is long. That said, the list of measures can be classified into three broad categories. Two of these categories include summary financial measures of performance, expressed either in market (stock price) or accounting terms, and the third category includes combinations of measures.

The *summary measures* reflect the aggregate or *bottom-line* impacts of multiple performance areas (e.g. accounting profits reflect the aggregate effects of both revenue- and cost-related decisions). The first category of summary measures contains *market measures*; that is, those that reflect changes in stock prices or shareholder returns. The second category contains *accounting measures*, which can be defined in either residual terms (such as net income after taxes, operating profit, residual income, or economic value added) or ratio terms (such as return on investment, return on equity, or return on net assets). These two categories of summary financial (market-based or accounting-based) measures of performance are the focus of this chapter. These measurement categories represent *financial* measures of performance because they are either denominated in currency (e.g. quarterly profits of $19.2 million); as a ratio of financial numbers, such as $0.12 earnings per share (EPS) or 12% return on equity (ROE); or as a change in financial numbers, such as 11% earnings growth.

The third measurement category consists of *combinations of measures*. These combinations can involve the use of either type of summary measures, or both, plus some *dis*aggregated financial measures (e.g. revenues, expenses) and/or *nonfinancial* measures (e.g. market share, customer satisfaction, employee turnover). We discuss the use of combinations of measures in Chapter 11. In both chapters, we use the evaluation criteria introduced in Chapter 2, notably *congruence*, *controllability*, *precision*, *objectivity*, *timeliness*, *understandability*, and *cost efficiency* to evaluate and to compare and contrast each measurement category.

Most organizations base their higher managerial-level results controls to a great extent on summary accounting measures of performance. Earlier chapters (particularly Chapters 2 and 7) have discussed the reasons why accounting measures of performance are in such common use. They have some significant advantages over other measurement alternatives. In particular, at minimal incremental cost, they provide a useful summary of the results of the many actions and decisions that managers take. It must be recognized, though, that even the best accounting measures are not perfect; they are only surrogate or proxy indicators of changes in firm value.

The use of accounting performance measures as a proxy for changes in firm value creates some significant control problems. This chapter describes one of the most significant problems accounting measures cause: a tendency to make managers excessively short-term oriented, or *myopic*. This chapter also discusses the issue of *suboptimization*, a form of behavioral displacement caused particularly by the use of accounting-based ROI-type (ratio or return) measures. The next chapter focuses on how the myopia problem can be alleviated, at least to some extent. A whole chapter is devoted to this subject because of its importance and complexity. The final chapter in this section, Chapter 12, discusses how to deal with the problems caused when employees are held accountable for results they cannot completely control.

VALUE CREATION

It is generally understood that the primary objective of for-profit organizations is to *maximize the value of the firm*, subject to some constraints, such as compliance with laws and adequate concern for employees, customers and other stakeholders.[1] As Michael Jensen phrases it, "200 years' worth of work in economics and finance indicate that social welfare is maximized when all firms in an economy attempt to maximize their own total firm value."[2] Ideally, then, to reflect success properly, performance measures should *go up when value is created and go down when it is destroyed*.[3]

The value of any economic asset can be calculated at any specific time by discounting the future cash flows that the firm is expected to generate for the time value of money and for risk. Employees can increase value by increasing the size of future cash flows of the firm, by accelerating the timing of those cash flows (due to the time value of money), or by making them more certain or less risky (thus allowing a lower discount rate). The change in firm value over any given period is called *economic income*. Therefore, *maximization of economic income* is an alternative way of phrasing the basic corporate financial objective of value maximization. As we will see, *economic income* is different from *accounting income*, and the difference has important management control implications.

MARKET MEASURES OF PERFORMANCE

One way of assessing value changes is by using market measures of performance, which are based on changes in the market value of the firm or, if dividends are also considered, return to shareholders. The value created (return to shareholders) can be measured directly for any period (yearly, quarterly, monthly) as the sum of the dividends paid to shareholders in the measurement period plus (or minus) the change in the market value of the stock. For publicly traded firms whose stock is traded in actively traded, efficient capital markets, the *market value* of the firm is generally viewed as the closest although imperfect measure of (hence, proxy for) the firm's *true intrinsic value*. As we have seen in Chapter 9, firms often employ a variety of stock-based compensation plans, such as stock option and restricted stock plans, which link incentive payments to stock price. In this way, employees who are eligible for equity-based compensation plans are rewarded for shareholder returns as defined above, or at least its most significant component – changes in the value of common stock.

In that sense, market measures have broad appeal in part because they provide relatively direct indications of changes in firm value. Such measurement *congruence* allays political pressure that otherwise might be brought on the company by outsiders. Who is to complain if managers share rewards in synch with those enjoyed by the firm's owners? If the market value changes are measured in terms of recent transaction prices in an actively traded, efficient market, the market measures also have other advantages. For publicly traded firms, market values are available on a *timely* (daily) basis. They are *precise* (no or little random error) and relatively *accurate* (no or little systematic biases, assuming an efficient information environment), and the values are usually *objective* (not manipulable by the managers whose performances are being evaluated, or at least not nearly as manipulable as some other measures). They are *understandable*, at least in terms of what the measures represent. They are *cost effective* as they do not require any company measurement expense.

Market measures do have limitations, however. First, market measures suffer from *controllability* problems. They can generally be affected to a significant extent only by the top few managers in the organization, those who have the power to make decisions of major importance. They say little about the performances of individuals lower in the organization, even those with significant management responsibilities, except in a collective sense. Individually, the efforts of virtually all employees below the very top level of management have an infinitesimally small impact on stock prices, which is captured pertinently by the following quote: "So many things can affect stock-price performance that have nothing to do with the individual employee – employees may actually be demotivated upon realizing that it can be like a lottery; we should only ask employees to control things they can influence, like earnings."[4]

But even for the top management team, market measures may be far from being totally controllable. Stock market valuations are affected by many factors that the managers cannot control, such as changes in macroeconomic activity (economic growth), political climate (e.g. election results), monetary policy (e.g. interest rate policy), industry events, and actions of competitors, as well as the general stock market mood (bearish or bullish). It is also difficult to explain all market valuations without considering some behavioral factors.[5] When this is the case, stock prices are less informative about even top-level managers' performances. Therefore, one reason why accounting information is import-ant in incentive contracting is that earnings can shield executives against the market risk inherent in firms' stock prices.[6]

It is possible, however, to "improve" the market measures to make them more informa-tive of the controllable elements of performance, such as by using *relative performance evaluations*. For example, managers can be held accountable for generating market returns greater than those of the overall market or greater than those of a chosen peer group of companies. (We discuss methods of making adjustments for the effects of uncontrollable factors in more depth in Chapter 12.)

Second, market values are also not always reflective of *realized* performance; instead the values are merely representing *expectations*, and it can be risky to base incentives on expectations because those expectations might not be realized. Indeed, markets can overreact to news (in either direction, positive or negative), such as to the appointment of a new chief executive or to news about a merger or a major project, or even to regular earnings announcements. For example, Microsoft chief executive Steve Ballmer said that he was "surprised" by the market reaction to the software giant's web search deal with Yahoo in July 2009. Microsoft's share price was hammered on Wall Street. "Watching the market reaction, nobody gets it," Mr. Ballmer said, even though he argued that the deal was a win–win strategic partnership that would create economic value for the shareholders of Yahoo and Microsoft.[7] Who is right – Mr. Ballmer or the markets – is hard to tell in advance, but it shows that managers' and market expectations are not always aligned, and that expectations are not to be equated with realizations. Market valuations do not always fully reflect the underlying value of the firm, and, hence, decisions or transactions on any given day, such as stock option grants or exercises, can be affected by the difference. Worse, as we discussed in Chapter 9, the possibility for such differences may even trigger *opportunistic* motivations by the executives to try to affect stock prices coincident with certain decisions or transactions, such as by selectively disclosing information to which the markets are expected to (over)react either with a downward or upward effect on stock prices, to bring about more favorable conditions for the granting or exercising of stock options, respectively.[8]

A third, and related, problem with market measures of performance is actually a potential *congruence* failure. Markets are not always well informed about a company's plans and prospects, and hence, its future cash flows and risks. For competitive reasons, companies often treat information about R&D productivity, pricing and sourcing strategies, product and process quality, customer satisfaction, and layoff intentions as confidential. Market valuations cannot reflect information that is not available to it. If sizable rewards are linked to market valuations, managers might be tempted to disclose this information to affect valuations, even if such disclosures could be harmful to their company.

But even market valuations with well-informed participants might not always be correct. Over the years, a number of valuation *anomalies* – such as the "Monday effect" and the "January effect" just to name two – have been documented, although these tend to be relatively small and temporary in duration. Moreover, these are anomalies only because they cannot be explained within the existing efficient markets hypothesis paradigm, so they may not be anomalies at all. More significant for incentive purposes are some other, larger market imperfections and lags, which are particularly likely, and more likely to be significant, in developing countries where stocks are not as actively traded. Indeed, in developing countries suggestions to reward managers based on stock market valuation changes are met with skepticism. Because regulations in certain countries are not as well established and not as well enforced as those in developed countries, managers can time or slant their disclosures to affect market valuations and large investors can manipulate the markets. This, therefore, raises a fourth problem with market measures – that is, their *feasibility* in certain circumstances. Market measures are also only readily available for publicly traded firms; they are not available for either privately held firms or wholly owned subsidiaries or divisions,[9] and they are not applicable to not-for-profit organizations.

To summarize the limitations, market measures are only *available*, and hence reasonably feasible, for publicly traded firms. They are largely *uncontrollable* by any employees except the top few individuals in the management hierarchy. Even for those few individuals, the measures are buffeted by many uncontrollable influences, making the market measures *noisy* indicators of performance. And, changes in stock price on any given day can be misleading for several of the reasons discussed above. All told, then, a company's stock price at any point in time can be a poor guide to long-term value, and thus, although an emphasis on shareholder value seems highly congruent conceptually, the use of short-term changes in stock price as a proxy for it can cause problems. These significant limitations of market measures cause organizations to look for surrogate measures of performance. Accounting measures, specifically accounting profits and returns, are the most important surrogates used, particularly at management levels below the very top management team.

ACCOUNTING MEASURES OF PERFORMANCE

Traditionally, most organizations have based their managers' evaluations and rewards heavily on standard accounting-based, summary financial measures. Accounting-based, summary or *bottom-line* performance measures come in two basic forms: *residual* measures (or *accounting profit* measures), such as net income, operating profit, earnings before interest, tax, depreciation and amortization (EBITDA), or residual income; or *ratio* measures (or *accounting return* measures), such as return on investment (ROI), return on equity (ROE), return on net assets (RONA), or risk-adjusted return on capital (RAROC). These measures are typically derived from the rules defined by standard setters for financial reporting purposes.

Summary accounting-based measures have some appealing advantages. They satisfy many of the measurement criteria. First, accounting profits and returns can be measured on a *timely* basis (in short time periods) relatively *precisely* and *objectively*. Accounting rules for assigning cash inflows and outflows even to very short measurement periods have been set and described in great detail by accounting rule makers, such as the International Accounting Standards Board (IASB) or the US Financial Accounting Standards Board (FASB). It is possible to measure accounting profits in short time periods, such as a month, with considerable precision. Precision stems from the existence of accounting rules, and hence, different people assigned to measure the profit of an entity for any given period will arrive at approximately the same number. Further, independent auditors provide an objectivity check of the accounting calculations. Objectivity is important when incentives are linked to measures because it eliminates, or at least sharply reduces, the potential for arguments about measurement methods.

Second, as compared with other quantities that can be measured precisely and objectively on a timely basis, such as cash flows, shipments, or sales, accounting measures are at least conceptually *congruent* with the organizational goal of profit maximization. In this respect, accounting profits provide an advantage over cash flows because accounting accruals are designed to provide a better matching of cash inflows and outflows over time.

Third, accounting measures usually can be largely *controlled* by the managers whose performances are being evaluated. The measures can be tailored to match the authority limits of any level of manager, from the CEO down to lower management levels. As such, entity managers are typically held accountable for fewer of the income statement and balance sheet line-items that they can control, compared to managers with more authority higher in the organizational hierarchy. Because of this, the profit performance of an entity within the organization is almost certainly more controllable by the entity manager than is the change in the company's overall stock price. Accounting profits also are not, or not as severely, affected by some of the uncontrollable factors discussed above that affect stock prices.

Fourth, accounting measures are *understandable*. Accounting is a standard course in every business school, and managers have used the measures for so long that they are well familiar with what the measures represent and how they can be influenced. Finally, accounting measures of performance are *inexpensive* because most firms have to measure and report financial results to outside users already, certainly when they are publicly traded, but also in many countries when they exceed a certain size. And even when these conditions do not apply, to obtain funding of any kind (debt or equity) requires the reporting of at least some financial information to the providers of the funds.

For all these reasons, pioneer manager Alfred P. Sloan may have had a point when he proclaimed that "no other financial principle with which I am acquainted serves better than [accounting] rate of return as an objective aid to business management."[10] Nonetheless, accounting measures of performance are far from perfect indicators of firm value and value changes. While research has shown that the correlations between annual accounting profits and stock price changes are positive, the correlations are small. They are far from the 1.0 correlation that would signify a perfect surrogate. The correlations are usually in the range of 0.20 to 0.30, depending on the sample of firms studied.[11] Thus, across a broad sample of firms, annual accounting profit measures must be said to be only imperfect surrogates for economic income.

In some types of firms, accounting profit measures are essentially meaningless. A good example is start-up firms. These firms almost inevitably report significant accounting losses early in their life cycle. The losses are just an artifact of conservative accounting rules that require the immediate or rapid expensing of long-term focused business-building investments (such as investments in research and development (R&D) and product and market development). In these cases, which include virtually all start-up firms, managers are not, or should not be, greatly concerned with short-term accounting profits (or rather losses) because the need for a long-term focus reduces the degree of *congruence* between earnings and firm value.

More generally, *measurement congruence*, or the correlation between accounting profits and firm value, does increase with the length of the measurement period. One large-sample study found that the correlations between profits and market values for periods of one, two, five, and ten years were, respectively, 0.22, 0.39, 0.57, and 0.79.[12] This pattern clearly illustrates tradeoffs between the congruence and timeliness measurement evaluation criteria. The increasingly higher correlations with increasingly longer measurement windows occur primarily because accounting profits provide a lagged indicator of economic income.[13] When economic income changes, those changes are often reflected only some time later in the profit measures. How much later depends on both what caused the economic income change and what type of accounting measurement rules is being used.

There are thus various reasons why accounting profit measures fail to reflect economic income far less than perfectly. Many things affect accounting profits but not economic income, and vice versa. First, accounting systems are *transactions-oriented*. Accounting profit is primarily a summation of the effects of the transactions that took place during a given period. Most changes in value that do not result in a transaction are not recognized in accounting profit. When a firm receives a patent or regulatory approval for a new drug, the expectation of economic income is affected, but there is no transaction, no accounting entry, and, thus, no effect on accounting income.

Second, accounting profit is highly dependent on the *choice of measurement methods*. Multiple measurement methods are often available to account for identical economic events. Depreciation accounting choices (straight-line vs. accelerated methods) are but one example. These methods also often require that some judgments are made, such as in this example, about the depreciable lives of the assets. Longer lives spread the costs over more years, and thus affect the accounting profits recorded over those years.

Third, accounting profit is derived from measurement rules that are often *conservatively biased*. Accounting rules require slow recognition of gains and revenues but quick recognition of expenses and losses. For example, accounting rules define strict criteria that must be satisfied before revenue (and the associated profit) can be recognized, and expenditures on intangible assets are generally expensed immediately. Thus, accounting measures do not always match revenues and expenses well, and this problem is particularly acute where measurement periods are shorter than the firms' investment payoff horizons.

Fourth, profit calculations *ignore some economic values and value changes* that accountants feel cannot be measured accurately and objectively. Investments in major categories of companies' intangible assets, such as research in progress, human resources, information systems, and customer goodwill, are expensed immediately. Consequently, these types of assets do not appear on the balance sheet. The omission of intangible assets occurs even though for many companies these types of assets are much more important than the old industrial-era-type assets of plant, equipment and land.[14] The physical assets of companies like Apple and Google, for example, are only a relatively small portion of the company's total market value. Profit also *ignores the costs of investments in working capital*. Managers sometimes increase their sales and profits by making bad investments in extra inventory, the costs of which do not appear on the income statement.

Fifth, profit reflects the cost of borrowed capital (through interest deductibility) but *ignores the cost of equity capital*. Firms earn real income only when the returns on capital are greater than the cost of that capital, and ignoring the cost of equity capital overstates the difference between returns and costs (that is, profit). This omission is serious because equity capital is typically more expensive than borrowed capital, and the cost of equity capital is even higher for companies with risky (volatile) stocks. Failure to reflect the cost of equity capital also hinders comparisons of the results of companies with different proportions of debt and equity in their capital structures.

Sixth, accounting profit *ignores risk and changes in risk*. Firms, or entities within firms, that have not changed the pattern or timing of their expected future cash flows but have made the cash flows more certain (less risky) have increased their economic value, and vice versa. This value change is not reflected in accounting profits.

Finally, profit figures also *focus on the past*. Economic value is derived from future cash flows, and there is no guarantee that past performance is a reliable indicator of future performance.

The multiple reasons why accounting income and economic income diverge have caused some critics to make strong statements against the use of accounting performance measures. Most managers, however, have found that the advantages of accounting measures outweigh their limitations, and they continue to use them. But they must be aware that motivating managers to maximize, or at least produce, accounting profits or returns, rather than economic income, can create a number of behavioral displacement problems. *Myopia* is probably the most potentially damaging. Managers whose focus is on accounting profits or returns measured in short periods tend to be highly concerned with increasing (or maintaining) monthly, quarterly or annual profits. When managers' orientations to the short-term become excessive – that is, when they are more concerned with short-term profits or returns rather than with long-term value creation – the managers are said to be myopic, which we discuss in the next section.

In summary, then, the major failure of accounting measures of performance is in terms of the congruence criterion for evaluation. Accounting measures do not reflect well changes in entities' economic values, particularly in shorter measurement windows. They also suffer some controllability problems, but the controllability problems can be addressed using the same methods that can be used to adjust the market measures, which we discuss in more detail in Chapter 12. Accounting measures, however, rate highly in terms of the other evaluation criteria – timeliness, accuracy, understandability, cost effectiveness, and feasibility.

INVESTMENT AND OPERATING MYOPIA

Accounting performance measures can cause managers to act myopically in making either investing or operating decisions. Holding managers accountable for short-term profits or returns may induce managers to reduce or postpone investments that promise payoffs in future measurement periods, even when those investments have a positive net present value and meet other criteria to make them worthwhile. This is *investment myopia*.

Investment myopia stems directly from two of the problems with accounting measures described above: their conservative bias and their ignoring of intangible assets with predominantly future payoffs. Accounting rules do not allow firms to recognize gains until they are realized; that is, until the critical income-producing activities (such as a sale) have taken place and the earnings can be measured in an objective, verifiable way. On the other hand, the rules require firms to begin recognizing costs when the investments are made. The understatement of profits in early measurement periods is magnified because accounting rules are purposely conservative. Projects with uncertain returns and little liquidation value, such as R&D projects and employee training, must be expensed as the costs are incurred, and capital investments must be expensed over periods that are typically shorter than those in which returns will be realized.

The motivational effect of these measurement rules is perverse because managers who are motivated to produce accounting profits or returns can (in the short-term) do so by *not* making worthwhile investments. By not making the investments, the managers reduce expenses in the current period and do not suffer the lost revenue until future periods. Even worse, the quest for short-term profits and returns sometimes induces managers to engage in manipulative *earnings management* practices, such as not booking "operating expenses" immediately, but instead pushing them into the future as "capital investments." We discuss such manipulative behaviors in more detail in Chapter 15.

Managers can also boost current period profits and returns by destroying goodwill that has been built up with customers, suppliers, employees, and so on. They can force employees to work overtime at the end of a measurement period to finish production so that the product can be shipped and the revenues and profits booked. But if the product is of lower quality, customer satisfaction (and future sales) may diminish; the costs of service repairs or customer returns may increase; and some employees may be demotivated and tempted to leave. Another common "trick" is known as *channel stuffing*, which involves boosting near-term sales by extending lower prices to distributors, encouraging them to load up while potentially hurting later sales. These are examples of *operating myopia*, sometimes also colloquially referred to as "shipping bricks and other tricks."

In many cases, determining whether managers are acting myopically is difficult. At Knight Ridder, a newspaper company that owns such respected names as the *Philadelphia Inquirer* and the *Miami Herald*, Tony Ridder, the company's CEO was accused of myopic behavior. He was said to be "chasing profits at the expense of good journalism" because he ordered sharp reductions in his company's workforce and other cost categories in order to boost margins, net income, and, hopefully, the stock price. Mr. Ridder can be said to be acting myopically if the cost cuts are compromising the company's newspapers' abilities to cover the news effectively. Decreased newspaper quality would probably lead to decreased readership and, hence, decreases in revenues, profits, and shareholder returns over time. If, on the other hand, the cost cuts were merely eliminating "fat" from the organization, resources that were costing more than they were worth, then Mr. Ridder can be said to have acted wisely. Judgments as to whether the cuts were myopic varied widely. Many employees concluded that Mr. Ridder's myopic focus on the bottom line was ruining the company, and a number of respected employees resigned in protest of the cuts. But some analysts concluded that the cuts were long overdue because the company's papers had long been overstaffed. Where does the truth lie? The stock market does not provide an unequivocal answer to this question. While Knight Ridder's stock outperformed that of most of its competitors in the year after the cost cutting, the company's price/earnings ratio was still lower than that of most of its major competitors.[15]

The Knight Ridder example illustrates the difficulty of making judgments that involve short-term vs. long-term tradeoffs. Managers in all businesses have to make these judgments, though, and all firms face a potential myopia problem. Investment myopia occurs only in businesses where investments are being made in the future, but operating myopia is a potential problem for all businesses, even those with, seemingly, only short operating horizons. Any business can treat customers in an insensitive manner, such as by refusing to refund money when the product sold does not meet expectations. Such actions may harm future performance if these customers shift their business to a competitor.

We discuss several ways to address the myopia problem in Chapter 11. But first we turn to another set of problems created by relying on return on investment (ROI) measures of performance, a specific form of accounting performance measure that is in common use in large, divisionalized firms.

RETURN-ON-INVESTMENT MEASURES OF PERFORMANCE

Divisionalized organizations are comprised of multiple responsibility centers, the managers of which are held primarily accountable for profit or some form of accounting return on investment (ROI). The divisionalized form of organization dates back to the 1920s when it was introduced in the DuPont Company, but its use spread particularly quickly after World War II as one response to increased organizational size and complexity. To this day, the divisionalized form of organization is used by many firms above minimal size.

As we discussed in Chapter 7, divisionalization and decentralization are related concepts, but the two words are not synonymous. An organization is said to be *decentralized* when authority for making decisions is pushed down to lower levels in the organization. All divisionalized organizations decentralize authority, at least to some extent, in specified areas of operations, notably a line of business or a geographical area. But the converse is not true – not all decentralized organizations are divisionalized. When decentralization is done along functional lines of authority (such as production and marketing), the responsibility centers are usually cost and revenue centers, not profit or investment centers (divisions).

Divisionalization provides several advantages. Large, complex organizations are not able to control behaviors effectively with action-dominated control systems involving, for example, the direct guidance of a central leader or the enforcement of standard operating procedures by a central administration. No central management can know everything about a complex organization's many product-market combinations and operational capabilities and constraints. Even if it could, it would take time for central management to direct its attention to each issue that arises, become informed about the details, and reach a decision. Decision-making would be unnecessarily delayed, even if it were informed.

When an organization is divisionalized, local managers become experts in their products and markets, and they are able to make informed decisions more quickly. Because they control their own success to a significant extent, the local managers are likely to be more motivated and entrepreneurial. Their involvement in decision-making helps them acquire experience that will benefit them as they move to higher organization levels. Top management's time becomes available to focus on strategic decisions.

Divisionalization is not without its problems and challenges, however. Many of the issues, particularly, relate to the problems created by the measurement of performance in terms of ROI.

Return-on-what?

ROI is a ratio of the accounting profits earned by the division divided by the investment tied up in the division. Divisionalized corporations typically use some form of various possible ROI measures to evaluate division performance.

Variances from plans can be analyzed using formula charts (*ROI trees*) such as the one shown in Figure 10.1. Such analyses might show that a division's actual ROI of 15% was below the planned level of 20% even though sales profitability (profit as a percent of sales) was on plan but asset turnover (sales divided by total investment) was worse than forecast:

Planned ROI (20%) = profit as percent of sales (20%) × asset turnover (1.0)
Actual ROI (15%) = profit as percent of sales (20%) × asset turnover (0.75)

The measures can then be further decomposed to understand whether, in this example, the variance was due primarily to a decline in sales or an increase in a specific kind of assets.

ROI formula charts are also useful for linking performance at various organizational levels. The chart can be expanded out to the right to show specific measures that can be used for control purposes right down to the lowest levels of the organization. Sales performance can be disaggregated into sales volume and price factors. These factors can be further disaggregated by product, geographical region, customer segment, or sales team.

The actual forms of ROI-type ratios that companies employ vary widely, as do the labels companies put on their bottom-line investment center measures. Among the most

FIGURE 10.1 Formula chart showing relationship of factors affecting ROI

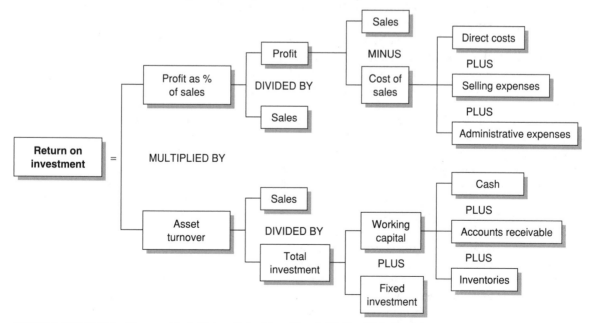

Source: K. A. Merchant, *Modern Management Control Systems: Text and Cases* (Upper Saddle River, NJ: Prentice Hall, 1998), p. 543.

common are *return on investment* (ROI), *return on equity* (ROE), *return on capital employed* (ROCE), and *return on net assets* (RONA). In these ratios, both the numerator and denominator can include all or just a subset of the line items reflected on the corporate financial statements. The profit measure in the ROI calculation can be a fully allocated, after-tax profit measure, or it can be a before-tax operating income measure. Similarly, the denominator can include all the line items of assets and liabilities, including allocations of assets and liabilities not directly controlled by the division managers, or it can include only controllable assets, which generally include, at a minimum, receivables and inventories. The variations are innumerable.

ROI-type measures are in widespread use because they provide some significant advantages. First, they provide a single, comprehensive measure that reflects the tradeoffs managers must make between revenues, costs, and investments. Second, they provide a common denominator that can be used for comparing returns on dissimilar businesses, such as divisions and outside competitors, or types of investments. Third, because they are expressed in percentage terms, they give the impression that ROI figures are comparable to other financial returns, such as those calculated for stocks and bonds, although this impression is sometimes false (as we explain later). Finally, because ROI measures have been in use for so long in so many places, virtually all managers understand both what the measures reflect and how they can be influenced.

Problems caused by ROI-type measures

Relying heavily on ROI measures in a results-control system can cause some problems, however. One problem is that the numerator in the ROI measure is accounting profit. Thus, ROI has all the limitations of profit measures, such as the tendency to produce management myopia, the common form of behavioral displacement that we discussed above. A second limitation is a tendency for the measures to induce *suboptimization*. A narrow focus on ROI can lead division managers to make decisions that improve division ROI even though the decisions are not in the corporation's global best interest. Finally, ROI measures sometimes provide *misleading signals* about the performance of the investment centers (divisions) because of difficulties in measuring the fixed asset portion of the denominator. These misleading signals can cause poor investment and performance evaluation decisions, as is explained below.

Suboptimization

ROI measures can create a suboptimization problem by encouraging managers to make investments that make their divisions look good even though those investments are not in the best interest of the corporation. Put simply, this problem arises because division managers are unlikely to propose capital investments that are expected to yield returns below their divisional return objectives, even if those investments are good ones from the company's perspective. Table 10.1 shows a simplified suboptimization example of this type. Assume the corporate cost of capital is 15%. If an investment opportunity arises promising a 20% return, the investment should be made (assuming the opportunity is consistent with the corporate strategy). The manager of Division A, whose performance targets reflect historical performance of 10%, would be willing to make this investment, but the manager of Division B, operating at 40%, would not.

Conversely, ROI measures can cause managers of unsuccessful divisions to invest in capital investment projects promising returns below the corporate cost of capital. This problem is illustrated in Table 10.2, which changes the Table 10.1 example only slightly by assuming the corporate cost of capital is 25%. In this situation, Division A would be

TABLE 10.1 Example of suboptimization: failure to invest in a worthwhile project

Assume: corporate cost of capital = 15%

	Division A	Division B
Base situation		
Profit before tax	$100,000	$400,000
Investment	$1,000,000	$1,000,000
Return on investment	10%	40%

Assume an investment opportunity that is good for the company: invest $100,000 to earn $20,000/year.

	Division A	Division B
New situation		
Profit before tax	$120,000	$420,000
Investment	$1,100,000	$1,100,000
Return on investment	10.9%	38.2%

Source: K. A. Merchant, *Modern Management Control Systems: Text and Cases* (Upper Saddle River, NJ: Prentice Hall, 1998), p. 545.

TABLE 10.2 Example of suboptimization: investment in a project that is *not* worthwhile

Assume: corporate cost of capital = 25%

	Division A	Division B
Base situation		
Profit before tax	$100,000	$400,000
Investment	$1,000,000	$1,000,000
Return on investment	10%	40%

Assume an investment opportunity that is *not* good for the company: invest $100,000 to earn $20,000/year.

	Division A	Division B
New situation		
Profit before tax	$120,000	$420,000
Investment	$1,100,000	$1,100,000
Return on investment	10.9%	38.2%

Source: K. A. Merchant, *Modern Management Control Systems: Text and Cases* (Upper Saddle River, NJ: Prentice Hall, 1998), p. 546.

willing to make this investment promising a 20% return, even though this investment does not cover the corporation's cost of capital.

Unless managers guard against these problems, the effect of situations like the examples shown in Tables 10.1 and 10.2 is that the firm's capital will gradually be allocated away from its most successful or, at least, highest-earning divisions and towards its least successful divisions, which is incongruent with the objective to maximize firm value, all else equal.

Where division managers have the authority to make financing decisions (to finance their investment decisions), ROI-type measures can also lead to suboptimization at that level. For example, return-on-equity (ROE) measures may induce managers to use debt financing (i.e. to reduce the equity put into the denominator of the ratio). This may push their entity's leverage to levels in excess of the desired corporate leverage.[16]

Misleading performance signals

Difficulties in measuring the denominator of the ROI measure, particularly pertaining to fixed assets, can provide misleading signals about the performance of an investment

TABLE 10.3 Example showing ROI overstatement when denominator is measured in terms of net book value

	Division C	Division D
Profit before depreciation	$110,000	$110,000
Depreciation	$10,000	$20,000
Profit after depreciation	$100,000	$90,000
Assets (net book value)	$500,000	$3,000,000
ROI	20%	3%

Source: K. A. Merchant, *Modern Management Control Systems: Text and Cases* (Upper Saddle River, NJ: Prentice Hall, 1998), p. 547.

TABLE 10.4 Example showing increase in ROI due merely to passage of time

	Division E		
	Year 1	Year 2	Year 3
Profit before depreciation	$110,000	$110,000	$110,000
Depreciation	50,000	50,000	50,000
Profit after depreciation	$60,000	$60,000	$60,000
Assets (net book value)	$500,000	$450,000	$400,000
ROI	12%	13.3%	15%

Source: K. A. Merchant, *Modern Management Control Systems: Text and Cases* (Upper Saddle River, NJ: Prentice Hall, 1998), p. 547.

center (division). The asset values reflected on the balance sheet do not always represent the real value of the assets available to managers for earning current returns. The assets were added to the business at various times in the past, under varying market conditions and varying purchasing power of the monetary unit. As such, the book values of the various assets accumulated over time on the balance sheet may say little about the economic value of the assets; that is, their ability to generate future cash flows. Nonetheless, many firms use net book values (NBV) to compute divisional ROI. When NBV is used, ROI is usually overstated. The overstatement is larger if the entity includes a relatively large number of older assets. Assuming inflation, the NBV of older assets are below their replacement values because they were bought in a period of lower prices and because they have been depreciated longer.

This ROI-overstatement problem is illustrated in Table 10.3. Assume that Divisions C and D are identical operating units except that Division C purchased most of its fixed assets many years ago and Division D has mostly new assets. For the sake of simplicity, assume there have been no technological advancements; the old assets perform the same tasks as efficiently as the new assets. Profit before depreciation is identical, but Division D's depreciation is twice that of Division C, so C's profit after depreciation is slightly higher. But C's ROI is dramatically higher than D's, mostly because its assets have a lower NBV. The difference between 20% and 3% ROI is not real; it is just an artifact of the measurement system.

Another quirk of ROI measures is that ROI calculated using NBV automatically increases over time if no further investments are made. This is illustrated in Table 10.4. Assume that Division E is operating in a steady state, earning in year 1 an ROI of 12%. Because the assets are being depreciated, the ROI increases to 13.3% in year 2, and 15% in year 3. This ROI increase is not real either.

These measurement quirks can cause managers who are using ROI-type measures to make bad decisions:

- They encourage division managers to retain assets beyond their optimal life and not to invest in new assets which would increase the denominator of the ROI calculation. This dysfunctional motivational effect is particularly strong if the managers expect their job tenures to be short. (This situation is another example of the myopia problem discussed above.)

- They can cause corporate managers to over-allocate resources to divisions with older assets because they appear to be relatively more profitable.

- They can contribute to the problem illustrated in Tables 10.1 and 10.2: the tendency for capital to be allocated toward the inherently least successful divisions, at the expense of the potentially most value-creating divisions.

- If corporate managers are not aware of these distortions or do not adjust for them, they can cause errors in evaluating division managers' performances.

Measuring fixed assets at gross book value (GBV) – that is, gross of depreciation for financial reporting purposes – minimizes some of these problems because GBV is closer to replacement value than is NBV, but it does not solve them. In periods of inflation, as is almost always the case, old assets valued at gross book value are still expressed at lower values than new assets, so ROI will still be overstated. Moreover, valuing assets at gross book value adds another risk, a risk that division managers will scrap useful equipment that is temporarily idle or underemployed in the short run in order to increase their ROI.

A final potential problem is that ROI measures create incentives for managers to lease assets, rather than buying them. Leased assets accounted for on an operating-lease basis are not recognized on the balance sheet, so they are not included in the ROI denominator. Managers can increase their divisional ROI by gaming the system in this way. Of course, corporations can easily include the capitalized value of assets employed in division ROI calculations even when those leases are not required to be capitalized for financial reporting purposes. This adjustment avoids this potential problem, but adjustments are costly and may complicate the administration of different books for different purposes. The idea of "adjusting" accounting measures of performance, however, leads us to the next section.

RESIDUAL INCOME MEASURES AS A POSSIBLE SOLUTION TO THE ROI MEASUREMENT PROBLEMS

A number of researchers and consultants have argued that the use of a residual income measure can help overcome the suboptimization limitation of ROI. *Residual income* is calculated by subtracting from profit a capital charge for the net assets tied up in the investment center. The capital is charged at a rate equal to the weighted average corporate cost of capital. Conceptually, an argument can be made to adjust the capital charge rate for each investment center's risk, thus making the performance measurement system consistent with the capital budgeting system. For the sake of focus, we do not carry this suggestion through in our discussion below, although it is straightforward to apply as it does not change the basic residual income calculations; it just causes them to be matched to the risk profile of each of the divisions.

If the residual income charge is made equal to the required corporate investment rate of return, then the residual income measures give all investment center managers an

TABLE 10.5 Example of suboptimization with residual income: failure to invest in a worthwhile project

Assume: corporate cost of capital = 15%

	Division A	Division B
Base situation		
Profit before tax	$100,000	$400,000
Investment	$1,000,000	$1,000,000
Return on investment	10%	40%
Residual income	$(50,000)	$250,000

Assume an investment opportunity that is good for the company: invest $100,000 to earn $20,000/year.

	Division A	Division B
New situation		
Profit before tax	$120,000	$420,000
Investment	$1,100,000	$1,100,000
Return on investment	10.9%	38.2%
Residual income	$(45,000)	$255,000

Source: K. A. Merchant, *Modern Management Control Systems: Text and Cases* (Upper Saddle River, NJ: Prentice Hall, 1998), p. 548.

identical incentive to invest, thereby addressing the suboptimization problem inherent in ROI measures. Regardless of the prevailing levels of return in each of the divisions, the division managers are motivated to invest in all projects that promise internal rates of return higher than, or at least equal to, the corporate cost of capital. This is illustrated in Table 10.5, which is a modified version of Table 10.1 with a row added for residual income. In both divisions, residual income is increased if the worthwhile investment is made.

Residual income also addresses the financing-type suboptimization problem. By considering the cost of both debt and equity financing (as by using a weighted average corporate cost of capital), residual income removes the managers' temptations to increase their entity's leverage through debt financing.

Residual income does not address the distortions often caused when managers make new investments in fixed assets, however. Many desirable investments initially reduce residual income, but then the residual income increases over time as the fixed assets get older and are depreciated.

One consulting firm, Stern Stewart & Company, recommends a measure called *Economic Value Added* (EVA™) that combines several of the modifications to the standard accounting model in a residual income-type measure.[17] The generic EVA formula is:

EVA = Modified net operating profit after tax − (modified total capital × weighted average cost of capital)

The word "modified" refers potentially to over 100 adjustments to standard accounting treatments, such as the capitalization and subsequent amortization of intangible investments such as for R&D, employee training, and advertising and the expensing of goodwill. Just which modifications should be implemented in any given situation is subject to judgment. The *weighted average cost of capital* reflects the weighted average cost of debt and equity financing.

Because it addresses some of the known weaknesses of accounting profit or return measures, EVA should better reflect economic income than accounting profit does in many settings. It should mitigate the investment myopia problem discussed above because it involves capitalization of the most important types of discretionary expenditures managers might try to cut if they were pressured for profits (such as on R&D, employee training, and customer acquisition). EVA also has all the advantages of a residual income-type measure.

It must be recognized, however, that despite its name, EVA is *not* economic income. It does not address all of the problems that differentiate accounting income from economic income. In particular, EVA still reflects primarily the results of a summation of transactions completed during the period, and, most importantly, EVA still focuses on the past, while economic income reflects changes in *future* cash flow potentials. Thus, EVA is still likely to be a poor indicator of value changes for organizations that derive a significant proportion of their value from future growth.

EVA also has some other measurement limitations. It suffers from *objectivity* problems as the EVA adjustments require considerable judgment. Managers can bias EVA just as they can accounting numbers. EVA also is probably not differentially affected by any of the usual *controllability* problems. EVA, however, is more likely to create some additional *understandability* problems, as the measures can be complex and are not as widely familiar. Many of the firms that have decided not to use EVA or similar "new" measures developed mainly by consulting firms, such as *cash flow return on investment* (Holt Value Associates), *total business return* (Boston Consulting Group), *economic profit* (McKinsey & Co.), and *shareholder value added* (LEK/Alcar), or which have tried such a measure and then abandoned it, seem to have done so mainly because of understandability failures.[18] EVA can also be quite *expensive*, requiring considerable assistance from consultants and much management development and training time.

In summary, EVA may have better congruence characteristics in some industry settings when a carefully chosen (and not too complicated) set of adjustments are made to the traditional accounting profit measures. EVA also exhibits the features of any generic residual income measure. That said, and perhaps not surprisingly, EVA is hardly a measurement panacea, an ideal that, as we discussed, is hard for any measure to meet.

CONCLUSION

The primary goal of managers of for-profit firms should be to maximize shareholder or firm value, which is a long-term, future-oriented concept. Short-term accounting profit and return measures provide imperfect, surrogate indicators of changes in firm value. *Management myopia*, an excessive focus on short-term performance, is an almost inevitable side-effect of the use of financial results control systems built on accounting measures of performance. In the next chapter, we discuss six alternatives that can be used individually or in combination to eliminate or reduce myopia.

In this chapter, we also discussed the issue of *suboptimization*, another form of behavioral displacement caused particularly by the use of accounting-based ROI-type measures. Managers who still rely on ROI-type measures do so probably because the conceptual weaknesses of ROI are well understood and the potential suboptimization problems can be monitored through the company's capital budgeting and strategic planning processes. Managers of highly profitable divisions can be encouraged to make more investments, and proposed investments from less profitable divisions can be scrutinized carefully. And even the managers evaluated by these measures should understand that when they "run down" their business by not investing in it or by not replacing their old assets this will eventually hamper their ability to generate revenues from these assets, thereby hurting the numerator of their ROI measure – assuming of course that they plan to be around long enough in the company for that to be a worry for them. In that sense, ROI measures have – although only over time – a self-disciplining mechanism built into them.

It is true that the suboptimization problems can be avoided or mitigated to some extent through the investment review processes, as well as through their inherent self-disciplining mechanism. By using these processes, companies can use ROI-focused results control systems with some degree of effectiveness. One might ask: Why use a measurement system that works effectively only in conjunction with bureaucratic oversight and processes (or other balancing control mechanisms) that are needed to prevent managers from taking undesirable actions? The answer to that question in many settings is that the net benefits of such a system are greater than those of several other feasible alternatives. There is no panacea, and better control is likely to arise from a set of mutually reinforcing and balancing mechanisms. An all-purpose performance measure (or performance measurement system) that meets all control objectives effectively without triggering any potentially harmful side effects simply does not exist.

Notes

1. "Shareholders vs. Stakeholders: A New Idolatry," *The Economist* (April 24, 2010), pp. 65–6.

2. M. Jensen, "Value Maximization, Stakeholder Theory, and the Corporate Objective Function," *Journal of Applied Corporate Finance*, 14, no. 3 (Fall 2001), p. 11.

3. The arguments presented in this chapter are based on the assumption of value maximization as the ultimate organizational objective in the context of for-profit corporations. We note, however, that corporations have responsibilities to a broader set of stakeholders, including employees, customers, suppliers, and society, and that fulfilling these stakeholder responsibilities requires tradeoffs. Although it is beyond the scope of this chapter to debate the question as to the ultimate (balance of) objective(s) of corporations, we reckon that the evaluation framework presented in this and earlier chapters, and the *congruence* criterion in particular, can be used to evaluate performance measures whatever an organization's purpose(s), and can be conceptually applied to even non-profit settings (as we discuss in Chapter 17) where the organizational purposes (e.g. provide healthcare, education, or affordable housing) are not directed towards maximizing shareholder value.

4. "Options for Everyone," *Business Week* (July 22, 1996), p. 84.

5. See, for example, N. Barberis and R. Thaler, "A Survey of Behavioral Finance," in G. Constantinides, M. Harris, and R. Stultz (eds.), *Handbook of the Economics of Finance* (North-Holland, Amsterdam: Elsevier, 2003).

6. R. Sloan, "Accounting Earnings and Top Executive Compensation," *Journal of Accounting and Economics*, 16, nos. 1–3 (1993), pp. 44–100.

7. "Microsoft CEO Surprised at Yahoo Deal Reception," *Reuters* (July 31, 2009), online (www.reuters.com).

8. See, for example, D. Aboody and R. Kasznik, "CEO Stock Option Awards and the Timing of Corporate Voluntary Disclosures," *Journal of Accounting and Economics*, 29, no. 1 (February 2000), pp. 73–100; L. Bebchuk, Y. Grinstein, and U. Peyer, "Lucky CEOs and Lucky Directors," *Journal of Finance*, 65, no. 6 (December 2010), pp. 2363–401.

9. See, for example, B. Schindler, "Understanding Private Company Incentive Pay Practices," *Workspan* (March 2008), pp. 44–8.

10. A. P. Sloan, Jr., *My Years with General Motors* (Garden City, NY: Doubleday, 1964), p. 140.

11. B. Lev, "On the Usefulness of Earnings: Lessons and Directions from Two Decades of Empirical Research," *Journal of Accounting Research*, 27 (Supplement 1989), pp. 153–92.

12. P. Easton, T. Harris, and J. Ohlson, "Accounting Earnings Can Explain Most of Security Returns: The Case of Long Return Intervals," *Journal of Accounting and Economics*, 15, nos. 2–3 (June–September 1992), pp. 119–42.

13. See, S. P. Kothari and R. G. Sloan, "Price-Earnings Lead-Lag Relation and Earnings Response Coefficients," *Journal of Accounting and Economics*, 15, nos. 2–3 (June–September 1992), pp. 143–71.

14. B. Lev, *Intangibles: Management, Measurement, and Reporting* (Washington, DC: Brookings Institution Press, 2001); C. D. Ittner, "Does Measuring Intangibles for Management Purposes Improve Performance? A Review of the Evidence," *Accounting and Business Research*, 38, no. 3 (May 2008), pp. 261–72.

15. "Tony Ridder Just Can't Win," *Fortune* (December 24, 2001), pp. 99–106.

16. See, for example, "The Best Way to Measure Company Performance," *Business Week* (March 5, 2010), online (www.businessweek.com).

17. G. B. Stewart, III, *The Quest for Value* (Harper Collins, 1991); and A. Ehrbar, *EVA: The Real Key To Creating Wealth* (Wiley, 1998).

18. See, for example, B. Birchard and A. Nyberg, "On Further Reflection," *CFO Magazine* (March 1, 2001).

Case Study

Behavioral Implications of Airline Depreciation Accounting Policy Choices

Most managers have significant discretion in choosing their accounting policies. The managers of some companies choose sets of policies that are relatively "conservative;" others choose sets that are relatively "liberal." Conservatism results in delay of the recognition of some revenues or gains and/or acceleration of the recognition of some expenses or losses. Liberal accounting policies do the opposite. The effect of conservatism is that profits are reported later than they would have been had more liberal accounting policies been adopted.

If one wants to determine whether an airline company is being conservative or liberal in its choice of accounting policies, one obvious place to look is in the area of accounting for property, plant and equipment (PP&E). PP&E usually constitutes more than 50% of the total assets of an airline. Interestingly, airlines' accounting policies for PP&E vary significantly.

Consider, for example, the aircraft depreciation practices used at four major airlines.

DELTA AIRLINES[1]

- straight-line over estimated useful lives;
- 20-year life (from the date the equipment was placed in service) on substantially all aircraft;
- residual value = 5% of cost.

AMR CORPORATION (PARENT OF AMERICAN AIRLINES)[2]

- straight-line;
- 25-year life (30-year life for Boeing 777s);
- residual value = 10% of cost.

SINGAPORE AIRLINES[3]

- straight-line;
- 15-year life;
- residual value = 10% of cost.

LUFTHANSA

- straight-line;
- 12-year life;
- residual value = 15% of cost.

OTHER FACTS

1. An aircraft can fly indefinitely, assuming the aircraft is properly maintained.

2. The cost of maintaining an aircraft tends to increase over time. Exhibit 1 shows a typical function relating the cost required to maintain the airframes of commercial jetliners, commonly referred to as the "maturity factor," as the jetliners' cumulative flight hours increase.

---

[1] These policies were adopted on April 1, 1993. From July 1, 1986, to April 1, 1993, Delta's policy had been to depreciate equipment to residual values (10% of cost) over a 15-year period. Prior to July 1, 1986, the company's policy was to depreciate equipment to a 10% residual value over a 10-year period.

[2] Prior to January 1, 1999, AMR used an estimated useful life of 20 years and a residual value of 5%. For the year ended December 31, 1999, the effect of this change was to reduce depreciation expense by approximately $158 million.

[3] These policies were adopted on April 1, 2001. From April 1, 1989 to April 1, 2001, Singapore's policy had been to depreciate over a 10-year period to a residual value of 20% of original cost. Prior to April 1, 1989, at Singapore Airlines, the operational lives of the aircraft were estimated to be eight years with 10% residual values.

This case was prepared by Professor Kenneth A. Merchant.

Copyright © by Kenneth A. Merchant.

3. The useful economic life of an aircraft is finite, but it is often difficult to estimate. Some DC-3 aircraft are still flying cargo routes commercially, even though this aircraft made its debut in 1935. But these aircraft, and some that followed them (such as the Boeing 707, which had its maiden flight in 1957), are no longer competitive for use in passenger markets.

4. New aircraft prices tend to rise over time. Fair market values for *used* aircraft decrease over time, but unless the aircraft are made obsolete by a technological breakthrough in new aircraft, which is rare, the values tend to decrease slowly. Some aircraft maintain 90% or more of their original value even after decades of use. Used aircraft values do fluctuate sometimes significantly depending on, for example, market demand and supply conditions

in the air travel and aircraft production industries, technological innovations, and changes in laws (e.g. governing noise pollution or allowable tax deductions). However, rarely do used aircraft market values drop below 50% of their original purchase price.

5. In many countries, including the United States, the rules governing the depreciation allowable for tax purposes are quite different from those that determine the depreciation that can be taken for financial reporting purposes. The tax rules allow ultra-conservative accounting to ensure that companies do not have to pay the tax before they have collected cash from their customers. Corporations should and do take advantage of these rules and depreciate the aircraft as quickly as possible to defer the taxes that need to be paid (assuming positive income).

EXHIBIT 1 Airframe labor and material maturity factors

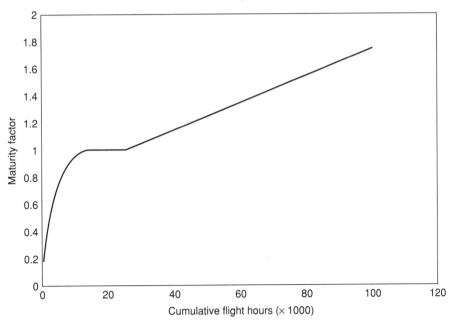

431

Case Study

Las Ferreterías de México, S.A. de C.V.

We had been operating our company like a family, but maybe we're too big to operate that way. I think some of our people have gotten lazy, and our performance has suffered. That is why I asked for the design of a new incentive compensation plan. We need to be more competitive to survive. I want our people to focus on what they can do to improve company performance, and if we're successful, I am quite willing to share a good proportion of the proceeds of our success.

Fernando Gonzalez, Chairman and CEO,
Las Ferreterías de México, S.A. de C.V.

THE COMPANY

Las Ferreterías de México, S.A. de C.V. (Ferreterías) was the second largest retailer of lumber, building materials, and home improvement products and equipment in Mexico. Ferreterías operated 82 stores in Mexico City and throughout most of the northern regions of Mexico. Each of Ferreterías' stores offered between 10,000 to 20,000 stock keeping units (SKUs) in a retail sales area, an outside lumberyard area, and a garden center. The total store areas ranged from 10,000 to 35,000 square feet.

Ferreterías was founded in 1902 in a suburb of Mexico City by Fernando Gonzalez' grandfather. Over the years, the company added more locations. It was listed on the Mexican Stock Exchange in 1983. In 2002, Ferreterías had sales of 2,210 million pesos and profits of almost 120 million pesos (see summary financial statements in Exhibits 1 and 2).[1]

Starting in the late 1980s, Fernando Gonzales launched a major company expansion to take advantage of the growth in the Mexican economy. He thought that his company needed to emulate the methods of the large American homebuilding retailers, such as Home Depot and Lowe's, in order to survive. Thus, improving market share and improving operating efficiencies became Ferreterías' strategic priorities.

The store managers enjoyed considerable autonomy. They were responsible for hiring, firing, and supervising their store's personnel. While the stores had the same architectural designs and some basic stock keeping requirements, the individual store managers were allowed to adapt their merchandise offerings, their inventory levels, and their advertising and promotional activities to their local markets, which were quite diverse. The store managers were given considerable latitude to reduce prices to move excess inventory or to meet competition. They were responsible for making credit-granting decisions, although for large accounts they were expected to ask finance personnel at headquarters to perform a credit check. And some aggressive store managers tried to generate new business by calling on prospective customers themselves.

The 82 stores were organized into nine geographical regions. The regional managers, each of whom was a former store manager, provided oversight and advice. Their role was seen as an important part of the management structure because most of the store managers had little formal education. Only a few were college educated, and few of those had formal business education. Each region also contained a regional sales office with specialists who worked with larger customers, primarily larger contractors, in selecting materials and estimating costs. Sales to these customers, though, were made through the store nearest to the job.

The corporate staff of Ferreterías provided a range of centralized functions, including purchasing, human resources, marketing, real estate, and investor

---

[1] At the time of the case, one Mexican peso was worth approximately US$0.10.

This case was prepared by Professors Kenneth A. Merchant and Wim A. Van der Stede with the research assistance of Sung-Han (Sam) Lee.

Copyright © by Kenneth A. Merchant and Wim A. Van der Stede.

relations. Inventory was shipped to the stores from one of three regional warehouses.

All Ferreterías' employees were paid a base salary or hourly wage plus a bonus based on a share of the company's overall profits. These bonuses were small, usually in the range of 2–5% of base salary, depending on organization level. In addition, Fernando Gonzalez typically provided some discretionary bonus awards to employees whose performance in a given year was exemplary. Generally, though, these types of bonuses were not considered to be effective at motivating behavior, as was indicated in the comment by Mr. Gonzalez presented at the beginning of the case.

A NEW INCENTIVE PLAN

In July 2002, Mr. Gonzalez hired a consulting firm to design a new performance-based compensation plan. He asked his chief financial officer and head of human resources to assist the firm with its work.

Mr. Gonzalez's original intent was to include all company salesmen, buyers, and managers in the new incentive plan. After a series of interviews, however, the consulting firm reported that it would not be easy to measure the performances of either salesmen or buyers. While most customers were assigned to one particular salesperson, it was difficult to assess whether a sale came from the assigned salesperson's efforts. Many customers had dealt with Ferreterías for years, and they placed their orders regardless of whether or not they received a call from a Ferreterías salesperson. Some of the large contractors had also established personal relationships with one or more corporate or regional staff, and oftentimes they called their friends for advice, rather than relying on the salesperson formally assigned to them. Measuring the performances of the buyers was similarly problematic. The primary aspect of buyer performance that could be measured – the prices paid for items purchased – was affected by many factors over which the buyer had little control. These included the order size and market conditions. Because of these measurement problems, the consultants concluded that the measures that could be tracked would not provide meaningful bases on which to assign bonus awards. They recommended that they work first on designing an incentive plan for managers, which included the individual store managers (82), regional managers (9), and corporate

staff managers (5). (Neither Fernando Gonzalez nor his chief operating officer was to be included in this plan; the compensation committee of the company's board of directors determined their bonuses.)

All other employees would continue to earn the same profit sharing awards that they had been earning. Those included in the new management incentive plan would no longer earn the profit sharing awards.

The consultants' suggestion for the management incentive plan included the following features:

1. **Bonus pool**. A total bonus pool would be created according to the following formula: 4 million pesos plus 8 percent of the corporate income before bonuses and taxes in excess of 120 million pesos. The total bonus pool would be divided into three classes as follows:

Store managers	70%
Regional managers	15%
Corporate staff managers	15%

2. **ROI measure of performance**. The bonus pools would be assigned to managers based on their entity's return on investment (ROI), defined as bonus-eligible revenues minus expenses divided by total store investments. The following guidelines were provided to facilitate the calculation of the ROI for bonus purposes:

- The **revenues** eligible for bonuses included all shipments from the store except those stemming from sales orders written by regional or headquarters personnel.

- The **expenses** include all direct store costs and all regional and headquarters costs. The costs of significant regional and headquarters activities traceable directly to a given store (e.g. cost of preparing a customer credit report, cost of a building upgrade) would be charged directly to that store. All other costs would be allocated to the stores. Activity-based allocations would be used where possible, such as in using the stores' relative proportions of receipts into inventory to allocate purchasing expenses. All other expenses would be allocated based on a proportion of bonus-eligible store revenues.

- The **investment** at each store would include the annual average of the month-end balances of cash, inventory in stock, accounts receivable associated with the bonus-eligible revenues, equipment, furniture, fixtures, buildings, and land. (If the property is rented, the rent would be recognized as an expense.)

3. **Allocation of the bonus pool**. The store managers' bonus pool would be divided among the store managers based on the their relative proportion of bonus units earned. All managers whose stores earned at least 5% ROI would earn one bonus unit. For each full percentage point above five, the managers would earn an additional bonus unit, up to a maximum of six bonus units.

In 2002, the distribution of the stores' ROI was as follows:

ROI	N
<5%	6
5–6%	6
6–7%	9
7–8%	11
8–9%	20
9–10%	15
10–11%	8
11–12%	4
>12%	3
	82

For store managers who had been in that position for less than the full year and managers who transferred between stores during a year, bonus units would be assigned by the relevant regional manager(s) by applying the basic bonus unit award philosophy as closely as possible.

The regional managers' bonus pool would be divided among the regional managers based on a proportion of the bonus units earned by the stores in their region divided by the total bonus units earned by all stores.

The allocation of the corporate staff bonus pool would be decided by Fernando Gonzales based on the corporation's annual ROI performance.

4. **Form of the awards**. Bonuses were to be paid in cash as soon as the financial statements were prepared and audited and the amounts could be calculated.

CONCERNS BEFORE IMPLEMENTATION

As Mr. Gonzalez looked over the consulting firm's design, he had some concerns. First, it was obvious to him that the new plan would increase the company's compensation expense. How much would that expense increase, and would the benefits of the plan be worth that expenditure? Second, he knew that he would have to be the one to announce the implementation of the plan. He had to anticipate what his managers' reactions would be. What were they mostly likely to complain about? Is this plan fair to all of the managers? And, finally, he still lamented the fact that personnel in the regional sales and corporate purchasing organizations were not included in this plan. If their individual performances could not be measured objectively, was there some other way he could motivate them and reward them for performing their roles, which were critical to the company's success?

Exhibit 1 Las Ferreterías de México, S.A. de C.V.: income statement as of 12/31/2002 (Ps 000)

Net sales	2,216,540
Costs of sales	1,582,670
Gross margin	633,870
Selling, general and administrative expenses	377,580
Depreciation expense	65,740
Interest expense	14,320
Total expenses	457,640
Earnings before taxes	176,230
Income tax provision	58,240
Net earnings after taxes	*117,990*

Exhibit 2 Las Ferreterías de México, S.A. de C.V.: balance sheet as of 12/31/2002 (Ps 000)

Assets

Current assets

Cash and cash equivalents	79,880
Short-term investments	5,430
Accounts receivable	16,550
Merchandise inventory	387,550
	489,410
Property, less accumulated depreciation	857,650
Long-term investments	8,720
Other assets	14,060
Total assets	*1,369,840*

Liabilities

Accounts payable	211,260
Other current liabilities	57,860
Long-term debt	384,350
Other long-term liabilities	67,140
	720,610

Shareholder' equity

Preferred stock ($10 par; 300,000 shares issued)	30,000
Common stock ($20 par; 1,000,000 share issued)	200,000
Retained earnings	419,230
	649,230
Total liabilities and shareholder' equity	*1,369,840*

Case Study

Industrial Electronics, Inc.

My division had another great year last year. We all worked hard, and the results were there. But again we got no reward for our hard work. It's very frustrating.

Division Manager, General Products Division,
Industrial Electronics, Inc.

Industrial Electronics, Inc. (IE) produced a wide range of electronic equipment, including signal sources, test equipment, communications systems, and various piece parts and subassemblies such as motors, generators, and probes. Total annual sales were in excess of $8 billion. IE's stock was listed on the New York Stock Exchange.

The company's objective was to maximize shareholder value. In most of its business areas, IE had to be innovative to stay ahead of the competition. However, price competition was also significant, so the company also had to maintain tight control over costs.

The company was organized by product line. Its 16 relatively autonomous divisions were managed as profit centers. The division managers reported to one of four Business Group managers who, in turn, reported to the company's CEO.

Thirty managers, including all line managers at the level of division manager and above plus ▶

This case was prepared by Professor Kenneth A. Merchant.

Copyright © by Kenneth A. Merchant.

key corporate staff managers, were eligible for an annual management bonus award. (Many lower-level employees were included in a separate "management-by-objectives" incentive plan.) The management bonuses were based on company-wide performance. Each year, a bonus pool equal to 10% of the corporation's profit after taxes in excess of 12% of the company's book net worth was set aside for assignment as bonuses to managers. This amount was divided by the total salary of all the executives eligible for a bonus. This yielded an "award per dollar of salary." The maximum bonus paid was 150% of salary.

Historically IE's managers had been earning bonuses that ranged from of 30–120% of salary, with the average approximately 50%. But because of the recession in the years 2000 and 2001, the bonus pool was zero.

Complaints about the management bonus system had been growing. Most of them stemmed largely from division managers whose divisions were performing well, even while the corporation as a whole was not performing well. These managers believed that the current bonus system was unfair because it failed to properly recognize their contributions. The quote cited at the beginning of the case was representative of these complaints.

In response, top management, with the assistance of personnel in the corporate Human Resources and Finance departments, proposed a new management bonus plan with the following features:

1. Bonuses would be determined by the performance of the entity for which each manager was responsible. That is, division manager bonuses would be based 100% on division performance; group manager bonuses would be based 100% on group performance; and corporate manager bonuses would be based 100% on corporate performance.

2. For bonus award purposes, actual performance would be compared with targets negotiated during IE's annual budgeting process. IE's philosophy was to try to set budget targets at "threshold" levels that were likely to be achieved if the management teams performed effectively. Corporate managers knew that IE was a "high tech" company that operated in many business areas in which there was significant operating uncertainty. It was often difficult to forecast the future accurately. They thought that the relatively highly achievable budget targets provided the operating managers with some insurance against an operating environment that might turn out to be more harsh than that seen at the time of budget preparation.

3. Each division would be given an "economic profit" objective equal to budgeted operating profit minus budgeted operating assets multiplied by 12%, which was assumed to be approximately IE's weighted average cost of capital. For example, a division with an operating profit budget of $100,000 and budgeted operating assets of $500,000 would be given an economic profit objective of $100,000 − 60,000 = $40,000.

4. The actual investment base was calculated as follows:

Cash	Assumed to be 10% of cost of sales
Receivables and inventories	Average actual month-end balances
Fixed assets	Average actual end-of-month net book values

5. If an entity's actual economic profits were exactly equal to its objective, the manager would earn a bonus equal to 50% of salary. The bonus would increase linearly at a rate of five percentage points for each $100,000 above the objective and be reduced linearly at a rate of five percentage points for each $100,000 below the objective. The maximum bonus would be 150% of salary. The minimum bonus would be zero.

Haengbok Bancorp

In 2009, Haengbok Bancorp, one of Korea's smaller nationwide banks, opened its first foreign branch in New York. It opened the branch for multiple reasons. This would be an important step in fulfilling the Haengbok's objective of being an international bank. Having a US presence would allow the bank both to provide better support to its Korean partners and to generate additional business from primarily US-based Korean-owned, but also related, businesses. Most of Haengbok's customers were small and medium-sized businesses, but many of those businesses had some international operations. In addition, having some employees based overseas would allow the bank to be better informed about worldwide banking trends.

Haengbok managers knew that the competition for US-based Korean customers was fierce. Many Korean banks, some of them much larger than Haengbok, had well-established operations in the United States. Nevertheless, they thought the time was right to open the US branch because many smaller businesses were having difficulty raising capital as a result of the financial crisis. The branch was located in New York both because it was the largest US money center and because the New York/New Jersey metropolitan area contained a relatively high concentration of Korean-owned and Korean-oriented businesses.

Haengbok's New York branch was a wholesale operation. The primary goal was to make US dollar loans to Korean or US companies. To limit foreign exchange risk, the branch had to raise all of its money, except for a small capital contribution from Haengbok Bancorp, in the US money markets. Only a few retail accounts were maintained for the convenience of Haengbok's multinational clients. No special services were offered to build the retail side of the business. Check clearing services were outsourced to a major US, New York-based bank.

MANAGEMENT OF THE BRANCH

Hyun Ki Kim, an experienced Haengbok account manager previously based in Seoul, was appointed as Senior Manager of the New York branch. Mr. Kim quickly hired five experienced account managers with track records of success at other banks in the United States. The account managers began identifying clients in need of loans. For the most part, the account managers were assigned defined geographical territories to develop. Two were based on the east coast, two on the west coast, and one in the Midwest. However, two of the account managers had had significant, specific prior industry experiences, and they were given responsibility for developing opportunities with a few specifically identified prospective clients in those industries that were located outside their assigned territory.

Mr. Kim knew that the account managers he hired had varied corporate experiences and operating styles, but that did not concern him at all. He put few constraints on their activities. He told the account managers that he did not care how they identified and cultivated their clients as long as they eventually "booked good deals."

For monitoring and incentive purposes, Mr. Kim set each account manager up as a "mini profit center." Their profit centers were credited with the interest earned on the loans initiated, and they were charged for the expenses incurred, including the cost of funding the loans. This was not the system used by Haengbok Bancorp in Korea, but Mr. Kim thought that such a system was needed to encourage the account managers' entrepreneurialism, which would be needed to be able to grow the branch rapidly.

In addition to their base salaries, which branch studies showed to be slightly below comparable bank averages, the account managers were paid a bonus of 10% of the aggregate profits generated in ▶

This case was prepared by Professor Kenneth A. Merchant. Assistance was provided by Jong Hwan Kim.

their mini profit centers each year. They were not penalized for aggregate losses that might be incurred in any given year, but it was understood that losses would not be tolerated for extended periods of time. The bonuses were paid out in full in cash shortly after the fiscal year end. Mr. Kim thought that after the account managers had built their loan portfolios to their envisioned levels, their total compensation would be competitive with those of the established banks.

Mr. Kim thought that as the branch matured, he might begin to set goals for each account manager and to provide bonuses based on achievement of those goals, but in the start-up phase, he did not have enough knowledge of either the market potentials or the account manager capabilities to set meaningful goals. He worried that short-term profits provided only an imperfect measure of success in the whole-sale banking industry. For one thing, the loans were typically granted for terms of 5–10 years, and no loan ever granted had a zero chance of default. But he thought that the rather rudimentary system put in place would suffice during the branch's start-up period. A more sophisticated reward system would probably emerge over time.

Managing time productively was a critical skill for the account managers. In all the geographical territories the number of potential clients was huge. But competition was also stiff. Many Korean banks, including Hanmi, Nara, Wilshire, Center, Saehan, Pacific City, Shinhan, Woori, and Mirae, were already well established in the United States, and some Korean-oriented businesses also raised money from non-Korean banks. The Haengbok account managers had to identify and solicit business from their best prospects. The best clients were businesses who wanted larger loans with higher spreads and, importantly, also had the ability to pay the loans back. The account managers also had to consider the costs of finding the prospects, analyzing their situations, and preparing the loan applications as well as the probabilities of getting the loans approved.

After the account managers identified loan prospects, they prepared a credit application. The loan application package needed to include a description of the client and its business, the proposed use of the loan funds, the proposed loan terms (e.g., size, payments, fees, security, covenants), and an analysis of the loan's risk. Risk was addressed in many ways, but market prospects and the client's financial statements were always considered.

Applications for loans less than $1 million could be approved by Mr. Kim. If the proposed loan exceeded $1 million, the application had to be approved by the branch's Credit Committee, which was comprised of Mr. Kim, the branch CFO/Treasurer, and two of the most experienced account managers. If the proposed loan exceeded $5 million, then the Haengbok Bancorp Corporate Credit Committee, based in Seoul, would also have to give approval before the loan could be made.

After loans were made, they were reviewed on a regular basis by management, national bank examiners, and external auditors. Management also regularly monitored clients for signs of possible problems, which might be indicated by declining business conditions, violations of covenants, and missed payments.

A REJECTED LOAN APPLICATION

In early 2010, Jae Lee, an account manager assigned to the southwestern US territory, submitted a credit application for an $11 million, seven-year term loan for Far East Trading Corporation (FETC), a company that had significant business activities in Korea. The pricing included a 1% fee at closing and a variable rate of 5% above the prime lending rate. The loan was fully collateralized with inventory. Because of the size of the loan, Jae spent considerable care in preparing the application. He was pleased with it:

> I thought this was a good deal for Haengbok. I priced it with a relatively large spread, so we were going to make good money over the life of the loan. FETC is a good company that has been in business for many years, and it has an experienced management team. They have found good business opportunities even in the current recessionary period. So I concluded that the loan was relatively low risk.

The branch's Credit Committee, of which Jae was not a part, quickly approved the loan. At the time, committee members noted that Jae's application was well prepared and that they trusted Jae's judgments about the merits of the deal. Jae happened to be one of the more experienced account managers. He had worked for several years for two major US banks before joining Haengbok's New York branch.

Since the proposed size of the loan exceeded $5 million, the application also had to be approved by the corporate Credit Committee in Seoul. When the corporate committee met, Jae joined part of the meeting by telephone. The committee members asked Jae a number of questions asking for both clarifications and more detail. Jae thought that he was able to answer all the questions satisfactorily.

A couple of days later, however, Jae and Mr. Kim were informed that corporate had decided that the loan should not be made. The committee spokesman explained that the problem was not with either Jae's analysis or the loan terms. A concern arose because some members of the Credit Committee had heard allegations that FETC was involved in some transfer pricing disputes with the tax authorities. These disputes could lead to protracted legal costs, possibly hefty fines, or an expensive settlement. While they could not confirm the allegations and did not know if the legal settlements, if any, might hinder FETC's ability to meet its cash flow obligations, when it came time to vote on this application, a majority of the committee members decided to err on the side of caution.

Case Study

Berkshire Industries PLC

We had to do something different. The company was doing great according to all the performance indicators we monitored, and our managers were earning nice bonuses, but the shareowners weren't benefiting.

William Embleton

William Embleton, managing director of Berkshire Industries PLC, explained why his company had implemented a new incentive system based on an "economic profit" measure of performance starting in the year 2000. In 2002, however, Berkshire managers were questioning whether their new system had had its desired effects. The new economic profit measure did not seem to be any better in reflecting shareowner returns than did the old measure – accounting earnings – on which Berkshire managers had previously focused. And the new system was causing some management confusion and a perceived unfairness issue. Mr. Embleton had to decide whether to modify the new system, and if so how, or to replace it with something else.

THE COMPANY

Berkshire Industries PLC (Berkshire) was founded in 1852 as a brewery serving local pubs. Over the years it had grown, both internally and by acquisition. In 2002, Berkshire was a medium-sized, publicly held corporation focused on the beverages and snack foods industry. It had annual turnover of about £500 million and it employed nearly 3,500 people in six countries. Berkshire was listed on the London Stock Exchange. The company headquarters were still located in Manchester, England, where the company was founded.

Berkshire had four operating divisions: beer, spirits, soft drinks, and snack foods. The managing directors of each of these divisions had considerable autonomy because Berkshire operated in a decentralized fashion. The small headquarters staff was primarily responsible for coordinating the finance, human resources, and various administrative functions (e.g., legal, information systems).

MEASUREMENT AND INCENTIVE SYSTEMS

Since the company had gone public, the primary performance emphasis at Berkshire had been on corporate earnings per share (EPS). The company's long-term EPS growth target was 8%, but the target was modified each year based on anticipated market conditions and pending acquisitions, if any. ▶

This case was prepared by Professors Kenneth A. Merchant and Wim A. Van der Stede, with the research assistance of Xiaoling (Clara) Chen.

The company's annual planning process was a bottom-up process, which first involved the operating divisions proposing their earnings targets for the year and their means of achieving them. The division's draft plans were consolidated and compared with Berkshire's corporate EPS growth target. Typically the difference between the divisions' plans and the corporate target was material. This "planning gap" was eliminated in a series of discussions among corporate and division managers, typically by increases in some or all divisions' targets.

Because top management considered it so important to meet analysts' EPS expectations, they also established a corporate "profit reserve" of approximately 10% of planned earnings. This reserve was established to ensure that the corporation would achieve its targets even if one, or perhaps even two, of its divisions failed to achieve their targets. If, later in the year, management determined that the company would achieve its targets, they would release this reserve to the Investments Committee for spending on discretionary projects, most of which had relatively long-term payoffs. But in 2000 and 2001 none of this reserve was released to the Investments Committee. All of it was turned in to meet the corporate EPS targets.

Senior managers at Berkshire, a group of about 40 people, participated in an annual incentive compensation plan. Performance was evaluated based on achievement of earnings targets in the entity to which the manager was assigned: a division in the case of division-level personnel or the entire corporation in the case of corporate-level personnel. The target bonuses ranged from 20–90% of base salary, depending on the manager's level of seniority. The plan allowed for subjective overrides of bonus awards if superiors, or the compensation committee of the board of directors in the case of top management, felt that performance shortfalls were caused by factors beyond the manager's control.

THE MOTIVATION FOR A NEW INCENTIVE PLAN

In 1999 Berkshire's board of directors asked William Embleton to explore the desirability of a new performance measurement and incentive system based on an "economic profit" measure of performance, a concept that had received many popular reviews in the management press.

The board's motivation for a new plan stemmed from two concerns. First, they were concerned that managers' interests were not aligned with those of shareowners. They were particularly concerned that EPS was not a good measure of performance in the new era where the management mantra had become "maximization of shareowner value." They noted that while Berkshire's EPS had been improving steadily, at an average annual growth rate of 9% in the last decade, the company's shareowners had not benefited. The company's share price had increased only slightly over that period of time.

Second, the board wanted to force more objectivity into the performance evaluation and reward system. Some board members believed that too many subjective bonus awards were being made, giving managers bonuses even in years where their entity did not perform well. One effect of allowing subjective judgments was that bonus awards were only loosely correlated with the realized operating performances. Another effect was a lot of misspent time, as managers engaged in "politicking." They tried to convince their evaluators that they had performed well, even though the results were disappointing. The board members in favor of change thought that a new incentive system should place sharp limits on the use of subjectivity in granting bonus awards, if not eliminate it entirely.

THE NEW SYSTEM

In response to the board's request, William Embleton asked three consulting firms to submit proposals for an engagement to design a new measurement and incentive system. After a series of meetings, the Berkshire management team and board selected the large New York-headquartered firm of Corey, Langfeldt and Associates (CLA). The consulting engagement was staffed by CLA associates based in London.

The CLA approach was based on the firm's proprietary "economic profit" measure of performance. The CLA formula for economic profit was:

Economic profit = Adjusted Net Operating Profit after Taxes − [Capital × Cost of Capital]

Net operating profit after taxes (NOPAT) excluded all nonoperating noncash charges, such as depreciation, amortization, asset write-offs and write-downs, and reserves. Cost of capital was determined annually for each business unit based on the yield on long-term government obligations plus a risk premium calculated based on an assumed capital structure and risk factor (β value) for comparable peer firms. Since Berkshire's business units were all seen as being in relatively stable industries, all were given the same cost-of-capital rate of 10%.

In each of their engagements, CLA would propose a specific combination of adjustments to NOPAT to make the economic profit measure "better," to better match costs and benefits and, hence, to improve the relationship between economic profits and share prices. The CLA system designers had identified well over 100 adjustments that might be used in certain situations. But in Berkshire's case, the consultants proposed only two adjustments because they wanted "to keep the model simple." First, they suggested that the company's consumer advertising expenses should be capitalized and amortized on a straight-line basis over three years. The current year's expense was added back to operating profits, and the capitalized amount was added to net operating assets. Exhibit 1 shows an example.

Second, the CLA consultants suggested that the goodwill that had arisen from the company's acquisitions should not be amortized.[1] Hence, they suggested that cumulative goodwill which had been amortized to date should be added back to net operating assets, and all goodwill amortization expense should be added back to operating earnings.

In their presentations, the CLA consultants explained that their economic profit measure was superior to all other measures, particularly accounting earnings, that Berkshire could use. The consultants presented charts showing that their measure of economic profits was highly correlated with returns to shareowners in a broad range of corporations. Thus, they claimed, it is the one measure that provides "the right signals to management all the time." Motivating managers to maximize their entity's economic profit would induce them to invest in their entities' futures. They would make all investments promising returns greater than the corporation's cost of capital. It would also motivate them to recognize the full cost of tying up the company's capital and, hence, to reduce their employed assets where the returns are inadequate.

Knowing their competition, the CLA consultants also directed some of their critique at systems that tried to link management incentives to elaborate combinations of measures. The multiple-measurement systems, they explained, were usually hopelessly complex. The systems typically incorporated measures that were not directly linked with shareowner value. They included performance concepts that were vague (for example, personnel development) and supported by weak measures. And they rarely made the trade-offs among the multiple measures clear. The overall effects were diffusion of management attention and loss of understandability and accountability.

The CLA consultants also recommended against the implementation of a stock-based incentive program. They pointed out that stock prices are affected by many external factors and are highly volatile in the short term. They further explained that stock-based incentives are not an effective tool for motivating division- and lower-level managers who can have, at best, a modest impact on share prices.

The measurement-focus of the CLA presentation was highly convincing to some of the board members. One remarked:

> This is what we need, one simple measure that goes up when shareowner value is created and that goes down when value is destroyed. If we get our managers focused on this measure, they will be working in the best interest of our shareowners. With earnings, we just don't know what we're getting.

A second element of the CLA system involved the automatic ratcheting of performance targets. In the CLA system managers were compensated directly for improving their entity's economic profits. In the first year the performance targets were set based on a projection of the unit's historical economic profit growth rate, if that growth rate was deemed to be good performance, multiplied by 75%. Thereafter performance targets were set automatically based on improvements from the actual performance of the prior year. Each business unit's performance target was ratcheted up (down) by 75% of the amount by which actual performance exceeded (fell short of) the unit's prior year's performance. The CLA consultants explained that this method of setting targets avoided the need to renegotiate performance targets each year and, hence, the politics and game playing that was almost inevitably associated with these negotiations. It also incorporated the desired management philosophy of continuous improvement.

A third element of the system was the explicit elimination of payout thresholds and caps. Managers were assigned a target bonus, a fixed percentage

---

[1] In the United Kingdom, companies can disclose goodwill amortization charges on the income statement, and they can also present goodwill-adjusted earnings per share figures.

of base pay, that would be earned if their units just achieved their performance targets. These targets were increased slightly from the bonus levels that were earned under Berkshire's old system to encourage managers' acceptance of change. The target bonuses ranged from 20% of base salary for functional managers within a division to 100% for Berkshire's managing director. If the units exceeded their performance targets, managers would earn larger bonuses. The slope of the line determining the payoffs for each level of economic profit was based on each unit's historical growth rate. This slope was intended to remain the same from year to year, although it was subject to board review. The maximum bonus that could be earned was unlimited (see Exhibit 2).

The fourth element of the system was a "bonus bank" that was intended to reduce manager risk by smoothing out the bonus awards, to reduce managers' short-term gaming behaviors, and to improve manager retention. If a unit's economic profit performance exceeded the performance target, the "excess" bonus earned (calculated as the slope of the payoff function times the amount by which the actual economic profit exceeds the target) was credited to the bonus bank. Managers were then paid their target bonus plus one-fourth of the amount in the bonus bank. If economic profit fell below the target amount a negative entry (obtained as the slope of the payoff function times the amount by which the actual economic profit fell short of the target) was made to the bonus bank. If managers changed divisions, their bonus bank amounts would follow them. Managers who left Berkshire voluntarily forfeited the amounts in their bonus bank accounts.

PROBLEMS AND CONCERNS

While Berkshire's board members' and managers' hopes were high after the company's introduction of the new economic profit system in 2000, early experiences with the system were disappointing. The new system had caused several problems and concerns. The board and the top management team were considering whether the system needed fixing. Some even questioned whether the new system should be continued.

One problem was that the new system had created considerable management confusion, which persisted even after all the operating managers had attended a series of training sessions. Corporate managers thought that the operating managers would quickly learn how the economic profit measure worked, since their bonuses now depended on it. But a number of the managers seemed not to understand how the economic profit measure was computed, and some of them continued to manage their entities based on their old earnings-based management reports.

A second problem was discouragement and demotivation in the Spirits Division (Spirits). In both 2000 and 2001 economic profits in Spirits were poor. In the recessionary times, consumers were drinking less spirits. With consumer demand down some of the Spirits Division's competitors cut prices significantly and Spirits had to match their reductions. This had a disastrous effect on margins. Spirits failed to achieve both its 2000 performance target and its ratcheted-down 2001 target, by wide margins. As a consequence bonus awards for Spirits managers were significantly below target levels, and all Spirits managers had sizable negative balances in their bonus bank accounts.

Ian Dent, Spirits' managing director, asked William Embleton for some special adjustments. He requested that the Spirits Division performance targets be adjusted retroactively to reflect the economic conditions that were actually faced. He did not think it was fair for his managers to suffer the negative effects of factors over which they had no control. He explained that his team had worked very hard in the trying conditions they had faced, and they had made the hard decisions that were called for, including cutbacks in discretionary expenses and layoffs. He also requested that the economic profit system not be applied to his division because it was not responsive to changing market conditions. Ian was worried that his division would suffer some significant management losses because of his managers' negative bonus bank balances.

A third problem was a widely shared perception of a basic failure of the economic profit measure itself. Overall, Berkshire's performance, as measured in terms of economic profit, seemed excellent. Economic profit had improved since 2000, but the company's stock price had actually declined over this period (see Exhibit 3). The CLA consultants had sold the new system based on a promise of a high correlation between the company's economic profit numbers and returns to shareowners, but to date, at least, the economic profits did not seem to be moving in parallel with the stock price. The shareowners had not benefited.

EXHIBIT 1 Example showing effect of capitalization and amortization of consumer advertising expenditure (£000s)

			First year of use of new system		
		1998	1999	2000	2001
Advertising expense as reported on income statement		900	1,200	1,800	2,400
Amortization for economic profit report	1998	300	300	300	
	1999		400	400	400
	2000			600	600
	2001				800
Advertising expense on economic profit report				1,300	1,800
Cumulative advertising expense (on income statement)		900	2,100	3,900	6,300
Less: cumulative amortization (economic profit report)		300	1,000	2,300	4,100
Capitalized advertising for economic profit calculation of capital for economic profit report				1,600	2,200

EXHIBIT 2 Link between economic profit performance and bonus awards

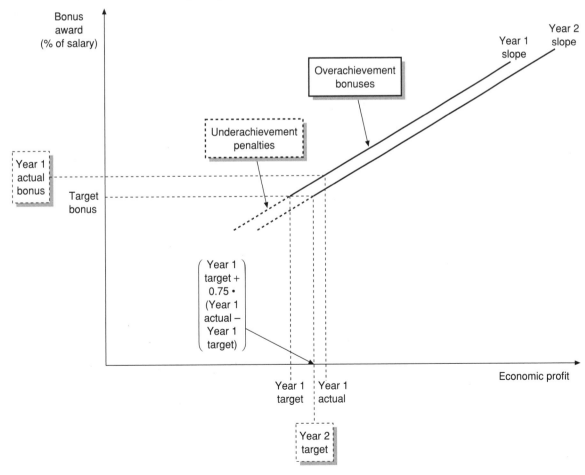

Exhibit 3 Berkshire Industries' earnings, economic profit, and stock price, 1997–2002

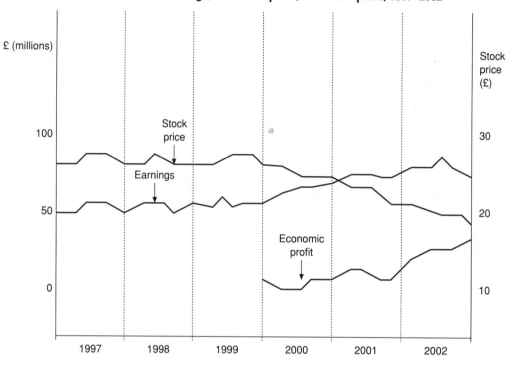

Chapter 11

REMEDIES TO THE MYOPIA PROBLEM

In Chapter 10 we explained how the use of financial results controls that emphasize current-period accounting profits can cause managers to become excessively short-term oriented, or *myopic*, in their decision-making. Myopia is a well-known dysfunctional side-effect of financial results control systems. In this chapter, we first discuss the pressures that cause managers to act myopically. We then discuss six financial results control remedies that can be used to alleviate the myopia problem. These remedies include: (1) reducing the pressure for short-term profits; (2) using preaction reviews (action controls) to control developmental, long-term investments; (3) lengthening the horizon over which performance is measured and rewarded (using long-term incentives); (4) changing what is measured (other proxies for shareholder value creation instead of accounting income); (5) adjusting or improving accounting measures to better reflect economic income; and (6) replacing (or complementing) accounting measures with (nonfinancial) value drivers of performance (that is, using *combination-of-measures systems*).

PRESSURES TO ACT MYOPICALLY

Managers, particularly top-level managers, must understand the ever-present tension between short-term and long-term results, and continually guard against unwise tradeoffs between them. What promotes one often hinders the other, or so it may seem. Every manager must continually strive for both: performing well today while, at the same time, developing the business for a sustainable future. As Peter Drucker is credited to have said, a manager "must keep his nose to the grindstone while lifting his eyes to the hills, which is quite an acrobatic feat."[1] "Lifting the eyes to the hills" is particularly hard when managers believe that the stock market will react vigorously to short-term earnings reports. Managers, then, may be inclined to take steps to try to maintain a smooth, steady earnings growth pattern and to meet or beat market earnings expectations at almost any cost.[2]

To suggest that stock markets only react to earnings, however, is an overstatement at best and misguided at worst, as research indicates that stock markets also react to announcements of strategic significance, such as investments in capital or research and development (R&D) projects, new management hires, and mergers and divestments. In other words, if management is deemed to be taking sound long-term decisions, the market seems to be able to compound into its valuations what the long-term impacts on earnings will be, even though the results may not be reflected fully, or even adequately, in short-run profits with immediate effect. Indeed, as we discussed in Chapter 10, stock valuations should reflect estimates of businesses' long-term cash generation potentials, even though they are imperfect estimates, as we discussed too.

Nonetheless, pressures for short-term results remain present. Acting myopically is one common response to the pressures arising from the belief in the need to prop up short-term profits. Another common response is to engage in *gamesmanship*, such as by altering judgments about reserves, which we discuss in more detail in Chapter 15. Myopia and gamesmanship are the two most common forms of what is generally referred to as *earnings management*.

Some companies are known for earnings management. For example, an article in *Fortune* explained that, "Though earnings management is a no-no among good-governance types, [General Electric] has never denied doing it, and GE Capital [GE's large capital division that has helped finance GE's vast array of businesses] is the perfect mechanism. Since financial assets are, under normal conditions, far more liquid than tangible assets, the company can buy or sell them in the final days of a quarter so that reported earnings rise with comforting smoothness, right in line with Wall Street expectations."[3] As such, GE Capital "has become such a necessary part of GE's legendary earnings results that General Electric could not perform as well or consistently if anything happened to it," according to Michael Lewitt, president of Harch Capital Management, a hedge fund.[4]

Some chief executives, however, appear to steadfastly object to such pressures and simply refuse to smooth or manage earnings, and over the long term their companies' stock performance does not seem to have been hurt by it. For example, Progressive, an Ohio-based insurance company, seems to have been able to maintain strong stock performance although its chairman, Peter Lewis, refused to try to smooth earnings zigzags: "It is not honest," he said, "Besides, when companies manage their earnings they mar their own business intelligence: the accounting stuff that is required to smooth things out causes management to mislead itself."[5]

Nonetheless, pressures exist to smooth or manage earnings as "investors [appear to] happily pay extra for companies whose profits rise steadily rather than erratically, so this function is valuable."[6] And so it takes resolve, even perhaps some stubbornness, to resist pressures to act myopically. There are, however, several management control system (MCS) approaches that can help mitigate myopia. In addition to the approaches discussed in Chapter 10 to try to offset the tendencies of accounting measures to cause myopia, we discuss a further six possible approaches here.

REDUCE PRESSURES FOR SHORT-TERM PROFIT

Sometimes the best myopia-avoidance solution might be merely to relax the pressure for generating short-term profits. The reductions in pressure can be affected in either of two basic ways. The weighting placed on the annual (or quarterly) profit targets can be reduced, perhaps even to zero, while other, longer-term performance indicators, such as market share or technical breakthroughs, are emphasized. At Johnson & Johnson, for example, the large and successful health care and pharmaceuticals company, profits are not directly linked with rewards:

> Our company philosophy is to manage for the long term. We do not use short-term bonus plans. Salary and bonus reviews are entirely subjective and qualitative and are intended to reward effort and give special recognition to those who have performed uniquely.[7]

Alternatively, the short-term profit targets can be made easier to achieve. Profit targets that are more highly achievable create some room for managers to be preoccupied by longer-term initiatives. The risk of doing so, however, is that relaxing short-term profit pressure may trigger slackness – a loss of concentration on short-term results – without necessarily a sharper long-term focus. Therefore, when relaxing the pressures for the short term, the managers whose pressures are being relaxed must be trusted, or otherwise (or in addition), the needed pressure must be imparted in other ways, such as through timely nonfinancial performance evaluations (which we discuss further below).

CONTROL INVESTMENTS WITH PREACTION REVIEWS

To control *investment myopia*, some companies find it useful to use financial result controls to reward improvements in short-term *operating performance* only. The costs of longer-term investments are considered *below* the income statement line for which the managers are held accountable, so managers feel no pressure, or less temptation, to cut these investments to boost short-term profits.

This approach is illustrated in Table 11.1. Panel A of this figure shows the aggregated income statement for a profit center, say. Panel B shows the segregation of short-term (or operating) income from total income. The key to implementing this approach is to distinguish between *operating expenses*, which are necessary to produce current-period revenues, and *developmental expenses*, which are incurred in order to generate revenues in future periods. If this distinction can be made, the profit center managers are asked to maximize *operating income*, which provides a good indicator of short-term performance: current period sales and operating efficiency. The managers are asked to propose ideas for developmental investments, those that will produce revenues and profits in future operating periods. The quality of those investment ideas and the payoffs from the expenditures is then monitored with other forms of control, such as preaction reviews of expenditure or investment proposals and monitoring of accomplishments against predefined milestones (as discussed in Chapter 3).

Some companies use variations of this approach, such as by not charging operating units for some developmental expenses that benefit them. Instead, they fund certain types of business development at higher organization levels (such as corporate or business group levels) until the investments begin to generate revenues in order to cushion lower-level entities' earnings from the impact of these expenses. Some corporations have split

TABLE 11.1 Separating developmental investments from short-term operating performance

Panel A. Standard income statement

Revenues	$100
Expenses	90
Net income	10

Panel B. Income statement with short-term operating performance isolated

Revenues	$100
Operating expenses	50
Operating margin	50
Developmental investments	40
Net income	10

Source: K. A. Merchant, *Modern Management Control Systems: Text and Cases* (Upper Saddle River, NJ: Prentice Hall, 1998), p. 463.

themselves into what could be called *today* businesses and *tomorrow* businesses. In the today businesses, managers are charged with making their businesses lean, efficient, and profitable in their competitive environment. Managers of tomorrow businesses are charged with developing new business opportunities (products, markets) that might one day augment or replace the existing today businesses. Today businesses are controlled through tight financial result controls. Tomorrow businesses are controlled with a combination of nonfinancial performance indicators and action controls.

This approach of separating and protecting developmental expenditures has two major limitations, however. One is that a clear distinction between operating expenditures and developmental expenditures may not exist, or that the distinction can be blurred. For example, manufacturing process improvements and market development programs will probably provide benefits (cost reductions or additional revenues) in current *and* future periods. Consequently, managers have some latitude to incur expenses either above or below the operating margin line, and they can use this latitude to game the system. In particular, when their entity is performing well in comparison with budget targets, they can choose to fund development expenditures within their current operating budget.

Another limitation of this approach is that it passes final decisions about which developmental expenditures to fund to corporate (or dedicated) management. Relative to entity managers, corporate managers in large, diversified corporations, particularly, are almost inevitably less well informed about the prospects of each specific business and the desired type and level of funding. This may harm the quality of resource allocation decisions to key investments in the future.

EXTEND THE MEASUREMENT HORIZON (USE LONG-TERM INCENTIVES)

Lengthening the period of measurement is a third alternative for improving the congruence of the accounting measures of performance. As discussed in Chapter 10, the longer the period of measurement, the more congruent the accounting measures of performance are likely to be with economic income (changes in shareholder returns). Annual accounting income is, on average, a better indicator of annual economic income than quarterly accounting income is of quarterly economic income, and three-year accounting income is a better indicator than is annual accounting income.

As discussed in Chapter 9, long-term incentive plans are common. These plans come in a variety of forms, but they usually provide rewards either for stock appreciation or for the attainment of performance targets, such as earnings per share or accounting return on equity measured over a three- to five-year period say.

As an example, consider the long-term performance awards (LTPA) plan in use at General Electric Company, as approved in February 2006. The awards were made in 2009 to 600 select executives based on performance in the 2006–08 three-year time period. The awards were based on four performance measures: average earnings per share growth rate, average revenue growth rate, cumulative return on total capital, and cumulative cash flow from operating activities. GE's board compensation committee selected these performance measures:

> [. . .] because they are the best measurement of the company's ability to compete and grow, to efficiently use its financial capital to generate earnings and to produce cash to reinvest or return to shareowners – and as such, these goals are aligned with our shareowners' interests.[8]

Each measure was to be adjusted to remove the effects of unusual events (a topic we discuss in Chapter 12), if any, and the effects of pensions on income. Each measure was weighted equally. Payments would be made for achieving any of three goals – threshold, target, or maximum – for any of the four measures. For example, the executives would receive only one-quarter of the threshold-level payment if at the end of the three-year period the company only meets a single threshold goal for a single measure. The awards were based on a multiple of the sum of the executive's base salary in 2006 plus the bonus assigned to him/her for 2005 performance (x). For the top two executives, and presumably for the others included in the plan, the multiples were as follows:

Threshold payment	0.75x
Target payment	1.50x
Maximum payment	2.00x

Payments were prorated for performance falling between these goal levels.

Looking at GE's 2009 proxy statement, we can see that the goal was (1) not achieved for average earnings per share growth rate (4.5% relative to the threshold level that was set at 10%); (2) achieved at the maximum level for average revenue growth rate (10.1% relative to the maximum target set at 10%); (3) achieved at the threshold level for cumulative return on total capital (17.3% relative to the threshold target set at 16%, but below the target level set at 18%); and (4) achieved at the target level for cumulative cash flow from operating activities ($66.2 billion relative to the target level set at $60 billion, but short of the maximum target level set at $70 billion). Because the company exceeded the goals in three of the four measurements, the executives were entitled to receive payments of $46.6 million in February 2009. In February 2009, however, Mr. Immelt (GE's chief executive) and the board agreed to modify the actual payments related to the LTPA for certain executives. Specifically, although Mr. Immelt was entitled to receive $11.7 million, his entire award was canceled. Similarly, half of the awards of Messrs. Sherin (GE's chief financial officer) and Neal (the executive in charge of GE's Capital Finance business) were canceled, which portion would have entitled them to $2.6 million and $2.9 million, respectively. As a result of these actions, the total payout to the named executives was reduced from $46.6 million to $29.4 million. In addition, payments to the other executives were made in 50% stock and 50% cash. The request to cancel these earned payments was mainly to heed the principle that GE's "compensation programs take into account the general business and political environment in which compensation decisions are made" – that is, considering the adverse circumstances and considerations of reasonableness during the challenging times that followed the 2008–09 financial and economic crisis.[9]

Although it is hard to determine definitively, one could reasonably conclude from the above example that the long-term incentive plan likely had the desirable effect of lengthening managerial horizons and, hence, of combating management myopia. As such, extending the measurement period can avoid some of the congruence problems of accounting measures of performance. To have noticeable positive motivational effects, however, the expected payoffs from long-term incentives must reflect the additional discounting that employees apply to deferred compensation. As discussed in Chapter 9, it has been suggested that, indeed, the mental discount rate employees apply to delayed rewards is greater than the time value of money.[10] Hence, extending the time horizon of incentives has a cost in terms of providing higher payoffs in expectation. If the firm fails to compensate for this by roughly offering an equal weighting in monetary units for the potential payoffs of the long-term and short-term rewards, it will provide motivational effects that are still skewed towards the short-term.

Another issue to be addressed in designing accounting-based long-term incentive plans is the performance standard. Firms commonly use the numbers included in the long-term strategic plan as the standard. But this practice can cause problems. It can drive much of the creative thinking out of strategic planning. It tends to make managers conservative in their aspirations (out of fear of subsequently being held against meeting those aspirations), exactly what most firms do not want in their strategic planning processes. And the standards themselves can become obsolete, either too easy or too difficult to achieve, because the assumptions embedded in the setting of the long-term plan might later prove to have been incorrect. Particularly in fast-moving, competitive environments, many things change over a three- to five-year period, or less.

MEASURE CHANGES IN VALUE DIRECTLY

A fourth possible remedy to the myopia problem is to try to measure *economic income* or shareholder value creation directly by estimating future cash flows and discounting them to the present value. This direct measurement of the value of an entity can be made both at the beginning and the end of a measurement period. The difference between the beginning and ending values is a direct estimate of the value created during the period, and thus of economic income.

The idea of measuring economic income directly and then using it in a financial result control system to motivate managers' behaviors is fraught with difficulties, however. As Henry Ford once said, "you can't build a reputation on what you are *going* to do" [emphasis in original].[11] Will the cash flow forecasts prove to be accurate? Who should prepare the forecasts? Certainly some measurement difficulties need to be faced, but there are those who believe that measuring changes in economic income directly might be workable within usable levels of accuracy in some situations.

Estimating future cash flows is not a new management concept. Most companies have considerable experience in preparing estimates of future cash flows and in reviewing the estimates for reasonableness. Analyses of future cash flows are a standard part of investment and acquisition proposals, and some companies are also accustomed to using discounted cash flow methods for strategic planning purposes. The discounting of cash flow estimates also is an important part of several accounting rules (such as those related to long-term receivables, leases, asset impairments, and pension liabilities) despite the importance accountants place on measurement precision. One of the significant trends in accounting actually seems to be a greater tolerance for this so-called softer, forward-looking, but potentially more relevant, data.

That said, measurement precision and objectivity are significant stumbling blocks to the use of direct measures of economic income. If rewards are linked to the cash flow estimates, managers may be tempted to bias their estimates. These biases could perhaps be controlled by having the estimates prepared, or at least reviewed, by an independent third party, such as a consulting firm or auditor. To do their work, however, these outsiders would have to be given access to considerable amounts of information the firm might consider sensitive (such as competitive analyses and marketing plans), and the process would undoubtedly be expensive. Nonetheless, if these problems can be overcome, direct estimates of economic income (changes in cash flow potentials) could be given some practical use in results control systems, at least on a less frequent basis (e.g. every three years rather than annually).

IMPROVE THE ACCOUNTING MEASURES

A fifth approach to mitigate investment myopia involves changing the measurement rules to make the accounting income measures *better*; that is, more congruent with economic income. These improvements address one or more of the deviations between accounting income and economic income.

Some measurement improvements provide a better matching of revenues and expenses. Companies can choose depreciable lives for fixed assets that are close to the useful economic lives of the assets, not conservatively short, as is typical. Similarly, companies can capitalize all, or at least more, categories of expenditures made for the express purpose of generating cash flows (revenues or cost savings) in future periods (developmental expenditures). Capitalization of investments such as for R&D, customer acquisition and employee development will provide a better matching of revenues and expenses if the future cash flows (revenues) are forthcoming from these investments, as they should if the investments are good ones.

Some measurement improvements recognize profits (and losses) more quickly, which makes the performance indicators more timely. The value changes are recognized as soon as they can be measured or estimated, rather than waiting for the completion of a transaction. Variations of this concept already exist, such as in *mark-to-market* accounting in certain industries (e.g. banks), where certain assets on the balance sheet are held at their market value rather than their historical cost, thus causing profits and losses to be recorded when the changes in value are observed and not just when the assets are sold.[12] A further example is where oil companies could provide rewards to their explorationists, geologists and geophysicists as soon as it is clear that they have created value for the firm; that is, when oil or gas is discovered. In this case, the rewards (bonuses, say) would be based on estimates of the value of the discovery; they would be paid years in advance of the production of the reserves and, hence, the cash flows to the firm and the accounting recognition of the gains.

Another possible adjustment involves charging depreciation for older assets that, for financial reporting purposes, are considered fully depreciated. Doing so recognizes that these assets, which are in use, still have market values that should be protected and that managers should be given an incentive to replace the assets when the decline in the assets' service potentials warrants the replacement.

Some accounting measure improvements are designed to reflect the company's entire cost of capital. Companies concerned about this problem include an imputed cost of equity capital on their income statements. Other accounting measure improvements are designed primarily to improve the denominator of return-on-investment measures (as discussed in Chapter 10). For example, some companies put all of their entities' leases on the balance sheet, regardless of whether they qualify under accounting rules as capital leases.

Note that such adjustments to accounting measures of performance, and many more, are akin to those proposed by Stern Stewart & Company, the consulting firm that recommends the Economic Value Added (EVA™) measure, which we discussed in Chapter 10.

However, most of these measurement improvements deviate from prevailing accounting rules and, hence, their implementation will cause the performance reports used for management control purposes to be different from those prepared for financial reporting purposes. The accounting measure improvements, then, necessitate the use of a third set of financial records, a management set, to supplement the books designed for financial reporting and tax purposes. Managers must be aware that these improvements, then, are not without costs. There are added processing, reporting, and reconciliation costs, and possibly costs of confusion that might not be inconsequential.

MEASURE A SET OF VALUE DRIVERS

The short-term, backward-looking, completed-transaction orientation of accounting measures (as we discussed in Chapter 10) can be balanced by focusing also on other performance measures that are more future-oriented. For example, well-chosen nonfinancial measures can provide signals about what is likely in the future. Accomplishments in areas such as R&D, new product development, product quality and customer satisfaction are often *value drivers*, and, hence, *leading indicators* of future financial performance. Thus, *supplementing* the accounting measures with some combination of these value drivers can be used to mitigate managers' tendencies to prop up short-term financial measures at the expense of future performance. Indeed, many firms have found it useful to focus on a set of value drivers in their measurement systems. Because carefully selected value drivers are leading indicators of forthcoming cash flows and profits, value drivers focus managers' attention on actions and decisions they should worry about today in order to create value in the reasonably-distant future.

One commonly used measurement combination is of market and accounting measures, each of which we discussed separately in Chapter 10. This particular combination of measures is often a key element of *performance stock* or *performance options* that we discussed in Chapter 9, and which also constitute long-term incentives, a myopia-problem remedy that we discussed above.

A second commonly used measurement combination involves the use of either summary accounting measures or specific, disaggregated financial elements (e.g. revenues, expenses, margins, assets, liabilities), or both, with any of a number of *nonfinancial* measures (e.g. product quality, yields, customer satisfaction, days since last lost-time accident). These combinations can be as simple as including a second parameter in an incentive contract. A division manager's bonus, for example, might be based 50% on return on assets and 50% on sales growth in units. But measurement combinations can also be quite complex.

Numerous stylized combination systems with a variety of trade names have been developed and publicized in recent years, such as *Performance Prisms*[13] and *Balanced Scorecards*,[14] just to name two. Kaplan and Norton's balanced scorecard is undeniably the most widely adopted of these. Specifically, it proposes a combination of short-term measures and leading indicators framed into the following four perspectives:[15]

- Financial perspective: *How do we look to shareholders?* Examples of measures in this category include operating income and ROE.

- Customer perspective: *How do our customers see us?* Examples of measures in this category include on-time delivery and percent of sales from new products.

- Internal perspective: *What must we excel at?* Examples of measures in this category include cycle time, yield and efficiency.

- Innovation and learning perspective: *Can we continue to improve and create value?* Examples of measures in this category include time to develop next generation, new product introductions vs. competition.

The first perspective is primarily short-term oriented and financial in nature, whereas the other three are prominent categories of nonfinancial, leading indicators of future financial performance.

The generic concept of combination-of-measures systems is not new, however. Many companies have used a variety of measures of value drivers. In the 1950s, when General Electric was decentralizing its organization into over a hundred profit centers, its managers developed a measurement system comprised of eight key measures: short-term profitability, market share, productivity, product leadership, employee attitudes, personnel development, public responsibility, and balance between short-range and long-range objectives. The eighth item was not a measure but a reminder that the short/long-term balance was indispensable. GE's managers ran their complex organization using this set of key performance indicators for much of the 1950s and 1960s.[16] Similarly, given the importance of new product development at 3M Corporation, all 3M divisions were required to have new products account for at least 30% of their sales. At Emerson Electric, 10% of division (profit center) managers' bonuses was tied to keeping their plants union-free, which they believed was critical to maintain the needed flexibility to implement product and process innovations.[17] In the airline industry, important value drivers have traditionally included measures of on-time performance, mishandled baggage, ticket over-sales, and in-flight service, all of which are believed to affect customer satisfaction.[18] Empirical evidence, much focused on customer satisfaction, appears to support the premise that some nonfinancial measures are significantly associated with future financial performance and contain additional information not reflected in past financial measures.[19]

The core idea behind combination-of-measures systems is that if the organization tracks the right set of leading indicators and gives them proper importance weightings, then profits will inevitably follow. Some studies document that both nonfinancial and financial performance improve following the implementation of performance measurement and incentive systems that include nonfinancial performance measures.[20] But to make the value-driver sets effective, managers must carefully consider which leading indicators to use and how the chosen indicators should be weighted, individually and in total.

In essence, then, a measurement combination approach including leading indicators of future performance, or value drivers, should reflect the economic effects on shareholder value of specific management accomplishments and failures more quickly than do accounting measures. Hence, holding managers accountable for some combination of leading indicators shifts the balance of incentives toward longer-term concerns because it forces the managers today to make tradeoffs between short-term profits and the drivers of future profits. As such, this balancing of short-term and long-term concerns can be seen as an attempt to make the performance indicators more *timely*. This is desirable because financial performance measures are generally thought to be lagging indicators of performance. The goal is to provide the information needed in a *feedforward* control system, which strives to alert managers of potential problems before they occur.

Besides the forward-looking feature, another key argument supporting the use of measurement combination approaches is that no single measure, no matter how good it is, can reflect organizational performance sufficiently well to motivate proper management decision making. As such, the multiple measures might provide a more *complete*, and hence more *congruent*, reflection of performance by capturing aspects of performance that are not reflected, or are not weighted highly enough in importance, in a summary performance measure. Measurement combinations are also more *flexible*. With summary financial measures, every dollar of inflows (revenues) and outflows (expenses) is weighted the same in importance. As a consequence, valuable information can be lost in the aggregation. If, however, the summary measures are decomposed, different financial elements can be given different weightings of importance. For example, revenues from new products can be weighted more highly than those from mature products and, if it is appropriate, controlling general and administrative expenses (overheads) can be given more importance than controlling raw material costs.

Another version of the completeness argument reflects a *stakeholder* view of the firm. That is, market and accounting measures reflect mainly the interests of the organization's financial claimants; the shareholders or owners. Hence, other measures can help reflect the interests of other stakeholders, which might include employees, customers, suppliers, conservationists, governments, and society at large.

Finally, combination-of-measures systems can address an *understandability* problem that exists in some settings. Some managers do not understand fully or near-completely what they should do to increase their entity's value. Combination-of-measures systems give managers more direction than do the systems based on summary performance measures, either market or accounting in nature. If the combination systems are well designed, they impart a better understanding as to what should be done to create value. The causal linkages in a balanced scorecard, for example, whether real or merely assumed, provide managers with some guidance as to what they must do to influence the financial performance measures, which are at the end of the *causal chain*. In the words of Kaplan and Norton:

> [A] properly constructed balanced scorecard should make explicit the sequence of hypotheses about the cause-and-effect relationships between outcome measures and performance drivers of those outcomes. Every measure selected for a balanced scorecard should be an element in a chain of cause-and-effect relationships that communicates the meaning of the business unit's strategy to the organization.[21]

But while balanced scorecard systems provide guidance to managers as to how to produce the desired ends, they can also erode their sense of decision authority.

Do these combination-of-measures systems work? Conceptually, it is difficult to argue against the combination-of-measures idea. They are infinitely flexible. If a summary performance measure has a weakness (e.g. too short-term oriented), managers can add another measure that minimizes that weakness (e.g. one that emphasizes returns in the future, such as new product development successes or the building of market share). If the combination of those two measures leaves out a concern for the environment, a measure can be added that induces managers to have that concern. And so on. Combination-of-measures systems are in widespread use, which suggests strongly that many companies have found them useful. However, because combination-of-measures systems exist in so much variety, they are difficult to subject to rigorous empirical tests. Much is yet to be learned about these systems.[22]

Inevitably, some companies' combinations-of-measures systems are not effective. Some companies uncritically implement boilerplate frameworks of measures without much consideration as to whether those frameworks fit the specific situation in which they are used. Other companies focus on the wrong measures. For example, managers of a fast food company thought that employee turnover was a key performance indicator, but subsequent analyses revealed that what explained the differing profitability of restaurants was, specifically, the turnover of supervisors, not that of front-line employees.[23] Even when the correct measurement concept is identified, decisions must still be made as to how to measure that concept. For example, in a retail environment, should customer satisfaction be measured by a survey of customers, by ratings from mystery shoppers, or in terms of a measure of customer retention? Different measurement methods can yield quite different answers.[24]

Another difficult question to address is how many measures are needed to define performance completely, or at least completely enough. For example, balanced scorecard systems are said ideally to contain 23–25 measures.[25] For motivational purposes, however, 20 or more measures are probably too many. When so many measures are used, each of the individual measure's importance is likely to become diluted, thereby causing employees to not pay sufficient attention to that, or possibly even any, measure.

Perhaps not surprisingly because of the ease of working with summary financial performance measures, one study by a compensation consulting firm found that where companies use a balanced scorecard, the financial dimension of performance – one of the four performance dimensions – is weighted heavily, 55% of the total in their sample of balanced scorecard firms.[26] Should this seemingly heavy weighting of financial measures be considered *balanced*? Will the lesser emphasis on the nonfinancial measures be sufficient to mitigate myopic behaviors induced by the financial measures?

There is also some evidence that managers may apply their own implicit weights to the various measures. For example, one study documented that even after a large financial services firm implemented a balanced scorecard system, most of the company's managers continued to base performance evaluations on factors other than those included in the balanced scorecard.[27] Other studies found that cognitive biases or information overload frequently causes evaluators to overemphasize the common measures, those used throughout an organization or based on a common methodology, as compared to the unique measures included in a balanced scorecard.[28]

The importance weightings would be difficult to set even if the performance factors were independent, but they are not independent. Many, if not most, of the performance factors *interact*. For example, consider just two factors – labor productivity and production throughput. Throughput can be increased by working employees harder, but at some point fatigue sets in, causing productivity to decrease. Similar tradeoffs occur with many, if not most, of the combinations of measures that might be considered.

Many of the payoff relationships are also *nonlinear*. For example, customer satisfaction may be particularly important if a company has not been paying attention to it. At some point, however, after the firm has spent enough, or maybe even overspent, on customer satisfaction, further improvements in customer satisfaction are not good investments. Greater satisfaction beyond that point might not generate any additional sales. Similarly, the effect of staff turnover on performance might be nonlinear. Turnover can be too high, as the firms need experienced personnel to staff their jobs. But zero, or close to zero, turnover is not desired either. Some turnover is good to keep the organizational hierarchy in balance and to lower staff costs. The payoff relationship is nonlinear and the inflection point is hard to determine.

About all that can be said in a general sense about the importance weightings placed on the performance factors is that they must vary across organizational settings, such as with the business strategy. They must vary over time as conditions change. And they must vary depending on the quality of the measures and the cost of measuring. With the current state of understanding, setting the importance weightings is more an art than a science. But it is an important art. If the weightings are flawed, the combination-of-measures system will have the same effect as if the wrong measures were chosen, meaning that the weighted combination of measures does not reflect, or is *incongruent* with, the organization's true objectives.

Kaplan and Norton argue that the choices of measures and their weights in a balanced scorecard require an explicit articulation of a *business model* or strategy that describes the hypothesized drivers of the desired business results.[29] But note the use of the word *hypothesized*. Most of these choices of measures and their weights are based on untested assumptions, not hard evidence of causal linkages between the measures and the desired ends.[30] A notable exception was Sears, the large US retailer, which identified various metrics organized into three performance domains called the *three compellings* – employee relations (*compelling place to work*), customer satisfaction and loyalty (*compelling place to shop*), and results for shareholders (*compelling place to invest*). They found that when employee attitudes on 10 essential counts improved by 5%, customer satisfaction improved by 1.3%, driving a one-half percent increase in revenues. But not all of these measures that they thought would be important proved to be important. At one stage of the analysis, for example, the analysts found that measures of *personal growth and development* and *empowered teams* showed no significant relationship with any customer data. The problem could lie either with the concepts or the measures of those concepts (as discussed above). So they tried both other concepts and alternative measures. In the end, they identified a relatively small number of factors that they believed were in fact driving performance.[31]

Cost is also a concern. The cost of designing and implementing a simple combination-of-measures system involving the use of just a few measures that are already in existence might be minimal. In many organizations, however, the development of a balanced scorecard often involves consultants to help with both the development and implementation processes and possibly the development of new measures. Some individual measures can also be quite expensive to use. It is expensive to administer customer satisfaction surveys, to employ mystery shoppers to evaluate operations from a customer perspective, or to conduct safety audits.

CONCLUSION

As discussed in Chapter 10, the primary goal of managers of for-profit organizations should be to maximize shareholder value. Value is a long-term concept. Short-term accounting profits and returns provide imperfect, surrogate indicators of shareholder value changes (economic income). Management myopia, an excessive focus on short-term performance, is an almost inevitable side-effect of the use of financial results control systems built on accounting measures of performance.

Myopia can be mitigated at top management levels by holding these managers accountable for increasing market valuations. Shares of stock are priced, although surely also imperfectly, based on a corporation's expected future cash flows, not just on current-period results. But the task of reducing myopia is more difficult at middle management levels. This chapter described six alternatives that can be considered to mitigate myopia. None of the alternatives is a panacea. But still it is important to understand where each of the alternatives falls short of perfection and how those shortfalls can be addressed. Choosing the "right" amount of pressure for short-term results to apply, the "right" control mix to use, and/or the "right" measurement alternative to adopt requires detailed analyses and complex judgments. Each approach has advantages and disadvantages, and possibly the best effects are to be had from employing a combination (of aspects) of these approaches.

Notes

1. D. Dodd and K. Favaro, *The Three Tensions: Winning the Struggle to Perform Without Compromise* (Jossey-Bass, 2007); "Managing the Short Term/Long Term Tension: How Small Changes to Traditional Strategic Planning Processes Can Make a Big Difference," *Financial Executive* (December 1, 2006), online (www.financialexecutives.org).
2. J. Graham, C. Harvey, and S. Rajgopal, "The Economic Implications of Corporate Financial Reporting," *Journal of Accounting and Economics*, 40, nos. 1–3 (December 2005), pp. 3–73; "Corner Office Thinks Short Term: Managers' Focus is to Hit Targets, Smooth Earnings,

Sacrificing Future Growth," *The Wall Street Journal* (April 14, 2004), p. C3.
3. "GE Under Siege," *Fortune* (October 15, 2008), online (http://money.cnn.com/magazines/fortune).
4. Ibid.
5. "Executive Critical of 'Managed' Earnings Doesn't Mind if the Street Criticizes Him," *The Wall Street Journal* (April 16, 1999).
6. "GE Under Siege," op. cit.
7. R. Simons, "Codman & Shurtleff, Inc.: Planning and Control System," Harvard Business School Case No. 9-187-081, p. 8.

8. GE Proxy Statement (www.ge.com/investors/financial_reporting/proxy_statements.html), March 2006.

9. Ibid., March 2009.

10. "Hard to Get," *CFO Europe* (April 2009), pp. 38–41.

11. "Thoughts on the Business of Life," *Forbes* (February 28, 1994), p. 140.

12. For a broader and recent discussion, see C. Laux and C. Leuz, "The Crisis of Fair-Value Accounting: Making Sense of the Recent Debate," *Accounting, Organizations and Society*, 34, nos. 6–7 (August–October 2009), pp. 826–34.

13. A. Neely, C. Adams and M. Kennerley, *The Performance Prism* (London, UK: Financial Times/Prentice Hall, 2003).

14. R. Kaplan and D. Norton, *The Balanced Scorecard* (Boston, MA: Harvard Business School Press, 1996).

15. Ibid., among various other publications by these authors.

16. See, for example, R. Greenwood, *Managerial Decentralization: A Study of the General Electric Philosophy* (Lexington, MA: D.C. Heath, 1974).

17. "A Knight with Thick Armor for IBM," *Business Week* (August 23, 1993).

18. B. Behn and R. Riley, "Using Nonfinancial Information to Predict Financial Performance: The Case of the U.S. Airline Industry," *Journal of Accounting, Auditing & Finance*, 14, no. 1 (Winter 1999), pp. 29–56; A. Davila and M. Venkatachalam "The Relevance of Nonfinancial Performance Measures for CEO Compensation: Evidence from the Airline Industry," *Review of Accounting Studies*, 9, no. 4 (December 2004), pp. 443–64.

19. Ibid. See also, for example, C. Ittner and D. Larcker, "Are Nonfinancial Measures Leading Indicators of Financial Performance? An Analysis of Customer Satisfaction," *Journal of Accounting Research*, 36, Supplement (1998), pp. 1–35.

20. See, for example, R. Banker, G. Potter, and D. Srinivasan, "An Empirical Investigation of an Incentive Plan that Includes Non-financial Performance Measures," *The Accounting Review*, 75, no. 1 (January 2000), pp. 65–92.

21. Kaplan and Norton, *The Balanced Scorecard*, op. cit., p. 31.

22. See, for example, F. de Geuser, S. Mooraj and D. Oyon, "Does the Balanced Scorecard Add Value? Empirical Evidence on its Effect on Performance," *European Accounting Review*, 18, no. 1 (2009), pp. 93–122.

23. C. Ittner and D. Larcker, "Coming Up Short on Nonfinancial Performance Measurement," *Harvard Business Review*, 81, no. 11 (November 2003), pp. 88–95; see also G. Cokins, "The Promise and Peril of the Balanced Scorecard," *Journal of Corporate Accounting and Finance*, 21, no. 3 (March/April 2010), pp. 19–28.

24. For an article and some evidence in respect of how firms struggle to measure nonfinancial performance, see P. Zingheim and J. Schuster, "Measuring and Rewarding Customer Satisfaction, Innovation and Workforce Engagement," *WorldatWork Journal* (Fourth Quarter 2007), pp. 8–22.

25. D. Norton, "BEWARE: The Unbalanced Scorecard," *Balanced Scorecard Report* (March 15, 2000).

26. Towers Perrin, "Inside the 'Balanced Scorecard,'" *Compuscan Report* (January 1996), pp. 1–5.

27. C. Ittner, D. Larcker, and M. Meyer, "Subjectivity and the Weighting of Performance Measures: Evidence From a Balanced Scorecard," *The Accounting Review*, 78, no. 3 (July 2003), pp. 725–58.

28. R. Banker, H. Chang and M. Pizzini, "The Balanced Scorecard: Judgmental Effects of Performance Measures Linked to Strategy," *The Accounting Review*, 79, no. 1 (January 2004), pp. 1–23; M. Lipe and S. Salterio, "The Balanced Scorecard: Judgmental Effects of Common and Unique Performance Measures," *The Accounting Review*, 75, no. 3 (July 2000), pp. 283–98.

29. R. Kaplan and D. Norton, "Using the Balanced Scorecard as a Strategic Management System," *Harvard Business Review*, 74, no. 1 (January–February 1996), pp. 75–85; R. Kaplan and D. Norton, *The Balanced Scorecard: Translating Strategy into Action* (Boston, MA: Harvard Business School Press, 1996); R. Kaplan and D. Norton, "Having Trouble with Your Strategy? Then Map It," *Harvard Business Review* (September–October 2000), pp. 3–11.

30. Ittner and Larcker, "Coming Up Short on Nonfinancial Performance Measurement," op. cit.

31. A. Rucci, S. Kirn, and R. Quinn, "The Employee-Customer-Profit Chain at Sears," *Harvard Business Review*, 76, no. 1 (January–February 1998), pp. 82–97.

Case Study

Catalytic Solutions, Inc.

We're a young company, and this is an exciting place to work. But the work is intense. People are here at work 24 hours a day, seven days a week. Our employees would probably be motivated even without our bonus plan. But the plan is still important. It is a tool to focus people's attention on the right things ... Being a young company, we're still in a "preprofit" stage of operation. Thus our performance measures are primarily nonfinancial. The nonfinancials are what we need to pay attention to.

Michael Redard, Vice President of Finance and Administration for Catalytic Solutions, Inc., was commenting on his company's performance measurement and incentive systems. Mike was confident that his company's systems were working effectively, but he also knew that the systems would have to evolve significantly over time as the company grew and matured.

COMPANY HISTORY AND STRATEGY

Catalytic Solutions, Inc. (CSI) was founded in Santa Barbara, California, in 1996 by Steve Golden and Bill Anderson. Steve, who had a Ph.D. in material sciences, developed a new coating formulation and proprietary manufacturing processes that produced catalytic converters with better performance and substantially lower prices than competing products. Catalytic converters are used to reduce the pollution caused by combustion engines. Bill, formerly the CEO of a publicly held company, had over 30 years of experience as a senior executive. He became the CEO of CSI shortly after raising seed money to finance the first few years of operation.

Exhibit 1 presents a timeline of the company's early history. CSI's first patents were issued in 1999 and its first sales were recorded as CSI started producing converters for stationary engines. These early sales proved that the technology was viable. But CSI's managers' immediate goal was to supply

converters to the huge automotive sector that spent over $7 billion (estimate for 2001) on catalytic converters, primarily because of tightening worldwide emissions regulations.

CSI's technological advantage was mainly due to the fact that its converters used 50–80% less Platinum Group Metals (PGMs) than did competitors' converters. Standard converters typically contained large amounts of PGMs platinum, palladium, and rhodium. As pollution standards became increasingly stringent (Exhibit 2), the demand for, and the price of, PGMs had risen dramatically (Exhibit 3). In 2001, about 60% of the world supply of PGMs was used to produce converters. Further, there was uncertainty about the supply of palladium, most of which came from Russia.[1] The average converter cost per vehicle tripled between 1990 and 2001, becoming the third largest automobile component cost after the engine and transmission. The savings resulting from CSI's lower usage of PGMs could range from $40 for a small-vehicle converter to as much as $200 for those used in large sports utility vehicles (SUVs). In an industry where manufacturers "kill for pennies," this presented an enormous cost saving potential. At the same time, CSI's proprietary technology was shown to have superior performance characteristics. CSI converters were able to withstand extremely high temperatures in exhaust systems and meet increasingly stringent emissions standards worldwide.

For years, three companies had dominated the supply of catalytic converters to the automobile market. However, CSI managers thought that the risk of one of these companies being able to appropriate CSI's technology was relatively low, for several reasons. First, CSI had patent protection. CSI had been issued two patents, and three others

---

[1] Source: http://www.detnews.com/2001/autos/0103/22/-202706.htm

This case was prepared by Professors Michal Matějka, Kenneth A. Merchant, and Wim A. Van der Stede.

Copyright © by Michal Matějka, Kenneth A. Merchant, and Wim A. Van der Stede.

were pending. (Each patent establishes a protection period of 17 years.) Second, CSI had developed some innovations, such as the coating composition and a proprietary manufacturing process, that CSI managers thought would be hard to imitate, even based on a finished product analysis (reverse engineering). Third, CSI continued to expend significant resources to improve its technology and to maintain its lead. And finally, suppliers to the automobile industry faced substantial barriers to entry. It had taken CSI several years to get established in the auto industry. New entrants copying CSI's technology would face similar challenges and would not be able to demonstrate a substantial cost advantage over CSI.

Suppliers for new platforms had to cooperate with car manufacturers several years before new models were launched. Winning a new original equipment (OE) commitment translated into sales, but with a one to five-year lag, depending on the customer and the platform. In the meantime, CSI had to work closely with the engine development teams of major car companies. Strict schedules had to be met during several rounds of preparing, testing, and shipping samples. Consistency and perfect quality were crucial. Further, it was a prerequisite for auto industry suppliers to obtain the QS-9000 quality certificate, which was a more demanding equivalent of the ISO-9000 certification. It was hard to obtain business without demonstrating technical skills, a commitment to flawless production, and reliable on-time deliveries.

CSI managers were also in the process of developing applications for other markets. One was the growing light duty diesel market, which management estimated would total $2.2 billion by 2008. Outside the transportation industry, the power-generating sector was likely to become the next major opportunity. More stringent emission regulations required pollution reductions of more than 50% of the existing standards by as early as 2003. The market for natural gas turbine converters was estimated to grow to nearly $1.3 billion by 2008. Other markets could include alternative fuel vehicles and fuel cells that may someday revolutionize the transportation industry.

EARLY SUCCESSES

CSI's early revenue stemmed largely from sales in the auto industry after-market, a $50 million market for converter replacements. OE commitments were to follow.

Honda Motor Company became the early OE adopter. It started evaluating CSI's technology in 1999, and in October 2000 it took an initial 10% stake in CSI. Production for the Honda Stepwagon model began in December 2000. Two additional vehicle programs were added in 2001. In late 2001, CSI was assigned to a high-volume platform for General Motors scheduled to begin in 2004. In early 2002, the company signed a strategic agreement with Ford to evaluate several high-volume platforms.[2] By this time, CSI was cooperating at some level with most of the major automakers of the world.

In June 2002, CSI received the *Gratitude Award for Excellency in Research and Development* by Honda Motor Company. During a special award ceremony at CSI, Mr. Tsuneo Tanai, Senior Vice President/General Manager of Honda R&D Americas, Inc., stated:[3]

> In early testing, everyone at Honda was very impressed by the great performance of the CSI product. Honda realized the huge potential that this technology promised. On behalf of Honda, I would like to express my deepest gratitude to everyone at CSI.

This award attested to CSI's success in the early years of the company's existence. CSI's converter product had won acceptance in one of the toughest markets in the world. Mike Redard explained: "It is extremely hard to penetrate the automotive market, change is slow in this industry."

CSI's product design had clearly won acceptance from the industry. The next step was to get ready to produce several million perfect quality converters each year. Production quality was important because the auto market was unforgiving.

THE COMPANY IN 2002

Most of CSI's senior management team had been with the company for several years (see Exhibit 4). The newest member was CFO Kevin McDonnell, who joined in 2002. CSI's board consisted of three of the executive officers and four outside directors.

---

[2] Source: http://www.tcbizreview.com/currentissue/06-02/catalytic.htm

[3] Source: http://www.pressreleasenetwork.com/pr-2002/june/mainpr1280.htm

In 2000, CSI employed 38 people. That number grew quickly to 110 in 2001, and 125 in 2002. In 2002, about half of the employees worked in manufacturing and quality control; one third were engineers assigned to R&D, and the rest were in sales and administration. Given that the main part of the research had been carried out earlier, recent efforts concentrated largely on the development of applications in close cooperation with the customers. Many of the engineers were new, young Ph.D.s with little industry experience. The company policy was to attract open-minded people who were not burdened with taken-for-granted approaches established in the converter industry. Mike Redard explained: "This is an exciting place to work with lots of opportunity, but there is also an element of risk due to the early stage of the company. We tend to attract ambitious people who are comfortable taking some risks."

People came to CSI because they believed in its future success. They were highly committed and hard working. Further, there was a strong spirit of team membership and cooperation, and personnel turnover was relatively low. CSI's human resource practices were designed to encourage this cooperation and to attract long-term employees. Managers were closely involved with operations and knew their employees well, which contributed to the collective spirit and informal culture.

As CSI was preparing for mass production, however, it became clear that some more formal managerial structures and policies were necessary. The company needed measurement devices to keep track of progress on a number of dimensions. The emphasis was mainly on nonfinancial performance indicators. Critical drivers of long-term success were quality, on-time delivery, and production efficiency. It was also crucial to win new sales commitments from OE car manufacturers. CSI managers believed that the initial focus on nonfinancial targets would later translate into financial success.

Getting new OE commitments was the responsibility of top executives. Suppliers' reputations and prices were the key determinants of success in the bidding process. Reputation was important because each OE commitment required several years of development work that had to meet the high standards of the auto industry. CSI also had to demonstrate significant cost savings over its more established competitors in order to have a good chance of winning new contracts. CSI's bids were based on estimates of unit costs derived from product specifications provided by the customer.

CSI's sales had climbed steadily through 2001, but the company was still perhaps a year or two from becoming profitable. The managers hoped to issue a public stock offering within a few years, but there was no pressure to rush the IPO. The company had adequate capital to fund its immediate product and process development and operating needs. In January 2002, it raised $29.6 million from private sources.[4] And with the public stock market valuations quite low in 2002, the cost of raising capital from private sources was not significantly higher than could be expected in a public stock offering.

COMPENSATION SYSTEMS

Every employee's compensation package consisted of three components: base salary, stock options, and a bonus (since 2001). **Base salaries** were set to be at or slightly below the industry median. Mike Redard noted that "In many instances people who joined CSI from larger, established companies took a pay cut to do so." The spread between the top and bottom salaries in the company was not large, and salary raises were modest, typically in the 4–5% range.

The first year they joined CSI, each employee was given **stock options**. These options vested over the first four years at 25% per year and expired 10 years after granting (or within 30 days of leaving the company). While a formal plan for annual stock option grants had not yet been implemented, follow-on grants were awarded on an ad hoc basis to ensure that employees' stock holdings were in line with their current position and contribution to the company. The value of the stock option component varied substantially depending on tenure, position in the company and value to the organization.[5] By 2002, employees (most of them were hired during the 2000–02 period) had on average accumulated value in stock options worth 50% of their annual salary. The employees, in total, owned on a fully diluted basis about 24% of CSI shares.

---

[4] This and other financial and operational figures in the case are disguised.
[5] The exercise price of stock options was based on independent valuations obtained during recent financing rounds.

One problem that Mike Redard had observed regarding the options was that "many people don't understand them and don't know how to value them." The options were, indeed, difficult to value. They could become quite valuable if the company went public and was successful. But they could also become near worthless if the company did not go public or if its performance languished.

The **annual bonus** plan was put in place in 2001 to communicate the importance of some short-term goals to employees and to align their interests with firms' objectives. Some employees also appreciated the cash bonuses, which were more immediate and "tangible" than the stock options. The target bonus could be from 5% to 15% of an employee's base salary depending on level within the company. All bonuses were awarded based on corporate, not individual, performance because, as Mike explained, "We want a team effort. We all win or all lose together."

Each year the senior managers discussed what elements they should be focusing on, why focus on those elements was important, and what weight each element should carry. These discussions established the list of performance areas on which the bonus assignments would be based. Because reliable, objective measures were important, managers recognized that the company needed to make rapid progress in improving some of its systems of measurement.

Exhibit 5 shows the performance areas linked to bonuses in 2001. The measures reflected company-wide achievements in three areas: receipt of new OE commitments, execution of existing business, and building of infrastructure.

1. In the area of **OE commitments**, managers identified a number of specific programs that CSI felt they had the opportunity to bid for in 2001. If the manufacturer made the order commitment to CSI, CSI employees would earn a designated portion of their target bonus. The two largest of these programs were given an importance weight of 20% each. This meant that if customers committed to both of these programs, employees would earn 40% of their target bonus amount just from this result. Also identified were three other large programs, each of which would add 10% of the target bonus and two smaller programs each with a weight of 5%. Each additional, significant, unidentified OE commitment would add 5%, up to a maximum of 15%, of the target bonus. If all of these OE commitments were made in 2001, CSI employees would earn 95% of their target bonuses. These programs were given a high weighting of importance because, as Mike Redard explained, "absent some problem, an assignment means you are designed into the vehicle platform, thus providing a high degree of visibility to future revenue."

2. **Execution of existing business** was assessed in terms of two elements: shipment volumes to two major customers and shipment quality. Maximum shipments to each major customer could produce 40% of the target bonus. The measures of quality were scrap, shipment errors, and on-time delivery. For each of these measures, performance ranges were set to result in bonuses of minus 5% to plus 5% for scrap, minus 10% to plus 5% for shipment errors, and zero to 10% for on-time delivery performance.

3. Finally, in 2001, the **building of infrastructure** referred to the attainment of QS-9000 certification. If this certification was attained, employees would earn 20% of their target bonuses.

Overall, the performance targets were set so that employees would have "a decent shot" at earning 100% of the target bonus. Performance ranges were set to allow bonus assignments to range from 0–215% of the target amounts, but Mike Redard explained that if the actual bonus earned was extreme, say either 20% or 200% of the target bonus, then "you'd have to question whether the performance targets were set correctly."

In 2001, after what Mike Redard described as "a lot of hard work," actual performance resulted in employees earning 117.9% of their target bonus. New OE commitments accounted for 50% of the total, execution for 32.9%, quality for 15%, and QS-9000 certification for 20% (see Exhibit 5). The QS-9000 quality certificate was actually awarded to CSI in January 2002, but since the timing was so close to the end of the year, management counted it as a successful accomplishment of the goal for 2001.

Mike Redard explained that management reserved the right to make subjective adjustments to the bonus plan, and this QS-9000 timing issue was one example where they exercised that right. But he quickly explained that: "We don't want to make subjective changes to provide rewards when the company has clearly not achieved its targets. Our employees understand that there can be some variance in the bonus awards. There will be good years and bad years."

In 2002, the performance areas linked to bonus awards were changed, as is shown in Exhibit 6. **Financial targets**, with a weight of 0–60% of the target bonus, were added. The focus was on increasing revenues and reducing operating losses. As in 2001, CSI continued emphasizing new **OE commitments** (0–105% of the target bonus) and **quality** as reflected in scrap, shipment errors, and on-time delivery (total weight of minus 15% to plus 20% of the target bonus). **Building infrastructure** was defined in 2002 as the upgrading of production to full automation, increasing safety standards, and obtaining QS-14001 certification (total weight 0–20%). Having the automated production line operational by the end of 2002 was a major challenge. Nevertheless, management had little doubts that the target would be met because it had to be – mass production was crucial for future growth.

CSI executives knew even this new list of measures omitted some important performance indicators. For example, it did not include a measure of new patents. While patents were unquestionably important, this particular measure was not included in the bonus plan because patents occurred infrequently and were the focus of only a few people in the company. But more importantly, CSI managers believed strongly that too many indicators would leave employees uncertain as to where the priorities should be. Mike Redard thought that the optimum number of measures was 4–6.

The performance targets for 2002 were again set so that 100% of the target bonus was realistically achievable. Entering the last quarter of 2002, the projected outcome for the year was for payments of 75–100% of the target bonus.

In addition to these three compensation elements, Mike Redard explained that management had additional ways of rewarding top performers, including special raises and promotions.

THE FUTURE

Overall, Mike Redard and the rest of the CSI management team was confident that the company's compensation system, and in particular its bonus plan, was fulfilling its objectives:

> We have benefited from the variety of backgrounds of our management team. We all worked for different companies with different compensation policies, and we all have experience with both good and bad bonus systems. The nice thing about working for CSI is that here we have the chance to do it right from the start. Sure, we are still wrestling with how many performance measures to include and which ones are most relevant, but I think the overall structure is working. The bonus plan communicates in simple terms to our employees what is important . . .
>
> We met most of our targets last year and I think in general people are quite happy with the bonus they received.

Mike expected that the financial measures would probably account for about 30% of the target bonus in 2002. He thought that the importance of financial measures would probably increase in the future as CSI became closer to becoming a public company. However, he also said he "would be shocked if their importance ever exceeded 50%."

Exhibit 1 Company history

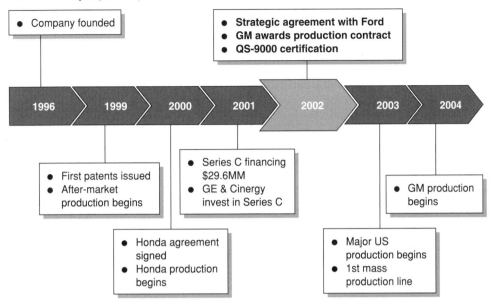

Exhibit 2 Tightening NO$_x$ emissions* standards in the US

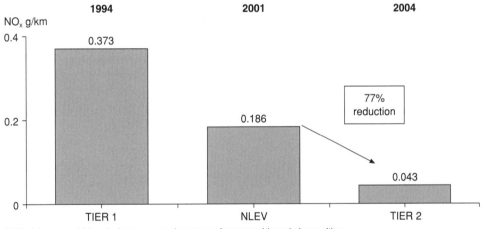

* NO$_x$ (nitrogen oxide) emissions are a major cause of smog problems in large cities.

Exhibit 3 Volatile cost of metals

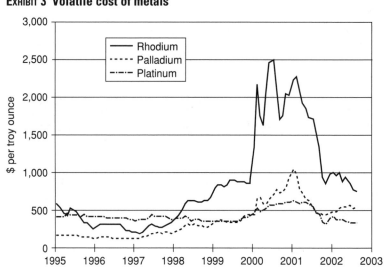

Exhibit 4 Management team

Stephen Golden, Ph.D.	CTO, Chairman, Cofounder
William Anderson	CEO, Cofounder
Daniel McGuire	President, COO
Kevin McDonnell	CFO
Michael Redard	VP, Finance and Administration
Timothy Truex, Ph.D.	VP, Technical Marketing
Steven Shotwell	VP, Operations and Manufacturing

EXHIBIT 5 2001 bonus objectives and actual results

	Target bonus %	Actual result %
OE program commitments[1]	0–95	50
Execute existing business		
Unit shipments[2]	0–80	32.9
Quality[3]	(15)–20	15
Build infrastructure	0–20	20
Total	215%	117.9%

Objective	Target bonus %
[1]**OE program commitments**	
New program A	5
New program B	5
New program C	10
New program D	10
New program E	10
New program F	20
New program G	20
Other OE commitments	each 5%
	(max. 15%)
[2]**Shipments**	
Customer A	0–40
Customer B	0–40
[3]**Quality**	
Scrap	(5)–5
Shipment errors	(10)–5
On-time delivery	0–10

EXHIBIT 6 2002 bonus objectives

	Target bonus %
Financial	0–60
Revenue	
Operating income	
OE program commitments	0–105
Quality	(15)–20
Scrap	
Shipment errors	
On-time delivery	
Build/improve infrastructure	0–20
Mass production	
QS-14001 certification	
Safety	
Total possible	205%

Case Study

First Commonwealth Financial Corporation

To meet the current requirements of corporate governance, board directors must make a transition to a more complete and modern set of management tools. Our board has learned that the best tool to accomplish this task is the Balanced Scorecard system.

E. James Trimarchi, Chairman of the Board

First Commonwealth Financial Corporation, headquartered in Indiana, Pennsylvania, the hometown of actor Jimmy Stewart, was the fifth-largest financial institution in Pennsylvania and in the top 100 in the United States (see summary financial statements in Exhibit 1). Its 1,600 employees operated from 92 branches in 18 central and southwestern Pennsylvania counties, a mostly rural region with blue-collar industries and slow population growth.

Jim Trimarchi and David Tomb, Jr. obtained the first new state bank charter in Pennsylvania in 50 years when they founded a small bank in nearby Blairsville in 1963. After selling their bank to 1st National Bank in Indiana, Pennsylvania, Trimarchi and Tomb became the senior managing executives for 1st National. During the next 20 years, Trimarchi expanded the bank by opening single bank branches in neighboring towns and changing the name to National Bank of the Commonwealth. In 1983, he reorganized the bank into First Commonwealth Financial Corporation, a bank holding company, and chose Pat McCarthy as the first chairman of the corporation. After McCarthy passed away in 1988, Trimarchi succeeded him as chairman and began an acquisitions program that eventually led to purchasing nine local community banks. The acquisitions, usually financed by stock, ranged in assets from $200 million to $1 billion. The most recent acquisition, in August 2003, was BankPittsburgh, with assets of $400 million. To expand its product mix, First Commonwealth established a trust company and an insurance agency, purchased a Pittsburgh-based financial planning company, and set up a joint-venture credit/life insurance company. It also centralized information technology processes by forming an independent company to service the bank's internal needs.

First Commonwealth initially allowed each acquisition to retain its local identity and its existing personnel, bank committees, and board of directors. The corporation imposed centralized policies and procedures, but each operating company had its own plans, budgets, and performance targets for traditional banking measures, including net income, loan growth, deposit growth, delinquency, cost control, noninterest income growth, net interest margin, and loan review and audit ratings. First Commonwealth published internally a monthly ranking of the 10 community banks along each performance measure, a process that fostered much competition among the individual banks' executive teams. The company also did an annual assessment of each employee according to his or her contributions to revenue growth, expense management, continuous improvement, and risk management. The bank believed that even tellers or back-office personnel could contribute to revenue growth through personal referrals. The operating philosophy was summarized by the phrase "add up big"; if each individual and each bank achieved its performance targets, the overall First Commonwealth results would be impressive.

In the mid-1990s, the bank experienced a slowdown in interest income and was generating little noninterest income despite its new trust, insurance, and financial advising businesses. Trimarchi and Joseph O'Dell, CEO, decided to reorganize all operating units under a single brand, First Commonwealth. The transition to a single brand began in 1995 when First Commonwealth consolidated the separate boards and committees of the 10 banks into a single charter

---

This case was prepared by Professor Robert S. Kaplan with the assistance of Michael Nagel of the Balanced Scorecard Collaborative.

and set of committees but maintained the 10 bank names in 10 divisions. The company completed the branding transition to one name in October 2002, at which time First Commonwealth consisted of a growth division made up of six growth regions, with banking, trust, insurance, and financial planning services and two support companies for professional services and data processing (see organizational chart in Exhibit 2).

The retail and commercial banking units had historically operated with local "product push" strategies. Each department promoted its own product, such as a deposit account, a loan product, a credit card, a financial planning solution, or an insurance product. The new strategy required account representatives to profile individual customers and businesses so that they could offer them a tailored mix of First Commonwealth-branded financial solutions. The bank had been averaging only two products or relationships per customer, so the new client-focused strategy offered opportunities for growth even in its low-population and economic-growth communities.

INTRODUCING THE BALANCED SCORECARD

In the transition to becoming one bank, the company had eliminated the standard measures for the 10 separate banks and the individual assessments for all employees. But results suffered, and Trimarchi was searching for a method to reintroduce a performance culture into the company. In 2000, Dave Dahlmann, CEO of Southwest Bank, recommended that Trimarchi consider using the Balanced Scorecard. Trimarchi read several *Harvard Business Review* articles about the Balanced Scorecard and saw how it could help FCFC make the transition from a product-driven bank to a banking service company: "The scorecard can get management and all employees on the same page for driving the strategy. Everyone can help us implement the strategy, but they first need to understand what the strategy is and where they fit and can make a contribution."

The First Commonwealth executive team established the following objectives for a Balanced Scorecard project:

- Sustain our ability to consistently perform in the top 25% of our peer group.

- Accelerate our efforts to become a world-class sales organization that can generate revenue growth organically, not from acquisitions.

- Clarify the First Commonwealth Financial Corporation strategy and client-value propositions.

- Establish a greater sense of urgency and accountability at all levels.

- Engage all employees in understanding and implementing strategy.

In 2001, Jerry Thomchick, senior executive vice president and chief operating officer, drew up an initial strategy map that described how First Commonwealth would compete through its new strategy. Thomchick took the strategy map and Balanced Scorecard to the holding company's executive committee, which approved it for use in strategic planning and reporting. Trimarchi, however, was not completely satisfied with the scorecard. In January 2002, Thomchick led a new project, assisted by consultants from the Balanced Scorecard Collaborative. The team went through eight drafts of the FCFC strategy, and in April 2002 the executive committee and the First Commonwealth Board approved a new strategy map (see Exhibit 3), along with objectives, measures, targets, and initiatives. In July 2002, the executive team received the first scorecard report, showing the second quarter results.

In Phase II of the project, from April to August 2002, the team cascaded the enterprise scorecard to the Growth and Support Divisions. The Support Division embraced the approach, and the concept rapidly cascaded down to the next level, with scorecards for the professional resources company, headed by Thomchick, and the data processing company, headed by Sue McMurdy. The Growth Division also developed a scorecard and began using it in October 2002. Linking the individual operating companies – bank, insurance, trust, financial planning – with the right set of financial and nonfinancial priorities, however, proved to be a more challenging task. A project to link the Growth Division operating companies was launched in February 2003.

John Glass, president of the Growth Division, commented on the impact:

> Before, each division had a different measurement system. As we consolidated into a single entity, the Balanced Scorecard gave us a common measurement system that we could deploy across the entire organization. This has been a significant development.

The nonfinancial measures have helped us understand the new strategy. But we are still getting used to the new measures and how they track retail consumer relationships to deliver bottom-line profitability.

CEO O'Dell reflected on progress with the new reporting framework: "Initially we focused on getting the tool developed and in place. Now we are learning how it delivers value. I like best that it is simple and keeps us focused on the core drivers and critical issues; we don't get lost in minutiae and details."

Trimarchi added: "By automating the measurements, we put data at management's fingertips with a process that is not obtrusive."

The final step in acceptance occurred when the company linked executive pay to the Balanced Scorecard. O'Dell recalled: "This sealed the deal. Executives began to cascade the scorecard to their direct reports. We're going to get good at this. We'll get even better as we identify the right drivers. The concept is accepted; it's not resisted."

Rolling forecasts

John Dolan (CFO), Angela Ritenour (head of strategic planning), and Thomchick introduced an innovative feature into the FCFC Balanced Scorecard by demonstrating and gaining approval for a six-quarter rolling forecast that would replace the annual budgeting process. Under their process, executives reforecasted six quarters of Balanced Scorecard metrics each month. The November forecast for the four quarters in the following year became the annual plan, which was required for regulatory purposes. O'Dell had been trying to get rid of the tedious and static annual budgeting process for five years. He hoped that the continual reforecasting of Balanced Scorecard measures would move First Commonwealth off its budget mentality:

Some of our financial metrics are red now and will be red one year from now because of the interest rate environment and the state of our local economy. There is nothing in the short term that we can do about these external conditions. With our monthly forecasts of future financial and nonfinancial Balanced Scorecard metrics, we can now see where these metrics will likely be one year from now, and we can put in initiatives to address objectives in the yellow or red zones.

The Balanced Scorecard makes sure that we don't do anything to deal with short-term problems that will damage the company in the long term. If earnings are off, we don't just think about how to cut costs. It has given us a tool, during this current down period, to drive long-term improvements.

The First Commonwealth executive team would evaluate managers' performance based on two factors: their achievement against the targets set in the November forecast, and their ability to reforecast and develop new initiatives that would link to long-term objectives and the strategy, not just to fix short-term problems.

A BALANCED SCORECARD FOR THE BOARD OF DIRECTORS

Trimarchi, from the beginning of the project, wanted the Balanced Scorecard to be incorporated into the governance process with the board of directors. The board had been asking him for more strategic information about the company, and Trimarchi wanted to get the board more involved in the company's strategy. The existing board packet consisted of the official financial measures required for regulatory purposes: historical financial statements, delinquency ratios, bad loans, and loan reserves. O'Dell observed: "By the time we presented all the historical information to the board and had some minor discussion, that was the board meeting. We needed a mechanism like an enterprise Balanced Scorecard, with rolling six-quarter forecasts, to put the board in a more forward-looking frame of mind so that we could have an active dialogue about the company's future."

In addition, the Sarbanes-Oxley Act of 2002, passed in the aftermath of the accounting and governance scandals at companies such as Enron, WorldCom, and Tyco, had placed new requirements on a company's senior executives and board of directors. Trimarchi felt that applying the Balanced Scorecard to governance would enable First Commonwealth to get ahead of the regulatory curve; it would not only help in compliance but also enable it to be a leader in corporate governance processes. He believed this capability would help First Commonwealth's acquisition strategy. Small community banks that were now struggling to meet the more onerous requirements of Sarbanes-Oxley could join a company that had a well-functioning governance process that drove value creation simultaneously with regulatory compliance.

First Commonwealth operated with four board committees: governance, compensation, audit, and executive. Each committee established its own charter that set forth the purposes, goals, and responsibilities of the committee; the qualifications for membership; and procedures for appointment and removal of committee members, structure and operations, and reporting to the board. (Exhibit 4 provides a summary of the purposes of the governance, compensation, and audit committees.) Trimarchi wanted to integrate the Balanced Scorecard into the operation of the entire board and each board committee, helping them fulfill the requirement that the board and each committee evaluate its performance annually. (Exhibit 5 shows the composition of the board in December 2002.)

The Board Balanced Scorecard project

Trimarchi shared articles about the Balanced Scorecard with the board members to get them familiar and comfortable with the concept. Some expressed concern about giving up the old reports. Trimarchi promised to continue to send the previous board package for them to review but indicated that this would not be part of the normal board discussion.

In February 2003, Trimarchi asked Michael Nagel, the consultant from the Balanced Scorecard Collaborative, to facilitate a process to apply the Balanced Scorecard framework to the board. Nagel used a recent report on how boards of directors could benefit from the Balanced Scorecard.[1] In addition to the board's reviewing the enterprise scorecard at each meeting, Nagel proposed the creation of a separate Board Balanced Scorecard that would define the strategic contributions of the board, provide the board with a tool to manage its performance and that of its committees, and clarify the strategic information required by the board. Nagel also proposed a third set of scorecards, Executive Balanced Scorecards, to provide accountability between each senior executive and the board. (Exhibit 6 shows the objectives for the three different scorecards and the relationships among them.)

---

[1] Marc J. Epstein and Marie-Josée Roy, *Measuring and Improving the Performance of Corporate Boards*, Management Accounting Guideline, Society of Management Accountants of Canada (Mississauga, Ontario: 2002).

Nagel interviewed the four internal and eight external board members individually and led several workshops with them. Most board members attended in-person interviews and workshops; others – particularly those who resided outside the First Commonwealth marketplace and had other responsibilities as CEOs, professionals, or business owners – participated by phone and had pre-workshop briefings.

The discussions on board responsibilities, performance, and composition were sensitive. Trimarchi sent a memo to all board members expressing his objectives for the Board Balanced Scorecard and stressing the confidentiality of all interview comments. He followed up with a personal phone call to address any concerns. At the conclusion of the interview and workshop process, all board members – even those originally opposed to the effort – noted that the process had been highly beneficial and had produced three valuable documents that clearly articulated director and CEO responsibilities and challenges.

Exhibit 7 describes the five director responsibilities and challenges: approve strategic decisions, oversee financial activities, counsel the CEO by providing decision support and performance advice, select and motivate executives, and ensure compliance.

Exhibit 8 provides a similar list of CEO objectives: define and communicate strategy, manage financial resources, align the talent, and manage execution.

These two lists sharpened the collective awareness of governance roles and clarified the information requirements and future skill sets needed by the board. Dave Dahlmann, vice chairman of the FCFC Board, believed that the challenge was to have these complementary roles of boards and CEOs performed well. A strong board with weak management would lead to poor execution of the strategy. A weak board and strong management would lead to weak governance. A strong board that understood the company's strategy could add value to a strong management team through excellent governance.

The third document was the board strategy map (see Exhibit 9), which was discussed and approved by the board at its April 2003 meeting. The financial perspective replicated the FCFC enterprise strategy map, since the board's success for shareholders was ultimately measured by the company's financial performance. The board scorecard used a stakeholder rather than a customer perspective to reflect the board's responsibilities to shareholders, regulators, and communities. The three objectives in the stakeholder perspective were:

S1: approve, plan, and monitor corporate performance;
S2: strengthen and motivate executive performance;
S3: ensure corporate compliance.

The objectives in the internal perspective were organized into three themes that would deliver the desired performance for stakeholders and that also could be assigned to a board committee for primary oversight and responsibility.

Internal perspective theme	Board committee with primary responsibility
Performance oversight	Governance Committee
Executive enhancement	Compensation Committee
Compliance and communication	Audit Committee

Objectives in the learning and growth perspective related to board skills and knowledge, productive board discussions, and access to appropriate strategic information about the company. Exhibit 10 shows the Balanced Scorecard report that supported the strategy map. It contained the initial measures and their corresponding performance, the board committee responsible for the measure, and commentary or description of the measure. For the board's learning and growth measures, the project team designed a survey that each board member would complete after each meeting to assess the quality of the meeting and board processes (Exhibit 11). Semiannually, each board member would complete a self-evaluation survey of his or her board performance (see Exhibit 12).

Dahlmann noted: "The board surveys will help us determine if we have the right skills to help the company in its strategic direction, the right strategic information at the right time, and the right climate to encourage discussion and dissent. We still might need some coaching, though, on how to have productive board discussions around the enterprise and board Scorecards."

The third leg of the new governance process (see Exhibit 4) required executive Scorecards. O'Dell stressed the importance of the executive enhancement theme of the board Scorecard: "The board's compensation committee has the responsibility to develop the compensation plan for senior executives. It must approve the specific measures and targets for each executive's compensation."

Each executive developed a personal scorecard, using the subset of measures on the enterprise Scorecard that he or she could influence. (Exhibit 13 shows the executive Scorecard produced for Glass, CEO of the Growth Unit.) All executive scorecards included measures and targets for people development and succession plans. O'Dell met quarterly to discuss each executive's performance on his or her Scorecard. Annually, the compensation and governance committees reviewed all executive Scorecards. O'Dell felt that a new compensation system, based on the executive scorecards, would be a big improvement:

> Before, we had a one-dimensional scorecard for executive compensation that hadn't paid much in recent years. Executives were becoming frustrated that they couldn't earn bonuses even when their individual performance had been excellent. They are now accountable for measurements based on clients, processes, and people. I am confident that if everyone hits their targets for these measures, the company and its shareholders will do well.

Dahlmann strongly supported executive scorecards: "We carved out specific executive responsibility for particular enterprise scorecard objectives and measures. Executive Scorecards take away places to 'hide' executive performance; they will help the board deliver on its second Scorecard theme, executive enhancement."

Board reaction to the Balanced Scorecard

During the process with the board, Trimarchi had reduced the number of board members from 23 to 12. Trimarchi believed that those board members most skeptical about introducing the Balanced Scorecard into board deliberations and evaluations had tended to leave. The remaining board members were those who embraced the new governance approach. O'Dell concurred: "We now have a good core of board members. They have accepted the responsibility to be more active and accountable for their performance. All our outside directors want to serve on the governance committee so that they can be actively involved in the process."

Tomb, board member and corporate secretary, noted:

> The enterprise Balanced Scorecard provides uniformity for board meetings. Directors show up knowing what

will be discussed. We spend less time on presentations and reviewing the statutory financials, though the details are still there. More time is spent discussing sales and customer relationships. The forecasts for Scorecard measures for next year lead to discussions on how management is dealing with underperformance in the future. Overall, the Balanced Scorecard has streamlined board processes; the outside directors can focus a lot faster on the key issues affecting the company.

In addition, Sarbanes-Oxley requires the board to do a self-evaluation of itself and of each board member. The Board Balanced Scorecard and the directors' self-assessments provide us with a framework for that evaluation. These will be used when deciding whether to ask a current board member to stand for reelection.

Laurie Singer and Jim Newill, former directors at Southwest Bank, were now serving on the board of First Commonwealth and on its governance and audit committees. Newill, chairman of the audit committee, reflected on the impact of the Scorecard on his role:

I still need to look at the financials to see whether the results are being delivered, especially in expense control and risk management. The risk management financial objective, and the communications and compliance internal process on the board scorecard, provide a good reminder of what the audit committee should be addressing. But we are just at the start, and I am still unsure what it means to us.

Singer commented:

We have seen many different Balanced Scorecards from various areas of the organization. The board strategy map makes the most sense to me with its three internal themes corresponding to the roles for the governance committee, the compensation committee, and the audit committee. It provides us with an opportunity to improve the performance of the First Commonwealth Board.

I appreciate the updates on the initiatives so we can see what is happening now to affect the future. It helps me track and assess the progress of the strategy. It's an evolutionary process; we're still learning how to use it.

Both were intrigued that Trimarchi, the founder and former CEO of First Commonwealth and, at 81, still a strong board chairman, had embraced the Balanced Scorecard for the board. Singer commented: "It makes his performance more visible, and he becomes more vulnerable. But he believed strongly in the process. It gave him a process to

imbue his philosophy and strategy into the company so that it can be sustained beyond his tenure. It should help us with succession planning when Trimarchi and O'Dell retire."

Newill added: "We still need a process to evaluate the chairman and develop a succession strategy for him. Also, to make the governance process truly effective, the chairman of the governance committee should be an independent director."

JULY 2003 BOARD MEETING

On Monday morning, July 14, 2003, Trimarchi, chairman of the governance committee, called the committee to order (see agenda in Exhibit 14). Trimarchi (agenda item 6) summarized the history of the Balanced Scorecard at the corporation and its present status. He noted:

The Scorecard has evolved a great deal since the start of the project. The format for the current enterprise, board, and related Scorecards, all of which are included in the board packet, should now stay about constant, though information on the Scorecard can change as circumstances change. There is not some other system out there; the Balanced Scorecard is what we will use to run the company. It is a good tool for explaining our strategy and our strengths. Companies that join us through our merger and acquisitions activity will have the benefit of joining a Balanced Scorecard organization.

Dahlmann provided some additional education on the Balanced Scorecard to the committee members and attendees, reminding them that it was launched to help First Commonwealth make the transition from a product to a customer-centric strategy:

The BSC will continue to make us think outside the box about our strategy and its success. Is it the right strategy for both parts of our business – commercial and consumer? We don't know yet; these are discussions that the executive management team continues to have. The BSC gives the board an opportunity to participate in and understand management's plans. It helps us understand what is happening in the organization, in a way that we could not do in the past when we just reviewed historical financial numbers.

Executive scorecards will help both the governance and compensation committees. The governance committee, in its deliberations on succession plans for key executives, now has guidelines for the strategic objectives required for each executive. It can track the performance of all members of the executive team. This information will also assist the compensation committee in decisions about executive compensation.

Thomchick and Ritenour then led the committee through the board scorecard and explained the color coding they had assigned to each objective. They had color coded as red (inadequate) two board objectives: *approve and monitor funding for strategic initiatives* and *ensure board skills and knowledge match the strategic direction*, since neither objective had an existing initiative in place. The committee recommended that this gap be remedied by the next meeting. The committee also decided that, going forward, the chairperson of each committee would be responsible for reporting on performance on the board Scorecard.

The committee discussed how to generate data for several of the board Scorecard measures. Thomchick reviewed the new full board evaluation and individual director self-assessment documents (Exhibits 11 and 12), pointing out that these evaluations should help the board comply with Sarbanes-Oxley. The governance committee reviewed the executive Scorecards of Thomchick and McMurdy and discussed how the governance and compensation committees would actively use these reports starting in 2004.

The full board met the following afternoon (see agenda in Exhibit 15). Thomchick, for agenda items 4 and 5, reviewed the contents in the major sections of the new board reporting package:

1. Board of Directors Balanced Scorecard Report.

2. Full Board Self-Evaluation Form.

3. Individual Director Self-Evaluation Form.

4. Board Resolution on Criteria for Board Membership.

5. Executive Balanced Scorecards: Thomchick forecasted that about a dozen executive scorecards should soon be available for the compensation committee.

6. Succession Plans: section still blank; forms needed to be developed. One board member noted that if a leader did not produce a succession plan, the board might have to produce one for that executive.

Thomchick used the enterprise strategy map to present the company's performance in the second quarter. Trimarchi asked the outside directors for their reaction. One commented how the Balanced Scorecard was growing in importance and value to the company. Another described it as a "work in process." The board meeting then turned to a discussion of a proposed acquisition.

Exhibit 1 Summary financial information: First Commonwealth Financial Corporation

	2002	2001	2000	1999	1998
Interest income	$275,568	$308,891	$311,882	$296,089	$282,067
Interest expense	122,673	167,170	174,539	152,653	148,282
Net interest income	**$152,895**	**$141,721**	**$137,343**	**$143,436**	**$133,785**
Provision for credit losses	12,223	11,495	10,030	9,450	15,049
Net interest income after provision for credit losses	**$140,672**	**$130,226**	**$127,313**	**$133,986**	**$118,736**
Securities gains	642	3,329	1,745	565	1,457
Other operating income	36,564	36,895	31,938	33,660	27,929
Nonrecurring charges	14,140	0	0	0	8,875
Other operating expenses	111,301	105,007	99,461	95,569	93,980
Income before taxes and extraordinary items	**$52,437**	**$65,443**	**$61,535**	**$72,642**	**$45,267**
Applicable income taxes	8,911	15,254	14,289	19,612	11,893
Net income	**$43,526**	**$50,189**	**$47,246**	**$53,030**	**$33,374**
At end of period					
Total assets	$4,524,743	$4,583,530	$4,372,312	$4,340,846	$4,096,789
Investment securities	1,680,609	1,762,408	1,636,337	1,592,389	1,525,332
Loans and leases, net of unearned income	2,608,634	2,567,934	2,490,827	2,500,059	2,374,850
Allowance for credit losses	34,496	34,157	33,601	33,539	32,304
Deposits	3,044,124	3,093,150	3,064,146	2,948,829	2,931,131
Company-obligated mandatory redeemable capital securities of subsidiary trust	35,000	35,000	35,000	35,000	0
Other long-term debt	544,934	629,220	621,855	603,355	630,850
Shareholders' equity	401,390	370,066	334,156	286,683	355,405
Key ratios					
Return average assets	0.96%	1.11%	1.10%	1.25%	0.85%
Return on average equity	11.09%	13.85%	15.65%	15.44%	9.13%
Net loans to deposits ratio	84.56%	81.92%	80.19%	83.64%	79.92%
Dividends per share as a percent of net income per share	80.67%	67.24%	68.90%	58.52%	82.41%
Average equity to average assets ratio	8.64%	8.01%	7.00%	8.10%	9.28%

Source: Company Annual Report, 2002.

EXHIBIT 2 First Commonwealth Financial Corporation: organizational chart

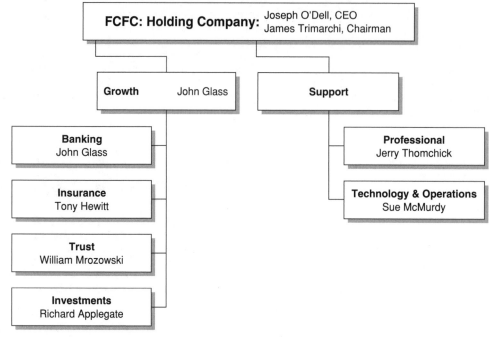

Source: internal company document.

Exhibit 3 First Commonwealth enterprise strategy map

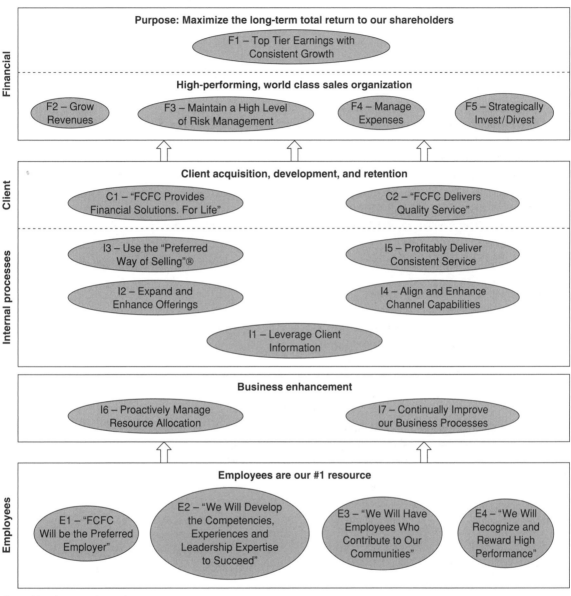

Source: internal company document.

Exhibit 4 Summary of board committee purposes

Governance Committee

● Identify individuals qualified to become board members and recommend director nominees to the board.

● Recommend director nominees for each board committee.

● Monitor, oversee, and review compliance by directors, officers, and employees with the corporation's code of conduct and ethics.

● Lead the board in its annual review of the board's performance.

● Develop a succession plan for the CEO; assist the compensation committee in the annual evaluation of the CEO and senior executive officers.

Compensation Committee

● Review and approve corporate goals and objectives relevant to CEO and senior executive officer compensation.

● Review annually and determine the compensation of all directors, senior executive officers, and the CEO, including incentive-compensation plans and equity-based plans.

● Produce an annual report on executive compensation for inclusion in the corporation's proxy statement.

Audit Committee

● Oversee and monitor the corporation's financial reporting process on behalf of the board and report to the board about:

   ● the integrity of the financial statements of the corporation;

   ● the independent auditor's qualifications and independence;

   ● the performance of the corporation's internal audit function and independent auditors;

   ● the compliance of the corporation with legal and regulatory requirements.

Source: http://www.snl.com/cache/1001117199.pdf; http://www.snl.com/cache/1001117227.pdf; http://www.snl.com/cache/1001117200.pdf.

Exhibit 5 First Commonwealth board of directors, December 2002

Name	City of residence	Position
Ray Charley	Greensburg, PA	President, Thomi Co.
Edward T. Côté	Rector, PA	Associate, The Wakefield Group
David S. Dahlmann	Greensburg, PA	Associate Professor, St. Vincent College; Former CEO, Southwest Bank, and Vice Chairman of FCFC Board
Alan R. Fairman	Punxsutawney, PA	Business Manager, Fairman Drilling Company
Johnston A. Glass	Indiana, PA	Vice Chairman, FCFC; President and CEO, First Commonwealth Bank
Dale P. Latimer	New Alexandria, PA	Chairman, R&L Development Co.
James W. Newill	Highland Beach, FL	CPA; Former President, J. W. Newill Company
Joseph E. O'Dell	Indiana, PA	President and CEO, FCFC
John A. Robertshaw, Jr.	Greensburg, PA	Former Chairman, Laurel Vending, Inc.
Laurie Singer	Allison Park, PA	President, Allegheny Valley Development Corporation
David R. Tomb, Jr.	Indiana, PA	Attorney
E. James Trimarchi	Indiana, PA	Chairman of Board, FCFC

Source: First Commonwealth Annual Report, 2002, p. 11.

EXHIBIT 6 Enterprise, Board, and Executive Scorecards

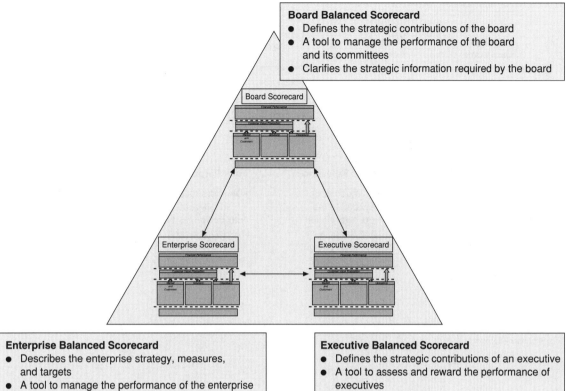

Board Balanced Scorecard
- Defines the strategic contributions of the board
- A tool to manage the performance of the board and its committees
- Clarifies the strategic information required by the board

Board Scorecard

Enterprise Scorecard

Executive Scorecard

Enterprise Balanced Scorecard
- Describes the enterprise strategy, measures, and targets
- A tool to manage the performance of the enterprise
- A key information input to the board

Executive Balanced Scorecard
- Defines the strategic contributions of an executive
- A tool to assess and reward the performance of executives
- A key information input to the board

Source: Balanced Scorecard Collaborative document.

Exhibit 7 Directors' responsibilities and challenges

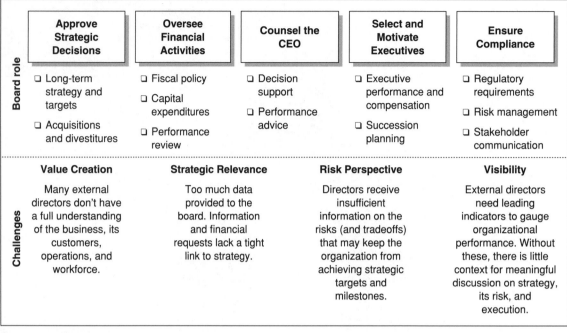

	Approve Strategic Decisions	Oversee Financial Activities	Counsel the CEO	Select and Motivate Executives	Ensure Compliance
Board role	□ Long-term strategy and targets □ Acquisitions and divestitures	□ Fiscal policy □ Capital expenditures □ Performance review	□ Decision support □ Performance advice	□ Executive performance and compensation □ Succession planning	□ Regulatory requirements □ Risk management □ Stakeholder communication
	Value Creation	**Strategic Relevance**	**Risk Perspective**	**Visibility**	
Challenges	Many external directors don't have a full understanding of the business, its customers, operations, and workforce.	Too much data provided to the board. Information and financial requests lack a tight link to strategy.	Directors receive insufficient information on the risks (and tradeoffs) that may keep the organization from achieving strategic targets and milestones.	External directors need leading indicators to gauge organizational performance. Without these, there is little context for meaningful discussion on strategy, its risk, and execution.	

Source: company document.

Exhibit 8 CEO responsibilities and challenges

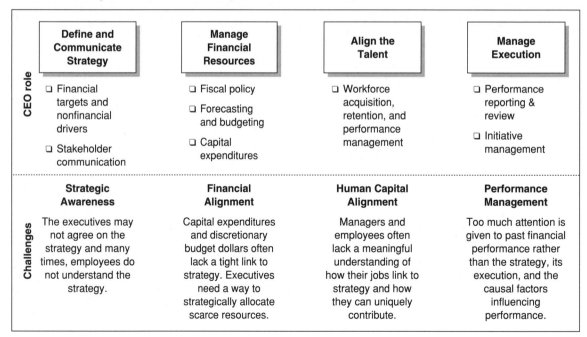

	Define and Communicate Strategy	Manage Financial Resources	Align the Talent	Manage Execution
CEO role	□ Financial targets and nonfinancial drivers □ Stakeholder communication	□ Fiscal policy □ Forecasting and budgeting □ Capital expenditures	□ Workforce acquisition, retention, and performance management	□ Performance reporting & review □ Initiative management
	Strategic Awareness	**Financial Alignment**	**Human Capital Alignment**	**Performance Management**
Challenges	The executives may not agree on the strategy and many times, employees do not understand the strategy.	Capital expenditures and discretionary budget dollars often lack a tight link to strategy. Executives need a way to strategically allocate scarce resources.	Managers and employees often lack a meaningful understanding of how their jobs link to strategy and how they can uniquely contribute.	Too much attention is given to past financial performance rather than the strategy, its execution, and the causal factors influencing performance.

Source: company document.

EXHIBIT 9 First Commonwealth Financial board of directors strategy map

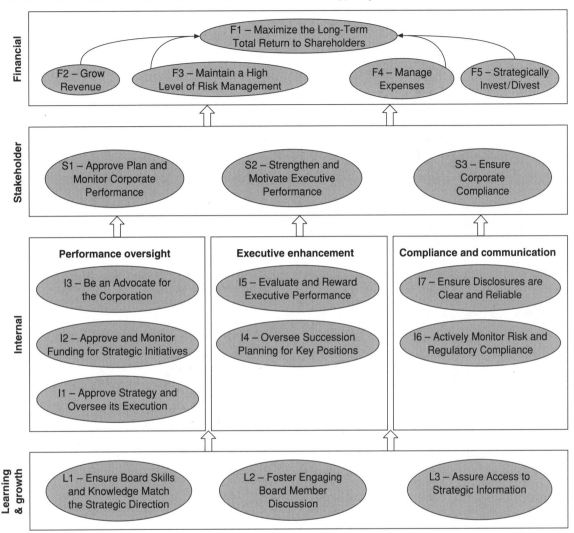

Exhibit 10 Board of directors Balanced Scorecard Report

Objective	Measure(s)	Performance	Owner	Performance analyses
S1 – Approve Plan and Monitor Corporate Performance	• Is the BSC used for decision-making?	G	Governance	• BSC is used in executive leadership meetings. Decision-making results shown in rolling reforecast and rolling plan.
S2 – Strengthen and Motivate Executive Performance	• Are executive officers and affiliate CEOs on track with development plans? • Have executive compensation packages resulted in expected corporate performance?	Y	Executive Compensation	• Executive officers and CEOs of affiliates are developing executive scorecards. • Executive compensation committee to review new long- and short-term incentive alternatives.
S3 – Ensure Corporate Compliance	• Regulatory Score (index of CAMELS rating, NYSE, SEC, CRA)	G	Audit	• Regulatory scores all favorable.
I1 – Approve Strategy and Oversee its Execution	• Completeness of strategic planning process • Is BSC linked to strategic plan?	Y	Full Board	• Strategic planning linked to the Balanced Scorecard through the rolling plan and rolling reforecast. • More work needs to be done on strategic plan, re: competitive, internal, and external analysis.
I2 – Approve and Monitor Funding for Strategic Initiatives	• % of strategic initiatives in plan that meet pro forma	R	Full Board	• Regular progress reports on strategic initiatives for 2003 plan not being done.
I3 – Be an Advocate for the Corporation	• # of strategic relationships referred to FCFC	Y	Full Board	• Need to develop report to determine.
I4 – Oversee Succession Planning for Key Positions	• Do all executive officers and affiliate CEOs have a succession plan in place?	Y	Governance	• Succession plans have been developed but probably need additional updating.

Exhibit 10 *continued*

Objective	Measure(s)	Performance	Owner	Performance analyses
I5 – Evaluate and Reward Executive Performance	• Do all executive officers and affiliate CEOs have an executive scorecard?	Y	Executive Compensation	• Scorecards in development for July; full use in 2004
I6 – Actively Monitor Risk and Regulatory Compliance	• Was the quarterly risk report reviewed and discussed? • Do key risks have a plan in place to enhance mitigants? • # of ethical or regulatory violations?	G	Audit	• Quarterly risk report done and reviewed • Key risks determined, with mitigants, at risk committee • No known ethical or regulatory violations
I7 – Ensure Disclosures are Clear and Reliable	• # of regulatory agency reviews • # of disputes with auditors	G	Audit	• No regulatory reviews • No disputes with auditors
L1 – Ensure Board Skills and Knowledge Match the Strategic Direction	• Strategic skills gap assessment	R	Governance	• Need to do skills assessment for board
L2 – Foster Engaging Board Member Discussion	• Meeting attendance • Board member survey on quality of board discussion	Y	Full Board	• Board attendance 100% • Survey attached. Please review and comment if this survey is OK.
L3 – Assure Access to Strategic Information	• Board member survey on relevance of information presented • # of days in advance that board packet is sent	Y	Full Board	• Survey attached. Please review and comment if this survey is OK. • Material out one week in advance

Source: company document.

Exhibit 11 Full board self-evaluation survey

Director's Name: _____   Board Meeting Date: _____

Scale:

1 = Strongly Agree	2 = Agree	3 = Disagree	4 = Strongly Disagree

1. Board member had input to the meeting's agenda.   _____

2. Board member discussion was encouraged.   _____

3. Board members were encouraged to express different viewpoints.   _____

4. The board meeting discussion focused on key strategic issues.   _____

5. In the past quarter, executive sessions were held without management.   _____

6. The board packet information was relevant and helped the board in its decision-making.   _____

7. Decisions were made based on how they impacted the FCFC Balanced Scorecard.   _____

8. The skill set of the board matches the strategic direction of the corporation.   _____

9. Board members have a thorough understanding of FCFC's long-term strategy.   _____

10. Board members have a thorough understanding of FCFC's planning process.   _____

11. Board members have a thorough understanding of FCFC's fiscal policy.   _____

12. In the past quarter, directors held discussions with executive management outside
    the quarterly board meeting.   _____

13. In the past quarter, the board updated stakeholders on the activities of FCFC.   _____

14. During the past quarter, I have referred potential clients to the organization.   _____

15. I use the Balanced Scorecard as a central tool to fulfill my governance responsibilities.   _____

_____

_____

_____

How could board meetings be more constructive?

_____

_____

_____

Is there any additional information you need to help you in your role? If so, what?

_____

_____

_____

Is there any additional training you would like to receive? If so, what?

_____

_____

_____

Additional comments:

_____

_____

_____

Source: company document.

Exhibit 12 Individual director self-evaluation

Name:	Performance Period:	Date Completed:

Purpose *(Define how your role contributes to FCFC's strategy)*
As a member of the FCFC Board of Directors, I will oversee the performance of the organization, strive to enhance the performance of executive management and ensure compliance to all regulatory requirements.

Scale: 1 – Performance does not meet position expectations
2 – Performance occasionally meets position expectations
3 – Performance consistently meets position expectations
4 – Performance far exceeds position expectations

Key strategic objectives from Board Balanced Scorecard	*Measure of performance*	Weight	Rating (1–4)	Weighted rating
S1 – Approve Plan and Monitor Corporate Performance	I have reviewed the strategic plan and monitored corporate performance relative to the plan.			
I1 – Approve Strategy and Oversee its Execution	I understand the link between the strategic plan and the Balanced Scorecard.			
I2 – Approve and Monitor Funding for Strategic Initiatives	I actively monitor the progress of stategic initiatives to ensure that the strategic plan will succeed.			
I3 – Be an Advocate for the Corporation	I have referred at least one strategic relationship to FCFC during the past quarter.			
S2 – Strengthen and Motivate Executive Performance	I have sought out members of executive management and discussed performance and/or motivational issues.			
S2 – Strengthen and Motivate Executive Performance	I have assessed the performance of executive management relative to their development plan.			
	I have assessed the performance of executive management relative to corporate performance.			
I4 – Oversee Succession Planning for Key Positions	I have taken an active role in assuring that succession plans are completed and appropriate individuals are nominated.			
I5 – Evaluate and Reward Executive Performance	I have taken an active role in assuring that executive management is regularly assessed and rewarded appropriately.			
S3 – Ensure Corporate Compliance	I regularly review our regulatory scores and recommend appropriate action.			
I6 – Actively Monitor Risk and Regulatory Compliance	I have reviewed the quarterly risk report and ensured that risk mitigants are in place.			
I7 – Ensure Disclosures are Clear and Reliable	I have taken an active role in assuring that disclosures are accurate and reliable.			
L1 – Ensure Board Skills and Knowledge	My skills will enable the organization to reach its long-term strategic goals.			
L2 – Foster Engaging Board Member Discussion	I take an active role in board meeting discussions.			
L3 – Assure Access to Strategic Information	I understand the information presented to the board and how it supports the strategic direction of the organization.			
Please give comments based on committee memberships if you feel your answers should be weighted more toward any certain committee responsibilities:				

Source: company document.

Exhibit 13 Executive Scorecard: John Glass, CEO of Growth Unit

FCFC Executive Performance Commitment

Name and Title: John Glass, President of Growth
Reviewer Name:

Performance Period:
Date Completed:

Purpose *(Define how your role contributes to FCFC's strategy)*
As the President of the Growth Unit, I will grow revenues, transition the organization into a sales-driven culture, and ensure that the Growth Unit has the right management team to execute the FCFC strategy.

Scale: 1 – Performance does not meet position expectations
2 – Performance occasionally meets position expectations
3 – Performance consistently meets position expectations
4 – Performance far exceeds position expectations

Key strategic objectives from FCFC Balanced Scorecard	Measure of performance	Target	Progress to date	Weight	Rating
Financial					
F1 – Top-Tier Earnings with Consistent Growth	ROA ROE Net Income				
F2 – Grow Revenues F4 – Manage Expenses	Revenue Growth/Expense Management				
F3 – Maintain a High Level of Risk Management	Overall Risk Rating				
Client					
C1 – "FCFC Provides Financial Solutions. For Life."	Client Acquisition, Development and Retention by Retail and Commercial Clients – Progress Report				
Internal Processes					
I3 – Use the "Preferred Way of Selling"®	Sales Rate of Profiled Households Closing Percentage				
Employees					
E1 – Ensure That We Have the Right People in the Right Executive Positions	Progress on Management Team Development/Succession Plans				
E2 – Transition the Organization to a Sales Culture	Progress on Actions Taken to Move to a Sales-Oriented Culture (narrative)				
E3 – We Will Have Employees who Contribute to Our Communities	Civic Involvement				

Composite Score _____

Exhibit 13 *continued*

Areas of strength *(Identify areas of strength by referring to the individual's accomplishments and demonstrated leadership competencies.)*	Areas of improvement *(Identify areas where competencies could be strengthened for further growth.)*

Summary of performance *(Describe overall performance, focus on major accomplishments, competencies demonstrated, and areas where improvement may be needed. Include specific examples.)*

Development Plan

Development goals *(Leadership Competencies to be developed and initiatives to be completed.)*
Board member may suggest development opportunities for leadership competencies or increased action regarding specific initiatives which support key objectives.

Development Action Steps *(For next review period)*

Key objectives	Actions	Progress update

Leadership competencies *(Rate performance level on leadership competencies relative to the requirements of the position.)*	Rating
• Establishes leadership standard for affiliate and its employees; promotes teamwork between other FCFC affiliates and employees; promulgates corporate values by example.	
• Focuses on long-term growth of the affiliate; promotes and reinforces mission and vision of the affiliate and FCFC.	
• Encourages an organizational environment that enables employees to achieve their fullest potential.	
• Displays innovation in own thinking; open to new experiences and ideas; encourages innovation among affiliate staff.	
• Demonstrates ability to be an eager decision maker; effectively motivates and persuades staff to adopt new ideas and processes.	
• Serves as a champion for the Balanced Scorecard; communicates the Balanced Scorecard concept within the organization.	

Employee Comments

Employee comments about the review

Source: company document.

Exhibit 14 First Commonwealth Governance Committee Agenda: July 14, 2003

Monday, July 14

10:30 a.m.   First Commonwealth Trust Company

1. Review and approve minutes of April 21, 2003 committee meeting.
2. Review succession plan of each CEO of the corporation: FCFC, FCB, FCIA, FCTC, FCSC, FCPRI, CTCLIC.
   a. Does action of replacement need to be taken within the next 3 to 6 months?
   b. Accept each succession plan, report the results to the FCFC Board of Directors at their next meeting.
3. Review and approve the Audit, Compensation and Governance charters.
4. Quarterly report on Code of Ethics.
5. Review and approve criteria for the appointment of new members to the FCFC Board of Directors.
6. Process followed by Governance Committee to implement for them the most beneficial application of the Balanced Scorecard system for its use to them and the Board of Directors for evaluating the Corporation's annual plan and budget, and the plan and budget reforecast provided to the Board for the second and third quarter of each year.
7. Good of the Order.
8. Adjourn.

11:45 a.m.   Lunch.

Enclosures: 1. Minutes of April 21, 2003 meeting.
2. Copies of Succession Plan forms from each CEO.
3. Criteria for the appointment of new members to the FCFC Board.
4. Copies of Audit, Compensation and Governance Charters.

Source: company document.

Exhibit 15 Agenda, board of directors meeting: First Commonwealth Financial Corporation

Board of Directors Meeting
Tuesday, July 15, 2003 – 1:30 p.m.
Agenda

1. Approval of Board minutes of April 2003 – sent.
2. Committee minutes not previously sent – sent now.
3. Introductory remarks by Chairman/President.
4. Balanced Scorecard Reports, sent in separate notebook.
5. Thomchick's narrative – Questions/comments – sent.
6. Acquisition update – discussion at meeting.
7. Capital management recommendations – overview attached, more information at meeting.
8. Special Reports and Resolutions:
   – Dividend report – at meeting
   – Loan Loss Reserve and Provision Approval – at meeting
   – Approve Policies and Procedures – sent separately
   – Ratify Loans over $10 MM – attached
   – Securities Firms and Banks – approved lists – attached.
9. Committee Reports – at meeting:
   – Governance
   – Audit
   – Executive Compensation.
10. President's Report.
11. Chairman's Report.
12. Good of the Order:
   – Annual calendar for 2004 draft for review – attached.
13. Adjourn.

Source: company document.

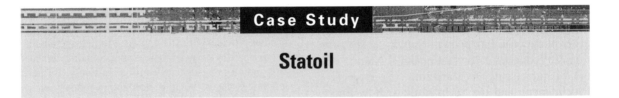

Case Study

Statoil

We have a management model that is very well-suited to dealing with turbulence and rapid change. It enables us to act and reprioritize quickly so that we can fend off threats or seize opportunities. This is much more difficult in a "traditional budget" world.

Helge Lund, CEO, Statoil

Statoil, the large Norwegian energy company, used an innovative performance management process called "Ambition-to-Action" to translate the company's overall strategies into strategic objectives, key performance indicators, needed actions, and individual goals. It combined two management concepts – the "balanced scorecard" and "beyond budgeting" – in a unique way.

The implementation of the Ambition-to-Action process had taken a long time, but by 2010 it had been fully implemented across Statoil. In August 2010, Bjarte Bogsnes (Vice President, Performance Management Development), reported that:

> One of our core values is to challenge accepted truths. We threw out our annual budgeting process back in 2005. In 2010, we decided to throw out the calendar. We are for instance implementing event-driven dynamic forecasting. No longer do we require any forecasts to be prepared at any fixed time, and the planning horizons vary depending on the business or operation. We are striving to make our entire process – strategic planning, target setting, action planning, forecasting – totally dynamic, done as needed. We want our management process to be business-driven, not calendar-driven. This is not accounting. Our aim is to create the conditions required for teams in Statoil to perform to their full potential.

The new Ambition-to-Action process had already provided many benefits. But Bjarte acknowledged that some Statoil managers were still uncomfortable with the Ambition-to-Action process. "It's a long journey, and it should be. Changing mindsets is not a quick fix," he said.

COMPANY BACKGROUND

Statoil, headquartered in Stavanger, Norway, was a large, multinational energy company.[1] The company was formed in 1972 by the Norwegian government and was wholly state owned until 2001 when its shares were listed on both the Oslo and New York stock exchanges. After the 2007 merger with the oil and gas division of Hydro, a Norwegian competitor, Statoil became the world's largest offshore energy producer, the world's third largest seller of crude oil, and Europe's second largest gas supplier. Statoil was also the largest company based in Scandinavia measured by market capitalization (nearly US$70 billion) and annual sales (US$70 billion). The company employed 20,000 people in 34 countries.

Statoil's original focus was on the exploration, production and development of oil and gas on the Norwegian continental shelf. The company's distinctive competency was deep water offshore drilling in harsh environments. Over the years, it diversified into refining and retailing of petroleum products and production of alternative forms of energy, such as wind power. In October 2010, Statoil spun off its retail business to create a separate public corporation, Statoil Fuel & Retail.

Statoil's strategy was to grow its long-term oil and gas production profitably while gradually building a position in renewable energy production. The oil reserves on the Norwegian continental shelf, on which the company had relied for many years, were being depleted. International growth was a key strategy. Statoil managers knew that the company was entering a new more competitive and more unpredictable era, so faster responsiveness to change was deemed critical.

---

[1] More information on the company can be found at www.statoil.com.

This case was prepared by Professor Kenneth A. Merchant and Wim A. Van der Stede.

The Statoil organization structure was relatively flat. It consisted of six main business units: (1) Exploration & Production – Norway; (2) Exploration & Production – International; (3) Natural Gas; (4) Manufacturing & Marketing; (5) Projects & Procurement; and (6) Technology & New Energy (see Exhibit 1).[2]

AMBITION-TO-ACTION

Statoil's Ambition-to-Action was a process that was designed to provide integration from organizational strategy to employees' actions, while providing sufficient freedom and flexibility. It was designed around five basic principles:

1. Performance is ultimately about *outperforming peers*.

2. *Do the right thing* in the actual situation, guided by the *Statoil Book*,[3] the Ambition-to-Action, decision criteria and authorities, and sound business judgment.

3. Within this framework, *resources* are made available or allocated case-by-case.

4. Business follow up is *forward looking* and *action* oriented.

5. Performance evaluation is a *holistic* assessment of delivery *and* behavior.

Strategic objectives, performance indicators, and actions

The Ambition-to-Action process was built around a key performance indicator (KPI) scorecard system that was originally introduced at the company in 1997. In 2002 additional information was added, to the KPI-dominated scorecard – a mission, strategic objectives, and needed actions – to provide a broader and richer language for describing and evaluating performance than could be provided by focusing just on KPI measures. Bjarte Bogsnes explained:

> Ambition-to-Action is the cornerstone of how we manage our business. It is how we exercise leadership, and it is the core of our business review meetings. It is a much better tool than a budget for integrating

the strategic processes with financial and operational measurement activities and people processes. A budget cannot provide a holistic approach to management as it has a narrow financial focus, and accounting numbers are getting more distant from our business. Because oil prices are so volatile, accounting reports tell us very little about performance unless we benchmark. You can't read strategy out of a budget, but you can read strategy out of a good scorecard.

All the Ambition-to-Action information was displayed together on a single page. Exhibit 2 shows an Ambition-to-Action example, that for the entire corporation. The overall mission is shown at the top: "Globally competitive – an exceptional place to perform and develop." The left column shows the *strategic objectives*, which answered the question: "Where are we going?" The center column showed the *performance indicators*, which answered the question: "How do we measure progress?" The right column described the *key actions* to be taken, which answered the question: "How do we get there?"

The corporation's two key financial performance indicators were relative total shareholder return and relative return on average capital employed (RoACE). Exhibit 3 shows back-up detail for these two KPIs, which compare Statoil performance with that of the other major energy companies.

Exhibits 4, 5 and 6 show other examples of Ambition-to-Action documents. These examples are for organizations at Levels 2 and 4 in the Projects & Procurement organization and at Level 3 in the Exploration & Production – Norway organization. The examples show the wide variety in the chosen strategic objectives and KPIs.

In 2010, over 1,100 Ambition-to-Action documents were in use within Statoil. Managers were encouraged to try the Ambition-to-Action process, but there was no corporate mandate imposing its use. Most, but not all, organizational entities above a certain size used it. The number of Ambition-to-Action documents had grown significantly over the years, more than doubling in just the last two years, simply because most Statoil managers wanted to use the process.

The *strategic objectives* had a medium-term time horizon. They were designed to describe "what success looks like on a medium term time horizon." To test the objectives they had developed, managers were asked to consider the following questions:

---

[2] Statoil announced a new organization effective January 1, 2011 that carved out North America as a seventh major business unit.

[3] The *Statoil Book* explained the company's most important operating principles, policies, and requirements. It set standards for "our behavior, our delivery and our leadership."

- Do they reflect ambition and strategy; i.e., areas that are *both* important and need change?

- Do they provide clear guidance and direction?

- Are they written in a language that makes you tick, without too many buzzwords?

- Do they support each other (cause and effect, from people and organization to finance)?

- Is the time horizon right, within an appropriate delivery period?

The lists of *performance indicators* (KPIs) were organized using five perspectives, the four traditional balanced scorecard perspectives – finance, market, operations, and people and organization – plus a fifth perspective of particular importance to Statoil: health, safety and environment (HSE). Statoil's conventional order for display of the perspectives was different from that of the standard balanced scorecard. Instead of starting with the financial perspective at the top, Statoil placed the people and organization perspective on top, followed by HSE, operations, and market, ending with finance. This was done to secure sufficient focus on the performance drivers found in the first four perspectives, as Finance was seen as the ultimate consequence of performing well in the other perspectives.

The managers of each entity selected the set of KPIs that they believed would work best for their organization. There were relatively few attempts to use the same KPIs at multiple levels of the organization if it did not make sense to do so, although some corporate entities from time to time tried to "push" their own favorites. Managers were aware of the strategic objectives, performance indicators and actions of the entities above them in the corporate hierarchy, as all of this information was made available on the common management information system (MIS) that maintains all Ambition-to-Actions. But Statoil did not want a mechanical "cascading" of the objectives, performance indicators, and actions throughout the organization. What they wanted was for each entity to run its own strategy process and to "translate" higher-level strategies into strategy themes that were actionable at each organization level. The goal was to secure ownership and have local teams manage themselves effectively in their local environment while moving in the right direction as defined by the strategies of entities higher in the organizational hierarchy. The measures were changed to fit the circumstances being faced, as

Baard Venge (Controller, Drilling & Well) explained: "We change measures when strategy changes or when we find better ones. If a measure is easy to manipulate, it is useless. We take it out."

Statoil wanted managers to define KPIs that were *relative*, rather than absolute. Relative KPIs linked inputs with outputs (e.g., cost per barrel) and, where possible, they compared the organization's performance with some benchmarks – performance relative to other entities. Statoil managers thought that relative KPI targets were more robust and "evergreen," meaning that they did not need to be updated as often. They also drove performance by stimulating a competitive mindset and peer pressure to perform and encourage learning from the best performers and the sharing of best practices. Regarding the question as to how challenging to set to targets, Geir Slora (Senior Vice President, Drilling & Well) clarified, "We want achievement of the targets to be possible. In most cases we are not aiming at world records. We are aiming at being in the top 25%."

Bjarte Bogsnes noted:

Absolute KPIs, such as a cost figure, is just measuring one side of the equation and is not in relation to what you want to get out of those costs. Is meeting an absolute cost target good or bad? Well, it depends on what you get back from those costs. Perhaps you should have spent more, as you lost value by missing business opportunities by not doing so. Or maybe you should have spent less because some expected opportunities did not come true. In any case, you will only know afterwards and not beforehand what the "right" cost level is. It is however not possible to find good relative KPIs in all areas, so we also use absolute cost targets. These should however be set at an overall level, not a detailed level, to secure flexibility for teams to take the right decisions.

Finally, the *actions* listed on the Ambition-to-Action documents were those considered to be the most important for achievement in the areas of performance reflected by the KPIs.

Regarding the advice he tended to give managers who were working on their Ambition-to-Action documents, Bjarte Bogsnes proffered:

Teams must spend quality time defining strategic objectives before moving on to the KPIs. The strategic objectives translate strategy into success using language that people understand. When scorecards only show KPIs, what strategies do they communicate? Making strategy more concrete through strategic objectives can also reveal lack of clarity in the strategy . . .

Don't search for the perfect KPI; it doesn't exist. I've spent 10 years looking for it. There are good KPIs and good combinations of KPIs, but there's no perfect KPI. The problem is that we often forget what the "I" in KPI stands for – *indicator*. It's only an indication of whether we are moving towards our strategic objectives. It's not a goal by itself. Therefore, de-emphasize KPI targets and heighten objectives and actions.

The Ambition-to-Action documents were intended to be updated only as required, not on a periodic (e.g., annual) basis.

Performance targets, forecasts, and capital allocations

Statoil previously used a traditional annual budgeting process but, inspired by the beyond budgeting principles,[4] the company's Executive Committee approved its discontinuance on May 9, 2005.[5] Statoil managers had many reasons for believing that budgeting was harmful to the corporation; for example:

- The budget forced three different purposes into one set of numbers – target setting, forecasting, and

resource allocation – hurting the quality of each purpose as these are different things. The budget as a forecast became biased because the same number also served as a target, or as an application for resources. An ambitious sales target cannot be the same number as a 50/50 sales forecast.

- The budget became obsolete shortly after it was prepared because the assumptions on which it was prepared were no longer accurate. Nonetheless, some operating managers tended to view the budgeted costs as entitlements that should be spent anyway: "Nobody ever gives anything back." Other operating managers were limited by the cost budget ceiling that prevented them from doing additional things that would be value-creating.

- Detailed budgets became centralized micro-management of highly competent and educated knowledge workers, which the company claimed were its most important asset.

- Managers spent a lot of budget review time looking backwards, explaining variance, rather than focusing on the future. Even though the budget reference points became more irrelevant as the months in the year went by, they were still compared with actual costs monthly with "accounting accuracy."

- Budgeting was done on an annual cycle, but an annual cycle is not optimal for all parts of Statoil's business. For some that is too often, but others should be evaluating performance and re-forecasting more frequently.

- The budget preparations were predicated on the assumption that financial capital is the main constraint. In many areas of Statoil, other constraints, particularly expertise (human resources), were more salient.

Bjarte Bogsnes explained that all these problems with budgeting undermined the power of their scorecards:

A key reason why many scorecard implementations fail is because they compete with the budget as a management tool, which confuse the organization over what's the most important. As long as we had both, the budget normally won because it had the longest tradition, and managers were most familiar with it. When we removed the budget, no one was in doubt about the role of the scorecard. We got an amazing turbo-charging of the process.

The Ambition-to-Action process is shown in diagram form in Exhibit 8. The process started with

---

[4] Beyond budgeting is a management model aimed at overcoming the problems caused by traditional budgeting. The model, first developed at the Swedish bank Handelsbanken, has been developed and refined as its use has spread to several other organizations around the world, including Toyota, Southwest Airlines, Whole Foods Markets, and Nokia.

  The aim of the beyond budgeting management model is to increase the adaptability of enterprises. Exhibit 7 shows the 12 core beyond budgeting principles. The first six principles are focused on taking the right leadership actions to address the drivers of change. The second six principles align management processes with leadership actions. Companies that follow the beyond budgeting principles have simple organizational structures, flat hierarchies, and flexible peer-to-peer networks. They operate with an assumption that organizations, like natural systems, are capable of self-organization and self-regulation. Their managers do not require negotiation of fixed performance targets, as is done in a traditional budgeting system. Allocations of resources are event-driven, not calendar-driven. Allocated resources are not treated as entitlements that must be spent. Unconstrained by a fixed and outdated plan, employees strive to improve their performance relative to their peers or some other benchmark. Creativity and rapid response to customer needs and unpredicted events are encouraged. The 12 principles are closely inter-related. Beyond budgeting proponents caution that adopting a few principles while ignoring the others could lead to unsatisfactory outcomes.

[5] Bjarte Bogsnes noted that "When you work with external partners [companies on large projects, say], you are often required to provide traditional budgets. When you aren't preparing budgets to operate internally, this can be confusing for those managers who have this external interface. So, we haven't completely eradicated budgets for those purposes." Baard Venge agreed: "It is hard to be dynamic if our partners are not also dynamic. Most of them want to see an annual budget."

strategic planning. Strategic themes and issues out to a ten-year horizon were discussed when needed as well as at the two Executive Committee meetings held each year. The ambition statements and strategic objectives developed out of the strategy discussions. They remained relatively stable over time.

Statoil managers separated the functions typically served by traditional budgeting processes – target setting, forecasting, and resource allocation – from each other in order to help improve the quality of each of these activities. Statoil used three distinct processes separated in time, or by KPIs used, to accomplish these very different purposes.

Performance *target setting* was done first. Performance targets were set to be both ambitious and, if possible, relative. Ideally, relative targets both connected inputs with outputs (e.g., cost per unit of production) and allowed performance comparisons with that of other like organizations (e.g., "above average in the industry"). For example, targets for the health, safety and environment measure of "serious incidence frequency" (SIF) commonly used in the exploration areas of the company were set relative to other like-entities within Statoil. Relative performance targets provided several advantages: there was no need to negotiate targets each year; managers set more ambitious targets for themselves because no one likes to be a laggard; and they motivated managers to be interested in learning from those who performed better on a relative basis.

Forecasts were designed to reflect expected outcomes, to provide early warnings of problems that might be occurring so that corrective actions could be taken if necessary. Statoil managers knew that there would always be noise in the forecasts, but they wanted the forecasts to be honest and unbiased. The forecasts were intended to reflect expected outcomes realistically, whether favorable or unfavorable. When visibility into the future was poor, the forecasts could include scenarios and ranges of outcomes.

The frequency, lead time and time horizon of the forecasts were intended to be driven by the business – not the calendar. In the first years of use of Ambition-to-Action, however, the process was more calendar-driven. Entities did strategic planning, KPI selection and target setting in the spring; action planning and forecasting in the fall, and performance evaluations at the end of the year.

Thus, starting in 2010 and 2011 respectively, Statoil changed the process to require use of *dynamic*

(or *event-based*) *forecasting and target setting*. Bjarte Bogsnes explained that, "An event is either something that happens around us or an action we take ourselves that has an effect that should be reflected in our targets and forecasts." Deciding when to update was a local manager decision. Forecasts were updated when an "event" happened or when important new information became available, but the time horizon was whatever local managers believed was relevant for their entity. Forecast updates were noted in a *forecast log* that was available for everyone to see in the MIS system. Strategic objectives, KPI selection, and target setting could be changed when necessary. However, major changes required approval one level up; minor changes were only reported as information. If changes affected other entities, the entity initiating the change was responsible for informing those entities. Changing targets did not happen frequently, but they were intended to happen at natural points in time instead of directed by the calendar. Performance evaluation still took place once a year as before, but against Ambition-to-Actions that varied from very stable to very dynamic.

As a result, Statoil's forecasts were approximately correct at all times, rather than being correct only at one fleeting point in time as is true in companies with a traditional annual planning and budgeting process. But since the targets were set to be ambitious and the forecasts were made to be realistic, it was common to have a gap between the two sets of numbers. This was seen as natural, as managers aimed high but had a realistic view of where they were.

Forecasts were not intended to be performance commitments, because targets had been set earlier. Cost forecasts were also not applications for resources for funds, as discussed next.

Allocations of resources at Statoil were not a mechanical function of either targets or forecasts. Managers had the freedom to commit resources up to limits defined by their scope of responsibility. The definition of a limit was however significantly redefined.

The problem with the conventional annual budget process was that it forced entities to decide on funding once a year, not only the total level but also the funding composition, which was not always the right time. Statoil did still allocate funds to projects or major decisions involving costs, but only when the project was ready for a decision.

Additional allocations were made dynamically, when the resources were needed, rather than far in advance as was typically done in a periodic budgeting process. Resources were "in principle" available whenever they were needed, if the project was good enough and if fresh forecasting information indicated sufficient capacity. "The bank is open year round," Bjarte Bogsnes exclaimed, "but you can still get a no on your request for money."

The intention with dynamic resource allocation was to cause a different managerial mindset. Instead of asking "Do I have the budget for this?" managers should ask whether spending the money was the right thing to do. Was it within their decision authority, could they justify the expenditure, was the spending necessary, and, last but not least, was the spending within the framework defined by Ambition-to-Action? This framework might include KPI targets like profit targets, unit cost targets or an overall absolute cost target. Some entities had no cost KPIs at all, instead addressing cost through strategic objectives or actions, combined with a continuous monitoring of their own actual spending development.

BUSINESS REVIEWS

Performance reviews provided a structured assessment of actual performance. The reviews focused on the Ambition-to-Action documents, which were produced monthly. Each document (examples are shown in Exhibits 2, 4, 5 and 6) provided a quick summary of recent performance. The circles to the right of each performance indicator and each action showed whether forecasted (not actual) performance was meeting targets or schedules. A circle with a plus sign (coded green) indicated yes; one with an exclamation point (colored yellow) was questionable; one with a minus sign (coded red) indicated no. The arrows to the right of the circles indicated if the last forecast update reflected a positive or negative trend since the last reporting period. This format created much more forward-looking business reviews.

The reviews typically started with an evaluation of KPIs and necessary action performance vs. targets. This was not as straightforward as it might first appear, as Geir Slora (Senior Vice President, Drilling & Well) explained:

> We can live with some red circles, as we look at the reasons for misses. Were there unforeseen problems? If the KPIs are all green, we get suspicious that the manager was too conservative in target setting. For example, one manager in the drilling business was able to show "all green" on his Ambition-to-Action because his cost targets were set in absolute terms. His entity was able to come in below the cost targets because they failed to do all the drilling that was expected for the period which, of course, was not good. At the end of the day, all we really want to see is whether the organization is headed in the right direction.

As a matter of fact, comparing the performances vs. targets was only a starting point. More important were the answers to the following five questions to "pressure test" the KPI results:

- *Did the KPI results contribute to the strategic objectives?* What were they unable to pick up? If we look beyond the KPI results, how would we evaluate performance?

- *How ambitious were the targets?* With hindsight, would we say that they were stretched?

- *Were there changes in assumptions that should be taken into account?* Were the results affected by a tail-wind or head-wind that had nothing to do with performance?

- *Were agreed-upon or necessary actions taken?*

- *Were the results sustainable?* Or had the managers made themselves look better in the short-run at the expense of the long-run?

Eldar Saetre, the CFO, said:

> Some uninformed observers might fear the prospect of cost anarchy. I disagree. Many businesses within Statoil have KPI targets on profitability and/or unit costs, benchmarked against peers where possible. Here, costs are managed by setting unit (rather than absolute) cost targets. Entity managers cannot spend wildly without a return or a good business case. In other areas we give overall guiding on acceptable cost levels. Across all businesses, we monitor cost trends carefully, at least monthly, and intervene at any time if a negative trend has no good explanation.

INDIVIDUAL PERFORMANCE EVALUATIONS

Individual performances evaluations were done holistically and with the advantage of hindsight. All Statoil employees had individual goals for both delivery (*what*) and behavior (*how*). Performance was judged 50% on delivery, as defined by Ambition-to-Action, and 50% on behavior and living up to Statoil values. Delivery performance was evaluated subjectively, taking into consideration relevant hindsight information. Statoil used 360-, 180- and 90-degree behavior evaluations plus a people survey and day-to-day observations to learn how managers and employees were living up to the company's values. Delivery and behavior evaluations were each scored on a 1–5 scale and weighted equally in determining salary increases and bonuses on top of the common bonus for everybody, which was linked to Statoil's financial performance vs. competitors.

Elder Saetre explained:

> We have broken the automatic link between fixed KPI targets, performance evaluation and bonuses, not just by introducing behavior as a key element, but also by broadening our definition of delivery. Delivery used to be solely defined by KPIs, but they seldom provide the whole picture. That is why you need a more holistic assessment. We now look at Ambition-to-Action as a whole and make qualified judgments with hindsight. It takes a few years for employees to understand how it works, but then it can be very credible.

IMPLEMENTATION

KPI-dominated scorecards were first introduced as a local initiative on one of the offshore platforms in the late nineties. Their popularity grew rapidly, both sideways and upwards in the organization, and by 2003 all of Statoil used them. Then the broader Ambition-to-Action process was introduced, emphasizing also strategic objectives and actions. In 2005 the company abolished traditional budgets, starting out with some pilots. The 2007 merger with Hydro, which added 10,000 people in new roles in a new organization, meant starting all over again in many entities. In 2010 the decision was taken to kick out the calendar.

Statoil managers did not wait until they had nailed down every detail. They designed the major features of the system and implemented it. They knew they were entering unfamiliar territory and did not believe that everything could be designed up front.

Some Statoil employees were worried about the change, as Bjarte Bogsnes recalled:

> The skeptical ones fall in two categories. Some are skeptical because they are confused. These just need time to learn and understand. But there will always be a group of hard-core skeptics that you cannot convince up front. Instead of arguing against them, tell them you accept that there is a risk that it will not work. But what is actually the risk if throwing out budgets fails? Most companies can go back to budgeting overnight. Nobody will have forgotten how to do it. So ask them to compare that minimal downside risk with the upside if it works as intended. That tends to calm people down.

By 2010, the Ambition-to-Action process was fully operational throughout Statoil. All of the major business units had implemented the process, and virtually all senior managers thought that it was a success. Exhibit 9 summarizes the major changes from the old command-and-control management style to the new more dynamic and flexible style.

Corporate managers did not impose the Ambition-to-Action process on any entity. They concluded that local managers needed to have the freedom to adapt the principles and practices of the process to fit their entity's needs, and they needed to find it useful themselves. If they did not, they would not use it anyway. Corporate managers needed to impose only enough structure to maintain a coherent vision and direction from the top to the bottom of the organization. They asked only that if the process was being used, all the documents be kept fully up-to-date at all times. They did try to communicate the purposes of the process and stood ready to train the managers to use it more effectively. They expected that as the managers became more comfortable with the system, its use was likely to increase and improve.

Even though all the major entities had chosen to implement Ambition-to-Action, not all implementations were equally effective. The quality of implementation at lower organization levels, particularly, was uneven because the levels of understanding, quality, and commitment varied considerably. Some managers used the process as it was designed, as a "leadership tool." But others used it merely as a "reporting tool," as a budget in disguise. Numerous problems were apparent. For example, some of the strategic objectives and KPIs were poorly chosen or defined or not changed often enough. Some performance standards were absolute when they could have been relative. Some KPIs and performance targets were dictated to subordinates by higher-level managers through cascading processes. Some important performance qualities, such as "capabilities and competencies" in an internal consulting entity, could not be measured effectively. Too many forecasts were only updated with a year-end horizon. Too many targets had end-of-December delivery dates.

THE FUTURE

It was inevitable that refinements to the process would be made over the years. The company was just beginning to incorporate risk heat maps into Ambition-to-Action. Bjarte Bogsnes thought that the system could become even more dynamic. In 2010, action planning, resource allocations, and forecasting were all done dynamically, and from 2011 setting the strategic objectives, determining the KPIs and KPI targets would also be event- and business-driven.

Looking forward Bjarte thought that, for example, performance evaluations might also be more closely linked to the completion of projects or activities.

He added:

I still have my dark days when I observe practices or behaviors reflecting what we wanted to leave behind. My medicine is, however, both simple and effective. I think back to how things were when we started out some years ago. If we can make similar progress in the coming years, we will have moved mountains.

Exhibit 1 Statoil: organization chart

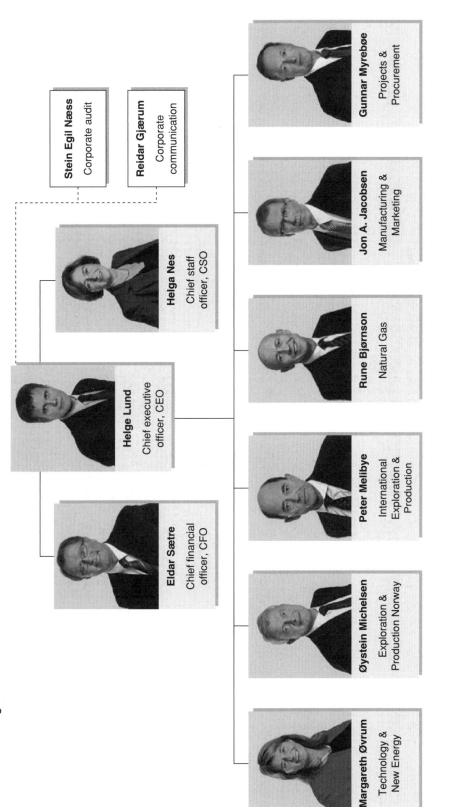

Stein Egil Næss
Corporate audit

Reidar Gjærum
Corporate communication

Helga Nes
Chief staff officer, CSO

Helge Lund
Chief executive officer, CEO

Eldar Sætre
Chief financial officer, CFO

Gunnar Myrebøe
Projects & Procurement

Jon A. Jacobsen
Manufacturing & Marketing

Rune Bjørnson
Natural Gas

Peter Mellbye
International Exploration & Production

Øystein Michelsen
Exploration & Production Norway

Margareth Øvrum
Technology & New Energy

EXHIBIT 2 Ambition-to-Action example – Statoil Corporation

Globally competitive – an exceptional place to perform and develop

Strategic objectives	Performance indicators	Actions (top 5)
People and organisation		
A values-based and performance driven organisation	Living the values	Ensure a strong position in talent markets (31.12.2010)
Secure compliance and learning	P@S process	Build a global organisation and common processes (31.12.2010)
		Accelerate people and leadership performance and development (31.12.2010)
		Continued focus on ethics and anti-corruption compliance (31.12.2010)
		Prepare for the Statoil 2011 organisation (20.12.2010)
Health, safety and environment		
Industry leader in HSE	Serious incident frequency	Ensure active use of HSE risk management in all activities at all levels (01.10.2010)
Industry leader in carbon efficiency	Climate	Improve technical integrity at our plants (11.01.2011)
	TTS Observations and actions	Secure a working environment promoting health and well-being (31.12.2010)
		Make climate ambition and strategy operational in the short, medium and long time frame (31.12.2010)
		Analyse and learn from GOM accident and recommend actions (01.03.2011)
Operation		
Operational and functional excellence	PE EPN	Deliver Peregrino and Leismer Demo as well as a road-map for oilsands (31.12.2010)
Apply technology to create value	Production oe Statoil Share	Ensure successful NCS integration process and value capture (31.12.2010)
High quality and cost efficient project development	Production cost (NOK/boe)	Implement actions to reach NCS Production / PE target (31.12.2010)
	Finding cost exploration (USD/boe)	Implement fast-track approach to develop NCS resources (31.12.2010)
		Mature and add value to GoM paleogene resource base (31.12.2010)
Market		
Exploration success among the best in the industry	New resources (equity, mmboe)	Actively secure petroleum business activities in Northern areas of the NCS (31.12.2010)
Maximise value creation through our value chains	Reserves to DG3 (equity, mmboe)	Create opportunities from exploration strategy (31.12.2010)
Secure competitive long term value creation	Downstream NOI (NOK bn)	Drive communication and stakeholder dialogue to strengthen reputation (31.12.2010)
		Mature Shah Deniz value chain (31.12.2010)
		Optimise value from gas flexibility and contract modernisation (31.12.2010)
Finance		
Competitive shareholder return and profitability	Relative RoACE	Actively manage cash position and balance sheet (15.12.2010)
Realise the full potential from the merger	Relative Shareholder Return	Drive overall cost performance according to targets (31.12.2010)
Retain financial robustness		Mature relevant inorganic and restructuring opportunities such as Peregrino, Marcellus and Shakespeare (31.12.2010)

Exhibit 3 Relative Statoil performance

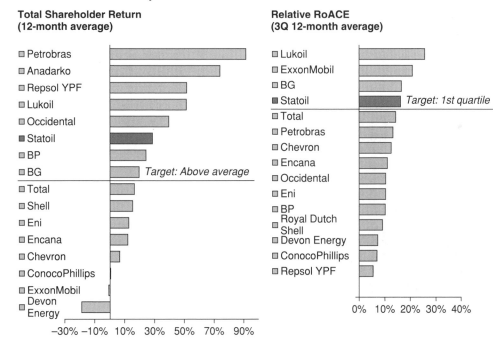

**Total Shareholder Return
(12-month average)**

**Relative RoACE
(3Q 12-month average)**

EXHIBIT 4 Ambition-to-Action example – Exploration & Production-Norway, Drilling & Well Organization (Level 3)

Professional delivery and innovation

Strategic objectives	Performance indicators	Actions (top 5)
People and organisation		
Competitive edge through a value based and performance driven culture	Indicator for safe and efficient operations	Actively use the P@S-process for development, deployment and reward (30.11.2010)
An efficient organisation with clear roles, responsibilities and best practice work processes	Manning on/offshore	Ensure alignment with the standardized operational model and secure safe, compliant and efficient operations (30.11.2010)
	People@Statoil process	Further develop a professional relationship with the unions and together ensure a good working environment (30.11.2010)
		Optimize organisational competence, capacity and flexibility (30.11.2010)
		Prioritize leadership- and leadership team development in EPN (10.12.2010)
Health, safety and environment		
Prevent unintentional discharges to sea and reduce the environmental impact of any environmental incidents	TRIF	Strengthen HSE culture, risk management and compliance (31.12.2010)
Secure a working environment that promotes well-being and good health	Accidental oil spills	Total risk assessment in D&W (30.09.2010)
Strengthen risk management in order to achieve an high HSE level	Accidental spills other	Verification of well control equipment (15.11.2010)
	Well control incidents	Ensure satisfying technical integrity of our facilities (31.12.2010)
	SIF	Risk management of safety issues focusing on prevention of incidents related to crane and lifting operations and Falling Objects (31.12.2010)
	Falling objects	
Operation		
Develop D&W to a competent supplier of drilling and well solutions by utilising our values and talents to the full potential	Production EPN – SØA	Assessment of 2011 – wells (15.10.2010)
	Rig availability	Business units to analyze the high level of downtime (30.09.2010)
	Ops(f) Total	Risk- and contingency planning with management involvement (30.05.2010) ✓
	Drilling Performance m/day	Performance management through measurement, daily/weekly target setting and accountability (A-standard) (30.09.2010)
	Intervention success	Defined customer–supplier relationships with mutual clarification of expectations (31.12.2010)
	Completion success	
Market		
Environmental relations: D&W will be presented as an efficient vendor of wells.	Number of new wells	Customer and supplier meetings (30.06.2010)
Reputation – develop a good reputation.		IOR potential – D&W proactive in idea development phase of AMAP (VC) (30.11.2010)
Finance		
More for less	Total cost ex rig rate per meter	D&W reduce total spending by 3 BNOK – BU's to propose concept (01.12.2010)
	Variance cost and time new wells	Initiate inventory project (01.10.2010)

EXHIBIT 5 Ambition-to-Action example – Projects & Procurement (Level 2)

Building for Tomorrow. Together.

Strategic objectives	Performance indicators	Actions (top 5)
People and organisation		
PRO Leadership implemented and demonstrated through a commercial mindset and culture	Deployment	Strategic workforce planning – operational people and competence strategy (30.06.2010)
A value-based and performance-driven organisation	GPS Living our values	Increase quality in project deployment (30.06.2010)
	P@S process	Evaluation of future manning needs and priorities (30.04.2010)
		Improve quality of P@S process, clarify and implement roles and responsibilities (30.12.2010)
		Increase quality of project teams (30.09.2010)
Health, safety and environment		
Industry Leader in HSE	Serious Incident Frequency	Improve work processes and establish standard A for HSE management in projects (01.12.2010)
PRO Leadership implemented and demonstrated through HSE top performance in operational line	SIF benchmark – projects	Secure a working environment promoting health and well-being (30.10.2010)
	TRIF benchmark – projects	Ensure active use of HSE risk management in all activities at all levels (01.12.2010)
		Implementation of revised HSE requirements in procurement (01.10.2010)
		Stimulate energy optimization prior to DG2/3 (01.10.2010)
Operation		
Implemented platform for compliance, standardisation and industrialisation	Estimate development	PEOPS (01.12.2010)
Successful completion of projects	Estimate Development Benchmark	Sheringham Shoal contingency plan (30.09.2010)
	Main milestones	Sheringham Shoal Schedule Risk Analysis (31.08.2010)
	Mitigating red risks	Frame agreements (01.06.2010)
	Progress benchmark	Top 10 risk register 2010 (15.12.2010)
Market		
Best value for Statoil in a global supplier market	Customer Satisfaction	Define expectations and content of PEOPS discussions in PRO MC (30.04.2010)
A professional and commercially oriented project provider		Establish a structured interaction between PRO and the customers (12/31/2010)
		Execute PEOPS improvement program (12/31/2010)
Finance		
Top 30% performer among peers within projects and procurement	Estimate development – early phase. DG2 → DG3	Enforce commercial mindset in PRO (01.03.2010)
	Procurement synergy impact PSR	
	Strategic rig capacity vs license committed capacity	
	Value Capture	

Exhibit 6 Ambition-to-Action example – Projects & Procurement, Sheringham Shoal (Level 4) (Offshore Wind)

Sheringham Shoal: Creating sustainable energy and shaping the future

Strategic objectives	Performance indicators		Actions (top 5)	
People and organisation				
A project organisation known for open, friendly and truthful communication	Work environment survey	⊕ ⇧	Execute self assessment of working environment within project team (31.12.2010)	⊕
Develop wind farm competence through project execution			Two teambuildings yearly (31.12.2011)	⊕
Health, safety and environment				
Zero harm to people and environment	SIF	● ↗	HSE Program and HSE Activity list (31.12.2011)	⊕
	Harmful discharge to sea	⊕ ⇧	Establish and follow up Authority plan (31.12.2011)	⊖
	TRIF	● ↘	HSE reviews and monitoring plan (31.12.2011)	⊕
		○ ⊖	Dropped objects campaign (31.12.2011)	⊕
			HSE training (VC) (01.03.2011)	⊕
Operation				
Pursuing opportunities, ensuring predictable results	Estimate Development	⊖ ⇧	Top 10 risk register (31.03.2012)	⊕
Combine Statoil's offshore experience with best practise from the wind industry	Main milestones	● ↗	Target cost actions (31.03.2012)	⊕
	Progress	○ ⊖		
Market				
Develop stakeholder relations	Claims from contractors	⊕ ⇧	Monitor interface register and avoid delay to agreed dates (31.12.2011)	⊕
Pursue cost reduction and optimisation opportunities	Timely consent approval	⊕ ⇧	Timely closing of Variation orders (31.12.2011)	●
Finance				
Build cost awareness throughout the entire value chain	SOX Compliance	⊕ ⇧	Execute SOX self assessment yearly (31.03.2012)	⊕

Exhibit 7 The 12 principles of beyond budgeting

Change in leadership	*Change in processes*
1. **Values** – Govern through a few clear values, goals, and boundaries, ***not*** *detailed rules and budgets.*	7. **Goals** – Set relative goals for continuous improvement, ***don't*** *negotiate fixed performance contracts.*
2. **Performance** – Create a high performance climate based on relative success, ***not*** *on meeting fixed targets.*	8. **Rewards** – Reward shared success based on relative performance, ***not*** *on meeting fixed targets.*
3. **Transparency** – Promote open information for self-management, ***don't*** *restrict it hierarchically.*	9. **Planning** – Make planning a continuous and inclusive process, ***not*** *a top-down annual event.*
4. **Organization** – Organize as a network of lean, accountable teams, ***not*** *around centralized functions.*	10. **Coordination** – Coordinate interactions dynamically, ***not*** *through annual planning cycles.*
5. **Autonomy** – Give teams the freedom and capability to act; ***don't*** *micro-manage them.*	11. **Resources** – Make resources available as needed, ***not*** *through annual budget allocations.*
6. **Customers** – Focus everyone on improving customer outcomes, ***not*** *on hierarchical relationships.*	12. **Controls** – Base controls on relative indicators and trends, ***not*** *on variances against plan.*

Exhibit 8 A pictorial representation of the Ambition-to-Action process

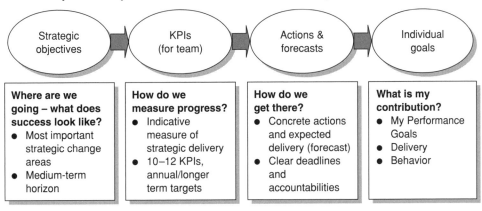

Strategic objectives	KPIs (for team)	Actions & forecasts	Individual goals
Where are we going – what does success look like? • Most important strategic change areas • Medium-term horizon	**How do we measure progress?** • Indicative measure of strategic delivery • 10–12 KPIs, annual/longer term targets	**How do we get there?** • Concrete actions and expected delivery (forecast) • Clear deadlines and accountabilities	**What is my contribution?** • My Performance Goals • Delivery • Behavior

Exhibit 9 Summary: "a *systematic* change of the *whole* process"

	"Annual command and control"	*More dynamic & flexible* *A new performance language*
Target setting	• Equal to plan – "what we can deliver" • KPI targets • Absolute targets	• Aspiration driven – "what we must deliver". Targets before plan • "Ambition-to-Action" • Relative targets

Planning	• Plan = target, forecast and resource
	  allocation
	• Gaps vs. targets hidden
	• One outcome only
	• Very detailed
		• Plan = forecast only (actions and *expected*
		  performance)
		• Gaps vs. targets visible
		• Main uncertainty spans
		• Less detailed

Resource allocation	• Annual pre-allocation through
	  budgets
	• Budgets "an entitlement – my money"
		• Resources available when needed, but
		  within KPI targets + mandates + decision
		  criteria. Monitoring of development

Business reporting	• Backward looking • Variance vs. YTD budget	• Forward looking • Forecast vs. targets, and actions to close gaps
Evaluation/rewards	• Only based on budgets and KPIs	• A broader evaluation: "Ambition to action" + Behavior

Chapter 12

USING FINANCIAL RESULTS CONTROLS IN THE PRESENCE OF UNCONTROLLABLE FACTORS

The effects of unpredictable, uncontrollable events have been ubiquitous following the 2008–09 financial and economic crisis where the business environment was fraught with financial instability and economic adversity. Add to that, for example, events like the closure of most of the airspace over Europe for several days in mid-April 2010 over concerns that ash from the Eyjafjallajökull volcano in Iceland could damage aircraft engines. This caused airplanes to remain grounded, thereby severely disrupting business not just for the airline industry, but also wreaking havoc for tourism, deliveries, supplies, and so on. And then, a few days later, there was the Macondo oil well blowout in the Gulf of Mexico, also known as the BP or Deepwater Horizon oil spill, and the temporary offshore drilling moratorium that was imposed because of it, which severely impacted not only BP, but also the entire oil industry and related sectors as the knock-on effects became apparent. And the list goes on. Business is rife with uncontrollables.

Against that backdrop, consider the following situation. The manager of a hi-tech subsidiary of a medium-sized publicly traded company was asked to grow annual sales and profit by 20% during the upcoming fiscal year. After the budget was prepared, however, a large client-company, which was projected to buy more than 15% of the subsidiary's total output, faced financial difficulty and later in the year went out of business. As a consequence, the subsidiary's actual performance was flat, and the subsidiary missed its budget target by a substantial margin. Almost everyone familiar with the situation agreed that, although bankruptcy is a common occurrence in fast-growing, hi-tech industries, it was virtually impossible to forecast at budget time that this customer would have gone out of business as quickly as it did. Considering this, should you expect the subsidiary manager to have had a contingency plan for such occurrences? Should the subsidiary manager be held accountable for not meeting the budget target? Would you forgive this subsidiary manager for the poor performance? Would that forgiveness include allowing the subsidiary manager to keep her job? Earn a nice salary increase? Collect a bonus?

If one adheres to the *controllability principle* in a strict sense, one would give the subsidiary manager in this situation all, or most, of the promised rewards. The results shortfall was not her fault. The controllability principle, which was introduced in Chapter 2, states that employees should be held accountable only for what they control. A measure is totally controllable by an employee if it is affected only by his or her actions or decisions. The logic behind the controllability principle is obvious: employees should not be penalized for bad luck. Neither should they be given rewards for mere good luck.

To implement the controllability principle, performance evaluators can reduce, and sometimes even eliminate, some of the distorting effects of uncontrollable factors on measured performance. This chapter discusses several ways in which this can be done.

Use of such distortion-reducing procedures is rarely unproblematic, however. Many important results measures, particularly at managerial levels in an organization, are only *partially* uncontrollable. Even though the measures are affected by occurrences outside the managers' control, such as supply shortages, changing cost factors, competitors' actions, or even business calamities, managers can take actions, to *react* to these factors to try to mitigate their impact on the results measures. If managers are protected against the uncontrollables, they might not be motivated to wield the influence they have. Moreover, even when it is clear that a given factor is largely uncontrollable, the extent of the distortion in the results measures because of it is often difficult to estimate. Combined then, organizations must determine both whether, and to what extent, they should adjust the results measures for the influence of uncontrollable factors.

Dealing with the effects of uncontrollable factors is also prone to misjudgments. Organizations sometimes fail to protect managers from the effects of uncontrollable factors when they should be protected; and sometimes they do protect them when they should not. Sometimes the protections that are provided are ill-conceived. If judgments about how to deal with uncontrollables are not made correctly, the advantages of results controls will be diminished, and potentially serious morale problems can arise from poor results-based performance evaluations.

This chapter discusses the problem of evaluating performance when measures are affected by uncontrollable factors. It presents the basic rationale for the controllability principle and describes the types of uncontrollable factors that can be faced. It then discusses the various methods organizations can use to implement the controllability principle and the applicability, advantages, and disadvantages of each of the methods.

THE CONTROLLABILITY PRINCIPLE

Several related arguments explain why employees should not be asked to bear uncontrollable business risks. Organizations that hold employees accountable for uncontrollable factors bear the costs of doing so because the vast majority of employees are *risk averse*; that is, employees prefer that their performance-contingent rewards stem directly from their efforts and not be affected by the vagaries of uncontrollables.

To illustrate risk aversion, assume the following two compensation contracts. The first provides a fixed salary of €100,000 per year. The second provides an opportunity to earn €200,000 if a performance target is met, and all involved agree that the likelihood of meeting the target is 50%. If the target is not achieved, however, there will be no compensation. The expected value of both contracts is €100,000, but most people will choose the fixed salary, the guarantee of €100,000. They do not want to bear the risk of earning nothing.

People's degrees of risk aversion vary with personal and various other characteristics. Although it is hard to generalize, sales and marketing personnel perhaps are, or are said to be, relatively more risk tolerant than are accounting and finance personnel, who are said or believed to be more prudent, and who are often selected into accounting, auditing, and control-related jobs because of that trait. For sales people, on the other hand, working on commission, rather than salary, may be some indicator of their relative risk tolerance. Personnel near retirement are sometimes believed to be more risk averse than are mid-career people who likely have greater career concerns. Employees at the start of their career, who still can recover from a job mishap if it were to happen, and who may not have any dependants to provide for and no mortgage payments or other major financial commitments yet, are more likely to be more risk tolerant or even risk seeking, depending on their personality and ambitions, as they can "afford" to be. So, too, can people at the other end of their career, who may have become independently wealthy through years of hard work and strong earnings power, although for them reputation concerns are still likely to affect their attitudes towards risk.

The extent of a person's risk aversion can be assessed by varying the parameters in the example above. For example, if the amount of the salary guarantee was lowered to €90,000, some relatively risk tolerant (less risk averse) people would be tempted enough by the higher expected value of compensation of the performance-contingent alternative offer (€100,000) that they would be willing to take the 50% risk of earning nothing. If the salary guarantee was lowered to €80,000, another group of people would be willing to take the risk. But the key point is that employees, on average, cannot be assumed to be risk neutral.

Risk aversion is the basis for the primary argument supporting the controllability principle. Firms that hold risk averse employees accountable for the effects of factors they cannot completely control will bear some costs of doing so. First, to compensate for the risk, firms will have to provide risk-bearing employees with a higher expected value of compensation. If they fail to do so, the firms will bear some costs in alternate forms, such as an inability to hire talented employees, a loss of motivation from their employees, and, probably eventually, turnover.

Second, firms holding employees accountable for uncontrollables will bear the costs of some employee behaviors designed to lower their exposure to uncontrollable factors, possibly at the expense of firm value. Employees may fail to develop or implement ideas for investments that are in the firm's best interest but that involve some risk. They may also engage in gameplaying behaviors, such as managing earnings or creating budgetary slack, to protect themselves against the effects of the uncontrollable factors.

Third, firms may bear the cost of lost time, as employees whose performances are evaluated in terms of measures that are distorted by uncontrollable influences are prone to develop excuses. They will spend time arguing about the extent of the distortions, at the expense of doing their jobs. The scheming, discussions, and "politicking" are not only unwelcome, they may trigger needless job-related stress and tension.

Essentially, then, business risks should be left with the business owners. Owners are better able to bear the risk as investors or because they have chosen to do so by virtue of being entrepreneurs. Unlike employees, owner-investors can diversify risk in their investment portfolios. Owner-entrepreneurs' rewards stem directly from the risk-bearing function they perform, and chose to perform, as their fortunes go up and down with the success or failure of the business.

TYPES OF UNCONTROLLABLE FACTORS

Before describing the methods managers can use to control for the distorting effects of uncontrollable factors, it is useful to categorize the types of factors that can be, to a greater or lesser extent, uncontrollable by management. They include (1) economic and competitive factors, (2) *force majeure*, and (3) interdependencies.

The first uncontrollable factor includes a broad range of *economic and competitive factors* that affect one or more results measures. One important results measure – profit – is affected by many factors that change: consumer demand, product/service prices, and/or the costs of doing business (factor costs). Among the factors that affect consumer demand and prices are business cycles, competitor actions, changing customer tastes, customer boycotts, changing laws and regulations, and foreign exchange rates. Among the factors that affect costs are the supply and demand of raw materials, labor and capital, foreign exchange rates, regulations, and taxes. Virtually every other results measure also can be affected by multiple, uncontrollable economic and competitive factors. For example, company stock prices are affected by market cycles, rumors, and investor tastes or even moods. On-time delivery measures can be adversely affected by supply shortages and changing customer demands. Customer satisfaction measures can be affected by, among other things, the quality of the products and services provided by competitors or the arrival of an online competitor with a quite different business model to provide essentially the same service.

Changes in economic and competitive factors are difficult for performance evaluators to deal with because while most of these factors appear to be uncontrollable, managers can, and should, usually make responses to these changes to positively influence the results measures. When raw material prices increase, managers can consider substituting alternate materials. When the cost of capital increases, they can consider delaying capital investments and reducing inventories. When exchange rates change, they can consider sourcing or selling in different countries. When customer tastes change, they can alter their product design or change their marketing strategy. Indeed, responses such as these are a key part of being a *manager*. As a consequence, most evaluators do not buffer managers from changes in economic and competitive factors, although they might take steps to have the organization share some of the risk with the managers, such as by corporate hedging to try to mitigate fluctuations in raw material prices.

A second type of uncontrollable factors includes *acts of nature*, *acts of God*, *acts of man*, or *acts of parliament*, all meant to indicate unpredictable and unreasonably severe events caused by natural or other forces over which employees have no control, also sometimes referred to as *forces majeures*. Such "major forces" are large, unexpected, one-off, totally uncontrollable events, such as hurricanes, earthquakes, floods, riots, terrorist attacks, key executive deaths, and, if they are not caused by negligence, fires, accidents, major installation breakdowns, thefts, and toxic torts. Even unexpectedly good or bad weather can cause problems for some businesses; such as for airlines and tourism. Most acts of nature involve negative surprises, but positive surprises sometimes also occur. For example, while hurricanes can destroy many businesses in their path, they create opportunities for other businesses, such as construction companies. And while severe weather can keep airplanes grounded at a cost of millions of dollars a day in lost business and subsequent damages, they boost hotel bookings in the airport's vicinity. Similarly, while airlines were grounded in April 2010 due to volcanic ash, P&O cross-Channel ferries and Eurostar trains were fully booked, and a group of business people paid a taxi driver £700 to take them from Belfast to London after they became stranded.[1]

Many organizations are inclined to protect employees from the downside risks caused by *force majeure*, but only if the events are deemed to be clearly uncontrollable and if steps are taken to motivate those responsible to recover from the adversity as expeditiously as possible. Controllability is sometimes an issue, as controversy can develop over the causes of fires, accidents, breakdowns, and thefts. Also potentially controversial is the extent to which a manager could have reduced exposure to these effects by purchasing insurance protection.

Even some of the most unprecedented, uncontrollable events, such as the 9/11 (September 11, 2001) terrorist attacks on the United States, needed an immediate response from management. Within days of the attacks, Boeing Company, the aerospace giant, scaled back production in its commercial airplanes unit, while planning for faster growth in defense-related units. Similarly, Bill Marriott, chairman and chief executive of Marriott

International, a large hotel group, made his first cost cutting decision on the afternoon of September 11 by canceling the firm's advertising based on the expectation that panicked customers were going to have fear of flying and would stay away from hotels in droves for at least several weeks.[2] Similarly, many companies are investing heavily to protect themselves from the effects of weather. Better forecasts and better scenario planning helped insurer Swiss Re to spread its risk better and FedEx to route its planes more robustly to deliver packages with minimal delays.[3] These examples illustrate clearly that managers must react when even mostly uncontrollable types of events happen. While the events themselves are uncontrollable, managers have influence over the effects that will be felt.

A third type of uncontrollable factor is caused by *interdependence*. Interdependence signifies that an entity is not completely self-contained, causing the measured results of the entity to be affected by other entities within the organization. Interdependencies can be pooled, sequential, or reciprocal.

Pooled interdependencies exist where a firm's entities use common resources or resource pools, such as shared staff or facilities (e.g. shared human resources support, shared research and development). Pooled interdependencies raise the question of whether managers should be put at risk for the poor performance of shared resource pools, such as corporate staff activities, on which they must rely. In many large firms, managers in the resource-dependent entities are protected from cost increases by the terms of an annual contract, negotiated during the annual planning process, which stipulates the services to be provided and their costs. The expected costs are impounded in a fixed allocation rate and unexpected rate increases cannot be passed on to internal customers until the next contract negotiation. But they are not necessarily protected from the poor performance of the shared activity.

Sequential interdependencies exist when the outputs of one entity are the inputs of another entity. Organizations that are high in sequential interdependence are vertically integrated firms, such as paper and steel companies. *Reciprocal interdependencies* are bi-directional sequential interdependencies. That is, organizational entities both produce outputs used by other entities and use inputs from them. Reciprocal interdependencies are high in some related-diversified firms. Most corporations deal with both sequential and reciprocal interdependencies by setting up internal *transfer pricing* systems that try to approximate the conditions found in external markets. These systems, which we discussed in Chapter 7, make these interdependencies act much like the economic and competitive uncontrollables described above, and evaluators then can deal with them in much the same way.

Another type of interdependency stems from *interventions from higher-level management*. Higher-level managers can force a decision on an entity manager and in so doing significantly affect a results measure linked to one or more forms of rewards. For example, corporate managers might order a division to sell to a particular customer at a money-losing price in return for other benefits that will accrue to other entities in the firm. Corporate managers can also affect results measures simply by not approving decisions initiated by an entity manager. They might not approve a proposed expenditure or a production schedule change. If these decisions are imposed on the entity managers, some organizations will make an adjustment for such arguably uncontrollable interventions. Others, however, argue that these interventions are not always totally uncontrollable. The entity managers might be involved in the discussions leading up to the decision and should, therefore, be held responsible for the effects of the negotiations and deliberations with their corporate superiors.

CONTROLLING FOR THE DISTORTING EFFECTS OF UNCONTROLLABLES

Managers can reduce (and sometimes even eliminate) some of the distorting effects of some of these uncontrollable factors by using either or both of two complementary approaches. *Before* the measurement period begins, they can define the results measures to include only those items that employees can control or at least significantly influence. *After* the measurement period has ended, they can calculate (or estimate) and adjust for the effects of any remaining uncontrollable factors using techniques such as variance analysis, flexible budgeting, relative performance evaluations, or subjective performance assessments.

Both of these methods of controlling for the effects of uncontrollable factors have costs. These costs must be balanced against the benefits of reducing the risks employees must bear. We discuss each of the methods of controlling for uncontrollables and their cost–benefit tradeoffs next.

Controlling for uncontrollables *before* the measurement period

Two primary methods can be employed to control for uncontrollables before the measurement period: purchasing insurance and design of responsibility structures.

Insurance

Many uncontrollable events, such as physical damage to company assets, employee-caused damage, product liability suits, employee errors and defalcations, riots, and vandalism, are insurable. A detailed discussion of insurance generally, and insurable events and insurance policies specifically, is outside the scope of this book. However, the key concept underlying insurance is that the company (the insured party) accepts a known relatively small "loss" (cost) in the form of a regular payment in exchange for being covered by the insurer for possibly large (although relatively unlikely) losses. Insurance might, therefore, be especially pertinent for what are sometimes called "low frequency–high impact" events. As such, the key benefit from purchasing insurance derives from a transfer of risk from the insured to the insurer. In addition to being able to transfer the risk of uncontrollable events at the cost of a predictable and contractually agreed regular payment, the company also benefits because it does not have to pay the employees a premium for bearing this risk.

Responsibility structures

The controllability principle underlies most of the logic guiding the design of responsibility structures. In Chapter 7, which focused on financial responsibility structures, we presented a key concept in the design of responsibility centers which is but a slight modification of the controllability principle: *hold employees accountable for the performance areas that management wants them to pay attention to.*

This general concept is widely applied. Organizations do not hold salespeople or production managers accountable for the results of corporate financing or major asset acquisition decisions. There is no need for these managers to pay attention to these decisions that are clearly outside their purview, and thus outside their control.

Performance reports often segregate controllable from uncontrollable items. As an illustration, Table 12.1 shows such a segregated performance report with four profit measures. A control system built on this report would hold this profit center manager

TABLE 12.1 Divisional income statement segregating controllable and noncontrollable items

	$
Sales	xxx
Less: variable costs	(xxx)
Sales margin	xxx
Less: controllable division expenses	(xxx)
Controllable profit	xxx
Less: noncontrollable division expenses	(xxx)
Less: allocations of central expenses	(xxx)
NET PROFIT	xxx

Source: K. A. Merchant, *Modern Management Control Systems: Text and Cases* (Upper Saddle River, NJ: Prentice Hall, 1998), p. 576.

responsible for *controllable profit*. Everything below the controllable profit line is deemed to be uncontrollable by that manager. In other words, companies thus aim to "match" an entity manager's *scope of decision authority* with the line-item for which they hold the entity manager accountable.

But are the items below the controllable profit line really uncontrollable? Maybe not entirely, thus raising the issue: When should managers be expected to pay attention to things over which they have less than complete control? In other words, can there be grounds for charging entity managers with the effects of corporate financing decisions or corporate research and development (R&D)? Assigning them the costs as a line-item on their entity's budget or profit-and-loss statement would, in effect, hold them accountable for that line item. If these managers are not involved in the corporate decisions regarding financing and R&D, say, and if there is no need for them to be aware of how much the corporation is spending on interest expense or R&D, then there is no need to assign them a share of those costs.

As an alternate example, should entity managers be assigned a share of corporate administrative (overhead) costs, such as those incurred in the corporate personnel and information systems departments? Here the answer may be yes. Charging these costs is likely to empower the entity managers to challenge the size of the costs or the quantity or quality of the services rendered in exchange for the costs. In other words, allocating these overhead costs to the entities will stimulate the entity managers to put pressure on corporate to control service costs and to provide a valuable, "competitive" service. These charges, however, violate the strict controllability principle, but they are consistent with the rule presented above; that is, to hold managers accountable for the performance areas you want them to pay attention to. You want them to exercise some *influence* even though they have less than direct control over these areas.

When employees are held accountable for many performance areas over which they have little influence, the organization will bear the increased costs of making employees bear the risk. At some point, these costs outweigh the benefits. As such, this approach is bounded by the limits of holding employees accountable for *too many* things over which they have *too little* influence.

Controlling for uncontrollables *after* the measurement period

Removing the distorting effects of uncontrollable factors from the results measures can also be attempted *after* the measurement period (but before the rewards are assigned). This can sometimes be done *objectively* (through numerical calculation) using variance analysis, flexible performance standards or relative performance evaluations. Alternatively, it can be done *subjectively* through exercising evaluator judgment. There are benefits and costs to each approach.

Variance analysis

A *variance analysis* is a systematic analysis designed to explain how and why two numbers are different. In MCS applications, variance analyses are used to explain why actual results are different from predetermined standards, budgets or expectations. They can help segregate controllable from uncontrollable variances and help explain who should be held accountable for the controllable variances, which may be either positive (favorable) or negative (unfavorable).

Variance analysis techniques as applied to manufacturing operations are described in great detail in every cost accounting textbook. To explain why actual manufacturing costs are different from standards, variance analysis segregates material, labor, and overhead cost variances, and then breaks each down into price, mix, yield, volume, and potentially other variance components. (Most cost accounting textbooks explain these variances, and the formulas for calculating them, in great detail.)[4] The variance analysis technique can be usefully applied to many settings other than production, however, as it essentially involves varying one performance factor at a time from expected to actual levels within a computational model to see what caused overall actual performance to be different from expected performance.

As an illustration, Table 12.2 shows how variance analysis can be applied to a sales territory in a foreign country. Assume that managers have determined that sales are largely dependent on four factors (industry volume, market share, price in local currency, and the currency exchange rate), and so they prepare a sales plan (a model) based on estimates of each of these factors. At the end of the measurement period, almost inevitably, actual sales will be different from the plan. An analysis such as that shown in Table 12.2 can then be developed to understand the bases of the sales variances.

The original sales plan is reflected in the left-hand column of Table 12.2, which shows the planned value for each of the key factors. The first analysis involves changing one of the factors from the planned to the actual value. Table 12.2 segregates the effect of industry volume first.[5] The difference between the sales plan and the amount shown in Analysis #1 is the *industry volume variance*. The second analysis changes a second factor, here market share, from the planned to the actual value, while holding the previously changed value (industry volume) at actual. This identifies a *market share variance*. This process continues for each of the remaining two factors, identifying a *sales price variance* and an *exchange rate variance*, respectively. The sum of the four variances will equal the

TABLE 12.2 Application of variance analysis to a marketing and sales setting

Sales plan	Analysis #1	Analysis #2	Analysis #3	Actual sales
Expected industry volume (IV$_P$)	IV$_A$	IV$_A$	IV$_A$	IV$_A$
Planned market share (MS$_P$)	MS$_P$	MS$_A$	MS$_A$	MS$_A$
Planned price (local currency) (PLC$_P$)	PLC$_P$	PLC$_P$	PLC$_A$	PLC$_A$
Planned foreign exchange rate (FX$_P$)	FX$_P$	FX$_P$	FX$_P$	FX$_A$
	Industry volume variance	Market share variance	Sales price variance	Exchange rate variance

$_P$ = planned.
$_A$ = actual.

Source: K. A. Merchant, *Modern Management Control Systems: Text and Cases* (Upper Saddle River, NJ: Prentice Hall, 1998), p. 578.

Figure 12.1 Illustrating the Table 12.2 example with a set of numbers

Assume:
IV_p = 1 million
IV_a = 1.4 million
MS_p = 10%
MS_a = 5%
PLC_p = 1.00
PLC_a = 1.10
FX_p = 1 home currency: 1 foreign currency
FX_a = 2 home currency: 1 foreign currency

Sales (in home currency)

Planned = 100,000
Actual = 154,000
Total Sales Variance = 54,000 favorable

Variances (in home currency)

Industry volume variance = 40,000 favorable
Market share variance = 70,000 unfavorable
Price variance = 7,000 favorable
Foreign exchange variance = 77,000 favorable

Source: K. A. Merchant, *Modern Management Control Systems: Text and Cases* (Upper Saddle River, NJ: Prentice Hall, 1998), p. 579.

total *sales variance* (the amount by which actual sales are different from the sales plan). This is illustrated with numbers in Figure 12.1.

Variance analyses such as these have two purposes. One is to segregate uncontrollable from controllable factors in explaining the difference between actual and planned results. In this example, the industry volume variance would probably be considered uncontrollable. The other purpose of variance analyses is to isolate certain controllable performance factors from others so that specific individuals (or groups of individuals) can be held accountable for them. In the above example, it is likely that the market share and price variances are deemed to fall within the responsibility of the marketing and sales department. However, further analyses might show that the accountability for these variances should be shared with other departments, such as engineering (product design) or production (production quality, schedule attainment). The exchange rate variance might be the responsibility of the corporate finance function if personnel in this department were charged with currency hedging. If not, this variance might be considered uncontrollable.

Flexible performance standards

Flexible performance standards, which we introduced in Chapter 8, can also be used to protect managers from the effects of uncontrollable factors. Flexible standards define the performance that employees are expected to achieve *given the actual conditions faced during the measurement period*. Flexible performance standards might be made to vary with any of a number of uncontrollable factors; for example, industry sales volumes, plant production volumes, or the levels of interest or exchange rates.

Flexible budgets, which are flexible performance standards expressed in financial terms, can be used when there is a dominant volume-of-activity indicator (e.g. production units or direct material usage) and when many of the costs are associated with this activity indicator. These requirements are not descriptive of many industries, however. Although costs in many firms vary with, say, direct material usage, and hence the cost of those materials, few production processes are dominantly dependent on any given material or input. Therefore, firms conventionally expect that managers will be able to manage or compensate unfavorable price movements for some materials against favorable price movements for some other materials, or, if that is not the case, they expect that managers will somehow be able to mitigate the adverse effects of unfavorable price movements. This probably explains why flexible budgets are relatively rarely used in practice.[6]

When environments are less predictable and managers wish to embed various assumptions about the future into their planning, they sometimes engage in what is called *contingency*, *scenario*, or *what-if* planning exercises. These exercises define how the company's resource requirements, risks, and performance will vary if macroeconomic and competitive conditions change. The Royal Dutch/Shell Group, the giant oil company, is long renowned for its contingency planning approach called *War Gaming*.[7] Shell managers prepare for the unexpected by developing strategies to safeguard the company against a broad range of possible risks defined in terms of scenarios. For example, two scenarios that Shell planned out to a 20-year horizon were called *Sustainable World* and *Global Mercantilism*. The first scenario assumed solutions were found to the major international economic disputes and thus greater attention was devoted to environmental issues, such as global warming trends, conservation, recycling, and emission controls. The major implication for Shell was an energy industry mix change towards more use of natural gas and less use of oil. The *Global Mercantilism* scenario assumed a gloomier future with numerous regional conflicts, a destabilized world, an increase in protectionism, and world recession. This scenario implied less focus on environmental issues and greater oil consumption.

Proponents of contingency planning maintain that it improves a company's ability to cope with (possibly radical) variations in key aspects that impact on the business, allows dealing with complex risk and control issues, and prepares to take pre-emptive action.[8] As such, scenario planning provides another way to apply flexible performance standards. At the beginning of the measurement period, managers prepare plans for each possible scenario in the future. Then managers are held accountable for achieving the plan associated with the scenario that actually unfolds.[9]

However, drawing up plans for a range of scenarios is not costless, particularly when done frequently, such as for annual budgeting purposes. Moreover, some events are just difficult to imagine as a plausible scenario. For example, even the managers at General Electric (GE), who have the reputation of being number-crunching and data-loving, found economic forecasts and historical antecedents like the Gulf War almost useless as they were trying to grapple with the uncertainty following the September 11 terrorist attacks on the United States. Mr. Immelt, then newly minted chairman and CEO at GE, commented that "In some ways, this event is so unprecedented that I'm as expert as anybody else."[10] That said, and perhaps due to recent events that had become nearly unthinkable in living memory, such as the bankruptcy of major banks, "People are trying to move beyond historic notions that tail risk events are so infrequent on the one hand, and so extreme on the other hand, that there is nothing you can do about them," said Eugene Ludwig, founder of the Washington-based risk management firm Promontory Financial Group.[11]

Another way to make performance standards more flexible is simply to update them more frequently. Any time a performance standard is set there is a chance that the assumptions underlying the preparation will prove to be inaccurate, rendering the standard obsolete. Obsolete standards subject managers to uncontrollable risks. Potential obsolescence is easy to see in a budgeting context. Budgets are prepared under the assumption of a given set of planning parameters, such as economic forecasts. The budget targets then remain fixed for the duration of the planning horizon (typically one year). The managers are at risk for all the *forecasting errors*; that is, they are asked to achieve their budget targets regardless of the conditions actually faced. To mitigate this, firms might evaluate managers' performances monthly or quarterly (rather than annually) and then prepare an updated, but hopefully more realistic, budget for the next month or quarter. *Rolling budgets* are an application of this approach, where there is a 12-month budget though it is updated each month or quarter and an additional budget month or quarter is added as each month or quarter passes. As such, the 12-month budget is "rolling" forward on a monthly or quarterly basis.

But updating standards more frequently is not a panacea either. One problem is cost. Updating standards can be time-consuming depending on how elaborate the budget preparation process is. Measuring results in short time periods creates some other potential problems. It is not always possible to determine in a short time period whether the results generated by some individuals, such as managers or research scientists, are good or bad. As such, the short time horizon may exacerbate the myopia problem, as we discussed in Chapter 11.

Relative performance evaluations

Another method of protecting employees from the distorting effects of uncontrollable factors is by way of *relative performance evaluations* (RPE). RPE means that employees' performances are evaluated not in terms of the absolute levels of the results they generate, but in terms of their results relative to each other or relative to those of their closest outside competitors. For RPE to be effective, all parties in the comparison or *peer group* must be performing roughly the same tasks and/or face roughly the same sets of opportunities and constraints. These conditions are sometimes met in companies with numerous comparable entities, such as in banks or fast food chains.

Consider a pizza parlor example. When at one time the price of mozzarella cheese rose sharply, the increase caused a profit squeeze at virtually all pizza parlors because cheese accounts for nearly half of a pizza's cost, and pizza prices are roughly fixed. As a spokesman for Domino's Pizza put it, "customers are accustomed to 'three-digit pricing' – people buy lots more pizza at $9.99 than at $10.99."[12] Consequently, profits at virtually all pizza parlors fell sharply over this period. If the evaluations of the managers of pizza outlets were based on their achievements vis-à-vis pre-established targets, such as budget targets not flexed with the change in cheese prices (as discussed above), then all the managers would be evaluated as poor performers. If those evaluations were linked to rewards, then, presumably, these managers' bonuses would be quite low, if not zero. But in this case, since all pizza outlets suffered the same uncontrollable shock, their performances can be compared relative to each other. As such, RPE would be an easy way for large pizza chains to adjust for the effects of this uncontrollable economic factor.

In most settings, however, good comparison groups do not exist, which may explain why RPE is not in widespread use, at least in a formal, objective sense. That said, the RPE *concept* often does influence subjective performance evaluations or justifications for target adjustments after-the-fact. Changes in targets with hindsight are often made with reference to *industry effects*.[13] In a loose sense, this is RPE where the comparison group is the company's relevant industry. It is not *formal* RPE, however, in the sense that targets were not RPE-based in the original plan but rather adjusted *after-the-fact* in an arguably *discretionary* way to reflect unforeseen industry changes. Which takes us to the next section.

Subjective performance evaluations

Many *subjective performance evaluations* take into consideration all the logic embodied in the objective methods of adjusting for uncontrollables. However, instead of making a formal, numerical calculation, the evaluator makes a judgment as to whether the results generated reflect good or bad performance. Proper subjective performance evaluations have undeniable advantages.[14] Most importantly, they can correct for flaws in the results measures. Results measures rarely reflect controllable performance completely and accurately, or in the words of compensation expert Edward Lawler:

> There are simply no hard, objective measures that would allow the [performance] appraisal to be based only on objective data. Thus, a judgment call is necessarily involved.[15]

Put differently, a rigid linking of evaluations to results measures inevitably implies penalizing employees for bad luck and rewarding them for good luck. When adding judgment, evaluators can use both the results measures and their knowledge of the situations faced by the employees to evaluate whether they performed well in any given period.

Subjectivity in evaluations creates its own problems, however. First, in applying judgment, subjective evaluations vest a source of power in superiors over their subordinates,[16] which may create tension and resentment. Second, subjective evaluations are likely to be biased.[17] One such bias is known as the *outcome effect*.[18] This effect is manifested, for example, when evaluators' performance evaluations are influenced by outcomes they know their evaluatees have little or no control over. An experimental study in this area, for example, documented how making results known to evaluators significantly influenced their performance evaluations even though the results measures were set up *not* to be informative of the individuals' performance.[19] Another possible bias is known as the *hindsight effect*. Hindsight-effect research shows that evaluators with knowledge of results tend to assume information about the pre-result circumstances that was not available to those being evaluated when they faced the circumstances. In other words, hindsight effects arise when an evaluator sees events that have occurred as being more controllable than they were when they took place; that is, the bias arises from inaccurate assessments of reality ex post facto.[20]

Thus, while subjectivity is intended to lower employees' reward-related risks, it can sometimes raise the risk of performance evaluations that are unfair, inconsistent, or biased. Third, subjectivity often leads to inadequate, or perhaps even no, feedback about how performance was evaluated. This lack of feedback inhibits learning and mitigates the motivation of the evaluatee to improve performance in subsequent periods. Fourth, even when the evaluations are fair, employees often do not understand or trust them. A mere perception of bias, whether accurate or not, can create morale and motivational problems. This is particularly salient when the evaluators *renege* on reward promises that were (presumably) made but not documented in writing.

Fifth, subjectivity often leads to creation of an *excuse culture*.[21] Humans seem to have an inherent trait that causes them to make excuses for poor performance. This trait has been studied under the rubric of a psychological theory called *attribution theory*, which maintains that individuals tend to attribute their success to their own efforts, abilities, skills, knowledge, or competence, while they attribute their failures to bad luck, task difficulty, or a variety of other environmental or situational factors at least partially out of their control. In other words, they tend to make excuses when things are not going well. In an excuse culture, instead of focusing on generating good results and being committed to achieving targets, employees spend considerable amounts of time making excuses and lobbying their evaluators for forgiveness of poor or mediocre results. They aim to beat the evaluation system rather than to work within it. These negotiation processes, as well as the appeal processes through which the employees often contest their performance evaluations, distract employees from the real tasks at hand.

Finally, and as a consequence of many of the issues raised above, if they are done well, subjective performance evaluations can be expensive, especially in terms of the time committed to them by both evaluators and evaluatees. Evaluators must often spend considerable time informing themselves about the circumstances their employees faced during the performance period. If performance targets were not reached, the evaluators must sift through considerable information that will enable them to separate the legitimate from the illegitimate excuses. If performance exceeded targets, they must search for evidence of good, but uncontrollable luck which might have accounted for the high performance. In this latter circumstance, they are unlikely to get much, if any, help from the employees being evaluated. And if the performance evaluations are rather negative, evaluators must be prepared for dealing with a fair dose of disgruntlement.

OTHER UNCONTROLLABLE FACTOR ISSUES

Organizations face other issues when considering adjustments for uncontrollables. One is the *purpose* for which the adjustments are made. Uncontrollables should not be treated identically for all reward purposes. Evaluators are likely to be forgiving when considering job retention decisions; rarely is an employee fired for being unlucky. However, evaluators are much less forgiving when considering compensation, particularly bonus, issues. If performance is down, organizations are less likely to have the financial resources to pay the additional compensation, so employees are asked to share the organization's burden.

A second issue is regarding the *direction* of the adjustments. Most evaluators seem to adjust for uncontrollables after the measurement period *asymmetrically*; that is, they make their adjustments in only one direction: to protect the employees from suffering from bad luck, but not to protect the owners (shareholders) from paying out undeserved rewards for good luck. The evaluators find it difficult to deny rewards, particularly bonuses, to employees when the organization has done well. Moreover, the managers face no pressure to make downward adjustments in rewards for good luck because the employees do not raise the issue, whilst the owners (shareholders) are probably not aware of the issue. Even if they are aware, they are already benefiting from the good performance. So who is to complain? But aside from the discomfort involved in "denying" employees rewards, no good reason exists as to why the adjustments should not be symmetric. Organizations should not have to reward employees for uncontrollable windfall gains. If employees cannot control the events, then the rewards provide no motivational benefits.

CONCLUSION

The controllability principle, holding employees accountable only for what they can control, seems so simple, yet implementing the principle is far from unproblematic. There are many complications. Most results measures are only partially uncontrollable and estimating the extent of uncontrollability is often less than an exact science. Moreover, organizations want employees to respond properly to many factors that influence the measures even if these factors are partially uncontrollable. In general, however, the controllability principle, or perhaps more accurately the *influenceability principle* – hold employees accountable for what they can sufficiently influence – provides good general guidance.

When decisions are made to protect employees from the effects of uncontrollables, each of the methods for doing so involves tradeoffs. If the adjustments are made after the performance period has ended, some of the advantages of having fixed, preset performance standards will be lost. Adjustments that involve subjective judgments can create bias and inconsistency. If complex procedures are implemented to deal with the many types of possible uncontrollable factors, simplicity is lost, raising the possibility that some employees will fail to understand what they are being asked to achieve. But regardless of the complexity, the stakes are high, as significant problems can arise if uncontrollables are not dealt with properly.

Notes

1. "Volcanic Ash Keeps Flights across Europe Grounded," *The Guardian* (April 17, 2010), online (www.guardian.co.uk).

2. "Uncertainty, Inc.: CEOs Find There is No Playbook for War and Ailing Economy," *The Wall Street Journal* (October 16, 2001), p. A1.

3. "Getting Ahead of the Weather," *Fortune* (February 7, 2005), pp. 87–94.

4. Variance analysis is covered in great detail in, for example, C. Horngren, S. Datar, G. Foster, M. Rajan, and C. Ittner, *Cost Accounting: A Managerial Emphasis*, 13th edn. (Prentice Hall, 2008).

5. The order in which the factors are analyzed is unimportant. The actual variance amounts will be slightly different because of the placement of what is referred to in many textbooks as the "joint variance." Regardless of the ordering, the total variance will be explained and the magnitude of each the variances will be indicative of the effect of that factor on the total.

6. See, for example, L. Serwen, "Solutions for Better Planning: What a National Survey Reveals," *Financial Executives Institute Research Foundation* (January 2002), pp. 17–18.

7. "Shell Gets Rich by Beating Risk," *Fortune* (August 26, 1991), pp. 79–82; "An Executive Risk Handbook," *Fortune* (October 3, 2005), pp. 69–70.

8. "Deloitte Acquires *Simulstrat* from King's College London to Bolster its Resilience and Testing Practice," *Deloitte* (March 1, 2010), online (www.deloitte.com).

9. W. Van der Stede and T. Palermo, "Scenario Budgeting: Integrating Risk and Performance," *Finance & Management*, no. 184 (January 2011), pp. 10–13.

10. "Uncertainty, Inc.," op. cit.

11. "Pimco Sells Black Swan Protection as Wall Street Markets Fear," *Bloomberg* (July 10, 2010), online (www.bloomberg.com).

12. "Pizza Chains in Cheese Squeeze," *The Los Angeles Times* (September 3, 2001), p. C4.

13. "Performance Bonus out of Reach? Move the Target," *The Wall Street Journal* (April 29, 2003), p. B1.

14. For an overview, see J. Bol, "Subjectivity in Compensation Contracting," *Journal of Accounting Literature*, 28 (2009), pp. 1–24; see also M. Gibbs, K. Merchant, W. Van der Stede, and M. Vargus, "Determinants and Effects of Subjectivity in Incentives," *The Accounting Review*, 79, no. 2 (April 2004), pp. 409–36.

15. E. E. Lawler, *Strategic Pay* (San Francisco, CA: Jossey-Bass, 1990), p. 90.

16. C. Prendergast, "A theory of 'Yes Men'," *American Economic Review*, 83, no. 4 (September 1993), pp. 757–70.

17. C. Prendergast and R. Topel, "Discretion and Bias in Performance Evaluation," *European Economic Review*, 37, nos. 2–3 (April 1993), pp. 355–65; F. Moers, "Discretion and Bias in Performance Evaluation: The Impact of Diversity and Subjectivity," *Accounting, Organizations and Society*, 30, no. 1 (January 2005), pp. 67–80.

18. D. Ghosh, "Alternative Measures of Managers' Performance, Controllability, and the Outcome Effect," *Behavioral Research in Accounting*, 17 (2005), pp. 55–70.

19. T. Mitchell and L. Kalb, "Effects of Outcome Knowledge and Outcome Valence on Supervisors' Evaluations," *Journal of Applied Psychology*, 66 (1981), pp. 604–12.

20. For a review of hindsight bias findings, see S. Hawkins and R. Hastie, "Hindsight: Biased Judgments of Past Events after the Outcomes Are Known," *Psychological Bulletin*, 107, no. 3 (May 1990), pp. 311–27.

21. C. Prendergast and R. Topel, "Favoritism in Organizations," *Journal of Political Economy*, 104 (1996), pp. 958–78; and P. Milgrom, "Employment Contracts, Influence Activities, and Efficient Organization Design," *Journal of Political Economy*, 96 (February 1988), pp. 42–60.

Olympic Car Wash

The Olympic Car Wash Company owned and operated 30 car washes in Belgium. The general managers of each of the 30 locations reported to Jacques Van Raemdonck, Olympic's chief operating officer.

At the end of each quarter, Jacques had to evaluate the performances of each of the car wash locations. His evaluations determined the size of a bonus pool that was allocated to personnel at the location. If the location achieved its budgeted profit target, €3,000 was put into the bonus pool. The pool was also augmented by €1 for every €10 the location exceeded its profit target.

However, the bonus contract gave Jacques the right to make subjective adjustments for the effects of factors he deemed outside the control of personnel at the location. In the past few years, Jacques had made such adjustments for the adverse effects on revenue of construction taking place on the street just in front of one car wash location and to cover the costs of vandalism at another location.

By far the largest uncontrollable factor that Jacques had to consider was, however, the weather. In particular, sales volume dropped sharply when it rained, and it rained frequently in Belgium. The budget, which was updated quarterly, was prepared based on an assumption of hours of good weather. Inevitably, though, those assumptions were not accurate.

During the Spring quarter 2002, it rained many more hours than were assumed in the company's budget, and actual profits for all of the locations were far below the budgeted profit level. The results for

TABLE 1 Profit vs. budget for Aalst location for spring 2002 quarter

	Budget	Actual	Variance
Revenue	€184,000	€124,080	€(59,920)
Variable expenses (50% of revenue)	92,000	62,040	29,960
Fixed expenses	53,820	55,000	(1,180)
Total expenses	145,820	117,040	28,780
Profit	38,180	7,040	(31,140)

TABLE 2 Operating statistics for Aalst location for spring 2002 quarter

	Budget assumption	Actual
Average number of vehicles washed in a good weather hour	23	24
Average revenue per vehicle	€10.00	€11.00
Total hours in quarter	920	920
Hours of bad weather	120	450
Hours of good weather	800	470

the Aalst location are shown in Table 1. Table 2 shows some operating assumptions and statistics for the quarter. The Aalst location is open every day, 10 hours per day when it is not raining. The car wash employees are paid the legally required minimum wage plus a fixed amount for each car wash completed, so labor costs are largely variable with revenues.

How large should the bonus pool be for the Aalst location?

This case was prepared by Professors Kenneth A. Merchant and Wim A. Van der Stede.

Case Study

Southern California Edison

In September 2003, John Cogan, director of compensation and benefits for Southern California Edison (SCE), reflected back on his company's administration of its incentive plans during the California energy crisis of 2000–01, which had brought SCE to the brink of bankruptcy.

> It was a difficult period. Our traditional financial measures of performance became meaningless. We were working the regulators, trying to get relief, doing the best we could. But we were operating in an era in which it was impossible to set goals, and we were losing money.
>
> As a public utility, we live under constant and intense public scrutiny. It is tough to pay bonuses in such a period. It's hard for the public to understand, and some parties are quick to scream out in protest. But we also had a need to retain our key people. Looking back, I think we did the best we could. We were balancing a number of considerations, and I think we did it quite well.

THE COMPANY

SCE, the major operating subsidiary of Edison International (NYSE: EIX), was one of the largest investor-owned electric utilities in the United States. Headquartered in Rosemead, California, the company served a 50,000 square mile area of central, coastal, and southern California. Included in this area were approximately 800 cities and communities and 12 million people. The company served 4.2 million business and residential customers. At December 31, SCE had consolidated assets of $18.2 billion and total shareholders equity of $4.4 billion. Annual revenues were in excess of $8 billion (see Exhibit 1). SCE had over 12,000 employees. The company was organized into 20 major operating and staff units.

SCE's history can be traced to 1886, but the company was incorporated with the SCE name in 1909 as a power generation and transmission company.

In the late 1990s SCE began to reduce its power generation activities. It still owned and operated two nuclear power generation units, 36 hydroelectric plants, two coal-fueled plants, and one diesel-fueled plant, as well as minority interests in several other power generation facilities. But as part of the restructuring of the electric industry in California in the late 1990s, SCE sold 12 other fossil fuel generating stations, and it was in the process of decommissioning its nuclear power facilities. The company purchased most of its power through the California Power Exchange and a variety of other utilities and independent power producers. SCE's main roles were becoming power transmission and distribution.

Between 1998 and 2003, SCE invested more than $3 billion in its transmission and distribution system, and company management expected to invest an additional $11 billion in electricity infrastructure replacement and improvement in the next decade. This upgrading of existing equipment was intended to accommodate the significant customer growth expected.

INCENTIVE PROGRAMS

SCE offered its employees several incentive programs. All permanent SCE employees except the top executive group, including all unionized employees, were included in a Results Sharing Program. Some levels of management participated in any of a variety of other plans, including a bonus plan, a stock option plan, and a performance share plan. These are described below.

A. Results sharing program

This program was designed to help focus employees on activities that have an impact – direct and

This case was prepared by Professors Kenneth A. Merchant and Wim A. Van der Stede. Financial support from the KPMG Foundation is gratefully acknowledged.

TABLE 1 Targeted results sharing payouts by employee category

Employee category	Target payout (%)	Maximum payout (%)
Nonexempt and unionized	4	6
Exempt employees	8	12
Nonexecutive managers	10–15	22–30

TABLE 2 SCE performance multiplier translation table (example)

Operating income vs. goal (%)	Payout multiplier
94	0.50
100	1.00
106	1.50

indirect – on the company's success and give them a stake in the achievement of company goals. Table 1 shows the targeted Results Sharing payouts as a percentage of base salary by employee category.

The Results Sharing payouts were determined by both business unit and SCE performance. The performance of the **business unit** to which the employee was assigned was measured in terms of the degree of accomplishment of a "balanced scorecard" comprised of goals in five areas. Performance on the financial dimension was always weighted 25% of the total. The key financial performance indicator was typically accomplishment of the budget for operating income excluding extraordinary items, but some subgoals, such as for specific income or expense line items, might also be identified. The other four goals were chosen and weighted by division management. Common measures were safety, service reliability, customer satisfaction, and specific key performance indicators such as program accomplishments.

The performance in each area was assessed in terms of whether the goal was achieved, or not. Thus, for example, if a business unit's safety goal was given a 20% importance weighting and the goal was not achieved, then personnel in that business unit would receive only a 0.80 business unit rating even if all of the other goals were achieved.

SCE performance was measured in terms of percent achievement of the annual operating income. This percentage was translated into a multiplier of the business unit award rating based on a translation table set annually. Table 2 shows an example of the type of translation table used.

The multiplier was interpolated for performance between these end points. Exhibit 2 shows a hypothetical example of a Results Sharing payout calculation.

B. Executive compensation programs

The executive compensation program at SCE was intended to: (1) attract and retain qualified employees, (2) motivate performance to achieve specific strategic objectives of the company, and (3) align the interests of senior management with the long-term interests of the company's shareholders and ratepayers. The program was designed for executives at vice-president levels and above, just over 30 individuals, but some lower-level managers participated in some elements of the program.

The program had three elements: base salaries, bonuses, and long-term incentives. The award levels for all three elements were targeted at median levels for comparable jobs among industry peers. For senior executives the peer group was comprised of comparable managers in 13 deregulated, diversified electric utilities.

Bonus payments were based on the basis of the achievement of both overall corporate and individual objectives. Target bonuses ranged from 30% of base salary for some subsidiary vice presidents to 80% of base salary for John Bryson (chairman, president/CEO). Maximum opportunity levels were set at 200% of target award levels. The bonus plan also allowed for the possibility of additional awards for "special recognition of accomplishment and for retention purposes."

For the top executive group, the long-term incentive awards were comprised 75% of 10-year nonqualified stock options and 25% performance shares. The goal of the long-term incentive awards was to link a significant portion of the executives' compensation directly to the value provided to shareholders. The long-term award amounts were not formula driven; i.e. based on performance.

Stock options, which were granted to executives, plus 300 other non-executive managers and individual contributions, expired 10 years after the date of the grant and vested over a period of up to five years. Some of the options included a dividend equivalent feature, but that feature was not used for awards after the year 1999. The weighted average fair value of options granted during 2000 and 2001 were $7.86 and $4.53 per share option, respectively.

The **performance shares** were awarded in different amounts to personnel at the various management levels based on SCE's total shareholder return (TSR) as compared to peer utility companies over a three-year period. Executives earned some performance shares if SCE's TSR was at least at the 40% percentile (from the bottom) on the ranked peer company list. At 60% they would earn their target award. If SCE was ranked on top, they would earn 300% of their target award.

The long-term incentive awards could be significant. Exhibit 3 shows a summary of the compensation given to top executives for the years 1998–2000.

THE CALIFORNIA ENERGY CRISIS

In September 1996, Pete Wilson, then-governor of California, signed a power deregulation plan into law. At the time, Wilson and many in the legislature viewed the electric utility industry as a monopoly taking advantage of consumers. The plan was designed to open up the state's electricity industry to competition, to provide increased customer choice, customer protection, and lower wholesale prices. The legislation deregulated the retail electricity market, effective in March 1998, for all but city-owned utilities.

The deregulated market operated fairly smoothly until May 2000, but then it collapsed. Fueled by increasing population and a strong economy, demand for electricity in California was growing by an average annual rate of 6%. Because of the high demand but no increases in supply – no new major power plants had been built in the prior 10-year period – supply became short. Power reserves dipped so low that the utilities had to implement rotating blackouts during the winters of 2000–01 to stabilize the power grid. Wholesale energy prices, which were now deregulated, rose dramatically. The imbalance between supply and demand was a major cause of the price increases, but evidence of manipulations of the California electricity market by power suppliers also came to light. Some companies allegedly created the false impression of congestion on power lines in the state when none existed; others withheld transportation of natural gas needed to fuel electricity

generators to exacerbate the supply problem; and still others reneged on contracts to supply emergency power in order to sell the power instead on the soaring spot market. The total effect of these market failures was that in 2000 California paid $28 billion for electricity, as compared to $7 billion in 1999. It paid another $26 billion for power in 2001.

Most of California's power utilities, including Southern California Edison, were squeezed. The rates they could charge to retail customers were fixed, but their costs were rising sharply. The state regulatory policy had forced them to sell most of their fossil fuel power plants, so they had to buy the needed electricity on the volatile spot market at rates that were soaring. In 2000, the utilities were buying electric power at costs that were, on average, five times higher than the rates they could charge their customers. The utilities appealed to the Federal Energy Regulatory Commission (FERC) and the California Public Utilities Commission (CPUC) for wholesale price controls and retail rate adjustments, but the relief was not immediately forthcoming.

The utilities had no choice but to borrow money to buy power. With their procurement debt exceeding $13 billion and their credit lines exhausted, SCE and PG&E, the large Bay Area power utility, suspended payments to creditors and suspended dividend payments for the first time in their histories.

In 2001, to keep the power flowing, the California legislature authorized the state Department of Water Resources to make purchases on behalf of utility customers. The state spent more than $8 billion on such purchases. To finance these purchases, the CPUC authorized two retail rate surcharges.

In the spring of 2001, frustrated with the progress of relief negotiations, PG&E declared Chapter 11 bankruptcy. SCE stayed out of bankruptcy but sought relief through the courts. The company filed suit seeking the authority to recover $3.6 billion dollars in uncollected power procurement costs. In October 2001, SCE and the CPUC announced an agreement that would allow the utility to increase its rates to generate the cash to pay off its creditors.

By early March 2002, the signs of recovery were evident. SCE credit ratings began to rise significantly. Its corporate credit rating rose from D to BB. The first quarter earnings of $8 million were well above the prior year, and the stock price was 73% higher than a year earlier. The power procurement-caused debt was repaid in full midway through 2003.

Since the 2000–01 crisis, the US Congress and California legislature have passed legislation to try to stabilize the electricity market. Among other things, these laws give the electric utilities long-term contracting authority to minimize their exposure to the spot market. They provide trigger mechanisms to ensure the timely recovery of electricity procurement costs. They ban some manipulative trading and marketing tactics and increase the penalties for violations. And they provide greater incentives for the development of new sources of power and the requisite transmission infrastructure.

ADMINISTRATION OF COMPENSATION SYSTEMS, 2000–02

The compensation and executive personnel committees of the board of directors concluded that the company had had an outstanding year in 1999, contributing above targeted profit levels and achieving nearly every performance objective. At the beginning of the year 2000, salaries for senior management were increased 8% over 1999 levels. After this increase, the committees concluded, the base salaries in the aggregate for the executive officers were 1% below the peer group median levels.

By the standards of the Results Sharing Program, company performance in 2000 was also excellent, even though 2000 marked the first year of the energy crisis. The payouts for 2000, however, were to be made in early 2001. By that time, SCE was teetering on the edge of bankruptcy. The board and management were reluctant to make the Results Sharing payments due, approximately $65 million, at the same time they were "screaming bankruptcy." Thus, they decided to delay the payments, citing the "uncertainty" to the employees. Then in May–June 2001, they decided to pay out only minimum amounts. No employee objections were heard because "everyone knew we were in deep trouble."

In January 2001, SCE management instituted a hiring freeze and pruned the workforce. John Cogan described this layoff of 700 people as "like trying to bail out the *Titanic* with a teacup." The CPUC actually asked SCE not to have a layoff because it would "threaten service reliability." As John Cogan noted, "The CPUC deliberations are influenced by the public. It is a political process."

The board committees approved no base pay increases for executives for 2001, and while they approved an average of 4% increases for lower-level employees, they delayed those increases by three–four months.

The committees decided not to pay executive bonuses for the year 2000. The following explanation appeared in the May 14, 2001, Annual Meeting Proxy Statement:

> The financial effects of the California energy crisis have overshadowed all other aspects of Company and individual performance. Notwithstanding the Companies' strong operating performance in many areas, the Committees determined that no bonuses will be paid to Executive Officers for 2000 under the annual incentive plan.

However, they did approve "special" bonus payments to two executives. The special recognition awards were made to two executive officers "in recognition of their significant contributions in 2000 to preserving the viability of Company during the financial crisis, and for retention purposes."

All of the long-term incentive awards that had been granted suffered dramatic decreases in value. The fall in the stock price (see Exhibit 4) destroyed all embedded value in outstanding stock options and, combined with the suspension of dividends, rendered the performance shares valueless.

In March 2001, the board committees changed the bonus plan into a retention incentive plan. These awards were not tied to performance because goals were seen to be "quite unclear." The payments were earned if an executive remained actively employed by SCE through the performance period. The retention incentives were set equal to target bonus levels (30–80% of base pay). For lower level executives, these awards were paid quarterly in cash. For more senior executives, the payments were in the form of 50% cash and 50% deferred stock units (DSUs). DSUs were convertible into shares of SCE stock after two years. At the most senior level, all of the awards were in the form of DSUs.

John Cogan explained why the link between performance and bonuses was severed:

> The financial measures of performance were meaningless. We knew we needed to keep the lights on, so our traditional operating goals (reliability, customer satisfaction, and safety) remained important, and our performance there remained excellent. But we were in a new world where cash flow was king, and the challenge was so enormous that we couldn't cost-cut our

way out of it. More important was creating a path to resolution via the political/regulatory process, rather than pursuing bankruptcy.

The first stock option grant in 2000 was made at $25 per share, but the stock price quickly fell from that level (see Exhibit 4). In May 2000, the board attempted to counter the drop in stock price by issuing a second option grant. (This is the May 18, 2000, grant, the results of which can be seen in Exhibit 5.) This grant pulled forward the grants that were to be made in 2001 and 2002. There were to have been no additional grants in those years. In addition, the compensation committees removed the TSR metric requirement from the grants of 2000 and 2001 performance shares, but they limited the size of the awards to target levels. But the stock price continued to fall.

In October 2001, SCE made a "stock option retention exchange offer" to personnel who had received option grants in 2001. Employees could turn in their options and receive DSUs equivalent in value to the Black-Scholes value of the option at the point of exchange, which was lower than the value at the grant date. These DSUs could be converted to shares of stock between 2002 and 2005.

In the year 2001, SCE's performance was not good. The company faced serious issues, such as the failure of a turbine in the San Onofre nuclear power plant and a significant unscheduled power outage in southern California. The company failed to achieve its financial targets. As a consequence, all incentive awards for 2001 were paid at minimum amounts. However, 2001 did mark the end of the crisis. SCE had greater clarity about the supplemental prices and payments the company was to receive. The company eventually received full relief totaling $3.6 billion, and a supplemental Results Sharing award was made making up 100% of the amounts employees lost in 2000.

The year 2002 was a good one, and incentive awards were expected to return to "good" levels. For example, in 2002 John Bryson earned $6 million in salary, bonus, stock, and other compensation, up from $2.7 the year before.

The political pressure related to incentives continued unabated. For example, Doug Heller of the Foundation of Taxpayer and Consumer Rights criticized the company's 2002 compensation payments

at a time when SCE customers were paying high rates to settle the debts from the crisis just ended. He was quoted as saying, "The executives at these companies, no matter how much they fail their consumers, they continue to pad their wallets."[1] Company management countered the charges by labeling the accusations "totally false." They cited comparable pay at peer companies, the company's stock performance, and a long list of managerial accomplishments, including strong earnings, leadership through the energy crisis, the favorable settlement with regulators, and a series of effective cost cutting and restructuring actions.

In July 2003, SCE reduced rates by an annualized $1.2 billion. The reductions ranged from 7.6% for some residential customers to as much as 25.7% for some big industrial power users.[2]

CONCLUSION

In reflecting back, John Cogan thought that the company managed its incentive plans quite well during the crisis. He did not think that company management could have done better in dealing with the extreme circumstances they faced:

You can't anticipate things like this. How do you prepare for tsunamis? But I think what we did was pretty rational, and the results speak for themselves – we suffered no key personnel losses. (I am sure this was partly due to the fact that the economy was so bad at the time.)

However, I can tell you that at the time it felt very uncomfortable. There was a lot of emotion. Many of our employees thought that this crisis was an attack on their families.

We knew when we were making these changes that we were going to receive some criticism from the public. When incentive systems don't pay out and you change the plan, there's the perception that you changed to get a payout, which feeds into the popular perception of executive greed. But as a business you need to retain the people you have to retain, so we did what we had to do.

---

[1] N. Rivera-Brooks, "Edison CEO's Total Pay Doubles," *The Los Angeles Times* (April 8, 2003).
[2] R. Smith, "Southern California Edison to Cut Utility Rates," *The Wall Street Journal* (July 11, 2003), p. B2.

Exhibit 1 Southern California Edison: consolidated statements of income (loss), for years ending December 31 ($ millions)

	2002	2001	2000	1999	1998
Operating revenue	**$8,706**	**$8,126**	**$7,870**	**$7,548**	**$7,500**
Fuel	243	212	195	215	324
Purchased power	2,016	3,770	4,687	3,190	3,262
Provisions for regulatory adjustment clauses – net	1,502	(3,028)	2,301	(763)	(472)
Other operation and maintenance	1,926	1,771	1,772	1,933	1,891
Depreciation, decommissioning and amortization	780	681	1,473	1,547	1,546
Property and other taxes	117	112	126	122	128
Net gain on sale of utility plant	(5)	(9)	(25)	(3)	(542)
Total operating expenses	6,579	3,509	10,529	6,242	6,136
Operating income (loss)	2,127	4,617	(2,659)	855	918
Interest and dividend income	262	215	173	69	67
Other nonoperating income	82	57	118	162	129
Interest expense – net of amounts capitalized	(584)	(785)	(572)	(483)	(485)
Other nonoperating deductions	2	(38)	(110)	(107)	(117)
Income (loss) before taxes	**1,889**	**4,066**	**(3,050)**	**973**	**964**
Income tax (benefit)	642	1,658	(1,022)	464	449
Net income (loss)	**1,247**	**2,408**	**(2,028)**	**509**	**515**
Dividends on preferred stock	19	22	22	26	25
Net income (loss) available for common stock	**$1,228**	**$2,386**	**$(2,050)**	**$484**	**$491**

Exhibit 2 Southern California Edison: hypothetical example of results sharing payout

1. Business unit award

	Weighting	Goal achieved?		Award
Financial	.25	Yes	.25	
Safety	.25	Yes	.25	
Reliability	.15	Yes	.15	
Customer satisfaction	.15	Yes	.15	
Key performance indicators	.20	No	—	
			.80	
Nonexempt and unionized	4%	times	.80	= 3.2%
Exempt employees	8%	times	.80	= 6.4%

2. SCE multiplier

Actual operating income = 104% of target
Interpolating on the payout chart = 1.33 multiplier

3. Results sharing payouts

	Business unit award	×	SCE multiplier	Results sharing award
Nonexempt and unionized employees	3.2%	×	1.33	= 4.3% (<6%)
Exempt employees	6.4%	×	1.33	= 8.5% (<12%)

Exhibit 3 Southern California Edison: summary of compensation given to top executive officers, 1998–2000

			Annual compensation			Long-term compensation awards		Payouts	
(a)	(b)	(c)	(d)	(e)	(f)	(g)	(h)	(i)
Name and principal position at December 31, 2000	Year	Salary ($)	Bonus ($)	Other annual compensation[1] ($)	Restricted stock ($)	Securities underlying options/SARs[2]	LTIP payouts ($)	All other compensation[3] ($)
John E. Bryson, Chairman of the Board, President and CEO of Edison International	2000	950,000	0	91,938[4]	–	1,273,600	–	579,115
	1999	900,000	1,260,000[6]	78,422	–	267,800	–	461,909
	1998	860,000	1,000,000	70,550	–	160,000	–	481,899
Stephen E. Frank, Chairman of the Board, President and CEO of SCE	2000	617,000	0	76,538[5]	–	321,600	–	65,831
	1999	593,000	711,600	1,114	–	117,700	–	49,793
	1998	565,000	559,400	1,109	–	69,600	–	61,255
Alan J. Fohrer, President and CEO of Edison Mission Energy	2000	477,000	0	49,797	–	497,800	–	57,342
	1999	397,000	486,000	–	–	83,100	–	39,310
	1998	367,000	393,800	–	–	44,700	–	60,810
Theodore F. Craver, Jr., Senior Vice President, CRO and Treasurer of Edison International	2000	375,000	100,000[6]	–	–	244,800	–	36,824
	1999	305,000	347,100	–	–	53,000	–	24,189
	1998	290,000	228,400	–	–	25,000	–	24,084
Bryant C. Danner, Executive Vice President and General Counsel of Edison International	2000	470,000	0	109,718[7]	–	483,100	–	61,361
	1999	435,000	534,000	84,187	–	83,100	–	44,328
	1998	415,000	433,500	77,935	–	44,700	–	70,530
Harold B. Ray, Executive Vice President of SCE	2000	390,000	50,000[6]	–	–	171,200	–	43,280
	1999	372,000	446,400	–	–	73,800	–	43,176
	1998	355,000	372,800	–	–	43,700	–	54,294
Robert G. Foster, Senior Vice President of Edison International and SCE	2000	322,500	0	–	–	171,200	–	55,595
	1999	284,000	242,800	–	–	73,800	–	48,363
	1998	270,000	194,400	–	–	43,700	–	57,231
John R. Fielder, Senior Vice President of SCE	2000	272,500	0	–	–	103,400	–	32,390
	1999	260,000	231,400	–	–	45,200	–	23,810
	1998	245,000	192,900	–	–	20,000	–	26,079
Richard M. Rosenblum, Senior Vice President of SCE	2000	265,000	0	–	–	102,500	–	21,721
	1999	250,000	197,500	–	–	43,400	–	15,997
	1998	230,000	175,950	–	–	20,000	–	269,581

[1] Includes perquisites if in total they exceed the lesser of $50,000 or 10% of annual salary and bonus, plus reimbursed taxes. Each perquisite exceeding 25% of the total is separately described in footnotes below.

[2] The awards shown in column (g) are Edison International nonqualified stock options for each Named Officer. SARS = stock appreciation rights.

[3] The amounts shown in column (i) for 2000 include contributions to the SSPP (pension plan) and a supplemental plan for eligible participants who are affected by SSPP participation limits imposed on higher paid individuals by federal tax law, preferential interest (that portion of interest that is considered under SEC rules to be at above-market rates) accrued on deferred compensation, vacation sale proceeds, Employee Stock Ownership Plan ("ESOP"), dividend incentives (the ESOP is a component of the SSPP), electric vehicle incentives, benefit forfeiture allocations and forgiven loans.

[4] Includes the following costs of providing Mr. Bryson's benefits: $33,149 under the Executive Survivor Benefit Plan and $22,076 for survivor benefits under the Executive Deferred Compensation Plan.

[5] Includes the following costs of providing Mr. Frank's benefits: $23,100 under the Executive Survivor Benefit Plan, $22,500 under the estate and Financial Planning Program, and $17,074 for survivor benefits under the Executive Deferred Compensation Plan.

[6] Although no bonuses were paid under the Executive Incentive Compensation Plan to Executive Officers for 2000 performance, Mr. Craver and Mr. Ray received special recognition awards in acknowledgement of their significant contributions in 2000 to preserving the viability of the Companies during the financial crisis, and for retention purposes.

[7] Includes $30,633, which is the cost of providing Mr. Danner's survivor benefits under the Executive Deferred Compensation Plan.

Source: Proxy Statement for May 14, 2001, Annual Meeting.

Exhibit 4 Southern California Edison: Edison International (EIX) stock price performance

1. Weekly close

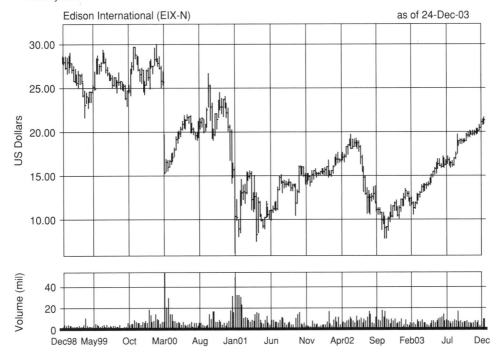

Edison International (EIX-N)   as of 24-Dec-03

2. Percent change vs. Dow-Jones utility average, 1999–2003

—— EIX Daily
—— DJUA

—— Volume   ©BigCharts.com

Exhibit 5 Southern California Edison: option/SAR grants to top executives in 2000

Name	Number of securities underlying options/SARs granted (#)[1]	% of total options/SARs granted to employees in 2000 (%)	Exercise or base price ($/share)	Expiration date[2]	Grant date present value ($)[3]
John E. Bryson	273,600[4]	2	$25.1875	01/04/2010	1,444,308
	1,000,000[5]	7	$20.0625	05/18/2010	5,820,000
Stephen E. Frank	106,600[4]	1	$25.1875	01/04/2010	562,848
	215,000[5]	2	$20.0625	05/18/2010	1,251,300
Alan J. Fohrer	83,100[4]	1	$25.1875	01/04/2010	438,768
	14,700[6]	<1	$27.1250	01/04/2010	84,231
	400,000[5]	3	$20.0625	05/18/2010	2,328,000
Theodore F. Craver, Jr.	43,900[4]	<1	$25.1875	01/04/2010	231,792
	20,900[6]	<1	$27.1250	01/04/2010	119,757
	180,000[5]	3	$20.0625	05/18/2010	1,047,600
Bryant C. Danner	83,100[4]	<1	$25.1875	01/04/2010	438,768
	400,000[5]	3	$20.0625	05/18/2010	2,328,000
Harold B. Ray	56,200[4]	<1	$25.1875	01/04/2010	296,736
	115,000[5]	1	$20.0625	05/18/2010	669,300
Robert G. Foster	38,900[4]	<1	$25.1875	01/04/2010	205,392
	90,000[5]	1	$20.0625	05/18/2010	523,800
John R. Fielder	33,400[4]	<1	$25.1875	01/04/2010	176,352
	70,000[5]	1	$20.0625	05/18/2010	407,400
Richard M. Rosenblum	32,500[4]	<1	$25.1875	01/04/2010	171,600
	70,000[5]	1	$20.0625	05/18/2010	407,400

[1] Edison International nonqualified stock options granted in 2000 may be exercised when vested to purchase one share of Edison International Common Stock. In January 2000, the annual Option Awards were made, and in May 2000, special Option Awards were made in lieu of the 2001 and 2002 annual Option Awards. Non dividend equivalents were included with these option grants.

[2] All Option Awards are subject to earlier expiration upon termination of employment as described in footnotes 4 and 5 below.

[3] The estimated grant data values are based on the Black-Scholes Model, a mathematical formula used to value options. The grant date value of each Edison International stock option for the January 3, 2000, Option Award was calculated to be $5.28 per option share with the following assumptions: a volatility rate of 23.48%, a risk-free rate of return of 5.58%, a dividend yield of 4.02%, a risk of forfeiture factor of 0.9039, and an exercise date of ten years after the date of the grant.

The value for the January 18, 2000, Option Award was calculated to be $5.73 per option share with the following assumptions: a volatility rate of 23.48%, a risk-free rate of return of 5.65%, a dividend yield of 4.02%, a risk of forfeiture factor of 0.9039, and an exercise date of 10 years after the date of the grant.

The value of the May 18, 2000, Option Award was calculated to be $5.82 per option share with the following assumptions: a volatility rate of 36.67%, a risk-free rate of return of 6.01%, a dividend yield of 4.21%, a risk of forfeiture factor of 0.9039, and an exercise date of 10 years after the date of the grant.

[4] The January 3, 2000, Option Awards are subject to a four-year vesting period with one fourth of the total award vesting and becoming exercisable annually beginning on January 2, 2001.

[5] The May 18, 2000, Option Awards are subject to a five-year vesting period with one fourth of the total award vesting and becoming exercisable annually beginning on May 18, 2002.

[6] The January 18, 2000, Option Awards granted an additional increment of Edison International stock options to Mr. Fohrer and Mr. Craver upon their elections as president and Chief Executive Officer of Edison Mission Energy and Chief Executive Officer of Edison Enterprises, respectively.

Source: Proxy Statement for May 14, 2001, Annual Meeting.

Beifang Chuang Ye Vehicle Group

On January 1, 1999 the municipal government of Beijing (People's Republic of China) mandated a new vehicle emission control standard. The new law, in essence, required all passenger vehicles sold within the Beijing city limits to be equipped with a fuel injection system, rather than an older carburetor system.[1]

This new law did not come as a surprise to the managers of Beifang Chuang Ye Vehicle Group, a large group of companies that included four automobile dealership locations in Beijing. They had become aware of the impending new law about a year earlier. However, like most other Beijing dealers and the manufacturers who supplied the vehicles, they did not believe that the Beijing government would actually enforce the new law. But it did! The government would not register any vehicles that did not meet the new, tighter emission standards. As a consequence, in early 1999 the Beifang dealers had no cars meeting the legal requirements to sell. In January 1999, their new car sales fell to zero.

Now, in early February 1999, Ming Zhou (vice director and general manager) had to decide, among other things, whether he should compensate his dealership managers and sales personnel as if this unfortunate external circumstance had not happened or whether they should be made to share the company's losses, and if so to what extent.

THE COMPANY

Beifang Chuang Ye Vehicle Group (Beifang) was a holding company comprised of 14 companies, most of which operated in segments of the transportation market in northern China. Among the Beifang companies were three taxi companies (operating 3,600 vehicles), a car rental company, an automobile association (with 160,000 members in northern China), an advertising company, a vehicle importer, three automobile dealerships, and an automobile repair company.

Beifang was formerly 100% owned by the Chinese central government, but the company was privatized. By the year 2000 the government owned only 10%. The other 90% was owned by private investors, the most prominent of which were members of Ming Zhou's family.

The three automobile dealerships were all 100% privately owned. The largest dealership company, Beijing Munitions Vehicle Trade Head Company (Beijing Munitions), sold and serviced four brands of vehicles, all of which were manufactured in China: Volkswagen, Citroën, Jeep, and Jin Bei. It maintained four locations in the greater Beijing area. Beijing Munitions had 90 employees. It also had indirect responsibility for the personnel servicing its customers' Citroën vehicles. However, the Citroën service personnel were formally considered employees of one of the car rental companies, which maintained a fleet of 2,000 Citroën vehicles.

The other two automobile dealership companies sold new cars only.[2] North Zhi Xing Car Trade Head Company, with 20 employees, sold imported cars (particularly Volkswagens and Audis) at one Beijing location. Qun Xing Car Lian Suo Dian, with 70 employees, sold domestic vehicle brands from locations in the Changan area in the northeast of China.

---

[1] A similar law was made effective across the entire People's Republic of China on September 1, 2001.

[2] Separation of the functions of new car sales, used car sales, and car servicing was still the norm in China, although some large dealerships, such as Beijing Munitions, were beginning to combine the activities. Still, even Beijing Munitions was not involved in used car sales or financing and insurance.

This case was prepared by Professors Thomas W. Lin, Kenneth A. Merchant, and Wim A. Van der Stede. They gratefully acknowledge funding support provided by the Center for International Business Education and Research at the Marshall School of Business, University of Southern California.

All of the dealership companies were organized by function. Beijing Munitions had a general manager and managers of sales, accessories, service, parts, marketing, and administration. The other two companies had fewer departments because they were just sales companies.

Net profit was the primary performance measure tracked within Beifang. Until 1999 all of the dealership companies were profitable. The dealerships were also all growing at healthy rates, 20% or more annually. Beifang managers predicted that the growth rate would increase significantly, particularly for imported brands of vehicles, if and when China was granted admission to the World Trade Organization.

EMPLOYEE COMPENSATION

In each of the car dealership companies, an incentive compensation pool was created based on the company's net profit performance, as shown in Table 1.

Taking money from this pool, the general manager of each company was expected to earn about 2% of the company's total net profit (8% of the total bonus pool) if the company just achieved its net profit target. He[3] would earn 1.5% of the profit if profit was positive but below target. And he would earn 4% of the profit if profits exceeded the target. The general managers decided how to allocate the remainder of the bonus pool to their subordinates.

The bonus potentials were a significant proportion of total compensation. The general managers' monthly base salaries ranged from 7,000–10,000 yuan.[4] In typical years their total monetary compensation ranged from 160,000–200,000 yuan. In the best year the highest paid general manager earned 360,000 yuan. The managers were also given some fringe benefits, including an apartment and a car.

The sales manager in Beijing Munitions earned a monthly base salary of 8,000 yuan, plus a car, which

is all he earned if net profit targets were not met. If the targets were met he would earn approximately 10,000 yuan per month.

The entire bonus pool would not necessarily be paid out immediately each month, however. Beifang and dealership company managers could, and typically did, reserve up to 3% of the pool both to provide lunar new year "bonuses," which were typically one month's base salary, and to smooth out the month-to-month and year-to-year fluctuations in incentive payments.

The net profit targets were set based on history and expected market changes. The target-setting processes started in early November with the submission of bottom-up budgets. The negotiation process culminated in an annual planning meeting held near the end of December. The targets could be, and typically were, revised each half-year. The monthly bonuses in the second half of the year were based on the revised targets.

DECISIONS TO BE MADE

In February 1999 Ming Zhou had to make a number of immediate decisions. He did not expect any cars to be available for sale until March at the earliest. The dealership companies were all losing money, and it was already obvious that they would not achieve their annual net profit plans. These losses were coming right out of Mr. Zhou's personal wealth, and that of his partners. Because Beifang was somewhat diversified, the company could stand to bear the losses in the dealerships for a short period of time. But should it?

Mr. Zhou had empathy for his employees. This problem was not their fault. They did not have great personal wealth, and most of them had families to support. Should he keep his employees on the payroll, prepare a revised plan, and then reward them if the revised plan was achieved? Should he keep them on the payroll but at a lower salary rate, perhaps even down to the government-mandated salary of approximately 500 yuan per month? Or should he lay off all or some off the employees until cars were available to be sold? If he did the latter he would still have to pay them the government-mandated unemployment rate of approximately 300 yuan per month, and he would risk the possibility that many of them would find alternative employment, as the Beijing economy was quite healthy.

TABLE 1 Calculation of bonus pool

Monthly net profit	Bonus pool share of total net profit
< 0	0
> 0 but < target	25%
> target	27%

---

[3] In all cases, the general managers were male.
[4] One yuan equals approximately US$0.12.

Case Study

Hoffman Discount Drugs, Inc.

In January 1996 a small fire broke out in the back-room of a drugstore in Downey, California owned and operated by Hoffman Discount Drugs, Inc. The fire department concluded that the fire was started by a fault in the store's electrical system. Luckily, the sprinkler system worked, and fire damage was held to a minimum. However, the water from the sprinklers damaged some of the inventory. Jane Firstenberg, the store's general manager, completed a Damage Report that described the situation and calculated the resulting losses. The losses were calculated as follows:

Total losses incurred
= value of inventory lost + cleaning expenses
+ payroll used in clean-up process

The losses incurred were not charged to their ordinary line item (for example, payroll). Instead they were charged to an account called *Noninsured Losses*. In this case the loss totalled $9,720.

Jane was discouraged when she saw the amount of the loss. If the loss had been greater than $10,000 a corporate adjustment would have been made to offset the effects of this *uncontrollable event* for net income bonus purposes. But since the loss was less than $10,000 no adjustment would be made. Jane commented:

This really hurts. My store is having a great year in sales, but our margins have been down. Now this. This loss might cause us not to achieve our net income objective for the year. We were right on the edge as it was. It takes a lot of sales to make up for a nearly $10,000 loss. I was looking forward to a nice bonus check. Even worse, if our bonuses are cut, I'm worried I may lose part of my management team. A couple of them have already been considering offers from competitors.

THE COMPANY

Hoffman Discount Drugs, Inc. (HDDI) was a large retail drug store chain that operated over 400 stores located throughout the western United States. It operated over 180 stores in the southwestern region that included southern California, Arizona, and Nevada. HDDI stores were typically located in large shopping centers that also included a supermarket chain store.

HDDI's recent performance had been mixed. For the last few years sales levels had been increasing and were currently the highest in the company's history. However, because of intense competition in the company's major markets, operating earnings were barely above breakeven. In late 1995 HDDI's president was fired, after only two years on the job, and Matt LeGeyt was appointed president.

Matt immediately started negotiating with several major insurance carriers to have HDDI be the sole distributor of prescriptions to individuals who hold policies with those carriers. By obtaining those prescription distribution rights Matt believed HDDI stores would benefit from increased customer traffic. But Matt believed HDDI's real key to success was to improve operations at the store level. He thought the company needed more effective local marketing, better customer service, and more efficient operations. He did not want to change the company's decentralized mode of operation, however. He believed it was potentially one of HDDI's advantages over its more centralized competitors.

STORE OPERATIONS

A typical large HDDI store carried $1 million of inventory, served nearly 800,000 customers per year, and generated annual sales of approximately $10 million ▶

This case was prepared by Professor Kenneth A. Merchant.

Copyright © by Kenneth A. Merchant.

and net income of $500,000. In computing net income all corporate expenses except interest and income taxes were traced or allocated to the stores. In addition the stores were charged a carrying cost on their inventory based on an annual approximation of the corporation's marginal cost of capital.

HDDI stores offered a wide range of products. The average percentage of total store sales was as follows:

Category	% of sales
General merchandise	64
Pharmacy	29
Liquor	7
Total	100

General merchandise items included health and beauty aids, detergent and soap products, baby supplies, greeting cards, toys, and seasonal items.

Many functions, such as purchasing, human resources, investor relations, and real estate, were centralized within HDDI, and inventory was shipped to the stores from one of three regional warehouses. Each store had the same basic look, and each store was required to carry a basic set of pharmacy-related inventory.

Other than these constraints, however, the stores were relatively autonomous. Store managers were allowed to adapt their merchandise offerings to their local market. So, stores located near the beach stocked many sun- and water-related items, such as sunscreen, beach towels, and boogie boards. Those located near retirement communities carried large stocks of age-related items, such as pain killers, laxatives, and blood pressure monitors. And those in neighborhoods dominated by upper-income professionals with young families carried large stocks of baby- and child-related products, as well as videocassette recorders, stereos, and cameras.

The store managers were also allowed to make decisions about local advertising. That is, they selected the amount and type of local advertising (newspaper, radio, and television), although newer managers typically asked for and received considerable guidance in this area from corporate specialists and their district managers. A typical large store spent nearly $400,000 per year on local advertising.

STORE MANAGEMENT BONUS PLAN

HDDI's policy was to pay store-level managers salaries that were slightly below market levels but to provide bonus opportunities that made the total compensation package competitive. The bonuses were intended to motivate the managers to work hard and to act in the company's best interests.

The HDDI Store Management Bonus Plan was based on achievement of predetermined objectives for sales and net income for each store.[1] These objectives were set in a *top-down* fashion. In a series of discussions that considered historical performance, demographic and competitive trends, and corporate initiatives, corporate and regional managers established sales and profit objectives for the corporation. They then broke these objectives down into objectives for the three regions. The regional managers, in consultation with the district managers, disaggregated the objectives into districts. And the district managers then had the responsibility to set objectives for the individual stores in their districts.

Because the company was constantly adding some new stores and improving some store locations the corporate, regional, and district objectives were usually increased, typically by an average of 4–7% annually. But the growth objectives for individual stores were generally more modest. Sometimes store objectives would even be lowered, as would be the case, for example, if the major supermarket store in the HDDI store's shopping center was closed.

The objectives for each store were disaggregated into monthly periods using historical seasonality patterns and, if necessary, some management judgment. Each month during the year store managers received reports comparing their store's sales, net income, and inventory performance with their objectives for the month and the year to date. Line-item detail was also provided for analysis purposes.

HDDI's fiscal year ended March 31. In early March, at the end of the company's annual planning process, each member of each store management team was presented with a Store Management Compensation Letter (see example in Exhibit 1). Managers had to signify receipt and understanding of this letter by signing a copy of the letter and returning it to the corporate Human Resources Department.

---

[1] The only other compensation plan offered to store- and lower-level employees was a stock purchase plan. Employees could have a portion of their check withheld for the purpose of purchasing stock. The stock was sold to the employees at the current market price, but the employees would not have to pay any commission fees on their purchases.

The Management Compensation Letters listed the individual's base salary, bonus objective, and total compensation objective. The bonus objectives were set as follows:

Role	Bonus objective (% base salary)
General manager	15–20
Assistant general manager	7–10
Assistant manager	3–5

The managers would earn their bonus objective if they exactly achieved their predetermined sales and net income objectives.

The bonus objective was broken down into a net income (before bonus) objective and a sales objective. Reflecting HDDI's belief in the importance of high profits, the net income objective was given three times the weight of the sales objective. That is, 75% of the bonus was based on achievement of net income objectives. The other 25% was based on achievement of sales objectives.

Exhibit 2 shows the description of the bonus plan as provided annually to participants. The bonus earned based on net income performance was calculated by adding/subtracting a percentage of the variance to/from the net income bonus objective according to the following formula:

$$B_N = O_N + A = O_N + (V \times S)$$

where:

B_N = bonus earned based on net income performance

O_N = net income objective

A = adjustment to net income bonus objective

V = net income variance = actual net income minus net income objective

S = sharing percentage (see the following).

The sharing percentage depended on the manager's level in the store, as follows: general manager (10%), assistant general manager (3%), assistant manager (1.5%). These percentages were set to reflect the different levels of responsibility associated with each job.

The effect of this net income bonus formula was that for every dollar of income the store earned above its predetermined objective, the general manager earned in bonus 10 cents more than his/her bonus objective. Conversely, for every dollar actual income

fell below the objective, the general manager earned 10 cents less than his/her bonus objective.

The sales portion of the bonus was based on the percent of annual sales objective achieved. The effect on the bonus objective was determined by using one of the charts shown at the bottom of Exhibit 2. The chart on the left was used if net income before bonus was above budget; the chart on the right was used if net income before bonus was below budget. These two charts differ only when sales exceed budget. If sales exceeded the objective but net income was below budget, then the managers' sales bonuses were set at lower limits.

Exhibit 3 shows a bonus calculation example.

Shortly after the midpoint of the appraisal period (that is, at the end of the 26th week of the year), HDDI gave each manager a bonus check equal to one half of the expected yearend bonus. This was done to provide the managers more timely reinforcement in hopes that they would stay focused throughout the entire year. This aspect of the plan seemed to work. Managers who received a large interim check were excited and were motivated to earn another large check at yearend. Those who received a small check were motivated to make up the difference in the second half of the year.

ADJUSTMENTS FOR UNCONTROLLABLE EVENTS

HDDI corporate managers reserved the right to make subjective adjustments to bonuses earned in case actual performance was distorted by uncontrollable events. They considered only three types of uncontrollable events: natural disasters (for example, fires, floods, earthquakes), robberies, and rioting and looting. In large (AAA classification) stores, adjustments were considered only if the damage resulting from the uncontrollable event exceeded $10,000. Events causing less than $10,000 damage were considered to be *immaterial*. Losses were considered only individually, not cumulatively, but in any case it was quite rare that an individual store would experience more than one or two uncontrollable events in a single year.

One example of an uncontrollable event was described in the introduction to this case. Here are three others:

1. In February 1996 heavy rains and a stopped-up sewer drain caused flooding around the HDDI store in Van Nuys, California. The store suffered approximately $8,000 in inventory damage as water came

into the stockroom, and clean-up expenses totalled $2,000 more. A more serious problem, however, was that a sinkhole developed in the major street artery in front of the store, and the street was closed for three days for repairs. The store manager argued that customers' difficulties in getting to the store caused sales for the month to be down more than $100,000, costing the store approximately $25,000 in net income. Corporate managers readily agreed to an adjustment for the inventory damage, but their opinions were mixed as to whether to make the adjustment for the *lost profits* because they thought the estimates were *soft*. However, they eventually did agree to an adjustment totalling $35,000.

2. In December 1995 an armed robbery occurred in a HDDI store in Glendale, Arizona. Since only $190 was stolen, no adjustment was made for bonus purposes.[2]

---

[2] The losses associated with robberies average between $100 and $200. Store managers are generally able to limit the amount of robbery losses by following the company policy of collecting money from the cash registers at regular intervals.

3. In the April 1993 riots in Los Angeles looters stole nearly $200,000 worth of merchandise from HDDI's Watts store and caused another $100,000 loss in structural damage to the building. Corporate managers awarded managers of this store their full bonus objectives as was their policy when stores suffered *heavy* damage.

MANAGEMENT CONCERNS

Matt LeGeyt, the new president, who believed the company's key to success was in improving store operations, had already expressed interest in having a thorough evaluation done of the Store Management Compensation Plan. When Jane Firstenberg complained to her superiors about unfairness of the situation described in the introduction to this case HDDI managers agreed to move this task up the agenda. The corporate Human Resources Department was asked to conduct a thorough analysis of the plan and to present its recommendations at the July management meeting.

Exhibit 1 Store management compensation letter

Ralph Williams　　　　　　　　　　　　　　　　　　　　　PERSONAL AND CONFIDENTIAL
General Manager
Store No. 142
Store Classification: AAA

The following pertains to your assignment for fiscal year 1996 as of 03/31/96

BASE PAY:	$44,400
BONUS OBJECTIVE:	$7,900
TOTAL COMPENSATION OBJECTIVE:	$52,300
THE PERFORMANCE RATING USED FOR PAY REVIEW PURPOSES WAS:	08

25% OF YOUR BONUS OBJECTIVE IS BASED ON STORE SALES AND 75% IS BASED ON BUDGETED NET INCOME BEFORE BONUS.

YOUR STORE IS CURRENTLY ON THE REGULAR PLAN (Refer to your 1996 Store Management Compensation Booklet for Plan details)

MINIMUM % OF BONUS OBJECTIVE PAYABLE:	0%
MAXIMUM % OF BONUS OBJECTIVE PAYABLE:	500%

The following information pertains to your Store Management assignments for fiscal 1996 to date and your most recent salary history:

				ANNUAL COMPENSATION OBJECTIVE			STORE	NIBB* BUDGET	
EFFECTIVE DATE	STORE	DIST	POSI.	BASE	BONUS OBJECTIVE	TOTAL	CLASSIFICATION	SALES BUDGET	PLAN
03/31/96	142	LO2	GM	44,400	7,900	52,300	AAA	872,777 10,700,143	REG.
02/03/95	142	LO2	GM	42,600	7,900	50,500	AAA	872,777 10,700,143	REG.

PRIOR COMPENSATION HISTORY:

02/04/95	142		GM	42,600	6,800	49,400
04/23/94	89		AGM	31,100	2,400	33,500
03/26/94	111		AGM	31,100	2,400	33,500
01/29/94	111		AGM	28,200	2,400	30,600
03/27/94	111		AGM	28,200	2,000	30,400
01/31/94	111		AGM	27,400	2,000	29,400
12/06/93	111		AGM	27,400	1,500	28,900
03/29/93	89		AM	26,000	1,000	27,000

These are the facts according to our records as of this date. Changes after this date will be sent to you in a separate carrier. No other considerations or adjustments will be made at any time unless stated and authorized in writing by the Regional Vice President of Operations.

If any of this information varies from what you understand your compensation plan to be, please contact your District Manager immediately for an explanation. Otherwise, please confirm your understanding of this information (including Appendix A, which is attached to your Store Management compensation letter, and the bonus payment table) by promptly signing one page of this letter and returning it to the Corporate Human Resources Department within two weeks.

I understand the compensation program explained above and have received a copy of Appendix A and understand the contents.

Signed: _____　　Date: _____

* net income before bonus

Exhibit 2 Net income/bonus function for regular plan

This plan is broken down into two pieces – NET INCOME BEFORE BONUS and SALES. The minimum payout is 0 and the maximum is 500% of your bonus objective for the combined pieces.

NET INCOME BEFORE BONUS (NIBB) PORTION OF BONUS OBJECTIVE:
  Bonus calculations are based on variance from budget. Your NIBB bonus objective will be adjusted by the amount of the variance multiplied by the sharing rates as follows:

GENERAL MANAGERS	+ or – 10.0% OF VARIANCE
ASSISTANT GENERAL MANAGERS & SENIOR MERCHANDISE ASSISTANTS	+ or – 3.0% OF VARIANCE
ASSISTANT MANAGERS, MERCHANDISE ASSISTANTS & SERVICE MANAGERS	+ or – 1.5% OF VARIANCE

SALES PORTION OF BONUS OBJECTIVE
  Bonus calculations are based on the percent of Sales budget achieved using the following charts:

If Net Income before Bonus is Above Budget:		If Net Income before Bonus is Below Budget:	
% of Sales Budget Achieved	% of Sales Objective Earned	% of Sales Budget Achieved	% of Sales Objective Earned
90.0	0.0%	90.0	0.0%
91.0	10.0	91.0	10.0
92.0	20.0	92.0	20.0
93.0	30.0	93.0	30.0
94.0	40.0	94.0	40.0
95.0	50.0	95.0	50.0
96.0	60.0	96.0	60.0
97.0	70.0	97.0	70.0
98.0	80.0	98.0	80.0
99.0	90.0	99.0	90.0
100.0	100.0	100.0	100.0
101.0	120.0	101.0	110.0
102.0	140.0	102.0	120.0
103.0	160.0	103.0	130.0
104.0	180.0	104.0	140.0
105.0	200.0	105.0	150.0
106.0	220.0	106.0	160.0
107.0	240.0	107.0	170.0
108.0	260.0	108.0	180.0
109.0	280.0	109.0	190.0
Max. 110.0	300.0	Max. 110.0	200.0

In the event a person transfers into a store, earnings are referred as the higher of the person's adjusted earnings after a transfer of the store's adjusted earnings.

DEDUCT 5% FROM THE PAYOUT ON SALES FOR EACH 1% STORE EARNINGS ARE BELOW 97%; DEDUCT 5% FROM THE PAYOUT ON STORE EARNINGS FOR EACH 1% ACTUAL SALES ARE BELOW 100%.

Exhibit 3 Bonus calculation example

Assume:

General manager

Base salary	$45,000	Bonus objective breakdown:	
Bonus objective	8,200	Net income	$6,150
Total compensation objective	$53,200	Sales	2,050

Net income portion of bonus:

actual 1995 net income	$995,041
− 1995 net income objective	758,936
variance	236,105
sharing percentage	10%
adjustment to NI bonus objective	$23,610.50

net income bonus objective + adjustment = net income bonus earned
$6,150 + 23,610.50 = $29,760.50

Sales portion of bonus:

actual 1995 sales	$9,642,910
1995 sales objective	9,304,473
actual % objective	103.6%

Since the store achieved its net income objective, use the left-side chart in Exhibit 2.
Interpolating on the chart, the percent objective earned is 172%.

sales bonus objective × percent objective earned = sales bonus earned
$2,050 × 172% = $3,526

Total compensation earned:

Base salary	$45,000.00
Net income bonus earned	29,760.50
Sales bonus earned	3,526.00
Total compensation	$78,286.50

Case Study

Formosa Plastics Group

For many years managers at Formosa Plastics Group (FPG) used a management control system with an element that was somewhat unique for a large corporation – all employees were evaluated subjectively. In making their judgments, evaluators looked at objective performance measures but subjectively made many adjustments for factors they deemed to be beyond the employee's control. One effect of this system was that bottom-line profit was not even considered in the evaluations of some profit center managers: these managers were evaluated only in terms of the controllable factors driving profit, such as meeting production schedules, efficiency, cost control, inventory control, and quality.

The FPG system seemed to work; the company had grown and thrived over the years. A sample of FPG managers who were interviewed in November 1991 were virtually unanimous in their praise of the company's control system. For example, Mr. C. T. Lee (senior vice president and general manager of the Plastics Division) said, "We are as close to perfect today as we can be. If we have good ideas, we implement them. We are continually refining our system."

COMPANY HISTORY, ORGANIZATION, AND STRATEGY

FPG was a diversified chemical company headquartered in Taipei, Taiwan (ROC). It produced and sold a broad range of products, including high density polyethylene (HDPE), chlorofluorocarbons, finished plastic products (e.g. shopping bags, garbage bags), intermediate raw materials for plastics production (e.g. polyvinyl chloride, caustic soda), carbon fiber, acrylic acids and esters, processed PVC products (e.g. flexible and rigid film, pipes, window frames), processed polyester products (e.g. polyester staple fiber, polyester chips, polyester preoriented yarn), electronic products (e.g. copper-clad laminate,

printed circuit boards), plasticizer, and textile products (e.g. rayon staple fiber, rayon and blended yarn and cloth, nylon tire cord yarn). It also ran a 6,000-bed hospital, a medical college (500 students), a nursing school (1,333 students), and a technical college (1,700 students).

Founded in 1954 with a capitalization of NT$5 million, FPG had grown over the years into the largest private company in Taiwan, with over 47,000 employees. Exhibit 1, which presents operating highlights for 1992, shows that 1992 revenues for the total FPG group exceeded US6.7 billion. Mr. Y. C. Wang (FPG's current chairman) still owned a significant portion of FPG's stock.

FPG management was projecting relatively difficult times in the early 1990s because of "the shortage of quality labor, rising wages, and the radicalization of the environmental movement." But the company had earned a profit for 30 consecutive years, even through some difficult periods, such as the 1973 oil embargo, which had a major negative effect on FPG and other petrochemical producers.

FPG was organized into three main corporations – Formosa Plastics, Nan Ya Plastics, and Formosa Chemicals & Fibre Corp. – and more than a dozen other affiliated companies located in Taiwan and abroad (notably the United States). The major corporations were composed of multiple divisions (see Exhibit 2), each responsible for one product line. The divisions, which were organized functionally, were reasonably autonomous; their managers were able to make their own plans and arrange all production and marketing aspects of their business within the scope of their approved authorizations. The division managers, who ranged in age from 40–60 years, were invariably career FPG employees (as were most other employees).

Many administrative functions, including engineering and construction management, technology

This case was prepared by Professor Kenneth A. Merchant with the assistance of Professor Anne Wu.

Copyright © by Kenneth A. Merchant.

(research and development), accounting, finance, procurement, data processing, legal, public relations, and personnel were centralized to take advantage of economies of scale. A unique feature of the corporate organization was a large (340-person) *president's office* comprising 15 *teams* of specialists whose function was to help division management. The president's office form of organization began when the corporation was small. The central staff personnel set up procedures, trained management, monitored performance, and facilitated the spreading of effective practices from one division to others. At times some of the central staff/division dealings had been confrontational; some division managers had referred to the staff as *the Red Guard*. But more recently, with increased management professionalization, the staff teams placed greater emphasis on cooperating with division management. They still ensured that the division's operating systems (e.g. accounting, procurement, construction, warehousing) conformed to corporate standards. But they allowed the divisions to operate with production systems that were different in virtually every plant, and they left division management alone if no significant negative performance variances existed.

Most of FPG's chemical divisions sold commodity products, so their strategy was to be the low cost producer in their market segment(s). It was important for them to produce at full capacity because most production costs were fixed; the only significant variable costs were for raw material and selling. On average, labor costs were only 20% of the total production cost, but since Taiwanese labor costs were rising along with the country's higher standard of living, FPG managers were constantly looking for ways to automate production processes to improve productivity. More than 80% of their products were exported.

FPG was making sizable investments to improve existing products, product quality, and production efficiency, and to prevent pollution. It was also increasing its investments to develop new products. Over the years, FPG had developed some new, lower volume, but higher value-added, products (e.g. carbon fiber), but these products still accounted for a very small proportion of total company sales. FPG employed 600 people in its central technology department, and its expenditures for new product development accounted for 3.6% of its total sales.

FINANCIAL CONTROL SYSTEM

Within FPG, companies and divisions were measured on a return-on-investment basis. The profit element of the ROI measure (the numerator) included allocations of all corporate expenses including interest, but profit was measured before taxes. The investment element of the ROI measure (the denominator) included only the investments that could be traced to the divisions (e.g. equipment, buildings, inventory, working capital). No corporate assets were allocated to the divisions. Within the divisions, plants and product groups were considered as profit centers; distinct production processes and group of machines were cost centers; and nonproduction-oriented units (e.g. sales, technology, management) were expense centers.

A key element of FPG's financial control system was a detailed cost accounting and reporting system. Standard costs were set for every aspect of manufacturing (e.g. labor, raw material, steam, packing, waste). The manufacturing processes tended to be stable, so the company had extensive historical records, and the cost standards were highly refined and accurate. Indirect costs were allocated to entities and products using a variety of allocation bases (e.g. number of people, production quantity). Where necessary, transfer prices for products sold internally were set either at market price less costs not incurred on internal transfers (e.g. selling costs, duties), or at full standard cost (less costs not incurred) plus a mark-up.

The cost standards were revised promptly when conditions warranted, and they were used to motivate continuous improvement. For example, if an investment project aimed at improving productivity was scheduled to be completed in July, the cost standards were changed in July. If the project was delayed or improvement was not as expected, the problem would show on an irregularities (variance) report. The company produced an extensive set of performance reports on a monthly basis (see Exhibit 3). These reports allowed management to attack problems quickly.

FPG's president monitored performance closely. Each month, he met with 30 senior managers (including division managers) in a detailed performance review meeting that typically lasted two to three hours. Every business was discussed at this meeting, and the president asked questions about sales, the competitive situation, future trends, and future products. About this meeting, one division manager said, "The president learns the details of our businesses. Sometimes we get new ideas from one or more of the managers at the meeting. Sometimes we get yelled at."

Performance-related bonus plans were also an important part of FPG's control system. All personnel in the company were included in one or more plans, and the plans were structured the same in all countries in which FPG operated. These were the major plans being used:

1. Year-end bonuses were given to everybody in the corporation based on the performance of the corporation. These bonuses were usually in the range of three–five months of base salary; the recent average was 4.2 months. About this plan, one corporate manager said, "This form of payment is typical in the Chinese culture. It is used by all companies in Taiwan. Most give a bonus of one or two months of *total compensation*, which is roughly equivalent to what we do, although we base the payments on *base salary*."

2. All people under section chief level (one level below a functional manager in a division) were included in a performance bonus program. Under this program their bonus was calculated based both on their position and the percentage of their performance targets reached. Staff and personnel in service departments were given either the same amount of bonus as these in direct departments or the average amount of bonuses given to direct departments. The purpose of this bonus program was to increase employee morale and efficiency. The bonuses awarded averaged approximately 20–26% of the employees' salaries.

3. All employees at section chief level and above were evaluated annually. A portion of these employees' salaries were reserved to create Management's Special Bonus Fund, which was used to award a special bonus immediately after the close of the year. The special bonus was calculated based both on the individual's performance and on the performance of the employee's corporation. Different bonus potentials were set for different levels of management, such as section chief, plant manager, and division manager.

4. FPG also provided incentive awards for employees, such as R&D staff, who generated good ideas that increased company value.

In all cases, top management decided subjectively the sizes of the awards and the bases on which to give the awards. The factors considered in making the performance evaluations and their relative weightings varied across roles and divisions. Among the performance-related factors considered in evaluating division managers were profit as compared to plan, production efficiency, quality, new product development, production quantity, production cost, and safety and environmental factors. Evaluators often also considered the person's ability and potential for the future, years in the company, teamwork, cooperation, and the situation faced. The evaluations were done subjectively because, as one manager explained, "Some factors are not easy to evaluate because it's hard to separate the controllable factors from the uncontrollable. It's certainly not easy to put all these items in a formula."

The total bonus amounts paid did not vary much over time. A corporate manager explained that:

> These (total) amounts are put in the budget at a fixed number and are not varied by the actual profit for the year. If the corporation earns a big profit, corporate managers take a portion of the bonus and reserve it for another year. If this year is no good and next year is no good, then maybe we will consider a lower bonus. It makes the situation more steady.

PERFORMANCE STANDARDS AND EVALUATIONS

One-year profit, revenue, and cost targets were set during a bottom-up planning process that started in September and ended in December.[1] The process began with division-level functional managers producing a sales plan and then a production plan. Labor cost parameters were sent to the divisions from corporate, and division managers were involved early in the planning process to make some key planning assumptions (e.g. selling price, key raw material costs). Generally every section in every plant was expected to reduce its costs every year (continuous improvement), which was not unreasonable because each was supported with improvement-project monies. The functional plans were reviewed and approved by division managers, the corporate accounting department, and corporate management.

---

[1] FPG managers did not use the word budget because "That is a term used by the government. It gives the impression that you will have less budget each year."

Corporate managers wanted the division targets to have an 80–90% probability of achievement. The divisions' first plan submission was rarely accepted because, as one corporate manager expressed it, "While the division managers understand their businesses better than does top management, they have a tendency to be very conservative about the figures." Thus in the review process top management generally asked the division managers to raise their profit targets. (Sometimes, however, typically in recessionary periods, they asked for the targets to be lowered.) Often the division managers had to revise their plans several times before top management approved them. However, even at the end of the discussions, the division managers did not always share corporate managers' perceptions of target achievability; for example, in 1991 one manager said he believed his chances of achieving his profit target were only 30–40%; he said, "The president squeezed very hard this year."

At the corporate level, the annual plans had proved to be quite accurate, with usually less than a 3% deviation between budgeted and actual expenses. If necessary, the performance targets could be revised during the year, monthly at the plant level and semiannually at division level.

Annually, the corporate accounting department performed a detailed analysis of each division's performance to understand where the profit came from and to know if the profit produced was reasonable given the circumstances faced. Among the items normally factored out as uncontrollable:

- Prices of products sold (in commodity product divisions only). In some divisions the market price was treated as controllable because the division managers set their products' prices.
- Raw material prices.
- Effects of raw material (e.g. oil, power) supply problems.
- Major problems deemed to be outside the manager's control (e.g. a fire caused by lightning).
- Expenditures approved by top management after the plan was finalized. A corporate manager explained, "If it's approved we don't care about the financial problems it causes to the budget. We want to encourage new ideas."

Because selling prices and raw material prices were considered uncontrollable in commodity product divisions, managers of these divisions were evaluated basically on quantity of product sold, product quality, consumption of materials, and production efficiency. This is well illustrated by describing the situation in 1991 in the Polyolefin Division.

1991 AT THE POLYOLEFIN DIVISION

The Polyolefin Division produced polyethylene, a commodity petrochemical used in a broad range of products, including plastic packing materials (e.g. shopping bags, bottles), rope, fishing nets, toys and athletic equipment. Because Taiwan's polyethylene import duty of 2.5% was the lowest in the world, the division had to compete, primarily on the basis of price, with competitors from all over the world and especially Korea. Division sales were not growing because the high density polyethylene output of the division was limited due to a shortage of ethylene supply from CPC, the only local ethylene supplier.

Ethylene was the only raw material used in polyethylene production, and it was *the* major cost item for the division, accounting for 60–65% of the total production cost. (Direct labor accounted for less than 3% of total production cost.) There was only one local ethylene supplier, CPC, a government corporation, and importing was difficult and expensive because ethylene had to be stored at high pressure and at $-104°C$. Freight for importing ethylene to Taiwan was approximately US$60–80 per ton from Japan or Korea, and approximately US$120 per ton from the United States. The Taiwanese government set ethylene prices at the average of the US and European prices. In 1991 FPG was paying ethylene prices that averaged 4–5% higher than US prices.

Ethylene caused the Polyolefin Division supply problems because a severe shortage existed in Taiwan. FPG had been trying for many years to secure permission to build its own ethylene plant, but the government had not given the permission because of worries about overcapacity. CPC (the government firm) was permitted to build another ethylene plant, but construction had been delayed because of environmental concerns, and FPG managers knew that a supply shortage would still exist even when this plant was completed.

Ethylene also caused financial planning problems because the Taiwanese ethylene prices fluctuated significantly, as is shown in Exhibits 4 and 5. Furthermore, the ethylene and polyethylene prices did not fluctuate together; both prices varied with market supply conditions. Lags of varying lengths existed before changes in ethylene prices were reflected in polyethylene prices. Thus division profits also fluctuated significantly.

Mr. Hsiao Chi-Hsiung, the division general manager, described his thinking in setting the plan for 1991:

> The Gulf War had just started when we began to pre-pare our plan, and we knew that would have a major effect on our business because ethylene is a petro-chemical. We had to assess how long the war would last and what it would do to our selling prices and our ethylene costs. We thought the Gulf War would not last very long, so we forecast that the average ethylene price would be around US$500 for the year. We concluded that our customers would worry about supply, so we forecast a higher selling price in January and then assumed a decrease. Starting this year, material from our Korean competitor should be very competitive.
>
> I did the work to forecast our selling prices and ethylene costs. We had to revise our production and sales plan several times according to the current market situation before we reported it to our top management for approval.

Mr. Hsiao knew, however, that he would also be evaluated in terms of each of the items on a list of controllable factors, not solely on achievement of the profit plan. He recalled that, "Sometimes we earn a nice profit, but it's not only from our endeavor. It's mainly influenced by the market prices." Mr. Hsiao could not explain exactly the bases on which his performance rating would be based, but he guessed they would be similar to the controllable factor list which he used to evaluate his plant manager:

- production efficiency (output/input);
- quality (proportion of output meeting customer specifications);
- unit consumption of important elements of cost (e.g. ethylene, solvents, labor[2]);
- cost of maintenance;
- leadership (including union relations, responses to employee suggestions, management of the monthly plant employee meeting, maintenance of hard work).

When pressed as to how these factors were weighted in relative importance, Mr. Hsiao said the first factor would be weighted about 40%, the second about 30%, and the other three about 30% in total. But he emphasized, "The weightings are not made very clear to anybody." It was clear to Mr. Hsiao, however, that achievement of his division's profit plan was certainly not the only factor on which he was evaluated.

---

[2] Labor was considered to be almost fixed in the short run, so controlling labor costs primarily meant controlling overtime.

Exhibit 1 1992 operating highlights (US$000s)

Company	Capital	Total assets	Operating revenue	Net income before tax	Profit ratio (%)	Return on capital (%)	Number of employees
Formosa Plastics Corp.	623,932	1,377,876	1,219,993	154,396	12.66	24.75	3,979
Nan Ya Plastics Corp.	701,437	1,931,335	2,512,532	229,114	9.12	32.66	14,803
Formosa Chemicals & Fibre Corp.	776,459	1,855,087	1,025,227	202,029	19.71	26.02	7,446
Others	1,914,697	6,207,220	1,955,440	163,265	8.35	8.53	21,093
Total	4,016,525	11,371,518	6,713,192	748,804	11.15	18.64	47,321

The operating revenue comparison (US$ millions)

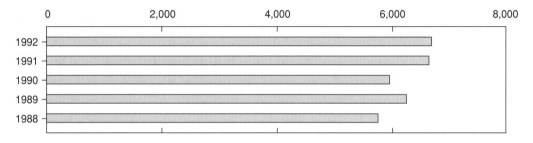

Exhibit 2 Formosa Plastics Group organization chart, 1991

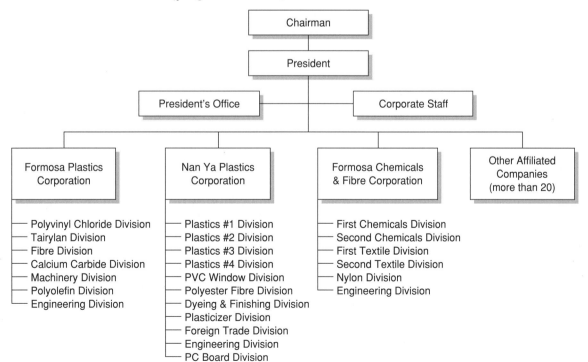

Exhibit 3 Operational performance reports

I. Financial Reports

FUNCTION	To show the complete operational conditions of a company and its divisions, including income statements, balance sheets, inventory reports, and labor costs reports.

CONTENT	1. Income Statement (corporate)
	2. Income Statements (by divisions)
	3. Balance Sheets (corporate and by divisions)
	4. Inventory Reports
	  (1) Raw Materials Report
	  (2) Supplies Report
	  (3) Work-in-Process Report
	  (4) Finished Goods Report
	  (5) Consigned-out Materials Report
	5. Labor Cost Reports
	  (1) Labor Costs Analysis Report
	  (2) Cooperative Administrative Expenses Report
	  (3) Comparative Selling Expenses Report
	6. Comparative Cash Flow Report

II. Income Statement/Cash Report by Plants

FUNCTION	1. Analyze the contents of variations between the actual and target incomes of each Profit Center. 2. Reports on the rate of achievement on efficiency and on the operational irregularities.
CONTENT	1. Income Statement by plants 2. Unit Cost Comparison Report 3. Fixed Manufacturing Cost Comparison Report 4. Selling/Adm./Fin. Expenses Allocation Report 5. Financial Expenses Calculation Report

III. Income Statements and Efficiency Variation Reports by Plant

FUNCTION	1. Analyze the contents of variations between the actual and target incomes of each Profit Center. 2. Reports on the rate of achievement on efficiency and on the operational irregularities.
CONTENT	1. Sum-up reports on income variations. 2. Analytical Reports on income variations. 3. Sum-up reports on efficiency evaluation of plants.

IV. Irregularities Report

FUNCTION	1. Listing of the efficiency items that have been achieved for three consecutive months for revision of targets. 2. Listing of the efficiency items which exceed the control standards for the analysts of the President's Office and Divisional Manager's Offices to investigate and follow up. 3. Listing of the cost items that exceed the control standards for the departments concerned to investigate and improve.
CONTENT	1. Efficiency Achievement Report 2. Efficiency Loss Report 3. Cost Variations Report

Exhibit 4 Sampling of ethylene prices in Taiwan

Year	Month	Price per ton ($US)
1990	November	781[1]
	July	494
	January	501
1989	July	678
	January	701
1988	July	612
	January	436

[1] Gulf War started.

Exhibit 5 1991 ethylene prices

Month	Price per ton (US$)
January	695
February	658
March	589
April	508
May	462
June	443
July	415
August	422
September	427
October	462

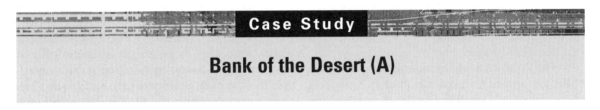

Case Study

Bank of the Desert (A)

In late 2001 Annette Lo, president of Branch Network of the retail banking division of Bank of the Desert (BoD), a large regional bank, was pondering the adequacy of the bank's branch performance measurement and evaluation system. Having the right performance indicators was important because BoD had an aggressive sales culture. Annette and her management team focused much of their attention on improving the performances of branches that were not achieving their growth targets. The performance evaluations were also important because they affected the assignments of annual bonuses for branch personnel.

Annette's discomfort with the bank's current system stemmed from several sources. She had heard grumbling from some of the branch managers, particularly about their performance targets. At least some of the branch managers did not understand how their targets were set, and those who thought that their targets were unfair were prone to complain about them. Annette had also heard claims that the bank's performance measures and evaluations, which were more sensitive to customer acquisition than to customer retention, had led to relatively high "customer churn" rates.

Annette discussed her concerns informally with Dave Phillips, a consultant friend. Dave said that it sounded to him like the system did have some significant weaknesses. BoD's performance measures both seemed to be incomplete and not to direct management attention to the areas with the greatest payoff potential. Annette decided that she should conduct a thorough review of the system.

THE COMPANY

Bank of the Desert, headquartered in Phoenix, Arizona, was a diversified financial services company that provided banking, insurance, investments, mortgage, and consumer finance services to customers located throughout the southwestern region of the United States. BoD competed in virtually every segment of the financial services industry and, in its regional market, it was among the market leaders in many. ▶

This case was prepared by Professors Kenneth A. Merchant, Wim A. Van der Stede, and research assistant Xiaoling (Clara) Chen.

Copyright © by Kenneth A. Merchant and Wim A. Van der Stede.

In 2001 BoD's size ranked it among the largest US banks. It had assets of approximately $30 billion and more than 10,000 employees.

BoD managers had observed the wave of consolidations in the banking industry, which were motivated to increase profits through greater economies of scale, but they were highly motivated to keep BoD independent. They believed that BoD could serve its customers best by remaining a smaller bank focused on the needs of the fast-growing Southwest region. To discourage potential acquirers so that they could remain independent BoD's managers knew that they needed to keep the company's stock price high. Thus, they set an aggressive 10% annual earnings-per-share growth rate target. BoD had not managed to meet this target each and every year, but it had reached the target over the long term: the bank's annualized growth rate since 1990 was 11.1%.

BoD's Retail Banking Division offered a full range of deposit, investment, loan and insurance products to consumers and small businesses in metropolitan and community markets. It served nearly 2 million households through the third largest retail banking network in the region, with approximately 250 branches and 2,700 automated teller machines (ATMs). Net income from retail banking exceeded $800 million in the year 2001. The division's mission was to satisfy all of its customers' financial needs and to help the customers succeed financially. The major components necessary to turn this vision into reality were all in place.

While some important decisions, such as regarding branch locations, product offerings, pricing, and promotions, were made at division headquarters, the day-to-day operations of the division were highly decentralized (see organization chart in Exhibit 1). Each of the regional presidents was responsible for approximately 50 branches, so the time they had available to help any one branch was limited. Thus, personnel in the branches were responsible for identifying their own customers and satisfying those customers' needs for financial services. Division-level staff provided some product training, marketing, and financial analysis support.

PERFORMANCE MEASURES AND INCENTIVES

For managers at the top of the retail division's management hierarchy, from the division president

down to the regional presidents, the performance measurement and incentive system focused on financial performance, in particular *growth in profits*. As mentioned above, BoD's profit growth target was 10% per year. During BoD's annual planning and budgeting process this overall target was disaggregated into targets for the branch network and each region. Given the importance of the branch network to BoD's total profits, the division and branch network annual profit goals were typically very close to 10%. In recent years the profit growth goals for the *regions* had varied, however, from 7% to 13% depending, particularly, on each region's economic prospects and the number of new branches that would be opened in that region.

Although BoD produced an extensive set of profit reports down to the level of individual branches, product types (e.g. demand deposits), and customers, profits were seen to be largely uncontrollable at the branch and lower organization levels. Branch profits were highly affected by interest rates. The branch managers also had little or no control over many of the revenue and expense items on the branch income statements. For example, the branch managers had no control over decisions regarding product offerings, prices, or facility leasing costs. Division-level managers even set branch staffing levels, which they did based on volumes of transaction activity.

What the branch managers could control, however, was the management of their employees for the purpose of generating bank revenues. Thus BoD's branch incentive compensation system focused on what were perceived to be the two most important, controllable profit drivers at the branch level. Both were revenue-focused. The first measure included in the incentive system was the *number of product sales*, scaled by the number of full-time-equivalent employees (FTE) in the branch to make the measure comparable across branches of different size. Product sales included both sales to new customers and new accounts opened by current customers. The measure was *number* of sales, rather than the profitability of the sale, because the profits of any given sale to the bank could vary significantly, for example depending on how much customers eventually deposited in an account or how long they kept the account open. But new sales were very important to the branch because they could provide a stream of profits to the bank that could last many years.

The second measure included in the incentive plan was the *cross sell/total retail accounts ratio*. "Cross sell" was defined as the proportion of customers who purchased products in more than one product category (e.g. loans, deposit accounts, mortgages, credit cards) per customer. The cross sell ratio was seen as a useful indicator of the effectiveness of the branches' marketing and sales efforts.

All performances within the division were evaluated by comparing actual results relative to targets set during the annual planning process. The goal setting process was primarily top-down. In September of each year BoD's corporate-level managers sent preliminary global profit targets to division managers. These preliminary targets were designed to ensure that the bank achieved its minimum 10% annual profit growth rate. Division-level staff then set preliminary goals for each region and branch, primarily by extrapolating trends in the branches' past performances. These preliminary goals were consolidated, reconciled with

the bank's target for the division, and presented to the top management team. Top management made adjustments based on their knowledge of market trends and promotion and investment plans for the year. Then the goals were presented to the branch managers, whose inputs led to a final round of negotiations.

At the end of the year, bonuses were paid to branch personnel based on their percent achievement of targets for the number of product sales per FTE (weighted 75%) and cross sell/total retail accounts ratio (weighted 25%). The number of product sales measure was given a higher weight because it was seen to be a more important driver of total profits. No bonuses were paid on performance dimensions where performance was below target. Personnel whose branches exactly achieved their targets would earn bonuses ranging from 10–50% of base salary. If performances exceeded targets by 50% or more, personnel could be paid bonuses of up to twice the target bonus levels.

Exhibit 1 Bank of the Desert organization chart – Retail Banking Division

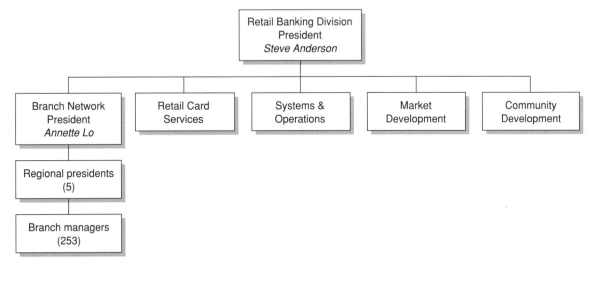

Bank of the Desert (B)

In October 2001 Annette decided to hire a management consulting firm to evaluate BoD's system of branch performance measures and evaluations. Dave Phillips, an experienced partner, was the lead consultant on the job. At the end of a four-month examination period Dave's consulting team presented its preliminary findings.

The consultants' findings startled Annette and her management team. Among other things, the consultants presented a list of the "10 branches with the largest improvement opportunities." Surprisingly, that list included several branches that the BoD management team thought were among its best performers. The manager of one of these branches had even been recently singled out for promotion.

Annette knew that the consultants' findings would have to be studied very carefully. If they were correct, major changes would probably have to be made to the bank's performance measurement and evaluation system.

PERFORMANCE STANDARDS

One of the consulting team's recommendations was that each branch's performance should be compared with what they called its *market opportunity potentials*, rather than with budget targets that were primarily extrapolations from the past. The consultants argued that large performance increases relative to past performance might only indicate low starting points. Market opportunity potentials, instead, would reflect the level of performance that each branch should reasonably be able to reach given its size, location, and operating conditions.

But how should those potentials be measured? BoD's branches were quite diverse. They operated in many different locales, some urban, some suburban, and some in small towns. Some of the branches were located in affluent communities, and some were located in poor communities. Some were old, established branches, and some were newly opened. And some had served customers for many years, while others served more transient communities. After considerable discussion the consulting team concluded that the branch performance potentials varied most significantly with the number and mix of customers in the regions they served and that market potentials could be measured reasonably accurately on that basis.

BoD staff had previously analyzed a broad range of customer demographics and behavior patterns and classified the bank's retail customers into 30 customer types, which they summarized into 10 broad segments, which included categories such as "Well Off," "Newly Secure," and "Future Potential." The customers in these categories varied in terms of their mix of purchases of various products and services and in current and future profit potentials.

The consulting team took these data on the mixes of customer types served by each of the 253 branches and, using a sophisticated statistical clustering program, grouped the branches into 10 clusters. The clusters were labeled:

1. Young Professionals
2. Experienced Investors
3. Middle-class Workers
4. Transaction Customers
5. New Wealth
6. Old Wealth
7. New Investors
8. Small Branches
9. Small Business Banking
10. Priority Banking.

Branch clusters 1 through 7 were based solely on the mix of consumer segments. For example, the average branch in the "Old Wealth" cluster (6) was comprised of 17.4% of "Well Off" customers, 11.5% of "Newly Secure" customers, 42.5% of "Future

---

This case was prepared by Professors Kenneth A. Merchant, Wim A. Van der Stede, and research assistant Xiaoling (Clara) Chen.

Potential" customers, 1.8% of "Core Bankers," 0.7% of "Traditional Bankers," 8.1% of "New Investors," 7.3% of "Getting There" customers, 6.7% of "Checks and Mortgages" customers, 0.7% of "Middle Stable" customers, and 3.3% of "Anomalies and Unclassified" customers.

Information on consumer characteristics was unavailable for some specialized branches. These branches were clustered based on balance sheet and transaction characteristics. Clusters 8 through 10 fell into this category. Among them, cluster 8 included branches with less than 3,500 customers, and clusters 9 and 10 were highly focused branches.

The branch clustering was important because it could be used to set more reasonable performance standards. Branch performances could be compared only with the performances of other BoD branches in the same cluster, i.e. those facing roughly the same business environment.

The consultants decided to set the branch performance standards based on the current performance of the *average* branch in each cluster. Dave Phillips explained:

> We did not want to pick some theoretical performance standard. It's too easy to argue with those. We chose to set standards based simply on how the average branch in each cluster was currently performing. The opportunity for improvement, then, was simply calculated based on bringing the poor-performing branches up to average. Everybody can understand that. Once they pick that "low hanging fruit," then maybe the bank managers can get more sophisticated and figure out how to move the higher-performing branches up.

PERFORMANCE OPPORTUNITY METRICS

Another key element of the consultants' engagement involved the development of a metric that could be used to distinguish the high and low performing branches in each cluster. They decided to take a customer focus. They based their performance model on the simple logic that the bank, and indeed any business, can improve its profits by: (1) acquiring new customers; (2) improving the profit potential of each of its customers (e.g. by selling them multiple products and, particularly, the most profitable products); and (3) retaining each customer as long as possible. They called the combination of the first two factors the *market opportunity*. They called the third factor the *customer retention opportunity*.

The team also sought to develop metrics that would quantify both opportunities on a common measurement dimension – profits. They thought that the common metric would help division managers bridge the gap between the financial performance focus at upper management levels and the operational focus at the branch level.

A. MARKET OPPORTUNITY METRIC

Each branch's market opportunity was the product of two factors: a customer value mix opportunity and a market penetration opportunity. Underlying the calculation of the *customer value mix opportunity* were some cost accounting analyses that had recently been conducted by BoD staff. These analyses estimated profitability by product and by customer. The *product profitability* analyses estimated the average profits the bank earned from the sale of each of a broad range of products. These included, for example, loans of various types, current accounts, savings accounts, credit cards, and certificates of deposit with various maturity lengths. Only averages could be estimated because the profitability of bank products can be dramatically different depending on how the customers use the products. For example, some current account customers maintain large balances; others do not. Some make considerable use of tellers for their transactions, while others use only the relatively inexpensive automated teller machines (ATMs). And some manage their accounts carelessly (e.g. bouncing checks), making it possible for the bank to charge them fees, while others do not.

Customer profitability was based on the profitability of the mix of products purchased by customers of different types. The customer profitability analysis first involved ranking the ten customer types described above in terms of desirability (i.e. both current profitability and growth potential). These categories were then reclassified into one of four more aggregate categories. Category 4 included all unprofitable customers. This category included, surprisingly, 18% of all the bank's customers. Category 3 included customers who generated some profits but who, because they offered limited growth potential, were not the type that bank managers wanted their line officers searching for. Categories 1 and 2 included the "outstanding" and "excellent" customer types. BoD managers only sought customers in Categories 1 and 2. The consultants calculated that the Category 1 and 2 customers, which comprised only 25% of the BoD's customers, provided 84% of the Retail Banking Division's total profits.

Based on these analyses and data on the mix of products purchased by customers in Categories 1 and 2, the consultants calculated a "standard profit per household," that is, what a branch could be expected to earn by attracting one more customer in either Category 1 or 2.

For example, Branch 188 served a total of 6,075 households, but only 19% were in the top two tiers (outstanding or excellent) in terms of profitability, as compared to the average percentage of top-tier customers in its cluster of 21%. Thus, Branch 188 can be said to have a customer value mix opportunity of 2%. The difference in profitability between the top two tier customers (outstanding and excellent profitability) and bottom two tier customers (moderate and potential profitability) is $543 for Branch 188. Therefore, the customer value mix opportunity of 2% translates into a profit potential of about $66,000 (i.e. 0.02 • 6,075 • $543, rounded).

The other element of the market opportunity metric, the *market penetration opportunity*, was more difficult to calculate. BoD had never measured market penetration or share at the branch level. The branch and ATM network was designed so that the individual service locations would work in a complementary manner to serve customers and to capture market share. Thus bank managers did not believe that the market share of any particular individual location was particularly meaningful. However, BoD staff had previously defined 48 distinguishable "market areas" served by the bank's branches. The consulting team used these data and calculated BoD's penetration rate in each market area by dividing the BoD retail households in the market area by the total potential households in that particular market. They then assumed that the penetration rate was the same for all BoD branches located in this market area.

For example, there were 135,176 households in the South Tucson area of Arizona (market area 1), in which Branch 188 was located. Within this market area BoD served a total of 32,442 households, so BoD's penetration rate was 24%. This figure was compared to BoD's overall average penetration rate of 29%. This led to the conclusion that the BoD branches in the South Tucson market area had a penetration opportunity rate of 5%.

Branch 188 currently served 6,075 households. Assuming that the branch's customer mix stayed the same at an average profit per household of $132, if the branch could increase its market penetration by 5%, thus bringing in an additional 304 households as customers, it could expect to earn an additional profit of about $40,000 (i.e. 0.05 • 6,075 • $132, rounded).

The total market opportunity was the sum of the customer value mix opportunity and the market penetration opportunity. For Branch 188, this was approximately $106,000.

B. CUSTOMER RETENTION OPPORTUNITY METRIC

The consultants knew that good customer service was one of the primary profit drivers in a bank branch and, indeed, most types of businesses. But BoD did not have good measures of customer satisfaction or customer feedback. It did, however, track a primary outcome of good customer service – customer retention. From the bank's customer retention statistics the consulting team calculated the profit opportunity that would be derived from improving each branch's customer retention rate to the average of its cluster. The formula was:

Customer retention profit opportunity = number of households currently served • retention improvement opportunity (%) • number of years of improved retention[1] • cluster average customer profit opportunity

For example, Branch 188 has a customer retention rate of 81.2%, as compared to the average retention rate in its cluster of 82.8%. Branch 188's customer retention opportunity, then, is 1.6%. Branch 188 serves 6,075 households in total and the profit per household is $132. Therefore, in dollar terms Branch 188's customer retention opportunity is $38,000 (i.e. 0.016 • 6,075 • $132 • 3, rounded).

THE CASE OF BRANCH 992

To illustrate how the new proposed evaluation systems yielded results that contrasted with those

---

[1] Assumed to be 3. This is to recognize that retention improvements generate streams of profits over more than a single year.

TABLE 1 Branch 992 performance vs. cluster 5 averages

	Cluster 5 average	Branch 992
Customers in top 2 tiers (%)	31.5%	24.1%
Customer retention (%)	88.2%	87.6%

of the evaluation system BoD was currently using, consider the consultants' conclusions regarding the performance of Branch 992. Branch 992 had been in operation for 36 years, and it served a total of 9,128 households.

Based on the operational metrics used for incentive purposes, Branch 992 had a cross sell/total retail accounts ratio of 95.3% and 5.6 sales per FTE per day, as compared to a target cross sell ratio of 93% and 5.4 sales per FTE per day. Since it exceeded both of its targets, Branch 992 was considered a superior performer under BoD's current evaluation system; it was ranked 44th best of the 253 branches.

Under the consultants' proposed evaluation system, however, Branch 992 was not ranked nearly as highly. In fact, in terms of the opportunity metrics, it ranked 218th out of the 253 branches.

Under the proposed segmentation Branch 992 belonged to cluster 5 ("New Wealth"). As shown in Table 1, Branch 992's performance was below the cluster average for both the customer mix and customer retention metrics. The penetration rate in Branch 992's market area was 28%, as compared to the overall bank average of 29%, so Branch 992 also failed to achieve that performance standard.

The consultants translated these performance opportunities into dollars and concluded that if Branch 992 could be brought up to average performance its profits would increase by $411,068 (27.5%) from a stronger customer value mix; $14,932 (1%) from better market penetration; and $26,317 (1.8%) from increased customer retention. With a total profit opportunity of $452,318, Branch 992 had the largest opportunity for improvement in the "New Wealth" branch cluster. It was far from being a top performer!

THE CONSULTANTS' PRESENTATION

Dave Phillips presented his report to BoD's retail division management on February 4, 2002. He described his team's approach and the rationale behind it. He showed that the new approach would lead to some significant differences in branch evaluations. Branch 992 was one of the examples that he presented. And he concluded his presentation with some overall statistics about how much money BoD had been "leaving on the table." Dave claimed that bringing the weaker performing branches in each cluster up to average would yield an additional bank profit of about $8.8 million from the customer value mix opportunity, $5.9 million from the market penetration opportunity, and $4.2 million from the customer retention profit opportunity. Taken as a whole, the division's profit would increase by approximately $18.9 million (7%), just from bringing all the poor-performing branches up to the current average within each cluster.

The division managers were stunned by the consultants' overall conclusions and, especially, by some of the specific branch examples. They wondered why the consultants' findings suggested that maybe they should be thinking about firing a branch manager, the one of Branch 992, whom they were preparing to promote because his branch had consistently met its performance targets.

In the days following the meeting Dave noted that the bank managers quickly started asking useful questions that they had not been asking, such as: Why do some branches do so well on the metrics we have been using but so poorly on the opportunity metrics? How should we be setting goals? If we implement this system, will the improvement automatically happen, or would we have to do something else to bring the poor performing branches up to at least average performance levels?

Dave knew that his team's analysis was not the final answer. They had completed only the first phase in what would have to be a lengthy analysis and change process. Nonetheless, Dave thought that they had achieved their primary purpose, which was to stimulate the BoD managers to ask some of the right questions. He considered the opportunity metrics primarily as a diagnostic tool that was particularly valuable for internal learning and improvement. However, he also thought that the opportunity metrics would encourage the branch managers to take a broader view of the business and focus their attention on the dimensions of performance that were critical to the long-term success of the company. In Dave's words:

They are in the earliest stages of figuring out the implications of seeing their business from this new perspective. Over time they will refine the perspective, and will begin to relate my findings to their day-to-day behavior. But the most important thing to note is that they were stunned. That was the primary value. I showed them that their perceptions of performance and their decision-making processes were less effective than they had thought because they didn't have a complete context for either.

However, Dave pointed out to the bank managers that while his system was relatively simple it might not be the ultimate answer to all their evaluation problems. The analyses were based on a number of marketing and cost accounting analyses. Even if these analyses were correct today – which Dave's team assumed they were at face value – the studies would have to be updated on a regular basis. He also pointed out that the three suggested metrics (customer mix, market penetration, customer retention) did not define branch performance completely. For example,

those metrics did not reflect how well branch managers controlled the expenses that they could control or how well they developed their employees' skill sets. Bank managers would have to decide whether focusing only on the three suggested metrics would cause branch managers to ignore other important but unmeasured aspects of their jobs.

DECISIONS TO BE MADE

Annette and BoD's other retail bank managers knew they had to make some important decisions. Was the consultants' approach superior to the system they had been using? If it was superior, how fast should they try to implement it? They had already communicated the terms of the 2002 bonus plan, using the old evaluation criteria, to branch personnel. Could they change now? If so, how would they explain the new system to the branch personnel? What should they do next?

Section V

CORPORATE GOVERNANCE, IMPORTANT CONTROL-RELATED ROLES, AND ETHICS

Chapter 13

CORPORATE GOVERNANCE AND BOARDS OF DIRECTORS

The term *corporate governance* refers to the sets of mechanisms and processes that help ensure that companies are directed and managed to create value for their owners while concurrently fulfilling responsibilities to other stakeholders (e.g. employees, suppliers, society at large). Many mechanisms and institutions can have corporate governance effects, and their effects vary considerably across countries. In Anglo-American economies, the primary governance mechanisms are provided by equity markets and the structures that support them or result from them, including laws and regulations, boards of directors, external auditors, governance ratings, and takeover threats. In some Western European and Asian economies, relatively more governance influence is provided by concentrated ownership patterns, such as the *Keiretsu* in Japan, the *Chaebols* in Korea, institutional investors in India, and state ownership in China. Governance in German companies is heavily influenced by national banks, insurance companies, and labor unions. Scandinavian countries rely more on social norms and expectations. Islamic countries rely on *Sharia* law.[1]

Beyond the legal and social influences, corporate governance practices in all countries are influenced by what is thought to be "best practice." Some of the broad pronouncements about best practice are based on the recommendations of expert panels, such as the Cadbury Committee in the United Kingdom[2] and the Treadway Commission in the United States.[3] Lists of best practices are published by the many corporate governance ratings organizations, such as ISS, the Corporate Library, and Governance Metrics International, and in publications by many actual or self-appointed experts. However, knowledge of what constitutes best practice, either in general or in any specific setting, is incomplete and uncertain. In the meantime, regulations are frequently changing, and corporations must do the best they can in environments that are often dynamic.

Whatever the source of the corporate governance forces, corporate governance systems and management control systems (MCSs) are inextricably linked. A corporate governance focus is slightly broader than is an MCSs focus. An MCSs focus takes the perspective of top management and asks what can be done to ensure the proper behaviors of employees in the organization. The corporate governance focus is on controlling the behaviors of top management (the executives) and also, although less directly, those of all the other employees in the firm. Thus, corporate governance adds to management control both the concern for controlling the behaviors of top management and, particularly, the monitoring roles of the company's board of directors. But the links are obvious. Changes in corporate governance mechanisms and practices will usually have direct and immediate effects on MCS practices and their effectiveness.

Primarily because of the major business scandals that were uncovered in the early-2000s – including Enron, WorldCom, Tyco, Parmalat, and Royal Ahold, to name just a few; the mismanagement, misreporting and fraud that contributed significantly to the financial crisis of 2008; and other abuses, such as late trading, market timing and option backdating – interest in corporate governance has skyrocketed.[4] This chapter provides a brief introduction to this complex and broad subject. The chapter begins by providing an overview of the legal and regulatory environment within which corporate governance practices must operate. The regulations are difficult to summarize because they vary considerably across legal jurisdictions, and even within a single jurisdiction they are fragmented. For example, many of the regulations are specific to an industry (such as banks) or to a goal (such as accurate financial reporting). The US Sarbanes-Oxley Act of 2002 is described in some detail in this chapter because it is the most significant piece of legislation affecting corporate governance practices to be passed in the United States since the Securities Act of 1934. Its importance also extends beyond US borders because it has inspired, and is similar to, other corporate governance reforms that have taken place around the world in recent years. The chapter then discusses the roles of boards of directors and, particularly boards' audit and compensation committees. Chapter 14 then discusses two other important organizational roles with both corporate governance and MCS significance, those of controllers and auditors.

LAWS AND REGULATIONS

Corporations are legal entities. As such, they are subject to the laws and regulations of the government jurisdictions in which they operate and those of the stock markets on which their shares are traded. Corporate governance approaches and mechanisms vary widely across countries. Generally, though, the world is said to be divided into two corporate governance orientations, the Anglo-American system, which focuses on the primacy of shareholders as the beneficiaries of fiduciary duties, and the Continental European/Japanese system, which has a broader concern also for the rights of other stakeholders. But even within these two broad types of systems, considerable variation exists in the governance mechanisms used (e.g. board composition and structure) and the contexts in which the mechanisms must work (e.g. laws, extent of merger and acquisition activity).[5]

The legal system in the United States creates a fiduciary obligation for managers and directors to act in the best interest of shareholders. The directors, the elected representatives of the shareholders, are charged with overseeing the actions of management. Since the shareholders are viewed as the residual claimants of the cash flows generated, the primary goal is to maximize the value of the corporation. In the United States, corporations are incorporated in an individual state and are bound by the laws and court decisions of that state. The Chancery Court in Delaware is particularly influential because many large corporations are incorporated in that state. The US federal government began regulating financial markets and their participants (e.g. corporations, securities exchanges, brokers, dealers, advisors) after the stock market crash of 1929. The US Congress passed the Securities Acts of 1933 and 1934 that, among other things, created the Securities and Exchange Commission (SEC), the agency primarily responsible for enforcement of US federal securities laws. These acts require that publicly traded corporations disclose certain types of information on a regular basis to the SEC and to the company's shareholders. The disclosures are intended to promote efficiency and transparency in the financial markets and provide the additional benefit of discouraging bad behavior.

The Continental European/Japanese system of governance is aimed at ensuring that the corporation is managed for the good of the enterprise, its multiple stakeholders, and the society at large. The shareholders are only one of many affected stakeholder groups.

One important effect of this legal difference is in the composition of the boards of directors. Large German corporations, for example, are required to have a two-tier board structure, one tier that provides strategic oversight and another tier that provides operational management oversight. In German corporations with more than 2,000 employees, the strategic oversight board must be comprised of equal numbers of employees' and shareholders' representatives.[6] In Japan, banks are often represented on the boards of directors of companies with which they do business.

Regardless of their home country, all corporations are bound by the rules and regulations of the stock exchange on which their shares are traded. Large exchanges, such as NYSE Euronext and NASDAQ, maintain extensive sets of rules to regulate their listed companies, to prevent manipulative practices and to promote fair principles of trade. Overall, then, corporations are subject to a complex array of laws and regulations designed to direct and constrain their activities. Many parties independent of management and the board of directors monitor corporate governance practices. These include auditors, regulators, analysts, credit-rating agencies, self-appointed watchdogs, and whistleblowers.[7]

A pertinent example of legislation specifically aimed at strengthening corporate governance generally, as practiced in the United States, is the Sarbanes-Oxley Act of 2002, to which we now turn.

THE SARBANES-OXLEY ACT OF 2002

In July 2002, in response to some major corporate failures, most notably Enron and WorldCom, the US Congress passed the Sarbanes-Oxley Act. Sarbanes-Oxley imposed new requirements on corporations listed in the United States and their auditors. The explicit goal of Sarbanes-Oxley was to improve the transparency, timeliness, and quality of *financial reporting*. But since improved controls over financial reporting also have beneficial management control effects, understanding the elements of Sarbanes-Oxley, and also those of other financial reporting regulations, is important for those interested in MCSs.

Sarbanes-Oxley has had effects beyond the US borders. All companies registered with the US Securities and Exchange Commission (SEC) must comply with Sarbanes-Oxley regardless of whether their headquarters are based in the United States or abroad. In addition, some countries, such as Canada and Japan, have adopted regulations similar to Sarbanes-Oxley.[8]

Figure 13.1 provides a summary of some of the key provisions of Sarbanes-Oxley. Among other things:

- The *external auditing* industry, which was formerly self-regulated, became highly regulated by the federal government. Sarbanes-Oxley created the Public Company Accounting Oversight Board (PCAOB) and gave it the authority, with oversight from the SEC, to set auditing standards and to monitor auditors' actions.

- The members of audit committees of companies' boards of directors are required to be independent and financially literate.

- Senior company managers, usually the CEO and CFO, are required to certify that they had reviewed their company's quarterly and annual financial statements; that the financial statements are fairly presented, with no untrue statements or omissions of material facts; that they acknowledged responsibility for disclosure controls and procedures and internal controls over financial reporting; and that they have evaluated those controls and procedures and disclosed any material changes or deficiencies to the auditors and audit committee. Penalties for fraud and for obstructing an investigation were broadened and made more severe.

Figure 13.1 Key provisions of the Sarbanes-Oxley Act of 2002

Section(s) of the Act	Key provision(s)
101 102 104	Creates the Public Company Accounting Oversight Board (PCAOB) to oversee the audit of public companies. ● The PCAOB will register accounting firms that audit public companies. ● It has the authority to establish standards for auditing, quality control, ethics, and independence relating to the preparation of audit reports. ● It will conduct a continuing program of inspections to assess the degree of compliance of each registered public accounting firm with professional standards. ● It will hold disciplinary proceedings and impose sanctions against firms whose acts, practices, or omissions violate the Act, the Board's rules, professional accounting standards, or the federal securities laws.
105	Increases penalties for accountants who fail to testify, produce documents, or cooperate with an investigation.
201	Prohibits auditors from providing certain non-audit services (including bookkeeping, financial information systems design and implementation, appraisal or valuation services, actuarial services, internal audit, management, human resources, investment advice, legal services) to the companies they audit.
202	Requires audit committee pre-approval of all services provided by audit firm.
203	Requires lead and second (review) audit partner rotation every five years.
204	Increases required communications between auditors and audit committee on critical accounting policies and practices, alternative accounting treatments, and other material written communications with management.
206	Requires a one year "cooling-off" period if audit firm employees who worked on the account are hired by the client into certain key financial oversight positions. Their former firm is prohibited from performing any audit services for the new employer for one year.
301	● Gives audit committee sole authority for the appointment, compensation, and oversight of auditors and approval of any significant non-audit work. ● Limits audit committee membership to independent directors. ● Requires development of channels of communication for complaints from whistleblowers and others to the audit committee.
302	Requires management (CEO and CFO) certifications that: ● They reviewed financial reports (quarterly and annual). ● Financial statements do not contain any untrue statements or omission of material facts and that they fairly present the financial condition and results of the operations of the company as of, and for, the periods presented in the report. ● They are responsible for the company's internal controls, have designed the controls to that material information is made known to them, have evaluated the effectiveness of the internal controls, and have presented their conclusions about the effectiveness of the internal controls in the report. They evaluated the disclosure controls and procedures as of period end and disclosed any material changes in internal control during the period. ● They disclosed to auditors/audit committee if control deficiencies and/or fraud exist.

Figure **13.1** *continued*

Section(s) of the Act	Key provision(s)
304	Includes a "claw-back" provision requiring CEOs and CFOs to forfeit certain bonuses received and profits realized on the sale of securities following a financial report that is later restated due to material non-compliance with securities laws as a result of misconduct.
402	New company loans to directors or executive officers are prohibited.
404	• Requires that annual report include management's assessment of the effectiveness of the company's internal control over financial reporting. • Auditors must attest to and report on management's internal control assessment.
406	Requires annual disclosure as to whether the company has adopted a code of ethics for its CEO and senior financial officers (e.g., CFO, controller). If it has a code, it must make it publicly available. If it does not have a code, it must explain why it does not.
407	Requires company to disclose whether it has a financial expert on the audit committee and if not, to explain the reasons why it does not.
409	Requires "rapid and current" disclosure of material changes in financial condition or operations.
802 806 807 902 906 1102 1007	Increases penalties. Imposes fines of up to $5 million and/or up to 25 years imprisonment for such actions as: • The knowing alteration, destruction, or concealment of documents with the intent to impeding an official investigation; • For retaliation against whistleblowers; • For knowingly or willfully filing a false certification; • For willful violations of various white collar criminal laws.

Source: The full text of the Act can be accessed on the Public Company Accounting Oversight Board website: http://pcaobus.org/About/History/Documents/PDFs/Sarbanes_Oxley_Act_of_2002.pdf.

But one of the most significant, and clearly the most expensive, provisions in the Act was contained in the internal control-related section of the Act, Section 404. Even prior to Sarbanes-Oxley, good internal controls were said to be good business practice. Not only did good controls help ensure fair and accurate financial reporting, they helped ensure that managers would have good information with which to make their business decisions and they helped reduce the incidence of fraud and loss of assets. Sarbanes-Oxley made good internal controls a legal requirement, at least for companies publicly traded in the United States.

Section 404 mandated an evaluation of the effectiveness of a company's internal controls by both management and the company's external auditor and formal written opinions about the effectiveness of those controls. In doing this evaluation, managers and auditors are required to examine a broad range of internal controls over financial reporting, including policies and procedures, audit committee effectiveness, integrity and ethical behavior programs, whistleblower programs, and tone at the top.

The existence of a single "material weakness" – a deficiency in internal control so major that it could result in a material misstatement of a company's actual financial situation (see definitions in Figure 13.2) – requires managers and auditors to conclude that the

Figure 13.2 Definitions of control deficiencies

> A *control deficiency* exists when the design or operation of a control does not allow management or employees, in the normal course of performing their assigned functions, to prevent or detect misstatements on a timely basis. A deficiency in *design* exists when (a) a control necessary to meet the control objective is missing or (b) an existing control is not properly designed so that, even if the control operates as designed, the control objective is not always met. A deficiency in *operation* exists when a properly designed control does not operate as designed, or when the person performing the control does not possess the necessary authority or qualifications to perform the control effectively.
>
> A *significant deficiency* is a control deficiency, or combination of control deficiencies, that adversely affects the company's ability to initiate, authorize, record, process, or report external financial data reliably in accordance with generally accepted accounting principles such that there is more than a remote likelihood that a misstatement of the company's annual or interim financial statements that is more than inconsequential will not be prevented or detected.
>
> A *material weakness* is a significant deficiency, or combination of significant deficiencies, that results in more than a remote likelihood that a material misstatement of the annual or interim financial statements will not be prevented or detected.

Source: PCAOB Auditing Standard No. 2, *An Audit of Internal Control Over Financial Reporting Performed in Conjunction With an Audit of Financial Statements*, online (http://pcaobus.org/Standards/Auditing/Pages/Auditing_Standard_2.aspx).

company's internal controls are not effective. Companies have no obligation to disclose the existence of any deficiency less severe than a material weakness, although they and their auditors are required to evaluate them to determine whether they could result in a material weakness.

Figure 13.3 shows the written 2010 opinion of Steve Jobs, Apple Inc.'s CEO, concluding that his company's internal control over financial reporting was effective. Figure 13.4 shows the 2010 opinion of Ernst & Young regarding Apple's financial statements and internal control over financial reporting. The two internal control opinions are consistent: both express the opinion that Apple's internal controls were effective, meaning that no material weaknesses were found.

The documentation and testing of internal controls as required by Section 404 is expensive. Estimates of the total cost of compliance in the first year were as high as $35 billion.[9] General Electric Company alone spent $30 million in the first year of 404 compliance.[10] But the costs of compliance declined significantly in year two – an average reduction of 44% for larger companies (those with a market capitalization over $700 million).[11] Those declines resulted because most of the documentation of existing controls was completed in year one, and all involved parties had become more familiar with the new requirements. Further, companies focused their attention on *key controls*, those that, by definition, are needed to prevent or detect a material error that is at least likely. In larger companies, the average number of key controls tests by auditors declined more than 19%, from 669 in year one to 540 in year two.[12]

In 2007, the PCAOB and SEC provided additional guidance both to auditors and companies regarding best ways to comply with Section 404. A study from the SEC's Office of Economic Analysis in 2009 showed that after the guidance the average Section 404 compliance costs dropped by 19% from the pre-guidance cost for companies that were already complying with Section 404. But the average total Section 404 compliance cost following the issuance of the SEC guidance was still $2.33 million per year.[13]

While the costs of compliance are significant, the Sarbanes-Oxley Act affected companies' MCSs in positive ways. It improved companies' internal control structures, audit

FIGURE 13.3 Certification of annual financial statements of Apple Inc. by the company's CEO

I, Steven P. Jobs, certify that:

1. I have reviewed this annual report on Form 10-K of Apple Inc.;

2. Based on my knowledge, this report does not contain any untrue statement of a material fact or omit to state a material fact necessary to make the statements made, in light of the circumstances under which such statements were made, not misleading with respect to the period covered by this report;

3. Based on my knowledge, the financial statements, and other financial information included in this report, fairly present in all material respects the financial condition, results of operations and cash flows of the registrant as of, and for, the periods presented in this report;

4. The registrant's other certifying officer(s) and I are responsible for establishing and maintaining disclosure controls and procedures (as defined in Exchange Act Rules 13a-15(e) and 15d-15(e)) and internal control over financial reporting (as defined in Exchange Act Rules 13a-15(f) and 15d-15(f)) for the registrant and have:

    (a) Designed such disclosure controls and procedures, or caused such disclosure controls and procedures to be designed under our supervision, to ensure that material information relating to the registrant, including its consolidated subsidiaries, is made known to us by others within those entities, particularly during the period in which this report is being prepared;

    (b) Designed such internal control over financial reporting, or caused such internal control over financial reporting to be designed under our supervision, to provide reasonable assurance regarding the reliability of financial reporting and the preparation of financial statements for external purposes in accordance with generally accepted accounting principles;

    (c) Evaluated the effectiveness of the registrant's disclosure controls and procedures and presented in this report our conclusions about the effectiveness of the disclosure controls and procedures, as of the end of the period covered by this report based on such evaluation; and

    (d) Disclosed in this report any change in the registrant's internal control over financial reporting that occurred during the registrant's most recent fiscal quarter (the registrant's fourth fiscal quarter in the case of an annual report) that has materially affected, or is reasonably likely to materially affect, the registrant's internal control over financial reporting; and

5. The registrant's other certifying officer(s) and I have disclosed, based on our most recent evaluation of internal control over financial reporting, to the registrant's auditors and the audit committee of the registrant's board of directors (or persons performing the equivalent functions):

    (a) All significant deficiencies and material weaknesses in the design or operation of internal control over financial reporting which are reasonably likely to adversely affect the registrant's ability to record, process, summarize, and report financial information; and

    (b) Any fraud, whether or not material, that involves management or other employees who have a significant role in the registrant's internal control over financial reporting.

Date: October 27, 2010

By: /s/ Steven P. Jobs
Steven P. Jobs
Chief Executive Officer

Source: 10-K Report, Apple Inc., for fiscal year 2010.

committees' confidence in the company's internal controls, and companies' ability to prevent and detect fraud. However, even following all the tenets of Sarbanes-Oxley will not guarantee an infallible control system. In fact, most experts have concluded that the extreme examples of fraud and corporate failure that motivated legislators to pass the Act would have occurred even if Sarbanes-Oxley had existed at the time. For example:

Figure 13.4 External auditor's opinion on Apple, Inc.'s financial statements and internal control over financial reporting, for fiscal year 2010 (ended September 25, 2010)

The Board of Directors and Shareholders of Apple Inc.

We have audited Apple Inc.'s internal control over financial reporting as of September 25, 2010, based on criteria established in *Internal Control – Integrated Framework* issued by the Committee of Sponsoring Organizations of the Treadway Commission ("the COSO criteria"). Apple Inc.'s management is responsible for maintaining effective internal control over financial reporting, and for its assessment of the effectiveness of internal control over financial reporting included in the accompanying Management's Annual Report on Internal Control over Financial Reporting. Our responsibility is to express an opinion on the Company's internal control over financial reporting based on our audit.

We conducted our audit in accordance with the standards of the Public Company Accounting Oversight Board (United States). Those standards require that we plan and perform the audit to obtain reasonable assurance about whether effective internal control over financial reporting was maintained in all material respects. Our audit included obtaining an understanding of internal control over financial reporting, assessing the risk that a material weakness exists, testing and evaluating the design and operating effectiveness of internal control based on the assessed risk, and performing such other procedures as we considered necessary in the circumstances. We believe that our audit provides a reasonable basis for our opinion.

A company's internal control over financial reporting is a process designed to provide reasonable assurance regarding the reliability of financial reporting and the preparation of financial statements for external purposes in accordance with generally accepted accounting principles. A company's internal control over financial reporting includes those policies and procedures that (1) pertain to the maintenance of records that, in reasonable detail, accurately and fairly reflect the transactions and dispositions of the assets of the company; (2) provide reasonable assurance that transactions are recorded as necessary to permit preparation of financial statements in accordance with generally accepted accounting principles, and that receipts and expenditures of the company are being made only in accordance with authorizations of management and directors of the company; and (3) provide reasonable assurance regarding prevention or timely detection of unauthorized acquisition, use, or disposition of the company's assets that could have a material effect on the financial statements.

Because of its inherent limitations, internal control over financial reporting may not prevent or detect misstatements. Also, projections of any evaluation of effectiveness to future periods are subject to the risk that controls may become inadequate because of changes in conditions, or that the degree of compliance with the policies or procedures may deteriorate.

In our opinion, Apple Inc. maintained, in all material respects, effective internal control over financial reporting as of September 25, 2010, based on the COSO criteria.

We also have audited, in accordance with the standards of the Public Company Accounting Oversight Board (United States), the 2010 consolidated financial statements of Apple Inc. and our report dated October 27, 2010 expressed an unqualified opinion thereon.

/s/ Ernst & Young LLP

San Jose, California
October 27, 2010

Source: 10-K Report, Apple, Inc., 2010.

The existence of SOX would not have, and does not now, prevent fraudulent acts from being perpetrated, does not prevent pervasive internal and external collusion to cover up the fraud, and does not prevent decisions being made at the highest levels inside a company in contravention of stated corporate practices and policies.[14]

But while it is not perfect, Sarbanes-Oxley has had significant effects on the activities and responsibilities of all those in financial reporting- and control-related roles. In the remainder of this chapter, we discuss one of the most important roles, that of members of boards of directors and, in particular, the boards' audit and compensation committees.

BOARDS OF DIRECTORS

In publicly traded companies, shareholders typically diversify their risks and own a portfolio of shares in numerous firms. Individually, they rarely have an incentive large enough to devote resources to ensure that management is acting in the best interest of the shareholders. The common solution is for shareholders collectively to delegate their authority to monitor management's actions to a board of directors. Boards of directors (and also corporate officers) have a fiduciary duty to foster the long-term success of the corporation for the benefit of shareholders, and also sometimes for debt holders. In the United States, this basic fiduciary duty is deemed to have multiple elements:

1. *Duty of care* – duty to make/delegate decisions in an informed way.

2. *Duty of loyalty* – duty to advance corporate over personal interests.

3. *Duty of good faith* – duty to be faithful and devoted to the interests of the corporation and its shareholders.

4. *Duty not to "waste"* – duty to avoid deliberate destruction of shareholder value.

All of these duties are defined by, and enforced through, the US legal system. In court cases involving all but the duty of loyalty, directors are somewhat protected by the *business judgment rule*. This rule is a legal presumption that a corporate fiduciary has endeavored in good faith to exercise care in the corporation's interest. It places the burden on the party complaining of breached duty to prove gross negligence.

To carry out their responsibilities, boards must ensure that they are independent and accountable to shareholders, and they must exert their authority for the continuity of executive leadership with proper vision and values. Boards are given ultimate control over management. They are singularly responsible for the selection and evaluation of the corporation's chief executive officer (CEO), and they also must ensure the quality of senior management (the corporate executives). Boards also can review and approve the corporation's long-term strategy and important management decisions, such as the design of equity and compensation plans that motivate management to achieve and sustain superior long-term performance.

Boards of directors have two main control responsibilities. First, they safeguard the equity investors' interests, particularly by ensuring that management seeks to maximize the value of the shareholders' stakes in the corporation. Second, they protect the interests of other corporate stakeholders (such as employees, suppliers, customers, competitors, or the society at large) by ensuring that the employees in the corporation act in a legally and socially responsible manner. Among other things, they help ensure fair financial reporting, fair compensation, fair competition, protection of the environment, and proper conduct of business by the corporation overall.

Many characteristics of boards and their members can affect their effectiveness. It is widely believed that a majority of board members should be *independent* of management. Interlocking directorates, situations where board members serve on each others' boards, is one particular problem many have lamented. Charles Elson, director of the Center for Corporate Governance at the University of Delaware, commented as follows on the "clubby nature" of boards, where companies' boards are populated with business partners and individuals with direct financial ties:

> Directors shouldn't be consultants. Their only financial ties to the companies they oversee should be through stock ownership, and they should own enough company stock that if they lost it, it would really hurt.[15]

Obviously, incentives are important, too, and especially the ways in which the incentive plans are set by a presumably independent board, a presumption that has been profoundly debated.[16] Issues such as these are a major reason why recent regulations, including those by stock exchanges, have strengthened the requirements for independent directors.

It is also obvious that board members must be competent and must be able to devote the needed time to the role. Douglas Austin, a Toledo, Ohio-based consultant, described an extreme situation:

> [The] worst board [I've ever seen] was five people strong, and two of them had to be brought in on stretchers. One was 87 [years old] and one was 83. They just laid them on a table in the back of the room, and that's how they got their quorum.[17]

Some board members are ineffective because they are serving on too many boards for the time they have available.

The many examples of board failures illustrate that firms should be concerned about the functioning of their boards. There is a burgeoning literature on the functioning of corporate governance systems and boards of directors. However, corporate governance systems are complex, and how the various governance mechanisms interact with one another and with characteristics of the situations in which they operate to produce good (or bad) outcomes is not well understood. Many research findings conflict. These conflicts reflect the incomplete state of knowledge in this complex area.[18]

In the meantime, board members have to do the best job they can. But in deciding how to structure their activities and how to act, boards of directors should follow some basic principles. First, they must comply with the relevant laws and regulations. To ensure this compliance, they often have to rely heavily on their company's lawyers both to inform them of the relevant laws and to educate them about the implications of those laws. If they are accused of wrongdoing, they will be judged in light of the extent they upheld their duties of care, loyalty, and so on.

Second, they should try to follow what they believe to be best practice. Consultants often play an important role in spreading and advocating such (various) practices. That said, board members should keep in mind that so-called experts often provide conflicting advice. Equally, evidence in many basic board-related areas, including the desirability of splitting the chairman and CEO roles, the optimum amount of equity involvement by board members, the right set and mix of board member skills, and the right board size, is still equivocal.

For possible guidance, board members could also examine the criteria used in any of the many corporate governance ratings. Among the most commonly cited ratings are those published by Institutional Shareholder Services (ISS), Standard & Poor's (S&P), the Corporate Library, and Governance Metrics International (GMI). A company's ISS Corporate Governance Quotient is based on 61 specific scores in eight core governance areas: board structure and composition, audit issues, charter and bylaw provisions, laws of the state of incorporation, executive and director compensation, qualitative factors, directors and officers' stock ownership, and director education. But these ratings also often conflict. For example, in 2002, S&P gave Fannie Mae a 9 out of 10 rating and a "gold star" for its corporate governance practices, whereas GMI rated it below average. In 2003, S&P indicated that HealthSouth outperformed 92.3% of its industry peers, whereas GMI rated the company's governance only average. What's more, these ratings appeared only a short period of time before major governance failures were uncovered at both Fannie Mae and HealthSouth.[19]

The final guide to director behavior must involve judgment. Oftentimes there is no specific law that must be followed, and the best-practice advice is conflicting or vague, but directors must endeavor to make the right choices. Many of these examples involve situations where directors are not quite comfortable with something in the company, but they also do not want to overstep their bounds to interfere in the day-to-day management of the company. Where should the line be drawn between the management and oversight roles in the organization? For example, if the board asks the CEO for a management succession plan but some board members are not comfortable with some of the choices of successors, how forcefully should they voice their objections?

Boards put in place a number of structures and processes that enable them to carry out their responsibilities effectively. Some issues are delegated to board committees both because many issues are too complex and too time-consuming to be dealt with by the entire board and to allow directors to make maximum use of their expertise. The board can delegate certain decisions to the relevant committee, or it can ask the committee to study the issue and develop recommendations to bring to the full board.

Most corporations have at least the following standing committees: audit committee, compensation committee, and nominating and governance committees. Some also have other committees, such as finance, investment, technology, public policy, and/or risk management committees that fit the needs of the company's industry or operating situation.

The following sections discuss two virtually universal board committees with significant management control-related responsibilities: audit committees and compensation committees.

AUDIT COMMITTEES

Audit committees provide independent oversight over companies' financial reporting processes, internal controls, and independent auditors. They enhance a board's ability to focus intensively and relatively inexpensively (without involving the full board) on the corporation's financial reporting-related functions. Although detailed regulations vary across countries, in most developed capital markets, audit committees are required to be comprised of outside (non-executive) or *independent* directors with a further requirement that they be *financially literate*.[20]

Furthermore, an audit committee's charter typically specifies the scope of the committee's responsibility and how it carries out those responsibilities, including structure, processes, and membership requirements. Audit committees also establish procedures for handling complaints regarding accounting, auditing, and internal control matters, including procedures for the confidential, anonymous submission by employees of concerns regarding questionable accounting practices. Audit committees also are typically responsible for the appointment, compensation, retention, and oversight of the work of the external auditors. The external auditors, in turn, discuss and address the quality, not just the acceptability, of the company's accounting principles with the audit committee.

As such, audit committees are intended to be informed, vigilant, and effective overseers of their companies' financial reporting processes and internal control systems. Audit committees generally assume the board's responsibilities relating to the organization's financial reporting, corporate governance, and control practices. In the financial reporting area, audit committees provide assurance that the company's financial disclosures are reasonable and accurate. In the corporate governance area, audit committees provide assurance that the corporation is in compliance with pertinent laws and regulations, is conducting its affairs ethically, and is maintaining effective controls against fraud and employee conflicts of interest. In the corporate control area, audit committees monitor the company's management and internal control systems that are designed to safeguard assets and employ them to achieve established goals and objectives. In fulfilling these responsibilities, audit committees hire the company's external auditors and monitor their performance. They maintain lines of communication between the board and the company's external auditors, internal auditors, financial management, and inside and outside counsel. Since they have limited resources directly available to them, audit committees must rely on the resources and support of other groups within the organization, and particularly the internal auditing function.[21]

Independence from management, in both fact and appearance, is one essential, and in many countries a legally required, characteristic of an audit committee. Before Sarbanes-Oxley was passed in the United States, company CEOs were known to select the audit committee members, determine their rotation policies, define their duties, routinely attend their meetings, and review and approve reports given to the audit committee. Such direct influence by the CEO or other key executives, such as the CFO, poses an obvious threat to the independence of the audit committee in their oversight role. Indeed, many corporate fraud cases involve the CEO or CFO, or both. When independence is lacking, employees and auditors will be reluctant to bring serious problems to the committee's attention, and the committee's effectiveness will be severely undermined. But other factors, such as directors' financial expertise and tenure, also affect the strength of the safeguards that audit committees provide.

The foci of audit committee oversight have changed significantly over the years. The Sarbanes-Oxley legislation placed a premium on documentation and testing of internal controls. The financial crisis of 2008 caused many audit committees to broaden their charters to include a focus on oversight of management's risk management practices, broadly defined. That is, the focus is often no longer just on financial statement risk. Many audit committees now also provide oversight of their companies' scenario planning, enterprise risk management, and investment risk decisions.

More research on audit committee effectiveness is needed, and it is clear that audit committees and their processes must be adapted to the requirements and resources of their company and board. That said, some common practices suggest that audit committees be advised to:

● Gain support and direction from the entire board of directors.

● Use agendas and follow formal work programs; keep minutes of meetings and distribute them to the full board of directors; schedule meetings in advance so participants have time to prepare.

● Have at least three members, but not too many more so that all members can be active participants.

● Ensure that the committee is comprised of the "right" individuals. Define the members' responsibilities and expect members who no longer contribute appropriately to step down. Ensure that all members are independent of management, financially literate, and engaged.

● Meet at least four times per year, including a pre-audit meeting and a post-audit meeting. (Some experts consider the frequency and duration of meetings to be highly reliable indicators of audit committee effectiveness.)

● Send a clear instruction to the independent auditor that the board of directors, as the shareholder's representative, is the auditor's client and that management is not. (This is a legal requirement of Sarbanes-Oxley.)

● Review all financial information; review interim, as well as annual, financial reports.

● Discuss with the independent auditor their qualitative judgments about the appropriateness, not just the acceptability, of the organization's accounting principles and financial disclosure practices.

- Go beyond a "check-the-box" orientation to compliance with legal requirements. Deal with the real issues of developing effective oversight and risk management practices.

- Be proactive. Participate in setting policies. Monitor the corporate code of conduct and compliance with it. Ensure that the internal auditing involvement in the entire financial reporting process is appropriate and properly coordinated with the independent auditor.

- Secure access to resources as needed, such as for responding to crises or conducting special investigations.

COMPENSATION COMMITTEES

The rules of some stock exchanges require listed companies to have compensation of top executives approved by a majority of independent directors. Most publicly held companies delegate such issues to a board *compensation committee* comprised solely of independent directors. In fact, New York Stock Exchange rules require the formation of such a compensation committee.

Compensation committees deal with issues related to the compensation and benefits provided to employees, and particularly top executives. In some companies, the compensation committee also provides oversight regarding the design and operation of retirement plans, although in other companies this function is delegated to an investment committee of the board.

Compensation committees have fiduciary responsibilities for ensuring that the company's executive compensation programs are fair and appropriate to attract, retain, and motivate managers and that they are reasonable in view of company economics and the relevant practices of comparable companies.

Compensation committees typically rely on the company's human resource function for staff support. In addition, because the design of compensation plans can raise many complex issues, such as relating to performance measures, pay forms (e.g. cash, stock options) and structures (e.g. performance thresholds, vesting provisions), external and internal compensation equity, and legal and tax considerations, compensation committees often employ outside consultants to provide data or expertise that the company does not have internally. Consultants often conduct industry compensation benchmarking studies or provide advice regarding the design of compensation plans. Compensation committees should retain full responsibility for overseeing the work of any compensation consultants they hire.

Much criticism is currently being directed at compensation committees. Much of this criticism stems from the large compensation, severance and/or retirement packages that have been offered to top executives. Examples of companies that have been scorned for "excessive pay" have recently been in the business press on almost a daily basis, especially since the financial crisis of 2008, when public outcry turned to the pay packages of "greedy bankers." Much of the criticism is leveled at boards who seem either unwilling or powerless to rein in the pay of their executives. A 2009 survey of directors by Corporate Board Member/PricewaterhouseCoopers revealed that 60% of the directors surveyed indicated that US company boards are having trouble controlling the size of CEO compensation.[22] Other critics are more concerned with the weak links in many companies between rewards and controllable performance, such as when many executives are well compensated when economic conditions are good even though their companies' performance lagged behind those of their closest competitors.[23] Some experts are predicting that compensation and the functioning of compensation committees will be the next area for additional regulation in the corporate governance arena.

CONCLUSION

This chapter has provided a brief introduction to the complex topic of corporate governance. It discussed the laws and regulations that govern its practice, and the important control-related roles played by members of boards of directors and, particularly, its audit and compensation committees. Boards of directors are important parts of companies' corporate governance systems and, hence, MCSs. Laws and regulations require some practices deemed to be desirable, such as the independence of board members who serve on audit and compensation committees. But the laws and regulations cannot define everything. In the best-run corporations, what is not defined by laws and regulations is shaped by a desire to emulate what is commonly called "best practice." The problem is that there is far from universal agreement as to what constitutes best practice. Multiple governance rating agencies define sets of practices that they deem to be best practice, but their suggested best practices do not always agree. And many books and articles provide advice about aspects of corporate governance, but those ideas, too, do not always converge.

Although they are important, it must be recognized that there are limits to what boards can do. It is common to blame boards of directors when companies suffer improprieties and ethical lapses. But independent directors only serve their organizations part-time. They cannot be held responsible for the day-to-day company management. They can only provide oversight. Good corporate governance must depend on managers' building a culture of integrity that involves an open and candid relationship with their engaged and supportive, but challenging, boards.

It also must be remembered that boards of directors and their committees are comprised of groups of individuals. Each individual has his/her own perceptions and understandings of roles and responsibilities. Thus, the functioning of these bodies is heavily dependent on group dynamics, which includes concerns such as how the agendas get set, how the issues get presented, how people get along, and whether members tolerate confrontation and/or compromise.[24] These are complex issues, and much is yet to be learned about what makes boards and board committees effective.

Notes

1. See, for example, "Corporate Governance," *The Economist* (September 7, 2009), online (www.economist.com); C. de Kluyver, *A Primer on Corporate Governance* (New York, NY: Business Expert Press, 2009); W. Judge, "Corporate Governance Mechanisms Throughout the World," *Corporate Governance: An International Review*, 18, no. 3 (2010), pp. 159–60; K. Balachandran, A. Dossi, and W. Van der Stede, "Corporate Governance Research in 'The Rest of the World'," *Journal of Accounting Auditing & Finance*, 25, no. 3 (Fall 2010), pp. 523–9.

2. See, for example, *The UK Corporate Governance Code* (Financial Reporting Council, June 2010), online (www.frc.org.uk).

3. See, for example, Committee of Sponsoring Organizations of the Treadway Commission (COSO), online (www.coso.org); and, specifically, *The COSO Financial Controls Framework* (2004 Version) and the original 1992 COSO Report: *Internal Control – An Integrated Framework*.

4. See, for example, N. Rajagoplan and Y. Zhang. "Recurring Failures in Corporate Governance: A Global Disease?," *Business Horizons*, 52 (2009), pp. 545–52; G. Kirkpatrick, "The Corporate Governance Lessons from the Financial Crisis," *Financial Market Trends*, 96, no. 1 (2009), online (www.oecd.org).

5. See, for example, J. Coffee, *Gatekeepers: The Professions and Corporate Governance* (New York, NY: Oxford University Press, 2006), particularly Chapter 4.

6. de Kluyver, *A Primer on Corporate Governance*, op. cit.

7. Coffee, *Gatekeepers*, op. cit.

8. P. Ali and G. Gregoriou, *International Corporate Governance after Sarbanes-Oxley* (New York, NY: Wiley Finance, 2006).

9. "How Much is it Really Costing to Comply with Sarbanes-Oxley?" *The Wall Street Journal* (June 16, 2005), online (http://online.wsj.com).

10. L. Rittenberg and P. Miller, *Sarbanes-Oxley 404 Work: Looking at the Benefits* (Altamonte Springs, FL: The

Institute of Internal Auditors Research Foundation, January 2005).

11. CRA International, *Sarbanes-Oxley Section 404 Costs and Implementation Issues: Spring 2006 Survey Update* (Washington, DC: CRA International, April 17, 2006).

12. Ibid.

13. US Securities and Exchange Commission, Office of Economic Analysis, *Study of the Sarbanes-Oxley Act of 2002, Section 404 Internal Control Over Financial Reporting Requirements* (September 2009).

14. S. Ernst, "CPA Corner: Sarbanes-Oxley and Corporation Fraud – Does One Size Fit All?," *AICPA CPA Insider* (May 8, 2006).

15. "Safeguards Failed to Detect Warnings in Enron Debacle," *The Wall Street Journal* (December 14, 2001).

16. For this alleged problem with corporate governance and boards, as well as many other issues, see, for example, L. Bebchuk and J. Fried, "Pay Without Performance: Overview of the Issues," *Journal of Corporation Law*, 30 (2005), pp. 647–73; L. Bebchuk and J. Fried, *Pay Without Performance: The Unfulfilled Promise of Executive Compensation* (Cambridge, MA: Harvard University Press, 2004).

17. "Now Hear This," *Fortune* (May 2, 1994), p. 16.

18. See, for example, D. Larcker, S. Richardson, and I. Tuna, "Corporate Governance, Accounting Outcomes, and Organizational Performance," *The Accounting Review*, 82, no. 4 (July 2007), pp. 963–1008. See also "Corporate Constitutions," *The Economist* (October 28, 2010), p. 74.

19. J. Sonnenfeld, "Good Governance and the Misleading Myths of Bad Metrics," *Academy of Management Perspectives*, 18, no. 1 (2004), pp. 108–13.

20. See, for example, US Securities and Exchange Commission, *Final Rule: Standards Relating to Listed Company Audit Committees: Rel. No. 33-8220* (December 18, 2007), online (www.sec.gov).

21. For a more detailed discussion of the audit committee charter, see publications by the major accounting firms, such as Deloitte & Touche, *Audit Committee Resource Guide* (Deloitte, 2010), online (www.deloitte.com).

22. "What Directors Think," *Corporate Board Member* (Special Supplement, 2009), p. 11.

23. See note 16.

24. See, for example, K. Merchant and K. Pick. *Blind Spots, Biases and Other Pathologies in the Boardroom* (New York, NY: Business Expert Press, 2010).

Case Study

Vector Aeromotive Corporation

John Pope, a member of the board of directors of Vector Aeromotive Corporation, had a lot on his mind as he drove to his office. It was March 22, 1993, the day Vector's board had agreed to ask formally for the resignation of the company's president and founder, Gerald A. (Gerry) Wiegert. Gerry had already been informed that if he did not resign he would be fired. John hoped that Gerry would step down gracefully and not provoke a confrontation. Gerry had been the mastermind of the company for many years, but now John believed the board had little choice but to remove him because Vector was in a crisis. It was not able to pay either its employees or its payroll taxes; checks were bouncing; and outstanding accounts payable were being ignored. John and the other board members were convinced that the crisis was the result of Gerry's management style and excessive spending and that it was the board's moral and legal obligation to the shareholders to remove Gerry as president.

When John reached Vector headquarters, however, he was greeted by armed guards barring entry to the building. His efforts to enter the building through a rear entrance were futile because all the locks had been changed. Gerry had barricaded himself inside. Clearly this was not going to be an amicable management succession process. Gerry Wiegert had declared war.

▶

This case was prepared by research assistant Michelle Wright under the supervision of Professor Kenneth A. Merchant.

Copyright © by Kenneth A. Merchant.

VECTOR AND THE EXOTIC SPORTS CAR INDUSTRY

Vector Aeromotive Corporation (hereafter Vector) designed, manufactured, and sold exotic sports cars. Cars are defined as exotic by their price range ($150,000–$500,000), their speed (in excess of 160 mph), their driving performance, their technologically superior, high performance components, their extensive use of hand manufacturing, and their appearance. Exotic sports cars are offered to a select, wealthy clientele. Vector management estimated the total worldwide market for exotic sports cars was approximately 5,500 vehicles per year. The company's major competitors were Ferrari and Lamborghini, who together held a 75% market share.

Vector, located in Wilmington, California, was the only US-based manufacturer of exotic sports cars. Gerry Wiegert's vision was to design an automobile using the finest technology in America – aerospace technology. Indeed the company's motto was "Aerospace Technology for the Road." In designing cars, performance was paramount; cost was no object.

Vector's standard model, the W8 Twin Turbo "luxury supercar", priced at $448,000, had received considerable critical acclaim in automotive magazines such as *Road & Track*. The W8 was powered by a 6.0 liter, all-aluminum engine with twin turbochargers that generated over 600 horsepower at 5,700 rpm. It could accelerate from 0 to 60 mph in 3.9 seconds and reach speeds of 260 mph. The car made considerable use of aerospace technology, including advanced composite materials for body panels, military specification electrical systems, and advanced tactical fighter instrumentation and displays. It also contained numerous safety and luxury features, such as an integrated rollcage, energy-absorbing crush zones, a spacious, "high-tech, jet-aircraft-like leather cockpit", and a custom, 10-disk compact disk changer.

From 1978 to 1987 the company operated as Vector Car, a privately funded limited partnership founded by Gerry Wiegert. Vector Aeromotive Corporation was formed in September 1987. It completed its Initial Public Offering in November 1988, selling approximately 35% of the company's stock for $6 million. Vector delivered its first car to a paying customer in September 1990, and as of March 1993, it had sold a total of 13 cars, to an international clientele. In its peak month the company employed 45 people.

Because of its low sales volumes Vector had reported substantial financial losses since its inception (see statements of operations in Exhibit 1). In an attempt to build volume Vector was developing two other models, the Avtech WX3-R roadster and WX3-C coupe. Gerry Wiegert wanted to price these models in the $700,000–$800,000 range, but some of the members of the board of directors thought the new models should be more modestly priced, at perhaps around $200,000.

THE BOARD OF DIRECTORS

At its incorporation in 1987 Vector Aeromotive had three members on its board of directors. Gerry Wiegert was the board chairman. The two other directors, John Pope and Barry Rosengrant, had been consultants to Vector Car and business associates of Gerry for many years. Barry's background was in real estate. John was a financial consultant who acted as Vector's chief financial officer from 1988–90 on a part-time basis.

The board's primary role was to act as a fiduciary body, to oversee management decisions and protect shareholders' interests. The board was not involved in the formation of company strategy, but it did ratify major financial and policy decisions, such as advertising and promotion budgets. When actual expenses were greater than budgeted expenses (as they often were), Gerry Wiegert, in his role as president, had to explain the variances to the other board members. Although the outside board members recognized that Gerry's effectiveness as president would probably decline as the company grew in size they did not identify or train possible successors, partly because the company was so small and partly because Wiegert would be strongly opposed to such actions.

The board of directors met quarterly on a regular basis, and additional special meetings were called occasionally to deal with specific issues, such as the signing of corporate documents. Vector management rarely provided information to board members prior to the meetings, but they shared considerable data and progress reports during the meetings. The atmosphere of the board meetings was generally congenial.

In 1991 Dan Harnett was added to the board of directors. Dan was an attorney and another long-time associate of Gerry Wiegert's. According to John Pope:

> Gerry wanted to shift the balance of power on the board. By 1991 Barry and I were not agreeing with him on some of the things that he wanted to do. He was getting voted down in some situations, and he wasn't particularly happy about that. I think he felt bringing Dan in would help shift the balance in his favor a little bit.

EARLY SIGNS OF TROUBLE

In June 1990 Don Johnson was hired as vice president, finance. Don quickly began to feel uncomfortable with Gerry's management style. Don said, "Gerry hires good people who think they will be able to make a difference. But after about six months I realized that he doesn't give anyone the freedom to be effective." Don thought Gerry was excessively focused on raising money and promoting the company while neglecting attention to engineering and production. He also believed that Gerry's management style, which was shaped by "a compulsive, obsessive personality and a foul mouth," imposed undue stress on employees. Don confronted Gerry about his concerns, but he was not able to change either Gerry's priorities or management style. Don also informed the board members of his concerns, but he received no support. For many months Don felt he was the sole voice of dissent, noting that "obviously the board was pretty much hand-picked."

Until 1992 the outside board members were not seriously concerned about Gerry Wiegert's management style, although they considered him eccentric. John Pope explained that:

> At some point in his schooling, Gerry must have stayed up all night preparing for an exam or a presentation and received an "A" for his effort. Since then he has decided that's the way life works, that if you let everything wait until the last minute and cram all your preparation into two days, you get better performance than if you spread it out over the month beforehand. That's how he functioned.

In retrospect, John attributed much of the outside board members' support of Wiegert to the fact that most of the information they received was designed to elicit agreement. He said:

Gerry Wiegert was, and is, literally a master of giving everybody, including the board, just enough information to support the conclusion he wants them to reach. The boardroom presenters were well coached, and we never received all of the relevant information.

The board finally took serious issue with some of Gerry's management actions early in 1992. Within three months of joining the board Dan Harnett became a strong adversary of Gerry because of some issues brought to his attention by Vector employees. In a board meeting, he charged that Gerry was misusing expense reports, using company funds for personal home improvements, and participating in other forms of self-dealing at the company's expense. The board asked Don Johnson to look into these issues. Three weeks later a board meeting was called to formally discuss the charges and to decide on a course of action. Dan Harnett called for Gerry's immediate removal.

But Dan did not get the board's support. The outside board members did not think the charges of illegal activity could be substantiated. Don Johnson did a study but found no evidence that Gerry had diverted any company assets to his home. He did question approximately $17,000 of items charged on Gerry's American Express card because he had provided inadequate documentation. But Gerry explained that all the expenses were legitimate because, as the president of an exotic car company, he "had an image to maintain."

The board did conclude that Gerry had participated in some questionable business deals. For example, Gerry lent an associate $25,000 of company money that was secured by a personal note made payable to himself. He also negotiated a lease at a below-market price and attempted to release the property to Vector at the market price. The board insisted that Gerry charge Vector the lower price for the lease, arguing that he should not realize personal gain at the expense of the company. Gerry reluctantly succumbed to the board's wishes on the lease issue. Since the loan was repaid and neither of these deals ended up hurting Vector the directors felt they did not warrant Gerry's termination. John Pope said:

> By this time I think that the board was concerned about Gerry's management style, how he ran things and his excessive spending, but he hadn't done anything illegal. He also had an employment contract (see excerpts in Exhibit 2) that says he's allowed to be a bad manager. He just isn't allowed to do anything illegal.

The outside directors also believed it was not in the company's best interests for them to agree with Dan Harnett's call for firing Gerry because there was no obvious successor. In the words of John Pope:

> One of the concerns at that time too was that Dan had no Act II. Act I was "get rid of Wiegert." Act II was, "What do we do now?" There had to be something in place as far as I was concerned. You don't just throw the guy out. You have to have a plan to move forward.

One outcome of this board meeting was an agreement to change the process for reimbursing Gerry for personal expenses. Previously, Vector had paid Gerry's entire credit card bill. After the meeting, Gerry was required to submit formal expense reports to the accounting department.

Later that year Dan Harnett resigned from the board and subsequently died. He was replaced on the board by George Fencl, a self-employed consultant and businessman, and another long-time associate of Gerry Wiegert.

AN INDONESIAN INVESTOR

In June 1992 Vector obtained $2 million in financing from Setiwan Djody, an Indonesian investor. Djody bought 4 million shares at $0.50 and also paid $118,000 for an option to buy an additional 6 million shares at $0.50. Mr. Djody advanced the money to Vector before completing a due diligence review. The board members perceived this quick advance as unusual and not very businesslike, but they later discovered that Djody customarily did business on the basis of trust. Included in Djody's purchase agreement was the right to appoint a director to the board. Thus a fifth director, Baduraman Dorpi, was added to protect Mr. Djody's interests in the company. Barry Rosengrant resigned shortly afterwards to make room for Mr. Dorpi, leaving the board still comprised of four members. Gerry had said that Mr. Djody insisted that the board not be increased in size, thus leaving him only a 20% vote. But the remaining board members later found out that this was not true; Gerry and Mr. Djody had never discussed the board size issue.

In September 1992 Gerry Wiegert negotiated a new employment contract. It included an option to buy 1 million shares of stock at $0.21875, the market price on the date the option was issued.

By December 1992 Vector was out of money again, and some employees had to be laid off. Mr. Djody was unwilling to exercise his stock purchase option, but he agreed to exercise Gerry's stock option if Gerry would transfer that option to him. Mr. Djody sent $220,000 to Vector in accordance with this agreement. But then, despite an agreement signed to the contrary, Gerry tried to renege on this deal, claiming that he had not intended that his option be transferred but just used as collateral for a loan. This disagreement breached the Indonesians' trust in Gerry. After this they had no interest in making additional investments in Vector, but they did keep Mr. Dorpi on as a director to protect the money they had already invested.

EVENTS LEADING TO GERRY WIEGERT'S TERMINATION

As Vector's financial position worsened tension between Gerry and the board of directors increased. The company's payroll taxes for the period September through December 1992 were not paid on time. This caused a debate over disclosures in the company's 10-K report for the fiscal year ended September 30, 1992. According to John Pope:

> Although the 10-K report is required to be filed within 90 days of the fiscal year end, Gerry would not allow it to be filed with the required disclosure that we hadn't paid our payroll taxes. But I would not allow it to be filed without that disclosure. So Gerry and I compromised. We had a sales prospect who was expected any day to give us a $100,000 check as a deposit on a car. That money could be used to pay the payroll taxes. We decided to let the 10-K be late.

In February 1993 John Pope was invited to Gerry Wiegert's house for a baby shower for the accounting manager who was preparing to go on maternity leave. This was his first visit to the house, and when he arrived, he was shocked to find the house was decorated in "modern Vector." Cabinets, floor tiles, and wall tiles were all identical to those used in Vector headquarters. John recalled:

> When I went into the house I couldn't believe it. I looked around and saw what looked like a mirror image of our office. On Monday morning I said to Don Johnson, I know you've examined all of the company invoices, but I have now been in Gerry's house and you're never going to convince me that

company money wasn't used in that house. I don't know how we're going to prove it, but I will guarantee you that he has diverted company assets.

That same month Don Johnson informed the board that the business plan Gerry was showing potential investors was, in the opinion of the heads of the marketing, finance, and production departments, wildly optimistic. He believed that Gerry's continued use of the business plan to solicit funds was fraudulent.

By March Vector's financial position was critical. Employees weren't being paid; the 10-K still had not been issued because the payroll taxes had not been paid; $14,000 in checks had bounced; and remaining accounts payable were being ignored. But Gerry Wiegert was focused on other things: he and some of his managers were out of the country, at the Geneva car show.

John Pope was ready to take action. He was convinced that with Gerry Wiegert at the stern Vector was heading for disaster. But before John could take any action against Gerry he needed George Fencl's support. George had also become increasingly disenchanted with Gerry. George's primary charge was to assist Vector in obtaining financing, but he was finding it difficult to do so because the potential investors he had contacted did not trust Gerry. John brought up the issue over lunch. He explained:

> George talked about his inability to raise any money because of Gerry's management style. I told him about my concerns regarding the probable diversion of funds. I also explained that I had pulled out a couple of Gerry's American Express bills and found out that the procedure we thought had been put into place had not been implemented. Gerry instead told the accounting department that they were now to pay off from only the face page of the bill. They were no longer going to get the individual tickets.

John Pope and George Fencl agreed to call the company's SEC counsel for advice. The lawyers acknowledged that the board did have authority to terminate Gerry for cause, and they further acknowledged that there appeared to be sufficient cause, most particularly the fraudulent business plan and

diversion of company assets. John called Mr. Dorpi, and he agreed to support the other outside board members in their decision to terminate Gerry.

John hand-delivered to Gerry notice of a special board meeting to be held on Friday, March 19, 1993. This notice, which contained no explanation of the purpose of the meeting, was given 24 hours in advance of the meeting, as required by company by-laws. After receiving this notice Gerry called Mr. Dorpi, and Dorpi told him that the purpose of the meeting was to terminate Gerry as president. Gerry immediately called George Fencl and demanded an explanation.

George and Gerry met for the entire day on Thursday the 18th. John Pope was there for part of the day. At this meeting George confirmed what Mr. Dorpi had said and added that the board planned to give him the opportunity to resign in the best interests of the shareholders. If Gerry chose to resign the board would send out a press release explaining that Gerry "wanted to devote himself to creative aspects of the business." If Gerry chose not to resign the board would terminate him and sue him for conversion of funds.

Gerry questioned both why this was happening and why now. He said he needed to go to New Jersey for the opening of a new dealership, and he had a financing meeting set up in New York. But George and John did not want him to make the trip. They did not think he should act as president when he was soon to be fired, and they did not want him to raise money by using the fraudulent business plan.

Finally, Gerry asked that the special board meeting be postponed 30 days. The board members refused this request, but they did agree to postpone until Monday to give Gerry the weekend to decide if he would *resign* or be terminated. The meeting was scheduled for Monday, March 22, at 5.00 p.m. On Monday morning Gerry responded by moving into the headquarters' building and barring all outsiders, including the board members, from the building. A newspaper account the next day labeled the affair *Wall Street Waco*, as it occurred at the same time as the Branch Davidians cult members' standoff with the federal agents in Waco, Texas.

Exhibit 1 Statements of operations

	Years ended September 30			September 12, 1987 (Inception) to September 30, 1992 (Cumulative)
	1992	1991	1990	
Sales, net (Note 15)	**$1,287,866**	$754,800	$20,000	$2,062,666
Costs of sales	**974,966**	579,800	20,000	1,574,766
Gross profit	**312,900**	175,000	–	487,900
Costs and Expenses				
Salaries and wages (Note 3)	**917,350**	1,533,199	1,253,554	4,251,037
Rental expense (Note 3)	**96,358**	112,972	128,558	529,088
Utilities expense	**91,793**	116,578	64,264	316,575
Research and development	**1,275,841**	718,346	2,340,818	4,878,034
Depreciation and amortization	**429,394**	466,316	241,437	1,266,813
Advertising and promotion	**566,121**	535,023	655,194	1,890,137
Professional fees	**613,015**	324,411	580,852	1,833,288
General and administrative	**528,275**	917,726	427,820	2,153,405
Warranty expense	**27,564**	31,157	–	58,721
Provision for loss contingency (Note 7)	–	633,167	–	633,167
Abandonment of property and equpiment	–	234,911	–	234,911
Total costs and expenses	**4,545,711**	5,623,806	5,692,497	18,045,176
Other income (expense)				
Other income	**231,299**	88,489	214,179	836,211
Other expense	**(35,400)**	(15,862)	(26,373)	(119,523)
	195,899	72,627	187,806	716,688
Net loss	**$(4,036,912)**	$(5,376,179)	$(5,504,691)	$(16,840,588)
Net loss per share (Note 12)	**$(0.39)**	$(1.11)	$(1.90)	
Weighted average common shares outstanding (Note 12)	**10,245,056**	4,832,556	2,890,329	

EXHIBIT 2 Excerpts from Gerry Wiegert's employee contract

EMPLOYMENT AGREEMENT

EMPLOYMENT AGREEMENT, effective July 1, 1992, by and between VECTOR AEROMOTIVE CORPORATION, a Nevada corporation (the "Company") and GERALD A. WIEGERT (the "Employee").

WHEREAS, the Company has, prior to the date of this Agreement, employed the Employee as the Company's President, and

WHEREAS, the Company desires to continue to employ the Employee on a full-time basis, and the Employee desires to be so employed by the Company, from and after the date of this agreement.

NOW THEREFORE, in consideration of the mutual covenants contained herein, the parties agree as follows:

Article I

EMPLOYMENT DUTIES AND BENEFITS

Section 1.5 Expenses. The Employee is authorized to incur reasonable expenses for promoting the domestic and international business of the Company in all respects, including expenses for entertainment, travel and similar items. The Company will reimburse the Employee for all such expenses upon the presentation by the Employee, from time-to-time, of an itemized account of such expenditures.

Section 1.6 Employee's Other Business. Employee shall be allowed to participate in outside business activities provided (i) such activities do not interfere with Employee's performance of his duties as a full-time employee of the Company; and (ii) the outside business is not a Business Opportunity of the Company, as defined herein. A Business Opportunity of the Company shall be a product, service, investment, venture or other opportunity which is either:

(a) directly related to or within the scope of the existing business of the Company; or

(b) within the logical scope of the business of the Company, as such scope may be expanded or altered from time-to-time by the Board of Directors.

The Employee's current outside business activities, which activities are hereby irrevocably approved by the Company, include investments in Ram Wing and the Wet Bike.

Article II

COMPENSATION

Section 2.1 Base Salary. The Company shall pay to the Employee a base salary of not less than the amount specified on Schedule 1. This amount may be adjusted for raises in salary by action of the Board of Directors.

Section 2.2 Bonus. The Employee shall be entitled to receive a bonus at such time or times as may be determined by the Board of Directors of the Company.

Article III

TERM OF EMPLOYMENT AND TERMINATION

Section 3.1 Term. This Agreement shall be for a term which is specified on Schedule 1, commencing on its effective date, subject, however, to termination during such period as provided in this Article. This Agreement shall be renewed automatically for succeeding periods of one year on the same terms and conditions as contained in this Agreement unless either the Company of the Employee shall, at least 30 days prior to the expiration of the initial term or of any renewal term, give written notice of the intention not to renew this Agreement. Such renewals shall be effective in subsequent years on the same day of the same month as the original effective date of this Agreement.

Section 3.2 Termination by the Employee Without Cause. The Employee, without cause, may terminate this Agreement upon 90 days' written notice to the Company. In such event, the Employee shall not be required to render the services required under this Agreement. Compensation for vacation time not taken by Employee shall be paid to the Employee at the date of termination.

Section 3.3 Termination by the Company With Cause. The Company may terminate the Employee, at any time, upon 90 days' written notice and opportunity for Employee to remedy any non-compliance with the terms of this Agreement, by reason of the willful misconduct of the Employee which is contrary to the best interests of the Company. Upon the date of such termination, the Company's obligation to pay compensation shall terminate. No compensation for vacation time not taken by Employee shall be paid to the Employee.

Exhibit 2 *continued*

Schedule 1

DUTIES AND COMPENSATION

Employee: Gerald A. Wiegert

Position: President

Base Salary: $275,000 per year, payable bi-weekly and quarterly performance payment equal to 10% of improvements over annual budget as approved by Board from time to time

Bonus: As determined by the Board of Directors

Term: December 31, 1997

Duties and Responsibilities: Supervision and coordination of all operations of the Company; supervision of all other operating officers of the Company.

APPROVED:

THE COMPANY: EMPLOYEE:

By: _____   *Gerald A. Wiegert*
    John Pope, Compensation Committee   Gerald, A. Wiegert

Date: _____, 1992   Date: _____*May 1*_____, 1992

Case Study

Golden Parachutes?

A special conference-call meeting of the compensation committee of the board of directors of Database Technologies, Inc. (DTI) was scheduled for the morning of February 23, 2007. DTI, headquartered in Sunnyvale, CA, was a leader in database-related software. The company's main products helped customers monitor, forecast, and manage data growth in enterprise resource planning (ERP) system environments.

The main agenda item for the special compensation committee meeting was discussion and possible approval of a proposed Change in Control Severance Agreement. In November 2006, a large, European-based technology company had expressed interest in acquiring DTI. Because of this inquiry, John Hoffman, DTI's chairman/CEO, had asked Alan Adamson, chair of DTI's compensation committee, to have his committee consider the implementation

---

This case was prepared by Professors Kenneth A. Merchant and Wim A. Van der Stede.

of a severance agreement. Mr. Adamson agreed. There was some urgency to the request because DTI management expected to receive the formal acquisition offer sometime in the first half of 2007.

After a series of discussions with Mr. Hoffman and Mr. Adamson, DTI's outside counsel drew up a proposed severance agreement. The agreement, if enacted, would provide payments under certain conditions (explained below) to a "select group of management or highly compensated employees" of DTI. Included in this select group were five executives: DTI's CEO, COO, CFO, chief technology officer (CTO), and general counsel/secretary.

The materials sent to the committee members in advance of the meeting explained that the severance agreement was –

> intended for the benefit of both the key DTI executives and the company. It would protect the executives against significant negative personal as well as financial consequences that could result from a change in control. Further, having this severance agreement in place would help to keep the executives employed and focused on shareholders' interests, rather than on their own interests. That is, it would help to ensure that the company would be able to rely upon the executives to continue in their positions without concern that they might be distracted by the personal uncertainties and risks created by the possibility that they might lose their jobs.

Under the terms of the severance agreement, the named executives would be entitled to receive benefits if the executive received a Qualifying Termination following a Change in Control of the company. *Change in Control* was deemed to have occurred as of the first day that 40% or more of the then-outstanding voting securities changed hands. A *Qualifying Termination* was deemed to have occurred if any one or more of the following events occurred within a 24 calendar month period following the date of a Change in Control:

1. An involuntary termination of the executive's employment for reasons other than Cause. *Cause* was defined as the occurrence of either or both of the following: (a) the executive's conviction for committing a felony or (b) the executive's willful engagement in misconduct that is significantly injurious to the company.

2. A voluntary termination of the employment by the executive for Good Reason. *Good Reason* was defined as the occurrence, without the executive's

express written consent, of any one or more of the following:

(a) A material reduction in the nature of status of the executive's authorities, duties, and/or responsibilities or a diminution of the executive's reporting relationship.

(b) A reduction in the executive's base salary.

(c) A reduction in the executive's relative level of participation in and relative level of coverage in the company's employee benefit plans. (The company can eliminate and/or modify existing programs, but the executive's level and amounts of coverage under all such programs must be at least as great as is provided to executives who have the same or lesser levels of reporting responsibilities within the company's organization.)

(d) The executive is informed by the company with less than 180 days' notice that his/her principal place of employment for the company will be relocated to a location that is greater than 35 miles away from the executive's principal place of employment for the company immediately prior to the Change in Control.

3. The company or any successor company repudiates or breaches any of the provisions of the Severance Agreement.

The executive's right to terminate employment for good reason was not affected by the executive's incapacity due to physical or mental illness.

Each Qualifying Termination would entitle the affected executive to receive:

1. A lump sum payment equal to twice (2×) the executive's highest annualized base salary in effect at any time on or before the effective date of termination.

2. A lump sum payment equal to twice (2×) the highest aggregate bonus(es) paid by the company to the executive for any one of the three full fiscal years of the company immediately preceding the executive's effective date of termination.

3. A lump-sum payment equal to the portion of the executive's account under the company's qualified retirement plan, nonqualified deferred compensation plan, or any other supplemental retirement plan that has not become vested as of the effective date of termination. Included in this provision was an immediate vesting of all of the executives' stock options.

4. A continuation of the executive's car allowance or other company perquisites for 24 months following the effective date of termination.

5. A continuation of the executive's and his/her family's medical coverage, dental coverage, and group term life insurance for 24 months following the executive's effective date of termination.

6. A reimbursement of up to $18,000 for outplacement services obtained during the 24-month period following the effective date of termination.

7. If the payments exceeded the safe harbor amount set by the US Congress, the payments would be "grossed up" so that the executives would not have to pay an excise tax sometimes referred to as a "golden parachute" tax.[1]

The executive would not be entitled to receive severance benefits if employment terminated, regardless of the reason, more than 24 months after the date of a Change in Control.

An estimate of the amounts that would be paid to the five key executives if the payments were triggered in 2007 is shown in Exhibit 1. CEO John Hoffman was the only executive who would be subject to the so-called "golden parachute" tax. John's proposed severance payments exceeded the allowed base amount because when John was recruited to DTI, he had been given a large number of options with a 10-year vesting period. If a Change in Control occurred, all of these options would immediately vest. The value of these options would comprise approximately half of the Change in Control Payments that John would be paid.

The materials sent in advance of the meeting presented a statement that most companies of DTI's size or larger had such an agreement in place, with the range of severance payments typically set between one and a half to three times the executives' base salary plus bonuses. However, the committee members were not provided with any formal benchmarking data.

A COMMITTEE MEMBER'S REACTIONS

As Dennis Feingold, one of DTI's three compensation committee members, read the proposed severance agreement, he had mixed feelings about it. Dennis believed that the purposes of such plans were valid. DTI's interests could be badly hurt if key executives, fearing for their jobs, left the company before the acquisition was consummated. Most, if not all, of these executives would probably not be retained by the management of the acquiring company. A severance agreement would probably keep them on the job until the end, and the payments would probably enable them to sustain their lifestyles until they could obtain another comparable job.

Dennis had particular empathy for DTI's CTO who was recruited to DTI just a few months earlier from a firm located in New York. Losing his job not long after a disruptive personal relocation would be difficult for the CTO and his family.

Dennis was not particularly concerned about the total cost of the severance payments. While the severance payments would reduce the acquisition price, they probably were not large enough to have a negative effect on the consummation of the transaction itself. Even if all of the severance payments were paid, the total cost would probably only be about $12 million, not a large amount of money in comparison with the company's acquisition price, which probably would be close to $2 billion.

But Dennis did have some concerns about the payments. Some of the individual payments would be quite large. Some of these executives were already quite wealthy, and they would be given millions of dollars more in severance payments. Dennis knew that shareholders did not have to approve such payments and probably would not even become aware of them, but he was concerned that if they, or rank-and-file employees, became aware of them, there would be some resentment.

Dennis also asked himself whether the company's performance warranted these payments. While the company's stock price had risen over the

---

[1] If the present value of the severance payments ("parachute payments") exceeded three times the individual's average annual compensation in the most recent five taxable years, a federal "golden parachute tax" would have to be paid. This tax legislation was passed to try to discourage what the US Congress considered to be "excessive" severance payments. The amount of the golden parachute tax was calculated as 20% of the excess of the parachute payments over the executive's average base salary over the prior five-year period.

If the company grossed up the payment, the paid tax amount would also have to be treated as part of the parachute payment, and a golden parachute tax would have to be paid on this amount also. As a consequence, grossing up the payments could be quite costly. The need to pay taxes on the excess and the need to pay additional taxes on the gross-up amounts was sometimes likened to a dog "chasing its tail."

years, by most objective metrics DTI's performance in recent years could be rated only mediocre, perhaps slightly below the median as compared to similar technology-intensive companies. A part of him thought that, with the exception of the newly hired CTO, the executives had been amply rewarded for their efforts over the years. In return, perhaps they should owe loyalty to the company.

Dennis wondered why these five employees, as key as they were, should have severance arrangements different from those of any other employee in the company. Other corporate officers (e.g. VP-operations, VP-sales and marketing, VP-human resources, controller) were not included in the severance agreement. In fact, Dennis noted that since no DTI employees were represented by a union, all DTI employees had always been considered to be employed "at will," meaning they could be fired at any time without cause.

Dennis knew that severance payments were a political hot button. Many management critics had focused much attention on what they perceived as "outrageous" management compensation packages, with large severance payments and potential payments seen as part of the problem.[2] Dennis knew that some corporate governance rating agencies and other "watchdogs" would be observing. He did not want to see DTI listed as being among a "rogue's gallery" of firms whose boards did not exercise their fiduciary responsibilities in the compensation area. Dennis was also concerned about his personal reputation. He enjoyed his board service and wanted to serve on other boards.

On the other hand, Dennis knew that if he raised objections, the other committee members would undoubtedly point to the fact that most companies have a severance agreement, and the terms of this agreement probably should be judged as reasonable by current corporate standards. Dennis himself, the CEO of a large company in the food processing industry, was covered by a severance agreement. His was not quite as lucrative as the one being proposed at DTI, but Dennis certainly did not want to go on record as being against severance agreements.

So as Dennis prepared to go to the meeting, he was mulling over all of these issues, which accumulated into one big question. Should he just "go along" with the other two compensation committee members and vote to approve the severance agreement as proposed, or should he voice his concerns? If the latter, how forcefully should he press his concerns if the other committee members did not immediately agree with him?

---

[2] In 2005 the average parachute payment for CEOs of the top 100 US corporations was $28 million. Some payments were much larger, such as the $188 million that Gillette's CEO James Kilts received when his company was sold to Procter & Gamble, and the $162 million that William McGuire, CEO of United Health, would receive if his company were sold. See "Golden Parachutes are Excessive," <lawprofessors.typepad.com/business_law/2006/01/golden_parachut.html> and M. Brush, "You're Fired. Here's Your $16 Million," *MSN Money* (April 9, 2003), <moneycentral.msn.com/content/p44954.asp>.

Exhibit 1 Estimate of DTI parachute payments if paid in 2007 ($000)

Executive	Change in control payment	Excess parachute payment	Total payment
CEO	$4,474	$1,670[3]	$6,144
COO	2,110	–	2,110
CFO	1,685	–	1,685
CTO	1,400	–	1,400
General counsel	623	–	623
Total	$10,292	$1,670	$11,962

[3] **Test for the need for a golden parachute tax payment:**

Total change in control payments	$4,474
Safe harbor amount (3x limit)	3,402
Difference	$1,072 (Since the difference is positive, a golden parachute tax must be paid.)

Calculation of the amount of the golden parachute tax:

Total change in control payments	$4,474
Base amount (ave. salary over last 5 years)	1,134
Excess parachute	3,340
Golden parachute tax (20%)	668
Grossed up golden parachute tax	$1,670

Case Study

Pacific Sunwear of California, Inc.

As a publicly owned company in the United States, Pacific Sunwear of California, Inc. (PacSun) was required to comply with the provisions of the Sarbanes-Oxley Act of 2002 (SOX). Among other things, SOX required top management to test their company's system of internal controls and to certify that it is effective. It also required the company's external auditors to conduct independent tests of those controls and to express their independent opinion about the effectiveness of the company's system.

In 2006, after their second year of complying with SOX, PacSun management looked back and concluded that the process had provided a few benefits, but they thought that the compliance costs far exceeded the benefits, at least to the company. With the compliance processes now well controlled and the costs of compliance having been sharply reduced, they were turning their attention back to issues of more business relevance, such as business continuity planning and, more generally, controlling business risks.

THE COMPANY

PacSun's mission is to be "the leading lifestyle retailer of casual fashion apparel, footwear and accessories for teens and young adults." The company's origins were as a small surf shop that started in 1980 in Newport Beach, California. The company was incorporated in August 1982, and it went public in 1993. Its stock is traded on NASDAQ using the symbol PSUN. By 2006, PacSun was a large company, with annual sales of almost $1.4 billion (see Exhibit 1). Over the years, the company's stock was split 3-for-2 six times, and was one of the fastest growing stocks on the NASDAQ stock exchange.

PacSun operated chains of mostly mall-based stores with three distinct retail concepts. As of July 29, 2006, it ran 826 PacSun stores, 102 PacSun Outlet stores, 201 d.e.m.o. stores and six One Thousand Steps stores, for a total of 1,112 stores located in all 50 states of the US and Puerto Rico. PacSun and PacSun Outlet stores specialized in board sport-inspired casual apparel, footwear, and related accessories. d.e.m.o. specialized in fashion-focused streetwear. One Thousand Steps, a new concept started in 2006, targeted 18- to 24-year-old customers and featured an assortment of casual, fashion-forward, branded footwear and related accessories.

In its stores, PacSun offered a wide selection of well-known board-sport inspired name brands, including Quiksilver, Roxy, DC Shoes, Billabong, Hurley, and Volcom. The company supplemented the name brand offerings with its own proprietary brands. The company had its own product design group that, in collaboration with the buying staff, designed the proprietary brand merchandise. The company also had a sourcing group that oversaw the manufacture and delivery of its proprietary brand merchandise with manufacturing contracted out both domestically and internationally.

PacSun's merchandising department oversaw the purchasing and allocation of its merchandise. Its buyers were responsible for reviewing branded merchandise lines from new and existing vendors, identifying emerging fashion trends, and selecting branded and proprietary brand merchandise styles in quantities, colors, and sizes to meet inventory levels established by company management. The planning and allocation department was responsible for management of inventory levels by store and by class, allocation of merchandise to stores, and inventory replenishment based upon information generated by its merchandise management information systems. These systems provided the planning

---

This case was prepared by Professors Kenneth A. Merchant, Wim A. Van der Stede and research assistant Fei Du.

department with current inventory levels at each store and for the company as a whole, as well as current selling history within each store by merchandise classification and by style.

All merchandise was delivered to the centralized distribution facility in Anaheim, California, where it was inspected, received into its computer system, allocated to stores, ticketed when necessary, and boxed for distribution to its stores or packaged for delivery to its internet customers. Each store was typically shipped merchandise three to five times a week, providing it with a steady flow of new merchandise. The company used a national and a regional small package carrier to ship merchandise to its stores and internet customers. The company occasionally used airfreight to ship merchandise to stores during peak selling periods.

PacSun's expansion pace was steady and fast. In 2005, the company opened 115 net new stores, which included 67 PacSun stores, 12 PacSun Outlet stores, and 36 d.e.m.o. stores, and also expanded or relocated an additional 34 existing stores.

The store operating structure was relatively flat. Each store had a manager, one or more co-managers or assistant managers, and approximately six to 12 part-time sales associates. District managers supervised approximately seven to 12 stores. Regional directors supervised approximately six to 10 district managers.

District and store managers and co-managers participated in a bonus program based on achieving predetermined metrics, including sales and inventory shrinkage targets. The company had well-established store operating policies and procedures and an extensive in-store training program for new store managers and comanagers. It placed great emphasis on loss prevention programs in order to control inventory shrinkage. These programs included the installation of electronic article surveillance systems in all stores, education of store personnel on loss prevention, and monitoring of returns, voids, and employee sales. As a result of these programs, PacSun's historical inventory shrinkage rates were below 1.5% of net sales at retail (0.6% at cost).

PacSun's merchandise, financial, and store computer systems were fully integrated. Its software was regularly upgraded or modified as needs arose or changed. Its information systems provided company management, buyers, and planners with comprehensive data that helped them identify emerging trends and manage inventories. The systems included purchase order management, electronic data interchange, open order reporting, open-to-buy, receiving, distribution, merchandise allocation, basic stock replenishment, interstore transfers, inventory and price management. Company management used weekly best/worst item sales reports to enhance the timeliness and effectiveness of purchasing and markdown decisions. Merchandise purchases were based on planned sales and inventory levels and were frequently revised to reflect changes in demand for a particular item or classification.

All of the PacSun stores had a point-of-sale system operating on in-store computer hardware. The system featured bar-coded ticket scanning, automatic price look-up, electronic check and credit/debit authorization, and automatic nightly transmittal of data between the store and corporate offices. Each of the regional directors and district managers could instantly access appropriate or relevant company-wide information, including actual and budgeted sales by store, district and region, transaction information, and payroll data.

The company's culture was lean and frugal. To illustrate, PacSun's CFO explained, "We never succumbed to management entitlements. Very few employees have company paid-for Blackberries, cell phones, and credit cards. No one travels by first class airfare."

COMPLYING WITH SECTION 404 OF THE SARBANES-OXLEY ACT OF 2002

As a company whose securities were sold publicly in the US, PacSun was bound by the provisions of the Sarbanes-Oxley Act of 2002. PacSun was first obligated to comply with the full provisions of SOX in its 2004 fiscal year (ended January 29, 2005).

The most difficult and expensive provisions in the Act to comply with were those contained in Section 404. Section 404 dealt with internal controls over financial reporting (ICOFR) – the processes that are designed to ensure the reliability of the financial reporting process and, ultimately, the preparation of financial statements. Section 404, with later clarifications by the SEC and the PCAOB, required management to (1) accept responsibility for the effectiveness of the company's ICOFR;

(2) evaluate the effectiveness of the company's ICOFR using suitable control criteria;[1] (3) support the evaluation with sufficient evidence, including documentation of the design of controls related to all relevant assertions for its significant financial statement accounts and disclosures; and (4) present a written assessment of the effectiveness of the company's ICOFR as of the end of the company's most recent fiscal year. The company's CEO and CFO personally had to certify the results of the evaluation.

As part of its assessment, management had to determine if identified internal control deficiencies – individually or in combination – constituted significant deficiencies or material weaknesses. An internal control *deficiency* exists when the design or operation of a control does not allow management or employees, in the normal course of performing their assigned functions, to prevent or detect misstatements on a timely basis. An internal control deficiency may be either a design or operating deficiency. A *significant deficiency* is a control deficiency, or combination of control deficiencies, that adversely affects the company's ability to initiate, authorize, record, process, or report external financial data reliably in accordance with generally accepted accounting principles such that there is more than a remote likelihood that a misstatement of the company's annual or interim financial statements that is more than inconsequential will not be prevented or detected. A *material weakness* is a significant deficiency, or combination of significant deficiencies, that results in more than a remote likelihood that a material misstatement of the annual or interim financial statements will not be prevented or detected. The existence of even a single material weakness is grounds for an *adverse* 404 opinion.

Management then communicated the findings of their tests to the external auditor. The company's auditors then had to attest to management's assertion on the effectiveness of internal controls – whether they had done enough work to have the basis to express their opinion – and to express their own opinion. If management had not fulfilled its

responsibilities, the auditor was required to issue a disclaimer opinion.

THE FIRST YEAR – FY 2004

The PacSun SOX compliance process for FY 2004 began in mid 2003. At that time, the company had a lean accounting staff and had not previously had an internal audit function. The company created its internal audit function in mid 2003 (one manager) and outsourced the initial direction of the 404 compliance work to a Big-4 auditing firm as an "audit consultant."[2] By late 2004, the internal audit function had been expanded to include a director, a manager, and two staff auditors. The audit consultant designed a five-step process:

1. **Scope and plan the evaluation**. This required scoping the entire internal control evaluation process. What controls and locations/units would be included in the study? What would be the approach, milestones, timeline? What resources would be needed?

2. **Document the controls**. All of the controls over relevant financial statement assertions related to all significant accounts and disclosures had to be documented. Documentation of controls could take many forms and could include a variety of information, including policy manuals, process models, flowcharts, job descriptions, documents, and forms.

3. **Evaluate the design and operating effectiveness of the controls**. Tests of the key controls had to be designed and carried out, and the results of the tests had to be documented.

4. **Identify, assess, and correct deficiencies**. Findings should be communicated, and deficiencies corrected, if possible.

5. **Report on internal control**. Management had to prepare a written assertion about the effectiveness of internal control over financial reporting.

The audit consultant and PacSun personnel identified 21 major business processes that the company used, such as involving property, plant and equipment, payroll, and taxes (see Exhibit 2). Each of the processes was assigned an "owner," and deadlines were set for the development of detailed process narratives.

---

[1] Most companies and auditors, including PacSun and PacSun's auditor (Deloitte & Touche LLP), relied on the language, concepts, and evaluation criteria described in the integrated internal control framework developed by the COSO (Committee of Sponsoring Organizations).

[2] The company could not have outsourced the work to its primary auditor. Doing so would have compromised the primary auditor's audit independence.

The documentation included detailed descriptions of the process objectives, the risks that threatened achievement of the objectives, the controls used to minimize the risks, and the process owners who were responsible for maintaining and documenting the process. The process narratives varied significantly in length depending on the complexity of the process. For example, some supply-chain narratives were 20–25 pages in length, while the equity narrative was only five pages in length.

Each of the 21 major business processes was disaggregated into subprocesses. Exhibit 3 shows the business objectives, and risks for the Merchandise Accounting process, a part of major process number 9 (Supply Chain Processes/Merchandise Accounting) (see Exhibit 2). The narrative of the process is shown in Exhibit 4. The two controls associated with this subprocess that were designated as *key* are shown in bold type in this narrative.

In FY 2004, a total of 238 key controls were identified across the 21 major business processes (as is shown in Exhibit 2). PacSun's CFO, explained:

> We did a good job in year one paring down the number of key controls. (Some big companies have identified 10,000 or more key controls.)[3] But our task was also easier than that of some other companies. We have a simple business model; a simple organization; and all of our major operations are located in Anaheim.

PacSun and the audit consultant's personnel jointly performed the tests of the controls.

In FY 2004, one significant deficiency was identified by Company management. This deficiency was caused by a variance between PacSun's accounting and that suggested in a February 2005 interpretation letter from the SEC's chief accountant. This new interpretation affected virtually all firms in the retail industry. The CFO explained:

> There were several parts to the problem. First, when most retailers buy a store in a mall, they sign a 120-month lease. They start construction three months

before opening but do not have to pay rent expense until the store opens. The SEC, though, decided that the lease should be expensed over 123 months. Second, if we received a landlord incentive allowance, which is designed to help us fund improvements, we treated that allowance as a reduction in capital expeditures, rather than a deferred lease incentive liability. The SEC ruled that it should be treated as a deferred lease incentive liability and amortized as a reduction in rent expense rather than as a reduction in depreciation expense, as we had been doing.

The adoption of the new accounting policy resulted in an immaterial reduction in net income of less than $25,000 for each period presented. However, these corrections did result in multi-million dollar reclassifications between rent expense (within cost of goods sold) and depreciation expense (within selling, general and administrative expenses), cumulative adjustments to the property, plant and equipment and deferred rent amounts on the balance sheet, and reclassifications between cash flows from investing activities and cash flows from operating activities on the company's statements of cash flow.

The CFO explained what these changes meant from his perspective:

> In 2005, we had to restate our prior two years' financial statements, which resulted in no material change to net income. What purpose did that restatement serve? I think the fact that we caught and fixed the problem is indicative of good internal control. But auditors judge restatements as deficiencies. But what type of deficiency? Here there is no consistency in the auditing industry. Two of the Big-4 firms, judged this particular type of restatement as only a significant deficiency. The other two judged it to be a material weakness.

CERTIFICATIONS

Section 302 of SOX required both the company's CEO and CFO to personally certify the "appropriateness of the financial statements and disclosures contained in the periodic report" and to guarantee that "financial statements and disclosures fairly present, in all material respects, the operations and financial condition of the issuer." Exhibit 5 shows the CFO's certification that appeared in the company's 10-K for FY 2004. About the certification requirement, the CFO said, "I feel confident about my certifications here."

PacSun top management required their subordinates to share the certification responsibility. All PacSun officers (vice president level or higher)

---

[3] A survey commissioned by the Big-4 accounting firms found that the average number of key controls identified in year one of Section 404 compliance by larger firms, those with over $700 million in capitalization, was 669. For smaller firms, those with a market capitalization between $75 million and $700 million, the average was 262 key controls (CRA International, *Sarbanes-Oxley Section 404 Costs and Implementation Issues: Spring 2006 Survey Update*, Washington, DC, April 17, 2006, pp. 4–5). PacSun's market capitalization was greater than $1 billion.

were required to certify that the controls in their area were effective (see Exhibit 6). Process owners also had to sign a similar certification (see Exhibit 7). The CFO noted that there was no resistance to the sharing of the certification requirements. He said, "This should not just be an accounting exercise; you've got to get the whole organization engaged."

In FY 2004, PacSun received "clean" opinions from its external auditors, Deloitte and Touche, LLP, both for the fair presentation of its financial statements and for the effectiveness of the company's internal control system (see Exhibit 8).

THE YEAR 2 PROCESS – FY 2005

In the second year of complying with SOX Section 404, the process was much easier. Everybody involved – audit consultant, PacSun, and primary auditor personnel – had already been through the process once. Most of the needed documentation had already been created. Rather than involving the audit consultant's personnel, the testing of controls was done by the PacSun internal audit staff, which had now grown to four persons. The testing was spread more evenly throughout the year, as the company was able to anticipate better what needed to be done. And the primary auditor was able to combine its financial statement opinion work with the 404 audit.

In SOX year two, most companies were able to make significant reductions in the number of key controls they tested,[4] but PacSun's reductions were relatively small. The number of key controls tested was reduced from 238 to 222 in FY 2005, only a 7% reduction. The CFO explained that this was not surprising to him. He argued that PacSun had a tight, effective control system even before SOX was implemented; the control environment at PacSun was not particularly complicated because the company operated primarily from a single business location and, from a control perspective had a simple business model; and PacSun and the audit consultant personnel did a good job in identifying the key control points in the first year.

But in FY 2005, The company discovered a new significant internal control deficiency. The issue related to the accounting for the liabilities created by the company's loyalty program called "Pac Bucks." In the Pac Bucks program, shoppers earn $25 in Pac Bucks for each $50 they spend. To use their PacBucks, the shoppers must spend at least another $50 in the stores within a set period of time. In FY 2005, the external auditors concluded that PacSun's accounting was not recognizing the liabilities and expenses in the proper accounting quarter (the full fiscal year was unaffected). This accounting problem was deemed to be a significant deficiency, but not a material weakness. In FY 2005, PacSun received clean financial statement and 404 opinions.

THE COSTS OF COMPLYING

The cost to PacSun of SOX compliance was significant. Exhibit 9 shows an estimate of the costs of 404 compliance and, for comparison purposes, the costs of the annual financial statements audit for fiscal years 2004 and 2005. These figures show that in FY 2004 the total cost of compliance – financial statement audit and 404 compliance – was an estimated $2 million, of which only a small portion of the cost was attributed to the standard financial statement audit. In year two, the costs declined by almost 40%. This reduction is comparable to that reported by other companies.[5]

But there were also some other, implicit costs. For example, the CFO noted that SOX had made it more burdensome to serve on the Audit Committee of the Board of Directors. At PacSun, the Audit Committee played an active role in the SOX 404 compliance process. While PacSun's director of internal audit, reported administratively to the CFO, he reported functionally directly to the Audit Committee. The director of internal audit met with the Committee five times a year and had conference calls with the committee members at least once a quarter. The CFO noted, however, that the relationship with the Audit Committee had become much

---

[4] A survey found that larger companies (those with greater than $700 million in market capitalization) reduced their numbers of key controls tested by more than 19%, from 669 in year one to 540 in year two (CRA International, 2006, p. 4).

[5] Large companies (those with greater than $700 million in market capitalization) reported that their total costs of complying with SOX Section 404 declined from $8.5 million in year one to $4.8 million in year two, a reduction of almost 44% (CRA International, 2006, p. 3).

more formalized, and time-consuming in a sense, due to SOX. "What took 30 minutes a couple of years ago takes 2–3 hours now. Everyone now asks checklists of questions. If you don't ask the questions, there is no record; and you need to create the record."

There also were costs associated with training. Although PacSun did not have a formal, dedicated SOX training program for rank-and-file personnel, several SOX orientation sessions were offered in combination with other training programs, such as for store personnel.

MANAGEMENT REFLECTIONS AND PLANS FOR THE FUTURE

Overall, PacSun management thought that the costs of the SOX compliance process far exceeded the benefits. The CFO explained:

> There were some benefits. When you go through an elaborate documentation process, it is inevitable that you will see some gaps and some redundancies. We did plug some gaps in our payroll and information systems areas. Most of the changes we made involved better segregation of duties. For example, we had some

payroll clerks who had access to too many systems. But the process was very expensive and, for the most part, not very useful for us. This company has always been tightly controlled, so we did not uncover any major issues, and the process forced us to create a lot of documentation that was not needed.

> I also wonder about the effectiveness of this legislation for its intended purposes. This process will not stop crooks from being crooks. For example, it won't stop people from doing off-balance sheet transactions . . .

When asked if the public disclosure of the significant internal control deficiencies had an effect on the company's stock price, the CFO responded that he could not detect any.

Going into year three of the SOX process, the role of the PacSun internal audit function was evolving. The focus of the first two years of its existence was on financial reporting and ensuring compliance with SOX. In FY 2006, the focus was shifting to a broader focus on controlling business risks. The department was spending a lot less time on SOX compliance and a lot more time worrying about business continuity planning. It was also preparing to conduct some operational audits.

EXHIBIT 1 Pacific Sunwear of California, Inc.: consolidated statements of income and comprehensive income

| | (in thousands, except share and per share amounts) | | |
FISCAL YEAR ENDED	January 28, 2006	January 29, 2005	January 31, 2004
Net sales	**$1,391,473**	**$1,229,762**	**$1,041,456**
Cost of goods sold, including buying, distribution and occupancy costs	884,982	781,828	668,807
Gross margin	**506,491**	**447,934**	**372,649**
Selling, general and administrative expenses	309,218	277,921	244,422
Operating income	**197,273**	**170,013**	**128,227**
Interest income, net	5,673	1,889	732
Income before income tax expense	202,946	171,902	128,959
Income tax expense	76,734	64,998	48,759
Net income	**$126,212**	**$106,904**	**$80,200**
Comprehensive income	$126,212	$106,904	$80,200
Net income per share, basic	$1.69	$1.41	$1.05
Net income per share, diluted	**$1.67**	**$1.38**	**$1.02**
Weighted average shares outstanding, basic	74,758,874	75,825,897	76,595,758
Weighted average shares outstanding, diluted	75,713,793	77,464,115	78,849,651
(See notes to consolidated financial statements.)			

Source: Pacific Sunwear of California, Inc. Annual Report 2005.

EXHIBIT 2 SOX 404 compliance project process index as of 2/10/2005

Reference		Business process	Narrative	Owner	Key controls
1	A	Control environment	–		11
2	B	IT general controls	1/16/2004		25
3	C	Budgeting process/financial planning	11/9/2004		2
4	D	General ledger maintenance	11/9/2004		13
5	E	Retail store operations and retail accounting	7/26/2004		8
6	F	Retail IT	11/9/2004		7
7	G	Retail store leasing acitvities	11/9/2004		5
8	H	General accounting	11/9/2004		8
9	I	Supply chain processes/merchandise accounting	11/30/2004		32
10	J	PP&E	11/9/2004		9
11	K	Accounts payable – merchandise	12/3/2004		21
12	L	Accounts payable – non-merchandise	1/19/2004		2
13	M	Payroll	11/22/2004		31
14	N	Treasury	1/19/2004		11
15	O	Debt	1/19/2004		4
16	P	Goodwill	7/19/2004		2
17	Q	Consolidation process	11/9/2004		2
18	R	Taxes	11/9/2004		22
19	S	Legal matters	7/9/2004		2
20	T	Equity	1/19/2004		17
21	U	Financial reporting process	10/25/2004		4

238

EXHIBIT 3 Objectives and risks of the merchandise accounting process

PROCESS DOCUMENTATION:	MERCHANDISE ACCOUNTING
PROCESS OWNER:	
EFFECTIVE DATE:	MAY 25, 2005

CONTENTS:

A. Control Objectives
B. Risks Which Threaten Objectives
C. Computer Information Systems

A. CONTROL OBJECTIVES:

1. To initiate, process and accurately record appropriate purchases reserves for sales returns, markdowns, charge-backs, vendor allowances, transfers, adjustments (to units and prices) and related liabilities.
2. Develop and maintain relationships with suppliers that meet company requirements.
3. Obtain quality merchandise on a timely basis.
4. Ensure inventory is properly safeguarded from damage or theft.
5. Inventory settings within system are complete.
6. Only valid inventory master file information has been captured in the system.
7. Accurately record physical and cycle count adjustments.
8. Approve and accurately record price changes and unit adjustments.
9. All inventory movement between the distribution center and stores (and from store to store) are recorded completely and accurately.
10. Proper presentation of inventory related line items are reflected on the financial statements.

B. RISKS WHICH THREATEN OBJECTIVES:

A. Poor quality merchandise is not identified timely.
B. Reserves for sales returns, markdowns and vendor chargebacks are not adequately reflected in the financial statements (e.g. the reserve for sales returns does not reflect actual return rates).
C. The Company obtains poor quality merchandise and/or obtains it at a different time than needed.
D. The Company selects suppliers that fail to meet standards.
E. Configured tolerances for physical inventory re-counts are inadequate. Adjustments may be inaccurate and/or posted by inappropriate users. Physical and cycle counts, significant adjustments are not investigated for root-cause.
F. Changes in prices are not authorized and/or are not automatically activated, resulting in inaccurate prices assigned to products.
G. Improper cutoff procedures result in inaccurate inventory and liability balances at period-end.
H. Inadequate receiving procedures and system content allow for the receipt of unauthorized purchases.
I. Inadequate monitoring of imports in transit result in inaccurate inventory and liability balances.
J. DC outbound shipments are not reconciled to receipts at stores resulting in missing/damaged goods not properly reflected on the financial statements.
K. Inventory accounts (including RTV's) are not reconciled timely resulting in inaccurate inventory's AP balances.
L. Inventory is not properly safeguarded from damage or theft.
M. Shortages/discrepancies identified are not monitored or reflected in inventory balances and/or root-cause are not identified and addressed in a timely manner (e.g. supplier failing to meet standards, employee picking inaccuracies, etc.).
N. Financial statement presentation and disclosures is inaccurate and/or misleading.
O. Inventory movements between distribution center and the stores or between stores monitored, reconciled, or are not properly recorded.
P. Inappropriate inventory system settings may impact financial statements.
Q. Incomplete or duplicated master data could prevent the initiation or completion of transactions.
R. Slow moving inventories are not identified in a timely manner.
S. Vendor allowances are being allocated to the wrong class of inventory or to the wrong vendor, and/or allowance amount is improperly calculated.

C. COMPUTER INFORMATION SYSTEMS:

Island Pacific, PKMS, Travado POS System

Exhibit 4 Narrative describing the process and controls surrounding distribution center receiving, a merchandise accounting subprocess

---

SUBPROCESS: DISTRIBUTION CENTER RECEIVING

Once the PO is EDIed to the vendor, the vendor then fills the PO and requests an Advance Shipping Notice (ASN) from Pac Sun. The ASN details out what Pac Sun expects to receive at the case level detail (it is similar to the vendor's shipping document or packing slip). Currently, Pac Sun has vendors on two different types of EDI: (1) SPS Commerce EDI and (2) Traditional EDI. SPS Commerce is a web based EDI tool that allows the vendor to look at the PO online, input their shipping information online, and if the shipping parameters are within predefined tolerance levels, Pac Sun will automatically generate an ASN for the vendor.

The system will not accept any ASNs outside of the predefined tolerance levels without a manual override of the system (SCP6). Only Store Planning and Allocation Managers (SPAMs), the Sr. Programmer Analyst, and the Import Assurance Coordinator, at the direction of the buyer, have the ability (and the system access within the EDI user maintenance IP profile control) to perform these types of override (CP7).

With Traditional EDI, the vendor is subject to the same business rules regarding quantity and price that determine if the shipment is within tolerance, and if it is, an ASN is generated. The Senior Programmer Analyst monitors all transactions to ensure that none are hung up in the system. (SCP8) If an ASN is hung up, the Senior Programmer Analyst will contact the buyer so that the vendor can be contacted and any issues resolved. Once both Pac Sun and the vendor have accepted the ASN, all of the PO history can be seen in IP and the vendor can print labels for the cartons that will be delivered to Pac Sun.

The PKMS system is based on only allowing one SKU per case. PKMS can also handle prepacks (merchandise prepackaged in a set size run – for example, 5 small, 10 medium, 20 large, 12 x-large in a single prepack). The system has a subfile that identifies prepacks. Prepacks are still only allowed one SKU per box and they will show up in the system as size 1111 (instead of a valid size code). In the IP system, the prepacks are exploded into the individual sizes and everything is seen by individual SKU. PKMS takes care of all of the warehouse instructions regarding packing and picking of the merchandise. The PKMS software generates transactions called PIX's to bridge PKMS and IP. Based on instructions generated from PKMS, the PIX will update IP. A Never Ending Program (NEPS) is constantly running that scoops all of the instructions out of PKMS to IP using PIX's so that IP is continuously being refreshed and updated with the most recent movement activity in the warehouse.

When a valid ASN is accepted, it allows the vendor to call the distribution center (DC) and schedule a delivery appointment (CP9). When the goods arrive, the trucking company buzzes in at the security gate. In PKMS, the first PIX is the receipt of the merchandise.

Merchandise is only received and accepted if there is a valid PO, ASN and delivery appointment (CP10). In order to be able to enter the docking facility and be assigned a door number, the truck driver must provide a valid ASN/PO and have a delivery appointment. Once the security guard and the receiving office validate everything, the truck is instructed to go to a particular door. The truck is parked, the documents are presented to the receiving personnel and the truck is unloaded and the cartons scanned by RF gun. The RF scan creates a PIX in PKMS and a receipt in IP. PKMS records the number of cartons received and the units in each carton, which is then bridged (via a PIX) into the IP system. The IP system then automatically closes the PO if the PO has been filled (SCP11). **A receipt number is generated in IP (next available number in the sequence) and a purchase is generated in the stock ledger (SCP12).** The stock ledger represents the perpetual inventory record for the chain. This process helps to ensure that merchandise received is recorded accurately and all merchandise received is recorded.

A predetermined level of test cartons is set (currently set at every 10th carton) whereby the carton is opened on the dock to verify that the ASN agrees to the carton contents (SCP13). PKMS will instruct the receivers to conduct random audits of cartons by prompting them after a carton has been scanned. The receiving of the goods cannot continue until this audit has been completed and the information regarding the quantities in the carton have been input into the RF gun. This predetermined level can be adjusted at the vendor level if it has been determined that a vendor has a high incidence of discrepancies. If certain checks fail, then the carton will be segregated to the rework area to be resolved with the vendors. At this point, there is a 100% review of the shipment prior to it being received in the system (i.e. the entire contents of the trailer are sent to the rework area for review prior to receipt). Any unusual items are forwarded to one of the DC Supervisors who investigates the differences and ensures correct treatment.

Rejected merchandise is adequately segregated from good merchandise and regularly monitored to ensure timely return to vendors (CP14). If merchandise is known to have problems from the outset (i.e. no ASN) they are sent to the "hospital." Items in the hospital have been physically received, but they are not recorded in IP. (See discussion regarding proper cutoff below.) The hospital is the troubled goods area where the inventory is reviewed to determine whether it can be reworked or if it should be returned to the vendor. The buyer is contacted if the goods are damaged and the buyer obtains a return authorization (RA) number from the vendor. DC personnel (the RTV Supervisor) contact

---

Exhibit 4 *continued*

the buyer for RA information for merchandise in RT (RTV) status. Once an RA# has been received, the goods are shipped and PKMS and IP inventory are relieved.

Although the goods have been physically received, items in the hospital have *not* been received in the IP system due to the fact that there is something wrong with them. In order to ensure that all items are properly recorded in inventory at any quarter- or year-end cutoff warehouse management and either the Merchandise Accounting Manager or the Assistant Controller – Merchandise Accounting physically inspect the hospital area at these cutoff dates noting the PO information for merchandise in the hospital area so that the goods can be accrued for. (CP15). A reversing journal entry is posted to accrue the PO quantity and cost for the goods in the hospital area that have not been systemically received in IP.

Exhibit 5 CFO financial statement and internal control certification

I, _____, certify that:

1. I have reviewed this annual report on Form 10-K of Pacific Sunwear of California, Inc.;

2. Based on my knowledge, this report does not contain any untrue statement of a material fact or omit to state a material fact necessary in order to make the statements made, in light of the circumstances under which such statements were made, not misleading with respect to the period covered by this report;

3. Based on my knowledge, the financial statements, and other financial information included in this report, fairly present in all material respects the financial condition, results of operations and cash flows of the registrant as of, and for, the periods presented in this report;

4. The registrant's other certifying officer and I are responsible for establishing and maintaining disclosure controls and procedures (as defined in Exchange Act Rules 13a–15(e) and 15d–15(e)) and internal control over financial reporting (as defined in Exchange Act Rules 13a–15(f) and 15d–15(f)) for the registrant and have:

   a) Designed such disclosure controls and procedures, or caused such disclosure controls and procedures to be designed under our supervision, to ensure that material information relating to the registrant, including its consolidated subsidiaries, is made known to us by others within those entities, particularly during the period in which this report is being prepared;

   b) Designed such internal control over financial reporting, or caused such internal control over financial reporting to be designed under our supervision, to provide reasonable assurance regarding the reliability of financial reporting and the preparation of financial statements for external purposes in accordance with generally accepted accounting principles;

   c) Evaluated the effectiveness of the registrant's disclosure controls and procedures and presented in this report our conclusions about the effectiveness of the disclosure controls and procedures as of the end of the period covered by this report based on such evaluation; and

   d) Disclosed in this report any change in the registrant's internal control over financial reporting that occurred during the registrant's most recent fiscal quarter (the registrant's fourth fiscal quarter in the case of an annual report) that has materially affected, or is reasonably likely to materially affect, the registrant's internal control over financial reporting; and

5. The registrant's other certifying officer and I have disclosed, based on our most recent evaluation of internal control over financial reporting, to the registrant's auditors and the audit committee of the registrant's board of directors (or persons performing the equivalent functions):

   a) All significant deficiencies and material weaknesses in the design or operation of internal control over financial reporting which are reasonably likely to adversely affect the registrant's ability to record, process, summarize and report financial information; and

   b) Any fraud, whether or not material, that involves management or other employees who have a significant role in the registrant's internal control over financial reporting.

Date: April 7, 2005

_____

Senior Vice President and Chief Financial Officer

Exhibit 6 Officer quarterly disclosure certification

I, _____, certify that:

1. I have brought to the CFO's attention everything that I believe might be important for purposes of disclosure in the Company's financial statements, including those filed with the Securities and Exchange Commission;

2. I am not aware of any material transactions (over $5,000) or agreements that I have not already reported to Finance via the monthly accrual sheet or other mode of communication;

3. I have not entered into any transactions or agreements on behalf of the Company that are in violation of the Company's policies, including the Company's Code of Ethics;

4. I have not made any false statements of material fact or intentionally omitted facts that would make the information underlying the Company's financial statements misleading as to any material fact;

5. I am not aware of (a) any fraud involving management or employees who have significant roles in the system of internal control or any fraud involving others which could have a material effect on the financial statements, (b) any violations of laws or regulations whose effects have not been considered for disclosure in the financial statements or as a basis of recording a loss contingency, (c) any communications from regulatory agencies concerning noncompliance with or deficiencies in financial statements, or (d) any failure to comply with contractual agreements where such failure would have a material effect on the financial statements that has not been discussed or for which a provision has not been recorded; and

6. I know of no plans or intentions that may materially alter the valuation of any Company assets or liabilities.

_____

Signature

_____

Date

Exhibit 7 Process owner certification

I, _____, certify that:

1. I am the designated Process Owner for the processes listed below and, as such, I am responsible for maintaining the adequacy and accuracy of the Process Narrative which serves as the documentation of disclosure controls and procedures and internal control over financial reporting for those processes. I am responsible for the following processes:

_____ _____

_____ _____

_____ _____

2. The process narratives on file with the Internal Audit department for my designated processes accurately document the internal control over financial reporting in existence at the end of the quarter covered by this certification.

3. I have disclosed to the Director of Internal Audit any change in internal control over financial reporting that occurred during the most recent fiscal quarter that has materially, or is reasonably likely to materially affect internal control over financial reporting.

4. I have evaluated the effectiveness of the internal control over financial reporting for my designated processes and have concluded that such controls and procedures were effective as of the end of the quarter covered by this report.

5. Based on my evaluation, I have disclosed to the Director of Internal Audit any control deficiencies in the design or operation of internal control over financial reporting which are likely to adversely affect the company's ability to record, process, summarize, and report financial information.

6. I have disclosed to the Ethics Review Team or the Audit Committee any fraud, whether or not material, that involves management or other employees who have a significant role in the company's internal control over financial reporting.

_____

Signature

_____

Date

Exhibit 8 Report of independent registered public accounting firm, FY 2004

To the Board of Directors and Stockholders of
Pacific Sunwear of California, Inc.
Anaheim, California

We have audited the accompanying consolidated balance sheets of Pacific Sunwear of California, Inc. and subsidiaries (the "Company") as of January 29, 2005 and January 31, 2004, and the related consolidated statements of income and comprehensive income, shareholders' equity, and cash flows for each of the three years in the period ended January 29, 2005. These financial statements are the responsibility of the Company's management. Our responsibility is to express an opinion on these financial statements based on our audits.

We conducted our audits in accordance with the standards of the Public Company Accounting Oversight Board (United States). Those standards require that we plan and perform the audit to obtain reasonable assurance about whether the financial statements are free of material misstatement. An audit includes examining, on a test basis, evidence supporting the amounts and disclosures in the financial statements. An audit also includes assessing the accounting principles used and significant estimates made by management, as well as evaluating the overall financial statement presentation. We believe that our audits provide a reasonable basis for our opinion.

In our opinion, such consolidated financial statements present fairly, in all material respects, the financial position of Pacific Sunwear of California, Inc. and subsidiaries as of January 29, 2005 and January 31, 2004, and the results of their operations and their cash flows for each of the three years in the period ended January 29, 2005, in conformity with accounting principles generally accepted in the United States of America.

We have also audited, in accordance with the standards of the Public Company Accounting Oversight Board (United States), the effectiveness of the Company's internal control over financial reporting as of January 29, 2005, based on the criteria established in *Internal Control – Integrated Framework* issued by the Committee of Sponsoring Organizations of the Treadway Commission and our report, dated April 4, 2005, expressed an unqualified opinion on management's assessment of the effectiveness of the Company's internal control over financial reporting and an unqualified opinion on the effectiveness of the Company's internal control over financial reporting.

As discussed in Note 2, the accompanying consolidated financial statements as of January 31, 2004 and for the years ended January 31, 2004 and February 1, 2003 have been restated.

Deloitte & Touche LLP

Costa Mesa, California
April 4, 2005

Exhibit 9 PacSun estimated audit and SOX compliance costs, FY 2004 and FY 2005 ($000)

	FY 2004	FY 2005
Primary auditor		
Standard financial statement audit	240	225
SOX 404 audit	470	345
Audit consultant		
Documentation and testing – non-IT	100	
Documentation and testing – IT	600	70
PacSun		
Setting up the Internal Audit dept.; started with SOX implementation	200	315
Other costs (rough guess by CFO)	500	300
Total financial statement audit and SOX 404 compliance costs	$2,110	$1,255

Case Study

Entropic Communications, Inc.

In 2009, Entropic Communications, a small but growing semi-conductor company headquartered in San Diego, California, was implementing a new Enterprise Risk Management (ERM) process. Lance Bridges, Entropic's VP/General Counsel, had taken the lead in developing the process and was coordinating its implementation. The first full process cycle was completed at the end of 2009. Lance was contemplating how effective it had been.

Lance was sure that the process had raised issues, stimulated discussion, and resulted in some tangible measures to mitigate risk. But he had a few areas of concern. He thought the risks that were identified might have been better aligned with company objectives. He knew that some department heads had not taken the process seriously. He was not sure either if there had been enough communication between departments or if the departments had applied risk scores consistently. Lance also wondered if a process like ERM might be most helpful in dealing with already known risks, and less useful for identifying and analyzing new risks that could arise in the dynamic industry in which Entropic operated. And he was unsure of the value of the final output of the ERM process – a risk management matrix. Some managers in the company had shown little or no interest in it. As Entropic headed into 2010, Lance was considering how the company might improve the process going forward.

COMPANY BACKGROUND

Entropic Communications, Inc. was a fabless semi-conductor company (meaning that it specialized in the design and sale of hardware devices while outsourcing the fabrication or "fab" of the devices to a specialized manufacturer) focused on ground-breaking system solutions for connected home entertainment. Entropic was incorporated in Delaware in 2001 and went public in 2007. The company's stock traded on NASDAQ under the symbol ENTR. In 2009, revenues totaled $116 million (see Exhibit 1). At the end of 2009, Entropic employed approximately 300 people. The organization was structured by functional department (e.g., sales, marketing, engineering, human resources).

Entropic sold products in four product lines: home networking, DBS outdoor unit solutions, broadband access, and TV Tuners. Entropic's home networking solutions enabled service providers to deliver multiple streams of high definition (HD) video throughout the home using the existing coaxial cable infrastructure. Applications of this technology allowed end users to download and share or "place-shift" video and personal content (e.g., photos, games) throughout the home. A demonstration of Entropic's home networking solutions can be seen at www.entropic.com/products/mocaanimation.htm.

Entropic's DBS outdoor unit solutions supported multiple tuners and simultaneous reception of multiple channels, from multiple satellites, over a single cable. Formerly each tuner required a unique cable, but with Entropic technology a single cable could support 12 tuners. The simplified cabling structure allowed satellite broadcasters to roll out new services without expensive installation and retrofitting, while improving aesthetics for the homeowner.

Entropic's broadband access solution was a cost-effective delivery system for broadband data, video networking, and voice services, designed to deliver "last kilometer" connectivity to customers in areas with fiber optic networks that terminated up to 600 meters from their home.

Entropic also sold silicon tuners with support for multiple analog and digital standards for terrestrial and cable applications.

This case was prepared by Professor Kenneth A. Merchant and research assistant Michelle Spaulding.

Most of Entropic's customers were original equipment manufacturers (OEMs) that sold equipment incorporating Entropic technologies to service providers, such as telecommunications companies (e.g., Verizon), cable companies (e.g., Comcast), and direct broadcast satellite (DBS) companies (e.g., DISH Network, DirecTV). Entropic worked closely with OEMs and service providers to develop customized solutions, and to increase the adoption of solutions that included Entropic technology. In 2009, four OEM customers accounted for 58% of Entropic's net revenues.

Entropic's products all provided technological advantages, but they competed in extremely dynamic markets characterized by rapid technological advancements, evolving industry standards and new demands for features and performance of multimedia content delivery solutions. Many of Entropic's competitors had longer operating histories and significantly more resources.

ENTERPRISE RISK MANAGEMENT

In 2010, risk was a hot topic in business management. Throughout the preceding decade, stricter regulatory compliance requirements, rating agency attention, and risk reporting requirements all promoted interest in the subject. Enterprise Risk Management (ERM) emerged as one of the leading management tools used to address risk.

A string of accounting scandals, most notably Enron and WorldCom, led to the passage of the Sarbanes-Oxley Act in 2002. Sarbanes-Oxley focused on internal controls related to fraud, compliance, and financial reporting risks. Under Section 404 of the Act, management was required to produce an annual "internal control report" verifying the effectiveness of internal controls over financial reporting. To meet the compliance requirements, many managers organized their documentation and tests of internal controls using the Internal Control Framework developed by the Committee of Sponsoring Organizations of the Treadway Commission (COSO).

In 2004, COSO developed a framework for Enterprise Risk Management that incorporated the widely used Internal Control Framework, but addressed a much broader range of risks. ERM encompassed operational and strategic risks, as well as the more easily defined financial, reporting and compliance risks. COSO defined ERM as "a process, effected by an entity's board of directors, management and other personnel, applied in strategy setting and across the enterprise, designed to identify potential events that may affect the entity, and manage risk to be within its risk appetite, to provide reasonable assurance regarding the achievement of entity objectives." The COSO framework categorized objectives as strategic, operational, reporting, and compliance. The framework outlined eight "components" or process steps to analyze, manage, and monitor risks (see Exhibit 2). The ERM framework was designed to align a corporation's actual risk exposure with its risk appetite. The goal of ERM was to reduce negative surprises and improve risk response decisions, ultimately improving an enterprise's financial performance.

In 2008, the global financial crisis led many to question whether risk was being adequately addressed in financial institutions specifically, but also in publically traded companies more generally. Standard and Poor's Rating Services (S&P) had incorporated risk management into their ratings for financial and insurance companies since 2005. In the latter part of 2008 they began to incorporate ERM discussions into regular meetings with non-financial companies as well. After interviewing more than 300 non-financial companies, they released preliminary findings regarding ERM in July 2009 (see Exhibit 3).

In early 2010, the Securities Exchange Commission (SEC) amended its proxy statement requirements to require a discussion of the board's role in risk oversight. (See Exhibit 4 for SEC's final rule.) The stated purpose was to "improve corporate disclosure regarding risk, compensation and corporate governance matters when voting decisions are made." While a formal ERM process was not specifically required, the new SEC rule put pressure on boards and management to create a structured risk management process of some kind and in some form.

It was in this environment that Entropic's management decided to implement ERM, in part to help the board of directors discharge its fiduciary duties. Entropic's finance department already reported financial risks to the board's audit committee quarterly; the board reviewed operational risks in connection with the SEC filings quarterly; and the board regularly discussed strategic risks at quarterly Board meetings, but Lance believed a more comprehensive summary of the company's risk assessment and management practices would be helpful. Lance had completed a risk management process for the legal department because he wanted an organized, systemic approach to identify and address risks in his area of responsibility. Lance presented his method and findings to the audit committee of the board in the fall of 2008, and recommended rolling out the process to the entire company the following year. Patrick Henry, Entropic's president and CEO, agreed with Lance's recommendation, so Lance embarked on the creation of a comprehensive ERM process at Entropic.

THE ERM PROCESS AT ENTROPIC

Implementing an ERM process generally involved five steps: event identification, risk assessment, risk response, communication, and monitoring.

Event identification

Lance began the event-identification process with the risks discussed in the SEC 10-K filings (see summary in Exhibit 5). Like all publicly traded corporations, Entropic was required to disclose its risk factors, including business, financial, and liquidity risks, in its annual report on Form 10-K. Lance sorted those risks by department and then charged each department head to develop a more comprehensive list of risk events for their respective department, using his list as a starting point.

Each department approached the event identification task slightly differently. Some used frameworks to make the process more systematic and comprehensive. Human Resources developed a matrix of functional department (benefits, payroll, recruitment) and the lifecycle of an employee (recruit, hire, separation) as a framework for identifying risks. Marketing chose to identify risks by functional department, by product line, and by risk type (competitive, company, and customer risks). Legal used a risk template from an outside source to make certain its list was comprehensive. The departments that were not as engaged in the process relied heavily, and in some cases exclusively, on Lance's initial list of risks. The final output was a catalogue of almost 150 potential risk events, sorted by department. (See Exhibit 6 for an excerpt from the Risk Management Matrix.)

The department heads who invested time in the process believed that it was helpful to go through the event identification exercise, although most agreed that the process itself was more useful than the output. Many found it beneficial to spend time analyzing the business in terms of risk. They believed that the process provided assurance that known risks were clarified and were being addressed. For example, Lance was able to pinpoint and clarify legal obligations in areas that he did not deal with everyday (e.g., facilities and certain labor laws) and to make sure that those risks were being monitored by an appropriate department manager.

Most of the risks identified were well known. The lack of new findings was not usually considered a failure of the process, but was more often attributed to management already actively addressing risks. As Patrick Henry stated, "If there had been big surprises, it would have meant we were asleep at the wheel." However there was some acknowledgement that there could be flaws inherent in the process itself. Suzanne Zoumaras, VP Human Resources, explained, "The list is only as good as the people who create it. The same people who create a list of risks, aren't going to be surprised by it."

Risk assessment

Risk assessment or quantification involved prioritizing and rating the potential severity of the risks. To that end, Lance developed a simple two-dimensional scoring method that was used by all of the departments. To locate each item on a "risk heat map," a severity score and a likelihood score were assigned to each risk event. The product of the scores became the overall score. Severity and likelihood were quantitatively defined, as explained in Figure 1 below. Severity was defined in terms of cash impact. Likelihood was defined in terms of a probability of occurrence in a given timeframe.

Entropic considered the risk events independently; there was no attempt to identify or quantify correlations between them. Every department used the same scoring system, but the scoring was done solely within each department. Individual risk scores were not aggregated into an overall company risk score that could be tracked over time. Top management had no enthusiasm to introduce an aggregate score into the process.

FIGURE 1 Risk Heat Map

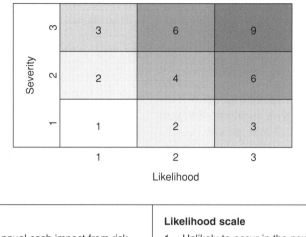

Severity scale

1 = Not significant (likely annual cash impact from risk occurring < $1 million)
2 = Significant but not material (likely annual cash impact from risk occurring is $1–$3 million)
3 = Material (likely annual cash impact > $3 million OR likely to affect stock price)

Likelihood scale

1 = Unlikely to occur in the next 12 months
2 = Potential for minor occurrences in the next 12 months
3 = Minor occurrences happening now OR potential for significant occurrences in next 12 months

Most managers were happy with the scoring system. They found it easy to implement and useful. In some cases, quantifying risks helped department managers realize that they didn't have high-level risks. In other cases, quantifying risks enabled managers to prioritize and focus. As Vinay Gokhale, Senior VP – Marketing and Business Development, explained, "Having metrics really helped. Otherwise it would have just been a big worry session." Nevertheless, Lance wondered if everyone applied the scoring method consistently and rigorously. He suspected that some participants might have just backed into the numbers they wanted.

Mitigation measures were summarized in a Risk Management Matrix for risks with a score of 4 or less. The 16 risks with scores of 6 or 9 received more attention, and in some cases risk-mitigation programs were initiated or improved.

Risk response/control activities

In most cases, mitigation plans were designed to reduce risk. For example, the legal department identified the lack of a formal document-retention policy and related procedures for preserving or destroying documents as a risk. As part of the risk response effort, IT and Legal collaborated, ultimately developing a Document Retention Policy that was subsequently implemented at Entropic. As a direct result, e-mails were moved to a new server and were only retained for one year rather than indefinitely, resulting in potentially significant savings and enhancing the company's ability to comply with electronic discovery orders in litigation. In Human Resources, ERM stimulated a higher level of compliance to existing standards. For instance, Human Resources developed measures to ensure that job descriptions were updated when people changed positions internally.

In other cases, a choice was made merely to accept certain risks. One of the few risks assessed as 9 was competitive risk, specifically relating to inadequate information on competitor's plans and products. Although managers at Entropic aggressively sought public information on competitors, they recognized that often reliable competitive information was just not available or hard to come by in the emerging industries in which they operated. This risk was accepted as inherent to the business. As Patrick explained, "Any company with a viable business model has competitive risk. You can't mitigate it completely, unless you have a tiny uninteresting market."

A third option, avoiding a risk by eliminating the risky event altogether, was not employed by any of the departments.

Communication

The majority of communication throughout the process took place between Lance and the department heads. No company-wide meeting dedicated to discussion of either the ERM process or the output was scheduled. Informally, however, some of the issues identified in the ERM process made their way into discussions at other formal company-wide meetings, such as the Annual Operating Plan (AOP) meetings. In December 2009, Lance presented the final output – the Risk Management Matrix with a summary of mitigation measures – to Patrick Henry and Entropic's Board of Directors.

Monitoring

The last step in the process was to decide how risks would be monitored on an ongoing basis. Lance and Patrick agreed that it would probably make sense to monitor existing risks on a semi-annual basis and to update the Risk Management Matrix on an annual basis.

DEPARTMENTAL PARTICIPATION

Department heads were given flexibility to tailor their department's level of participation in the ERM process to fit their departmental needs. As a result, the amount of commitment to the process varied greatly from department to department.

The Engineering department was at one end of the spectrum. Engineering already had a robust quality control process in place that governed not only manufacturing but also new product development and testing processes. Consequently, engineering managers saw the ERM initiative as largely "make-work." The department's culture, which stressed innovation and creativity, tended to resist formal process and bureaucracy.

Management in the Finance department didn't see a great need for ERM either. In 2008, the Finance department had updated its internal controls to comply with requirements imposed by Sarbanes-Oxley and the SEC for public companies. As a result, the department had recently been through

a detailed review of its risk management practices. With regard to this new ERM process, CFO David Lyle explained,

> It's not something that we put a lot of time into. When you're a smaller company and you have a smaller department, you tend to have fewer resources than are needed to do everything you need to do. A separate ERM program is lower on the priority for this department because we don't have a lot of time to spend on it. But I'm a huge fan of process. I don't want to discount its value, just because I didn't participate so much in it. We already manage risk well. We talk about risk every day. I just don't think Lance's forms helped us.

On the other end of the spectrum were Human Resources and Marketing, two departments that participated actively in ERM and that found it useful. Suzy Zoumaris explained, "I'm a process person; having the right processes and controls in place frees me up to do more strategic things."

Patrick Henry was not troubled by the varying levels of commitment to the ERM process. Participation in the ERM process had no bearing on performance reviews or capital allocations. Patrick had a pragmatic perspective. He was not interested in championing processes for process sake. He recognized the need for good systems, but was also cognizant of the downside of adding too much process too quickly. He explained,

> It's important to layer on process at the right thickness and to scale it appropriately to the size of the company. One of the key benefits of being a small company is speed of decision making. We don't want to become too bureaucratic and become a slave to process, as opposed to designing processes that serve us.

FINAL THOUGHTS

Lance and Patrick were largely satisfied with the ERM process. They thought that the time spent going through the process was valuable and reasonable. But they didn't see a pressing need to further expand or elevate ERM in the near future.

Lance considered improving the process by changing to the COSO organizing framework – strategic, operational, reporting, and compliance risks – to identify and describe types of risk in future iterations. He thought that categorizing risks by objective could help particularly in identifying risks that intersected multiple departments. He also considered improving the process through further work on the back-end of the process, particularly analyzing how risks were interrelated and the extent to which mitigating or addressing one risk might increase other risks or lead to new risks not previously identified.

Despite Lance's and Patrick's overall satisfaction with ERM, they recognized some of its limitations. The process was redundant for some departments. Not all risks could be mitigated. In fact, the most severe risk was inherent to the business. Not all risks could be anticipated; in the same year that ERM was implemented, Entropic mitigated a serious business risk that was not on the ERM

matrix. A service provider insisted on using technology that Entropic engineers were sure wouldn't meet quality standards. Entropic management could refuse the service providers's request, or move forward with a sub-optimal solution, but either way they ran the risk of losing an important customer. Entropic management was ultimately able to work out a solution, but the risk of losing the service provider's business dwarfed any of the risks in the ERM matrix. Patrick felt strongly that responding well to surprises was as, or more, important than trying to identify and mitigate everything upfront. Nevertheless, Entropic planned to continue to refine and use the ERM process in the future.

Exhibit 1 Entropic Communications, Inc., income statements (2005–2009)

	Years Ended December 31				
	2009	2008	2007	2006	2005
	(in $ thousands, except per share data)				
Consolidated Statement of Operations Data:					
Net revenues	$116,305	$146,033	$122,545	$41,471	$3,719
Cost of net revenues	57,399	79,411	76,196	31,099	1,979
Gross profit	58,906	66,622	46,349	10,372	1,740
Operating expense:					
Research and development	45,161	55,769	35,235	11,601	9,574
Sales and marketing	13,955	16,262	10,348	4,112	2,247
General and administrative	10,868	12,752	8,685	2,192	1,846
Write off of in-process research and development	–	1,300	21,400	–	–
Amortization of intangible assets	16	2,735	2,634	–	–
Restructuring charges	2,173	1,259	–	–	–
Impairment of goodwill and intangible assets	208	113,193	–	–	–
Total operating expenses	72,381	203,270	78,302	17,905	13,667
Loss from operations	(13,475)	(136,648)	(31,953)	(7,533)	(11,927)
Other income (expense), net	142	229	31	482	(269)
Income tax (benefit) provision	(93)	(49)	44	–	–
Net loss	(13,240)	(136,370)	(31,966)	(7,051)	(12,196)
Accretion of redeemable convertible preferred stock	–	–	(118)	(126)	(89)
Net loss attributable to common stockholders	$(13,240)	$(136,370)	$(32,084)	$(7,177)	$(12,285)
Net loss per share attributable to common stockholders – basic and diluted	$(0.19)	$(2.01)	$(2.47)	$(1.66)	$(3.70)
Weighted average number of shares used to compute net loss per share attributable to common stockholders	69,834	67,733	13,011	4,325	3,317

Source: 2009 Form 10-K.

Exhibit 2 COSO Enterprise Risk Management Integrated Framework – objectives and components

This enterprise risk management framework is geared to achieving an entity's objectives, set forth in four categories:

- *Strategic* – high-level goals, aligned with and supporting its mission
- *Operations* – effective and efficient use of its resources
- *Reporting* – reliability of reporting
- *Compliance* – compliance with applicable laws and regulations

Components of enterprise risk management

Enterprise Risk Management consists of eight interrelated components. These are derived from the way management runs an enterprise and are integrated with the management process. These components are:

- *Internal environment* – The internal environment encompasses the tone of an organization, and sets the basis for how risk is viewed and addressed by an entity's people, including risk management philosophy and risk appetite, integrity and ethical values, and the environment in which they operate.
- *Objective setting* – Objectives must exist before management can identify potential events affecting their achievement. Enterprise Risk Management ensures that management has in place a process to set objectives and that the chosen objectives support and align with the entity's mission and are consistent with its risk appetite.
- *Event identification* – Internal and external events affecting achievement of an entity's objectives must be identified, distinguishing between risks and opportunities. Opportunities are channeled back to management's strategy or objective-setting processes.
- *Risk assessment* – Risks are analyzed, considering likelihood and impact, as a basis for determining how they should be managed. Risks are assessed on an inherent and a residual basis.
- *Risk response* – Management selects risk responses – avoiding, accepting, reducing, or sharing risk – developing a set of actions to align risks with the entity's risk tolerances and risk appetite.
- *Control activities* – Policies and procedures are established and implemented to help ensure the risk responses are effectively carried out.
- *Information and communication* – Relevant information is identified, captured, and communicated in a form and timeframe that enable people to carry out their responsibilities. Effective communication also occurs in a broader sense, flowing down, across, and up the entity.
- *Monitoring* – The entirety of enterprise risk management is monitored and modifications made as necessary. Monitoring is accomplished through ongoing management activities, separate evaluations, or both.

Source: ERM – Integrated Framework, Executive Summary, September 2004.

EXHIBIT 3 S&P Progress Report: Integrating Enterprise Risk Management Analysis Into Corporate Credit Ratings, July 22, 2009, Preliminary Findings

Based on our discussions, we note that:

- The level of adoption, formality, maturity, and engagement of ERM varies widely within and across sectors and regions. We haven't seen many companies provide clear examples of definitions for risk tolerance or risk appetite. While that's not surprising (since ERM is still relatively new), a preliminary conclusion could be that many companies find it difficult to ensure uniform behavior across the enterprise.

- Many companies exhibit an active management of risks with ongoing risk reviews and the assessment of high-impact/high-probability risks.

- The way the risk management function fits in the organizational structure indicates how integrated a company's approach is to risk management. We observe that "silo-based" risk management, focused only at the operational managers' level, continues to be prevalent.

- There appears to be a link between transparency and disclosure and companies' confidence about ERM; many companies have been willing and able to provide considerable detail about risk management practices.

- Companies with a true enterprise-wide approach to ERM appreciate the importance of going beyond only quantifiable risks or even top 10 risks. They increasingly understand the importance of emerging risks.

- Companies often facilitate their ERM execution via separate structures, with associated roles and responsibilities clearly defined. The ERM function's reporting line is typically to the CFO or the CEO, often with a direct line of communication to the board of directors, commonly to the audit committee. However, we have also seen numerous examples of risk-management structures that lack stature and influence in their organizations.

- Companies in industries with more quantifiable and hedgeable risks are generally more comfortable discussing ERM, but they tend to focus on controls of those specific risks. Examples include: energy, pharmaceuticals, agribusiness, and some manufacturers.

Just as a company's introduction of ERM is unlikely to radically change its current decision-making processes, we don't see ERM analysis radically altering our existing credit rating opinions. We expect its value to be incremental in many cases, negligible in a few, and eye opening in some.

Exhibit 4 SEC rule amendments, summary and excerpt

PROXY DISCLOSURE ENHANCEMENTS AGENCY: Securities and Exchange Commission.

ACTION: Final rule.

SUMMARY: We are adopting amendments to our rules that will enhance information provided in connection with proxy solicitations and in other reports filed with the Commission. The amendments will require registrants to make new or revised disclosures about: compensation policies and practices that present material risks to the company; stock and option awards of executives and directors; director and nominee qualifications and legal proceedings; board leadership structure; the board's role in risk oversight; and potential conflicts of interest of compensation consultants that advise companies and their boards of directors. The amendments to our disclosure rules will be applicable to proxy and information statements, annual reports and registration statements under the Securities Exchange Act of 1934, and registration statements under the Securities Act of 1933 as well as the Investment Company Act of 1940. We are also transferring from Forms 10-Q and 10-K to Form 8-K the requirement to disclose shareholder voting results.

EFFECTIVE DATE: February 28, 2010

C. New Disclosure about Board Leadership Structure and the Board's Role in Risk Oversight

3. Final Rule

The final rules also require companies to describe the board's role in the oversight of risk. We were persuaded by commenters who noted that risk oversight is a key competence of the board, and that additional disclosures would improve investor and shareholder understanding of the role of the board in the organization's risk management practices. Companies face a variety of risks, including credit risk, liquidity risk, and operational risk. As we noted in the Proposing Release, similar to disclosure about the leadership structure of a board, disclosure about the board's involvement in the oversight of the risk management process should provide important information to investors about how a company perceives the role of its board and the relationship between the board and senior management in managing the material risks facing the company. This disclosure requirement gives companies the flexibility to describe how the board administers its risk oversight function, such as through the whole board, or through a separate risk committee or the audit committee, for example. Where relevant, companies may want to address whether the individuals who supervise the day-to-day risk management responsibilities report directly to the board as a whole or to a board committee or how the board or committee otherwise receives information from such individuals.

Exhibit 5 Risk factors identified and described in Entropic's 10-K report

Investing in our common stock involves a high degree of risk. Before deciding to purchase, hold or sell our common stock, you should carefully consider the risks described below in addition to the other cautionary statements and risks described, and the other information contained, elsewhere in this Annual Report and in our other filings with the SEC. The risks and uncertainties described below are not the only ones we face. Additional risks and uncertainties not presently known to us or that we currently deem immaterial may also affect our business. If any of these known or unknown risks or uncertainties actually occurs, our business, financial condition, results of operations and/or liquidity could be seriously harmed. In that event, the trading price of our common stock could decline and you could lose some or all of your investment.

Risks related to our business

We have had net operating losses for several years, had an accumulated deficit of $242.0 million as of December 31, 2009 and only recently became profitable, and we are unable to predict whether we will remain profitable.

We face intense competition and expect competition to increase in the future, with many of our competitors being larger, more established and better capitalized than we are.

We depend on a limited number of customers, and ultimately service providers, for a substantial portion of our revenues, and the loss of, or a significant shortfall in, orders from any of these parties could significantly impair our financial condition and results of operations.

If we fail to develop and introduce new or enhanced products on a timely basis, our ability to attract and retain customers could be impaired, and our competitive position may be harmed.

Our results could be adversely affected if our customers or the service providers who purchase their products are unable to successfully compete in their respective markets.

If the market for HD video and other multimedia content delivery solutions based on the MoCA standard does not develop as we anticipate, our revenues may decline or fail to grow, which would adversely affect our operating results.

Even if service providers, ODMs and OEMs adopt multimedia content delivery solutions based on the MoCA standard, we may not compete successfully in the market for MoCA-compliant chipsets.

The semiconductor and communications industries have historically experienced cyclical behavior and prolonged downturns, which could impact our operating results, financial condition and cash flows.

Our operating results have fluctuated significantly in the past and we expect them to continue to fluctuate in the future, which could lead to volatility in the price of our common stock.

Our operating results may be harmed if our 2009 restructuring plan does not achieve the anticipated results or causes undesirable consequences.

Adverse U.S. and international economic conditions have affected and may continue to adversely affect our revenues, margins and profitability.

The success of our digital broadcast satellite outdoor unit products depends on the demand for our products within the satellite digital television market and the growth of this overall market.

Market-specific risks affecting the digital television, digital television set-top boxes and digital television peripheral markets could impair our ability to successfully sell our silicon tuners.

The success of our silicon tuners is highly dependent on our relationships with demodulator manufacturers.

The market for our broadband access products is limited and these products may not be widely adopted.

We intend to expand our operations and increase our expenditures in an effort to grow our business. If we are not able to manage this expansion and growth, or if our business does not grow as we expect, we may not be able to realize a return on the resources we devote to expansion.

Any acquisition, strategic relationship, joint venture or investment could disrupt our business and harm our financial condition.

We may not realize the anticipated financial and strategic benefits from the businesses we have acquired or be able to successfully integrate such businesses with ours.

The average selling prices of our products have historically decreased over time and will likely do so in the future, which may reduce our revenues and gross margin.

Our product development efforts are time-consuming, require substantial research and development expenditures and may not generate an acceptable return.

Our products typically have lengthy sales cycles, which may cause our operating results to fluctuate, and a service provider, ODM or OEM customer may decide to cancel or change its service or product plans, which could cause us to lose anticipated sales.

Exhibit 5 *continued*

Fluctuations in the mix of products we sell may adversely affect our financial results.

If we do not complete our design-in activities before a customer's design window closes, we will lose the design opportunity, which could adversely affect our future sales and revenues and harm our customer relationships.

Our products must interoperate with many software applications and hardware found in service providers' networks and other devices in the home, and if they do not interoperate properly, our business would be harmed.

Our customers may cancel their orders, change production quantities or delay production, and if we fail to forecast demand for our products accurately, we may incur product shortages, delays in product shipments or excess or insufficient product inventory.

Our ability to accurately predict revenues and inventory needs, and to effectively manage inventory levels, may be adversely impacted due to our use of inventory "hubbing" arrangements.

We extend credit to our customers, sometimes in large amounts, but there is no guarantee every customer will be able to pay our invoices when they become due.

We depend on a limited number of third parties to manufacture, assemble and test our products, which reduces our control over key aspects of our products and their availability.

When demand for manufacturing capacity is high, we may take various actions to try to secure sufficient capacity, which may be costly and negatively impact our operating results.

We believe that transitioning certain of our silicon products to newer or better manufacturing process technologies will be important to our future competitive position. If we fail to make this transition efficiently, our competitive position could be seriously harmed.

We rely on sales representatives to assist in selling our products, and the failure of these representatives to perform as expected could reduce our future sales.

Our products may contain defects or errors which may adversely affect their market acceptance and our reputation and expose us to product liability claims.

We depend on key personnel to operate our business, and if we are unable to retain our current personnel and hire additional qualified personnel, our ability to develop and successfully market our products could be harmed.

If we fail to comply with environmental regulatory requirements, our operating results could be adversely affected.

Certain of our customers' products and service providers' services are subject to governmental regulation.

Our failure to raise additional capital or generate the significant capital necessary to expand our operations and invest in new products could reduce our ability to compete and could harm our business.

Our costs have increased significantly as a result of operating as a public company, and our management is required to devote substantial time to comply with public company regulations.

Our effective tax rate may increase or fluctuate, and we may not derive the anticipated tax benefits from any expansion of our international operations.

Our ability to utilize our net operating loss and tax credit carryforwards may be limited, which could result in our payment of income taxes earlier than if we were able to fully utilize our net operating loss and tax credit carryforwards.

If we fail to manage our exposure to global financial and securities market risk successfully, our operating results could be adversely impacted.

Risks related to our intellectual property

Our ability to compete and our business could be jeopardized if we are unable to secure or protect our intellectual property.

Our participation in "patent pools" and standards setting organizations, or other business arrangements, may require us to license our patents to competitors and other third parties and limit our ability to enforce or collect royalties for our patents.

Any dispute with a MoCA member regarding what patent claims are necessary to implement MoCA specifications could result in litigation which could have an adverse effect on our business.

Possible third-party claims of infringement of proprietary rights against us, our customers or the service providers that purchase products from our customers, or other intellectual property claims or disputes, could have a material adverse effect on our business, results of operation or financial condition.

Our use of open source and third-party software could impose limitations on our ability to commercialize our products.

Because we license some of our software source code directly to customers, we face increased risks that our trade secrets will be exposed through inadvertent or intentional disclosure, which could harm our competitive position or increase our costs.

EXHIBIT 5 *continued*

Risks related to international operations

We expect a significant portion of our future revenues to come from our international customers, and, as a result, our business may be harmed by political and economic conditions in foreign markets and the challenges associated with operating internationally.

Our products are subject to export and import controls that could subject us to liability or impair our ability to compete in international markets.

Our third-party contractors are concentrated primarily in areas subject to earthquakes and other natural disasters. Any disruption to the operations of these contractors could cause significant delays in the production or shipment of our products.

Risks related to ownership of our common stock

Our stock price is volatile and may decline regardless of our operating performance, and you may not be able to resell your shares at or above the price at which you purchased such shares.

Future sales of our common stock or the issuance of securities convertible into or exercisable for shares of our common stock may depress our stock price.

Anti-takeover provisions in our charter documents and Delaware law might deter acquisition bids for us that you might consider favorable.

Our principal stockholders, executive officers and directors have substantial control over the company, which may prevent you and other stockholders from influencing significant corporate decisions and may harm the market price of our common stock.

If securities or industry analysts publish inaccurate or unfavorable research about our business, our stock price and trading volume could decline.

We do not expect to pay any cash dividends for the foreseeable future.

Our stock may be delisted from The NASDAQ Global Market if the closing bid price for our common stock is not maintained at $1.00 per share or higher.

Source: Entropic, Inc. 10-K for fiscal year ending Dec 2009.

EXHIBIT 6 Risk management matrix

Note: The following matrix is an excerpt from the matrix created by Entropic. Actual likelihood and severity scores assigned by the company have been disguised.

	Risk Description	Likelihood	Severity	Risk Score
Engineering	Failing to follow industry "best practices" in product development & designs	2	2	4
	Risk of missing a design window due to product development delays	2	3	6
	Being unaware of requirements for or failing to obtain government certifications related to our products (e.g., compliance with FCC standards, safety regulations for consumer products)	1	1	1
	Risks re: our products failing to achieve timely certification by a standards body or an operator	2	2	4
	Risk that our products will not interoperate fully with software or hardware in a customer's product or a service provider network	2	2	4
	Risks re: failing to acquire the most appropriate chip design software tools	1	3	3
	Infringing patents held by third parties	1	3	3
	Infringing third party copyrights	1	2	2
	Risk of currency fluctuations increasing our cost of labor in overseas development sites	1	1	1
Operations	Product quality – unanticipated warranty returns	2	3	6
	Export control (proper permits and licenses, export of encrypted product, US Gov't boycotts)	1	3	3
	Product quality – low manufacturing yields	2	2	4
	Risk of cost increases from our suppliers that cannot be passed on to customers	2	2	4
	Risks of supply constraints	2	2	4
	Inadequate inventory controls or inability to sell products in inventory due to how they are marked or manufactured	2	2	4
	Product quality – latent defects	1	3	3
	Risk that our MRP systems will prove inadequate for our needs or fail to provide necessary functionality	1	3	3
	Failing to comply with environmental regulations (worldwide)	1	2	2
	General product safety	1	1	1
	Risks of supply interruption (e.g., act of god or war)	1	1	1
	Risk of currency fluctuations affecting our cost to build product	1	1	1
	Failing to maintain ISO certification or pass customer quality audits	1	1	1
Marketing & Business Development	Assuring that product features, costs and availability date meet customer requirements	2	3	6
	Assuring that length of product life cycle and sales volume will be sufficient for required ROI	1	2	2
	Pricing products to achieve target gross margins	3	2	6
	Accurately assessing market size and forecasting market share for the company's products	2	2	4
	Risks re: customer acceptance of products (performance, bugs, integration, documentation, etc.)	1	3	3
	Risks associated with penetrating new markets or new applications	2	2	4
	Inadequate G2 on competitor's products, plans	3	3	9
	Infringement of trademarks held by third parties	1	1	1
	Loss of key customer or operator relationships due to personnel changes	2	3	6
	Building excessive inventory	1	2	2

Exhibit 6 *continued*

Sales	Failing to accurately forecast product demand, future orders, deployment rates and inventories of customers/operators	2	2	4
	Not being able to accurately track existing orders or price commitments	1	2	2
	Risks associated with use and management of sales reps and distributors	1	2	2
	Risks associated with long sales cycles	1	2	2
	Sales seasonality	1	1	1
	Loss of relevant personnel	3	1	3
	Conflicting Sales/Marketing service models	2	3	6
	Shipment Terms & Conditions disputes	1	2	2
	Risks associated with customer collections & disputes	2	2	4
	Risks associated with contract violations & disputes	1	2	2
	Failure to meet customer audit requirements	1	1	1
	Failure to hire qualified regional Sales/TAM personnel	1	2	2
	Product quality/customer returns	1	2	2
CTO	Risks associated with participation in standards bodies (MoCA, ITU, etc.) – Notice of IP, RAND license obligations	2	2	4
	Risks associated with identifying and addressing competing technologies and evolving industry standards	2	3	6
	Failure to timely identify new and emerging markets and complementary technologies	2	3	6
	Failure to develop core technology competencies over the long term	1	3	3
Human Resources	Negligent hiring/background checks	1	1	1
	Risks related to "on-boarding" new employees and consultants	1	1	1
	Compliance with immigration laws at hire and ongoing	1	1	1
	Workplace safety and health	1	1.5	1.5
	Health and benefit plans	1	1	1
	Privacy protection for employees	1	2	2
	COBRA Administration	1	1	1
	Discrimination and Sexual Harrassment in the workplace	1	1	1
	Risks related to "exiting" employees and consultants	1	1	1
	Retaliation/wrongful discharge	1	2	2
	Recruiting risk	1	2	2
	Risks associated with identifying resource needs early enough to timely fill them and ensuring all required competencies are identified	1	2	2
	Retention risk	2	2	4
	Employee compliance with laws	1	1	1
	Ethical business conduct	1	1	1
	Compliance with labor laws	1	1.5	1
Facilities	Facilities planning risk	1	2	2
	Design & maintenance risks	1	1	1
	Special needs risks (e.g., cooling for computer servers, rooftop use, network infrastructure, etc.)	1	2	2
	Compliance with (i) building codes, (ii) local regulations & (iii) lease obligations	1	1	1
	Workplace safety and health	2	2	4
	Physical security & monitoring of premises	1	2	2
	Use & disposal of hazardous materials	1	1	1

EXHIBIT 6 *continued*

IT	Risk that company proprietary information will be compromised due to hacking or industrial espionage	2	2	4
	Theft/misuse of proprietary information by current or former employees and consultants	2	2	4
	Service gaps, unscheduled computer downtime or slow network impacting productivity	1	1	1
	Disaster recovery (e.g., earthquake/fire)	1	3	3
Finance and Accounting	Financial statements/earnings management and manipulation	1	3	3
	Risk that all transactions are not accurately recorded or accounted for	1	3	3
	Adequate accounting controls (Sarbane-Oxley internal controls of financial reporting)	1	3	3
	Adequate disclosure controls	1	2	2
	Awareness of new accounting rules or pronouncements	1	1	1
	Changes in accounting policies required by auditors	1	1	1
	Revenue recognition issues	1	3	3
	Collection of revenues from customers who take goods on credit	3	2	6
	Theft risk for cash accounts	1	1	1
	Cash management – loss of principal/illiquidity	1	2	2
	Taxes – awareness of tax obligations	1	1	1
	Taxes – timely and accurate domestic & int'l filings	1	1	1
Legal	Antitrust & Trade Reg. Compliance; FCPA Compliance	1	3	3
	Litigation – patent infringement (including customer indemnification claims)	2	3	6
	Litigation – wrongful termination; discrimination; whistleblower claims	1	2	2
	Litigation – warranty or product defect claim	2	1	2
	Contracts – creating binding obligations without proper review or authorization	2	2	4
	Contracts – onerous contract obligations, breach of contract	2	2	4
	Awareness of new laws or regulations affecting the company	1	3	3
	Retention of Documents During Litigation	1	3	3
	Management/destruction/return of third party confidential information	1	2	2
	Obtaining, maintaining and enforcing intellectual property rights (includes patents, trademarks, trade secrets) in the US and in foreign countries	2	3	6

Case Study

Financial reporting problems at Molex, Inc.

In mid-November 2004, Molex's board of directors met to decide the future of Joe King and Diane Bullock, the company's CEO and CFO respectively. Molex's external auditors, Deloitte & Touche, had accused both of failing to disclose an $8 million pretax inventory valuation error in a recent letter of representation to the auditors. In response, King and Bullock argued that at the time of their letter they had determined that the financial impact of the error was immaterial. Despite an inquiry by the Audit Committee, which concluded that management had not deliberately withheld information from the auditors, Deloitte & Touche was not satisfied. The audit firm insisted that it could no longer rely on Bullock's and King's representations, and would be unable to complete its review of the first quarter results until representations were received from a new CFO and in all likelihood a new CEO.

MOLEX BACKGROUND AND MANAGEMENT

Founded in Lisle, Illinois in 1938 by Frederick Krehbiel, Molex Inc. designed, manufactured and distributed electronic connectors that were used by a wide range of industries.[1] For example, in the computer industry its connectors were used to produce computers, servers and printers; in the telecommunications industry they were used to produce mobile phones and networking equipment; the consumer products industry used Molex connectors to manufacture CD and DVD players, cameras, plasma and LCD televisions; and the automotive industry used them for the production of engine control units and adaptive breaking systems. In 2003, Molex was the second largest firm in the connector industry, with a worldwide share of 6.9%, and production and distribution facilities located throughout the world.[2]

In July 2001, Molex's board of directors appointed Joe King as vice chairman and chief executive officer. Trained as an engineer in Ireland, King had joined Molex as a quality control manager in 1975. Initially responsible for overseeing manufacturing quality at the company's Shannon plant and for working with customers on technical issues, he soon took over material management, including planning, purchasing and inventory control. King was subsequently promoted to assistant head of international operations, which covered the US Export Group and Computer Systems, and then to vice president of operations, where he oversaw most of the company's technical systems and was in charge of developing and implementing a strategic plan for international operations. From 1985 to 1988, as corporate vice president and president of the Far East south region, he opened an operating facility in Malaysia, initiated discussions on operations that would later open in Thailand and China, and developed the region's marketing and engineering capabilities. As competition in the region intensified during the late 1980's, King stressed customer service, quality, and new product development as ways for Molex to compete more effectively. In 1988, he was appointed group vice president-international, responsible for sales and manufacturing operations in Europe, the Far East and new international ventures. Eight years later, King

---

[1] The Krehbiel family continued to have a controlling interest in Molex. Brothers Frederick A. Krehbiel and John H. Krehbiel, Jr. were Co-Chairs of the board of directors and former CEOs, and Fred L. Krehbiel, the son of John H. Krehbiel, Jr. was a member of the board.

[2] The number one firm in the industry was Tyco Electronics, with a 19.7% market share. See "Top 100 Connector Manufacturers," Market Research Report, Bishop & Associates, September 2004.

This case was prepared by Professor Paul Healy.

became executive vice president for functional groups worldwide, where he played a key role in integrating domestic and international operations, consolidating global staff functions, and assigning all regions to report to one person, the president and chief operating officer.[3]

In contrast, Molex's chief financial officer, Diane Bullock, had a very brief history with the firm. She had been hired in October of 2003 to replace Bob Mahoney as CFO effective January 1, 2004. Bullock had previously held a variety of global financial positions in the automotive components industry and in public accounting.

MOLEX FINANCIAL PERFORMANCE

2002 and 2003 were challenging years for Molex. The company experienced a sharp downturn in demand for its products, particularly from technology customers. Molex management reacted by reducing its workforce and expenses, and by directing investment into products less affected by recession. Management's task was further complicated by heavy short selling of Molex's stock during the downturn. For example, during 2003, average short-interest was 8 million shares, roughly 12.5 days of average daily share volume.[4]

The first sign of a recovery came during the quarter ended December 31, 2003 (the second quarter of the June 30, 2004 fiscal year), when sales and earnings increased by 21% and 46% respectively over the same quarter one year earlier. In response, Molex's stock price jumped by 6% relative to the Nasdaq Composite Index.

However, the stock price increase proved to be temporary. On February 17, an online research firm, CashFlowNews.com, observed that Molex's free cash flow (defined as cash flow from operations minus capital expenditures) had declined 52% for the 12 months ended December 31, 2003, from $240 million to a six-year low of $114 million. Following publication of the report, Molex's stock fell by 8% relative to the Nasdaq Composite Index (see Exhibit 1 for a graph of Molex's stock price performance).

Molex showed steady financial improvement during the first six months of 2004. Revenues for the year ended June 30, 2004 increased by almost 22%, and net income more than doubled from $84.9 million to $176.0 million (see Exhibit 2 for a 10-year summary of Molex's financial performance). The company reported fourth quarter earnings per share of $0.30, exceeding its own prior estimates of $0.27 to $0.29, and analyst estimates of $0.28.[5]

In a July 27, 2004 press release and in the 2004 10-K filed on September 10, 2004, management estimated that earnings per share for the first quarter of the following year would be between $0.26 and $0.29, compared to analyst forecasts of $0.29. In discussing the company's future prospects, management noted that:

> The outlook in the majority of the Company's global markets remains strong. . . . The Company expects revenue growth of 16% to 19% during fiscal 2005 and net income is expected to grow faster than revenues due to leverage from the higher volume. Earnings per share are expected in the range of $1.24 to $1.34, an increase of 35 to 45%.

Yet despite increased sales and earnings for 2004, and management's expectation of continued sales and earnings growth, Molex's stock price lagged the market and short interest in its stock remained high (8 million shares in August 2004).

AUDIT INDUSTRY CHALLENGES

2002 and 2003 were also challenging years for the audit industry. Its reputation for independence and high quality audits plunged following a wave of corporate accounting scandals that included Enron, Worldcom, Adelphia, Global Crossing and Freddie Mac in the US, and Ahold and Parmalat in Europe.

In mid-2002, Enron's auditor, Arthur Andersen, the fifth largest auditing firm, was convicted of obstruction of justice for shredding documents related to its Enron audit. Since US Securities and Exchange Commission (SEC) rules prohibited convicted felons from auditing public companies, Arthur Andersen was forced to surrender its licenses and its right to practice before the SEC, leaving only four large accounting firms (in order of size,

---

[3] Source: Joseph King Bio on http://www.ttiinc.com/object/ME_ExecIntKing.html

[4] Source: Bloomberg.

[5] Analyst estimates are from Thomson First Call.

Deloitte & Touche, PriceWaterhouseCooper, Ernst & Young, and KPMG).

Although Arthur Andersen was the audit firm most closely identified with the accounting scandals, many of the other leading firms were also affected. For example, several of Deloitte & Touche's largest clients (notably Adelphia, Fortress Re, Parmalat, and Ahold) were hit with fraud and accounting problems, leading the accounting firm to face a string of law suits claiming billions of dollars in potential damages.

Following the scandals and the collapse of Arthur Andersen, new regulations were adopted to improve the independence and quality of audits. For example, the Sarbannes Oxley Act of 2003 created a new oversight board (the Public Company Accounting Oversight Board) that was assigned responsibility for reviewing and disciplining accounting firms' audit quality, ethical standards, and independence. In addition, the act required audit partners to be rotated every five years. Audit firms, which had developed large consulting practices during the 1980s and 1990s, were prohibited from selling many of these services (including information systems design and implementation; appraisals, valuation, and actuarial services; and internal audit services) to their audit clients. Finally, audit committees, rather than management, were assigned responsibility for appointing and overseeing the external auditor, and for pre-approving the purchase of any material nonbanned consulting services.

MOLEX'S ACCOUNTING PROBLEM

In mid-July 2004, Molex's corporate finance group identified a potential problem with inventory that had affected results for several years. Profits on inventory sales between Molex subsidiaries (but which had not been sold to an external customer by period-end) had not been excluded in computing the consolidated firm's earnings and inventory. Consequently, earnings, inventory and retained earnings were most likely overstated.

After the discovery, disclosure of the misstatements to top management, the auditors, the audit committee, and investors took place as follows:

July 21, 2004: Diane Bullock (the company's CFO) brought the matter to the attention of other top management at a meeting that included Joe King (the Vice Chairman of the Board and CEO). A decision was made to investigate the matter further to assess whether and to what extent there was a problem. But based on subsequently gathered information, management concluded that the amounts involved were not material.[6]

July 27, 2004: Fourth quarter results were released with no mention of the problem.

September 10, 2004: The management representation letter for the annual financial statements and 10-K, dated August 20 2004 and signed by King and Bullock, was delivered to the external auditors (Deloitte & Touche LLP).[7] The letter made no mention of the inventory error.

October 15, 2004: Prior to releasing results for the first quarter ending September 30, 2004, Molex's management discussed the error for the first time with Deloitte & Touche and proposed recognizing $2 million of the adjustment during the current quarter with additional amounts recognized in subsequent quarters throughout the year.

October 19, 2004: At an Audit Committee meeting where the issue was discussed, Deloitte & Touche disagreed with management's October 15 proposal and argued that the entire error amount should be recorded in the first quarter. The Audit Committee requested that management and Deloitte & Touche work to determine the appropriate accounting.

October 20, 2004: Molex announced its first quarter results: revenues $640 million, net income $55.6 million, and earnings per share $0.29. The full amount of the accounting error ($8 million before tax and $5.8 million after tax, of which approximately $3.0 million before tax and $2.2 million after

---

[6] For financial reporting purposes, materiality was defined as "the magnitude of an omission or misstatement in the financial statements that makes it probable that a reasonable person relying on those statements would have been influenced by the information or made a different judgment if the correct information had been known" (FASB Concept Statement Number 2). Interpreting this definition frequently involved the exercise of professional judgment.

[7] A management representation letter is required as part of the audit engagement. The letter is drafted by the auditor, given to the client's management to print on its letterhead, and signed by the CEO and CFO. In the letter, management acknowledges that it is responsible for the financial statements, and commits in writing to prior oral representations made to the auditor that were relied on in conducting the audit. The representations are intended to reduce any misunderstandings between the auditors and management. Exhibit 3 provides a sample representation letter.

tax was related to the year ended June 30, 2004) was included as an adjustment to current operating results, but the error was considered immaterial and not disclosed (see Exhibit 4 for a summary of the first quarter results).

October 21, 2004: After the adjournment of a meeting of the Audit Committee, the engagement partner from Deloitte & Touche questioned Diane Bullock as to whether she was aware of the inventory error before signing the September 10, 2004 representation letter. When she confirmed that she had been aware of the problem at that time, Deloitte & Touche expressed concern about the significance of the omission to the Audit Committee. Bullock and King responded that, since the error's effect on the firm's financial performance was deemed immaterial, they did not think that it needed to be addressed in the letter. In an attempt to resolve the dispute, the Audit Committee held an inquiry with the help of independent legal and accounting advisors. The inquiry revealed no additional adjustments were required and that management had not deliberately withheld information from the auditors.

THE BOARD'S CHALLENGE

Deloitte & Touche continued to express dissatisfaction over top management's representations. It argued that management had known about the magnitude of the restatement as early as the July 21 meeting. Based on admissions from Bullock and King that they had expressly decided not to inform Deloitte & Touche of the errors at that time, the auditors

concluded that they were no longer willing to rely on Bullock and King's representations, and would only be able to complete their review of the first quarter results in connection with the company's 10-Q filing when representations were received from a new CFO and in all likelihood a new CEO.

In November, Molex's Board convened to discuss the situation (see Exhibit 5 for information on the board of directors). It appeared to face three options. (1) It could accede to the auditor's request to remove the CFO and/or CEO as executive officers so that they would not have any influence over financial reporting or internal controls. (2) It could ignore Deloitte & Touche's demand, forcing the auditor to either refuse to review the quarterly financial statements or to resign. In either case, Molex would be unable to file its quarterly results on time with the SEC and NASDAQ, violating the Exchange's listing requirements.[8] (3) It could dismiss Deloitte & Touche and hire a new auditor, in which case an 8-K would have to be filed with the SEC to explain the change.

---

[8] When NASDAQ determined that a company was delinquent in meeting its listing requirements, it notified the company that it had seven days to issue a press release announcing the delinquency and to file for a hearing with the NASDAQ Hearing Panel. At the hearing, the company was required to present a plan for how it intended to regain and subsequently maintain compliance. If the Panel found the plan convincing, it granted the company a conditional listing (called a limited-duration exception) and added an identifying letter "E" after the company's ticker. If the Panel decided not to grant an exception, the company's securities were delisted or transferred to The NASDAQ SmallCap Market.

EXHIBIT 1 Molex stock price performance relative to NASDAQ from Jan. 1, 2004 to Nov. 15, 2004

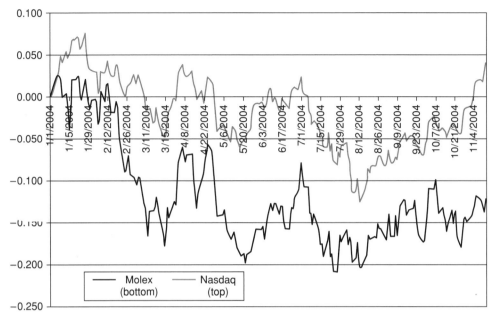

Source: Thomson Financial's Datastream.

Exhibit 2 Molex Incorporated, 10-year financial highlights summary, (in thousands, except per share data)

	2004	2003	2002	2001	2000	1999	1998	1997	1996	1995
Operations										
Net revenue	$2,246,715	$1,843,098	$1,711,497	$2,365,549	$2,217,096	$1,711,649	$1,622,975	$1,539,712	$1,382,673	$1,197,747
Gross profit	776,746	579,248	536,551	859,610	853,892	668,125	670,266	640,895	562,731	512,498
Income before income taxes	239,892	110,042	93,167	291,416	323,694	230,214	274,823	262,369	228,953	214,492
Income taxes	63,571	24,762	16,684	87,424	100,810	52,363	92,490	95,581	83,300	90,273
Net income [a]	175,950	84,918	76,479	203,919	222,454	178,029	182,243	166,716	145,586	124,035
Earnings per share: [b]										
Basic	0.93	0.44	0.39	1.04	1.13	0.92	0.93	0.85	0.74	0.63
Diluted	0.92	0.44	0.39	1.03	1.12	0.91	0.92	0.84	0.74	0.63
Net income – % of net revenue	7.8%	4.6%	4.5%	8.6%	10.0%	10.4%	11.2%	10.8%	10.5%	10.4%
Financial Position										
Current assets	1,168,644	962,113	915,343	891,865	1,023,009	881,338	867,791	873,614	734,589	773,036
Current liabilities	428,464	356,148	359,593	374,106	475,449	342,441	336,275	342,026	275,182	278,046
Working capital	740,180	605,965	555,750	517,759	547,560	538,897	531,516	531,588	459,407	494,990
Current ratio	2.7	2.7	2.5	2.4	2.2	2.6	2.6	2.6	2.7	2.8
Property, plant and equipment, net	1,022,378	1,007,948	1,067,590	1,092,567	980,775	809,602	676,161	665,468	613,125	567,303
Total assets	2,572,346	2,329,870	2,253,920	2,213,627	2,247,106	1,902,012	1,639,634	1,636,931	1,460,999	1,441,020
Long-term debt	10,243	13,137	14,223	19,351	21,593	20,148	5,566	7,350	7,450	8,122
Capital leases	3,796	3,731	3,626	6,114	–	–	–	–	–	–
Shareholders' equity	2,065,994	1,896,568	1,827,652	1,765,640	1,705,804	1,500,537	1,261,570	1,235,912	1,131,271	1,107,268
Return on beginning equity	9.3%	4.6%	4.3%	12.0%	14.8%	14.1%	14.7%	14.7%	13.1%	14.1%
Dividends per share [b]	0.1	0.1	0.1	0.1	0.09	0.05	0.05	0.04	0.03	0.02
Average common shares: [b]										
Basic	190,207	191,873	194,327	195,471	196,060	194,340	195,750	196,389	196,768	195,343
Diluted	192,186	193,229	195,986	197,633	198,208	195,631	197,971	198,349	198,819	197,414

[a] Fiscal 2003 results include a charge of $35.0 million ($24.8 million after tax) for restructuring costs and $5.1 million ($3.8 million after tax) for write-down of investments. Fiscal 2002 results included a restructuring charge of $24.2 million ($18.8 million after tax) and a charge for investment impairment of $10.0 million ($6.5 million after tax). Fiscal 2001 results included a restructuring charge of $30.8 million ($21.4 million after tax) and a charge for excess and slow moving inventory of $12.7 million ($8.9 million after tax).

[b] Restated for the following stock dividends: 25% – January 2000; 25% – November 1997; 25% – February 1997; 25% – August 1995; 25% – November 1994.

Source: Company 10-K, September 10, 2004.

EXHIBIT 3 Sample management representation letter, written on client letterhead

(Date)
(To the Auditor)

We are providing this letter in connection with your review of the financial statements of (name of entity) as of (dates) and for the (periods of review e.g. for the years then ended) for the purpose of expressing limited assurance that there are no material modifications that should be made to the statements in order for them to be in conformity with generally accepted accounting principles. We confirm that we are responsible for the fair presentation in the financial statements of financial position, results of operations, and cash flows in conformity with generally accepted accounting principles.

Certain representations in this letter are described as being limited to matters that are material. Items are considered material, regardless of size, if they involve an omission or misstatement of accounting information that, in the light of surrounding circumstances, makes it probable that the judgment of a reasonable person relying on the information would be changed or influenced by the omission or misstatement.

1. We confirm, to the best of our knowledge and belief, [as of (the date of the auditor's review report)] the following representations made to you during your review.

2. The financial statements referred to above are fairly presented in conformity with generally accepted accounting principles.

   We have made available to you all:

   a. Financial records and related data.

   b. Minutes of the meetings of stockholders, directors, and committees of directors, or summaries of actions of recent meetings for which minutes have not yet been prepared.

3. There are no material transactions that have not been properly recorded in the accounting records underlying the financial statements.

4. We acknowledge our responsibility to prevent and detect fraud.

5. We have no knowledge of any fraud or suspected fraud affecting the entity involving management or others where the fraud could have a material effect on the financial statements, including any communications received from employees, former employees or others.

6. We have no plans or intentions that may materially affect the carrying amounts or classification of assets and liabilities.

7. There are no material losses (such as from obsolete inventory or purchase or sales commitments) that have not been properly accrued or disclosed in the financial statements.

8. There are no:

   a. Violations or possible violations of laws or regulations, whose effects should be considered for disclosure in the financial statements or as a basis for recording a loss contingency.

   b. Unasserted claims or assessments that our lawyer has advised us are probable of assertion that must be disclosed in accordance with Financial Accounting Standards Board (FASB) Statement No. 5 [AC section C59], Accounting for Contingencies.

   c. Other material liabilities or gain or loss contingencies that are required to be accrued or disclosed by FASB Statement No. 5.

9. The company has satisfactory title to all owned assets, and there are no liens or encumbrances on such assets, nor has any asset been pledged as collateral.

10. We have complied with all aspects of contractual agreements that would have a material effect on the financial statements in the event of noncompliance.

11. The following have been properly recorded or disclosed in the financial statements:

    a. Related party transactions, including sales, purchases, loans, transfers, leasing arrangements, and guarantees, and amounts receivable from or payable to related parties.

    b. Guarantees, whether written or oral, under which the company is contingently liable.

Exhibit 3 *continued*

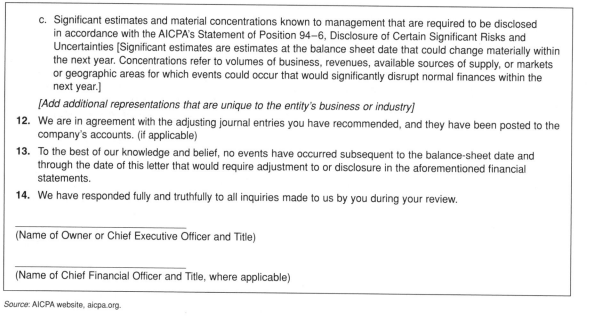

c. Significant estimates and material concentrations known to management that are required to be disclosed in accordance with the AICPA's Statement of Position 94–6, Disclosure of Certain Significant Risks and Uncertainties [Significant estimates are estimates at the balance sheet date that could change materially within the next year. Concentrations refer to volumes of business, revenues, available sources of supply, or markets or geographic areas for which events could occur that would significantly disrupt normal finances within the next year.]

[Add additional representations that are unique to the entity's business or industry]

12. We are in agreement with the adjusting journal entries you have recommended, and they have been posted to the company's accounts. (if applicable)

13. To the best of our knowledge and belief, no events have occurred subsequent to the balance-sheet date and through the date of this letter that would require adjustment to or disclosure in the aforementioned financial statements.

14. We have responded fully and truthfully to all inquiries made to us by you during your review.

_____

(Name of Owner or Chief Executive Officer and Title)

_____

(Name of Chief Financial Officer and Title, where applicable)

Source: AICPA website, aicpa.org.

Exhibit 4 Molex first quarter financial results for September 30, 2004

FISCAL FIRST QUARTER RESULTS

Revenue of $640.2 million increased 29% from last year's first quarter of $496.8 million. Revenue in local currencies increased 25%, as currency translation increased net revenue by approximately $19 million when compared with last year's first quarter. Revenue for the first quarter included $18 million from the automotive acquisition in Europe that was completed on April 2, 2004. Excluding the acquisition, revenue increased 25% from last year's first quarter. Net income was $55.6 million compared with last year's first quarter of $32.1 million, an increase of 74%. Earnings per share of $0.29 increased 71%, compared with $0.17 reported for the first quarter a year ago.

Joe King, Vice Chairman and Chief Executive Officer, said, "Revenue growth compared with last year's first quarter revenue was very strong. Revenue also increased sequentially, an excellent result in this seasonally challenging quarter. We believe we are growing significantly faster than the overall connector market, primarily due to our ongoing investment in new products and our global capabilities. We were also pleased with the strong growth in earnings after absorbing higher costs for many of our raw materials."

REGIONAL RESULTS

Revenue in the Far East South region was $190 million, an increase of 33%, primarily driven by the digital consumer, PC, and mobile communication markets. In this region, we continue to gain market share, based on our many new products and increased penetration into our global customers who continue to transfer production to the region. Revenue in the Far East North region (Japan and Korea) was $132 million, an increase of 13% in dollars and 6% in local currencies. This growth was primarily due to new products for the digital consumer and communication markets. Revenue in the Americas region was $177 million, an increase of 17%, due to stronger demand for high-speed, industrial and medical electronics products, which more than offset lower demand in automotive. Revenue in Europe was $128 million, an increase of 73% in dollars and 61% in local currencies. Excluding the previously mentioned automotive acquisition, revenue increased 49% in dollars, as the region recovers from recession.

Exhibit 4 *continued*

OPERATING RESULTS

Gross profit margin was 35.7% compared with last year's first quarter margin of 33.8%. Pretax return on sales was 12% compared with 8.9% in the year ago quarter. The effective tax rate for the first quarter was 27%, the same rate as last year's first quarter. The Company now anticipates an effective tax rate of 27% for the 2005 fiscal year, compared with previous guidance of 27.5% and a 2004 fiscal year rate of 26.5%. Net return on sales was 8.7% compared with 6.5% in last year's first quarter. Cash and marketable securities were $331.4 million at September 30, 2004.

The Company's order backlog on September 30, 2004 stood at $313.6 million, a 51% increase compared with $208 million for the same period last year. Without the impact of changes in currency rates, the order backlog would have increased 48%. New orders for the first quarter were $622.4 million, an increase of 21% compared with last year's first quarter. This was a reasonable result, considering an estimated $25 million in orders were advanced by customers into the June quarter, as discussed in the June 30, 2004 earnings release.

RESEARCH AND DEVELOPMENT EXPENDITURES AND CAPITAL SPENDING

Research and development expenditures for the first quarter were $33.4 million, an increase of 24% when compared with the same period last year. Capital expenditures were $48.4 million for the quarter versus $45.3 million last year.

FISCAL SECOND QUARTER OUTLOOK

King continued, "Our operations in the Far East continue to drive our results. We expect this trend to continue, based on the magnitude of production transferred by our global customers to the region and supported by our technical capabilities and long term history of working in the region."

"It is apparent that many of our customers in the Americas are in the process of adjusting their finished goods inventory to more conservative levels. However, we believe that the amount of actual connector inventory within these channels is reasonable, and therefore the outlook in the majority of our markets remains encouraging. In addition, we expect to gain market share based on our positions within key market segments – such as digital consumer, mobile communication and mobile computing – that are growing faster than the overall connector market, as well as our focus on the emerging medical electronics market."

Based on these facts, the Company expects that revenue for the fiscal second quarter ending December 31, 2004, will be in a range of $635–$650 million. This represents an increase of 16–18% over last year's fiscal second quarter. The Company expects that earnings per share will be in a range of $0.29–$0.31, an increase of 38–48% over last year's fiscal second quarter earnings per share.

STOCK BUYBACK ACTIONS

During the quarter, the Company purchased 875,000 shares of MOLXA common stock, at a total cost of $21.9 million. These purchases were done under a $100 million Board authorization for the full fiscal year ending June 30, 2005.

Exhibit 4 (*continued*) Consolidated balance sheet (unaudited, in thousands)

	Sept. 30, 2004	*June 30, 2004*
ASSETS		
Current assets:		
Cash and cash equivalents	$238,292	$234,431
Marketable securities	93,153	104,223
Accounts receivable, net	544,736	529,630
Inventories	283,417	265,344
Other current assets	40,027	35,016
Total current assets	1,199,625	1,168,644
Property, plant and equipment, net	1,009,163	1,022,378
Goodwill	164,969	164,915
Other assets	194,930	216,409
Total assets	$2,568,687	$2,572,346
LIABILITIES AND SHAREHOLDERS' EQUITY		
Current liabilities:		
Accounts payable	$225,731	$234,823
Accrued expenses	132,625	143,160
Other current liabilities	47,508	50,481
Total current liabilities	405,864	428,464
Other non-current liabilities	9,361	10,487
Accrued pension and postretirement benefits	51,435	52,151
Long-term debt	10,075	10,243
Obligations under capital leases	3,143	3,796
Minority interest in subsidiaries	3,383	1,211
Shareholders' equity:		
Common Stock	10,747	10,734
Paid-in capital	376,518	369,660
Retained earnings	2,209,211	2,160,368
Treasury stock	−532,216	−509,161
Deferred unearned compensation	−32,722	−32,180
Accumulated other comprehensive income	53,888	66,573
Total shareholders' equity	2,085,426	2,065,994
Total liabilities and shareholders' equity	$2,568,687	$2,572,346

ᴇxʜɪʙɪᴛ 4 (*continued*) Consolidated income statement (unaudited, in thousands, except per share data)

	September 30	
	2004	*2003*
Net revenue	$640,230	$496,763
Cost of sales	411,558	328,739
GROSS PROFIT	228,672	168,024
Selling, general and administrative expenses:		
Selling	54,020	44,416
General and administrative	102,192	83,048
Total selling, general and administrative expenses	156,212	127,464
INCOME FROM OPERATIONS	72,460	40,560
Other (income) expense:		
Equity income	(2,029)	(2,183)
(Gain)/loss on investments	(1,152)	
Interest, net	(925)	(1,235)
Total other (income) expense	(4,106)	(3,418)
INCOME BEFORE INCOME TAXES AND MINORITY INTEREST	76,566	43,978
Income taxes and minority interest	20,924	11,916
NET INCOME	$55,642	$32,062
EARNINGS PER SHARE:		
Basic	$0.29	$0.17
Diluted	$0.29	$0.17
AVERAGE COMMON SHARES OUTSTANDING:		
Basic	188,763	190,679
Diluted	190,617	192,372
CASH DIVIDENDS PER SHARE	$0.04	$0.03

Source: Company press release, 20 October 2004.

Exhibit 5 Molex board of directors

Frederick A. Krehbiel Co-Chairman of the Board of Molex. Director since 1972 and member of the Executive Committee. Age 63. Elected Vice Chairman and Chief Executive Officer in 1988 and Chairman of the Board of Directors in 1993. Became Co-Chairman in 1999 and served as Co-Chief Executive Officer from 1999–2001. Owned 28.0% of voting common stock. Also served on the boards of Tellabs, Inc., W. W. Grainger, Inc. and DeVry Inc.

John H. Krehbiel, Jr. Co-Chairman of the Board of Molex. Director since 1966 and member of the Executive Committee. Age 67. President of Molex 1975–1999 and Chief Operating Officer 1996–1999. Became Co-Chairman in 1999 and served as Co-Chief Executive Officer from 1999–2001. Owned 32.8% of voting common stock.

Michael J. Birck Director since 1995. Member of the Audit Committee[a] and the Executive Committee. Age 66. Founder and Chairman of the Board of Tellabs, Inc. (telecommunications equipment). Also served on the board of Illinois Tool Works Inc.

Douglas K. Carnahan Director since 1997 and Chairman of the Audit Committee. Age 63. Retired former executive of Hewlett-Packard Company (computers, computer peripherals and instrumentation).

Michelle L. Collins Director since 2003 and member of the Nominating and Corporate Governance Committee. Age 44. Co-founder and Managing Director of Svoboda, Collins LLC (private equity firm), and former partner of William Blair & Company, LLC (1992–97). Also served on the board of CDW Corporation.

Edgar D. Jannotta Director since 1986. Chairman of the Nominating and Corporate Governance Committee and member of the Executive Committee. Age 73. Investment banker and Chairman of William Blair & Company, LLC. (securities and investment banking). Also served on the boards of Bandag, Incorporated, Aon Corporation and Exelon Corporation.

J. Joseph King Vice Chairman of the Board and Chief Executive Officer of Molex. Director since 1999 and member of the Executive Committee. Age 60. Owned 0.2% of voting common stock, and 201,293 stock options. Also served on the board of Cabot Microelectronics Corporation.

Fred L. Krehbiel Director since 1993. Age 39. President of Molex Connector Products Division (Americas). Worked at Molex since 1988 in various engineering, marketing and managerial capacities. Previously served as Assistant to the Regional President (Americas) for the Global Desktop Business (1998–2000) and President of the Automotive Division (Americas) (2000–2003). Owned 1.0% of voting common stock and 6,250 stock options.

Joe W. Laymon Director since 2002 and member of the Compensation Committee. Age 51. Group Vice President, Corporate Human Resources & Labor Affairs of Ford Motor Company (automobile manufacturer). Previously worked for U.S. State Department-Agency for International Development, Human Resource at Xerox Corporation (1979–1996) and Eastman Kodak Company (1996–2000).

Donald G. Lubin Director since 1994 and member of the Nominating and Corporate Governance Committee. Age 70. Partner of Sonnenschein Nath & Rosenthal (private law practice). Also served on the board of McDonald's Corporation.

Masahisa Naitoh Director since 1995 and member of the Compensation Committee. Age 66. Chairman and CEO of The Institute of Energy Economics, Japan (private think tank). Previously held senior positions at The Institute of Energy Economics and Itochu Corporation (a Japanese global trading firm). Also served on the board of E. I. DuPont de Nemours and Company.

Robert J. Potter Director since 1981. Chairman of the Compensation Committee and member of the Audit Committee. Age 71. President and Chief Executive Officer of R. J. Potter Company (consulting business). Also served on the boards of Cree, Inc. and Zebra Technologies Corporation.

Martin P. Slark Director since 2000 and member of the Executive Committee. Age 49. President and Chief Operating Officer of Molex. Worked at Molex since 1976 filling various administrative, operational and executive positions both internationally and domestically. Served as Executive Vice President from 1999–2001, and assumed the post of President and Chief Operating Officer on July 1, 2001. Owned 0.1% of voting common stock and 137,623 stock options. Also served on the board of directors of Hub Group, Inc.

[a] Molex's Audit Committee does not have a "Financial Expert" as defined (but not required) by the applicable SEC Rules. In its Proxy Statement, the company explained that, "given the level of financial sophistication and business experience of the Audit Committee members, the board of directors believes that the Audit Committee members can perform the audit committee functions as required."

Source: Company Proxy Statement, September 15, 2004.

Chapter 14

CONTROLLERS AND AUDITORS

This chapter discusses the roles and challenges of personnel in two important corporate governance- and management control system (MCS)-related roles that both require financial measurement expertise: controllers and auditors. Personnel in these roles *within the firm*, such as corporate and division controllers and internal auditors, must serve two important roles. One role is *management service*, which involves helping line managers with their decision-making and control functions, to help create firm value. The other role is *oversight*, which involves ensuring that the actions of everyone in the organization, and especially the managers, are legal, ethical, and in the best interest of the organization and its owners. Fulfilling both roles often creates tension, as these two roles can, and often do, conflict. This chapter discusses this conflict and some other issues faced in making individuals in these roles effective.

The chapter also discusses the control roles of *external* auditors. External auditors provide an important independent check on managers' financial reporting, disclosure, and internal control practices. They face a different set of role conflicts, those between the need to serve their clients, to serve the public interest, and to earn profits for their own employer, the audit firm.

CONTROLLERS

The finance and accounting functions in a corporation are typically managed by a person with the title of *chief financial officer* (CFO) or *vice president finance* (VP Finance). (Terms vary across countries. In the United Kingdom this role is typically referred to as the *finance director*.) In recent times, particularly since the early 2000s, this role has gained in status.[1] For example, Fazal Chaudhri, group financial director at Exelco, a Belgian diamond concern, said the crisis has done his job profile "a favor" – where once local managers would wait for him to approach them about performance, Mr. Chaudhri now fields calls from throughout the organization seeking strategic advice, he said.[2] In other words, the crisis may have strengthened the importance of the financial executive's *management service* role. It, and the corporate scandals of the early 2000s, have also strengthened the importance of the financial executive's *oversight* role. For example, the passing of the Sarbanes-Oxley Act in the United States added status, but also risk, to the senior financial officer role in publicly held firms because CFOs must co-sign both the financial statement certifications and the opinions as to the effectiveness of their firm's internal control systems.

FIGURE 14.1 Corporate financial management roles

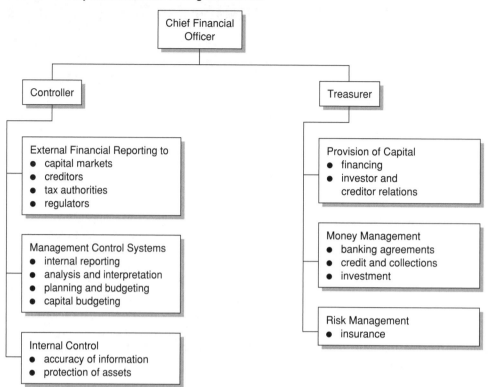

Source: K. A. Merchant, *Modern Management Control Systems: Text and Cases* (Upper Saddle River, NJ: Prentice Hall, 1998), p. 640.

As Figure 14.1 shows, the senior financial executive role commonly encompasses two domains, which in larger firms typically exist as specific roles with dedicated personnel for each: controller and treasurer. (In smaller firms, these roles may be combined.) The *controller* function deals primarily with financial record keeping, reporting, and control. The *treasury* function deals primarily with raising and managing capital. The treasury function is generally highly centralized. The controllership function is often decentralized in large divisionalized corporations with controllers in most or all of the profit centers (business units, divisions) and some of the larger cost centers (e.g. manufacturing plants).

Controllers play key roles in line management and in the design and operation of a management control system (MCS). They are the financial measurement experts within their firm (or their entity), and most of them are key members of the management team. As such, they are involved in preparing plans and budgets, challenging operating managers' plans and actions, and participating in a broad range of management decisions, including allocating resources, pricing, setting policies regarding receivables and payables, making acquisitions and divestments, and raising money.[3]

Evidence suggests that controllers have become more and more highly involved in helping managers make good business decisions. As recent views suggest, "Coming into the 21st century, financial professionals saw the emphasis of their responsibilities shift from recording various aspects of a corporation's financial health to joining top executives in a broad-based partnership, a trend accelerated by the 2008 financial crisis."[4] But being highly involved in management decision making is not the only role controllers must play; they are also their entity's "chief accountant." They and others in their organizations play an "oversight" and "scorekeeping" role. They, and their subordinates, record transactions, prepare performance reports, and fulfill financial, tax, and government reporting obligations. They establish and maintain internal control systems that help ensure both the reliability of information and the protection of the company's assets. And, depending on the organization, the controller also might supervise the internal audit and management information system functions. Experts, then, not surprisingly, also caution that "as [the financial professionals] become ever closely connected with the business, they must also ensure to not become subservient to it."[5]

Indeed, as chief accountants for their entities, controllers also must stay appropriately *independent* of their entity's managers. They have a *fiduciary responsibility* to ensure that the information reported from their entity, particularly that of a financial nature, is accurate and that the entity's internal control systems are adequate. They have a management *oversight responsibility* to inform others in the organization if individuals in their entity are violating laws or ethical norms.

Can controllers who are highly involved as part of the management team maintain the requisite degree of independence to fulfill their fiduciary and management oversight responsibilities effectively? In other words, can controllers *wear two hats*; one of a *team member* and *confidant*, and the other of a *watchdog* or *police cop*? In one sense, controllers' fiduciary responsibilities are quite consistent with their management oversight responsibilities – both sets of responsibilities require a constructively critical mindset and a sense of independence from management. That said, the fiduciary and management oversight responsibilities can conflict with the controllers' management service responsibilities, and, if not that, they certainly can create tension. Recent survey evidence of over 5,000 financial professionals from countries across the globe suggests, indeed, that the respondents recognized "concerns" from their expanding roles ranging from increased pressure from management to fears about their own objectivity.[6]

It is often claimed that *corporate controllers* may tend to put the interests of their corporate management, with whom they are closely connected as a management team, before the interests of the shareowners and other stakeholders. Similarly, *business-unit* or *division controllers* (*entity controllers*, for short), those located in a decentralized entity, such as a business unit, division, or operating unit, can easily become emotionally attached to their local, decentralized entity and the people they work with in the entity. They want to be part of the team. Indeed, entity controllers who are included in an incentive compensation plan based on entity performance can have motivations to "go along" with their entity management and, worse, condone gamesmanship that affect the results measures which they are assumed to oversee and report to corporate. To maintain the integrity of the controller's role, firms can, and probably should, implement several additional safeguards to ensure that controllers fulfill their management oversight and fiduciary duties effectively.

First, audit committees of boards of directors and internal auditors can be used to oversee the controller function. Audit committees were discussed in Chapter 13, and the roles and activities of internal auditors are discussed below. Second, controller behaviors can be shaped through personnel or cultural controls, such as selection and training. Some controllers have better judgment, have a better sense of ethical integrity, and are better able to function effectively in situations with strong role conflict than others.[7] Individuals who must follow strong and relevant professional ethics responsibilities may be good choices for controller positions. For example, the American Institute of Certified Public Accountants (AICPA) bolstered its professional code of ethics by requiring CPAs who work in corporations (rather than in public accounting) to report material misstatements of their company's financial statements to their superiors. If the superiors fail to respond,

FIGURE 14.2 Possible reporting relationships in the controller's organization

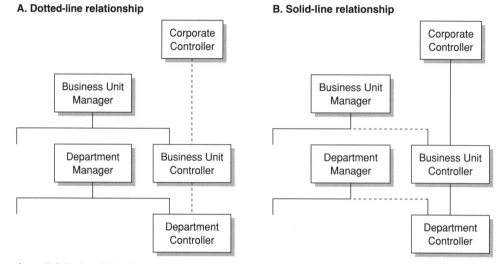

Source: K. A. Merchant, *Modern Management Control Systems: Text and Cases* (Upper Saddle River, NJ: Prentice Hall, 1998), p. 642.

the CPA should report the misstatements to the company's outside auditors or to regulators, such as the Securities and Exchange Commission (SEC). Professional codes such as this one add weight to the fiduciary responsibility of controllers who are also CPAs. Finally, training programs can be used to remind controllers of their multiple responsibilities and to give them the interpersonal skills useful in maintaining the proper balance between their management service versus management oversight and fiduciary roles.

Designing incentive systems that do not create temptation is a third way of ensuring that controllers fulfill their management oversight and fiduciary duties effectively. In particular, controllers probably should not be rewarded for performance defined by measures they can manipulate.

Finally, some firms have found that *solid-line* reporting in the controller's organization is effective for controlling entity controllers' activities. As shown in Figure 14.2, solid-line reporting means that the entity controller's primary reporting relationship is to the corporate controller (or in the case of a lower-level operating unit, a higher-level entity controller). In this controllership structure, the corporate controller – not the local entity managers – determine the entity controller's tasks, priorities, and performance evaluations.

Solid-line reporting is designed to reduce the emotional attachment between entity controllers and the local entity management to which they are assigned. It signals to the entity controllers that their most important roles are to protect the corporation's assets and to ensure that financial reports are accurate. This reminder is perhaps more important if the entity is located at great distance from headquarters. But for all entity controllers, it provides a heightened emphasis on their management oversight and fiduciary responsibilities. Indeed, evidence suggests that changing the controllers' reporting relationships does alter entity controllers' job priorities and loyalties.[8] The primary cost of solid-line reporting is a potential reduction in the quality of the entity controller's management service function. Entity controllers reporting on a solid-line to corporate can come to be viewed in the local entity as *corporate spies* rather than as members of the entity management team. This "cost" should not be seen as trivial, as recent research suggests that solid-line reporting may cause role conflict, which, in turn, and opposite to the aims of instituting solid-line reporting, may enhance rather than mitigate data misreporting.[9]

All told, designing an effective controllership function is both difficult and important. Poor controllership has been shown on more than one occasion to be a contributing factor in corporate scandals and failures, although flaws in aspects of *organizational culture* inarguably have a lot to do with it, too. The Walker Review of corporate governance in UK banks and other financial industry entities following the financial crisis of 2008, for example, pertinently observed that structural arrangements alone might not be sufficient to mitigate a repeat of the consequences of poor control and oversight, but also that a "material change of culture [is needed] so that disciplined but rigorous challenge on substantive issues comes to be seen as the norm."[10]

AUDITORS

When the word *audit* is mentioned, most people think first of either a *financial audit*, in which a public accounting firm expresses an opinion about the fairness of presentation of a company's financial statements, or a *tax audit*, in which government auditors test to see if taxpayers have followed the laws and reported taxable income truthfully. Historically these common audit forms have played only limited roles in management control systems, whereas other types of audits, such as *internal audits*, *operational audits*, and *performance audits*, have been seen as much more critical to the effective operation of internal control systems. Nonetheless, since the passing of the Sarbanes-Oxley Act in the United States, for example, the external financial audit, and in particular the portion of it that is designed to express an opinion on the effectiveness of a company's system of *internal controls*, has become more relevant for MCSs.

Audits

An audit can be defined as a *systematic process* of (1) *objectively obtaining and evaluating evidence* regarding *objects of importance*, (2) *judging* the degree of correspondence between those objects and certain *criteria*, and (3) *communicating* the results to relevant users. This definition is broad so as to cover all types of audits. It is useful to elaborate on the meaning of the key (italicized) terms.

The phrase *systematic process* is used to connote the fact that audits are not done randomly. They involve an orderly sequence of interrelated steps, all designed with one or more audit objectives in mind. Every audit starts with what is commonly called a planning phase. The planning phase involves developing an understanding of the established criteria of the groups who will use the audit report and the required scope of the audit. It is used to design an audit program that identifies the specific tasks to be performed and, if appropriate, the schedule for starting and completing each task and the persons assigned to each task.

The second phase of the audit process, which is typically the most time consuming, involves *obtaining and evaluating evidence*. This process is *objective* because auditors are, by definition, independent of those being audited. Non-independent reviews, such as superiors inspecting the work of their subordinates for which they are also held responsible, are not audits, despite the obvious similarities. Depending on the focus and scope of the audit, the evidence gathering may involve some or all of the following: observation, interviews, reviews of reports, re-computations, confirmations, and analyses. As evidence is gathered, alterations to the original audit program may be necessary.

Differences in the *objects of importance* provide the major reason for the varied labels being put on different types of audits. Compliance audits are designed to test for compliance with rules about behavior or results, such as specific company policies, laws, or loan covenants. Marketing audits focus on the effectiveness and efficiency of the marketing function. Financial statement audits provide a basis for the external auditors to express an opinion as to whether the financial statements fairly present the financial status and performance of the entity involved.

The third phase of an audit requires a *judgment*, based on the evidence, as to whether or not (or to what extent) the criteria have been met. These judgments are fallible, though, as in all but the simplest situations some probability exists that the judgments will subsequently be proven incorrect. All of the evidence necessary to make an infallible judgment may not be available, or the judgment may involve an assessment about an uncertain future.

The *criteria* for comparison can vary widely across audit types. They may be very narrow and specific, such as those used in procedure-related compliance audits (e.g. requirement of two signatures on checks). Or they may be no more specific than a vague definition of a desired characteristic, such as the "efficiency" of a given process or function.

Communicating the results to relevant users concludes the audit process. The audit report is the primary tangible product of the audit. At a minimum, the audit report describes the evidence examined and presents an opinion as to whether the established criteria were met. In issuing the report with the stated opinion, the auditor is, in essence, assuming responsibility for the opinion, with the risk of economic or reputation loss if the opinion is subsequently determined to be less than correct. Sometimes the report highlights areas where improvements can be made, and it may go as far as to make specific recommendations.

External and internal auditors

Auditors can be classified as either external or internal. *External auditors* are independent of management because they are employed by professional service firms with no business ties to the auditee except performance of the audit and, perhaps, a few, ancillary advisory services (e.g. tax). Those performing financial audits (described below) are generally accountants employed by a public accounting firm or so-called *audit firms*. They have professional training and experience and are licensed by a professional association. Those executing performance audits (also described below) are employed by a public accounting or consulting firm. These auditors can have any of a variety of backgrounds, including general management, risk management, finance, information systems, engineering, or computer science.

Internal auditors are employees of the company they are auditing. They are often referred to as "the eyes and ears of management." Internal audit staffs can operate with either narrow or broad charters, and the breadth of charter is one of the major determinants of the size of the staff. A narrow charter, which would necessitate a relatively small internal audit staff only, leads to mostly compliance audits and performance of some functions for the external auditors (such as preparation of audit schedules and documentation of internal controls) to reduce external audit fees. At the other extreme, some staffs operate with a broad charter that can include many forms of performance auditing, involvement in the design and improvement of business processes and internal control systems, and other forms of what would usually be classified as management consulting.

The size of internal audit staffs varies widely across firms. Small firms typically have no internal auditors. Large firms may have a small or a large staff. One study, however, found that the internal audit function is often prone to "the axe" in difficult economic times, ironically when firms might be most benefiting from the audits. In that survey, specifically, 19% of the respondents (700 internal auditors, 69% of whom are from companies with $1 billion or more in revenues) reported budget reductions in 2008 compared with 10% in 2007, 49% expected budgets to remain flat, and 36% expected a decrease for 2010. In addition, 51% of Fortune 500 respondents believed that there was a medium-to-high risk of the economic downturn causing a reduction in the internal audit budget during 2009.[11]

Internal auditor backgrounds vary with their staff's charter. Many internal auditors have an accounting background, but as internal audit charters have broadened, many firms' audit staffs have become more diverse and include, among others, information system specialists, computer experts, and consultants. Moreover, and mainly because the charter of internal audit can be so varied, internal audit functions frequently turn to subject matter experts to assist in audit coverage requiring deeper knowledge of the specific business, process, or function. What most internal audit staffs have in common, however, is that they are typically headed by experienced professionals: the vast majority of chief audit executives and internal audit managers have over eight years of experience (nearly 80% and 60% of them, respectively).[12]

Most internal auditors have ties to a professional association. In the United States, the Institute of Internal Auditors, a professional association with more than 75,000 members, has defined professional standards and responsibilities, a code of ethics, and a common body of knowledge for internal auditors. It has also instituted a certification program (Certified Internal Auditor).

Organizationally, the internal audit function operates in a staff capacity and almost always reports high in the organization, at least to the corporate controller or CFO/VP Finance. However, experts recommend that the internal audit staff should report directly to the audit committee of the board of directors to enhance their independence, credibility, and visibility. Related, many internal audit functions are said to be still heavily stuck in the past, focusing on financial and compliance audits (see below), presumably still hallmarks of the earlier Sarbanes-Oxley period. One survey suggests that only 13% of respondents indicated that their departments allocated at least 25% of resources to strategic and business audits (which we categorize as *performance audits* below), while a majority (57%) assigned this degree of resources to traditional financial audits. The survey also suggests, however, that strategic, business, and operational audits are among the fastest-growing areas of internal audit focus.[13]

Common audit types

While the mechanics and techniques are basically the same among all types of audits, the motivations and end results are different. This section briefly describes some of the most common types of audits that serve various control purposes.

Financial audits

In a financial audit, independent, external auditors are asked to express an opinion as to whether the financial statements prepared by management are fairly presented in accordance with applicable accounting standards, such as International Financial Reporting Standards (IFRS) in many countries or Generally Accepted Accounting Principles (GAAP) in the United States. The guidelines that external auditors must follow in performing an audit in the United States are known as Generally Accepted Auditing Standards (GAAS). These guidelines are established by the Public Company Accounting Oversight Board (PCAOB), which was born out of the Sarbanes-Oxley Act. Similarly,

International Standards on Auditing (ISAs) are developed by the International Auditing and Assurance Standards Board (IAASB) of the International Federation of Accountants (IFAC). These acronyms aside, financial audits essentially provide a tool by which outside regulators (such as stock exchanges, government bodies) can enforce standards for the preparation and presentation of accounting information to interested parties who are outside the organization, which is critically important for the efficient functioning of capital markets, among other purposes. A detailed discussion of financial audits, however, is outside the scope of this book.

Compliance audits

Organizations are responsible for complying with many laws, rules, procedures, and administrative policies set down by various authorities. In a compliance audit, the auditors are asked to express an opinion as to whether actual activities or results are in compliance with the established standards, rules, and regulations. As such, compliance audits generally involve a narrower scope of investigation than do other types of audits. Despite their rather narrow scope, compliance audits nonetheless often manage to unearth fraud and irregularities even though that is not their primary purpose. Both external and internal auditors perform compliance-type audits. Compliance audits vary widely in the amount of evidence to be gathered and the auditor expertise needed. Audits for compliance with more complex rules, such as some tax laws, may require considerable specialized knowledge and a large amount of professional judgment.

Performance audits

Performance audits, which go by various names such as *operational audits*, *management audits*, or *strategic audits*, are used to provide an overall evaluation of the general performance, or some specific aspect of the performance of an activity, function, entity, or company and its management. Performance audits can be performed by broad-scope internal auditors or external auditors in a consulting role. The criteria for comparison are vague in many performance audits, often only loosely referring to assessing an activity, function, or entity's effectiveness. Accordingly, an important part of performance audits often involves defining the criteria in more specific terms. In many cases, the scope is usefully limited by virtue of focusing on a specific activity, function, or entity, or a specific performance dimension thereof (e.g. quality, delivery, information systems). In addition to making a judgment as to whether or not performance meets the set criteria, performance auditors usually also produce an important by-product through identifying areas for improvement. Although performance auditors generally have broader training and experience than other types of auditors, they typically also turn to internal or external subject matter experts, depending on the needed coverage on any given assignment. The audit reports may be directed to management, government regulatory agencies (such as environmental protection agencies), or a prospective acquiring firm.

The value of audits

Audits create value in two primary ways. First, the audit report adds credibility to the information provided to user groups. The auditors are providing an independent check against criteria reflecting users' needs for whom presumably the knowledge as to whether or to what extent the criteria have been met is valuable. As a by-product of this evaluation process, auditors often provide what can be an equally valuable benefit through identifying areas for improvement and providing specific recommendations where practices need to be redressed or issues need to be addressed. These recommendations can deal with minor procedural changes or major management policy changes. It should be noted, however, that some argue that recommendations should not be part of the audit function. They argue that recommendations compromise audit independence, if not in the first audit, certainly in all audits performed by the same auditors after the recommendations are (or are not) implemented. The independence of external auditors, particularly, who often also provide performance audits, tax services or various types of consulting to their clients as an extension of their financial statement audits, has been a thorny issue and the subject of increased regulatory attention.[14]

The second benefit of audits is provided not by the audit itself but by the *anticipation* of an audit. Knowing that an audit will or might take place can have strong motivational effects on the individuals involved to conform to the standards they reckon the auditors will use in their evaluation. In 1995, an embezzlement of more than $900,000 was discovered at the University of California. Investigators discovered that auditors had not visited the university for more than a decade. Gray Davis, then lieutenant governor of California and a university regent, reacted as follows: "Everyone performs better if they know someone is looking over their shoulder. When you put out the word that no one is looking, it's an invitation to disaster."[15]

Audits are not equally valuable in all situations. One factor that affects the potential value of an audit is the importance of the area to be audited. The greater the potential consequences (the higher the stakes), the greater the potential value of the audit. Audits are also potentially more valuable if the probability is high that either the established criteria are not being met or would not be met in the absence of the audit. Audits are also potentially more valuable when other control mechanisms are not feasible. For example, reviews by independent auditors are necessary when the user group is not able to satisfy itself directly as to whether the established criteria have been or are being met. This inability may be caused by the complexity of the subject matter, physical remoteness, institutional barriers preventing access to some of the evidence needed (such as in a joint venture), or just reasonable suspicion that self-interest (of those being audited) will prevail over the interests of the relevant user group(s) in the absence of an independent, objective audit.

Audits can be valuable tools in many management control situations. Auditors can serve as the "eyes and ears" of management in assessing what is happening within the organization, and they can also share their expertise by providing recommendations for improvement. For management purposes, the potential value of an audit is greatest if the criteria to be used for comparison are those set by management. Audits commissioned by outsiders, such as financial or environmental audits, are designed to serve the interests of those outsiders, although the auditors may provide some observations of use to management. But even for those audits, the benefits can come in seemingly unexpected ways. For example, a report commissioned by the UK government (to decide if emissions reporting will be mandatory) found that companies that measure their carbon emissions do not find the exercise arduous or expensive – some even said it brings benefits. Just over half the firms surveyed said reporting emissions carried a net benefit for their business. Indeed, although there may be no obvious direct benefits from the act of reporting emissions, reporting emissions forces a company to first measure them, and that does bring benefits as measuring emissions produces an incentive to reduce them, which might be done by spending less on energy.[16]

Where audits are feasible, they can be an important alternative or supplement to other management control mechanisms, such as direct supervision or incentives. Audits can test whether the desired behaviors were in fact taken, and they often have powerful influences on behavior at acceptable cost. Auditors can usually reach an informed judgment by examining just a small proportion of the relevant evidence, and in many situations just the threat of an audit can be a powerful deterrent against undesirable behavior.

But audits have limitations. One is that they are done only on a periodic basis and thus provide little protection against problems occurring in the interim except to the extent that they provide a deterrent effect. This limitation of audits is pertinent in situations where something must be done properly the first, or every, time. Audits also can create negative reactions, such as defensiveness, especially when individuals feel their integrity is questioned or their autonomy is jeopardized. Audits can be costly. They consume considerable time from expert auditors, as well as from company employees who have to prepare information for the auditors to review. Moreover, audits can assess only the past. Thus, audits of one-time occurrences have value only if they provide some useful insights about situations that might occur in the future.

All told, audits are invaluable in many situations and have likely increased in importance following the financial and economic crisis of 2008–09, as the following quote signifies:[17]

> Financial scandals, the rise in new worldwide regulations, and the nascent economic recovery have created a climate in which companies should be elevating the role of their Chief Audit Executives (CAEs) to that of a *strategic business partner* with the senior executive team. With risk now a core focus for Boards of Directors and senior executives, the CAE, who has traditionally been relegated to the tactical execution of an annual audit plan, is uniquely positioned to play a central role in the risk-intelligent company, thanks to his or her visibility into, and understanding of, the enterprise's holistic risk-management activities. For companies to maximize the strategic contributions of the CAE, however, they must have both a *business-aware* auditor and an *audit-aware* board and leadership group. [Italics added.]

However, the elevation of the role of auditors, as the quote suggests, implies that *business-aware auditors* will face similar role duality, and possibly role conflicts, as controllers do in the execution of their management *service* vs. *oversight* roles.

CONCLUSION

This chapter focused on the important control-related roles of controllers and auditors, both internal and external. These are important and difficult roles. Auditors' roles are challenging because, in a limited amount of time, they must examine business processes and employees' (e.g. accountants, managers) work and make judgments as to whether the work meets the set standards. Some standards, such as those defining significant and material internal control weaknesses, as described in Chapter 13, or fairness of presentation, are sometimes ill-defined, thus inevitably requiring judgment. The controller and internal auditor roles are particularly challenging because they involve an inherent conflict of interest. Individuals in these roles are asked to serve their organization and its management while at the same time providing a management oversight role on behalf of the organization's owners and other stakeholders. Their role may require them to take actions that are quite costly to their organization in the short run, such as exposing a fraudulent financial reporting scheme. It takes strong, courageous individuals with excellent interpersonal skills to perform such roles effectively. But building and maintaining a strong finance function is an important foundation of a management control system.

Notes

1. See, for example, "McKinsey Global Survey Results: How Finance Departments Are Changing," *The McKinsey Quarterly* (April 2009), online (www.mckinseyquarterly.com).

2. J. Karaian, "Business Outlook Survey," *CFO Europe* (April 2, 2009), pp. 13–14.

3. See, for example, *The New Value Integrator: Insights from the IBM Chief Financial Officer Study*, IBM Global Business Services (March 2010).

4. See W. Van der Stede and R. Malone, *Accounting Trends in a Borderless World* (Chartered Institute of Management Accountants, November 2010), online (www.cimaglobal.com); J. Banks, "Value Creation – Support Network," *Excellence in Leadership* (November 2010), pp. 12–15.

5. Ibid.

6. See Van der Stede and Malone, "Accounting Trends in a Borderless World," op. cit.

7. W. Blais, "Personality Types of Controllers," *Strategic Finance* (June 2000), pp. 89–92.

8. V. Sathe, *Controller Involvement in Management* (Englewood Cliffs, NJ: Prentice-Hall, 1982).

9. V. Maas and M. Matejka, "Balancing the Dual Responsibilities of Business Unit Controllers: Field and Survey Evidence," *The Accounting Review*, 84, no. 4 (July 2009), pp. 1233–53.

10. D. Walker, *A Review of Corporate Governance in UK Banks and Other Financial Industry Entities: Final Recommendations* (London: The Walker Review Secretariat, November 26, 2009).

11. *Business Upheaval: Internal Audit Weighs its Role Amid the Recession and Evolving Enterprise Risks* (PricewaterhouseCoopers, 2009), online (www.pwc.com).

12. Ibid.

13. Ibid.

14. See, for example, *Auditors: Market Concentration and Their Role*, Uncorrected Evidence Before the Economic Affairs Committee of the House of Lords (December 7, 2010), online (www.parliament.uk).

15. "UC Sues Official Over Alleged Embezzlement," *The Los Angeles Times* (August 25, 1995), p. A3.

16. "Carbon Counting is 'Good for Business'," *BBC* (November 30, 2010), online (www.bbc.co.uk).

17. "Leadership in the Risk-Intelligent Organization," *Business Week* (September 30, 2010), online (www.businessweek.com).

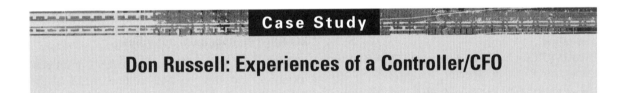

Case Study

Don Russell: Experiences of a Controller/CFO

In February 1991 Don Russell, chief financial officer (CFO) at Eastern Technologies, Inc. (ETI) was mulling over a critical decision. Don had joined ETI only 14 months earlier and had gradually become convinced that the company's financial accounting was excessively aggressive. He thought a sizable correcting entry should be made immediately. But if the correction was made ETI would report a large loss that would trigger violations of debt financing covenants and place the company's survival in jeopardy.

ETI's chairman and president were strongly against making the correcting entry. They reminded Don that the company had a plan to shore up its operations and to get cheaper financing in place and that the plan needed time to work. But Don was not convinced that top management's plan was viable.

Don felt that ETI's accounting reports were misleading to decision-makers both outside and inside the company. This caused him particular concern because he had seen the dangers of manipulating earnings reports at his previous employer. But he knew that if he forced the change now he would lose his job. Even if ETI survived he was sure he would be fired for "not being a team player." As he noted to an observer:

▶

It is frightening to know that you're going to be out the door almost immediately after you make the decision. It's even more frightening to me right now because I've just gone through a divorce and remarriage, and now I've got six kids and annual alimony payments of $60,000.

He also thought about the effect the decision would have on the value of the tens of thousands of ETI stock options he had been given. The options would be worth several hundred thousand dollars when exercised, and half of them could be exercised in two months.

EARLY CAREER

Don Russell joined the audit staff of the Chicago office of Touche & Young (T&Y) in July 1973 immediately upon graduation from the University of Illinois. His advancement was rapid. In 1983 he was promoted to senior manager and was given indications that he was on track toward partnership. Over the 1975–80 period Don attended DePaul University's evening MBA program and earned his degree in management information systems. T&Y gradually shifted his work responsibilities to take advantage of his systems expertise. By 1984 Don's time was split almost equally between auditing and systems consulting.

In 1985 Don left T&Y to become corporate controller for Cook & Spector, Inc. (C&S), a large ($4 billion sales) consumer products division of Queen's Industries, a major British corporation. C&S had been acquired by Queen's in 1984. Don was familiar with C&S because it was one of his major audit clients. He explained why he decided to take the job:

> When the headhunter first approached me about the job I wasn't interested. C&S had an antiquated accounting system. It was a huge company, but they still had a manual accounts receivable system. They did no planning; no budgeting. It was ridiculous. But C&S's top managers told me, "You have carte blanche to make whatever changes you think are necessary. You have complete control." So I was intrigued by the challenge.
>
> It was also a great career opportunity. C&S was a large, reasonably profitable corporation with some outstanding brand names. And my job was significant. I had 250 people working for me. I reported to the CFO, and the only other person reporting to him was the Treasurer who had eight people working for him. So I thought I would probably be next in line for the CFO job.

CONTROLLERSHIP EXPERIENCES AT COOK & SPECTOR

Systems development activities

Don started at C&S in August 1985. He spent his first six months planning the changes he wanted to make to the firm's accounting information systems. Then over the next three years he implemented major changes. He changed the chart of accounts so that the firm could produce profit and loss statements down to the product level; the new system had 500,000 account/cost center combinations. He installed new general ledger, accounts receivable, and accounts payable systems that would operate in a modern database environment. And he implemented a standard cost system in the firm's 42 factories. About the cost system change, he observed, "C&S had had only an actual cost system. The monthly costs fluctuated wildly and weren't useful. They didn't provide a reflection of what was going on."

After the accounting systems were computerized Don found it easy to reduce costs in the controller's department. He reduced his accounting staff from 250 to 110 and saved the company over $4 million per year.

Earnings management activities

In 1985, for a variety of reasons, C&S's profit performance was running $45 million ahead of the $200 million plan. To *save* the profit for periods when it might be needed Don established several types of large reserves. For example, C&S had been aggressive in expensing the acquisition costs incurred as part of the Queen's acquisition process, so Don set up a large reserve ($53 million) for taxes, in case the IRS disallowed the expense deductions. He also set up reserves for unknown liabilities because, "Everybody realized that the company had a poor accounting system." Don believed at the time that the reserves were justified and that, "It's better to be safe than sorry. If it turns out that we were overly conservative, it's no big deal."

These reserves had to be spread across the 34 line items in the income statements of each of the over 600 product lines in 60 divisions in a way that would not attract the attention of the analysts on Queen's corporate staff or the auditors. Don accomplished this task without significant questions being raised.

In 1986 company sales and profits were below forecast and top management told Don they wanted to use some of the reserves. They said they wanted to report an 8% increase in earnings and to increase significantly the amount of expenditures on new product development to help the company grow in the future. Don was able to free up the reserves to satisfy these requests.

Corporate recognition

Don's superiors were ecstatic about his efforts. He had modernized the company's accounting systems; had saved the company $4 million in overhead annually; and had demonstrated great skill in managing the accounting profit numbers. After a year with the company he was promoted to Vice President/Controller.

Don was flushed with success:

> Every management meeting I was held up as the ideal. I remember one top-level meeting when they flashed my picture on the screen and said, "Follow this guy's lead. This is the way you should manage your department." One time the president called me *the Monet of the accounting profession*.
>
> My head was exploding. At T&Y they keep telling you you are worthless to keep you there and to keep your salary down. All of a sudden I'm important, and I'm making a lot of money. After I had been at C&S six months I gave them my six-month plan, and I got a $30,000 bonus right there on the spot. I was in shock. I had never had that much free money in my life. Plus I was involved. I attended all the key management meetings.

Concerns about earnings management

During his third year at C&S Don began to have concerns about his manipulations of reserves. He said:

> I hadn't really thought much about my manipulations of reserves. I thought I was being a team player. This is how the company had been run for years. It had a record of 33 consecutive years of increasing quarterly earnings. But real results, with recessions and everything else that happens, don't happen that way. So I hadn't invented earnings management at C&S, although we were probably now doing it on a grander scale than had been done before.
>
> But it suddenly dawned on me that something was horribly wrong. We were pristine in reporting for taxes because I sent my tax manager to the operating units to make sure real data were going to the IRS. But

we didn't care if real data were going to Queen's. All of a sudden we had two years that weren't comparable and we really didn't know where we were. When people looked back at trends they were looking at distorted numbers. And because we spread the reserves around we had distorted all the product P&Ls.

Don attempted to drain the reserves out of the product-level profit and loss statements, but the complexity was overwhelming because each of the 60 divisions and over 600 product lines would now have two P&Ls each. Plus the draining provoked a number of arguments with the operating managers because the divisions had been manipulating the numbers on their own. They had not really spent the promotion expense by product as was reported, and they had their own buried reserves. In fact, the division reserves probably totalled more than those created at corporate. So even if Don could eliminate the distortions he had caused, the product statements that would result still would not yield accurate information.

Don's concern about the earnings management activities rose in 1988:

> The year 1988 looked like another down year and everybody was saying, "We need more product development because last year's development didn't work." And the president, of course, was saying we need another 8% increase in income.
>
> I told the president that we can't allow the reserves within the division. Every year we'd have something like a $200 million target, but we'd have $40 million in reserves ready to help us. So everybody would get their bonuses; the executive parking lot was filled with BMW 750s and Mercedes. I was doing well also. My regular salary was around $130,000, but my total compensation was nearly $230,000.
>
> While the company was reporting profits, I thought we were headed in a downward spiral. The old products were still extremely profitable, but we were spending a huge amount of money on new products and were disguising the fact that the new products were a lot less profitable. There was no linkage between bonuses and a strategic plan, just a link to an accounting number that was not tied to a plan. It was just an accounting game. We were getting our bonuses for nothing – actually worse than nothing because we were making bad decisions.

Attempts to change the company's financial goals and measurement system

To improve company decision-making and reduce the temptations to manage earnings Don decided to try to change C&S's financial goals and measurements system. He was particularly concerned that the potentially lucrative bonuses, ranging up to 70–100% of base salary, were based on operating profit numbers that were too easy to manipulate.

He began a fact-finding study. He began interviewing all the C&S division heads on his own and soon realized that the company was not doing any real strategic planning. He found that company planning involved just settling on a set of revenue and profit numbers that looked reasonable. C&S operating managers were unwilling to tell Queen's about their real plans, such as for new products, because they were worried that they would *have egg on their face* if they weren't able to accomplish their plans.

Among the questions Don asked in the interviews was, "What are the most important decisions you make on a monthly and annual basis, and what information do you use in making those decisions?" The manager of the largest operating unit said, "On a monthly basis, one of the most important decisions I make is how much profit to recognize."

Don's reaction:

> I was floored. This is one of the most senior managers in a huge company, and he was telling me that one of his most important decisions is how to manipulate the numbers. His operating decisions are secondary. His first role, he viewed, was to give the president the profit number he wanted that month.
>
> And this guy wasn't unique. Everyone else I talked with reinforced this message. Managers who missed their monthly budget targets would take a lot of flak. The president would quickly call them and ask, "What are you doing? How are you correcting the problem? Cut your advertising! Fire some people! . . ." This drilled into me what happens when you allow manipulations. People don't focus on real problems.

Don planned to take his interview observations to the president and tell him:

> We've got a big problem here because we're not managing the company the way we should be. We're spending four times the amount of product development and capital expenditures we need because it's easy to get Queen's to approve them. But Queen's assumes we are making good decisions, and we're not.

But Don wanted to be able to propose an alternative, and he set out looking for "the Holy Grail of more reasonable financial reporting."

Don learned that some companies were experimenting with an approach to planning that focused on changes in shareholder value. This focused measurement attention on hard numbers – cash flows – rather than the easily manipulatable operating profit. He studied these approaches and proposed their use to top management, but they were completely opposed to any changes. They did not understand why they would want to make such a drastic change when the company and its management team were doing so well.

The decision to leave

As the pace of accounting systems change slowed Don's job became more routine, and he became bored. He began listening for other career opportunities. He thought he wanted to become a chief financial officer so that he could work more in finance areas where he had had no experience. And he thought he would like eventually to move into a line management position.

In early 1989 a headhunter approached Don with an opportunity to interview for the position of CFO of Eastern Technologies, Inc. (ETI), a public communications services company. ETI was growing rapidly and was raising large amounts of money both from banks and direct placements. He was interviewed for the job and accepted it when it was offered. He joined ETI on December 1, 1989.

CFO EXPERIENCES AT EASTERN TECHNOLOGIES

The company

ETI, headquartered in Stamford, Connecticut, was founded in 1978 as a cable television firm. It had several cable franchises in New England and the New York metropolitan area. The company had been profitable since the early 1980s. It went public in 1984 with an initial offering price of $11.00 per share. For the 1988 fiscal year (ended June 30), revenues were $30 million and profits were just above $1 million. The 1988 yearend stock price was $8.75.

In 1987 ETI's founder, a skilled electronics engineer, decided to diversify the company's operations into the fast-growing area of satellite broadcasting. This business involves sending broadcast signals, such as from a concert or a sporting event, to a broadcast satellite that relays the signal to a network of large dish antennas on the ground. These antennas then distribute the signals to users, such as local television stations.

To finance the construction of antennas and distribution networks throughout the Northeast ETI raised considerable bank financing. By the end of 1987 ETI's debt–equity ratio was 4 to 1, but management figured the company still needed $10 million of additional capital. They approached a prominent investment banking firm to make a bond offering. The investment bankers showed ETI management how easy it was to raise money with high yield bonds, and the company eventually made a much larger offering – of $25 million. When the bonds sold, the company had considerable cash but a debt–equity ratio of 6 to 1.

ETI management used the extra cash to accelerate the expansion of facilities and to acquire a Baltimore-based broadcasting firm of similar size to ETI. Growth exploded as the company signed more and more long-term contracts with customers. Revenues totalled $81 million in 1989, almost three times the 1988 level. But after-tax profits were just under $1 million, as the company had to book a large loss in the fourth quarter of the year to cover *one-time start-up problems* with the new technology.

ETI made another acquisition in February 1990. This was of a Southern California-based consulting firm that provided specialized communications services primarily to firms in the defense industry. The two acquired companies were run as largely autonomous divisions within the ETI corporate structure.

Transition of power

When Don joined ETI his major concern was whether ETI's president, Joe Blevins, would allow him autonomy in his CFO role. Joe was a former T&Y audit partner who had joined ETI in 1987. But Don found Joe's approach to the transition of power to be quite reasonable. Joe asked Don to focus his initial attention on improving the company's operating systems: ETI had no computerized systems, no planning, and no budgeting, and the controller was weak. But Joe let Don sit in on the discussions with bankers and investment bankers to

help him learn the treasury functions that he would eventually assume.

Don quickly found that ETI's financial focus was on earnings per share, and he vowed to change the focus to cash flow. Joe said, however, "You don't really understand the market. I'll listen to your thoughts, but EPS is what the analysts care about. Cash flow may be the latest *voodoo* thought, but it's not very realistic." Still, Don thought Joe would be open-minded, and he believed he could convince Joe to change.

Don, however, had a lot of work to do before he could focus on changes in the company's planning and measurement processes. He focused his attention first on ETI's chart of accounts. Billing was done manually, and expenses were assigned only to highly aggregated accounts. For example, the company paid huge bills for satellite rental and telephone services with no attempt to trace the expenses to contracts or even product lines. Another complicating factor: many of the charges were not billed regularly, so expenses had to be accrued. But the bases on which the accruals were done were not well thought out, and the company's monthly profit figures fluctuated wildly. Don knew he could not prepare a credible budget without a better understanding of where the expenses were coming from and what lines of business were more profitable than others. That understanding required a better accounting system. He wanted eventually to be able to produce reliable budgets and operating reports at department, and even project, levels of the organization.

Changing the chart of accounts proved to be a difficult process because few people in the company understood what Don was trying to do. The controller was not supportive. He was comfortable with the current chart of accounts and liked the fact that it was easy to work with. Don observed that, "It didn't matter to him that it did not provide meaningful information. He thought of accounts just as pots that you throw expenses into. If you make the system more complex the assignment of expenses takes more thought."

Don also had to spend time integrating the systems of the newly acquired subsidiaries. He found ETI to be much more dynamic than C&S. At C&S he had time to plan what he wanted to do. At ETI he had to implement changes quickly and hope to fine-tune the systems later.

ETI's first budgeting process

Don led ETI through its first formal budgeting process in June–July 1990. Most of the numbers work was done by accounting personnel after they had consulted with the operating managers. Budgets were prepared for each division using the categories in Don's new chart of accounts.

When the budget for fiscal year 1991 was consolidated it showed a $2 million loss. But nobody was sure if the budget was realistic. This was the first budget that had been prepared at the division level, and no division-level historical reports were available for comparison purposes. It also quickly became apparent that budgeting mistakes had been made. For example, management soon discovered that a major contract had been left out of the budget. Operating managers had failed to pass the information to accounting personnel, and two months into the year some significant unbudgeted expenses had to be paid.

ETI's financial reporting strategy

After the budget was prepared Don began an analysis of why the budget showed a loss for FY 1991 even though ETI had been reporting profits for years. It became obvious to him that the satellite communications business was in reality very unprofitable. ETI had been reporting profits because the company had implemented an extremely aggressive financial reporting strategy. Joe Blevins had a theory that all start-ups are unprofitable in the beginning and that aggressive accounting policies are necessary to make the company look profitable so that money can be raised. The profits catch up later.

Joe used a number of methods of boosting earnings, including the following:

1. Virtually all repairs and maintenance were capitalized. Because there was so much development going on Joe's position was that all the engineers' and technicians' time was spent working on construction or making modifications that add capability to the equipment. Therefore all the costs were capitalizable.

2. Most interest was capitalized because it was deemed to be the cost of financing the construction in progress. For example, Don found that "We had deferred $3.5 million in interest for construction of a new video control center. We claimed it hadn't been put into service until May 1990 because we were still getting the bugs out of it, but it had actually been up and running since mid-1988 and certainly met the GAAP criterion of *substantially complete*." Don also found that "Nothing ever came out of construction in progress. They just kept capitalizing more and more interest."

3. Most equipment was being depreciated on a 12-year life. But electronic equipment, which comprised the bulk of the equipment, probably has a maximum five-year life, and some of the expensive tubes have a maximum 24-month life.

4. As many expenditures as possible (for example travel) were classified as being related to one of the acquisitions so that they would add to goodwill and be amortized over 40 years instead of being expensed immediately. Also, if any parts of the acquired businesses were suffering operating losses, those losses were capitalized. On the other hand, a gain of over a half million dollars on the sale of a portion of a communications relay station acquired in an acquisition was recorded directly as profit instead of as an adjustment to the price of the acquisition. Don noted, "We told the auditors we were just selling the rights to that asset since the buyers obviously couldn't take the asset with them. The auditors swallowed hard but accepted it."

The auditors had not objected strenuously to ETI's financial reports because they did not understand the technology. Satellite communications was a relatively new business that was just starting to grow. Few equipment retirements had taken place as yet, so it was difficult to tell what the true equipment lives were. Don found out that, "When the auditors asked questions about the 12-year depreciation lives Joe would always point to the large antennas and say, 'They will be there for 100 years.' That's true, but not much of the company's equipment cost is in the antennas."

Don also noted:

The auditors had a feeling that there were some repairs and maintenance being capitalized, but they never really found it. When they did their investigations the engineers would tell them, "We're just fine-tuning the equipment, getting it ready to use." The auditors weren't thorough enough. If they had studied it carefully they would have found, for example, that it takes $400,000 per year to maintain each of the fancy video tape decks. If the company doesn't do the maintenance Sony won't guarantee the machines.

By the end of FY 1990 Don judged that of the $10 million in capital additions for the year $3.5 million was in interest and another $2 million was for items that should have been classified as repairs and maintenance expense and engineering salaries. If those expenses were moved to the income statement ETI would show a huge loss. But as long as ETI management could get funds for more capital additions they would keep deferring those expenses.

Year end 1990

Don went to Joe and proposed a large accounting adjustment, of nearly $2 million, approximately twice the amount ETI would otherwise report as 1990 profit. But Joe was in the middle of an important series of negotiations that had begun in 1989 with National Telephone Corporation (NTC), a large telecommunications company. NTC had offered to buy a new offering of ETI stock at a substantial premium over market prices and to allow ETI to participate as a partner in the start of a whole new type of business – satellite telephone communications. This business, which was in an early development stage, involved having special telephones manufactured by NTC send a signal to a satellite positioned to handle such transmissions. The satellite would relay the call to a ground station that fed it into the regular phone network. This business was seen to have a large potential market in providing easy telephone communications to remote areas and to passengers in airplanes throughout the world. NTC was attempting to set up a worldwide satellite communications network and was promising to give ETI the East Coast franchise. ETI managers knew that the NTC deal was important both for the opportunity to enter a new business and for the infusion of cash that would allow the retirement of some expensive bonds.

So when Don proposed the accounting adjustment Joe said,

> No! No! No! You don't understand. We've got NTC going to hand us an enormous amount of money, and that will solve the problem. We must report the profits they're expecting or they'll back away from us. Let's get through this year and digest these acquisitions. Our interest costs will be lower next year because we will be able to renegotiate our loans. Let's focus on the future. I'll talk to the auditors.

Don attended the meeting with the auditors, but said, "I had to leave the room because it was so outrageous."

The auditors gave the ETI 1990 financial statements an unqualified opinion, although they told the board of directors that the statements were *pushing the edge on aggressive reporting*. In response to a question about how the auditors approved the statements, Don replied:

> When I was at T&Y I felt relatively certain that nobody could get anything by me. By the time I'd left C&S I realized that auditors provide *no* safety net. There is no way you can have relatively untrained people (even those with up to five years' experience), no matter how many you have, come up against financial people in a company with similar backgrounds but with a lot more experience and a full year to decide how they want to shape the financial picture they want to present to the world.
>
> I think Joe also had an effect on the auditors. He has an explosive personality. I have watched him call the auditors, even the partner, into his office and literally shriek at them. He grossly overreacts to things; he's not emotionally mature. I think they're afraid of him. Even when they realize their mistakes they feel a natural pressure to go along to keep their client afloat. They hope it works out.

Even though Don felt ETI should not be reporting as it did he knew he did not know what the proper accounting should be because he had spent his time focusing on improving the company's systems. Furthermore, he felt that the problem would be fixed in 1991 as a lot of goodwill amortization and depreciation of equipment put in service would have to be recognized as expense. Don was also appeased because management had agreed to limit expenditures, and Joe had finally agreed to let him change the company's measurement focus from EPS to cash flows.

Don wrote the management discussion and analysis section of ETI's 1990 annual report. In it he indicated that fiscal year 1991 would be a year of restructuring, that the company would be amortizing its expenses over a much shorter period and, consequently, that profits would be much lower. His feeling at the time:

> I felt that I had done a reasonable job of telling people what was going on. I was signalling that the trend should not be plotted from these results. I thought if people looked at cash flows they would understand what

was going on. We had disclosed how much interest we had capitalized. I thought that someone who was smart and took the time would be able to draw the right conclusions from our disclosures.

Fiscal year 1991

The budget proved to be reasonably accurate in the first quarter of fiscal year 1991, and Don was convinced that the company would actually report something close to the $2 million loss that had been forecast unless changes were made. He showed his analysis to top management and made them promise to make significant cuts in expenditures. They committed to cut people and travel, to delay the capital additions, and even to sell some assets.

But at the end of the second quarter (January 1991) the manager of the satellite video division dropped his $3.5 million operating profit projection for the year to $1.5 million, so company profits were now forecast at a $4 million loss for the year. Don visited the presidents of all the divisions and asked

them to raise their profit forecasts for the year, but they said that was impossible. For example, the president of the most profitable division said he had made a bad error and fired a couple of salespeople and his sales were below plan. Plus he said he had budgeted an aggressive level of sales that he had known from the beginning he could not deliver.

Don was now quite concerned. The rest of ETI's top management team still did not put great faith in the budget numbers, and they had not cut costs as sharply as Don would have liked. And they still believed that the negotiation with NTC pointed the way to the company's future. Don knew their stance perpetuated the pressures for aggressive financial reporting.

Don wondered what he should do. Should he continue to work on improving the company's accounting and budgeting systems and keep trying to convince top management that ETI had a serious financial problem on its hands? Or should he force the issue by making the accounting adjustment and hope that the company (and his job) survived the loss?

Case Study

Desktop Solutions, Inc. (A): Audit of the St. Louis Branch

In 1995 a team of auditors from the Internal Audit staff of Desktop Solutions Inc., an electronic distributor, audited the St. Louis branch of the Operations Group. Their audit report included the following overall judgment:

> In our opinion, the St. Louis branch's administrative process was unsatisfactory to support the attainment of branch business objectives.

The auditors noted that many of the branch procedures were working effectively, but they found major deficiencies existed in the branch's equipment control and order entry processes.

This case focuses on the areas of the audit that led to the Unsatisfactory audit judgment. It describes

what the auditors did, what they found, and how management responded.

DESKTOP SOLUTIONS, INC.

Desktop Solutions produced a broad line of printing and scanning systems for desktop printing/publishing applications. In 1995 the company's revenues were over $400 million (see Exhibit 1). The company's printers and scanners were available for rental or purchase. All rental plans in the United States included maintenance, service and parts. For equipment purchase, Desktop Solutions offered financing plans over two- to five-year periods with competitive interest rates. Some equipment was

---

This case was prepared by Professor Kenneth A. Merchant with the assistance of Research Assistant Howard Koo.

Copyright © by Kenneth A. Merchant.

sold with trade-in privileges. The company also sold supplies, such as toner, developer, and paper.

Desktop Solutions' worldwide marketing and sales organization marketed directly to end-user customers. The company also used some alternate channels, including retail stores, direct mail and sales agents. It also maintained worldwide networks of regional service centers (for servicing products) and distribution centers (for sales of parts and consumable supplies).

OPERATIONS GROUP

The Operations Group (OG) was the North American sales, marketing and service operation within Desktop Solutions' Operations Division. Within the OG the most important line organizations were the branches. They represented Desktop Solutions' direct interface with customers and were responsible for fulfilling all their equipment and servicing needs.

Until the late 1980s the management of the branches in OG had been highly decentralized. The decentralized organization was abandoned in the late 1980s and early 1990s in favor of a functional type of organization, which allowed for more direct control over branch functions by regional headquarters. Under the functional organization each branch was run by three parallel functional managers – a branch sales manager, a branch control manager (or branch controller), and a branch technical service manager – each of whom reported directly to the respective functional manager at the regional level (see Exhibit 2). The sales manager was responsible for all sales and leasing of Desktop Solutions' products in the branch territory. The control manager was in charge of all the internal operating, administrative, and financial reporting systems, such as order entry, accounts receivable, equipment control, and personnel. The technical service manager was responsible for the installation, servicing, and removal of sold and leased equipment.

The most difficult challenge with the new functional organization was maintaining good communication between personnel in the different functions of the branch. Frequent and effective communications were also important for achieving customer satisfaction, which was the most important branch success factor. Good communications were required to ensure that equipment would be installed promptly, that billings would be accurate, and that problems would be resolved with a minimum of hassle.

INTERNAL AUDIT

Internal audit had been a centralized function at Desktop Solutions since 1980. The function was centralized in order to increase auditor independence and to improve the professionalism of the staff. In 1995 the internal audit organization consisted of 15 people, headed by Steve Kruse, who reported to the chief financial officer, Scott Pepper.

Two features of the Desktop Solutions' Internal Audit (IA) organization were unique as compared with the internal audit groups in most corporations. First, the IA personnel had diverse backgrounds, and internal audit was not considered a career objective for most of them. The accounting/auditing personnel, who predominated on many corporate internal audit staffs, were in the minority; only three of the IA personnel were CPAs. The others were trained in a variety of disciplines, including engineering, marketing, computer science and liberal arts. Nine of the staff came into IA from outside Desktop Solutions. An initial assignment in IA was perceived as a good introduction to the company and a good training ground for moving into line operations. Most staff auditors did, in fact, move into the operations side of the company after gaining a few years' IA experience.

Second, the IA charter was very broad. The listing of IA functions (see Exhibit 3) showed that IA was expected to be involved in the development, not just the testing, of operational and internal controls. Exhibit 4 describes the different types of audits the IA staff performed and the allocation of audit resources among them in 1995.

Most of the audits were planned at headquarters, as part of the review of the company's controls. However, IA also received requests for services from line managers. In recent years the number of such requests had exceeded IA's capacity. Balancing the needs for regular audit cycles with the needs for special services requested was the difficult part in preparing the IA plan. Audit plans were approved by the audit committee of the board of directors, which was given regular progress reports throughout the year on each audit.

After executing an audit IA staff gave formal presentations to senior line management detailing their results and recommendations. They also followed up at a later date to see if the deficiencies had been corrected and the recommendations had been implemented.

AUDIT OF THE ST. LOUIS BRANCH

The St. Louis branch was selected for audit in 1995 for three reasons. First, the 1995 Master Audit Plan called for a number of large branch audits. The St. Louis branch, which served customers in Missouri, Illinois, and Kansas, was one of the largest of OG's 52 branches. In 1995 it earned revenue of $7.6 million and had a sale/lease equipment inventory of 7,710 machines. Second, a 1993 audit of the St. Louis branch had uncovered deficiencies in branch equipment control, and IA management thought this would be a good time to verify if improvements had been implemented. And third, a new branch control manager (branch controller) was recently hired, and the audit would give the new control manager a chance to work with the auditors and learn about the branch's systems and problems. The IA audit team and the new controller arrived at the St. Louis branch on the same day.

The objective of the audit was to determine whether the branch administrative/control processes were well defined, executed, and managed to ensure: (1) controlled and documented equipment movement and tracking; (2) timely and accurate order entry; (3) proper customer billing and adjustment; and (4) effective collections activity.

On the St. Louis audit, like most branch audits, the auditors focused most of their attention on equipment inventory and accounts receivable. These were the two largest branch balance sheet items, and both were under the direct control of the branch managers.

EQUIPMENT CONTROL/BILLING

Equipment control (EC) involved the tracking of equipment movements in and out of the branch's physical inventory and the simultaneous triggering of changes in customer billings. EC was critical to the branch's ability to schedule, deliver and install machines for Desktop Solutions customers, and to be paid for the equipment the customers used.

The key control personnel in EC were the order administrators (OAs), the equipment administrator

(EA), and the schedulers. The OAs were responsible for editing incoming orders, entering the orders into the computer system, keeping track of the orders after they were sent to scheduling, and processing the install transactions (install date, serial number, meter reads).

The EA was responsible for the accuracy of inventory records, and the timely resolution of equipment discrepancies that delayed orders (thus billing) from being completed. The EA maintained the Non-Revenue Report (NRR), a computer-generated inventory listing (by equipment serial number) of all branch equipment not installed at a customer location. The NRR was updated daily with information about new installations and cancellations. At the beginning of each month the EA took a physical inventory of all equipment at the warehouse, matched it with the NRR, and reconciled the differences. Equipment on the NRR not found at the warehouse was reclassified as uninventoriable (lost). If it was not found within 90 days the branch was charged for the net book value of the lost equipment. The process for cancellation and deinstallation of equipment was very similar.

The schedulers matched the orders with the equipment shown as available on the NRR. A target delivery date (ideally two days) was transmitted to the rigger who delivered the equipment (by serial number indicated).

Exhibit 5 shows a simplified flowchart of the process used in the St. Louis branch for order-entry and installation of the high-end printing and scanning systems. Personnel in the control function of the branch played a central communication role, transmitting the order information from the sales representatives to the rigger (warehouse) personnel and branch technical service personnel. They also processed the information about installations so as to trigger the customer billing.

Some low-end systems were delivered and installed by the sales representatives (reps). When this was done the equipment control process was simplified because the rep was responsible for delivering the order paperwork and the printer serial number to the OA for entry into the computer system.

While their operations were quite similar, the branches used slightly different administrative processes and personnel roles. OG management elected not to use a detailed, centralized set of administrative processes for all branches. They preferred allowing the branch managers to tailor their branch's processes to the local conditions.

AUDIT PROCEDURES

The audit fieldwork at the St. Louis branch took a team of six auditors approximately two months to complete. Exhibit 6 describes the tests performed on the equipment control process. About 40% of the audit time was devoted to equipment control procedures. Initially the IA personnel conducted background interviews with key branch personnel. They also reviewed organization charts and prepared detailed flow charts of the order entry, scheduling and equipment control processes. This was done to understand how the branch operated, to determine the degree of compliance with company procedures, and to determine the efficiency of branch personnel. Potential problem areas were noted for special attention during the audit fieldwork.

In addition to equipment control the auditors also tested several other areas, including customer billings for equipment, supplies and servicing (for accuracy and timeliness), price plan conversion (for compliance with company procedures), order entry and cancellation processes (for accuracy and efficiency), credit and collections, and order-to-installation time lag. Each of these areas represented a cycle or process activity that was important to the operation of a branch.

FINDINGS – EQUIPMENT CONTROL

The auditors found that management failed to define responsibilities clearly or hold the EA accountable for his performance. Branch management was not involved in the monitoring and maintenance of the equipment control process. And control management did not maintain effective contact with marketing and service management to ensure that the equipment control process was operating properly. Exhibit 7 describes some of the deficiencies found.

However, the branch was rated very good in other areas, and the auditors noted that the negative impacts from the deficiencies in the equipment control area seemed to be effectively minimized:

> Although the delayed equipment transaction processing contributed to incorrect billings and an increased rate of costly billing adjustments, overall the billing function was sufficiently well organized and controlled

to be able to absorb the pressures generated. The billing adjustments reviewed were highly accurate, and resolution of customer inquiries was satisfactory. The credit and collection program was well administered; performance budgets were consistently met, and adjustment and write-off activity was well controlled.

RECOMMENDATIONS AND FOLLOW-UP

On July 14, 1995 the audit team presented a final listing of the recommendations to the branch managers. Shortly thereafter they prepared a formal audit report to all OG management responsible for the St. Louis branch operations.

In the audit report the auditors presented a list of 46 recommendations. Most of these were directed to the new branch control manager, and generally related to one or more of the following:

1. The reconciliation between the physical inventory and the inventory records (NRR) should be completed.
2. The deficient equipment processes should be studied, refined, and documented.
3. The individuals involved in equipment control should be given clearly defined responsibilities, and be held accountable for the accuracy of the equipment reports and billings.

Ultimate responsibility for correcting deficiencies rested with line management (branch managers), not with IA. Company policy required the branch managers to prepare an action plan to address each of the deficiencies and recommendations made in the audit report. The last written response to the auditors' recommendations came from the St. Louis branch control manager on December 15, 1996. He addressed each of the auditor's recommendations and noted that most of them had already been implemented.

Company policy also required that someone independent of both IA and branch management be assigned to monitor progress in implementing the audit recommendations. In OG this was usually someone from the headquarters finance staff.

REACTIONS

Martha Sorensen (IA manager) reflected on the audit:

> The St. Louis branch had been recognized for some time as a problem branch. In most of the branches

many of the systems and administrative procedures go back to the days when the branches were run by a single branch manager, and the branches that were not well run in those days tended not to get going well when we switched to the functional organization. So going into this audit, we had a good idea we would find some problems, and the results of the audit confirmed this judgment. I hope we're now well on the way to getting the problems ironed out.

Phil Phillips, Region 3 manager, responded to the disclosure of the St. Louis branch's ongoing equipment control problem:

We can't blame these problems on the system because it works well in other branches. The problems occur for a combination of reasons including people, management, the sheer volume of work that was handled, and the fact that St. Louis is larger and has a more diverse organization structure than most of the other branches. These all create problems. We believe the problems are manageable, but it will take time to whittle away at them. We're making progress, but at this point we have not given the St. Louis branch a specific time deadline to clear up all their problems.

Exhibit 1 Summary income statements, Desktop Solutions Inc. ($ millions)

| | Year Ended December 31 | |
	1994	1995
Operating revenues		
Rentals and services	$228.1	$262.2
Sales	156.6	176.3
Total operating revenues	387.7	438.5
Cost and expenses		
Cost of rentals and services	101.6	116.2
Cost of sales	77.9	80.6
Research and development expenses	25.9	30.1
Selling, administrative and general expenses	144.6	159.8
Total cost and expenses	350.0	386.7
Operating income	37.6	51.8
Other income (deductions), net	(9.4)	(2.4)
Income before income taxes	28.2	49.4
Income taxes	7.8	13.6
Income before outside shareholders' interests	20.4	35.8
Outside shareholders' interests	3.5	5.9
Income from continuing operations	16.9	29.9
Discontinued operations	2.6	1.2
Net income	$19.5	$31.1

Exhibit 2 Operations Group organization chart

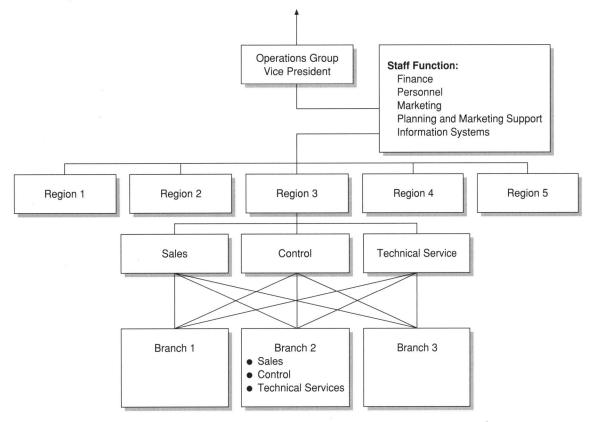

Exhibit 3 Internal audit functions

1. Develop and implement a program of operational, financial, and information systems audits that best meet the requirements of the corporation; assure the integrity of operational and internal controls in protecting the assets of the company and improve operational effectiveness.

2. Assist corporate and operating unit management in identifying and developing operational, financial, and systems policies and procedures necessary to accomplish the goals and objectives of the corporation; evaluate activities through audit report findings and recommend actions to eliminate problems uncovered during audits.

3. Perform special audits in any functional area and for all levels of management as required.

4. Present the audit plan and related audit findings to the Audit Committee of the Board of Directors and corporate management.

5. Coordinate external audit activities and control-related audit fees. Ensure an optimum balance between internal and external audit work in fulfilling the basic audit objectives and obtaining annual certification of Desktop Solutions' consolidated financial statements.

6. Develop new concepts of auditing responsive to the changing business and technological environment within Desktop Solutions and maintain a professional staff skilled in the required disciplines.

Exhibit 4 Audit types and 1995 plan for allocation of resources

Control Environment Audits (24% of resources in 1995)

Control Environment audits evaluate the organizational arrangements; financial planning and analysis; personnel policies and practices; and policy definition and communication within operating organizations. The objective is to assess the basis on which responsibility is assigned, accountability is determined, performance is measured, and overall specific controls are established.

Business Entity Audits (39%)

These are reviews of specific business cycle controls in a business entity such as a branch or small to medium subsidiary.

Business Cycle Audits (17%)

These are reviews of the seven business cycles as set forth in the Desktop Solutions Compendium of Internal Controls to determine if the overall and individual cycle control objectives stated there are being met. The overall objectives tested are: authorization; accounting transaction processing; and safeguarding of corporate assets. The cycle reviews will also include reviews of applicable control environment functions and tests of supporting computer controls.

Financial Audits (11%)

Financial audits, unless otherwise indicated, are in direct support of the annual audit by our external auditors and represent independent evaluation for the purpose of attesting to the fairness, and reliability of the financial data.

Systems Audits (8%)

System audits are pre-implementation and post-implementation reviews and data center audits. Pre-implementation audits consider the integrity, control, performance, security and conformance with policies and standards of each system reviewed during the design and development process. Post-implementation audits determine whether cost and performance objectives are met and test the system's integrity, including controls, in its live environment. Audits of data centers assess overall performance and the data control function and address security, scheduling and utilization, control, documentation, organization, training and cost effectiveness.

EXHIBIT 5 Simplified flowchart of order entry and installation process for high-end systems

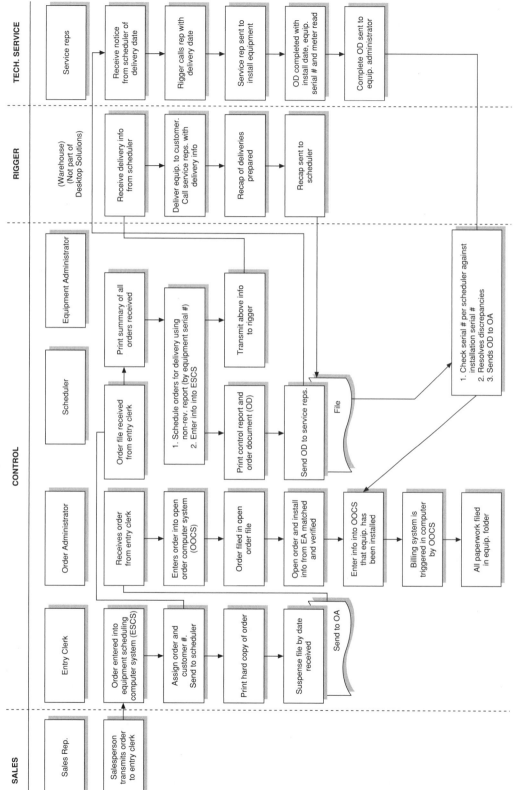

Exhibit 6 Audit tests performed on Equipment Control at the St. Louis branch

1. *Physical inventory.* A total sample of 1387 equipment units was examined, including a complete (100%) examination of the units of one single product. The audit team recorded all the serial numbers of the sample units found at the rigger (warehouse) and matched the numbers with those shown on the NRR. Serial numbers not matching up were given to the equipment administrator for reconciliation.

2. *Scheduling process.* The auditors examined the paperwork for a sample of 243 installations to see how the schedulers notified the riggers about what equipment to install.

3. *Install lag test.* A sample of 46 machines was examined for the timeliness of the steps in the order-to-install process, including how long the sales reps held on to orders before submitting them, how long the OAs took to enter the order correctly, how long it took the schedulers to get the machine out to the customer site and then the delay before the technical service reps installed the machine; and how long the OAs take to enter the final install information correctly into the system to trigger the billing process.

4. *Cancel lag test.* A sample of 33 cancellations was examined for proper adherence to contract terms and cancellation policies. The auditors were looking to see if the customer cancellation notification policy was followed, if the stop billing date was appropriate, if the removal charges were correctly billed, and if the processing was done on a timely basis.

5. *Low-volume copier installations.* A sample of 23 low-volume copier installations was examined to see if transmission of information from the sales reps to the OAs was adequate.

6. *Trials.* A sample of 22 machines out for customer trial was tested for adherence to company duration guidelines and approval procedures.

Exhibit 7 Partial list of internal audit findings at the St. Louis branch

1. The responsibilities of branch personnel were found to be slightly unusual in order entry and scheduling/equipment control. Some special order transactions (e.g. maintenance agreements, price plan conversions) were processed by customer service assistants, not OAs. The OAs did not track orders through the order-to-install process. And the information about installations and status changes went to the EA, instead of the scheduler, as at most other branches.

2. The physical inventory of 1387 mainframe and sorter units showed over 633 discrepancies when compared to the NRR. Seven weeks after the audit results were turned over to the branch, the EA had only reconciled 382 of these items, leaving 251 items unreconciled – 76 units potentially lost, 15 units potentially found, and 160 location and/or status discrepancies. At other branches, 95–100% of the inventory discrepancies were typically reconciled within the first two weeks.

3. The schedulers had learned they could not rely on the NRR, so they kept their own equipment inventory records. They manually assigned serial numbers to incoming orders. To move equipment quickly they sometimes directed the rigger to deliver products directly from the receiving dock before the serial numbers had been recorded in the branch's inventory by the EA. They kept track of movements in or out of the inventory based on information received from service personnel, but the auditors found that this listing was also inaccurate.

4. It took seven days on average from the date a machine was installed to the time the system recognized it as a valid install so that billing could begin. In addition, some documentation was missing: 3 of the 46 sampled had no credit approval; 2 had no service agreement; 4 had no valid installation date stamp.

5. The cancellation procedure was not working effectively. One hundred machines that had been returned by the customer and sent to the refurbishing center had not been noted as canceled by the OAs, and this number had increased sharply in the prior three months.

6. The low-end printing equipment was not well controlled. Units to be delivered by the sales reps were taken from regular inventory, rather than from a special pool of machines in "consignment to sales" status. In nine cases (39%), the sales reps did not send the serial numbers of the equipment to the OAs. In one case the rigger tried to deliver a machine to a customer who had received his a week before from the sales rep.

7. Of the machines out for customer trial only 3 of the 22 tested complied with company policy, and 5 had no approval signature. For four successful trials (i.e. the customer wanted to keep the machine), the ending date was recorded improperly, resulting in 29 days of unbilled rental revenue. For eight unsuccessful trials, the removal was scheduled two days past the trial expiration. Four trials were extended without approval. The average length past the normal trial duration was 17 days, while the average length past the extension deadline was 9.5 days.

8. Management failed to define responsibilities clearly or hold the EA accountable for his performance. Management did not get involved in the monitoring and maintenance of the equipment control process. Finally, control management did not maintain effective contact with marketing and service management to ensure that the equipment control process was operating properly as it affected those areas.

Desktop Solutions, Inc. (B): Audit of Operations Group Systems

In September 1995 Don Lindsay, the newly appointed manager of the Systems department of the Operations Group (OG) of Desktop Solutions, Inc., believed that some deep-rooted problems were hindering his unit's operational effectiveness. Systems had a long-standing reputation as being expensive and resistant to change, and systems planning in OG was generally recognized as deficient. As one manager put it:

> Don's predecessor tended to allow the user organizations to tell him what to do. The Systems personnel work closely with the various users, so closely, in fact, that it really became a direct-line relationship to the user managers and a dotted-line relationship to the Systems managers. That does not allow for a very effective operation because you really don't have control of the organization. All the users had their own parochial demands. They built their own databases, and there was very little sharing of files even between individuals in the same branch. The result was that the number of Systems personnel needed to meet the increasing number of user needs ballooned. People became resistant to change, and they were protective of what they had created. Virtually no planning or coordination was occurring.

Don thought that personnel from Desktop Solutions's corporate Internal Audit (IA) staff could help him by providing an independent opinion as to how well Systems was performing, identifying problems that might have gone unnoticed, and making suggestions for improvement. He also thought that an audit with recommendations for change would increase the support he would get from upper-level OG management and user organizations for implementing changes. He therefore requested a special audit from the IA organization. The purpose was to assess OG-Systems' ability in performing its centralized system support functions.

OG-SYSTEMS

Systems was a centralized systems support organization charged with two primary tasks: (1) maintaining and enhancing existing OG information systems; and (2) planning and implementing replacement systems. Because of OG's diversity these tasks were formidable. OG had 10 regional offices responsible for a total of 52 branch offices. Each region and branch operated their own unique information systems with different procedures and databases. Requests for system maintenance and development could come from any of several management levels in the user (i.e. branch or regional offices) organizations, and they were allowed to go directly to the first-line (lowest level) Systems managers responsible for their particular systems.

In 1995 Systems' budget was $15.8 million, of which about 60% was to be spent on systems maintenance, planning and development, and the rest on data processing operations. All work was fully charged back to the user organizations. Systems employed 155 people, 93 of whom were directly involved in code-creation activity (i.e. programmers, analysts).

The Systems organization, which reported directly to the OG vice president, was divided into three parts: Operations, Planning and Systems Architecture, and Control and Administration (see Exhibit 1). The Operations organization was responsible for creating new software and running three regional data processing centers. The Planning and Systems Architecture organization was responsible for long-range planning of both software and hardware. It also provided technical expertise to user-organizations and reviewed all new system designs for hardware compatibility. The Control and Administration organization was responsible for financial planning, analysis and reporting.

▶

This case was prepared by Professor Kenneth A. Merchant with the assistance of research assistant Howard Koo.

AUDIT PROCEDURES AND FINDINGS

The OG-Systems audit was planned and executed by two auditors who spent approximately 1,600 hours each on the entire project. One of the auditors had an extensive systems background, and was familiar with the operation and history of the Systems organization. Exhibit 1 describes the audit steps performed and the percent of time spent on each.

The auditors confirmed that systems planning and coordination in the OG organization were inadequate. They observed that many systems implementation decisions were being made at lower levels of management of the user organizations, without reference to related decisions in other areas. They found that Systems did not guide and coordinate the systems and programming personnel in the user organizations in the development of long-range or annual work plans, but they concluded that this problem was partly beyond the control of the Systems organization. One of the comments in their report was, "Generally, the current OG group-level business planning process does not result in formal management-approved output that is sufficiently integrated and detailed to direct a long-range systems development process."

To improve systems planning, the auditors suggested that OG senior management should:

1. Designate an information controller in each functional area to be responsible for providing an interface between strategic business planning and strategic systems planning. This person would also be responsible for integrating information needs within the function and between functions and for ensuring that all systems development activities flowed through OG-Systems. Once senior OG management had decided on a strategic business direction and the information needs, Systems personnel could develop compatible systems within each user organization to satisfy those needs.

2. Establish a process of recording and reporting of systems benefits to improve systems investment appraisal decisions and performance evaluations.

They suggested that the vice president of OG-Systems (Don Lindsay) should:

1. Establish and document responsibilities and procedures to ensure that the systems/user interface took place as needed and at the appropriate managerial levels within each organization.

2. Prepare detailed descriptions of the automated portions of the existing OG information processing cycles to support OG function and group-level business process planning. These documents should also be analyzed in order to identify opportunities to integrate existing processes and resources and to reduce costs.

3. Develop and maintain a description of the OG Systems Architecture, including hardware, software, databases, and networks that is sufficiently detailed to guide Systems planners in the development of the Long Range Systems Plan, as well as to direct operations managers in the development of application systems.

4. Establish and document responsibilities and procedures to ensure that Systems planners develop a Long Range Systems Plan based on an understanding of the OG Long Range Business Process Plan, the OG Systems Architecture, current OG information cycles, and future business requirements.

5. To ensure the promotion of the Long Range Systems Plan, ensure that the first year of the Long Range Systems Plan be sufficiently detailed to serve as the next year's Annual Work Plan; assign accountability for the execution of the Annual Work Plan to management in the user organizations; establish and document procedures to ensure the review and approval by the Systems planning staff of adjustments to the Annual Work Plan; and assign specific responsibility within the planning function for review of all new applications systems for adherence to the Long Range Systems Plan.

In the area of line operations, the auditors concluded that a diversity of operational practices existed within Systems, due to "a general lack of discipline and definition in operational practices within user first-line operations, as well as the absence of common operational procedures, measures and tools at the group level." This diversity restricted management's ability to monitor and assess the quality and efficiency of software production activities, and hindered the realization of economies of scale.

The auditors also concluded that key elements of the software creation process were not sufficiently controlled to ensure the efficient production of high-quality software products. To remedy these deficiencies they presented a long list of specific recommendations. These included suggestions for developing and implementing procedures for job requests and authorizations, scheduling jobs, ensuring better software security, and evaluating and documenting changes.

MANAGEMENT REACTIONS

The reactions to the audit were generally favorable. Larry Parton, manager of OG Planning and Systems Architecture, expressed his feelings:

> You can treat auditors either as outsiders or as a resource for management. Desktop Solutions has a very strong audit staff, and we like to take advantage of their expertise. We have some problems, and we have an awful lot to gain by asking them to come in and do an audit. That is the way we treated it and that is the way it turned out. We needed an independent look at what we were doing, and the audit group gave us that.

Don Lindsay was also satisfied:

> The reason I invited corporate audit to come in and do this audit was relatively straightforward. I had my own diagnosis of the problems in the Systems Department and an action plan for solving them. I just needed to get someone else's perception of the problems and their recommendations. IA is really the only group we have to do this kind of work. They are not a Gestapo organization; they are a support group that has the ability to get into this kind of work.
>
> I feel very good about the audit report. I agree with their base identification of the issues. They confirmed my analysis. I don't feel they came up with a lot of strong recommendations, however. I think the solution to many of our problems is a better focus on systems planning within the entire OG, and that is something that I, by myself, cannot solve. That is probably the single most important issue in OG, and the audit report dealt with it only superficially. It discussed planning but seemed to place more emphasis on day-to-day operating issues.
>
> It was not my original intention to use the audit report as additional leverage to plead my case, but that has certainly turned out to be an important benefit. After we realized how deeply ingrained our problems were we realized that we had to use every means available to get the message across. The audit report was one such forum.

EXHIBIT 1 Audit steps performed and the percentage of time spent on each on the OG-Systems audit

1. *Scoping* (30%). Conducted preliminary independent interviews with users and Systems managers about their systems procedures and working relationships.

2. *Planning* (15%). Reviewed the results of the scoping phase and discussed them with Don Lindsay. Formulated a model of how the operations work and developed a set of problem hypotheses. Developed fieldwork questionnaires.

3. *Fieldwork* (25%). Sent questionnaires to a sample of involved or affected personnel, including 11 first-line managers and 10 analysts and programmers, all in the Systems organization, and 12 first-line user managers. Followed up the questionnaires with personal interviews and prepared a summary of responses. Interviewed 5 second-line and 3 third-line Systems managers and prepared a summary of these responses.

4. *Clearing and Summarizing* (15%). Verified interview responses where necessary. Developed conclusions drawn from fieldwork summaries and proposed recommendations. Presented conclusions and recommendations to OG-Systems management.

5. *Formal Report to Systems Management* (15%). Prepared formal written audit report with conclusions and recommendations for Systems management (Don Lindsay).

Case Study

Landale PLC

In January 2002 Patrick Kirk, vice president/ controller of Landale PLC, appointed a committee, called the Finance and Accounting Strategy and Training (FAST) committee, to review the effectiveness of the company's Finance and Accounting Development Program. The program, which had been in place since 1990, was a job rotation program designed to enhance the skills of Landale's finance and accounting professionals so that the corporation could select its controllers from among a set of competent internal candidates.

While most people considered the program to have been successful a number of issues had arisen over the 11 years of its existence. These included questions as to what jobs should be included as rotational assignments, how fast individuals should be rotated through various jobs, what constituted the optimal recruiting mix, how large the program should be, whether formal training should be a part of the program, and whether the program should have a purpose broader than development of just controllers. The FAST committee was asked to review the program, present recommendations about each of these issues, and develop a written program charter by September 2002.

THE COMPANY

Landale PLC (Landale) was founded in 1938. The company took its name from the highly successful Landale brand of laundry-cleaning product that its founder had developed. Over the years Landale managers expanded their product offerings, both internally and through a series of acquisitions, so that the company's fortunes would not depend on just one product.

In 2002 Landale, headquartered in London, was a large, diversified, international company with over 65,000 employees and annual sales of over £12 billion. The company's principal business still involved the development, manufacture, and marketing of premium quality household products that were sold in grocery stores and other retail outlets. Some of these products were also marketed to wholesale customers, such as restaurants, schools, and hotels. But the company also manufactured and sold a broad range of other products, including crop chemicals, food and food processing equipment, fuel additives, and tobacco filters. Landale marketed its brands in 93 countries and produced its products in 57 manufacturing facilities located throughout the world. It also participated in joint ventures in Saudi Arabia, Spain, Egypt, Colombia, Argentina, Malaysia, and the Dominican Republic.

Landale's performance over the years had been good, with a long-term earnings growth rate in excess of 10%. However, in 2001 Landale suffered disappointing earnings primarily because of a £90 million write-off. It had launched an expensive roll out of a new personal care product that failed miserably. While analysts noted the failure, which caused an end to a significant string of double-digit annual increases in earnings, they gave Landale's management credit for taking risks and challenging competitors even larger than themselves. One analyst observed, "They [Landale managers] are not afraid to take on the big cats. They are fearless, and tenacious."

ORGANIZATIONAL STRUCTURE

As the corporate organization chart in Exhibit 1 shows, the company was organized into one international division and six product divisions:

1. Home Care and Professional Cleaning Products Division (HCC) – home and laundry cleaning products;

This case was prepared by Professors Kenneth A. Merchant and Wim A. Van der Stede, with the research assistance of Sung-Han (Sam) Lee.

2. Personal Care Division (PCD) – skin cleansers, deodorants, and antiperspirants;

3. Basic and Fine Chemicals Division (BFC) – crop protection agents, plastics, and chemicals for manufacturing electronic components;

4. Food Service Products Division (FSPD) – food and food processing equipment for institutional and restaurant use, with emphasis on the dry and frozen food categories;

5. Fuel Additives Division (FAD) – petroleum additives and specialty chemicals;

6. Tobacco Filters Division (TFD) – cellulose acetate filters.

Each product division was run as if it were its own company, with its managers responsible for the development, manufacturing, and marketing of its products. The product divisions were organized functionally. The division controllers reported on a solid-line basis to the division general managers, but they also reported on a strong dotted-line basis to Patrick Kirk, Landale's corporate controller.

FINANCE AND ACCOUNTING DEVELOPMENT PROGRAM

Purpose

In 1990 Michael Shaw, then Landale's chief financial officer, implemented the Finance and Accounting Development Program to develop new controllers internally so that the company would no longer have to hire them from outside. Michael patterned the Landale program after a similar program that had been successful at his former employer, a large competitor of Landale.

The program was set up to provide Landale employees on-the-job training by rotating them through a series of finance and accounting (F&A) assignments designed to give them the skills and exposure necessary to handle a division controllership position effectively within a time frame of 8–12 years.[1] The job assignments, about 95% of which were located in the London headquarters building, were rotated every 12–18 months until the individual reached a managerial level, at which

time the length of the assignments could increase. Exhibit 2 shows some representative F&A job descriptions and the approximate timing for the career progression of a new employee.

While many different types of jobs could be included as rotation assignments, program administrators considered it essential, or at least strongly preferred, for everyone in the program to have at least one assignment in each of five major areas that were generally seen as providing essential experiences for someone in a controller role: general accounting, cost accounting, forecasting, financial analysis, and internal auditing. These common elements were included because of the belief that, as one senior financial manager expressed it, "At the senior financial manager level, we try to have roughly interchangeable parts. All senior managers should have all the important experiences." Some participants complained about the restrictiveness of the program, particularly the requirements for audit and general accounting experiences. But Patrick Kirk defended the program's design:

Not many people enjoy auditing. Nobody with controllership potential wants to be an auditor for life, and many people don't see it as important in their development. But I think an auditing experience is vital. You get across division lines, meet many different kinds of people, and get to perform some operational audits . . .

Similarly, nobody wants to do general accounting, but managing 30 clerks is good experience. As you move up, your job is more and more dependent on the effective management of people . . .

In cost accounting you learn how the business is built and how good management decisions should be made . . .

You need to be a good forecaster to succeed as a controller. To be a good forecaster you have to have good business knowledge; you need to understand how the numbers fit together; and you need to know how to set up the pads to cover your rear end if volume falls off. If you blow it, it's serious.

In the mid-1990s the focus of the program was expanded to include the development of virtually all F&A professionals up to the division controller level. As one manager put it, "You don't graduate from the program. We continue to watch and manage everybody's career." The only exceptions were a few people who decided to leave the program either because they believed that they had "found their niche" or because they did not like the types

---

[1] None of the other functions within Landale (e.g. brand management, manufacturing management) had their own development programs. In those areas, "People earn their stripes and move up."

of jobs the program offered, and some people who were considered to have peaked in their careers at a managerial level (five to ten years in the company). These people were no longer formally rotated. In 2002 a total of 90 people were considered to be in the program.

Recruiting

In an average year, 10 new employees were recruited into the program. Most of the new recruits were recent college graduates or MBA graduates with a maximum of two to three years' work experience. MBAs were hired at a higher job grade and paid about £10,000 per year more. The only exception to this recruiting profile occurred in a 13-month period in 1999–2000 when the company recruited 17 employees with prior accounting firm experience (typically three to five years) to fill some immediate needs.

When the program was started the company hired exclusively new MBA graduates, but the emphasis on MBAs declined over the years because top managers came to believe that the MBAs were, in general, not worth the premium that they had to be paid over new university graduates. In 2002 the recruiting goal was 60% university graduates, 20% MBA graduates, and 20% employees with prior experience. The new university graduates were 70% finance majors and 30% accounting majors (even though two out of three of the jobs in the program were more accounting oriented than finance oriented).

Job assignments

For entry-level employees up through job grade 16 (generally individuals with three to five years' experience), a group totaling about 30 people, a Rotational Committee determined the job assignments. This committee, comprised of four managers from different divisions, met twice per month. Each committee member was responsible for the rotations of a specific group of employees. Membership on the committee rotated completely each year; every three months one committee member was replaced.

The committee made its rotation recommendations after looking at each individual's education, experiences, strengths, and developmental needs and soliciting input from the employees' current managers. The recommendations had to be approved by the division controllers affected by the moves, and frequently the assignments had to be reworked several times before the controllers could reach agreement. The individuals being rotated had virtually no influence on their assignments until they had worked at Landale for five years. After that they were given some influence, particularly if they were among the better performers.

An assignment example

In many cases conflicts existed between the controllers' desires to assemble a team of people who would perform well and the rotational committee's desires to develop the individuals in the program. This type of conflict can be illustrated by describing the assignment choices the committee had to make in August 2001. Four people had to be placed:

Dan –   A new university graduate (finance major).
Debra – 17 months at Landale. One assignment in HCC cost accounting.
Mary – 14 months at Landale. Three assignments, all in general accounting.
John – Three years at Landale. In most recent 12 months, consolidated HCC division forecasts and analyzed monthly profit-and-loss statements.

The committee recommended that:

1. John be given a cost accounting assignment. He would work with the 13 plants in HCC, resolve problems in the inventory control system, analyze variances by plant and by product, and perform the monthly general ledger close for inventory and cost of sales.

2. Mary be given John's old forecasting position. The committee wanted to give her a prime and stable assignment since her first year had been so tough (three assignments in 14 months).

3. Dan be given an entry-level forecasting position in HCC, reporting to Mary.

4. Debra be given a corporate general accounting assignment.

Most of the division controllers agreed that these assignments made sense, but Linda Marshall, the HCC controller, vetoed the recommendation. She said:

I can't afford to lose Debra. She's the only experienced cost accountant I've got in the division. The only accountant I would have left is brand new [two months]. Plus my manager of cost accounting left six months ago, and I had to promote my inexperienced assistant manager and bring in a new assistant manager. I need Debra's experience because I'm implementing a new cost and resource planning system in the plants. And, remember, cost accounting assignments typically last longer than other types of assignments [closer to 18 months, on average], so she has not been in her current position an abnormally long period of time.

To accommodate Linda, the committee altered its recommendation as follows:

1. They restructured John's current position so that it would provide Debra with useful experience, yet allow her to stay in the HCC division and make her expertise available to the accounting department when needed.

2. Dan would take the corporate general accounting assignment originally slotted for Debra. This position was better for a second rotational assignment because it required a good understanding of the company and the supervision of a clerk. But the committee thought the position would provide Dan with a good challenge.

3. Mary would take the forecasting position originally intended for Dan, but the job would be restructured to eliminate some of the clerical tasks to make it more challenging.

4. John would still take the cost accounting assignment.

The committee members thought that while the new assignments were not ideal they represented a reasonable compromise between company and individual needs.

Overall program evaluation

Virtually everybody in the company agreed that the development program had been a success. All of Landale's current set of F&A managers and controllers had come through the program, and the program was credited with upgrading the Landale F&A function. Here are some representative observations about the program.

Patrick Kirk (VP/corporate controller):

When the program started, marketing and sales had driven the company, while finance and accounting were clearly weaker functions. Managers even tended to put in F&A people who were not doing well elsewhere. Now we are equal. We are no longer seen as "green eyeshade" people. We are asked our opinions on business issues, and one of the last three people appointed as a general manager came out of the accounting function . . .

The best F&A people are equal to the best people in any function. On average, though, I think we still have to conclude that the quality of marketing people is higher. They recruit MBAs from the best universities and have a faster career progression early on; they get to manager level more quickly, in three years, as opposed to 10 years in F&A. But they also force attrition.

Jeff Thompson (manager of internal auditing):

The program has been successful. We have raised our own controllers. People percolate up that are right for our jobs.

Kevin Fisher (controller, PCD):

On net, the rotations are advancing the company. It is a good recruiting tool, and it gives us lower turnover and better people.

ISSUES FOR THE FAST COMMITTEE TO CONSIDER

Over the years a number of program issues had arisen, and they provided Patrick Kirk with the motivation to appoint the FAST committee. These issues concerned the selection of assignments to be included in the program, the speed of rotation, the recruiting mix, the size of the program, the formal training to be used, and the ultimate purpose of the program.

1. Selection of acceptable assignments

One broad set of issues related to the types of jobs to be included as potential rotation assignments. Some people saw a problem in that, as Timothy Freeman, an assistant manager in HCC expressed it, "In some jobs you don't learn much, and in others what you learn is not useful." Many specific questions had arisen. For example, should tax positions be included in the program, or is tax a totally separate skill? And would an assignment in employee benefits, computer systems, or treasury be beneficial?[2]

Jobs in the international division were seen as particularly problematic because they were quite

---

[2] No corporate treasury assignments were currently available. The current treasurer was not a supporter of the program because he thought the F&A people were rotated through jobs too quickly, and he did not like not having control over the rotations through his area.

different from those in other parts of the company. Jeff Thompson explained:

> International is a beast unto itself. There is a premium on risk assessment and risk taking. There is more finance context, such as currency translations and risks, hedging, and raising local currency. Tax planning is very important. You have to be diplomatic in dealing with our many joint venture partners. And not all the accounting skills come into play.

With regard to his own Landale experiences Kevin Fisher, current International Division controller, concluded: "Nothing I did trained me for this job." Kevin was not even sure that the International Division benefited much from being a part of the program because skills and orientations needed in the division were different. He thought that if International were to continue in the program he needed some of his positions to be classified as "continuity" positions, i.e. staffed by permanent employees. Some other controllers had also argued for having some continuity positions in their divisions.

Another issue was that of remote assignments (i.e. those located away from the headquarters building). Some people believed that everyone in the program should have at least one such assignment to allow them to see, for example, the differences in perspectives and cultures at the plant level of the corporation and the new team approaches being developed in manufacturing. But Patrick Kirk noted:

> Most people won't go. These jobs are manufacturing oriented and not glamorous. It's hard on employees with families. Plus our people have seen that many have succeeded without taking these assignments. But I do think these jobs provide a great learning experience.

Finally, some people questioned the need for requiring the five basic areas of experience. For example Martin Edwards, a finance manager in PCD, described his experiences to make the case for allowing less traditional career paths:

> I've been with the company ten years. I spent a year in internal audit, 18 months as a plant accountant, a year in corporate financial planning, two years in BFC in Birmingham, two years on an MRP II implementation project, and I've been in my current job for six months. (I plan to stay in this job for two to three years.) Mine was not a traditional path. I did not hit the five key areas. I missed traditional general accounting and cost accounting jobs, and this has sometimes caused a steeper than desirable learning curve. But my path is more advantageous for a generalist, as opposed to somebody with a hardcore accounting orientation. For example, does it really matter if you know all the particulars about closing the books (e.g. how to reconcile all the accounts)? . . .

> At BFC I got to see a business fall apart without having to worry about losing my job, and the systems job was somewhat unique. I think those skills will be more important in the next ten years. My goal is to become a controller, and I got a broad perspective from a *business*, not accounting, standpoint, including plant and remote site experience. Audit was the least useful experience. It was hard to feel fulfilled. I didn't feel I made any contributions except to save time on the Ernst & Young audit.

The pressures for allowing variances from the policy of requiring experiences in the five key areas were accentuated because assignment constraints sometimes made it difficult for the company to provide all individuals with all of the required experiences early in their careers. Exhibit 3 shows the job experiences of six F&A professionals. Only the first two individuals followed the desired career paths by receiving an additional required job experience in each of their early assignments.[3] If the area requirements were taken seriously these individuals would probably have an advantage over the others. But most of the young program participants believed that their assignments were beyond their control: "Turning down a rotation assignment, even one that is not in your best interest, is not viewed positively."

One suggestion that had been made was to permit greater variety in people's job rotation patterns by allowing different developmental tracks for people with different interests. For example, among the tracks that might be offered were generalist (controller), international, systems, and treasury.

---

[3] Some of the assignments that did not formally satisfy the requirements of a required area of experience provided experiences related to those of a required area. For example, the person referred to as No. 3 in Exhibit 3 took her first assignment as a staff accountant in corporate information systems. In this job she did some general accounting, but she was not given credit for having fulfilled the general accounting requirement because she did not learn the entire general ledger system, the chart of accounts, and the closing process.

2. Speed of rotation

Another set of program issues pertained to the speed of job rotations. More rapid rotations provided a steeper learning curve, but they also caused more organizational continuity problems and increased the individuals' risk of failure. Individuals in the program had differing views on the rotational speed issue. For example, Shirley Freeman said:

I would slow down some of the rotations. In all of the positions I've had I had just climbed the learning curve to proficiency and then had to leave. There is not as much of a sense of accomplishment or contribution. It's frustrating.

But Martin Edwards disagreed:

If you don't move people fast enough, they'll leave the company, believing that they are not progressing fast enough.

Raymond Allen, manager of corporate analysis and control, agreed with Martin:

People want to build career skills. This is especially true when times are tougher and the company is not growing as fast. People seek to build their skills because they are not convinced that the company will be a good place to spend their whole career. There may be a generation gap here, with the more junior F&A professionals having less loyalty to the company and a greater interest in the development of their career skills.

Some people suggested that rapid rotation be provided for only a few "stars." But if that was attempted it was not clear what criteria should be used to identify the stars.

3. Recruiting mix

A third issue concerned the ideal recruiting mix. Most people believed that on average the MBAs had risen fastest in the organization because, as Kevin Fisher noted:

Most had another experience before Landale before they were employed. It's a sorting process. They have experience, some perspective, and more aggressiveness. But we also find incompetence quickly because MBAs are put in higher positions more quickly.

But most did not think the success of the MBAs should mean that Landale should recruit only MBAs into the F&A program. As Jeff Thompson noted:

Having an MBA-oriented program would cost more. Plus we would have fewer jobs that would interest MBAs, so we would probably have to have shorter rotations. This would be bad for most of the company because we would have no continuity in the operating units.

And one manager thought that many MBAs, particularly those from the better universities and those with experience, would not find the rotation aspect of the program appealing.

Few people wanted to resume large-scale recruiting from public accounting firms. The turnover statistics from the accounting firm group were not different from those of the other groups, but this group's average performance ratings were lower because some of them did not perform well. Patrick Kirk explained:

We brought these people in through internal audit, but then we faced the issue about how to put them in a division. They are good accountants, but many of them didn't work well in a business environment, and we had trouble placing them. They want and need forecasting experience, but inside people want it too. So we do the best we can. We'll give them a chance, and if it doesn't work we'll let them go. Some of them have asked to be "red-circled," to go to a lower level job to catch up.

Others agreed with this position. Kevin Fisher said, "In general, those we have hired from public accounting have not made the transition well. They don't have the broad business background, and they're too passive. We want people to challenge the cocky marketing and sales people." And Jeff Thompson commented: "Folks who come in from the outside must learn the company and how to compete in it. In a forecasting job they are behind from day one. They are managing people who know more than they do. Some do well. Others die."

But Jane Gruber, who spent $5\frac{1}{2}$ years with a public accounting firm before joining Landale and was currently manager of general accounting in BFC, thought that the "insiders," those who joined Landale straight from a university campus, and the "outsiders," those who joined Landale after working at an accounting firm, each brought some strengths to the company:

The insiders' strengths are more experience from the ground up. They had time to get down to the detail level, and they have had a better opportunity to be known by the controllers. If they are strong performers, that can be an advantage, but if they are poor it is a disadvantage. The MBAs are more successful if they bring in relevant prior business experience because they know how to work with people, communicate, and structure their time . . .

Outsiders have to prove themselves quickly. But the outsiders are accustomed to moving from client to client to learn businesses and issues quickly. They have good interviewing skills. They know how to learn something from scratch. And they know how different companies do different things, so they bring fresh ideas to spice up the company's environment. The insiders say, "Outside people don't know anything." The outsiders say, "They don't give me a chance."

4. Size of program

In 2002 the development program included 90 people. Some people were concerned that this number was too large because the number of good rotation assignments was too small to accommodate everyone. One suggestion was to scale back the program to focus rotations only on high potential people. Others, however, thought everyone should have the chance to move around and be challenged. Kevin Fisher said, "People tend to get cynical when they don't have a chance to move. And there is a visibility issue. The guys upstairs have to be comfortable with you, and you can't get visibility without rotation."

5. Formal training

Some people suggested that the program add some formal training sessions. Some on-site courses were offered at Landale, but none of these were in accounting. Recently the controller's organization had begun sponsoring monthly informal lunches for F&A professionals to chat about various topics. Typical attendance was about 45–50% of the F&A staff.

6. Basic purpose of program

There was lack of agreement about the basic purpose of the program. Jeff Thompson (manager of internal auditing) explained:

Like any program that evolves, people have different expectations of it. Different people see it different ways. A number of lower- and middle-level folks see it differently from the leadership [the corporate controller and the seven division controllers]. We've tried not to define the purpose precisely, but my bias is not for more definition than we have. I think the purpose is to create the senior-level financial managers (division controllers) of the future. But many of my colleagues have other ideas.

Two broad questions had arisen about the basic purpose(s) of the program. One was an issue as to whether the program should continue to aim to develop controllers or whether it should also strive to develop general managers or other types of professionals (e.g. information technology specialists). Some of the impetus for the idea of using the program to help F&A personnel become general managers stemmed from line manager comments such as, "If you're not telling people you're training general managers, it's limiting. Good people shouldn't aspire to less." But if the purpose of the program were broadened to include the development of other specialties, many of the other issues described above (e.g. types of assignments considered acceptable, recruiting mix) would have to be reconsidered.

A second purpose question was whether the finance and accounting functions should be merged in one program. Some people suggested that the tasks were really separate because "accounting is a staff function, and finance is a line function."

THE COMMITTEE'S TASK

As the September deadline for the FAST committee's presentation of a proposed program charter neared, the committee members contemplated their task. They knew that many of the issues raised were related. They would have to address various combinations of them concurrently in order to provide suggestions to maximize the program's contribution to the corporation.

Exhibit 1 Landale PLC organization chart, August 2002

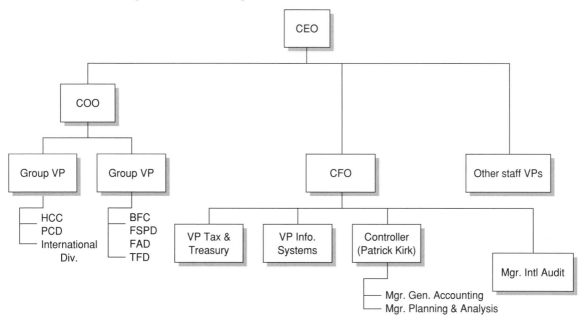

Key:

HCC = Home Care and Professional Cleaning Products Division
PCD = Personal Care Division
BFC = Basic and Fine Chemicals Division
FSPD = Food Service Products Division
FAD = Fuel Additives Division
TFD = Tobacco Filters Division

Exhibit 2 Representative F&A job descriptions

Staff Accountant (1–2 years' experience)

Prepare journal entries, control monthly profit center accounting close, prepare accurate financial statements and supporting schedules, analyses and other financial data for management review. Reconcile and analyze accounts. Manage clerical employees.

Cost Analyst (2–4 years' experience)

Prepare and publish monthly detailed and summary production costs and inventory data, assist in analyses of variances against standards and budgets. Maintain computerized inventory system. Organize and direct monthly cost accounting close.

Senior Financial Analyst (3–5 years' experience)

Analyze and evaluate financial impact of marketing proposals using internal rate of return and net present value techniques. Participate in preparation of and explain key strategic documents, such as the long-range plan, to upper management.

Assistant Manager (4–5 years' experience)

Ensure accuracy of monthly profit center income statement and balance sheet providing information for controlling manufacturing costs. Assist in establishing manufacturing budgets and controls. Supervise professional and clerical people.

Manager – General Accounting (5–8 years' experience)

Coordinate and direct preparation of the division P&L, balance sheet, and supporting schedules. Direct the preparation of the division balance sheet and cash flow statements and identified opportunities for managing working capital to achieve financial goals. Manage the interface of other corporate accounting, distribution, sales, treasury, and other systems to the division's general ledger and recommend improvement to these systems. Manage professional and clerical staff.

Manager – Analysis and Control (5–8 years' experience)

Coordinate, develop, and analyze financial implications of profit center short-term and long-term business plans. Interpret forecasts for profit center and corporate top management. Determine financial feasibility of projects to assist profit center and corporate top management in allocating company resources among numerous spending proposals. Monitor and report on actual performance against the plans, measuring progress against financial goals and objectives. Manage professional and clerical staff.

Profit Center Controller (8–12 years' experience)

Participate in both the establishment of strategic objectives for the profit center and in the detailed plan to achieve those objectives. Serve as primary financial advisor to the profit center. Participate in evaluation of major plans, including capital expenditure projects, feasibility studies, and new product introductions. Ensure timeliness, accuracy, and integrity of financial reports and records. Serve on profit center management committee.

EXHIBIT 3 Job experiences of six F&A professionals, 1997–2002

Assignments	Required areas covered*
Person 1: hired April 1997; 4 of 5 required areas covered	
1. Auditor I	Audit
2. Staff accountant, Corporate general accounting	General
3. Financial analyst, PCD	Forecasting
4. Senior cost analyst, PCD	Cost accounting
Person 2: hired June 1997; 4 of 5 required areas covered	
1. Auditor I	Audit
2. Staff accountant, Corporate	Forecasting
3. Financial analyst, HCC general accounting	General accounting
4. Senior cost analyst, HCC	Cost accounting
Person 3: hired June 1997; 1 of 5 required areas covered	
1. Staff accountant, Corporate information systems	–
2. Cost accounting, HCC	Cost accounting
3. Plant accountant, HCC	–
Person 4: hired June 1997; 1 of 5 required areas covered	
1. Cost accountant, HCC	Cost accounting
2. Budget accountant, HCC	–
3. Plant accountant, HCC	–
Person 5: hired July 1997; 2 of 5 required areas covered	
1. Staff accountant, Tech Center	–
2. Cost accountant, HCC	Cost accounting
3. Senior financial analyst, HCC	Forecasting
4. Assistant manager, International	–
Person 6: hired September 1997; 2 of 5 areas covered	
1. Staff accountant, Corporate	Forecasting
2. Staff accountant, BFC	Forecasting
3. Financial systems analyst, Corporate	–
4. Senior financial analyst, FSPD	–
5. Assistant manager, HCC	Financial analysis

* Required areas of responsibility before reaching controller level are: cost accounting, general accounting, internal audit, forecasting, and financial analysis.

Chapter 15

MANAGEMENT CONTROL-RELATED ETHICAL ISSUES

Managers involved in designing and using management control systems (MCSs) should have a basic understanding of ethics. Ethics is the field of study that is used to prescribe morally acceptable behavior. It provides methods of distinguishing between "right" and "wrong" and of systematically determining the rules that provide guidance as to how individuals and groups of individuals should behave. Its systematic nature goes beyond what even thoughtful people do in making sense of their own and others' moral experiences. Ethics is important for managers involved with MCSs because ethical principles can provide a useful guide for defining how employees should behave. Further, employees' ethics are an important component of personnel or cultural controls. If good ethics can be encouraged in an organization, they can substitute for, or augment, actions or results controls.

Ethics is a difficult subject for many managers to understand. One reason for this is that many managers' basic discipline training is in economics or business.[1] Two common assumptions in economics are that rational people should act to maximize their own self-interest and that the primary purpose of employees in for-profit organizations is to maximize shareholder value.[2] Ethics, however, provides alternative assumptions about how people should and do behave. It assumes that ethical individuals must consider the impact of their actions on other *stakeholders* – those affected by their actions – including employees, customers, local communities and other users of shared resources, such as people and animals that might be affected by corporate use of land, water, and air.

Ethical behavior and value-maximizing behavior are not equivalent. While the commonly cited aphorism, "good ethics is good business," is usually true, it is not always true. Good ethics does *not* always "pay" either for the individuals or organizations involved; and definitely does not always "pay" in the short-run. Ethical individuals sometimes must take actions that are not in their own self-interest or their organization's owners' best interest because of some legitimate interests of other stakeholders. They are accountable to these non-ownership stakeholders as well, and no group, not even owners, automatically has priority over the other stakeholders. Indeed, it is the struggles between being selfish and doing "what is right" that provides the most interesting and important ethical issues that we must consider.

It would be comforting to think that people will be rewarded for doing what is right, at least in the long run. But that does not always happen. Many employees who do what is right sometimes earn lower bonuses, are passed over for promotions, or are fired. It is for this reason that laws (such as, say, the whistleblower protection provisions in the Sarbanes-Oxley Act) are created to protect the rights of employees who expose fraud in their organization. Conversely, employees who act unethically sometimes benefit from their unethical actions because they are not caught, a probability which is sometimes quite low.

The potential for personal sacrifice while acting ethically is reflected in many codes of professional conduct. The preamble of the Code of Professional Conduct of the American Institute of Certified Public Accountants (AICPA) states, "The Principles call for an unswerving commitment to honorable behavior, even at the sacrifice of personal advantage."[3] But when are the ethical principles so important that one must consider other than self-interest or one's organization's best interest? That is a core ethical question.

This chapter provides an introduction to the complex subject of ethics. It discusses the importance of good ethical analyses and describes some models of ethical behavior that can be used to analyze ethical issues related to MCSs. The chapter concludes with some suggestions for encouraging ethical behavior in organizations.

THE IMPORTANCE OF GOOD ETHICAL ANALYSES

Unethical behaviors are costly to individuals, organizations, markets, and societies. They create needs for extra laws and standards from governments and regulatory agencies, and extra rules, reviews, or supervision within organizations. These extra enforcement mechanisms are incomplete, imperfect, and expensive, and have the typical drawbacks of rigid action controls. Good ethics is the glue that holds organizations and societies together. It causes people not to be "unreservedly opportunistic [but to] constrain their own behavior out of an ethical sensibility or conscience."[4]

Lapses in ethics are often precursors of more serious problems, such as fraud. For example, "aggressive" financial reporting, which many interpret as less than ethical but maybe not quite illegal, often appears to be one step on a "slippery slope" that eventually culminates into costly, fraudulent activities. Indeed, many of the worst corporate failures had aggressive accounting practices in common in the years leading up to their eventual ruin.[5] And even if aggressive accounting practices do not lead to ruin, they can be costly. For example, in August 2009, GE paid $50 million to settle federal charges that it committed accounting fraud over a two-year period. The alleged violations included the company's accounting for certain loans and sales of trains and aircraft parts, which presumably enabled GE to boost earnings by hundreds of millions of dollars. "GE bent the accounting rules beyond the breaking point," said Robert Khuzami, director of the SEC's Division of Enforcement, adding that the "overly aggressive accounting distorted [the] company's true financial condition and mislead investors." GE said it had corrected its financial statements and spent $200 million in legal and accounting expenses to fix the problems raised by the SEC.[6] All told, and as Warren Buffett, chairman of Berkshire Hathaway, puts it:

> Once a company moves earnings from one period to another, operating shortfalls that occur thereafter require it to engage in further accounting maneuvers that must be even more "heroic." These can turn fudging into fraud.[7]

To control unethical behaviors within an organization, managers need perceptive ethical reasoning skills. Just as they need good skills in their technical disciplines in order to make good business judgments, managers need moral expertise to make good ethical judgments. Senior managers should serve as *moral exemplars*, or role models, within their organizations. They should also design their MCSs to promote moral points of view and ethical behaviors. A number of highly specific controls, including some policies and procedures and elements of measurement and reward systems, stem from ethical analyses. But these need to be supplemented with some other controls that help ensure ethical behaviors in areas where totally precise organizational prescriptions are impossible, including training sessions, codes of conduct, and credos that help employees identify, appreciate, and assess ethical issues.

Managers who are ignorant about ethics can make any of a number of mistakes that can lead to high probabilities of unethical behaviors within their organizations. First, they sometimes fail to recognize ethical issues when they arise. One common problem is that managers sometimes equate ethical and legal issues; they conclude that if an action is not illegal, it must be ethical. This is clearly not true. While many laws do indeed prohibit immoral practices, it is impossible to write laws to prohibit all unethical behaviors. Lying is usually considered immoral; however, laws prohibiting lying would be hard and inefficient to enforce.[8] As a consequence, lying is against the law only in the most important circumstances, such as perjury. On the other hand, many would argue that some laws themselves, such as those allowing abortion or those causing huge payments to be made to victims of relatively minor accidents, are not morally defensible.

Second, ethical issues often are addressed with amateurish rules, such as "always tell the truth," "do no harm" or "do unto others as you would have them do unto you." Such simple, conscience-based rules only work when the values of the person invoking the rule are shared by the others who are or might be affected. As a consequence, they rarely provide guidance for ethical behaviors in specific (management control) situations because people's values often vary widely.

Ethical models

The first challenge in adapting ethical thinking to managerial settings is in recognizing the existence of the ethical issues that do or might exist. The ethics literature includes numerous normative models of behavior. Almost all of these models recognize that, in a social context, ethics is about how actions affect the interests of other people. Every ethical issue involves multiple parties, some of whom benefit while others are harmed, slighted, or put at risk by a particular action. The characterizations of harm, slight, or risk are made in terms of one or more ethical principles, rules or values that are embedded in the various normative models of behavior. The following sections describe briefly four commonly cited ethical models – utilitarianism, rights and duties, justice/fairness, and virtues.[9] Each model has merits, but none is perfect; each also has its limitations.

Utilitarianism

Using the *utilitarianism* (or *consequentialism*) model, the rightness of actions is judged on the basis of their consequences.[10] Utilitarian-type thinking has been adopted by many businesses because of its tradition in economics, and it has been embedded in many public policy decision procedures, such as welfare economics and cost–benefit analyses. In this model, an action is morally right if it maximizes the total of good in the world; that is, if it produces at least as much *net good* (benefits less costs and harms) as any other action that could have been considered. Sometimes this objective is phrased as "the greatest good for the greatest number of people." Utilitarianism does not mean that the right action is the one that produces the most good for the person performing the act, but rather the one that produces the most good for all parties affected by the action.

Utilitarian models are not without their limitations, however. Quantifying *net good* is difficult because the benefits of some actions or decisions, such as job satisfaction, freedom from stress, or a risky possibility of additional profits sometime in the future, are difficult to measure, aggregate, and compare across individuals. Further, using utilitarian-type reasoning makes it easy to sacrifice the welfare of a few individuals for the benefit of others. For example, in a famous case from the 1970s, Ford Motor Company's management decided not to do a safety retrofit of the company's Pinto subcompact car to prevent the gas tank from rupturing in rear-end collisions. They used the logic that the expensive retrofit of 11 million Pintos would save only a maximum of 180 deaths, so it would not be cost effective from a societal point of view. Nonetheless, some people did die in horrible accidents.[11]

Rights and duties

The rights and duties model maintains that every individual has certain moral entitlements in virtue of their being human. Commonly cited basic rights in most modern societies include the rights to dignity, respect and freedom. Some societies also accept that people should have welfare rights, such as the right to be educated, to have access to health care and good housing. Regardless of what is on the list, every right that an individual has creates a duty for someone else to provide, or at least not to interfere. So if an individual is said to have a right to privacy, then others have a duty not to interfere with that person's privacy. If top management has a right to be given informative performance reports from lower-level managers, then those lower-level managers have the duty to provide those reports. In other words, rights and duties need to be *mutually* observed by those participating in the group to which those rights and duties apply.

Like all the other models, rights and duties models have their limitations. It is sometimes difficult to get agreement as to what rights different individuals or groups of individuals should have. Rights can proliferate. They can also conflict. Do smokers have the right to smoke, or do others have the right to be free of secondhand smoke? Does top management really have a right to receive totally informative performance reports, or should lower-level managers have the right to retain some of their private information to themselves in order to, for example, protect themselves from some risk, up to some limit?

Justice/fairness

The justice or fairness model maintains that people should be treated the same except when they are different in relevant ways. Most societies conclude that *processes*, not necessarily outcomes, should be fair. Most people are not concerned when the richest person in a country wins a lottery when the process was fair. Having a fair process, such as in evaluating employee performance, depends on such things as impartiality and consistency.

But people differ in many ways, and determining which of these differences should be considered relevant is a core issue that must be dealt with in applying the justice/fairness model. Employees may not be concerned when their compensation packages differ when it arises from differences in the nature of the job. It is seen as fair for people with jobs that are more difficult, more stressful or riskier to be paid commensurately. But some may not deem it is fair for people who have greater needs, such as a single parent, to be paid more than others performing like jobs by virtue of being a single parent. They feel such hardship needs should be taken care of elsewhere, such as through government support programs.

Another limitation of the justice/fairness model is that it is easy to ignore effects on both aggregate social welfare and specific individuals. Perceived justice for one group may harm another group. For example, when pharmaceutical companies are ordered to pay large damages to plaintiffs who allegedly suffered physical ills even in cases where there is little direct evidence of the drugs causing those ills, could one submit that justice has been done for the plaintiffs but not for the companies?

Virtues

A final commonly used model of moral behavior is rooted in *virtues*. Prominent examples of virtues are integrity, loyalty, and courage. Individuals with *integrity* have the intent to do what is ethically right without regard to self-interest. Integrity has many components, including honesty, fairness, and conscientiousness. *Loyalty* is faithfulness to one's allegiances. People have many loyalties, to other persons, organizations, religions, professions, and even "causes." When loyalties conflict, their relative strength dictates how the conflict is resolved. *Courage* is the strength to stand firm in the face of difficulty or pressure.[12]

Virtues are often reflected in both professional and corporate codes of conduct. For example, the Statement of Ethical Professional Practice from the Institute of Management Accountants is organized into four areas of virtue: competence, confidentiality, integrity, and credibility.[13] The Financial Executives International's Code of Ethics also uses virtue concepts as it requires members to conduct their business and personal affairs with honesty and integrity.[14] Similarly, the document describing the Code of Conduct for Google Inc., the large search-engine, cloud computing, and internet-based products and services company, starts by describing the company's informal corporate motto – "Don't be evil." It then goes on to describe a number of corporate principles or values. In the area relating to "Serving Our Users," Google employees are asked to have their actions guided by the following principles: *usefulness* (of products, features, and services), *integrity*, *responsiveness* (to users), and *taking action*.[15] Parts of many corporate codes of conduct define how individuals ought to behave; in other words, in terms of duties. Virtue theory does not deal directly with duties, although often duties can be derived quite logically from virtues.

Virtues provide their own *intrinsic rewards*. Virtuous individuals appreciate, and hence pursue, these rewards. But not all employees in organizations should be taken as virtuous *prima facie*, which is why other forms of controls are necessary. As such, publicized sets of virtues can be a valuable part of an organizational control system. However, action controls, such as policies and procedures, cannot always be made both specific and complete. This limitation is reflected in Google's Code of Conduct:

> It's impossible to spell out every possible ethical scenario we might face. Instead, we rely on one another's good judgment to uphold a high standard of integrity for ourselves and our company. We expect all Googlers to be guided by both the letter and the spirit of this Code. Sometimes, identifying the right thing to do isn't an easy call. If you aren't sure, don't be afraid to ask questions of your manager, Legal or Ethics & Compliance.[16]

Virtues fill in the gaps and provide guidance as to what is the right thing to do. They are an element of personnel or cultural control.

Virtue-based approaches, however, also have limitations. One problem is that the list of potential virtues is long. For example, in addition to those mentioned in the codes mentioned above, one might consider character, generosity, grace, decency, commitment, frugality, independence, professionalism, idealism, compassion, responsibility, kindness, respectfulness, and moderation. Critics of the virtue model argue that it is not obvious which set of virtues should be applied in any given setting. In addition, some characteristics considered virtues can actually impede ethical behavior. Courage, for example, is sometimes essential to commit fraud, and respect for elders (superiors) might actually stop someone from exposing a fraud. It is also difficult to know whether particular virtues exist in any individuals, how to develop virtues in individuals and groups of individuals, and how to recognize when day-to-day pressures are eroding the virtues.

Analyzing ethical issues

Good ethical behavior needs to be guided by more than opinions, intuitions, or gut feeling. Where the ethics of an action is in question, individuals should structure their situational analysis by using a proper reasoning or decision model. Various models exist, but most involve the following steps:

1. **Clarify the facts**. What is known, or what needs to be known, to help define the problem? The facts should identify what, who, where, when, and how.

2. **Define the ethical issue**. What about the situation causes an ethical issue to be raised? This logic should be phrased using the terms of one or more of the ethical models. What *stakeholders* are harmed or put at risk? Are there conflicts over *rights*? Is someone being treated *unfairly*? Is someone acting dishonestly (lacking *integrity*)?

3. **Specify the alternatives**. List the alternative courses of action, including those that represent some form of compromise.

4. **Compare values and alternatives**. See if there is a clear decision. If one course of action is so compelling, then the analysis can be concluded.

5. **Assess the consequences**. Identify short- and long-term, positive and negative consequences for the major alternatives. This step will often reveal unanticipated results as, for example, short-term benefits will be shown to be dwarfed by long-run costs.

6. **Make a decision**. Balance the consequences against the primary ethical principles or values and select the alternative that best fits.

It is important to recognize that different people can consider identical situations and reach different conclusions even after structuring their decision processes equally carefully and thoroughly. This can occur because they prioritize the various ethical principles differently. None of the ethical models is perfect and complete, and the models sometimes lead to different conclusions. That insight is important by itself. Managers need to be open to different approaches because different people will be viewing and judging their actions through different lenses.

WHY DO PEOPLE BEHAVE UNETHICALLY?

People behave unethically for several reasons. There are some people who unscrupulously act as *bad apples*. They are essentially dishonest. For them, the burden of good ethics is greater than what they are willing to bear. Others are merely *morally disengaged* or ignorant. They might not recognize an ethical issue when they face one, so their conscience does not stop them from behaving unethically. Yet others who recognize ethical issues develop *rationalizations* to justify their possibly unethical behaviors. These rationalizations include such "justifications" as "if we don't manage earnings this quarter, we'll have to lay off some valued employees;" "aggressive financial reporting may not be totally honest, but everyone does it – we're only shooting ourselves in the foot if we don't;" "I shouldn't be taking office supplies home for the kids, but some of my colleagues are doing much worse things than I do, and it isn't really hurting anybody;" "we're uncomfortable about the aggressive estimates of our tax liabilities, but we decided as a team that this was all right;" and "my boss knows about it – she said we'll be ok." Some of these rationalizations stem from a poor corporate culture. Unethical behaviors are contagious.

Finally, some people who know they are doing something wrong are not able to stop because they *lack moral courage*. Moral courage is the strength to do the right thing despite fear of the consequences. It is well known that those who insist on acting ethically can suffer any of many negative consequences, including shame, ostracism, and even dismissal. People with poorly formed ethical beliefs and/or little moral courage may easily "capitulate." Those who wish to build up their moral courage should clarify their core values, those they are willing to uphold regardless of the consequences. Those who recognize that they do not have the needed moral courage should choose their work environments carefully. They should choose environments in which it is unlikely they will be pressured into decisions that require good ethical judgment. They may not be suitable for the financial controller-type jobs we discussed in Chapter 14, as indeed one commentator noted that for these jobs around the globe:

> [I don't] know of a senior financial professional who is not under pressure from others around their organization. The difference may be that in the West they face pressure from the executives to show bigger returns for stock markets, whereas in the East they may be under pressure from a powerful majority shareholder to pinch profits from minority shareholders. But they are always between a rock and a hard place. The rock and the hard place are just different parties."[17]

SOME COMMON MANAGEMENT CONTROL-RELATED ETHICAL ISSUES

Many ethical issues arise in the context of MCSs. Some even use ethical arguments to question the basic foundations of management "control" and, all the same, "capitalist systems" that "coerce" management into make decisions on "economic" grounds (only). They argue that "value" is put before "values" and that corporate restructurings and downsizings, say, are unethical because they put "profits" before "welfare." Others counter, however, that the restructurings are necessary responses to changes in the environment. While they may cause pain to displaced employees, they help ensure that the restructured businesses remain competitive and, thus, able to gainfully employ their remaining employees. They call this "creative destruction" – that is, a painful yet necessary condition for innovation and progress. Such political economy-related ethics debates are, however, beyond the scope of this book. Instead, the following sections identify and briefly discuss four narrower, but common and important, MCS-related ethical issues: (1) creating budget slack; (2) managing earnings; (3) responding to flawed control indicators; and (4) using controls that are "too good." These issues are important, and the analyses required to deal with them are representative of those that could be used to analyze similar issues that might arise.

The ethics of creating budget slack

Many performance targets, particularly those used at managerial organization levels, are negotiated between the budgeters and their higher-ups. Negotiation processes provide opportunities for those proposing their budget – the budgeters – to "game" the process; that is, to distort their positions in order to be given more easily achievable targets against which they subsequently will be evaluated and on the basis of which they typically stand to earn performance-contingent rewards (as we discussed in Chapters 8 and 9).[18] This distortion is often colloquially referred to as *sandbagging* or *creating slack*. As we discussed in Chapter 5, building slack into budgets is quite common. But is it ethical?

When employees create slack, they are exploiting their position of superior knowledge about their entity prospects. They are failing to disclose to their superiors all of their available information and informed insights and are, as such, presenting a distorted picture of their entity's business. Therefore, creating budget slack can be deemed in violation of several of the obligations listed in the Statement of Ethical Professional Practice from the Association for Accountants and Financial Professionals in Business.[19] For example, the credibility standard requires management accountants to "communicate information fairly and objectively."

Analysis from the tenets of utilitarianism also suggests that slack creation constitutes an ethical issue. Typically, employees creating budget slack will benefit personally from it. Slack protects employees against unfavorable occurrences such as an increase in costs, thus mitigating the probability that performance targets would be missed and performance-contingent rewards left unearned. If the reward-performance function is continuous (i.e. not capped), slack will also increase the size of the rewards that will be earned. Whereas the budgetee benefits, the slack creation can be costly to some stakeholders, especially the firm and its owners. Budgets containing slack are often less than optimally motivating. When achievement of the target is assured, employee effort may be waning. Moreover, the budgetees may not want to exceed their target by too much because that might cause them to be given a higher, more difficult target for the following period. They may not work as hard; they may make unnecessary expenditures to consume the excess; or they may be motivated to play games to "save" the profit not needed in the current year. Slack creation also can be deemed less than correct from the standpoint of the users of the budget submissions – higher-level management – as they will rely on the information in the budget to make investment, resource allocation, and performance evaluation decisions that will become distorted.

On the other hand, some arguments can be raised to support the position that slack creation is ethical, or at least can be seen as justifiable. Many managers argue that creating slack is a rational response within a results control system. They do not view slack as a distortion but as a means of protecting themselves from the downside risks of an uncertain future. Viewed this way, slack serves a function identical to that of the accepted management accounting practices of variance analysis and flexible budgeting, both of which are used to eliminate the effects on the performance measures of some uncontrollable factors, and in so doing shield managers from the risk these factors create. This protection from risk is particularly valuable in firms that treat the budget forecasts as "hard promises" from the budgetee to the corporation with little or no tolerance for missed targets or "under-performance" with possible dismissal as a consequence when it occurs. In the same way, some managers argue that budget slack is sometimes necessary to address the imbalance of power that is inherent in a hierarchical organization. It helps protect budgetees from evaluation unfairness that may arise from imperfect performance measures or evaluation misuse by superiors.

Finally, managers who defend the creation of slack also often point out that it is an accepted practice in their organization's budget negotiating process. Managers at all levels of the organization negotiate for slack in their budgets, and everyone is aware of the behavioral norm. Indeed, they point out, many senior managers were promoted into their positions precisely because they were good at negotiating for slack and, hence, for achieving their budget targets consistently over time. In many organizations, superiors may actually (implicitly) encourage their subordinates to create slack because they also benefit from it. The superiors' targets are usually consolidations of the targets of their subordinates, so they enjoy the same reduction in risk and increase in the expected values of their rewards as the slack creators. When creation of slack is widespread and the practice is encouraged, can we say that the organizational culture is encouraging unethical behavior, or does it indicate that in this community, at least, creation of slack is an acceptable behavioral norm?

Combined, then, in making judgments as to whether slack creation is ethical in any specific setting, many factors must be considered, including the following:

- How good the performance measures are (the extent to which they reflect "true" performance and are unaffected by factors the managers cannot control).
- Whether budget targets are treated as a rigid promise from managers to the corporation.
- Whether the manager's intent in creating the slack primarily reflects self-interest.
- Whether (or how much) superiors are aware of the slack.
- Whether the superiors encourage the creation of slack.
- Whether the amount of slack is "material."
- Whether the individual(s) involved are bound by one or more of the sets of standards of professional conduct. (Most accountants are, whereas most managers are not.)

The ethics of managing earnings

A second ethical issue involves the data manipulation problem discussed in Chapter 5. A common form of manipulation is *earnings management*, which includes any action that changes reported earnings (or any other income statement or balance sheet item) while providing no real economic advantage to the organization and, sometimes, actually causing harm. Generally, earnings management actions are designed either to *boost* earnings, such as to achieve a budget target or increase stock price, or to *smooth* earnings patterns to give the impression of higher earnings predictability and, hence, lower risk. Some actions might also be designed to *reduce* earnings, such as to "save" profits for a future period when they might be needed or to lower stock price to facilitate a management buyout or to coincide with a stock option grant.[20]

Earnings management can be deemed unethical for several reasons. First, most of the actions are not apparent to either external or internal users of financial statements or the reported information more generically. Thus, those engaging in earnings management may be deriving personal advantage through deception. Second, professional managers and accountants can be said to have a duty to disclose fairly presented information. Indeed, most professional associations state so in their codes of ethics. Specifically, the Statement of Ethical Professional Practice referenced above requires to "disclose all relevant information that could reasonably be expected to influence an intended user's understanding of the reports, analyses or recommendations."[21] Hence, the distortions can be interpreted as not being consistent with a professional's obligation to report and disclose information credibly. Third, the rewards earned from managing earnings are not fair when the reported performance is only cosmetic, not real.

Managers may have several justifications for managing earnings, however. They might be using their private information about company prospects to smooth out some meaningless, short-term perturbations in the earnings measures to provide more, rather than less, informative performance signals to financial statement users. As with slack creation, they might argue to be taking these actions merely to protect themselves from rigid, unfair performance evaluations. They might also be taking actions that make it unnecessary for them to take other possibly more damaging actions, such as laying off employees or suspending research and development expenditures.[22]

Curiously, most people judge *accounting methods* of managing earnings more harshly than *operating methods* even though the purposes of the two earnings management methods are identical, and the economic effects of the operating methods are typically far more costly to the firm.[23] (As discussed in Chapter 5, *accounting methods* of managing earnings involve the selection of accounting methods and the flexibility in applying those methods to affect reported earnings. *Operating methods* involve the altering of actual operating decisions, such as the timing of sales or discretionary expenditures.) Clearer standards for judging accounting performance (i.e. accounting standards) could explain this finding. As such, employees may be less likely to engage in earnings management (or other questionable behaviors) when they believe it violates *established rules*, which accounting standards are, suggesting that people use clarity of laws, rules, standards, or procedures as a basis for reaching an ethical conclusion.

Several situational factors are likely to influence judgments as to whether earnings management actions are deemed (un)ethical, including (1) the direction of the manipulation (boost, shrink or merely smooth earnings); (2) the size of the effect (materiality); (3) the timing (quarter- vs. year-end, random timing vs. immediately preceding a bond offering or stock option grant); (4) the method used (adjust reserves, defer discretionary expenditures, change accounting policies); (5) the managers' intent regarding the informativeness of the numbers (and disclosures); (6) the clarity of the rules prohibiting the action; and (7) the degree of repetition (one-time use vs. ongoing use even after a warning).

Making judgments about earnings management is complex, although in so doing it is probably judicious to err on the side of caution rather than rationalization. Speaking out against what he deemed unrelenting earnings management practices, Arthur Levitt, former chairman of the Securities and Exchange Commission (SEC), called these practices so serious that "we need to embrace nothing less than a cultural change."[24] The incidence and size of various corporate scandals and failures, including in major financial institutions such as Bear Stearns and Lehman Brothers, in only the first decade of the twenty-first century seem to have proven him right.[25]

The ethics of responding to flawed control indicators

Results targets and action prescriptions provide signals to employees as to what the organization considers important, be it profits, growth, quality, or any other desired performances. When the targets and prescriptions are not defined properly, they can actually motivate behaviors that employees know are not in the organization's best interest. The employees earn rewards for doing what they are asked to do, but the organization suffers. Indeed, many fraud cases involve employees taking unethical and illegal actions that they perceive to be "necessary" for their company to thrive or survive, sometimes under pressure from higher-ups,[26] but that they are ashamed or embarrassed about to tell their relatives.

We discussed one common flawed-response example in detail in Chapter 11 – that of *myopia*. It occurs when companies place a high emphasis on the achievement of short-term profit targets, even though some profit-increasing activities (such as reducing investments in training, maintenance, or R&D) may diminish shareholder value in the long run. Relevant to the discussion here, the managers who engage in the myopic behaviors often know that they are causing long-term harm to their entity and their company, yet perhaps under pressure, they decide to do it anyway.

What should employees do if they know the results measures or action prescriptions are flawed? Should they act to generate the results for which they will be rewarded, or should they sacrifice their own self-interest in favor of what they believe to be "truly" best for the organization? When they face this conflict of interest, most employees will choose to follow the rules of the reward system, perhaps while lobbying to get the measures changed. This behavioral norm might not be ethical. Financial professionals have standards of ethical conduct (duties) that require them to further their organization's "legitimate interests." For example, the Financial Executives International's Code of Ethics requires to "Act in good faith, responsibly, with due care, competence and diligence, without misrepresenting material facts or allowing one's independent judgment to be subordinated."[27] Managers not bound by those professional standards perhaps should be bound by a sense of loyalty (a virtue) to their organization.

The ethics of using control indicators that are "too good"

Another ethical issue relates to the use of control indicators that are "too good." Highly, perhaps excessively, tight control indicators have been made possible by advances in technology. For example, computer surveillance programs that allow companies to monitor their employees' personal computer screens, data use, and internet traffic are widespread today. Supervisors can listen in on employees' sales calls; cameras can record all the actions some employees take; computers can count the number of keystrokes by data entry clerks and telephone operators to gauge productivity; and location devices can track an employee's whereabouts throughout the work day.

What is the ethical issue? The number of correct keystrokes and reports of employees' locations-by-time may be good results measures in certain situations. They may describe what the organizations want from their employees, and they can be measured accurately and on a timely basis. That said, there is a fine line between the employer's right to monitor and the employees' rights to autonomy, privacy, or freedom from oppressive controls that suggest they are working in *electronic sweatshops*. Thus, questions relevant to determinations of whether use of such measures is ethical probably include:

- Is the use of the measures disclosed to employees?
- Are safeguards in place to protect the collected data?
- Are safeguards in place to ensure that the data are used for their intended purposes only (e.g. for quality monitoring of customer calls; for monitoring employees in training, not experienced employees)?
- When supervisors use these tight controls, do they emphasize quality rather than just quantity ("grab everything")?

But some companies also make the news with allegations of subjecting their employees to conditions that presumably resemble an era of *physical sweatshops*. For example, when 11 employees committed suicide in a short period in early 2010, the Taipei-based company Foxconn "was introduced to much of the world in the worst terms imaginable – as an *industrial monster* that treats workers like machines [. . .] to make products like the iPhone at seemingly impossible prices." For the image-conscious businesses that Foxconn supplies, including IBM, Cisco, Microsoft, Nokia, Sony, HP, and Apple, the suicides were a public-relations nightmare and a challenge to the "off-shoring strategies" that were essential to their bottom lines.[28] But whether Foxconn's controls were "too tight" is actually difficult to judge. "[Foxconn] pays workers on time and for overtime according to the regulations, and that's why workers always queue to work there," said Geoffrey Crothall, spokesman for Hong Kong-based China Labor Bulletin, a worker-rights organization, adding that "despite [. . .] the intense nature of the work, it's still better than a small workshop with no guarantee you'll get paid."[29] An anonymous former employee said: "The factories themselves are top notch although they are fairly intense working environments. Westerners would find it very difficult to work there."[30]

Clearly what is acceptable to some is not acceptable to others, and, as the last quote suggests, views may differ across (national) cultures (which we discuss in Chapter 16). What is clear, however, is that when controls are "too good" or "too tight" – or "oppressive" as some would argue – they are likely to induce unintended and/or undesirable consequences, such as by triggering job-related tension and even stress-related health complaints. This may be especially true for action controls, as indeed at Foxconn it was said that "obviously work is tiring and there's pressure; there are lots of rules here."[31] But results controls can also be "too tight" in that they induce myopia and pressures for earnings management, as we discussed above and elsewhere in this book.

SPREADING GOOD ETHICS WITHIN AN ORGANIZATION

Ethical progress within an organization typically proceeds in stages. In an early stage, when the organization is small, the organization becomes an extension of the founder or the top management group. The founder acts as a role model, setting the ethical tone, and is usually able to monitor employees' compliance with that tone.

In a later stage of development, organizations predominantly use action accountability-type controls. Part of these are standards, rules, and regulations embodying desired behaviors. Organizations communicate these standards either through corporate policies and procedures manuals, corporate codes of conduct, or less formal sets of memoranda. The rules clarify the meaning of good ethics, make it clear that ethical behavior is valued, and provide guidance to employees to think through ethical issues. The rules may need updating from time to time, even though the underlying principles of good ethical conduct may remain largely the same. For example, at Google, the document that lays out the company's "Ten Things" of their corporate philosophy states at the bottom: "We first wrote these '10 things' several years ago. From time to time we revisit this list to see if it still holds true. We hope it does – and you can hold us to that."[32]

After the rules are communicated, the organization takes steps to ensure that its employees follow the rules. Oftentimes companies ask their employees to sign a statement certifying that they understand and will abide by the rules. At Boeing, the large aircraft manufacturer, employees are asked to certify annually that they will adhere to the company's Code of Conduct, which outlines the ethical business conduct required of employees in the performance of their company responsibilities. The company website explains that "Individuals certify that they will not engage in conduct or activity that may raise questions as to the company's honesty, impartiality or reputation or otherwise cause embarrassment to the company."[33]

However, even the best laid out codes of ethics and signed employee certification statements may not be sufficient. Consider the following excerpt from the Statement of Vision and Values Principles of a large publicly traded corporation:

> Because we take our responsibilities to our fellow citizens seriously, we act decisively to ensure that all those with whom we do business understand our policies and standards. Providing clearly written guidelines reinforces our principles and business ethics. [Our] employees at all levels are expected to be active proponents of our principles and are trained to report without retribution anything they observe or discover that indicates our standards are not being met.
>
> Compliance with the law and ethical standards are conditions of employment, and violations will result in disciplinary action, which may include termination. New employees are asked to sign a statement indicating that they have read, understand and will comply with this statement, and employees are periodically asked to reaffirm their commitment to these principles.

Which company, do you reckon, espoused these principles and required signed statements certifying understanding and compliance with the principles? Enron, a corporation now held up as the epitome of corporate evil![34]

It is obvious that merely having a set of ethical standards and rules and taking steps to ensure that employees have read them is not sufficient. Top management must set a credible "tone at the top," and they must endeavor to maintain a good internal MCS so that potential violators know that there is a good chance that they will be caught. Monitoring should be done by both employees' superiors, colleagues (mutual control), and internal auditors. Violators of the rules should be sanctioned. These sanctions help give employees the courage to resist counter pressures. Companies also often appoint a designated ombudsperson to help employees facing ethical issues.

Tone at the top can be an effective form of cultural control when it is consistent, and supervision and mutual monitoring can be effective when given teeth in an otherwise trusting organizational climate. Under effective corporate cultures, ethical behaviors are "shaped" rather than merely "enforced" from time to time, often after a major violation has occurred and damage has been done.

CONCLUSION

This chapter has provided a brief introduction to the topic of ethics as it relates to the design and use of MCSs. To create the right ethical environment, management must have moral expertise and know where and how to provide it.

The sampling of issues discussed in this chapter should have made it obvious that many important ethical issues are not black or white. One cannot conclude unequivocally that, for example, creating budget slack is always unethical or that controls are "too good" or "not tight enough." The "greyness" of the judgments, however, makes it all the more important for managers to subject the various ethical issues to a formal analysis. That said, many situational factors must be considered in making ethical judgments. For example, judgments of what is ethically acceptable vary across national cultures, suggesting that multinational companies wishing to achieve similar levels of ethicalness across entities located in different countries should probably rely on different ethical models or implement different controls. We discuss this further in Chapter 16.

Employees face many pressures and temptations that can cause them to act unethically. They can easily bow to performance deadlines and crises, reward temptations, pressures for conformity, and even counterproductive orders from their bosses. Unless managers act to deflect these pressures and temptations on a fairly consistent basis, their company's ethical climate will be weakened. Managers must help guide the behaviors of their employees who are incapable of thinking through ethical issues (distinguishing right from wrong) themselves. They must understand how and why individuals will reach different ethical conclusions, and, importantly, they must take a stance as to how they want employees in their organization to behave.

Every organization has an ethical climate of some sort; either good, bad, or mixed. It is important for managers to build a good ethical climate, one that respects the rights, duties, and interests of stakeholders inside and outside the firm. An organization that fosters unethical behaviors from its employees, even those that benefit the company in the short run, will probably eventually find itself the victim of its own policies. Such organizations are more likely to attract people who feel comfortable bending the rules; they may even entice sincere people to bend the rules. Bad cultures are contagious. Yet, weakened or poor ethical climates can lead to unethical behaviors that can damage or destroy individual and organizational reputations. Once ethical climates are weakened and reputations are damaged, they can be quite difficult to rebuild.

Notes

1. See, for example, H. Mintzberg, *Developing Managers, Not MBAs* (Harlow, UK: Financial Times/Prentice Hall, 2005).

2. See, for example, "Shareholders vs. Stakeholders: A New Idolatry," *The Economist* (April 24, 2010), pp. 65–6.

3. *AICPA Code of Professional Conduct* (American Institute of Certified Public Accountants, June 1, 2010), online (www.aicpa.org/Research/Standards/CodeofConduct).

4. E. Noreen, "The Economics of Ethics: A New Perspective on Agency Theory," *Accounting, Organizations and Society*, 13, no. 4 (1988), pp. 359–69.

5. See, for example, "Findings on Lehman Take Even Experts by Surprise," *The New York Times* (March 12, 2010), online (www.nytimes.com).

6. "GE to Pay $50 Million to Settle SEC Fraud Charges," *The Washington Post* (August 5, 2009), online (www.washingtonpost.com).

7. See, for example, "Why Honesty is the Best Policy," *The Economist* (March 9, 2002), p. 9.

8. See, for example, "How to Tell When Your Boss is Lying," *The Economist* (August 19, 2010), p. 52.

9. For an overview and more detailed treatment of some of these ethical models, see J. Gaa and R. Ruland (eds.), *Ethical Issues in Accounting* (Sarasota, FL: American Accounting Association, 1997); see also J. Driver, *Ethics: The Fundamentals* (Wiley-Blackwell, 2006).

10. See also, J. Driver, *Consequentialism* (New York: Routledge, 2011).

11. See, for example, D. Birch and J. Fielder, *The Ford Pinto Case: A Study in Applied Ethics, Business, and Society* (Albany, NY: State University of New York Press, 1994).

12. See also J. Gaa and R. Ruland, "Ethics in Accounting: An Overview of Issues, Concepts and Principles," in J. Gaa and R. Ruland (eds.), *Ethical Issue in Accounting* (Sarasota, FL: American Accounting Association, 1997).

13. The Statement of Ethical Professional Practice from the IMA, now called The Association for Accountants and Financial Professionals in Business, is available at www.imanet.org/PDFs/Statement of Ethics_web.pdf.

14. The Financial Executives International (FEI) Code of Ethics can be found at www.financialexecutives.org/about/FEICodeofEthics.pdf.

15. See Google, Inc. website: http://investor.google.com/corporate/code-of-conduct.html (April 8, 2009).

16. Ibid.

17. *Global Perspectives on Governance: Lessons from East and West* (Chartered Institute of Management Accountants, 2010), online (www.cimaglobal.com), op. cit., p. 8.

18. See also M. Jensen, "Corporate Budgeting is Broken: Let's Fix it," *Harvard Business Review* (November 2001), pp. 94–101; and M. Jensen, "Why Pay People to Lie?," *The Wall Street Journal* (January 8, 2001), p. A32.

19. See note 13.

20. For a more extensive discussion of earnings management practices, see C. Mulford and E. Comiskey, *The Financial Numbers Game: Detecting Creative Accounting Practices* (Chichester, UK: John Wiley & Sons, 2002).

21. See note 13.

22. See, for example, J. Graham, C. Harvey, and S. Rajgopal, "Value Destruction and Financial Reporting Decisions," *Financial Analysts Journal*, 62, no. 6 (November 2006), pp. 27–39.

23. K. Merchant and J. Rockness, "The Ethics of Managing Earnings: An Empirical Investigation," *Journal of Accounting and Public Policy*, 13, no. 1 (Spring 1994), pp. 79–94. For another study of how ethical judgments of earnings management vary across different user groups (shareholders vs. non-shareholders), see S. Kaplan, "Further Evidence on the Ethics of Managing Earnings: An Examination of the Ethically Related Judgments of Shareholders and Non-Shareholders," *Journal of Accounting and Public Policy*, 20, no. 1 (Spring 2001), pp. 27–44.

24. A. Levitt, *The Numbers Game*, Speech at New York University Center for Law and Business (September 28, 1998).

25. See, for example, "Findings on Lehman Take Even Experts by Surprise," op. cit.

26. See, for example, "WorldCom Official Tried to Quash Employee's Accounting Concerns," *The Wall Street Journal* (August 27, 2002), p. B6.

27. See note 14.

28. "Everything is Made by Foxconn in Future Evoked by Gou's Empire," *Business Week* (September 9, 2010), online (www.bloomberg.com).

29. Ibid.

30. "Foxconn Suicides: 'Workers Feel Quite Lonely'," *BBC* (May 28, 2010), online (www.bbc.co.uk).

31. Ibid.

32. See Google, Inc. website: www.google.com/intl/en/corporate/tenthings.html (September 2009).

33. See Boeing website at www.boeing.com/companyoffices/aboutus/ethics/hotline.html. See also Boeing's "Policies & Procedures" at www.boeing.com/companyoffices/aboutus/ethics/epolicy.htm, such as that regarding Ethical Business Conduct (January 26, 2009).

34. Enron's Code of Ethics (July 2000), online (no longer available).

Case Study

Two Budget Targets

In the three years since he had been appointed manager of the Mobile Communications Division (MCD) of Advanced Technologies Corporation (ATC), Joe supervised the preparation of two sets of annual budget numbers. When ATC's bottom-up budgeting process began, Joe instructed his subordinates to set aggressive performance targets because he believed such targets would push everyone to perform at their best.

Then, before Joe presented his budget to his superiors, he added some *management judgment.* He made the forecasts of the future more pessimistic, and he added some allowances for *performance contingencies* to create what he called the *easy plan.* Sometimes the corporate managers questioned some of Joe's forecasts and asked him to raise his sales and profit targets somewhat. However, MCD operated in a rapidly growing, uncertain market that Joe understood better than his superiors, and

Joe was a skillful and forceful negotiator. In each of the past three years the end result was that the targets in the official budget for MCD were highly achievable. MCD's performance had exceeded the targets in the easy plan by an average of 40%, and Joe earned large bonuses. Joe did not show his superiors the targets his subordinates were working toward, but some of Joe's direct reports were aware of the existence of the easy plan.

In his subjective evaluations of his subordinates' performances for the purposes of assigning bonuses and merit raises Joe compared actual performance with the aggressive targets. In the last three years only approximately 25% of the aggressive targets had been achieved. Joe did not fire any of his managers for failing to achieve their targets, but he reserved the vast majority of the discretionary rewards for the managers who had achieved their targets.

This case was prepared by Professor Kenneth A. Merchant.

Copyright © by Kenneth A. Merchant.

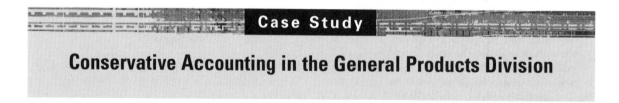

Case Study

Conservative Accounting in the General Products Division

The year 1991 was a good one for the General Products Division (GPD) of Altman Industries, Inc., a large industrial products manufacturer. Sales and profits in the division were significantly above plan due largely to unexpectedly brisk sales of a new product introduced at the end of last year. The good fortune started Robert Standish, the GPD general

manager, thinking about how he could save some of this year's profits for periods in which he might need them more. He believed that GPD's plan for next year would be tough to achieve because the corporation as a whole was not doing well, and corporate managers would expect GPD to show growth even above this year's abnormally high sales and

This case was prepared by Professor Kenneth A. Merchant.

Copyright © by Kenneth A. Merchant.

profit levels. And already in September he was sure that his division's profit would exceed the level above which no additional bonuses were awarded for higher performance – 120% of plan – and he wanted to save some of this year's profits so that he could report them in a year in which they would augment his bonus and those of his direct reports.

Robert asked his staff to do what they could before the end of the year to *stash some acorns* that he could use in future years. He suggested to Joanne, his controller, that she start preparing the pessimistic scenarios that could be used to justify additional reserves and start thinking about how expenses could be accelerated and revenues deferred at yearend.

Joanne was uncomfortable. She reminded Robert that among the company accounting policies was a statement that assets and reserves should be fairly reported based on the existing facts and circumstances and not be used to manage income. Furthermore, because of continuing order declines, the company was looking for ways to report higher, not lower, profits in the current year and that if the situation did not turn around quickly layoffs were threatened.

But Robert explained that GPD would still be reporting very high profits; he just wanted to save a portion of the excess above plan. And in any case, GPD couldn't help the corporation much because it was so small in comparison with the entire corporation.

Case Study

Education Food Services at Central Maine State University

Pam Worth, Manager of Education Food Services at Central Maine State University (CMSU), is meeting with a researcher to explain some apparent discrepancies in last year's budgeted figures and the actuals. The researcher, a faculty member at another university, is doing field studies in the food service business. Pam is explaining why she always tries to hide some slack in her numbers when she prepares her budget. She says that it is her understanding that she is just doing what others in her company and in her industry do. She agreed to speak to the researcher only with guarantees of strict confidentiality.

> I like to have a moderate cushion in my budget. The stakes are high. If I make my budget my performance review will be good, almost regardless of whatever else I do during the period, and I will earn my 20% bonus. If I miss my budget without valid reasons I may not be allowed to keep my job.

More than that, however, the cushion in the budget allows me to do a better job. I don't have to worry that my staff is working at peak efficiency all the time, so I don't have to supervise every action. That is better for the staff, also; they hate it when I'm looking over their shoulders. The cushion also allows me to buy things that I can use to provide the university with better service. For example, this year I was able to buy several portable bars that we have used already for some parties.

Pam, an accounting graduate of Northern University, is an employee of Contract Food Services Corporation (CFSC), a large corporation that provides food on a contract basis to universities, hospitals, and businesses. Pam runs a profit center that provides services only to one university – CMSU. Her operation provides food at two major, on-campus cafeterias serving 12,000 students and nearly 2,000 faculty and staff. Pam also has responsibility for ▶

This case was prepared by Professor Kenneth A. Merchant.

the vending machine business on campus, and her employees sometimes provide catering services for on-campus business meetings. Pam's operation employs 59 regular employees and between 150 and 180 students on a part-time basis. Annual revenues are slightly in excess of $3 million.

Relations between CFSC and CMSU are governed by a contract that is renegotiated each January for the following academic year. The contract defines the responsibilities of each party. For example, CMSU administrators are given the power to review and approve CFSC's service plans and prices. The university provides all equipment costing over $100. CFSC sets the menus and hires the employees.

The contract also defines limits on the profits CFSC can earn from the CMSU operation. CFSC earns 100% of the profits from the food operation up to a limit of 10% profit on sales. Beyond that limit, profits are split equally with CMSU. The contract is set this way as an incentive to CFSC managers to provide extra quality and services after they have ensured themselves a reasonable profit.

Budgets are prepared on a bottom-up basis. In July corporate headquarters personnel send planning guidelines and assumptions (e.g. employee benefits, inflation) to all operating units. The operating managers forecast their customer counts, which determines their food requirements, and then estimate their operating costs for the 18-month period starting in January. Since the university owns the buildings and equipment the bulk of CFSC's costs are for food and labor.

After the units' budgets are prepared a series of budget *challenge* rounds are held to review the numbers at successively higher CFSC consolidation levels – district, region, division, group, and corporate. If the numbers meet the managers' profit expectations the budgets are accepted. Typically, however, each of the managers in the hierarchy is asked to raise his or her profit targets. These requests lead to a series of meetings designed to explore whether revenue projections should be raised or cost projections cut. The size of these profit increase requests are not predictable, but in recent years they have ranged from zero to 15%.

Pam explains that she routinely hides some cushion in both labor and food costs:

I can build the budget cushion in a lot of places. This year for example:

- I kept the proportion of meals served on board contracts (which are more lucrative for us) equivalent to last year's level even though I know that proportion will be growing because the trend is to have more students living on campus.

- I planned for a number of labor hours at $7.15 when I knew that I would hire students for those hours, and students don't earn that much.

- I planned no efficiency improvements when I know we almost always improve our efficiency. There is a learning curve in this business. My superiors know about this learning curve too – they ran operations just like this – but they don't object to my having a cushion. It is to their advantage to have me meet my budget too.

These types of things add up. I put just enough in so that I am sure I will be able to meet my budget targets even after corporate management squeezes some of my cushion out in their reviews.

I know more about what is happening at CMSU than anyone else. My bosses can't come here and check every assumption that I have in the plan. They don't have the time. My immediate boss, for example, is responsible for nine units spread over a fairly large geographic area.

You can easily identify new managers – they submit budgets that are realistic. Experienced managers build in pads for themselves. It's a bit devious, sure, but it's not theft. It's just playing with projections. The money's there. Besides, if you don't build a cushion for yourself you're not going to survive for long in this business.

The "Sales Acceleration Program"

In early October, Priscilla Musso, general manager of the Specialty Products Division (SPD) of Consolidated Furniture Corporation (CFC), was studying the division's third quarter financial reports. Sales were running significantly below plan, and it became quite clear to Priscilla that SPD would need strong performance in the last quarter of the year in order to reach its annual profit target. Meeting budget was very important to Priscilla and her management team because they were included in CFC's lucrative executive bonus program, and they would lose all of their bonus opportunities if SPD did not achieve the profit targets.

To brainstorm for ideas, Priscilla called her management team together. At first the managers on the team expressed only discouragement. Everybody had been working hard, but the market was softening, and competitors were being very aggressive.

Then, after some delay with nobody else suggesting any options, Jonathan Robbins, SPD's manager of sales and marketing, suggested that the division could implement a new sales program to pull some sales that might ordinarily be made next year into the current year. Any customers who accepted delivery in the fourth quarter would not have to pay their invoice for six months. (Normally payments in the industry were to be made within 30 days.)

Priscilla's first reaction was favorable; this program might, indeed, achieve the desired result. But she asked the members of her team for their reactions.

Shirley Covey, manager of human resources noted that if this program was successful, it would probably cause SPD's employees to have to work overtime at the end of the year, and that was something they traditionally did not want during the holiday season. But Priscilla reminded Shirley that the employees would be paid time-and-a-half for all the overtime hours that they worked.

Priscilla asked Bill Bennett, SPD's controller, if this program would violate any accounting rules. Bill said there would be no problem recording the sales as long as the items were shipped and billed before December 31. The accounting would be consistent with GAAP. But Bill cautioned that this program was probably only providing a short-term, cosmetic profit improvement. While it might well make the current year look better, it would probably cause significantly lower sales to be recorded in the first quarter of next year. So next year the division would start in a deep hole. They would be scrambling all year to trying to dig themselves out of that hole, with no guarantees that they could pull it off. It was just postponing the problem. In addition, Bill reminded the team that this program would be very expensive. On top of the overtime expense that would have to be incurred in the production areas, the program would greatly increase SPD's accounts receivable. CFC was currently paying about 12% on its lines of credit, so this increase in working capital would be quite expensive for the corporation.

But Priscilla cut Bill short. She reminded him that CFC did not allocate interest expenses to SPD, so she was not particularly concerned about the corporation's increased borrowing costs. She was more worried with her superiors' negative reactions if she did not make this year's profit plan than she was about their reactions to her allowing the receivables' balance to increase in the early part of the year. And while she acknowledged that they might be creating a problem for next year, she suggested it would be best to worry about that problem when, and if, it became real.

With no other options on the table to solve the current year's budget problem, the SPD managers decided, unanimously, to implement what they called the "Sales Acceleration Program."

This case was prepared by Professor Kenneth A. Merchant.

Case Study

The Expiring Software License

On September 30, Jianxin (Jimmy) Wu, manager of the Information Systems Department for Southwest Industries (SWI), was in panic mode. SWI was a medium-size manufacturer of portable shelters, tents, and awnings. Jimmy was panicking because the company's Citrix software had just died. Because of his oversight, an invoice had not been paid, and the SWI's license to use the software had expired.

Jimmy knew that something had to be done very quickly. Many of the company's information systems users, who were situated at three different locations, relied heavily on the Citrix software. All of SWI's applications ran under Citrix. The Citrix software gave all employees access to the SWI applications they needed no matter where they were, as long as they had access to the Internet. The Citrix license renewal would cost $3,600, but going through the purchasing department to get a requisition issued would take several days. The users could not be without the Citrix capability for that long.

Then Jimmy thought about using his purchasing card. The card, which worked like a credit card, was intended for small purchases, not including travel, hotels, or food. SWI issued the card to some of its key personnel to avoid the costs of processing the paperwork required for many small, incidental purchases. The company only had to make one single payment to the credit card company, and the credit card company did all the processing.

The maximums placed on Jimmy's card were $2,000 for any single purchase, and $5,000 per month. Jimmy knew that these limits were strictly enforced. Personnel in the accounting department scanned the bills monthly looking for violations. But Jimmy thought that he could get Citrix to split the bill in two, and then the accounting department personnel would not raise any objections.

With no other apparent options at hand, Jimmy decided to try to use his card to renew the license. The Citrix salesman agreed to charge the card in two transactions of $1,800 each. The license was renewed quickly, and few of SWI's Citrix users were ever aware that there had been a problem.

This case was prepared by Professors Kenneth A. Merchant and Leslie R. Porter.

Case Study

Lernout & Hauspie Speech Products

This case is a tragic blow not just for Belgium but also for all of Europe. It shows how badly we need much greater transparency and a sense of corporate governance. For too long, banks and businesses did not feel they should be held accountable to shareholders. That has to change.[1]

Philippe De Buck, Executive Director, Belgium Federation of Industries

Mr. De Buck was referring to the demise of Lernout & Hauspie Speech Products (L&H), which had been considered a world leader in speech-recognition technology and one of Belgium's most promising hi-tech companies. The company declared bankruptcy in October 2001 after the discovery of a massive accounting fraud that implicated many L&H managers, including the top management team. Like many others, Mr. De Buck wondered how this could have happened and what might be done to avoid other scandals like this in the future.

THE COMPANY

The entrepreneurs

L&H was founded in 1987 when Jo Lernout, then a sales executive with the Belgian arm of Wang Laboratories, Inc., grew intrigued by an early Wang voice-mail system. The system was not selling well because many Europeans still had rotary phones and could not use them to select amongst the voice-mail choices. Mr. Lernout's idea was to create software that allowed users to make voice-mail selections by speaking into the phone. He set up a company to commercialize speech technology. Pol Hauspie,

who owned a small firm that made accounting software, joined him. Belgium seemed a good location from which to operate the company because the country was home to many software engineers fluent in multiple languages. The two partners based their company in Ieper, Belgium.

To finance the business, Mr. Hauspie sold his software firm and Mr. Lernout sold his house. Mr. Lernout, an ebullient chain-smoker with ruddy cheeks and a mop of sandy-blond hair, recalled in an interview that convincing his wife "was the hardest road show I've had."[2] The company barely survived several early financial crises. At one point, it couldn't make the payroll and bailiffs came to seize property, Mr. Lernout recalled. But he seemed to thrive on crisis. One of his favorite sayings is, "The grass is always greener on the other edge of the precipice."[3]

Starting any new company is difficult, but two factors helped L&H survive in its early years. The first was Belgium's national pride. Like much of Europe, Belgium envied America's great hi-tech engine of wealth. And now here were two guys with ambitions to turn a rural corner of Flanders into a Silicon Valley of language technology. In L&H's early years, Flanders, Belgium's Dutch-speaking region, formed a tax-exempt zone in Ieper – which gradually became known as the "Flanders Language Valley" – and showered L&H with research grants. The Flanders regional government became a major L&H investor through a venture capital arm. During one of L&H's cash crunches, it guaranteed 75% of a bank loan to the company. "Without that,"

---

[1] William Drozdiak, "Lost in the Translation; Voice-Recognition Firm's Failure Holds Painful Lesson for Europeans," *The Washington Post* (December 17, 2000).

[2] Mark Maremont, Jesse Eisinger, and John Carreyrou, "Muffled Voice: How High-Tech Dream at Lernout & Hauspie Crumbled in Scandal," *The Wall Street Journal* (December 7, 2000), p. A1.

[3] Ibid.

This case was prepared by Professors Kenneth A. Merchant, Wim A. Van der Stede, and research assistant Xiaoling (Clara) Chen. The case was revised with the help of Professor Martine Cools.

Mr. Lernout says, "we would have gone broke."[4] Stefaan Top, a Belgian venture capitalist, says the combination of ambitious entrepreneurs and a government that sorely wanted "a local tech champion was a combustible mix – it was dangerous."[5]

The second was a series of complex financing plans dreamed up by Mr. Hauspie. The taciturn former tax accountant set up an intricate holding-company structure that let the founders retain control while selling various minority interests. Devising such structures is "Pol's forte," Mr. Lernout says. "He's very creative. Legally it's all right, and it helps you survive."[6]

In late 1995, the company went public with a listing on the Nasdaq Stock Exchange, even though it had never been profitable and had just a few million dollars in annual revenue. As with many hi-tech firms, the hope lay in a glittering future. "Natural speech interface is the next technology wave," one securities analyst wrote, "a potential multimillion dollar market."[7] L&H's managers dreamed of creating software that would let computers effortlessly understand human speech, speak back, and translate among the world's tongues.

The company seemed to face many challenges. Technical development was painstakingly slow, as the systems had to cope with many different accents and speech patterns, not to mention the need to sort out homonyms such as "wait" and "weight." And industry demand was sluggish. Many rivals struggled. One, Kurzweil Applied Intelligence, Inc., in Massachusetts, imploded after auditors found that its managers had faked a large proportion of the company's sales. Another Massachusetts rival, Dragon Systems, Inc., eked out only slow growth in the mid-1990s. At L&H, however, sales quadrupled in 1996 to $31 million. Though some small acquisitions produced part of the growth, L&H seemed to be relying on sales to customers with which it had financial ties.

Over the years, many of L&H's customers received investments from Flanders Language Valley Fund (FLV Fund), a venture-capital pool that Mr. Lernout and Mr. Hauspie helped create the year L&H went public. Mr. Lernout and Mr. Hauspie were directors

of the fund's management arm until 1997, and even afterward they maintained considerable sway over its affairs. Michael Faherty, a former L&H salesman in the US, says he and others were encouraged to refer potential customers who were cash-poor to the FLV Fund. "If FLV invests $1 million in the customer," he says, "it was understood that we'd get about $300,000" [in the form of license fees paid by that customer to L&H].[8] Though the FLV Fund denied financial links between L&H and FLV, the close dealings between the two were evident to some informed parties from the start. In 1995, for example, FLV took a 49% stake in the Belgian unit of Quarterdeck Corp., a high-flying California software company. This Belgian unit became L&H's largest customer, accounting for 30% of revenue that year, and Quarterdeck in California accounted for another 6.5% of L&H's sales.[9]

The CEO

In late 1996, Gaston Bastiaens was hired as L&H's president and CEO. Mr. Bastiaens was an engineer who led the failed Newton project at Apple Computer, Inc. But he flourished at L&H. Around the time Mr. Bastiaens joined L&H, the company discovered a new and unusual source of revenue: its own research-and-development needs. This required an intricate accounting maneuver, one that L&H had continued to lean on throughout its tenure as a public company. L&H knew it was trailing competitors in developing software to recognize words spoken at an ordinary clip. "If we didn't catch up, we were cooked," Mr. Lernout recalled in an interview. "But we couldn't catch up, because we didn't have enough R&D dollars."[10]

The solution was to start a company and have it contract with L&H to develop the software. L&H said it gathered outside investors to fund the start-up, called Dictation Consortium, NV. But L&H employees wrote its business plan and did the software work under contract. When the software was finished, L&H had an option to buy the Dictation Consortium at a profit to the investors. The arrangement ensured that L&H could claim to be growing at a rapid pace. Dictation Consortium provided L&H

---

[4] Ibid.
[5] Ibid.
[6] Ibid.
[7] Ibid.

[8] Ibid.
[9] Ibid.
[10] Ibid.

with $26.6 million in revenue in 1996 and 1997, about one-quarter of its 1996 sales and 19% of its 1997 sales. Since Dictation Consortium bore the R&D costs, they didn't burden L&H's bottom line. In 1998, L&H bought Dictation Consortium for $40 million, gaining control of the software it so badly wanted. Since Dictation Consortium had few assets and almost the entire price represented goodwill, it could be amortized over seven years, further shielding L&H's bottom line.

Buoyed by such deals and a spate of fresh acquisitions, L&H's revenue mushroomed to $211.16 million in 1998, more than double 1997's. The stock soared. Mr. Lernout and Mr. Hauspie became entrepreneurial celebrities, Belgium's answer to Microsoft's Bill Gates and Paul Allen.

With the stock price up, Mr. Bastiaens bought technology leaders such as Kurzweil Technologies, Inc., a speech-recognition company in Wellesley Hills, Massachusetts, and Mendez Translation Group of Brussels, Belgium. In 1997, a year after he came on board, Mr. Bastiaens landed an important investor: Bill Gates. Microsoft invested $45 million in L&H, ending up with an 8% stake. The early Microsoft investment gave L&H much needed credibility and revenues. In 1999, Intel invested $30 million in L&H and formed a venture with it to develop e-commerce and telecommunications products.

Though all seemed well from the outside, internally there were continuing glitches with L&H's technology. A 1998 presentation Mr. Lernout gave to French executives in Paris turned into a debacle when the software failed to recognize many words, an L&H insider recalled. "The bottom line was that the technology wasn't ready and the market wasn't ready," this person says, "but management had to deliver every quarter."[11] Under Mr. Bastiaens, it did. L&H kept reporting growth. Its sales rose 63% in 1999 to $344 million. Its Asian sales exploded to more than $150 million from less than $10 million in 1998. In March 1998, its stock hit $72.50, up 2,500% from its initial offering price four and a half years earlier.[12]

However, financial analysts had been suspicious of L&H's financial results as far back as 1997. In February 1997, Lehman Brothers' Brian Skiba issued a report, claiming that L&H's growth in the US and Europe was much lower than investors had assumed, and that the company was not coming clean. Mr. Bastiaens denied it, but in a conference call, he refused to give a geographic breakdown of sales.[13]

Still, investors ignored financial analysts' warnings and applauded the year-2000 acquisitions of Dictaphone, based in Stratford, Connecticut, and Dragon Systems, of Newton, Massachusetts. The future did, indeed, look bright. L&H seemed to have a lock on some of the best speech-recognition software, and the company was powerfully positioned as the Web migrated into phones and cars, where people would talk to machines and machines would talk back. At the time, Mr. Bastiaens assured anybody who would listen, "This market is going to explode."[14] With the purchase of the company's two main US rivals, L&H was suddenly a software company with $1 billion in annual sales, and it was poised to follow SAP and Nokia Corp. into Europe's technology elite.

The Dictaphone purchase, however, meant more than half of L&H's business was in the US. This obliged the company to file detailed accounts with the SEC. Analysts learned that sales in Korea had soared from a mere $97,000 in 1998 to $58.9 million in the first quarter of 2000, some 52% of the total sales of the company. Suspecting an attempt to pump up results, investors began to dump the stock in 2000.[15]

THE WALL STREET JOURNAL REPORT

In August 2000, *The Wall Street Journal* reported that some Korean companies L&H described as customers denied doing business with it, while some others said they had bought less than L&H said they had:

> In all, the *Journal* contacted 18 of about 30 companies claimed by L&H as customers. Three of the companies said they weren't, in fact, L&H customers . . . Three more companies said their purchases from L&H over the past three quarters were smaller than figures provided by Mr. Bastiaens or Sam Cho, vice president of L&H Korea. One additional company said it is in a joint business with L&H that produces

11 Ibid.
12 Ibid.
13 Ibid.
14 William Echikson and Ihlwan Moon, "How to Spook Investors," *Business Week* (September 18, 2000), pp. 69–72.
15 Ibid.

considerably less revenue than L&H claims. Officials from an eighth company initially said it had formed a joint venture with L&H and that the joint venture, not the company itself, had purchased products from L&H . . .

Of the other 10 companies, three confirmed they were customers but wouldn't give the size or timing of their purchases. Officials at another six confirmed total purchases totaling $450,000 to $5.5 million in the period since [September 1999]. One company says it signed a $10 million contract with L&H and paid in May 2000.

All told, of the 12 companies that responded to inquiries about their purchases from L&H in the period since [September 1999], the revenue tallied roughly $32 million. From all of its customers in Korea, in 1999 and the first quarter of 2000, L&H posted $121.8 million of Korea sales, and it had said that it expected second-quarter revenue from that country to exceed the first quarter's $58.9 million.[16]

L&H responded with a statement saying that comments attributed to L&H customers were "misquoted or factually incorrect" and that other information in the article was "distorted."[17] To buttress its case, L&H commissioned a mid-year audit by KPMG.

After the Korea scandal broke, Mr. Bastiaens rushed to restore confidence. He contacted several of the Korean customers interviewed for the *Journal* story, and they publicly said they were misquoted. A trip to Korea was arranged for two financial analysts, both of whom were impressed with the company's business there. "I met customers and saw L&H products really being used," says Kurt Janssens of KBC Securities in Brussels.[18] Most important, Mr. Bastiaens asked for the KPMG special audit. "He wouldn't be so stupid as to ask for an audit if he had something to hide," says Pierre-Paul Verelst, an analyst at Brussels brokers Vermeulen Raemdonck.[19]

By this time, founders Lernout and Hauspie thought Mr. Bastiaens had become a liability. On August 25, 2000, he was replaced with John Duerden, a British-born US citizen who had worked at Xerox Corp. and Reebok International, Ltd., before running Dictaphone.[20] In November 2000, L&H admitted for the first time that "mistakes and irregularities" had slipped into the annual accounts. Mr. Hauspie resigned as an officer, and in March 2001, Mr. Lernout was dismissed. In November 2000, L&H filed for bankruptcy protection.[21]

DISCOVERY OF A MASSIVE FRAUD

In January 2001, Philippe Bodson replaced Mr. Duerden as L&H's chief executive, and PricewaterhouseCoopers (PwC) was brought in for an investigation. The PwC report was released on April 6, 2001. It revealed that 70% of the nearly $160 million in sales booked by L&H's Korean unit between September 1999 and June 2000 were fictitious. In an effort to earn rich bonuses tied to sales targets, the Korean unit's managers developed highly sophisticated schemes to fool L&H's regular auditor, KPMG International. One especially egregious method involved funneling bank loans through third parties to make it look as though customers had paid when in fact they had not.

L&H's new chief executive, Philippe Bodson, said that upon learning of PwC's findings he "was very impressed by the level of sophistication" of the fraud and "the amount of imagination that went into it."[22]

To fool auditors, L&H Korea used two types of schemes. The first involved factoring unpaid receivables to banks to obtain cash up front. Side letters that were concealed from KPMG gave the banks the right to take the money back if they couldn't collect from L&H Korea's customers. Hence, the factoring agreements amounted to little more than loans.

The second, more creative scheme was set in motion after auditors questioned why L&H Korea wasn't collecting more of its overdue bills from customers. L&H Korea told many customers to transfer their contracts to third parties. The third parties then took out bank loans, for which L&H Korea provided collateral, and then "paid" the overdue bills to L&H Korea using the borrowed money. The upshot is that L&H Korea was paying itself. When the contracts were later cancelled, L&H Korea paid

---

[16] Mark Maremont, Jesse Eisinger, and Meeyoung Song, "Tech Firm's Korean Growth Raises Eyebrows," *The Wall Street Journal* (August 8, 2000), p. C1.

[17] Mark Maremont, "Lernout & Hauspie Shares Fall 19% as it Attacks Article," *The Wall Street Journal* (August 9, 2000), p. A16.

[18] William Echikson and Ihlwan Moon, "How to Spook Investors," *Business Week* (September 18, 2000), pp. 69–72.

[19] Ibid.

[20] Ibid.

[21] "Dossier Lernout en Hauspie," *De Standaard* (January 2011), online at www.standaard.be.

[22] John Carreyrou, "Lernout Unit Book Fictitious Sales, Says Probe," *The Wall Street Journal* (April 9, 2001), p. B2.

"penalties" to the customers and the third parties to compensate them "for the inconvenience of dealing with the auditors."[23]

The probe also found that the bulk of L&H Korea's sales came from contracts signed at the end of quarters, so managers could meet ambitious quarterly sales targets and receive large bonuses. For instance, 90% of the revenue recorded by L&H Korea in the second quarter of 2000 was booked in 30 deals signed in the final nine days of the quarter. But L&H Korea was forced to subsequently cancel 21 of those contracts because the customers – most of them tiny start-ups – didn't have the means to pay.

The fraud appears to have begun in earnest when L&H bought a small Korean firm called Bumil Information & Communication Co. in September 1999 and put Bumil's management, headed by Joo Chul Seo, in charge of L&H Korea. L&H Korea, which had been reporting negligible sales until then, recorded nearly $160 million in license revenue between the time Bumil was acquired and June 30, 2000. Mr. Seo made $25 million from the sale of Bumil to L&H and earned another $25 million in bonuses for meeting sales targets while at the head of L&H Korea.[24]

WHERE WERE THE AUDITORS?

In the aftermath of the accounting scandal at L&H, angry investors turned their gaze on KPMG International, the giant accounting firm that audited L&H's books and gave the company clean opinions in 1998 and 1999. KPMG also gave a clean 1999 opinion regarding the accounting for L&H's South Korean operations, where sales had grown improbably to $62.8 million from just $245,000 in the previous year. Michael G. Lange, a partner at a Boston law firm that was leading one of the shareholder lawsuits seeking class-action status against L&H, said that the accounting irregularities at L&H "were so pervasive and included so many aspects of the business" that "there had to be red flags" that KPMG auditors missed.[25]

KPMG, in its defense, accused the former top management of L&H of signing off on revenue over-inflation tactics, of lying about key business structures within the company, of influencing others to give false information to KPMG auditors and of orchestrating a campaign to minimize their involvement in the events that had led to the calamitous downfall of the company. In April 2001, a few hours before the release of an abridged version of PwC's report, KPMG filed a lawsuit against L&H's former management in a Belgian court. The complaint alleged that former senior L&H executives "deliberately" provided "false or incomplete information" to KPMG and conspired to obstruct the firm's audits.[26]

In its complaint, KPMG said that L&H's former top management "was fully aware and actively involved in the irregularities and that these people have wittingly given false information to KPMG."[27] KPMG alleged that Mr. Hauspie was implicated in a scheme to illegally raise money for a fund he participated in. The scheme involved a complex web of Korean banks, L&H subsidiaries, and Joo Chul Seo, the company's former head of Korean operations. KPMG also alleged that the company co-founder Jo Lernout, at the very least, participated in the campaign to conceal information from its auditors.

In addition, KPMG commented that the practice of inflating revenues was a common one at L&H. "Afterwards [referring to a period in 1999] it appeared that the antedating of contracts to increase the turnover of the relevant quarter was common practice," said the KPMG report.[28] "The company, on a regular basis, increased its turnover of a particular year or quarter by means of various kinds of irregularities."[29]

THE AFTERMATH

In April 2001, Mr. Lernout and Mr. Hauspie were arrested in Belgium and placed under custody for nine weeks on charges of forgery and market manipulation. The arrests came after a new round

---

23 Ibid.
24 Ibid. According to the PwC report, investigators have been unable to track down Mr. Seo since L&H fired him in November 2000. Mr. Bodson said Mr. Seo was last spotted in China.
25 Mary Maremont, "KPMG, Former Auditor of L&H, May Draw Investor Ire," *The Wall Street Journal* (January 18, 2001).
26 Robert Conlin, "KPMG: Lernout & Hauspie Top Management Lied," *www.CRMDaily.com* (May 11, 2001).
27 Ibid.
28 Ibid.
29 Ibid.

of audit uncovered an additional $96 million in fictitious sales, which brought the tally of fake sales from early 1998 to mid-2000 to $373 million, or 45% of reported revenue.[30]

L&H was declared bankrupt in October 2001 after the commercial court in Belgium rejected the company's request for bankruptcy protection. US-based Scansoft purchased the speech technology and kept some L&H personnel in employ, but the name L&H was axed.

KPMG and its Belgian affiliate settled a lawsuit for $115 million brought against it by shareholders. KPMG stated that they settled to avoid a protracted legal trial, and maintained that they had acted appropriately in their audit of L&H at all times.[31]

The court hearings started in May 2007 against Mr. Lernout, Mr. Hauspie, and 19 others, including former senior corporate and subsidiary managers. In September 2010, a Belgian court found the company's co-founders, Mr. Hauspie and Mr. Lernout, as well as former CEO Bastiaens and another senior

manager, guilty on various charges relating to financial fraud, including falsification of annual accounts, forgery, and market manipulation. Mr. Hauspie, Mr. Lernout, and the senior manager were all sentenced to five years in prison, of which three years effective and two years probationary. Mr. Bastiaens was sentenced to two years effective imprisonment. Under Belgian prison terms, however, they were unlikely to have to clock any jail time.[32]

While KPMG was cleared, its partner responsible for the accounting supervision at L&H was fined €2,478.93. The court declared that the professional fault held against him was not intentional, but he was found guilty of negligence.[33]

These charges, however, covered the criminal liability of those involved in the company's fraud only. The question of compensation was to be tackled in pending civil proceedings, which were slated to start by the end of 2011.[34]

---

[30] John Carreyrou, "Lernout & Hauspie Figures Are Arrested," *The Wall Street Journal* (April 30, 2001).

[31] Mark Maremont, "KPMG to Settle Suit over Audit of Lernout," *The Wall Street Journal* (October 8, 2004).

[32] Charles Forelle, "Lernout Founders Guilty of Fraud," *The Wall Street Journal* (September 2, 2010), p. B.1.; Mark Eeckhaut, "L&H-Toplui Wellicht Nooit Naar de Cel," *De Standaard* (September 22, 2010); www.deminor.com (September 23, 2010).

[33] www.deminor.com (September 23, 2010).

[34] Ibid.

Exhibit 1 Appendix to the August 8, 2000 *The Wall Street Journal* report

A Kick from Korea

Lernout & Hauspie's sales by region or country for the three months ended March 31, 2000 ($000). The company's South Korean business soared after an acquisition in September 1999.

	1999	2000
Europe (excluding Belgium)	22,435	19,748
US	20,154	19,939
Belgium	14,739	9,178
Singapore	10,430	501
Other Far East	2,853	2,396
South Korea	97	58,932

Source: *The Wall Street Journal* (August 8, 2000), p. C1.

Exhibit 2 10 steps to Chapter 11

A Lernout & Hauspie Chronology

June 30, 2000	L&H reveals that nearly all of its overall growth in recent quarters came from South Korea and Singaporean business.
Aug. 8, 2000	*The Wall Street Journal* reports that some Korean customers claimed by Lernout & Hauspie do no business with the company. Others said their purchases were smaller than L&H reported.
Aug. 25, 2000	CEO Gaston Bastiaens steps down; former Dictaphone CEO John Duerden steps in. The company's stock falls 9% to $31.
Sept. 20, 2000	The SEC launches a formal investigation of L&H's accounting practices.
Sept. 22, 2000	*The Wall Street Journal* reveals that 25% of L&H's 1999 revenue came from start-up companies that it helped create.
Sept. 25, 2000	Europe's Easdaq launches a formal investigation into L&H.
Sept. 27, 2000	L&H issues a profit warning for the third quarter.
Nov. 9, 2000	L&H says it will revise financial statements for 1998, 1999, and the first half of 2000 to make up for past accounting "errors and irregularities;" cochairmen Jo Lernout and Pol Hauspie resign their executive posts; trading of L&H stock is suspended.
Nov. 16, 2000	The company's accounting firm KPMG International withdraws its audits of 1998 and 1999 results.
Nov. 29, 2000	L&H files for Chapter 11 bankruptcy protection along with its Dictaphone unit, after $100 million is discovered missing in the firm's South Korean unit.

Source: *The Wall Street Journal* (November 30, 2000), p. A3.

Exhibit 3 Accounting for auditing problems: recent large settlements paid by auditors

Auditor	Company audited	Year	Allegations	Settlement amount ($ millions)
Ernst & Young	Cendant	1999	Inflated revenue, understated expenses	$335
Ernst & Young	Informix	1999	Inflated revenue	$34
Arthur Anderson	Waste Management	1998	Overstated assets and other accounting problems	$75
Coopers & Lybrand*	Centennial Technologies	1998	Bogus sales	$20

* Now part of PwC.
Source: The Wall Street Journal (January 18, 2001), p. C1.

Section VI

SITUATIONAL INFLUENCES ON MANAGEMENT CONTROL SYSTEMS

Chapter 16

THE EFFECTS OF ENVIRONMENTAL UNCERTAINTY, ORGANIZATIONAL STRATEGY, AND MULTINATIONALITY ON MANAGEMENT CONTROL SYSTEMS

A basic premise that pervades this book is that there is no universally best management control system (MCS) that applies to all situations in any organization, much less all organizations. Managers involved in designing, implementing and using MCSs must consider a large number of *situational factors* that, individually and collectively, affect either the costs or the effectiveness of the various management controls. Figure 16.1 depicts the general contingency framework within which MCS design should be considered. This figure shows that the effects of the various elements and characteristics of MCSs on the various MCS outcomes are contingent upon any of a number of situational factors.

Because the range of organizational settings is large, many relevant situational factors exist. Examples of factors that affect one or more MCS choices include differences in aspects of national culture; differences in the structure, stability, size, growth, competition, and regulation of the industry or market; differences in aspects of the ownership, size, strategy, and culture of the organization; differences in production or service process complexity, technology, interdependence, or routineness; and differences in management and employee experience, skills, and training. Although this list is inevitably incomplete, failure to consider even one of these situational factors can make the difference between an excellent and a suboptimal MCS choice.[1]

Determining the relevant aspects of the situational context and their effects on MCS elements is difficult because (1) many of the situational factors are related (e.g. technological change can affect production process complexity, and organization size can affect organizational culture); and (2) many of the factors interact with each other to produce MCS-related effects (e.g. technological change might not have the same impact on the MCSs in large and small organizations).[2]

Research has only begun to sort out the many complex MCS-related relationships. But even if all of the effects of each of these, and other, factors on MCS elements and

FIGURE 16.1 A general MCS contingency framework

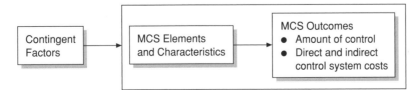

Source: K. A. Merchant, *Modern Management Control Systems: Text and Cases* (Upper Saddle River, NJ: Prentice Hall, 1998), p. 728.

MCS-related outcomes were well understood, space constraints would not permit their detailed discussion in a general-purpose book. A few of these factors that have not been discussed in prior chapters but that are important in a broad range of settings merit highlighting. That is the purpose of this chapter. It focuses on the effects of three important situational factors: (1) environmental uncertainty; (2) organizational strategy; and (3) multinationality.

ENVIRONMENTAL UNCERTAINTY

Environmental uncertainty refers to the broad set of factors that, individually and collectively, make it difficult or impossible to predict the future in a given area. Uncertainty can stem from changes (or potential changes) in natural conditions (e.g. weather), the political and economic climate, or the actions of competitors, customers, suppliers (including labor), and regulators. Uncertainty is higher where the pace of technological change is higher. Uncertainty is also generally higher the farther one tries to look into the future. Thus, uncertainty is higher in organizations where the natural business cycle – the lag between investment and the payoff from that investment – is longer.

Uncertainty has some potent effects on MCSs. Uncertainty makes action controls difficult to use. Action controls are effective only if there is knowledge as to which actions are desirable and if those actions are consistently desirable. If managers want to use action controls in uncertain situations, they have to develop knowledge about the desirable actions, which usually implies that they must become personally involved in the activities being controlled. They must use more intensive preaction reviews, get involved in more face-to-face meetings with the employees being controlled, and/or use more direct observation and supervision.

As discussed in the early chapters of this book, when action controls are deemed infeasible or impractical, managers generally tend to place a higher reliance on results controls. Results controls can be used even in highly uncertain settings, as employees can be rewarded for generating more of what is known to be desirable.[3] However, uncertainty makes result controls more difficult to use as well, for a number of reasons.

First, result controls are not effective when employees do not understand how to generate the desired results. Uncertainty often hinders their abilities to know. Second, even when employees know how to respond, result controls will not be optimally effective unless properly challenging performance targets are set. In uncertain situations, it is difficult to calibrate performance targets. It is almost inevitable that fixed targets (i.e. those that do not adjust to changing conditions and are not relative to the performance of peers facing like business conditions) will be too easy or too challenging to meet. Because information asymmetry between superiors and subordinates is likely to be relatively high, subordinates can add slack to their budgets relatively easily. In addition, the targets will include many uncontrollables caused by forecasting errors regarding, for example, the state of the economy, competitors' actions, and sources and prices of supplies. These uncontrollables will adversely affect the reliability of the performance evaluations.

Third, uncertainty combined with the use of results controls causes employees to bear risk, which brings into play all the conditions discussed in Chapter 12. The organization will either have to compensate employees for bearing the risk or take steps to limit the risk. To limit the risk, organizations facing an uncertain environment might choose not to regard managers' budget targets as firm commitments to the organization and, thus, might not interpret unfavorable budget variances as clear indicators of poor performance.

But if they do so, organizations will give up some short-term performance pressure, and with it its motivational effects.[4] Alternatively, if organizations decide to treat budget targets as performance commitments from their managers, they will likely find it desirable to implement systems using contingency (scenario) planning, flexible performance targets or subjective performance evaluations; to use shorter planning and measurement periods; or to increase their reliance on environmental scanning mechanisms and forecasting procedures to reduce the uncertainty (as discussed in Chapter 12).[5]

Fourth, high uncertainty tends to have some broad effects on organization structures and decision-making and communication patterns, and these effects increase the complexity of the management task. Organizations facing relatively high uncertainty will tend to decentralize their operations, have more participative, relatively bottom-up planning and budgeting processes, and make important decisions only after relatively intensive consultations among larger groups of managers.

The broad effects of uncertainty are well illustrated with a production example. In the old mass production system invented by Henry Ford, the production function of the organization was buffered from the environment. Thus the uncertainty faced by managers in that area of the company was, in the short run, effectively zero. This buffering was possible because customer demand was relatively predictable, competition low, and product variety limited (e.g. all Ford T-models were black). Thus, production managers could standardize behaviors and processes and produce in large runs or batches. Tasks were divided into many separate parts; labor was specialized; employees' actions were dictated by rules; decision-making was centralized; and many vertical levels of management were used to provide coordination.

However, most organizations today operate in vastly more uncertain (less programmable) environments, ones that require agility to respond to rapidly changing customer-driven demands. Customer-driven organizational processes also require multi-functional, cross-departmental problem solving and coordination characterized by greater interdependencies across tasks and entities within organizations. Many firms have responded to these challenges by implementing so-called "new" manufacturing processes, including flexible manufacturing systems (FMS), just-in-time production (JIT), total quality management (TQM), and elimination of non-value-added activities. While these new processes are designed to streamline production processes and eliminate buffers (inventories), they have also shifted the control focus. In order to be responsive, line personnel must exercise more control. As a result, firms that use the new manufacturing processes tend to have flat organization structures and use few formal work rules and less hierarchical control. Jobs lose much of their formal definition; duties are continuously redefined; the number of middle managers is reduced; and the workforce is asked to be adaptive. There is less top-down monitoring; more teamwork; more coordination through personal, lateral channels rather than by standard operating procedures; less rewards based on individual performance; and greater use of control through socialization mechanisms. The result is that the production environment is more adaptive as the workforce is encouraged to solve problems and implement solutions. But the MCS must be implemented more loosely, particularly with respect to behavior-constraining action controls, because actions are less programmable.

Uncertainty is not only prevalent in many contemporaneous manufacturing environments; it also is a significant situational factor that affects MCS design in many other organizations, particularly service organizations, such as professional service firms that provide legal, accounting, business consulting, or financial services, where coordination and knowledge integration is critical for effective service delivery. Early research findings in this area indicate that effective controls in such organizations evolve around carefully chosen *combinations* of controls, including extensive planning and budgeting processes (to perform preaction reviews and to ensure coordination), individual and team measures of performance and associated incentives (to ensure individual and team accountability commensurate with decision autonomy), personnel controls (such as selective recruiting and staffing of teams to ensure the presence of the requisite knowledge as well as knowledge sharing), and cultural controls (to provide reinforcements of the core organizational values, such as teamwork, customer focus, and knowledge sharing).[6]

ORGANIZATIONAL STRATEGY

Larger, more complex organizations often specify two levels of strategy: a corporate strategy (often called *diversification strategy*) and a business strategy within each of their so-called strategic business units (often called *competitive strategy*). Strategies at both levels constrain organizations to focus on what they do best and constitute important situational factors for the design of effective MCSs.[7]

Corporate strategy

An organization's corporate strategy determines what businesses it wants to be in and how resources should be allocated among those businesses. One way of viewing corporate strategies is to array them along a continuum from related to unrelated diversification. Firms pursuing *related diversification* do not stray far from their "core business." They diversify in order to exploit *economies of scope* stemming from relationships among their entities (business units). Firms pursuing *unrelated diversification* are not concerned with restricting their focus to their core business. They pursue a portfolio of unrelated businesses to exploit *internal capital market* benefits that stem from internal decision makers' relative information advantages for resource allocations compared to external capital markets. However, to fully realize the benefits of either the related or unrelated forms of diversification, firms must adopt appropriate and effective administrative systems, including MCSs.

An important distinguishing characteristic of firms that are diversified into *related* businesses is high *interdependence* among their business units. Related-diversified firms therefore typically design their MCSs to take advantage of this interdependence to exploit synergies and reap economies of scope. Hence, related-diversified firms often have relatively elaborate planning and budgeting systems; that is, those requiring large amounts of interpersonal communication. These systems force the business unit managers to communicate with each other and make it more likely that the managers can keep their interrelated activities coordinated to exploit synergies. Further, to signal that cooperation among entities is important, related-diversified firms are more likely to use incentive compensation systems that base some portion of business unit managers' bonuses on the performance of the next higher-level entity in the organization, which may be a division, region, business group, or the entire corporation. Related-diversified firms are also likely to spend considerable resources addressing transfer pricing problems, as we discussed in Chapter 7. Transfer pricing problems become particularly acute if some business units supply others and no competitive price is observable from outside markets.

An important distinguishing characteristic of firms that are diversified into *unrelated* businesses is relatively high *information asymmetry* between corporate and business unit management as corporate managers are unable to remain well informed about all the developments in all of their diverse business units' operating areas. Decentralization and heavy reliance on financial results controls are common responses to information asymmetry. Corporate managers can reduce their information processing requirements by pushing the locus of decision making lower in the organization. And they can obtain good management control by relying on financial results controls built around profit and investment center responsibility structures (as discussed in Chapter 7). The financial measures help the corporate managers in comparing diverse businesses.

These choices will, however, cause many performance discussions among corporate and business unit managers to be largely in financial terms. Because they do not have the detailed knowledge about the activities and idiosyncrasies of the business units, the corporate managers will also tend to judge the performances of the diverse business units objectively and award formula bonuses based on what they monitor – financial performance. They will tend to use relatively little subjectivity in their performance evaluations. With such a system, the business unit managers usually have considerable pressure for financial performance, but they also have relatively high autonomy. They tend to participate heavily in the setting of their performance targets, and they have considerable discretion as to how to achieve their financial targets. But if the autonomy is combined with the use of less-than-perfect financial measures, the business unit managers are likely to engage in some dysfunctional behaviors, such as slack creation, thereby undoing some of the benefits of internal capital markets that unrelated diversification strategies purport to generate.

Finally, because business units of unrelated diversified corporations have few operational synergies and are essentially autonomous, corporate performance is a noisy measure that provides relatively little information about any individual business unit manager's actions. Therefore, business unit managers in these firms more commonly receive bonuses that are relatively highly, or even strictly, based on the financial performance of their own units, rather than those based on corporate performance.[8]

Business strategy

Business strategy, also sometimes called *competitive strategy*, defines how a firm or entity within the firm (often called a *strategic business unit*) chooses to compete in its industry and tries to achieve a competitive advantage relative to its competitors. The strategy literature distinguishes two primary competitive strategies: cost leadership and differentiation.[9] A *cost leadership* strategy involves offerings of relatively standardized, undifferentiated products; vigorous pursuit of cost reductions; generation of volume to exploit economies of scale and to move down the learning curve; acquisition of process engineering skills; and, as much as possible, establishment of a routinized task environment. A *differentiation* strategy involves the creation of a product or service that customers perceive as uniquely differentiated from competitors' offerings. Such differentiation can focus on one or more dimensions, including product innovation, product functionality, quality, brand image, customization, or customer service. Regardless of the chosen focus, a likely requirement is intensive coordination and collaboration across a broad array of employees and organizational entities. For example, success in improving customer service is likely to depend on the free flow of information and coordinated efforts among marketing, product design, production and delivery. Such interdependency increases uncertainty, as decision-making processes become more unprogrammable due to the decision context in one functional area being affected by the decisions made in other areas. Another feature of differentiation initiatives is that they often require substantial time to translate into financial results, as it involves prospecting new markets and/or developing new product or services.

An extensive strategy literature discusses the conditions that lead a business to adopt a particular competitive strategy, but these are outside the scope of this book. What is important here is the impact of whatever strategy that has been selected on one more MCS characteristics. So-called *contingency* logic maintains not only that competitive strategy (as well as other *contingency factors*) should drive the design of MCSs, but also, and more importantly, that organizational effectiveness depends on the extent to which both are *aligned*; that is, on the extent to which the MCSs "fit" the competitive strategy.[10]

Competitive strategy, then, should be directly related to the results measures included in a results control system. Businesses endeavoring to be cost leaders, and those defending existing businesses, will tend to control their employees' behaviors through relatively tight, formal financial controls and standardized operating procedures designed to maximize efficiency. For motivating managers in that context, the results measures emphasize cost reductions (process innovation) and budget achievement. Conversely, businesses competing on the basis of differentiation, and those prospecting for new markets, would tend to have a more informal control system, a participative decision-making environment, and incentive systems that include growth, measured either in financial or unit terms, or any of a number of forward-looking, nonfinancial performance indicators, such as product innovation, market development, and/or customer service. Moreover, some of the key dimensions of differentiation strategies, such as those focused on knowledge sharing and cooperativeness, are difficult to quantify, and thus may need to be evaluated subjectively.

In summary, organizational strategies are important to MCS designers because they define what is critical to success. An organization's critical success factors should drive the various MCS design choices. Organizations that align their choice of MCSs with their strategy are more likely to affect better control, and, thus, are more likely to exhibit superior performance.[11]

MULTINATIONALITY

Multinational organizations (MNOs), those that operate in more than one country, must understand how they must adapt their management practices, including management control practices, to make them work in each of their international locations. MNOs have many similarities with large domestic organizations in that they are usually characterized by a high degree of decentralized decision making and by management control through financial results controls. That said, controlling MNOs is often more difficult than is controlling domestic organizations because MNOs face a multidimensional organizational problem: they are organized not only by function and/or product line, but also by geography. The geography dimension requires managers to be sensitive to each of the national (and perhaps even regional) cultures in which they operate. This section provides a discussion of, primarily, three sets of factors that have been shown to affect MCS choices or outcomes across countries: national culture, institutions, and local business environments. We also discuss the additional problem of evaluating the performance of managers whose results are measured in different currencies and currencies that are different from that in the firm's home country.

National culture

Some of the effects, benefits, and costs of management controls are universal because, at a certain basic level, people in all countries have similar physiological needs and desires for achievement and financial security, say. But despite some basic similarities in people around the world, there are also many differences. One important set of factors with potentially important influences on MCSs can be explained under the rubric of *national culture*. National culture has been defined as "the collective programming of the mind that distinguishes the members of one group or society from another."[12] As such, the national culture concept essentially recognizes that people's tastes, norms, values, social attitudes, personal priorities, and responses to interpersonal stimuli vary across nations. By extension, and of particular importance here, it can be argued that people from different national cultures are likely to have different preferences for, and reactions to, management controls because control problems are behavioral problems. When groups of employees perceive things differently, or react to things differently, different control choices may have to be made. Thus, an important factor that contributes to the effectiveness of MCSs is whether the employees perceive them as *culturally appropriate*; that is, whether they suit the shared values maintained by the society in which they operate.

Several taxonomies of national culture have been proposed. The most commonly cited taxonomy consists of the four cultural dimensions identified in a study by Geert Hofstede: individualism, power distance, uncertainty avoidance, and masculinity. The *individualism* (vs. collectivism) dimension of national culture relates to individuals' self-concept; that is, whether individuals see themselves primarily as an individual or as part of a group. Individuals from an individualistic culture tend to place their self-interests ahead of those of the group and prefer interpersonal conflict resolution over conflict suppression. Individuals in a collectivist culture are motivated by group interests and emphasize maintenance of interpersonal harmony. The *power distance* dimension relates to the extent to which members of a society accept that institutional or organizational power is distributed unequally. Individuals who score high in *uncertainty avoidance* feel uncomfortable when the situation they face is ambiguous. The *masculinity* dimension relates to the preference for achievement, assertiveness, and material success (traits labeled masculine), as opposed to an emphasis on relationships, modesty, and the quality of life (traits labeled feminine).[13]

Hofstede showed that people from different countries vary considerably on these cultural dimensions. For example, Hofstede showed that, as compared to the Taiwanese culture, the US culture is much more individualistic and more masculine, while the Taiwanese culture is higher in both power distance and uncertainty avoidance.[14] If that is true, then each of the cultural dimensions can be said to have MCS implications. For example, employees high in individualism are possibly more likely to prefer individual rather than group-oriented work arrangements, performance evaluations, and pay. Similarly, given the high value placed on individualism in the United States, it should perhaps not be surprising to observe that organizations in the United States make relatively high use of individual performance-based incentives as compared to organizations in other countries.[15]

People who are high in power distance are likely to prefer, or at least more likely to accept, greater centralization of decision authority and less participation in decision processes. Thus, when power distance is high, employees may be more willing, say, to accept greater discretionary power or subjectivity exercised by their superiors in performance evaluations and incentive determination. People high in uncertainty avoidance are likely to want to avoid or reduce risk and ambiguity. When designing MCSs in high uncertainty-avoidance settings, organizations might therefore consider using less subjectivity in performance evaluations. Finally, and merely providing more examples, employees' desire for achievement and competition in masculine cultures may be conducive to an effective use of relative performance evaluations where employees' performances are directly compared, and, hence, are competing with one another. But whereas employees high in masculinity may prefer rewards based on "hard" performance, those low in masculinity may prefer more "equitable" allocations based on need. And so on.

These four dimensions, however, do not explain all aspects of national culture and their differences across countries. For example, one aspect of cross-cultural differences not directly picked up by any of the four Hofstede dimensions relates to corporate goals. Managers in some countries, particularly those in Asia, are often more concerned with the interests of non-owner groups than are US managers.[16] To illustrate, when the executives and middle managers of large Japanese firms were asked what their company's objectives were, the executives ranked pursuit of shareholder profit only in fourth place. Both executives and middle managers ranked employees first among those entitled to the organization's profits.[17] Managers running a business for the benefit of many *stakeholders*, and not primarily its *shareholders*, will make different decisions. With regards to MCS design, they are likely to choose different performance measures (e.g. employee safety) and use different ways of rewarding employees (e.g. job security and employee benefits).

Local institutions

Corporate governance regulations, employment law and contract law, as well as banking systems and governance interventions, just to name a few "institutions," also vary significantly across nations. Just as with national culture, such institutional factors can influence both the design and effects of an organization's management control system.[18] For example, organizations in countries with strong labor unions may find it difficult to provide incentive pay as unions often prefer seniority-based pay systems.

One set of institutional factors with potentially important MCS implications are those descriptive of the financial markets in various countries, their importance in raising capital, and the extent of disclosures and types of information they demand.[19] The state of the capital markets in various countries may affect the extent to which organizations provide stock-based incentives, such as restricted stock or stock options. Indeed, where capital markets are less "efficient" and/or where trading is "thin," stock market valuations are less likely to reflect firm value adequately, rendering stock-based incentives impotent if not incongruent. The quality of the required disclosures of (financial) information by publicly traded firms also varies across countries, in part because of differences in the organization and regulation of their auditing. Just as poor stock valuations may hamper the use of stock-based incentives, so may poor earnings quality affect the use of accounting-based incentives, such as by the parent company for incentive purposes of its managers in the foreign entity with weak auditing. The strength of regulation, auditing, and enforcement also may affect managers' abilities and propensities to engage in earnings management. Moreover, not all countries require the reporting of quarterly financial performance, which may affect managers' focus on short-term financial performance, and hence, their propensity to engage in myopic decision making to meet or beat publicly announced earnings targets on a quarterly basis to affect stock price valuations.

Differences in local business environments

Business environments also differ significantly across countries. Elements of these environments can affect environmental uncertainty, inflation, and the availability of qualified personnel. Each of these factors, and many other factors in this realm, has MCS implications.

Uncertainty

Country-specific environmental uncertainty can be caused by many things. Some countries are inherently more risky places in which to do business. Military conflicts, kidnappings, terrorism, and extortion threats can create major security problems. Some countries are also prone to corporate espionage and theft of corporate secrets by local competitors, perhaps even with the tacit consent of the host government. Risk also differs across countries because of the stage of economic development. As discussed, developing countries tend to have limited access to capital, relatively poor accounting regulation and oversight, weaker legal enforcement of contract violations, and other obstacles to doing business.

Government interventions also affect business risk. Governments have, to a greater or lesser extent, powers that enable them to serve certain objectives. These powers can have major effects on the value of companies' assets and the expected returns on those assets. For example, governments can exercise bureaucratic control in issuing business permits, controlling prices, and restricting currency flows. They can implement laws that restrict foreign firms' activities and/or favor domestic firms. They can design tax laws that redistribute income or affect the value of monetary compensation and other reward arrangements. They can apply constraints through labor policies designed to reduce unemployment such as by rigid labor laws to restrict layoffs.

In general, in nations where the governments have greater powers and tend to use them more frequently, business risk is higher. However, governments can also act to lower business risk. Tariff barriers can protect corporations from competitive market forces. Governments can buy some of the companies' products to stabilize prices. They can provide subsidies. They can provide support for research and investment activities through grants or tax provisions. They can provide economic data that can be used for planning purposes as well as competitive data that can be used for benchmarking and relative performance evaluations.

Company growth patterns also can affect risk through their influence on organizational learning. Managers of MNOs have one important MCS-related advantage over their domestic counterparts: they are able to learn more quickly and more thoroughly about potentially desirable practices used in foreign countries. Those practices are known by employees in their foreign entities, and some of those practices can be readily adapted across countries. Firms that grow by acquisition learn from the management systems, including MCSs, being used in the organizations they acquire. When firms grow by acquisition, they are likely to have to use, at least for a period of time, several variations of MCSs. The MCS variations may persist if they are superior for controlling the acquired businesses, even though it can be costly to maintain multiple sets of MCSs. But what is important is that the acquisitions enhance organizational learning. The companies are exposed to multiple MCSs, and they can adapt the features that suit them best. This enhanced learning can improve management control and lower uncertainty. In the absence of acquisitions, it is possible to derive much of the same benefits by entering into joint ventures with companies in other countries.[20]

Inflation

Inflation is another environmental factor that differs significantly across countries. Inflation and fluctuations in inflation, which affect the relative values of currencies, create financial risk. Valued in terms of a fixed currency, high inflation can cause a company's assets or an individual's compensation to deteriorate significantly in value in a short period of time.

High inflation – at the extreme, *hyperinflation* – affects the congruence of financial measurement systems. It can lead to the adoption of some form of inflation accounting which involves either the expressing of accounts and financial statements in terms of real (rather than nominal) amounts or expressing all assets and liabilities at current (or replacement) values. It can also lead to the use of some form of flexible budgeting, to shield managers from uncontrollable inflation risk, or the partial abandonment of accounting measures of performance in favor of some nonfinancial measures.

Talent

Organizations operating in developing countries often face limited availability of skilled and educated personnel. When employees are not highly educated, decision-making structures are usually more centralized, and MCSs tend to be more focused on action controls, rather than results controls. Small offices may contain only a few educated people. This makes it difficult to implement one of the basic internal control principles: separation of duties. All told, when talent is in short supply, both the firm's ability to do business, as well as its capacity to affect good control, are more likely to be compromised.

Personnel mobility also differs across countries. In the United States, managers tend to change companies often over the course of their career. In many other countries, including Japan, most managers in the larger companies, particularly, spend their entire career with one company. Using a quote to illustrate such differences:

> Japanese workers introduce themselves by their company name first and their own name second, and are far more likely to define themselves by whom they work for than by what they do. This is true even in Japan's most global companies. In the United States you are always "dating" the company; in Japan, employees "marry" their company.[21]

When personnel mobility is low, there is less need for implementing long-term incentive plans that motivate managers both to think long-term and to stay with the firm to earn their rewards.

Foreign currency translation

MNOs also face currency exchange and translation problems. At first glance, it is not obvious that results controls in MNOs should be complicated by the fact that the firms' profits are earned in multiple currencies. Results controls over foreign entities can be implemented using the same practices employed in most domestic firms, by comparing performance measured in terms of the local currency with a pre-set plan also expressed in the local currency. However, MNOs bear economic risk caused by fluctuating currency values. The values of foreign investments appreciate or depreciate based on the relative values of the home and foreign currencies. Through their performance evaluation practices, MNOs can make their entity managers bear this risk or can shield them from it.

Some MNOs evaluate the managers of their foreign entities in terms of results measured in home-country currency; that is, the currency of the parent company. The home-country currency is the unit of measure in which the corporate financial objectives are stated; it is usually the currency that most of the shareholders will be spending; and it is the unit of measure used to evaluate the top executives. As such, it is natural for corporate management to want to encourage entity managers to take actions to increase profits denominated in the currency of the parent company. Use of home-country currencies, however, can cause problems. If the foreign currency is appreciating relative to the home currency, foreign entities can comfortably earn the target rate of return or show impressive sales gains even though they may not be performing near the potential that is offered by foreign market opportunity. The converse is also true.

In other words, evaluating managers of foreign entities in terms of the amount of home-country currency they earn subjects those managers to *foreign currency translation risk*. The risk arises because the managers earn their profits in the foreign currency that fluctuates in value in comparison to the home currency. Thus, when measured in home-country currency, the foreign entities' reported profits are subjected to an extra uncontrollable factor: the relative change in the two monetary units over the measurement period. If the home currency appreciates in value relative to the local currency, then foreign entity profits expressed in home currency will be lower than they otherwise would have been; that is, the foreign entity incurs a *foreign currency translation loss*. If the local currency appreciates in value relative to the home currency, then the converse is true: a *foreign currency translation gain* will be incurred.

The amount of translation gain or loss can vary significantly depending on the accounting convention used. The current US convention, since June 2009 described as Topic 830 in the FASB Accounting Standards Codification (ASC 830) requires translation of assets and liabilities at the exchange rate *at the time of the financial statement*. ASC 830 is based on Financial Accounting Statement No. 52 (FAS 52), which became effective on January 1, 1983. From 1976 to 1982, the US accounting rule for translation was expressed in FAS 8, which required translation of "real" assets, such as inventories and plant and equipment, at the rates in effect *when the assets were booked*; that is, they were accounted for at *historical* rather than at *current* exchange rates. Companies reporting under International Financial Reporting Standards (IFRS) are subject to International Accounting Standard No. 21, The Effects of Changes in Foreign Exchange Rates (IAS 21), which is similar to ASC 830 (and FAS 52).

The most important control decision in this area, however, is whether to hold managers accountable for foreign exchange gains and losses, thus subjecting them to foreign currency translation risk. The issues involved here are identical to those discussed in Chapter 12 regarding uncontrollable factors. The extra measurement noise caused by uncontrollable foreign exchange risk, and various methods of measuring the gains and losses, can affect judgments about the entity managers' performances.

One could argue that entity managers who can influence the amount of the foreign exchange gains or losses should bear the foreign exchange risk. Some entity managers can take actions that have foreign currency implications. Some have the authority to make significant cross-border investments, product sourcing or marketing decisions. Some have the authority to write purchasing or sales contracts denominated in one currency or another. Some even have the authority to enter into foreign exchange transactions, such as hedging, currency swaps, or arbitrage. But most of these specialized hedging transactions require special skills most operating managers do not have, and, thus, authority in this area commonly resides with the finance department at corporate.

If corporate managers decide that the managers of their foreign entities should not bear the foreign exchange risk, they can instead use any of four essentially identical methods:

1. Evaluate the manager in terms of local currency profits as compared to a local currency plan or budget.
2. Treat the foreign exchange gain or loss as "below" the income-statement line for which the manager is held accountable.
3. Evaluate the manager in terms of profits measured in home currency, but calculate a "foreign exchange variance" and treat it as uncontrollable.
4. Re-express the home currency budget for the entity in local currency using the end-of-year, not beginning-of-year, exchange rate or some average for the period. This procedure creates a budget that "flexes" with exchange rates.

CONCLUSION

This chapter has identified some of the situational factors that can influence MCS choices and the effects of those choices. Clearly, the appropriateness of each MCS choice depends on the situation. The chapter also described some of the most salient MCS-related effects of three important situational factors: environmental uncertainty, organization strategy, and multinationality. Similar discussions could be presented with respect to other factors, such as the impacts of technology and organizational structure and size.

Some of these factors can create MCS design *conflicts*. For example, a business unit in an uncertain environment but with a cost leadership strategy faces conflicts between the desire to stay focused and efficient and the need to scan the environment to gather information that might indicate a structural change in the industry. Similar conflicts can arise with respect to national culture. For example, employees in cultures characterized by high uncertainty avoidance may not react favorably to the ambiguity associated with subjective performance evaluations used to award discretionary bonuses. The amount of dissatisfaction with subjective performance evaluations, however, will depend in part on the amount of trust and respect for the evaluator, which is an element of power distance. Hence, uncertainty avoidance and power distance may interact and cause mutually reinforcing or opposing effects on the preference for MCSs. Furthermore, employees with a high aversion for uncertainty may prefer group, as opposed to individual, performance-based incentives because they facilitate the sharing of risk. But the reaction to group rewards, however, also depends on the degree of individualism. In short, multiple cultural dimensions may affect an employee's preferences for, and reactions to, MCSs in interactive ways.

Adapting MCSs is particularly challenging in multinational environments. MNO managers almost invariably face high information asymmetry between themselves and personnel in the foreign locations. The foreign personnel have specialized knowledge about their environments (such as about local norms, tastes, regulations, and business risks). The high information asymmetry limits the corporate managers' abilities to use action controls, such as preaction reviews, because the corporate managers have limited knowledge to make the needed judgments. MNO managers also face the barriers of distance, time zones and language, which limit the use of direct monitoring. They cannot easily visit their foreign-based subordinates, although advancing technologies have made communications easier. On top of that, they must deal with the significant problem of measuring performance in multiple currencies.

Despite the incomplete state of knowledge about the effects of various forms of MCSs in various situations, managers must cope. The main message in the chapter is that managers must be sensitive to these situational factors. They must be aware of the key dimensions of the situations in which they are managing and either adapt their MCS to the situational contingencies they face or find ways to alter the situation. In that sense, companies are both *shaped by*, but also *shaping*, their contexts. A delicate task indeed.

Notes

1. For a review article, see R. H. Chenhall, "Management Control Systems Design Within its Organizational Context: Findings from Contingency-Based Research and Directions for the Future," *Accounting, Organizations and Society*, 28, nos. 2–3 (February–April 2003), pp. 127–68.

2. J. Gerdin and J. Greve, "Forms of Contingency Fit in Management Accounting Research: A Critical Review," *Accounting, Organizations and Society*, 29, nos. 3–4 (April–May 2004), pp. 303–26; see also see T. Malmi and D. Brown, "Management Control Systems as a Package – Opportunities, Challenges and Research

Directions," *Management Accounting Research*, 19, no. 4 (December 2008), pp. 287–300.

3. See, for example, M. Raith, "Competition, Risk, and Managerial Incentives," *American Economic Review*, 93 (2003), pp. 1425–36; M. Raith, "Specific Knowledge and Performance Measurement," *Rand Journal of Economics*, 39 (2008), pp. 1059–79.

4. See, for example, W. Van der Stede, "The Relationship Between Two Consequences of Budgetary Controls: Budgetary Slack Creation and Managerial Short-Term Orientation," *Accounting, Organizations and Society*, 25, no. 6 (August 2000), pp. 609–22.

5. See, for example, W. Van der Stede and T. Palermo, "Scenario Budgeting: Integrating Risk and Performance," *Finance & Management*, no. 184 (January 2011), pp. 10–13.

6. See, for example, J. Whalen, "Bureaucracy Buster? Glaxo Lets Scientists Choose its New Drugs," *The Wall Street Journal* (March 27, 2006), p. B1. For research articles, see A. Ditillo, "Dealing with Uncertainty in Knowledge-Intensive Firms: The Role of Management Control Systems as Knowledge Integration Mechanisms," *Accounting, Organizations and Society*, 29, nos. 3–4 (April–May 2004), pp. 401–21, as well as several articles in the Special Issue on "Accounting, Innovation and Entrepreneurship," *European Accounting Review*, 18, no. 2 (2009), pp. 277–405.

7. For an overview of, and various perspectives on, the management control literature in this respect, see C. Chapman, *Controlling Strategy: Management, Accounting, and Performance Measurement* (New York, NY: Oxford University Press, 2005).

8. See, for example, R. Bushman, R. Indjejikian, and A. Smith, "Aggregate Performance Measures in Business Unit Manager Compensation: The Role of Intra-Firm Interdependencies," *Journal of Accounting Research*, 33 (Supplement 1995), pp. 101–27; and A. S. Keating, "Determinants of Divisional Performance Evaluation Practices," *Journal of Accounting and Economics*, 24, no. 3 (December 1997), pp. 243–73.

9. The seminal reference here is M. E. Porter, *Competitive Strategy* (New York: Free Press, 1980). Another oft-cited competitive strategy typology is that of "defenders" vs. "prospectors" as developed by R. Miles and C. Snow, *Organizational Strategy, Structure and Process* (New York: McGraw-Hill, 1978). Although both Porter's "low cost vs. differentiation" and Miles & Snow's "defender vs. prospector" strategy typologies have their own nuances, they also exhibit overlap. For this reason, and for brevity, we primarily use Porter's terminology in this chapter.

10. Chenhall, "Management Control Systems Design Within its Organizational Context," op. cit.; Gerdin and Greve, "Forms of Contingency Fit in Management Accounting Research," op. cit.

11. Chapman, *Controlling Strategy*, op. cit.

12. G. Hofstede, *Culture's Consequences: International Differences in Work-Related Values* (Beverly Hills, CA: Sage Publications, 1980), p. 25; G. Hofstede, *Culture's Consequences: Comparing Values, Behaviors, Institutions and Organizations Across Nations* (Thousand Oaks, CA: Sage Publications, 2001).

13. Ibid. Hofstede's original data on which his original national culture taxonomy was based are over 30 years old now and were obtained from employees in only one multinational firm (IBM). Despite its wide use, Hofstede's framework also has been criticized. For a debate, see R. Baskerville, "Hofstede Never Studied Culture," *Accounting, Organizations and Society*, 28, no. 1 (January 2003), pp. 1–14; G. Hofstede, "What is Culture? A Reply to Baskerville," *Accounting, Organizations and Society*, 28, nos. 7/8 (October–November 2003), pp. 811–13.

14. Hofstede, *Culture's Consequences*, op. cit.

15. For a sample of several studies in this area, see C. Chow, M. Shields and A. Wu, "The Importance of National Culture in the Design of and Preference for Management Controls for Multinational Operations," *Accounting, Organizations and Society*, 24, nos. 5/6 (July–August 1999), pp. 441–61; W. Van der Stede, "The Effect of National Culture on Management Control and Incentive System Design in Multi-Business Firms: Evidence of Intra-corporate Isomorphism," *The European Accounting Review*, 12, no. 2 (2003), pp. 263–85; and E. P. Jansen, K. Merchant, and W. Van der Stede, "National Differences in Incentive Compensation Practices: The Differing Roles of Financial Performance Measurement in the United States and the Netherlands," *Accounting, Organizations and Society*, 34, no. 1 (January 2009), pp. 58–84.

16. See, for example, "Shareholders vs. Stakeholders: A New Idolatry," *The Economist* (April 24, 2010), pp. 65–6.

17. Survey results cited in *Nihon Sangyo Shimbun* (July 5, 1990). P. Milgrom and J. Roberts, *Economics Organization and Management* (Englewood Cliffs, NJ: Prentice-Hall, 1992), p. 41.

18. See, for example, K. Balachandran, A. Dossi and W. Van der Stede, "Corporate Governance Research in 'The Rest of the World'," *Journal of Accounting Auditing & Finance*, 25, no. 3 (Fall 2010), pp. 523–9.

19. See, for example, C. Leuz, "Different Approaches to Corporate Reporting Regulation: How Jurisdictions Differ and Why," *Accounting and Business Research*, 40, no. 3 (Special Issue, 2010), pp. 229–56.

20. See, for example, T. Groot and K. Merchant, "Control of International Joint Ventures," *Accounting, Organizations and Society*, 25, no. 6 (August 2000), pp. 579–607; P. Chalos and N. O'Connor, "Determinants of the Use of Various Control Mechanisms in US-Chinese Joint Ventures," *Accounting, Organizations and Society*, 29, no. 7 (October 2004), pp. 591–608.

21. "Insiders and Outsiders," *The Economist* (November 18, 2010), pp. 7–9.

Case Study

ConAgra Grocery Products Company

In January 1999 managers at ConAgra Grocery Products Company (CAGP) revamped their system of allocating and controlling trade-marketing spending. CAGP annually spent over $400 million on trade marketing expenditures – expenditures aimed at helping grocery retailers promote CAGP's products. Because of the size of the expenditures and the impact they had on the success of the business, CAGP managers were understandably concerned as to whether that money was allocated wisely. They were also concerned about their controls over trade spending because the company had recently overspent its trade-spending budget.

Among the major changes in the new system were the giving of increased responsibility for allocating trade spending dollars to the sales organization, the assignment of volume-variable budgets called "case rates" (rather than fixed dollar budgets), a lengthening of the budget period (to semiannual rather than quarterly periods), the creation of a new customer marketing manager role to improve communications between the marketing and sales organizations, and modifications to the incentive systems that were designed to induce sales personnel to pay more attention to cost control.

In late 1999 Ken Sobaski, president of CAGP's Grocery Products Brand Company, reflected on the system changes:

At its highest level this change is all about trade marketing managers giving up some control and empowering field sales managers, giving them more flexibility and responsiveness in meeting the needs of their customers. Our assumption is that by pushing funding control out closer to the customer, with greater lead time and better planning and strategic direction from headquarters, we will be more effective and efficient with our spending.

COMPANY HISTORY AND BACKGROUND

CAGP was a subsidiary of ConAgra, Inc. ConAgra, headquartered in Omaha, Nebraska, was one of the largest food conglomerates in the world (fiscal year 1999 sales of almost $25 billion; 85,000 employees). ConAgra's businesses operated across the entire food chain. Its products included fertilizers, crop protection chemicals, and seeds for farmers; food ingredients, such as flour and spices, for manufacturers; and a wide range of branded products for consumers, including shelf-stable and frozen foods, meat and fish products, tablespreads, cheeses, and dessert toppings. ConAgra was a successful company. Its 19 consecutive years of earnings-per-share growth at an annual rate of 14.6% was unequaled by any major food company.

CAGP, formerly Hunt-Wesson, Inc., was one of 11 major operating companies in ConAgra. CAGP was founded by the Hunt Brothers in 1890 as a canning business in Santa Rosa, California. CAGP's current headquarters were in Fullerton, California. CAGP was itself a large business with over 8,000 employees nationwide and annual sales of $2.5 billion.

CAGP's mission was to provide "the finest-quality and best-tasting products to consumers." The company operated manufacturing plants, distribution centers and sales offices in more than 30 states across the United States. CAGP produced, marketed, and sold a wide variety of products, including tomato paste and sauces, canned tomatoes, ketchup, pasta, barbecue sauces, soups, cereals, chili, canned beans, canned beans and weiners, sloppy joe sauces, meat snacks, peanut butter, popcorn products, puddings, fruit snacks, gels, cooking and salad oils, Oriental and Mexican foods, hot cocoa mixes, bread mixes, flour, grain snacks, dry beans, peas, lentils, rice, ground

---

This case was prepared by Professor Kenneth A. Merchant and research assistants Lay Khim Ong and Liu Zheng.

black pepper, preserves, jams, jellies, syrups, cookies, and salad dressings. Among the company's 17 food brands were Hunt's, Wesson, Orville Redenbacher's, Peter Pan, Van Camp's, Swiss Miss, Knott's Berry Farm, Chun King, La Choy, and Rosarita.

CAGP sold to more than 300 customers ("buying points"). But the largest 7–10 customers (e.g. Wal-Mart, Kroger, Albertsons) accounted for over half of the total sales volume.

ORGANIZATION

Since April 1999, when a major reorganization was made and a new management team took over, responsibility for the US grocery business was divided between Ken Sobaski, who was responsible for marketing, and Doug Knudsen, who was responsible for sales. CAGP's organization chart is shown in Exhibit 1.

Ken Sobaski, president of the Grocery Brands Company, was head of the marketing function for products sold in the United States through grocery store outlets. Ken's organization (see Exhibit 2) encompassed brand marketing, trade marketing, and customer marketing. The *brand marketing* managers were responsible for consumer promotion, advertising, market research, packaging, brand strategy, and the overall profit and loss management of each of the brands. The brand marketing organization was organized into four SBUs: ingredients, snacks, meals, and functional foods.

The trade marketing and customer marketing organizations both reported to Howard Bowne, VP trade marketing (see Exhibit 3). *Trade marketing* managers developed the national trade strategies and objectives within the volume and case rate parameters established together with brand marketing. The trade marketing managers were responsible for the customer profit and loss statements, although their actions really only affected sales volume, sales mix, and trade marketing expenditures.

Customer marketing, a newly created role, provided a liaison between sales and trade marketing. The customer marketing managers helped sales managers plan promotion events within the assigned volume and rate parameters and resolved planning issues with trade marketing. They also identified local market opportunities, assisted account managers in calling on accounts, and educated field sales on brand and trade strategies.

The president of CAGP's *Sales Division* was Douglas Knudsen (see Exhibit 4). Each of the five sales vice presidents was responsible for Corporate, Major, or Regional accounts. *Corporate accounts* (e.g. Wal-Mart, Albertsons, Safeway, Kroger) were customers that were corporately owned and spanned across multiple markets. These accounts were centralized and made their purchasing and merchandising decisions at the headquarter levels rather than at the store or geographical level. *Major accounts* (such as Ralphs, Vons) and smaller *regional accounts* were customers that were not corporately owned and that covered a particular limited geographical area.

Reporting to each sales vice president were customer directors who managed the field sales teams and the field sales force. The field sales organization included key account managers (KAMs), account managers (AMs) and regional account managers (RAMs). KAMs and AMs called on the headquarters accounts of corporate or major customers. RAMs called on the headquarters accounts of regional customer teams. The sales force was responsible for the day-to-day management of store-level activity, with the emphasis on securing distribution of new items and selling additional cases of items already being sold.

The profiles of the personnel in the various functions were quite different. The brand marketing personnel were typically MBAs who had concentrated their studies on marketing. Most of the brand marketing personnel, even up to the brand manager level, were quite young (still in their 20s). They had little or no field experience. Most sales personnel were college graduates who had worked their way up the sales organization. Only a few of them had MBAs. The trade marketing organization was less homogeneous. It included both some younger, MBA-type personnel and some sales personnel who were doing a stint at headquarters.

These educational and experience differences contributed to a natural tension in the organization. Field sales personnel were reluctant to accept theories from a new, young marketing person. They believed that the marketers' "book learning with no real world experience" did not help them understand how customers really think. The marketing personnel, on the other hand, thought that sales personnel were, in general, too volume-focused and lacked the numbers skills to calculate the profit effects of various decisions that might be made.

BUSINESS STRATEGY

The new CAGP management team was changing the company's strategy and the employees' mindsets as to how best to sell the company's products. In the old marketing approach the focus was on growth. CAGP marketing and sales personnel sought to fill customers' warehouses with CAGP products. They hoped that consumer advertising would pull the product through the warehouses and, if CAGP prices were discounted, that the retailers would pass the discounts on to the consumers, creating larger demand.

Recent results had been disappointing, however. In 1999 unit sales volumes declined slightly from 1998 levels, and CAGP missed its profit target for the first time in 12 years. More ominous was the fact that some of CAGP's share positions and brand equity had been eroding.

The new marketing approach involved more of a focus on the building of brand equity, which meant getting consumers to prefer CAGP products even, potentially, at a higher price. The new approach stemmed from a desire to build a foundation for long-term success and a realization that CAGP was not, and probably never would be, among the lowest cost producers in the industry. Marketing managers were attempting to build the equity of the various CAGP brands through a variety of methods, including product and packaging design and advertising and promotions.

MARKET SEGMENTATION AND ALLOCATION OF TRADE SPENDING DOLLARS

As part of brand and trade strategies aimed at selling products to retailers and, ultimately, to consumers, CAGP managers allocated monies for any or all of four promotion tactics. These were temporary price reductions, major advertisements, coupon advertisements, and displays. *Temporary price reductions* were discounts off the everyday price of an item for a set time period (e.g. a bonus buy). *Major advertisements* and *coupon advertisements* were advertisements run by an account. They could be delivered in-store or via newspapers or direct mail. *Displays* involved prominent placement of in-store stocks, such as at the end of an aisle ("end cap"), an in-aisle stack, a special rack, or a "wall of values." Each display event required a certain dollar allocation.

CAGP's marketing strategy involved the segmentation of markets both to match promotional spending with geographic opportunities and to align promotion tactics with important characteristics of the accounts within the designated market. The domestic national market was divided into more than 50 geographical market zones (e.g. Chicago, Seattle, Los Angeles). Then, for each brand, trade marketing grouped the market zones into different market segments.

The market segmentation often influenced the amount of trade funds allocated. CAGP's allocations of trade spending dollars had to be tailored both to the brand characteristics and to the grocery retailers' strategies. In considering the brand characteristics, marketing managers asked "What does it take to have competitive performance at the retail level?" Among the relevant factors that had to be considered were market size and growth, competition, brand strengths, and product profitability. For example, CAGP would do most of its promoting of the Van de Camp's pork and beans products in the central and southern portions of the United States where the market potential was larger because per capita consumption was much higher than on the coasts. Sometimes, however, marketing managers made strategic decisions to invest heavily to build the position of new or weak products. And sometimes where they had a dominant market share they cut their promotional expense because of a belief that there was little to be gained.

Market segmentation varied by brand. For example, the trade marketers responsible for Peter Pan peanut butter segmented the market zones into core markets and noncore markets. Core markets provided the highest volume and therefore received the highest concentration of trade marketing funding.

In contrast, the trade marketers responsible for Hunt's spaghetti sauce segmented the brand's markets into four categories: profit contributor, profit maximizer, battlefield, and underdeveloped. *Profit contributors* were market segments in which the CAGP brand already had share leadership and growth was difficult. In such segments a defend strategy, with moderate trade and marketing funding and with the elimination of inefficient trade promotions, was adopted to maintain market share. *Profit maximizers* were market segments where the business was stable or declining and with little potential for further growth. In such markets CAGP adopted a maintain strategy, to maintain distribution and share of shelf space, to deliver profitable volume. *Battlefields* were market segments where both a high level of competition and a high growth potential existed. In such segments an invest strategy, with the highest concentration of trade and marketing funding, was adopted to strengthen the competitive position. In *underdeveloped* markets, where brand growth opportunity existed, a growth opportunity strategy was employed to grow share and volume.

The allocations of trade funds also varied with the timing of product consumption. For Orville Redenbacher microwaveable popcorn, for example, many different display events might be needed over the course of a year timed, perhaps, to major television-watching periods (e.g. Super Bowl). Another brand might need only two events.

A final factor that had to be considered was differences in the retailers' strategies. The retailers who sold CAGP products employed many different strategies to distinguish themselves from their competitors. Some were high-end retailers, while others operated low cost (e.g. warehouse outlet) stores. Some emphasized consumer memberships, while others did not. Some used "everyday low prices," while others used normally higher prices but featured many temporary special prices. CAGP's marketing and sales managers had to tailor their promotions to the customers' needs because the retailers decided both which products and brands they would promote and when they would offer the promotions.

THE OLD SYSTEM OF ALLOCATING AND CONTROLLING TRADE SPENDING

Up until 1999 CAGP's budgeting process started in January, when managers in the corporate trade marketing organization developed national volume objectives and a national trade-spending budget. After top management approved these targets the trade marketing managers disaggregated the targets. They established volume objectives and lump sum trade spending budgets by quarter for each of the 300+ grocery buying points.

Trade marketing also set up deal parameters as guidelines for sales when they planned and executed merchandising deals with accounts. Deal parameters could relate to the lowest unit price at which a product could be offered to a customer, the

dates of a deal, or the values allowed on the discount coupons retailers ran in their own in-store advertisements. Before implementing exceptions to the established deal parameters sales managers had to secure the approval of the appropriate trade marketing manager.

The quarterly spending budgets and parameters usually did not change during the year. Sales personnel had to try to tailor their promotion events to their accounts' needs while at the same time working within the guidelines given to them by trade marketing. If sales personnel identified promotion opportunities that exceeded the account's budget or violated one or more of the deal parameters they had to obtain approval from trade marketing. As one sales manager explained, "They can't just cut their own special deals. That is grounds for dismissal."

The sales organization had its own planning process. Sales volume quotas were generated by a computer information system that was independent of the system that generated the volume objectives for trade marketing. During the year the company's and trade marketing's volume targets were held fixed; sales updated theirs.

The incentive compensation systems for trade marketing and sales personnel were quite different. Incentives for trade marketing personnel were based on CAGP profit before tax (PBT) (40% weighting), the profit contribution of the brands managed (20%) and other objectives tailored to the role (40%). In contrast, incentives for field sales personnel were based on sales volume (75%) and CAGP PBT (25%). Target bonuses were generally around 15% of base salary for lower-level marketing personnel and 20–22% for lower-level sales personnel. Managers at higher organization levels had higher target bonuses. The bonus opportunities were highly leveraged. No bonuses were paid for if targets were not close to being achieved (e.g. 90% of target). Exceeding targets could result in bonus payouts several times the target bonus (e.g. exceeding the target by 5% would sometimes more than double the bonus payout).

Sales personnel were sometimes also offered *spiffs* – special incentives for accomplishment of specific short-term incentives. For example, if the company wished to boost profits or reduce inventories in a given quarter, sales personnel might be offered a $1,500 bonus if their performance exceeded 105% of their quarterly quota.

PROBLEMS WITH THE OLD SYSTEM

CAGP managers did not believe that the old system of allocating and controlling trade spending dollars was effective. CAGP, in general, had not been meeting its performance targets. A general erosion in the market position of CAGP products suggested that the allocation of trade spending dollars was not optimal, and the recent overspending of the trade spending budgets provided evidence that control of the allocated dollars was ineffective.

The overspending problem was perceived to have two basic causes. First, because sales incentives were based solely on sales volumes, sales personnel were not greatly concerned with staying within the budgeted spending limits. Second, while sales personnel had to secure approval from trade marketing to exceed budget, some of them had learned how to evade the control by biasing their volume estimates in a downward direction. Then, when actual volume was higher than was forecast, overspends were inevitable. A trade marketing manager explained:

> Let's say I allocated $600,000 to use on programs during a given period. Not infrequently the sales manager would call me and say, "Sorry I overspent. I assumed we would sell 10,000 cases, but we actually sold 20,000 cases. Isn't that great?" My reply was "No that's horrible. Now I've sold 20,000 cases at a discount." Last year that cost us a 20% spending overrun "by accident." But the sales manager would not be held accountable for the overspend as long as he met his volume objectives.

Considerable tension existed between the marketing and sales organizations. Personnel in both organizations were concerned about whether personnel in the other organization "really had a grasp on what it takes to drive the customers." Some sales personnel felt that it was very tiring and frustrating for them to have to fight for money for promotion events that were ultimately for the company's benefit. The incompatibility of incentives magnified this problem. For example, some trade marketing managers complained that the sales managers "just wanted to sell" irrespective of whether the additional volume generated was profitable or not.

The incompatibility of the volume targets set for the trade marketing and sales organizations caused some problems. For example, some trade marketing managers were irked that the sales organization could be meeting its volume targets and getting its bonuses even though profit targets were not being met. The opposite situation could also happen, as one sales director explained:

> Sometimes marketing rejects the opportunity to fund potentially profitable events proposed by a customer because they have already met their national profit objectives. But sales may not have met their volume targets yet!

The old system of allocating and controlling trade spending also aggravated the problems of forward buying and diverting, which were prevalent in the industry. *Forward buying* occurred where accounts bought larger quantities of products being offered at special prices than they could sell during the promotional period. They would then sell the excess inventory to consumers at regular prices after the deal period and obtain a higher profit margin. The accounts knew when the promotions were scheduled, and they sometimes acted so as to pay the full list price as little as possible. *Diverting* occurred where accounts bought extra product (more than their consumers would buy) at special prices and then sold the product to other accounts that were not offered similar pricing. The accounts were very up-front about this practice. Many had "diverter buyers" who would even openly talk to CAGP (and other manufacturers) and tell them what they were buying.

Both forward buying and diverting were harmful to CAGP. These practices reduced the amount of trade spending that was effectively merchandising the products. Under the old system of allocating and controlling trade spending sales personnel had little direct incentive to police forward buying and diverting activities by their accounts because the bonuses for sales managers were based on volume targets.

NEW SYSTEM OF ALLOCATING AND CONTROLLING TRADE SPENDING

In January 1999 CAGP implemented a new system for allocating and controlling trade spending. The new system involved five main changes. First, the old lump-sum trade spending allocation system was replaced by a new variable allocation system called a *case rate* system. Under this rate system the trade promotion funds available for each account increased automatically with an increase in shipments. Trade marketing managers allocated a case rate (e.g. $2.00/case) to the 25 sales teams, and the sales team directors allocated the case rates down to the account (buying point) level.

The budgeted case rate was determined by taking the total planned trade marketing budget for a brand divided by the planned volume expressed in terms of *equivalent cases*. The case equivalencies were needed to adjust for the volumes in the different product package sizes so that cases containing different quantities or sizes could be added for reporting purposes. For example, Orville Redenbacher popcorn was sold in 3-packs and 10-packs. The 3-packs were sold in cases of 12 – a total of 36 consumer servings. The 10-packs were sold in cases of 6 – a total of 60 servings. Dividing the volume in one package size case by the volume in another created what was called a *conversion factor*. The factor for converting the volume of popcorn in 10-pack cases to 3-pack cases was 1.667 (= 60 ÷ 36). In other words sales of cases of 10-packs of popcorn were multiplied by 1.667 when comparing them to sales of 3-packs of popcorn.[1]

The actual (realized) case rate was calculated by dividing actual trade spending by actual total shipments. Actual total shipments include promoted as well as nonpromoted volume. Sales managers were held accountable for ensuring that the actual case rate did not exceed the budgeted case rate. For example, suppose that Hunt's spaghetti sauce had a budgeted brand case rate of $2 per case and that sales planned a promotion event with an account to spend trade dollars at a rate of $2 per case and also provided an account with a lump sum amount of $2,000. Also assume that the volume sold to the account during the promotion was 1,000 cases and that the volume sold to the account outside the promotion period was 1,000 cases. The actual case rate would then be $2 (=1,000 cases*$2/case + $2,000)/2,000 cases).

Many factors could affect the actual case rate. Sales could reduce its realized case rate by including a case cap[2] or a scan event,[3] as opposed to paying on all cases purchased by an account. Using the Hunt's spaghetti sauce example, suppose that sales planned a promotion event and was able to monitor an account's activities to decrease occurrences of forward buy. Under such circumstances the account might purchase fewer products on deal during the promotion and might purchase more products without the deal. Assume in the example above that the amount of shipments under the promotion decreased to 600 cases (e.g. with a decreased forward buy) and the shipments in the nonpromotion period increased to 1,200. Thus the total shipments would be 1,800 cases. Again, if the merchandising funds were spent at a rate of $2 per case and a lump sum amount of $2,000, realized case rate would be reduced to $1.80 (=600 cases*$2/case + $2,000)/1,800 cases).

On the other hand the realized case rate would increase if there was an unrealistically high volume estimation, a large lump sum payment, or customer forward buying or diverting. For example, suppose an account bought product diverted from another account. In this case the nonpromoted volume that the account would purchase would decrease, perhaps to zero. Assuming the same deal as above, with a purchase of 1,000 cases of promoted product but with zero nonpromoted volume, the realized case rate would be $4 (=1,000 cases*$2/case + $2,000)/1,000 cases).

The above examples show that requiring sales to stay within budgeted case rates in effect held sales personnel responsible for tracking all the items (e.g. forward buying, diverting, volume estimates) that could affect the realized case rate.

The second major change encompassed in the move to the new system was to allow the 25 sales teams, rather than trade marketing managers, to set volume and spending objectives for each of the 300+ buying points. This change was important both because it passed significant authority and responsibility to the sales organization and because it ensured that the volume objectives set for sales personnel tied directly to the volume targets set by trade marketing.

The third change was to plan the volume targets and trade spending allocations on a semiannual, rather than a quarterly, basis. This change was made because quarterly planning was believed to engender a short-term focus. The longer horizon also allowed sales and their accounts more flexibility in planning promotional events. Most events required about

---

[1] The volume equivalencies usually were not the same as profit equivalencies. It was not a simple matter to calculate profits by product and customers. For example, larger volume packages usually provided savings on unit packaging costs, but the prices offered a volume discount. CAGP was developing a system to measure profit by product (and customer) and then to communicate those measures to the sales force, but that system was not yet in place.

[2] A case cap was a limit on the amount of promoted product a customer can order. It was used to help control forward buys and diverting.

[3] A scan event was one in which a per-unit allowance was paid to an account for products *sold to consumers*, i.e. scanned at check-out.

12–15 weeks lead time to implement. At the mid-year point the original profit plan was not changed; that was committed to ConAgra in February. Many trade promotion tactics could change, however, and trade spending dollars could also be reallocated between brands and accounts.

The fourth change was the creation of a new role: customer marketing manager. The customer marketing managers served as liaisons between the marketing and sales organizations. It was hoped that the customer marketing managers would improve communications and both ease the transition to the new system and relieve the cross-organizational tensions. This new organization was costly, however. The total cost of the new customer marketing organization was in excess of $10 million per year.

The fifth change involved several modifications to the monetary incentives for sales personnel. The bonus plan was changed to emphasize achievement of the overall company objectives. Starting in FY 2000 bonuses for sales personnel were based 50% on CAGP PBT (measured annually) and 50% on national cumulative product market share (measured semiannually). This change was made to align goals, to make everyone feel a part of one company, and to encourage sales personnel to learn the company's profit drivers (e.g. equity value, volumes, margins, costs).

Second, the criteria to be used in making the annual Performance Planning Appraisals (PPAs) of *sales* personnel, which were used to determine annual salary increases, were changed to include a specific importance weighting on achievement of case rate objectives. The importance weighting placed on achievement of the case rate objectives varied by role, but it was significant. For key account managers, for example, the PPAs were 17.5% based on achievement of case rate objectives. A weekly case rate tracking report was produced, and managers paid considerable attention to actual case rates. In recent years the pool for annual salary increases was approximately 4% of base salaries. Actual increases given to employees were typically in the 2–7% range.

Third, spiffs were discontinued. CAGP managers believed that in many cases spiffs had contributed to bad, excessively short-term oriented business decisions. For example, in one situation a KAM who earned a quarterly spiff sold at a discount eight months of inventory to a customer who had plans to put up large display advertising. But the display advertising promotion was never implemented.

Fourth, some contests among customer sales teams were offered. For example, at certain times the team with the highest increase in customer profitability would win a contest, and everyone on the team would be awarded a trip.

REMAINING PROBLEMS AND ISSUES

In general CAGP managers were pleased with the new system. In particular they thought that tensions between marketing and sales had eased because the new system had personnel in both organizations working toward the same objectives.

Many still had some significant concerns about the new system, however, and some believed that further changes would have to be made. Among the concerns expressed were those regarding the increased work and skill load placed on the sales organization, the tendency to make sales personnel conservative in their use of promotions, the lack of customization of the system to significant product, geographical, and customer characteristics, and inflexibilities caused by the still-short semiannual planning horizon.

The sales organization faced the greatest challenges in adapting to the new case rate system. Many sales managers had been in the field for 20 or 30 years, and up to now they had been primarily volume focused. They had tended to focus on short-term objectives and getting product into the customers' warehouses. Under the new system they still had to perform all the tasks they had been performing, and now they were being asked to do more planning and forecasting and to manage budgets – to plan promotional events and arrange deals that stay within the case rates. Some sales personnel struggled with this challenge.

To help the sales personnel CAGP managers formed a Trade Promotion Effectiveness Team to teach the sales force how to spend promotional monies wisely. The salespeople were being taught how to influence end-user consumption of the products through distribution (i.e. what products are on the retailer's shelf), shelving (i.e. where on the shelf the product was located; eye-level was best); merchandising (e.g. displays, feature advertisements), and pricing (i.e. understanding competition and price points). Some, but not all, sales personnel looked forward to the increased responsibilities and the potential for having more dialogue with trade marketing managers, particularly in the initial stages of trade and brand planning. But some trade marketing managers thought that the new workload and its challenges were beyond the capabilities of some personnel in the sales organization, even with the new training assistance.

One particular concern of many was that the case rate system was causing sales personnel to be overly conservative. It was difficult to anticipate the volume that would be generated through the various trade spending programs so, as a customer marketing director noted: "Sales is tending to cancel promotion programs if they feel uncertain about the volumes that the program could generate."

Another concern, particularly from some sales managers, was that the planning process was not adequately customized to differences in product, geographical and customer characteristics. On the product issue, for example, a customer marketing manager, commented:

> The case rate system allows flexibility to plan at account level, but it may not be suitable for certain brands and products. Some products such as Hunt's spaghetti sauce may need only a simple strategy such as an everyday low-price strategy. Other products, such as Van Camp, only contribute small volumes. It may not be worthwhile to manage such products through the complicated case rate system. Perhaps the case rate system should only be used for the larger growth brands, such as Orville Redenbacher.

Many CAGP sales personnel and customer marketing personnel hoped that CAGP could move to an annual, rather than a semiannual, planning process. Some customers, particularly, were concerned about the inflexibility in the use of excess funds that were generated late in the six-month period. For example, one thought that the lack of "carryover" of unspent funds to the next period "spoiled an otherwise good program." Most sales and account personnel also did not like the fact that case rates often changed at the six-month point, sometimes significantly. For retailers who planned their promotions far in the future this change and uncertainty was annoying. Some sales personnel also

noted that an annual planning process would further reduce the paperwork requirements. But many trade marketing managers admitted to be struggling with even the six-month horizon. As one said, "Everything out that far in the future gets foggy."

Finally, the new system did not provide a complete solution to the problems of forward buying, diverting, and lack of customer compliance. *Lack of customer compliance* manifested itself in many different ways. For example, some customers would take deductions they did not earn (i.e. they did not implement the promotion, did not pay in time to earn the discount). Some would deduct for unsaleables without supporting documentation. Some, if a shipment were short, would order from a competitor and bill CAGP for the difference in price. In many of these cases CAGP managers concluded that they had little recourse unless they were willing to shut off the customer's supply of product.

CAGP managers had discussed implementing *national* case rates to further reduce the diverting problem. National case rates would reduce the ability of CAGP personnel to tailor its promotional offerings. But with mergers in the grocery industry and the growth of larger customers (e.g. Wal-Mart), applying case rates on a national, or at least a larger regional, basis was now perhaps easier to do.

ONGOING REVIEW PROCESSES

Ken Sobaski thought that the new system was a positive step but that considerable work remained to be done. The Trade Promotion Effectiveness Team was charged both with helping to solve the problems associated with the adoption of the new system and investigating whether the new case rate system was leading to more effective use of the trade funds and the building of brand equity. Ken also knew that the company had to build its capability to better measure product and customer profitability. But while he could perhaps envision a better system he also had to concern himself with the organization's ability to absorb what had been significant change in a relatively short time period.

Exhibit 1 ConAgra Grocery Products Company executive organization chart

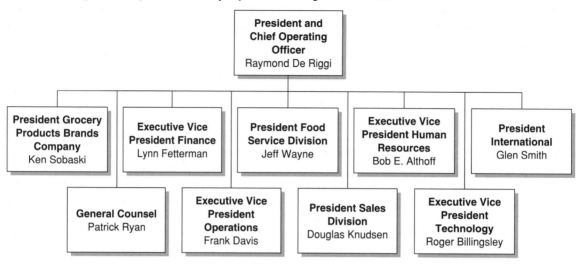

Exhibit 2 Marketing organization chart

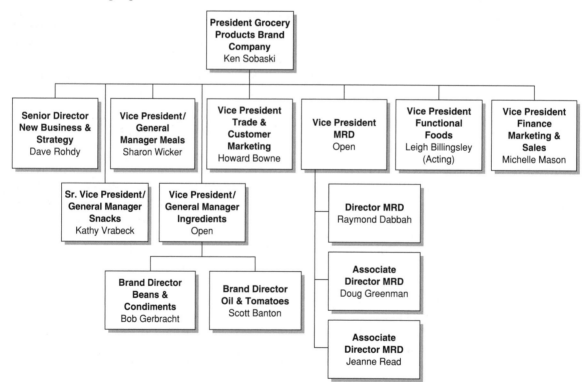

Exhibit 3 Trade marketing and customer marketing organization chart

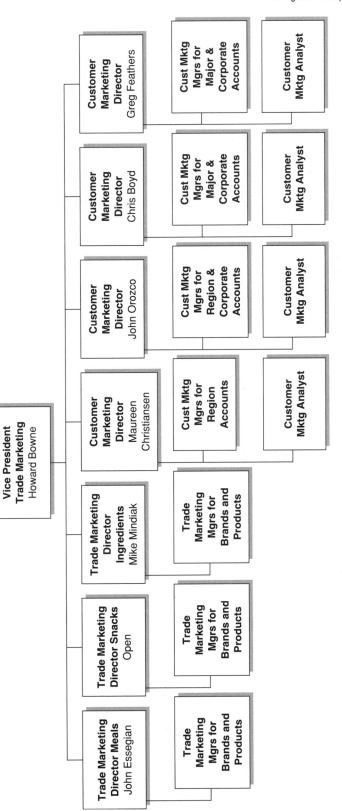

Exhibit 4 Sales division organization chart

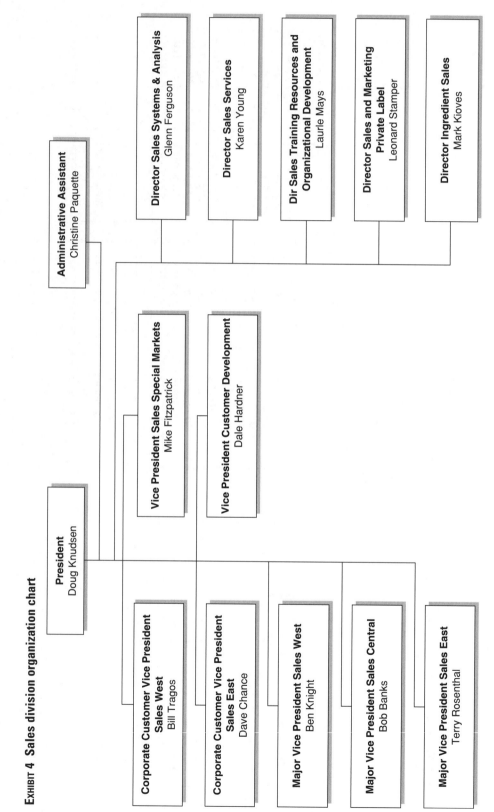

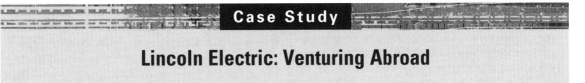

Case Study

Lincoln Electric: Venturing Abroad

Returning late to his half-finished lunch of rice and stir-fried vegetables, Michael Gillespie, president for the Asia region of The Lincoln Electric Company, reviewed his plans to expand the company's production base in his area. Although this venerable US-based manufacturer of welding machinery and consumables had sold products throughout Asia for decades, these had been produced at plants in Australia, the United States, and Europe. Anthony Massaro, Lincoln's new CEO and – like Gillespie – a newcomer to the company, had encouraged the Asia president to develop plans to open welding consumables factories in several Asian countries. Such facilities would enable Lincoln to take advantage of low labor costs and avoid trade barriers.

Specifically, Gillespie now turned his attention to plans for Indonesia. He faced several sets of choices. The first concerned whether to build a factory in Indonesia at all, given the particular political and economic conditions in that country, the nature of the market for welding products, and the competitive situation. If he decided this in the affirmative, he would need to choose whether to enter the market through a wholly-owned factory or a joint venture. Finally, Gillespie wondered whether the planned operation should adopt Lincoln Electric's famous incentive system, credited with rapid, steady increases in productivity in the company's flagship plant in Cleveland, Ohio. Although no immediate deadline loomed for these decisions, he would be asked to discuss his plans at the September 1996 meeting between Massaro and the presidents of Lincoln's five worldwide regions, scheduled for the following Monday in Cleveland.

LINCOLN IN THE UNITED STATES[1]

Founded by John C. Lincoln in 1895 in Cleveland to manufacture electric motors and generators, Lincoln

Electric introduced its first machine for arc welding in 1911. The company eventually became the world leader in sales of welding equipment and supplies (such as welding electrodes). (Exhibit 1 gives more detail on welding technology and Lincoln's products.) James F. Lincoln, John's younger brother, joined in 1907 and complemented his older brother's flair for technical innovation with a proficiency in management and administration. The company remained closely held by the family and employees until 1995, when a new share issue put 40% of its equity into the hands of the general public. These new shares acquire voting rights in the year 2005.

Founding philosophy

James F. Lincoln's independent ideas about human motivation formed the basis of Lincoln Electric's management methods and incentive compensation system. At the foundation of his philosophy was an unbounded faith in the individual and a belief in the equality of management and workers. He also believed that everyone could develop to his or her fullest potential through a system of proper incentives designed to encourage both competition and teamwork. In 1951 he wrote in his company-published monograph, *Incentive Management*:

> There will always be greater growth of man under continued proper incentive. The profit that will result from such efficiency will be enormous . . . How, then, should the enormous extra profit resulting from incentive management be split? . . . If the worker does not get a proper share, he does not desire to develop himself or his skill . . . If the customer does not have part of the savings in lower prices, he will not buy the increased output . . . Management and ownership must get a part

¹ This section draws on The Lincoln Electric Company (HBS No. 376-028) by Professor Norman Berg.

▶

This case was prepared by research associate Jamie O'Connell under the direction of Professor Christopher A. Bartlett.

of the savings in larger savings and perhaps larger dividends . . . All those involved must be satisfied that they are properly recognized or they will not cooperate – and cooperation is essential to any and all successful application of incentives.

Incentive system

James F. Lincoln implemented his philosophy of "incentive management" through an unusual structure of compensation and benefits. He wrote, "There never will be enthusiasm for greater efficiency if the resulting profits are not properly distributed. If we continue to give it to the average stockholder, the worker will not cooperate." The system had four key components: wages for most factory jobs based solely on piecework output; a yearend bonus that could equal or exceed an individual's regular pay; guaranteed employment; and limited benefits.

Piecework

Nearly all production workers – about half of Lincoln's total US workforce – received no base salary but were paid on the basis of the number of pieces they produced. A Time Study Department established piecework prices that stayed constant until production methods were changed. The prices enabled an employee working at what was judged to be a "normal" rate to earn, each hour, the average wage for manufacturing workers in the Cleveland area. (Rates were adjusted annually for local wage inflation.) Each worker also had to ensure his or her own quality, however, repairing any defects identified by quality control inspectors before being paid for the piece in question. But there was no limit on how much could be earned by those who worked faster or harder than the normal rate.

Annual bonus

Since 1934 Lincoln had paid each worker a bonus at the end of each year based on his or her contribution to the company's total performance. The US *Employee's Handbook* explained, "The bonus is not a gift and it does not happen automatically. The bonus is paid at the discretion of the Board of Directors of the Company. It is a sharing of the results of efficient operation and is based upon the contribution of each person to the overall success of the Company for that year." Until the 1980s, the annual bonus averaged nearly as much as the total wages of those eligible: the average worker in an average year received a bonus that almost doubled his or her base pay. In the 1980s and 1990s higher base wages and competitive pressures reduced bonuses to 50% to 60% of base pay.

Nearly all Lincoln employees were eligible for a bonus, including office workers and managers whose regular compensation was not based on piecework. Each individual's share of the bonus pool was determined by a semiannual "merit rating" that measured his or her performance compared to those of others in the same department or work group. The rating depended on four factors: output, ideas and cooperation, dependability, and quality. (Exhibit 2 explains these factors in further detail.) Each department received a pool of points for each factor that would allow employees in each department to average 25 points on each factor. Supervisors then allocated the points among individuals according to their relative performance. Merit ratings varied widely, with some workers receiving total ratings as low as 50 and some as high as 150. Each individual's share of the bonus pool was determined entirely by the ratio of his or her points to the total awarded.

The combination of piecework and the annual bonus enabled Lincoln's best employees to earn much more than their counterparts at other manufacturing companies. In 1995 the highest paid production worker at Lincoln's US operations received $131,000 in base pay and bonus, while the average employee received $51,911 in pay and bonus – 82.8% above the Cleveland average for manufacturing workers.

Guaranteed employment

James F. Lincoln saw guaranteed employment as an essential part of his system, writing: "Higher efficiency means fewer man-hours to do a job. If the worker loses his job more quickly, he will oppose higher efficiency." He also believed that the costs of recruiting and training the highly motivated, creative workers who thrived in his system would outweigh any savings achieved by cutting the payroll during downturns. In 1958 he introduced the Guaranteed Continuous Employment Plan, which assured employment for at least 75% of the standard

40-hour week to every full-time employee who had been with the company at least three years.[2]

James F. Lincoln's successors agreed broadly with these views. When orders dropped, the company took advantage of falling materials prices to produce for inventory. If demand still did not pick up, management could cut hours to 30 per week and redeploy workers to maintenance and other tasks. During the deep recession of 1982, for example, production workers were retrained and sent out as salespeople, selling $10 million-worth of a new product in their first year alone. Such techniques had enabled Lincoln to avoid laying off a single employee in the United States, even one with less than three years' experience, since 1948.

Limited benefits

James F. Lincoln's radical individualism also led him to minimize company-paid benefits under the rationale that fewer benefits enhanced profits and, thereby bonuses and worker compensation. While Lincoln employees received paid vacation, they had no paid holidays off, even Christmas. (They could, however, stay home on recognized holidays without their merit rating suffering.) Taking a day off for sickness also meant giving up a day's pay. The company did not oppose benefits as such – it provided employees with access to a group health insurance policy if they paid the full premium – but it preferred to pay employees with higher cash wages and bonuses, rather than fixed benefits, to give them maximum choice.

Management style and culture

James Lincoln strove to erase hierarchical distinctions, and management's approachable style combined with the system of rational incentives to build a spirit of cooperation between management and employees. The mutual respect was reinforced by the workers' recognition that management worked as hard as they did, often putting in 60- to 70-hour weeks. Through its constant monitoring of the incentives and other work systems, Lincoln managers strove to build a

sense of trust with the workforce. There were no reserved parking places in the company parking lot and executives ate in the same institutional cafeteria as janitors.

Open communication was regarded as essential, and management from the CEO down historically had spent hours of each work day on the shop floor. Furthermore, executives followed James Lincoln's "open-door" policy toward all employees, encouraging them to bring suggestions for improvement and complaints straight to the executive offices, which were located adjacent to the Cleveland plant. Since 1914, an Advisory Board of elected employee representatives had met twice a month with Lincoln's top executives. It provided a forum in which employees could bring issues to top management's attention, question company policies, and make suggestions for their improvement. Advisory Board representatives also communicated management's perspectives to their fellow employees, and minutes of all meetings were posted on bulletin boards throughout the plant and discussed among employees.

The culture that resulted from Lincoln's incentive program and unusual management style seemed to encourage individual employees to produce and innovate. For example, over the years, Lincoln's engineers and operators had collaborated to modify most equipment to run at two to three times its original rate, and had even developed some proprietary machinery. Lester Hillier, a welder with 17 years' experience at Lincoln, was a good example. In 1994 he told *The New York Times*, "I don't work for Lincoln Electric – I work for myself. I'm an entrepreneur." Hillier had put forward some 50 suggestions for cost reductions during the first half of 1994, about 30 of which management had accepted. Chief Financial Officer H. Jay Elliott gave his view of the atmosphere:

> If I go down to the cafeteria, the guy in grubby clothes sitting next to me is just as proud of his job as the chairman in a suit – who's sitting next to him! I think this is the best thing that piecework, the bonus system, guaranteed employment, and many employees' participation in our stock purchase plan have created: a sense of ownership of the company from top to bottom.

Performance

Since 1911 Lincoln Electric executives and employees had attributed much of the company's financial health

---

[2] Although there was very high turnover in the first three years of employment – and particularly in the first 12 months – overall, Lincoln's turnover rate had historically been less than 1% compared to 4–5% for all manufacturing companies.

to its innovative management style and, particularly, its incentive system. The company grew quickly, even as giants such as Westinghouse and General Electric entered the US welding market. Although Lincoln maintained a significant cost advantage over its competitors, during World War II, a patriotic James Lincoln offered to share the company's proprietary methods and equipment designs in order to boost industry productivity. Although its competitors' costs were close to Lincoln's in the immediate postwar period, company data showed Lincoln's productivity per worker was increasing at twice the rate of benchmark manufacturing companies.

Eventually, Lincoln's competitors began to wither in the face of the company's high productivity growth, and by the 1980s the large companies had withdrawn from the market entirely. When Lincoln acquired British Oxygen's US welding company, Airco, management was able to confirm that they had again outdistanced the competitors. In a similar facility, Lincoln was achieving three times the output with half the people. George Willis, Lincoln's CEO in the late 1980s and early 1990s, summarized the company's competitiveness this way: "We're not a marketing company, we're not an R&D company, and we're not a service company. We're a manufacturing company, and I believe that we are the best manufacturing company in the world."

By 1995, Lincoln Electric estimated that it held 36% of the $1.5 billion US market for welding equipment and supplies, making it the leading competitor in an otherwise fragmented industry. "It's a simple strategy," explained one manufacturing manager. "We strive for high productivity based on employee effort, continuous improvement in production processes, and seven-day-a-week utilization of equipment. By passing on cost savings to our customers, we generate very high demand that allows you to send everything you make straight out the door."

EARLY VENTURES ABROAD

Canada

Lincoln started exporting from Cleveland early on, and in 1916 established a sales organization for electric motors in Toronto, Canada. In 1925, it opened a manufacturing plant there and produced the full line of Lincoln products, almost solely for the Canadian market, until the early 1990s. At that time, the advent of the North American Free Trade Agreement (NAFTA) led the US and Toronto plants to specialize in different product lines.

The operation quickly adopted most of the US incentive system, including an annual bonus starting in 1940 and piecework beginning in 1946. Like the US company, Lincoln Canada did not pay piecework employees for sick leave. Holidays were paid, however, as required by Canadian law, and a guarantee of employment was never introduced. A senior executive who had spent most of his career with the subsidiary believed that piecework and the bonus had played a key role in motivating employees to high productivity. Executives' open-door policy and the worker Advisory Council ensured communication among the subsidiary's 200 employees. These workers, like the US ones, resisted unionization, turning it down in a vote in the 1970s.

Australia

Lincoln continued gradually to expand its international manufacturing presence. In 1940, William Miskoe, a disciple of James Lincoln, moved from the United States to Australia to manage a plant Lincoln had opened in 1938. He introduced piecework for most production jobs and an annual bonus that usually amounted to between 25% and 35% of prebonus compensation. Although a commitment was never formalized, employees considered their jobs to be secure, and management cut employees' hours during several recessions to avoid layoffs. Australia was one of the most highly unionized societies in the world, but Lincoln workers rebuffed organizing attempts on several occasions. A senior Lincoln Australia executive believed that Miskoe's introduction of the incentive system when the operation had fewer than 100 employees had facilitated its initial acceptance; later hires embraced the system because their factory-floor colleagues liked it.

High Australian tariffs led Lincoln Australia to diversify into a nearly complete range of welding equipment and consumables. The company eventually began exporting to Asian countries, developing relationships with distributors and building the Lincoln brand-name.

France

In 1955, Lincoln responded to a request from the French government for US manufacturing investment under the Marshall Plan and opened a factory that made welding consumables, and later, equipment. It sold its products throughout western Europe, along with ones made by Lincoln in the United States, through one of Lincoln's US distributors that also had rights to sell into Europe.

Expatriates from Cleveland helped implement the incentive system – including piecework, merit ratings, and a bonus that averaged 10% to 15% of prebonus compensation – in the late 1950s. A formal guaranteed employment policy was in effect from then until its repeal in the early 1970s. (Vacation, holiday, and sick pay were either mandated by law or by industry norms to which Lincoln adhered, varying the US model.) Although Lincoln France had not studied its workers' productivity, its executives believed that it had created a much greater enthusiasm for the work and commitment to the company than existed at other French companies. "There is no question in my mind that the incentive system is a major source of Lincoln France's success. I am deeply convinced that it is essential to our competitiveness," one remarked. From its founding through the late 1980s, the subsidiary had just one unprofitable year, after the oil crisis of the early 1970s, and paid a bonus every year except that one.

Despite this international growth, the Cleveland factory accounted for approximately 85% of worldwide production and monopolized new product development through the late 1980s. The three foreign factories manufactured on a small scale for local and regional markets and relied on US plants for a number of key parts. Corporate executives, based in Cleveland, paid them little attention, content with their healthy, if modest, financial contribution.

INTERNATIONAL EXPANSION, 1988–94

Upon James Lincoln's death in 1965, William Irrgang became the first nonfamily member to lead the company. Under Chairman Irrgang, however, Lincoln launched no new international ventures. Having fled Nazi Germany in the 1930s for the United States, Irrgang had a deep mistrust of all governments but that of his adopted country. This led him to turn down several oversees expansion proposals over the years, many from his President, George Willis.

Following Irrgang's death in 1986, Willis became CEO and finally had the freedom to expand the

company's international manufacturing presence aggressively. He believed that a slowdown in US market growth, as manufacturing's share of the country's economy continued to decline, would force Lincoln to find most future growth abroad. In the mid-1980s the importance of regional trade blocs, such as the European Community and the Andean Pact appeared to be increasing. The new chairman felt that his company needed manufacturing facilities inside each major bloc to ensure that external trade barriers did not render it uncompetitive with local producers. The European Community's (EC's) planned elimination of internal tariffs in 1992 was a source of particular interest.

Believing that the opportunity for immediate market presence made acquisitions more attractive than new "greenfield" factories, between 1988 and 1992 Willis acquired plants in nine countries. Finding no appropriate acquisition candidates, he also built new ones in Japan and Venezuela. In anticipation of European market integration in 1992, prices of many target acquisitions had been bid up to record level. As a result, Lincoln incurred long-term debt for the first time in its history. (Exhibit 3 lists the locations of Lincoln factories as of 1986 and 1992.)

Managing the new subsidiaries

After years of domestic focus under Irrgang's leadership, Lincoln's corporate headquarters contained no managers with substantial international experience. As a result, Willis retained the existing managers of most of the acquired companies to take advantage of their local knowledge, but directed them to implement Lincoln's incentive and manufacturing systems. To help them, he sent out US managers who knew the system in Cleveland, and also linked overseas supervisors and foremen with mentors among their US counterparts. Beyond this, however, corporate headquarters largely left the new subsidiaries to manage on their own.

Most of Lincoln's acquisitions were unionized, and at each relations between management and labor historically had been less cordial than at Lincoln. Corporate executives felt that this would change with time. William Miskoe, the former Lincoln Australia chief, who had become corporate senior vice president for international sales, told a reporter for *Cleveland Enterprise*:

[Workers in the acquisitions] have to learn to trust management, which is not something they are accustomed to doing. That means we have to be completely honest and not pull any punches. We give them the facts, and let them make their own decisions.

Resistance from many quarters hindered the implementation of key elements of the incentive system, however. Many of the European managers and workers were philosophically opposed to piecework and seemed to value vacation time more highly than extra income from bonuses. Regulations presented additional obstacles: in Brazil any bonus paid for two consecutive years became a legal entitlement and in Germany piecework was illegal.

Financial trouble

In 1991, while internal reworking was still in progress, the new subsidiaries' sales were hit hard by a severe recession in Europe and Japan. By 1992, nearly all of the newly acquired plants, plus France, were operating in the red. Nevertheless, corporate executives, still focused primarily on Cleveland, paid little attention. They remained optimistic that modified versions of the incentive system would eventually help most plants abroad achieve rapid productivity growth similar to Cleveland's. Mexico had successfully implemented the system already and Willis told an interviewer that he expected the European operations to have some form of it in place within two years. Fred Stueber, the firm's outside counsel and later its senior vice president and general counsel, recalled, "In 1992, Lincoln was in denial about the severity of the financial problems. They didn't realize their full scale until 1993."

When the 1992 results were reported in early 1993, the situation was plain: the new plants, especially those in Europe, were dragging the whole corporation down, and Lincoln Electric had lost money for the first time in its history. Despite strong performance in the United States, 1993 saw another loss. (Exhibit 4 shows net sales and profits for Lincoln's operations by geography.) Recalled Stueber, "The company was almost in a death spiral: it had shareholders' equity approaching $300 million, and had lost over $80 million in two years. It was hemorrhaging so severely in Europe that prospects were scary." $217 million in long-term debt made the 1993 financial statements terrifying reading for Lincoln's historically cautious board of directors. (Exhibit 5 shows Lincoln's income statements and Exhibit 6 its balance sheets from 1987 through 1995.)

A new broom . . .

In 1992, company president Don Hastings was named CEO, in the middle of what he later called "the nightmare years." His first move was to assemble an International Strategic Liaison Team to analyze the foreign operations and set attainable goals and performance guidelines for which local management would be held accountable. Despite its efforts, the team, comprised entirely of Cleveland-based managers, was unable to stanch the losses.

Recognizing that Lincoln lacked the expertise needed to handle the crisis, Hastings decided to look outside for executives with international experience. In April 1993, he hired Tony Massaro, former worldwide group president at Westinghouse Electric, as a consultant and brought him on permanently in August as director of international operations. Jay Elliott, former international vice president for finance at Goodyear Tire and Rubber Corporation, joined Lincoln in August as international chief financial officer to work closely with Massaro. The two were the first senior executives Lincoln had ever hired from outside the company. Hastings also added four heavyweight outsiders to the board of directors, including Edward E. Hood, Jr., former vice chairman of General Electric and Paul E. Lego, former chairman of Westinghouse.

Massaro's first priority was to conduct an intensive examination of Lincoln's new overseas subsidiaries. With Elliott's help, he quickly identified several causes of the subsidiaries' poor financial performance. First, they recognized that because most attention had been focused on the quality of the acquisition target's manufacturing facilities, several of the newly acquired European companies had small market shares and weak sales organizations.

Another problem was that fragmented production had kept costs high. Instead of concentrating manufacturing of each product in one factory to take advantage of the EC's elimination of intra-European tariffs in 1992, each European factory had continued to manufacture a nearly full line of welding products. In the resulting Balkanized organization, many plants suffered from overcapacity and competed with each other. Ray Bender, a Cleveland veteran, appointed director of manufacturing for Europe, had realized upon arrival that rather than increase production – the classic Cleveland approach – he had to squeeze costs. "Managers ran operations like national fiefdoms," Elliott noted, "and Lincoln lacked the confidence to bring them to heel. Headquarters let the subsidiaries do their own thing and never said 'no.'"

In Venezuela and Brazil, Massaro and Elliott found different problems. There, the company had replaced inherited managers with former Lincoln distributors who were enthusiastic about Lincoln's manufacturing and incentive systems but who had no manufacturing experience. Cleveland had given them little assistance, leaving them to succeed or fail on their own. "The Lincoln culture was so focused on individualism that corporate took a 'sink or swim' attitude with the subsidiaries," commented Elliott. The new executives' analysis concluded that Lincoln's lack of international experience had led management to believe that the new acquisitions and the greenfield in Japan would accept its unusual incentive systems and management style easily. Massaro remarked, "Part of the problem was that they tried to do things the Lincoln way everywhere, rather than adjust to local conditions." With the benefit of hindsight, Hastings agreed:

> We found that operating an international business calls for a lot more than just technological skill. And to be candid, in many cases we didn't truly understand the cultures of those countries where we expanded. For example, we had an incentive program that was based on the belief that everybody in the world would be willing to work a little harder to enhance their lives and their families and their incomes. It was an erroneous assumption.[3]

... Sweeps clean

With firm support from Hastings and the board of directors, Massaro and Elliott set about restructuring international operations to achieve profitability. Massaro explained,

> The cleanup had two main stages. Some subsidiaries could not be saved and we had to shut these down. After that, we rationalized the product lines of the remaining plants in Europe and improved the sales force to increase volume.

---

[3] Quoted in Richard M. Hodgetts, "A conversation with Donald F. Hastings of The Lincoln Electric Company," *Organizational Dynamics*, January 1997.

The plants in Germany, Japan, Venezuela, and Brazil were judged too troubled to keep. In Germany, for example, sales costs were out of control, yet labor laws limited Lincoln's flexibility to respond. Massaro noted that the plant's militant union, IG Metall, was especially resistant to proposed changes, and the company ended up closing the subsidiary in 1994 at the cost of 464 jobs. Elsewhere in Europe, approximately 200 administrative and other non-production workers lost their jobs, leaving European operations' overhead costs 20% below their 1993 level. Plant closings in Brazil, Venezuela, and Japan the same year eliminated another 120 positions.

The process of rationalizing production within Europe proved contentious. In the hope of preventing their production being moved elsewhere, subsidiary managers argued incessantly about whose costs were lower. When incompatible accounting systems made comparison impossible at first, Massaro developed an approach to solving the problem, as Elliott explained:

> Tony did not follow the historical Lincoln practice of imposing a solution from on high. Instead, he created a European management team, comprised of the general manager of each European subsidiary, plus himself, me, Ray Bender, and Cleveland's former head of internal audit. We were collectively responsible for gathering comparable data, then analyzing them to determine which plants would close and how production would be shifted around.

A variety of other efforts boosted volume and, through it, profitability. For example, Massaro replaced several managers deemed unable to handle the changes, and hired new European sales and marketing staff who had experience in international business. He negotiated long-term supply agreements with key customers and arranged for some products being manufactured in the United States for export to Europe to be transferred to the European plants. These moves increased volume and utilization and cut tariff costs. Increasing reliance on local materials also reduced tariff bills. Finally, at Massaro's behest, Lincoln's engineering department developed new products that met European customers' needs better than the US designs the company had been offering.

Significantly, Massaro and Elliott also gave up trying to implement the full Lincoln incentive system in the acquired plants. After the restructuring, most plants stopped focusing on incentive-based compensation systems. Employees in most locations received bonuses based on their factory's results, but these comprised relatively small percentages of total compensation. However, a new bonus program was created for approximately 40 top European managers. Based on pan-European results, it was designed to encourage their cooperation in the service of the corporation as a whole. "Previously, they had no incentive to do anything but maximize their local profitability. The new system ensures that they aren't penalized for contributing to other Lincoln subsidiaries' production and efficiency," Massaro explained.

Following the restructuring, the overseas subsidiaries rebounded. In 1994 European operations made a profit as the continent emerged from recession and their profits grew through 1995 and 1996. The plant in Mexico followed a similar trajectory, while Canada boomed following the NAFTA-related rationalization.

A NEW APPROACH, 1996

In March 1996, Massaro was named President and Chief Operating Officer of The Lincoln Electric Company, and in November succeeded Hastings as CEO. The first outsider among the company's six CEOs and the only one with substantial international experience, Massaro looked to expand Lincoln's presence abroad. Two years earlier, foreign customers had accounted for 36% of the company's sales, but with the international operations in crisis, the newcomer had questioned whether the figure could reach 50% by the turn of the millennium.

Massaro's approach differed dramatically from that of George Willis, the CEO who had overseen the rapid international expansion of the late 1980s and early 1990s. The new CEO judged that the mature North American and European markets would grow only half as fast as those in less-developed countries. Therefore, in 1995, Lincoln had begun extending its sales and distribution networks in Latin America and Asia, and Massaro's next priority was to build manufacturing capacity in the developing markets.

As part of the new strategy, the new CEO also planned to oversee the international ventures more actively. In preparation for further expansion, he created a new structure for the company's international operations, naming a president for each of five regions: North America (including the United States and Canada), Europe, Russia/Africa/Middle East, Latin America, and Asia (including Australia). With vice-presidential rank in the corporate structure, these presidents supervised sales staff in their territories, advised Massaro on whether Lincoln needed to create manufacturing capacity in their regions, and developed plans for new factories. The five met as a group with the CEO every two months to discuss global strategy. Their compensation reflected Massaro's desire for interregional cooperation. A sophisticated bonus system motivated each to develop profitable production operations and maximize sales within his or her territory, but made it most personally rewarding to source goods from the Lincoln factory that could provide them most profitably, even if it was located in another territory.

Finally, Massaro was more flexible than his predecessors about how Lincoln workers abroad would be compensated. He believed that Lincoln's incentive system was an important source of competitive advantage in the United States, but was not convinced that it made sense everywhere. He gave his international managers full freedom to employ only the elements of the system that they judged appropriate for their countries' particular cultural and economic contexts, saying, "If the incentive system makes sense in a particular plant, we'll use it, but we'll also feel free to operate more traditionally or to pick and choose to create an appropriate mixture."

LINCOLN ELECTRIC – ASIA

As of mid-1996, plans to expand Lincoln's international presence in manufacturing had proceeded farthest in the Asia region. Gillespie, a 13-year veteran of ESAB, a Swedish manufacturer of welding products, had already spent six years in Asia when he was recruited in 1995 by Massaro, then Lincoln's director of international operations.

Strategy

As president of Lincoln Asia, Gillespie had developed an integrated sales and manufacturing strategy that would build on the company's existing relationships with distributors and customers. While continuing to source equipment from Australia and elsewhere, Gillespie planned to build factories in Asian countries to manufacture consumables for their local markets. (Trade barriers and the cost of transport made consumables more difficult to import profitably than equipment.) He estimated that each factory would take two to three years to break even.

The strategy was that Lincoln consumables would build brand awareness and loyalty, generating new sales of imported Lincoln equipment. It targeted the construction and manufacturing industries, which were large consumers of welding products and accounted for much of Asian economies' rapid growth. Ray Bender – former head of manufacturing for Europe who now had been appointed to the same post for Asia – summarized the situation:

> Local production of basic consumables will build our market share and thereby enable us to pull higher-end consumables and equipment from other Lincoln factories. In this way, the local production, on which we will earn a modest but reasonable return, will boost higher-margin activities outside Indonesia and increase Lincoln's global return on equity.

Indonesia

Country and market

Indonesia was one of Gillespie's first targets for a new factory. The country's market for welding products was large, but unsophisticated. Most customers used handheld stick welders rather than the semiautomatic or fully automatic machines more common in developed countries. About 50,000 tons (50 million kilos) per year of stick welding consumables were sold each year in Indonesia, representing a market about one-fourth the size of those of more developed countries, such as South Korea. To date, Lincoln had been confined to the equipment and automatic consumables segments, while its participation in the stick consumables market was negligible. (Exhibit 7 shows approximate market shares in each segment for Lincoln and key competitors.)

The bulk of the stick consumables market was served by two multinationals that had local factories and well-developed distribution networks – although some reports of distributor problems had been circulating. Several local firms had significant market shares, but their products were of lower quality. Tariffs of approximately 30% and shipping costs of approximately 7% of factory cost made it impossible for Lincoln to compete in the low-margin stick consumables segment without a local manufacturing base.

Lincoln's reputation as a high-quality producer was well established, and Gillespie believed that customers would switch to Lincoln stick consumables if these were offered at a competitive price. He envisioned a factory that could produce about 7,500 tons of electrodes per year at full capacity. Although only one shift's worth of production workers would be hired initially, others would be added as sales grew, and the plan anticipated using a full three shifts within about three years.

In addition to welding market, Gillespie had to consider broader political and economic risks in deciding whether to enter Indonesia. Political power in the country was concentrated in the hands of President Suharto, a former general who had seized power in a 1965 coup. In the months of civil strife and violence after the coup, up to one million Indonesians had been killed. By 1996, the 76-year-old Suharto's health was deteriorating, but he had designated no successor and continued to repress political opposition. During riots in July, government opponents had burned 10 buildings, including two state-run banks, and some analysts feared that a bloody succession struggle might follow the president's eventual death.

Indonesia's economy was growing rapidly but presented significant challenges to foreign investors. Suharto's relatives controlled large portions of it through personal conglomerates. *Business International* consistently cited the government as one of the world's most corrupt, and officials at all levels routinely demanded "gratuities" to process imported goods, grant licenses, and perform other functions. Local companies dominated the import, export, and distribution businesses, partly for these reasons but also because local customers seemed to prefer dealing with their own countrymen. Another major concern was the economy's stability. Some observers had expressed concern that financial troubles or economic bottlenecks – mismatches in capacity between interlocking sectors of the economy – could cause the overheated economy to stumble. A slump could cause the currency to drop, reducing demand for Lincoln's imports and the dollar value of profits from the local factory.

Economic and political risks were serious, but Indonesia's regulatory environment had been improving. While distribution companies had to be joint ventures with local partners, 100% foreign ownership of manufacturing ventures was now permitted. Furthermore, the government imposed no restrictions on repatriation of profits and the rupiah was freely convertible. As a result, foreign direct investment in the country was booming, having risen 13.3% in the first quarter of 1996. (Exhibit 8 provides economic and social data on Indonesia.)

Entry strategies

If Gillespie decided to enter Indonesia, he could choose from a variety of methods. While 100% ownership of a manufacturing venture would give Lincoln full control and the right to all its profits, a joint venture would provide access to a partner's local expertise and relationships with key people in business and government. Gillespie knew that such contacts could be important during the process of constructing the factory as well as for operations and distribution. His marketing manager described a good local partner as "essential" to provide the company with local knowledge and contacts.

The most obvious possible joint venture partners were Lincoln's two local distributors: Tira Austenite (Tira) and Suryiasurana Hidupjaya (SSHJ). The two were very different. The Indonesian-owned Tira had a network of 14 offices throughout the country and sold a full range of hardware products, including welding equipment and supplies. It had been distributing Lincoln products in Indonesia since 1991, and while it had good access to medium-sized and large customers in a variety of industries, its sales force tended to sell from Tira's vast catalog of products it had sold for decades, servicing their existing clients' established needs. The company's high-level relationships with government officials enabled it to circumvent the bureaucratic obstacles that routinely presented themselves to businesses in Indonesia. However, having to hold inventories of many different products, Tira seemed to be spread thin financially, and management felt it probably would not be able to invest much equity in a joint venture.

SSHJ was a subsidiary of Sin Soon Huat, a Singaporean-Chinese family firm that had distributed Lincoln products in Singapore for nearly 20 years. Its operations in Vietnam, Burma, and China also sold Lincoln products. Founded in 1994 after Lincoln gave Sin Soon Huat permission to distribute its products in Indonesia, SSHJ had only two offices in the country. However, the Lincoln sales staff found the new distributor had adopted a more professional sales style than Tira. SSHJ salespeople visited potential customers and demonstrated the technical advantages and cost savings that Lincoln products could bring them, persuading them to switch from their current brands. SSHJ sold few products other than Lincoln welding equipment and supplies, and its managers from Singapore had years of experience with these. Finally, although it lacked Tira's extensive government contacts, SSHJ's financial strength made it attractive as a joint venture partner. On previous occasions, the parent, Sin Soon Huat, had taken a loss to help Lincoln enter new markets. Because the Lincoln franchise brought the distributor prestige, Gillespie believed that SSHJ would be willing to put up some of the cost of building the new factory and help cover early operating losses.

Gillespie recognized that he could invite one, or both companies to become joint venture partners. Or he could set up a wholly owned manufacturing company and continue to employ them as distributors, although such a move might reduce their commitment to Lincoln. The decision was a difficult one since Gillespie already found it challenging to modulate relationships between two distributors and keep their competition energizing rather than destructive.

Compensation

Beyond these strategic questions, Gillespie also pondered the issue of compensation and incentives, ever important at Lincoln. If he did build a factory, should he pay production workers prevailing wages or introduce some form of incentive system? The only legal requirement was that the company pay the legal minimum wage of 170,000 rupiah per month. At an exchange rate of 2,342 rupiah per US dollar, this represented the lowest wage rate in the Lincoln factory system. However, the prevailing rate at large manufacturing companies was 250,000 rupiah per month, plus an annual bonus equal to two months' salary. At a minimum, Gillespie felt he would have to match this rate, but his inclination was to go further.

Echoing James Lincoln's individualist philosophy, he stated, "I believe strongly in rewarding people for the quality and quantity of their work." Reflecting this belief, Gillespie felt that another option was to make the annual bonus merit-based and link it directly to factory performance, an approach that would require workers to put part of their compensation at risk. He envisioned a scheme based on the Cleveland model, but simplified for the less educated Indonesian workforce. His thought was to offer a merit-based bonus that could reach 30% of the worker's base pay in good years, but which could disappear if the plant were not profitable.

In discussions with Ray Bender, who had joined Lincoln Asia as head of manufacturing, a third option emerged. On the basis of his experience in Cleveland and in Europe, Bender felt that most factory workers did not connect bonuses to their daily work practices. "People think about bonuses twice a year when they get their merit rating," he said. In his view, the real power of the Lincoln incentive system came from piecework. He was convinced that if selected and trained properly, workers in most countries would embrace such a compensation system, because it would provide them the opportunity to earn substantially more money through individual effort. From the company's perspective, he argued that once the workers became familiar with the system, their higher productivity would yield 20% to 40% more output from the same equipment. (Exhibit 9 summarizes the impact of such an increase on gross margins.)

Although his experience with Indonesian labor practice was limited, Gillespie knew of no factory in that country that was using piecework. However, he believed it would not be illegal as long as workers earned the prescribed minimum monthly wage. As a relative newcomer to Lincoln, he was less committed to the approach than veterans like Bender were, and his initial reaction was skeptical. "My experience with Indonesian workers is that they are more effectively managed with traditional management methods," he said, "I'm not sure that the systems that work in Cleveland would be effective there."

Finally, in considering the options, Gillespie realized that ethical and public relations considerations added another wrinkle to these calculations. A number of western multinationals had come under fire for paying employees in developing countries prevailing wages that seemed low to observers in their home countries. Indonesian manufacturing workers generally lived in poor conditions and some supported large families. Gillespie expected that most Lincoln workers in Indonesia would earn more through piecework than under a wage system, but some could earn less. Even a merit-based bonus scheme could put the earnings of the lowest-ranked workers below what they might have earned with a traditional two-month guaranteed bonus. Should these factors affect the compensation system he designed?

As Gillespie discarded his empty styrofoam plate and returned to a stack of reports, he wondered what plans he would report the next week to his colleagues and Tony Massaro.

EXHIBIT 1 Arc welding

Arc welding is a group of joining processes that utilize an electric current produced by a transformer or motor generator (electric or engine powered) to fuse various metals. The temperature at the arc is approximately 10,000 Fahrenheit.

The welding circuit consists of a welding machine, ground clamp, and electrode holder. The electrode carries electricity to the metal being welded and the heat from the arc causes the base metals to join together. The electrode may or may not act as a filler metal during the process; however, nearly 60% of all arc welding that is done in the United States utilizes a covered electrode that acts as a very high quality filler metal.

The Lincoln Electric Company manufactured a wide variety of covered electrodes, submerged arc welding wires and fluxes, and a unique self-shielded, flux-cored electrode called Innershield. The company also manufactured welding machines, wire feeders, and other supplies that were needed for arc welding.

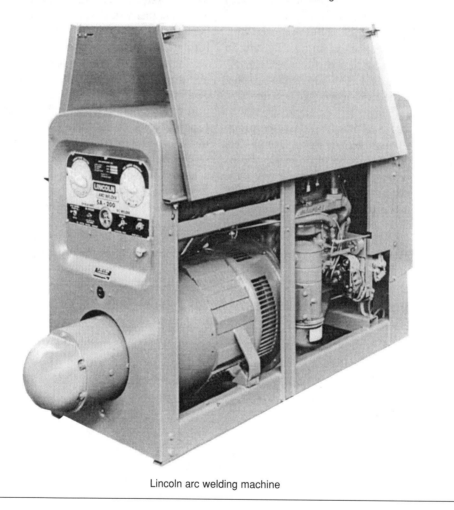

Lincoln arc welding machine

Exhibit 2 Criteria for merit rating for annual bonus (US plants)

The section of Lincoln Electric's *Employee's Handbook* concerning the annual bonus described the four criteria on which supervisors rated employees. (Employees received a rating card for each criterion.)

1. Dependability

This card rates how well your supervisors have been able to depend upon you to do those things that have been expected of you without supervision. It also rates your ability to supervise yourself, including your work safety, performance, orderliness and care of equipment, and effective use of your skills.

2. Quality

This card rates the quality of the work you do. It also reflects your success in eliminating errors and in reducing scrap and waste.

3. Output

This card rates how much productive work which conforms to Lincoln standards you actually complete. It reflects your willingness to maintain high standards of effort and efficiency. It also takes into account your attendance record. Your rating score on "Output" is affected by absence from your job. A deduction of four-tenths of one point from your "Output" rating will be made for each day of absence other than [jury duty, military service, injury on the job, bereavement, vacation, and attendance at company events, but not sickness]. For any one incident of absence a deduction will be made for no more than four days, or a maximum of 1.6 points. If absences are habitual or excessive, regardless of the reasons, other action, including further reduction in merit rating and/or termination, will be considered. The output card will show the number of incidences of absence, total countable days missed in the rating period and the total point deduction.

4. Ideas and cooperation

This card rates your cooperation, ideas and initiative. New ideas and methods are important to the Company in its continuing effort to reduce costs, increase output, improve quality, improve safety and enhance our relationship with our customers. This card credits you for your ideas and initiative as well as your acceptance of change. It also rates your cooperation including how well you work with others as a team. Factors considered include your attitude toward supervision, co-workers and the Company; your efforts to share your expert knowledge with others; and your cooperation in installing new methods smoothly.

Exhibit 3 Locations of Lincoln Electric manufacturing facilities, 1986 and 1992

	1986	*1992*
North America	United States	United States
	Canada	Canada
Asia and Australia	Australia	Australia
		Japan[a]
Europe	France	France
		Germany[a]
		Ireland
		Italy
		Netherlands
		Norway
		Spain
		United Kingdom
Latin America		Brazil[a]
		Mexico
		Venezuela[a]

[a] Plants in these countries were closed in 1993 and 1994.

Exhibit 4 Lincoln Electric financial growth by geography (figures in US$000s)

	1987	1988	1989	1990	1991	1992	1993	1994	1995
Net sales to unaffilitated customers[a]									
US	$363,857	$442,605	$474,060	$500,992	$461,876	$487,145	$543,458	$641,607	$711,940
Europe	29,454	52,401	135,923	215,378	288,251	275,520	211,268	156,803	201,672
Other	57,029	89,639	98,576	94,788	93,560	90,342	91,273	108,194	118,786
Corporate total	450,340	584,645	708,559	811,158	843,687	853,007	845,999	906,604	1,032,398
Income before taxes and extraordinary items[b]									
US	49,874	55,910	53,039	28,205	30,806	24,860	42,570	71,650	87,044
Europe	1,480	3,099	4,423	2,057	(14,377)	(52,828)	(68,865)	3,945	11,350
Other	1,321	1,960	(555)	(6,780)	(2,949)	(7,183)	(22,903)	5,520	10,246
Eliminations	(2,781)	(5,102)	(8,369)	6,878	20,931	721	2,248	(947)	(605)
Corporate total	49,894	55,867	48,538	30,360	34,411	(34,430)	(46,950)	80,168	108,035

[a] For 1987–91 net sales includes interest and other income of between 1.2% and 2.5% of corporate total.

[b] For 1987–91 includes income from interest and other income. For 1992–94 does not include income form interest and other income. 1995 income figures are for operating profit equal to net sales minus cost of goods sold; sales, general and administrative expenses; and foreign exchange loss.

Source: Lincoln Electric SEC filings.

Exhibit 5 Lincoln Electric Company consolidated income statements, 1987–95 (US$ millions)

	1987	1988	1989	1990	1991	1992	1993	1994	1995
Net sales	443.2	570.2	692.8	796.7	833.9	853.0	846.0	906.6	1,032.4
Interest income	5.9	12.3	12.7	11.4	6.0	3.1	1.6	1.4	1.7
Other income	1.2	2.2	3.1	3.1	3.8	4.4	2.9	3.1	2.2
	450.3	584.6	708.6	811.2	843.7	860.5	850.5	811.1	1,036.3
Costs and expenses									
Cost of goods sold	279.4	361.0	441.3	510.5	521.8	553.1	532.8	556.3	634.6
Selling, general & administrative expenses and freight out	72.6	100.7	149.1	190.6	214.1	298.3	276.8	258.0	287.9
Restructuring charges (income)	0	0	0	0	0	23.9	70.1	(2.7)	0
Yearend incentive cash bonus	41.1	50.4	51.8	53.7	45.0	a	a	a	a
Payroll taxes paid by company on bonus	2.1	2.4	3.1	3.5	3.1	a	a	a	a
Hospital and medical expense	5.2	6.7	7.0	7.6	8.3	a	a	a	a
Foreign exchange loss	0	7.7	7.6	3.8	1.2	0.9	0.2	3.7	1.9
Interest expense				11.1	15.7	18.7	17.6	15.7	12.3
	400.4	528.8	660.0	780.8	809.3	894.9	897.5	831.0	936.7
Income before income taxes and extraordinary items	49.9	55.9	48.5	30.4	34.4	(34.4)	(47.0)	80.2	99.6
Provision for income taxes	22.3	21.5	21.0	19.3	20.0	11.4	(6.4)	32.2	38.1
Extraordinary items	0	0	0	0	0	0	2.5[b]	0	0
Net income	27.6	34.4	27.6	11.1	14.4	(45.8)	(38.1)	48.0	61.5

[a] Incentive bonus, all payroll taxes, and medical expenses included in selling, general and administrative expenses after 1992.

[b] Effect of change in method of accounting for income taxes.

Source: Lincoln Electric Company Annual Reports and 10-K filings.

EXHIBIT 6 Lincoln Electric Company consolidated balance sheets, 1987–95 (US$ millions)

	1987	1988	1989	1990	1991	1992	1993	1994	1995
ASSETS									
Cash and equivalents	61.0	23.9	19.5	15.5	20.3	20.6	20.4	10.4	10.1
Net receivables	61.7	90.9	100.8	127.3	118.0	111.3	110.5	126.0	140.8
Inventories	74.7	116.3	120.5	164.4	206.3	171.3	143.7	155.3	182.9
Other current assets	9.1	12.0	14.4	14.5	17.5	18.0	51.1	21.7	23.3
Total current assets	206.4	243.1	255.1	321.7	362.1	321.2	325.7	313.4	357.1
Gross property, plant, and equipment	195.7	274.8	328.2	387.7	422.9	435.2	406.7	444.5	490.6
Accumulated depreciation	121.2	148.6	170.2	193.1	213.3	226.8	237.0	260.3	285.0
Net property, plant, and equipment	74.5	126.3	158.0	194.7	209.6	208.4	169.7	184.2	205.6
Investments at equity	0.3	0.0	0.0	0.0	0.0	0.0	0.0	0.0	0.0
Intangibles, including goodwill	0.0	10.6	26.8	38.0	41.2	50.3	40.1	41.9	40.7
Other assets	13.4	23.2	15.8	17.9	27.4	23.4	24.1	17.3	14.4
TOTAL ASSETS	294.7	403.2	455.8	572.2	640.3	603.3	559.5	556.9	617.8
LIABILITIES									
Current debt, including notes payable and long-term debt due within one year	6.6	39.2	41.6	40.6	50.7	27.1	33.4	18.1	29.8
Accounts payable	23.4	36.8	40.0	44.3	46.6	44.2	43.5	54.8	53.9
Other current liabilities	32.7	38.1	41.0	52.5	61.4	77.2	99.0	71.2	85.0
Total current liabilities	62.7	114.2	122.6	137.4	158.7	148.5	175.9	144.1	168.7
Long-term debt	0.0	17.5	30.2	109.2	155.5	221.5	216.9	194.8	93.6
Deferred taxes	7.0	10.1	9.8	7.4	7.9	8.5	6.1	6.6	7.1
Minority interest	11.9	31.4	42.6	47.4	41.7	16.8	7.9	6.8	5.5
Other liabilities	8.4	5.1	6.8	16.7	12.4	9.2	9.2	10.3	13.0
Total liabilities	90.0	178.4	211.9	317.9	376.1	404.6	416.0	362.7	287.8
Total stockholders' equity	204.7	224.8	243.8	254.3	264.1	198.7	143.5	194.1	329.9
TOTAL LIABILITIES AND EQUITY	294.7	403.2	455.8	572.2	640.3	603.3	559.5	556.9	617.8

Source: Standard & Poor's Compustat PC Plus.

Exhibit 7 Indonesian welding market segments, 1996

	Automatic welding process		Semiautomatic welding process		Stick welding process	
	Equipment	Consumables	Equipment	Consumables	Equipment	Consumables
Size (per year, in metric tons)	n.a.	1,500	n.a.	5,000	n.a.	50,000
Annual growth rate	n.a.	12%	n.a.	12%	n.a.	9%
Market shares (%)						
Lincoln Electric[a]	55%	50%	15%	0%	30%	1%
International company #1	0	5	0	40	0	45
International company #2	30	25	30	20	35	15
Indonesian companies	0	0	0	0	0	35
Imports by other companies	15	20	55	40	35	4

n.a. Not available.

[a] Imported from plants outside Indonesia.

Notes: All Lincoln products were imported. The two major international and the local competitors manufactured stick consumables locally, but imported nearly all of their semiautomatic and automatic consumables and stick equipment, and all of their semiautomatic and automatic equipment.

Source: Lincoln Electric estimates.

Exhibit 8 Indonesia: economic and social characteristics

GDP, 1995	US$ 186 billion[a]
Population, 1995	196,600,000
GDP per capita, 1995	US$ 945[a]
Real GDP growth, average per year, 1991–95	7.3%
Consumer price inflation, average per year, 1991–95	9.0%
Exchange rate, September 1, 1996	US$1 = 2,342 rupiah
Rupiah, average annual depreciation, 1991–95	3.5%
Construction industry growth, 1996	12.4%
Manufacturing industry growth, 1996	11.0%
Prevailing monthly pay for full-time production workers in manufacturing as of September 1996 (Lincoln estimate)	250,000 rupiah
Legal minimum monthly pay for full-time workers (September 1996)	170,000 rupiah
Adult literacy (est.)	84%
Unemployment, official figures, 1994	3%
Underemployment, unofficial estimates, 1994	40%

[a] Converted at market exchange rate.

Sources: The Economist Intelligence Unit, *EIU Country Profile*; The Economist Intelligence Unit, *EIU Country Report*; The Economist Intelligence Unit, *Business Asia*; Central Intelligence Agency, *The World Factbook 1996*.

Exhibit 9 Cost structure for one kilogram of stick welding electrodes manufactured and sold in Indonesia

Scenario	Plant running three shifts, normal labor productivity	Piecework boosts labor productivity by 20%	Piecework boosts labor productivity by 40%
Price	$1.35	$1.35	$1.35
Costs			
Materials	0.70	0.70	0.70
Share of fixed costs (including SG&A, depreciation)	0.20	0.17	0.14
Variable cost (including energy, lubricants)	0.08	0.08	0.08
Direct labor	0.02	0.02	0.02
Profit	0.35	0.38	0.41
Gross margin	**25.9%**	**28.1%**	**30.4%**

Notes: Figures are US dollars. Figures do not represent a single kind of stick welding electrode, but rather a composite of high- and low-margin electrodes, weighted according to their approximate share of the Indonesian market.

Source: Lincoln Electric estimates (disguised).

Case Study

TECO Electric & Machinery Co. Ltd.

In July 1995 Mr. T. S. Hsieh, president of TECO Electric & Machinery Co., Ltd., explained that he thought much of the company's success over the years was due to the "spirit of TECO." The TECO spirit existed because top-level managers hired good people, ran the corporation in a democratic way, encouraged employees to perform as a team, and made sure successes were enjoyed not only by shareholders but also employees, the society, and the corporation itself.

Mr. Hsieh thought one important factor helping to create the TECO spirit was a management decision to evaluate performance using *value-added*, rather than profit, as the primary corporate measure of success. Value-added was calculated by subtracting from sales revenues all payments to outsiders (for example, suppliers, subcontractors). TECO managers believed that the use of value-added focused attention on the right issues and created less conflict between shareholders and employees.

In the last few years, however, some issues regarding the use of value-added had arisen. Mr. Fred P. C. Wang, vice chairman of the TECO board, was quick to explain that, "We are not considering abandoning value-added. The concept is perfect. But maybe we need to adjust it." The issues being discussed related to the calculation of value-added, the optimal way for sharing value-added between employees and shareholders, and employee understanding and acceptance of the measure.

▶

This case was prepared by Professor Kenneth A. Merchant with the assistance of Professor Anne Wu.

Copyright © by Kenneth A. Merchant.

THE COMPANY

TECO was founded in 1956 as Tong-Yuen Electric Company[1] in San Chung City, a suburb of Taipei, Taiwan (Republic of China) with an initial capitalization of NT$3 million (US$200 thousand). Its initial product was induction motors.

Since its inception, TECO's stated mission was to generate customer satisfaction, create profit, and promote social prosperity. To fulfill the company's mission TECO's management endeavored to build an excellent organization that emphasized technology and the creation of "a harmony between managers and employees." The basic strategy involved both continuous improvement of core businesses and expansion of long-term horizons through well-considered diversification into businesses that leveraged core strengths.

Guided by these principles and strategies, TECO management responded in the early 1970s to the development of a more affluent society in Taiwan and the international oil crisis in 1972 by shifting the company's focus more toward home appliances and high-technology information systems products, both of which were designed to increase energy savings and efficiencies. This led to the introduction of a broad range of new products, including refrigerators, clothes washers and dryers, air conditioners, televisions, video cassette recorders, calculators, computer monitors and terminals, printers, robots, facsimile machines, and personal computers.

In addition to developing technology and marketing strengths internally, over the years TECO formed alliances with leading international companies to enhance its strategic position. Among its alliance partners were General Electric, Whirlpool, Westinghouse, Toshiba, Ericsson, Pitney Bowes, and Royal Co. Ltd. of Japan.

By 1994 TECO had grown to become one of the 20 largest private-sector companies in Taiwan with more than 3,500 employees and sales of NT$17.1 billion.[2] It had established a network of overseas subsidiaries and affiliates to serve markets in Southeast Asia, Australia, North America, and Europe. Exhibit 1 shows highlights of TECO's 13-year financial results.

The company made its initial public stock offering in 1973. The number of shareholders grew from 437 in 1973 to more than 50,000 in 1995. Unlike many Taiwanese firms, no single family controlled a significant proportion of TECO stock.

ORGANIZATION

Throughout its early history TECO operated with a functional form of organization. In 1978, facing an increased number of product lines that made it difficult to coordinate manufacturing and sales for each product line centrally, management tried to implement a decentralized profit center form of organization. But this early attempt failed because the organization proved to be too complex. It had too many profit centers; every product line and the sales and marketing functions within each product line were set up as profit centers. A number of conflicts arose, such as about transfer prices. Top management was too busy at the time to resolve these problems, so the profit center organization was discontinued after a one-year test period.

In 1985 TECO management began the implementation of a more modest form of divisionalization. They divided the company into three divisions – home automation, factory automation, and information technology – each of which was to be run as a profit center. It took three years to design the performance measures and reports, to allocate the assets to divisions and, most importantly, to train the managers to use the new system. The system was formally introduced at the end of 1987. Exhibit 2 shows TECO's 1991 organization chart.[3]

THE VALUE-ADDED MEASURE OF PERFORMANCE

Value-added was the most important measure of performance within TECO. It was used for evaluating management performances and for distributing bonus monies. Value-added was calculated by subtracting from revenues the amounts of value provided to

---

[1] The company adopted TECO as its official English name in 1978.
[2] At the time of the case NT$1 = approximately US$.04.

[3] The Information Systems division was spun off in 1989 as TECO Information Systems Co. Ltd., with TECO still owning 70% of the stock. This separation was made to allow the division to respond better to the dynamic nature of the information product markets and technologies. TECO managers found that the information systems personnel, who were more creative, needed different systems and higher pay scales.

outsiders, which included direct materials, utility expenses, depreciation, indirect expenses (excluding payroll), and subcontract fees and other purchases from outsiders. What remained were the amounts of value provided to:

1. employees (salaries, bonuses, benefits);
2. shareholders (dividends, directors' compensation, retained earnings);
3. society (taxes, donations, interest) ("Banks are social shareholders").

Regarding the value contributed to society: TECO's management recognized that much of the company's success was due to Taiwan's considerable success. In TECO's 1993 Annual Report, in a section titled "The Company's Ideals: Contributing to the Good of Society and Country," they acknowledged that, "Our debt to society must be repaid" and that "We measure our enterprise's success in terms of how this debt is repaid."

TECO implemented the value-added concept in 1966. Mr. Shieh, TECO's president, was quick to explain, however, that "We didn't invent value-added; we borrowed it from the Japanese." TECO's chairman had visited a Japanese university, read about the system, and adapted it for use in TECO.[4]

Value-added was used within TECO for deciding "how big the pie is for employee bonuses". In the opinion of TECO management value-added was superior to profit as a measure of entity performance both because it was more consistent with the company's values and because it generated less conflict between shareholders and employees. The basic difference between profit and value-added is that with the profit concept the residual goes to the shareholders; with the value-added concept the residual goes both to the shareholders and to the people whose efforts created the value-added (the employees).

After the "size of the value-added pie" was calculated management had to decide how it should be divided between employees and shareholders. Initially 25% was allocated to employees. Over the years, however, more competitive market conditions had caused TECO's value-added return to decrease, and prices and incomes in Taiwan had increased. In response to these changes TECO managers gradually

raised the employees' share of the value-added. The last change, made in 1990, raised the employee's share from 40 to 43%. The sharing rule was changed only infrequently. The shares were generally fixed for at least five years and were changed only when they were challenged.

TECO used the value-added system in all of its domestic and foreign locations. TECO managers believed it worked equally well in all locations except Southeast Asia. Mr. Shieh, said, "US and Australian managers love it. But managers in South-east Asia seem to have trouble understanding the company's philosophy of sharing the value created."

INCENTIVE COMPENSATION

The employee's share of the corporate value-added created a pool of funds to be allocated to individuals as bonuses. The pool was translated into an average number of days of salary to be given in bonuses and was allocated to individuals according to the following formula:

> Individual bonus
> = average bonus (number of days of salary)
> × individual's daily salary × number of days
> employed in the current year × entity performance
> percent × individual performance percent
> × (1 + extra-job pay percentage).

Explanation of the last three factors in the individual bonus formula:

1. The entity performance percentage was based 50% on corporate value-added and 50% on the performance of the subunit to which the employee was assigned, both as compared to plan. For division managers and division-staff managers the subunit was the division. Subunit performance was measured using a variety of indicators. For example, in 1995 for the top-level managers in one division the factors considered in calculating the entity performance percentage and the factor weightings were:

Performance as compared to plan	Factor weighting (%)
Corporate value added	50
Sales	15
Sales growth rate	7.5
Return on assets	15
Value added per NT$ payroll	12.5
	100% (max.)

---

[4] The value-added measure was not in widespread use in either Japan or Taiwan, although a few companies did use it.

Entity performance was also measured in 18 subunits that were smaller than a division. Eight of these subunits were within the factory automation division; four were within the home automation division; and six were within corporate staff.

Plans for each of these elements of performance were set in a mostly top-down manner by corporate managers. But as part of the planning process the corporate managers solicited input from division and corporate staff managers.

No automatic adjustments were made for the effects of uncontrollable factors (for example, typhoon damage to a plant), but the president was given the power to adjust the entity performance percent upward by up to 5% if uncontrollable circumstances so warranted or if he wanted to reward managers for aspects of their performance that had not yet been reflected in the financial measures (for example, effective implementation of a new system, development of a useful social relationship). To date, however, he had never exercised this adjustment right.

2. The individual performance percent was based on each individual's performance rating, on a scale from 1 (highest) to 5 (lowest), based on achievement of tailored MBO targets. The list of MBO performance areas for a representative division manager are shown in Exhibit 3, and those for a representative product manager are shown in Exhibit 4. These lists show that the individual performance evaluations were based on a combination of quantitative indicators and subjective assessments.

The evaluations were then forced into an approximately normal distribution, with 5% of the employees earning the highest rating of *one*, 20% earning a *two*, 50% earning a *three*, and so on. These ratings were then translated into a performance percent for use in the bonus formula as follows:

Performance rating	Performance percent
1	140
2	130
3	120
4	110
5	100

It was a conscious management decision to give the lowest rated employees a performance percentage of 100%, not a lower figure such as zero. Mr. Michael S. F. Liu, senior manager in the corporate planning department, explained, "This is part of Chinese philosophy, to make people feel good."

3. The extra-job pay percent was designed to ensure that higher level employees received larger bonuses. The extra-pay percentages were:

Division manager	40%
Manager	20%
Product-line manager	10%
All lower-level employees	0%

These calculations resulted in average bonuses for all types of employees that were approximately 40% of salary in a good year for the corporation, 35% in a normal year, and 30% in a bad year. In 1994 TECO awarded its employees 176 days of base pay in bonus, the highest in the company's history.

CURRENT ISSUES

While they judged that the value-added system was generally working well, TECO managers were preparing to discuss three issues that had arisen. One related directly to the formula for calculating value-added. Some within the firm had raised questions as to whether depreciation and interest expense should be included or excluded from value-added and whether adjustments should be made for uncontrollable changes in the company's situation. Depreciation was becoming a more significant expense item as the company automated its production processes. Interest expense had become a concern because debt levels were no longer roughly constant, as they had been a decade ago. Furthermore, the company was taking on different kinds of debt, such as overseas convertible bonds rather than bank loans. Finally, some employees worried that uncontrollable changes in, for example, Taiwan's GDP or TECO's competition, could have significant, unfair effects on the value-added measure.

A second issue was created by uncertainty about the optimal sharing of the corporate value-added. Among the questions the managers were discussing were: Should the allocation percentage be changed more frequently to adapt to changing conditions? Should the company have a formula that automatically determined the allocation percentage? If so, what factors should be in the formula? For example, should the degree of automation be considered?

Could the formula be used to provide incentives for employees to increase productivity, such as by dropping the employee's share if automation efforts were lagging? Should labor market conditions be considered? Labor was currently tight in Taiwan, and a higher percentage might enhance the company's ability to attract the best employees.

The third issue related to how best to explain the value-added system to lower-level employees, particularly those with low levels of education. The system had not worked particularly well with manufacturing personnel in the factory automation division. These employees had low education levels: they had trouble understanding the system;

and they did not think that the goals given them were reasonable. In recent years these employees' bonuses had been based only on division subunit performance, and managers believed that the failure to link bonuses to individual performance had hindered efforts to improve productivity in the plant.

On the other hand, the system had worked well with the manufacturing people in the home automation division. As compared with those in factory automation these employees were younger, better educated (most had graduated at least from junior high school), and were engaged in more simpler, assembly-type work, the outputs of which were easier to distinguish for evaluation purposes.

Exhibit 1 TECO 13-year financial highlights (NT$ billion)

	Sales	Gross margin	Net income after tax	Total assets	Equity
1982	NT$3.7	NT$0.8	NT$0.2	NT$4.1	NT$2.0
1983	5.0	1.2	0.4	4.7	2.2
1984	7.0	1.6	0.7	5.9	2.7
1985	6.7	1.5	0.5	5.6	3.0
1986	7.5	1.6	0.7	6.6	3.3
1987	9.3	2.0	1.0	8.7	4.1
1988	11.2	2.3	1.1	10.6	4.9
1989	12.2	2.3	0.9	12.9	7.0
1990	9.6	2.3	1.1	12.1	7.7
1991	10.3	2.7	1.3	13.4	8.7
1992	11.9	2.9	1.3	14.8	9.4
1993	14.2	3.4	1.6	16.4	10.4
1994	17.1	4.0	2.0	21.2	12.1

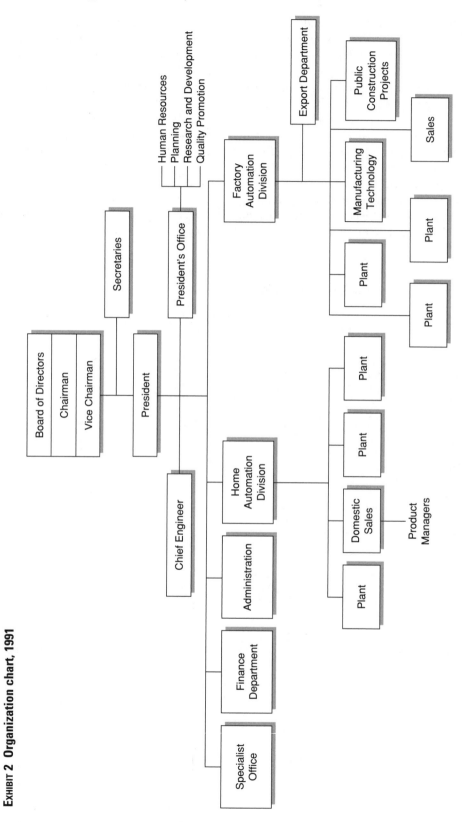

EXHIBIT 2 Organization chart, 1991

Exhibit 3 MBO performance areas for a representative division manager (importance weighting shown in parentheses)

A. Short term (60%)
1. Return on assets
2. Competitive power
   a. Market share
   b. Sales growth
3. Productivity
   a. Labor (value-added/payroll expense)
   b. Asset (value-added/total assets)

B. Long term (40%)
1. Planning
   a. Middle–long term planning (5–10 years); subjective evaluation of the direction the business is taking
   b. Market planning; subjective evaluation of the near-term strategic direction for the business unit, given the competition and industry situation
2. Merchandise
   a. New products/models
   b. Strategic product sales*/total sales
   c. Technology (e.g. productivity, product standardization, waste reduction)
3. Human resource development (education, training, rotation)

---

* Strategic products tended to be high volume, profitable products or products that promised high profits in the near future.

Exhibit 4 MBO targets for a representative product manager within the Home Automation Division (importance weighting shown in parentheses)

1. Product sales attained (35%)
2. Growth in gross profit for product line (17%)
3. Market share (17%)
4. Inventory turnover (14%)
5. Sales development of a strategic product (14%)
6. Control of marketing and promotion expenses (3%)

Case study

Kooistra Autogroep

When he took over as CEO of the Kooistra Autogroep in 2002, Tom Kooistra made significant changes to his company's management control system. Most significantly, he decentralized decision-making authority, developed a performance reporting system that included both financial and nonfinancial information, and introduced a pay-for-performance system for the company's dealership and department managers. Tom explained:

> My father had been running this company like a family, but we've become too big to operate like this. Besides, we need to be more competitive to survive. That's why I am so keen on implementing the new pay-for-performance plan. With decentralization comes accountability for performance. If our people are willing to accept that accountability, then I am quite willing to share with them a fair proportion of the company's success.

But while the company's managers seemed to value the increased authority and performance-related information, their feelings regarding the pay-for-performance system were mixed. In 2007, Tom was considering whether he should try to reinforce the system by telling the managers that the system was here to stay and that they needed to learn how to make it work, or whether he should revise, or possibly even abandon, the system.

THE COMPANY

Kooistra Autogroep was a family-owned automobile retailing company founded in 1953. Over the years, Kooistra grew from a small company that sold and serviced cars of only one or two brands from a single location to a top-20 player in the Dutch car dealership market. In early 2007, it owned and operated 13 dealership locations selling 10 brands of automobiles and employed approximately 325 people.

The Kooistra dealerships were located in the city of Tilburg and in smaller surrounding towns in the southern part of the Netherlands. Kooistra owned five Opel dealerships, three Toyota dealerships, one Citroën dealership, one Suzuki dealership, one Saab dealership, one Alfa Romeo dealership, and one combined Chevrolet, Cadillac, Corvette, and Hummer dealership. Opel (a brand of General Motors) had been the market leader in the Netherlands since the 1970s, with a market share of almost 10% in 2006. Toyota was the sixth largest brand, with a 7% market share. Citroën had a market share of 4% and Suzuki and Chevrolet had market shares of about 2–3%. The other brands sold by Kooistra – Saab, Alfa Romeo, Cadillac, Corvette, and Hummer – all had market shares of less than 1%. For these smaller brands, the nearest competing dealership was typically located far away. In addition to the car dealerships, the Kooistra Autogroep also owned a body repair shop and a car lease company.

In the context of Dutch automobile retailers, Kooistra was large. Even in 2007, the typical Dutch car dealership sold and serviced cars of only one brand from a single location. Most dealerships were family-owned with about 20 employees on average.

In the early 2000s, as a consequence of the weak economic conditions and increased competition, the financial performance of most Dutch car dealers deteriorated. This performance deterioration gave rise to many changes in the industry. One important change was industry consolidation. Many larger car dealerships expanded through acquiring several formerly family-owned dealerships. Kooistra Autogroep was among the first to expand the number of brands sold, standardize operating procedures, and exploit economies of scale.

In 2002, Tom Kooistra's father retired, and Tom took over as the company's CEO. Tom chaired the

---

This case was prepared by Professors Pieter Jansen (University of Groningen), Kenneth A. Merchant (University of Southern California), and Wim A. Van der Stede (London School of Economics).

TABLE 1 Average return on sales in the Dutch car dealership sector (2001–05)

	2001	2002	2003	2004	2005
Average Netherlands	1.02%	1.35%	1.19%	1.05%	0.31%

Source: BOVAG Autodealers 2006. Reproduced with permission.

company's top-management team (see Exhibit 1). Also on the top-management team were Anna Lubbers, CFO, and eight managers. Five of the managers were dealership managers, each responsible for several dealership locations selling between one to five brands. Each dealership location employed a sales manager, a service manager, a workshop manager,[1] and a parts manager. The other three top-level managers were responsible for the body repair shop,[2] the car lease company, and the group's central after-sales department.[3] These managers supervised receptionists, salesmen, technicians, and warehousemen. Also in the company was a central corporate staff responsible for finance and accounting, marketing, quality management, personnel and organization, used car auctions,[4] and fleet sales.[5]

---

[1] Some of the dealerships were located in close proximity. For these dealerships, Kooistra Autogroep maintained one central workshop managed by the after-sales department (see Exhibit 1), which serviced several brands. The dealerships in the other locations had their own workshop. The workshops essentially serviced both the sales and service departments. For service jobs, customers went through the service department which determined the work that needed done as well as the (estimated) cost and time for completion of the work. In addition, the workshop performed get-ready work for new cars sold by the sales department, installation of accessories on new cars, and service and reconditioning work on used cars for resale by the dealership.

[2] Like the service workshop, the body repair shop obtained business internally through the service department and from used car sales for reconditioning body work. The body repair shop, however, also had its own reception for walk-in customers as not all Dutch car dealerships provided car body repair work. Another significant source of business consisted of contracts with insurance companies for repairs related to car accidents.

[3] Because the centralized service workshop was quite large, the role of after-sales manager was created to oversee several workshop supervisors who, in turn, supervised the mechanics (see Exhibit 1).

[4] Customers who bought a car often expected the dealership to purchase their old car. Like most dealerships, Kooistra Autogroep classified these used cars into two categories. Cars that were in good enough condition were offered for sale by the dealership to used car customers. Cars in poor condition, however, considering the reputation of the dealership, were auctioned off in batches by the auction sales department to other companies that specialized in selling these (cheaper) cars outside of a brand name dealership network.

[5] The fleet sales department was responsible for establishing and maintaining relationships with, and selling cars to, companies that bought cars in large numbers.

Although some of its dealerships had been performing quite well, recent overall performance of the Kooistra Autogroep was sub-par, but still in line with industry averages. To ensure adequate resources necessary for business continuity, a rule of thumb in the Dutch car dealership business was that the return on sales (net profit over sales) should be at least 2%. However, due primarily to generally poor economic conditions, the average returns of Dutch car dealerships had not been near this level since the late-1990s (see Table 1).

THE NEW MANAGEMENT CONTROL SYSTEM

As Kooistra Autogroep became a larger and more complex organization, Tom Kooistra concluded that the company's management control system needed to change. Tom's father used to make most of the significant decisions across all the company's operations. Tom, however, believed that he needed to decentralize decision-making. Tom thought that the dealership managers should have substantial authority for the critical decisions in their business, including the hiring, firing, and supervising of their dealership personnel; advertising investments; sales promotions in their local markets; and price reductions that might be needed to move excess inventory or to meet the competition.

But Tom also believed that with decentralization came results accountability. To make this accountability possible, Tom implemented three new systems when he took over as the CEO in 2002: performance reporting, budgeting, and pay for performance. These new systems were to be implemented by fiscal year 2003.

1. Performance reporting

The new performance reporting system included both financial and nonfinancial information. It was used as an instrument to communicate the company's most important objectives to the dealership and department managers; to provide these managers with the information they needed to do their jobs; and to provide feedback to top management so that they could monitor the lower-level managers' performances. Tom explained:

> My father needed to inform the dealership managers and the department managers only about the most important performance indicators because he made most of the operational decisions. I decentralized an important part of his decision-making authority. But when I made the operating managers responsible for achieving the required performance, I also had to communicate much more detailed performance information to them.

One type of performance report, which was referred to as the "Balanced Scorecard" within the Kooistra organization, was distributed to the managers on a weekly basis. It reported year-to-date summary performance on key metrics for each individual manager's operations (e.g. a dealership) with an indication of progress towards budget target accomplishment. Exhibit 2 shows this so-called Balanced Scorecard for the Toyota dealership. In addition to the weekly balanced scorecards, the managers also received far more detailed monthly reports, with sometimes up to hundreds of line-items pertaining to their areas of operation.

The dealership and department managers apparently used the performance reports actively. Tom explained:

> Every Thursday at 2 o'clock, the dealership and department managers receive their Balanced Scorecards by email. When I walk through the company on Thursday afternoon and the reports have not yet been e-mailed, department managers ask me what's up. The department managers are interested in their performance and, particularly, in comparing their performance *vis-à-vis* target.

2. Budgeting

At the same time, Tom introduced a formal annual budgeting process. Although various types of financial and nonfinancial information was considered during the budgeting process, the main focus was on determining net profit targets for the forthcoming year.

Net profit was defined as revenues minus controllable expenses, which in practice meant that most corporate overhead allocations were "below the line" on which the operating managers focused. However, Tom felt that continued decentralization would eventually lead the company to improve its methods of allocating shared service costs to obtain more

inclusive net profit numbers and, thus, to allow even better accountability at lower organizational levels.

The budgeting process was intended to be bottom-up. The responsible managers prepared their own budget proposals. The budget proposals were then reviewed by Tom and the CFO, Anna Lubbers, followed by what they both described as "rather tough, sometimes vociferous, discussions" with each manager. Tom and Anna decided the final budgets.

The budget discussions served several useful purposes. Most managers were inexperienced with budgeting and only few of them had had any formal business education. Anna noted that,

> For these and other reasons we can't always trust the initial budget proposals, so we have to have a very hard look at them. In the end, however, I believe that we find the proverbial happy median for targets that we feel the manager should be willing to commit to.

But not only did the budgeting discussions serve a training role, they also were a valuable communication tool to focus discussions about the business, which allowed Tom and Anna to solicit information from those who were closest to the day-to-day operations from which they themselves had become farther removed.

Tom and Anna monitored performance through weekly reviews of the Balanced Scorecards. When they saw performance patterns that were of concern to them because they were not consistent with the budget targets and/or the performance of other company entities, they had conversations with the managers. The entire top-management team also held monthly meetings to review performance issues and discuss other company-wide business matters.

The net profit budget targets were believed to be achievable with considerable effort. As Exhibit 2 shows, the Toyota dealership had almost achieved its 2006 net profit target even though there were still five weeks to go in the budget year. When asked, the Toyota dealership manager estimated that at the time his budget was approved his likelihood of achieving the net profit target was around 90%. He also pointed out that "Although I've made my budget in each of the past three years, it was rather close. But not all of my department managers met their budget each year. My workshop department had some cost control issues and did not always achieve its net profit targets." The Toyota dealership was among the best performing entities in the Kooistra Autogroep.

Some of the other dealership managers, however, complained that they had trouble meeting their budget targets due to factors outside of their control. For example, the combined Chevrolet, Cadillac, Corvette, and Hummer dealership complained that recent hikes in fuel prices had negatively impacted car sales beyond what could have been foreseen at budget time. He wasn't sure though that Tom would be sympathetic if he failed to meet his budget, which he likely would this year.

But Tom also could sometimes "help" the dealerships make their target. Kooistra Autogroep had a sizable contract with a big rental car company that specified the number and type of cars (e.g. small cars, medium-sized family cars, vans), but not the brand, that the rental car company purchased. Thus, when the Opel dealership was close to making its target but needed "a little help," Tom could offer the Opel Astra model to the rental car company. Alternatively, if the Toyota dealership needed some help, he could propose the Toyota Corolla instead. Tom noted that, because of this leverage, he faced considerable lobbying from the dealership managers to go with their brand. He said, "I never hear any complaints when good fortune comes their way. It's only when they miss their targets that I hear them grumbling."

3. Pay for performance

A third major change was the expansion of a pay-for-performance system for salespeople and the implementation of a pay-for-performance system for dealership and department managers. Some salespeople already received a bonus. But now Tom introduced a pay-for-performance bonus plan for the managers.

Traditionally, compensation for nearly all personnel in the Netherlands was not performance-dependent. It was based on a job rating, an assessment of the training and experience needed for executing a job, rather than on the individual performance of the employee. The job ratings were linked to preestablished salary increases. Hence, the relationship between levels of compensation and actual employee performance was usually weak.

To bypass the limits of salary increases for a certain job grade, top-performing individuals often were promoted to jobs with a higher job rating, when those positions became available. For example, sometimes excellent car salespeople were promoted to

sales manager positions. These promotions sometimes happened even when the dealership would have benefited more from the individual's continued selling efforts than it would from their management skills.

For years at Kooistra, salespeople had had monthly sales targets, defined in terms of the number of (new and used) cars sold. Some of the salespeople were eligible for bonus payouts. In 2007, these bonus-eligible salespeople earned €18.50 per car sold. In addition, when the salesperson met his or her monthly sales target, the bonus amount was doubled to €37.00 per car for the month. On average, bonus payments were about 25% of salary for salespeople who met their targets.

However, not all salespeople were yet eligible for bonuses. Of the 45 salespeople at Kooistra Autogroep, only 25 were bonus-eligible because some of them had negotiated a compensation package without a bonus contingency when they were hired, sometimes at a dealership that had been acquired. These contracts could not easily be renegotiated. Considering these factors, Kooistra's top managers admitted that the sales bonus plan was limited in scope. It also was still subject to change. Anna Lubbers, CFO, explained that management was considering fine-tuning the sales bonus plan by incorporating other performance criteria, perhaps gross, or even net, profit per car.

Tom's new pay-for-performance system for managers added a bonus element to the managers' compensation package. The bonuses were added on top of the managers' salaries. Target bonuses for dealership managers were set between 10 and 20% of annual salary. Target bonuses for department managers were set at 8% of annual salary. For dealership and department managers, the bonuses were based on the extent to which the managers met their annual net profit targets as set during the budgeting process. Only managers who met their net profit target earned their target bonus. No bonuses were paid for below- or above-target performance.

Both Tom and Anna believed that the bonus plan specifically, and the idea of pay for performance more generally, was putting the company on the right track. Tom explained:

> I introduced bonuses primarily to make managers conscious of the fact that something had changed [. . .] that department managers were not only given more decision-making authority but that their responsibilities to meet expected performance also had changed. I think the plan had that desired effect.

Management also had the authority to reduce any or all bonus awards. However, in the first three years since implementation of the system such discretion had never been applied. Moreover, the criteria that might justify a bonus reduction were not yet clear, as Tom explained:

> Theoretically we might reduce bonuses because, for example, administrative procedures were not followed or customer satisfaction ratings were too low. But a bonus reduction would be a very subjective decision. We need to articulate the criteria for such decisions more clearly. This is a priority for the coming year.

ISSUES

Pay for performance was a relatively unknown phenomenon in Dutch companies. For example, one study showed that in 2001 only 10% of the department managers in Dutch car dealerships received a formula bonus and only 7% received a "discretionary" (subjectively assigned) bonus (see Exhibit 3). For sales managers, these percentages were somewhat higher: 20% and 7%, respectively (not tabulated in Exhibit 3).

However, several studies had shown that Dutch companies (not just car dealerships) were increasingly relying on pay-for-performance practices, which was commonly attributed to increased international competition. One study concluded that although only a minority of Dutch companies applied some form of pay for performance, the trend towards doing so was upward with 33%, 36%, and 40% of a sample of Dutch firms using some form of pay for performance in 1997, 1999, and 2001, respectively.[6]

Because such systems were rare in Dutch dealerships, perhaps not surprisingly Kooistra Autogroep faced considerable skepticism from its employees when it first introduced its pay-for-performance system. A survey conducted by a consultant showed that the vast majority of Kooistra employees preferred a salary raise over a bonus, even if the raise was significantly lower than the expected bonus. To illustrate this point, Edwin Vliering, a dealership manager, recounted the following conversation he had had with one of his salesmen:

> In terms of profit and sales volume, the last three–four years were generally bad years for Dutch car dealerships. At the beginning of 2006, one of my top salesmen asked for a salary raise. I offered her a bonus instead. In her situation the bonus would have resulted in more money than the raise she had asked for, even in the poor last couple of years. Nevertheless, she was unhappy. She clearly valued the security of a fixed income. I'd say that she is quite representative of the vast majority of employees around here.

Did the pay-for-performance system provide a significant motivational boost? Edwin thought the answer to this question was *no*:

> Due to the economic situation, the last couple of years were not good years. Consequently, my dealership and some of my department managers did not make their targets and did not receive their bonus. In my opinion, however, this has not affected the motivation of any of us. We are all still working hard. On the other hand, even in good years the level of the bonuses is, I think, too low to motivate, particularly for the department managers. In all truth, I wouldn't mind if we abolished the bonuses for department managers.

On the other hand, Tom Kooistra and Anna Lubbers were convinced that the bonuses could, and did, affect motivation. Tom explained:

> Our managers are certainly highly motivated. This was true in recent years even though, due to the poor economic situation, some of them were unable to realize their performance targets. But I am convinced that they make considerable extra effort when they have a chance to meet their targets. For example, they organize extra sales activities when realization of the target is possible. I also know that they feel good when they achieve their targets. That is part of the motivation. But the money is obviously important as well.

Anna Lubbers agreed that the bonuses could provide strong motivational effects, although she believed that that depended strongly on the likelihood that the managers can meet their targets:

> It is important to set realistic targets. Only bonuses that are based on realistic targets have a motivating effect. Setting realistic targets is particularly important in years of an economic slump, like in recent years. When the target is a *pie in the sky*, the bonus will not work.

---

[6] For example, Bekker, S., D. Fouarge, M. Kerkhofs, A. Román, M. de Voogd-Hamelink, T. Wilthagen and C. de Wolff, *Trend-rapport: Vraag naar Arbeid 2002* (Tilburg, August 2003, ISBN 906566 0623).

EXHIBIT 1 Kooistra Autogroep: organization structure

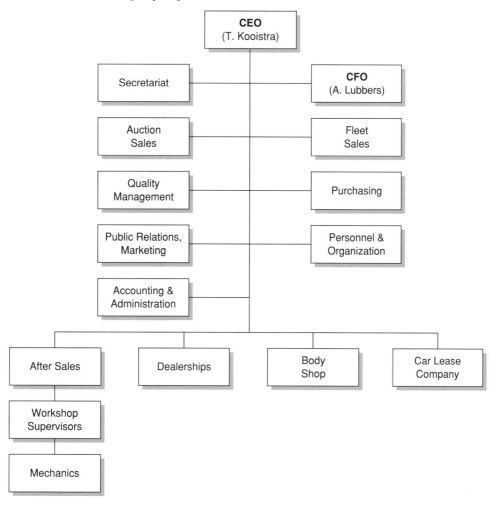

Exhibit 2 Kooistra Autogroep: sample summary performance report for a dealership (2006)

Eindhoven Toyota 1 Jan–17 Nov 2006 (47 wks)		2006 Target	2006 Actual	2006 Percent	2005 Actual
				47/52 wks = 90%	
Sales Department					
New car units		250	229	92	221
Used cars units		225	231	103	225
New car revenues		5,900,000	5,467,522	93	5,298,521
Used car revenues		3,100,000	2,978,644	96	2,906,335
Sales revenues		9,000,000	8,446,166	94	8,204,856
New car net		125,000	112,135	90	107,154
Used car net		5,000	3,504	70	−982
Sales net [1]		130,000	115,639	89	106,172
Sales net margin		1.44%	1.37%		1.29%
New car net/unit		500	490		485
Used car net/unit		22	15		−4
Used car warranty expenses		84,275	82,364	98	90,264
Warranty expense/used car		375	357		401
Manufacturer incentives		150,000	122,687	82	165,922
Service Workshop					
Service revenues		860,000	815,367	95	845,648
Service net [2]		215,000	191,819	89	201,087
Service net margin		25.00%	23.53%		23.78%
Number of orders		1,650	1,621	98	1,648
Number of cars handled		1,050	1,002	95	1,010
Capacity (number of hours)	a	8,800	8,745	99	8,800
Productive hours	b	8,350	8,328	100	8,319
Invoiced hours	c	7,400	7,149	97	7,380
Productivity	b/a	95%	95%		95%
Invoiced hours percentage	c/a	84%	82%		84%
Parts Department					
Parts revenues		1,325,000	1,318,879	100	1,291,820
Parts net [3]		275,000	276,312	100	256,562
Parts net margin		20.75%	20.95%		19.86%
Parts rev./invoiced hrs workshop		179	184		175
Interest Expenses [4]		245,000	216,560	88	232,487
Total revenues		11,185,000	10,580,412	95	10,342,324
Total net [1] + [2] + [3] − [4]		375,000	367,210	98	331,334
Total net margin		3.35%	3.47%		3.20%
Inventory					
New cars in stock		50	47		58
New cars average days in stock		45	40		51
New cars in stock >90 days		10	8		14
Number of backorders		50	62		49
Used cars in stock		60	55		60
Used cars average days in stock		50	45		60
New cars in stock >90 days		0	1		12
Used cars stock (euros)		475,000	424,954		287,469
Parts in stock (euros)		135,000	133,659		136,953

(Numbers are disguised.)

Eхнiвiт 3 US vs. Netherlands comparison of compensation plans used in car dealerships

	US sample (1998)				Netherlands sample (2001)			
	Base salary	Formula bonus	Discretionary bonus	Spiffs	Base salary	Formula bonus	Discretionary bonus	Spiffs
General Managers	[N = 250] Avg. Tot. Comp. = $190,658 (n = 240)				[N = 61] Avg. Tot. Comp. = €58,303 (n = 61)			
Comp. package breakdown	56.8%	36.5%	3.9%	2.9%	96.9%	2.6%	0.4%	0.1%
Number receiving	n = 238	n = 170	n = 49	n = 110	n = 61	n = 9	n = 3	n = 1
Percent receiving	95.2%	68.0%	19.6%	44.0%	100%	14.8%	4.9%	1.6%
Average amount	$82,262	$136,724	$36,449	$10,458	€56,029	€13,079	€6,000	€3,000
Avg. pct. of total comp.	58.2%	51.5%	18.9%	6.3%	96.9%	17.5%	8.1%	5.1%
Department Managers	[N = 526] Avg. Tot. Comp. = $72,390 (n = 510)				[N = 145] Avg. Tot. Comp. = €36,318 (n = 145)			
Comp. package breakdown	49.8%	36.2%	4.2%	9.9%	98.7%	0.9%	0.2%	0.3%
Number receiving	n = 433	n = 338	n = 118	n = 323	n = 145	n = 15	n = 10	n = 30
Percent receiving	82.3%	64.3%	22.4%	61.4%	100%	10.3%	6.9%	20.7%
Average amount	$35,757	$53,751	$15,149	$4,585	€35,745	€3,992	€940	€457
Avg. pct. of total comp.	58.7%	54.6%	18.0%	15.6%	98.7%	8.6%	2.7%	1.2%

Capital "N" indicates the total number of managers in each sample; small "n" indicates those managers in each sample receiving the particular compensation element. Averages are computed for those that receive the respective compensation element (n), as opposed to being computed on the total sample (N). TOTAL COMPENSATION is the sum of BASE SALARY, FORMULA BONUS, DISCRETIONARY BONUS, and SPIFFS. SPIFFS are miscellaneous rewards, such as the use of promotional vehicles and certain incentives provided by the car manufacturers (e.g. vacation trips). All numbers are annualized.

Source: Jansen, E. P., K. A. Merchant and W. A. Van der Stede (2006), "A Comparative Study of Incentive Plan Designs in US and Dutch Car Dealerships," Working Paper.

Chapter 17

MANAGEMENT CONTROL IN NOT-FOR-PROFIT ORGANIZATIONS

In prior chapters, we focused on management control systems (MCSs) in for-profit organizations. Not-for-profit organizations deserve some specific focus because they are in some ways quite different than for-profit organizations. They are also important. Not-for-profit organizations fill a number of important societal roles. All (or virtually all) government organizations, museums, labor unions, and political and fraternal organizations are not-for-profit organizations. Many, if not most, schools and hospitals are too. Collectively, not-for-profit organizations comprise a considerable portion of the economy the world over.

Not-for-profit organizations have many things in common with for-profit organizations. Most of them provide services (or, less commonly, products) and have to compete with other organizations to be the chosen provider. They have professional managers who develop objectives, strategies, and budgets. Many not-for-profit organizations are large, and so their managers delegate authority and hold their employees accountable in specific performance areas. But not-for-profit organizations' MCS alternatives and challenges are often quite different than those faced by for-profit organizations.

DIFFERENCES BETWEEN FOR-PROFIT AND NOT-FOR-PROFIT ORGANIZATIONS

Ironically perhaps, but strictly speaking, the defining difference between for-profit and not-for-profit organizations does not lie in how much profit they can generate, but instead in how it is distributed. A not-for-profit organization's profit cannot be paid out to the owners or anyone else associated with the organization; instead it must be dedicated to the purpose of the organization. Hence, the major defining characteristic of a not-for-profit organization is the *organization's purpose*; its mission or goal. As such, a not-for-profit organization is an organization whose primary purpose is typically to provide some kind of public service. The not-for-profit category, however, includes a large and diverse set of organizations, so the types of services provided vary widely. They can be charitable, religious, scientific, educational, or even political. Included in the not-for-profit category are *governmental organizations* and their various institutions, authorities, agencies, and programs. Also included are a large number of private organizations operated for *public benefit*, such as museums, hospitals, universities, and schools. Some not-for-profit organizations, such as religious organizations and charitable foundations, serve various *private benefit* purposes. And some, such as cooperatives, and labor, fraternal, trade, and homeowners' associations, are operated for the *mutual benefit* of their members.

Unlike for-profit organizations, not-for-profit organizations do not have any outside equity interest. However, like all organizations they do have to generate revenues to fund their operations. Many not-for-profit organizations earn revenues by selling services or products, such as by charging admissions to see a museum exhibit or a theatrical presentation. Others are given money by a third party in exchange for providing their service. For example, a government entity might provide a school a fee or subsidy for every child enrolled in the school. However, money (that is, cash flows and surpluses of revenues over expenses) is only a constraint; it is not normally the overriding goal of a not-for-profit organization. That said, some entities within not-for-profit organizations do have goals to earn profits. For example, governments run lotteries, hospitals run gift shops, and universities sell books, meals, and athletic tickets. In earning their profits they compete with for-profit organizations. But whatever profits they earn are meant to be used to further the organizations' overriding purpose and not to be paid out to the owners or anyone else associated with the organization. Not-for-profit organizations do not pay dividends. All the resources they acquire must be used to further the organizations' primary purpose.

In sum, all not-for-profit organizations have in common the above *purpose* and *profit distribution* (ownership) characteristics. However, although not-for-profit organizations are sometimes perceived as relatively small organizations working for altruistic purposes, such as food banks and community charities staffed by a small number of dedicated managers and unpaid volunteers, being not-for-profit does not necessarily mean being small or being charitable.[1] Many not-for-profit organizations are major employers and a large part of the revenues they generate is needed to cover their overheads. In other words, besides the not-for-profit purpose and the lack of shareholders, it is often difficult to tell some of these not-for-profit organizations from their for-profit counterparts. Nevertheless, not-for-profit organizations tend to have some characteristics with MCS implications that apply to them far more than they apply to for-profit organizations. The following sections describe these characteristics and their MCS implications.

GOAL AMBIGUITY AND CONFLICT

As discussed earlier, MCSs should be designed to enhance the probability that the organization's goals will be achieved, and assessments about MCS effectiveness should be predicated upon judgments of the likelihood (or degree of) goal achievement. Although put somewhat simplistically, goal clarity exists in for-profit organizations. In Anglo-American corporations, for example, the primary goal is commonly taken to be focused on maximizing shareholder value subject to some constraints and other stakeholder interests.[2] And although again somewhat simplified, managers of publicly-traded firms can obtain timely feedback on their goal achievement by monitoring their firm's stock performance and comparing it to that of their competitors and the overall market.

This level of goal clarity, however, does usually not exist in not-for-profit organizations. Many *constituents* typically have an interest in the organization, its goals, and its performance. But these constituents often do not agree; their values and interests conflict. The board of trustees of a museum may perceive their primary goal is to inspire a diverse public through the collection and exhibition of works of art of the highest quality. Other stakeholders, such as the local community and government officials, might be more interested in having the museum present exhibitions aimed at children. Still others, such as religious leaders, might be most concerned about whether or not the art is, in their view, socially and morally acceptable. Resolving these conflicts and differences in perceptions requires unique decision-making mechanisms.

Conflict is also inevitable in government organizations. These organizations are often directed from a number of sources, including the executive, legislative, and judicial branches of government and, possibly, from various levels of government, some national and some local. Law enforcement agencies, for example, have to respond to laws passed and rulings made by all levels of legislatures. Their funding, and their consequent accountability, may also be to multiple authorities. Managers of these organizations face external pressure because the press and public in democratic societies have access to considerable information. Some key officials may face re-election pressures and, thus, may feel a need to please the public at large and campaign donors. This diffusion of direction and potential conflict greatly complicates management. At a minimum, it provides for more goal complexity.

As an example, consider the Los Angeles Department of Water and Power (DWP), which had long regarded itself more as a private company than as the city's public utility, causing a chronic source of tension with city officials. City controller Laura Chick had repeatedly accused DWP officials of wasting hundreds of thousands of dollars on community events, staff perks and parties. DWP officials, however, rebutted that the city bureaucrats just misapprehend the organization, which at the time raised more than $3 billion in revenues for the city annually. "The parties may seem like unnecessary expenses, but they are essential for supporting the community and boosting the morale of DWP employees," said the utility's general manager David Wiggs. Separately, state attorney general Bill Lockyer filed a claim against the DWP alleging that the utility gouged customers during the energy crisis by overcharging ratepayers, to which Wiggs retorted that "[we] sold power for less than the maximum but more than the cost." Although the DWP received high marks for power quality and reliability, customer service, price, value and company image in an independent survey by J.D. Power and Associates, city officials and DWP management seemed to disagree about the organization's goals. "They are neither behaving like a Fortune 500 company that is accountable to shareholders, nor like a public utility that is accountable to ratepayers," said Laura Chick. But even city officials disagree, as one councilman said: "[The DWP] takes in $3 billion worth of people's money; who wouldn't expect them to give some back to the community."[3]

Without clarity as to what goals should be achieved and how tradeoffs among them should be made, it is difficult, if not impossible, to judge how well the organization's control system or, indeed, how well the management team, is performing. Some not-for-profit organizations struggle with these fundamental problems of goal ambiguity and conflict. They must be addressed to aid in designing an effective control system and in assessing the effectiveness of the control system in place, while reflecting the legal, regulatory, policy, and resource environment within which the particular not-for-profit organization operates.

DIFFICULTY IN MEASURING PERFORMANCE

Even if not-for-profit organizations' goals are quite clear, managers of these organizations typically do not have at their disposal any single, quantitative bottom-line performance indicator, like the profit and return measures available to for-profit organizations. The degree of achievement of the organization's overall goals – the provision of quality service to its constituents – usually cannot be measured accurately in financial terms. If a hospital's goal is to save lives or to cure the ill, for example, how is success to be judged? By time to attend to patients brought to the emergency ward? By death rates among emergency patients experiencing heart attacks? By cancer survivor rates? Or should there be measures of prevention rather than merely curing? And how about costs? And because one focus can be compromised in favor of another (e.g. cost vs. care; prevention vs. cure), what importance is to be placed on each?

Without a small set of quantifiable performance indicators, the tasks of management and management control become more complicated. It becomes difficult to:

- measure organizational performance in light of the overall goals and, thus, to use results controls (including performance-based incentives) even at a broader organizational level;
- analyze the benefits of alternative investments or courses of action;
- decentralize the organization and hold entity managers accountable for specific areas of performance that relate exactly to the organization's overriding goal; and
- compare the performances of entities performing dissimilar activities.

The boards of directors, trustees, or overseers of not-for-profit organizations have been especially criticized for their inattention to performance measures. They are commonly unable to do their jobs effectively because they fail to determine "what matters most."[4] Thus, they do not have the performance measures they need to assess the organization's health and to signal potential problems.

Interest in increasing the use of performance measurements by public-service organizations and in disseminating more such data to the general public has been growing, however. The goal of these initiatives is to supplement the traditional input-focused measures (such as expenditures, staffing levels) with results-oriented measures (such as output, quality, timeliness), and in so doing, to improve governmental efficiency and effectiveness by increasing public managers' accountability.[5] Such "government accountability" and public management "reforms" have been introduced in almost all sectors of government in many countries around the world. To quote an example from the National Health Service (NHS) in the United Kingdom:

> Hundreds of new quality measures in over 150 different areas of care will be published in the coming years to help the NHS in England improve care. The vision is that these are to be used by managers or possibly GPs [doctors] if they take on responsibility for managing budgets, where those services that do not meet the standards will struggle to attract funding. Patients may also use the standards to demand they get the best quality care.[6]

One must caution, however, that such increased focus on measurement may produce some of the same dysfunctional side-effects that are also common in for-profit organizations, such as behavioral displacement (concentration on the areas measured to the exclusion of other important but unmeasured areas) and gaming (misrepresentation of data).

An oft-cited success story in the United States is that of the United States Postal Service (USPS), which implemented its so-called Pay-for-Performance Program in 1995 for white-collar employees, covering about 75,000 USPS employees. In the 10 years since 1995, the program was credited with nothing short of a complete turnaround of the then perennial lackluster performance picture: net income increased enough to offset the previous 24 years of net losses, and indicators of both customer service (such as measured by on-time delivery of mail) and employee welfare (such as measured by workplace safety and employee opinion surveys) and employee productivity rose to record levels in USPS's history. One article quoted the program's success as follows: "If the Postal Service, with 75,000 employees and operating with a history of losses, can achieve success, consider what organizations in the not-for-profit and for-profit sector can do."[7]

Various academic studies have provided supporting evidence in some settings as well. For example, one study of not-for-profit hospitals found that profit-based incentives can lead to increases in charity care, suggesting that such incentive contracts may attract managers who are more talented at generating profits and achieving not-for-profit objectives.[8] A number of not-for-profit organizations also have reported success with combination-of-measures approaches (e.g. balanced scorecards) to manage their operations effectively.[9] All told, then, when carefully designed, and when good performance measures can be found, performance measurement and incentive systems might have many similarities between for-profit and not-for-profit organizations, both in their purported functional, but possible also dysfunctional, effects.

ACCOUNTING DIFFERENCES

The financial statements prepared by not-for-profit organizations vary widely from those used in for-profit organizations in both form and content. A comprehensive standard for general-purpose external financial statements provided by not-for-profit organizations did not exist in the United States until the Financial Accounting Standards Board issued Financial Accounting Statement No. 117 in 1993 (FAS 117). Up until that time, some not-for-profit organizations provided consolidated financial statements whereas others did not. Some not-for-profit organizations provided cash flow information, but most did not. FAS 117 was intended to improve the relevance, understandability, and comparability of not-for-profit organizations' financial statements. At the time of the writing of this book, a revision of the International Financial Reporting Standards (IFRS) for not-for-profit organizations was being proposed.[10]

The individual accounting standards used by not-for-profit organizations for operating transactions have also historically been different from those used in for-profit organizations. Depreciation is probably the single most important area of difference. In the United States, depreciation of long-lived tangible assets was required for not-for-profit organizations starting only in 1990 by FAS Nos. 93 and 99. Government organizations are still exempted; they recognize depreciation expense only in their funds that account for business-like activities. Most experts, however, now conclude that the accounting principles used in not-for-profit organizations should be identical to those used in for-profit organizations, with one exception: not-for-profit organizations need separate accounts, called funds, to segregate operating transactions from contributed capital transactions. Indeed, one of the ideas behind the proposed revisions of IFRS for not-for-profit organizations is to use a "cut down" version of the financial reporting standards for small and medium-sized entities (SMEs), although one could argue here that, as mentioned above, not all not-for-profit organizations are necessarily small.

For-profit organizations acquire their resources by selling stock, borrowing money, and earning profits through the selling of the goods and services they provide. Their managers can use those resources any legal way they wish. Most of the resources obtained by not-for-profit organizations, on the other hand, are donated or granted to the organization. The terms of the donation or grant can *restrict* the purposes for which those resources can be used. The restriction may involve use of the resources for a specific purpose (such as to conduct cancer research), a particular type of expenditure (such as for a new building), or a particular time period (such as not until after the year 2015).

Ensuring that each of these donations or grants is used for only its intended purpose places extra demands on the managers of not-for-profit organizations. Some of these restrictions are legal obligations; others are moral obligations from the organization to the donor. To satisfy the extra dimension of accountability that these restrictions involve, most not-for-profit organizations use *fund accounting*. Fund accounting separates resources restricted for different purposes from each other. Each fund has its own set of financial statements: balance sheet and statement of changes in fund balances. Each not-for-profit organization also has a *general fund* that is used to account for all operating transactions and resources not included in any of the restricted funds.[11]

Most not-for-profit organizations prepare consolidated financial reports. The fund accounting counterpart of the for-profit organizations' income statement (which can be called a *statement of activities*, *operating statement*, or *statement of income and expenses*) provides important information about the financial performance of the not-for-profit organization. Figure 17.1 shows a representative operating statement, in this case for the University of Southern California (USC). The statement shows that USC, a private university, raised about $3.1 billion in revenues in fiscal year 2010, but nearly $160 million of those revenues were restricted, either temporarily or permanently (the two middle columns). Expenses totaled $2.7 billion. Thus, USC was able to invest the surplus of about $430 million in its assets, most particularly buildings and various other kinds of restricted and unrestricted investments.

The statement of activities is quite informative because if resource inflows are persistently less than resource outflows, the not-for-profit organization will not survive. On the other hand, having inflows exceed outflows consistently by too great a margin is not by itself desirable either. It may indicate that the organization is not fulfilling its primary mission as well as it could with the resources it has available to it.

It must be recognized, however, that consolidated financial statements for not-for-profit organizations can be misleading. Consolidation obscures the resource restrictions. A consolidated cash balance, for example, may not be usable for paying the organization's operating expenses if the use of that cash is restricted.

EXTERNAL SCRUTINY

Most not-for-profit organizations do not directly serve, and do not have to answer to, a group with ultimate authority, like a shareholder group. They do, however, have to answer to a number of external constituencies, often including donors, government entities, alumni, and even the society at large to some extent. These external constituencies often are demanding. This is natural because most not-for-profit organizations were established precisely to provide valuable social services. In that context, performance reports can provide valuable information that helps the constituents make informed choices, such as regarding which school to send their children to, which hospital to entrust their health with, or which charity to donate their money to. To help inform the public, public websites have been developed, such as Charity Navigator (www.charitynavigator.org), which claims to be "America's premier independent charity evaluator, [which] works to advance a more efficient and responsive philanthropic marketplace by evaluating the financial health of over 5,500 of America's largest charities."

High societal expectations lead to high demands for accountability, as we have seen above. Sometimes benefactors, or the general public, bring direct political pressure on the organization. If an organization is perceived not to be performing suitably, donations can be withheld, and managers and board of directors can be forced out of office. Government regulators can shut the organizations down or place additional restrictions on them. For example, when the Los Angeles convention center's occupancy rate dropped from 83% in 2001 to 72% in 2002; city officials, hotel owners, and regional business advocates rapidly pressed for changes and reforms at the Visitor Bureau, the not-for-profit group responsible for renting the city-owned convention center and promoting regional tourism. The various constituents threatened to monitor the bureau's activities more closely,

FIGURE **17.1 Consolidated statement of activities, University of Southern California, for the year ended June 30, 2009**

	Unrestricted Net Assets	Temporarily Restricted Net Assets	Permanently Restricted Net Assets	Year Ended June 30, 2010 Total Net Assets	Year Ended June 30, 2009 Total Net Assets
Revenues	A	B	C	D	E
1 Student tuition and fees	$1,152,480			$1,152,480	$1,065,342
2 Less financial aid	(325,467)			(325,467)	(320,161)
3 Net student tuition and fees	827,013			827,013	745,181
4 Endowment income	49,720		$374	50,094	62,397
5 Investment and other income	10,654		231	10,885	7,174
6 Net appreciation (depreciation) in fair value of investments	99,810	$183,448	13,198	296,456	(903,089)
7 Government contracts and grants	285,571			285,571	255,864
8 Recovery of indirect costs	118,896			118,896	111,588
9 Gifts and pledges	414,557	14,003	62,749	491,309	392,898
10 Sales and service	31,221			31,221	32,513
11 Auxiliary enterprises	225,363			225,363	226,972
12 Net patient service revenues	592,669			592,669	101,599
13 Professional services agreements	108,625			108,625	102,983
14 Clinical practices	11,997			11,997	80,427
15 Other	89,813			89,813	81,068
16 Present value adjustment to annuities payable		(4,600)	(6,164)	(10,764)	23,208
17 Net assets released from restrictions/ redesignations	103,965	(99,023)	(4,942)		
18 **Total Revenues**	**2,969,874**	**93,828**	**65,446**	**3,129,148**	**1,321,283**
Expenses					
19 Educational and general activities	1,800,354			1,800,354	1,766,739
20 Health care services	714,606			714,606	273,526
21 Depreciation and amortization	142,471			142,471	120,044
22 Interest on indebtedness	40,842			40,842	31,360
23 **Total Expenses**	**2,698,273**			**2,698,273**	**2,191,669**
24 **Increase (Decrease) in Net Assets**	**271,601**	**93,828**	**65,446**	**430,875**	**(870,386)**
25 **Beginning Net Assets**	**2,016,713**	**945,644**	**1,343,700**	**4,306,057**	**5,176,443**
26 **Ending Net Assets**	**$2,288,314**	**$1,039,472**	**$1,409,146**	**$4,736,932**	**$4,306,057**
Nature of specific net assets:					
27 Internally designated	$52,049			$52,049	$4,883
28 Gift and departmental	444,993			444,993	366,138
29 Externally restricted		$47,425	$34,234	81,659	71,377
30 Pledges		117,212	59,883	177,095	193,813
31 USC/Norris Cancer Center Foundation					102
32 Unexpended endowment income	163,490			163,490	152,098
33 Annuity and living trusts		38,915	75,848	114,763	109,669
34 True endowment and net appreciation		835,920	1,239,181	2,075,101	1,914,485
35 Funds functioning as endowment	872,877			872,877	756,941
36 Debt service funds	70,887			70,887	69,886
37 Invested in plant	684,018			684,018	666,665
38	$2,288,314	$1,039,472	$1,409,146	$4,736,932	$4,306,057

Source: University of Southern California, Financial Report 2010. Reproduced with permission.

set performance benchmarks, or else cut ties with the Visitors Bureau.[12] The scrutiny from parties external to the organization places extra control system-related demands on not-for-profit organizations. In particular, the organizations' governing body, such as its board of directors, trustees, or overseers, which represents the external constituencies, must be informed and act responsibly and fiscally.

Members of not-for-profit organizations' boards are sometimes selected, however, for reasons that do not qualify them to exercise organizational oversight optimally. For example, they may have been selected because they are potentially large donors to the organization or because they are good friends of a high-ranking government official. In addition, most not-for-profit board members are paid little or nothing for their services, so they can be easily distracted from their tasks. The consequence is that, as one set of authors concluded, "Effective governance by the board of a not-for-profit organization is a rare and unnatural act."[13] When the organization's internal oversight fails, direct pressure is more likely to be brought from external constituencies.

The sometimes-intense external scrutiny can also shape some decision-making processes, including some MCS-related processes. Planning and budgeting processes are likely to be more important and more time-consuming because the external parties must be heard and their concerns must be accommodated. Management and employee compensation in not-for-profit organizations is also often subject to considerable political pressure. In the words of a Los Angeles city official who commented on the city's review of employee bonuses: "A big piece of the process is not just money; it's inspiring confidence. People don't have confidence [city officials] are spending tax dollars wisely. You've got to be hyper-focused in the attention to detail."[14]

A related concern, and one which naturally takes us into our next section, was voiced by Michael DeLucia, director of charitable trusts and senior assistant attorney general at the New Hampshire Attorney General's Office: "in the charitable sector, there tends to be more trust and less scrutiny." "The Achilles heel in the charitable sector is that people appear to be more trusting and have less internal controls and oversight. That is a weakness."[15] A trustee or board member must act in good faith and exercise the degree of diligence, care, caution, and skill that an ordinary prudent individual would use under similar circumstances in a similar position.

EMPLOYEE CHARACTERISTICS

Employees of not-for-profit organizations often have some characteristics that distinguish them from those in for-profit organizations, and those characteristics can have both positive and negative control implications. The sizes of the compensation packages of employees in many not-for-profit organizations are not competitive with those offered at for-profit organizations. This can cause control problems if employee quality is diminished, as one of the main control problems – personal limitations – may be more salient. For example, when an audit revealed that the Los Angeles County Department of Mental Health had sloppy bookkeeping, weak controls over its expenditures, and spotty compliance with county contract regulations, the Department's chief deputy director replied that "it was essentially a lack of training and lack of adequate controls; [. . .] we need to make sure that our staff understands what the requirements are and follow them."[16]

To address some of the personnel-related control problems, the mayor of Los Angeles and other city leaders have defended large salaries to lure top managers away from private companies, while government critics have called these high salaries "an outrageous waste of taxpayer money." The mayor, however, stood by his policy of hiring good people and holding them accountable, even "if that means paying top dollar." "If you think it's expensive to hire talented people, try hiring untalented people; it's penny wise and pound foolish," Deputy Mayor Ben Austin said.[17]

On the other hand, many not-for-profit organizations tend to attract employees who are highly committed to their organization's goals. They find it easier to relate personally to the organization's goal, whether that is providing shelter for the homeless, food for the hungry, or a cure for AIDS, than to a goal merely to create more value for shareholders. Some not-for-profit employees even work with an idealistic fervor. This high commitment minimizes the other control problems: lack of direction and lack of motivation. Control, then, can be more easily achieved through personnel/cultural means.

CONCLUSION

Control in not-for-profit organizations has both similarities with, and differences from, control in for-profit organizations. The basic needs for good control are the same. Managers of not-for-profit organizations have to address the same set of control problems – lack of direction, lack of motivation, and lack of ability (personal limitations) – as do their for-profit counterparts. They also have basically the same set of control tools – action, results, and personnel/cultural controls – at their disposal. They also face many of the same problems, including the need to implement goal-congruent performance measurement and incentive systems, and the need to avoid many of the same dysfunctional side effects that we discussed elsewhere in this book.

However, MCSs in not-for-profit organizations are sometimes not as well developed as those in for-profit organizations for a number of reasons, such as relating to the types of personnel that they attract and manage to retain, as well as resource constraints and public or even political pressure, to name a few. On the other hand, many larger and perhaps more professional not-for-profit organizations implement many of the control features used in for-profit organizations.

That said, MCSs often must differ appreciably in not-for-profit organizations. Managers of these organizations often find that a command-and-control style of management is not effective. They must spend considerable time managing elaborate, open decision processes designed to build consensus. Even then the decisions often get tied up in a lengthy approval process involving multiple regulators and overseers. Managers cannot easily define results measures and motivate behavior through financial incentives. The goals are not always clear; the important results are often difficult to measure; internal auditors cannot just be ordered into a department to do a performance audit; and the provision of incentives may be unfeasible or unaffordable. There are no stock options to offer. Bonuses are often specifically prohibited by law or labor contracts, and if not that, subject to public scrutiny and scorn.

There are, however, several success stories that suggest lessons not-for-profit managers can learn from for-profit managers. Richard Riordan, a successful businessman who went on to serve two terms as the mayor of Los Angeles, implemented mission statements for various departments and formal results-oriented performance evaluations backed up by, in some cases, merit pay. A study revealed that his city officials – "executives" as he called them – ranked among the most richly compensated public officials in the country. Mr. Riordan's organizational changes produced some successes, although he kept lamenting that "in government there is too much talk about process and not enough talk about results."[18] But many not-for-profit or public sector organizations are not run by business-people, sometimes for good reasons, although that can cause problems and frictions of its own. One of the alleged reasons why the "One Laptop per Child" charity – a group founded by Professor Negroponte at MIT with the audacious goal of transforming learning by supplying millions of the world's poorest children with laptops – was facing difficulties was blamed on "how hard it is for a not-for-profit made up largely of academics to operate like a business and compete with powerful companies."[19]

Add to that how not-for-profit organizations often face legal constraints that are more extensive than those faced by for-profit organizations, where compliance with these constraints almost certainly calls for the use of action controls, and it is easy to see how not-for-profit organizations in many cases must rely on a unique combination of action, results and personnel/cultural controls that "fit" the pursuit of their primary purpose quintessential to their existence, and survival.

Notes

1. See, for example, "How to Be Bold: A Former Fund Raiser Argues for Capitalistic Charity," *The Economist* (January 22, 2009), pp. 88–9.

2. See, for example, "Shareholders vs. Stakeholders: A New Idolatry," *The Economist* (April 24, 2010), pp. 65–6.

3. "DWP's Spending Comes under Scrutiny," *The Los Angeles Times* (March 31, 2002), p. B1.

4. B. Taylor, R. Chait and T. Holland, "The New Work of the Non-Profit Board," *Harvard Business Review*, 74, no. 5 (September–October 1996), p. 7.

5. See, for example, K. Cavalluzzo and C. Ittner, "Implementing Performance Measurement Innovations: Evidence from Government," *Accounting, Organizations and Society*, 29, nos. 3–4 (April–May 2004), pp. 243–67.

6. "New Goals to Replace NHS Targets," *BBC* (July 1, 2010), online (www.bbc.co.uk).

7. J. Schuster, P. Weatherhead, and P. Zingheim, "Pay-for-Performance Works: The United States Postal Service Presents a Powerful Business Case," *World-at-Work Journal* (First Quarter 2006), p. 31.

8. L. Eldenburg, F. Gaertner and T. Goodman, "The Influence of Profit-Based Compensation on Non-Profit Objectives," *Working Paper* (University of Arizona, 2010). For a similar study, see W. Baber, P. Daniel, and A. Robert, "Compensation to Managers of Charitable Organizations: An Empirical Study of the Role of Accounting Measures of Program Activities," *The Accounting Review*, 77, no. 3 (July 2002), pp. 679–93.

9. See, for example, A. Gumbus, D. Bellhouse, and B. Lyons, "A Three Year Journey to Organizational and Financial Health Using the Balanced Scorecard: A Case Study at a Yale New Haven Health System Hospital," *Journal of Business and Economic Studies*, 9, no. 2 (Fall 2003), pp. 54–64.

10. See, for example, *International Financial Reporting Standards and Not-For-Profit Entities: A Cross-Sector Review of the Potential Impact of Recent Proposals* (BDO, March 2010), online (www.bdo.co.uk).

11. Many for-profit organizations also have some funds, such as pension funds, trust funds, and charitable foundation funds that must be kept separate from the firm's main operating accounts. These restricted funds, however, typically comprise a small fraction of the firm's total assets.

12. "Officials Target Visitors Bureau," *The Los Angeles Times* (April 7, 2002), p. B1; "Audit Urges Major Reforms of Visitors Bureau Spending," *The Los Angeles Times* (October 15, 2002), p. B1.

13. B. Taylor, R. Chait, and T. Holland, "The New Work of the Non-Profit Board," *Harvard Business Review*, 74, no. 5 (September–October 1996), p. 36.

14. "Public Enemy No. 1: Bonuses," *The Daily News* (March 9, 2006), p. 1.

15. "Blumenthal May Investigate Charities Ripped Off By Madoff," *Forbes* (December 22, 2008), online (www.forbes.com).

16. "Audit Finds Myriad Woes in Department of Mental Health," *The Los Angeles Times* (August 15, 2003), p. B3.

17. "Riordan OKs Raises for Top Officials," *The Los Angeles Times* (January 30, 2001), p. B1.

18. Ibid.

19. "One Laptop Meets Big Business," *Business Week* (June 5, 2008), online (www.businessweek.com).

Case Study

City of Yorba Linda, California

Arthur Simonian, the city manager of Yorba Linda, California, introduced some refinements in the city's budget process and content for the budget cycle for the fiscal years 1991–92 and 1992–93 (ended June 30). The city's department directors were given more responsibility for making their expenditure projections; a budget manual was created by the Finance Department to assist department personnel with budgeting duties; and more detail was required regarding the purposes of the programs proposed and measurements used to evaluate the programs.

The budgeting cycle encompassed the period January–June 1991. On June 18, 1991 the City Council of the City of Yorba Linda approved the budget. For only the second time in city history, however, the budget was not unanimously approved. The final vote was four in favor and one abstention. The abstaining council member raised several issues, the most important of which was a 24.9% increase in police service costs.

BACKGROUND

The city of Yorba Linda, located in northern Orange County, California, was incorporated in 1967 as a general law city.[1] Yorba Linda is known as the birthplace of Richard Nixon, the 37th president of the United States, and is the home of the Nixon Presidential Library. Since 1980 Yorba Linda had been growing at a rate of about 3,000 people per year. In 1991 the city had 53,000 residents living in approximately 18.5 square miles.

Yorba Linda used a city manager form of government. Mr. Simonian, the city manager, was a full-time employee appointed by the City Council

to manage all city departments except Legal Services (see organization chart in Exhibit 1). The city's budget included 68 full-time employee positions for general city operations and 17 for library operations.

A City Council set city policy. The council was comprised of five city residents elected on an at-large basis for a four-year, part-time term. The council met twice each month, and sessions, except those dealing with personnel or litigation matters, were open to the public. Council members were paid $500 per month for their services. One council member was elected by the council to serve a one-year, largely ceremonial term as mayor. A mayor pro tem performed the mayoral duties when the mayor was unavailable.

Yorba Linda was a contract city, meaning that the city contracted with public and private agencies to provide many of its services. The neighboring City of Brea provided police protection. The County of Orange provided fire, paramedic, public bus transportation, and sewage treatment services. And private agencies provided a variety of other services, including water, trash collection, cable television, engineering, legal, maintenance, public construction, and recreation program instruction. The contract approach enabled the city to cut back or delay noncritical services or projects when revenues were not available.

City revenues, which totalled slightly less than $30 million per year, were derived primarily from state and local sources. State funds included state subventions and grants. In the subvention process the state collected fees and taxes (e.g. motor vehicle license fees, petrol (gas) taxes, cigarette taxes) and redistributed the funds back to the cities, usually on the basis of population. The state also awarded grants intended for specific purposes, such as the improvement of park facilities. Some grants were

---

[1] A general law city is governed by the laws of the state of California. The alternative, a charter city, is governed by its own laws.

This case was prepared by research assistant Patrick Henry and Professor Kenneth A. Merchant.

awarded on a per-capita basis, while others were awarded based on a competition. Yorba Linda's primary local sources of revenues were property taxes, sales taxes, franchise fees and building permit fees. US federal government monies were also available to cities, but the City of Yorba Linda rarely applied for them.

California state law required cities to use fund accounting. Fund accounting creates a clear separation between operating and capital transactions and helps ensure that the restrictions placed on revenues (e.g. use only for parks, traffic safety, or library improvement) were adhered to. Yorba Linda summarized its operations in six major fund categories: general fund, special revenue funds, capital revenue funds, special assessment funds, reserve funds, and restricted funds. Exhibit 2 shows estimates of fund balances at the end of fiscal year 1990–91 and estimates of revenues and expenditures for fiscal year 1991–92. Each fund had its own self-balancing set of accounts. Revenues not restricted to a specific purpose were put into the city's general fund.

THE BUDGETING SYSTEM

Purposes of budgeting

All cities in California were required by state law to have an annual budget. These budgets had two primary purposes. They provided city managers with the authority to make expenditures. Without this budget authority the City Council would have to approve expenditures individually. The budgets also provided control over expenditures by providing benchmarks against which to compare reports of actual expenditures.

By law, city budgets had to be balanced, but Yorba Linda maintained reserves to ensure a balanced budget even when faced with nonrecurring expenses, such as capital additions and unexpected emergencies. The Yorba Linda City Council established a goal of maintaining a general fund reserve level equal to 50% of the operating budget. This assured the city's capability of continuing operations for six months in the event of a major catastrophe. In view of Yorba Linda's many contractual arrangements (e.g. fire, police), the Council also thought it wise for the city to be prepared to deliver services if a contractor defaulted or otherwise became unable to perform vital services. Because Yorba

TABLE 1 City Council members and their occupations

Mark Schwing (Mayor)	Aerospace company manager
Irwin M. Fried (Mayor pro tem)	Lawyer
John M. Gullixson	Lawyer
Henry W. Wedaa	Book company owner
William E. Wisner	Shoe store owner

Linda had enjoyed a sustained period of prosperity city managers had come close to achieving the City Council's goal for general fund reserves: the 1991 ending balance was exactly 50% of the operating budget; the lowest balance was 41% in 1988; and the projection for fiscal 1993 was 53%.

Mr. Simonian had three basic goals for the city's budgeting process, all intended to ensure that the process provided a forum for discussion leading to the establishment of good city policies and priorities. First, he wanted the budget to be easy for members of the City Council to understand. The Yorba Linda council members had little or no formal training in public administration or policy. (Table 1 shows the full-time occupations of the 1991–92 Yorba Linda city councillors.) Second, he wanted the budget to be understandable by members of the community. The citizens were the ultimate customers of the city services, and Mr. Simonian wanted them to understand city priorities and to get involved in the budget-setting process. Typically only two or three citizens attended a budget hearing. Third, he wanted to encourage the city department directors to analyze current and projected activities and their available resources so that priorities could be evaluated.

Comparisons of actual program performance as compared to budget were not considered in department performance evaluations. These evaluations tended to be totally subjective. The evaluations were not linked to monetary awards. The city had no bonus system, and the salaries of most managers and their subordinates were at maximum for their job classification. These personnel received cost-of-living salary increases only.

Evolution of the budgeting system

The Yorba Linda city budgeting system had been evolving over the last decade. In 1986 Mr. Simonian implemented a program budget to replace the line-item budget that had been used for many years.

With the line-item budget, amounts of most line-items were quite small, and the city manager found that the council members had a tendency to get lost in the detail. The Council would ask questions such as, "Why are telephone charges going up 13% next year?" and lose focus on the programs being planned and their objectives. The program budget identified the objectives of every major project/program and resources required.

In 1986 the city also began using a multiyear budgeting approach. Mr. Simonian thought that planning for two years was better than annual planning since many programs and most capital projects lasted longer than one year. Thus in odd years city administrators issued a new two-year budget to the City Council for approval. In even years qualified revisions were made and submitted for approval.

In odd years the budgeting process took place over the period November–June in two distinct phases. The first phase involved preparation of the capital improvement projects (CIP) budget, a five-year capital plan designed to make council members aware of upcoming capital expenses. City managers submitted the CIP budget to Council in December for approval by March. The second phase involved the preparation of the two-year operating budget. Mr. Simonian presented the operating budget to Council in mid-April. The council had to approve a budget by mid-June since Yorba Linda's fiscal year ended on June 30.

Mr. Simonian designed the budget to facilitate the setting of policies and priorities. It presented the council members with options. If, for instance, the council members wanted to accelerate construction of a community center in the 1991–92 fiscal year, the budget showed them where the money could come from. The City Council established final priorities.

During the year Mr. Simonian tried to keep budget revisions to a minimum. But as part of a midyear financial performance review the City Council sometimes authorized additional expenditures for projects that occurred after the budget was prepared. Typically departmental budgets were not changed unless, for example, a major piece of equipment broke and needed replacing. At the midyear review Council also looked at the second year of the budget, sometimes making changes, such as to accelerate the commencement of a particular project.

Several changes were made to the budgeting process and budget content for the 1991–93 cycle. First, the department managers were given responsibility for making all their expenditure projections, including personnel costs. Second, a budget manual, with guidelines, samples, forms, standard costs, and the chart of accounts, was distributed to assist department personnel in the preparation of their budgets. Third, the budget instructions called for more detail than had been asked for in the past about the purpose of each departmental program, program accomplishments over the past budget cycle, objectives for the next two years, and the criteria that department managers believed should be used for measuring achievement of the objectives. (Exhibits 3 and 4 show two program budget examples. Exhibit 3 shows the budget submission for the Contract Classes program of the Parks & Recreation Department. Exhibit 4 shows the submission for the Records/Office Automation Management Program of the City Clerk's Office.) And fourth, the budget calendar was expanded for three weeks to allow managers more time to define the program portion of the budget.

THE PROCESS OF SETTING THE 1991–92 AND 1992–93 BUDGETS

Revenue projections

Revenue projections were made by Gordon Vessey, finance director. Mr. Vessey typically projected revenues conservatively to ensure that the city exceeded its revenue goals. For 1991–93, however, he and the city manager endeavored to make the revenue projections "more realistic." They knew finances would be tight during this period and did not want to cut programs unnecessarily.

As is shown in Exhibit 5, Yorba Linda's revenues were expected to decline from fiscal year 1991. General fund revenues, the most significant component of revenues, had been declining since fiscal 1988–89, but personnel in the city manager's office were pursuing four major initiatives to increase general fund revenues. First, programs and incentives to encourage commercial development were continued. The city manager expected the Yorba Linda Auto Plaza, Price Club, and other new commercial developments to generate additional sales tax revenues in future years. Second, franchise fees were expected to increase, due in large part to a restructuring of the cable television franchise fee. Third, building permit fees were expected to return in 1989–90 levels within the next two years. And fourth, property taxes, the largest single revenue source, were expected to continue to increase. Property taxes generated $3.6 million in revenues in 1991–92 and $4.0 million in 1992–93. Overall, Mr. Vessey projected general fund revenues for 1991–92 and 1992–93 to increase by 16.6% and 7.9%, respectively.

Mr. Vessey expected special revenues to remain constant over the next two years. He knew petrol tax revenues would increase because of a recent 5% gallon state petrol tax increase, but he expected gains from the petrol tax to be offset by a decline in special revenue grant monies. He expected capital revenues to decline considerably in 1991–92 because of a sharp reduction in developer fees. Special assessments, fees charged to residents for landscaping and street lights in their district, had provided a reliable source of revenue in past years with consistent increases each year, and Gordon expected these revenues to continue to grow. Mr. Vessey projected increases in public library revenues in 1991–92 and 1992–93 of 13.9% and 11.3%, respectively. The city established a dedicated fund for library revenues as a result of the Library District's merger with the city in 1985. As part of the transition process the City Council committed to guarantee the monies for library operations. Virtually all the library revenues were collected from property taxes. So overall, Mr. Vessey projected moderate increases in total city revenues to $23.2 million in 1991–92 and $25.5 in 1992–93.

Expenditure projections

As was discussed above, the Yorba Linda department directors prepared all aspects of their expenditure budgets in the 1991–93 budget cycle. In a letter included within the budget manual, Mr. Simonian cautioned the directors to be conservative in their plans. He reminded them that the city had expended 20% of General Fund Reserve balances in the 1990–91 fiscal year and that this trend could not continue if the city was to maintain its healthy fiscal base. Thus he asked them to take a "*hard* and *realistic* look at their current level of operations," to make a "critical evaluation of existing services and programs," and to make a review and prioritization of general operations. Mr. Simonian realized that department directors tended to budget on a line-item basis: if they spent $1,000 last year, they tended to budget $1,000, plus inflation, for the next year. Because finances were tight he asked the directors to look carefully at each item and eliminate or reduce items when possible.

The initial expenditure budget submission was too high, so Mr. Simonian asked the directors to identify potential reductions of 5% and 10% from original requests. He thought it was *prudent* to involve the department managers in the cutting process. The potential reductions were discussed in a series of management meetings. Final cuts did not fall equally on all departments. City management attempted to preserve services and programs traditionally preferred by the residents of Yorba Linda. Plus, reductions were easier to make in larger departments and in departments where directors were inclined to build in slack. Many of the targeted reductions in the budget focused on capital outlay items that city and department managers believed could be deferred to future years without significant impact on operations or services. Exhibit 6 shows a comparison of expenditures by department for fiscal year 1990–91 compared with budgeted figures for fiscal years 1991–92 and 1992–93.

The proposed budget contained several significant changes in the operating expenses of the City Council, city manager, city clerk, police, and Parks and Recreation Department. The City Council's budget was higher than normal in 1990–91 due to public relations efforts associated with the dedication of the Nixon Library. The city manager's office incurred an expense of $100,000 in 1990–91 for consulting fees associated with waste management plans, but Mr. Simonian knew the city would require fewer services of this type over the next two years. The city clerk's budget was increased 9% in 1992–93 to allow for administration of the November 1992 election. The budget for police services was increased by 24.9% in 1991–92 and 10% in 1992–93 because of proposed salary increases and additional patrol hours to improve response times and enhance enforcement of the most serious accident-causing traffic violations. The Parks and Recreation budget for 1992–93 was increased in anticipation of the opening of a new community center projected to be constructed.

Budget changes were also made for capital improvements, capital projects, and the library. Yorba Linda undertook many capital improvements in 1991. Significant expenses were for remodeling the library, land acquisition for and design of the community center, street maintenance, and street improvements. The library was scheduled for completion in early 1992 and the community center for early 1993, which accounted for the 42.5% decrease in the budget for 1992–93. The capital project account differed from the capital improvement account in that capital projects were funded with bonded debt. One of the most prominent capital projects in the city's history, the Gypsum Canyon Bridge, was completed in the 1990–91 budget cycle. As a result, the absence of expenditures related to this project accounted for a large portion of the 63.2% decrease in capital projects for 1991–92. The Yorba Linda Public Library had been operating in a temporary facility since April 1990. Upon completion of the library remodel, library services were to be increased in operating, maintenance, and capital expense, which accounted for the projected 16.0% increase.

As in past years, Mr. Simonian proposed a balanced operating budget (as required by law). But this budget cycle differed from past budgets in the property tax monies in the amount of $1.4 million in 1991–92 and $1.1 million in 1992–93 were allocated to the general fund in order to balance the operating budget. The city had begun receiving property tax money in 1984, and the city manager's goal had been not to rely on property tax money to operate the general fund. But this goal was temporarily abandoned in this budget cycle because of the recession.

In total, city expenditures proposed for 1991–92 and 1992–93 were $32.9 million and $24.1 million, respectively, as shown in Exhibit 7. The general fund balance was projected to be $8.6 million (Exhibit 2) at fiscal year end 1991–92 and $9.5 million at fiscal year end 1992–93.

BUDGET APPROVAL

After the proposed budget was prepared, Mr. Simonian met with City Council members individually to answer questions and resolve objections. In addition, he held a departmental budget staff work session with the Council in early May. This session was open to the public.

Council member John Gullixson voiced disagreement with portions of the budget, particularly proposed increases in the cost of police services. According to terms of the five-year contract approved in 1991 with the neighboring city of Brea, Yorba Linda was charged for police patrol hours, traffic control hours, detective hours, and an allocated portion of overhead for the Brea police force. Brea police overhead was charged to Yorba Linda based on the proportion of police force person-hours used. In 1991 this charge was 48% of Brea police department overhead costs. A 24.9% increase in police service costs was projected for fiscal year 1991–92 because of projections of expanded services provided to Yorba Linda and an average 7.5% salary increase for police force personnel. This increase in police service costs was of concern to Mr. Gullixson. He believed police personnel were overpaid, and he was disturbed that Brea was "making money" on the contract since Brea did not have to cover the full overhead costs for a police force.

Mr. Simonian, however, believed that the police contract was an equitable arrangement and that using Brea services was a good way to provide services to Yorba Linda. He explained, for example, that if Yorba Linda had its own police force it would have to employ full-time detectives for vice and narcotics, but by contracting, the city only had to pay for the hours of detective service actually used. He noted that if Yorba Linda had its own police force it would have to cover all the overhead costs associated with the force. And he pointed out that Yorba Linda's police costs were low in comparison with most other cities in Orange County. So he pressed for approval of the budget over Mr. Gullixson's objections.

The City Council met formally on June 18, 1992 to consider the budget. Because of the earlier budget sessions there was little discussion at this meeting. Mr. Gullixson had not changed his mind about his objection to increased costs of police service. But the budget was approved and adopted with four favorable votes and with Mr. Gullixson abstaining.

Exhibit 1 City of Yorba Linda, California: organization chart

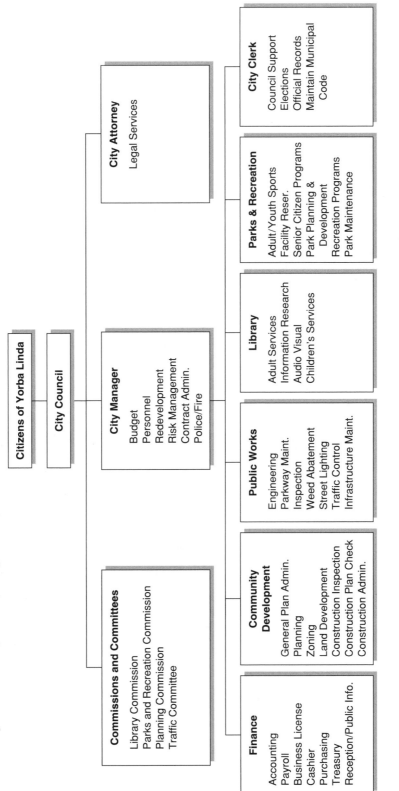

Exhibit 2 Annual budget fund analysis

Fund	Description	Estimated fund balance 6/30/91	Projected revenues 91/92	Total available 91/92	Projected expenditures 91/92	Fund transfer in (out)	Estimated fund balance 6/30/92
					Fiscal Year 91/92		
General Fund							
001	General Fund	9,097,067	13,541,300	22,638,367	12,007,000	(2,020,756)	8,610,611
							*Library loan balance $800,000
Special Revenue Funds							
002	Gas Tax	874,388	887,500	1,761,888	0	(1,420,171)	341,717
003	Aid to Cities	57,872	760,500	818,372	0	(351,771)	466,601
004	Traffic Safety	36,101	225,000	261,101	0	(225,000)	36,101
006	Housing & Community Development	0	15,000	15,000	0	(15,000)	0
026	Street Light Energy	470,765	20,000	490,765	0	0	490,765
	*Total Special Revenue Funds	1,439,126	1,908,000	3,347,126	0	(2,011,942)	1,335,184
Capital Improvement Fund							
008	Capital Improvements	(272,707)	0	(272,707)	14,391,900	10,719,498	(3,945,109)
Capital Projects Funds							
005	Street Improvements	221,861	0	221,861	0	(50,000)	171,861
010	Traffic Signal Development	344,172	0	344,172	0	(234,600)	109,572
014	Park In-Lieu West	366,545	20,000	386,545	0	(225,827)	160,718
014	Park In-Lieu East	359,702	1,500,000	1,859,702	0	(1,562,169)	297,533
014	Park In-Lieu (Designated)	450,000	0	450,000	0	0	450,000
011 & 015	Master Plan of Drainage & Sewers	621,203	820,000	1,441,203	115,000	(1,013,440)	312,763
027	Public Improvement East	417,528	35,000	452,528	0	(348,000)	104,528
Debt Service Funds							
007	Weir Canyon 79-1 Redemption	114,250	0	114,250	0	0	114,250
028	Atwood 85-1 Redemption	0	6,200	6,200	6,200	0	0
030	Savi 83-1 Refund Issue Redemption	1,186,842	458,000	1,644,842	1,431,000	0	213,842
031	Savi 83-1 Redemption	306,017	175,000	481,017	350,000	0	151,017
033	Pub Fin Auth/Cop Redemption Fund	1,433,288	0	1,433,288	0	0	1,433,288
	*Total Capital Projects Funds	5,821,408	3,014,200	8,835,608	1,882,200	(3,434,036)	3,519,372

Exhibit 2 *continued*

Fund	Description	Fiscal Year 91/92					
		Estimated fund balance 6/30/91	Projected revenues 91/92	Total available 91/92	Projected expenditures 91/92	Fund transfer in (out)	Estimated fund balance 6/30/92
012	Street Lighting District #2	284,089	576,500	860,589	615,000	(61,500)	184,089
016	Greenbelt Maintenance District #1	31,364	22,900	54,264	47,800	(4,780)	1,684
017	Landscape Maint Assmt District #5	218,326	34,400	252,726	29,900	(2,990)	219,836
019	Landscape Maint Assmt District #3	58,485	993,200	1,051,685	906,300	(90,630)	54,755
020	Landscape Maintenance District #7	25,289	24,800	50,089	46,200	(4,620)	(731)
021	Landscape Maintenance District #8	18,420	7,400	25,820	11,400	(1,140)	13,280
022	Landscape Maintenance District #9	35,362	17,800	53,162	20,100	(2,010)	31,052
023	Landscape Assessment District #1	(73,957)	846,700	772,743	611,600	(61,160)	99,983
024	Landscape Assessment District #2	11,572	388,600	400,172	328,700	(32,870)	38,602
025	Sewer Maintenance District #1	77,122	77,500	154,622	56,600	(5,660)	92,362
	*Total Special Assessment Funds	686,072	2,989,800	3,675,872	2,673,600	(267,360)	734,912
Reserve Funds							
034	Continuation Wages Reserve	33,787	100,000	133,787	15,000	15,000	133,787
035	Liability Insurance Reserve	1,024,631	100,000	1,124,631	470,000	372,000	1,026,631
037	Savi 83-1 Bond Reserve	79,228	5,000	84,228	0	0	84,228
038	Unemployment Insurance Reserve	20,000	2,000	22,000	2,000	2,000	22,000
039	Liability Benefit Reserve	263,238	19,000	282,238	0	0	282,238
041	Pub Fin Auth/Cop Reserve Fund	403,986	0	403,986	0	0	403,986
042	Savi 83-1 Refund Issue Bond Reserve	188,590	0	188,590	0	0	188,590
045 & 047	Sinking Funds Reserve	695,834	75,000	770,834	0	125,000	895,834
046	Community Center Reserve	232,230	205,000	437,230	0	0	437,230
048	Bridge Restoration Reserve	876,247	70,000	946,247	0	0	946,247
051	Library Remodel Reserve	382,432	0	382,432	0	(845,706)	(463,274)
	*Total Reserve Funds	4,200,203	576,000	4,776,203	487,000	(331,706)	3,957,497
Restricted Funds							
050	Yorba Linda Public Library	301,546	1,705,000	2,006,546	1,514,000	(466,747)	25,799
Redevelopment Agency (Memo Entry)							
069	Redevelopment Agency					(2,186,951)	
						2,186,951	
						ref: RDA Fund Bal	
	***Total All Funds	21,655,147	23,734,300	45,389,447	32,955,700		13,774,992

757

EXHIBIT 3 Budget submission for Contract Classes Program, Parks and Recreation Department

STATEMENT OF PURPOSE:

The purpose of the Contract Classes Division is to provide varied and comprehensive recreational opportunities for City residents of all ages based upon a self-supporting fee basis.

ACTIVITY SUMMARY:

89/90 & 90/91 Accomplishments:

1. Increased Tennis program's enrollment by over 20%.
2. Established Aquatics program with 520 participants.
3. Initiated "Santa Visits" program.
4. Coordinated July 4th Fireworks Spectacular celebration with attendance of 5,000 in 1989 increasing to 10,000 in 1990.
5. Provided over 100 different classes to the public during each quarterly session.
6. Generated over $225,000 in revenue from contract classes participation.

91/92 & 92/93 Goals:

1. Continue to offer a variety of contractual programs to meet the diversified interests of the community.
2. Expand the aquatics program to include water safety awareness.

OBJECTIVES:

1. Increase department's knowledge of community's interest areas.
2. Provide qualified contract instructors for new classes/activities.
3. Provide water safety awareness instructional lessons for children and adults and other information to general public regarding safe pool practices at the home.

MEASUREMENTS:

1. Conduct community survey regarding their interest by June 1992.
2. Provide a minimum of two new contract instructors per quarterly session.
3. Publish and provide a pool safety flyer to the general public and all participants in the Aquatics program.

	Actual expenditures 06/30/1990	Actual expenditures 03/31/1991	Department requests 1991/92	City Mgr proposed 1991/92	Department requests 1992/93	City Mgr proposed 1992/93
Personnel services	17,602	34,825	46,900	49,200	49,800	52,300
Maintenance & operations	18,259	10,450	21,800	21,600	22,800	22,800
Contractual services	114,264	125,474	140,000	140,000	146,000	146,000
Capital outlay						
TOTAL DEPARTMENT	150,125	170,750	208,700	210,800	218,600	221,100
CONTRACTUAL SERVICES (Line-Item Detail)						
Recreation/instructors			7,000	7,000	8,000	8,000
Recreation/classes	103,429	95,406	115,000	115,000	119,000	119,000
Special events	10,835	30,069	18,000	18,000	19,000	19,000
TOTAL CONTRACTUAL SERVICES	114,264	125,474	140,000	140,000	146,000	146,000

EXHIBIT 4 Budget submission for Records/Office Automation Management Program, City Clerk's Department

DEPARTMENT: City Clerk   Department No 001.4.132
DIVISION/PROGRAM: Records/Office Automation Management

STATEMENT OF PURPOSE:

The purpose of the Records/Office Automation Management Division is to improve productivity and provide a cost-effective use of resources in the City Clerk's Department by maintaining an effective Records Management System for the storage, preservation and retrieval of official City/RDA records.

ACTIVITY SUMMARY:

89/90 & 90/91 Accomplishments:

1. Completed physical inventory of records.
2. Separated RDA from City records.
3. Established file patterns and master File indexes with cross reference system for City and RDA records.
4. Attended graduate level "Managing Successful Records Management Programs" seminar.
5. Implemented new computer system.
6. Attended computer hardware/software application workshops.

91/92 & 92/93 Goals:

1. Complete Comprehensive Records Management System.
2. Implement database software on computer system.
3. Develop Legislative History Program.

MEASUREMENTS:

1. Development of Records Retention and Destruction Schedules, and written policy regarding disposition of records.
2. Installation of database and development of Legislative History Program.

OBJECTIVES:

1. Continue implementation of systematic records plan for retention, storage, destruction, and microfilming of records.
2. Selection and acquisition of database for implementation of records program.

	Actual expenditures 06/30/1990	Actual expenditures 03/31/1991	Department requests 1991/92	City Mgr proposed 1991/92	Department requests 1992/93	City Mgr proposed 1992/93
Personnel services	17,650	14,063	27,700	26,600	29,500	28,100
Maintenance & operations	7,236	4,277	9,600	9,600	9,900	9,900
Contractual services	113		3,100	3,800	3,300	4,000
Capital outlay			1,300	1,300		
TOTAL DEPARTMENT	24,998	18,341	41,700	41,300	42,700	42,000
CONTRACTUAL SERVICES (Line-item detail)						
Misc other contract services	113		3,100	3,800	3,300	4,000
TOTAL CONTRACTUAL SERVICES	113		3,100	3,800	3,300	4,000

Exhibit 5 Annual budget revenues

Account number	Account title	Actual revenues 87/88	Actual revenues 88/89	Actual revenues 89/90	Actual revenues 90/91	Projected revenues 91/92	Projected revenues 92/93
Revenue Summary							
	General Fund	9,919,107	13,234,564	12,326,222	12,966,927	13,541,300	14,604,300
	Special Revenue Funds	1,174,402	1,046,333	1,201,358	1,947,536	1,908,000	2,084,500
	Capital Revenue Funds	23,313,834*	4,038,583	5,445,348	6,777,323**	3,014,200	2,431,800
	Special Assessment Funds	1,851,858	2,113,953	2,380,172	2,798,568	2,989,800	4,131,500
	Reserve Funds	2,236,324	170,074	235,021	279,549	576,000	318,000
	Public Library Fund	1,313,905	1,494,073	1,733,987	1,855,724	1,705,000	1,897,000
	***Total City Revenues	39,809,430	22,097,580	23,322,108	26,625,627	23,734,300	25,467,100

* Includes a bond sale of $16,027,794.
** Includes bond proceeds of $3,949,850.

Exhibit 6 Expenditures by department

Department	1990/91 projected expenditures	1991/92 proposed expenditures	% change	1992/93 proposed expenditures	% change	Average % change (2 years)
City Council	$153,000	$94,200	−38.4%	$95,900	1.8%	−18.3%
City Manager	$580,400	$473,600	−18.4%	$483,100	2.0%	−8.2%
City Clerk	$206,600	$212,900	3.0%	$232,100	9.0%	6.0%
Finance	$344,300	$352,800	2.5%	$360,400	2.2%	2.3%
Legal Services	$132,000	$133,000	0.8%	$140,600	5.7%	3.2%
Government Buildings	$174,700	$142,600	−18.4%	$156,200	9.5%	−4.4%
Continuation Wages	$10,000	$15,000	50.0%	$15,000	0.0%	25.0%
Liability Insurance	$470,000	$470,000	0.0%	$490,000	4.3%	2.1%
Unemployment Insurance	$2,000	$2,000	0.0%	$2,000	0.0%	0.0%
Police	$3,773,600	$4,713,200	24.9%	$5,184,500	10.0%	17.4%
Community Development	$1,652,400	$1,651,400	−0.1%	$1,442,200	−12.7%	−6.4%
Public Works	$2,684,500	$2,669,900	−0.5%	$2,734,200	2.4%	0.9%
Parks & Recreation	$1,447,100	$1,574,900	8.8%	$1,871,100	18.8%	13.8%
Total Operating Budget	$11,630,600	$12,505,500	7.5%	$13,207,300	5.6%	6.6%
Capital Improvements	$11,013,600	$12,663,000	15.0%	$7,275,000	−42.5%	−13.8%
Capital Projects	$2,669,900	$982,200	−63.2%	$898,800	−8.5%	−35.9%
Special Assessments	$2,201,700	$2,670,400	21.3%	$3,531,900	32.3%	26.8%
Library	$1,302,100	$1,510,100	16.0%	$1,550,200	2.7%	9.3%
Total Expenditures	$28,817,900	$30,331,200	5.3%	$26,463,200	−12.8%	−3.8%

Exhibit 7 Annual budget expenditures

Account number	Account title	Actual revenues 87/88	Actual revenues 88/89	Actual expenditures 89/90	Actual expenditures 90/91	Adopted expenditures 91/92	Adopted expenditures 92/93
	Expenditure Summary						
	Operating Budget	7,995,958	9,374,920	10,176,504	11,327,782	12,494,000	13,172,500
	Capital Improvements	5,774,384	3,515,392	5,135,104	10,018,072	14,391,900	5,005,000
	Capital Projects	10,495,508	13,100,277	6,081,755	4,051,292	1,882,200	898,800
	Special Assessments	1,622,488	1,870,539	2,188,885	2,373,050	2,673,600	3,531,900
	Public Library	1,054,484	1,133,702	1,365,748	1,264,025	1,514,000	1,540,000
	***Total City Expenditures	26,942,822	28,994,830	24,947,996	29,034,221	32,955,700	24,148,200

Case Study

Waikerie Co-Operative Producers Ltd.

The 1993 Budget Report for Waikerie Co-Operative Producers Ltd., an Australian citrus co-operative, listed "the four singularly most important factors in the operation of the co-operative":

1. Are we making a profit and close to budget on our cash flow?

2. Are we paying a competitive price for all produce supplied?

3. Is our volume of handling near or better than our estimate?

4. Are our sales targets being achieved?

The budget for fiscal year 1993 was calculated "with these factors uppermost in all considerations," but Duncan Beaton, general manager of the cooperative, had concerns in each of these areas. The cooperative had had a negative operating surplus in each of the last two fiscal years and its managers were forecasting another, in large part because it was operating at less than 50% of its capacity. Some grower-members were complaining that the cooperative was not paying a competitive price for produce (although Duncan was not convinced that their criticisms were valid). And Waikerie managers found it difficult to prepare even reasonably accurate sales and budget targets both because of volatility in the produce markets and less than complete cooperation from the grower-members.

THE COOPERATIVE

Waikerie Producers was the largest citrus packer in Australia. Because Australia produced only 1% of the world's citrus, however, it was still a small organization; 1992 revenues totalled A$8.4 million (excluding fruit revenue of approximately A$20 million paid directly to growers).[1] (Exhibit 1 shows

an organization chart.) The cooperative was located at Waikerie, a town of 5,000 people approximately 150 kilometers northeast of Adelaide, South Australia. Waikerie, and the small towns around it, were in a region called the *Riverland*, the largest of five citrus growing regions in Australia.

The cooperative existed to serve its grower-members. It was founded in 1914 to pack dried fruit (e.g. apricots, raisins). It began packing oranges in 1920, and the operating emphasis shifted gradually to citrus, rather than dried fruit, reflecting the agricultural production in the region. The peak year for packing dried fruit was 1944. The cooperative had been exporting citrus fruit under the *Riverland* brand since 1936.

The cooperative's most important functions were the packing and marketing of fruit, primarily oranges, but also grapefruit, lemons, mandarins, and dried fruit. It also provided its members with a broad range of other services, including fruit price forecasts, growing advice (e.g. how to minimize mold infestations, how to reduce irrigation to reduce fruit blemishes), bulk (e.g. fertilizer) and hardware supplies, transport, and equipment sales and servicing. All of the grower-members were relatively small: the average grower's holdings in the Riverland area were 20–25 acres; the largest was 500 acres.

The grower-members delivered citrus fruit to the cooperative in 60-bushel bins. The major packing seasons were as follows: Navel oranges – primarily April to September; Valencia oranges – August to May; grapefruit – June to November; lemons – May to October; mandarins – May to October; dried fruit – December to February. Waikerie Producers chose a fiscal year ending March 31, in the slow season, toward the end of the Valencia season but before the beginning of the Navel season.

▶

---

[1] At the time of the case, A$1 was worth approximately US$.70.

This case was prepared by Professor Kenneth A. Merchant.

Copyright © by Kenneth A. Merchant.

The larger, higher quality citrus fruit was washed, dipped in fungicide, waxed, sorted by grade (export or standard) and size, stamped with the *Riverland* logo, and packed in 30-liter (4/5 bushel) boxes or 3-kilo mesh bags. This fruit was sold either directly to larger retailers or to sales agents. Smaller, lower quality (e.g. blemished) fruit was sold by the truck-load to be made into juice. Waikerie Producers maintained a strict quality standard to protect its brandname: about 70% of the product sent was sold to be made into juice; this compared to approximately 60% at other packers.

To join the cooperative members were required to purchase at least A$300 worth of cooperative shares, the current market value of which was approximately A$67 per share. If the cooperative earned a surplus, 50% of the surplus was rebated to the members, and 50% was held back as a rotating reserve.

The members elected a board of directors, comprised of seven grower-members, to a two-year term. The board met not less than once a month; in 1991 it met 20 times. The board members usually had altruistic and prestige motives for serving. They were paid little for their services: the members earned $1,000 a year; the chairman earned $5,000.

Waikerie Producers had the capacity to sort and pack 6,500 cases per day, but it was operating at an average of only 2,000–2,500 cases per day. In 1989 Waikerie managers made what was, in retrospect, a strategic error. They added more automated sorting and packing equipment to reduce unit costs through economies of scale, but the additions coincided with a downturn in the market for Australian fruit and a dramatic rise in interest charges. Because of the industry overcapacity they were unable to sell the excess equipment.

The whole Riverland area had significant citrus packing overcapacity. Virtually every small town in the Riverland area had its own citrus packing cooperative. The area also contained a few private packers, each of which was a small, privately owned family business. The packing cooperatives generally abided by the six internationally accepted principles of cooperation shown in Exhibit 2. The last of these principles prohibited competition among cooperatives, so the packing co-operatives tended to specialize geographically and were looking for ways to share resources (e.g. marketing,

administration) to reduce unit costs. The private packers had some operating advantages over the cooperatives because, for example, they could discriminate among growers (e.g. offer special terms to large growers), they could choose not to accept all the fruit the growers wanted to send them, and they could keep their strategic information confidential. Despite these advantages, however, the private packers were also suffering from the decline in the industry. For example, the town of Waikerie alone used to have 20 private packers, but competition had driven all but one out of business.

CITRUS MARKETING

Waikerie Producers sold its packed fruit at market prices that were set (by variety and size) weekly. Table 1 shows the market prices being offered in July 1992. Juice prices were lower than, but were closely linked to, the local market price. The co-operative paid the growers the market price less packing and freight costs which, in 1992, averaged approximately A$5.50 and $1.00 per 4/5 bushel, respectively. The prices paid to growers were identical for all fruit (in any one grade and size) processed in a pool (of a week or fortnight in duration). Assignment to a pool depended on the delivery date to the cooperative. All growers with fruit in a given pool were paid the same prices for each specific grade. The growers were paid 30 days after the month of delivery.

In 1992 Waikerie producers began offering its grower-members supply contracts. Growers who committed to deliver a certain quantity of fruit to the cooperative were guaranteed a minimum price. If the market price turned out to be greater than the guaranteed minimum the growers would be paid the market price. The contract system was designed both to provide the grower-members with some pricing stability and to encourage them to ship more fruit in a more consistent stream to the cooperative.

The cooperative supplied the growers' juice-quality citrus to their associate cooperative,

TABLE 1 **Orange prices per 30-liter box, July 1992**

Export, large fruit	A$11.00
Export, small fruit	A$9.50
Local	A$7.00–10.00

Berrivale Orchards, the largest orange juicer in Australia and located in a town adjacent to Waikerie. Approximately 50% of the juicer's daily capacity was used for fresh-squeezed juice; the balance was for concentrate. The price for the deliveries for fresh-squeezed juice was set at $170/T.[2] The balance of the juice oranges were sold at the prevailing market price, which in July 1992 was $60/T.

FINANCIAL PLANNING

Waikerie Producers' managers prepared an annual plan in considerable detail. (They planned beyond one year only sketchily.) The annual plan was seen as important because, as was stated in the 1992 Budget Report, "At this crucial period in the life of our co-operative, we must elucidate where we go and how we plan to get there, and then have a consensus which we can pursue for the ultimate benefit of our co-operative and members."

The annual planning process began in November with a grower survey. The grower-members were asked for an estimate of how much tonnage, by variety, they would be sending the cooperative in the forthcoming fiscal year (starting April 1). A field officer visited each grower to inspect the orchards and to impress upon them the importance of completing the questionnaire. Even so, estimates were received from only about 60% of the members. After they received the questionnaires Waikerie managers consolidated the estimates, extrapolated them to an estimate of total fruit receipts, and added their judgment. Duncan Beaton described the planning philosophy:

> We try to be realistic to the best of our ability. There are so many external factors, such as frost, drought, sooty mold infestations, and changes in the levels of duties. We look at a moving average for the last five years and add our knowledge of the current market and a factor for optimism/pessimism.

Despite the attention paid to the crop estimates, however, Waikerie managers were not satisfied with the accuracy of these estimates. Most years the actual volume of fruit sent to the cooperative was less than estimated, as can be seen in Table 2.

Concurrently, Cliff Carthew, Waikerie's chief financial officer, worked with the department

TABLE 2 Total tonnage: estimate versus actual received

Fiscal year	Estimate	Actual
91/2	44,520	41,810
90/1	56,524	54,317
89/90	44,316	40,273
88/9	49,407	46,512
87/8	53,520	57,890

managers to estimate costs and cash flows for the coming fiscal year. Considerable time was spent thinking about how to reduce costs to ensure that the cooperative could make payments to members that are "competitive and worthy of support." As a result, staffing levels were reduced, and no capital expenditures were planned for 1993.

Cliff then set the unit packing costs to be charged to grower-members, which were based on estimates of the full cost of the service plus a modest profit margin. Cliff estimated the costs for many different packing types, 14 for oranges alone. He began by estimating the standard labor cost per minute. This calculation is shown in Exhibit 3. Then he multiplied the standard labor costs per minute by the standard labor minutes per operation, as calculated in a time-and-motion study conducted in 1990. Third, he estimated material costs, which varied with the size of the package and the types of materials used, by requesting quotations from suppliers of major items (e.g. cartons) and estimating the costs of other materials for each pack type (see Exhibit 4). Fourth, he added an allocation of overhead (see Exhibit 5) and transportation. These allocations were crude. For example, the transportation charge of 6 cents per carton had not been reestimated in several years. The packing costs also included an allocation of interest, and because of Waikerie's high borrowing to buy automated equipment, this was a relatively large number that caused Waikerie's packing costs to be higher than many of the other packers. Finally, Cliff added a small profit margin as a cushion. A summary of the costs of three representative pack types is shown in Exhibit 6.

Duncan admitted that Waikerie's system of estimating costs was crude, but he thought it was ahead of most packers. "A lot of packers don't do any costing at all. They don't know their costs."

[2] One ton of fruit was equivalent to 48 30-liter (4/5 bushel) boxes.

Despite the potential for inaccuracies, Waikerie managers tried to keep the packing charges constant for the whole fiscal year. A few times, however, the costs had varied because of significant changes in volumes or large cost factors.

The ideal was to plan for, and then deliver, a small surplus of, perhaps, less than A$500,000. That small surplus would ensure a satisfactory cash flow while providing the opportunity to reduce interest costs and exposure to adverse market conditions plus provide a small rebate. Duncan Beaton said, "It would be nice to have a big surplus year to recoup the losses we have had recently, but it is not our goal to increase our surplus each year." However, because times were tough, losses were forecast in both 1992 and 1993.

The Waikerie board of directors approved the budget in the middle of March. As they had been apprised of financial issues during the preparation of the budget there were usually no last minute issues to be settled. The original budget remained fixed for the year, but managers prepared frequent updates of volume forecasts. The cooperative produced an extensive set of formal reports comparing actual with budgeted numbers on a monthly basis.

PERFORMANCE EVALUATIONS AND INCENTIVES

Performance evaluations at Waikerie Producers were done informally. Even for manager-level personnel, there was no formal annual review. Waikerie's practices stemmed from Duncan Beaton's philosophy. He described formal performance evaluations as "a bit traumatic." He preferred to talk to his subordinates about performance-related issues "somewhat steadily."

The cooperative offered no bonuses of any kind. Duncan Beaton explained:

> I have thought about it a lot, but I would want to base bonuses on performance, and I can't do it based on profit. In production areas, we have done a lot of one-off projects which are hard to evaluate. In the hardware store, I have evaluated the manager based on sales, but even there evaluations are difficult. Profit is not a good performance measure because he can't really raise profit margins when he is supplying shareholders in a small town, but I don't want him to cut prices excessively to increase sales either.

CONCERNS FOR THE FUTURE

As fiscal year 1993 began Waikerie managers knew that difficult operating conditions were continuing. The market for Australian citrus was shrinking, and prices were very competitive. The bad market conditions forced Waikerie managers to put some growers on quota. They were allowed to ship only the quantity remaining in their original volume estimate.

Some citrus growers in the Riverland were being encouraged to move to alternate crops, such as grapes, potatoes, carrots, leaf vegetables, melons, or tomatoes, which were even more risky than oranges. But these crops provided greater flexibility because the grower could make annual decisions on what to grow. Citrus growers, typically, can replant only approximately 10% of their crop each year. If this crop shift took place Waikerie Producers could face a gradually shrinking market for some time.

During the difficult times grower loyalty to the cooperative was declining, and there was a lot of "co-op bashing." Duncan Beaton explained that, "The growers complain about everything – the board, management, prices." In particular he noted that the growers had become increasingly insistent on high returns, and they did not think the cooperative was offering competitive prices. Duncan believed Waikerie Producers was within 10% of the best price available to the growers, but he found it difficult to verify the growers' claims because packers in the Riverland area, both cooperative and private, did not willingly disclose their prices and packing charges. He was aware of some attempts that some growers were trying to "beat the co-op," for example by getting an estimate from the cooperative and then taking it to private packers to see if they would better it.

It was clear to Duncan that Waikerie Producers would have to become more efficient to get an increasing share of a smaller market. He thought that Waikerie Producers was large enough to build more special relationships with supermarkets in order to sell directly, rather than on the open market. He also wanted the cooperative to provide consistently superior service and to offer special promotions so that the Riverland product could compete without always being sold at the lowest price.

It was also clear that Waikerie management was handicapped by their inability to prepare reasonably accurate annual financial plans. The summary income statement comparisons of budget versus actual shown in Exhibit 7 reveals some significant variances. Crop forecasts were one part of the problem. Consequently, in a note to members accompanying the 1993 budget, Waikerie managers wrote:

> Crop forecasting, particularly of citrus, has become more difficult and more time-consuming, and ultimately has proved less accurate each year . . . Our projection of volumes in all activities is critical to the budgetary process, and it is only as a result of this exercise that we can propose a budget . . . Each year we spend more time and effort to create our estimates, which appear to be less accurate through varying levels of support from our grower suppliers. As the estimate is the singularly most critical factor in the calculations, this causes us much concern.

EXHIBIT 1 Waikerie Co-Operative Producers Ltd.: organization chart

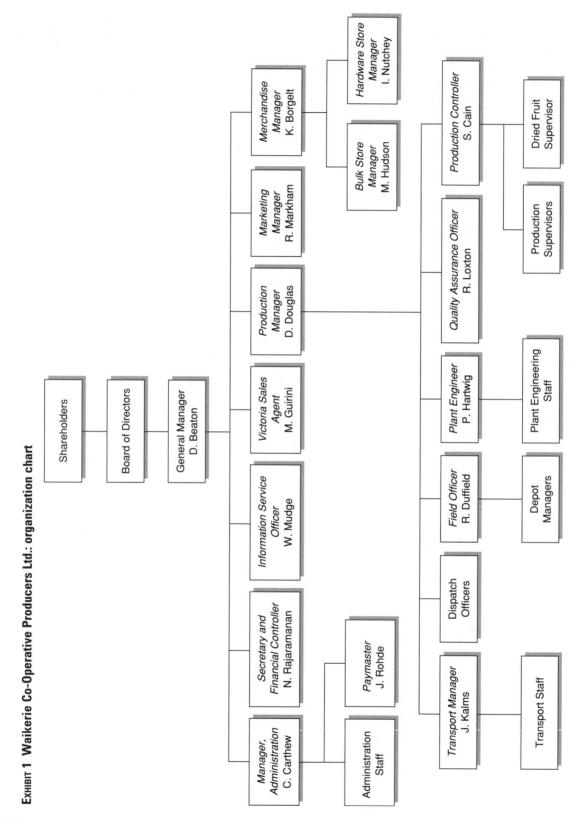

Exhibit 2 International principles of co-operation

1. OPEN AND VOLUNTARY MEMBERSHIP
   Membership of a co-operative society should be voluntary and available without artificial restriction or any social, political, racial, or religious discrimination, to all persons who can make use of the co-operative's services and are willing to accept the responsibilities of membership.

2. DEMOCRATIC CONTROL
   Co-operative societies are democratic organizations. Their affairs should be administered by persons elected or appointed in a manner agreed by the members and accountable to them. Members of primary societies should enjoy equal rights of voting (one member, one vote) and participation in decisions affecting their societies. In other than primary societies, the administration should be conducted on a democratic basis in a suitable form.

3. LIMITED INTEREST ON SHARES
   Share capital should only receive a strictly limited rate of interest, if any.

4. EQUITABLE DISTRIBUTION OF SURPLUS
   Surplus or savings arising out of the operations of a society belong to the members of that society and should be distributed in such a manner as would avoid one member gaining at the expense of others. This may be done by decision of the members at the Annual General Meeting as follows:
   a. By provision for development of the business of the co-operative (rotation reserves, 5 years);
   b. By provision of common service;
   c. By distribution among members in proportion to their transactions with the Society.

5. CO-OPERATIVE EDUCATION
   All co-operative societies should make provision for the education of their members, officers, and employees and of the general public, in the principles and techniques of co-operation, both economic and democratic.

6. CO-OPERATION AMONGST CO-OPERATIVES
   All co-operative organisations, in order to best serve the interest of their members and their communities should actively co-operate in every practical way with other co-operatives at local, national, and international levels.

Exhibit 3 Estimate of standard cost of labor for fiscal year 1993

Labour rate at 31/1/90	A$9.00/hr
+increase in January	.36
	9.36
+increases during year (8.16%)	10.12/hr
+cost of operating at only 50% efficiency	10.12
	20.24
+oncost* of 35%	7.09
Standard hourly rate	A$27.33
Standard minute rate	A$0.4556
In fiscal year 1992:	
Standard minute rate = $.383	
Increase = .0726 or 19%	

* Employee benefits.

Exhibit 4 Cost of packing materials for three representative types of packages

	C6 CTN*	3KG P/P**	Bulk wood†
Carton-top	A$.5153	A$.9565	
Carton-tray	.6381		
Glue	.0150		
Wraps			
Labels			
Taping			
Fungicides	.1700		
Wax	.0600	.2300	A$.2300
Tags		.3360	
Headers		.1200	
Enclosures		.0850	
Make-up		.3000	
Total materials	A$1.3984	A$2.0275	A$.2300
Assume 20% inflation on all	A$1.6781	A$2.4330	A$.2760

* A C6 CTN is a 30 liter (or 0.8 bushel) export carton.

** A 3KG/P/P is 3 kilogram net bags in prepack cartons, 6 to a carton, and equivalent to 0.8 bushels/carton.

† Bulk wood is loose oranges in a wooden bin. Each bin holds 20 0.8-bushel-equivalent units.

Exhibit 5 Overhead cost budget (A$)

	1993	1992
Direct labour-related	606,300	454,020
Direct labour oncost	212,205	158,907
Indirect labour	231,673	210,794
Repair labour	98,518	70,514
Indirect and repair labour oncost	115,567	98,460
Variable costs	398,215	335,256
Other income	(42,180)	(33,074)
Fixed costs	1,119,890	1,108,130
Total overhead costs	2,740,188	2,403,007
Packed cases	885,800	1,007,300
Needed overhead cost recovery/case	3.09	2.36

Exhibit 6 Packing costing summary for three representative pack types

	C6 carton	3KG P/P	Bulk wood
Std. mins.	1.85	1.71	0.50
Labour per pack	0.8429	0.7791	0.2278
Matl. per pak	1.6781	2.4330	0.2760
Pack overhead	3.09	3.09	3.09
Transportation to shed @ 4¢	0.060	0.060	0.060
Profit @ 20¢	0.20	0.20	0.20
Total packing cost	5.8710	6.5621	3.8538

Note: A C6 CTN is a 30 liter (or 0.8 bushel) export carton.
A 3KG P/P is 3 kilogram net bags in prepack cartons, 6 to a carton, and equivalent to 0.8 bushels/carton.
Bulk wood is loose oranges in a wooden bin. Each bin holds 20 0.8-bushel-equivalent units.

EXHIBIT 7 Income statement budget versus actual – citrus packing only

	Total 1992 Act.	Total 1992 Budg.	March Act.	March Budg.	February Act.	February Budg.	January Act.	January Budg.	December Act.	December Budg.	November Act.	November Budg.
Sales/packing charges income	$3,681.6	$4,075.8	$125.6	$97.2	$226.7	$251.8	$201.5	$254.1	$245.5	$247.0	$172.3	$301.4
cost of goods/services sold	1,035.7	1,332.3	(122.3)	41.9	76.6	81.4	70.1	78.7	77.0	79.6	98.3	97.3
Added value/gross margin	2,645.9	2,743.5	247.9	55.3	150.1	170.4	131.5	175.5	168.5	167.3	74.0	204.1
Direct labour and oncost*	1,282.5	1,501.7	49.0	45.0	90.3	81.9	91.5	81.7	93.3	91.6	136.6	110.6
Gross contribution margin	1,363.5	1,241.8	198.9	10.2	59.9	88.6	40.0	93.7	75.2	75.7	(62.6)	93.5
Indirect & repair labour and oncost*	351.6	354.3	24.2	29.4	27.0	29.5	26.6	29.4	24.9	29.4	32.7	29.5
Net contribution margin	1,011.9	887.5	174.7	(19.2)	32.9	59.2	13.3	64.2	50.4	46.3	(95.3)	64.0
Variable costs**	352.3	346.3	18.4	18.7	22.7	23.0	30.1	23.8	22.5	24.6	26.7	35.2
Other income†	(143.9)	(21.3)	(105.5)	(1.7)	(12.1)	(1.8)	(2.6)	(1.8)	(.9)	(1.8)	1.0	(1.7)
Divisional contribution	803.4	562.6	261.6	(36.1)	22.4	38.0	(14.2)	42.2	28.7	23.4	(122.8)	30.6
Fixed costs††	928.5	971.6	11.9	79.7	77.2	79.8	77.3	77.6	79.7	80.8	83.3	81.0
Net operating surplus	($125.1)	($409.0)	($249.7)	($115.8)	($54.8)	($41.8)	($91.6)	($35.4)	($50.9)	($57.4)	($206.2)	($50.3)

	October Act.	October Budg.	September Act.	September Budg.	August Act.	August Budg.	July Act.	July Budg.	June Act.	June Budg.	May Act.	May Budg.	April Act.	April Budg.
Sales/packing charges income	$308.7	$373.0	$491.8	$415.0	$491.7	$768.1	$506.6	$672.2	$381.3	$482.1	$332.0	$115.6	$197.8	$98.3
cost of goods/services sold	85.9	133.6	152.5	135.3	176.3	243.4	145.8	205.2	111.7	163.8	102.0	36.5	61.8	35.6
Added value/gross margin	222.7	239.4	339.4	279.7	315.4	524.7	360.7	467.0	269.7	318.4	230.0	78.9	136.0	62.8
Direct labour and oncost*	60.0	159.4	147.7	137.7	146.8	236.3	148.3	218.2	156.4	166.5	78.9	144.8	83.7	27.9
Gross contribution margin	162.7	80.0	191.7	142.0	168.6	288.4	212.4	248.8	113.3	151.9	151.1	(65.9)	52.3	34.9
Indirect & repair labour and oncost*	24.3	29.5	36.2	29.5	29.9	29.4	31.0	29.5	39.7	29.9	24.5	29.7	30.6	29.6
Net contribution margin	138.4	50.5	155.5	112.5	138.7	259.0	181.4	219.3	73.6	122.0	126.6	(95.6)	21.7	5.3
Variable costs**	22.3	31.3	37.7	30.3	36.7	45.0	47.1	42.0	32.8	30.2	29.6	23.6	25.7	18.6
Other income†	(.8)	(1.8)	(5.6)	(1.8)	(.7)	(1.8)	(.6)	(1.8)	3.5	(1.7)	(43.3)	(1.8)	(23.7)	(1.8)
Divisional contribution	116.8	21.0	123.4	84.1	102.7	215.7	134.9	108.3	37.3	93.5	140.3	(117.4)	(27.7)	(11.5)
Fixed costs††	78.9	82.0	84.5	82.0	82.9	81.9	84.1	82.5	81.3	81.9	80.8	81.8	106.6	80.6
Net operating surplus	$38.0	$61.1	$38.9	$2.0	$19.8	$133.9	$50.8	$96.5	$44.0	$11.7	$59.5	($199.1)	$134.3	($92.2)

* Oncost includes the costs of employing labour (e.g. annual leave, sick leave, holidays, superannuation, payroll taxes).
** General costs over which the supervisor has control (e.g. advertising, repair and maintenance, power, stationery).
† Income gained not as a direct result of selling (e.g. rebates, rental, commissions, recharges).
†† Costs incurred irrespective of the level of activity (e.g. depreciation, interest, rent).

Boston Lyric Opera

Mission		
Loyal and Generous Contributors	National and International Opera Scene	Greater Boston Community

Janice Mancini Del Sesto, general director of the Boston Lyric Opera company, explained the writing on the white board in BLO's conference room: "I write the three strategic themes from our Balanced Scorecard on the board before each weekly staff meeting. I want our conversations to relate to activities that support the themes. That way, we will stay focused on achieving our objectives."

OPERA AND THE PERFORMING ARTS

Opera was one of the fastest growing segments in the performing arts, increasing its audience from 4 million patrons in the 1970s to more than 20 million by CY 2000. Performing arts and other cultural institutions, such as museums and libraries, generated 3.5% of all jobs in the New England region and supported an annual payroll of $4.3 billion.

Over the past decade, arts organizations faced steeply rising operating costs – from salaries to building maintenance. At the same time, corporate donations for unrestricted operating funds have decreased and been replaced by company branding of specific events and programs. These trends have increased the pressure on cultural institutions to generate high donations from their board members. For example, the Los Angeles Philharmonic recently raised the annual minimum gift expected from directors from $10,000 to $25,000.[1] Opera was the most expensive art form to produce. Fully staged opera productions were multimedia, and

required classically trained singers, a symphony orchestra, professional choreography, elaborate sets and costumes, and often a full chorus.

Performing arts institutions generated revenue from gifts, charitable foundations, ticket sales, and individual contributions. While gifts from charitable foundations were on the rise, individual support remained the largest single source of funding for the arts in the United States – up an estimated 19% in the last 10 years to $8.3 billion.[2] Also, many performing arts institutions had limited seating capacity so that price increases represented the only option for increasing revenues from ticket sales.

OPERA IN BOSTON

Opera in Boston had a checkered history. Several opera companies had come and gone, and the dominant force in Boston opera from 1960 up to early 1990 was Sarah Caldwell. Her Opera Company of Boston was known for putting on lavish artistic performances without sufficient funds. Caldwell scraped for money from show to show. When the money was not there, she spent it anyway, borrowing against the building, deferring maintenance, and not paying bills.[3] Financial difficulties as well as personal illness led Caldwell to cancel entire seasons. Ticket holders often found that shows were canceled, performance dates were changed, and even entire productions were replaced without notice. A December 1999 article in the *Boston Globe* recalled: "It sounds ridiculous, but the simple fact that you could buy a ticket to, say, 'La Bohème' and actually get to see that opera on the date printed on the ticket was an important step [for opera in Boston]."

---

[1] *Wall Street Journal*, May 7, 1999.

[2] Ibid.
[3] *Opera News*, September 1996.

This case was prepared by Professor Robert S. Kaplan and doctoral student Dennis Campbell.

Copyright © 2001 President and Fellows of Harvard College. Harvard Business School Case 9-101-111.

In addition, opera in Boston existed in the shadow of the prestigious Metropolitan Opera Company, nearby in New York City. Many patrons traveled to New York or waited for the Met's touring productions to come to Boston to satisfy their opera interests.

Boston Lyric Opera

The Boston Lyric Opera company was founded in 1976 by the merger of three New England opera companies. The BLO had a unique commitment to bridge the gap between an artist's advanced training and his or her professional career. It featured world-class emerging singers, conductors, directors, and designers. In the mid 1990s, the BLO had launched a "Fund for Emerging Artists," which underwrote the costs of talent search and audition expenses, coaching, travel, and housing for promising young artists. Many of the artists who debuted at the BLO – including Deborah Voigt, Lorraine Hunt Lieberson, Paul Groves, David Daniels, Gregory Turay, and Patricia Racette – achieved successful careers and won prestigious national awards.

In addition to its main stage productions, the BLO operated a variety of education and community outreach programs with the goal of making opera available and accessible to communities in the greater Boston area. In 1998, it acquired Opera New England, making this youth-oriented focused opera company the BLO education and community programs division. Opera New England presented 60-minute versions of popular operas for children in grades 3–7, reaching over 24,000 students from 275 schools. In addition, the BLO actively encouraged interaction between professionals and students by, for example, bringing world-class artists to the community to give public lectures and master classes for young singers. The BLO also offered educational programs designed for adults through free preopera lectures prior to all performances. For the 2000/2001 season, the BLO expected to reach approximately 40,000 people through its education and community outreach programs. The BLO mission statement, adopted in 1993 (see Exhibit 1), communicated the company's three major goals of producing high quality professional opera productions, developing future opera talent, and promoting opera appreciation through educational

and community outreach. The BLO, in FY2001, had a 46-person Board of Directors and a separate 51 person Board of Overseers.

Janice Mancini Del Sesto, as general director of the BLO, supervised the company's five operating departments (see organization chart in Exhibit 2) and interfaced with its two boards. Del Sesto had studied voice at the New England Conservatory and sang opera for several years before becoming a consultant and administrator of arts-oriented organizations. In 1992, she had been appointed general director of the BLO, shortly after another failed opera company – the Boston Opera Theater – ceased operations, with several of its board members elected to the BLO board. Del Sesto and the expanded board knew that Boston's recent history of expensive opera productions and large losses required the BLO to adopt a new philosophy: operate in a fiscally prudent manner, and offer excellent artistic quality but not spectacular productions.

The subsequent seasons offered a good blend of traditional and contemporary operas (see Exhibit 3) and the BLO built a loyal, enthusiastic base of opera subscribers and supporters. In September 1998, the BLO made a major transition from the limited 890 seat Emerson Theater to the 1,500 seat Shubert Theater, enabling the BLO to reach a larger audience and expand the number of performances it offered. In addition to increased seating capacity, the Shubert also offered a larger orchestra pit and improved stage house amenities. One BLO board member remarked, however, that an opera company needed 1,800–2,400 seats to do standard repertory and remain fiscally solvent.

In the 2000/2001 season, the BLO offered 26 performances of four main stage productions attended by 39,000 people. Its season was broadcast regionally on a local FM radio station. The BLO audience had a median age of 45, 80% resided in Massachusetts, 70% had graduate degrees, and more than 60% had household incomes above $60,000. Its budget had grown from 64th in size ($1 million in FY1992) to 15th ($7 million in FY2000) out of 95 US opera companies. With subscribers increasing more than 100% and the number of performances by 50% from 1995 to 2000, the BLO had become the fastest-growing opera company in North America. The company had operated continually with a balanced budget or a small surplus (see summary statistics in Exhibit 4).

Del Sesto's leadership and direction were widely credited by the local media and her colleagues in the Boston opera community as the driving force behind opera's success in Boston. Sue Dahling-Sullivan, an MBA graduate from Dartmouth's Tuck School and deputy director of the BLO, described Del Sesto as an unusual nonprofit leader, "a visionary who ran her organization like a business."

A NEW PLANNING PROCESS

The main concern of the BLO Board in the late 1990s had been the company's transition from the Emerson to the Shubert Theater. The board wondered whether sufficient interest existed in the Boston area to fill the large increase in available seats. By September 1999, the board had its answer. The move to the Shubert had been successfully accomplished. The subscriber base had increased to fill the new capacity and the retention rate for the following season was more than 80%. The near-term future of the BLO was ensured.

The company now faced the challenge of what it should become. Even with the higher audience base, revenues from ticket sales remained less than 40% of operating expenses. The BLO needed to convert more subscribers to donors, attract significant funding from its supporters and foundations, and contemplate a 2,200-seat facility that would permit even more ambitious artistic productions and provide greater financial stability through increased ticket sales.

Ken Freed, a BLO board member since 1992, was cochairman of the strategic planning committee. He had seen BLO's staff and budget grow rapidly during the 1990s and felt that its informal, kitchen-cabinet style governance structure was no longer sufficient. He believed that a more formal strategic planning process was essential. An active participant in several arts organizations, Freed had seen organizations fail because leaders had not actively involved the board in strategy and planning deliberations.

In September 1999, the BLO convened senior administrative staff, the Board of Directors, and the Board of Overseers for a weekend, off-site strategic retreat. They summarized the deliberations with a broader and sharper mission statement:

Boston Lyric Opera's mission is to ensure the future or the art form by: (1) building a community that is

knowledgeable about, appreciative and supportive of opera; and (2) developing the next generation of professionals, audience, supporters and volunteer leadership. This will be achieved by providing education and community programs and activities, and access to the highest quality productions of diverse repertoire of artistically excellent, musically and theatrically innovative and fiscally sound opera.

Del Sesto now faced the challenge of developing a strategy to deliver on the mission. Through the fall, she met with focus groups from BLO's constituencies, senior staff, chairs of standing and ad hoc board committees, and key supporters.

Dahling-Sullivan had recently returned to the BLO as Deputy Director after spending a sabbatical year as Associate Director of Planning at Harvard Business School. She had seen various HBS program offices use a new management tool, the Balanced Scorecard, to set strategic objectives and measure their performance against those objectives.[4] She felt that the BLO could use the Balanced Scorecard to focus its planning process. Dahling-Sullivan approached Ellen Kaplan, a new Board of Overseers member, who she knew had had experience adapting the Balanced Scorecard to nonprofit organizations such as New Profit, Inc., The May Institute, and United Way. Kaplan readily agreed to facilitate a process with the staff and the board to build a Balanced Scorecard for the BLO.

DEVELOPING THE BLO BALANCED SCORECARD

During a several month period in the first half of CY 2000, a group consisting of Del Sesto, Dahling-Sullivan, Kaplan, senior department heads, artistic leaders, board members and financial donors met periodically. The meetings were the first time that these diverse groups engaged in open dialogue about what the BLO was and what it wanted to become. Kaplan challenged the group to define its strategy, its competitive advantage, and distinguishing characteristics that would make the Boston Lyric Opera Company unique. Board Chairman, Sherif Nada, enthusiastically endorsed the approach:

---

[4] R. S. Kaplan and D. P. Norton, *The Balanced Scorecard: Translating Strategy into Action* (Boston: HBS Press, 1996), and *The Strategy-Focused Organization: How Balanced Scorecard Companies Thrive in the New Business Environment* (Boston: HBS Press, 2001).

I was on the Board of Citizens School, an organization funded by New Profit, Inc., and I had seen the Balanced Scorecard work effectively there. During our meetings, Ellen [Kaplan] brought in examples from other organizations but demanded that the audience participate actively in the discussion to reflect their views about the BLO. She kept telling us, "I write on the board, but it's your plan." She brought all the people around the table into the process.

The group's discussions led to defining three high-level strategic themes, each relating to a key customer group:

- Develop loyal and generous individuals who feel a strong sense of ownership in BLO's future.
- Build the BLO reputation on the national and international opera scene.
- Reach the Boston-area community.

Loyal and generous supporters

With the BLO now ensconced at the 1,500-seat Shubert Theater for the foreseeable future, and a new facility a distant vision, the planning group realized that the future of the opera company depended on continuing to receive almost 70% of each year's operating budget from sources other than ticket sales. This created an intense focus on how to attract new donors and increase the support from existing donors.

Two customer objectives were created for the first strategic theme:

- Target loyal and generous contributors and prospects.
- Enhance involvement and recruitment of board members.

The first objective was obvious, but the second objective was not. In the past, board members had been chosen because of past or potential financial support. Now, board members would be recruited and selected for their ability to help the BLO accomplish its strategic objectives.

Del Sesto realized that the BLO already had many initiatives under way for subscribers and potential donors, but had no process for assessing the effectiveness of these programs.

For several years, we hosted a VIP room prior to a performance at a hotel near the theater where we invited individuals for cocktails and hors d'oeuvres.

We had never measured the impact of the program. As our discussions progressed, I asked our staff, "are we attracting the right people to the VIP room," and "are we converting the guests to high-contributing board members?" The staff liked running these events but hadn't been accountable for follow-up actions to track the outcomes and demonstrate a return on investment from the VIP room.

The staff had invested a lot in the VIP room and were frustrated that they couldn't answer Del Sesto's challenge to demonstrate tangible results. Del Sesto cut the program off, but didn't criticize the staff:

The BLO strives to be a learning organization and we attract wonderful young talent with that philosophy. That means we experiment, and it's OK to fail. But the staff got the message that they have to be more analytical in what they are trying to accomplish and to quantify the outcomes from their processes.

It's important with a young staff not to reject "bad ideas." I try to question them and take them through the process so they learn to see weaknesses in their proposals and come to their own conclusions. This is a more time-consuming process for me and I have a continual tension between making the decisions myself versus having long interactive discussions with young staff to help them understand all the relevant issues. The BSC's strategic objectives have helped the staff understand how they can contribute with their day-to-day activities to deliver value for our most important constituents.

Another recent program was Opera Express, which had been targeted at the young, professional segment. While direct expenses had been funded by a two-year foundation grant, virtually all of BLO's marketing resources had been committed to marketing and putting on its many events, which reached only 100 individuals. No Opera Express participant ended up as a donor or even a subscriber. Dahling-Sullivan noted that at the time of the grant, the company had no strategic basis for rejecting the money, leading to the dissipation of its scarce human resources for two years.

National and international opera scene

The board and staff did not want the BLO to be just a regional producer of traditional opera for local audiences, or to define success only by subscriber renewals. Del Sesto wanted the BLO to do exciting things that would make an impact. But she and the Board would have to redefine what they meant by "world class." The BLO, as a young, small and resource-constrained opera company, could not hope to compete with the great opera houses of the world: The Metropolitan, Covent Garden, La Scala, or Vienna State Opera. It needed, however, to differentiate itself from the many apparently similar regional companies in North America.

Two customer objectives developed for this theme reflected the BLO strategy since 1992:

● Launch a unique, comprehensive residency program that would attract the best young talent – singers, conductors, directors, production and stage personnel, and administrators – who would subsequently perform with the most prestigious opera companies in North America and the world.

● Present a diverse and exciting repertory that included popular, lesser known, and contemporary works.

The strategic discussions introduced a third customer objective for this theme, one that would further contribute to BLO's differentiation strategy:

● Institutionalize an artistic/production style and set of standards, characterized by "crisp and clean, simple and strong, elegant" that would become identified with BLO productions.

And to leverage BLO's limited resources, while still delivering high-quality operating productions, the group proposed a fourth strategic objective:

● Collaborate with prestigious partners to strengthen BLO's position in the international and national opera scene.

Collaborations could include relationships with major opera companies to develop and train their best new talent, coproductions with distinguished companies, and local collaboration with other arts organizations. For example, the 1999/2000 BLO season featured an Egyptian theme (*Aïda*, *Akhnaten*, and *The Magic Flute*) in conjunction with major Egyptian exhibitions at Boston's Museum of Fine Arts and Museum of Science, and Egyptian programming at the Boston Ballet Company.

Community

The discussions on the third strategic theme, engaging and educating a diverse community centered in Boston about opera, were among the most active of all. Opera had to continually attract new generations of audiences. Few children were exposed to high-quality opera, and the art form risked obsolescence if it could not convert younger generations into opera fans. Also, community support would be essential if the BLO were to ever gain approval for a new facility. Ken Freed knew that obtaining a new facility in the Boston area was more a political issue than a financial one. Stephen Lord, Music Director and principal conductor, was eloquent in pointing out the importance of the community strategy:

> Opera in the past was for the masses. Working people came in their everyday clothes to see and hear great productions. We need to break down the image that opera is only for the elite, dressed in their finest. We should be striving to make opera part of people's every day lives. Let's bring opera to the Public Garden, the Hatch Shell, even Fenway Park!

The group identified two high-level customer objectives for the community strategic theme:

● Build community support for BLO as an important part of the greater Boston community.

● Develop value-added opera education programs, targeting greater-Boston children, their families, and their schools.

The discussion on community, like the one on loyal and generous individuals, forced the board and staff to address existing programs. For example, when the BLO had acquired Opera New England (ONE) in July 1998, it had agreed not to change ONE's events for the first two years. ONE had five productions, which it rotated from year to year. In FY 2000, it put on 33 events in venues from Western Connecticut to central Maine. The former head of ONE was now a BLO board member and a participant in the Balanced Scorecard strategic process. The group discussed how ONE's existing programs supported the BLO strategy. The discussions revealed that the New England market was probably too diffuse and expensive for the BLO. The group concluded that it would be more cost effective for the BLO to focus on communities within the Boston capture area. Freed commented on how the consensus got built:

> We had a cooperative process – open, transparent and rational – that enabled our members from Opera New

England to get on board with the BLO strategy and the role for ONE in that strategy. This worked much better than if a decision had been dictated by Janice or imposed by long-time BLO board members.

Starting in 2002, ONE would focus its productions on Boston city and metropolitan area schools. The BLO would continue to support interested venues outside this immediate capture area, but such events would be repriced to enable the BLO to recover its costs.

COMPLETING THE BALANCED SCORECARD

The group then turned to the critical internal processes that would help the company achieve its strategic customer objectives in the three strategic themes. This led to identifying three high-level business processes at which the BLO must excel and nine internal strategic objectives for the three processes:

Increase Brand Awareness

- Develop new value-added educational and community programs as well as special events that target community, supporters, and ticket buyers.
- Launch a comprehensive public relations program that creates "buzz" and strengthens the BLO strategic position, locally and globally.

Enhance Customer Relationships

- Streamline ticketing and gift acknowledgment processes.
- Increase one-on-one contact with donors, board and prospects.
- Improve board support, communication, and education systems.
- Develop web-based services and products, easy to use, that provide access to valuable information.

Insure Operational Excellence

- Improve product quality by identifying, recruiting, and contracting "best-in-class" artistic, production, and administrative talent.
- Develop an innovation review process that supports initiatives with strategic importance.
- Increase cost effectiveness and quality assurance with departmental three-year operational plans.

These internal process objectives provided specific guidance to BLO departments and staff for what

should be done to help the company achieve its mission and its constituents' objective.

The group then proceeded to develop objectives for three enabling Learning & Growth themes and two Financial themes (see Exhibit 5 for the full Balanced Scorecard strategy map and Exhibit 6 for a description of the Learning and Growth and Financial objectives).

While most members of the group were enthusiastic about the process and the outcome, several of the board members expressed concerns. Dahling-Sullivan noted:

> In times of change, people – especially those new to the organization – are looking for focus and the boundaries of the strategy. Some of our long-time supporters, however, were slower to embrace the new process.

Del Sesto also observed that some board members and artistic staff, accustomed to the financial measures, were unsure about why, all of a sudden, the company had to measure things beyond subscription revenues and renewals.

DEPLOYING THE BALANCED SCORECARD

After the BLO strategy map and strategic objectives had been formulated, Dahling-Sullivan asked each department – finance and administration, marketing, development, and artistic productions – to develop its own Scorecard. The departmental Scorecard would describe how the department would do its own work effectively and efficiently and also contribute to the high-level BLO strategic themes.

Development office

Fundraising was clearly a major priority for an organization that obtained almost 70% of its annual operating budget from donations. Del Sesto, with many years of fundraising experience and knowledge, saw how the Balanced Scorecard could enhance the development function by linking the staff, the board, and donors to the company's mission and strategy.

> Earlier in my career, I owned a consulting firm that helped businesses identify and negotiate sponsorship opportunities and set clearly defined measures for their support. I have seen the development field

become more professional over the past thirty years. Companies and foundations are now more strategic and focused in their grant-making and sponsorship. They are forcing organizations to deliver measurable results.

Of measuring their success only through the attainment of financial goals even though these are just one component of a comprehensive fundraising plan. The Balanced Scorecard requires that the staff and board think strategically about the desired outcomes of every relationship-building and fund-raising activity we do. During the process of creating our BSC, the entire staff was constantly reminded that each person's work contributes, in some way, to the overall success of our fundraising.

Del Sesto noted that many seasoned professionals in the fundraising field plan initiatives and run events that have few measures of success and little linkage to strategy. BLO's younger development staff, however, seemed eager for the structure and framework that the Balanced Scorecard offered. With the Scorecard, they could set priorities for their work and position their day-to-day activities within a larger and more strategic context. Staff could see how their success would be measured. They started to focus on initiatives and events that were likely to have the highest impact on organizational objectives.

For example, one junior staff person took the initiative to design a database application linking quantifiable donor data (gift and ticketing history) to qualitative information about donor meetings and personal information. This application streamlined information collection as well as increased the success of solicitation activities. The Corporate and Grants Manager implemented a strategy to increase one-on-one contact with corporate and foundation prospects. The development began to work more closely with the marketing/box office department of VIP seating and donor education initiatives.

A former director of development commented:

Often, the development office is "out there," quite separate from the rest of the organization. The Balanced Scorecard ties development into the heart of the organization. The development staff now has a much deeper understanding of the mission and priorities of the BLO. Everyone in the department understands the critical role of "loyal and generous donors" to the BLO's success.

Production and artistic administration

Steve Steiner was director of Production and Artistic Administration for the company, the department that executed the company's artistic vision, including contracting with singers, designers, stage hands, unionized workers and trade people:

Many different and complex things have to happen before the curtain goes up. And then everything has to be coordinated to occur within the same three hour period.

Steiner's staff were typically young people with artistic backgrounds. He explained the BLO Scorecard to his staff and could see the lights go on:

It's easy for our young artistically trained people to go off in many different directions. The Scorecard gave them an understanding about both the mission and the business aspects of the company. It was eye opening to them. It gave them context and focus. They now understand how their work affects the business aspects, and we now have a common terminology for sharing ideas and communicating.

From these discussions, Steiner's staff proposed an initiative to educate the board, donors, and subscribers about what goes on behind the scenes. In April 2000, the BLO offered a guided tour of how the magic in *The Magic Flute*, the current production, was accomplished. Steiner believed:

The more the board member understands what goes on behind the scene, the more loyal and committed the board member becomes.

Melanie Muradian, a young staff member in the Artistic Productions department, told how the Balanced Scorecard helped her generate some new ideas to support the strategy.

After every production, we always have some leftover merchandise – t-shirts, CDs, etc. I suggested that we give these as gifts to the artistic staff – singers, chorus, orchestra players – as a way of saying "thank you". They were very appreciative.

Also, I decided to write an article in the BLO newsletter about a supernumerary, who had just participated in his 25th production.[5] The article made

---

[5] A supernumerary performs a small, non-speaking, non-singing (and often unpaid) role in operas, such as a spear-carrier in the triumphal march of *Aïda*.

him feel good about his contribution to the BLO, and, unexpectedly, helped us when the article triggered a bunch of calls from volunteers asking how they could become supernumeraries in future productions.

THE BALANCED REPERTORY

In attempting to quantify the quality of the actual opera programming, the tension among the BLO's strategic themes would be the highest. Many existing and potential opera patrons liked the accessibility and familiarity of the classical repertory, including the popular works of Mozart, Donizetti, Bellini, Bizet, Verdi, and Puccini. But exclusive production of these classics would not appeal to knowledgeable opera subscribers and supporters, nor would it expose and educate the current audience about the wide range of lesser-known or even new works that also had significant artistic merit. In addition, seasons filled with "top ten" operas would not give the BLO much distinction or visibility in the national and international opera scene. The premieres of new work and productions of lesser-known operas not only led to international media attention, they also attracted more established singers who wished to broaden their repertoire.

Dahling-Sullivan prepared a Repertory Planning Template that would provide the basis for discussions of future year's programming with the company's two artistic leaders, Stephen Lord, Music Director and principal conductor since 1991, and Leon Major, Artistic Director since 1998. Del Sesto noted the need to balance across multiple dimensions:

> We've always had to balance artistic goals with our financial goals. But our strategy requires us to also balance within artistic goals. In any season, we want different composers, different eras, and different types of operas. The orchestra and chorus could be large or small; the artists, both recognized and emerging; an experienced conductor matched with a rookie director, and vice versa. Our productions should have a mix of period and updated settings, traditional and modern approaches, and a mix of rented, coproduced and new productions.

Dahling-Sullivan proposed a points scoring scheme along each dimension of choice and established targets so that each year's four productions could present a balance among composers, music, styles, performances and artists. Exhibit 7 shows how the FY2000 programs would have been scored according to these criteria. Del Sesto wanted Lord and Major to fill in the template as they formulated their plans for future years. She thought it would help them think systematically about the artistic tradeoffs and in their programming plans.

Leon Major was skeptical initially. It looked as if he were being presented with a formula to plan and evaluate seasons. Lord, with his 21 years of experience at the St. Louis opera where he had worked with a formula about the company's operations, felt the template provided an excellent starting point for discussions:

> Jan, Leon and I come from three different places. The template provides a more objective place for us to start our planning. On a scale from 1 to 10, it enables us to start at about 5. But I would not want it to be at 10, the final point. We still need to leave room for artistic judgment and not have everything in the formula.

Del Sesto concurred:

> We must plan a repertory to meet the strategy. Occasionally, artistic people have trouble sticking to decisions they have already made. We need to lock in the programs 3–4 seasons in advance to get the artists they want and to do the coproducing. But I agree that we want the flexibility to incorporate emerging new talent for artists, designers and directors. So the artistic staff has to balance long-term commitments and short-term flexibility.

Lord felt comfortable with the approach as long as he could, in his discussions with Jan and Leon, say, "look, this suggestion fits within four of the five categories, so why shouldn't we try it out." Major felt it would be helpful to extend the new approach to a 5–7 year plan so that balance could be achieved over time, not just within a single season. Lord concluded:

> The discipline from this process has been wonderful. We all have dreamy minds and strong feelings about what we like and what we don't like. Now, we all start from the same point.

THE BOARD

Del Sesto felt the BLO board represented her greatest challenge. As she shared the new strategy and Scorecard with the board, she learned that even some long-time members were unfamiliar with the mission:

> They asked, "why can't we feature Pavarotti or Kiri Te Kanawa." I wondered how they could not know about our mission to identify new talent and launch their careers? The scorecard should help us communicate better our vision and mission to them.

Ken Freed, co-chair of the Board's strategic planning committee, described the Balanced Scorecard as "breathtakingly clarifying."

> It forces people to think about the tradeoffs that have to be confronted. If handled the right way, it should increase Board knowledge and involvement, which are the keys to success for nonprofits.
>
> I am not sure we have the right measures, and it could still evolve into a bureaucratic process. But with Jan and Sue's leadership, I am optimistic that our discussions will focus on "why are we doing this," and "how does this initiative get us to the future," not about the color of napkins at the next benefit. The scorecard gives me assurance that we have an approved mission and strategy. We can now build the trust and awareness in our constituencies about the BLO, and demonstrate that it is completely different from Sarah's opera company.

Del Sesto believed that the Balanced Scorecard would help her keep the board's attention on its proper role:

> Some of the board members come here to relax from the quantitative aspects of their business lives. They want to revel in the "art" and come to the BLO board to understand opera better. Also, boards typically have great difficulty deciding what **not** to do. The scorecard helps me focus the discussion back to the strategy that they, in fact, were involved in developing.

Del Sesto knew that Board members continually generated ideas about special events that they would like to sponsor. Each such event, however, required Del Sesto and senior administrative or artistic staff to participate. The Balanced Scorecard gave Del Sesto a framework to say "no" to such proposals unless they delivered a significant number of targeted constituents and had high potential for successful follow-up. The development staff was now working proactively to design events for targeted constituents, and, after they had been designed, search for appropriate hosts from the Board for the events.

The board had started to incorporate the Balanced Scorecard into some of its committee activities. For example, the committee to identify potential new board members developed a strategic needs chart that clearly outlined existing strengths and weaknesses in the existing board profile, and identified the gaps that needed to be filled by future recruiting activities.

Sherif Nada, Chairman of the Board, reflected on two contrasting methods for introducing the scorecard to nonprofit boards:

> At Citizen Schools, the two professional leaders worked closely with their staff to develop the Balanced Scorecard. Then they brought it to the board and Executive Committee, who reacted and modified the scorecard before approving it. At the BLO, the effort was done at a high level, with active involvement of the board, and then cascaded out to lower-level staff.
>
> As a board member, the BLO process makes more sense to me, though the degree of understanding of the BSC inside the organization was higher at Citizen Schools.

Not all board members, however, shared the enthusiasm for the Balanced Scorecard. Nada commented:

> The board is heterogeneous. Some were extremely involved, and loved the approach. Others were passive and reactive. A few became very concerned that the company was in danger of losing its soul. They didn't believe you could run a performing arts organization by the numbers.
>
> I've tried to run my life with a balanced philosophy represented, metaphorically, by the head, the heart, and the hand: the head, with the brain, has ideas and knowledge; the heart represents compassion and emotion; and the hand enables us to execute. The Balanced Scorecard tries to integrate all three components, but some on the board feel most deeply about the heart. They feel this component has been sacrificed by introducing the Scorecard.

NEXT STEPS

Dahling-Sullivan was beginning to develop the initial set of measures for all the objectives. These would be taken back to the Board for discussion and approval. She was also continuing to work closely with each department to help them formulate their own scorecards, and develop measures and targets for the upcoming year.

Del Sesto reflected on the recent journey and the path ahead. People are now thinking more strategically, and with greater clarity about our objectives. They are more willing to abandon initiatives that are not delivering on our measured objectives. I use the Balanced Scorecard to challenge people, "How will we achieve this target?" The process forces more self-assessment and more group problem solving.

But we can not take success for granted. We must remain steadfastly committed to the Balanced Scorecard, which will require continual analysis, assessment, and re-evaluation. We will applaud the little things and leverage our successes, accept but learn from our failures, and be prepared to modify strategies and measures as we go along.

EXHIBIT 1 Boston Lyric Opera mission statement (adopted 1993)

To offer audiences productions of the highest quality, of varied repertoire using primarily young, emerging singers, and important directors and designers.

To offer opportunities that help bridge the gap between the training of performing and creative artists and the professional career.

To present seasons which offer a well-known work, a less frequently performed work(s), and a 20th century American work.

To help build a body of American works of opera through the commissioning and production of such works and through educational and outreach programs that enable and encourage interactions between audiences and creative artists.

To extend our offerings and reach new audiences through collaborative productions with other American opera companies and cultural organizations.

To educate and expand audiences of all ages and diverse cultures through new productions of existing works, the presentation of new works, and education programs and special programs designed to build a better educated, informed, and risk-taking audience.

Exhibit 2 Boston Lyric Opera organizational chart

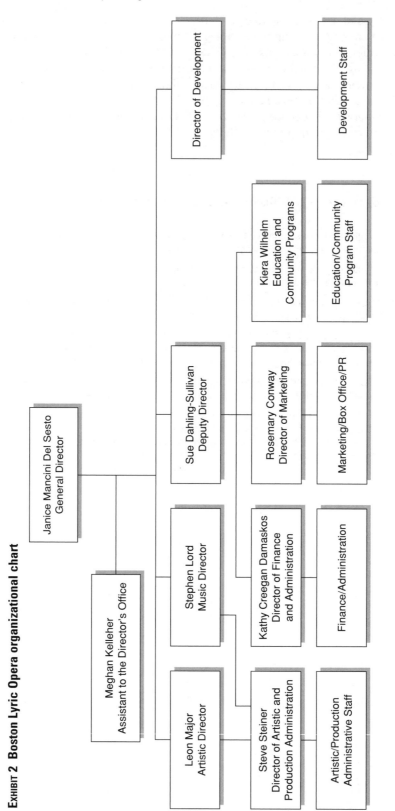

Exhibit 3 Boston Lyric Opera repertory history

1977/78	*Zaide*, Mozart
1979/80	*King for a Day*, Verdi
1980/81	*Amahl and the Night Visitors*, Menotti
	La clemenza di Tito, Mozart
	The Consul, Menotti
	The Coronation of Poppea, Monteverdi
1981/82	*Norma*, Bellini
	The Abduction from the Seraglio, Mozart
	Werther, Massenet
1982/83	*Der Ring des Nibelungen*, Wagner
	Ariadne auf Naxos, Strauss
	Il Trovatore, Verdi
	Madama Butterfly, Puccini
1984/85	*First the Music, Then the Words*, Salieri
	The Impresario, Mozart
1985/86	*Agrippina*, Handel
	Façade, Walton
	La Voix Humaine, Poulenc
	The Barber of Seville, Rossini
1986/87	*Rigoletto*, Verdi
	The Rake's Progress, Stravinsky
1987/88	*Maria Stuarda*, Donizetti
	The Turn of the Screw, Britten
1988/89	*The Portrait of Manon*, Massenet
	Therese, Massenet
	Dialogues des Carmelites, Poulenc
1989/90	*Tosca*, Puccini
	The Flying Dutchman, Wagner
	La Traviata, Verdi
1990/91	*The Daughter of the Regiment*, Donizetti
	Ariadne auf Naxos, Strauss
	Regina, Blitzstein

1991/92	*La Cenerentola*, Rossini
	Lost in the Stars, Weill
	The Tales of Hoffman, Offenbach
1992/93	*La Bohème*, Puccini
	Beatrice and Benedict, Berlioz
	Wuthering Heights, Floyd
1993/94	*I Puritani*, Bellini
	Carmen, Bizet
	The Postman Always Rings Twice, Paulus
1994/95	*Rigoletto*, Verdi
	Il Barbiere di Siviglia, Rossini
	Candide, Bernstein
1995/96	*Faust*, Gounod
	Falstaff, Verdi
	Xerxes, Handel
1996/97	*Tosca*, Puccini
	The Shepherd King, Mozart
	L'elisir d'amore, Donizetti
1997/98	*Deborah Voigt in Concert*
	Lucia di Lammermoor, Donizetti
	The Ballad of Baby Doe, Moore
	Werther, Massenet
1998/99	*La Traviata*, Verdi
	Romeo et Juliette, Gounod
	Le nozze di Figaro, Mozart
1999/00	*Aïda*, Verdi
	Akhnaten, Glass
	Die Zauberflöte, Mozart
2000/01	*Madama Butterfly*, Puccini
	Don Giovanni, Mozart
	Salome, Strauss
	The Daughter of the Regiment, Donizetti

EXHIBIT 4 Boston Lyric Opera financial statements

Income Statement for the Year Ended May 31, 2000

	2000	1999
Support:		
Contributions	$4,223,042	$2,619,338
Special events	372,110	218,062
Grants	205,710	393,055
Contributions-in-kind	34,970	61,438
Total support	$4,835,832	$3,291,893
Revenue:		
Ticket sales	$1,713,389	$1,431,620
Other Income	78,313	67,117
Interest	57,088	38,663
Unrealized gain	208	–
Total revenue	$1,848,998	$1,537,400
Total support and revenue	$6,684,830	$4,829,293
Expenses and Losses:		
Production expenses[a]	$3,774,179	$2,685,447
General and administrative	1,520,287	1,222,965
Development expenses	610,709	472,517
Education	274,691	317,132
Bad debt	153,828	–
Loss on sale of securities	8,737	5,098
Loss on disposal of assets	–	3,301
Unrealized loss	–	624
Total expenses and losses	$6,342,431	$4,707,084
Net Income	$ 342,399	$ 122,209

[a] Schedule of Production Expenses.

	2000	1999
Production salaries and fees	$2,082,376	$1,538,004
Other production costs	591,412	358,646
Advertising and promotion	358,775	359,298
Scenery and properties	322,928	52,491
Costumes	224,242	173,928
Theatre rental	159,052	176,421
Depreciation	35,385	26,659
Total production expenses	$3,774,179	$2,685,447

Balance Sheet as of May 31, 2000

	2000	1999
Current Assets:		
Cash	$1,886,090	$1,445,786
Unconditional promises to give	934,826	601,014
Inventory	7,495	7,065
Other current assets	360,993	66,013
Total current assets	$3,189,404	$2,119,878
Net book value of property and equipment	$ 314,091	$ 374,008
Other assets	31,575	95,901
Total assets	$3,535,070	$2,589,787
Current Liabilities:		
Accounts payable	$ 290,973	$ 152,951
Advance ticket subscriptions	1,382,014	922,569
Payroll taxes withheld and accrued	5,613	196
Total current liabilities	$1,678,600	$1,075,716
Net assets[a]	$1,856,470	$1,514,071
Total liabilities and net assets	$3,535,070	$2,589,787

[a] Net assets are contributed by donors and are equivalent to owners' equity in for-profit entities.

EXHIBIT 5 Boston Lyric Opera's strategy map

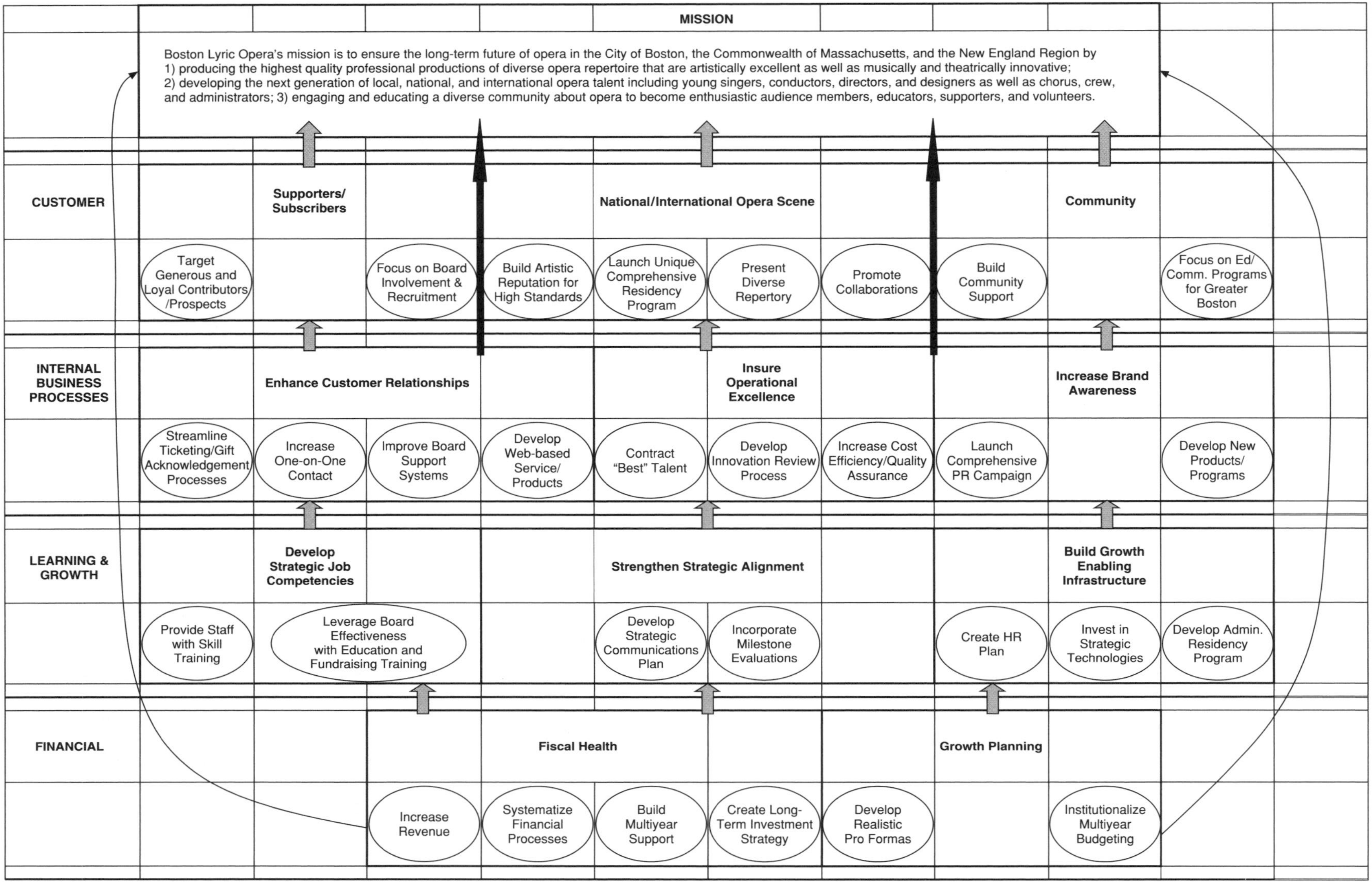

MISSION

Boston Lyric Opera's mission is to ensure the long-term future of opera in the City of Boston, the Commonwealth of Massachusetts, and the New England Region by 1) producing the highest quality professional productions of diverse opera repertoire that are artistically excellent as well as musically and theatrically innovative; 2) developing the next generation of local, national, and international opera talent including young singers, conductors, directors, and designers as well as chorus, crew, and administrators; 3) engaging and educating a diverse community about opera to become enthusiastic audience members, educators, supporters, and volunteers.

CUSTOMER

- Supporters/Subscribers
- National/International Opera Scene
- Community

- Target Generous and Loyal Contributors/Prospects
- Focus on Board Involvement & Recruitment
- Build Artistic Reputation for High Standards
- Launch Unique Comprehensive Residency Program
- Present Diverse Repertory
- Promote Collaborations
- Build Community Support
- Focus on Ed/Comm. Programs for Greater Boston

INTERNAL BUSINESS PROCESSES

- Enhance Customer Relationships
- Insure Operational Excellence
- Increase Brand Awareness

- Streamline Ticketing/Gift Acknowledgement Processes
- Increase One-on-One Contact
- Improve Board Support Systems
- Develop Web-based Service/Products
- Contract "Best" Talent
- Develop Innovation Review Process
- Increase Cost Efficiency/Quality Assurance
- Launch Comprehensive PR Campaign
- Develop New Products/Programs

LEARNING & GROWTH

- Develop Strategic Job Competencies
- Strengthen Strategic Alignment
- Build Growth Enabling Infrastructure

- Provide Staff with Skill Training
- Leverage Board Effectiveness with Education and Fundraising Training
- Develop Strategic Communications Plan
- Incorporate Milestone Evaluations
- Create HR Plan
- Invest in Strategic Technologies
- Develop Admin. Residency Program

FINANCIAL

- Fiscal Health
- Growth Planning

- Increase Revenue
- Systematize Financial Processes
- Build Multiyear Support
- Create Long-Term Investment Strategy
- Develop Realistic Pro Formas
- Institutionalize Multiyear Budgeting

Exhibit 6 Learning and growth and financial objectives

LEARNING AND GROWTH	FINANCIAL
Outcome #1: Strategic skill competencies for staff. *Driver objective:* ● Invest in training to develop stronger skills in management, budgeting, analysis, planning, project management, and technology applications. ● Career path development **Outcome #2:** Leveraged effectiveness of board and volunteers through education and fundraising training. *Driver objective:* ● Create an interactive education program that develops board knowledge about Boston Lyric Opera's vision and opera "operations." ● Develop and enhance board fundraising skills. **Outcome #3:** Integrated organizational alignment with strategic goals. *Driver objectives:* ● Develop a communications component to the strategic plan that educates and engages all constituents. ● Incorporate milestones to evaluate departmental, organizational, and board progress towards goals. **Outcome #4:** Ongoing investment in growth enabling infrastructure to support future vision. *Driver objectives:* ● Develop and launch administrative portion of BLO Residency Program. ● Create a human resources plan that focuses on recruitment, retention, and training of top-notch administrative talent. ● Invest in strategic technologies and training that will provide competitive advantages.	**Outcome #1:** Short-term and long-term fiscal health and stability. *Driver objectives:* ● Increase sustainable earned and unearned revenue levels through ticket income, fundraising, set rental/sales, and other new revenue streams. ● Systematize financial controls and monitoring systems. ● Develop multiyear support programs. ● Create a long-term investment strategy. **Outcome #2:** Strategically-driven and accurate financial growth models to support planning efforts. *Driver objectives:* ● Develop realistic pro formas that can be easily adapted to changes in the operating environment. ● Implement a multiyear budgeting process. ● Integrate long-term facility issues and alternatives into financial planning process.

EXHIBIT 7 BLO repertory planning template, FY 2001 draft/sample

Opera (Name)	Composer Version?	# of Performances	Casting and/or Conductor/ Director	Artistic Profile (S,M,L)	Production Profile	Artistic Style	Audience Appeal	Collaborations
Ratings:	1 point for different composer; 2 points for living composer; 2 for unusual version, etc. Avg. 4 Good: 5+	(for Budgeting Pro Formas)	Overall Rating on quality of cast and creative team. 1–10 (Ten is tops) Average: 5 Above Avg: 6 Good Quality: 7 Excellent: 8 Great: 9–10	(for Budgeting Pro Formas)	1 point for Rent 2 for Co-production 3 for New Average = 6 Good = 7 Excellent = 8+	2 for modern/ American 1 for top ten 1.5 for next tier 2 for lesser known Avg. Mix = 5 Good = 6+	1 point for Mass (top 10) 1 point for opera Fanatics 1.5 Mid-Appeal 2 Families Avg. = 5 Good = 6	Strategic Partnerships: 1 point for each Goal: 1 per year
Madama Butterfly (Oct)	Puccini 1	7	Actual: 7	Cast: Chorus: Orchestra: Supers:	1	1	1	
Don Giovanni (Nov.)	Mozart 1	7	Actual: 8.5	Cast: Chorus: Orchestra: Supers:	3	1	1	
Salome (Jan)	Strauss 1	6	Actual: 8	Cast: Chorus: Orchestra: Supers:	2	1.5	2	
Daughter of the Regiment (May)	Donizetti 1	6	Actual: 7	Cast: Chorus: Orchestra: Supers:	1	1.5	1.5	
ACTUAL RATINGS	**4**	**26**	**7.6 (avg.)**		**7**	**5**	**5.5**	

Season Planning Notes:

2000/2001 4 productions w/6 subscription performances; 2 single ticket performances (Total: 26 performances)
2001/2002 4 productions w/7 subscription performances; 2 single ticket performances (Total: 30 performances) 25th Anniversary Season
2002/2003 4 productions w/7 subscription performances; 2 single ticket performances (Total: 30 performances)
2003/2004 4 productions w/8 subscription performances; 2 single ticket performances (Total: 34 performances)
2004/2005 5 productions: 4 productions w/8 subscription performances; 1 production w/6 performances (January) (Total: 38 performances)

Case Study

University of Southern California: Responsibility Center Management System

In 1981 a major change was made to decentralize the management of the University of Southern California. Deans of schools and managers of administrative units were given the authority for most of the decisions that would determine the university's academic and fiscal success. To hold the operating managers accountable for the financial consequences of their decisions, the university implemented a financial control system originally called the Revenue Center Management System. Most people who were familiar with the system credited it with playing a significant role in USC's success over the years, particularly because it provided a high degree of financial transparency and encouraged academic deans to be entrepreneurial, market-savvy, and fiscally responsible.

This system, which over time became to be known as the Responsibility Center Management System (RCMS), was still being used in 2008, but critics complained that the system had a number of serious, unintended, dysfunctional side-effects. USC administrators had modified some of the RCMS elements over the years to try to maintain the advantages of the system while minimizing these side-effects. More changes were possibly forthcoming.

THE UNIVERSITY OF SOUTHERN CALIFORNIA

The University of Southern California (USC), established in 1880, was California's oldest private, research university. Located on the perimeter of downtown Los Angeles, USC was a diverse and complex organization. It ran 19 colleges and schools, more than any other private university in the United States. It enrolled over 33,000 students from all 50 US states and from 115 countries. The student body included almost 7,000 international students, more than at any other university in the United States. Undergraduate students could design degrees from 77 majors and 147 minors. Graduate students could earn degrees in 139 areas of study. The "Trojan Family" included over 194,000 living alumni. USC employed over 3,200 full-time faculty members, and had annual operating revenues of $2.5 billion. It was the largest private employer in Los Angeles and the third largest in the state of California. Exhibit 1 shows some quantified university highlights.

The university's academic and administrative programs were led by president Steven Sample (see Exhibit 2). All of the school deans and a number of senior academic administrators reported to the provost, Max Nikias, who was USC's chief academic officer (see Exhibit 3).

As a research university, USC's goals included both creation and transmission of knowledge (see the statement of mission and goals in Exhibit 4). Thus USC's faculty was expected to engage in basic or applied research as well as to perform their teaching. USC supported its activities primarily by generating tuition revenues, securing research sponsorship, and attracting philanthropic contributions. Because its endowment-per-student was relatively small, the university was heavily dependent on tuition revenues. However, it was successful in generating research funds. For example, USC ranked 17th among the nation's universities in receipts of federal research and development funds.

Overall, USC's top priority was to enhance its academic reputation, and there is evidence that it was doing so successfully. In recent years, USC had risen sharply in the many university rankings. For example, in 2008 *US News & World Report* ranked

This case was prepared by Professor Kenneth A. Merchant with the assistance of Sahil Parmar.

USC 27th in its list of "America's Best Colleges," up from a ranking of 41st just 10 years earlier.

STRATEGIES

On October 6, 2004, USC's Board of Trustees approved a new strategic plan called the Plan for Increasing Academic Excellence.[1] This plan stated the following objective: "USC intends to become one of the most influential and productive research universities in the world."

The strategic plan focused attention and resources on three areas that had to be addressed for USC to achieve its goal of providing leadership to the academic world and society as a whole:

1. meeting societal needs, through research and education that examines, anticipates and resolves pressing societal urgencies;

2. expanding USC's global presence, through collaboration with institutions around the world, especially in the Pacific Rim; and

3. promoting learner-centered education, through adaptive and flexible approaches that redefine learning, as the context and content of higher education change rapidly.

The plan also identified four strategic capabilities that should be developed to position USC for success. These were (1) span disciplinary and school boundaries to focus on problems of social significance, (2) link fundamental to applied research, (3) build networks and partnerships, and (4) increase responsiveness to learners.

THE MANAGEMENT SYSTEM PRIOR TO RCMS

Prior to implementation of RCMS, decision making power at USC was centralized. One senior administrative officer – the provost – played the key role in all major resource allocation decisions. Dennis Dougherty, USC's chief financial officer (CFO), remembered that "The old system relied on personal negotiation. The resource allocation decisions were made behind the scenes in a 'smoke filled room'."

Also in the old system, financial accountability for the unit heads was weak. Each university unit (schools and departments) had its own financial

statement, but the statements were not complete. Some revenues and costs were neither traced nor allocated to the units that generated them. Some deans felt that the more money their schools generated, the greedier the central administrators became.[2] Furthermore, unit heads were not sanctioned for producing unfavorable variances as compared to their budget. One finance manager recalled that:

> Some units would consistently overrun their budgets, and some had substantial overruns. Most of the overruns were due to under-generated revenues, rather than cost overruns. No one had any explicit incentives to manage differently.

Some deans were also seen as spendthrifts, and some in the central administration believed that one of their key roles was to protect the university and its units from financial ruin.[3]

RCMS DESIGN PRINCIPLES

Work on the RCMS began in 1981, at the beginning of a period that promised to be difficult because significant declines in the population of traditional college-aged persons necessitated budget cuts. The RCMS was designed by a Task Force on Budget Incentives appointed by then-university president, James Zumberge. The Task Force based much of the RCMS design on the system used at the University of Pennsylvania (Penn) which, in turn, was adapted from the system in use at the General Electric Company. Reginald Jones, GE's then-chairman, had been on the Board of Trustees at Penn, and he insisted that this kind of system would provide a better alignment of authority and responsibility and, hence, better university management.

The objectives of systems like that used at Penn included "clarifying roles and responsibilities between local and central units, linking cause and effect through revenue and indirect cost allocations, placing local academic planning decision making in a cost/benefit context, and unleashing entrepreneurship."[4] Overall, they allow universities

---

[1] The full text of the plan can be seen at www.usc.edu/about/core_documents/2004_strategic_plan.html.

[2] A. Rahnamay-Azar, "Revenue Center Management at the University of Southern California: A Case Study," unpublished doctoral dissertation, University of Pennsylvania, 2008.

[3] Ibid.

[4] J. R. Curry and J. C. Strauss (2002), *Responsibility Center Management: Lessons from 25 Years of Decentralized Management* (Annapolis Junction, MD: National Association of College and University Business Officials), p. 3.

to focus on outcome measures rather than relying on bureaucracies to administer process controls.

USC's design task force developed the following nine management principles to guide their development of the USC RCMS:[5]

1. Responsibility should be commensurate with authority, and vice versa.

2. Decentralization should be proportional to organizational size and complexity.

3. Locally optimal decisions are not always globally optimal: central leverage is required to implement corporate (global) priorities.

4. Outcome measures are preferable to process controls.

5. Accountability is only as good as the tools which measure it.

6. Quantitative measures of performance tend to drive out qualitative measures.

7. Outcomes should matter: plans that work should lead to rewards; plans that fail should lead to sanctions.

8. Resource-expanding incentives are preferable to resource-dividing ones.

9. People play better games when they own the rules.

The new RCMS system had to include three basic elements that would permit a decentralized management system within USC. First, the university had to be divided into responsibility centers. Second, the performance reports, including methods for tracing or allocating shared revenues and costs to the primary operating units, had to be designed. Third, the extent of decision authority to be delegated to the operating units needed to be clarified.

RESPONSIBILITY CENTERS

USC was comprised of two types of responsibility centers, revenue centers and administrative centers. *Revenue centers* were organizational units to which revenues could be uniquely attributed. Some of these, the colleges, schools, and research institutes, were called "academic" revenue centers. The other revenue centers, including athletics, residence halls, bookstores, parking operations, and food

services, were called "auxiliary" revenue centers. *Administrative centers* were entities that did not generate revenues directly but performed activities that supported the revenue centers. Examples included Admissions and Financial Aid, Business Affairs, Financial Services, Legal Services, Library, Office of the President, and Registrar.

Most of the responsibilities for raising revenues and expending resources were delegated to the revenue center managers. As noted in USC's 1985 Financial Report:

> At USC, we believe that the primary planning takes place at the operating unit level: the school or auxiliary enterprise, or the administrative unit. We believe that people closest to the action know their programs, their customers, and their markets best; they are best informed and, therefore, the most capable of strategic thinking. The role of central planners is primarily one of coordinating and monitoring.

The central administration maintained the power to hold the responsibility center managers accountable for attaining their targets. The academic revenue center managers (i.e., school deans) were evaluated in terms of their units' academic excellence (research and teaching), generation of sponsored research grants, faculty development, fundraising, and bottom line financial performance. Their performances were reviewed formally every five years.

PERFORMANCE REPORTS

USC produced an elaborate set of reports to facilitate control of each responsibility center's operations. A monthly financial report presented the current month's and year-to-date performance as compared to budget. Other reports provided information on gifts, grants, enrollments, student numbers, personnel, space usage, and the detailed items affecting the revenues and expenses of each responsibility center. The financial reports included four primary categories of accounts: revenues, direct expenses, indirect expenses, and participations/subventions.

Revenues

The revenue centers were allowed to keep the revenues they generated. The university generated two types of revenues: designated and undesignated. More than 25% of the total funds available to support operations were *designated*, meaning that they

[5] J. R. Curry (1991), Afterword: The USC Experience with Revenue Center Management, in E. L. Whalen, *Responsibility Center Budgeting: An Approach to Decentralized Management for Institutions of Higher Education* (Indiana University Press), p. 178.

were given to the university for a specific purpose or project. These funds came from grants and contracts from the federal government and other sponsors of specific research projects, from gifts from private donors and foundations, and from income from endowments to support specific individuals and/or activities. The designated revenue funds had to be used only for the specific purpose for which they were given and were not allowed to be transferred to an undesignated account without prior permission from the central administration.

The other revenues were *undesignated*. They came from tuition and fees, unrestricted gifts, and indirect cost recoveries from government contracts. Tuition revenue was credited 100% to the revenue center offering the course taken. Undergraduate student aid was administered centrally and charged to academic centers on a predetermined percent of undergraduate tuition. For FY08, that rate was set at 28%. The indirect cost recoveries were determined by formula negotiated with each funding source. For example, USC's indirect cost recovery rate on US government projects was 63% of direct costs. That is, for every dollar reported as the approved direct costs of a research project, the university received an additional 63 cents to help cover indirect costs. But on other projects, the recovery rate was lower. Those funded by the Kellogg Foundation, for example, provided only an 8% recovery rate, and some grants provided for no overhead cost recovery.

Expenses

Under RCMS, each revenue center was responsible for the full costs of its operations. The *direct expenses* of a revenue center included the costs of the people and the equipment directly assigned to that center. *Indirect expenses* included the costs of shared resources, such as buildings, utilities, and various kinds of support (e.g., libraries, computing, security, transportation, student aid) provided by the administrative centers.

Since the inception of RCMS, the university relied on a complex set of allocation methods. University administrators, in collaboration with revenue center managers, determined what centers shared what cost pools and how the costs would be spread across pool participants. Some cost allocations were based on actual usage, but others were based on approximations.

John Curry, USC's then-vice president of budget and planning, acknowledged that the allocations were based on:

> [. . .] imperfect rules, some of which were totally arbitrary. We used Federal government allocation guidelines as a guide, but we also put together a group of deans and administrators and hammered the rules out.

Dennis Dougherty concurred:

> Our allocations of indirect cost are done with thumbnail methods that are much less precise than precise. No study was done, but the allocations were somewhat thoughtful. We developed rules of thumb and tried to remove blatant inaccuracies.

Over time, the number of cost pools grew. By the late 1990s, the number of allocation bases in USC's indirect cost allocation system grew to more than 150.

Participations and subventions

University administrators used a system of participations and subventions to maintain a degree of control over university-wide resource allocation decisions and to even out the distribution of monies between revenue centers. *Participations* were contributions required from all academic revenue centers, based on an equal proportion of tuition and fees, sales or service income, and indirect cost recoveries, to further the objectives and well being of the entire university. In the revenue center financial reports, participations were shown as negative indirect income.

These contributions, along with revenues from other discretionary funds (investment income and income from endowment restricted to the provost), were redistributed back to revenue centers as block grants historically called *subventions*. Provost Nikias avoided use of the word "subventions" because, he believed, it made the grants sound like entitlements. He preferred to call them either Academic Initiatives or Provost's Initiatives. Academic Initiative funding was defined in USC's 2007 financial report as for "specific activities for a limited time period." Provost's Initiatives funding was allocated "to support university priorities."

When they made their allocations of subventions, the administrators, particularly the provost and president, tended to focus on three key factors: (1) differentials in the costs of educating students in different fields; (2) the revenue centers' cost/quality ratios; and (3) university priorities.

The cost of educating students varied widely between schools. Some schools could educate their students effectively by teaching them in large sections, while others had to provide instruction in small classes or in expensive laboratories. John Curry explained:

> The cost of educating a music major is large, especially in a conservatory-like program like ours. The dominant mode of instruction is one-on-one; a master pianist and pupil on the same bench. Business education is much less expensive, as accounting and finance can be taught well to classes of 25 or 50, or even more. But we as a university have decided to charge both music and business students the same tuition. Common price, but most uncommon "unit" costs!

Part of the subvention allocations was aimed at evening out this cost disparity.

The subjectively determined ratio of costs to academic excellence represented what the university administrators perceived they were receiving for their investment. This is illustrated in Figure 1. A school located near point 3, such as the Thornton School of Music, with both high cost of instruction and high academic excellence,[6] was most likely to get a disproportionately high subvention. It offered high quality programs and research productivity but was unable to cover its costs through tuitions. A school located near point 4 was valuable to the university because it offered high quality and financial independence. It could probably provide funds that can be used in other parts of the university, but administrators had to be careful to allow it to keep enough funds to maintain its excellence. A school located near point 2 was in trouble. It was a candidate for new leadership or program discontinuance.

To illustrate the wide disparity in subvention amounts, Table 1 shows the 2007 summary income statement numbers for the Marshall School of Business and the Thornton School of Music.[7] As can be seen, the Thornton School received much larger subventions, both in total and in a relative sense.

---

[6] *Rolling Stone Magazine* ranked the USC Thornton School of Music as one of the top five music schools in the United States.

[7] The entire USC 2007 financial report can be seen at www.usc.edu/private/factbook/USC.FR.2007.pdf. On pp. 20–23, this report shows revenue center summaries for all of USC's colleges, schools, centers, institutes, health care services, auxiliaries, and athletics.

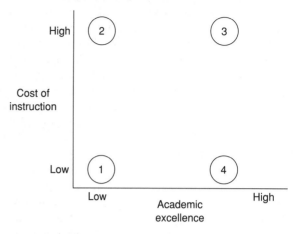

FIGURE 1 Cost/academic excellence ratios

INTERCENTER BANK

The RCMS included one other significant element, an Intercenter Bank. This bank provided revenue centers, but not administrative centers, the opportunity to carry unrestricted funds across fiscal year boundaries. It thus provided revenue center managers incentives to produce year end surpluses rather than just to meet a break-even bottom-line. It also reduced the "use-it-or-lose-it" mentality, present in some not-for-profit organizations, which causes managers to spend all the money that had been approved in their budget before the year-end.

The Intercenter Bank was used both by revenue centers reporting surpluses and by those reporting losses. If a revenue center had a surplus, it was given an account in the bank and provided interest on the account balance at the fiscal treasury-bill rate as of July 1 of the year just started. These revenue center managers were to spend their account balance in future years, but only up to a maximum of 20% of the balance each year. Conversely revenue centers with a deficit were assigned a loan from the bank that charged interest at the treasury-bill rate. They had to budget for repayment of the loan at a rate of at least 20% of the beginning balance each year.

CRITICISMS OF THE RCMS SYSTEM

Over the years, various faculty groups and other critics voiced a number of complaints about the RCMS. These included criticisms that the system discouraged innovation, multidisciplinary research,

TABLE 1 Individual revenue center summary (2007–08 budget) ($000)

	Marshall School of Business		Thornton School of Music	
	Undesignated	Designated	Undesignated	Designated
Revenues:				
Direct:	$126,866	$12,928	$22,044	$2,404
Center	156,799	12,928	28,862	2,404
UG Student Aid Fund	(25,434)		(6,012)	
Facilities Improvement Fund	(4,499)		(806)	
Indirect:	(8,485)		2,951	
Participation	(10,078)		(1,911)	
Academic Initiatives			4,500	
Provost's Initiatives	35		97	
Graduate Programs	1,558		265	
Total Revenues	**$118,381**	**$12,928**	**$24,995**	**$2,404**
Expenses:				
Direct	$85,846	$12,928	$17,106	$2,404
Indirect	32,535		7,889	
Allocated Central Costs	30,292		6,944	
Facilities Based	2,243		945	
Total Expenses	**$118,381**	**$12,928**	**$24,995**	**$2,404**

and the seeking of some outside grants and that it encouraged both the proliferation of redundant and inappropriate courses and end-of-period financial gameplaying. It also stimulated numerous debates about the fairness of allocations of indirect costs.

Discouragement of innovation

The discouragement-of-innovation criticism stemmed from the belief that the RCMS forced deans to think of their mission more in financial terms than in terms of their academic mission. An open letter sent by some faculty to President Sample stated:

> The system in place makes few allowances for the various missions and contributions of the academic units of the university. Those units unable to show a "profit" under current budgetary formulas are condemned to live in a deficit situation, to depend upon subventions given after demeaning negotiations, and to face inferior status among other units in the university.

Some believed that the financial pressure discouraged innovation and even teaching quality. One committee report noted that, "innovators whose ideas do not imply immediate income feel that no one in the system will give those ideas a sympathetic hearing and so are discouraged from innovating." Another added that, "Faculty under pressure to produce income are not focused on students." Some even believed that the emphasis on financial performance would lead university administrators to hire deans with, perhaps, more financial management abilities than leadership vision for their schools.[8]

Another group of critics believed that innovation and initiative were stifled because RCMS institutionalized decentralization only to the level of the deans and, thus, did not go far enough. Deans were unlikely to carry the delegation any further and, as a consequence, the university was stripped of the entrepreneurial energies of many faculty leaders.

Still another group of critics lamented that much of the power and discretionary funds had been taken from the USC's top-level managers, and their roles essentially became those of administrators, not leaders. One critic noted, "Neither [the president or provost at that time] has become identified with

---

[8] Indeed several of the new deans recently hired at USC (e.g., Medicine, Libraries) had MBA degrees in addition to the terminal degree for their field. But Provost Nikias argued that to be successful in the twenty-first century, deans needed both leadership vision and financial management skills, in that order.

any public position. All the leadership that is being exerted is coming from the [good] deans."

Discouragement of multidisciplinary research

Some faculty believed that the best research, particularly that of an applied nature, was multidisciplinary, involving researchers with different skills and perspectives. But since RCMS emphasized financial priorities, most deans could not see the financial benefits of multidisciplinary research.

In fact, it could be a burden trying to figure out how to share project revenues. If, for example, faculty from three schools were involved in a multidisciplinary research project, should the revenues be shared equally? If not, how much should be allocated to the school whose personnel conceived of the research idea? How much to the school whose personnel prepared the proposal? How much to the school that provided the facilities where the project was completed? What if facilities from two schools were used but the costs of these facilities were quite different? The effort required to answer all these questions could be sizable. And depending on how the revenues and costs of the cross-revenue center work were shared, the outcome could be a financial drain on a revenue center, not a benefit.

Critics noted that little multidisciplinary work was being done at USC. They blamed the RCMS, at least in part, and cited examples in which deans had reprimanded faculty members for getting involved in research with someone from outside their revenue center.

Discouragement of the seeking of outside grants

Some faculty were discouraged from seeking some outside funding grants because those grants appeared to be "unprofitable" to the revenue center. This is because those grants provided indirect cost recoveries at rates lower than the departments' actual spending rates. For example, even the US government's recovery rate of 63%, which was higher than the recovery rates allowed by many foundations, did not cover the overall USC average overhead rate, which was approximately 68% of direct costs. Furthermore, the indirect cost rates in some departments, such as those with expensive laboratories, were several times higher than the overall university average.

Encouragement of "inappropriate" courses

Some courses tended to proliferate across campus because tuition revenues were captured by the school who offered the course. Thus many schools offered similar or even identical courses (e.g., statistics, communications) in order to retain all of the tuition dollars at their school. Many schools created general education courses intended to have market appeal to large numbers of undergraduate students. Some schools were also accused of offering courses that were popular for the wrong reasons. Among the examples cited were "gut" (excessively easy) courses that fell below traditional university standards and the toleration of professors who graded "liberally" to keep their courses popular. Although proposals for new courses were subject to review and approval by the university's curriculum committee, this control was deemed by many not to have been effective.

Encouragement of end-of-period financial gameplaying

Many examples were cited of revenue center managers moving revenues and expenses between fiscal years depending on whether they were in a budget surplus or deficit position. For example, they could ask donors to accelerate or delay contributions, or they could deposit June donations immediately or wait until after July 1, the start of the new fiscal year. They could move expenses between years by, for example, accelerating or delaying discretionary expenditures or by asking faculty and staff members to submit requests for reimbursement of expenditures already made in the current or following fiscal year.

The deans and many others within the university did not consider such manipulations unethical because they had observed top-level university administrators taking the same types of actions. In its entire 126-year history, USC had never posted a fiscal year deficit. That record was seen as important because it provided evidence that the university was well-run, and it contributed to the high quality (Aa1) bond rating that USC was given by Moody's and Standard and Poor's. Both of these indicators facilitated the raising of capital and donations from alumni, foundations, and the investment community. As Dennis Dougherty noted, "Big donors will not give to a school running a deficit. They assume the people there can't handle the money."

Debates about the fairness of cost allocations

Under RCMS, each revenue center was responsible for the full costs of its operations, including its share of indirect costs, the allocated costs of centralized support services. Since the inception of RCMS, the university relied on a complex set of allocation methods. University administrators, in collaboration with revenue center managers, determined which centers shared which cost pools and how the costs would be spread across pool participants. Some cost allocations were based on actual usage, but others were based on one or more approximations. Eventually the number of allocation bases in USC's indirect cost allocation system grew to nearly 150. Doing all the calculations required a major effort.

Not surprisingly, the system caused much tension and many debates about the fairness of the allocations of indirect costs. Deans would closely examine their indirect costs and compare them with their perceived usage of central services. Then they would argue as to why they should not be charged with costs from a given pool, or charged only at a reduced rate perhaps because the central services duplicated services provided locally by the school or because they simply did not value the centralized services. Indeed, the students from some schools made little use of such services as the central library, computer labs, career services, and/or transportation services. These discussions consumed considerable time and effort, and the outcomes of the discussions often led to an even greater proliferation of cost pools and more complex calculations. Deans worried about their ability to predict what the allocation parameters and, hence, their indirect costs, would be in the forthcoming year.

REFINEMENTS OVER THE YEARS

Over the years, USC administrators made a number of changes to the RCMS to try to address some of the criticisms of it. These changes included the following:

Centralization of General Education courses

In fiscal year 1998 (FY98), the offering of all General Education (GE) courses for undergraduate students was centralized in the College of Letters, Arts and Sciences ("the College"). The various schools loved the opportunity to offer GE courses because they provided access to large numbers of students, many of whom were non-majors who might develop an interest in the School's offerings. But while most of the GE courses offered in various Schools were well designed and effectively delivered, these courses seemed to provide some of the greatest opportunities for offering courses seemingly only for revenue reasons. The decision to centralize the offering of GE courses was made to ensure academic quality.

This change created a large revenue boost for the College and significant revenue challenges for some other schools. To allow schools that were adversely impacted by this change to adjust their operations and priorities, the provost instituted a two-year phase-in period. Most schools quickly adapted and stabilized themselves financially, but a couple continued to struggle with largely fixed costs (e.g., tenured faculty) and sharply reduced revenues. The survival of one school was seriously threatened.

Centralization of doctoral program finances

In FY03, the finances related to doctoral education were centralized. This was done to encourage cross-school cooperation, to make sure that the best teaching and research assistants were employed. Formerly doctoral programs were treated like all other graduate programs. The schools were credited with the revenues generated from the courses they offered and were charged with the costs of teaching those courses.

But this policy created some revenue/expense mismatches. For example, many students from the Engineering School can serve quite effectively as teaching assistants in math or physics courses, which are offered by the College. Math has a large undergraduate population but few graduate students. Formerly, if engineering students worked as teaching assistants in math classes, engineering would get the revenue because the engineering students would probably take most, if not all, of their courses in engineering, but math would have to pay the teaching assistant cost. This type of mismatch discouraged schools from using PhD students from outside their school.

After the change, starting in FY03, all of the PhD revenue was captured centrally and used to cover all the costs of PhD student fellowships, teaching assistantships, and research assistantships. This change allowed schools to hire the best PhD student help for their courses and research projects without concern for possibly adverse financial consequences.

Removal of constraints on capital investments

In FY02, a major change was made to USC's capital-planning processes. In earlier years, a school had to raise nearly all of the money needed to build a new facility, plus funds to endow most of the costs of maintenance, before construction could start. This conservative requirement caused significant delays in building and often caused completed buildings to be smaller than the actual needs of the school.

In FY02, USC's trustees adopted a centralized capital program that enabled the university to use debt capital, as well as other resources, to build capital projects more quickly. Academic deans would still be responsible for fundraising, but gifts intended to fund an academic building would be heavily levered. The gift monies would actually be invested in USC's endowment pool to support the academic programs to be housed in the new facility. The facility would be built with funds from USC's new Capital Plan, with debt payments made from a number of sources, including subventions, indirect cost recoveries, and investment income. Although the Capital Plan originally sought to expand the university's research infrastructure, the Plan has since been used also to fund some seismic upgrades and renovations. Non-academic (i.e., auxiliary) units still had to pay for the entire costs of their capital projects through their fundraising efforts and operating budgets.

Early evidence suggested that many deans were reenergized in their efforts to seek new monies for construction of new facilities. Many new facilities were being built and planned.

Changing of the participation "tax"

When the RCMS was first implemented, the schools' participation rate was lowered. It started at 20% of tuition and fees, sales or service income, and indirect cost recoveries. At that participation

rate, all schools were put in a deficit unless they could negotiate with the provost for some subvention relief. Thus the focus of every dean during the bonus meetings was on how to increase their subvention.

Then-provost Lloyd Armstrong decided that he wanted to change the tenor of the budget meetings and to increase the decentralization level. Thus, at his direction the participation rate was lowered in FY95 to 10%. It was lowered again in FY00 to 3.4%. Since then the participation rate had been increasing gradually. It was 6.4% in both FY07 and FY08. When the participation rate was 5% or lower, most of the schools could balance their budgets even without receiving a subvention.

In FY08, the subvention pool was approximately $100 million. About $60 million of this amount was spent to balance the budget of some schools that could not do so on their own. The other $40 million was to be used to further the provost's strategic objectives.

Modifications of assignments of indirect costs

As mentioned earlier, the methods used to allocate indirect costs to revenue centers were complex and controversial. University officials sought to simplify the situation. In FY00, it was decided that the 157 cost pools would be collapsed into one. The allocations of indirect costs in FY99 would become the new baseline going forward. Future years' allocations were determined simply by applying the average rate increase in all the administrative cost pools, regardless of how much of the central services they and their students consumed. In recent years, growth in the overall pool of administrative center expenses was capped at 5%.

Margo Steurbaut, Associate Senior Vice President and University Budget Director, explained:

> The allocation of central costs is one of the most widely debated and most reviewed aspects of RCMS. Any allocation system needs to allocate costs in an efficient manner, yet the allocated costs should bear some resemblance to actual usage. Most of the allocations are based on averages. Since the averages do not represent actual for any individual unit, the methodologies can become dysfunctional over time.
>
> While there will always be a spirited discussion over allocation methodologies, most of the focus should be on *managing* the central costs – not allocating

them. Once the costs are established, the allocations of those costs then create a zero sum game on a consolidated level.

Over the years, the number of allocation pools used at USC was reduced from 157, to 5, to 1. Having fewer pools allowed revenue centers to predict future costs more accurately and allowed central administration to focus on controlling costs rather than trying to determine how to allocate those costs. We sacrificed a degree of accuracy for predictability, and this trade-off was well received by both revenue centers and central administration.

A major problem with the original allocation system with 157 pools was that it penalized any revenue center that was growing faster than the university. That revenue center would experience allocated indirect cost increases at a rate larger than the growth in overall costs. The pie wasn't becoming more caloric, but they had to take a larger slice of the pie. The move to a simplified methodology was driven by central administration's desire to encourage growth.

After the FY00 cost allocation method change, the revenue centers that were growing their operations faster than the growth in the indirect costs benefited from this change because the indirect costs would become a smaller proportion of their overall budgets. Those that were growing more slowly faced an increasingly large indirect cost burden.

In 2002, an attempt was made to devise a new indirect cost allocation system based on only five or six allocation bases. A number of analyses were completed that showed a different set of revenue center "winners" and "losers." In particular, schools with new buildings would have received significantly higher indirect costs. Then-provost Lloyd Armstrong decided at that time to stick with the one-pool system.

In 2007, updated numbers were input into the allocation model developed in 2002. This analysis showed quite a number of surprising differences in "winners" and "losers." But Provost Nikias decided not to implement an allocation change. He concluded that the one-pool system was achieving the desired goals: it enabled schools to be able to predict future costs easily, and it rewarded growth. Further, there was concern about the relatively large number of new deans – eight – who had been hired recently. Some senior managers did not think it was fair to confront these new deans with, possibly, a dramatically different financial picture than the one they were shown during the interviewing process.

More flexibility in the use of Intercenter Bank funds

The Intercenter Bank was originally intended to allow some cross-year flexibility in the use of funds. Academic units generating surpluses could put those surplus funds into the Intercenter Bank and withdraw a portion of the balance in a subsequent year to use for any purpose. In the original RCMS design, the dean had to withdraw 20% of the balance in the subsequent year. But the 20% withdrawal rate was not seen as enough of an incentive for deans to turn in their surplus. Thus the withdrawal amount was raised in a later year to 33% to allow the deans quicker access to their monies.

The vision of Max Nikias, who assumed the provost role in 2005, was that all of the surplus funds would be placed in a provost reserve account. Deans would have to submit a proposal to justify the withdrawal and spending of monies from that account. Details of this procedure were still being worked out. It was expected that before approving any withdrawal, Provost Nikias would examine the reasons why the surplus was generated. Was it for good reasons, such as an increase in the student retention rate? Or was it for bad reasons, such as the creation of a questionable new course that "stole" students from another school? He would also be looking for a good academic justification for spending these monies. In addition, he might require the schools to maintain a minimum balance of, perhaps, 8–10% of the school's operating budget as an emergency reserve.

SOME SENIOR MANAGEMENT OPINIONS ABOUT RCMS

Here are some opinions about RCMS from USC's CFO, an experienced dean, and a recently appointed dean:

Dennis Dougherty

Dennis Dougherty had been USC's CFO for the entire period that USC had used the RCMS. He was closely involved in the original RCMS implementation, and he thought the system had served its purposes well over the years.

One of the advantages of the system is that it's very transparent. You can see everybody's financial statements. But to make it work you need good information systems, which not all universities have.

Dennis also noted that the current provost, Max Nikias, was making some subtle shifts in the application of RCMS:

> We will be shrinking our undergraduate student population. Max is encouraging the deans to generate *new* money, such as from graduate education, sponsored research, intellectual property, and continuing professional education. The deans are not going to get subvention monies based on size. He will base them on the quality of the schools' academic plans and the degree to which they are in sync with the university's academic plan.

Elizabeth Daley

Elizabeth Daley had served as the dean of USC's School of Cinematic Arts (until 2006 named the School of Cinema-Television) since 1991.

> RCMS enables USC to attract people who like to build something. The key message in RCMS is very clear: you bring in the revenue, and you manage it, as long as what you do is academically sound. It allows a school to establish itself, grow itself, and manage itself. In industry, I had to make payments on time and balance a budget. Here too I am responsible for the bottom-line. I prefer it that way.
>
> [. . .] With a top-down management system, deans might have little control over their own destiny. For example, they might be forced to ask their provost questions like, "When can we get another faculty line assigned?" With [RCMS] we don't ask that question because we know the answer. If the faculty hire is appropriate for the academic program, then we can make the hire when we have raised the money to sustain that position! So, for example, if we want an animation program, we know that if we raise the money, prepare a solid curriculum, and show that there is demand for the program, then we can do it. This is important because I can go to potential donors knowing that we have the freedom to propose that they fund such a program. We can assure them that the funds they give us will indeed be used for that program.
>
> [. . .] Without a system like RCMS, I might not have been as interested in staying here because the cinema school needed a great deal of outside support that it did not have at the time I came. RCMS enabled us to take the entrepreneurial approach that was required to build the resources we needed.
>
> [. . .] Sure, there are things I don't like with any budget system. I don't like surprises. I don't like

unfunded mandates, as not every proposal from a central administration office fits every school equally well. And I don't like what I sometimes consider as "excessive" taxation. But the negatives are very minor compared with how much I like RCMS.

> [. . .] I do want to note that I have always believed that there are some programs, important programs for the university's academic mission, that probably can't be self-supporting. They need central funding help. There are other programs that don't fit in any revenue center but are necessary for the good of the whole university. They also need central funding and no doubt some of that funding has to come from the revenue centers. RCMS has to be balanced between self-sufficiency/independence and the good of the whole. It's a philosophy that I think is healthy as long as it is applied with some flexibility.

Jim Ellis

Jim Ellis, one of the eight USC deans appointed in 2007, was dean of the Marshall School of Business:

> It's a good system for a school like this one with critical mass. It carries with it an "eat-what-you-kill" philosophy. We know how much we need to raise to cover our expenses and to hire new faculty. It's tougher for some small schools. Those deans have to go hat in hand to the provost because they don't generate as much income, and their alumni are not as wealthy or as generous as some of ours are.
>
> [. . .] I don't worry about the arbitrary cost allocation bases as long as they are maintained on a consistent basis year to year. This is not like a business. We know our revenue stream. But the indirect costs are very significant for us. If the indirect costs change, our whole income statement can get screwed up. If I feel some uncertainty about the size of indirect cost allocations that we will have to cover, I will be very conservative in what I do. If I know the parameters, I will deal with them.
>
> [. . .] Some of the other deans yell at us for stealing their revenue. That is because the undergraduate business minor has become huge. But we require our students to take two courses in math and two in economics, and those are taught by professors in the college. So we give back. We understand that we are not just here for ourselves; we are part of the larger university community.

LOOKING TO THE FUTURE

RCMS was more than an accounting system; it defined a complete style of decentralized management in a large, complex academic setting. Almost no one connected with USC wanted to abandon that style of management. Some of USC's successes were attributed to the use of RCMS. The system tended to encourage deans to be entrepreneurial, yet fiscally prudent. Clearly further refinements were necessary, but USC administrators were loathe to make changes too quickly.

Exhibit 1 Highlights of the University

	June 30 2007	June 30 2006
Financial (in thousands)		
Total revenues	$2,523,525	$2,257,234
Total cash gifts and equipment gifts	$350,725	$379,471
Capital expenditures	$240,851	$283,869
Total assets at year end	$6,342,621	$5,533,079
Total debt at year end	$505,897	$406,771
Increase in net assets	$674,181	$461,496
Market value of endowment	$3,715,272	$3,065,935
Executed contracts, grants, subcontracts and cooperative agreements	$726,485	$794,363
Property, plant and equipment, net	$1,444,566	$1,293,549
Net Asset Balances:		
Unrestricted	$3,731,115	$3,147,924
Temporarily restricted	$209,520	$208,009
Permanently restricted	$1,266,961	$1,177,482
Students		
Enrollment (head count, autumn):		
Undergraduate students	16,729	16,897
Graduate and professional students	16,660	15,939
Degrees conferred:		
Bachelor degrees	4,676	4,269
Advanced	5,380	5,274
Certificates	209	188
Annual tuition rate	$33,314	$31,458
Faculty and Staff		
Faculty	4,596	4,510
Staff	7,992	7,855

Exhibit 2 USC organization chart

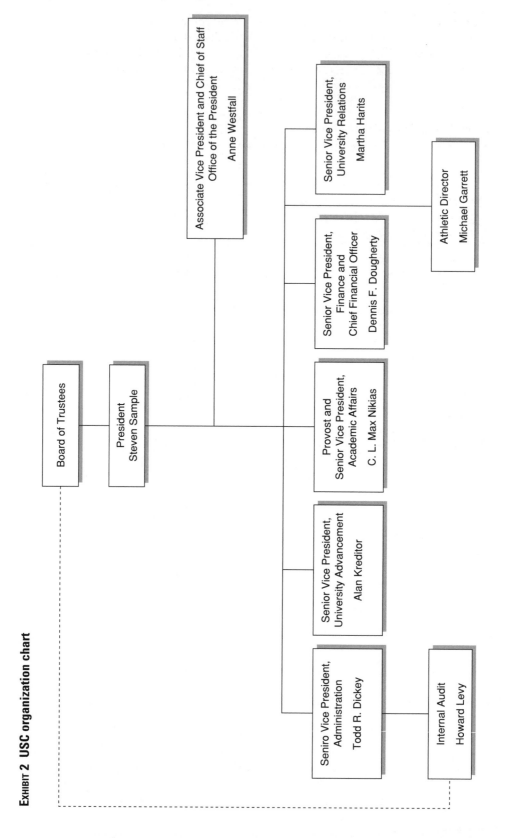

Exhibit 3 USC Provost organization

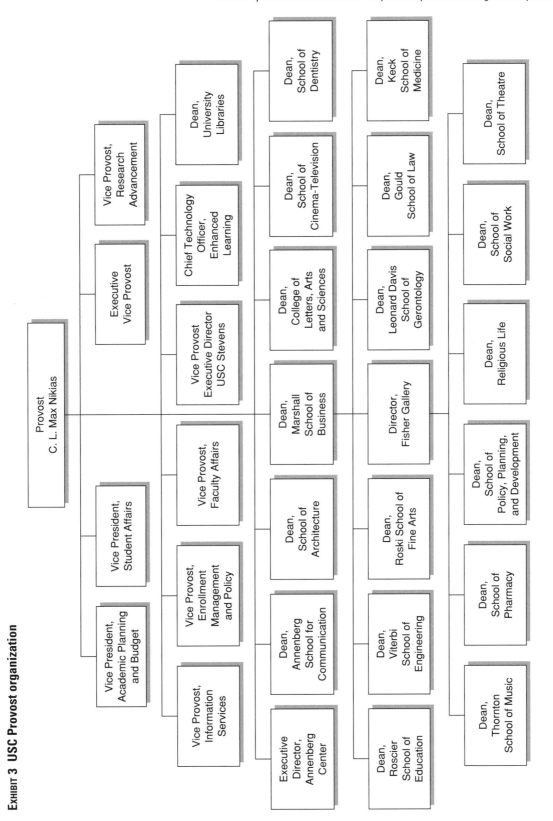

Exhibit 4 Role and mission of USC

The central mission of the University of Southern California is the development of human beings and society as a whole through the cultivation and enrichment of the human mind and spirit. The principal means by which our mission is accomplished are teaching, research, artistic creation, professional practice and selected forms of public service.

Our first priority as faculty and staff is the education of our students, from freshmen to postdoctorals, through a broad array of academic, professional, extracurricular and athletic programs of the first rank. The integration of liberal and professional learning is one of USC's special strengths. We strive constantly for excellence in teaching knowledge and skills to our students, while at the same time helping them to acquire wisdom and insight, love of truth and beauty, moral discernment, understanding of self, and respect and appreciation for others.

Research of the highest quality by our faculty and students is fundamental to our mission. USC is one of a very small number of premier academic institutions in which research and teaching are inextricably intertwined, and on which the nation depends for a steady stream of new knowledge, art, and technology. Our faculty are not simply teachers of the works of others, but active contributors to what is taught, thought and practiced throughout the world.

USC is pluralistic, welcoming outstanding men and women of every race, creed and background. We are a global institution in a global center, attracting more international students over the years than any other American university. And we are private, unfettered by political control, strongly committed to academic freedom, and proud of our entrepreneurial heritage.

An extraordinary closeness and willingness to help one another are evident among USC students, alumni, faculty, and staff; indeed, for those within its compass the Trojan Family is a genuinely supportive community. Alumni, trustees, volunteers and friends of USC are essential to this family tradition, providing generous financial support, participating in university governance, and assisting students at every turn.

In our surrounding neighborhoods and around the globe, USC provides public leadership and public service in such diverse fields as health care, economic development, social welfare, scientific research, public policy and the arts. We also serve the public interest by being the largest private employer in the city of Los Angeles, as well as the city's largest export industry in the private sector.

USC has played a major role in the development of Southern California for more than a century, and plays an increasingly important role in the development of the nation and the world. We expect to continue to play these roles for many centuries to come. Thus our planning, commitments and fiscal policies are directed toward building quality and excellence in the long term.

Adopted by the USC Board of Trustees, February, 1993.

INDEX